GLENCOE MATH

TEACHER WALKAROUND EDITION

McGraw Hill Education

McGraw Hill Education

GLENCOE MATH

Glencoe Math empowers you to engage every student, and develop a classroom of critical thinkers...

Show your students the fascinating world of math while teaching them all the skills they need to become mathematically proficient and excel on next generation assessments. With *Glencoe Math* you have the standards at your fingertips, with lessons ready to roll out or customize to your teaching style.

Whether you use one classroom computer, an interactive whiteboard, tablets, or 1:1 computing, you and your students will move easily between print and digital. ConnectED is your platform for all digital resources accessible from school or home. Wherever you are in the digital transition, *Glencoe Math* is there with you, offering the perfect blend of print and digital to fit into all your classroom needs.

...making math relevant, rigorous, and possible for every student.

Rigor

Built-in and supported throughout the program

The three components of rigor, conceptual understanding, applications, and procedural skill and fluency, are embedded in resources, lessons, and even assessments.

Relevance

Math in context so students see how math matters

Glencoe Math makes math real for students. Thousands of digital planning tools and interactive resources are available online in one, easy-to-use portal, ConnectED. Use these resources as is or make them your own to spark student thinking.

Results

Proficiency for all students is the goal

Meet students wherever they are in their learning. Assessments help you determine proficiency before, during, and after lessons, while differentiated-instruction resources ensure approaching-level students master concepts before moving on, while beyond-level students are challenged.

Meet the Demands of Standards...

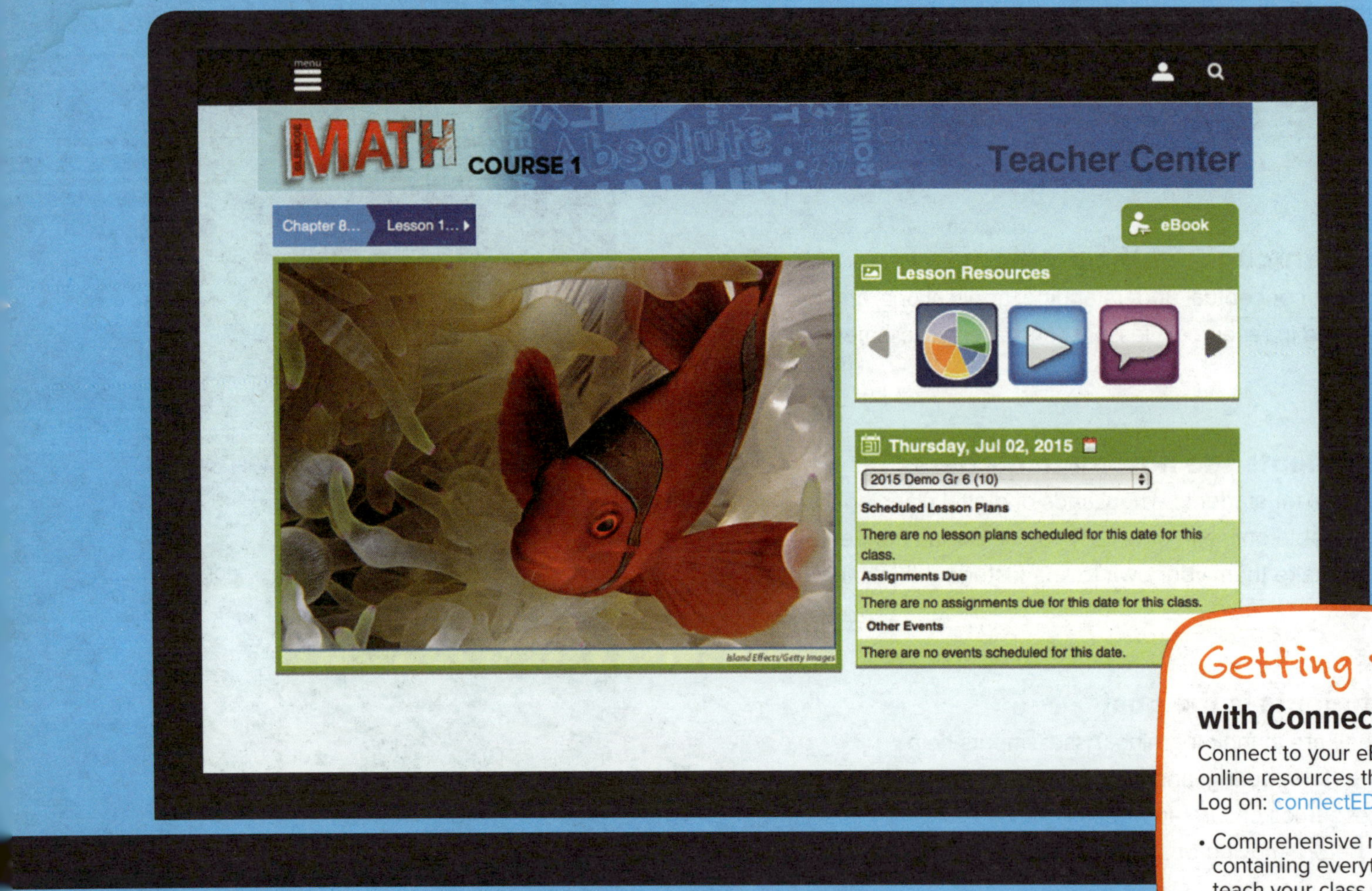

Getting Started
with ConnectED

Connect to your eBook and all your online resources through ConnectED. Log on: connectED.mcgraw-hill.com

- Comprehensive resources containing everything you need to teach your class.
- Accessible anywhere, from any computer, at any time.
- Use your device via ConnectED mobile available from your App Store. (See page v.)

Wesley Hitt/Photodisc/Getty Images

...instilling a deep appreciation for math.

Focus, coherence, and rigor are the driving forces behind *Glencoe Math*. Every lesson, activity, assessment, and resource is designed to build your students' mathematical understanding and connect learning to the Standards for Mathematical Practice.

Focus

Glencoe Math is built in a way that you can be confident you're covering everything your students need to succeed.

Coherence

Glencoe Math builds on knowledge gained in previous lessons and grades, guiding students through each concept with thoughtful progressions, while making connections that are natural extensions of what students have already learned.

Rigor

The three components of rigor, conceptual understanding, application, and procedural skill and fluency, are woven throughout *Glencoe Math* in equal intensity which, according to the Publishers' Criteria, allow your students to progress toward a higher level of achievement.

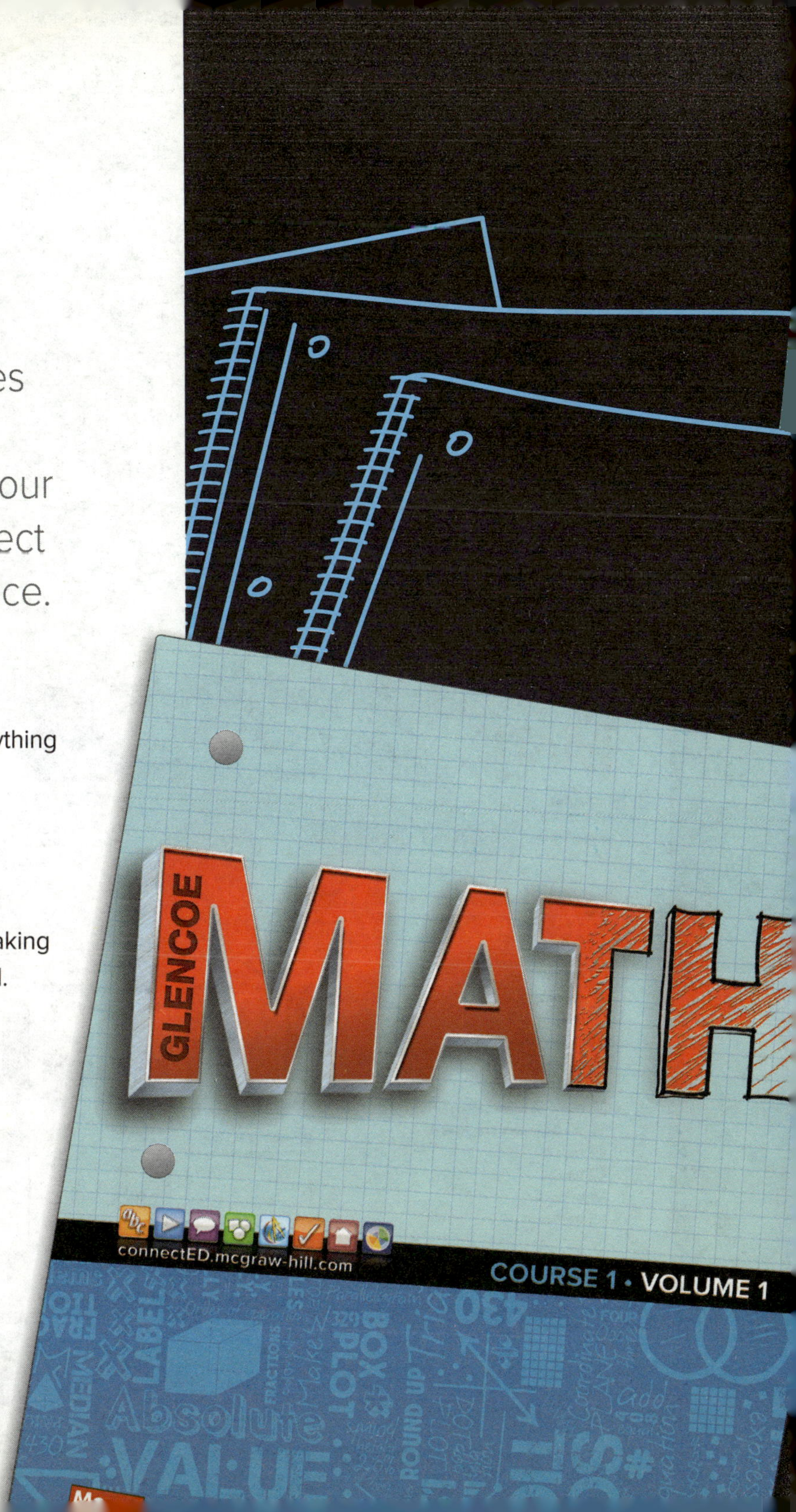

Expect high achievement...

Rigor isn't just about harder problems, it's about ensuring students acquire a deep understanding of mathematical concepts and the ability to apply them in real-world situations.

The three components of rigor are found throughout every chapter and in every activity.

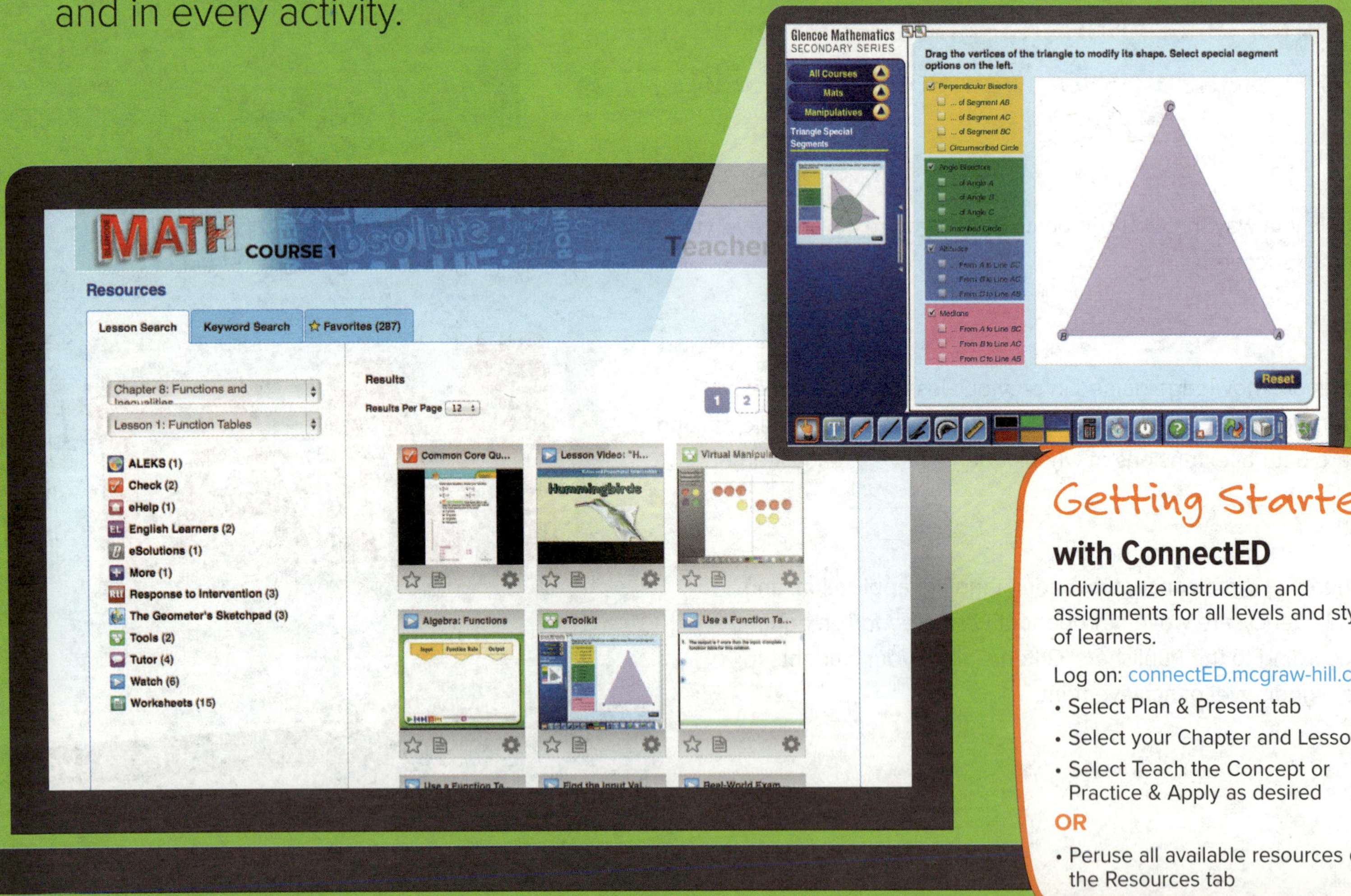

Getting Started

with ConnectED

Individualize instruction and assignments for all levels and styles of learners.

Log on: connectED.mcgraw-hill.com

- Select Plan & Present tab
- Select your Chapter and Lesson
- Select Teach the Concept or Practice & Apply as desired

OR

- Peruse all available resources on the Resources tab

...supporting rigor every step of the way.

Conceptual Understanding

Inquiry Labs Hands-on collaboration promotes critical thinking

H.O.T. Problems Higher-order thinking creates high level understanding

Virtual Manipulatives Interactive concept exploration providing problem-based learning opportunities

The Geometer's Sketchpad™ Interactive content enabling students to see and apply structures in appropriate lessons

Applications

Unit Projects Collaborative assignments promoting teamwork and research skills

21st Century Careers Exploration of varied career paths with relevant mathematical and analytical skills

Real-World Math Exercises with practical application of content knowledge and skills in everyday life

Problem-Solving Investigations Opportunities for students to solve non-routine problems in collaborative settings

STEM Projects Connections to mathematical content through the development of problem-solving skills and the engineering design process

Procedural Skill and Fluency

Guided Practice In-class practice of concepts that are presented in the text examples

Independent Practice Designed to be used for homework assignments and differentiated for each student's needs based on Levels of Complexity

Extra Practice Use for additional reinforcement or second-day assignments

Leveled Worksheets Available online, provide additional practice for approaching-, beyond-, and on-level students

Prepare for next-generation assessments...

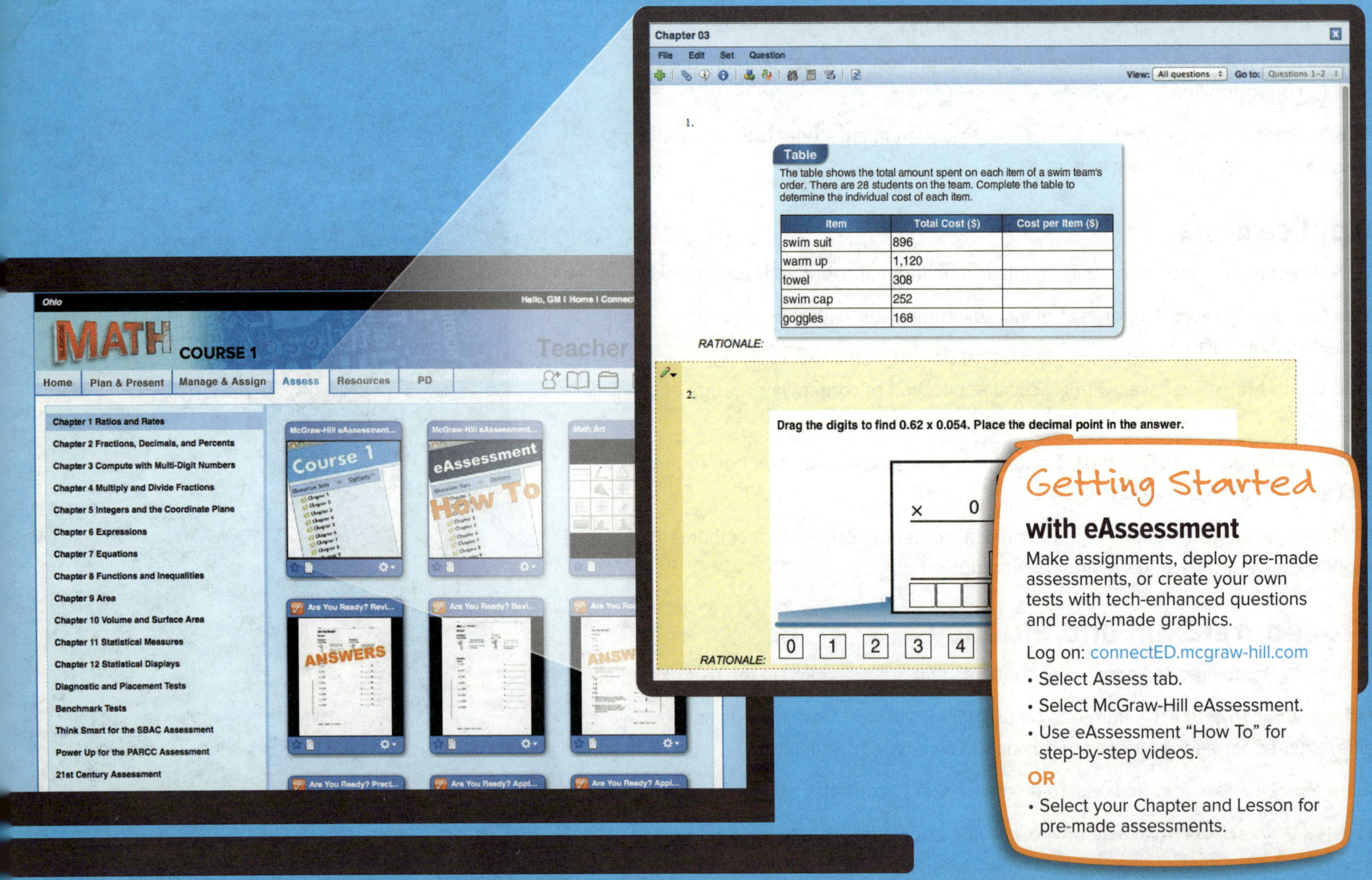

Getting Started

with eAssessment

Make assignments, deploy pre-made assessments, or create your own tests with tech-enhanced questions and ready-made graphics.

Log on: connectED.mcgraw-hill.com

- Select Assess tab.
- Select McGraw-Hill eAssessment.
- Use eAssessment "How To" for step-by-step videos.

OR

- Select your Chapter and Lesson for pre-made assessments.

...succeeding with confidence.

Your students will be prepared to excel on new kinds of assessment that measure deeper understanding, critical-thinking, and problem-solving skills. They will be able to practice the types of questions they can expect to face in an online testing environment.

Online Practice Tests allow students to become comfortable with how they'll be asked to demonstrate their mathematical understanding.

Performance Tasks at the end of each chapter require students to solve multi-step problems through abstract reasoning, precision, and perseverance.

Online Benchmark Tests in each chapter that are designed to check students' understanding before they are evaluated on summative assessments.

Test Practice in every lesson mirrors the types of questions found on the online assessments.

eAssessment helps you create your own online assessments including tests, quizzes and worksheets, while tech-enhanced questions mimic the types of questions found on thestate assessment tests.

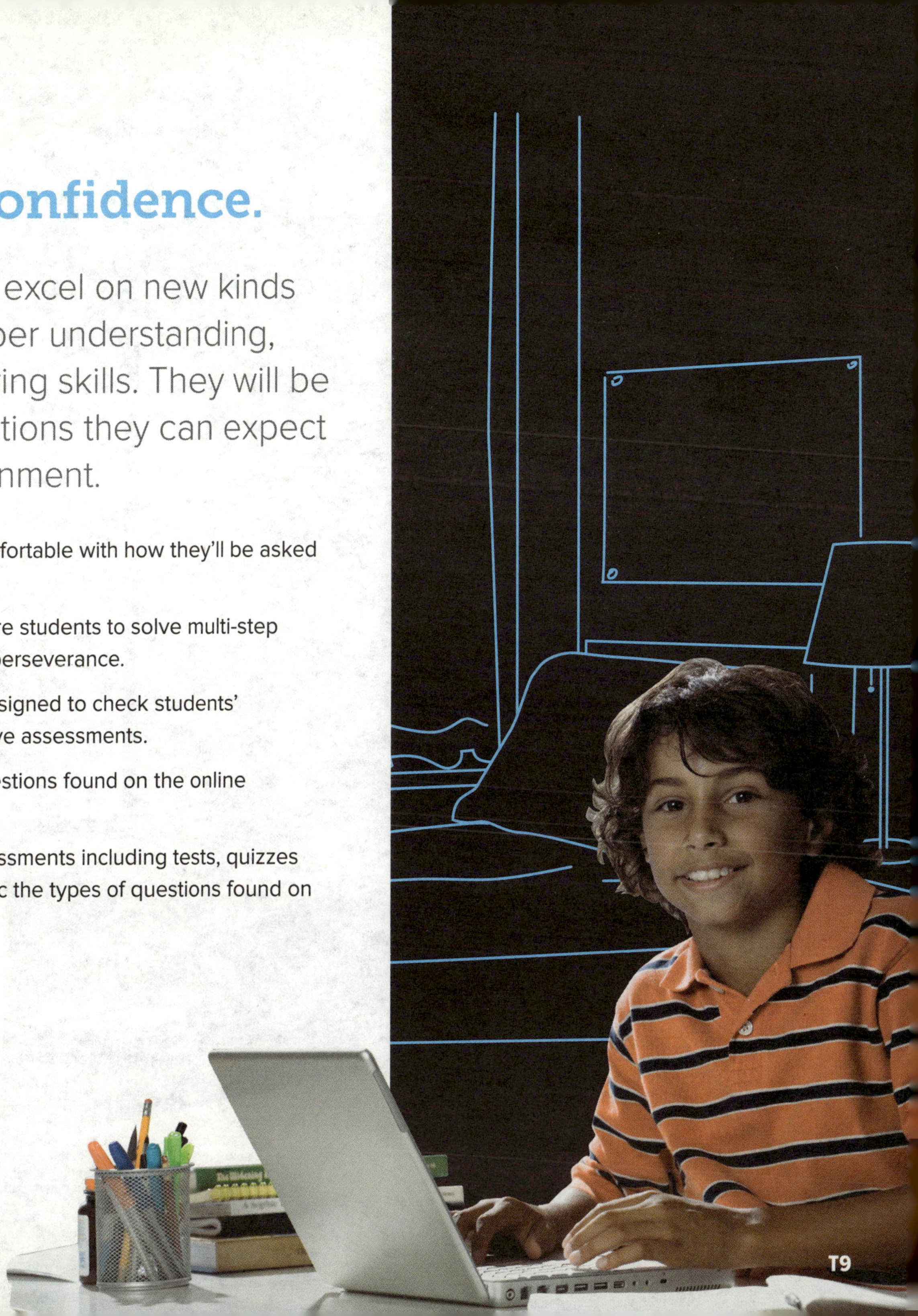

Engaging Resources...

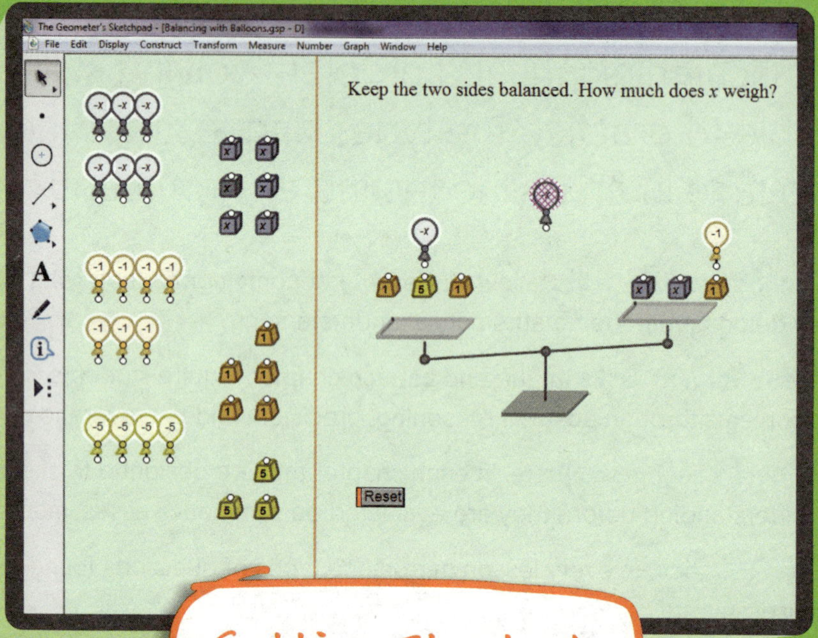

Getting Started

with THE GEOMETER'S SKETCHPAD®

Bring math concepts alive with point-of-use sketches within ConnectED.

- Embedded activities available from the eBook.
- Presentation sketches provide detailed notes for in-class use.
- Downloadable software for full product access available at MHEOnline.com/Sketchpad.

...learning that empowers students.

You've got lots of resources available to you, but it's your inspiration and energy that will bring them to life for your students.

Foldables® provide three-dimensional personalized graphic organizers.

Step-by-Step Examples allow you to walk through each solution of every example in the Student Edition.

Online Personal Tutors and **Animations** provide visual support of math concepts.

Virtual Manipulatives provide a visual approach to math without the classroom cleanup.

The Geometer's Sketchpad™ illustrates mathematical ideas in a tangible, visual way that increases student engagement, understanding, and achievement.

Inquiry Labs promote collaboration, conceptual understanding, and critical thinking.

Real-World Applications allow students to understand the everyday relevance of math.

21st Century Careers highlight the math skills needed to ensure real-world success.

Small Group Activities provide suggestions for collaborative learning to help you differentiate your instruction.

The **Interactive Student Edition**, available in print as well as digitally through the ConnectED online portal or the ConnectED Mobile App, allows students to get involved and take ownership of their work like never before.

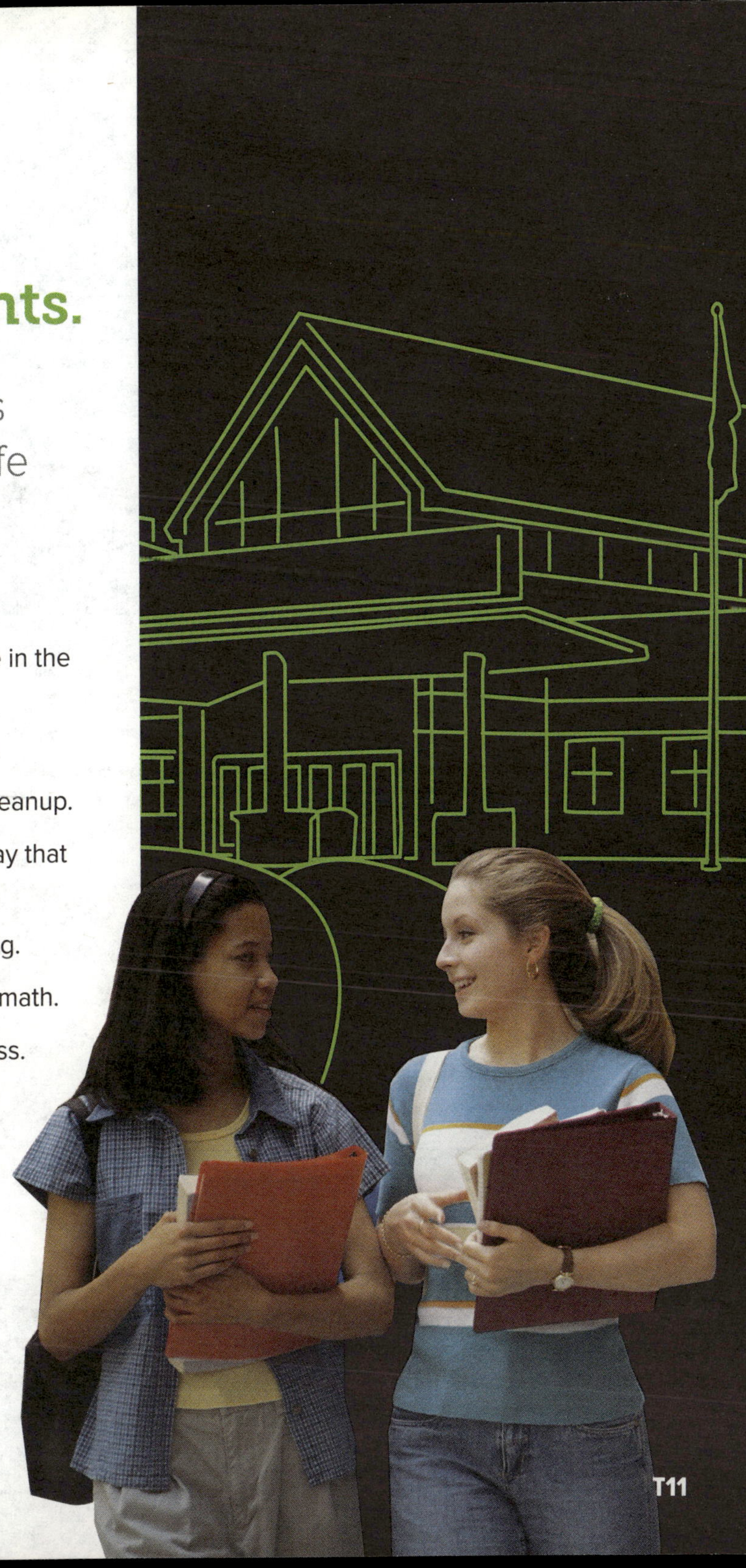

Plan easier...

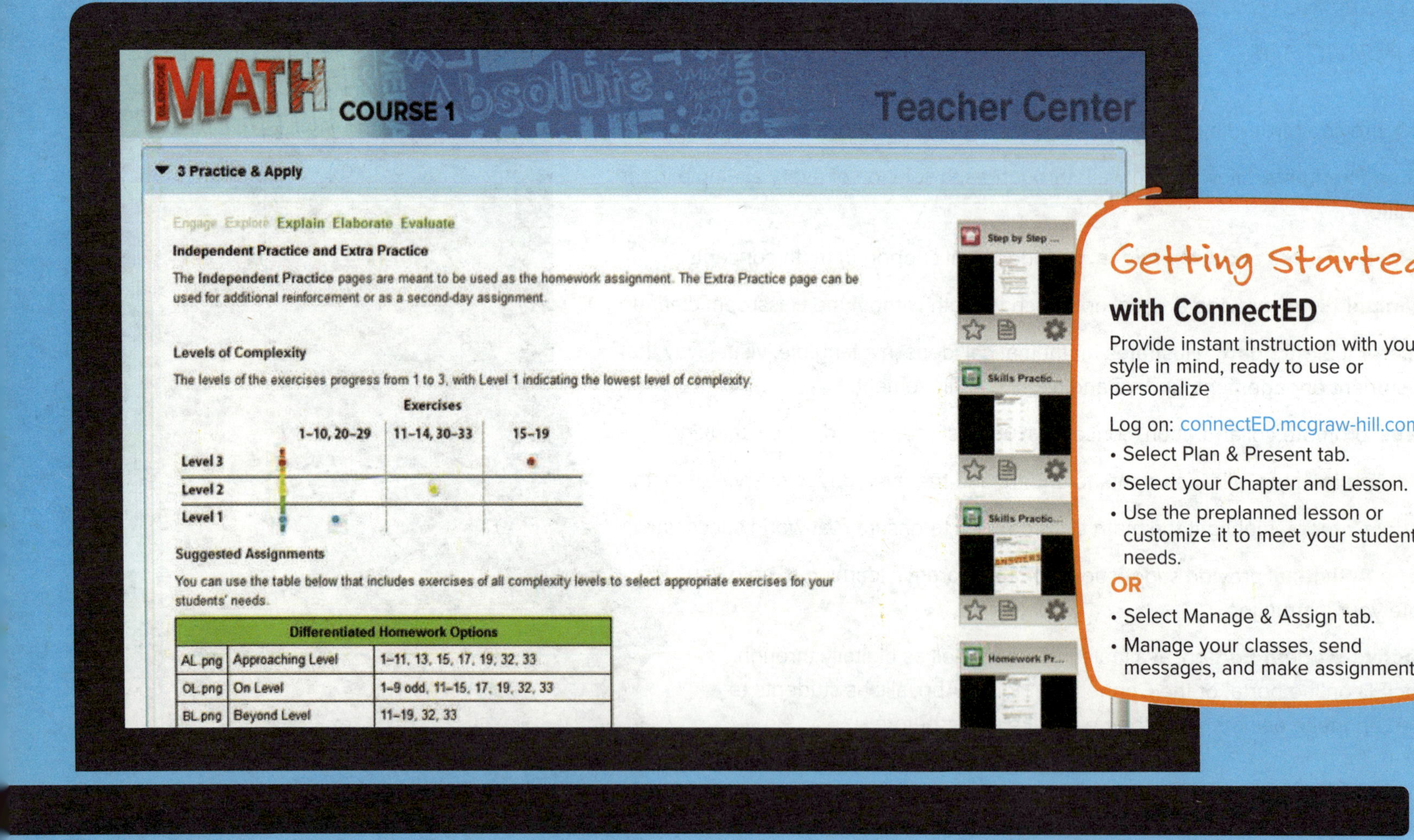

Getting Started

with ConnectED

Provide instant instruction with your style in mind, ready to use or personalize

Log on: connectED.mcgraw-hill.com

- Select Plan & Present tab.
- Select your Chapter and Lesson.
- Use the preplanned lesson or customize it to meet your students' needs.

OR

- Select Manage & Assign tab.
- Manage your classes, send messages, and make assignments.

...providing you more time and energy to teach.

Class periods are over in a flash but the planning and preparation that goes into each one is no small task. With *Glencoe Math* you'll spend less time searching for quality resources, ensuring you're covering the standards, making real-world connections, and putting it all together.

Online prepared lesson plans customize to meet your students' needs or use our recommended path.

The Calendar feature allows for long-term planning.

Homework and **Extra Practice** are included in the Student Edition, which save you time from having to print and copy worksheets from another source, while keeping your students organized.

Forgot to tell your students something or need to remind them of an upcoming test? **Send messages** or **make assignments** to students through the online Teacher Center.

Resources are located at point of use in your lesson plan, ready to project or print.

Interactive Lesson Presentations can be customized by adding your favorite resources to give the lesson your touch.

Practical Professional Development...

Glencoe Math includes relevant, research-based professional development delivered when you need it.

Before your first day of teaching with *Glencoe Math*, access your Quick-Start Course where you'll find videos of an expert consultant who will provide a digital walkthrough of everything you need to know to get started.

As you're planning your lessons, access PD videos modeling effective teaching strategies embedded at point-of-use within your online lesson plans.

When using *Glencoe Math* tools, be sure to check out collections of PD support for using Dinah Zike's Foldables, The Geometer's Sketchpad® and ALEKS®.

When you're seeking a trusted source, access PD video collections, white papers, and on-demand webinars featuring important topics, such as incorporating The Standards for Mathematical Practice, increasing rigor and student engagement, and teaching with technology.

To achieve program mastery and continue your professional development, access your online Professional Learning Environment where you'll find an in-depth Implementation Course and active community of *Glencoe Math* teachers.

PD

...the PD you need, when you need it.

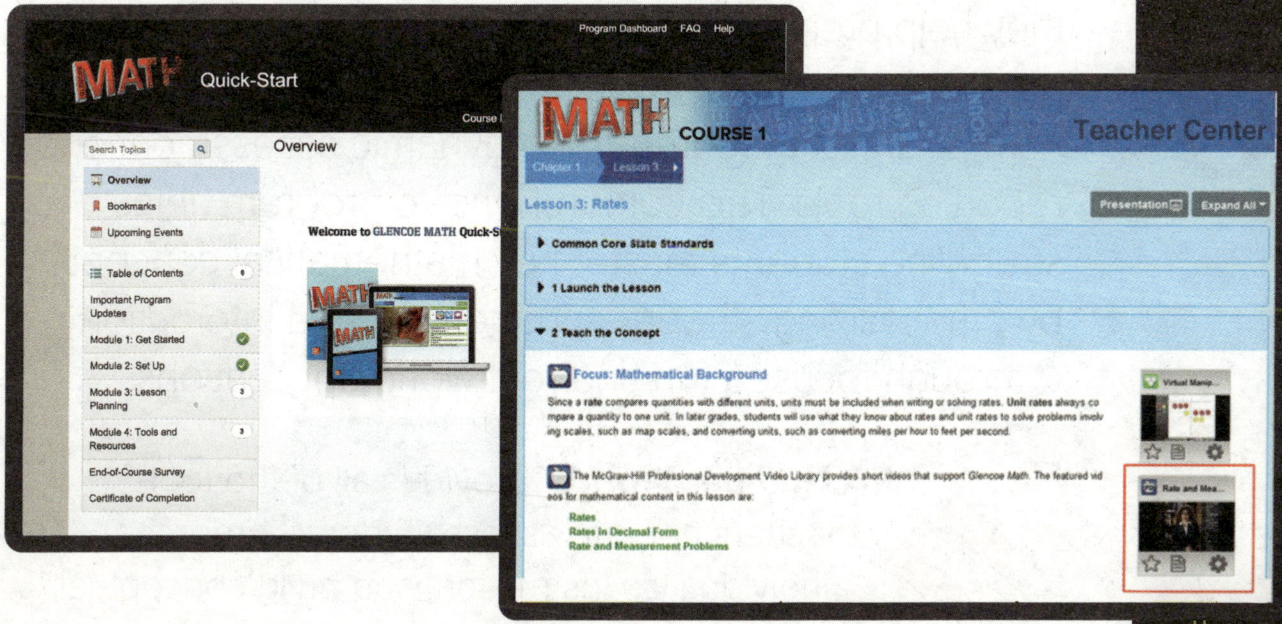

Take Advantage of Your *Glencoe Math* Professional Learning Environment

Track your progress and get credit for your work. The *Glencoe Math* Professional Learning Environment allows you to work at your own pace and tracks your progress as you go so you can see which resources you've accessed. Once you've completed a course, you'll earn a Certificate of Completion that serves as a record of time spent in the course.

Connect with other Glencoe Math teachers. Active discussion areas within the Glencoe Math Professional Learning Environment provide an opportunity for you to share your ideas, questions, and best practices.

Request additional courses. Contact your McGraw-Hill Education sales representative to learn about additional professional development courses available.

Proven to help struggling students.

Together with *Glencoe Math* and *SRA Number Worlds* they help prepare, engage and assess students' achievement with proven curriculum, interactive games, digital resources, and dynamic assessment and reporting tools. This comprehensive program helps struggling students master key mathematical concepts by emphasizing student engagement and interaction through focused fun and real-world applications.

SRA Number Worlds provides all of the tools teachers need to assess students' progress, individualize instruction, and build conceptual math understanding and computational fluency while making learning fun!

- Targeted instruction
- Flexibility for teachers and students
- Precise assessment
- Comprehensive, fully-integrated program

For more information, contact your sales representative.
MHEonline.com/NumberWorlds/

Simplifying differentiated instruction.

McGraw Hill Education | ALEKS®

Can be a challenge. It's ALEKS® to the rescue! This adaptive online resource uses open-responsive questioning to provide each student with a personalized learning path.

Support each student's unique needs

- Knowledge checks identify what a student knows and where there are gaps
- Personalized instruction allows students to progress at their own pace
- Robust reporting tools provide instructionally-actionable data
- Targeted instruction on Ready to Learn topics build learning momentum and confidence
- Open-response environment ensures students demonstrate understanding—no guessing!

Learn how ALEKS can enhance your current math curriculum. Contact your rep today.

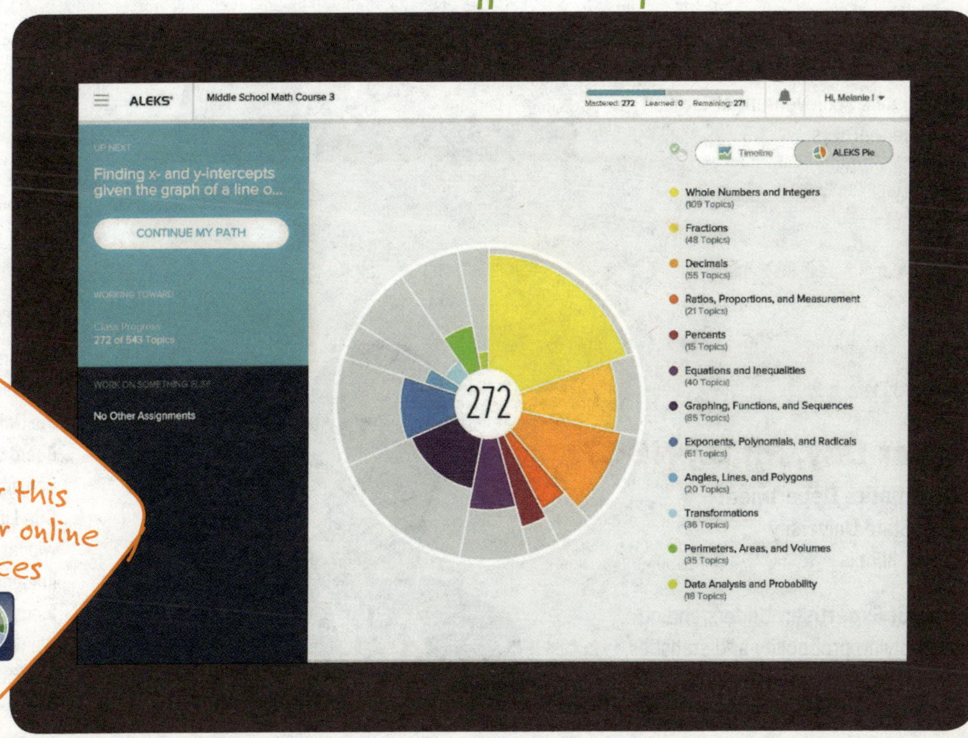

Look for this logo in your online resources

Meet the Authors

Lead Authors

Our lead authors ensure that the McGraw-Hill mathematics programs are truly vertically aligned by beginning with the end in mind - success in Algebra 1 and beyond. By "backmapping" the content from the high school programs, all of our mathematics programs are well articulated in their scope and sequence.

John A. Carter, Ph.D.

Principal
Westlake High School
Austin, Texas

Areas of Expertise: Using technology and manipulatives to visualize concepts; mathematics achievement of English language learners

Gilbert J. Cuevas, Ph.D.

Professor of Mathematics Education
Texas State University—San Marcos
San Marcos, Texas

Areas of Expertise: Use of technology in teaching geometry

Roger Day, Ph.D., NBCT

Mathematics Department
Illinois State University
Normal, Illinois

Areas of Expertise: Understanding and applying probability and statistics; mathematics teacher education

In Memoriam
Carol Malloy, Ph.D.

Dr. Carol Malloy was a fervent supporter of mathematics education. She was a Professor at the University of North Carolina, Chapel Hill, NCTM Board of Directors member, President of the Benjamin Banneker Association (BBA), and 2013 BBA Lifetime Achievement Award for Mathematics winner. She joined McGraw-Hill in 1996. Her influence significantly improved our programs' focus on real-world problem solving and equity. We will miss her inspiration and passion for education.

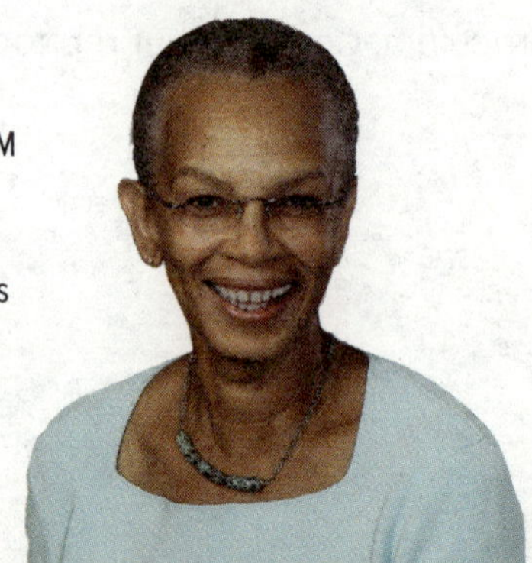

McGraw-Hill Education

Program Authors

Gladis Kersaint, Ph.D.
Professor of Mathematics Education, K–12
University of South Florida
Tampa, Florida

Mary Esther Reynosa
Instructional Specialist for Elementary Mathematics
Northside Independent School District
San Antonio, Texas

Robyn Silbey
Math Coach and Consultant
Gaithersburg, Maryland

Kathleen Vielhaber
Mathematics Consultant
St. Louis, Missouri

Contributing Author

Dinah Zike
Author, Consultant, Inventor of FOLDABLES
Dinah Zike Academy; Dinah Might Adventures, LP
San Antonio, Texas

McGraw-Hill Education; (tr)Courtesy of Dinah Zike; (bc)Aaron Haupt

Consultants and Reviewers

These professionals were instrumental in providing valuable input and suggestions for improving the effectiveness of the mathematics instruction.

Consultants

Instructional Technology

Cheryl Conley
Teacher
2011 Florida Teacher of the Year
2011 National Teacher of the Year Finalist
Vero Beach, FL

Atsusi "2C" Hirumi, Ph.D.
Associate Professor
University of Central Florida
Orlando, FL

James Jarvis
Division Manager, Science & Technology
Thomas Jefferson High School
Alexandria, VA

Kathy Schrock
Educational Technologist
Eastham, MA

Family Involvement

Paul Giganti, Jr.
Director, California Math Council Parent Outreach
California Mathematics Council
Albany, CA

Response to Intervention (RtI)

Margaret A. Searle
President, Searle Enterprises, Inc
Perrysburg, OH

English Language Learners (ELL)

Kathryn Heinze
Associate Professor
Hamline University, School of Education
Saint Paul, MN

Homework

Richard W. Herrig
Educational Consultant
Consulting Services International
Regina, Saskatchewan

Gifted and Talented

Shelbi K. Cole, Ph.D.
Mathematics Consultant
Connecticut State Department of Education
Hartford, CT

21st Century Skills and Vocabulary Development

Sue Z. Beers
President/Consultant for Tools for Learning, Inc.
ASCD Author and Speaker
Jewell, IA

Vocabulary Development

Timothy Shanahan, Ph.D.
Professor of Urban Education
University of Illinois at Chicago
Chicago, IL

Donald R. Bear, Ph.D.
Professor
University of Nevada, Reno
Reno, NV

Douglas Fisher, Ph.D.
Associate Professor in the College of Education
Department of Teacher Education
San Diego State University
San Diego, CA

Assessment

Cheryl Rose Tobey
Assessment Author and Consultant
Randolph, ME

Differentiated Instruction

Jennifer Taylor-Cox
Educational Consultant
Taylor-Cox Instruction
Severna Park, MD

STEM Education

Celeste Baine
Director
Engineering Education Service Center
Clinton, WA

Erleen Braton
Curriculum Integration Coordinator
Rogers, MN

Cindy Hoffner Moss, Ph.D.
Director of STEM
Charlotte-Mecklenburg Schools
Mount Holly, NC

Understanding by Design (UbD)

Jay McTighe
Educational Author and Consultant
Columbia, MD
Understanding by Design® is a registered trademark of the Association for Supervision and Curriculum Development ("ASCD").

Problem Solving

Dr. Stephen Krulik
2011 NCTM Lifetime Achievement Award in Mathematics
Professor Emeritus of Math Education
Temple University
Philadelphia, PA

Reviewers

Shawanna G. Anekwe, Ed.S, NBCT
Peer Mathematics Coach
Cleveland Metropolitan School District
Cleveland, Ohio

Kimberly Bess
Mathematics Teacher
Holland Elementary School
Springfield, Missouri

Karen M. Borghi
Mathematics Interventionist
Tracy Elementary School
Easton, Pennsylvania

Jill Carlson
Elementary Principal
Crownhill Elementary School
Bremerton, Washington

Lynda G. D'Angiolillo
Director of Curriculum and Instruction
Wanaque Schools
Wanaque, New Jersey

Patricia Erneste
Mathematics Instructional Coach
Park Hill School District
Kansas City, Missouri

Dana Ferguson
Mathematics Coordinator K-12
Columbia Public Schools
Columbia, Missouri

Tanjanika Foster
Mathematics Department Chairperson
Collinsville Middle School
Collinsville, Illinois

Robert Gyles, Ph.D.
Professor of Mathematics Education
Hunter College/CUNY
New York, New York

Sr. Helen Lucille Habig, RSM
Assistant Superintendent of Schools
Archdiocese of Cincinnati
Cincinnati, Ohio

Donna M. Hastie
Director of Curriculum and Instruction
North Haledon School District
North Haledon, New Jersey

Karen Henkes
Mathematics Teacher
Bluefield Middle School
Bluefield, West Virginia

Laura Hunovice
Mathematics Resource Teacher
Hampstead Elementary School
Linton Springs Elementary School
Carroll County, Maryland

Sandra Jenoure
Adjunct Professor of Mathematics/Science Education
Hunter College
New York, New York

Gail Karle
Lead Teacher
South Elementary
Mt. Healthy City School District
Cincinnati, Ohio

Traci A. Kimball
Mathematics Department Coordinator
Glenwood Middle School
Chatham, Illinois

Jennifer Ledbetter
Teacher
Crownhill Elementary School
Bremerton, Washington

Robert A. LeVien, Jr.
Teacher
Maud S. Sherwood Elementary School
Islip, New York

Stephanie Long
Mathematics Teacher/Curriculum Development Council Chairperson
Pleasant View Middle School
Springfield, Missouri

Sara Mahoski
Mathematics Specialist
Cheston Elementary School
Easton, Pennsylvania

Michael R. McGowan
Elementary Supervisor
Allegany County Board of Education
Cumberland, Maryland

Marcy E. Myers
Mathematics Resource Teacher
Robert Moton Elementary School
Westminster, Maryland

Jenni R. Parsons
Mathematics Teacher/Mathematics Specialist
Palmer Elementary School
Easton, Pennsylvania

Cary Sikes
Mathematics Chairperson, K-2
Sherwood Elementary
Springfield, Missouri

Liza Starkey
Mathematics Resource Teacher
Taneytown Elementary School
Taneytown, Maryland

Rebecca J. Wilkins
Mathematics Coach and Curriculum Specialist
Saginaw Public Schools
Saginaw, Michigan

Heather Youngblood
Teacher
Sherwood Elementary
Springfield, Missouri

Jan Youtz
Mathematics Specialist Interventionist
Easton Area School District
Easton, Pennsylvania

Built-in Differentiated Instruction

Embedded for easy use

Glencoe Math provides every student access and opportunity to learn.

- **AL** Approaching Level
- **OL** On Level
- **BL** Beyond Level
- **EL** English Learners

All levels of Differentiated Instruction are found at point-of-use online in the Launch the Lesson and Teach the Concept sections.

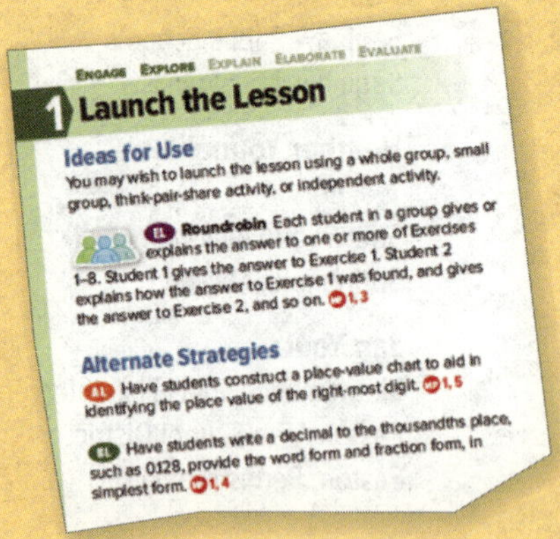

Weaved throughout *Glencoe Math*

- Each lesson offers great tools for Approaching Level, On Level & Beyond Level students, including three levels of differentiated instruction for English Language Learners
- Online Personal Tutors in English and Spanish
- Online Glossary with 13 Languages
- Tier 1 & 2 Intervention uses Hands-On activities followed by a Reteach practice page that allows them apply it and ensure conceptual understanding.
- Additional Response to Intervention resources are found online
- The Targeted Strategic Intervention is available online. Based on assessment results, teachers can find instruction to fill gaps in prerequisite skills.
- Intensive Intervention through SRA Number Worlds—a research proven curriculum (sold separately)

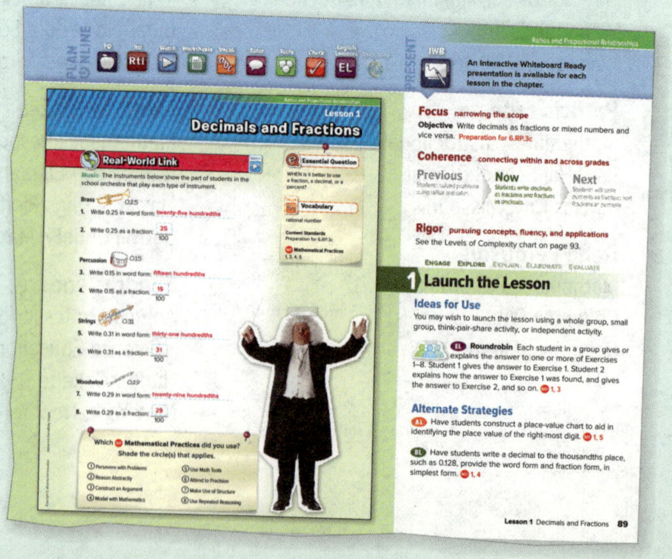

Mathematical Practices

Correlated to *Glencoe Math*, Course 2

For information about how to implement the Mathematical Practice Standards into your classroom, please view the professional development video *Standards for Mathematical Practice in Action* at connectED.mcgraw-hill.com.

Mathematical Practices	Student Edition	Page(s)
MP1 Make sense of problems and persevere in solving them. Mathematically proficient students start by explaining to themselves the meaning of a problem and looking for entry points to its solution. They analyze givens, constraints, relationships, and goals. They make conjectures about the form and meaning of the solution and plan a solution pathway rather than simply jumping into a solution attempt. They consider analogous problems, and try special cases and simpler forms of the original problem in order to gain insight into its solution. They monitor and evaluate their progress and change course if necessary. Older students might, depending on the context of the problem, transform algebraic expressions or change the viewing window on their graphing calculator to get the information they need. Mathematically proficient students can explain correspondences between equations, verbal descriptions, tables, and graphs or draw diagrams of important features and relationships, graph data, and search for regularity or trends. Younger students might rely on using concrete objects or pictures to help conceptualize and solve a problem. Mathematically proficient students check their answers to problems using a different method, and they continually ask themselves, "Does this make sense?" They can understand the approaches of others to solving complex problems and identify correspondences between different approaches.	A strong problem-solving strand is present throughout the textbook with an emphasis on strategies in the Problem-Solving Investigation lessons. Look for the **Persevere with Problems** head in the exercises.	14, 22, 30, 38, 41, 44, 50, 60, 70, 78, 86, 109, 108, 115, 116, 126, 133, 134, 137, 140, 148, 156, 164, 172, 196, 225, 228, 238, 268, 276, 288, 296, 297, 304, 307, 310, 316, 324, 332, 354, 362, 372, 380, 392, 400, 408, 420, 452, 462, 474, 486, 489, 492, 502, 510, 518, 540, 548, 560, 567, 590, 598, 618, 628, 636, 644, 647, 650, 658, 670, 682, 694, 716, 717, 726, 738, 746, 753, 756, 762, 770, 780, 781, 798, 806, 818, 821, 824, 834, 844
MP2 Reason abstractly and quantitatively. Mathematically proficient students make sense of quantities and their relationships in problem situations. They bring two complementary abilities to bear on problems involving quantitative relationships: the ability to *decontextualize*—to abstract a given situation and represent it symbolically and manipulate the representing symbols as if they have a life of their own, without necessarily attending to their referents—and the ability to *contextualize,* to pause as needed during the manipulation process in order to probe into the referents for the symbols involved. Quantitative reasoning entails habits of creating a coherent representation of the problem at hand; considering the units involved; attending to the meaning of quantities, not just how to compute them; and knowing and flexibly using different properties of operations and objects.	Students are routinely asked to write an equation or an expression in order to solve a real-world problem. Exercises that emphasize this practice are labeled as **Reason Abstractly**.	50, 60, 86, 134, 156, 164, 208, 232, 353, 354, 363, 366, 380, 392, 393, 400, 401, 407, 409, 420, 434, 442, 446, 452, 462, 467, 473, 487, 495, 501, 511, 517, 519, 561, 580, 612, 636, 645

Mathematical Practices	Student Edition	Page(s)
MP3 Construct viable arguments and critique the reasoning of others. Mathematically proficient students understand and use stated assumptions, definitions, and previously established results in constructing arguments. They make conjectures and build a logical progression of statements to explore the truth of their conjectures. They are able to analyze situations by breaking them into cases, and can recognize and use counterexamples. They justify their conclusions, communicate them to others, and respond to the arguments of others. They reason inductively about data, making plausible arguments that take into account the context from which the data arose. Mathematically proficient students are also able to compare the effectiveness of two plausible arguments, distinguish correct logic or reasoning from that which is flawed, and—if there is a flaw in an argument—explain what it is. Elementary students can construct arguments using concrete referents such as objects, drawings, diagrams, and actions. Such arguments can make sense and be correct, even though they are not generalized or made formal until later grades. Later, students learn to determine domains to which an argument applies. Students at all grades can listen or read the arguments of others, decide whether they make sense, and ask useful questions to clarify or improve the arguments.	Students are required to justify their reasoning in problems and to find the errors in samples of other's work. Look for these heads in the exercises: Justify Conclusions Reason Inductively Make a Conjecture Use a Counterexample Find the Error Which One Doesn't Belong Make a Prediction Multiple Representations Construct an Argument	8, 13, 14, 15, 22, 23, 30, 38, 39, 41, 51, 60, 61, 64, 70, 71, 78, 79, 86, 87, 101, 108, 117, 126, 127, 134, 137, 142, 148, 156, 157, 165, 171, 172, 176, 196, 208, 209, 220, 224, 238, 239, 242, 247, 248, 268, 276, 282, 288, 295, 296, 297, 303, 305, 316, 317, 324, 332, 333, 362, 366, 371, 372, 380, 381, 383, 392, 400, 408, 414, 420, 436, 441, 442, 446, 452, 453, 456, 461, 462, 468, 474, 475, 480, 485, 486, 489, 495, 502, 510, 540, 548, 549, 552, 560, 565, 566, 574, 580, 584, 590, 591, 598, 599, 612, 618, 622, 628, 629, 644, 647, 652, 658, 664, 670, 676, 682, 688, 693, 694, 695, 716, 720, 725, 726, 730, 732, 738, 746, 752, 753, 762, 763, 774, 780, 797, 798, 799, 806, 807, 812, 818, 819, 821, 826, 833, 838, 844 845
MP4 Model with mathematics. Mathematically proficient students can apply the mathematics they know to solve problems arising in everyday life, society, and the workplace. In early grades, this might be as simple as writing an addition equation to describe a situation. In middle grades, a student might apply proportional reasoning to plan a school event or analyze a problem in the community. By high school, a student might use geometry to solve a design problem or use a function to describe how one quantity of interest depends on another. Mathematically proficient students who can apply what they know are comfortable making assumptions and approximations to simplify a complicated situation, realizing that these may need revision later. They are able to identify important quantities in a practical situation and map their relationships using such tools as diagrams, two-way tables, graphs, flowcharts and formulas. They can analyze those relationships mathematically to draw conclusions. They routinely interpret their mathematical results in the context of the situation and reflect on whether the results make sense, possibly improving the model if it has not served its purpose.	Real-world applications in problem solving are woven throughout every lesson. In addition to the real-world examples in each lesson, look for Model with Mathematics heads in the exercises.	8, 29, 30, 38, 41, 49, 50, 54, 64, 70, 78, 86, 102, 107, 116, 120, 126, 134, 137, 142, 156, 163, 164, 176, 197, 202, 207, 208, 214, 220, 225, 232, 237, 238, 262, 268, 276, 288, 304, 307, 316, 324, 331, 354, 355, 361, 372, 383, 456, 462, 463, 468, 474, 480, 486, 489, 496, 502, 503, 518, 540, 559, 560, 567, 580, 590, 598, 618, 622, 628, 636, 643, 644, 669, 670, 676, 682, 687, 688, 694, 715, 732, 738, 745, 746, 747, 752, 769, 770, 780, 798, 806, 811, 817, 821, 834, 843, 844
MP5 Use appropriate tools strategically. Mathematically proficient students consider the available tools when solving a mathematical problem. These tools might include pencil and paper, concrete models, a ruler, a protractor, a calculator, a spreadsheet, a computer algebra system, a statistical package, or dynamic geometry software. Proficient students are sufficiently familiar with tools appropriate for their grade or course to make sound decisions about when each of these tools might be helpful, recognizing both the insight to be gained and their limitations. For example, mathematically proficient high school students analyze graphs of functions and solutions generated using a graphing calculator. They detect possible errors by strategically using estimation and other mathematical knowledge. When making mathematical models, they know that technology can enable them to visualize the results of varying assumptions, explore consequences, and compare predictions with data. Mathematically proficient students at various grade levels are able to identify relevant external mathematical resources, such as digital content located on a website, and use them to pose or solve problems. They are able to use technological tools to explore and deepen their understanding of concepts.	In addition to the traditional mathematical tools like estimating, using mental math, or measuring, students are encouraged to use software and the Internet in problem solving. Exercises utilizing this strategy are labeled with Use Math Tools.	14, 15, 30, 116, 140, 148, 164, 196, 219, 249, 262, 282, 288, 325, 333, 373, 380, 434, 436, 443, 486, 518, 554, 565, 572, 579, 581, 584, 652, 683, 739, 805, 812

Mathematical Practices	Student Edition	Page(s)
MP6 Attend to precision. Mathematically proficient students try to communicate precisely to others. They try to use clear definitions in discussion with others and in their own reasoning. They state the meaning of the symbols they choose, including using the equal sign consistently and appropriately. They are careful about specifying units of measure, and labeling axes to clarify the correspondence with quantities in a problem. They calculate accurately and efficiently, express numerical answers with a degree of precision appropriate for the problem context. In the elementary grades, students give carefully formulated explanations to each other. By the time they reach high school they have learned to examine claims and make explicit use of definitions.	Solutions are not just numbers, but include measurements to give the solution meaning. Look for Be Precise heads in the exercises.	22, 44, 147, 149, 221, 269, 307, 324, 392, 567, 570, 617, 650, 658, 664, 671, 824, 835
MP7 Look for and make use of structure. Mathematically proficient students look closely to discern a pattern or structure. Young students, for example, might notice that three and seven more is the same amount as seven and three more, or they may sort a collection of shapes according to how many sides the shapes have. Later, students will see 7×8 equals the well remembered $7 \times 5 + 7 \times 3$, in preparation for learning about the distributive property. In the expression $x^2 + 9x + 14$, older students can see the 14 as 2×7 and the 9 as $2 + 7$. They recognize the significance of an existing line in a geometric figure and can use the strategy of drawing an auxiliary line for solving problems. They also can step back for an overview and shift perspective. They can see complicated things, such as some algebraic expressions, as single objects or as being composed of several objects. For example, they can see $5 - 3(x - y)^2$ as 5 minus a positive number times a square and use that to realize that its value cannot be more than 5 for any real numbers x and y.	Emphasizing the structure of mathematics is present through use of classifying, explaining, giving examples as well as nonexamples. Exercises that emphasize this practice are labeled with Identify Structure.	208, 214, 220, 248, 268, 289, 372, 379, 380, 386, 452, 510, 539, 541, 549
MP8 Look for and express regularity in repeated reasoning. Mathematically proficient students notice if calculations are repeated, and look both for general methods and for shortcuts. Upper elementary students might notice when dividing 25 by 11 that they are repeating the same calculations over and over again, and conclude they have a repeating decimal. By paying attention to the calculation of slope as they repeatedly check whether points are on the line through (1, 2) with slope 3, middle school students might abstract the equation $(y - 2)/(x - 1) = 3$. Noticing the regularity in the way terms cancel when expanding $(x - 1)(x + 1)$, $(x - 1)(x^2 + x + 1)$, and $(x - 1)(x^3 + x^2 + x + 1)$ might lead them to the general formula for the sum of a geometric series. As they work to solve a problem, mathematically proficient students maintain oversight of the process, while attending to the details. They continually evaluate the reasonableness of their intermediate results.	Patterns in reasoning are demonstrated throughout leading students to sound mathematical conclusions. Exercises with Identify Repeated Reasoning heads exemplify this practice.	224, 225, 238, 262, 554, 619

Standards for Mathematics, Grade 7

Correlated to *Glencoe Math*, Course 2

Standards		Lesson(s)	Page(s)
Domain 7.RP Ratios and Proportional Relationships			
Analyze proportional relationships and use them to solve real-world and mathematical problems.			
7.RP.1	Compute unit rates associated with ratios of fractions, including ratios of lengths, areas and other quantities measured in like or different units. *For example, if a person walks 1/2 mile in each 1/4 hour, compute the unit rate as the complex fraction 1/2/1/4 miles per hour, equivalently 2 miles per hour.*	**IQL 1–1, 1–2**	**7–8, 17–24**
7.RP.2	Recognize and represent proportional relationships between quantities.	**IQL 1–1, 1–1, 1–3, 1–4, Ch. 1 PSI, 1–5, IQL 1–6, 1–6, IQL 1–7, 1–7, 1–8, 1–9, 2–4**	**7–8, 9–16, 25–32, 33–40, 41–43, 45–52, 53–54, 55–62, 63–64, 65–72, 73–80, 81–88, 129–136**
	a. Decide whether two quantities are in a proportional relationship, e.g., by testing for equivalent ratios in a table or graphing on a coordinate plane and observing whether the graph is a straight line through the origin.	**1–4, 1–5, IQL 1–6, 1–9**	**33–40, 45–52, 53–54, 81–88**
	b. Identify the constant of proportionality (unit rate) in tables, graphs, equations, diagrams, and verbal descriptions of proportional relationships.	**IQL 1–1, 1–1, 1–4, IQL 1–7, 1–7, 1–8, 1–9**	**7–8, 9–16, 33–40, 63–64, 65–72, 73–80, 81–88**
	c. Represent proportional relationships by equations. *For example, if total cost t is proportional to the number n of items purchased at a constant price p, the relationship between the total cost and the number of items can be expressed as* $t = pn$.	**1–6, 2–4**	**55–62, 129–136**
	d. Explain what a point (x, y) on the graph of a proportional relationship means in terms of the situation, with special attention to the points (0, 0) and $(1, r)$ where r is the unit rate.	**1–7**	**65–72**

IQL = Inquiry Lab for the lesson referenced **PSI** = Problem-Solving Investigation

Standards		Lesson(s)	Page(s)
7.RP.3	Use proportional relationships to solve multistep ratio and percent problems. *Examples: simple interest, tax, markups and markdowns, gratuities and commissions, fees, percent increase and decrease, percent error.*	**1–3, 1–6, IQL 2–1, 2–1, 2–2, IQL 2–3, 2–3, 2–4, Ch. 2 PSI, IQL 2–5, 2–5, 2–6, 2–7, 2–8, IQL 2–8, 4–7**	**25–32, 55–62, 99–102, 103–110, 111–118, 119–120, 121–128, 129–136, 137–139, 141–142, 143–150, 151–158, 159–166, 167–174, 175–176, 319–326**
Domain 7.NS The Number System			
Apply and extend previous understandings of operations with fractions to add, subtract, multiply, and divide rational numbers.			
7.NS.1	Apply and extend previous understandings of addition and subtraction to add and subtract rational numbers; represent addition and subtraction on a horizontal or vertical number line diagram.	**IQL 3–2, 3–2, IQL 3–3, 3–3, IQL 3–3, IQL 4–3, 4–3, 4–4, 4–5**	**199–202, 203–210, 211–214, 215–222, 223–224, 279–282, 283–290, 291–298, 299–306**
	a. Describe situations in which opposite quantities combine to make 0. *For example, a hydrogen atom has 0 charge because its two constituents are oppositely charged.*	**3–2**	**203–210**
	b. Understand $p + q$ as the number located a distance $\|q\|$ from p, in the positive or negative direction depending on whether q is positive or negative. Show that a number and its opposite have a sum of 0 (are additive inverses). Interpret sums of rational numbers by describing real-world contexts.	**3–2, IQL 4–3**	**203–210, 279–282**
	c. Understand subtraction of rational numbers as adding the additive inverse, $p - q = p + (-q)$. Show that the distance between two rational numbers on the number line is the absolute value of their difference, and apply this principle in real-world contexts.	**IQL 3–3, 3–3, IQL 3–3, 4–3**	**211–214, 215–222, 223–224, 283–290**
	d. Apply properties of operations as strategies to add and subtract rational numbers.	**3–2, 3–3, 4–3, 4–4, 4–5**	**203–210, 215–222, 283–290, 291–298, 299–306**
7.NS.2	Apply and extend previous understandings of multiplication and division and of fractions to multiply and divide rational numbers.	**IQL 3–4, 3–4, IQL 3–4, 3–5, 4–1, 4–2, 4–6, 4–7, 4–8**	**229–232, 233–240, 241–242, 243–250, 263–270, 271–278, 311–318, 319–326, 327–334**
	a. Understand that multiplication is extended from fractions to rational numbers by requiring that operations continue to satisfy the properties of operations, particularly the distributive property, leading to products such as $(-1)(-1) = 1$ and the rules for multiplying signed numbers. Interpret products of rational numbers by describing real-world contexts.	**3–4, IQL 3–4, 4–6**	**233–240, 241–242, 311–318**
	b. Understand that integers can be divided, provided that the divisor is not zero, and every quotient of integers (with non-zero divisor) is a rational number. If p and q are integers, then $-(p/q) = (-p)/q = p/(-q)$. Interpret quotients of rational numbers by describing real-world contexts.	**3–5, 4–2**	**243–250, 271–278**
	c. Apply properties of operations as strategies to multiply and divide rational numbers.	**3–4, IQL 3–4, 3–5, 4–6, 4–8**	**233–240, 241–242, 243–250, 311–318, 327–334**

IQL = Inquiry Lab for the lesson referenced **PSI** = Problem-Solving Investigation

Standards		Lesson(s)	Page(s)
	d. Convert a rational number to a decimal using long division; know that the decimal form of a rational number terminates in 0s or eventually repeats.	**4–1**	**263–270**
7.NS.3	Solve real-world and mathematical problems involving the four operations with rational numbers.	**1–2, IQL 3–2, 3–2, IQL 3–3, 3–3, Ch. 3 PSI, IQL 3–4, 3–4, 3–5, IQL 4–3, 4–3, 4–4, 4–5, Ch. 4 PSI, 4–6, 4–7, 4–8, Ch. 5 PSI**	**17–24, 199–202, 203–210, 211– 214, 215–222, 225–227, 229–232, 233–240, 243–250, 279–282, 283–290, 291–298, 299–306, 307–309, 311–318, 319–326, 327–334, 383–385**
Domain 7.EE	**Expressions and Equations**		
Use properties of operations to generate equivalent expressions.			
7.EE.1	Apply properties of operations as strategies to add, subtract, factor, and expand linear expressions with rational coefficients.	**5–3, 5–4, 5–5, 5–6, 5–7, IQL 5–8, 5–8**	**367–374, 375–382, 387–394, 395–402, 403–410, 411–414, 415–422**
7.EE.2	Understand that rewriting an expression in different forms in a problem context can shed light on the problem and how the quantities in it are related. *For example, $a + 0.05a = 1.05a$ means that "increase by 5%" is the same as "multiply by 1.05."*	**2–6, 5–3, 5–4, 5–5, 5–6, 5–7, 5–8**	**151–158, 367–374, 375–382, 387–394, 395–402, 403–410, 415–422**
Solve real-life and mathematical problems using numerical and algebraic expressions and equations.			
7.EE.3	Solve multi-step real-life and mathematical problems posed with positive and negative rational numbers in any form (whole numbers, fractions, and decimals), using tools strategically. Apply properties of operations to calculate with numbers in any form; convert between forms as appropriate; and assess the reasonableness of answers using mental computation and estimation strategies. *For example: If a woman making $25 an hour gets a 10% raise, she will make an additional 1/10 of her salary an hour, or $2.50, for a new salary of $27.50. If you want to place a towel bar 9 3/4 inches long in the center of a door that is 27 1/2 inches wide, you will need to place the bar about 9 inches from each edge; this estimate can be used as a check on the exact computation.*	**IQL 2–1, 2–1, 2–2, IQL 2–3, 2–4, Ch. 2 PSI, IQL 2–5, 2–5, 2–6, 2–7, 2–8, 3–2, Ch. 3 PSI, 3–4, 4–1, 4–2, 4–3, 4–4, 4–5, Ch. 4 PSI, 4–6, 4–8, Ch. 6 PSI**	**99–102, 103–110, 111–118, 119–120, 129–136, 137–139, 141–142, 143–150, 151–158, 159–166, 167–174, 203–210, 225–227, 233–240, 263–270, 271–278, 283–290, 291–298, 299–306, 307–309, 311–318, 327–334, 489–491**
7.EE.4	Use variables to represent quantities in a real-world or mathematical problem, and construct simple equations and inequalities to solve problems by reasoning about the quantities.	**IQL 6–1, 6–1, IQL 6–2, 6–2, IQL 6–3, 6–3, IQL 6–4, 6–4, IQL 6–5, 6–5, IQL 6–6, 6–6, 6–7, 6–8**	**433–436, 437–444, 445–446, 447–454, 455–456, 457–464, 465–468, 469–476, 477–480, 481–488, 493–496, 497–504, 505–512, 513–520**
	a. Solve word problems leading to equations of the form $px + q = r$ and $p(x + q) = r$, where p, q, and r are specific rational numbers. Solve equations of these forms fluently. Compare an algebraic solution to an arithmetic solution, identifying the sequence of the operations used in each approach. *For example, the perimeter of a rectangle is 54 cm. Its length is 6 cm. What is its width?*	**IQL 6–1, 6–1, IQL 6–2, 6–2, IQL 6–3, 6–3, IQL 6–4, 6–4, IQL 6–5, 6–5**	**433–436, 437–444, 445–446, 447–454, 455–456, 457–464, 465–468, 469–476, 477–480, 481–488**

IQL = Inquiry Lab for the lesson referenced **PSI** = Problem-Solving Investigation

Standards		Lesson(s)	Page(s)
	b. Solve word problems leading to inequalities of the form $px + q > r$ or $px + q < r$, where p, q, and r are specific rational numbers. Graph the solution set of the inequality and interpret it in the context of the problem. *For example: As a salesperson, you are paid $50 per week plus $3 per sale. This week you want your pay to be at least $100. Write an inequality for the number of sales you need to make, and describe the solutions.*	**IQL 6–6, 6–6, 6–7, 6–8**	**493–496, 497–504, 505–512, 513–520**
Domain 7.G Geometry			
Draw, construct, and describe geometrical figures and describe the relationships between them.			
7.G.1	Solve problems involving scale drawings of geometric figures, including computing actual lengths and areas from a scale drawing and reproducing a scale drawing at a different scale.	**Ch. 7 PSI, IQL 7–4, 7–4, IQL 7–4**	**567–569, 571–574, 575–582, 583–584**
7.G.2	Draw (freehand, with ruler and protractor, and with technology) geometric shapes with given conditions. Focus on constructing triangles from three measures of angles or sides, noticing when the conditions determine a unique triangle, more than one triangle, or no triangle.	**IQL 7–3, 7–3, IQL 7–3**	**551–554, 555–562, 563–566**
7.G.3	Describe the two-dimensional figures that result from slicing three-dimensional figures, as in plane sections of right rectangular prisms and right rectangular pyramids.	**7–6**	**593–600**
Solve real-life and mathematical problems involving angle measure, area, surface area, and volume.			
7.G.4	Know the formulas for the area and circumference of a circle and use them to solve problems; give an informal derivation of the relationship between the circumference and area of a circle.	**IQL 8–1, 8–1, IQL 8–2, 8–2, 8–3, Ch. 8 PSI**	**611–612, 613–620, 621–622, 623–630, 631–638, 647–649**
7.G.5	Use facts about supplementary, complementary, vertical, and adjacent angles in a multi-step problem to write and solve simple equations for an unknown angle in a figure.	**7–1, 7–2**	**535–542, 543–550**
7.G.6	Solve real-world and mathematical problems involving area, volume and surface area of two- and three-dimensional objects composed of triangles, quadrilaterals, polygons, cubes, and right prisms.	**8–3, 8–4, Ch. 8 PSI, IQL 8–5, 8–5, IQL 8–6, 8–6, IQL 8–6, 8–7, IQL 8–8, 8–8**	**631–638, 639–646, 647–649, 651–652, 653–660, 661–664, 665–672, 673–676, 677–684, 685–688, 689–696**

IQL = Inquiry Lab for the lesson referenced **PSI** = Problem-Solving Investigation

Standards		Lesson(s)	Page(s)
Domain 7.SP Statistics and Probability			
Use random sampling to draw inferences about a population.			
7.SP.1	Understand that statistics can be used to gain information about a population by examining a sample of the population; generalizations about a population from a sample are valid only if the sample is representative of that population. Understand that random sampling tends to produce representative samples and support valid inferences.	**10–1, 10–2, Ch. 10 PSI**	**793–800, 801–808, 821–823**
7.SP.2	Use data from a random sample to draw inferences about a population with an unknown characteristic of interest. Generate multiple samples (or simulated samples) of the same size to gauge the variation in estimates or predictions. *For example, estimate the mean word length in a book by randomly sampling words from the book; predict the winner of a school election based on randomly sampled survey data. Gauge how far off the estimate or prediction might be.*	**10–1, 10–2, IQL 10–2**	**793–800, 801–808, 809–812**
Draw informal comparative inferences about two populations.			
7.SP.3	Informally assess the degree of visual overlap of two numerical data distributions with similar variabilities, measuring the difference between the centers by expressing it as a multiple of a measure of variability. *For example, the mean height of players on the basketball team is 10 cm greater than the mean height of players on the soccer team, about twice the variability (mean absolute deviation) on either team; on a dot plot, the separation between the two distributions of heights is noticeable.*	**IQL 10–4, IQL 10–4**	**825–826, 837–838**
7.SP.4	Use measures of center and measures of variability for numerical data from random samples to draw informal comparative inferences about two populations. *For example, decide whether the words in a chapter of a seventh-grade science book are generally longer than the words in a chapter of a fourth-grade science book.*	**IQL 10–4, 10–4**	**825–826, 827–836**
Investigate chance processes and develop, use, and evaluate probability models.			
7.SP.5	Understand that the probability of a chance event is a number between 0 and 1 that expresses the likelihood of the event occurring. Larger numbers indicate greater likelihood. A probability near 0 indicates an unlikely event, a probability around 1/2 indicates an event that is neither unlikely nor likely, and a probability near 1 indicates a likely event.	**9–1, 9–5**	**711–718, 757–764**
7.SP.6	Approximate the probability of a chance event by collecting data on the chance process that produces it and observing its long-run relative frequency, and predict the approximate relative frequency given the probability. *For example, when rolling a number cube 600 times, predict that a 3 or 6 would be rolled roughly 200 times, but probably not exactly 200 times.*	**IQL 9–2**	**719–720**

IQL = Inquiry Lab for the lesson referenced **PSI** = Problem-Solving Investigation

Standards		Lesson(s)	Page(s)
7.SP.7	Develop a probability model and use it to find probabilities of events. Compare probabilities from a model to observed frequencies; if the agreement is not good, explain possible sources of the discrepancy.	**9–1, IQL 9–2, 9–2, IQL 9–2**	**711–718, 719–720, 721–728, 729–732**
	a. Develop a uniform probability model by assigning equal probability to all outcomes, and use the model to determine probabilities of events. *For example, if a student is selected at random from a class, find the probability that Jane will be selected and the probability that a girl will be selected.*	**9–1, IQL 9–2, 9–2, IQL 9–2**	**711–718, 719–720, 721–728, 729–732**
	b. Develop a probability model (which may not be uniform) by observing frequencies in data generated from a chance process. *For example, find the approximate probability that a spinning penny will land heads up or that a tossed paper cup will land open-end down. Do the outcomes for the spinning penny appear to be equally likely based on the observed frequencies?*	**9–2, IQL 9–2**	**721–728, 729–732**
7.SP.8	Find probabilities of compound events using organized lists, tables, tree diagrams, and simulation.	**9–3, 9–4, IQL 9–4, Ch. 9 PSI, 9–5, 9–6, IQL 9–7, 9–7**	**733–740, 741–748, 749–752, 753–755, 757–764, 765–772, 773–774, 775–782**
	a. Understand that, just as with simple events, the probability of a compound event is the fraction of outcomes in the sample space for which the compound event occurs.	**9–3, 9–5, 9–6, 9–7**	**733–740, 757–764, 765–772, 775–782**
	b. Represent sample spaces for compound events using methods such as organized lists, tables and tree diagrams. For an event described in everyday language (e.g., "rolling double sixes"), identify the outcomes in the sample space which compose the event.	**9–3, 9–5, IQL 9–7, 9–7**	**733–740, 757–764, 773–774, 775–782**
	c. Design and use a simulation to generate frequencies for compound events. *For example, use random digits as a simulation tool to approximate the answer to the question: If 40% of donors have type A blood, what is the probability that it will take at least 4 donors to find one with type A blood?*	**9–4, IQL 9–4, Ch. 9 PSI, IQL 9–7**	**741–748, 749–752, 753–755, 773–774**

IQL = Inquiry Lab for the lesson referenced **PSI** = Problem-Solving Investigation

connected.mcgraw-hill.com

STEM McGraw-Hill is committed to providing instructional materials in Science, Technology, Engineering, and Mathematics (STEM) that give all students a solid foundation, one that prepares them for college and careers in the 21st century.

Send all inquiries to:
McGraw-Hill Education
8787 Orion Place
Columbus, OH 43240

ISBN: 978-0-07-668323-9 (*Teacher Edition, Volume 2*)
MHID: 0-07-668323-0 (*Teacher Edition, Volume 2*)
ISBN: 978-0-07-668319-2 (*Student Edition, Volume 2*)
MHID: 0-07-668319-2 (*Student Edition, Volume 2*)

Printed in the United States of America.

3 4 5 6 7 8 9 LMN 21 20 19 18 17

CONTENTS IN BRIEF

Units organized by domain

Glencoe Math is organized into units based on groups of related standards called domains. The Standards for MP Mathematical Practices are embedded throughout the course.

Mathematical Practices Handbook

Tetra Images/Getty Images

UNIT 1

Richard Drury/Photodisc/Getty Images

UNIT 2

Gerald Nowak/Westend61/Photolibrary

UNIT 3

Jill Braaten/McGraw-Hill Education

UNIT 4

©Photo by Scott Bauer/USDA

UNIT 5

Back in the Pack dog portraits/Flickr/Getty Images

Online Student Center

Resources for students at school and on the go

Log on to connectED.mcgraw-hill.com. In addition to access to their eBook and electronic resources, students can view the homework assignments you have made and receive messages from you with reminders about upcoming events or plans for days when school is not in session.

Online Teacher Center

Log on to connectED.mcgraw-hill.com to access the online teacher center to create lesson plans, customize interactive whiteboard lessons, send messages and assignments to students, as well as view all of the available resources for each chapter.

The following icons appear throughout the online teacher center to alert teachers when additional support is available.

- You can view videos of model lessons and listen to testimonials concerning best practices for use in the classroom.
- RtI You can find resources to differentiate instruction to meet the needs of all students.

Everything you need,

anytime, anywhere.

With ConnectED, you have instant access to all of your study materials—anytime, anywhere. From homework materials to study guides—it's all in one place and just a click away. ConnectED even allows you to collaborate with your classmates and use mobile apps to make studying easy.

Resources built for you—available 24/7:

- Your eBook available wherever you are
- Personal Tutors and Self-Check Quizzes to help your learning
- An Online Calendar with all of your due dates
- eFlashcard App to make studying easy
- A message center to stay in touch

Go Mobile!

Visit mheonline.com/apps to get entertainment, instruction, and education on the go with ConnectED Mobile and our other apps available for your device.

GET IT ON Google play   Available on the App Store

Go Online!

connectED.mcgraw-hill.com

your Username

your Password

Vocab Learn about new vocabulary words.

Watch Watch animations and videos.

Tutor See and hear a teacher explain how to solve problems.

Tools Explore concepts with virtual manipulatives.

Sketchpad Discover concepts using The Geometer's Sketchpad®.

Check Check your progress.

eHelp Get targeted homework help.

Worksheets Access practice worksheets.

Online Resources
These icons appear throughout the interactive Student Edition to alert students that there are online resources to enhance their learning experience. The icons are also the navigation tools in the Student Center for easy access to their resources.

GO mobile
The McGraw-Hill Education apps headquarters is constantly updated with new apps that provide mobile ways to practice and review math skills through various forms of media.

Chapter 1 concentrates on the **Ratios and Proportional Relationships**. However, aspects of **The Number System** are also used in the study of ratios and proportional reasoning.

Ratios and Proportional Relationships

Analyze proportional relationships and use them to solve real-world and mathematical problems.

Standard	Lesson
7.RP.1	2
7.RP.2	1, 3, 4, Problem-Solving Investigation, 5, 6, 7, 8, 9
7.RP.3	3, 6

The Number System

Apply and extend previous understandings of operations with fractions to add, subtract, multiply, and divide rational numbers.

Standard	Lesson
7.NS.3	2

UNIT 1 Ratios and Proportional Relationships

UNIT PROJECT PREVIEW page 2

Chapter 1 Ratios and Proportional Reasoning

Essential Question

HOW can you show that two objects are proportional?

Chapter 2
Percents

Essential Question

HOW can percent help you understand situations involving money?

Chapter 2 concentrates on the **Ratios and Proportional Relationships**. However, aspects of **Expressions and Equations** are also used in the study of percents.

Ratios and Proportional Relationships

Analyze proportional relationships and use them to solve real-world and mathematical problems.

Standard	Lesson
7.RP.2	4
7.RP.3	1, 2, 3, 4, Problem-Solving Investigation, 5, 6, 7, 8

Expressions and Equations

Use properties of operations to generate equivalent expressions.

Standard	Lesson
7.EE.2	6

Solve real-life and mathematical problems using numerical and algebraic expressions and equations.

Standard	Lesson
7.EE.3	1, 2, 4, Problem-Solving Investigation, 5, 6, 7, 8

Chapter 3 concentrates on **The Number System**. However, aspects of **Expressions and Equations** are also used in the study of integers.

The Number System

Apply and extend previous understandings of operations with fractions to add, subtract, multiply, and divide rational numbers.

Standard	Lesson
7.NS.1	2, 3
7.NS.2	4, 5
7.NS.3	1, 2, 3, Problem-Solving Investigation, 4, 5

Expressions and Equations

Solve real-life and mathematical problems using numerical and algebraic expressions and equations.

Standard	Lesson
7.EE.3	2, Problem-Solving Investigation, 4

UNIT PROJECT PREVIEW page 185

Chapter 3 Integers

Essential Question

WHAT happens when you add, subtract, multiply, and divide integers?

Real World p. 233

Chapter 4
Rational Numbers

Essential Question

WHAT happens when you add, subtract, multiply, and divide fractions?

Explore the Ocean Depths

The Number System

Chapter 4 concentrates on **The Number System**. However, aspects of **Expressions and Equations** and **Ratios and Proportional Relationships** are also used in the study of rational numbers.

The Number System

Apply and extend previous understandings of operations with fractions to add, subtract, multiply, and divide rational numbers.

Standard	Lesson
7.NS.1	3, 4, 5
7.NS.2	1, 2, 6, 7, 8
7.NS.3	3, 4, 5, Problem-Solving Investigation, 6, 7, 8

Expressions and Equations

Solve real-life and mathematical problems using numerical and algebraic expressions and equations.

Standard	Lesson
7.EE.3	1, 2, 3, 4, 5, Problem-Solving Investigation, 6

Ratios and Proportional Relationships

Analyze proportional relationships and use them to solve real-world and mathematical problems.

Standard	Lesson
7.RP.3	7

Chapter 5 concentrates on the **Expressions and Equations**. However, aspects of **The Number System** are also used in the study of expressions.

Expressions and Equations

Use properties of operations to generate equivalent expressions.

Standard	Lesson
7.EE.1	1, 2, 3, 4, 5, 6, 7, 8
7.EE.2	1, 2, 3, 4, 5, 6, 7, 8

The Number System

Apply and extend previous understandings of operations with fractions to add, subtract, multiply, and divide rational numbers.

Standard	Lesson
7.NS.3	Problem-Solving Investigation

UNIT 3 Expressions and Equations

UNIT PROJECT PREVIEW page 344

Chapter 5
Expressions

Essential Question

HOW can you use numbers and symbols to represent mathematical ideas?

Chapter 6 Equations and Inequalities

Essential Question

WHAT does it mean to say two quantities are equal?

Chapter 6 concentrates on the **Expressions and Equations**.

Expressions and Equations

Solve real-life and mathematical problems using numerical and algebraic expressions and equations.

Standard	Lesson
7.EE.3	Problem-Solving Investigation
7.EE.4	1, 2, 3, 4, 5, 6, 7, 8

Chapter 7 concentrates on the **Geometry**.

Geometry

Draw, construct, and describe geometrical figures and describe the relationships between them.

Standard	Lesson
7.G.1	Problem-Solving Investigation, 4
7.G.2	3
7.G.3	5 (Preparation), 6

Solve real-life and mathematical problems involving angle measure, area, surface area, and volume.

Standard	Lesson
7.G.5	1, 2

UNIT 4 Geometry

UNIT PROJECT PREVIEW page 530

Chapter 7 Geometric Figures

Essential Question

HOW does geometry help us describe real-world objects?

Real World p. 535

Chapter 8
Measure Figures

Essential Question

HOW do measurements help you describe real-world objects?

Real World p. 623

Chapter 8 concentrates on the **Geometry**.

Geometry

Solve real-life and mathematical problems involving angle measure, area, surface area, and volume.

Standard	Lesson
7.G.4	1, 2, 3, Problem-Solving Investigation
7.G.6	Problem-Solving Investigation, 4, 5, 6, 7, 8

Chapter 9 concentrates on the **Statistics and Probability**.

Statistics and Probability

Investigate chance processes and develop, use, and evaluate probability models.

Standard	Lesson
7.SP.5	1, 5
7.SP.7	1, 2
7.SP.8	3, 4, Problem-Solving Investigation, 5, 6, 7

UNIT 5 Statistics and Probability

UNIT PROJECT PREVIEW page 706

Chapter 9 Probability

Essential Question

HOW can you predict the outcome of future events?

Chapter 10 Statistics

Essential Question

HOW do you know which type of graph to use when displaying data?

Chapter 10 concentrates on the **Statistics and Probability**.

Statistics and Probability

Use random sampling to draw inferences about a population.

Standard	Lesson
7.SP.1	1, 2, 3 (Extension), 5 (Extension)
7.SP.2	1, 2

Draw informal comparative inferences about two populations.

Standard	Lesson
7.SP.4	4

Standards for MATHEMATICS, Grade 7

***Glencoe Math*, Course** 2, focuses on four critical areas: (1) developing understanding of and applying proportional relationships; (2) operations with rational numbers and working with expressions and linear equations; (3) solving problems involving scale drawings, geometric constructions, and surface area, and volume; and (4) drawing inferences about populations.

Content Standards

Ratios and Proportional Relationships

- Analyze proportional relationships and use them to solve real-world and mathematical problems.

The Number System

- Apply and extend previous understandings of operations with fractions to add, subtract, multiply, and divide rational numbers.

Expressions and Equations

- Use properties of operations to generate equivalent expressions.
- Solve real-life and mathematical problems using numerical and algebraic expressions and equations.

Geometry

- Draw, construct and describe geometrical figures and describe the relationships between them.
- Solve real-life and mathematical problems involving angle measure, area, surface area, and volume.

Statistics and Probability

- Use random sampling to draw inferences about a population.
- Draw informal comparative inferences about two populations.
- Investigate chance processes and develop, use, and evaluate probability models.

MP Mathematical Practices

1. Make sense of problems and persevere in solving them.
2. Reason abstractly and quantitatively.
3. Construct viable arguments and critique the reasoning of others.
4. Model with mathematics.
5. Use appropriate tools strategically.
6. Attend to precision.
7. Look for and make use of structure.
8. Look for and express regularity in repeated reasoning.

Track Your Progress

These pages list the key ideas that you should be able to understand by the end of the year. You will rate how much you know about each one. Don't worry if you have no clue **before** you learn about them. Watch how your knowledge grows as the year progresses!

I have no clue. I've heard of it. I know it!

7.RP Ratios and Proportional Relationships	Before: I have no clue.	Before: I've heard of it.	Before: I know it!	After: I have no clue.	After: I've heard of it.	After: I know it!
Analyze proportional relationships and use them to solve real-world and mathematical problems.						
7.RP.1 Compute unit rates associated with ratios of fractions, including ratios of lengths, areas and other quantities measured in like or different units.						
7.RP.2 Recognize and represent proportional relationships between quantities. **a.** Decide whether two quantities are in a proportional relationship, e.g., by testing for equivalent ratios in a table or graphing on a coordinate plane and observing whether the graph is a straight line through the origin. **b.** Identify the constant of proportionality (unit rate) in tables, graphs, equations, diagrams, and verbal descriptions of proportional relationships. **c.** Represent proportional relationships by equations. **d.** Explain what a point (x, y) on the graph of a proportional relationship means in terms of the situation, with special attention to the points (0, 0) and $(1, r)$ where r is the unit rate.						
7.RP.3 Use proportional relationships to solve multistep ratio and percent problems.						

7.NS The Number System	Before: I have no clue.	Before: I've heard of it.	Before: I know it!	After: I have no clue.	After: I've heard of it.	After: I know it!
Apply and extend previous understandings of operations with fractions to add, subtract, multiply, and divide rational numbers.						
7.NS.1 Apply and extend previous understandings of addition and subtraction to add and subtract rational numbers; represent addition and subtraction on a horizontal or vertical number line diagram. **a.** Describe situations in which opposite quantities combine to make 0. **b.** Understand $p + q$ as the number located a distance $\lvert q \rvert$ from p, in the positive or negative direction depending on whether q is positive or negative. Show that a number and its opposite have a sum of 0 (are additive inverses). Interpret sums of rational numbers by describing real-world contexts. **c.** Understand subtraction of rational numbers as adding the additive inverse, $p - q = p + (-q)$. Show that the distance between two rational numbers on the number line is the absolute value of their difference, and apply this principle in real-world contexts. **d.** Apply properties of operations as strategies to add and subtract rational numbers.						

Grade 7

Track Your Progress

The content knowledge that your students will learn this year is listed on these pages.

Prior to beginning each chapter, you will be reminded to have your students rate their knowledge of each content standard covered in that chapter. Then, at the end of each chapter, you will be reminded to have your students return to these pages to rate their knowledge again. They should see their content knowledge increasing as the year progresses. Prior to taking the assessment, students can review their ratings and determine which standards, if any, with which they still need help.

Use the table below to reference the standards covered in each chapter.

Chapter	
1	7.RP.1, 7.RP.2*, 7.RP.2a, 7.RP.2b, 7.RP.2c*, 7.RP.2d, 7.RP.3*, 7.NS.3
2	7.RP.2*, 7.RP.2c*, 7.RP.3*, 7.EE.2*, 7.EE.3
3	7.NS.1*, 7.NS.1a, 7.NS.1b*, 7.NS.1c*, 7.NS.1d*, 7.NS.2*, 7.NS.2a*, 7.NS.2b*, 7.NS.2c*, 7.NS.3*, 7.EE.3
4	7.NS.1*, 7.NS.1b*, 7.NS.1c*, 7.NS.1d*, 7.NS.2*, 7.NS.2a*, 7.NS.2b*, 7.NS.2c*, 7.NS.2d, 7.NS.3*, 7.RP.3*, 7.EE.3
5	7.EE.1, 7.EE.2*, 7.NS.3*
6	7.EE.3, 7.EE.4, 7.EE.4a, 7.EE.4b
7	7.G.1, 7.G.2, 7.G.3, 7.G.5
8	7.G.4, 7.G.6
9	7.SP.5, 7.SP.6, 7.SP.7, 7.SP.7a, 7.SP.7b, 7.SP.8, 7.SP.8a, 7.SP.8b, 7.SP.8c
10	7.SP.1, 7.SP.2, 7.SP.3, 7.SP.4

*Students will learn these standards across multiple chapters. You may wish to have your students rate their knowledge before and after completing these standards.

7.NS The Number System *continued*	Before			After		
7.NS.2 Apply and extend previous understandings of multiplication and division and of fractions to multiply and divide rational numbers. **a.** Understand that multiplication is extended from fractions to rational numbers by requiring that operations continue to satisfy the properties of operations, particularly the distributive property, leading to products such as $(-1)(-1) = 1$ and the rules for multiplying signed numbers. Interpret products of rational numbers by describing real-world contexts. **b.** Understand that integers can be divided, provided that the divisor is not zero, and every quotient of integers (with non-zero divisor) is a rational number. If p and q are integers, then $-(p/q) = (-p)/q = p/(-q)$. Interpret quotients of rational numbers by describing real-world contexts. **c.** Apply properties of operations as strategies to multiply and divide rational numbers. **d.** Convert a rational number to a decimal using long division; know that the decimal form of a rational number terminates in 0s or eventually repeats.						
7.NS.3 Solve real-world and mathematical problems involving the four operations with rational numbers.						

7.EE Expressions and Equations	Before			After		
Use properties of operations to generate equivalent expressions.						
7.EE.1 Apply properties of operations as strategies to add, subtract, factor, and expand linear expressions with rational coefficients.						
7.EE.2 Understand that rewriting an expression in different forms in a problem context can shed light on the problem and how the quantities in it are related.						
Solve real-life and mathematical problems using numerical and algebraic expressions and equations.						
7.EE.3 Solve multi-step real-life and mathematical problems posed with positive and negative rational numbers in any form (whole numbers, fractions, and decimals), using tools strategically. Apply properties of operations to calculate with numbers in any form; convert between forms as appropriate; and assess the reasonableness of answers using mental computation and estimation strategies.						
7.EE.4 Use variables to represent quantities in a real-world or mathematical problem, and construct simple equations and inequalities to solve problems by reasoning about the quantities. **a.** Solve word problems leading to equations of the form $px + q = r$ and $p(x + q) = r$, where p, q, and r are specific rational numbers. Solve equations of these forms fluently. Compare an algebraic solution to an arithmetic solution, identifying the sequence of the operations used in each approach. **b.** Solve word problems leading to inequalities of the form $px + q > r$ or $px + q < r$, where p, q, and r are specific rational numbers. Graph the solution set of the inequality and interpret it in the context of the problem.						

7.G Geometry	Before 😞	Before 😐	Before 🙂	After 😞	After 😐	After 🙂
Draw, construct, and describe geometrical figures and describe the relationships between them.						
7.G.1 Solve problems involving scale drawings of geometric figures, including computing actual lengths and areas from a scale drawing and reproducing a scale drawing at a different scale.						
7.G.2 Draw (freehand, with ruler and protractor, and with technology) geometric shapes with given conditions. Focus on constructing triangles from three measures of angles or sides, noticing when the conditions determine a unique triangle, more than one triangle, or no triangle.						
7.G.3 Describe the two-dimensional figures that result from slicing three-dimensional figures, as in plane sections of right rectangular prisms and right rectangular pyramids.						
Solve real-life and mathematical problems involving angle measure, area, surface area, and volume.						
7.G.4 Know the formulas for the area and circumference of a circle and use them to solve problems; give an informal derivation of the relationship between the circumference and area of a circle.						
7.G.5 Use facts about supplementary, complementary, vertical, and adjacent angles in a multi-step problem to write and solve simple equations for an unknown angle in a figure.						
7.G.6 Solve real-world and mathematical problems involving area, volume and surface area of two- and three-dimensional objects composed of triangles, quadrilaterals, polygons, cubes, and right prisms.						

7.SP Statistics and Probability	Before 😞	Before 😐	Before 🙂	After 😞	After 😐	After 🙂
Use random sampling to draw inferences about a population.						
7.SP.1 Understand that statistics can be used to gain information about a population by examining a sample of the population; generalizations about a population from a sample are valid only if the sample is representative of that population. Understand that random sampling tends to produce representative samples and support valid inferences.						
7.SP.2 Use data from a random sample to draw inferences about a population with an unknown characteristic of interest. Generate multiple samples (or simulated samples) of the same size to gauge the variation in estimates or predictions.						
Draw informal comparative inferences about two populations.						
7.SP.3 Informally assess the degree of visual overlap of two numerical data distributions with similar variabilities, measuring the difference between the centers by expressing it as a multiple of a measure of variability.						

7.SP Statistics and Probability *continued*	Before 🙁	Before 😐	Before 🙂	After 🙁	After 😐	After 🙂
7.SP.4 Use measures of center and measures of variability for numerical data from random samples to draw informal comparative inferences about two populations.						
Investigate chance processes and develop, use, and evaluate probability models.						
7.SP.5 Understand that the probability of a chance event is a number between 0 and 1 that expresses the likelihood of the event occurring. Larger numbers indicate greater likelihood. A probability near 0 indicates an unlikely event, a probability around 1/2 indicates an event that is neither unlikely nor likely, and a probability near 1 indicates a likely event.						
7.SP.6 Approximate the probability of a chance event by collecting data on the chance process that produces it and observing its long-run relative frequency, and predict the approximate relative frequency given the probability.						
7.SP.7 Develop a probability model and use it to find probabilities of events. Compare probabilities from a model to observed frequencies; if the agreement is not good, explain possible sources of the discrepancy. **a.** Develop a uniform probability model by assigning equal probability to all outcomes, and use the model to determine probabilities of events. **b.** Develop a probability model (which may not be uniform) by observing frequencies in data generated from a chance process.						
7.SP.8 Find probabilities of compound events using organized lists, tables, tree diagrams, and simulation. **a.** Understand that, just as with simple events, the probability of a compound event is the fraction of outcomes in the sample space for which the compound event occurs. **b.** Represent sample spaces for compound events using methods such as organized lists, tables and tree diagrams. For an event described in everyday language (e.g., "rolling double sixes"), identify the outcomes in the sample space which compose the event. **c.** Design and use a simulation to generate frequencies for compound events.						

UNIT 3
Expressions and Equations

Essential Question

HOW can you communicate mathematical ideas effectively?

Chapter 5
Expressions

Algebraic expressions can be used to represent real-world situations. In this chapter, you will apply the properties of operations to simplify and evaluate algebraic expressions.

Chapter 6
Equations and Inequalities

An equation is a mathematical sentence stating that two expressions are equal. In this chapter, you will use the properties of equality to solve equations algebraically. Then you will apply what you learn to solve inequalities.

Expressions and Equations

Plan Online connectED.mcgraw-hill.com

You can use the resources available online to plan for this unit.

Essential Question

At the end of this unit, students should be able to answer "How can you communicate mathematical ideas effectively?"

Each chapter explores a different essential question that assists students in answering the unit question. The lessons in each chapter include exercises that lead students to various aspects of the essential question.

This unit focuses on the Expressions and Equations. The chapters address the following grade 7 standards:

Use properties of operations to generate equivalent expressions.

1. Apply properties of operations as strategies to add, subtract, factor, and expand linear expressions with rational coefficients. (7.EE.1)
2. Understand that rewriting an expression in different forms in a problem context can shed light on the problem and how the quantities in it are related. (7.EE.2)

continued on page 344

Solve real-life and mathematical problems using numerical and algebraic expressions and equations.

3. Solve multi-step real-life and mathematical problems posed with positive and negative rational numbers in any form (whole numbers, fractions, and decimals), using tools strategically. Apply properties of operations to calculate with numbers in any form; convert between forms as appropriate; and assess the reasonableness of answers using mental computation and estimation strategies. (7.EE.3)

4. Use variables to represent quantities in a real-world or mathematical problem, and construct simple equations and inequalities to solve problems by reasoning about the quantities. (7.EE.4)

- **a.** Solve word problems leading to equations of the form $px + q = r$ and $p(x + q) = r$, where p, q, and r are specific rational numbers. Solve equations of these forms fluently. Compare an algebraic solution to an arithmetic solution, identifying the sequence of the operations used in each approach. (7.EE.4a)
- **b.** Solve word problems leading to inequalities of the form $px + q > r$ or $px + q < r$, where p, q, and r are specific rational numbers. Graph the solution set of the inequality and interpret it in the context of the problem. (7.EE.4b)

Collaborate

Unit Project Preview

Have students record the results of their poll in a frequency table. They can then use the data in the frequency table to create the circle graph.

The Unit Project can be found on pages 527–528.

Collaborate

Unit Project Preview

Watch

Stand Up and Be Counted! The U.S. Census is a survey of the American people that is taken every 10 years. The census is used to collect data about the United States population and to determine the number of House of Representatives for each state.

Conduct your own mini-census. Survey twenty students about the typical way they come to school: by school bus, by car, on foot, or by some other means. Then make a circle graph of the data.

At the end of Chapter 6, you'll complete a project to find how the U.S. population affects the House of Representatives. This adventure will appeal to your "census."

PLAN ONLINE

PD | RtI | Watch | Worksheets | Vocab | Tutor | Tools | Check | English Learners | Sketchpad

PRESENT

IWB

An Interactive Whiteboard Ready presentation is available for each lesson in the chapter.

Expressions and Equations

Chapter 5 Expressions

Essential Question

HOW can you use numbers and symbols to represent mathematical ideas?

Content Standards
7.EE.1, 7.EE.2, 7.NS.3

MP Mathematical Practices
1, 2, 3, 4, 5, 6, 7

Math in the Real World

Meerkats live in burrows. Because meerkats have sharp claws, they are able to dig at a rate of 1 foot per second.

Suppose a meerkat digs for 3 seconds. Cross out the expression that does not represent the underground distance dug by the meerkat.

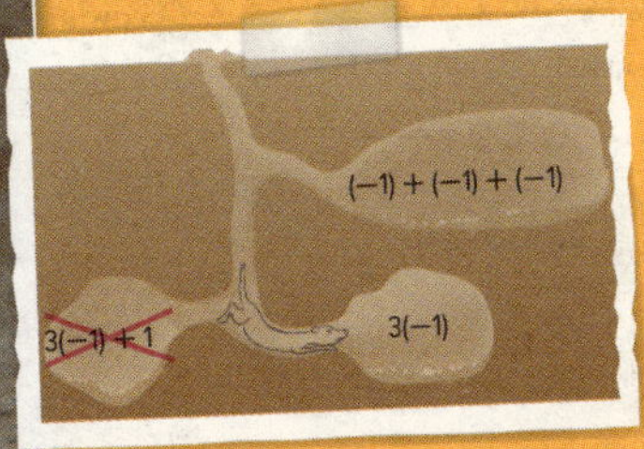

FOLDABLES Study Organizer

1. Cut out the Foldable on page FL3 of this book.
2. Place your Foldable on page 426.
3. Use the Foldable throughout this chapter to help you learn about expressions.

Focus narrowing the scope

This chapter focuses on content from the **Expressions and Equations** (EE) domain.

Mathematical Background Additional information about the mathematical background for this chapter can be found online at connectED.mcgraw-hill.com.

Coherence connecting within and across grades

Previous
Students added, subtracted, multiplied, and divided integers and fractions.

Now
Students use properties of operations to write and simplify expressions.

Next
Students will apply the use of expressions to writing and solving equations and formulas.

Rigor pursuing concepts, fluency, and applications

The Levels of Complexity charts located throughout this chapter indicate how the exercises progress from conceptual understanding and procedural skills and fluency, to application and critical thinking.

Launch the Chapter

Math in the Real World

Meerkats Students may forget to represent the distance a meerkat digs below the surface as a negative integer. Remind students that the word *below* indicates use of a negative sign.

What Tools Do You Need?

Vocabulary Activity

As you proceed through the chapter, introduce each vocabulary term using the following routine.

Define: Algebraic expressions are combinations of variables, numbers, and at least one operation.

Example: $14 + a$

Ask:

- *What makes the above example an algebraic expression?* There is a variable (a), a number (14), and an operation (+).

Review Vocabulary

Students should be familiar with the order of operations. If students have trouble using the graphic organizer to evaluate the expression, have students use a vertical table to evaluate the expression instead of the graphic organizer.

What Tools Do You Need?

Vocabulary

Additive Identity Property
algebra
algebraic expression
arithmetic sequence
Associative Property
coefficient
Commutative Property
constant
counterexample
define a variable
Distributive Property
equivalent expressions
factor
factored form
like terms
linear expression
monomial
Multiplicative Identity Property
Multiplicative Property of Zero
property
sequence
simplest form
term
variable

Review Vocabulary

Order of Operations The order of operations is a four-step process used to evaluate numerical expressions.

1. Evaluate the expressions inside grouping symbols.
2. Evaluate all powers.
3. Multiply and divide in order from left to right.
4. Add and subtract in order form left to right.

Use the order of operations to evaluate $3 + 5^2(4 + 4)$. Write each step in the organizer below.

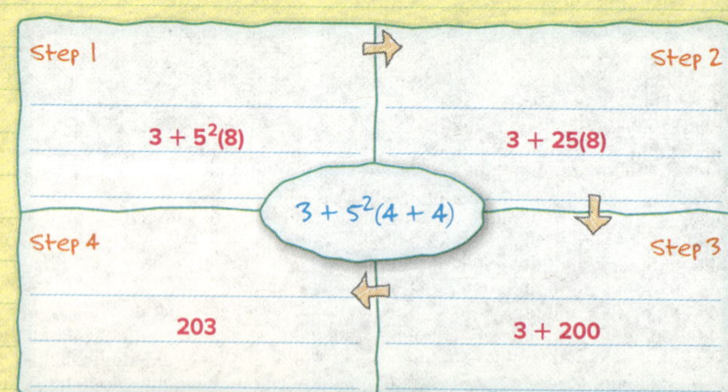

What Do You Already Know?

Read each statement. Decide whether you agree (A) or disagree (D). Place a checkmark in the appropriate column and then justify your reasoning. See students' work.

Expressions			
Statement	A	D	Why?
Like terms are terms that contain different variables.			
When addition or subtraction signs separate an algebraic expression into parts, each part is called a term.			
An algebraic expression is in simplest form if it has no like terms and no parentheses.			
A property is an example that shows that a conjecture is false.			
When you use the Distributive Property to combine like terms, you are simplifying the expression.			
Equivalent expressions have the same value.			

When Will You Use This?

Here are a few examples of how expressions are used in the real world.

Activity 1 Do you or your parents have a texting plan? If so, how much does it cost per text or per month? Ask your parents to help you research different texting plans. Then compare and contrast each plan.

See students' work.

Activity 2 Go online at connectED.mcgraw-hill.com to read the graphic novel ***Too Many Texts***. How many text messages are included in Dario's texting plan? 250 text messages

What Do You Already Know?

In this activity, students assess their prior knowledge by determining whether they agree or disagree with each statement about concepts in this chapter.

- You may want to add a third option of "I'm not sure" for those students who may not have much prior knowledge of the content of the statement.
- After completing the chapter, have students return to this page and see if any of their responses would change now that they have completed the chapter.

When Will You Use This?

Activity 1

Students find out that using an expression can demonstrate the cost of a texting plan per month.

Activity 2

Use the Graphic Novel to help students learn about using expressions to solve problems.

Ask:

- *If it costs $5.00 to send 250 text messages, how much does each text message cost?* $0.02

Are You Ready?

Use this page to determine if students have skills that are needed for the chapter.

Quick Review

Students with strong math backgrounds may opt to go directly to Quick Check.

QUICK REVIEW		
Example(s)	**Skill**	**Standard**
1, 2	Evaluate and Write Powers	6.EE.2c
3, 4	Multiply Integers	7.NS.2c

Quick Check

If students have difficulty with the exercises, present another example to clarify any misconceptions.

Exercises 1–3
Evaluate 7^4. 2,401

Exercise 4
Write $8 \cdot 8 \cdot 8 \cdot 8 \cdot 8 \cdot 8$ in exponential form. 8^6

Exercises 5–7
Find $6(-4)$. -24

RtI Response to Intervention
Go online at connectED.mcgraw-hill.com for resources to differentiate remediation for Tier 1, Tier 2, and Tier 3 students.

McGraw Hill Education ALEKS® can provide additional remediation support with personalized instruction and practice. See pages T8 and T9 for more information.

Are You Ready?

Try the Quick Check below.
Or, take the Online Readiness Quiz. Check

Quick Review

6.EE.2c, 7.NS.2c

Example 1

Evaluate 2^5.

$2^5 = 2 \cdot 2 \cdot 2 \cdot 2 \cdot 2$
$= 32$

Example 2

Write $3 \cdot 3 \cdot 3 \cdot 3 \cdot 3 \cdot 3 \cdot 3$ in exponential form.

3 is the base. It is used as a factor 7 times. So, the exponent is 7.

$3 \cdot 3 \cdot 3 \cdot 3 \cdot 3 \cdot 3 \cdot 3 = 3^7$

Example 3

Find 4(–2).

$4(-2) = -8$ The integers have different signs. The product is negative.

Example 4

Find –5(–8).

$-5(-8) = 40$ The integers have the same signs. The product is positive.

Quick Check

Exponents **Evaluate each expression.**

1. $2^4 =$ 16
2. $3^3 =$ 27
3. $4^2 =$ 16

Show your work.

4. Write $4 \cdot 4 \cdot 4 \cdot 4$ in exponential form. 4^4

Integer Operations **Multiply.**

5. $5(-10) =$ -50
6. $-9(-4) =$ 36
7. $-5^2 =$ -25

How Did You Do?

Which problems did you answer correctly in the Quick Check? Shade those exercise numbers below.

① ② ③ ④ ⑤ ⑥ ⑦

PLAN ONLINE

PD | RtI | Watch | Worksheets | Vocab | Tutor | Tools | Check | English Learners | Sketchpad

PRESENT

IWB

An Interactive Whiteboard Ready presentation is available for each lesson in the chapter.

Lesson 1

Algebraic Expressions

Vocabulary Start-Up

A **variable** is a symbol that represents an unknown quantity. An **algebraic expression**, such as $n + 2$, is an expression that contains variables, numbers, and at least one operation.

Variable → $n + 2$

Write each of the following phrases in the correct section of the Venn diagram: *contains an operation, has variables and numbers, has only numbers*.

Characteristics of Expressions

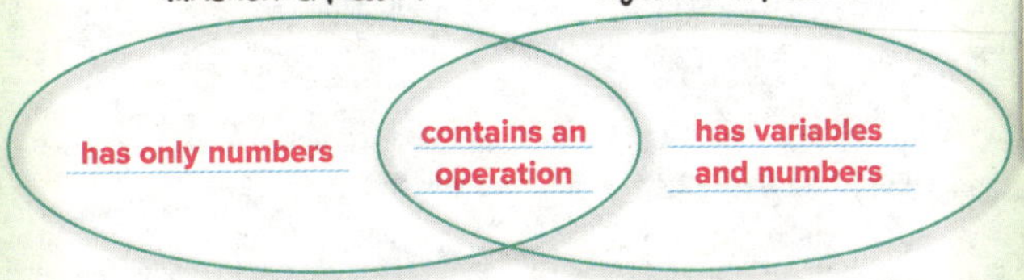

Essential Question

HOW can you use numbers and symbols to represent mathematical ideas?

Vocabulary

variable
algebraic expression
algebra
coefficient
define a variable

Content Standards
Preparation for 7.EE.1 and 7.EE.2

MP Mathematical Practices
1, 2, 3, 4

Real-World Link

The expression $(F - 32) \times \frac{5}{9}$ can be used to convert a temperature from Fahrenheit to Celsius. In this algebraic expression, the variable F represents the temperature in degrees Fahrenheit.

Which MP **Mathematical Practices** did you use? Shade the circle(s) that applies.

1. Persevere with Problems
2. Reason Abstractly
3. Construct an Argument
4. Model with Mathematics
5. Use Math Tools
6. Attend to Precision
7. Make Use of Structure
8. Use Repeated Reasoning

Michael Ventura/Alamy

Focus narrowing the scope

Objective Evaluate simple algebraic expressions.
Preparation for 7.EE.1 and 7.EE.2

Coherence connecting within and across grades

Previous Students used the order of operations to simplify numerical expressions.

Now Students evaluate algebraic expressions given values for the variables.

Next Students will add and subtract linear expressions.

Rigor pursuing concepts, fluency, and applications

See the Levels of Complexity chart on page 353.

ENGAGE EXPLORE EXPLAIN ELABORATE EVALUATE

1 Launch the Lesson

Ideas for Use

You may wish to launch the lesson using a whole group, small group, think-pair-share activity, or independent activity.

BL EL **Circle the Sage** Poll the class to find out who understands the difference between numerical and algebraic expressions. Those students, the sages, spread about the room. Divide the rest of the class into teams. Each student surrounds a sage while the sage explains what they know. The classmates listen and ask questions. Students return to their teams and discuss what they learned. MP 1, 2, 3

Alternate Strategy

AL Point out that the main difference between numerical and algebraic expressions is that an algebraic expression contains a variable and a numerical expression does not. MP 2, 7

ENGAGE EXPLORE **EXPLAIN** ELABORATE EVALUATE

2 Teach the Concept

Ask the scaffolded questions for each example to differentiate instruction.

Examples

IWB

1. Evaluate an algebraic expression.

AL
- *In what order do you perform operations on an expression?* parentheses, exponents, multiply and divide, add and subtract
- *What is the variable?* n

OL
- *What is the value of n?* -4
- *What is the first step in evaluating the expression?* Replace n with -4.

BL
- *Evaluate $2n + 6$ if $n = -4$. How does this answer compare to the answer in Example 1?* -2; It is the same.

Need Another Example?
Evaluate $3(t - 4)$ if $t = 6$. 6

2. Evaluate an algebraic expression.

AL
- *What are the variables?* w and v
- *What is the value of w? of v?* 5; 3

OL
- *What is the first step in evaluating the expression?* Replace w with 5 and v with 3.
- *What should you do next?* Multiply, then subtract.

BL
- *Can you evaluate the expression $2b + 3c$? Explain.* no; you don't know the value of b and c, so you can't evaluate the expression.

Need Another Example?
Evaluate $6s - 3t$ if $s = 4$ and $t = -2$. 30

3. Evaluate an algebraic expression.

AL
- *How do you find 3^3?* Multiply $3 \cdot 3 \cdot 3$.

OL
- *What is the first step in evaluating the expression?* Replace y with 3.

BL
- *Evaluate the expression if $y = -\frac{3}{4}$.* $\frac{5}{16}$

Need Another Example?
Evaluate $3m^2 - 4$ if $m = -3$. 23

Work Zone

Order of Operations
1. Evaluate the expressions inside grouping symbols.
2. Evaluate all powers.
3. Multiply and divide in order from left to right.
4. Add and subtract in order from left to right.

Evaluate an Algebraic Expression

The branch of mathematics that involves expressions with variables is called **algebra**. In algebra, the multiplication sign is often omitted.

$6d$	$9st$	mn	a^3
6 times d	9 times s times t	m times n	a times a times a

The numerical factor of a multiplication expression that contains a variable is called a **coefficient**. So, 6 is the coefficient of $6d$.

Expressions like $\frac{y}{2}$ can be written as $y \div 2$ or $y \times \frac{1}{2}$.

Examples

Watch Tutor

1. Evaluate $2(n + 3)$ if $n = -4$.

$2(n + 3) = 2(-4 + 3)$ Replace n with -4.
$= 2(-1)$ Evaluate inside the parentheses.
$= -2$ Multiply.

2. Evaluate $8w - 2v$ if $w = 5$ and $v = 3$.

$8w - 2v = 8(5) - 2(3)$ Replace w with 5 and v with 3.
$= 40 - 6$ Do all of the multiplication first.
$= 34$ Subtract 6 from 40.

3. Evaluate $4y^3 + 2$ if $y = 3$.

$4y^3 + 2 = 4(3)^3 + 2$ Replace y with 3.
$= 4(27) + 2$ Evaluate the power.
$= 110$ Multiply, then add.

Got It? **Do these problems to find out.**

Evaluate each expression if $c = 8$ and $d = -5$.

a. $c - 3$ **b.** $15 - c$ **c.** $3(c + d)$
d. $2c - 4d$ **e.** $d - c^2$ **f.** $2d^2 + 5d$

Show your work.

a. 5
b. 7
c. 9
d. 36
e. -69
f. 25

Real-World Example

Tutor

4. **Athletic trainers use the formula $\frac{3(220 - a)}{5}$, where a is a person's age, to find their minimum training heart rate. Find Latrina's minimum training heart rate if she is 15 years old.**

$\frac{3(220 - a)}{5} = \frac{3(220 - 15)}{5}$ — Replace a with 15.

$= \frac{3(205)}{5}$ — Subtract 15 from 220.

$= \frac{615}{5}$ — Multiply 3 and 205.

$= 123$ — Divide 615 by 5.

Latrina's minimum training heart rate is 123 beats per minute.

Fractions
The fraction bar is a grouping symbol. Evaluate the expressions in the numerator and denominator separately before dividing.

Got It? Do this problem to find out.

g. To find the area of a triangle, use the formula $\frac{bh}{2}$, where b is the base and h is the height. What is the area in square inches of a triangle with a height of 6 inches and base of 8 inches?

Show your work.

g. 24 in^2

Write Expressions

To translate a verbal phrase into an algebraic expression, the first step is to define a variable. When you **define a variable**, you choose a variable to represent an unknown quantity.

Real-World Examples

Tutor

5. **Marisa wants to buy a DVD player that costs $150. She already saved $25 and plans to save an additional $10 each week. Write an expression that represents the total amount of money Marisa has saved after any number of weeks.**

Words	savings of $25 plus ten dollars each week
Variable	Let w represent the number of weeks.
Expression	$25 \quad + \quad 10 \quad \cdot \quad w$

$25 + 10w$ represents the total saved after any number of weeks.

Examples

IWB

4. Evaluate an algebraic expression.

AL
- *What do you need to find?* Latrina's minimum training heart rate
- *What expression will you use to find the heart rate?* $\frac{3(220 - a)}{5}$

OL
- *What is the value of a? Why?* 15; a represents the age and Latrina's age is 15

BL
- *How does the order of operations apply when evaluating this expression?* Use the order of operations to evaluate the numerator. Then divide by the denominator.

Need Another Example?
The formula for rewriting a Fahrenheit temperature as a Celsius temperature is $\frac{5(F - 32)}{9}$, where F equals the temperature in degrees Fahrenheit. Find the Celsius equivalent of 77° Fahrenheit. 25°C

5. Write an algebraic expression.

AL
- *What is the unknown value in the problem?* the number of weeks Marisa has saved money
- *What variable could you use to represent the number of weeks?* w
- *How much has she saved already?* $25
- *How much does she save each week?* $10

OL
- *How can you find the total amount saved for any week?* Multiply 10 by the number of weeks and then add 25.

BL
- *How many weeks do you think Marisa needs to save in order to buy the DVD player? Explain how you arrived at your answer.* 13 weeks; Sample answer: The DVD player is $150 and she already has $25, so she needs to save $125. At $10 per week, she would need to save for 13 weeks. If she only saved for 12 weeks, she would have saved $120, which is not enough.

Need Another Example?
Leah read 20 pages of a book. She plans to read 5 pages each day from now on. Write an expression that represents the total number of pages she will have read in d days. $20 + 5d$

Example

IWB

6. Evaluate an algebraic expression.

AL
- *What do you need to find?* whether Marisa will have saved enough to buy the DVD player in 11 weeks
- *What value will you use for w? Explain.* 11; It represents the number of weeks she has saved.

OL
- *Explain how you would use the order of operations to determine how much money she has saved.* In the order of operations, addition comes after multiplication, so multiply 10 • 11, then add 25.
- *What do you need to do after you evaluate the expression?* Compare the amount saved to the cost of the DVD player.

BL
- *How much more does Marisa need to save?* $15
- *How many weeks will it take her to save that amount?* 2 weeks

Need Another Example?
Leah read 20 pages of a book. She plans to read 5 pages each day from now on. Use the expression from Need Another Example 5 to see if Leah will have read more than 60 pages in 7 days. Explain. No; $20 + 5 \cdot 7 = 55$ so, she will only have read 55 pages in 7 days.

Guided Practice

Formative Assessment Use these exercises to assess students' understanding of the concepts in this lesson.

If some of your students are not ready for assignments, use the differentiated activities below.

AL EL **Think-Pair-Solo** Divide students into teams of 4. Each team completes Exercise 1. Have students pair up to complete Exercise 2. The team regroups to discuss the solution. Have students complete Exercises 3 and 4 alone and regroup to share answers. Have them work together to find any errors. MP 1, 2, 4

BL EL **Find the Fib** Divide students into teams of 3–4. Have one student on each team create 3 problems similar to Exercises 1–3. Have them solve 2 correctly and 1 incorrectly. Have the team find the incorrect solution and solve it correctly. MP 3

6. Refer to Example 5. Will Marisa have saved enough money to buy the $150 DVD player in 11 weeks? Use the expression $25 + 10w$.

$25 + 10w = 25 + 10(11)$ — Replace *w* with 11.
$= 25 + 110$ — Multiply.
$= 135$ — Add.

Marisa will have saved $135 after 11 weeks. Since $\$135 < \$150$, Marisa will not have enough money to buy the DVD player.

Got It? **Do this problem to find out.**

h. An MP3 player costs $70 and song downloads cost $0.85 each. Write an expression that represents the cost of the MP3 player and *x* number of downloaded songs. Then find the total cost if 20 songs are downloaded.

Show your work.

h. $70 + 0.85x$; $87

Guided Practice

Check

Evaluate each expression if $m = 2$, $n = 6$, and $p = -4$. (Examples 1–4)

1. $3m + 4p$ -10
2. $n^2 + 5$ 41
3. $6p^3$ -384

Show your work.

4. A Web site charges $0.99 to download a game and a $12.49 membership fee. Write an expression that gives the total cost in dollars to download *g* games. Then find the cost of downloading 6 games. (Examples 5 and 6)
$12.49 + 0.99g$; $18.43

5. **Building on the Essential Question** Tell whether the statement below is *sometimes, always,* or *never* true. Justify your reasoning.
The expressions $x - 3$ and $y - 3$ represent the same value.
sometimes; Sample answer: $x - 3$ and $y - 3$ represent the same value only when $x = y$.

Rate Yourself!

How well do you understand algebraic expressions? Circle the image that applies.

Clear Somewhat Clear Not So Clear

For more help, go online to access a Personal Tutor.

Tutor

Name ______________________ My Homework ______________________

Independent Practice

Go online for Step-by-Step Solutions eHelp

Evaluate each expression if $d = 8$, $e = 3$, $f = 4$, and $g = -1$. (Examples 1 – 3)

1. $2(d + 9)$ **34**

2. $\frac{d}{4}$ **2**

3. $\frac{ef}{4}$ **3**

Show your work.

4. $4f + d$ **24**

5. $\frac{5d - 25}{5}$ **3**

6. $d^2 + 7$ **71**

7. $\frac{d - 4}{2}$ **2**

8. $10(e + 7)$ **100**

9. $\frac{2g}{2}$ **−1**

10. The expression $5n + 2$ can be used to find the total cost in dollars of bowling where n is the number of games bowled and 2 represents the cost of shoe rental. How much will it cost Vincent to bowl 3 games? (Example 4)

\$17

11. MP **Reason Abstractly** A car rental company's fees are shown. Suppose you rent a car using Option 2. Write an expression that gives the total cost in dollars for driving m miles. Then find the cost for driving 150 miles. (Examples 5 and 6)

$50 + 0.17m$; \$75.50

Car Rental Prices	
Option 1	Option 2
\$19.99 per day	\$50 fee
\$0.17 per mi	\$0.17 per mi

12. Refer to Exercise 11. Suppose you rent a car using Option 1. Write an expression that gives the total cost in dollars to rent a car for d days and m miles. Then find the cost for renting a car for 2 days and driving 70 miles. (Examples 5 and 6)

$19.99d + 0.17m$, \$51.88

ENGAGE EXPLORE EXPLAIN ELABORATE EVALUATE

3 Practice and Apply

Independent Practice and Extra Practice

The Independent Practice pages are meant to be used as the homework assignment. The Extra Practice page can be used for additional reinforcement or as a second-day assignment.

Levels of Complexity

The levels of the exercises progress from 1 to 3, with Level 1 indicating the lowest level of complexity.

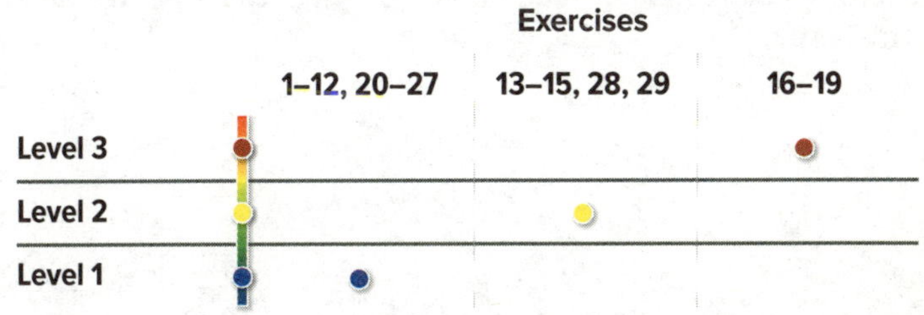

Suggested Assignments

You can use the table below that includes exercises of all complexity levels to select appropriate exercises for your students' needs.

Differentiated Homework Options		
AL	Approaching Level	1–13, 15–17, 28, 29
OL	On Level	1–11 odd, 13–17, 28, 29
BL	Beyond Level	13–19, 28, 29

McGraw Hill Education ALEKS® can provide additional remediation support with personalized instruction and practice.

Watch Out!

Common Error Some students may be confused as to the order of operations in expressions such as the one in Exercise 5. Remind students that the fraction bar acts as a grouping symbol. So, the expression above the bar must be evaluated before it is divided by the number below.

MP MATHEMATICAL PRACTICES	
Emphasis On	**Exercise(s)**
1 Make sense of problems and persevere in solving them.	18, 19
2 Reason abstractly and quantitatively.	11, 16
4 Model with mathematics.	17, 27

Mathematical Practices 1, 3, and 4 are aspects of mathematical thinking that are emphasized in every lesson. Students are given opportunities to be persistent in their problem solving, to express their reasoning, and apply mathematics to real-world situations.

Formative Assessment

Use this activity as a closing formative assessment before dismissing students from your class.

TICKET Out the Door

Have students describe a word problem with a variable (or variables). Make sure they define the variables(s).
See students' work.

Evaluate each expression if $x = 3.2$, $y = 6.1$, and $z = 0.2$.

13. $x + y - z$ **9.1**

14. $14.6 - (x + y + z)$ **5.1**

15. $xz + y^2$ **37.85**

H.O.T. Problems Higher Order Thinking

16. MP **Reason Abstractly** Write an algebraic expression with the variable x that has a value of 3 when evaluated.

Sample answer: $5x - 37$ if $x = 8$

17. MP **Model with Mathematics** Write a real-world problem that can be represented by the expression $5x + 10$.

Sample answer: The fee to rent a bicycle is \$10 plus \$5 for each hour. The expression $5x + 10$ represents the total cost for renting a bicycle for x hours.

18. MP **Persevere with Problems** To find the total number of diagonals for any given polygon, you can use the expression $\frac{n(n-3)}{2}$, where n is the number of sides of the polygon.

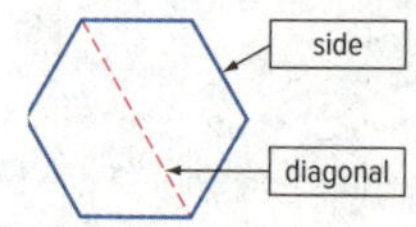

a. Determine the minimum value that n could be. **3**

b. Make a table of four possible values of n. Then complete the table by evaluating the expression for each value of n.

c. Check by drawing the diagonals of a pentagon and counting the diagonals.

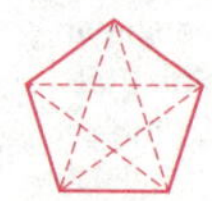

Sample answers given:

n	value
3	0
4	2
5	5
6	9

19. MP **Persevere with Problems** Franco constructed the objects below using toothpicks.

Figure 1 Figure 2 Figure 3

Write two different rules that relate the figure number to the number of toothpicks in each figure.

Sample answer: $2n + 4$; $2(n + 2)$

Name ______________________ My Homework ______________________

Extra Practice

Evaluate each expression if $d = 8$, $e = 3$, $f = 4$, and $g = -1$.

20. $10 - e$ 7

$10 - e$

$10 - 3 = 7$

Homework Help

21. $\frac{16}{f}$ 4

$\frac{16}{f}$

$\frac{16}{4} = 4$

22. $4e^2$ **36**

23. $8g - f$ **−12**

24. $\frac{(5 + g)^2}{2}$ **8**

25. $e^2 - 4$ **5**

26. The expression $\frac{w}{30}$, where w is a person's weight in pounds, is used to find the approximate number of quarts of blood in the person's body. How many quarts of blood does a 120-pound person have?

4 quarts

27. MP **Model with Mathematics** Refer to the graphic novel frame below. Let n represent the number of text messages. Evaluate the expression $0.15(n - 250) + 5$ to find the cost of 275 text messages. **$8.75**

Create Your Own Homework Online

eSolutionsManual can be used to create worksheets for the suggested assignments on page 353, or create your own worksheets for differentiated homework or review.

Power Up! Test Practice

Exercises 28 and 29 prepare students for more rigorous thinking needed for the state assessment.

28.

This test item requires students to support their reasoning or evaluate the reasoning of others by justifying their response and constructing arguments.	
Depth of Knowledge	DOK2
Content Standard	7.EE.1
Mathematical Practices	MP1, MP3, MP4
Online Experience	Students drag symbols to complete the model and type their response in the box.
Scoring Rubric	
2 points	Students correctly model, evaluate, and explain the expression.
1 point	Students correctly model and evaluate, but fail to explain the expression OR students evaluate and explain, but fail to model the expression.

29.

This test item requires students to reason abstractly and quantitatively when problem solving.	
Depth of Knowledge	DOK1
Content Standard	7.EE.1
Mathematical Practice	MP1
Online Experience	Students will be required to click on the bubbles to select all answers that are correct.
Scoring Rubric	
1 point	Students correctly answer each part of the question.

Power Up! Test Practice

28. Tonya has x quarters, y dimes, and z nickels in her pocket. Select the appropriate operations to complete the expression that represents the total amount of change Tonya has in her pocket.

×	÷
+	−

(\$0.25 [×] x) [+] (\$0.1 [×] y) [+] (\$0.05 [×] z)

Evaluate the expression for $x = 3$, $y = 5$, and $z = 2$. What does this value represent?

\$1.35; This is the amount of change Tonya has in her pocket if she has 3 quarters, 5 dimes, and 2 nickels.

29. The prices of magazines and books at the school book fair are shown in the table. Determine if each statement is true or false.

School Book Fair Prices	
Item	**Cost**
Magazines	\$4.95
Paperback books	\$7.95

a. The expression $7.95b + 4.95m$ represents the cost of buying b books and m magazines. ■ True □ False

b. The expression $12.90(b + m)$ represents the cost of buying b books and m magazines. □ True ■ False

c. The total cost of buying 3 books and 4 magazines is \$43.65. ■ True □ False

Spiral Review

Define a variable and write each phrase as an algebraic expression. 6.EE.2

30. 8 feet less than the height **Let h = the height; $h - 8$**

31. Sarah worked 8 more hours than Paida. **Let p = the number of hours Paida worked; $p + 8$**

32. Kumar has twice the number of goals as Jacob. **Let j = the number of Jacob's goals; $2j$**

33. Addison is 3 years younger than Nathan. **Let n = Nathan's age; $n - 3$**

34. The table shows the costs of different camping activities. Over the summer, Maura canoed 4 times and fished 3 times. Write and evaluate an expression that represents the total cost Maura spent canoeing and fishing. 5.OA.1

Camping Activity Costs	
Activity	**Cost**
Canoeing	\$8
Fishing	\$5

4(8) + 3(5); \$47

PLAN ONLINE

PD | RtI | Watch | Worksheets | Vocab | Tutor | Tools | Check | English Learners | Sketchpad

PRESENT

IWB

An Interactive Whiteboard Ready presentation is available for each lesson in the chapter.

Lesson 2

Sequences

Vocabulary Start-Up

A **sequence** is an ordered list of numbers. Each number in a sequence is called a **term**. In an **arithmetic sequence**, each term is found by adding the same number to the previous term.

Complete the graphic organizer below.

arithmetic sequences

Numbers	Words
Continue each sequence.	Describe each sequence.
1, 3, 5, 7, 9, ...	Add 2 to the previous term.
1, 1.5, 2, 2.5, 3, 3.5, ...	Add 0.5 to the previous term.

Essential Question

HOW can you use numbers and symbols to represent mathematical ideas?

Vocabulary

sequence
term
arithmetic sequence

Content Standards
Preparation for 7.EE.1 and 7.EE.2

MP Mathematical Practices
1, 2, 3, 4

Real-World Link

Horseback Riding The number of students who went on each horseback riding trip is shown. Do the numbers represent the terms of an arithmetic sequence? Explain.

Trip	1	2	3	4	5
Number of Students	15	16	18	21	25

no; The same number is not added to the previous term. The numbers increase by 1, 2, 3, and 4.

Which MP **Mathematical Practices** did you use? Shade the circle(s) that applies.

1. Persevere with Problems
2. Reason Abstractly
3. Construct an Argument
4. Model with Mathematics
5. Use Math Tools
6. Attend to Precision
7. Make Use of Structure
8. Use Repeated Reasoning

Focus narrowing the scope

Objective Describe the relationships and extend terms in arithmetic sequences. Preparation for 7.EE.1 and 7.EE.2

Coherence connecting within and across grades

Previous Students used the order of operations to evaluate expressions.

Now Students evaluate expressions involving absolute values.

Next Students will add integers with the same sign and add integers with different signs.

Rigor pursuing concepts, fluency, and applications

See the Levels of Complexity chart on page 361.

ENGAGE EXPLORE EXPLAIN ELABORATE EVALUATE

1 Launch the Lesson

Ideas for Use

You may wish to launch the lesson using a whole group, small group, think-pair-share activity, or independent activity.

AL EL **Think-Pair-Share** Have students work in pairs. Give students 3–5 minutes to complete the graphic organizer. Have them share their responses with their partner, then together complete the Real-World Link. Then call on one student to share their response within a small group or large group discussion. MP 5, 6

Alternate Strategy

BL Have students work in pairs to research *geometric sequences*. Ask them to compare and contrast them with arithmetic sequences by using a graphic organizer. Each pair can report their findings to a small group or to the entire class. MP 5, 6

2 Teach the Concept

Ask the scaffolded questions for each example to differentiate instruction.

Examples

IWB

1. Describe and extend sequences.

AL
- *What number do you need to add to 8 to get 13?* 5
- *What number do you need to add to 13 to get 18?* 5
- *What number would you add to each term to find the next term?* 5

OL
- *To find the fifth term, what should you do?* Add 5 to 23.

BL
- *What is the tenth term?* 53

Need Another Example?
Describe the relationship between the terms in the arithmetic sequence 7, 11, 15, 19, ... Then write the next three terms in the sequence. 4 is added to each term; 23, 27, 31

2. Describe and extend sequences.

AL
- *What number do you need to add to 0.4 to get 0.6?* 0.2
- *What number do you need to add to 0.6 to get 0.8?* 0.2
- *What number would you add to each term to find the next term?* 0.2

OL
- *To find the fifth term, what should you do?* Add 0.2 to 1.0.
- *What should you do next?* Continue adding 0.2 to the previous term.

BL
- *What is the tenth term? Describe how to find it.* 2.2; Sample answer: since you know the 7th term, you need to add 0.2 three more times to 1.6; $1.6 + 3(0.2) = 2.2$.

Need Another Example?
Describe the relationship between the terms in the arithmetic sequence 0.1, 0.5, 0.9, 1.3, ... Then write the next three terms in the sequence. Each term is 0.4 greater than the previous term; 1.7, 2.1, 2.5.

Work Zone

Describe and Extend Sequences

In an arithmetic sequence, the terms can be whole numbers, fractions, or decimals.

Examples

Tutor

1. Describe the relationship between the terms in the arithmetic sequence 8, 13, 18, 23, ... Then write the next three terms in the sequence.

8, 13, 18, 23, ...
+5 +5 +5

Each term is found by adding 5 to the previous term.

Continue the pattern to find the next three terms.

$23 + 5 = 28$ $28 + 5 = 33$ $33 + 5 = 38$

The next three terms are 28, 33, and 38.

2. Describe the relationship between the terms in the arithmetic sequence 0.4, 0.6, 0.8, 1.0, ... Then write the next three terms in the sequence.

0.4, 0.6, 0.8, 1.0, ...
+0.2 +0.2 +0.2

Each term is found by adding 0.2 to the previous term.

Continue the pattern to find the next three terms.

$1.0 + 0.2 = 1.2$ $1.2 + 0.2 = 1.4$ $1.4 + 0.2 = 1.6$

The next three terms are 1.2, 1.4, and 1.6.

Got It? **Do these problems to find out.**

Describe the relationship between the terms in each arithmetic sequence. Then write the next three terms in the sequence.

a. 0, 13, 26, 39, ...
b. 4, 7, 10, 13, ...
c. 1.0, 1.3, 1.6, 1.9, ...
d. 2.5, 3.0, 3.5, 4.0, ...

Show your work.

a. 13 is added to the previous term; 52, 65, 78

b. 3 is added to the previous term; 16, 19, 22

c. 0.3 is added to the previous term; 2.2, 2.5, 2.8

d. 0.5 is added to the previous term; 4.5, 5.0, 5.5

Expressions and Equations

Write an Algebraic Expression

In a sequence, each term has a specific position within the sequence. Consider the sequence 2, 4, 6, 8,...

Notice that as the position number increases by 1, the value of the term increases by 2.

Position	Operation	Value of Term
1	$1 \cdot 2 = 2$	2
2	$2 \cdot 2 = 4$	4
3	$3 \cdot 2 = 6$	6
4	$4 \cdot 2 = 8$	8

(+1 between successive positions; +2 between successive values of term)

You can also write an algebraic expression to represent the relationship between any term in a sequence and its position in the sequence. In this case, if n represents the position in the sequence, the value of the term is $2n$.

Arithmetic Sequences
When looking for a pattern between the position number and each term in the sequence, it is often helpful to make a table.

Real World

Example

Tutor

3. **The greeting cards that Meredith makes are sold in boxes at a gift store. The first week, the store sold 5 boxes. Each week, the store sells five more boxes. The pattern continues. What algebraic expression can be used to find the total number of boxes sold at the end of the 100th week? What is the total?**

Position	Operation	Value of Term
1	$1 \cdot 5$	5
2	$2 \cdot 5$	10
3	$3 \cdot 5$	15
n	$n \cdot 5$	$5n$

Each term is 5 times its position. So, the expression is $5n$.

$5n$ — Write the expression.

$5(100) = 500$ — Replace n with 100.

At the end of 100 weeks, 500 boxes will have been sold.

IWB

Example

3. Write and evaluate an algebraic expression.

AL
- *What do you need to find?* the number of boxes sold at the end of the 100th week
- *After Week 1, how many boxes of cards are sold?* 5
- *After Week 2, how many total boxes of cards are sold? Week 3? Week 4?* 10; 15; 20

OL
- *What is the relationship between the number of weeks and the number of boxes sold?* The number of boxes sold is equal to 5 times the number of weeks.
- *How can you represent this situation with an expression?* Sample answer: Let n represent the number of weeks and $5n$ represent the total number of boxes sold.

BL
- *Suppose the first week, the store sold 8 boxes, then each week after that, the store sells 5 more boxes. What expression could you write to describe the situation? Explain.* $5n + 3$; Sample answer: The terms are 8, 13, 18, 23, ... The value of each term is equal to 5 times the term position plus 3.

Need Another Example?
Mehmet started a new exercise routine. The first day, he did 2 sit-ups. Each day after that, he did 2 more sit-ups than the previous day. If he continues this pattern, what algebraic expression can be used to help find the number of sit-ups on the nth day? Use the expression to find the number of sit-ups on the tenth day. $2n$; 20 sit-ups

Guided Practice

Formative Assessment Use these exercises to assess students' understanding of the concepts in this lesson.

If some of your students are not ready for assignments, use the differentiated activities below.

AL EL Pairs Discussion Have students work in pairs to complete Exercises 1–3. If they are having trouble finding what needs to be added to each term, give them centimeter cubes to build figures represented by each term in the sequence. Then, each pair trades their solutions with another pair of students and discusses any differences. MP 1, 4, 5, 7

BL EL Trade-a-Problem Have students create their own arithmetic sequences, similar to Exercises 1–3. Challenge them to use fractions and mixed numbers in their sequences. Also challenge them to have a different first term than what they will use for their common difference. Students trade their problems, solve each other's problem, and compare solutions. If the solutions do not agree, students work together to find the errors. MP 1, 7

STOP and Reflect

Suppose Figure 1 had 3 circles, Figure 2 had 5 circles, and Figure 3 had 7 circles. What algebraic expression represents this situation?

$2n + 1$

Show your work.

e. $3n$; 150

Got It? Do this problem to find out.

e. If the pattern continues, what algebraic expression can be used to find the number of circles used in any figure? How many circles will be in the 50th figure?

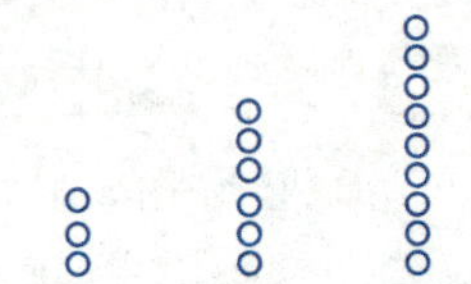

Figure 1 Figure 2 Figure 3

Guided Practice

Check

Describe the relationship between the terms in each arithmetic sequence. Then write the next three terms in each sequence. (Examples 1 and 2)

1. 0, 9, 18, 27, ...

Show your work.

9 is added to the previous term; 36, 45, 54

2. 4, 9, 14, 19, ...

5 is added to the previous term; 24, 29, 34

3. 1, 1.1, 1.2, 1.3, ...

0.1 is added to the previous term; 1.4, 1.5, 1.6

4. Hannah has a doll collection. The table shows the total number of dolls in her collection for three years. Suppose this pattern continues. Write an algebraic expression to find the number of dolls in her collection after n years. How many dolls will Hannah have after 25 years? (Example 3)

Year	Number of Dolls
1	6
2	12
3	18

$6n$; 150 dolls

5. **Building on the Essential Question** Explain why the following sequence is considered an arithmetic sequence.

5, 9, 13, 17, 21,...

Sample answer: It is arithmetic because each term is found by adding the same number, 4, to the previous term.

Rate Yourself!

How confident are you about sequences? Check the box that applies.

For more help, go online to access a Personal Tutor.

Tutor

Name ______________________ My Homework ______________________

Independent Practice

Go online for Step-by-Step Solutions eHelp

Describe the relationship between the terms in each arithmetic sequence. Then write the next three terms in each sequence. (Examples 1 and 2)

1. 0, 7, 14, 21, ...
7 is added to the previous term; 28, 35, 42

2. 1, 7, 13, 19, ...
6 is added to the previous term; 25, 31, 37

3. 26, 34, 42, 50, ...
8 is added to the previous term; 58, 66, 74

4. 0.1, 0.4, 0.7, 1.0, ...
0.3 is added to the previous term; 1.3, 1.6, 1.9

5. 2.4, 3.2, 4.0, 4.8, ...
0.8 is added to the previous term; 5.6, 6.4, 7.2

6. 2.0, 3.1, 4.2, 5.3, ...
1.1 is added to the previous term; 6.4, 7.5, 8.6

7. Refer to the table shown. If the pattern continues, what algebraic expression can be used to find the plant's height for any month? What will be the plant's height at 12 months? (Example 3)
$3n$; 36 in.

Month	Height (in.)
1	3
2	6
3	9

8. MP **Model with Mathematics** Explain how the number of text messages Dario sent and the cost form an arithmetic sequence. Then write an expression to find Dario's text messaging bill if he sends n text messages over 250.
Sample answer: For each text message over 250, the cost increases by $0.15; $0.15n + 5$.

ENGAGE EXPLORE EXPLAIN ELABORATE EVALUATE

3 Practice and Apply

Independent Practice and Extra Practice

The Independent Practice pages are meant to be used as the homework assignment. The Extra Practice page can be used for additional reinforcement or as a second-day assignment.

Levels of Complexity

The levels of the exercises progress from 1 to 3, with Level 1 indicating the lowest level of complexity.

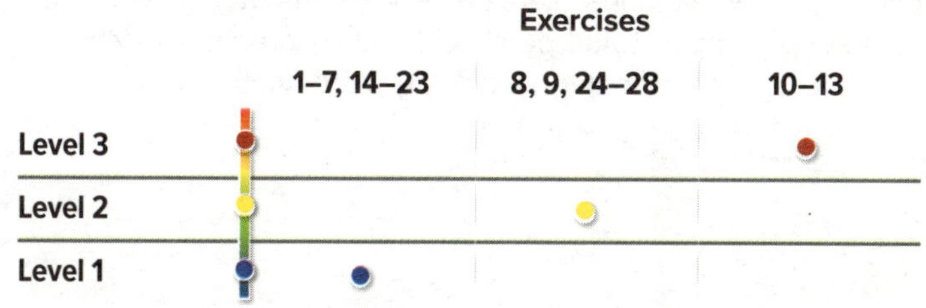

Suggested Assignments

You can use the table below that includes exercises of all complexity levels to select appropriate exercises for your students' needs.

Differentiated Homework Options		
AL	Approaching Level	1–7, 9, 10, 27, 28
OL	On Level	1–7 odd, 8–10, 27, 28
BL	Beyond Level	8–13, 27, 28

ALEKS® can provide additional remediation support with personalized instruction and practice.

Watch Out!

Common Error If the expression for finding the nth term of a sequence is incorrectly determined, the terms that are found using that expression will also be incorrect. Have students check their expressions using all of the numbers that were given to them in the sequence.

MATHEMATICAL PRACTICES

Emphasis On	Exercise(s)
1 Make sense of problems and persevere in solving them.	11–13
3 Construct viable arguments and critique the reasoning of others.	23
4 Model with mathematics.	9, 10
5 Use appropriate tools strategically.	8

Mathematical Practices 1, 3, and 4 are aspects of mathematical thinking that are emphasized in every lesson. Students are given opportunities to be persistent in their problem solving, to express their reasoning, and apply mathematics to real-world situations.

Formative Assessment
Use this activity as a closing formative assessment before dismissing students from your class.

TICKET Out the Door

Write the sequence 8, 16, 24, 32, ... on the board. Then have students find the 9th term of the sequence. 72

Watch Out!

In Exercise 9, remind students that the coordinate plane can be used to plot ordered pairs. The horizontal axis is the *x*-axis and the vertical axis is the *y*-axis. To plot an ordered pair (*x*, *y*), the *x*-coordinate corresponds to the number along the *x*-axis and the *y*-coordinate corresponds to the number along the *y*-axis.

9. **Multiple Representations** Kendra is stacking boxes of tissues for a store display. She stacks 3 boxes in the first minute, 6 boxes by the end of the second minute, and 9 boxes by the end of the third minute. Suppose the pattern continues for parts **a–d**.

a. Table Make a table of values for 1, 2, 3, 4, and 5 minutes.

x	1	2	3	4	5
y	3	6	9	12	15

b. Symbols Write an expression to find the *n*th term in the sequence.

$3n$

c. Graph Graph the table of values from part **a** on the coordinate plane. Let *x* represent the number of minutes and *y* represent the number of boxes. Then describe the graph.

Sample answer: The number of boxes increases by 3 each minute. The points appear to fall in a straight line passing through the origin.

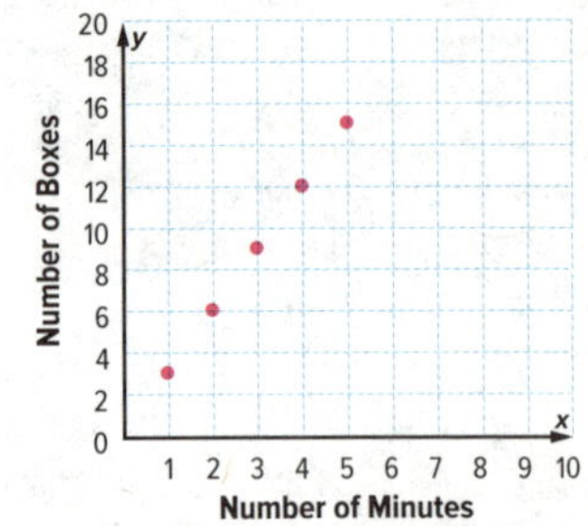

d. Numbers How many boxes will be displayed after 45 minutes?

135 boxes

H.O.T. Problems Higher Order Thinking

10. **Justify Conclusions** Write five terms of an arithmetic sequence and describe the rule for finding the terms.

Sample answer: 5, 6, 7, 8, 9, ...; $n + 4$, where *n* represents the position of the term

Persevere with Problems Not all sequences are arithmetic. But, there is still a pattern. Describe the relationship between the terms in each sequence. Then write the next three terms in the sequence.

11. 1, 2, 4, 7, 11, ...

+ 1, + 2, + 3, + 4, ...; 16, 22, 29

12. 0, 2, 6, 12, 20, ...

+ 2, + 4, + 6, + 8, ...; 30, 42, 56

13. **Persevere with Problems** Use an arithmetic sequence to find the number of multiples of 6 between 41 and 523. Justify your reasoning.

81; Sample answer: The multiples of 6 from 41 to 523 can be represented by the sequence 42, 48, 54, ... 522. The expression $6n + 36$ represents this sequence. When $n = 81$, the value of the expression is 522. So, the 81st term of the sequence is 522. There are 81 multiples of 6 between 41 and 523.

Name ____________ My Homework ____________

Extra Practice

Describe the relationship between the terms in each arithmetic sequence. Then write the next three terms in each sequence.

14. 19, 31, 43, 55, ...
12 is added to the previous term; 67, 79, 91

Homework Help

15. 6, 16, 26, 36, ...
10 is added to the previous term; 46, 56, 66

16. 33, 38, 43, 48, ...
5 is added to the previous term; 53, 58, 63

17. 4.5, 6.0, 7.5, 9.0, ...
1.5 is added to the previous term; 10.5, 12.0, 13.5

18. 1.2, 3.2, 5.2, 7.2, ...
2 is added to the previous term; 9.2, 11.2, 13.2

19. 4.6, 8.6, 12.6, 16.6, ...
4 is added to the previous term; 20.6, 24.6, 28.6

20. 18, 33, 48, 63, ...
15 is added to the previous term; 78, 93, 108

21. 20, 45, 70, 95, ...
25 is added to the previous term; 120, 145, 170

22. 38, 61, 84, 107, ...
23 is added to the previous term; 130, 153, 176

23. MP **Reason Abstractly** Refer to the figures for parts **a** and **b**.

Figure 1 Figure 2 Figure 3

a. Describe the relationship between the figures and the number of rectangles shown. Each figure is 8 less than the previous figure.

b. If the pattern continues, how many rectangles will be in the next 2 figures? 40, 32

The terms of an arithmetic sequence can be related by subtraction. Write the next three terms of each sequence.

24. 32, 27, 22, 17, ...
12, 7, 2

25. 45, 42, 39, 36, ...
33, 30, 27

26. 10.5, 10, 9.5, 9, ...
8.5, 8, 7.5

Create Your Own Homework Online

eSolutionsManual™ can be used to create worksheets for the suggested assignments on page 361, or create your own worksheets for differentiated homework or review.

Power Up! Test Practice

Exercises 27 and 28 prepare students for more rigorous thinking needed for the state assessment.

27.

This test item requires student to explain and apply mathematical concepts and solve problems with precision, while making use of structure.	
Depth of Knowledge	DOK1
Content Standard	7.EE.1
Mathematical Practice	MP1
Online Experience	Students will be required to click on the bubbles to select all correct answers.
Scoring Rubric	
1 point	Students correctly answer each part of the question.

28.

This test item requires student to analyze and solve complex real-world problems through the use of mathematical tools and models.	
Depth of Knowledge	DOK2
Content Standard	7.EE.1
Mathematical Practices	MP1, MP4
Online Experience	Students will draw points on the graph and type their responses in boxes.
Scoring Rubric	
2 points	Students correctly complete the table, plot the points, and find the number of photos.
1 point	Students correctly complete the table and find the number of photos but fail to plot the points OR students complete the table and plot the points but fail to find the number of photos OR students incorrectly complete the table but plot the points and find the number of photos based on the error in the table.

Power Up! Test Practice

27. The table shows the first 5 terms of a sequence. Determine if each statement is true or false.

Position	1	2	3	4	5	n
Value of Term	2	5	10	17	26	■

a. The expression $n^2 + 1$ can be used to find the nth term of the sequence. ■ True ☐ False

b. The 8th term of the sequence is 65. ■ True ☐ False

c. The table represents an arithmetic sequence. ☐ True ■ False

28. Katie is putting photos in an album. She puts five pictures on the first page. Each page after that contains five pictures. Suppose the pattern continues. Complete the table of values for 1, 2, 3, 4, and 5 pages. Then graph the table of values on the coordinate plane. Let x represent the number of pages and y represent the total number of photos.

Number of Pages	Total Photos
1	5
2	10
3	15
4	20
5	25

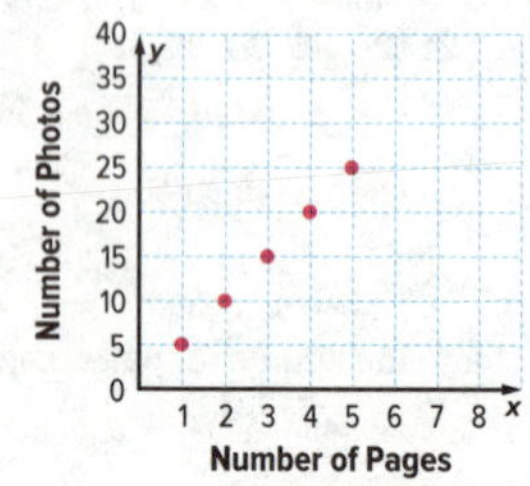

How many photos will Katie have on 20 pages? 100 photos

Spiral Review

Evaluate. 6.EE.1

29. $1^4 =$ 1

30. $3^3 =$ 27

31. $8^2 =$ 64

32. $10^4 =$ 10,000

33. $5^1 =$ 5

34. $7^5 =$ 16,807

35. Jayden goes to the batting cage. He purchases three tokens and rents a helmet. If he spends a total of $6.50, how much is each token? 6.EE.6

$1.50

Batting Cage Prices	
Tokens	■
Helmet Rental	$2

PLAN ONLINE: PD | RtI | Watch | Worksheets | Vocab | Tutor | Tools | Check | English Learners | Sketchpad

PRESENT: IWB — An Interactive Whiteboard Ready presentation is available for each lesson in the chapter.

Expressions and Equations

Inquiry Lab
Sequences

Inquiry HOW can geometric figures be used to model numerical patterns?

Content Standards
Preparation for 7.EE.2

MP Mathematical Practices
1, 3

A fencing company uses 4 planks of wood for one section of fencing, 7 planks for two sections, and 10 planks of wood for three sections. The fence sections are represented using the toothpicks shown. Determine how many planks would be used to create 5 sections of fencing.

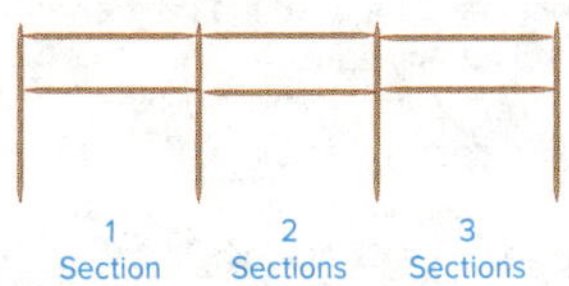

Hands-On Activity

Step 1 Find a pattern in the table. Then fill in the number of planks that would be in 4 and 5 sections of fencing.

Number of Sections	Number of Planks
1	4
2	7
3	10
4	13
5	16

Step 2 Check your work by using toothpicks to show 5 fence sections. Draw the result in the space below.

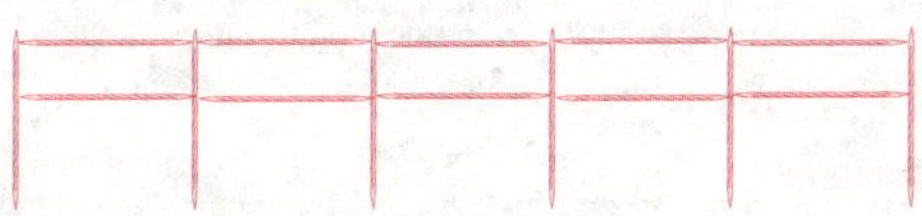

So, there will be 16 planks in 5 sections of fencing.

Focus narrowing the scope

Objective Explore patterns in sequences of geometric figures.
7.EE.2

Coherence moving from concrete to abstract

Now
Students examine sequences formed from geometric figures.

Next
Students create algebraic representations for geometric sequences.

Rigor pursuing concepts, fluency, and applications

See the Levels of Complexity chart on page 366.

ENGAGE EXPLORE EXPLAIN ELABORATE EVALUATE

1 Launch the Lab

The activity is intended to be used as a whole-group activity.

Hands-On Activity

AL EL Tell students that number of toothpicks represents the number of wood planks needed for each section.

Ask:

- *What number is added to the number of sections to find the next term?* 1
- *What number is added to the number of planks to find the next term?* 3

BL EL Have students work in pairs to alter the activity (and fence specifications) so that 5 planks are needed for 1 section, 9 planks are needed for 2 sectons, 13 planks are needed for 3 sections, and so on. Then have them complete a table similar to the one in the activity and use toothpicks to show 5 fence sections. There should be 21 toothpicks for 5 fence sections.

2 Collaborate

The **Investigate** section is intended to be used as a small-group investigation. The **Create** section is intended to be used as independent exercises

Levels of Complexity

The levels of the exercises progress from 1 to 3, with Level 1 indicating the lowest level of complexity.

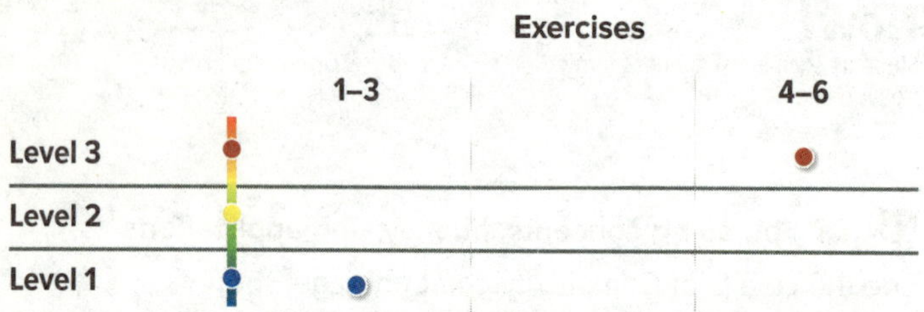

Investigate

Collaborate

AL EL **Pairs Discussion** Have students work in pairs to complete Exercises 1–3. Have them trade their solutions with another pair of students and discuss any differences. MP 1, 3, 7

Create

On Your Own

BL EL **Trade-a-Problem** Have students create their own pattern with toothpicks. Students trade their patterns with another student and write an expression for each other's pattern. MP 1, 7

Inquiry Students should be able to answer "HOW can geometric figures be used to model numerical patterns?" Check for student understanding and provide guidance, if needed.

Investigate

Collaborate

Work with a partner. Complete the table. You can use toothpicks to continue each pattern if needed.

1.

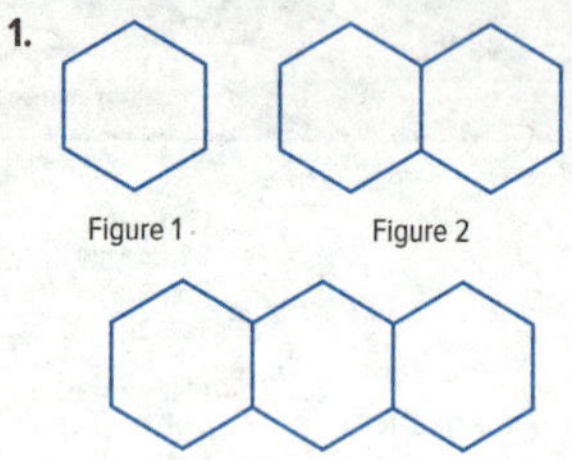

Figure 1 Figure 2 Figure 3

Figure Number	Number of Toothpicks
1	6
2	11
3	16
4	21
5	26

2. Refer to Exercise 1. Write an expression that could be used to find the number of toothpicks that would be needed for any figure.

$5n + 1$

3. Use your expression from Exercise 2 to find the number of toothpicks that would be needed to create Figure 10. Explain.

51 toothpicks; Evaluate $5n + 1$ for $n = 10$; $5(10) + 1 = 51$.

Create

On Your Own

4. MP **Reason Abstractly** Refer to the activity. Write an expression that could be used to find the number of planks in any number of sections.

$3n + 1$

5. MP **Justify Conclusions** Use the expression in Exercise 4 to find the number of planks that would be needed to create 10 sections of fencing. Explain.

31 planks; Evaluate $3n + 1$ for $n = 10$; $3(10) + 1 = 31$.

6. Inquiry HOW can geometric figures be used to model numerical patterns?

Sample answer: Using a geometric figure to represent each number in a pattern helps to visualize the pattern.

PLAN ONLINE

PD | RtI | Watch | Worksheets | Vocab | Tutor | Tools | Check | English Learners | Sketchpad

PRESENT

IWB

An Interactive Whiteboard Ready presentation is available for each lesson in the chapter.

Expressions and Equations

Lesson 3

Properties of Operations

Real-World Link

Driving Miss Ricardo drives up and down her street to complete different errands. Some of the places on her street are shown below. The number of blocks between the places are also shown.

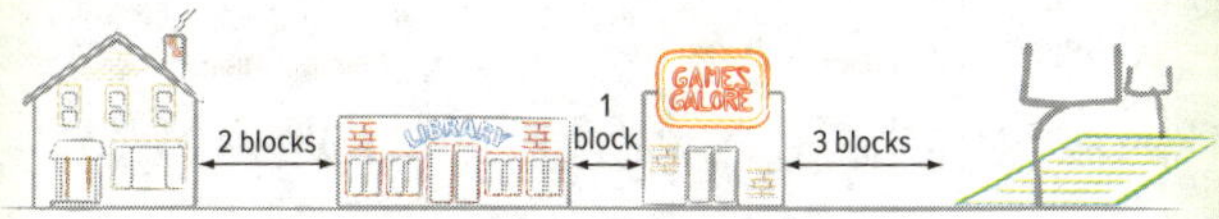

1. Suppose Miss Ricardo drives from home to the game store and back. Write an expression for each distance.

   from home to the game store: $2 + 1$ from the game store to home: $1 + 2$

2. Circle the property that is illustrated in Exercise 1.

   (Commutative) Associative

3. On Monday, Miss Ricardo drives from home, stops at the library, and then drives to the football field. On Tuesday, she drives from home, stops at the game store, and then drives to the football field. Write an expression for each distance.

   Monday: $2 + (1 + 3)$ Tuesday: $(2 + 1) + 3$

4. Circle the property that is illustrated in Exercise 3.

   Commutative (Associative)

Which MP **Mathematical Practices** did you use?
Shade the circle(s) that applies.

① Persevere with Problems
② Reason Abstractly
③ Construct an Argument
④ Model with Mathematics
⑤ Use Math Tools
⑥ Attend to Precision
⑦ Make Use of Structure
⑧ Use Repeated Reasoning

Essential Question

HOW can you use numbers and symbols to represent mathematical ideas?

Vocabulary

Commutative Property
Associative Property
property
Additive Identity Property
Multiplicative Identity Property
Multiplicative Property of Zero
counterexample

Content Standards
7.EE.1, 7.EE.2

MP **Mathematical Practices**
1, 3, 4, 5, 7

Focus narrowing the scope

Objective Identify and use mathematical properties to simplify algebraic expressions. 7.EE.1, 7.EE.2

Coherence connecting within and across grades

Previous Students wrote and evaluated algebraic expressions given a value for the variable.

Now Students use mathematical properties to simplify algebraic expressions.

Next Students will add and subtract linear expressions.

Rigor pursuing concepts, fluency, and applications

See the Levels of Complexity chart on page 371.

ENGAGE EXPLORE EXPLAIN ELABORATE EVALUATE

1 Launch the Lesson

Ideas for Use

You may wish to launch the lesson using a whole group, small group, think-pair-share activity, or independent activity.

BL EL **Think-Pair-Write** Have students work in pairs. Give them two minutes to think about the verbs *commute* and *associate* in everyday use. Have them discuss their ideas with their partner. Then have students write how the everyday uses of these verbs apply to the Commutative Properties and the Associative Properties. MP 1, 6

Alternate Strategy

AL Have students generate a list of words that are similar to *Commutative* and *Associative*, such as *commute, commuter, associates, associated,* and *association.* MP 1, 6

2 Teach the Concept

Ask the scaffolded questions for each example to differentiate instruction.

IWB

Example

1. Identify properties.

AL
- *What is the order of the numbers and variables on the left side of the equation?* **2, 5, *n***
- *What is the order of the numbers and variables on the right side of the equation?* **2, 5, *n***
- *Did the order change?* **no**
- *What changed?* **the grouping**

OL
- *What do the grouping symbols indicate?* **The parentheses indicate the operations that are to be performed first.**
- *What does each side of the equation simplify to?* **10*n***
- *What property does this statement illustrate?* **Associative Property of Multiplication**

BL
- *What properties are shown by the statement $5 + (0 + x) = x + 5$?* **Commutative Property of Addition and the Additive Identity Property**

Need Another Example?
Name the property shown by the statement $(3 \cdot m) \cdot 2 = 2 \cdot (3 \cdot m)$. **Commutative Property of Multiplication**

Key Concept

Properties of Operations

Watch

Work Zone

Words	The **Commutative Property** states that the order in which numbers are added or multiplied does not change the sum or product.	
	Addition	**Multiplication**
Symbols	$a + b = b + a$	$a \cdot b = b \cdot a$
Examples	$6 + 1 = 1 + 6$	$7 \cdot 3 = 3 \cdot 7$
Words	The **Associative Property** states that the way in which numbers are grouped when they are added or multiplied does not change the sum or product.	
	Addition	**Multiplication**
Symbols	$a + (b + c) = (a + b) + c$	$a \cdot (b \cdot c) = (a \cdot b) \cdot c$
Examples	$2 + (3 + 8) = (2 + 3) + 8$	$3 \cdot (4 \cdot 5) = (3 \cdot 4) \cdot 5$

A **property** is a statement that is true for any number. The following properties are also true for any numbers.

Property	Words	Symbols	Examples
Additive Identity	When 0 is added to any number, the sum is the number.	$a + 0 = a$ $0 + a = a$	$9 + 0 = 9$ $0 + 9 = 9$
Multiplicative Identity	When any number is multiplied by 1, the product is the number.	$a \cdot 1 = a$ $1 \cdot a = a$	$5 \cdot 1 = 5$ $1 \cdot 5 = 5$
Multiplicative Property of Zero	When any number is multiplied by 0, the product is 0.	$a \cdot 0 = 0$ $0 \cdot a = 0$	$8 \cdot 0 = 0$ $0 \cdot 8 = 0$

Example

Tutor

1. Name the property shown by the statement $2 \cdot (5 \cdot n) = (2 \cdot 5) \cdot n$.

The order of the numbers and variable did not change, but their grouping did. This is the Associative Property of Multiplication.

Got It? **Do these problems to find out.**

a. $42 + x + y = 42 + y + x$ **b.** $3x + 0 = 3x$

Show your work.

a. Commutative (+)

b. Identity (+)

You may wonder if any of the properties apply to subtraction or division. If you can find a **counterexample**, an example that shows that a conjecture is false, the property does not apply.

Example

2. State whether the following conjecture is *true* or *false*. If *false*, provide a counterexample.

Division of whole numbers is commutative.

Write two division expressions using the Commutative Property.

$15 \div 3 \stackrel{?}{=} 3 \div 15$ State the conjecture.

$5 \neq \frac{1}{5}$ Divide.

The conjecture is false. We found a counterexample. That is, $15 \div 3 \neq 3 \div 15$. So, division is *not* commutative.

Got It? Do this problem to find out.

c. The difference of two different whole numbers is always less than both of the two numbers.

Show your work.

c. false; Sample answer: $8 - 2 = 6; 6 \not< 2$

Real World Example

3. Alana wants to buy a sweater that costs \$38, sunglasses that costs \$14, a pair of jeans that costs \$22, and a T-shirt that costs \$16. Use mental math to find the total cost before tax.

Write an expression for the total cost. You can rearrange the numbers using the properties of math. Look for sums that are multiples of ten.

$38 + 14 + 22 + 16$

$= 38 + 22 + 14 + 16$ Commutative Property of Addition

$= (38 + 22) + (14 + 16)$ Associative Property of Addition

$= 60 + 30$ Add.

$= 90$ Simplify.

The total cost of the items is \$90.

Got It? Do this problem to find out.

d. Lance made four phone calls from his cell phone today. The calls lasted 4.7, 9.4, 2.3, and 10.6 minutes. Use mental math to find the total amount of time he spent on the phone.

Show your work.

d. 27 min

IWB

Examples

2. Find a counterexample.

AL
- *What is a conjecture?* Sample answer: A statement that has not been proven.
- *What is a counterexample?* an example that shows a conjecture is false

OL
- *Why does the Commutative Property not apply to division?* Sample answer: The order in which you divide matters.

BL
- *Write an equation, using the inverse operation of $15 \div 3$, that illustrates the Commutative Property of Multiplication.* $15 \cdot \frac{1}{3} = \frac{1}{3} \cdot 15$

Need Another Example?

State whether the following conjecture is *true* or *false*. If false, provide a counterexample: *Subtraction of whole numbers is associative.* false; Sample answer: $(12 - 5) - 3 \neq 12 - (5 - 3)$

3. Use mental math.

AL
- *What are compatible numbers in addition?* numbers that are easy to add mentally
- *In the example, what number is compatible with 38? Why?* 22; 38 and 22 have a sum of 60, which ends in 0
- *In the example, what number is compatible with 14? Why?* 16; 14 and 16 have a sum of 30, which ends in 0

OL
- *Look at the cost of each item. Which pairs of numbers can you add mentally? Explain.* 38 and 22, 14 and 16; Sample answer: The ones digits in each pair make a ten ($8 + 2 = 10$ and $4 + 6 = 10$).
- *What property will allow you to reorder the addition expression?* Commutative Property of Addition
- *What property will allow you to regroup the numbers in the expression?* Associative Property of Addition

BL
- *Give an example of a problem where you would want to change the order of the problem to find a product mentally.* Sample answer: $4 \cdot 18 \cdot 25 = 4 \cdot 25 \cdot 18$

Need Another Example?

In a garden, a decorative pool in the shape of a box is 2 feet deep, 17 feet long, and 5 feet wide. Use mental math to find the volume of water in the pool. 170 ft^3

IWB

Examples

4–5. Simplify expressions.

AL • *Refer to Example 4. What other term is like 7? Why?* 5; They are known values.

• *Refer to Example 4. Can you add 7 and g? Explain.* no; You don't know the value of *g*.

OL • *Refer to Example 4. How can you rewrite (7 + g) + 5 so that you can add 7 and 5?* Switch the order of 7 and *g*, then regroup so that 7 and 5 are added first.

BL • *Refer to Example 5. What does the exponent indicate?* The variable *m* is multiplied by itself.

Need Another Example?

Simplify $6 + (d + 8)$. Justify each step.

$6 + (d + 8) = 6 + (8 + d)$	Commutative (+)
$= (6 + 8) + d$	Associative (+)
$= 14 + d$	Simplify.

Guided Practice

Formative Assessment Use these exercises to assess students' understanding of the concepts in this lesson.

If some of your students are not ready for assignments, use the differentiated activities below.

AL EL **Numbered Heads Together** Assign students to 3- or 4-person learning teams. Each member is assigned a number from 1 to 4. Each team completes Exercises 1–4, making sure that every member understands. If students are having difficulty coming up with the steps in Exercise 4, supply the steps and ask students to give the reason. Call on a specific number from one team to present the team's solution to the class. MP 1, 6

BL EL **Think-Pair-Share** Have students work in pairs. Give students three minutes to write five conjectures, some true and some false, about properties of whole numbers. Have them share their conjectures with their partner. Each partner should identify the conjectures as true or false. If false, students must give a counterexample. Call on one student to share a conjecture within a small group or large group discussion. MP 1, 3, 7

Simplify Algebraic Expressions

To simplify an expression is to perform all possible operations.

Examples

Tutor

Simplify each expression. Justify each step.

4. $(7 + g) + 5$

$(7 + g) + 5 = (g + 7) + 5$	Commutative Property of Addition
$= g + (7 + 5)$	Associative Property of Addition
$= g + 12$	Simplify.

5. $(m \cdot 11) \cdot m$

$(m \cdot 11) \cdot m = (11 \cdot m) \cdot m$	Commutative Property of Multiplication
$= 11 \cdot (m \cdot m)$	Associative Property of Multiplication
$= 11m^2$	Simplify.

Got It? Do this problem to find out.

e. $4 \cdot (3c \cdot 2)$

Show your work.

e. $4 \cdot (3c \cdot 2) = 4 \cdot (2 \cdot 3c)$, Commutative (×); $(4 \cdot 2) \cdot 3c$, Associative (×); $8 \cdot 3c$, Simplify; $(8 \cdot 3) \cdot c$, Associative (×); 24c, Simplify

Guided Practice

Check

Name the property shown by each statement. (Example 1)

1. $3m \cdot 0 \cdot 5m = 0$ Multiplicative (0)

2. $7c + 0 = 7c$ Identity (+)

3. State whether the following conjecture is *true* or *false*. If *false*, provide a counterexample. (Example 2)

Subtraction of whole numbers is associative.

false; Sample answer: $(8 - 5) - 3 \neq 8 - (5 - 3)$

4. Simplify $9c + (8 + 3c)$. Justify each step. (Examples 3–5)

$= 9c + (3c + 8)$	Commutative (+)
$= (9c + 3c) + 8$	Associative (+)
$= 12c + 8$	Simplify.

5. **Building on the Essential Question** Explain the difference between the Commutative and Associative Properties. Sample answer: The Commutative Property allows you to add or multiply in any order whereas the Associative Property allows you to group the numbers in any way.

Rate Yourself!

Are you ready to move on? Shade the section that applies.

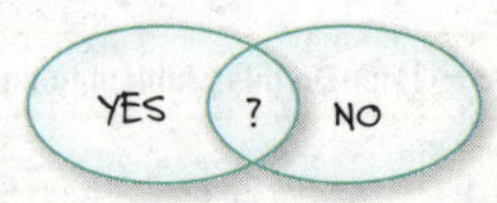

For more help, go online to access a Personal Tutor.

Tutor

Name ______________ My Homework ______________

Independent Practice

Go online for Step-by-Step Solutions eHelp

Name the property shown by each statement. (Example 1)

1. $a + (b + 12) = (b + 12) + a$
 Commutative (+)

2. $(5 + x) + 0 = 5 + x$
 Identity (+)

3. $16 + (c + 17) = (16 + c) + 17$
 Associative (+)

4. $d \cdot e \cdot 0 = 0$
 Multiplicative (0)

5. MP **Use a Counterexample** State whether the conjecture is *true* or *false*. If *false*, provide a counterexample. (Example 2)

 Division of whole numbers is associative.

 false; Sample answer: $(24 \div 4) \div 2 \neq 24 \div (4 \div 2)$

6. Darien ordered a soda for $2.75, a sandwich for $8.50, and a dessert for $3.85. Sales tax was $1.15. Use mental math to find the total amount of the bill. Explain. (Example 3) $16.25;

 Sample answer: $3.85 + $1.15 = $5 and $2.75 + $8.50 = $2.50 + $0.25 + $8.50 = $11.25, $11.25 + $5 = $16.25

Simplify each expression. Justify each step. (Examples 4 and 5)

7. $15 + (12 + 8a)$

$= (15 + 12) + 8a$	Associative (+)
$= 27 + 8a$	Simplify.

8. $(5n \cdot 9) \cdot 2n$

$= (9 \cdot 5n) \cdot 2n$	Commutative (×)
$= 9 \cdot (5n \cdot 2n)$	Associative (×)
$= 9 \cdot 10n^2$	Simplify.
$= (9 \cdot 10) \cdot n^2$	Associative (×)
$= 90n^2$	Simplify.

9. $3x \cdot (7 \cdot x)$

$= 3x \cdot (x \cdot 7)$	Commutative (×)
$= (3x \cdot x) \cdot 7$	Associative (×)
$= 3x^2 \cdot 7$	Simplify.
$= 3 \cdot 7 \cdot x^2$	Commutative (×)
$= (3 \cdot 7) \cdot x^2$	Associative (×)
$= 21x^2$	Simplify.

10. $(4m \cdot 2) \cdot 5m$

$= (2 \cdot 4m) \cdot 5m$	Commutative (×)
$= 2 \cdot (4m \cdot 5m)$	Associative (×)
$= 2 \cdot 20m^2$	Simplify.
$= (2 \cdot 20)m^2$	Associative (×)
$= 40m^2$	Simplify.

ENGAGE EXPLORE **EXPLAIN** **ELABORATE** **EVALUATE**

3 Practice and Apply

Independent Practice and Extra Practice

The Independent Practice pages are meant to be used as the homework assignment. The Extra Practice page can be used for additional reinforcement or as a second-day assignment.

Levels of Complexity

The levels of the exercises progress from 1 to 3, with Level 1 indicating the lowest level of complexity.

Exercises	1–10, 16–26	11, 27, 28	12–15
Level 3			●
Level 2		●	
Level 1	●		

Suggested Assignments

You can use the table below that includes exercises of all complexity levels to select appropriate exercises for your students' needs.

Differentiated Homework Options		
AL	Approaching Level	1–14, 27, 28
OL	On Level	1–9 odd, 11–14, 27, 28
BL	Beyond Level	11–15, 27, 28

ALEKS® can provide additional remediation support with personalized instruction and practice.

Watch Out!

Common Error Some students may think that Exercise 1 represents the Associative Property of Addition because the statement uses parentheses. Explain to students that the variables and numbers grouped together inside the parentheses would have to change for the Associative Property to apply, such as $a + (b + 12) = (a + b) + 12$.

MP MATHEMATICAL PRACTICES	
Emphasis On	**Exercise(s)**
1 Make sense of problems and persevere in solving them.	15
3 Construct viable arguments and critique the reasoning of others.	5, 13
4 Model with mathematics.	12
5 Use appropriate tools strategically.	21
7 Look for and make use of structure.	14

Mathematical Practices 1, 3, and 4 are aspects of mathematical thinking that are emphasized in every lesson. Students are given opportunities to be persistent in their problem solving, to express their reasoning, and apply mathematics to real-world situations.

Formative Assessment
Use this activity as a closing formative assessment before dismissing students from your class.

TICKET Out the Door

Ask students to give examples of the Associative Property and the Commutative Property. See students' work.

Watch Out!

Find the Error Students may need to be reminded in Exercise 13 that *associative* properties are related to *grouping*, while *commutative* properties are related to *order*.

11. Simplify the expression $(7 + 47 + 3)[5 \cdot (2 \cdot 3)]$. Use properties to justify each step.
$[7 + (47 + 3)][5 \cdot (2 \cdot 3)]$, Associative (+); $(7 + 50)[5 \cdot (2 \cdot 3)]$, Simplify; $57[5 \cdot (2 \cdot 3)]$, Simplify; $57[(5 \cdot 2) \cdot 3]$, Associative (×); $57 \cdot 10 \cdot 3$, Simplify; $(57 \cdot 10) \cdot 3$, Associative (×); $570 \cdot 3$, Simplify; 1,710

H.O.T. Problems Higher Order Thinking

12. **MP Model with Mathematics** Write about something you do every day that is commutative. Then write about another situation that is not commutative.
See students' work.

13. **MP Find the Error** Blake is simplifying $4 \cdot (5 \cdot m)$. Find his mistake and correct it.
Blake incorrectly multiplied both the 5 and *m* by 4. He should have used the Associative Property to group the 5 and 4 together, simplify and then multiply by *m*.
$4 \cdot (5 \cdot m) = 20m$

14. **MP Identify Structure** Does the Associative Property *always*, *sometimes*, or *never* hold for subtraction? Explain your reasoning using examples and counterexamples.
sometimes; Sample answer: It works for the expression $5 - (6 - 0)$. It does not work for the expression $5 - (6 - 6)$.

15. **MP Persevere with Problems** If you take any two whole numbers and add them together, the sum is always a whole number. This is the Closure Property for Addition. The set of whole numbers is *closed* under addition.

a. Is the set of whole numbers closed under subtraction? If not, give a counterexample.
no; Sample answer: $2 - 3 = -1$ and -1 is not a whole number

b. Suppose you had a very small set of numbers that contained only 0 and 1. Would this set be closed under addition? If not, give a counterexample.
no; Sample answer: $1 + 1 = 2$ and 2 is not a member of the set.

Name _______________ My Homework

Extra Practice

Name the property shown by each statement.

16. $9(ab) = (9a)b$

Associative (×)

Homework Help

17. $y \cdot 7 = 7y$

Commutative (×)

18. $1 \times c = c$

Identity (×)

19. $5 + (a + 8) = (5 + a) + 8$

Associative (+)

20. State whether the conjecture is *true* or *false*. If *false*, provide a counterexample.

Subtraction of whole numbers is commutative.

false; Sample answer: $10 - 4 \neq 4 - 10$

21. MP **Use Math Tools** The times for each leg of a relay for four runners are shown. Use mental math to find the total time for the relay team. Explain.

48 s; Sample answer: $12.4 + 12.6 = 25$ and $11.8 + 11.2 = 23$, $25 + 23 = 48$

Runner	Time (s)
Jamal	12.4
Kenneth	11.8
Bryce	11.2
Jorge	12.6

Simplify each expression. Justify each step.

22. $(22 + 19b) + 7$

$= (19b + 22) + 7$ Commutative (+)

$= 19b + (22 + 7)$ Associative (+)

$= 19b + 29$ Simplify.

23. $18 + (5 + 6m)$

$= (18 + 5) + 6m$ Associative (+)

$= 23 + 6m$ Simplify.

24. $11s(4)$

$= 11 \cdot 4 \cdot s$ Commutative (×)

$= (11 \cdot 4) \cdot s$ Associative (×)

$= 44s$ Simplify.

25. $10y(7)$

$= 10 \cdot 7 \cdot y$ Commutative (×)

$= (10 \cdot 7) \cdot y$ Associative (×)

$= 70y$ Simplify.

26. $(9 + 31 + 5)[(7 \cdot 5) \cdot 4]$

$[(9 + 31) + 5][(7 \cdot 5) \cdot 4]$, Associative (+); $(40 + 5)[(7 \cdot 5) \cdot 4]$, Simplify; $45[(7 \cdot 5) \cdot 4]$, Simplify; $45[7 \cdot (5 \cdot 4)]$, Associative (×); $45 \cdot 7 \cdot 20$, Simplify; $45 \cdot 20 \cdot 7$, Commutative (×); $(45 \cdot 20) \cdot 7$, Associative (×); $900 \cdot 7$, Simplify; 6,300, Simplify

Create Your Own Homework Online

eSolutionsManual™ can be used to create worksheets for the suggested assignments on page 371, or create your own worksheets for differentiated homework or review.

Power Up! Test Practice

Exercises 27 and 28 prepare students for more rigorous thinking needed for the state assessment.

27.

This test item requires students to explain and apply mathematical concepts and solve problems with precision, while making use of structure.	
Depth of Knowledge	DOK1
Content Standard	7.EE.1
Mathematical Practice	MP1
Online Experience	Students will be required to click on the bubbles to select all answers that are correct.
Scoring Rubric	
1 point	Students correctly answer the question.

28.

This test item requires students to reason abstractly and quantitatively when problem solving.	
Depth of Knowledge	DOK2
Content Standard	7.EE.1
Mathematical Practices	MP1, MP7
Online Experience	Students will drag phrases to the appropriate place in the table and to type their responses in boxes.
Scoring Rubric	
2 points	Students correctly place all seven values.
1 point	Students correctly place five or six of the seven values.

Power Up! Test Practice

27. The table shows the cost of different items at a bakery. Yolanda buys 2 doughnuts, a muffin, and 2 cookies. Which of the following expressions represents the total cost? Select all that apply.

Item	Cost ($)
Cookie	2.21
Doughnut	2.29
Muffin	2.50
Roll	1.15

- ■ 2(2.29) + 2(2.21) + 2.50
- ■ 2(2.29) + 2.50 + 2(2.21)
- □ 2(2.29 + 2.21 + 2.50)
- ■ 2.50 + 2(2.21 + 2.29)

28. Determine if the two expressions in each pair are equivalent. If they are equivalent, select the property that is illustrated.

Commutative Property | Identity Property | Associative Property | Multiplicative Property of Zero

	Equivalent?	Property
$9 \cdot 4 \div 20 = 9 \cdot 20 \div 4$	No	
$3b \cdot 0 \cdot c = 0$	Yes	Multiplicative Property of Zero
$35 + 2m + n = 35 + n + 2m$	Yes	Commutative Property
$12t \cdot 3v + 0 = 12t \cdot 3v$	Yes	Identity Property

Spiral Review

Evaluate each expression if $a = 6$, $b = 15$, and $c = 9$. 6.EE.2

29. $a + 2b$ 36

30. $c^2 - 5$ 76

31. $10 + a^3$ 226

32. $8c - 9 + 25$ 88

33. $14 + 8b \div 2$ 74

34. $3^3 \div (3a)$ 1.5

35. A package of pencils costs $1.25. A new eraser costs $0.45. Write an expression to find the total cost of 3 packages of pencils and 2 erasers. Then find the total cost. 6.EE.2

$1.25(3) + $0.45(2); $4.65

PLAN ONLINE

PD | RtI | Watch | Worksheets | Vocab | Tutor | Tools | Check | English Learners | Sketchpad

PRESENT

IWB

An Interactive Whiteboard Ready presentation is available for each lesson in the chapter.

Lesson 4

The Distributive Property

Real-World Link

School Supplies Jordan buys three notebooks that cost $5 each. He also buys three packages of pens for $6 each.

1. Write an expression that shows the cost of three notebooks added to the cost of three packages of pens.

   $3 \cdot 5 + 3 \cdot 6$

2. Write an expression that shows three times the cost of one notebook and one package of pens.

   $3(5 + 6)$

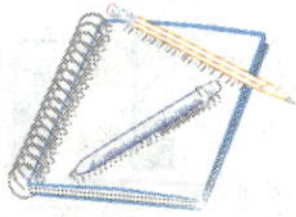

3. Evaluate both expressions. What do you notice?

   $33; $33; The expressions have the same value.

4. Suppose Jordan buys five notebooks that cost $3 each and five packages of pens that cost $1 each. Circle the expressions that represent Jordan's purchases.

   (circled) $5 \cdot 3 + 5 \cdot 1$ $5 \cdot 3 \cdot 5 \cdot 1$ (circled) $5(3 + 1)$

5. Suppose Jordan buys two rulers that cost $1 each and two folders that cost $1.50 each. Circle the expressions that represent Jordan's purchases.

   $2 + 1 + 2 + 1.50$ (circled) $2(1 + 1.50)$ (circled) $2 \cdot 1 + 2 \cdot 1.50$

Essential Question

HOW can you use numbers and symbols to represent mathematical ideas?

Vocabulary

Distributive Property
equivalent expressions

Content Standards
7.EE.1, 7.EE.2

MP Mathematical Practices
1, 3, 4, 5, 7

Which MP **Mathematical Practices** did you use?
Shade the circle(s) that applies.

① Persevere with Problems
② Reason Abstractly
③ Construct an Argument
④ Model with Mathematics
⑤ Use Math Tools
⑥ Attend to Precision
⑦ Make Use of Structure
⑧ Use Repeated Reasoning

Focus narrowing the scope

Objective Apply the Distributive Property to rewrite algebraic expressions. 7.EE.1, 7.EE.2

Coherence connecting within and across grades

Previous Students used properties to simplify algebraic expressions.

Now Students use the Distributive Property to simplify algebraic expressions.

Next Students will use the Distributive Property to factor linear expressions.

Rigor pursuing concepts, fluency, and applications

See the Levels of Complexity chart on page 379.

ENGAGE EXPLORE EXPLAIN ELABORATE EVALUATE

1 Launch the Lesson

Ideas for Use

You may wish to launch the lesson using a whole group, small group, think-pair-share activity, or independent activity.

BL EL **Pairs Discussion** Have students work in pairs to complete Exercises 1–5. Then ask them to consider how they could apply this concept to mentally multiply 54 by 22. Have them discuss their findings with another pair of students. MP 1, 7

Alternate Strategy

AL Give students two-sided counters. One side represents $5 for each notebook, and the other side represents $6 for each package of pens. Have students model the two different situations in Exercises 1 and 2. They can then assign different values to the counters to model Exercises 4 and 5. MP 1, 4, 7

ENGAGE EXPLORE **EXPLAIN** ELABORATE EVALUATE

2 Teach the Concept

Ask the scaffolded questions for each example to differentiate instruction.

IWB

Example

1. Evaluate expressions.

AL
- *What number is outside the parentheses?* 8
- *What does it mean that 8 is outside the parentheses?* Sample answer: 8 is being multiplied by both −9 and 4.
- *How can you use the Distributive Property in the Example?* Multiply each term by 8, then add.

OL
- *Do you need to multiply the first term, the second term, or both terms by 8?* both
- *After you distribute the multiplication, what should you do?* Add the two products.

BL
- *What does the word distribute mean in everyday use?* Sample answer: to spread something out
- *How does the everyday meaning of the word distribute relate to the Distributive Property?* Sample answer: When you use the Distributive Property, you spread the multiplication out over the addition or subtraction.

Need Another Example?

Use the Distributive Property to evaluate 7(3 + 12).

$7 \cdot 3 + 7 \cdot 12$; 105

Work Zone

Key Concept

Use the Distributive Property

Watch Tools

Words	The **Distributive Property** states that to multiply a sum or difference by a number, multiply each term inside the parentheses by the number outside the parentheses.	
Symbols	$a(b + c) = ab + ac$	$a(b - c) = ab - ac$
Examples	$4(6 + 2) = 4 \cdot 6 + 4 \cdot 2$	$3(7 - 5) = 3 \cdot 7 - 3 \cdot 5$

You can model the Distributive Property with algebraic expressions using algebra tiles. The expression $2(x + 2)$ is modeled below.

Model $x + 2$ using algebra tiles.

Double the amount of tiles to represent $2(x + 2)$.

Rearrange the tiles by grouping together the ones with the same shapes.

$2(x + 2) = 2(x) + 2(2)$ Distributive Property

$= 2x + 4$ Multiply.

The expressions $2(x + 2)$ and $2x + 4$ are **equivalent expressions**. No matter what x is, these expressions have the same value.

Example

Tutor

1. Use the Distributive Property to evaluate 8(−9 + 4).

$8(-9 + 4) = 8(-9) + 8(4)$ Expand using the Distributive Property.

$= -72 + 32$ or -40 Multiply. Then add.

Got It? **Do these problems to find out.**

a. $5(-9 + 11)$ **b.** $7(10 - 5)$ **c.** $(12 - 8)9$

Show your work.

a. 10

b. 35

c. 36

Examples

Tutor

Use the Distributive Property to rewrite each expression.

2. $4(x + 7)$

$4(x + 7) = 4(x) + 4(7)$ Expand using the Distributive Property.

$= 4x + 28$ Simplify.

3. $6(p - 5)$

$6(p - 5) = 6[p + (-5)]$ Rewrite $p - 5$ as $p + (-5)$.

$= 6(p) + 6(-5)$ Expand using the Distributive Property.

$= 6p + (-30)$ Simplify.

$= 6p - 30$ Definition of subtraction

4. $-2(x - 8)$

$-2(x - 8) = -2[x + (-8)]$ Rewrite $x - 8$ as $x + (-8)$.

$= -2(x) + -2(-8)$ Expand using the Distributive Property.

$= -2x + 16$ Simplify.

5. $5(-3x + 7y)$

$5(-3x + 7y) = 5(-3x) + 5(7y)$ Expand using the Distributive Property.

$= -15x + 35y$ Simplify.

6. $\frac{1}{3}(x - 6)$

$\frac{1}{3}(x - 6) = \frac{1}{3}[x + (-6)]$ Rewrite $x - 6$ as $x + (-6)$.

$= \frac{1}{3}(x) + \left(\frac{1}{3}(-6)\right)$ Expand using the Distributive Property.

$= \frac{1}{3}x + (-2)$ Simplify.

$= \frac{1}{3}x - 2$ Definition of subtraction

Got It? Do these problems to find out.

d. $6(a + 4)$ e. $(m + 3n)8$

f. $-3(y - 10)$ g. $\frac{1}{2}(w - 4)$

Show your work.

d. $6a + 24$

e. $8m + 24n$

f. $-3y + 30$

g. $\frac{1}{2}w - 2$

Examples

IWB

2–3. Write equivalent expressions.

AL
- *How are Examples 2 and 3 different?* Example 2 is the product of a number and a sum. Example 3 is the product of a number and a difference.
- *In Example 3, why is $p - 5$ changed to $p + (-5)$?* It helps us to remember to multiply 6 by -5, not 5. Subtracting a positive integer is the same as adding a negative integer.

OL
- *In Example 3, why is $6p + (-30)$ changed to $6p - 30$?* Since they are equivalent expressions, it is simplified when written as $6p - 30$.
- *In Example 3, can you subtract 30 from 6p? Explain.* No; they are not like terms.

BL
- *Refer to Example 3. What is another way you can rewrite the expression, without first changing the subtraction to addition?* Sample answer: You can distribute the multiplication over the subtraction and keep the subtraction sign; $6(p - 5) = 6p - 30$

Need Other Examples?

Use the Distributive Property to rewrite each expression.

a. $11(x + 5)$ $11x + 55$ **b.** $5(p - 8)$ $5p - 40$

4–6. Write equivalent expressions.

AL
- *In Example 4, do you distribute just the 2, just the negative sign, or the entire number -2 to both terms?* -2
- *In Example 4, what is $-2 \cdot (-8)$?* 16
- *In Example 6, what is $\frac{1}{3} \cdot x$?* $\frac{1}{3}x$

OL
- *In Example 5, can you add $-15x$ and $35y$? Explain.* no; Sample answer: They are not like terms since the variables are different.

BL
- *In Example 4, why was it beneficial to change subtraction to addition before distributing?* Sample answer: It helped to avoid making a sign mistake by remembering to multiply -2 by -8, and not by 8.

Need Other Examples?

Use the Distributive Property to rewrite each expression.

a. $-3(x - 2)$ $-3x + 6$ **b.** $\frac{1}{4}(x - 16)$ $\frac{1}{4}x - 4$

Example

7. **Simplify expressions.**

AL • *What do you need to find?* the total cost of 9 helmets

• *Why rename $19.95 as $20.00 − $0.05?* to be able to use the Distributive Property to mentally multiply 9 by $20.00 and 9 by $0.05

OL • *How does the Distributive Property allow you to use mental math in this example?* Sample answer: I can find 9 × $20 and 9 × $0.05 quicker than I can find 9 × $19.95.

BL • *Is there another way to solve this problem using the Distributive Property? If so, write the expression you could use.* yes; Sample answer: 19.95(10 − 1)

Need Another Example?

Fifteen students are buying T-shirts that cost $10.60 each. Use the Distributive Property to find the total cost of the shirts. $159; 15($10 + $0.60) = 15 • 10 + 15 • 0.6 = 150 + 9, or 159

Guided Practice

Formative Assessment Use these exercises to assess students' understanding of the concepts in this lesson.

If some of your students are not ready for assignments, use the differentiated activities below.

AL EL **Team Pair Solo** Divide students into teams of four. Each team completes Exercises 1 and 2. Then students pair up to complete Exercise 3. The team regroups to discuss the solution. Finally, students work alone to complete Exercise 4, return to the team, and share answers. If the solutions do not agree, students work together to find the errors. MP 1, 7

BL EL **Pairs Discussion** Have students work in pairs. Tell students the "official" names of the Distributive Property: the Distributive Property of Multiplication over Addition, and the Distributive Property of Multiplication over Subtraction. Ask students to consider the expression 5(3 • 6) and determine whether there is a Distributive Property of Multiplication over Multiplication. Then call on one student to share and justify their response within a small group or large group discussion. MP 1, 6, 7

Real World Example

7. **Mr. Ito needs to buy batting helmets for the baseball team. The helmets he plans to buy are $19.95 each. Find the total cost if Mr. Ito needs to buy 9 batting helmets for the team.**

Rename $19.95 as $20.00 − $0.05. Then use the Distributive Property to find the total cost mentally.

9($20.00 − $0.05) = 9($20.00) − 9($0.05)	Distributive Property
= $180 − $0.45	Multiply.
= $179.55	Subtract.

The total cost of the helmets is $179.55.

Got It? Do this problem to find out.

h. A sports club rents dirt bikes for $37.50 each. Find the total cost for the club to rent 20 bikes. Justify your answer by using the Distributive Property.

Show your work.

h. $750; 20($37.00 + $0.50) = 20 • 37 + 20 • 0.5

Guided Practice

Use the Distributive Property to evaluate or rewrite each expression. (Examples 1–6)

1. (8 + 11)(−3) = −57

2. −5(2x + 4y) = −10x − 20y

3. $\frac{1}{5}(g - 10) = \frac{1}{5}g - 2$

Show your work.

4. A housefly can fly about 6.4 feet per second. At this rate, how far can it fly in 25 seconds? Justify your answer by using the Distributive Property. (Example 7)

160 ft; 25(6 + 0.4) = 25 • 6 + 25 • 0.4

5. **Building on the Essential Question** Describe how the formula to find the perimeter of a rectangle is an application of the Distributive Property. Sample answer: You can find the sum of the length and width and then multiply by two, $2(\ell + w)$. You can also find the sum of twice the length and twice the width, $(2\ell + 2w)$.

Rate Yourself!

How confident are you about the Distributive Property? Check the box that applies.

For more help, go online to access a Personal Tutor.

Name ____________ My Homework ____________

Independent Practice

Go online for Step-by-Step Solutions eHelp

Use the Distributive Property to evaluate each expression. (Example 1)

1. $3(5 + 6) =$ **33**
2. $(6 + 4)(-12) =$ **−120**
3. $-6(9 - 4) =$ **−30**

Show your work.

4. $5(-6 + 4) =$ **−10**
5. $4(8 - 7) =$ **4**
6. $(5 - 7)(-3) =$ **6**

MP **Identify Structure** Use the Distributive Property to rewrite each expression. (Examples 2–6)

7. $3(-4x + 8) =$ **$-12x + 24$**
8. $4(x - 6y) =$ **$4x - 24y$**
9. $6(5 - q) =$ **$30 - 6q$**
10. $\frac{1}{2}(c - 8) =$ **$\frac{1}{2}c - 4$**
11. $-3(5 - b) =$ **$-15 + 3b$**
12. $(d + 2)(-7) =$ **$-7d - 14$**

13. Amelia bought roast beef for \$6.85 per pound. Find the total cost if Amelia bought 4 pounds of roast beef. Justify your answer by using the Distributive Property. (Example 7)
\$27.40; 4(\$7.00 − \$0.15) = 4 • 7 − 4 • 0.15

14. The table shows the different prices of items at a movie theater.
 a. Suppose Mina and two of her friends go to the movies. Write an expression that could be used to find the total cost for them to go to the movies and buy one of each item.
 3(2.25 + 3.25 + 4.50 + 7.50)
 b. What is the total cost for all three people?
 \$52.50

Movie Theater Prices	
Item	**Cost (\$)**
box of candy	2.25
drink	3.25
popcorn	4.50
ticket	7.50

ENGAGE EXPLORE **EXPLAIN** **ELABORATE** **EVALUATE**

3 Practice and Apply

Independent Practice and Extra Practice

The Independent Practice pages are meant to be used as the homework assignment. The Extra Practice page can be used for additional reinforcement or as a second-day assignment.

Levels of Complexity

The levels of the exercises progress from 1 to 3, with Level 1 indicating the lowest level of complexity.

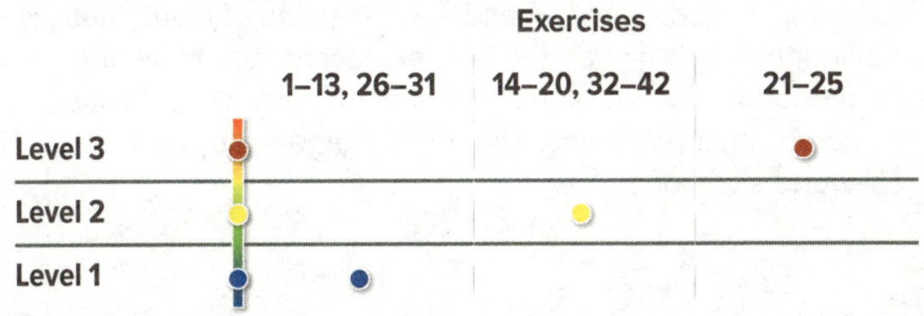

Suggested Assignments

You can use the table below that includes exercises of all complexity levels to select appropriate exercises for your students' needs.

Differentiated Homework Options		
AL	Approaching Level	1–13, 15–19 odd, 21, 22, 24, 41, 42
OL	On Level	1–13 odd, 14–22, 24, 41, 42
BL	Beyond Level	15–25, 41, 42

McGraw Hill Education **ALEKS**® can provide additional remediation support with personalized instruction and practice.

Watch Out!

Common Error Some students may make errors simplifying expressions such as $(x + 7)5$ because of the order. Have students use the Commutative Property of Multiplication to write the equivalent expression $5(x + 7)$.

MP MATHEMATICAL PRACTICES

Emphasis On	Exercise(s)
1 Make sense of problems and persevere in solving them.	23, 25
2 Reason abstractly and quantitatively.	21
3 Construct viable arguments and critique the reasoning of others.	24, 32
5 Use appropriate tools strategically.	15–20
7 Look for and make use of structure.	7–12, 22

Mathematical Practices 1, 3, and 4 are aspects of mathematical thinking that are emphasized in every lesson. Students are given opportunities to be persistent in their problem solving, to express their reasoning, and apply mathematics to real-world situations.

Formative Assessment
Use this activity as a closing formative assessment before dismissing students from your class.

TICKET Out the Door

Have students explain how they think today's lesson on the Distributive Property will help them with simplifying algebraic expressions. See students' work.

MP Use Math Tools Find each product mentally. Justify your answer.

15. $9 \cdot 35 =$ 315

$9(30 + 5) = 9(30) + 9(5)$
$= 270 + 45$

16. $8 \cdot 28 =$ 224

$8(20 + 8) = 8(20) + 8(8)$
$= 160 + 64$

17. $112 \cdot 6 =$ 672

$(100 + 12)6 = 100(6) + 12(6)$
$= 600 + 72$

18. $85 \cdot 8 =$ 680

$(80 + 5)8 = 80(8) + 5(8)$
$= 640 + 40$

19. $4 \cdot 122 =$ 488

$4(120 + 2) = 4(120) + 4(2)$
$= 480 + 8$

20. $12 \cdot 64 =$ 768

$12(60 + 4) = 12(60) + 12(4)$
$= 720 + 48$

H.O.T. Problems Higher Order Thinking

21. **MP Reason Abstractly** Write an expression that when using the Distributive Property can be simplified to $12a + 18b - 6c$.

Sample answer: $6(2a + 3b - c)$

22. **MP Identify Structure** Use the Distributive Property to rewrite the expression $7bx + 7by$ as an equivalent expression.

$7b(x + y)$

23. **MP Persevere with Problems** Use the Distributive Property to write an equivalent expression for the expression $(a + b)(2 + y)$.

$2a + ay + 2b + by$

24. **MP Find the Error** Julia is using the Distributive Property to simplify $3(x + 2)$. Find her mistake and correct it.

$3(x + 2) = 3x + 2$

Sample answer: Julia did not distribute the 3 to the second term inside the parentheses; the correct answer is $3x + 6$.

25. **MP Persevere with Problems** Is $3 + (x \cdot y) = (3 + x) \cdot (3 + y)$ a true statement? If so, explain your reasoning. If not, give a counterexample.

No; $3 + (4 \cdot 5) = 23$ but $(3 + 4) \cdot (3 + 5) = 56$

Name ________________ My Homework ________________

Extra Practice

Use the Distributive Property to evaluate each expression.

26. $(3 + 6)(-8) =$ -72

$3 \cdot (-8) + 6(-8) =$

$-24 + (-48) = -72$

Homework Help

27. $4(11 - 5) =$ 24

28. $(12 - 4)(-5)$ -40

Use the Distributive Property to rewrite each expression.

29. $-8(a + b) =$ $-8a - 8b$

30. $(2b + 8)5 =$ $10b + 40$

31. $(p + 7)(-2) =$ $-2p - 14$

32. MP **Justify Conclusions** Theresa is planning on making a fleece blanket for her nephew. She learns that the fabric she wants to use is $7.99 per yard. Find the total cost of 4 yards of fabric. Justify your answer by using the Distributive Property.

$31.96; 4($8.00 − $0.01) = 4 • 8 − 4 • 0.01

33. You are ordering T-shirts with your school's mascot printed on them. Each T-shirt costs $4.75. The printer charges a setup fee of $30 and $2.50 to print each shirt. Write two expressions to represent the total cost of printing *n* T-shirts.

$n(4.75 + 2.50) + 30; 7.25n + 30$

Use the Distributive Property to rewrite each expression.

34. $0.5x(y - z)$

$= 0.5xy - 0.5xz$

35. $-6a(2b + 5c)$

$= -12ab - 30ac$

36. $-4m(3n - 6p)$

$= -12mn + 24mp$

37. $3(2y + 4z)$

$= 6y + 12z$

38. $-2(3a - 2b)$

$= -6a + 4b$

39. $-6(12p - 8n)$

$= -72p + 48n$

40. Write two equivalent expressions for the area of the figure.

$8(x + 4); 8x + 32$

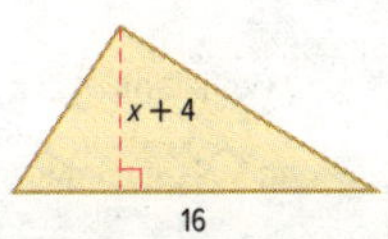

Create Your Own Homework Online

eSolutionsManual™ can be used to create worksheets for the suggested assignments on page 379, or create your own worksheets for differentiated homework or review.

Power Up! Test Practice

Exercises 41 and 42 prepare students for more rigorous thinking needed for the state assessment.

41.

This test item requires students to reason abstractly and quantitatively when problem solving.	
Depth of Knowledge	DOK1
Content Standard	7.EE.1, 7.EE.2
Mathematical Practices	MP1, MP3, MP4
Online Experience	Students will be required to type their responses in the boxes.
Scoring Rubric	
2 points	Students correctly model the situation and answer the question.
1 point	Students correctly model the situation OR students correctly answer the question.

42.

This test item requires students to support their reasoning or evaluate the reasoning of others by justifying their response and constructing arguments.	
Depth of Knowledge	DOK3
Content Standard	7.EE.1, 7.EE.2
Mathematical Practice	MP1
Online Experience	Students will be required to click on the bubbles to select all answers that are correct.
Scoring Rubric	
1 point	Students correctly answer the question.

Power Up! Test Practice

41. A group of 3 seniors, 3 adults, and 3 children bought tickets to the aquarium.

Type of Ticket	Cost ($)
Adult	18.95
Senior	14.95
Child	9.95

Fill in the boxes to model the total amount spent with an expression.

[3] × ([$18.95] + [$14.95] + [$9.95])

How much did the group spend on tickets altogether? How does applying the Distributive Property make it easier to find this amount?

$131.55; Sample answer: The ticket prices can be added first and then the sum can be multiplied by 3. This requires fewer steps and easier computations than multiplying each price by 3 and then adding the resulting products.

42. Celeste is going to summer camp. The table shows the cost of items she will need to purchase with the camp logo. She needs to buy four of each item.

Item	Cost ($)
T-shirt	8.00
Shorts	4.50
Socks	2.25

Which of the following expressions represents the total cost of the items? Select all that apply.

- [x] 4(14.75)
- [ ] 4(8.00) + 4.50 + 2.25
- [x] 4(8) + 4(4.50) + 4(2.25)
- [x] 4(8.00 + 4.50 + 2.25)

Spiral Review

Evaluate each expression if $x = 9$ and $y = 3$. 6.EE.2c

43. $x + y - 58$ -46

44. $y^3 + x^3$ 756

45. $y^4 - 128 =$ -47

46. In the expression below, identify the coefficient and the variable. 6.EE.2

$4x + 450$

coefficient: 4 variable: x

PLAN ONLINE: PD | RtI | Watch | Worksheets | Vocab | Tutor | Tools | Check | English Learners | Sketchpad

PRESENT: IWB — An Interactive Whiteboard Ready presentation is available for each lesson in the chapter.

MP **Problem-Solving Investigation**

Make a Table

Content Standards
7.NS.3

MP **Mathematical Practices**
1, 3, 4

Case #1 Mountain Biking

Hoshi wants to purchase a membership to a bike park. The cost depends on the number of people on the membership. It costs $55 for 5 people, $65 for 6 people, and $75 for 7 people.

Find the cost of a membership that includes 8 people.

1 Understand *What are the facts?*

The cost of a membership depends on the number of people included on the membership.

2 Plan *What is your strategy to solve this problem?*

Make a table that shows the number of people and the cost.

3 Solve *How can you apply the strategy?*

Make a table. Find the cost for 8 people.

Number of People (p)	Cost	
5	$55	+10
6	$65	+10
7	$75	+10
8	$85	

So, the cost for 8 people is $85.

4 Check *Does the answer make sense?*

The expression $10p + 5$ can be used to represent the situation.

Since $10(8) + $5 = $85, the solution is reasonable.

Analyze the Strategy

Tutor

MP **Justify Conclusions** Hoshi wants to purchase a membership for four people. Explain how the table would change and then solve.

Sample answer: The table would be set up in descending order. To solve for 4 people, subtract $10 from $55; $45.

Focus narrowing the scope

Objective Solve problems by making a table. This lesson emphasizes MP **Mathematical Practice 4.** Using tables, students model real-world situations. Then they justify conclusions with written explanations and computations.

Make a Table Making a table is a useful strategy for solving many kinds of problems. In this lesson, students will work with tables involving numbers, objects, and geometric figures.

Coherence connecting within and across grades

Now
Students solve non-routine problems.

Next
Students will apply the make a table strategy to find patterns.

Rigor pursuing concepts, fluency, and applications

See the Levels of Complexity chart on page 385.

ENGAGE EXPLORE EXPLAIN ELABORATE EVALUATE

1 Launch the Lesson

The problems on pages 383 and 384 are intended to be used as a whole-group discussion on how to solve non-routine problems and are designed to provide scaffolded guidance. The problem on page 383 walks students through the solution, while the problem on page 384 asks students to come up with their own solutions.

Case #1 Mountain Biking

BL Have students extend the problem by having them answer the questions below.

Ask:

- *Find the average cost per person using the cost for one person and the cost for four people.* The cost for one person is $15. The average cost per person for four people is $11.25.

Case #2 Financial Literacy

AL **EL** **Circle the Sage** Have students work in teams of 3–5 students to read through the problem. Poll the class to see who feels that they have a solid understanding on how to solve the problem. Those students (the sages) spread out around the room. Have the teams split up with each team member going to a different sage, if possible. Have the sages explain how they completed the exercises while the classmates listen, ask questions, and take notes. MP 1, 3,

BL **EL** **One Stray** Have students complete the problem in teams of 3 or 4. Call one or more students to stand. The standing student(s) move to a team with an empty seat. The student(s) who moved compare their team's responses with the new team's responses. As the student(s) return to their original team, give them time to change any of their responses, if necessary. MP 1

Need Another Example?

In a pyramid of balloons, there is one balloon at the top, four balloons in the second layer, and seven balloons in the third layer. The pattern continues for a total of six layers. How many balloons are in the sixth layer?

Layer	1	2	3	4	5	6
Number of Balloons	1	4	7	10	13	16

There are 16 balloons in the sixth layer.

Case #2 Financial Literacy

Latoya is saving money to buy a saxophone. After 1 month, she has $75. After 2 months, she has $120. After 3 months, she has $165. She plans to keep saving at the same rate.

How long will it take Latoya to save enough money to buy a saxophone that costs $300?

1 Understand

Read the problem. What are you being asked to find?

I need to find the number of months it will take Latoya to save $300 to buy a saxophone.

Underline key words and values. What information do you know?

After 1 month, Latoya has $75. After 2 months, she has $120. After 3 months, she has $165. She continues to save at the same rate.

Is there any information that you do *not* need to know?

I do not need to know that Latoya is saving to buy a saxophone.

2 Plan

Choose a problem-solving strategy.

I will use the make a table strategy.

3 Solve

Use your problem-solving strategy to solve the problem.

Months	1	2	3	4	5	6
Amount Saved ($)	75	120	165	210	255	300

+45 +45 +45 +45 +45

Latoya will have $300 saved in 6 months.

4 Check

Use information from the problem to check your answer. Sample answer: After the first month, she saves $45 dollars each month. Add the first month ($75) to the 5 other months ($45)5. $75 + ($45)5 = $300.

Expressions and Equations

Collaborate

Work with a small group to solve the following cases.
Show your work on a separate piece of paper.

Case #3 Carnivals

For a carnival game, containers are arranged in a triangular display. The top row has 1 container. The second row has 2 containers. The third row has 3 containers. The pattern continues until the bottom row, which has 10 containers.

A contestant knocks down 29 containers on the first throw. How many containers remain?

26 containers

Case #4 Budget

Tamara earns $2,050 each month. She spends 65% of the amount she earns. The rest of the money is equally divided and deposited into two separate accounts.

How many months until Tamara has deposited more than $2,500 in one of her accounts?

7 months

Case #5 Toothpicks

Write an expression that can be used to find the number of toothpicks needed to make any figure. Then find the number of toothpicks needed to make the eighth figure.

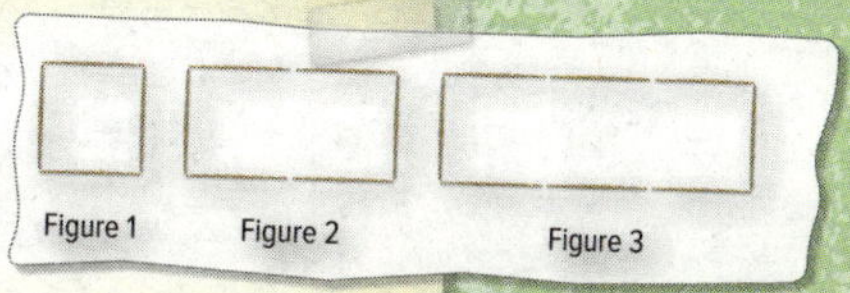

$2n + 2$; 18 toothpicks

Case #6 Diving

A diver descends to −15 feet after 1 minute, −30 feet after 2 minutes, and −45 feet after 3 minutes.

If the diver keeps descending at this rate, what is their position after 12 minutes?

−180 ft

ENGAGE EXPLORE **EXPLAIN** **ELABORATE** EVALUATE

2 Collaborate

Levels of Complexity

The levels of the exercises progress from 1 to 3, with Level 1 indicating the lowest level of complexity.

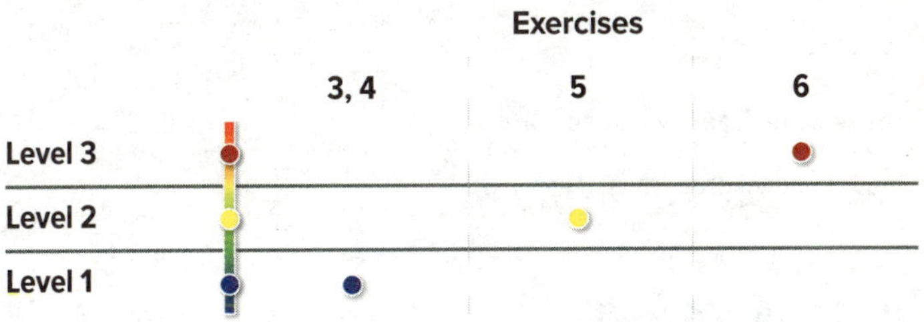

AL EL Rally Coach Have students work in pairs to complete Cases 1–4. Student 1 completes Case 1, talking through their solution process, while Student 2 watches, listens, coaches, and praises. Partners alternate roles until all exercises have been completed. MP 1, 6

BL EL Team Discussion In teams of 3–4, have students discuss how making a table can help them solve a problem involving a linear relationship. Have them study their tables in Cases 1–4 to determine if each relationship is linear. Have them justify their responses. MP 1, 6, 7

Ask:

- *How does making a table help you solve the problem?* **Sample answer: Making a table helps to organize the information to discover a pattern or see if there is a constant rate of change.**
- *How do you know if a relationship is linear, by studying the table?* **Sample answer: If the table shows a constant rate of change, the relationships is linear.**

Mid-Chapter Check

If students have trouble with Exercises 1–10, they may need help with the following concepts.

Concept	Exercise(s)
sequences (Lesson 2)	2–5
algebraic expressions (Lesson 1)	1, 10
Distributive Property (Lesson 4)	6–8
mathematical properties (Lesson 3)	9

Vocabulary Activity

EL **Pairs Discussion** Have students work in pairs to complete Exercise 2. One student makes a list of similarities between an arithmetic sequence and a geometric sequence. The other student makes a list of differences. Have them swap lists and discuss, modifying their lists if necessary. MP 1, 6, 7

ALEKS® provides additional remediation support with personalized instruction and practice for those who are struggling, while providing enhanced learning for those who have mastered the concepts.

Mid-Chapter Check

Vocabulary Check

1. Fill in the blank in the sentence below with the correct term. (Lesson 1)

A **variable** is a symbol that represents an unknown quantity.

2. Define *arithmetic sequence*. Then provide an example. (Lesson 2)

In an arithmetic sequence each term is found by adding the same number to the previous term. Sample answer: 5, 7, 9, 11, ...

Skills Check and Problem Solving

Describe the relationship between the terms in each arithmetic sequence. Then write the next three terms in each sequence. (Lesson 2)

3. 5, 8, 11, 14, ...

Add 3 to the previous term; 17, 20, 23

4. 4, 11, 18, 25, ...

Add 7 to the previous term; 32, 39, 46

5. 5.8, 10.8, 15.8, 20.8, ...

Add 5 to the previous term; 25.8, 30.8, 35.8

Show your work.

Use the Distributive Property to rewrite each expression. (Lesson 4)

6. $4(x + 9) =$ $\mathbf{4x + 36}$

7. $2(x + 5) =$ $\mathbf{2x + 10}$

8. $3(-2x + 4) =$ $\mathbf{-6x + 12}$

9. MP **Identify Structure** What property is shown by the statement $8x + 0 = 8x$? (Lesson 3)

Identity (+)

10. MP **Persevere with Problems** A coach bought some baseball bats and five baseball gloves. Let *b* represent the number of bats. Write an expression that can be used to find the total cost of the bats and gloves. Then find the total cost if he bought three bats. (Lesson 1)

5(48) + 35*b*; $345

PLAN ONLINE: PD | RtI | Watch | Worksheets | Vocab | Tutor | Tools | Check | English Learners | Sketchpad

PRESENT: IWB — An Interactive Whiteboard Ready presentation is available for each lesson in the chapter.

Lesson 5

Simplify Algebraic Expressions

Real-World Link

Music Store Patricia, Hugo, and Sun work at a music store. Each week, Patricia works three more than twice the number of hours that Hugo works. Sun works 2 less hours than Hugo.

1. Let x represent the number of hours that Hugo works each week. The number of hours that Hugo, Patricia, and Sun work can be modeled as shown below. Write an expression that represents each person's number of hours.

Expression: x Expression: $2x + 3$ Expression: $x - 2$

2. Model the total number of hours that Patricia and Sun work. Draw the result below. Then write an expression for the drawing.

Expression: $2x + 3 + x + (-2)$

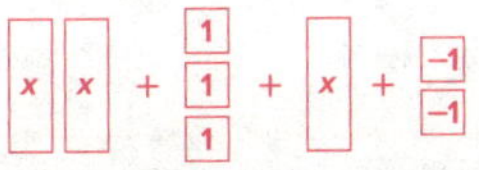

3. Like tiles are tiles that have the same shape. Group like tiles together and remove the zero pairs. Draw the result below. Then write an expression for your drawing.

Expression: $3x + 1$

Which MP Mathematical Practices did you use? Shade the circle(s) that applies.

① Persevere with Problems
② Reason Abstractly
③ Construct an Argument
④ Model with Mathematics
⑤ Use Math Tools
⑥ Attend to Precision
⑦ Make Use of Structure
⑧ Use Repeated Reasoning

Essential Question

HOW can you use numbers and symbols to represent mathematical ideas?

Vocabulary

term
like terms
constant
simplest form

Content Standards
7.EE.1, 7.EE.2

MP Mathematical Practices
1, 2, 3, 4, 6

Focus narrowing the scope

Objective Simplify algebraic expressions. 7.EE.1, 7.EE.2

Coherence connecting within and across grades

Previous Students used properties to simplify algebraic expressions.

Now Students simplify algebraic expressions with more than two terms by combining like terms.

Next Students will combine like terms when adding and subtracting linear expressions

Rigor pursuing concepts, fluency, and applications

See the Levels of Complexity chart on page 391.

ENGAGE EXPLORE EXPLAIN ELABORATE EVALUATE

1 Launch the Lesson

Ideas for Use

You may wish to launch the lesson using a whole group, small group, think-pair-share activity, or independent activity.

AL EL **Paired Heads Together** Have students work in pairs to complete Exercises 1–3, making sure each member understands how to arrive at the answer. Call on one member to present the team's solution in a small group or whole class discussion. MP 1, 4

Alternate Strategy

BL Tell students that terms with the same variable can be combined because of the Distributive Property. For example, $5x + 3x$ is the same as $(5 + 3)x$ or $8x$. They can combine those terms by performing the addition or subtraction indicated by the coefficients. MP 1, 7

2 Teach the Concept

Ask the scaffolded questions for each example to differentiate instruction.

IWB

Example

1. Identify parts of an expression.

AL
- *What are like terms?* terms that contain the same variable to the same power
- *What is a coefficient?* the numerical part of a term
- *What is a constant?* a term without a variable

OL
- *What terms are like terms?* $6n$, $-7n$, and n
- *What is the coefficient of n?* 1
- *How will you add the like terms?* add the coefficients

BL
- *Why do you think the term that is called constant got its name?* Since there is no variable, the value of the term does not change, it stays constant.

Need Another Example?

Identify the terms, like terms, coefficients, and constants in the expression $3x - 5 + 2x - x$. terms: $3x$, -5, $2x$, and $-x$; like terms: $3x$, $2x$, and $-x$; coefficients: 3, 2, and -1; constant: -5

Work Zone

STOP and Reflect

Circle the term below that is a like term with $-4x^3$.

$-4x^2$ x^3 -4

Identify Parts of an Expression

When addition or subtraction signs separate an algebraic expression into parts, each part is called a **term**. Recall that the numerical factor of a term that contains a variable is called the coefficient of the variable.

Like terms contain the same variables to the same powers. For example, $3x^2$ and $-7x^2$ are like terms. So are $8xy^2$ and $12xy^2$. But $10x^2z$ and $22xz^2$ are *not* like terms. A term without a variable is called a **constant**. Constant terms are also like terms.

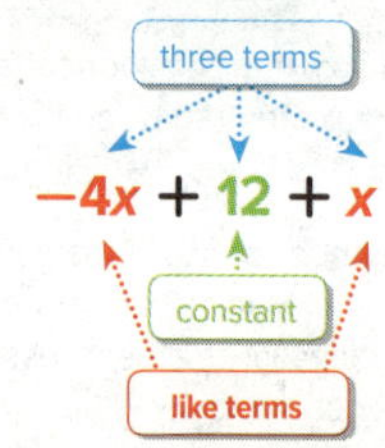

Example

1. Identify the terms, like terms, coefficients, and constants in the expression $6n - 7n - 4 + n$.

$6n - 7n - 4 + n = 6n + (-7n) + (-4) + 1n$ Rewrite the expression.

- Terms: $6n$, $-7n$, -4, n
- Like terms: $6n$, $-7n$, n All of these terms have the same variable.
- Coefficients: 6, -7, 1
- Constants: -4 This is the only term without a variable.

Got It? Do these problems to find out.

Identify the terms, like terms, coefficients, and constants in each expression.

a. $9y - 4 - 11y + 7$

b. $3x + 2 - 10 - 3x$

Show your work.

a. terms: $9y$, -4, $-11y$, 7; like terms: $9y$ and $-11y$, -4 and 7; coefficients: 9, -11; constants: -4, 7

b. terms: $3x$, 2, -10, $-3x$; like terms: $3x$ and $-3x$, 2 and -10; coefficients: 3, -3; constants: 2, -10

Simplify Algebraic Expressions

An algebraic expression is in **simplest form** if it has no like terms and no parentheses. Use the Distributive Property to combine like terms.

Examples

2. Write $4y + y$ in simplest form.

$4y$ and y are like terms.

$4y + y = 4y + 1y$ — Identity Property; $y = 1y$

$= (4 + 1)y$ or $5y$ — Distributive Property; Simplify.

3. Write $7x - 2 - 7x + 6$ in simplest form.

$7x$ and $-7x$ are like terms. -2 and 6 are also like terms.

$7x - 2 - 7x + 6 = 7x + (-2) + (-7x) + 6$ — Definition of subtraction

$= 7x + (-7x) + (-2) + 6$ — Commutative Property

$= [7 + (-7)]x + (-2) + 6$ — Distributive Property

$= 0x + 4$ — Simplify.

$= 0 + 4$ or 4 — Multiplicative Property of zero and Additive Identity Property of zero.

Equivalent Expressions

To check whether $4y + y$ and $5y$ are equivalent expressions, substitute any value for y and see whether the expressions have the same value.

Got It? Do these problems to find out.

c. $4z - z$ d. $6 - 3n + 3n$ e. $2g - 3 + 11 - 8g$

Show your work.

c. $3z$

d. 6

e. $8 - 6g$

Real World Example

4. The cost of a jacket j after a 5% markup can be represented by the expression $j + 0.05j$. Simplify the expression. Then determine the total cost of the jacket after the markup, if the original price is $35.

$j + 0.05j = 1j + 0.05j$ — Identity Property; $j = 1j$

$= (1 + 0.05)j$ — Distributive Property

$= 1.05j$ — Simplify.

$1.05j = 1.05(35)$ — Replace j with 35 to find the total cost.

$= 36.75$ — Multiply.

So, the cost of the jacket after a 5% markup is $36.75.

Got It? Do this problem to find out.

f. Write an expression in simplest form for the cost of the jacket in Example 4 if the markup is 8%. Then determine the total cost after the markup.

f. $1.08a$; $37.80

Examples

IWB

2–3. Simplify expressions.

AL
- *In Example 2, what are the like terms?* 4y and y
- *In Example 2, what are the coefficients of the like terms?* 4 and 1

OL
- *What are the like terms in Example 3?* 7x and −7x; −2 and 6
- *In Example 3, how would you combine the like terms?* For the x terms, add 7 and −7, for the constants, add −2 and 6.

BL
- *In Example 2, why is $4y + y = 5y$ and not $5y^2$?* Sample answer: You are adding the terms, so you add the coefficients 4 and 1 and keep the variable y. You do not multiply y by y.

Need Another Example?

Write $8z + z - 5 - 9z + 2$ in simplest form. -3

4. Simplify expressions.

AL
- *What are you trying to find?* the total cost of the jacket after the 5% markup
- *Why is the expression $j + 0.05j$ and not $j + 5j$?* The 5% markup should be expressed as a decimal, 0.05.
- *What are the coefficients of j in the terms j and 0.05j?* 1 and 0.05

OL
- *Does simplifying $j + 0.05j$ as $1.05j$ answer the question presented in the example? Explain.* no; Sample answer: The question asks for the total cost of the jacket after the markup. We need to replace j with 35 to find the total cost.

BL
- *Is it easier for you to simplify the expression first, then evaluate it for $j = 35$, or evaluate it for $j = 35$ first, then simplify? Explain.* See students' preferences.
- *Write an expression, in simplest form, that would represent the total cost of the jacket after a 15% markup. Then find the total cost.* 1.15j; $40.25

Need Another Example?

The cost of a set of DVDs after a 25% markup can be represented by the expression $c + 0.25c$. Simplify the expression. Then determine the total cost of the DVDs after the markup if the original price is $40. 1.25c; $50

Example

IWB

5. Simplify expressions.

AL
- *What do you need to find?* an expression for the total cost of some T-shirts and CDs
- *What do you know about the number of T-shirts and CDs purchased?* The number is the same.
- *How can you represent the number of T-shirts and CDs purchased?* with a variable

OL
- *What is the cost of one T-shirt? one CD?* \$12; \$7.50
- *Why can you combine 12x and 7.5x?* They are like terms.

BL
- *Suppose you bought 5 of each. How much did you spend?* \$97.50

Need Another Example?
Manfred buys some boxes of cereal for \$4.85 each and the same number of bags of pretzels for \$2.90 each. Write an expression in simplest form that represents the total amount spent. $7.75x$

Guided Practice

Formative Assessment Use these exercises to assess students' understanding of the concepts in this lesson.

If some of your students are not ready for assignments, use the differentiated activities below.

AL EL **Pairs Discussion** Have students work in pairs to complete Exercises 1–5. Have them trade their solutions with another pair of students and discuss any differences. MP 1, 2, 3

BL EL **Trade-a-Problem** Have students create their own problem, similar to Exercise 4. Students trade their problems, solve each other's problem, and compare solutions. If the solutions do not agree, students work together to find the errors. Challenge students to use more than one variable or variables raised to a power. MP 1, 2, 6

Real World

Example

Tutor

5. **At a concert, you buy some T-shirts for \$12.00 each and the same number of CDs for \$7.50 each. Write an expression in simplest form that represents the total amount spent.**

Let x represent the number of T-shirts and CDs.

$12x + 7.50x$	Write the expression.
$12x + 7.50x = (12 + 7.50)x$	Distributive Property
$= 19.50x$	Simplify.

The expression \$19.50x represents the total amount spent.

Got It? **Do this problem to find out.**

g. You have some money. Your friend has \$50 less than you. Write an expression in simplest form that represents the total amount of money you and your friend have.

Show your work.

g. $2x - 50$

Guided Practice

Check

1. Identify the terms, like terms, coefficients, and constants in $5n - 2n - 3 + n$. (Example 1)
   terms: $5n, -2n, -3, n$; like terms: $5n, -2n, n$; coefficients: 5, −2, 1; constant: −3

2. Write $4p - 7 + 6p + 10$ in simplest form. (Examples 2 and 3)
   $10p + 3$

3. The cost of a game g with 7% sales tax can be represented by the expression $g + 0.07g$. Simplify the expression. Then determine the total cost of the game after sales tax if the original price is \$52. (Example 4)
   $1.07g$; \$55.64

4. You go to a basketball game and buy 3 waters that cost x dollars each. Your brother buys a bottle of water and a bag of peanuts that costs \$4.50. Write an expression in simplest form that represents the total amount of money spent altogether. (Example 5)
   $4x + 4.50$

5. **Building on the Essential Question** Explain why $2(x - 1) + 3(x - 1) = 5(x - 1)$ is a true statement.
   $2(x - 1) + 3(x - 1) = 2x - 2 + 3x - 3$ or $5x - 5$, which is equivalent to $5(x - 1)$.

Rate Yourself!

Are you ready to move on? Shade the section that applies.

YES ? NO

For more help, go online to access a Personal Tutor.

Tutor

Name ______________ My Homework ______________

Independent Practice

Go online for Step-by-Step Solutions eHelp

Identify the terms, like terms, coefficients, and constants in each expression. (Example 1)

1. $2 + 3a + 9a$
   terms: 2, $3a$, $9a$; like terms: $3a$, $9a$; coefficients: 3, 9; constant: 2

2. $7 - 5x + 1$
   terms: 7, $-5x$, 1; like terms: 7, 1; coefficient: -5; constants: 7, 1

3. $9 - z + 3 - 2z$
   terms: 9, $-z$, 3, $-2z$; like terms: 9 and 3, $-z$ and $-2z$; coefficients: -1, -2; constants: 9, 3

Write each expression in simplest form. (Examples 2 and 3)

4. $n + 5n =$ $6n$

5. $12c - c =$ $11c$

6. $-4j - 1 - 4j + 6 =$ $-8j + 5$

7. The cost of a ticket t to a concert with a 3% sales tax can be represented by the expression $t + 0.03t$. Simplify the expression. Then determine the total cost after the sales tax if the original price is \$72. (Example 4)
   $1.03t$; \$74.16

Write an expression in simplest form that represents the total amount in each situation. (Example 5)

8. You rent x pairs of shoes for \$2 each. You buy the same number of drinks for \$1.50 each. You also pay \$9 for a bowling lane.
   $3.50x + 9$

9. You watch x minutes of television on Monday, the same amount on Wednesday, and 30 minutes on Friday.
   $2x + 30$

10. In a State Legislature, there were 119 more members in the House of Representatives than in the Senate. If there were m members in the Senate, write an expression to represent the total members in the State Legislature. $2m + 119$

11. Elian and his friends paid a total of \$7 for tickets to the school football game. While at the game, they bought 5 hot dogs at x dollars each, 4 boxes of popcorn at y dollars each, and 2 pretzels at z dollars each.
    a. Write an expression to show the total cost of admission and the snacks.
       $7 + 5x + 4y + 2z$
    b. Hot dogs cost \$4, popcorn cost \$3, and pretzels cost \$2. What was the total cost for admission and snacks? \$43

ENGAGE EXPLORE **EXPLAIN ELABORATE EVALUATE**

3 Practice and Apply

Independent Practice and Extra Practice

The Independent Practice pages are meant to be used as the homework assignment. The Extra Practice page can be used for additional reinforcement or as a second-day assignment.

Levels of Complexity

The levels of the exercises progress from 1 to 3, with Level 1 indicating the lowest level of complexity.

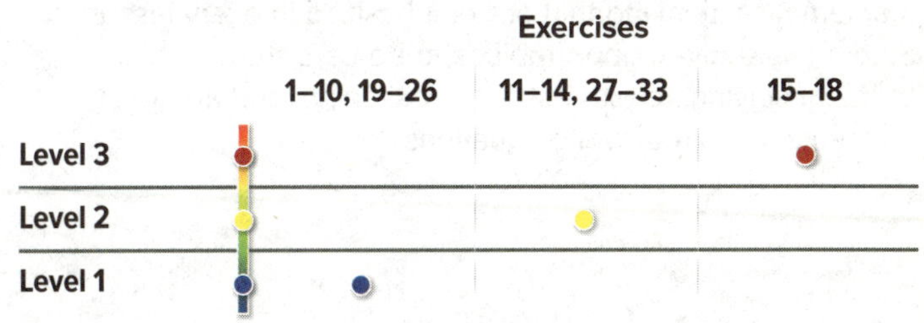

Suggested Assignments

You can use the table below that includes exercises of all complexity levels to select appropriate exercises for your students' needs.

Differentiated Homework Options		
AL	Approaching Level	1–11, 13, 15, 16, 18, 32, 33
OL	On Level	1–9 odd, 11–16, 18, 32, 33
BL	Beyond Level	11–18, 32, 33

ALEKS® can provide additional remediation support with personalized instruction and practice.

Watch Out!

Common Error Some students may overlook the coefficient of a variable if the coefficient is 1 or -1. Remind students that a coefficient of 1 is *not* usually written in an algebraic expression. For example, $8n + n$ means $8n + 1n$.

MATHEMATICAL PRACTICES

Emphasis On	Exercise(s)
1 Make sense of problems and persevere in solving them.	17
2 Reason abstractly and quantitatively.	12–14, 28
3 Construct viable arguments and critique the reasoning of others.	16, 18
6 Attend to precision.	15

Mathematical Practices 1, 3, 4, and 5 are aspects of mathematical thinking that are emphasized in every lesson. Students are given opportunities to be persistent in their problem solving, to express their reasoning, and apply mathematics to real-world situations.

Formative Assessment

Use this activity as a closing formative assessment before dismissing students from your class.

TICKET Out the Door

Have students explain how to simplify the expression $5n + n$. **Add the coefficients 5 and 1 to get $6n$.**

Reason Abstractly Write an expression in simplest form for the perimeter of each figure.

12.

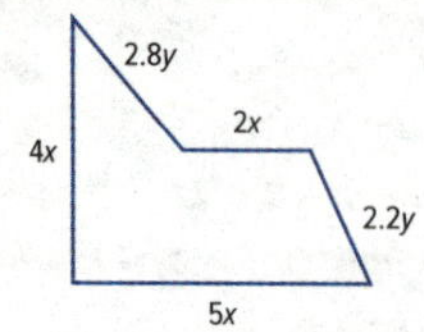

$11x + 5y$

13.

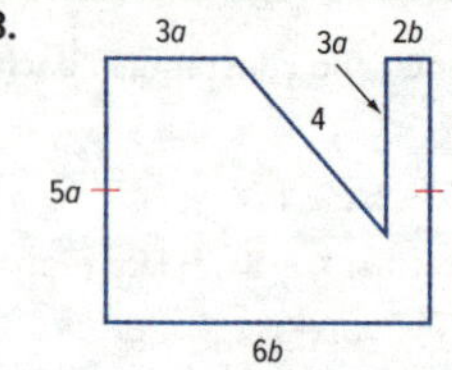

$16a + 8b + 4$

14.

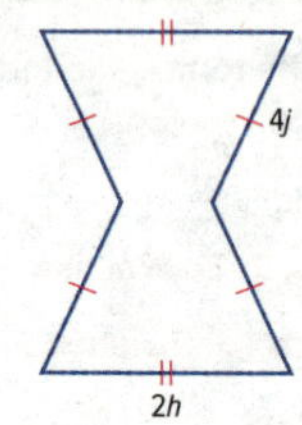

$4h + 16j$

H.O.T. Problems Higher Order Thinking

15. **Be Precise** Write an expression that has three terms and simplifies to $4x - 7$. Identify the coefficient(s) and constant(s) in your expression.

Sample answer: $3x + x - 7$; coefficients: 3, 1; constant: -7

16. **Which One Doesn't Belong?** Identify the expression that is not equivalent to the other three. Explain your reasoning.

$x - 2 + 3x$	$4(x - 2)$	$-2 + 7x - 3x$	$4x - 2$

$4(x - 2)$; Sample answer: $4(x - 2)$ is equivalent to $4x - 8$, while the other three expressions are equivalent to $4x - 2$.

17. **Persevere with Problems** Simplify the expression $8x - 2x + 12x - 3$. Show that your answer is true for $x = 2$.

$18x - 3$; $18x - 3 = 18(2) - 3 = 33$ and

$8x - 2x + 12x - 3 = 8(2) - 2(2) + 12(2) - 3 = 33$

18. **Justify Conclusions** Determine whether the following statement is *always*, *sometimes*, or *never* true. Explain your reasoning.

When using the Distributive Property, if the term outside the parentheses is negative, then the sign of each term inside the parentheses will change.

always; Sample answer: If the term outside the parentheses is negative and is multiplied by a term with a positive coefficient, the product will be negative. If the coefficient of the term in the parentheses is negative, then the product will be positive.

Name ______ My Homework ______

Extra Practice

Identify the terms, like terms, coefficients, and constants in each expression.

19. $4 + 5y - 6y + y$
terms: $4, 5y, -6y, y$
like terms: $5y, -6y, y$
coefficients: $5, -6, 1$
constant: 4

Homework Help

20. $n + 4n - 7n - 1$
terms: $n, 4n, -7n, -1$; like terms: $n, 4n, -7n$; coefficients: $1, 4, -7$; constants: -1

21. $-3d + 8 - d - 2$
terms: $-3d, 8, -d, -2$; like terms: $-3d$ and $-d$, 8 and -2; coefficients: $-3, -1$; constants: $8, -2$

Write each expression in simplest form.

22. $5x + 4 + 9x$
$= 14x + 4$

23. $2 + 3d + d$
$= 2 + 4d$

24. $3r + 7 - 3r - 12$
$= -6r - 5$

Write an expression in simplest form that represents the total amount in each situation.

25. You subscribe to *m* different magazines. Your friend subscribes to 2 fewer than you.
$2m - 2$

26. Today is your friend's birthday. She is *y* years old. Her brother is 5 years younger.
$2y - 5$

27. You spent *m* minutes studying on Monday. On Tuesday, you studied 15 more minutes than you did on Monday. Wednesday, you studied 30 minutes less than you did on Tuesday. You studied twice as long on Thursday as you did on Monday. On Friday, you studied 20 minutes less than you did on Thursday. Write an expression in simplest form to represent the number of minutes you studied in all.
$7m - 20$

28. MP **Reason Abstractly** Write a real-world situation for $7.50y + 9$.
Sample answer: You buy *y* movie tickets that cost \$7.50 each and spend \$9 at the concession stand.

Simplify each expression.

29. $3(4x - 5) + 4(2x + 6)$
$= 20x + 9$

30. $-8(2a - 3b) - 5(6b - 4a)$
$= 4a - 6b$

31. $10(5g + 2h - 3) - 4(3g - 4h + 2)$
$= 38g + 36h - 38$

Create Your Own Homework Online

eSolutionsManual™ can be used to create worksheets for the suggested assignments on page 391, or create your own worksheets for differentiated homework or review.

Power Up! Test Practice

Exercises 32 and 33 prepare students for more rigorous thinking needed for the state assessment.

32.

This test item requires students to analyze and solve complex real-world problems through the use of mathematical tools and models.	
Depth of Knowledge	DOK3
Content Standard	7.EE.1
Mathematical Practices	MP1, MP4
Online Experience	Students will drag algebra tiles to model expressions and type their response in a box.
Scoring Rubric	
2 points	Students correctly model the amount of cards each person has and write an expression to represent each amount.
1 point	Students correctly model all three but fail to write the expressions OR students write correct expressions for each but fail to model OR students correctly model and write the corresponding expressions for two of the people.

33.

This test item requires students to explain and apply mathematical concepts and solve problems with precision, while making use of structure	
Depth of Knowledge	DOK1
Content Standard	7.EE.1
Mathematical Practice	MP1
Online Experience	Students will be required to type their response in the box.
Scoring Rubric	
1 point	Students correctly answer the question.

Power Up! Test Practice

32. Vince, Neal, and Patrick collect baseball cards. Neal has 3 fewer cards than twice the number of cards Vince has. Patrick has 5 more baseball cards than Vince. Let x represent the number of baseball cards that Vince has. Use the algebra tiles to represent the number of cards each person has.

	Vince	Neal	Patrick
Model			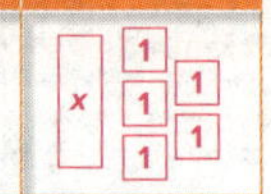
Expression	x	$2x - 3$	$x + 5$

Write an expression, in simplified form, for the number of baseball cards the three friends have altogether.

$4x + 2$

33. The table shows the number of tickets needed and the number of times Talia participated in different activities at a carnival. Write an expression, in simplified form, for the total number of tickets that Talia used.

Activity	Tickets	Times Completed
Balloon Pop	3	a
Dunk Tank	4	b
Ring Toss	2	a
Trampoline	5	b

$5a + 9b$

Spiral Review

34. Mica spends $5 for her lunch and $2 for breakfast each day Monday through Friday. Use the Associative Property to find how much money she spends on lunch and breakfast for 4 weeks. 7.EE.1

7(5)(4); $140

Define a variable. Then write each phrase as an algebraic expression. 6.EE.2

35. Anna has volunteered 9 more hours than Tricia

t = hours Tricia volunteered; $t + 9$

36. the cost of a pair of jeans is 4 times the cost of a book

b = cost of a book; $4b$

Evaluate each expression if $x = 2$, $y = 10$, and $z = 4$. 6.EE.2c

37. $5z - 10$ 10

38. $y \div 2 + x$ 7

39. $x^3 + (y \div x)$ 13

PLAN ONLINE

PD | RtI | Watch | Worksheets | Vocab | Tutor | Tools | Check | English Learners | Sketchpad

PRESENT

IWB

An Interactive Whiteboard Ready presentation is available for each lesson in the chapter.

Lesson 6

Add Linear Expressions

Real-World Link

Tools

Homework Luke has 20 math problems and 11 science questions for homework. Cameron has 23 math problems and 10 science questions for homework.

1. The expression below represents the types of exercises that Luke has for homework.

   20 math problems + 11 science questions

   Complete the expression that represents the types of exercises that Cameron has for homework.

   23 math problems + 10 science questions

2. Write an expression for the total number of math problems and science questions for both boys.

   43 math problems + 21 science questions

3. Suppose Luke has x math problems and 5 science questions for homework and Cameron has x math problems and 6 science questions. The algebra tiles below represent the total number of math problems and science questions for both boys. Write an expression in simplest form that represents the algebra tiles.

Expression: $2x + 11$

Which MP Mathematical Practices did you use? Shade the circle(s) that applies.

① Persevere with Problems
② Reason Abstractly
③ Construct an Argument
④ Model with Mathematics
⑤ Use Math Tools
⑥ Attend to Precision
⑦ Make Use of Structure
⑧ Use Repeated Reasoning

Essential Question

HOW can you use numbers and symbols to represent mathematical ideas?

Vocabulary

linear expression

Content Standards
7.EE.1, 7.EE.2

MP Mathematical Practices
1, 2, 3, 4

Focus narrowing the scope

Objective Add linear expressions. 7.EE.1, 7.EE.2

Coherence connecting within and across grades

Previous Students simplified algebraic expressions by combining like terms.

Now Students add linear expressions with more than two terms by combining like terms.

Next Students will combine like terms when subtracting linear expressions.

Rigor pursuing concepts, fluency, and applications

See the Levels of Complexity chart on page 399.

ENGAGE **EXPLORE** EXPLAIN ELABORATE EVALUATE

1 Launch the Lesson

Ideas for Use

You may wish to launch the lesson using a whole group, small group, think-pair-share activity, or independent activity.

AL EL **Trade-a-Problem** Ask each student to write an expression that can be simplified with six terms on a piece of paper. Then have them exchange papers with a neighbor and simplify the given expression. Repeat as time allows. If the solutions do not agree, students work together to find the errors. MP 1, 7

Alternate Strategy

BL Ask students to study the lesson to research the phrase *linear expression*. Ask them to identify if each of the following *is* or *is not* a linear expression, and to explain their reasoning. MP 1, 6

$3x^2 + x$ $5y - 3$ $6p + 7p + 4$ $15st$

2 Teach the Concept

Ask the scaffolded questions for each example to differentiate instruction.

Examples

IWB

1. Add linear expressions.

AL
- *What are the like terms?* $2x$ and x, 3 and 4
- *How does using algebra tiles help you add linear expressions?* Sample answer: I can visually see the like terms and determine the total number of x-tiles and the total number of 1-tiles.

OL
- *What is $2x + x$?* $3x$
- *Can you simplify $3x + 7$? Explain.* No; $3x$ and 7 are not like terms.

BL
- *What properties would you use to add the two expressions?* Commutative Property of Addition and Associative Property of Addition

Need Another Example?
Find $(6x + 2) + (x + 3)$. $7x + 5$

2. Add linear expressions.

AL
- *What are the like terms?* $2x$ and x, -1 and -5
- *How would you use algebra tiles to model this expression?* Use 2 x-tiles and one -1-tile to model $2x - 1$, then add one x-tile and five -1-tiles to model $x - 5$.

OL
- *What are the two coefficients of x?* 2 and 1
- *What are the two constants?* -1 and -5

BL
- *Can you simplify this expression another way? Explain.* Sample answer: Rewrite the expression so that like terms are together, then add; $2x + x + (-1) + (-5)$

Need Another Example?
Find $(4x - 2) + (x - 4)$. $5x - 6$

Work Zone

Add Linear Expressions

A **linear expression** is an algebraic expression in which the variable is raised to the first power and variable are not multiplied or divided. The table below gives some examples of expressions that are linear and some examples of expressions that are not linear.

Linear Expressions	Nonlinear Expressions
$5x$	$5mn$
$3x + 2$	$3x^3 + 2$
$x - 7$	$x^4 - 7$

You can add linear expression with or without models. Sometimes you will need to use zero pairs.

Examples

Tutor

Add.

1. $(2x + 3) + (x + 4)$

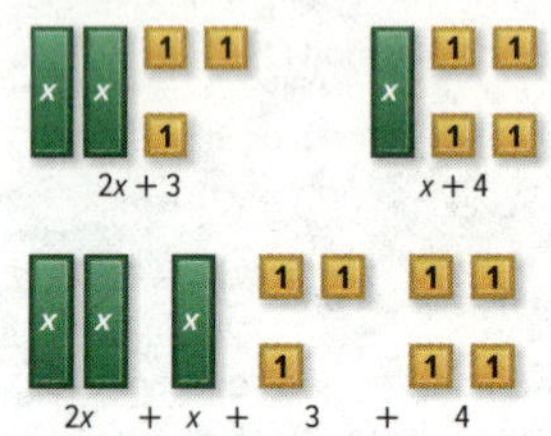

Model each linear expression.

Combine like tiles and write a linear expression for the combined tiles.

So, $(2x + 3) + (x + 4) = 3x + 7$.

2. $(2x - 1) + (x - 5)$

$(2x - 1) + (x - 5) = [2x + (-1)] + [x + (-5)]$ Definition of subtraction

$2x + (-1)$
$\underline{+\ x + (-5)}$ Arrange like terms in columns.
$3x + (-6)$ Add.

So, $(2x - 1) + (x - 5) = 3x + (-6)$ or $3x - 6$.

Got It? Do these problems to find out.

a. $(3x + 5) + (2x + 3)$ **b.** $(2x - 4) + (3x - 7)$

Show your work.

a. $5x + 8$

b. $5x - 11$

Examples

Tutor

3. **Find $(2x - 3) + (-x + 4)$. Use models if needed.**

Model each linear expression.

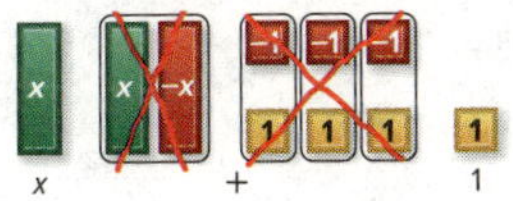

Combine like tiles. Then remove all zero pairs and write a linear expression for the remaining tiles.

So, $(2x - 3) + (-x + 4) = x + 1$.

4. **Find $2(x + 3) + (3x + 1)$.**

$2(x + 3) + (3x + 1) = (2 \cdot x + 2 \cdot 3) + (3x + 1)$ — Use the Distributive Property.

$= (2x + 6) + (3x + 1)$ — Simplify.

$$\begin{array}{r} 2x + 6 \\ +\ 3x + 1 \\ \hline 5x + 7 \end{array}$$

Arrange like terms in columns.

Add.

So, $2(x + 3) + (3x + 1) = 5x + 7$.

5. **Find $5(x - 4) + (2x - 7)$.**

$5(x - 4) + (2x - 7) = (5 \cdot x - 5 \cdot 4) + (2x - 7)$ — Use the Distributive Property.

$= (5x - 20) + (2x - 7)$ — Simplify.

$$\begin{array}{r} 5x - 20 \\ +\ 2x - \ \ 7 \\ \hline 7x - 27 \end{array}$$

Arrange like terms in columns.

Add.

So, $5(x - 4) + (2x - 7) = 7x - 27$.

Got It? **Do these problems to find out.**

Add. Use models if needed.

c. $(x - 1) + (2x + 3)$

d. $(x - 4) + (-2x + 1)$

e. $6(x + 7) + (x + 3)$

f. $(12x + 19) + 2(x - 10)$

Show your work.

c. $3x + 2$

d. $-x - 3$

e. $7x + 45$

f. $14x - 1$

IWB

Examples

3. Add linear expressions.

AL
- *What does each square red tile represent?* -1
- *What is a zero pair?* When one positive tile is paired with one negative tile, the result is 0.

OL
- *What are the two coefficients of x?* 2 and -1
- *What is the sum of $2x + (-x)$?* x

BL
- *What property allows you to switch the order of the algebra tiles to find zero pairs?* Commutative Property of Addition

Need Another Example?
Find $(3x - 6) + (-2x + 7)$. $x + 1$

4. Simplify expressions.

AL
- *How could you model this expression using algebra tiles?*
Set up two groups of one x-tile and three 1-tiles, and then add three x-tiles and one 1-tile.

OL
- *What should you do first?* Multiply x and 3 each by 2.
- *What are the like terms after you distribute?* $2x$ and $3x$, 6 and 1

BL
- *Is it easier for you to line up the expressions vertically or to work with them horizontally? Explain.* See students' preferences.

Need Another Example?
Find $4(x + 1) + (5x + 2)$. $9x + 6$

5. Simplify expressions.

AL
- *What does the 5 outside of the parentheses mean?* You need to multiply both terms inside the parentheses by 5.
- *What should you do first?* Multiply x and -4 by 5.

OL
- *After you distribute, what are the like terms?* $5x$ and $2x$; -20 and -7
- *What is $-20 + (-7)$?* -27

BL
- *Find $-3(5x - 1) + 2(3x + 1)$.* $-9x + 5$

Need Another Example?
Find $3(x - 8) + (4x - 5)$. $7x - 29$

Example

IWB

6. Simplify expressions.

AL • *What do you need to find?* the perimeter of the triangle

• *What do you know?* the lengths of the sides as algebraic expressions and the value of *x*

OL • *Look at the lengths of the sides of the triangle. What are the like terms?* 3*x*, 2*x*, and 5*x*; −3, and 9

• *What does the expression 10x + 6 represent?* the perimeter as an algebraic expression

BL • *Is there another way to solve this problem? Explain.* Sample answer: Replace *x* with 5 before you write an expression for the perimeter and simplify to find each side length. Then add the lengths of the sides.

Need Another Example?
The side length of a square is (5*x* + 1) inches. Write a linear expression in simplest form to represent the perimeter of the square. Then find the perimeter if *x* equals 4. 20*x* + 4; 84 in.

Guided Practice

Formative Assessment Use these exercises to assess students' understanding of the concepts in this lesson.

If some of your students are not ready for assignments, use the differentiated activities below.

AL EL **Think-Pair-Share** Have students work in pairs. Give them one minute to complete Exercise 1. One student should use algebra tiles, while the other uses pencil and paper. Have them share their responses with their partner and discuss any differences. Then for Exercise 2, have them switch roles. Call on one student to share the team's answers in a small group or large group discussion. MP 1, 4, 5

BL EL **Trade-a-Problem** Have students create their own problem, similar to Exercise 3, but involving finding the perimeter of a composite figure. Students trade their problems, solve each other's problem, and compare solutions. If the solutions do not agree, students work together to find the errors. Challenge students to use more than one variable or to include fractions in their expressions. MP 1, 2

Properties
The Commutative Property allows the terms of the expression to be reordered.

Real World

Example

Tutor

6. Write a linear expression in simplest form to represent the perimeter of the triangle. Find the perimeter if the value of *x* is 5 centimeters.

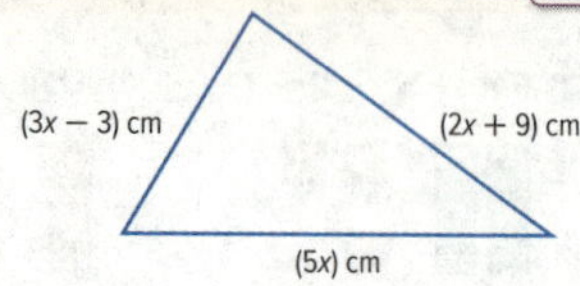

Write a linear expression for the perimeter of the triangle.

(3*x* − 3) + (2*x* + 9) + (5*x*) — Write each expression.

(3*x* + 2*x* + 5*x*) + (−3 + 9) — Rearrange to combine like terms.

10*x* + 6 — Add.

Find the perimeter.

10*x* + 6 = 10(5) + 6 or 56 — Replace *x* with 5. Simplify.

So, the perimeter of the triangle is 56 centimeters.

Got It? **Do this problem to find out.**

Show your work.

g. A rectangle has side lengths (*x* + 4) feet and (2*x* − 2) feet. Write a linear expression in simplest form to represent the perimeter. Find the perimeter if the value of *x* is 7 feet.

g. (6*x* + 4) ft; 46 ft

Guided Practice

Check

Add. Use models if needed. (Examples 1–5)

Show your work.

1. (2*x* + 3) + (*x* + 1) = 3*x* + 4

2. 10(*x* − 2) + (6*x* − 6) = 16*x* − 26

3. Write a linear expression in simplest form to represent the perimeter of the pentagon. Then find the perimeter if the value of *x* is 3 yards. (Example 6)

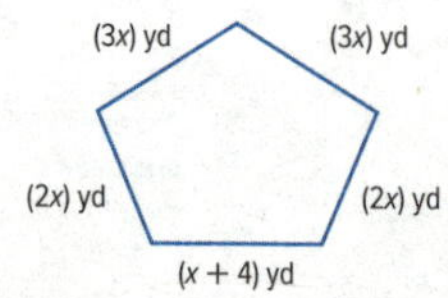

(11*x* + 4) yd; 37 yd

4. **Building on the Essential Question** Explain how adding linear expressions is similar to simplifying expressions.

Sample answer: You combine the like terms when adding or simplifying linear expressions.

Rate Yourself!

How confident are you about adding linear expressions? Check the box that applies.

For more help, go online to access a Personal Tutor.

Tutor

FOLDABLES Time to update your Foldable!

Name ______________________ My Homework ______________________

Independent Practice

Go online for Step-by-Step Solutions eHelp

Add. Use models if needed. (Examples 1–5)

1. $(4x + 8) + (7x + 3) =$ **$11x + 11$**

2. $(-3x + 7) + (-6x + 9) =$ **$-9x + 16$**

3. $(x - 10) + (3x - 6) =$ **$4x - 16$**

4. $(-3x - 7) + (4x + 7) =$ **x**

5. $2(x + 14) + (2x - 14) =$ **$4x + 14$**

6. $(11x - 8) + 7(x - 1) =$ **$18x - 15$**

7. Write a linear expression in simplest form to represent the perimeter of the triangle at the right. Then find the perimeter if the value of x is 10 millimeters. (Example 6)
$(22x + 10)$; 230 mm

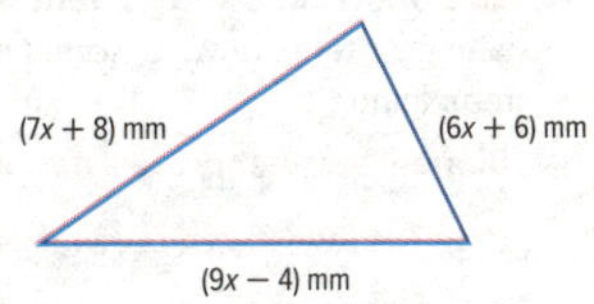

8. A rectangle has side lengths $(2x - 5)$ meters and $(2x + 6)$ meters. Write a linear expression in simplest form to represent the perimeter. Find the perimeter if the value of x is 12 meters. (Example 6)
$(8x + 2)$ m; 98 m

9. Find the sum of $(x + 5)$, $(-4x - 2)$, and $(2x - 1)$.
$-x + 2$

Add.

10. $(-3.5x + 1.7) + (9.1x - 0.3) =$ **$5.6x + 1.4$**

11. $(0.5x + 15) + (8.2x - 16.6) =$ **$8.7x - 1.6$**

ENGAGE EXPLORE **EXPLAIN** **ELABORATE** **EVALUATE**

3 Practice and Apply

Independent Practice and Extra Practice

The Independent Practice pages are meant to be used as the homework assignment. The Extra Practice page can be used for additional reinforcement or as a second-day assignment.

Levels of Complexity

The levels of the exercises progress from 1 to 3, with Level 1 indicating the lowest level of complexity.

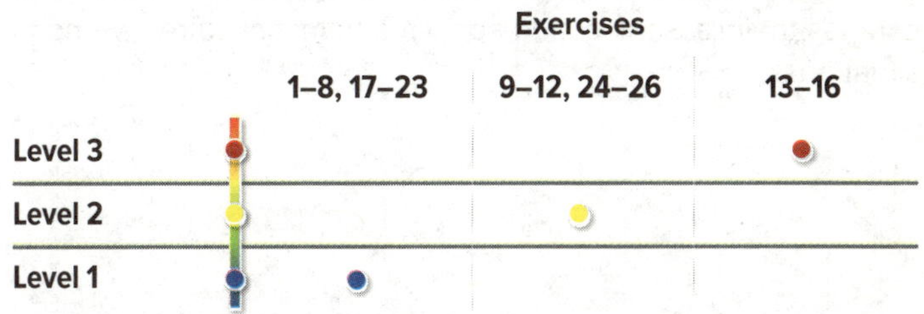

Suggested Assignments

You can use the table below that includes exercises of all complexity levels to select appropriate exercises for your students' needs.

Differentiated Homework Options		
AL	Approaching Level	1–9, 11, 13, 14, 16, 25, 26
OL	On Level	1–7 odd, 9–14, 16, 25, 26
BL	Beyond Level	9–16, 25, 26

ALEKS® can provide additional remediation support with personalized instruction and practice.

MATHEMATICAL PRACTICES

Emphasis On	Exercise(s)
1 Make sense of problems and persevere in solving them.	15, 17
2 Reason abstractly and quantitatively.	12, 24
3 Construct viable arguments and critique the reasoning of others.	13, 14, 16

Mathematical Practices 1, 3, and 4 are aspects of mathematical thinking that are emphasized in every lesson. Students are given opportunities to be persistent in their problem solving, to express their reasoning, and apply mathematics to real-world situations.

Formative Assessment
Use this activity as a closing formative assessment before dismissing students from your class.

TICKET Out the Door

Have students write an explanation of how to add two linear expressions. See students' work.

12. **Reason Abstractly** The table shows the breakdown of the points scored in last week's basketball game.

	1st Quarter Field Goal Points	2nd Quarter Field Goal Points	3rd Quarter Field Goal Points	4th Quarter Field Goal Points	Total Free Throw Points
Panthers	$2x - 6$	$x + 2$	$2x$	$x - 6$	9

a. Write a linear expression in simplest form to represent the total field goal points scored in the first two quarters.
$3x - 4$

b. Write a linear expression in simplest form to represent the total points scored in the game.
$6x - 1$

H.O.T. Problems Higher Order Thinking

13. **Reason Inductively** Write two linear expressions with a sum of $-5x + 4$.
Sample answer: $(10x + 2)$ and $(-15x + 2)$

14. **Construct an Argument** Will the sum of two linear expressions, each with an x-term, *always, sometimes,* or *never* have an x-term? Explain your reasoning.
Sometimes; sample answer: If the coefficients of the x-term are not opposites, then the statement is always true. If they are opposites, then the statement is false.

15. **Persevere with Problems** An integer can be represented by x. The next integer can then be represented as $(x + 1)$. Write a linear expression that represents the sum of any two consecutive integers. Show that the sum of any two consecutive integers is always odd.
$2x + 1$; The expression $2x + 1$ will always be odd when x is an integer because when an integer is doubled, the result is always even. Adding one to the result will give an odd number.

16. **Reason Inductively** Explain how algebra tiles represent like terms and zero pairs.
Sample answer: Algebra tiles that represent like terms have the same size and shape. When adding algebraic expressions, a red tile and a tile of any other color with the same size and shape form a zero pair and may be removed. The result is the sum of the algebraic expressions.

Name ______________________ My Homework ______________________

Extra Practice

Add. Use models if needed.

17. $(-x + 10) + (-3x + 6) =$ $-4x + 16$

Homework Help

$-x + 10$
$(+)\ -3x + 6$
$-4x + 16$

18. $(-4x + 3) + (-2x + 8) =$ $-6x + 11$

19. $(-6x + 5) + (4x - 7) =$ $-2x - 2$

20. $(-4x + 5) + (15x - 3) =$ $11x + 2$

21. $(-5x + 4) + -1(x - 1) =$ $-6x + 5$

22. $17(2x - 5) + (-x + 4) =$ $33x - 81$

23. Write a linear expression in simplest form to represent the perimeter of the trapezoid at the right. Then find the perimeter if the value of x is 7 yards. $(24x + 9)$ yd; 177 yd

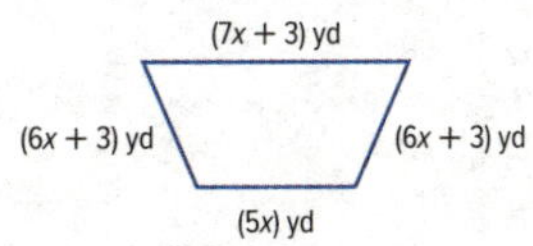

24. MP **Reason Abstractly** The table shows the points earned by a contestant in four rounds on a game show.

Round 1	Round 2	Round 3	Round 4
$2x + 40$	$5x + 12$	100	$6x - 10$

a. Write a linear expression in simplest form to represent the total points earned by the contestant in rounds 1 and 2.

$7x + 52$

b. Write a linear expression in simplest form to represent the total points earned in all four rounds.

$13x + 142$

c. If the value of x is 8, what is the total points earned in all four rounds?

246 points

Show your work.

Create Your Own Homework Online

eSolutionsManual™ can be used to create worksheets for the suggested assignments on page 399, or create your own worksheets for differentiated homework or review.

Power Up! Test Practice

Exercises 25 and 26 prepare students for more rigorous thinking needed for the state assessment.

25.

This test item requires students to reason abstractly and quantitatively when problem solving.	
Depth of Knowledge	DOK1
Content Standard	7.EE.1
Mathematical Practice	MP1
Online Experience	Students will be required to click on the bubbles to select all answers that are correct.
Scoring Rubric	
1 point	Students correctly answer each part of the question.

26.

This test item requires students to explain and apply mathematical concepts and solve problems with precision, while making use of structure.	
Depth of Knowledge	DOK2
Content Standard	7.EE.1
Mathematical Practice	MP1
Online Experience	Students will drag values to the appropriate place.
Scoring Rubric	
2 points	Students correctly place all eight values.
1 point	Students correctly represent two of the sides, but fail to correctly represent the third side and complete the answer accordingly OR students correctly represent all three sides, but fail to represent the perimeter.

Power Up! Test Practice

25. Karina makes x dollars per hour working at the grocery store. She makes y dollars per hour working at the library. One week she worked 9 hours at the grocery store and 12 hours at the library. Determine if each statement is true or false.

a. The expression $21x$ represents Karina's earnings from the library. ☐ True ■ False

b. The expression $9y$ represents Karina's earnings from the grocery store. ☐ True ■ False

c. The expression $9x + 12y$ represents Karina's total earnings for the week. ■ True ☐ False

26. A triangle has the side lengths represented by the expressions shown in the figure. Select the appropriate numbers and expressions to complete the model representing the perimeter of the triangle.

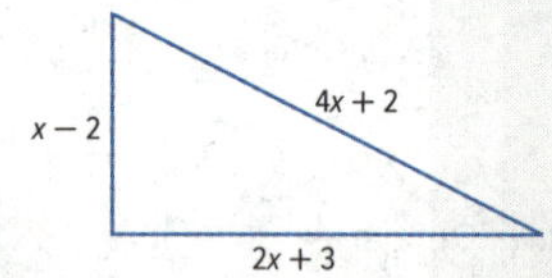

	x	+	-2
	$2x$	+	3
+	$4x$	+	2
+	$7x$	+	3

x	-1
$2x$	1
$4x$	2
$5x$	3
$7x$	7
-2	

Spiral Review

Use the Distributive Property to evaluate each expression. 6.EE.3

27. $7(9 - 4) =$ 35

28. $(9 + 2)6 =$ 66

29. $5(9 + 8) =$ 85

30. The number of students in each of the seventh grade homerooms that volunteer in the office are shown in the table. Use mental math to find the total number of students who volunteered. Explain. 6.EE.3

23 students; Sample answer:

$6 + 4 = 10, 5 + 8 = 13, 10 + 13 = 23$

Office Volunteers	
Homeroom	**Number of Students**
A	6
B	5
C	4
D	8

PLAN ONLINE: PD | RtI | Watch | Worksheets | Vocab | Tutor | Tools | Check | English Learners | Sketchpad

PRESENT

IWB An Interactive Whiteboard Ready presentation is available for each lesson in the chapter.

Expressions and Equations

Lesson 7

Subtract Linear Expressions

Real-World Link

Watch

Dog Sledding The Iditarod is a dog sledding race over 1,150 miles across Alaska. The table shows two winning times.

Iditarod				
	Days	Hours	Minutes	Seconds
Race 1	9	11	46	48
Race 2	9	5	8	41

1. What is the difference in hours, minutes, and seconds between the two races?

   6 h 38 min 7 s

2. Explain how you could find the difference in times between any two races, given the days, hours, minutes, and seconds.

   Subtract like units; keep the labels.

3. Describe another situation in which finding the difference involves subtracting like units.

   Sample answer: To compare the ingredient amounts in a recipe you would compare cups of flours and teaspoons of vanilla in one recipe to cups of flours and teaspoons of vanilla in another recipe.

Essential Question

HOW can you use numbers and symbols to represent mathematical ideas?

Content Standards
7.EE.1, 7.EE.2

MP Mathematical Practices
1, 2, 3, 4

Which MP **Mathematical Practices** did you use?
Shade the circle(s) that applies.

1. Persevere with Problems
2. Reason Abstractly
3. Construct an Argument
4. Model with Mathematics
5. Use Math Tools
6. Attend to Precision
7. Make Use of Structure
8. Use Repeated Reasoning

Focus narrowing the scope

Objective Subtract linear expressions. 7.EE.1, 7.EE.2

Coherence connecting within and across grades

Previous
Students added linear expressions by combining like terms.

Now
Students subtract linear expressions with more than two terms by combining like terms.

Next
Students will combine like terms when solving linear equations.

Rigor pursuing concepts, fluency, and applications

See the Levels of Complexity chart on page 407.

ENGAGE EXPLORE EXPLAIN ELABORATE EVALUATE

1 Launch the Lesson

Ideas for Use

You may wish to launch the lesson using a whole group, small group, think-pair-share activity, or independent activity.

AL EL **Pairs Discussion** Have students complete the Real-World Link in their texts, ensuring that each student understands that only like units, such as hours, can be combined. Call on one set of pairs to share their responses with the class. MP 1, 6

Alternate Strategy

BL Have students rewrite the rows as linear expressions. For example, the row for Race 1 could be written as $9d + 11h + 46m + 48s$. Then have them write and simplify a subtraction expression that models the situation. Have them compare their answer to the answer they determined in Exercise 1. MP 1, 7

ENGAGE EXPLORE **EXPLAIN** ELABORATE EVALUATE

2 Teach the Concept

Ask the scaffolded questions for each example to differentiate instruction.

IWB

Examples

1. Subtract linear expressions.

AL
- *When using algebra tiles, how do you show subtraction?* **by removing tiles**
- *Using algebra tiles, how would you model subtracting 2x from 6x?* **Remove two x-tiles from the six x-tiles.**
- *Using algebra tiles, how would you model subtracting 2 from 3?* **Remove two 1-tiles from the three 1-tiles.**

OL
- *What is $6x - 2x$?* **$4x$**
- *What is $3 - 2$?* **1**
- *What is $(6x + 3) - (2x + 2)$?* **$4x + 1$**

BL
- *Can you simplify $4x + 1$? Explain.* **No; 4x and 1 are not like terms.**

Need Another Example?
Find $(4x + 5) - (3x + 1)$. Use models if needed. **$x + 4$**

2. Subtract linear expressions.

AL
- *How do you represent -3 using algebra tiles?* **use three red -1-tiles**
- *How would you use algebra tiles to model this expression?* **Use two x-tiles and three -1-tiles, then remove one x-tile and two -1-tiles.**

OL
- *What is $2x - x$?* **x**
- *What is $-3 - (-2)$?* **-1**
- *What is $(2x - 3) - (x - 2)$?* **$x - 1$**

BL
- *Can you solve this problem another way? Explain.* **Sample answer: Yes, subtract each set of like terms.**

Need Another Example?
Find $(4x - 6) - (2x - 4)$. Use models if needed. **$2x - 2$**

Work Zone

Subtract Linear Expressions

When subtracting linear expressions, subtract like terms. Use zero pairs if needed.

Examples

Tools Tutor

Subtract. Use models if needed.

1. $(6x + 3) - (2x + 2)$

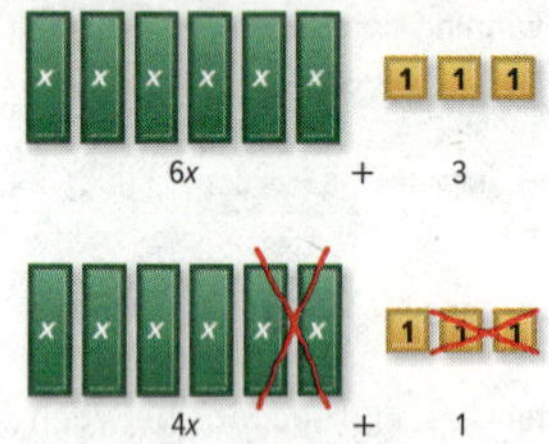

Model the linear expression $6x + 3$.

To subtract $2x + 2$, remove two x-tiles and two 1-tiles. Then write the linear expression for the remaining tiles.

There are four x-tiles and one 1-tile remaining.
So, $(6x + 3) - (2x + 2) = 4x + 1$.

2. $(2x - 3) - (x - 2)$

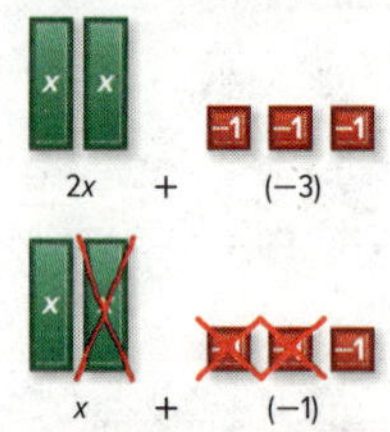

Model the linear expression $2x - 3$.

To subtract $x - 2$, remove one x-tile and two -1-tiles. Then write the linear expression for the remaining tiles.

There is one x-tile and one -1-tile remaining.
So, $(2x - 3) - (x - 2) = x - 1$.

Show your work.

Got It? Do these problems to find out.

a. $(5x - 9) - (2x - 7)$ b. $(6x - 10) - (2x - 8)$

a. $3x - 2$

b. $4x - 2$

Example

3. **Find $(-2x - 4) - (2x)$. Use models if needed.**

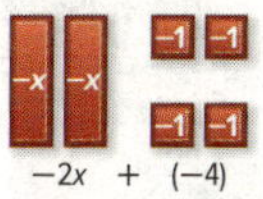

Model the linear expression $-2x - 4$.

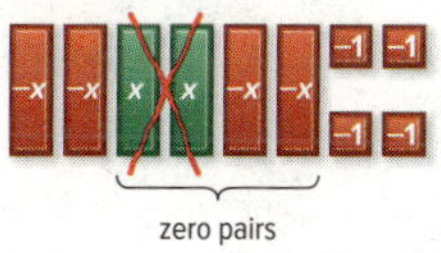

Since there are no positive x-tiles to remove, add two zero pairs of x-tiles. Remove two positive x-tiles.

So, $(-2x - 4) - (2x) = -4x - 4$.

Got It? **Do these problems to find out.**

c. $(3x - 2) - (5x - 4)$ d. $(4x - 4) - (-2x + 2)$

Show your work.

c. $-2x + 2$

d. $6x - 6$

Use the Additive Inverse to Subtract

When subtracting integers, you add the opposite, or the additive inverse. The same process is used when subtracting linear expressions.

Examples

4. **Find $(6x + 5) - (3x + 1)$.**

$$\begin{array}{r} 6x + 5 \\ (+)\ -3x - 1 \\ \hline 3x + 4 \end{array}$$

Arrange like terms in columns.
The additive inverse of $3x + 1$ is $(-3x - 1)$.

5. **Find $(-4x - 7) - (-5x - 2)$.**

$$\begin{array}{r} -4x - 7 \\ (+)\ 5x + 2 \\ \hline x - 5 \end{array}$$

Arrange like terms in columns.
The additive inverse of $(-5x - 2)$ is $(5x + 2)$.

Additive Inverse
The additive inverse is found by multiplying the linear expression by −1.

Got It? **Do these problems to find out.**

e. $(4x - 3) - (2x + 7)$ f. $(5x - 4) - (2x + 3)$

e. $2x - 10$

f. $3x - 7$

Examples

IWB

3. Subtract linear expressions.

AL
- *Name one way in which the model in Example 3 is different from the models in the previous examples.* **Sample answer: There are negative *x*-tiles in Example 3 and only positive *x*-tiles in Examples 1 and 2.**
- *How do you model −4?* **Use four red −1-tiles.**

OL
- *Why did you need to add two zero pairs of x-tiles to the model?* **There were no positive *x*-tiles to take away, so add two zero pairs. Then remove two positive *x*-tiles.**

OL
- *Does adding a zero pair change the value of the expression?* **No; a zero pair represents 0 which does not affect the value of the expression.**

BL
- *Rewrite $(-2x - 4) - (2x)$ as an addition expression. Then simplify.* $-2x + (-4) + (-2x) = -4x - 4$

Need Another Example?
Find $(-7x - 6) - (7x)$. $-14x - 6$

4. Use the additive inverse to subtract expressions.

AL
- *How could you model this expression using algebra tiles?* **Set up six *x*-tiles and five 1-tiles, and then remove three *x*-tiles and one 1-tile.**
- *What is $6x - 3x$? $5 - 1$?* $3x$; 4

OL
- *What is the additive inverse of $3x + 1$?* $-3x - 1$
- *After finding the additive inverse of $3x + 1$, what are the like terms?* **$6x$ and $-3x$, 5 and −1**

BL
- *How does the Distributive Property apply to finding the additive inverse of $3x + 1$?* **You find the additive inverse of each term.**

Need Another Example?
Find $(12x + 8) - (6x + 2)$. $6x + 6$

5. Use the additive inverse to subtract expressions.

AL
- *What is the additive inverse of $-5x$? of -2?* $5x$; 2

OL
- *After you find the additive inverse, what are the like terms?* **$-4x$ and $5x$; −7 and 2**

BL
- *Find $-2(x - 3) - 2(2x - 5)$.* $-6x + 16$

Need Another Example?
Find $(-5x - 9) - (-6x - 1)$. $x - 8$

Example

6. Use linear expressions.

AL • *What do you need to find?* how many more college hats were sold than professional hats

• *What do you know?* you know expressions for the number of each type of hat

• *What operation will you use?* subtraction

OL • *What is the additive inverse of 5m − 2?* $-5m + 2$

• *After you have simplified the expression, how will you evaluate the expression?* Replace m with 10 and simplify.

BL • *Is there another way to solve this problem? Explain.* Sample answer: Replace m with 10, in the expressions $6m + 3$ and $5m - 2$. Simplify, then subtract.

Need Another Example?

A bakery wants to know how many more chocolate chip cookies than sugar cookies were sold last month. The number of chocolate chip cookies sold is represented by the expression $(7n + 6)$. The number of sugar cookies sold is represented by the expression $(6n - 3)$. Write an expression to show how many more chocolate cookies were sold last month. Then evaluate the expression if n equals 15. $n + 9$; 24

Guided Practice

Formative Assessment Use these exercises to assess students' understanding of the concepts in this lesson.

If some of your students are not ready for assignments, use the differentiated activities below.

AL EL **Pairs Discussion** Have pairs complete Exercises 1 and 2. One student should use algebra tiles to model the expressions as the other student writes the problems vertically on their paper. Then, they discuss any differences in the answers. MP 1, 7

BL EL **Make a Game** Have students create a game to help practice adding and subtracting linear expressions. For example, they could write 20 linear expressions on index cards, and roll a die to determine if they need to add or subtract. The group at play determines if the player earns or loses a point. If the games are successful, the entire class can play. MP 1, 7

Real-World Example

6. **A hat store tracks the sale of college and professional team hats for m months. The number of college hats sold is represented by $(6m + 3)$. The number of professional hats sold is represented by $(5m - 2)$. Write an expression to show how many more college hats were sold than professional hats. Then evaluate the expression if m equals 10.**

Find $(6m + 3) - (5m - 2)$.

$$\begin{array}{r} 6m + 3 \\ (+)-5m + 2 \\ \hline m + 5 \end{array}$$

Arrange like terms in columns. The additive inverse of $5m - 2$ is $(-5m + 2)$.

Evaluate the expression if $m = 10$.

$m + 5 = 10 + 5$ Substitute 10 for m.

$= 15$ Simplify.

So, 15 more college team hats were sold.

Guided Practice

Subtract. Use models if needed. (Examples 1–5)

1. $(2x + 4) - (-x + 5) =$ $3x - 1$

2. $(6x + 9) - (7x - 1) =$ $-x + 10$

Show your work.

3. The number of runs scored by the home team at a baseball game is represented by $(x + 7)$. The number of runs scored by the visiting team is represented by $(3x - 7)$. Write an expression to find how many more runs the home team scored than the visiting team. Then evaluate the expression if the value of x is 6. (Example 6)

$-2x + 14$; 2 runs

4. **Building on the Essential Question** How can you use the additive inverse to help you subtract linear expressions?

Sample answer: If you multiply the second linear expression by −1, it makes it simpler to line up like terms and add.

Rate Yourself!

How well do you understand subtracting linear expressions? Circle the image that applies.

Clear Somewhat Clear Not So Clear

For more help, go online to access a Personal Tutor.

FOLDABLES Time to update your Foldable!

Name ________________ My Homework ________________

Independent Practice

Go online for Step-by-Step Solutions eHelp

Subtract. Use models if needed. (Examples 1–5)

1. $(9x + 5) - (4x + 3) =$ **$5x + 2$**

2. $(-x + 3) - (x - 5) =$ **$-2x + 8$**

3. $(3x + 4) - (x + 2) =$ **$2x + 2$**

4. $(7x + 5) - (3x + 2) =$ **$4x + 3$**

5. $(9x - 8) - (x + 4) =$ **$8x - 12$**

6. $(9x - 12) - (5x - 7) =$ **$4x - 5$**

7. MP **Reason Abstractly** The number of customers in a store on the first day is represented by $(6x - 3)$. The number of customers on the second day is represented by $(x - 1)$. Write an expression to find how many more customers visited the store on the first day. Then evaluate the expression if x is equal to 50. (Example 6)

$5x - 2$; 248 customers

8. The perimeter of the garden shown is $(6x + 2)$ units. Find the length of the missing side.

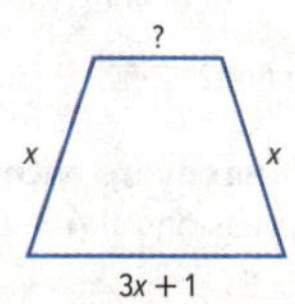

$x + 1$

9. The cost for shipping a package that weighs x pounds from Boise to Los Angeles is shown at the right. How much more does Shipping Central charge than Globe Delivery?

Company	Cost ($)
Shipping Central	$3x + 3.50$
Globe Delivery	$2x + 2.99$

$x + 0.51$

ENGAGE EXPLORE **EXPLAIN** **ELABORATE** **EVALUATE**

3 Practice and Apply

Independent Practice and Extra Practice

The Independent Practice pages are meant to be used as the homework assignment. The Extra Practice page can be used for additional reinforcement or as a second-day assignment.

Levels of Complexity

The levels of the exercises progress from 1 to 3, with Level 1 indicating the lowest level of complexity.

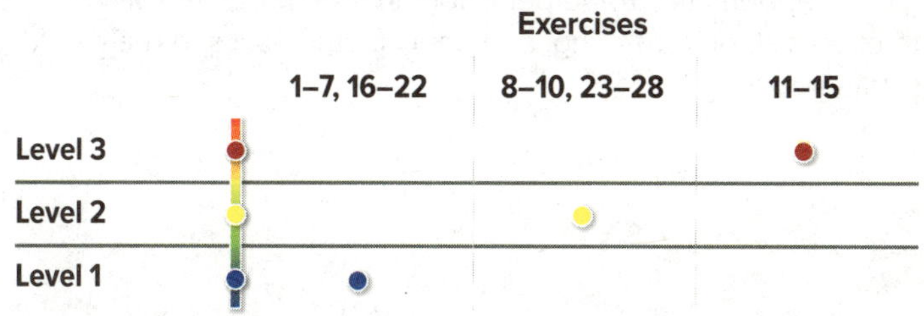

Suggested Assignments

You can use the table below that includes exercises of all complexity levels to select appropriate exercises for your students' needs.

Differentiated Homework Options		
AL	Approaching Level	1–7, 9, 11, 12, 15, 27, 28
OL	On Level	1–7 odd, 8–12, 15, 27, 28
BL	Beyond Level	8–15, 27, 28

McGraw Hill Education ALEKS® can provide additional remediation support with personalized instruction and practice.

Watch Out!

Common Error When subtracting linear expressions, students often forget to add the opposite of every term. Encourage them to show all of their work including sign changes in the subtrahend and to keep their work organized.

MP MATHEMATICAL PRACTICES

Emphasis On	Exercise(s)
1 Make sense of problems and persevere in solving them.	13, 14
2 Reason abstractly and quantitatively.	7, 22
3 Construct viable arguments and critique the reasoning of others.	11, 12, 15

Mathematical Practices 1, 3, and 4 are aspects of mathematical thinking that are emphasized in every lesson. Students are given opportunities to be persistent in their problem solving, to express their reasoning, and apply mathematics to real-world situations.

Formative Assessment
Use this activity as a closing formative assessment before dismissing students from your class.

TICKET Out the Door

Have students write an explanation of how to subtract two linear expressions. See student's work.

Watch Out!

Find the Error In Exercise 11, Theresa forgot to add the opposite of 1 in the second polynomial. Suggest that students highlight or circle each term in an expression that requires a change in sign when adding the opposite.

10. Find the difference in the given lengths of the polygons. $(x + 7)$ units

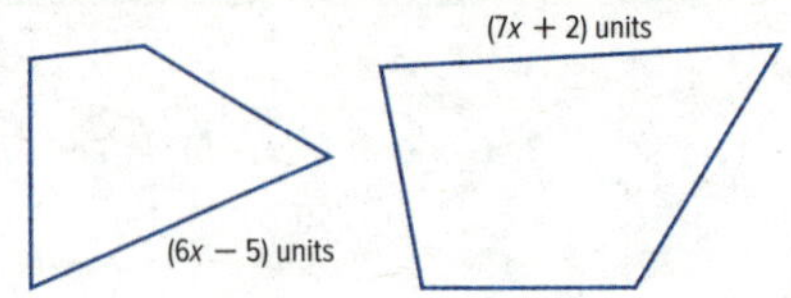

H.O.T. Problems Higher Order Thinking

11. MP **Find the Error** Theresa is finding $(5x + 3) - (2x + 1)$. Find her mistake and correct it.

Sample answer: The additive inverse of $(2x + 1)$ is $(-2x - 1)$.

$(5x + 3) - (2x + 1)$

$= (5x + 3) + (-2x - 1)$

$= 5x + 3 + (-2x) + (-1)$

$= 5x + (-2x) + 3 + (-1)$

$= 3x + 2$

12. MP **Reason Inductively** Name two linear expressions whose difference is $5x - 4$.

Sample answer: $(7x - 1) - (2x + 3) = 7x - 1 - 2x - 3 = 5x - 4$

13. MP **Persevere with Problems** One linear expression is subtracted from a second linear expression and the difference is $x - 5$. What is the difference when the second linear expression is subtracted from the first? $-x + 5$

14. MP **Persevere with Problems** Suppose A and B represent linear expressions. If $A + B = 2x - 2$ and $A - B = 4x - 8$, find A and B.

$A = 3x - 5$; $B = -x + 3$

15. MP **Reason Inductively** Explain how you can apply the rule for subtracting integers to linear expressions.

Sample answer: The rule is to add the inverse when subtracting integers, and is applied to each term in the linear expression that is subtracted.

Name ____________ My Homework ____________

Extra Practice

Subtract. Use models if needed.

16. $(-3x - 2) - (7x + 9) =$ $-10x - 11$

Homework Help

$-3x - 2$
$(+)\ -7x - 9$
$-10x - 11$

17. $(-2x - 1) - (x - 7) =$ $-3x + 6$

18. $(9x + 5) - (6x - 8) =$ $3x + 13$

19. $(-8x + 1) - (8x - 1) =$ $-16x + 2$

20. $(4x + 10) - (-3x + 5) =$ $7x + 5$

21. $(-6x - 11) - (-2x - 4) =$ $-4x - 7$

22. MP **Reason Abstractly** The number of questions on a math test is represented $(3x + 1)$. The number of questions on a spelling test is represented by $(x + 12)$. Write an expression to find how many more questions were on the math test. Then evaluate the expression if the value of x is 8.

$2x - 11$; 5 questions

Subtract.

23. $(5.7x - 0.8) - (4.9x - 1.4) =$ $0.8x + 0.6$

24. $\left(-\frac{5}{6}x + 5\frac{1}{2}\right) - \left(\frac{2}{3}x + 4\right) =$ $-1\frac{1}{2}x + 1\frac{1}{2}$

25. $2(x + 1) - 3x =$ $-x + 2$

26. $5(x - 3) - x =$ $4x - 15$

Create Your Own Homework Online

SolutionsManual™ can be used to create worksheets for the suggested assignments on page 407, or create your own worksheets for differentiated homework or review.

Power Up! Test Practice

Exercises 27 and 28 prepare students for more rigorous thinking needed for the state assessment.

27.

This test item requires students to reason abstractly and quantitatively when problem solving.	
Depth of Knowledge	DOK1
Content Standard	7.EE.1
Mathematical Practice	MP1
Online Experience	Students will drag values to model the equation.
Scoring Rubric	
2 points	Students correctly model the equation.
1 point	Students correctly place four or five of the six values.

28.

This test item requires students to explain and apply mathematical concepts and solve problems with precision, while making use of structure.	
Depth of Knowledge	DOK2
Content Standard	7.EE.1
Mathematical Practice	MP1
Online Experience	Students will be required to click on the bubbles to select all answers that are correct.
Scoring Rubric	
1 point	Students correctly answer each part of the question.

Power Up! Test Practice

27. The costs for a large pizza and each topping for two pizzerias are shown in the table.

Pizzeria	Cost per Pizza ($)	Cost per Topping ($)
Mario's Pizza	10	1.25
Pizza Palace	12	1.50

Select the appropriate values to complete the model to show how much more a pizza with *t* toppings costs at Pizza Palace than at Mario's Pizza.

0.25	2.75	1.25	1.50
2	10	12	22

[12] + [1.50] t − ([10] + [1.25] t) = [2] + [0.25] t

28. Mei wants to frame a picture. The picture is $(12x + 4)$ units long, and the frame is $(7x + 1)$ units long. Determine if each statement is true or false.

a. The picture is longer than the frame. ■ True □ False

b. The frame is longer than the picture. □ True ■ False

c. Mei will have to trim $(5x + 3)$ units from the picture to fit it in the frame. ■ True □ False

Spiral Review

29. Camilla wants to attach a string of lights to the edges of her patio for a party. She does not want the string to go across the edge with the steps. Write a linear expression that represents the length of string in feet she will need. Then find the length if $x = 3$. 7.EE.1

$(12x - 4)$ ft; 32 ft

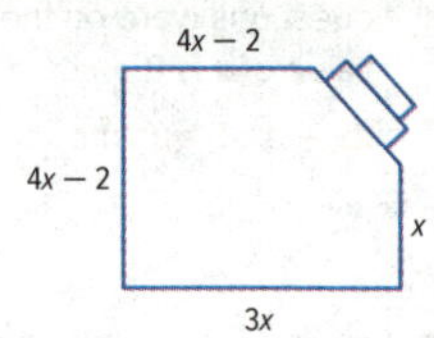

Evaluate each expression if $x = \frac{1}{2}$ and $y = \frac{3}{4}$. 6.EE.3

30. xy $\frac{3}{8}$

31. $x - y$ $-\frac{1}{4}$

32. $x + y$ $1\frac{1}{4}$

33. x^3 $\frac{1}{8}$

34. $3y + 2x$ $3\frac{1}{4}$

35. $x \div y$ $\frac{2}{3}$

PLAN ONLINE

PD | RtI | Watch | Worksheets | Vocab | Tutor | Tools | Check | English Learners | Sketchpad

PRESENT

IWB

An Interactive Whiteboard Ready presentation is available for each lesson in the chapter.

Inquiry Lab
Factor Linear Expressions

Inquiry HOW do models help you factor linear expressions?

Content Standards
7.EE.1

MP Mathematical Practices
1, 3

Max has enough 1 inch square glass tiles to create a rectangular piece of mosaic art that has an area of 24 square inches. Some of the possible dimensions of the rectangle are listed in the table. Write the two missing possible dimensions.

Length (in.)	Width (in.)
24	1
3	8
12	2
6	4

Each of the dimensions listed are factors of 24. Sometimes, you know the product and are asked to find the factors. This process is called *factoring*.

Hands-On Activity 1

Tools

Use algebra tiles to factor $2x + 6$.

Step 1 Model the expression $2x + 6$.

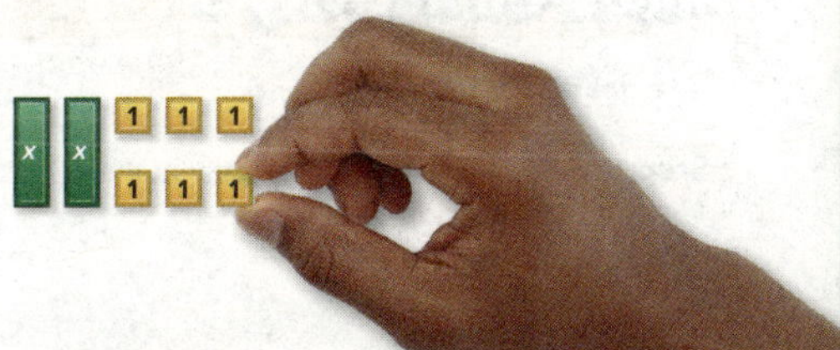

Step 2 Arrange the tiles into a rectangle with equal rows and columns. The total area of the tiles represents the product. Its length and width represent the factors.

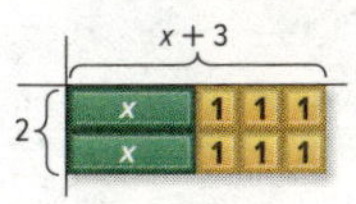

The rectangle has a width of two 1-tiles and a length of one x-tile and three 1-tiles.

So, $2x + 6 = 2(x + \boxed{3})$.

Focus narrowing the scope

Objective Factor linear expressions using models. 7.EE.1

Coherence moving from concrete co abstract

Now
Students use algebra tiles to model factoring linear expressions.

Next
Students will combine like terms when solving linear equations.

Rigor pursuing concepts, fluency, and applications

See the Levels of Complexity chart on page 413.

ENGAGE EXPLORE EXPLAIN ELABORATE EVALUATE

1 Launch the Lab

Activities 1–3 are intended to be used as whole-group activities. Activities 1 and 2 are designed to provide more guidance than Activity 3.

Hands-On Activity 1

AL EL Remind students that when using algebra tiles, a green x-tile is used to represent x, a yellow tile is used to represent 1, and a red tile is used to represent -1. Have students practice modeling integers like -4, 7, and 3 before moving on to the Activity. MP 1, 4, 5

Ask:

- *To model the expression, how many x-tiles do you need?* 2
- *To model the expression, how many 1-tiles do you need?* 6
- *In Step 2, what do the length and width of the rectangle represent?* the factors

BL Have students alter the model so that the factors are 2 and $x + 4$. Then have them determine the expression of the product that is modeled, $2x + 8$. MP 1, 4, 5

Hands-On Activity 2

AL **EL** If students have trouble understanding why they use negative 1-tiles in Activity 2, remind them that $2x - 8$ can be rewritten as $2x + (-8)$. This should help them see the connection between the tiles and the expression. **MP** 1, 7

Ask:

- *To model the expression, how many x-tiles do you need?* 2
- *To model the expression, how many negative 1-tiles do you need?* 8
- *In Step 2, what do the length and width of the rectangle represent?* the factors

BL Have students alter the model so that the factors are 3 and $x - 4$. Then have them determine the expression of the product that is modeled, $3x - 12$. **MP** 1, 4, 5

Hands-On Activity 3

AL **EL** Make sure students understand that the algebra tiles need to form a rectangle. If not, they cannot produce the correct *length* × *width* expression. **MP** 1

Ask:

- *To model the expression, how many x-tiles do you need?* 3
- *To model the expression, how many negative 1-tiles do you need?* 6
- *In Step 2, what do the length and width of the rectangle represent?* the factors

BL Have students alter the model so that the factors are 4 and $x - 4$. Then have them determine the expression of the product that is modeled, $4x - 16$. Then have them determine the factors of the expression $5x - 20$ without using a model. **MP** 1, 4, 5

Hands-On Activity 2

Use algebra tiles to factor $2x - 8$.

Step 1 Model the expression $2x - 8$.

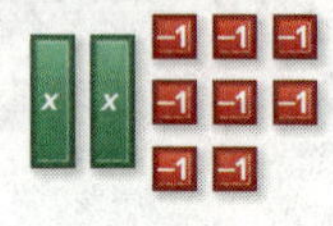

Step 2 Arrange the tiles into a rectangle with equal rows and columns.

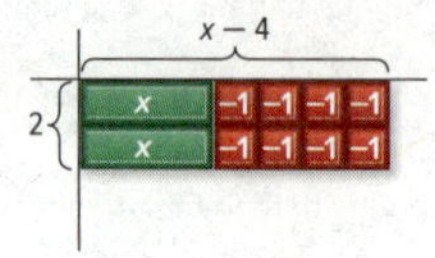

The rectangle has a width of two 1-tiles and a length of one x-tile and four −1-tiles.

So, $2x - 8 =$ $2(x - 4)$.

Hands-On Activity 3

Use algebra tiles to factor $3x - 6$.

Step 1 Draw the tiles that represent the expression $3x - 6$.

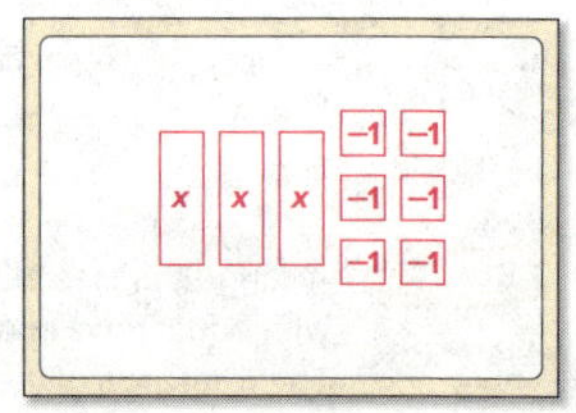

Step 2 Redraw the tiles into a rectangle with equal rows and columns.

The rectangle has a width of three 1-tiles and a length of one x-tile and two −1-tiles.

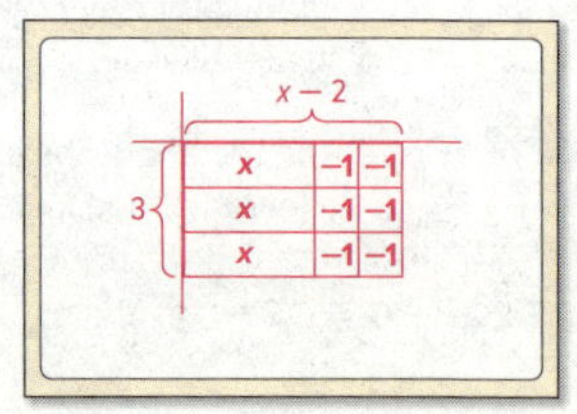

So, $3x - 6 =$ $3(x - 2)$.

Investigate

Collaborate

Work with a partner. Factor each expression by arranging the appropriate algebra tiles into equal rows and columns. Draw the finished product.

1. $4x + 6 =$ $2(2x + 3)$

Show your work.

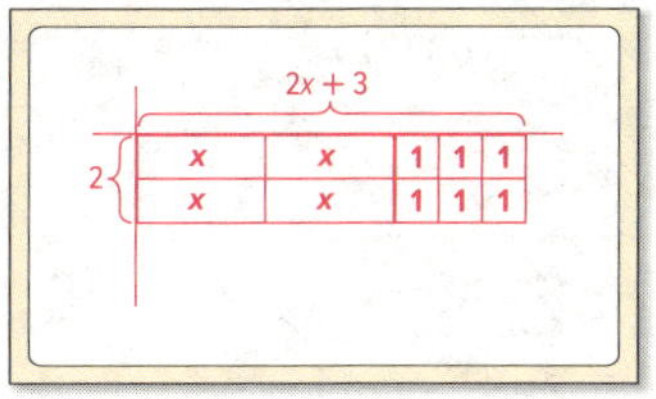

2. $5x + 10 =$ $5(x + 2)$

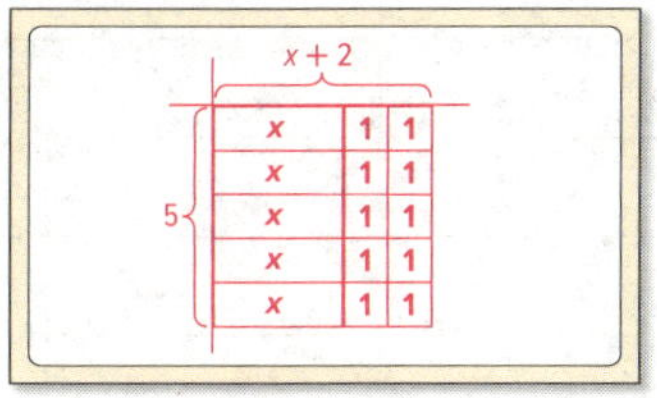

3. $3x + 12 =$ $3(x + 4)$

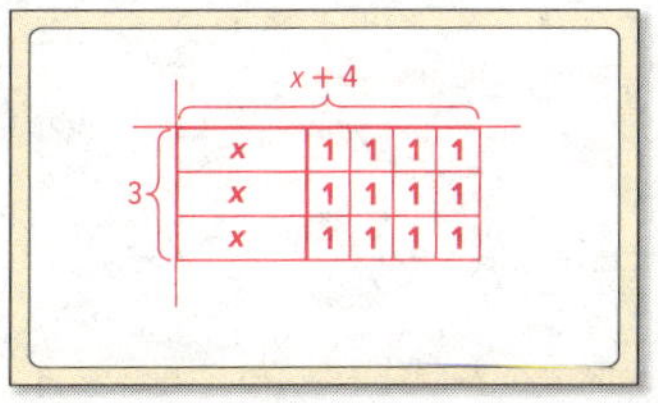

4. $4x - 10 =$ $2(2x - 5)$

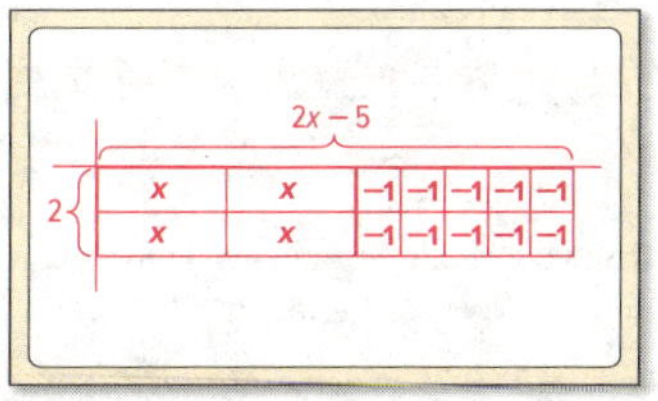

5. $3x - 9 =$ $3(x - 3)$

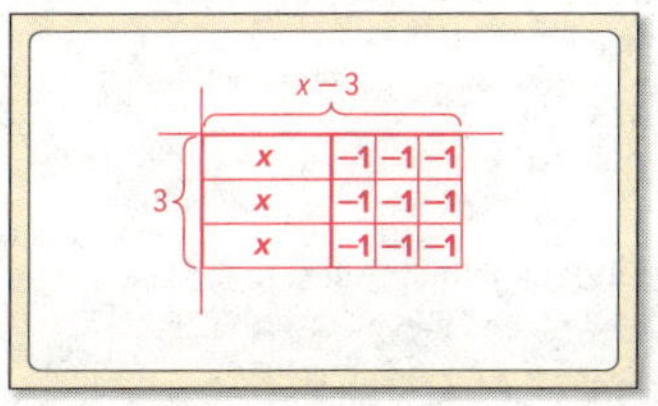

6. $2x - 4 =$ $2(x - 2)$

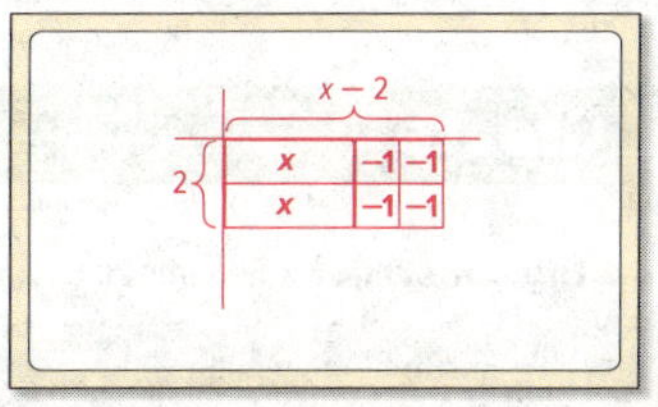

7. $4x + 2 =$ $2(2x + 1)$

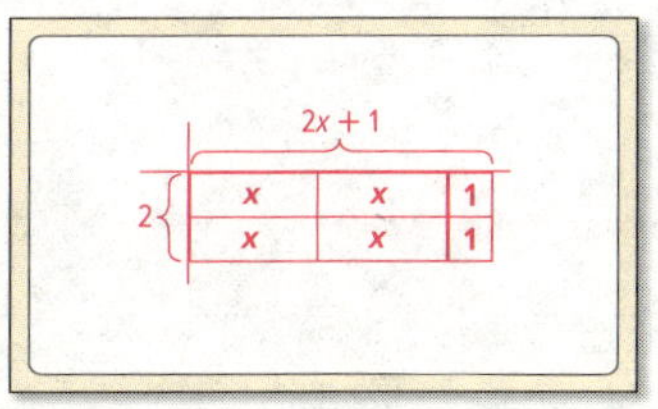

8. $5x - 5 =$ $5(x - 1)$

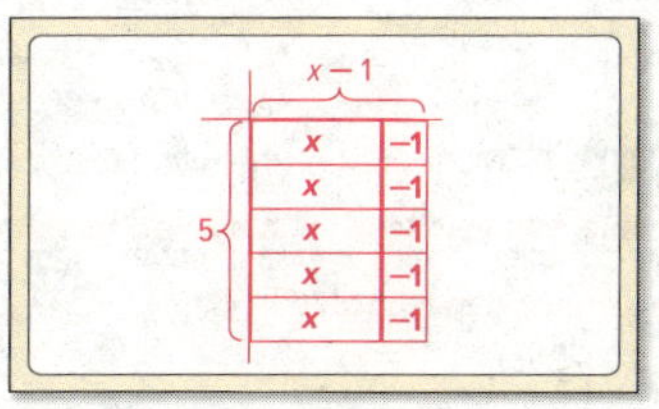

ENGAGE EXPLORE EXPLAIN ELABORATE EVALUATE

2 Collaborate

The **Investigate** and **Analyze and Reflect** sections are intended to be used as small-group investigations. The **Create** section is intended to be used as independent exercises.

Levels of Complexity

The levels of the exercises progress from 1 to 3, with Level 1 indicating the lowest level of complexity.

Exercises

	1–8	9–14	15, 16
Level 3			●
Level 2		●	
Level 1	●		

Investigate

Collaborate

AL **EL** **Pairs Discussion** Have students work in pairs to complete Exercises 1–8. Have them trade their solutions with another pair of students and discuss any differences. **MP 1, 4, 5**

BL **EL** **Trade-a-Problem** Have students create their own problem, similar to Exercises 1–8. Students trade their problems, solve each other's problem, and compare solutions. If the solutions do not agree, students work together to find the errors. **MP 1, 4, 5**

Analyze and Reflect

Collaborate

AL **EL** **Rally Coach** For Exercises 9–14, have students work in pairs. Student 1 should complete Exercise 1 while Student 2 watches, listens, coaches, and praises. Student 2 completes the next exercise while Student 1 watches, listens, coaches, and praises. Students take turns until the exercises are completed. MP 1, 7

BL **EL** After completing Exercises 9–14, ask students to give an example of an expression that cannot be factored. MP 1, 7

Create

On Your Own

BL **EL** **Trade-a-Problem** Have students create a word problem that could be solved by factoring a linear expression. Then have them trade their word problems, solve each other's problem using a model or diagram, and compare solutions. Ask them if there are any other ways to solve the problem. MP 1, 7

Inquiry Students should be able to answer "HOW do models help you factor linear expressions?" Check for student understanding and provide guidance, if needed.

Analyze and Reflect

Collaborate

Work with a partner to complete the table. Use algebra tiles if needed.

	Original Expression	Factored Expression	Distributive Property
	$2x + 8$	$2(x + 4)$	$2(x) + 2(4) = 2x + 8$
9.	$4x - 8$	$4(x - \boxed{2})$	$4(x) - 4(2) = 4x - 8$
10.	$6x + 2$	$2(\boxed{3}x + 1)$	$2(3x) + 2(1) = 6x + 2$
11.	$2x - 10$	$2(x - 5)$	$2(x) - 2(5) = 2x - 10$
12.	$8x + 6$	$2(4x + 3)$	$2(4x) + 2(3) = 8x + 6$

13. MP **Reason Inductively** How is factoring related to using the Distributive Property?

Sample answer: Factoring and using the Distributive Property are inverse processes. Check the solution of one by performing the other.

14. MP **Construct an Argument** Is the expression $2x - 2$ equivalent to the expression $2(x - 2)$? Explain.

They are not equivalent. Sample answer: $2(x - 2)$ is equivalent to $2x - 4$.

Create

On Your Own

15. MP **Justify Conclusions** Explain how you could use algebra tiles to factor $5x + 15$.

Sample answer: Arrange 5 rows of one x-tile and three 1-tiles. The resulting factors would then be 5 and $(x + 3)$.

16. Inquiry HOW do models help you factor linear expressions?

Sample answer: Models help you to visualize the factors as if they were the area of a rectangle.

An Interactive Whiteboard Ready presentation is available for each lesson in the chapter.

Expressions and Equations

Lesson 8

Factor Linear Expressions

Real-World Link

Yard Sale A rectangular yard is being separated into four equal-size sections for different items at a yard sale. The area of the yard is $(8x + 12)$ square meters.

1. How can you find the area of each section of the yard sale?
   Since there are 4 equal sections, divide $8x + 12$ by 4.

2. What is the area of each section? Explain your answer.
   $(2x + 3)$ m^2; Sample answer: Four multiplied by some number is $8x + 12$. Using the Distributive Property, $4(2x + 3) = 8x + 12$. So, the area of each section is $(2x + 3)$ square meters.

3. The algebra tiles represent the area of the entire yard sale. Fill in the length and width. Write an expression that represents the area in terms of the length and width of the model. **$4(2x + 3)$**

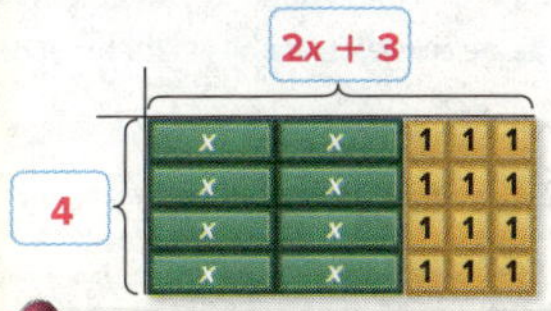

Which MP Mathematical Practices did you use? Shade the circle(s) that applies.

① Persevere with Problems
② Reason Abstractly
③ Construct an Argument
④ Model with Mathematics
⑤ Use Math Tools
⑥ Attend to Precision
⑦ Make Use of Structure
⑧ Use Repeated Reasoning

Essential Question

HOW can you use numbers and symbols to represent mathematical ideas?

Vocabulary

monomial
factor
factored form

Content Standards
7.EE.1, 7.EE.2

MP Mathematical Practices
1, 2, 3, 4

Focus narrowing the scope

Objective Read and write integers, and find the absolute value of an integer. 7.EE.1, 7.EE.2

Coherence connecting within and across grades

Previous	Now	Next
Students used the Distributive Property to multiply a sum or difference by a number.	Students use the Distributive Property to factor the GCF out of a sum or difference.	Students will combine like terms when solving linear equations.

Rigor pursuing concepts, fluency, and applications

See the Levels of Complexity chart on page 419.

ENGAGE EXPLORE EXPLAIN ELABORATE EVALUATE

1 Launch the Lesson

Ideas for Use

You may wish to launch the lesson using a whole group, small group, think-pair-share activity, or independent activity.

BL EL **Think-Write-Pair** Give students one minute to think about how the Distributive Property can be used to multiply a number and an algebraic expression, such as writing $5(3x + 1)$ as $15x + 5$. Ask them to write a rule that would use the Distributive Property backwards to write $15x + 5$ as $5(3x + 1)$. Have them share their rules with a partner. MP 1, 7

Alternate Strategy

AL Have students work in pairs. Give each pair a set of algebra tiles. Have them use the algebra tiles to equally separate $2x + 8$ into two groups, $3x - 6$ into three groups, and finally $4x + 12$ into four groups. MP 1, 4, 5

ENGAGE EXPLORE **EXPLAIN** ELABORATE EVALUATE

2 Teach the Concept

Ask the scaffolded questions for each example to differentiate instruction.

Examples

IWB

1. Find the GCF.

AL
- *What is the Greatest Common Factor of two numbers?* the greatest number that will divide evenly into both numbers
- *How would you find the GCF of 16 and 20?* Write the prime factorization of each number, circle the common factors, and then multiply the common factors.
- *What is the GCF of 16 and 20?* 4

OL
- *What is the prime factorization of 4x?* $2 \cdot 2 \cdot x$;
- *What is the prime factorization of 12x?* $2 \cdot 2 \cdot 3 \cdot x$
- *What are the common factors?* 2, 2, and x

BL
- *What is the GCF of $15x^2$ and 25x?* $5x$

Need Another Example?

Find the GCF of 48x and 28x. $4x$

2–3. Find the GCF.

AL
- *In Example 2, what is the prime factorization of 18a? 20ab?* $2 \cdot 3 \cdot 3 \cdot a$; $2 \cdot 2 \cdot 5 \cdot a \cdot b$
- *What factors are common to 18a and 20ab?* 2 and a
- *What is the GCF of 18a and 20ab?* $2a$

OL
- *In Example 3, what is the prime factorization of 12cd? of 36cd?* $2 \cdot 2 \cdot 3 \cdot c \cdot d$; $2 \cdot 2 \cdot 3 \cdot 3 \cdot c \cdot d$
- *What factors are common to 12cd and 36cd?* 2, 2, 3, c and d
- *What is the GCF of 12cd and 36cd?* $12cd$

BL
- *Why is it helpful to know the GCF when using the Distributive Property in reverse?* Sample answer: The GCF is the number that will appear outside of the parentheses.

Need Another Example?

Find the GCF of 14ab and 28ab. $14ab$

Work Zone

Find the GCF of Monomials

A **monomial** is a number, a variable, or a product of a number and one or more variables.

Monomials	**Not Monomials**
25, x, $40x$	$x + 4$, $40x + 120$

To **factor** a number means to write it as a product of its factors. A monomial can be factored using the same method you would use to factor a number.

The greatest common factor (GCF) of two monomials is the greatest monomial that is a factor of both.

Examples

Tutor

Find the GCF of each pair of monomials.

1. **$4x$, $12x$**

$4x = 2 \cdot 2 \cdot x$ — Write the prime factorization of $4x$ and $12x$.

$12x = 2 \cdot 2 \cdot 3 \cdot x$ — Circle the common factors.

The GCF of $4x$ and $12x$ is $2 \cdot 2 \cdot x$ or $4x$.

2. **$18a$, $20ab$**

$18a = 2 \cdot 3 \cdot 3 \cdot a$ — Write the prime factorization of $18a$ and $20ab$.

$20ab = 2 \cdot 2 \cdot 5 \cdot a \cdot b$ — Circle the common factors.

The GCF of $18a$ and $20ab$ is $2 \cdot a$ or $2a$.

STOP and Reflect

Which of the following is not a factor of $22x$? Circle your response.

(4) 2 11 x

3. **$12cd$, $36cd$**

$12cd = 2 \cdot 2 \cdot 3 \cdot c \cdot d$ — Write the prime factorization of $12cd$ and $36cd$.

$36cd = 2 \cdot 2 \cdot 3 \cdot 3 \cdot c \cdot d$ — Circle the common factors.

The GCF of $12cd$ and $36cd$ is $2 \cdot 2 \cdot 3 \cdot c \cdot d$ or $12cd$.

Got It? **Do these problems to find out.**

Find the GCF of each pair of monomials.

a. 12, 28c **b.** 25x, 15xy **c.** 42mn, 14mn

Show your work.

a. 4

b. 5x

c. 14mn

Factor Linear Expressions

You can use the Distributive Property and the work backward strategy to express a linear expression as a product of its factors. A linear expression is in **factored form** when it is expressed as the product of its factors.

$8x + 4y = 4(2x) + 4(y)$ The GCF of $8x$ and $4y$ is 4.

$= 4(2x + y)$ Distributive Property

Examples

Tutor

4. **Factor $3x + 9$.**

Method 1 **Use a model.**

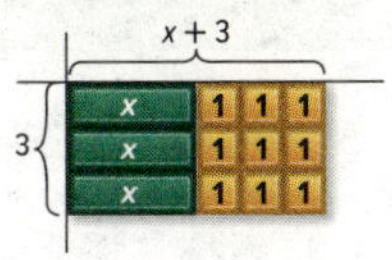

Arrange three x-tiles and nine 1-tiles into equal rows and columns. The rectangle has a width of three 1-tiles, or 3, and a length of one x-tile and three 1-tiles, or $x + 3$.

Method 2 **Use the GCF.**

$3x = 3 \cdot x$ Write the prime factorization of $3x$ and 9.

$9 = 3 \cdot 3$ Circle the common factors.

The GCF of $3x$ and 9 is 3. Write each term as a product of the GCF and its remaining factors.

$3x + 9 = 3(x) + 3(3)$

$= 3(x + 3)$ Distributive Property

So, $3x + 9 = 3(x + 3)$.

5. **Factor $12x + 7y$.**

Find the GCF of $12x$ and $7y$.

$12x = 2 \cdot 2 \cdot 3 \cdot x$

$7y = 1 \cdot 7 \cdot y$

There are no common factors, so $12x + 7y$ *cannot be factored.*

Got It? **Do these problems to find out.**

Factor each expression. If the expression cannot be factored, write *cannot be factored*. Use algebra tiles if needed.

d. $4x - 28$ **e.** $3x + 33y$ **f.** $4x + 35$

Factoring Expressions

To check your factored answers, multiply your factors out. You should get your original expression as a result.

Show your work.

d. $4(x - 7)$

e. $3(x + 11y)$

f. cannot be factored

Examples

4. **Factor algebraic expressions.**

AL
- *What does it mean to factor an expression?* If possible, write it as a product of its factors.
- *Using a model, what do the length and width of the rectangle represent?* the factors

OL
- *Using Method 2, what is the GCF of 3x and 9?* 3
- *What is the factored form of 3x + 9?* $3(x + 3)$
- *How can you check to see if the factored form is correct?* Use the Distributive Property to multiply. The answer should be the original expression.

BL
- *Do you prefer Method 1 or Method 2 when factoring an expression? Explain.* See students' preferences.

Need Another Example?
Factor $12x + 48$. $12(x + 4)$

5. **Factor algebraic expressions.**

AL
- *What is the prime factorization of 12x?* $2 \cdot 2 \cdot 3 \cdot x$
- *What the prime factorization of 7y?* $1 \cdot 7 \cdot y$ or $7 \cdot y$
- *Are there any common factors?* There are no common factors.

OL
- *Why can't 12x + 7y be factored?* There are no common factors.

BL
- *When an expression cannot be factored, it is considered prime. Is 12x + 7y prime?* yes
- *Compare and contrast prime expressions and prime numbers.* Sample answer: The only factors of each one are 1 and itself. A prime expression may have individual parts that are not prime numbers, but the entire expression is prime.

Need Another Example?
Factor $3x + 11$. cannot be factored

Example

6. Use linear expressions.

AL
- *What do you need to find?* the dimensions of the garden
- *What do you know?* the total area of the garden
- *How will you find possible dimensions?* factor $15x + 18$

OL
- *What is a possible width of the garden?* 3 ft
- *What the corresponding possible length of the garden?* $(5x + 6)$ ft

BL
- *Is there another possible solution to the problem? If so, name one.* yes; Sample answer: 2 ft by $(7.5x + 9)$ ft

Need Another Example?
Lily's favorite picture has an area of $(3x + 12)$ square inches. Find possible dimensions of the picture. 3 in. by $(x + 4)$ in.

Guided Practice

Formative Assessment Use these exercises to assess students' understanding of the concepts in this lesson.

If some of your students are not ready for assignments, use the differentiated activities below.

AL EL **Pairs Check** Have students work in pairs to completes Exercises 1–6. One partner completes the problem while the other partner coaches. Students switch roles for the next problem. After each section, the pairs check their answers with another pair and discuss any differences in the answers. MP 1

BL EL **Pairs Discussion** Have students work in pairs to complete the problem shown below. Have them trade their solutions with another pair and discuss any differences. MP 1, 7

Mindy's dog kennel sits in the corner of a field as shown in the diagram. The walkway around the kennel is 4 feet wide. Write an expression in factored form that represents the area of the walkway around the kennel. $8(x + 5)$ ft²

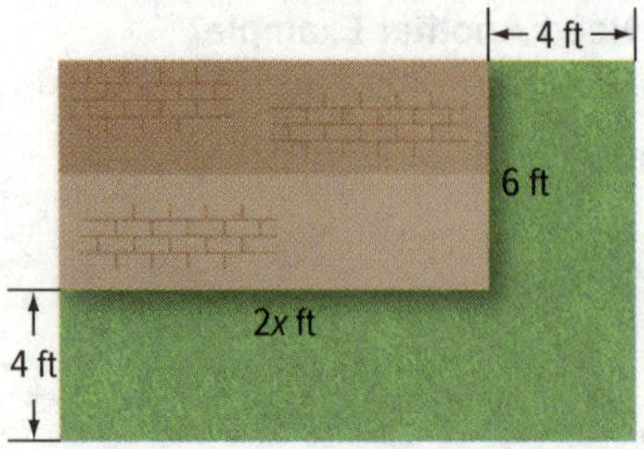

Real World Example

6. **The drawing of a garden at the right has a total area of $(15x + 18)$ square feet. Find possible dimensions of the garden.**

Factor $15x + 18$.

$15x = 3 \cdot 5 \cdot x$ — Write the prime factorization of 15x and 18.

$18 = 2 \cdot 3 \cdot 3$ — Circle the common factors.

The GCF of $15x$ and 18 is 3. Write each term as a product of the GCF and its remaining factors.

$15x + 18 = 3(5x) + 3(6)$

$= 3(5x + 6)$ — Distributive Property

So, the possible dimensions are 3 feet by $(5x + 6)$ feet.

Guided Practice

Find the GCF of each pair of monomials. (Examples 1–3)

1. $32x$, 18 **2**
2. $27s$, $54st$ **$27s$**
3. $18cd$, $30cd$ **$6cd$**

Show your work.

Factor each expression. If the expression cannot be factored, write cannot be factored. Use algebra tiles if needed. (Examples 4 and 5)

4. $36x + 24$ **$12(3x + 2)$**
5. $4x + 9$ **cannot be factored**
6. $14x - 16y$ **$2(7x - 8y)$**

7. Mr. Phen's monthly income can be represented by the expression $25x + 120$ where x is the number of hours worked. Factor the expression $25x + 120$. (Example 6)
$5(5x + 24)$

8. **Building on the Essential Question** Explain how the GCF is used to factor an expression. Use the term *Distributive Property* in your response.
Sample answer: The Distributive Property shows that $a(b + c) = ab + ac$. The GCF is the number that is distributed to each factor inside the parentheses.

Rate Yourself!
Are you ready to move on? Shade the section that applies.
YES ? NO

For more help, go online to access a Personal Tutor.

FOLDABLES Time to update your Foldable!

Name ______________________ My Homework ______________________

Independent Practice

Go online for Step-by-Step Solutions eHelp

Find the GCF of each pair of monomials. (Examples 1–3)

1. $24, 48m$ **24**
2. $32a, 48b$ **16**
3. $36k, 144km$ **36k**

Show your work

Factor each expression. If the expression cannot be *factored*, write *cannot be factored*. Use algebra tiles if needed. (Examples 4 and 5)

4. $3x + 6$ **$3(x + 2)$**
5. $2x - 15$ **cannot be factored**
6. $12x + 30y$ **$6(2x + 5y)$**

7. The area of a rectangular dance floor is $(4x - 8)$ square units. Factor $4x - 8$ to find possible dimensions of the dance floor. (Example 6)
4 units by $(x - 2)$ units

8. The area of a rectangular porch is $(9x + 18)$ square units. Factor $9x + 18$ to find possible dimensions of the porch. (Example 6)
9 units by $(x + 2)$ units

9. Six friends visited a museum to see the new holograms exhibit. The group paid for admission to the museum and $12 for parking. The total cost of the visit can be represented by the expression $6x + $12. What expression would represent the cost of the visit for one person?
$(x + 2)$ dollars

10. The diagram represents a flower border that is 3 feet wide surrounding a rectangular sitting area. Write an expression in factored form that represents the area of the flower border.
$6(3x + 11)$ ft^2

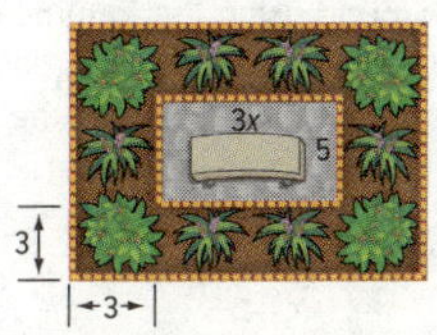

ENGAGE EXPLORE **EXPLAIN** **ELABORATE** **EVALUATE**

3 Practice and Apply

Independent Practice and Extra Practice

The Independent Practice pages are meant to be used as the homework assignment. The Extra Practice page can be used for additional reinforcement or as a second-day assignment.

Levels of Complexity

The levels of the exercises progress from 1 to 3, with Level 1 indicating the lowest level of complexity.

	Exercises 1–8, 18–31	Exercises 9–14, 32–39	Exercises 15–17
Level 3			●
Level 2		●	
Level 1	●		

Suggested Assignments

You can use the table below that includes exercises of all complexity levels to select appropriate exercises for your students' needs.

Differentiated Homework Options		
AL	Approaching Level	1–8, 9–13 odd, 15, 16, 38, 39
OL	On Level	1–7 odd, 9–16, 38, 39
BL	Beyond Level	9–17, 38, 39

McGraw Hill Education **ALEKS®** can provide additional remediation support with personalized instruction and practice.

Watch Out!

Common Error Students may attempt to factor an expression that cannot be factored. Remind them that they should always check their answers by using the Distributive Property to see if the product of their factors is equivalent to the original expression.

MATHEMATICAL PRACTICES

Emphasis On	Exercise(s)
1 Make sense of problems and persevere in solving them.	17
2 Reason abstractly and quantitatively.	11–14
3 Construct viable arguments and critique the reasoning of others.	15, 16

Mathematical Practices 1, 3, 4, and 5 are aspects of mathematical thinking that are emphasized in every lesson. Students are given opportunities to be persistent in their problem solving, to express their reasoning, and apply mathematics to real-world situations.

Formative Assessment
Use this activity as a closing formative assessment before dismissing students from your class.

TICKET Out the Door

Have students explain how to factor $54x + 18$ using the GCF. See students' work.

Watch Out!

Find the Error Point out that in Exercise 16, Jamar has the incorrect number of terms inside the parentheses. When factoring a simplified expression, there should be the same number of terms inside the parentheses as there were terms in the original expression.

MP Reason Abstractly Write an expression in factored form to represent the total area of each rectangle.

11.

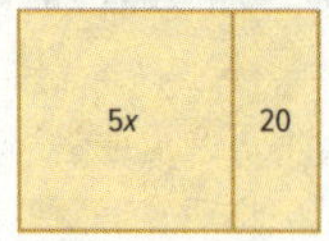

$5(x + 4)$ units^2

12.

$7(1 + 7x)$ units^2

13.

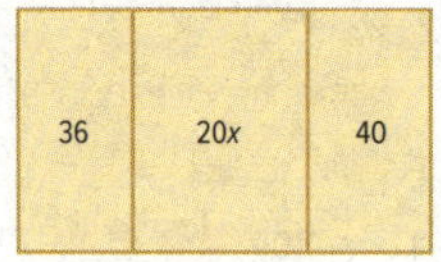

$4(5x + 19)$ units^2

14.

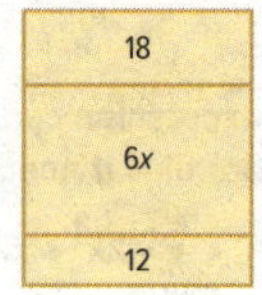

$6(x + 5)$ units^2

H.O.T. Problems Higher Order Thinking

15. **MP Reason Inductively** Write two monomials whose greatest common factor is $4m$.

Sample answer: $20m$ and $12mn$

16. **MP Find the Error** Jamar is factoring $90x - 15$. Find his mistake and correct it.

Sample answer: The GCF is 15. When he factored out 15, he wrote $6x$ instead of $6x - 1$. The correct answer should be $15(6x - 1)$.

17. **MP Persevere with Problems** The area of a rectangle is found using the formula $A = \ell w$, where ℓ is the length and w is the width of the rectangle. Write an expression in factored form that represents the area of the shaded region at the right.

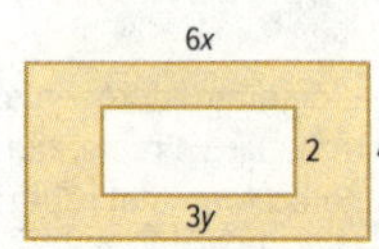

$6(4x - y)$

Name ______________ My Homework

Extra Practice

Find the GCF of each pair of monomials.

18. 63*p*, 84 **21**

$63p = 3 \cdot 3 \cdot 7 \cdot p$

$84 = 2 \cdot 2 \cdot 3 \cdot 7$

Homework Help: The GCF of 63*p* and 84 is $3 \cdot 7$ or 21.

19. 30*rs*, 42*rs* **6*rs***

$30rs = 2 \cdot 3 \cdot 5 \cdot r \cdot s$

$42rs = 2 \cdot 3 \cdot 7 \cdot r \cdot s$

The GCF of 30*rs* and 42*rs* is $2 \cdot 3 \cdot r \cdot s$ or 6*rs*.

20. 60*jk*, 45*jkm* **15*jk***

21. 40*x*, 60*x* **20*x***

22. 54*gh*, 72*g* **18*g***

23. 100*xy*, 75*xyz* **25*xy***

Factor each expression. If the expression cannot be factored, write *cannot be factored*. Use algebra tiles if needed.

24. $5x + 5$ **$5(x + 1)$**

25. $18x + 6$ **$6(3x + 1)$**

26. $4x - 7$ **cannot be factored**

27. $10x - 35$ **$5(2x - 7)$**

28. $32x + 24y$ **$8(4x + 3y)$**

29. $30x - 40$ **$10(3x - 4)$**

30. James has $120 in his savings account and plans to save $*x* each month for 6 months. The expression $6*x* + $120 represents the total amount in the account after 6 months. Factor the expression $6x + 120$.

$6(x + 20)$

31. A square scrapbooking page has a perimeter of $(8x + 20)$ inches. What is the length of one side of the scrapbooking page?

$(2x + 5)$ in.

Copy and Solve Write an expression in factored form that is equivalent to the given expression. Show your work on a separate piece of paper. **32–37. Sample answers given.**

32. $\frac{1}{2}x + 4$ **$\frac{1}{2}(x + 8)$**

33. $\frac{2}{3}x + 6$ **$\frac{2}{3}(x + 9)$**

34. $\frac{3}{4}x - 24$ **$\frac{3}{4}(x - 32)$**

35. $\frac{5}{6}x - 30$ **$\frac{5}{6}(x - 36)$**

36. $\frac{2}{5}x + 16$ **$\frac{2}{5}(x + 40)$**

37. $\frac{3}{8}x + 18$ **$\frac{3}{8}(x + 48)$**

Create Your Own Homework Online

eSolutionsManual™ can be used to create worksheets for the suggested assignments on page 419, or create your own worksheets for differentiated homework or review.

Power Up! Test Practice

Exercises 38 and 39 prepare students for more rigorous thinking needed for the state assessment.

38.

This test item requires students to analyze and solve complex real-world problems through the use of mathematical tools and models.	
Depth of Knowledge	DOK3
Content Standard	7.EE.1
Mathematical Practices	MP1, MP3, MP4
Online Experience	Students will drag values to complete the Venn Diagram and type their response in the box.
Scoring Rubric	
2 points	Students correctly complete the Venn Diagram, find the GCF and explain.
1 point	Students correctly complete the Venn Diagram, find the GCF, but fail to explain OR students correctly place 6–9 of the values in the diagram and find the GCF OR students correctly place 6–9 of the values in the diagram, find the GCF, and explain OR students fail to find the GCF, place 6–9 values on the diagram, and explain.

39.

This test item requires students to explain and apply mathematical concepts and solve problems with precision, while making use of structure.	
Depth of Knowledge	DOK1
Content Standard	7.EE.1
Mathematical Practice	MP1
Online Experience	Students will be required to click on the bubbles to select all correct answers.
Scoring Rubric	
1 point	Students correctly answer the question.

Power Up! Test Practice

38. Select the correct terms to fill in the Venn diagram to show the factors of 12 and 18x.

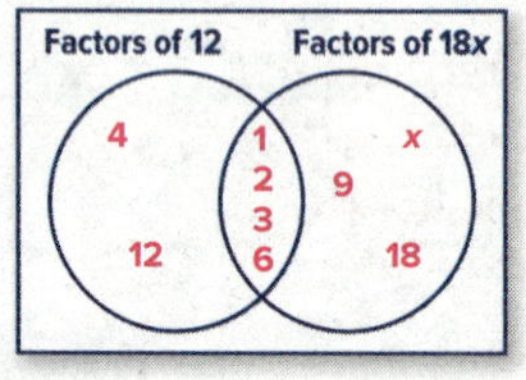

1	9
2	12
3	18
4	x
6	

What is the GCF of 12 and 18x? Explain how the Venn diagram helped you find the GCF.

6; Sample answer: You can use the Venn diagram to locate each factor of the monomials. The center overlapping region shows all of the common factors. To find the GCF, simply find the largest factor in the overlap region.

39. Which pairs of monomials have a GCF of 4a? Select all that apply.

- ☐ 8a, 18a
- ☐ 16a, 8b
- ☑ 16ab, 12a
- ☑ 28a, 20a

Spiral Review

Use the Distributive Property to rewrite each expression. 6.EE.1

40. $4(x + 1) =$ $4x + 4$

41. $3(a + 10) =$ $3a + 30$

42. $7(2b + 5) =$ $14b + 35$

43. The letters P, E, M, D, A, and S form PEMDAS. This is a mnemonic device that can be used to help you remember the order of operations. Each letter stands for something. Complete the organizer. 6.EE.3

- P → Parentheses
- E → Exponents
- M → Multiplication
- D → Division
- A → Addition
- S → Subtraction

PLAN ONLINE

PD | RtI | Watch | Worksheets | Vocab | Tutor | Tools | Check | English Learners | Sketchpad

PRESENT

College & Career READINESS

21ST CENTURY CAREER in Animal Conservation

Shark Scientist

Are you fascinated by sharks, especially those that are found around the coasts of the United States? If so, you should consider a career as a shark scientist. Shark scientists use satellite-tracking devices, called tags, to study and track the movements of sharks. By analyzing the data transmitted by the tags, scientists are able to learn more about the biology and ecology of sharks. Their research is helpful in protecting shark populations around the world.

College & Career READINESS

Is This the Career for You?

Are you interested in a career as a shark scientist? Take some of the following courses in high school.

- Algebra
- Calculus
- Physics
- Statistics

Find out how math relates to a career in Animal Conservation.

Focus narrowing the scope

Objective Apply mathematics to problems arising in the workplace.

This lesson emphasizes MP **Mathematical Practice 4** Model with Mathematics.

Coherence connecting within and across grades

Previous
Students use expressions to represent mathematical ideas.

Now
Students apply the content standard to solve problems in the workplace.

Rigor pursuing concepts, fluency, and applications

See the Career Project on page 424.

ENGAGE EXPLORE EXPLAIN ELABORATE EVALUATE

1 Launch the Lesson

Ask students to read the information on the student page about shark scientists and answer the following questions.

Ask:

- *What does a shark scientist do?* Sample answer: studies the biology and ecology of sharks
- *What courses should you take if you are interested in becoming a shark scientist?* Sample answers: Calculus, Algebra, Physics, and Statistics

College & Career READINESS

Help students connect what they do today to their futures. Direct them to the Internet or another source to explore, learn, and plan for college and future careers.

2 Collaborate

AL EL Think-Pair-Share Have students work in pairs to complete Exercises 1, 3, and 5 using the following scaffolded questions. Answers shown are for Exercise 1. MP 1, 2, 4

Ask:

- *What information from the note cards do you need to complete this exercise?* **The total length of a hammerhead shark is about 1.3 times the fork length.**
- *What variable is used to represent the fork length (or total length in Exercise 5)?* ***f***
- *What operation is indicated by the note card?* **multiplication**

BL EL Trade-a-Problem Have students alter Exercises 2, 4, and 6 using different given fork lengths for a hammerhead shark and sandbar shark, and total length of a white shark. Then have them trade their altered problems with another student. Each student solves the other's problems and compare solutions. If the solutions do not agree, students should work together to determine any errors. MP 1, 2, 3

Career Portfolio

When students complete this page, have them add it to their Career Portfolio.

Career Facts

Due to fisheries, unregulated catching of sharks, and habitat destruction, more than 50 percent of oceanic shark species are currently listed as *threatened with extinction*. Through their research projects, scientists help promote conservation of sharks worldwide.

MP Tag, You're It!

The *fork length* of a shark is the length from the tip of the snout to the fork of the tail. Use the information on the note cards to solve each problem.

1. Write an expression to represent the total length of a hammerhead shark that has a fork length of *f* feet. **$1.3f$**
2. Use the expression from Exercise 1 to find the total length of a hammerhead shark that has a fork length of 11.6 feet. **15.08 ft**
3. Write an expression to represent the average fork length of a tiger shark, given the average fork length s of a sandbar shark. **$2s - 55$**
4. Use the expression from Exercise 3 to find the average fork length of a tiger shark if the average fork length of a sandbar shark is 129 centimeters. **203 cm**
5. Write an expression to find the average fork length of a white shark with a total length of *t* centimeters. **$0.94t - 5.74$**
6. The total length of a white shark is 204 centimeters. Use the expression in Exercise 5 to find the approximate fork length of the white shark. **186 cm**

Tiger Shark
A study found that the average fork length of a tiger shark is 55 centimeters less than twice the average fork length of a sandbar shark.

White Shark
The fork length of a white shark is about 5.74 centimeters less than 0.94 times the total length t.

Hammerhead Shark
The total length of a hammerhead shark is about 1.3 times the fork length.

MP Career Project

It's time to update your career portfolio! Describe the skills that would be necessary for a shark scientist to possess. Determine whether this type of career would be a good fit for you.

List several challenges associated with this career.

-
-
-
-
-

Chapter Review

Check

Vocabulary Check

Vocab

In the puzzle below, write a vocabulary term for each clue.

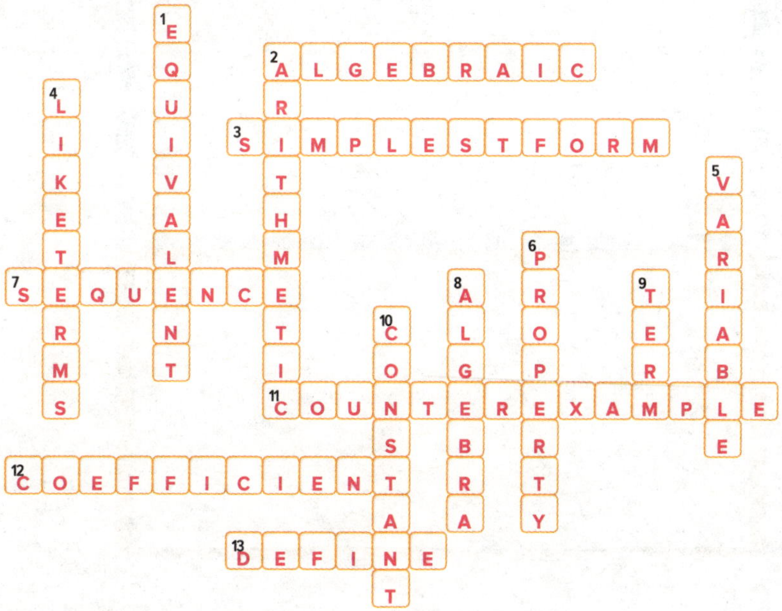

Across

2. a type of expression that contains a variable or variables
3. an algebraic expression that has no like terms and no parentheses is in this form (two words)
7. an ordered list of numbers
11. an example showing a statement is not true
12. the numerical factor of a multiplication expression
13. what is done to a variable to represent an unknown quantity

Down

1. expressions like $4(3 + 2)$ and $4(3) + 4(2)$
2. a sequence in which each term is found by adding the same number
4. terms that include the same variable
5. a letter or symbol
6. a statement that is true for any number or variable
8. a branch of mathematics that uses variables
9. a number in a sequence
10. a term that contains a number only

Vocabulary Check

EL **Numbered Heads Together** Assign students to 3- or 4-person learning teams. Each member is assigned a number from 1 to 4. Each team completes the Vocabulary Check, making sure every team member understands the terms and their definitions. Call on a specific number from one team to present the group's solution to the class. MP 1, 6

Alternate Strategy

AL **EL** To help students, you may wish to give them a vocabulary list from which they can choose their answers. A vocabulary list for this activity would include:

- algebra (Lesson 1)
- algebraic expression (Lesson 1)
- arithmetic sequence (Lesson 2)
- coefficient (Lesson 1)
- constant (Lesson 5)
- counterexample (Lesson 3)
- define a variable (Lesson 1)
- equivalent expression (Lesson 4)
- like terms (Lesson 5)
- property (Lesson 3)
- sequence (Lesson 2)
- simplest form (Lesson 5)
- term (Lessons 2 and 5)
- variable (Lesson 1)

Key Concept Check

FOLDABLES EL A completed Foldable for this chapter should include a review of adding, subtracting, and factoring linear expressions.

If you choose not to use the Foldable, have students write a brief review of the Key Concepts found throughout the chapter and give an example of each.

Ideas for Use

EL Have students work in pairs to discuss their Foldables. Have them practice speaking in a collaborative setting by sharing how they have completed their Foldable thus far and how they could finish it. Have each student complete their Foldable and trade with their partner to discuss any similarities and differences. MP 1, 3, 5

Got It?

If students have trouble with Exercises 1–5, they may need help with the following concepts.

Concept	Exercise(s)
Commutative Property (Lesson 3)	1
Distributive Property (Lesson 4)	2, 4
simplifying expressions (Lesson 5)	3
factoring expressions (Lesson 8)	5

ALEKS® provides additional support with personalized instruction and practice for those who are struggling, while providing enhanced learning for those who have mastered the concepts.

Key Concept Check

Use Your FOLDABLES

Use your Foldable to help review the chapter.

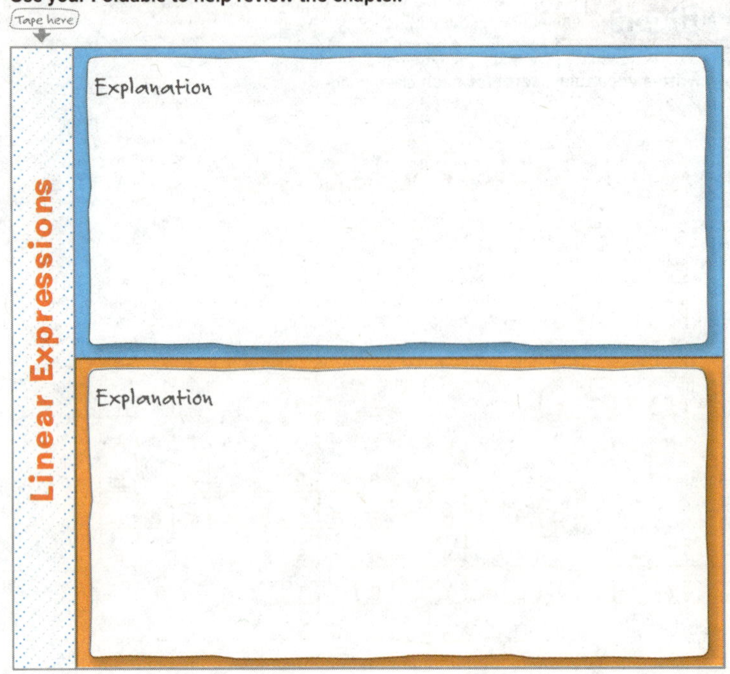

Got it?

Draw a line to match each expression with its equivalent expression.

1. $3 + 1$
2. $4(2 - x)$
3. $3x - 2 - x + 6$
4. $2(x + 2) + (3x + 1)$
5. $3x + 21$

a. $8 - 4x$
b. $5x + 5$
c. $3(x + 7)$
d. $1 + 3$
e. $2x + 4$

Expressions and Equations

Power Up! Performance Task

Movie Time

The Townsends, a family of five, are going to the local movie theater. The family consists of two adults and three children. Mr. Townsend wants to calculate the cost of the night out. He looks up the admission prices online.

Admission:

Adults — $10.50

Children — $6.50

All shows before 6 P.M. $\frac{1}{2}$ price

Before leaving, Mr. Townsend decides that he will get some items at the theater concession stand, a large drink for each person and a large tub of popcorn for everyone to share. He will not know the prices of the items at the concession stand until they arrive.

Write your answers on another piece of paper. Show all of your work to receive full credit.

Part A

Write an expression that represents the cost of the admission prices and the concession stand items based on the available information. Let *d* represent the cost for a large drink and let *p* represent the cost of the popcorn. The initial expression must include parentheses. Then simplify the expression by using the Distributive Property and combining like terms.

Part B

Two children from next door join the Townsends. The neighbor children have movie passes and have already eaten, so Mr. Townsend will only need to pay for two more large drinks. At the concession stand, one of the children gives Mr. Townsend a five dollar bill to help pay for the drinks. Write an expression that represents the cost of the drinks for the neighbor children and includes the money given to Mr. Townsend.

Part C

While at the concession stand, Mr. Townsend sees that the large tub of popcorn is $7.50, and large drinks are $6 each. Using your answers from Part A and Part B, write an expression that represents the total cost. Then substitute the values for the popcorn and drinks in your expression. What is the total cost for the evening?

Power Up! Performance Task

The Performance-Based Assessment requires students to solve multi-step problems through abstract reasoning, precision, and perseverance. This practice scenario can be used to help students prepare for the thinking skills that will be used on the State Assessment.

A complete scoring rubric with answers to the Exercises can be found on page PT1.

Answering the Essential Question

Before answering the Essential Question, have students review their answers to the **Building on the Essential Question** exercises found in each lesson of the chapter.

- Will the expressions $x - 3$ and $y - 3$ sometimes, always, or never represent the same value? (p. 352)
- Why is 5, 9, 13, 17, 21, ... considered an arithmetic sequence? (p. 360)
- What is the difference between the Commutative and Associative Properties? (p. 370)
- How is the formula for the perimeter of a rectangle an application of the Distributive Property? (p. 378)
- Why are the expressions $2(x - 1) + 3(x - 1)$ and $5(x - 1)$ equivalent? (p. 390)
- How is adding linear expressions similar to simplifying expressions? (p. 398)
- How can you use the additive inverse to help you subtract linear expressions? (p. 406)
- How is the GCF used to factor expressions? (p. 418)

Ideas for Use

EL **Think-Pair-Share** Have students work in pairs. Pose the Essential Question. Give students about one minute to think about how they could complete the graphic organizer. Then have them share their responses with their classmate before they complete the graphic organizer.

MP 1, 3, 5

Reflect

Answering the Essential Question

Use what you learned about algebraic expressions to complete the graphic organizer. Then answer the chapter's Essential Question below.

When do you use a variable?

Sample answer: A variable is a letter or symbol that represents a number or set of numbers. Variables are used to represent an unknown quantity. Suppose a real-world problem states that each pizza costs \$7, but the problem does not state how many pizzas are ordered. Let p represent the number of pizzas ordered and $7p$ represent the cost of the pizzas.

Essential Question

HOW can you use numbers and symbols to represent mathematical ideas?

How do you know which operation symbol to use?

Sample answer: Four operation symbols are: + for addition; − for subtraction; ×, •, or ( ) for multiplication, and ÷ for division. Read a real-world problem carefully to look for key words indicating which operation to use, such as *more than* or *increased by* for addition and less than or decreased by for subtraction. Then use the symbol for that operation.

Answer the Essential Question. HOW can you use numbers and symbols to represent mathematical ideas?

See students' work.

PLAN ONLINE

PD | RtI | Watch | Worksheets | Vocab | Tutor | Tools | Check | English Learners | Sketchpad

PRESENT

IWB

An Interactive Whiteboard Ready presentation is available for each lesson in the chapter.

Expressions and Equations

Chapter 6
Equations and Inequalities

Essential Question

WHAT does it mean to say two quantities are equal?

Content Standards
7.EE.3, 7.EE.4, 7.EE.4a, 7.EE.4b

MP Mathematical Practices
1, 2, 3, 4, 5, 7

Math in the Real World

Driving Suppose you live in a state where you must be at least 16 years of age to obtain a driver's license. Circle the statement that represents this age.

FOLDABLES® Study Organizer

1. Cut out the Foldable on page FL5 of this book.
2. Place your Foldable on page 524.
3. Use the Foldable to help you learn about equations and inequalities.

Focus narrowing the scope

This chapter focuses on content from the **Expressions and Equations** (EE) domain.

Mathematical Background Additional information about the mathematical background for this chapter can be found online at connectED.mcgraw-hill.com.

Coherence connecting within and across grades

Previous	Now	Next
Students used properties of operations to simplify expressions.	Students solve equations and inequalities.	Students will use expressions and equations to solve geometric relationships.

Rigor pursuing concepts, fluency, and applications

The Levels of Complexity charts located throughout this chapter indicate how the exercises progress from conceptual understanding and procedural skills and fluency, to application and critical thinking.

Launch the Chapter

Math in the Real World

Driving Remind students that the phrase *at least* indicates that you should use the ≥ symbol.

What Tools Do You Need?

Vocabulary Activity

EL As you proceed through the chapter, introduce each vocabulary term using the following routine. Ask the students to say each term aloud after you say it.

Define: A coefficient is the numerical factor of a term that contains a variable.

Example: In the term $\frac{1}{2}b$, $\frac{1}{2}$ is the coefficient.

Ask:

- *What is the coefficient in the equation $\frac{2}{5}t = \frac{12}{15}$?* $\frac{2}{5}$

Reading Math

EL Students identify key information in word problems. This is important in the understanding and solving of word problems. Have students read the steps to identify key information in the Reading Math section.

Ask:

- *How does putting the important information in one sentence help with solving a word problem?* **Sample answer: It helps to sort out what you know and what you need to find.**
- *What are some key words or phrases in Exercise 1?* **Sample answer: 3.1 million pounds more than, how many**

What Tools Do You Need?

Vocabulary

Addition Property of Equality
Addition Property of Inequality
coefficient
Division Property of Equality
Division Property of Inequality
equation
equivalent equation
inequality
Multiplication Property of Equality
Multiplication Property of Inequality
solution
Subtraction Property of Equality
Subtraction Property of Inequality
two-step equation
two-step inequality

Study Skill: Reading Math

Identify Key Information Have you ever tried to solve a word problem and didn't know where to start. Start by looking for key words in the text and images. Then write the important information in one sentence.

1. Highlight or circle key words in the following real-world problem.

   During a recent Super Bowl, millions of pounds of potato chips and tortilla chips were consumed. The number of pounds of potato chips consumed was 3.1 million pounds more than the number of pounds of tortilla chips. How many pounds of tortilla chips were consumed?

2. Write a sentence that summarizes the information provided. Include information from the text and the image. **Sample answer: 12.4 million pounds of potato chips were 3.1 million more than the number of pounds of tortilla chips.**

What Do You Already Know?

Place a checkmark below the face that expresses how much you know about each concept. Then scan the chapter to find a definition or example of it. See students' work.

☹ I have no clue. 😐 I've heard of it. ☺ I know it!

Equations and Inequalities				
Concept	☹	😐	☺	Definition or Example
inequalities				
solving one-step equations				
solving inequalities by addition or subtraction				
solving inequalities by multiplication or division				
solving two-step equations				
solving two-step inequalities				

When Will You Use This?

Here are a few examples of how equations are used in the real world.

Activity 1 Describe a situation when you only had a set amount of money to spend and you needed to buy a certain number of items. Then explain how you determined what you could buy.

See students' work.

Activity 2 Go online at connectED.mcgraw-hill.com to read the graphic novel ***Movie Night***. How much does each DVD cost? How much money do they need for popcorn? $19; $39

What Do You Already Know?

In this activity students assess their prior knowledge choosing a face to represent their knowledge about concepts in the chapter.

After completing the chapter, have students return to this page and have them reevaluate their knowledge level about the content.

When Will You Use This?

Activity 1

Students develop an understanding of the connection between a real-world situations and using equation to solve problems.

Activity 2

Use the Graphic Novel to help students learn about writing and solving equations.

Ask:

- *What information do you need to solve the problem?* the cost of popcorn, the cost of each DVD, and the amount of money they have to spend
- *Do you have enough information?* yes

Are You Ready?

Use this page to determine if students have skills that are needed for the chapter.

Quick Review

Students with strong math backgrounds may opt to go directly to the Quick Check.

QUICK REVIEW		
Example	Skill	Standard
1	Write algebraic expressions.	6.EE.2a
2	Identify solutions of equations.	6.EE.5

Quick Check

If students have difficulty with the exercises, present an additional example to clarify any misconceptions.

Exercises 1–3

Write the phrase *12 years older than his sister* as an algebraic expression. $s + 12$

Exercises 4–9

Is 28, 29, or 30 the solution of the equation $25 + d = 54$? 29

Response to Intervention

Go online at connectED.mcgraw-hill.com for resources to differentiate remediation for Tier 1, Tier 2, and Tier 3 students.

ALEKS® can provide additional remediation support with personalized instruction and practice. See pages T8 and T9 for more information.

Are You Ready?

Try the Quick Check below.
Or, take the Online Readiness Quiz.

Quick Review

6.EE.2a, 6.EE.5

Example 1

Write the phrase as an algebraic expression.

Phrase: five dollars more than Jennifer earned

Variable: Let *d* represent the number of dollars Jennifer earned.

Expression: $d + 5$

Example 2

Is 3, 4, or 5 the solution of the equation $x + 8 = 12$?

Value of x	$x + 8 = 12$	Are both sides equal?
3	$3 + 8 \stackrel{?}{=} 12$ $11 \neq 12$	no
4	$4 + 8 \stackrel{?}{=} 12$ $12 = 12$	yes ✓
5	$5 + 8 \stackrel{?}{=} 12$ $13 \neq 12$	no

The solution is 4 since replacing x with 4 results in a true sentence.

Quick Check

Words and Symbols Write the phrase as an algebraic expression.

1. 3 more runs than the Pirates scored $p + 3$
2. a number decreased by eight $n - 8$
3. ten dollars more than Grace has $g + 10$

Show your work.

One-Step Equations Identify the solution of each equation from the list given.

4. $8 + w = 17$; 7, 8, 9 9
5. $d - 12 = 5$; 16, 17, 18 17
6. $6 = 3y$; 2, 3, 4 2
7. $7 \div c = 7$; 0, 1, 2 1
8. $a + 8 = 23$; 13, 14, 15 15
9. $10 = 45 - n$; 35, 36, 37 35

How Did You Do?

Which problems did you answer correctly in the Quick Check? Shade those exercise numbers below.

① ② ③ ④ ⑤ ⑥ ⑦ ⑧ ⑨

PLAN ONLINE: PD | RtI | Watch | Worksheets | Vocab | Tutor | Tools | Check | English Learners | Sketchpad

PRESENT

IWB

An Interactive Whiteboard Ready presentation is available for each lesson in the chapter.

Expressions and Equations

Inquiry Lab

Solve One-Step Addition and Subtraction Equations

Inquiry **HOW can bar diagrams or algebra tiles help you solve an equation?**

Content Standards
7.EE.4, 7.EE.4a

MP **Mathematical Practices**
1, 2, 3, 5

In a recent year, 19 of the 50 states had a law banning the use of handheld cell phones while driving a school bus. Determine how many states did *not* have this law.

Hands-On Activity 1

You can represent this situation with an equation.

Step 1 The bar diagram represents the total number of states and the number of states that have passed a cell phone law. Fill in the missing information.

50 states	
states with a law	**states that do not have a law**
19 states	?

Step 2 Write an equation from the bar diagram. Let *x* represent the states that do not have a cell phone law for school bus drivers.

$$19 + x = 50$$

Step 3 Use the *work backward* strategy to solve the equation. Since $19 + x = 50$, $x = 50 - 19$. So, $x =$ 31.

Check $19 + 31 = 50$ ✓

So, 31 states did *not* have a law banning the use of cell phones by bus drivers.

Focus narrowing the scope

Objective Use models to write and solve addition and subtraction equations. 7.EE.4, 7.EE.4a

Coherence connecting within and across grades

Now
Students use bar diagrams and algebra tiles to write and solve one-step addition and subtraction equations.

Next
Students will use Properties of Equality to solve one-step equations.

Rigor pursuing concepts, fluency, and applications

See the Levels of Complexity chart on page 434.

ENGAGE EXPLORE EXPLAIN ELABORATE EVALUATE

1 Launch the Lab

Activity 1 is intended to be used as a whole-group activity. Activity 1 is designed to provide more guidance than Activity 2.

Hands-On Activity 1

AL EL Remind students that the bar diagram represents the sum of the states with a law and the states that do not have a law.

Ask:

- *How many states have this law?* 19 states
- *How can you use the bar diagram to write an equation?* The first section represents the 19 states with a law, the second section represents the states that do not. The sum of these is equal to 50.

BL Omit Activities 1 and 2 and proceed directly to the Investigate section. MP 1, 4, 5

2 Collaborate

The **Investigate** and **Analyze and Reflect** sections are intended to be used as small-group investigations. The **Create** section is intended to be used as independent exercises.

Levels of Complexity

The levels of the exercises progress from 1 to 3, with Level 1 indicating the lowest level of complexity.

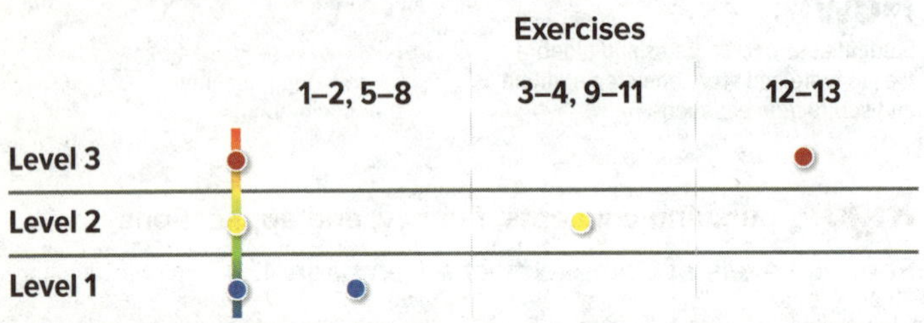

Investigate

AL EL Pairs Discussion Have students work in pairs to complete Exercises 1 and 2. Have them trade their solutions with another pair of students and discuss any differences. MP 1, 2, 4, 5

BL EL Trade-a-Problem Have students create their own problem, similar to Exercises 1 and 2. Students trade their problems, solve each other's problem, and compare solutions. If the solutions do not agree, students work together to find the errors. MP 1, 2, 4

Analyze and Reflect

AL EL Think-Pair-Share Have students work in pairs. Give students one minute to think through their responses to Exercises 3 and 4. Have them share their responses with their partner. Then call on one student to share their response within a small group or large group discussion. MP 1, 2, 5

Investigate

Work with a partner to solve each problem.

1. Draw a bar diagram and write an addition equation to represent the following situation. Then solve the equation.

   The sum of a number and four is equal to 18.

Equation: $x + 4 = 18$ Solution: $x = 14$

2. MP **Use Math Tools** Jack collects postage stamps. He sold 7 of his stamps and had 29 stamps left. Complete the bar diagram below. Then write and solve a subtraction equation to find the number of stamps Jack had at the beginning.

Equation: $n - 7 = 29$ Solution: $n = 36$

So, Jack had 36 stamps at the beginning.

Analyze and Reflect

3. Suppose Jack sold 15 stamps and had 21 stamps left. How would the bar diagram change?

   Sample answer: Since Jack sold 15 stamps instead of 7, the stamps sold bar would be longer.

4. MP **Reason Abstractly** Suppose Jack had 40 stamps in the beginning and sold 7 of them. How would the bar diagram change? What equation could you write to represent the situation?

   Sample answer: Write 40 stamps above the bar and use a variable for the number of stamps left; $7 + n = 40$.

Hands-On Activity 2

Tools

Solve $x - 3 = -2$ using algebra tiles.

Remember a 1-tile and −1 tile combine to make a *zero pair*. You can add or subtract zero pairs from either side of an equation without changing its value.

Step 1 Model the equation.

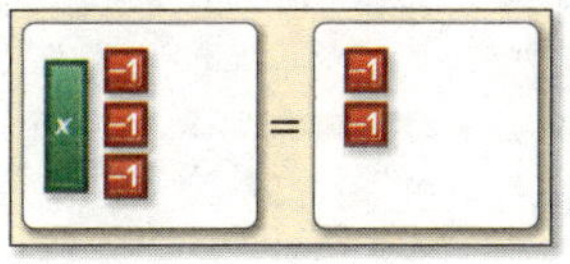

$x - 3 \quad = \quad -2$

Step 2 Add three 1-tiles to the left side of the mat and three 1-tiles to the right side of the mat to form zero pairs on each side of the mat.

$x - 3 + 3 \quad = \quad -2 + 3$

Step 3 Remove all of the zero pairs from each side. There is one 1-tile on the right side of the mat.

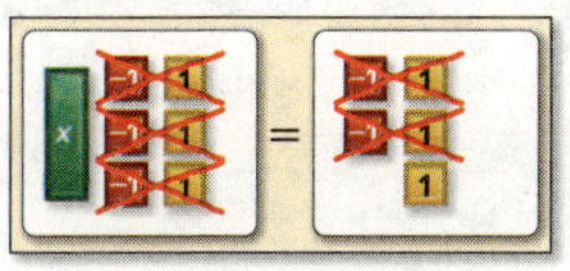

$x \quad = \quad 1$

Therefore, $x = 1$.

Check $1 - 3 = -2$ ✓

Hands-On Activity 2

AL EL Explain to students that a 1-tile and a −1-tile make a zero pair because when 1 and −1 are opposites. Zero pairs can be removed from or added to the equation mat without changing the value on that side of the equation.

Ask:

- *To isolate the variable, do you need to add 1-tiles or −1-tiles?* 1-tiles
- *How many 1-tiles need to be added to each side of the mat to isolate the variable?* 3
- *How many zero pairs are now on the left side of the mat?* 3
- *How many zero pairs are now on the right side of the mat?* ?
- *How many 1-tiles remain on the right side of the mat?* 1

Investigate

AL EL Rally Coach For Exercises 5–8, have students work in pairs. Partner A should answer the first Exercise while Partner B watches, listens, coaches, and praises. Partner B solves the next Exercise while Partner A watches, listens, coaches, and praises. Partners take turns until the Exercises are complete. MP 1, 2, 5

Analyze and Reflect

AL EL Numbered Heads Together Assign students to 3- or 4-person learning teams. Each member is assigned a number from 1 to 4. Each team completes Exercises 9–11 making sure that every member understands. Call on a specific number from one team to present the team's solution to the class. MP 1, 2

BL EL Trade-a-Problem Have students create their own problem, similar to Exercises 9–11. Students trade their problems, solve each other's problem, and compare solutions. If the solutions do not agree, students work together to find the errors. MP 1, 2

Create

BL EL Pairs Discussion Have students work in pairs to complete Exercises 12 and 13. Have them trade their solutions with another pair of students and discuss any differences. MP 1, 7

Inquiry Students should be able to answer "HOW can bar diagrams or algebra tiles help you solve an equation?" Check for student understanding and provide guidance, if needed.

Investigate

MP Use Math Tools Work with a partner to solve each equation. Use algebra tiles. Show your work using drawings.

5. $x + 4 = 4$ $x =$ 0

Show your work.

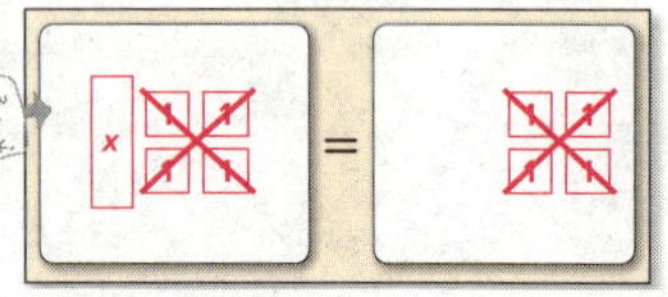

6. $-2 = x + 1$ $x =$ −3

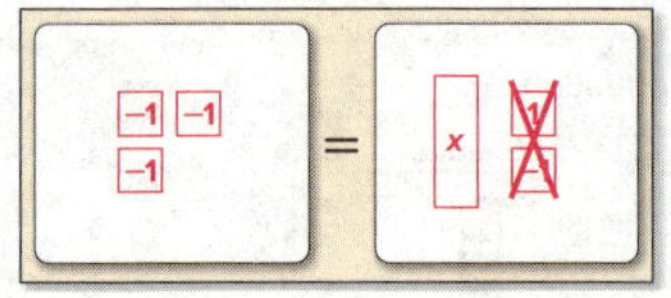

7. $x - 1 = -3$ $x =$ −2

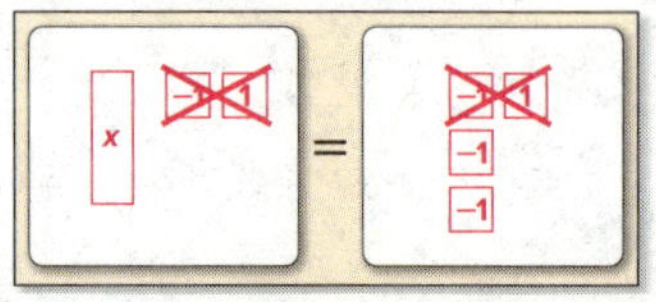

8. $4 = x - 2$ $x =$ 6

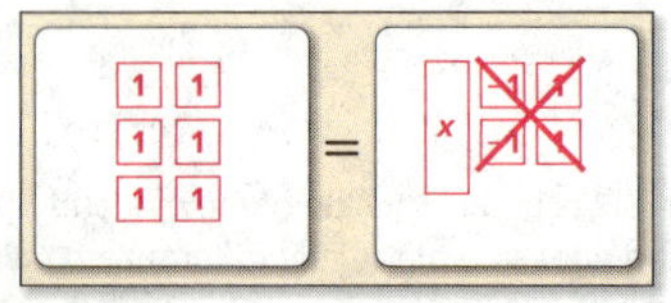

Analyze and Reflect

Work with a partner to complete the table. The first one is done for you.

	Equation	Related Equation
	$x + 3 = 4$	$x = 4 - 3$
9.	$6 + x = 10$	$x = 10 - 6$
10.	$x + 3 = -1$	$x = -1 - 3$
11.	$6 + x = -7$	$x = -7 - 6$

Create

12. **MP Construct an Argument** Write a rule that you can use to solve addition equations without using models or a drawing.

Sample answer: Write them as subtraction equations.

13. Inquiry HOW can bar diagrams or algebra tiles help you solve an equation?

Sample answer: A bar diagram or an algebra tile model provides a visual aid when deciding which operation to use.

PLAN ONLINE: PD · RtI · Watch · Worksheets · Vocab · Tutor · Tools · Check · English Learners · Sketchpad

PRESENT: IWB — **An Interactive Whiteboard Ready presentation is available for each lesson in the chapter.**

Lesson 1

Solve One-Step Addition and Subtraction Equations

Vocabulary Start-Up

An **equation** is a sentence stating that two quantities are equal. The value of a variable that makes an equation true is called the **solution** of the equation.

$$\begin{aligned} x + 2 &= 6 \\ -2 &= -2 \\ x &= 4 \end{aligned}$$

The equations $x + 2 = 6$ and $x = 4$ are **equivalent equations** because they have the same solution, 4.

Circle the equations below that are equivalent to $x = 3$. Use algebra tiles if needed.

$x + 3 = 6$ (circled)	$x + 1 = 6$	$x + 6 = 8$
$x + 3 = 3$	$x + 1 = 4$ (circled)	$x + 2 = 5$ (circled)

Essential Question

WHAT does it mean to say two quantities are equal?

Vocabulary

equation
solution
equivalent equation
Subtraction Property of Equality
Addition Property of Equality

Content Standards
7.EE.4, 7.EE.4a

MP Mathematical Practices
1, 2, 3, 4, 5

Real-World Link

Video Games Robyn had some video games, and then she bought 4 more games. Now she has 10 games. This scenario can be described using the equation $x + 4 = 10$.

1. What does x represent in the equation?
   The x represents the number of games Robyn started with.

2. Write two different equations that are equivalent to $x + 4 = 10$.
   Sample answer: $x = 6$ and $2x = 12$.

Which MP Mathematical Practices did you use? Shade the circle(s) that applies.

1. Persevere with Problems
2. Reason Abstractly
3. Construct an Argument
4. Model with Mathematics
5. Use Math Tools
6. Attend to Precision
7. Make Use of Structure
8. Use Repeated Reasoning

Focus narrowing the scope

Objective Solve addition and subtraction equations. 7.EE.4, 7.EE.4a

Coherence connecting within and across grades

Previous Students wrote and evaluated algebraic expressions.

Now Students write and solve one-step linear equations.

Next Students will solve two-step linear equations.

Rigor pursuing concepts, fluency, and applications

See the Levels of Complexity chart on page 441.

ENGAGE EXPLORE EXPLAIN ELABORATE EVALUATE

1 Launch the Lesson

Ideas for Use

You may wish to launch the lesson using a whole group, small group, think-pair-share activity, or independent activity.

EL AL **Think-Pair-Share** Have students work in pairs to complete the Vocabulary Start-Up. When they get to the vocabulary word *equivalent equations,* give students one minute to think about the word equivalent, what it means, and where they have used it before. Have them share their responses with their partner. Then call on one student to share their response within a small group or large group discussion. MP 1, 6

Alternate Strategy

BL Have students work in pairs. Have one student give an example of an equation. Then have the other student write an equation that is equivalent to the first equation. Challenge students to write more complex equations. MP 1, 4

2 Teach the Concept

Ask the scaffolded questions for each example to differentiate instruction.

Examples

IWB

1. Solve addition equations.

- **AL** *What is the variable?* x
- *What number is on the same side of the equals sign as the variable?* 6
- *What operation is used between x and 6?* addition
- *How do you undo addition?* subtraction
- **OL** *What is the first step to solving the equation?* subtract 6 from each side
- *What is 4 − 6?* −2
- **BL** *What property allows you to subtract 6 from each side of the equation?* Subtraction Property of Equality

Need Another Example?
Solve 14 + y = 20. Check your solution. 6

2. Solve addition equations.

- **AL** *What is the variable?* b
- *What number is on the same side of the equals sign as the variable?* 8
- *What operation is used between b and 8?* addition
- *How do you undo addition?* subtraction
- **OL** *What is the first step to solving the equation?* subtract 8 from each side
- *What is −5 −8?* −13
- *What property allows you to subtract 8 from each side of the equation?* Subtraction Property of Equality
- **BL** *How can you check your solution?* Replace b with −13 in the original equation, simplify, and determine if the final statement is true.

Need Another Example?
Solve −12 = 4 + c. Check your solution. −16

Key Concept

Subtraction Property of Equality

Words The **Subtraction Property of Equality** states that the two sides of an equation remain equal when you subtract the same number from each side.

Symbols If $a = b$, then $a - c = b - c$.

Work Zone

You can use bar diagrams and the *work backward* problem-solving strategy to solve equations arithmetically. Or, you can use the properties of equality to solve equations algebraically.

Solutions
Notice that your new equation, x = −2, has the same solution as the original equation, x + 6 = 4.

Examples

Tutor

1. Solve $x + 6 = 4$. Check your solution.

	$x + 6 = 4$	Write the equation.
	$-6 = -6$	Subtraction Property of Equality
	$x = -2$	Simplify.
Check	$x + 6 = 4$	Write the original equation.
	$-2 + 6 \stackrel{?}{=} 4$	Replace x with −2.
	$4 = 4$ ✓	The sentence is true.

So, the solution is −2.

2. Solve $-5 = b + 8$. Check your solution.

	$-5 = b + 8$	Write the equation.
	$-8 = -8$	Subtraction Property of Equality
	$-13 = b$	Simplify.
Check	$-5 = b + 8$	Write the original equation.
	$-5 \stackrel{?}{=} -13 + 8$	Replace b with −13.
	$-5 = -5$ ✓	The sentence is true.

So, the solution is −13.

Got it? Do these problems to find out.

Solve each equation. Check your solution.

a. $y + 6 = 9$ **b.** $x + 3 = 1$ **c.** $-3 = a + 4$

Show your work.

a. 3

b. −2

c. −7

Real World Example

Watch Tutor

3. **An angelfish can grow to be 12 inches long. If an angelfish is 8.5 inches longer than a clown fish, how long is a clown fish?**

Words	An angelfish is 8.5 inches longer than a clown fish.				
Variable	Let c represent the length of the clown fish.				
Equation	12	=	c	+	8.5

$12 = c + 8.5$ Write the equation.

$-8.5 = \quad -8.5$ Subtraction Property of Equality

$3.5 = c$ Simplify.

A clown fish is 3.5 inches long.

Solve Arithmetically

You can use a bar diagram to solve an equation arithmetically.

angelfish, 12 inches

clown fish

c — 8.5 inches

Work backward to solve for c.

$c = 12 - 8.5 = 3.5$

Got it? **Do this problem to find out.**

d. The highest recorded temperature in Warsaw, Missouri, is 118°F. This is 158° greater than the city's lowest recorded temperature. Find the lowest recorded temperature.

Show your work.

$118 = 158 + t$;

d. −40°F

Addition Property of Equality

Key Concept

Words The **Addition Property of Equality** states that the two sides of an equation remain equal when you add the same number to each side.

Symbols If $a = b$, then $a + c = b + c$.

Example

Tutor

4. **Solve $x - 2 = 1$. Check your solution.**

$x - 2 = 1$ Write the equation.

$+2 = +2$ Addition Property of Equality

$x = 3$ Simplify.

The solution is 3. Check $3 - 2 = 1$ ✓

Got it? **Do these problems to find out.**

e. $y - 3 = 4$ **f.** $r - 4 = -2$ **g.** $q - 8 = -9$

Show your work.

e. 7

f. 2

g. −1

IWB

Examples

3. Write and solve an addition equation.

AL
- *What do you need to find?* the length of the clown fish
- *What do you know?* the length of an angelfish is 8.5 inches longer than the clown fish and an angelfish can grow to 12 inches
- *The length of the clown fish plus what is the equal to the length of the angelfish?* 8.5

OL
- *What addition equation represents this situation?* $c + 8.5 = 12$
- *How would you solve this equation?* subtract 8.5 from each side of the equation

BL
- *Suppose a certain betta fish is $1\frac{1}{4}$ inches longer than the clown fish. How long is the betta fish?* 4.75 inches

Need Another Example?

A grapefruit weighs 11 ounces, which is 6 ounces more than an apple. Write and solve an equation to find the weight of the apple. $a + 6 = 11$; 5 oz

4. Solve a subtraction equation.

AL
- *What is the variable?* x
- *What number is on the same side of the equals sign as the variable?* 2
- *What operation is used between x and 2?* subtraction
- *How do you undo addition?* addition

OL
- *What is the first step to solving the equation?* Add 2 to each side.
- *What property allows you to add 2 to each side of the equation?* Addition Property of Equality

BL
- *Solve the equation $-12 = p - (-20)$.* −32

Need Another Example?

Solve 12 = z − 8. Check your solution. 20

Example

5. Write and solve a subtraction equation.

AL • *What do you need to find?* the cost of the jeans

• *What do you know?* A pair of shoes that are $25 is $14 less than the cost of the jeans.

• *The cost of the jeans minus what is equal to the cost of the shoes?* 14

OL • *What subtraction equation represents this situation?* $j - 14 = 25$ or $25 = j - 14$

• *How would you solve this equation?* Add 14 to each side of the equation and simplify.

BL • *Are the two equations $j - 14 = 25$ and $25 = j - 14$ equivalent? Explain.* yes; Both equations have the same solution, $j = 39$.

Need Another Example?
Vivian practiced the piano for 32 minutes. She practiced 11 minutes less than her brother did. Write and solve an equation to determine how long her brother practiced the piano. $b - 11 = 32$; 43 minutes

Guided Practice

Formative Assessment Use these exercises to assess students' understanding of the concepts in this lesson.

If some of your students are not ready for assignments, use the differentiated activities below.

AL EL **Pairs Discussion** Have students work in pairs to solve Exercises 1–4. Students can use algebra tiles if needed to model the equations. Have them trade their solutions with another pair of students and discuss any differences. MP 1, 2, 4

BL EL **Think-Pair-Share** Have students work in pairs. Give them a minute to think through their responses to the problems shown. Have them share their responses with their partner. Then call on one student to share their response within a small group or large group discussion. MP 1, 2

$-x + 5 = -7$ $\quad -3 - x = -4$ $\quad \frac{2}{3} + x = 2$ $\quad x - 5\frac{1}{2} = -7$

Models
A bar diagram can be used to represent this situation.

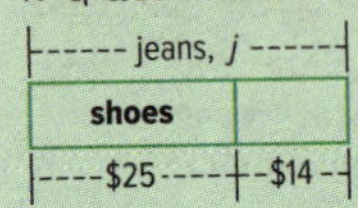

$j = 25 + 14 = 39$

Real World Example

5. A pair of shoes costs $25. This is $14 less than the cost of a pair of jeans. Find the cost of the jeans.

Shoes are $14 less than jeans. Let j represent the cost of jeans.

$25 = j - 14$	Write the equation.
$+14 = \quad +14$	Addition Property of Equality
$39 = j$	Simplify.

The jeans cost $39.

Got it? **Do this problem to find out.**

h. The average lifespan of a tiger is 17 years. This is 3 years less than the average lifespan of a lion. Write and solve an equation to find the average lifespan of a lion.

h. $\ell - 3 = 17$; 20 years

Guided Practice

Solve each equation. Check your solution. (Examples 1, 2, and 4)

1. $n + 6 = 8$ 2

2. $7 = y + 2$ 5

3. $-7 = c - 6$ -1

4. Orville and Wilbur Wright made the first airplane flights in 1903. Wilbur's flight was 364 feet. This was 120 feet longer than Orville's flight. Write an equation to represent the flights. Use a bar diagram if needed. Then solve to find the length of Orville's flight. (Examples 3 and 5)
$d + 120 = 364$: 244 ft

5. **Building on the Essential Question** What are two methods for solving a real-world problem that can be represented by an equation?
Sample answer: One method is to solve arithmetically using a bar diagram. Another method is to solve the equation algebraically using the properties of equality.

Rate Yourself!

☐ I understand how to solve one-step addition and subtraction equations.

Great! You're ready to move on!

☐ I still have some questions about solving equations.

No Problem! Go online to access a Personal Tutor.

Name ______________________ My Homework ______________________

Independent Practice

Go online for Step-by-Step Solutions eHelp

Solve each equation. Check your solution. (Examples 1, 2, and 4)

1. $a + 3 = 10$ **7**
2. $y + 5 = -11$ **−16**
3. $s - 8 = 9$ **17**
4. $5 = x + 8$ **−3**
5. $-2 = p - 1$ **−1**
6. $14 = s + 7$ **7**

Show your work.

Use a bar diagram to solve arithmetically. Then use an equation to solve algebraically. (Examples 3 and 5)

7. Last week Tiffany practiced her bassoon a total of 7 hours. This was 2 hours more than she practiced the previous week. How many hours did Tiffany practice the previous week?

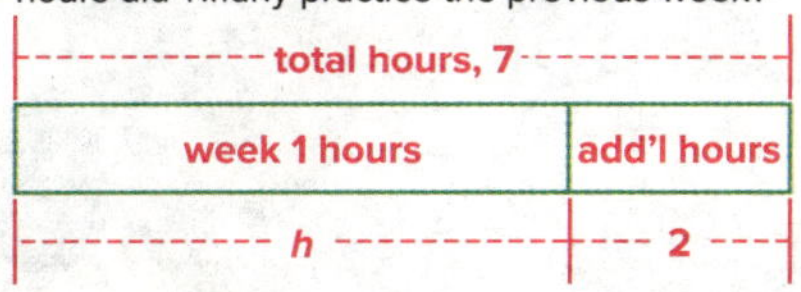

$7 = h + 2$; 5 h

8. In a recent presidential election, Ohio had 18 electoral votes. This is 20 votes less than Texas had. How many electoral votes did Texas have?

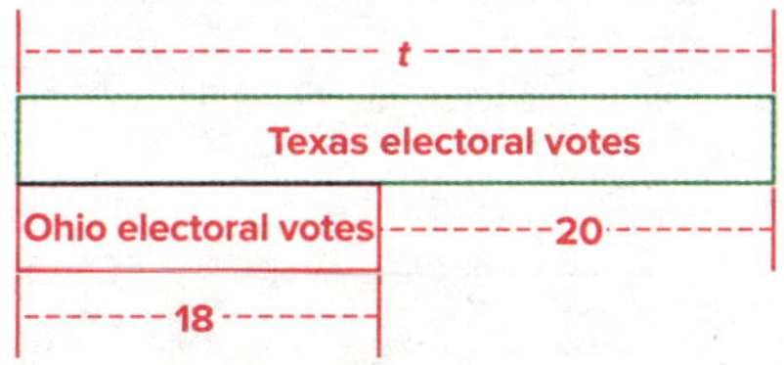

$18 = t - 20$; 38 votes

9. **MP Multiple Representations** Use the table to solve.

Tallest Wooden Roller Coasters	Height (feet)	Drop (feet)	Speed (mph)
Colossos	h	159	68
T Express	184	151	65
El Toro	181	176	s
Voyage	163	d	67

a. **Symbols** The difference in speeds of El Toro and T Express is 5 miles per hour. If El Toro has the greater speed, write and solve a subtraction equation to find its speed.

$s - 65 = 5$; 70 mph

b. **Diagram** Voyage has a drop that is 22 feet less than El Toro. Draw a bar diagram to the right and write an equation to find the height of Voyage.

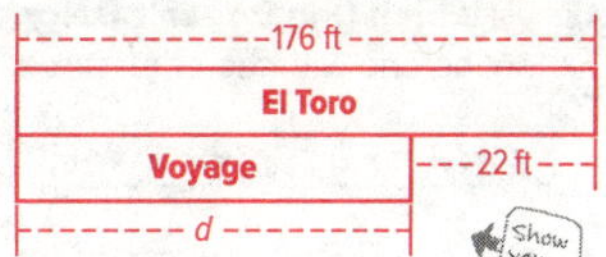

$d + 22 = 176$; 154 ft

Show your work.

c. **Words** Let h represent the height of the Colossos roller coaster. Explain why $h - 13 = 184$ and $h - 34 = 163$ are equivalent equations. Then explain the meaning of the solution.

The solution of each equation is 197; Colossos is 197 feet tall.

ENGAGE EXPLORE EXPLAIN ELABORATE EVALUATE

3 Practice and Apply

Independent Practice and Extra Practice

The Independent Practice pages are meant to be used as the homework assignment. The Extra Practice page can be used for additional reinforcement or as a second-day assignment.

Levels of Complexity

The levels of the exercises progress from 1 to 3, with Level 1 indicating the lowest level of complexity.

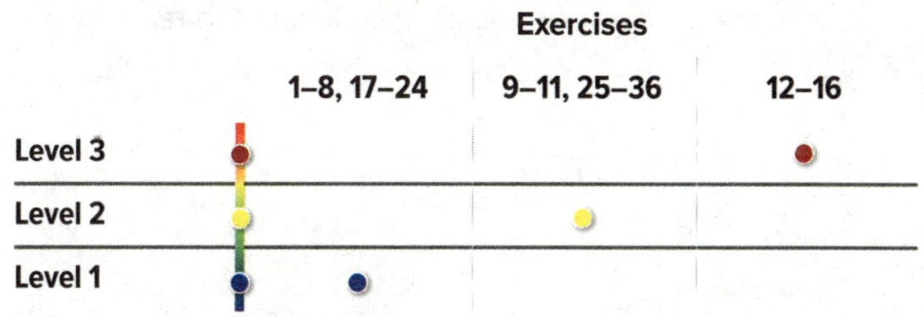

Suggested Assignments

You can use the table below that includes exercises of all complexity levels to select appropriate exercises for your students' needs.

Differentiated Homework Options		
AL	Approaching Level	1–9, 11–16, 35, 36
OL	On Level	1–7 odd, 9–16, 35, 36
BL	Beyond Level	9–16, 35, 36

McGraw Hill Education **ALEKS®** can provide additional remediation support with personalized instruction and practice.

Watch Out!

Common Error Students often forget whether to add or subtract to solve an addition or subtraction equation. Remind them to use the inverse of the operation in the equation. To solve an addition equation, use subtraction. To solve a subtraction equation, use addition.

MP MATHEMATICAL PRACTICES

Emphasis On	Exercise(s)
2 Reason abstractly and quantitatively.	14
3 Construct viable arguments and critique the reasoning of others.	9, 12, 13, 15, 16
5 Use appropriate tools strategically.	23, 24

Mathematical Practices 1, 3, and 4 are aspects of mathematical thinking that are emphasized in every lesson. Students are given opportunities to be persistent in their problem solving, to express their reasoning, and apply mathematics to real-world situations.

Formative Assessment
Use this activity as a closing formative assessment before dismissing students from your class.

TICKET Out the Door

Ask students to write the steps explaining how to solve $x - 3 = 19$. See students' work.

Watch Out!

Find the Error For Exercise 13, remind students to use inverse operation to solve equations. In this addition equation, they subtract in order to isolate the variable.

10. The sum of the measures of the angles of a triangle is 180°. Write and solve an equation to find the missing measure.

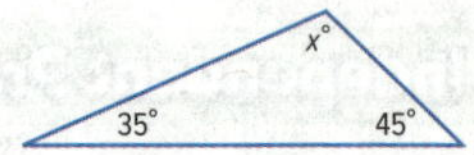

$35 + 45 + x = 180$; 100

11. The sum of the measures of a quadrilateral is 360°. Write and solve an equation to find the missing measure.

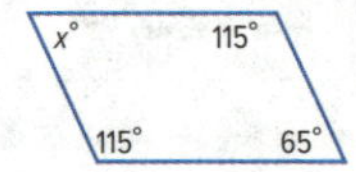

$115 + 115 + 65 + x = 360$; 65

H.O.T. Problems Higher Order Thinking

12. MP **Reason Inductively** Write an addition equation and a subtraction equation that have 10 as a solution.

Sample answer: $20 + x = 30$; $30 - x = 20$

13. MP **Find the Error** Aisha is finding $b + 5 = -8$. Find her mistake and correct it.

She should have subtracted 5 from each side; −13

14. MP **Reason Abstractly** Suppose $x + y = 11$ and the value of x increases by 2. If their sum remains the same, what must happen to the value of y? Justify your response

The value of y decreases by 2; Sample answer: $(x + 2) + (y - 2) = 11$ if $x + y = 11$, because if you add 2 and the sum remains the same, you must also subtract 2.

15. MP **Which One Doesn't Belong?** Identify the equation that does not belong with the other three. Explain your reasoning.

$x + 4 = -2$	$x + 5 = -1$	$x + 2 = 8$	$3 - x = 9$

$x + 2 = 8$; The solution for the other equations is −6.

16. MP **Reason Inductively** In the equation $x + y = 5$, the value for x is a whole number greater than 2 but less than 6. Find the possible solutions for y.

0, 1, 2

Name ____________________ My Homework ____________________

Extra Practice

Solve each equation. Check your solution.

17. $r + 6 = -3$

Homework Help
$r + 6 = -3$
$\underline{\;\; - 6 = -6}$
$r \;\; = -9$

18. $w - 7 = 11$ **18**

19. $k + 3 = -9$ **−12**

20. $-1 = q - 8$ **7**

21. $9 = r + 2$ **7**

22. $y + 15 = 11$ **−4**

MP Use Math Tools **Use a bar diagram to solve arthimetically. Then use an equation to solve algebraically.**

23. The Miami Heat scored 79 points. This was 13 points less than the Chicago Bulls. How many points did the Chicago Bulls score?

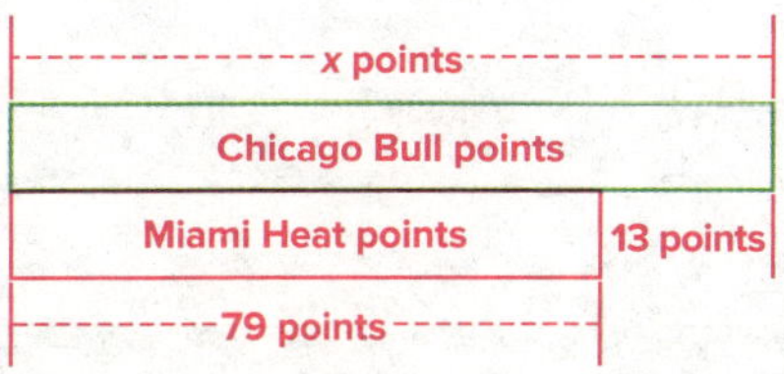

$x - 13 = 79$; 92 points

24. Zach is $15\frac{1}{2}$ years old. This is 3 years younger than his brother Lou. How old is Lou?

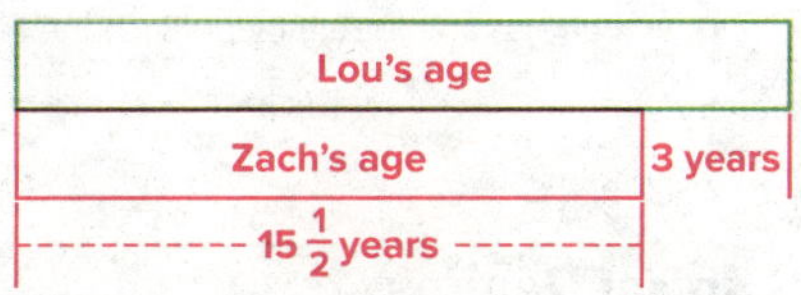

$15\frac{1}{2} = y - 3$; $18\frac{1}{2}$ years old

25. The table shows a golfer's scores for four rounds of a recent U.S. Women's Open. Her total score was even with par. What was her score for the third round?

$-1 + (-3) + s + 2 = 0$; +2

Round	Score
First	−1
Second	−3
Third	s
Fourth	+2

Copy and Solve **Solve each equation. Check your solution. Show your work on a separate piece of paper.**

26. $a - 3.5 = 14.9$ **18.4**

27. $b + 2.25 = 1$ **−1.25**

28. $-\frac{1}{3} = r - \frac{3}{4}$ $\frac{5}{12}$

29. $x - 2.8 = 9.5$ **12.3**

30. $r - 8.5 = -2.1$ **6.4**

31. $z - 9.4 = -3.6$ **5.8**

32. $m + \frac{5}{6} = \frac{11}{12}$ $\frac{1}{12}$

33. $-\frac{5}{6} + c = -\frac{11}{12}$ $-\frac{1}{12}$

34. $s - \frac{1}{9} = \frac{5}{18}$ $\frac{7}{18}$

Create Your Own Homework Online

eSolutionsManual™ can be used to create worksheets for the suggested assignments on page 441, or create your own worksheets for differentiated homework or review.

Power Up! Test Practice

Exercises 35 and 36 prepare students for more rigorous thinking needed for the state assessment.

35.

This test item requires students to reason abstractly and quantitatively when problem solving.	
Depth of Knowledge	DOK1
Content Standard	7.EE.4a
Mathematical Practice	MP1
Online Experience	Students will be required to click on the bubbles to select all answers that are correct.
Scoring Rubric	
1 point	Students correctly answer each part of the question.

36.

This test item requires students to analyze and solve complex real-world problems through the use of mathematical tools and models.	
Depth of Knowledge	DOK2
Content Standard	7.EE.4, 7.EE.4a
Mathematical Practice	MP1, MP4
Online Experience	Students drag symbols to complete the model and type their response in the box.
Scoring Rubric	
2 points	Students correctly model and solve the equation.
1 point	Students correctly model OR solve the equation.

Power Up! Test Practice

35. The model represents the equation $x - 2 = 5$. Determine if each statement is true or false.

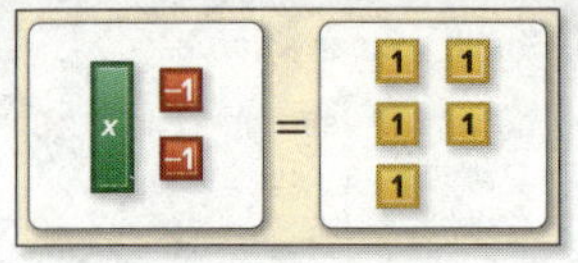

a. To solve the equation, add 2 positive counters to each side of the equation mat. ■ True □ False

b. To solve the equation, add 5 negative to each side of the equation mat. □ True ■ False

c. The value of x is 7. ■ True □ False

36. Britney practiced the piano a total of 7 hours this week. This is 3 hours less than she practiced last week. Select the correct labels to complete the bar diagram that is used to find the number of hours w Britney practiced last week.

this week
last week, w
3 hours
4 hours
7 hours
10 hours

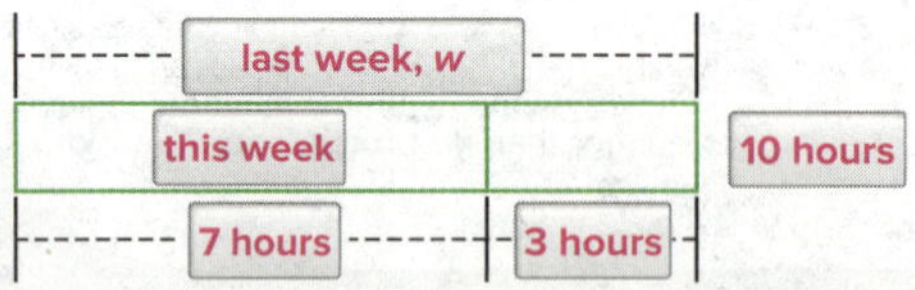

How many hours did Britney practice the piano last week? 10 hours

Spiral Review

Multiply or divide. 7.NS.2

37. $5(-4) =$ -20

38. $\frac{36}{-9} =$ -4

39. $(-10)(-6) =$ 60

40. $\frac{-42}{-7} =$ 6

41. $(-3)(12) =$ -36

42. $\frac{-54}{2} =$ -27

43. While playing a round of golf, Tina had a score of three under par after the first three holes. Write and solve an equation to find Tina's average score per hole h after three holes. 7.NS.3 $3h = -3; h = -1$

44. On Friday morning, the temperature dropped 2 degrees per hour for four hours. Write and solve an equation to find the total number of degrees d the temperature dropped on Friday morning. 7.NS.3 $-2 \times 4 = d; d = -8$

PLAN ONLINE

PD | RtI | Watch | Worksheets | Vocab | Tutor | Tools | Check | English Learners | Sketchpad

PRESENT

IWB

An Interactive Whiteboard Ready presentation is available for each lesson in the chapter.

Inquiry Lab

Multiplication Equations with Bar Diagrams

Inquiry **HOW do you know which operation to use when solving an equation?**

Content Standards
7.EE.4, 7.EE.4a

MP **Mathematical Practices**
1, 2, 3

Sakiya tutors students to earn money to buy a new Blu-ray™ player that costs \$63. She is able to tutor seven hours in a week. How much should she charge per hour to have enough money by the end of the week?

What do you know? the cost of the Blu-ray™ player, the number of hours Sakiya can tutor.

What do you need to find? the amount per hour Sakiya should charge

Hands-On Activity

Step 1 Draw a bar diagram that represents the money Sakiya needs to earn and the number of hours she is available to tutor that week.

\$ 63

hour 1	hour 2	hour 3	hour 4	hour 5	hour 6	hour 7

?

Step 2 Write an equation from the bar diagram. Let x represent the amount she should charge each hour.

$$7x = 63$$

Step 3 Use the *work backward* strategy to solve the equation. Since $7x = 63$, $x = 63 \div 7$. So, $x =$ 9.

Check $7 \times 9 = 63$ ✓

So, Sakiya should charge \$9 per hour.

Focus narrowing the scope

Objective Use bar diagrams to write and solve problems involving ratios. 7.EE.4, 7.EE.4a

Coherence connecting within and across grades

Now
Students used bar diagrams to write and solve one-step addition and subtraction equations.

Next
Students will use Properties of Equality to solve one-step equations.

Rigor pursuing concepts, fluency, and applications

See the Levels of Complexity chart on page 446.

ENGAGE EXPLORE EXPLAIN ELABORATE EVALUATE

1 Launch the Lab

The activity is intended to be used as a whole-group activity.

Hands-On Activity

AL EL Remind students that the bar diagram represents the total amount of money she needs to earn.

Ask:

- *Into how many sections should the bar diagram be divided? Why?* 7 sections; This represents the 7 hours that she can tutor.
- *How much money does she need?* \$63
- *What equation is represented by the bar diagram?* $7x = 63$

BL Omit the activity and proceed directly to the Investigate section. MP 1, 4

2 Collaborate

The **Investigate** and **Analyze and Reflect** sections are intended to be used as small-group investigations. The **Create** section is intended to be used as independent exercises.

Levels of Complexity

The levels of the exercises progress from 1 to 3, with Level 1 indicating the lowest level of complexity.

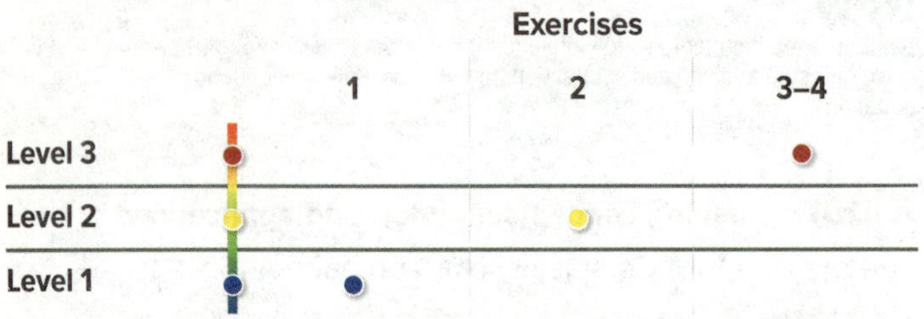

Investigate

AL EL **Pairs Discussion** Have students work in pairs to complete Exercise 1. Have them trade their solution with another pair of students and discuss any differences. MP 1, 2, 5

BL EL **Trade-a-Problem** Have students create their own problem, similar to Exercise 1. Students trade their problems, solve, and compare solutions. MP 1, 2, 4

Analyze and Reflect

AL EL **Think-Pair-Share** Have students work in pairs. Give students one minute to think through their responses to Exercise 2. Have them share their responses with their partner. Then call on one student to share their response. MP 1, 2, 5

Create

Inquiry Students should be able to answer "HOW do you know which operation to use when solving an equation?" Check for student understanding and provide guidance, if needed.

Investigate

Collaborate

Work with a partner to solve.

1. The screen on Lin's cell phone allows for 8 lines of text per message. The maximum number of characters for each message is 160. How many characters can each line hold? Complete the bar diagram below and write an equation. Then solve the equation.

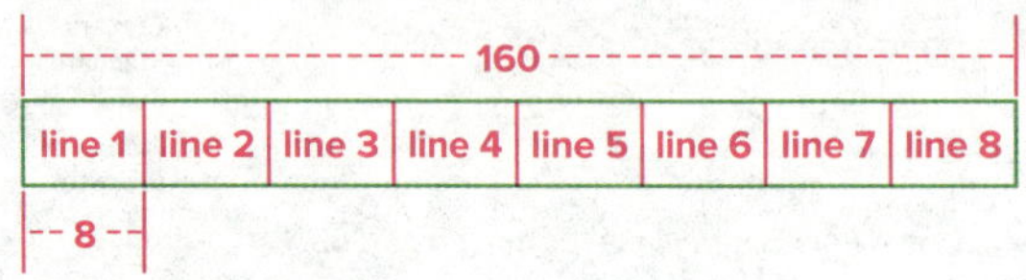

$8x = 160$; 20 characters

Analyze and Reflect

Collaborate

Work with a partner to answer the following question.

2. MP **Make a Conjecture** Refer to Exercise 1. Suppose Lin's cell phone allows 4 lines of text and a maximum of 80 characters for each text message. How would the bar diagram and equation change?

Sample answer: The bar would be divided into 4 sections instead of 8. The equation would be $4x = 80$.

Create

On Your Own

3. MP **Reason Abstractly** Keyani spent $70 for 4 hours of dance classes. How much did she spend per hour of dance class? Draw a bar diagram below and write an equation. Then solve the equation.

Show your work.

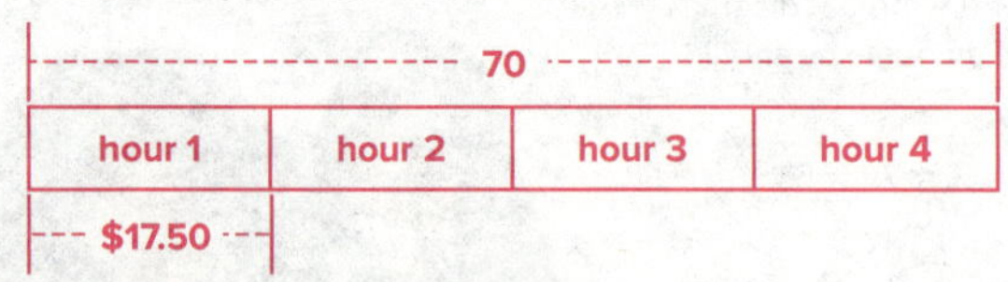

$4x = 70$; $17.50

4. Inquiry HOW do you know which operation to use when solving an equation?

Sample answer: Use the inverse operation. Division is the inverse of multiplication. So, use division to solve a multiplication equation.

PLAN ONLINE

PD | RtI | Watch | Worksheets | Vocab | Tutor | Tools | Check | English Learners | Sketchpad

PRESENT

IWB

An Interactive Whiteboard Ready presentation is available for each lesson in the chapter.

Lesson 2

Multiplication and Division Equations

Vocabulary Start-Up

Watch | Tools | Vocab

The expression $3x$ means *3 times the value of x*. The numerical factor of a multiplication expression like $3x$ is called a **coefficient**. So, 3 is the coefficient of x.

The figure below illustrates the multiplication equation $3x = 6$.

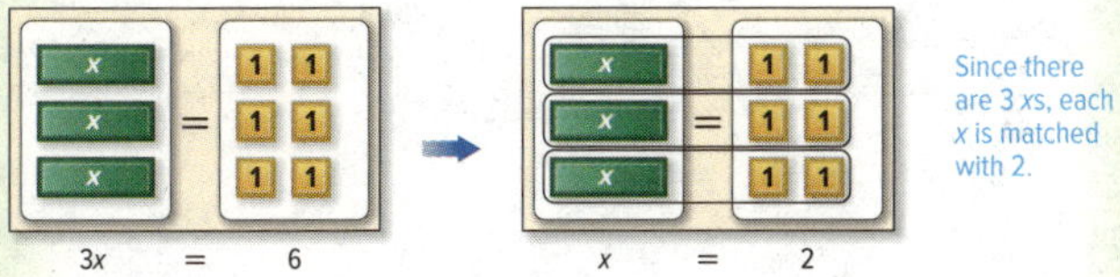

The solution of $3x = 6$ is 2.

Write an equation that represents each of the models below. Identify the coefficient in your equation. Then solve.

1.

Equation: $3x = 12$

Coefficient: 3

Solution: 4

2.

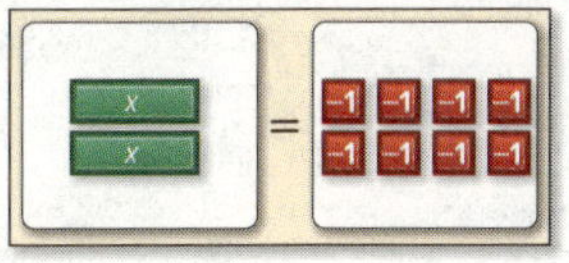

Equation: $2x = -8$

Coefficient: 2

Solution: -4

Essential Question

WHAT does it mean to say two quantities are equal?

Vocabulary

coefficient
Division Property of Equality
Multiplication Property of Equality

Content Standards
7.EE.4, 7.EE.4a

MP Mathematical Practices
1, 2, 3, 4, 7

Which MP **Mathematical Practices** did you use? Shade the circle(s) that applies.

① Persevere with Problems
② Reason Abstractly
③ Construct an Argument
④ Model with Mathematics
⑤ Use Math Tools
⑥ Attend to Precision
⑦ Make Use of Structure
⑧ Use Repeated Reasoning

Focus narrowing the scope

Objective Solve one-step multiplication and division equations. 7.EE.4, 7.EE.4a

Coherence connecting within and across grades

Previous Students solved one-step addition and subtraction equations.

Now Students write and solve one-step multiplication and division equations.

Next Students will solve two-step linear equations.

Rigor pursuing concepts, fluency, and applications

See the Levels of Complexity chart on page 451.

ENGAGE EXPLORE EXPLAIN ELABORATE EVALUATE

1 Launch the Lesson

Ideas for Use

You may wish to launch the lesson using a whole group, small group, think-pair-share activity, or independent activity.

AL EL **Pairs Discussion** Have students work in pairs to solve the Vocabulary Start-Up. After they have identified the coefficients, have them write a definition for coefficient using their own words. MP 1, 5, 6

Alternate Strategy

BL Have students think about what they learned in the previous lesson. Have them make a conjecture about how to solve multiplication and division equations, and what properties would be used. MP 1, 3, 6

ENGAGE EXPLORE **EXPLAIN** ELABORATE EVALUATE

2 Teach the Concept

Ask the scaffolded questions for each example to differentiate instruction.

IWB

Examples

1. Solve a multiplication equation.

AL
- *What is the variable?* x
- *What operation is used between x and 4?* multiplication
- *How do you undo multiplication?* division

OL
- *What is the coefficient in the expression 4x?* 4
- *What is the first step to solving the equation?* Divide each side by 4

BL
- *What property allows you to divide each side of the equation by 4?* Division Property of Equality

Need Another Example?
Solve $39 = 3y$. Check your solution. 13

2. Solve a multiplication equation.

AL
- *What is the variable?* y
- *What is the coefficient in the expression −8y?* −8
- *What operation is used between y and −8?* multiplication
- *How do you undo multiplication?* division

OL
- *What is the coefficient in the expression −8y?* −8
- *What is the first step to solving the equation?* Divide each side by −8
- *What property allows you to divide each side of the equation by −8?* Division Property of Equality

BL
- *How can you check your solution?* Replace y with −3 in the original equation, simplify, and determine if the final statement is true.

Need Another Example?
Solve $-4z = 60$. Check your solution. −15

Work Zone

Key Concept

Division Property of Equality

Words The **Division Property of Equality** states that the two sides of an equation remain equal when you divide each side by the same nonzero number.

Symbols If $a = b$ and $c \neq 0$, then $\frac{a}{c} = \frac{b}{c}$.

You can use the Division Property of Equality to solve multiplication equations.

Examples

Tutor

1. Solve $20 = 4x$. Check your solution.

$20 = 4x$ Write the equation.

$\frac{20}{4} = \frac{4x}{4}$ Division Property of Equality

$5 = x$ Simplify.

Check $20 = 4x$ Write the original equation.

$20 \stackrel{?}{=} 4(5)$ Replace x with 5.

$20 = 20$ ✓ This sentence is true.

So, the solution is 5.

2. Solve $-8y = 24$. Check your solution.

$-8y = 24$ Write the equation.

$\frac{-8y}{-8} = \frac{24}{-8}$ Division Property of Equality

$y = -3$ Simplify.

Check $-8y = 24$ Write the original equation.

$-8(-3) \stackrel{?}{=} 24$ Replace y with −3.

$24 = 24$ ✓ This sentence is true.

So, the solution is −3.

Got it? **Do these problems to find out.**

Solve each equation. Check your solution.

a. $30 = 6x$ **b.** $-6a = 36$ **c.** $-9d = -72$

Show your work.

a. 5

b. −6

c. 8

Real World Example

Tutor

3. **Lelah sent 574 text messages last week. On average, how many messages did she send each day?**

Let m represent the number of messages Lelah sent.

$574 = 7m$	Write the equation. There are 7 days in one week.
$\frac{574}{7} = \frac{7m}{7}$	Division Property of Equality
$82 = m$	Simplify.

Lelah sent 82 messages on average each day.

Solve Arithmetically

You can use a bar diagram to solve an equation arithmetically.

text messages in 1 week, 574

m	m	m	m	m	m	m

text messages in 1 day

Work backward to solve for m.

$m = 574 \div 7 = 82$

Got it? **Do this problem to find out.**

show your work.

d. Mrs. Acosta's car can travel an average of 24 miles on each gallon of gasoline. Write and solve an equation to find how many gallons of gasoline she will need for a trip of 348 miles.

d. $24x = 348$; 14.5 gal

Multiplication Property of Equality

Key Concept

Words The **Multiplication Property of Equality** states that the two sides of an equation remain equal if you multiply each side by the same number.

Symbols If $a = b$, then $ac = bc$.

You can use the Multiplication Property of Equality to solve division equations.

Example

Tutor

4. **Solve $\frac{a}{-4} = -9$.**

$\frac{a}{-4} = -9$	Write the equation.
$\frac{a}{-4}(-4) = -9(-4)$	Multiplication Property of Equality
$a = 36$	Simplify.

Got it? **Do these problems to find out.**

e. $\frac{y}{-3} = -8$ **f.** $\frac{m}{5} = -7$ **g.** $30 = \frac{b}{-6}$

e. 24

f. −35

g. −180

Examples

IWB

3. Write and solve a multiplication equation.

AL
- *What do you need to find?* the average number of text message she sent per day
- *What do you know?* the number of messages she sent last week
- *How many messages did she send altogether?* 574
- *How many days are in a week?* 7

OL
- *What multiplication equation represents this situation?* $7m = 574$
- *How would you solve this equation?* divide each side of the equation by 7

BL
- *How many text messages would you expect Lelah to send in 30 days?* 2,460 text messages

Need Another Example?

Serena mailed 138 letters during the last 6 days. Write and solve an equation to find, on average, how many letters she mailed each day. $6x = 138$; 23 letters

4. Solve a division equation.

AL
- *How do you know this is a division equation?* The fraction $\frac{a}{-4}$ means a divided by −4.
- *How do you undo division?* multiplication

OL
- *What is the first step to solving the equation?* Multiply each side by −4.
- *What property allows you to multiply each side of the equation by −4?* Multiplication Property of Equality

BL
- *Rewrite this equation as a multiplication equation.* $-\frac{1}{4}a = -9$.
- *How would you solve this equation?* Multiply each side of the equation by −4.

Need Another Example?

Solve $\frac{m}{2} = -10$. Check your solution. −20

Example

5. Solve a division equation.

AL
- *What is the variable?* d
- *What number is on the same side of the equals sign as the variable?* 3
- *What operation is used between d and 3?* division
- *How do you undo division?* multiplication

OL
- *How would you solve this equation?* Multiply each side of the equation by 3 and simplify.

BL
- *Use what you learned in this lesson to explain how to solve the equation $d = rt$ for the variable r. Then solve for r.* Use the Division Property of Equality to divide each side by t; $r = \frac{d}{t}$

Need Another Example?

The distance *d* that Lee travels on his bike at a rate of 20 miles per hour for 4 hours is given by the equation $\frac{d}{4} = 20$. How far did he ride? 80 mi

Guided Practice

Formative Assessment Use these exercises to assess students' understanding of the concepts in this lesson.

If some of your students are not ready for assignments, use the differentiated activities below.

AL EL **Team-Pair-Solo** Have students work in teams of 4 to solve Exercise 1, then break up in pairs to solve Exercise 2, and finally work alone to solve Exercise 3. Have them repeat the process to solve Exercises 4–6. Have them trade their pair and solo solutions with the rest of the group and discuss any differences. MP 1, 2

BL EL **Trade-a-Problem** Have students create their own problem, similar to Exercise 7, using either multiplication or division. Students trade their problems, solve each other's problem, and compare solutions. If the solutions do not agree, students work together to find the errors. MP 1, 2, 4

Distance Formula

The distance formula, distance = rate × time, can be written as $d = rt$, $r = \frac{d}{t}$, or $t = \frac{d}{r}$.

Real World Example

5. The distance *d* Tina travels in her car while driving 60 miles per hour for 3 hours is given by the equation $\frac{d}{3} = 60$. How far did she travel?

$\frac{d}{3} = 60$	Write the equation.
$\frac{d}{3}(3) = 60(3)$	Multiplication Property of Equality
$d = 180$	Simplify.

Tina traveled 180 miles.

Guided Practice

Solve each equation. Check your solution. (Examples 1, 2, and 4)

1. $6c = 18$ 3
2. $24 = -8x$ −3
3. $7m = -28$ −4

Show your work.

4. $\frac{p}{9} = 9$ 81
5. $\frac{a}{12} = -3$ −36
6. $\frac{n}{-10} = -4$ 40

7. Antonia earns $6 per hour helping her grandmother. Write and solve an equation to find how many hours she needs to work to earn $48. (Example 3) $6h = 48$; 8h

8. A shark can swim at an average speed of 25 miles per hour. At this rate, how far can a shark swim in 2.4 hours? Use $r = \frac{d}{t}$. (Example 5) 60 mi

9. **Building on the Essential Question** How is the process for solving multiplication and division one-step equations like solving one-step addition and subtraction equations?
Sample answer: The process always involves using the inverse operation.

Rate Yourself!

How confident are you about solving one-step multiplication and division equations? Check the box that applies.

For more help, go online to access a Personal Tutor.

Name ______________________ My Homework ______________________

Independent Practice

Go online for Step-by-Step Solutions eHelp

Solve each equation. Check your solution. (Examples 1, 2, and 4)

1. $7a = 49$ **7**

2. $-6 = 2x$ **−3**

3. $-32 = -4b$ **8**

4. $\frac{u}{6} = 9$ **54**

5. $-8 = \frac{c}{-10}$ **80**

6. $54 = -9d$ **−6**

7. $-12y = 60$ **−5**

8. $\frac{r}{20} = -2$ **−40**

9. $\frac{g}{10} = -9$ **−90**

10. Brandy wants to buy a digital camera that costs $300. Suppose she saves $15 each week. In how many weeks will she have enough money for the camera? Use a bar diagram to solve arithmetically. Then use an equation to solve algebraically. (Example 3) **$15w = 300$; 20 weeks**

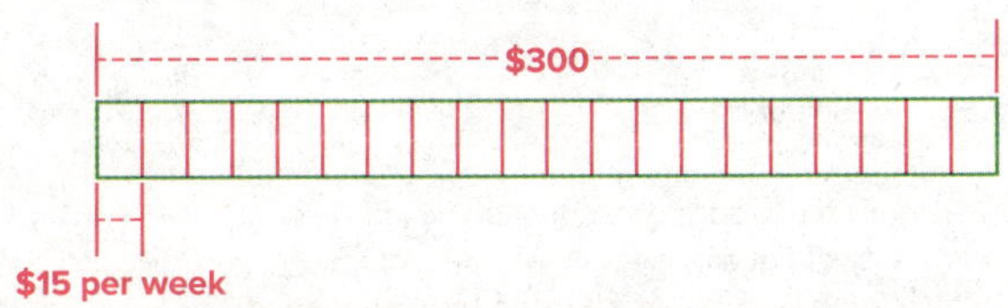

11. A race car can travel at a rate of 205 miles per hour. At this rate, how far would it travel in 3 hours? Use $r = \frac{d}{t}$. Write an equation and then solve. (Example 5)
$205 = \frac{d}{3}$; 615 mi

12. A certain hurricane travels at 20.88 kilometers per hour. The distance from Cuba to Key West is 145 kilometers. Write and solve a multiplication equation to find about how long it would take the hurricane to travel from Cuba to Key West.
$20.88h = 145$; 7h

ENGAGE EXPLORE **EXPLAIN** **ELABORATE** **EVALUATE**

3 Practice and Apply

Independent Practice and Extra Practice

The Independent Practice pages are meant to be used as the homework assignment. The Extra Practice page can be used for additional reinforcement or as a second-day assignment.

Levels of Complexity

The levels of the exercises progress from 1 to 3, with Level 1 indicating the lowest level of complexity.

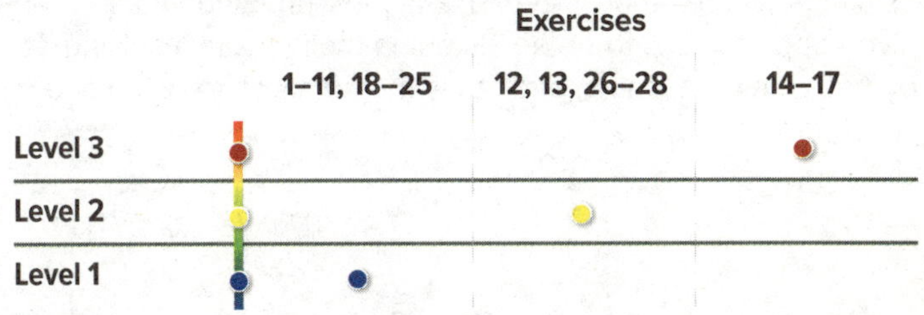

Suggested Assignments

You can use the table below that includes exercises of all complexity levels to select appropriate exercises for your students' needs.

Differentiated Homework Options		
AL	Approaching Level	1–11, 13–15, 27, 28
OL	On Level	1–11 odd, 12–15, 27, 28
BL	Beyond Level	12–17, 27, 28

ALEKS® can provide additional remediation support with personalized instruction and practice.

Watch Out!

Common Error Students may have trouble solving equations when the variable is on the right side of the equal sign. Remind them that if $30 = \frac{x}{-5}$, then $= \frac{x}{-5} = 30$.

MP MATHEMATICAL PRACTICES

Emphasis On	Exercise(s)
1 Make sense of problems and persevere in solving them.	16, 17
2 Reason abstractly and quantitatively.	14
3 Construct viable arguments and critique the reasoning of others.	13, 26
7 Look for and make use of structure.	15

Mathematical Practices 1, 3, and 4 are aspects of mathematical thinking that are emphasized in every lesson. Students are given opportunities to be persistent in their problem solving, to express their reasoning, and apply mathematics to real-world situations.

Formative Assessment

Use this activity as a closing formative assessment before dismissing students from your class.

TICKET Out the Door

Write the distance/time/rate formula $d = rt$ on the board. Have students write and solve their own rate problems.
See students' work.

13. MP **Multiple Representations** Kennedy saves \$5.50 for each hour she works. She needs to save an additional \$44 to buy an E-reader. How many more hours does Kennedy need to work to pay for the E-reader?

a. **Diagram** Draw a bar diagram that represents the situation.

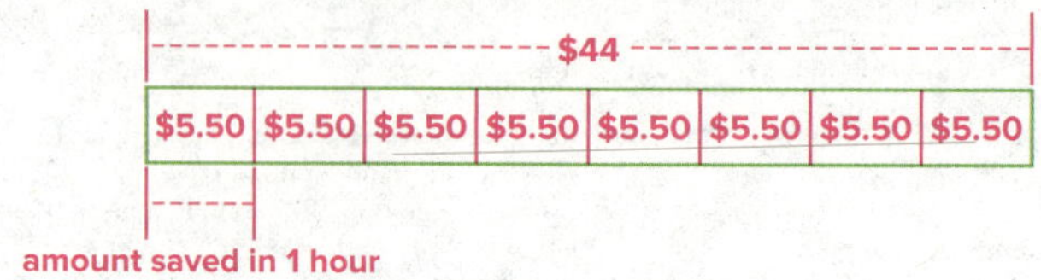

b. **Algebra** Write an equation that represents the situation.
$5.5x = 44$

c. **Words** Describe the process you would use to solve your equation. Then solve.
Sample answer: Divide each side by 5.5. Then simplify. $x = 8$

H.O.T. Problems Higher Order Thinking

14. MP **Reason Abstractly** Describe a real-world situation in which you would use a division equation to solve a problem. Write your equation and then solve your problem.

Situation: See students' work.

Equation: ______ Solution: ______

15. MP **Identify Structure** *True* or *false*. To solve the equation $5x = 20$ you can use the Multiplication Property of Equality. Explain your reasoning.
True; Sample answer: Multiply each side of the equation by $\frac{1}{5}$ instead of dividing each side by 5.

16. MP **Persevere with Problems** Solve $3|x| = 12$. Explain your reasoning.
The absolute value of a positive or negative number is always positive. So, $x = 4$ or $x = -4$.

17. MP **Persevere with Problems** Explain how you would solve $\frac{-30}{x} = 6$. Then solve the equation.
Sample answer: Multiply both sides by x, then divide both sides of the equation by 6; -5.

Name ______________________ My Homework ______________________

Extra Practice

Solve each equation. Check your solution.

18. $-4j = 36$

Homework Help

$-4j = 36$

$\frac{-4j}{-4} = \frac{36}{-4}$

$j = -9$

19. $-4s = -16$ **4**

20. $63 = -9d$ **−7**

21. $\frac{m}{10} = 7$

$\frac{m}{10} = 7$

$\frac{m}{10}(10) = 7(10)$

$m = 70$

22. $\frac{h}{-3} = 12$ **−36**

23. $\frac{g}{12} = -10$ **−120**

24. The width of a computer monitor is 1.25 times its height. Find the height of the computer monitor at the right. Use a bar diagram to solve arithmetically. Then use an equation to solve algebraically. **$1.25x = 15$; 12 in.**

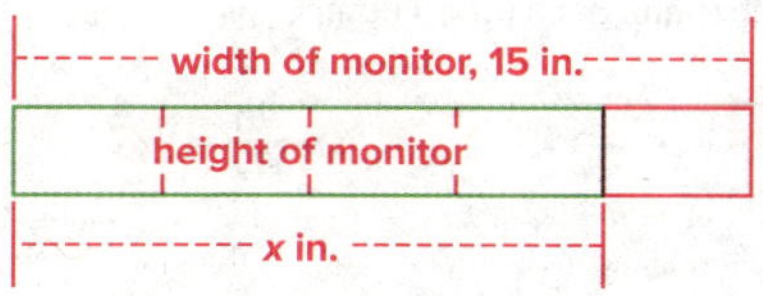

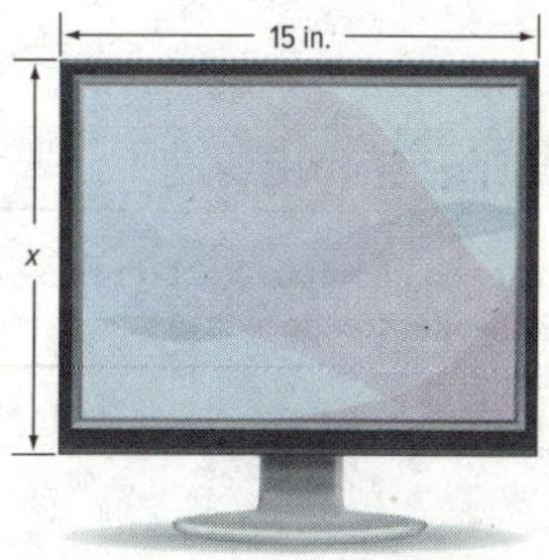

25. A dragonfly, the fastest insect, can fly a distance of 50 feet at a speed of 25 feet per second. Find the time in seconds. Write the equation in the form $d = rt$, then solve.

$50 = 25t$; 2 s

26. MP **Find the Error** Raul is solving $-6x = 72$. Find his mistake and correct it.

Sample answer: Raul divided by +6 and should have divided by −6.; $x = -12$

Create Your Own Homework Online

eSolutionsManual™ can be used to create worksheets for the suggested assignments on page 451, or create your own worksheets for differentiated homework or review.

Watch Out!

Find the Error For Exercise 26, remind students that when solving this equation for x, they must divide each side by the coefficient. The coefficient is −6, so divide each side of the equation by −6.

Power Up! Test Practice

Exercises 27 and 28 prepare students for more rigorous thinking needed for the state assessment.

27.

This test item requires students to explain and apply mathematical concepts and solve problems with precision, while making use of structure.	
Depth of Knowledge	DOK1
Content Standard	7.EE.4a
Mathematical Practice	MP1
Online Experience	Students will be required to type their response in the box.
Scoring Rubric	
1 point	Students correctly answer the question.

28.

This test item requires students to reason abstractly and quantitatively when problem solving.	
Depth of Knowledge	DOK2
Content Standard	7.EE.4, 7.EE.4a
Mathematical Practice	MP1, MP4
Online Experience	Students will drag values to model the equation and type their response in the box.
Scoring Rubric	
2 points	Students correctly model and solve the equation.
1 point	Students correctly model OR solve the equation.

Power Up! Test Practice

27. The formula $A = bh$ can be used to find the area A of a parallelogram with base b and height h. The parallelogram shown has an area of 56 square inches.

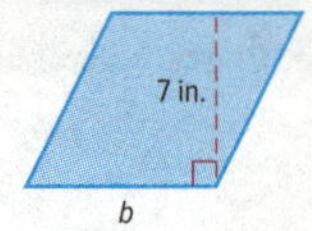

What is the length of the base? 8 in.

28. The table shows the prices of different satellite radio plans. Mrs. Freedman paid $99 for m months of satellite radio under Plan A. Fill in each box to write a multiplication equation to represent the situation.

Satellite Radio Plans	
Plan	Cost per Month ($)
A	16.50
B	14.35
C	11.99

16.50 × m = 99

m	16.50
11.99	99
14.35	

How many months of service did Mrs. Freedman purchase? 6 months

Spiral Review

Write each improper fraction as a mixed number and each mixed number as an improper fraction. 5.NF.3

29. $\frac{10}{3} = 3\frac{1}{3}$

30. $\frac{40}{7} = 5\frac{5}{7}$

31. $\frac{101}{100} = 1\frac{1}{100}$

32. $2\frac{2}{7} = \frac{16}{7}$

33. $3\frac{1}{4} = \frac{13}{4}$

34. $10\frac{5}{9} = \frac{95}{9}$

Divide. 6.NS.3

35. $6 \div 1.5 = 4$

36. $3.6 \div 0.4 = 9$

37. $2.73 \div 1.3 = 2.1$

Multiply. Write in simplest form. 5.NF.4

38. $\frac{2}{9} \times \frac{7}{5} = \frac{14}{45}$

39. $\frac{3}{4} \times 7 = \frac{21}{4}$ or $5\frac{1}{4}$

40. $\frac{5}{8} \times \frac{4}{15} = \frac{1}{6}$

PLAN ONLINE

PD | RtI | Watch | Worksheets | Vocab | Tutor | Tools | Check | English Learners | Sketchpad

PRESENT

IWB

An Interactive Whiteboard Ready presentation is available for each lesson in the chapter.

Inquiry Lab

Solve Equations with Rational Coefficients

Inquiry HOW can you use bar diagrams to solve equations with rational coefficients?

Content Standards
7.EE.4, 7.EE.4a

MP Mathematical Practices
1, 3

Two thirds of Chen's homeroom class plan to participate in the school talent show. If 16 students from the class plan to participate, how many students are in the homeroom class?

What do you know? the fraction and number of students participating in the talent show

What do you need to find? the number of students in Chen's homeroom class

Hands-On Activity

You can represent the situation above with an equation.

Step 1 Draw a bar diagram that represents the total number of students in the class and how many plan to participate.

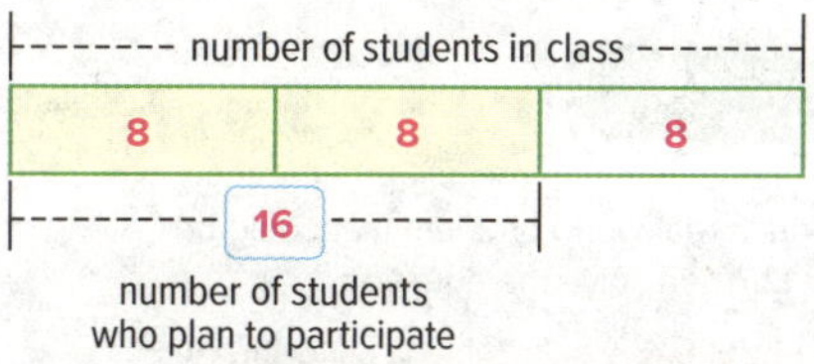

Step 2 Write an equation from the bar diagram. Let *c* represent the total number of students in the class. $\frac{2}{3}c = 16$

Step 3 Find the number of students represented by the sections of the bar. Write that number in each section of the bar in Step 1.

Since each section represents 8 students, there are 8 × 3 or 24 students in the class.

Check $\frac{2}{3} \times 24 = \frac{2}{3} \times \frac{24}{1}$

$= \frac{48}{3}$ or 16 ✓

Focus narrowing the scope

Objective Use bar diagrams to model and solve equations with rational coefficients. 7.EE.4, 7.EE.4a

Coherence connecting within and across grades

Now Students will use models to solve equations with rational coefficients.

Next Students will solve equations with rational coefficients.

Rigor pursuing concepts, fluency, and applications

See the Levels of Complexity chart on page 456.

ENGAGE EXPLORE EXPLAIN ELABORATE EVALUATE

1 Launch the Lab

The activity is intended to be used as a whole-group activity.

Hands-On Activity

AL EL **Paired Heads Together** Have students work in pairs to complete the activity. Assign each student a number. Pairs should ensure that both students understand how to draw a bar diagram, write an equation, and use the bar diagram to solve the equation. Students are responsible to ask for help, if needed. Call on one numbered student to share their responses with the class. MP 1, 2, 4, 5

BL EL **Pairs Discussion** Have students work with a partner to determine a different method that can be used to solve the problem. Have them present their method to the class. MP 1, 2, 7

2 Collaborate

The **Investigate** and **Analyze and Reflect** sections are intended to be used as small-group investigations. The **Create** section is intended to be used as independent exercises.

Levels of Complexity

The levels of the exercises progress from 1 to 3, with Level 1 indicating the lowest level of complexity.

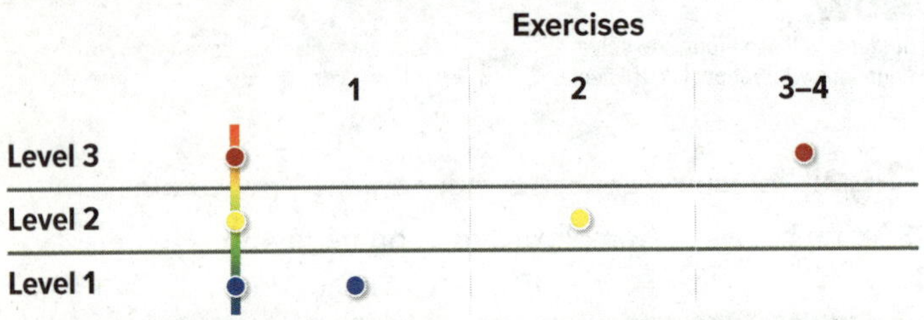

Investigate

Collaborate

AL EL Think-Pair-Write Give students one minute to think through how they would draw a bar diagram and write an equation to complete Exercise 1. Then have them work in pairs to complete the problem. Have students diagram the parts of the equation (coefficient, variable, constant) and write out in words what each part of the equation represents. For example, *three-fifths of Eliana's monthly allowance is the amount she wants to spend, $24.* MP 1, 2, 5

Analyze and Reflect

Collaborate

AL EL Think-Pair-Draw Give students time to think of a real-world problem that could be represented by an equation with a rational coefficient. Have them work in pairs to write equations that represent the problem. Have them draw bar diagrams that can be used to solve the equations. MP 1, 2, 4, 5

Inquiry Students should be able to answer "HOW can you use bar diagrams to solve equations with rational coefficients?" Check for student understanding. Provide guidance, if needed.

Investigate

Collaborate

Work with a partner to solve the following problem.

1. Eliana is spending $\frac{3}{5}$ of her monthly allowance on a costume for the talent show. She plans to spend $24. Draw a bar diagram to represent the situation. Then write and solve an equation to find the amount of Eliana's monthly allowance.

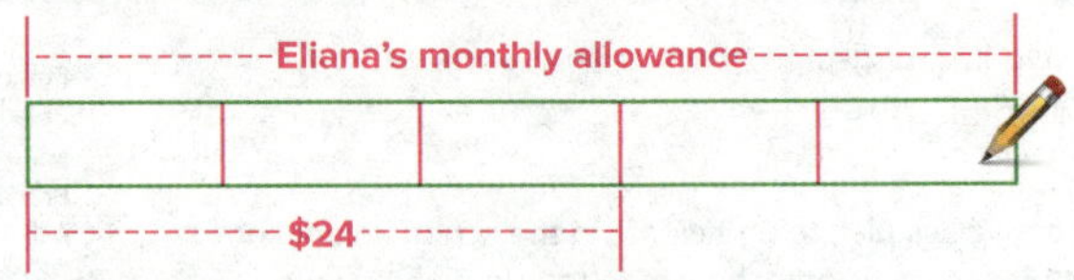

Equation: $\frac{3}{5}a = 24$ Solution: $40

Analyze and Reflect

Collaborate

Work with a partner to answer the following question.

2. MP **Make a Conjecture** Suppose Eliana planned on spending $\frac{3}{4}$ of her monthly allowance on a costume. How would the diagram and equation be different?

Sample answer: The bar would be divided into four equal sections. The equation would be $\frac{3}{4}a = 24$.

Create

On Your Own

3. MP **Model with Mathematics** Write a real-world problem that could be represented by the equation $\frac{2}{3}x = 12$. Then solve the equation.

Sample answer: Josefa sold $\frac{2}{3}$ of her video collection at a community yard sale. If she sold 12 videos, how many did she originally have to sell?; 18 videos

4. Inquiry HOW can you use bar diagrams to solve equations with rational coefficients?

Sample answer: You find the value of one section by dividing, then you multiply by the number of sections.

PLAN ONLINE

PD | RtI | Watch | Worksheets | Vocab | Tutor | Tools | Check | English Learners | Sketchpad

PRESENT

IWB

An Interactive Whiteboard Ready presentation is available for each lesson in the chapter.

Lesson 3

Solve Equations with Rational Coefficients

Real-World Link

Social Networks Three-fourths of the students in Aaliyah's class belong to a social network. There are 15 students in her class that belong to a social network.

1. Create a bar diagram and shade $\frac{3}{4}$, or 0.75, of it.

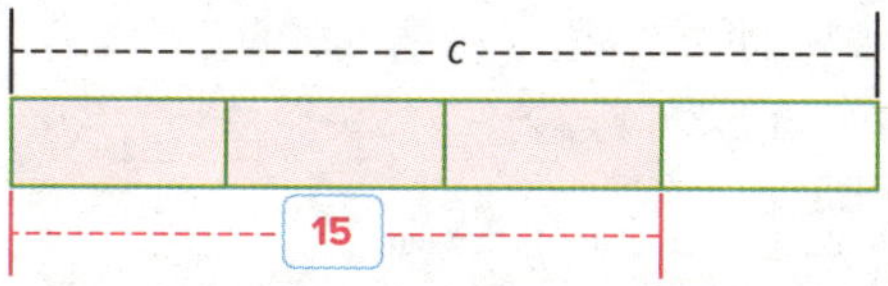

Label 15 along the bottom to show the amount of the bar that represents 15 students.

2. Based on the diagram, circle the equation that can be used to find c, the number of students in Aaliyah's class.

$15c = \frac{3}{4}$ $\qquad$ $0.75c = 15$ (circled) $\qquad$ $4c = 15$

3. Based on what you know about solving equations, explain how you could solve the equation you circled in Exercise 2.
Divide each side of the equation by 0.75.

4. How many students are in Aaliyah's class?
20 students

Essential Question

WHAT does it mean to say two quantities are equal?

Content Standards
7.EE.4, 7.EE.4a

MP Mathematical Practices
1, 2, 3, 4

Which MP **Mathematical Practices** did you use?
Shade the circle(s) that applies.

1 Persevere with Problems
2 Reason Abstractly
3 Construct an Argument
4 Model with Mathematics
5 Use Math Tools
6 Attend to Precision
7 Make Use of Structure
8 Use Repeated Reasoning

Focus narrowing the scope

Objective Solve one-step equations with rational coefficients.
7.EE.4, 7.EE.4a

Coherence connecting within and across grades

Previous Students wrote and solved one-step equations with integer coefficients.

Now Students solve equations with rational coefficients.

Next Students will model and solve two-step equations.

Rigor pursuing concepts, fluency, and applications

See the Levels of Complexity chart on page 461.

ENGAGE EXPLORE EXPLAIN ELABORATE EVALUATE

1 Launch the Lesson

Ideas for Use

You may wish to launch the lesson using a whole group, small group, think-pair-share activity, or independent activity.

EL **Talking Chips** Have students work in small groups to discuss and complete Exercises 1–4. Provide each student with 5 chips. Students must place a chip in the center of the table as they contribute to the discussion. After they have used all of their chips, they may not contribute. All students must use all of their chips. MP 1, 2, 4, 5

Alternate Strategy

AL Have students explain what is different about the equations $3c = 15$ and $\frac{3}{4}c = 15$. Ask them what operation is being performed on the variable in each equation and how they should solve each equation. MP 1, 3

ENGAGE EXPLORE **EXPLAIN** ELABORATE EVALUATE

2 Teach the Concept

Ask the scaffolded questions for each example to differentiate instruction.

Examples

IWB

1. Solve equations with decimal coefficients.

AL
- *What is a coefficient?* the number being multiplied by the variable
- *What is the coefficient in this example?* 0.25

OL
- *What operation is indicated by the coefficient?* multiplication
- *What is the inverse operation of multiplying by 0.25?* dividing by 0.25

BL
- *Describe a way to solve this equation mentally.* Sample answer: The coefficient is 0.25, which is one-fourth. One-fourth of a number is equal to 16, so that number must be 64.

Need Another Example?
Solve $10 = 0.5x$. Check your solution. 20

2. Solve equations with decimal coefficients.

AL
- *What does the variable represent?* the number of cones the coach can buy
- *What is the cost of each cone?* $2.40

OL
- *How do you know that the coefficient will be 2.4?* The cost, $2.40, will be multiplied by the number of cones, n.
- *How can you solve this equation?* Divide each side by 2.4.

BL
- *How can you use estimation to determine if your answer is reasonable?* Sample answer: Round 2.4 to 2. Since $30 \div 2 = 15$ and 12.5 is close to 15, the answer is reasonable.

Need Another Example?
Jamie wants to cut pieces of siding that are each 3.5 feet long to fit between a window and the end of the house. If the original piece of siding is 21 feet long, write and solve an equation to determine the total number of 3.5-foot-long pieces he can cut. $3.5x = 21$; 6 pieces

---

Work Zone

Division with Decimals

$$0.25\overline{)16.00} = 64.$$
$- 150$
100
$- 100$
0

Show your work.

a. 8

b. −1.5

c. 2.3

d. 15 cones

Decimal Coefficients

If the coefficient is a decimal, divide each side by the coefficient.

Example

Tutor

1. Solve $16 = 0.25n$. Check your solution.

$16 = 0.25n$	Write the equation.
$\frac{16}{0.25} = \frac{0.25n}{0.25}$	Division Property of Equality
$64 = n$	Simplify.
Check $16 = 0.25n$	Write the original equation.
$16 \stackrel{?}{=} 0.25 \cdot 64$	Replace n with 64.
$16 = 16$ ✓	This sentence is true.

The solution is 64.

Got it? Do these problems to find out.

a. $6.4 = 0.8m$ **b.** $-2.8p = 4.2$ **c.** $-4.7k = -10.81$

Real World Example

Tutor

2. Jaya's coach agreed to buy ice cream for all of the team members. Ice cream cones are $2.40 each. Write and solve an equation to find how many cones the coach can buy with $30.

Let n represent the number of cones the coach can buy.

$2.4n = 30$	Write the equation; $2.40 = 2.4.
$\frac{2.4n}{2.4} = \frac{30}{2.4}$	Division Property of Equality
$n = 12.5$	Simplify.

Since the number of ice cream cones must be a whole number, there is enough money for 12 ice cream cones.

Got it? Do this problem to find out.

d. Suppose the ice cream cones cost $2.80 each. How many ice cream cones could the coach buy with $42?

Fraction Coefficients

Recall that two numbers with a product of 1 are called multiplicative inverses, or reciprocals. If the coefficient in a multiplication equation is a fraction, multiply each side by the reciprocal of the coefficient.

Examples

Tutor

3. Solve $\frac{3}{4}x = \frac{12}{20}$.

$\frac{3}{4}x = \frac{12}{20}$ Write the equation.

$\left(\frac{4}{3}\right) \cdot \frac{3}{4}x = \left(\frac{4}{3}\right) \cdot \frac{12}{20}$ Multiply each side by the reciprocal of $\frac{3}{4}$, $\frac{4}{3}$.

$\frac{\overset{1}{\cancel{4}}}{\underset{1}{\cancel{3}}} \cdot \frac{\overset{1}{\cancel{3}}}{\underset{1}{\cancel{4}}}x = \frac{\overset{1}{\cancel{4}}}{\underset{1}{\cancel{3}}} \cdot \frac{\overset{4}{\cancel{12}}}{\underset{5}{\cancel{20}}}$ Divide by common factors.

$x = \frac{4}{5}$ Simplify. Check the solution.

4. Solve $-\frac{7}{9}d = 5$. Check your solution.

$-\frac{7}{9}d = 5$ Write the equation.

$\left(-\frac{9}{7}\right) \cdot \left(-\frac{7}{9}\right)d = \left(-\frac{9}{7}\right) \cdot 5$ Multiply each side by the reciprocal of $-\frac{7}{9}$, $-\frac{9}{7}$.

$\left(-\frac{9}{7}\right) \cdot \left(-\frac{7}{9}\right)d = \left(-\frac{9}{7}\right) \cdot \frac{5}{1}$ Write 5 as $\frac{5}{1}$.

$\left(-\frac{\overset{1}{\cancel{9}}}{\underset{1}{\cancel{7}}}\right) \cdot \left(-\frac{\overset{1}{\cancel{7}}}{\underset{1}{\cancel{9}}}\right)d = \left(-\frac{9}{7}\right) \cdot \frac{5}{1}$ Divide by common factors.

$d = -\frac{45}{7}$ or $-6\frac{3}{7}$ Simplify.

Check $-\frac{7}{9}d = 5$ Write the original equation.

$-\frac{7}{9}\left(-\frac{45}{7}\right) \stackrel{?}{=} 5$ Replace d with $-\frac{45}{7}$.

$\frac{315}{63} \stackrel{?}{=} 5$ Simplify.

$5 = 5$ ✓ This sentence is true.

Fractions as Coefficients

The expression $\frac{3}{4}x$ can be read as $\frac{3}{4}$ of x, $\frac{3}{4}$ multiplied by x, $3x$ divided by 4, or $\frac{x}{4}$ multiplied by 3.

Got it? Do these problems to find out.

e. $\frac{1}{2}x = 8$ f. $-\frac{3}{4}x = 9$ g. $-\frac{7}{8}x = -\frac{21}{64}$

Show your work.

e. 16

f. −12

g. $\frac{3}{8}$

Examples

IWB

3. Solve equations with fractional coefficients.

AL
- *What is the coefficient?* $\frac{3}{4}$
- *What operation is indicated by the coefficient?* multiplication

OL
- *Why can you multiply both sides by the reciprocal of the coefficient?* When you multiply any value by its reciprocal, the product is 1, which isolates the variable.
- *What is the reciprocal of $\frac{3}{4}$?* $\frac{4}{3}$

BL
- *What is another way to solve the equation?* Sample answer: Divide both sides of the equation by $\frac{3}{4}$, which is equivalent to multiplying both sides of the equation by $\frac{4}{3}$.

Need Another Example?

Solve $\frac{2}{3}x = \frac{6}{15}$. Check your solution. $\frac{3}{5}$

4. Solve equations with fractional coefficients.

AL
- *What is the coefficient?* $-\frac{7}{9}$
- *What is the inverse operation of multiplying by $-\frac{7}{9}$?* dividing by $-\frac{7}{9}$

OL
- *What is the reciprocal of $-\frac{7}{9}$?* $-\frac{9}{7}$
- *Why is dividing by common factors helpful in solving this equation?* Sample answer: Dividing by common factors makes the multiplication easier.

BL
- *What is another way to solve the equation?* Sample answer: Divide both sides of the equation by $-\frac{7}{9}$, which is equivalent to multiplying both sides of the equation by $-\frac{9}{7}$.

Need Another Example?

Solv $-\frac{2}{3}x = 12$. Check your solution. −18

IWB

Example

5. Write and solve an equation to solve a real-world problem.

AL
- *What are you trying to find?* how many hats Valerie can make with 6 yards of fabric
- *How much fabric is needed for one hat?* $\frac{2}{3}$ yd

OL
- *What equation can be used to represent the problem?* $\frac{2}{3}n = 6$
- *What is the reciprocal of the coefficient?* $\frac{3}{2}$

BL
- *How do you know if your answer is reasonable?* Sample answer: Valerie needs between $\frac{1}{2}$ yard and 1 yard to make one hat. So, to make 9 hats, she will need between $4\frac{1}{2}$ yards and 9 yards. 6 yards is between these two measurements, so the answer is reasonable.

Need Another Example?

Samantha answered $\frac{4}{5}$ of the questions on her science quiz correctly. If she answered 8 questions correctly, write and solve an equation to find the number of questions that were on the quiz. $\frac{4}{5}x = 8$; 10 questions

Guided Practice

Formative Assessment Use these exercises to assess students' understanding of the concepts in this lesson.

If some of your students are not ready for assignments, use the differentiated activities below.

AL EL **Three Stay, One Stray** Have students work in small groups to complete Exercises 1–3. Have one student stray to a new group to share responses and resolve any differences. Have the new group complete Exercises 4–6. Then have the students share responses in their original group. MP 1, 2

BL EL **Trade-a-Problem** Have students work in pairs to write a real-world problem that can be represented by a one-step equation involving a rational coefficient. Have them trade problems with a partner. Each partner solves the equation and checks each other's work. MP 1, 4

Bar Diagrams

A bar diagram can be used to represent this situation.

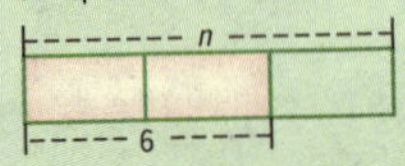

$n = 6 \div \frac{2}{3} = \frac{6}{1} \times \frac{3}{2} = 9$

Real World

Example

Watch Tutor

5. **Valerie needs $\frac{2}{3}$ yard of fabric to make each hat for the school play. Write and solve an equation to find how many hats she can make with 6 yards of fabric.**

Write and solve a multiplication equation. Let n represent the number of hats.

$\frac{2}{3}n = 6$	Write the equation.
$\left(\frac{3}{2}\right) \cdot \frac{2}{3}n = \left(\frac{3}{2}\right) \cdot 6$	Multiply each side by $\frac{3}{2}$.
$n = 9$	Simplify.

So, Valerie can make 9 hats.

Guided Practice

Check

Solve each equation. Check your solution. (Examples 1, 3, and 4)

1. $1.6k = 3.2$ **2**

2. $-2.5b = 20.5$ **−8.2**

3. $-\frac{1}{2} = -\frac{5}{18}h$ $1\frac{4}{5}$

Show your work.

Write and solve an equation. (Examples 2 and 5)

4. The average growth of human hair is 0.5 inch per month. Find how long it takes a human to grow 3 inches of hair.

   Equation: $0.5t = 3$ Solution: 6 months

5. Three fourths of the fruit in a refrigerator are apples. There are 24 apples in the refrigerator. How many pieces of fruit are in the refrigerator?

   Equation: $\frac{3}{4}n = 24$ Solution: 32 pieces of fruit

6. **Building on the Essential Question** What is the process for solving a multiplication equation with a rational coefficient? Sample answer: Divide by decimal coefficients. If the coefficient is a fraction, multiply by the reciprocal of the fraction.

Rate Yourself!

Are you ready to move on? Shade the section that applies.

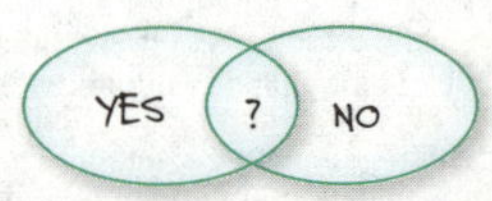

For more help, go online to access a Personal Tutor.

Tutor

Name ______________________ My Homework ______________________

Independent Practice

Go online for Step-by-Step Solutions eHelp

Solve each equation. Check your solution. (Examples 1, 3, and 4)

1. $1.2x = 6$ **5**

2. $14.4 = -2.4b$ **−6**

3. $-3.6h = -10.8$ **3**

Show your work.

4. $\frac{2}{5}t = \frac{12}{25}$ **$\frac{6}{5}$ or $1\frac{1}{5}$**

5. $-3\frac{1}{3} = -\frac{1}{2}g$ **$\frac{20}{3}$ or $6\frac{2}{3}$**

6. $-\frac{7}{9}m = \frac{11}{6}$ **$-\frac{33}{14}$ or $-2\frac{5}{14}$**

7. **Financial Literacy** Dillon deposited $\frac{3}{4}$ of his paycheck into the bank. The deposit slip shows how much he deposited. Write and solve an equation to find the amount of his paycheck. (Example 2)

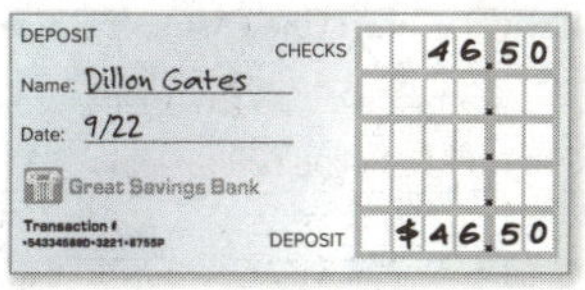

Equation: **$\frac{3}{4}p = 46.50$** Solution: **$62**

8. Twenty-four students brought their permission slips to attend the class field trip to the local art museum. If this represented eight tenths of the class, how many students are in the class? Use a bar diagram to solve arithmetically. Then use an equation to solve algebraically. (Example 5)

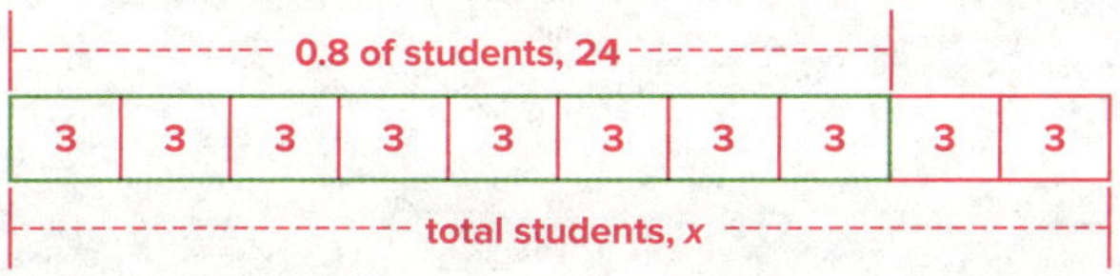

Equation: **$0.8x = 24$;** Solution: **30 students**

9. **MP Justify Conclusions** Seventy-five percent, or 15, of the students in Emily's homeroom class are going on a field trip. Two thirds, or 12, of the students in Santiago's homeroom class are going on the field trip. Which class has more students? Justify your answer. **Emily's homeroom class; Sample answer: Write and solve the equations $0.75e = 15$ and $\frac{2}{3}s = 12$; $e = 20$ and $s = 18$; Since $20 > 18$, Emily's homeroom class has more students.**

ENGAGE EXPLORE EXPLAIN ELABORATE EVALUATE

3 Practice and Apply

Independent Practice and Extra Practice

The Independent Practice pages are meant to be used as the homework assignment. The Extra Practice page can be used for additional reinforcement or as a second-day assignment.

Levels of Complexity

The levels of the exercises progress from 1 to 3, with Level 1 indicating the lowest level of complexity.

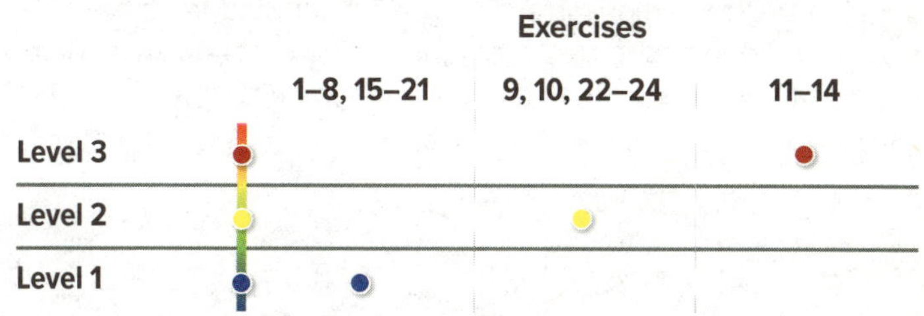

Suggested Assignments

You can use the table below that includes exercises of all complexity levels to select appropriate exercises for your students' needs.

Differentiated Homework Options		
AL	Approaching Level	1–9, 11, 12, 14, 23, 24
OL	On Level	1–7 odd, 9–12, 14, 23, 24
BL	Beyond Level	9–14, 23, 24

ALEKS® can provide additional remediation support with personalized instruction and practice.

MP MATHEMATICAL PRACTICES

Emphasis On	Exercise(s)
1 Make sense of problems and persevere in solving them.	13
2 Reason abstractly and quantitatively.	10
3 Construct viable arguments and critique the reasoning of others.	9, 11, 12
4 Model with mathematics.	14, 22

Mathematical Practices 1, 3, and 4 are aspects of mathematical thinking that are emphasized in every lesson. Students are given opportunities to be persistent in their problem solving, to express their reasoning, and apply mathematics to real-world situations.

Formative Assessment

Use this activity as a closing formative assessment before dismissing students from your class.

TICKET Out the Door

Have students explain in writing how what they learned about solving one-step equations will help them to solve two-step equations. Use the writing prompt below.

See students' work.

- Solving one-step equations will help me to solve two-step equations because...

Watch Out!

Common Error Students may have difficulty finding the reciprocal of whole numbers such as 5. Review that all whole numbers can be written as a fraction with a denominator of 1. For example, $5 = \frac{5}{1}$, so the reciprocal of $\frac{5}{1}$ is $\frac{1}{5}$.

10. MP **Reason Abstractly** Nora and Ryan are making stuffed animals for a toy drive. The table shows the fabric purchases they made. Who purchased the more expensive fabric?

Purchaser	Amount Purchased (yd)	Amount Paid ($)
Nora	$\frac{2}{3}$	4
Ryan	0.8	6

Explain your reasoning. Ryan; Sample answer: Write and solve the equations $\frac{2}{3}n = 4$ and $0.8r = 6$; $n = 6$ and $r = 7.5$; Since $7.5 > 6$, Ryan purchased the more expensive fabric.

H.O.T. Problems Higher Order Thinking

11. MP **Reason Inductively** Complete the statement: If $8 = \frac{m}{4}$, then $m - 12 = \blacksquare$. Explain. 20; Sample answer: Solve $8 = \frac{m}{4}$ to find that $m = 32$. So, replace m with 32 to find $32 - 12 = 20$.

12. MP **Which One Doesn't Belong?** Identify the pair of numbers that does not belong with the other three. Explain. $\frac{3}{5}$, 5; The other pairs of numbers are reciprocals.

$\frac{9}{6}, \frac{6}{9}$	$4, \frac{1}{4}$	$\frac{3}{5}, 5$	$\frac{2}{7}, \frac{7}{2}$

13. MP **Persevere with Problems** The formula for the area of a trapezoid is $A = \frac{1}{2}h(b_1 + b_2)$, where b_1 and b_2 are both bases and h is the height. Find the value of h in terms of A, b_1, and b_2. Justify your answer.
Sample answer: Multiply each side by 2. Then divide each side by $(b_1 + b_2)$. So, $\frac{2A}{b_1 + b_2} = h$.

14. MP **Model with Mathematics** Write a real-world problem that can be represented by the equation $224 = 3.5r$. Then solve the problem and explain the solution.
Sample answer: Audrey drove 224 miles in 3.5 hours. Find the rate r at which Audrey was traveling; 64 mph; She drove at a rate of 64 miles per hour.

Name ______________________ My Homework ______________________

Extra Practice

Solve each equation. Check your solution.

15. $0.4d = 2.8$

$0.4d = 2.8$

$\frac{0.4d}{0.4} = \frac{2.8d}{0.4}$

$d = 7$

Homework Help

16. $-5w = -24.5$ **4.9**

17. $-22.8 = 6n$ **−3.8**

18. $\frac{7}{8}k = \frac{5}{6}$

$\frac{7}{8}k = \frac{5}{6}$

$\left(\frac{8}{7}\right) \cdot \frac{7}{8}k = \left(\frac{8}{7}\right) \cdot \frac{5}{6}$

$k = \frac{40}{42}$ or $\frac{20}{21}$

19. $-6\frac{1}{4} = \frac{3}{5}c$ $-\frac{125}{12}$ or $-10\frac{5}{12}$

20. $-\frac{4}{7}v = -8\frac{2}{3}$ $\frac{91}{6}$ or $15\frac{1}{6}$

21. The Mammoth Cave Discovery Tour includes an elevation change of 140 feet. This is $\frac{7}{15}$ of the elevation change on the Wild Cave Tour. What is the elevation change on the Wild Cave Tour? Use a bar diagram to solve arithmetically. Then use an equation to solve algebraically.

$\frac{7}{15}$ of elevation, 140 ft

20	20	20	20	20	20	20	20	20	20	20	20	20	20	20

total elevation, *x* ft

Equation: $140 = \frac{7}{15}x$ Solution: **300 ft**

22. MP **Model with Mathematics** Refer to the graphic novel frame below. Write and solve an equation to find how many movies they have time to show.

Equation: $1.75\ m = 3.5$ Solution: **2 movies**

Create Your Own Homework Online

eSolutions Manual™ can be used to create worksheets for the suggested assignments on page 461, or create your own worksheets for differentiated homework or review.

Power Up! Test Practice

Exercises 23 and 24 prepare students for more rigorous thinking needed for the state assessment.

23. This test item requires students to explain and apply mathematical concepts and solve problems with precision, while making use of structure.

Depth of Knowledge	DOK1
Content Standard	7.EE.4, 7.EE.4a
Mathematical Practice	MP1
Online Experience	Students will be required to click on the bubbles to select all answers that are correct.
Scoring Rubric	
1 point	Students correctly answer the question.

24. This test item requires students to reason abstractly and quantitatively when problem solving.

Depth of Knowledge	DOK2
Content Standard	7.EE.4, 7.EE.4a
Mathematical Practice	MP1, MP7
Online Experience	Students will be required to type their responses in the boxes.
Scoring Rubric	
2 points	Students correctly write and solve an equation.
1 point	Students correctly write OR solve an equation.

Power Up! Test Practice

23. Which of the following high speed trains are traveling at a rate of 150 miles per hour? Select all that apply.

- [x] a train that travels 100 miles in $\frac{2}{3}$ hour
- [ ] a train that travels 160 miles in $\frac{5}{6}$ hour
- [ ] a train that travels 125 miles in $\frac{4}{5}$ hour
- [x] a train that travels 90 miles in $\frac{3}{5}$ hour

24. The table shows the results of a survey. Of those surveyed, 275 students said they prefer pop music.

Music Preference	
Type	**Fraction of Students**
Jazz	$\frac{1}{8}$
Pop	$\frac{5}{8}$
Rap	$\frac{1}{4}$

Write an equation that could be used to find the total number of students *s* who were surveyed. $s \cdot \frac{5}{8} = 275$

How many students were surveyed? 440 students

Spiral Review

Use the order of operations to evaluate each expression. 6.EE.2c

25. $6 \times 4 - 2 =$ 22

26. $70 - 5 \times 4 =$ 50

27. $18 \div 2 - 7 =$ 2

28. Write *add, divide, multiply,* and *subtract* in the correct order to complete the following sentence. 6.EE.2c
When using the order of operations to evaluate an expression, always multiply and divide before you add and subtract.

Write and evaluate an expression for each situation. 6.EE.1

29. Used paperback books are \$0.25, and hardback books are \$0.50. If you buy 3 paperback books and 5 hardback books, how much money do you spend?

Expression: 3 × \$0.25 + 5 × \$0.50 Solution: \$3.25

30. Suppose you order 2 pizzas, 2 garlic breads, and 1 order of BBQ wings. How much change would you receive from \$30?

Item	Cost
14" pizza	\$8
garlic bread	\$2
BBQ wings	\$4

Expression: $30 - (2 \times 8 + 2 \times 2 + 4)$ Solution: \$6

PLAN ONLINE: PD | RtI | Watch | Worksheets | Vocab | Tutor | Tools | Check | English Learners | Sketchpad

PRESENT: IWB — An Interactive Whiteboard Ready presentation is available for each lesson in the chapter.

Inquiry Lab

Solve Two-Step Equations

Inquiry HOW can a bar diagram or algebra tiles help you solve a real-world problem?

Content Standards
7.EE.4, 7.EE.4a

MP Mathematical Practices
1, 2, 3, 4

Latoya plays basketball and tennis. She has two basketballs and three tennis balls that weigh a total of 48 ounces. Each tennis ball weighs 2 ounces. What is the weight of a basketball?

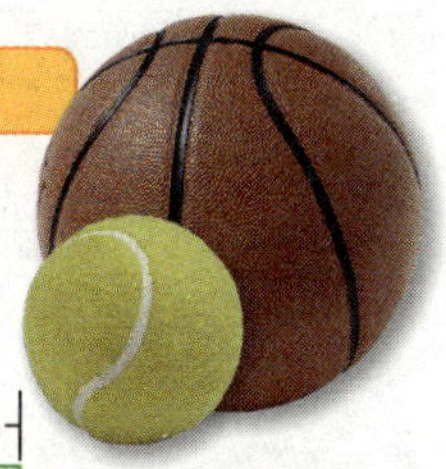

Hands-On Activity 1

You can use a bar diagram to represent the situation.

Step 1 Draw a bar diagram that represents the total weight.

48 oz

basketball	basketball	tennis	tennis	tennis
?	?	2 oz	2 oz	2 oz

Step 2 Write an equation that is modeled by the bar diagram. Let x represent the weight of a basketball.

$$2x + 6 = 48$$

total weight

2 basketballs

3 tennis balls

Step 3 Use the bar diagram to solve the equation. Subtract the weight of the tennis balls, 6 ounces, from the total weight, 48 ounces.

The two basketballs together weigh 48 − 6, or 42 ounces.

Divide the weight by 2 to find the weight of one basketball.

So, $x =$ 21. The weight of one basketball is 42 ÷ 2, or 21 ounces.

Check $2 \cdot 21 + 6 = 48$ ✓

The weight of one basketball is 21 ounces.

Focus narrowing the scope

Objective Use bar diagrams to model and solve two-step equations. 7.EE.4, 7.EE.4a

Coherence connecting within and across grades

Now Students model and solve two-step equations.

Next Students will solve two-step equations.

Rigor pursuing concepts, fluency, and applications

See the Levels of Complexity chart on page 467.

ENGAGE EXPLORE EXPLAIN ELABORATE EVALUATE

1 Launch the Lab

Activities 1 and 2 are intended to be used as whole-group activities. Activity 1 is designed to provide more guidance to students than Activity 2.

Materials: algebra tiles

Hands-On Activity 1

AL EL **Pairs to Groups** Arrange students to work in pairs to complete Steps 1–3, ensuring that each student understands how the bar diagram models the equation. Have pairs of students join up to form groups of 4. The group should share their responses and resolve any differences. Call on each group to share results with the class. MP 1, 2, 4, 5

Hands-On Activity 2

AL **EL** **Circle the Sage** Designate several "sages" for Activity 2. Sages should be proficient in using algebra tiles, solving one-step equations, and communication skills. Have the sages stand in the front of the room. Have one student from each group report to a sage, with no two students from the same group reporting to the same sage, if possible. Sages lead the discussion for the steps in the activity. Then have students report back to their original groups and compare what they learned from each sage. Students may use manipulatives, such as a paper bag and counters, if algebra tiles are not readily available. MP 1, 2, 5

BL **EL** **Pairs Discussion** Have students work with a partner to determine how to solve the equation without using algebra tiles, or other manipulatives. MP 1, 2

Hands-On Activity 2

Tools

You can use algebra tiles to model and solve the equation $4x - 2 = 10$.

Step 1 Model the equation.

$4x - 2 = 10$

Step 2 Add [2] 1-tiles to each side of the mat to form zero pairs on the left side.

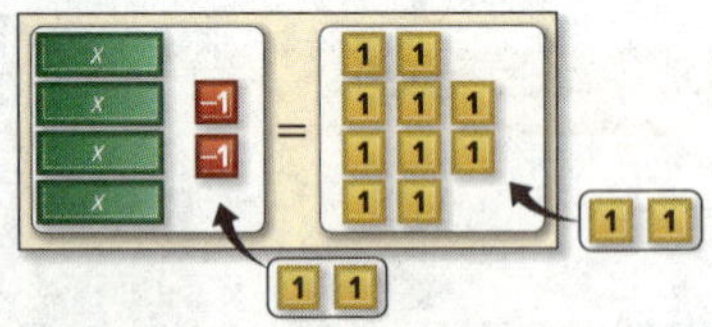

$4x - 2 + 2 = 10 + 2$

Step 3 Remove both zero pairs from the left side so that the variable is by itself.

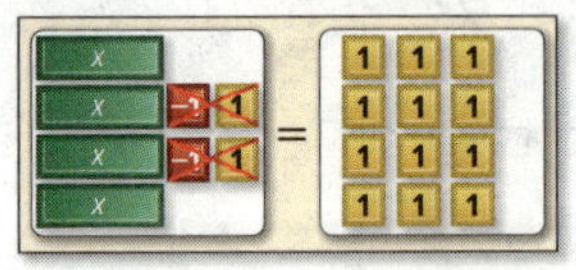

$4x = 12$

Step 4 Divide the remaining tiles into [4] equal groups.

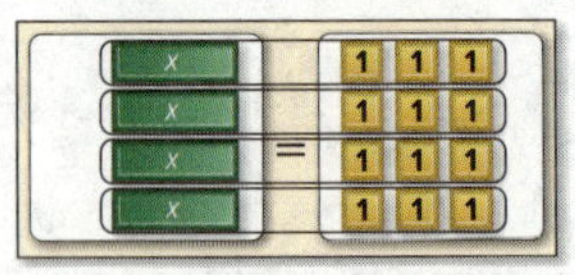

$\frac{4x}{4} = \frac{12}{4}$

So, $x =$ [3].

Check $4 \cdot$ [3] $- 2 = 10$ ✓

Investigate

Collaborate

Work with a partner to solve the following problem.

1. MP **Reason Abstractly** Ryan is saving money to buy a skateboard that costs $85. He has already saved $40. He plans to save the same amount each week for three weeks. Draw a bar diagram. Then write an equation. How much should Ryan save each week?

Show your work.

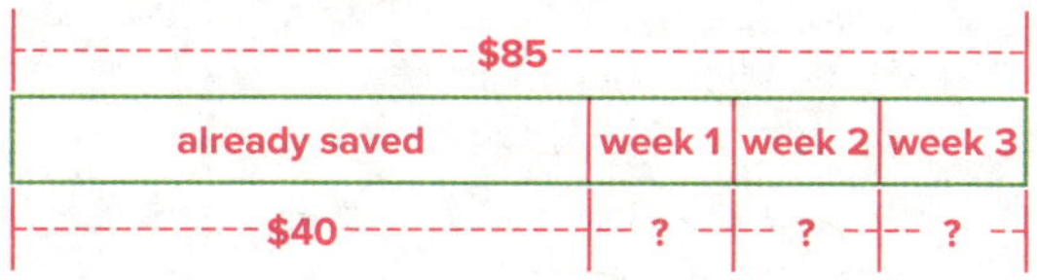

$3x + 40 = 85$; Ryan should save $15 each week.

Work with a partner to solve each equation. Use algebra tiles. Show your work using drawings.

2. $2x + 1 = 5$ $x =$ 2

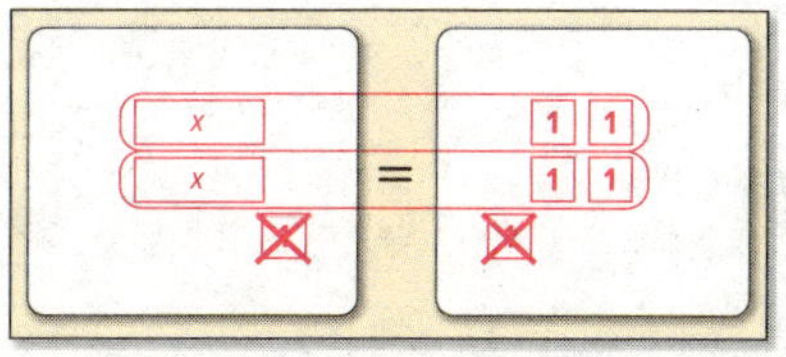

3. $3x + 2 = 11$ $x =$ 3

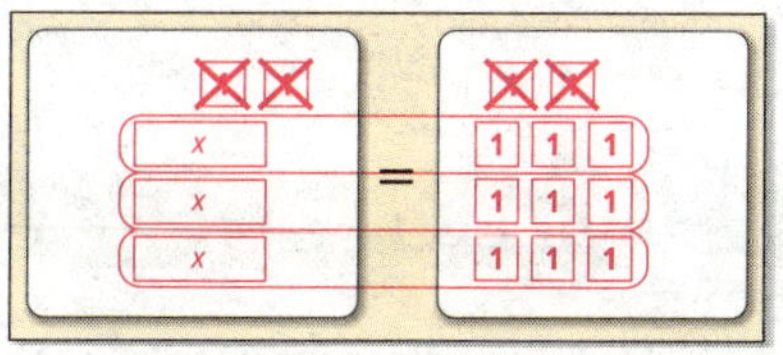

4. $4x + 3 = -5$ $x =$ -2

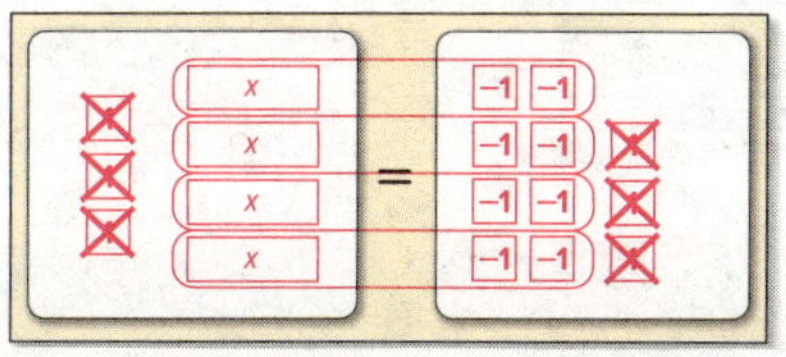

5. $2x - 1 = 7$ $x =$ 4

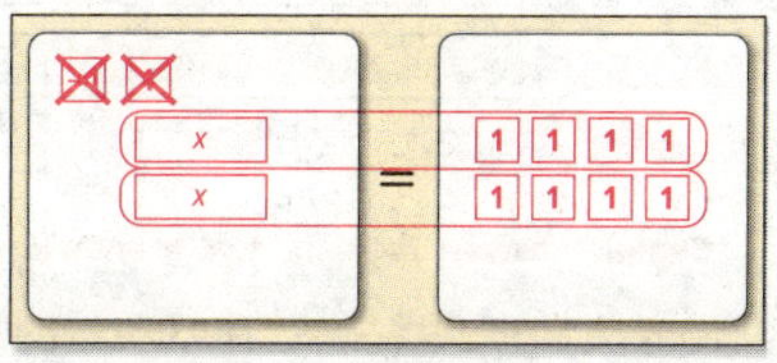

6. $5x - 2 = -7$ $x =$ -1

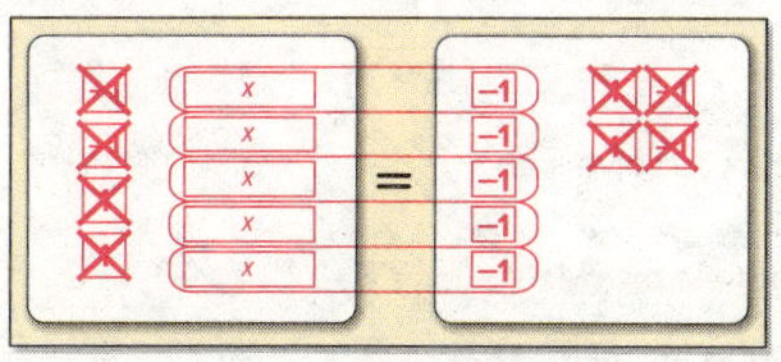

7. $3x - 4 = 5$ $x =$ 3

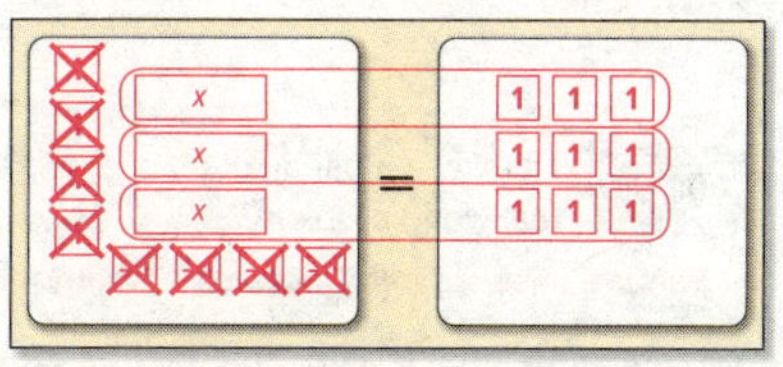

ENGAGE EXPLORE EXPLAIN ELABORATE EVALUATE

2 Collaborate

The **Investigate** and **Analyze and Reflect** sections are intended to be used as small-group investigations. The **Create** section is intended to be used as independent exercises.

Levels of Complexity

The levels of the exercises progress from 1 to 3, with Level 1 indicating the lowest level of complexity.

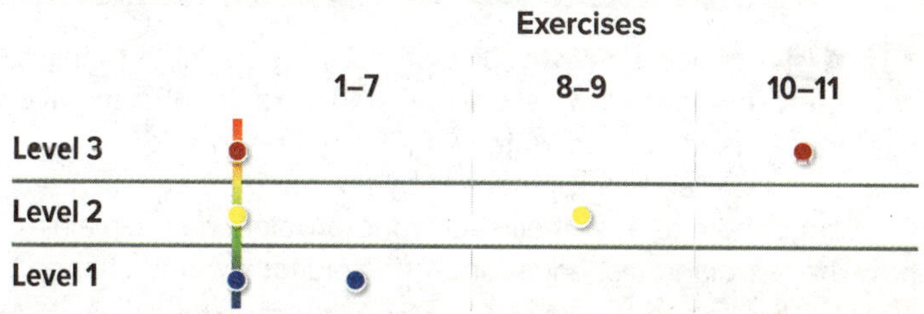

Investigate

Collaborate

AL **EL** **Rally Coach** Have students work in pairs to complete Exercises 1–7. Student 1 should read the problem aloud and talk through their steps to complete the problem, while Student 2 watches, listens, coaches, and praises. Students alternate roles for each exercise. MP 1, 2, 5

BL **EL** **Trade-a-Problem** Have students work in pairs to draw either a bar diagram or a diagram showing algebra tiles that model a two-step equation. Without including the equation, have students trade their diagrams with a partner. Each partner should determine the equation that is modeled and then solve the equation. The pair should discuss and resolve any differences. MP 1, 2, 5

Analyze and Reflect

Collaborate

AL **EL** **Pairs Discussion** Have students work with a partner to complete Exercises 8 and 9. Have Student 1 read the steps aloud, while Student 2 listens carefully and models the correct equation using algebra tiles. Students trade roles each exercise. Students may use paper bags and counters if algebra tiles are not readily available. MP 1, 2, 5, 7

Create

On Your Own

BL **EL** **Think-Pair-Write** Give students one minute to think about how they would write the real-world problem. Then have students work in pairs to write two different real-world problems that can be represented by the bar diagram. Challenge them to alter their real-world problem and explain how the bar diagrams, equations, and solutions would change. MP 1, 2, 4, 5

Inquiry Students should be able to answer "HOW can a bar diagram or algebra tiles help you solve a real-world problem?" Check for student understanding and provide guidance, if needed.

Analyze and Reflect

Collaborate

8. MP **Reason Inductively** Work with a partner. Read the steps to model and solve an equation using algebra tiles. Then circle each correct equation.

Steps to Solve	Choices of Equation		
• Add three 1-tiles to each side of the mat. • Divide tiles into two equal groups.	$2x + 3 = 15$	$3x + 2 = 15$	$2x - 3 = 15$
• Add four 1-tiles to each side of the mat. • Divide tiles into three equal groups.	$3x - 4 = 11$	$3x + 4 = 11$	$4x - 3 = 11$
• Remove seven 1-tiles from each side of the mat. • Divide tiles into three equal groups.	$7x + 3 = 10$	$3x + 7 = 10$	$3x - 7 = 10$
• Add two −1-tiles to each side of the mat. • Remove two zero pairs from the left side of the mat. • Divide tiles into five equal groups.	$5x - 2 = -8$	$5x + 2 = -8$	$2x + 5 = -8$

9. MP **Construct an Argument** What did you observe while choosing the correct equations in the table above?

Sample answer: The number of equal groups matches the coefficient of the variable in the equation.

Create

On Your Own

10. MP **Model with Mathematics** Write a real-world problem and an equation that the bar diagram below could represent. Then solve your problem.

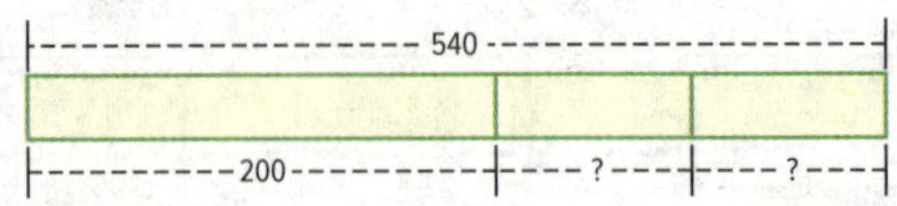

Sample answer: Jack and two friends downloaded 540 songs. Jack downloaded 200 songs. If the two friends downloaded an equal number of songs, how many songs did each download? $2x + 200 = 540$; 170 songs

11. Inquiry HOW can a bar diagram or algebra tiles help you solve a real-world problem?

Sample answer: Bar diagrams and algebra tile models provide visual representations to write an equation for a real-world problem. They also help you decide the steps needed to solve the equation.

PLAN ONLINE: PD | RtI | Watch | Worksheets | Vocab | Tutor | Tools | Check | English Learners (EL) | Sketchpad

PRESENT — IWB: An Interactive Whiteboard Ready presentation is available for each lesson in the chapter.

Lesson 4

Solve Two-Step Equations

Real-World Link

Watch

Balloons A company charges $2 for each balloon in an arrangement and a $3 delivery fee. You have $9 to spend. The equation $2x + 3 = 9$, where x is the number of balloons, represents the situation. Work backward to solve for x.

Start with the amount of money you have to spend. $9 → Subtract the $3 delivery fee. → $6 → Since each balloon is $2, divide by two. → 3

So, you can purchase 3 balloons.

Check your work by substituting your solution into the equation.

$$2(3) + 3 \stackrel{?}{=} 9.$$
$$6 + 3 \stackrel{?}{=} 9$$
$$9 = 9$$

1. How many balloons could you have purchased if there was a $1 delivery charge?

4 balloons

Start with the amount of money you have to spend. $9 → Subtract the $1 delivery fee. → $8 → Since each balloon is $2, divide by two. → 4

Which MP **Mathematical Practices** did you use? Shade the circle(s) that applies.

1. Persevere with Problems
2. Reason Abstractly
3. Construct an Argument
4. Model with Mathematics
5. Use Math Tools
6. Attend to Precision
7. Make Use of Structure
8. Use Repeated Reasoning

Essential Question

WHAT does it mean to say two quantities are equal?

Vocabulary

two-step equation

Content Standards
7.EE.4, 7.EE.4a

MP **Mathematical Practices**
1, 2, 3, 4

Focus narrowing the scope

Objective Solve two-step equations. 7.EE.4, 7.EE.4a

Coherence connecting within and across grades

Previous Students solved one-step equations with rational coefficients.

Now Students solve two-step equations.

Next Students will solve two-step equations in the form $p(x + q) = r$.

Rigor pursuing concepts, fluency, and applications

See the Levels of Complexity chart on page 473.

ENGAGE EXPLORE EXPLAIN ELABORATE EVALUATE

1 Launch the Lesson

Ideas for Use

You may wish to launch the lesson using a whole group, small group, think-pair-share activity, or independent activity.

EL **Think-Pair-Share** Give students one minute to individually think through their response to Exercises 1. Then have them complete the exercises with a partner, ensuring that each student understands how to set up the two-step equation. Call on one pair of students to share their response with the class. MP 1, 2

Alternate Strategy

AL Provide students with a partially completed bar diagram to model the problem. Have them highlight the number that represents the coefficient in the problem. MP 1, 4

2 Teach the Concept

Ask the scaffolded questions for each example to differentiate instruction.

Example

IWB

1. Solve a two-step equation.

AL
- *What two operations are being performed on the variable?* multiplication and addition
- *Which operation is being performed first on the variable?* multiplication

OL
- *What step will you do first? Why?* subtract 3 from both sides; Sample answer: Undo the operations in the reverse order of the order of operations.
- *After subtracting 3 from both sides, what is the next step?* divide both sides by 2
- *How can you use the number line to check your solution?* Sample answer: Start at 0. 2 groups of 3 is equal to 6. Then after adding 3, the result is 9, so the equation is true.

BL
- *Write a word problem that can be represented by the given equation.* See students' work.

Need Another Example?

Solve $4x + 3 = 19$. Check your solution. 4

Watch Out!

Common Error In exercises where the coefficient is negative, remind students to divide by the entire coefficient, including the negative sign for negative coefficients.

Work Zone

Solve Two-Step Equations

Recall that the *order of operations* ensures that numerical expressions, such as $2 \cdot 5 + 3$, have only one value. To reverse the operations, undo them in reverse order.

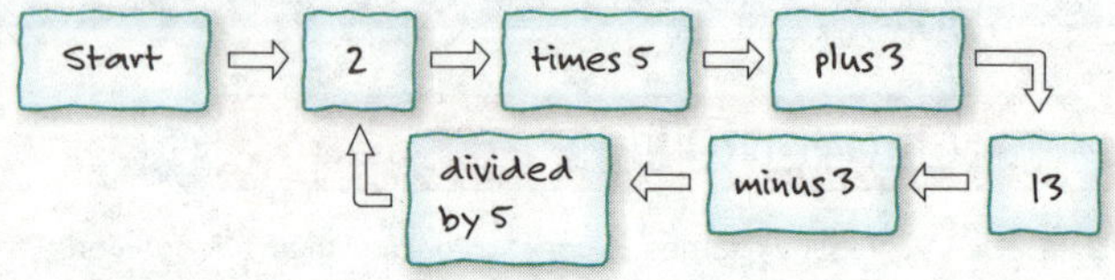

This equation is written as $px + q = r$, where p, q, and r are rational numbers.

A **two-step equation**, such as $2x + 3 = 9$, has two different operations, multiplication and addition. To solve a two-step equation, undo the operations in reverse order of the order of operations.

Step 1 Undo the addition or subtraction first.

Step 2 Undo the multiplication or division.

STOP and Reflect

What are the two operations you would perform to solve $3x - 4 = 8$? Write your answer below.

Add 4 and divide by 3.

Examples

Tutor

1. Solve $2x + 3 = 9$. Check your solution.

$2x + 3 = 9$ Write the equation.

$-3 = -3$ Undo the addition first by subtracting 3 from each side.

$2x = 6$

$\frac{2x}{2} = \frac{6}{2}$ Next, undo the multiplication by dividing each side by 2.

$x = 3$ Simplify.

Check $2x + 3 = 9$ Write the original equation.

$2(3) + 3 \stackrel{?}{=} 9$ Replace x with 3.

$9 = 9$ ✓ The sentence is true.

The solution is 3.

2. **Solve $3x + 2 = 23$. Check your solution.**

$3x + 2 = 23$	Write the equation.
$-2 = -2$	Undo the addition first by subtracting 2 from each side.
$3x = 21$	
$\frac{3x}{3} = \frac{21}{3}$	Division Property of Equality
$x = 7$	Simplify.
Check $3x + 2 = 23$	Write the original equation.
$3(7) + 2 \stackrel{?}{=} 23$	Replace x with 7.
$23 = 23$ ✓	The sentence is true.

The solution is 7.

3. **Solve $-2y - 7 = 3$. Check your solution.**

$-2y - 7 = 3$	Write the equation.
$+7 = +7$	Undo the subtraction first by adding 7 to each side.
$-2y = 10$	
$\frac{-2y}{-2} = \frac{10}{-2}$	Division Property of Equality
$y = -5$	Simplify.
The solution is -5.	Check the solution.

4. **Solve $4 + \frac{1}{5}r = -1$. Check your solution.**

$4 + \frac{1}{5}r = -1$	Write the equation.
$-4 = -4$	Undo the addition first by subtracting 4 from each side.
$\frac{1}{5}r = -5$	
$5 \cdot \frac{1}{5}r = 5 \cdot (-5)$	Multiplication Property of Equality
$r = -25$	Simplify.
The solution is -25.	Check the solution.

Equations

Remember, solutions of the new equation are also solutions of the original equation.

Got it? **Do these problems to find out.**

Solve each equation. Check your solution.

a. $2x + 4 = 10$ b. $3x + 5 = 14$ c. $5 = 2 + 3x$

d. $4x + 5 = 13$ e. $-5s + 8 = -2$ f. $-2 + \frac{2}{3}w = 10$

Show your work.

a. 3

b. 3

c. 1

d. 2

e. 2

f. 18

Examples

IWB

2. **Solve a two-step equation.**

- **AL** *What two operations are being performed on the variable?* **multiplication and addition**
- **OL** *What operation will you undo first? Why?* **Undo the addition by subtracting 2 from both sides; because you reverse the order of operations.**
- **BL** *Write a real-world problem that could be represented by the equation.* **See students' work.**

Need Another Example?
Solve $6 + 5y = 26$. Check your solution. **4**

3. **Solve a two-step equation.**

- **AL** *What two operations are being performed on the variable?* **multiplication and subtraction**
- **OL** *What operation will you undo first? Why?* **Undo the subtraction by adding 7 to both sides; because you reverse the order of operations.**
- *What does the equation become after adding 7 to both sides?* **$-2y = 10$**
- **BL** *Why is the solution -5 and not 5?* **A positive divided by a negative is a negative.**

Need Another Example?
Solve $-3c + 9 = 3$. Check your solution. **2**

4. **Solve a two-step equation.**

- **AL** *What two operations are being performed on the variable?* **addition and multiplication**
- **OL** *After subtracting 4, what does the equation become?* **$\frac{1}{5}r = -5$**
- **BL** *Why do you multiply by 5 to undo the multiplication of $\frac{1}{5}$?* **Multiplying by $\frac{1}{5}$ is the same as dividing by 5. The inverse of dividing by 5 is multiplying by 5.**

Need Another Example?
Solve $0 = 6 + \frac{1}{3}t$. Check your solution. **-18**

IWB

Example

5. Write and solve a two-step equation to represent a real-world problem.

AL • *What are you trying to find?* the number of friends at the party

• *What expression represents the cost of the tickets?* $8.5n$

OL • *What equation represents this situation?* $27 + 8.5n = 78$

• *What are the steps to solve the equation?* Subtract 27 from each side, and then divide each side by 8.5.

BL • *How much money was spent on movie tickets?* $51

Need Another Example?
Luis's cell phone plan costs $39 per month. Text messages cost an additional $0.15 each. If Luis's cell phone bill last month totaled $55.05, write and solve an equation to find the number of text messages he sent. $0.15m + 39 = 55.05$; 107 text messages

Guided Practice

Formative Assessment Use these exercises to assess students' understanding of the concepts in this lesson.

If some of your students are not ready for assignments, use the differentiated activity below.

AL EL **Roundrobin** Have students go around the room or around a circle responding to specific questions regarding each exercise. Some possible questions are given below. MP 1, 2, 7

- *What is the coefficient of the variable?* See students' work.
- *What operations are being performed on the variable?* See students' work.
- *Which operation will you undo first?* See students' work.
- *Which operation will you undo second?* See students' work.
- *What is the solution to the equation?* See students' work.

Solve Arithmetically

You can use a bar diagram to solve an equation arithmetically.

$78	
pizza	tickets
$27	$8.50n

Subtract 27 from 78. Then divide by 8.5.
78 − 27 = 51; 51 ÷ 8.5 = 6

Real World

Example

Tutor

5. Toya had her birthday party at the movies. It cost $27 for pizza and $8.50 per friend for the movie tickets. How many friends did Toya have at her party if she spent $78?

Words	Cost of pizza	plus	Cost of 1 friend	times	number of friends	equals	$78.
Variable	Let n represent the number of friends.						
Equation	27	+	8.50	·	n	=	78

$27 + 8.50n = 78$ Write the equation.

$-27 \quad = -27$ Subtract 27 from each side.

$8.50n = 51$

$\frac{8.50n}{8.50} = \frac{51}{8.50}$ Division Property of Equality

$n = 6$ Simplify.

Toya can have 6 friends at her party.

Guided Practice

Check

Solve each equation. Check your solution. (Examples 1–4)

1. $13 = 1 + 4s$ 3
2. $-3y - 5 = 10$ −5
3. $-7 = 1 + \frac{2}{3}n$ −12

Show your work.

4. Syreeta wants to buy some CDs that each cost $14, and a DVD that costs $23. She has $65. Write and solve an equation to find how many CDs she can buy. (Example 5)

Equation: $14c + 23 = 65$

Solution: 3 CDs

5. **Building on the Essential Question** When solving an equation, explain why it is important to perform identical operations on each side of the equals sign.
Sample answer: Any operations performed on one side must be performed on the other side to maintain equality.

Rate Yourself!

How well do you understand solving two-step equations? Circle the image that applies.

For more help, go online to access a Personal Tutor. Tutor

FOLDABLES Time to update your Foldable!

Name ______________________ My Homework ______________________

Independent Practice

Go online for Step-by-Step Solutions eHelp

Solve each equation. Check your solution. (Examples 1–4)

1. $3x + 1 = 10$ **3**

2. $-3 + 8n = -5$ $-\frac{1}{4}$

3. $4h - 6 = 22$ **7**

Show your work.

4. $-8s + 1 = 33$ **−4**

5. $-4w - 4 = 8$ **−3**

6. $5 + \frac{1}{7}b = -2$ **−49**

7. **MP Reason Abstractly** Cristiano is saving money to buy a bike that costs \$189. He has saved \$99 so far. He plans on saving \$10 each week. In how many weeks will he have enough money to buy the bike? Use a bar diagram to solve arithmetically. Then use an equation to solve algebraically. (Example 5)

Show your work.

$189 = 10x + 99$; 9 weeks

Solve each equation. Check your solution.

8. $2r - 3.1 = 1.7$ **2.4**

9. $4t + 3.5 = 12.5$ **2.25**

10. $8m - 5.5 = 10.1$ **1.95**

11. Temperature is usually measured on the Fahrenheit scale (°F) or the Celsius scale (°C). Use the formula $F = 1.8C + 32$ to convert from one scale to the other.
   a. Convert the temperature for Alaska's record low in July to Celsius. Round to the nearest degree.
   −9°C
   b. Hawaii's record low temperature is −11°C. Find the difference in degrees Fahrenheit between Hawaii's record low temperature and the record low temperature for Alaska in January.
   92.2°F

Alaska Record Low Temperatures (°F) by Month	
January	−80
April	−50
July	16
October	−48

ENGAGE EXPLORE EXPLAIN ELABORATE EVALUATE

3 Practice and Apply

Independent Practice and Extra Practice

The Independent Practice pages are meant to be used as the homework assignment. The Extra Practice page can be used for additional reinforcement or as a second-day assignment.

Levels of Complexity

The levels of the exercises progress from 1 to 3, with Level 1 indicating the lowest level of complexity.

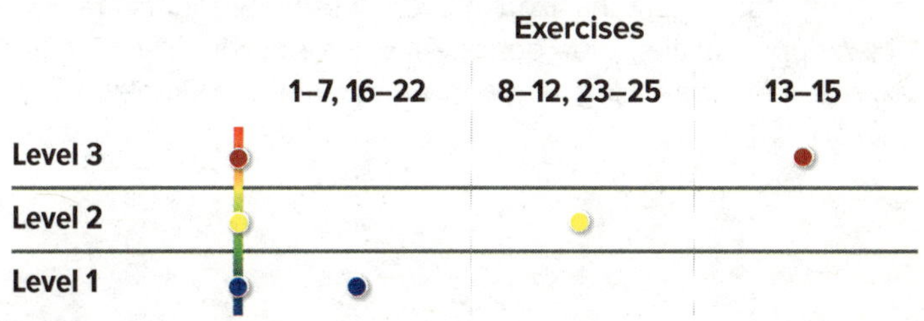

Suggested Assignments

You can use the table below that includes exercises of all complexity levels to select appropriate exercises for your students' needs.

Differentiated Homework Options		
AL	Approaching Level	1–11, 13, 14, 16, 29, 30
OL	On Level	1–11 odd, 12–14, 16, 29, 30
BL	Beyond Level	12–17, 29, 30

McGraw-Hill Education ALEKS® can provide additional remediation support with personalized instruction and practice.

MP MATHEMATICAL PRACTICES

Emphasis On	Exercise(s)
1 Make sense of problems and persevere in solving them.	14
2 Reason abstractly and quantitatively.	7
3 Construct viable arguments and critique the reasoning of others.	13, 23
4 Model with mathematics.	12, 15

Mathematical Practices 1, 3, and 4 are aspects of mathematical thinking that are emphasized in every lesson. Students are given opportunities to be persistent in their problem solving, to express their reasoning, and apply mathematics to real-world situations.

Formative Assessment
Use this activity as a closing formative assessment before dismissing students from your class.

TICKET Out the Door

Have students solve the equation $18 + \frac{6}{11}b = 96$. 143

12. MP **Model with Mathematics** Refer to the graphic novel frame below. Jamar figured that they will spend $39 for popcorn. Each movie cost $19. Write and solve an equation to find how many movies they can purchase.

$19x + 39 = 100$; $x = 3.21$; Since it is not possible to purchase part of a movie, they can purchase 3 movies.

H.O.T. Problems Higher Order Thinking

13. MP **Reason Inductively** Refer to Exercise 11. Is there a temperature in the table at which the number of degrees Celsius is the same as the number of degrees Fahrenheit? If so, find it. If not, explain why not.

No, none of the Fahrenheit temperatures convert to the same temperature in Celsius. Only −40°F = −40°C.

14. MP **Persevere with Problems** Suppose your school is selling magazine subscriptions. Each subscription costs $20. The company pays the school half of the total sales in dollars. The school must also pay a one-time fee of $18. Write and solve an equation to determine the fewest number of subscriptions that can be sold to earn a profit of $200.

$\frac{1}{2}(20x) - 18 = 200$; 22 subscriptions

15. MP **Model with Mathematics** Write a real-world problem that can be represented by the equation $\frac{(12 + 14) \times h}{2} = 52$. Then solve the problem.

Sample answer: Cameron found the area of a trapezoid to be 52 square inches. One base was 12 inches long and the other was 14 inches long. What is the height *h* of the trapezoid?; 4 in.

Name ______________ My Homework ______________

Extra Practice

Solve each equation. Check your solution.

16. $5x + 4 = 19$

Homework Help

$5x + 4 = 19$
$-4 = -4$
$\frac{5x}{5} = \frac{15}{5}$
$x = 3$

17. $6m + 1 = -23$ **−4**

18. $5 + 4d = 37$ **8**

19. $-7y + 3 = -25$ **4**

20. $25 + \frac{11}{12}b = 47$ **24**

21. $15 - \frac{1}{2}b = -3$ **36**

22. It costs $7.50 to enter a petting zoo. Each cup of food to feed the animals is $2.50. If you have $12.50, how many cups can you buy? Use a bar diagram to solve arithmetically. Then use an equation to solve algebraically.

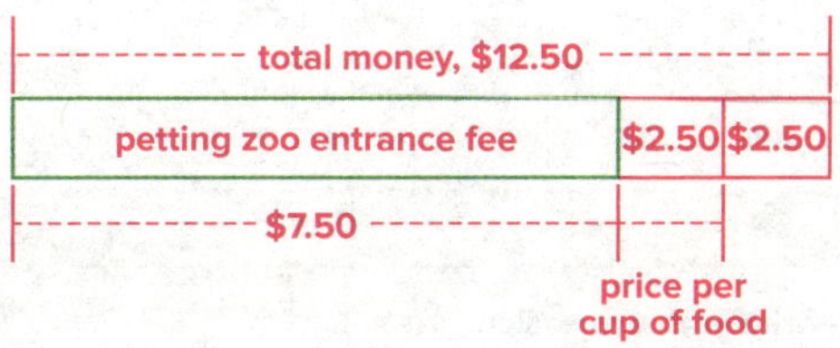

Show your work.

7.50 + 2.5p = 12.50; 2 cups

23. MP **Multiple Representations** The perimeter of a rectangle is 48 centimeters. Its length is 16 centimeters. What is the width *w*?

a. Draw a bar diagram that represents this situation.

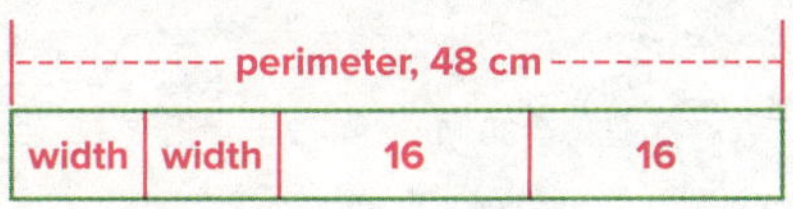

b. Write and solve an equation that represents this situation.

48 = 32 + 2w; 8 cm

c. How does solving the equation arithmetically compare to solving an equation algebraically?

Sample answer: Using either method, you would subtract first and then divide.

Create Your Own Homework Online

eSolutionsManual™ can be used to create worksheets for the suggested assignments on page 473, or create your own worksheets for differentiated homework or review.

Power Up! Test Practice

Exercises 24 and 25 prepare students for more rigorous thinking needed for the state assessment.

24.

This test item requires students to analyze and solve complex real-world problems through the use of mathematical tools and models.	
Depth of Knowledge	DOK2
Content Standard	7.EE.4, 7.EE.4a
Mathematical Practice	MP1, MP4
Online Experience	Students will drag values to complete the bar diagram and type their response in the box.
Scoring Rubric	
2 points	Students correctly model and solve the equation.
1 point	Students correctly model OR solve the equation.

25.

This test item requires students to reason abstractly and quantitatively when problem solving.	
Depth of Knowledge	DOK1
Content Standard	7.EE.4, 7.EE.4a
Mathematical Practice	MP1
Online Experience	Students will be required to type their responses in the boxes.
Scoring Rubric	
1 point	Students correctly answer the question.

Power Up! Test Practice

24. Admission to an amusement park costs \$15 and game tickets cost \$0.50 each. Craig has \$22 to pay for admission and game tickets. Select the correct labels to complete the bar diagram that can be used to find the number of game tickets t that Craig can purchase.

admission
game tickets
0.50
15
22
$0.50t$
t

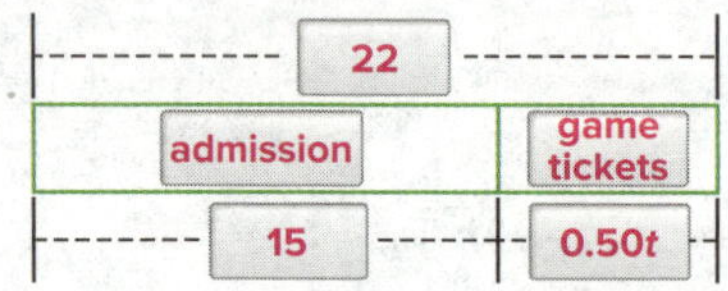

How many game tickets can Craig purchase? **14 game tickets**

25. A rental car company charges a fixed fee of \$30 plus \$0.05 per mile. Let c represent the total cost of renting a car and driving it m miles.

Write an equation that could be used to find the total cost of renting a car and driving it any number of miles. $c = 30 + 0.05m$

The Boggs family paid \$49.75 for their car rental. How many miles did they drive? **395 mi**

Spiral Review

Use the Distributive Property to rewrite each expression. 6.EE.3

26. $2(x + 7) =$ $2 \cdot x + 2 \cdot 7$ or $2x + 14$

27. $6(10 + n) =$ $6 \cdot 10 + 6 \cdot n$ or $60 + 6n$

28. $5(k - 4) =$ $5 \cdot k - 5 \cdot 4$ or $5k - 20$

Factor each expression. 6.NS.4

29. $5x + 5 \cdot 7 =$ $5(x + 7)$

30. $4n + 4 \cdot 2 =$ $4(n + 2)$

31. $10t + 10 \cdot 3 =$ $10(t + 3)$

32. $7v + 7 \cdot 8 =$ $7(v + 8)$

PLAN ONLINE: PD | RtI | Watch | Worksheets | Vocab | Tutor | Tools | Check | English Learners | Sketchpad

PRESENT: IWB

An Interactive Whiteboard Ready presentation is available for each lesson in the chapter.

Expressions and Equations

Inquiry Lab

More Two-Step Equations

Inquiry HOW are equations in $p(x + q) = r$ form different from $px + q = r$ equations?

Content Standards
7.EE.4, 7.EE.4a

MP Mathematical Practices
1, 3, 4

Mark has two summer jobs. He babysits and helps with the gardening. He works at each job three days a week and earns a total of $240. The table shows his earnings each day. How much does he earn each day babysitting?

Job	Daily Earnings ($)
Babysitting	x
Gardening	30

What do you know? gardening daily earnings: $30, total daily earnings: $240, he works 3 days per week.

What do you need to find? the amount earned each day from babysitting

Hands-On Activity 1

Step 1 Draw a bar diagram that represents the situation.

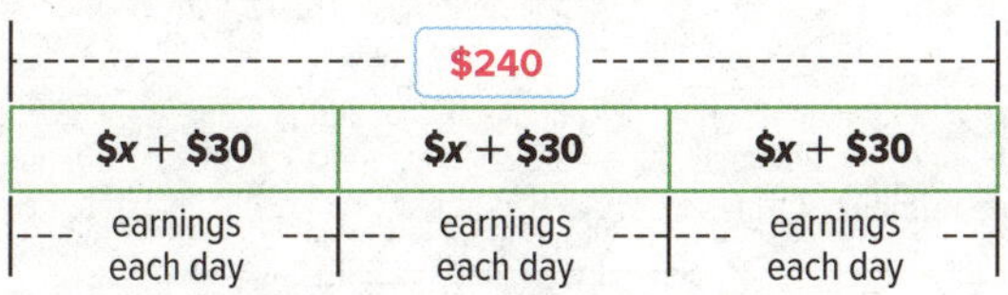

Step 2 Write an equation that is modeled by the bar diagram.

3($$x$ + $30) = $240

From the diagram, you can see that one third of Mark's total earnings is equal to $$x$ + $30. So, $$x$ + $30 = $\frac{\$240}{3}$ or $80.

Mark earns $80 − $30, or $50 each day babysitting.

Focus narrowing the scope

Objective Use models to write and solve two-step equations in $p(x + q) = r$ form. 7.EE.4, 7.EE.4a

Coherence connecting within and across grades

Now Students model and solve two-step equations in the form $p(x + q) = r$.

Next Students will solve two-step equations in the form $p(x + q) = r$.

Rigor pursuing concepts, fluency, and applications

See the Levels of Complexity chart on page 479.

ENGAGE EXPLORE EXPLAIN ELABORATE EVALUATE

1 Launch the Lab

Activities 1 and 2 are intended to be used as whole-group activities. Activity 1 is designed to provide more guidance to students than Activity 2.

Materials: algebra tiles, equation mats

Hands-On Activity 1

AL EL **One Stay, One Stray** In pairs, have students complete the activity. Students should discuss how the bar diagram helps them write the equation. Then, have one student stray to another pair to share responses and discuss differences. MP 1, 2, 4, 5

BL EL **Pairs Consult** Give students expressions in the $px + q$ form to translate into the form $p(x + q)$ form. Have them identify the property they are using. MP 1, 7

Hands-On Activity 2

AL **EL** **Roundrobin** Have students work in groups of 3 or 4. Have each student be responsible either for reading a step aloud or performing the actions in the step. Have students alternate roles for each step. MP 1, 2, 4, 5

BL **EL** **Pairs Consult** Have students model the equation $2x + 12 = 16$ using algebra tiles and explain why the models are the same. Have them identify the property that states that the expressions $2(x + 6)$ and $2x + 12$ are equivalent. MP 1, 5, 7

Vijay and his brother bought two hamburgers and two lemonades. The hamburgers cost $6 each. They spent a total of $16. How much did each lemonade cost?

Hands-On Activity 2

Tools

Use algebra tiles to model the situation described above.

Step 1 Model $2(x + 6) = 16$ using algebra tiles. Use 2 groups of $(x + 6)$ tiles.

$2(x + 6) = 16$

Step 2 Divide the tiles into 2 equal groups on each side of the mat. Remove 1 group from each side.

$x + 6 = 8$

Step 3 Remove the same number of 1-tiles from each side.

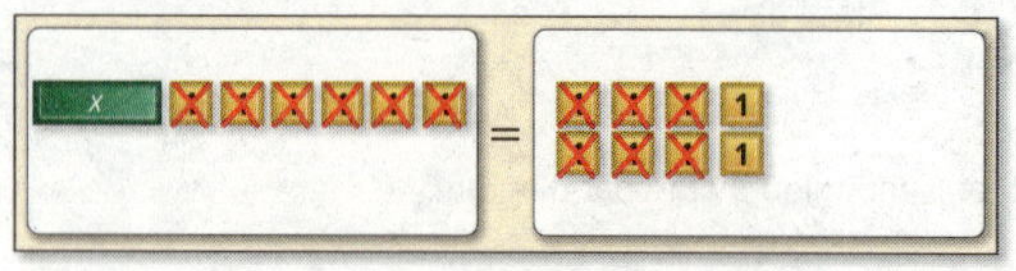

$x = 2$

So, $x =$ 2. Each lemonade costs $2.

Investigate

Collaborate

Work with a partner to model and solve each equation. Use a bar diagram for Exercises 1 and 2. Use algebra tiles for Exercises 3–6.

1. $3(x + 5) = 21$ $\quad x =$ 2

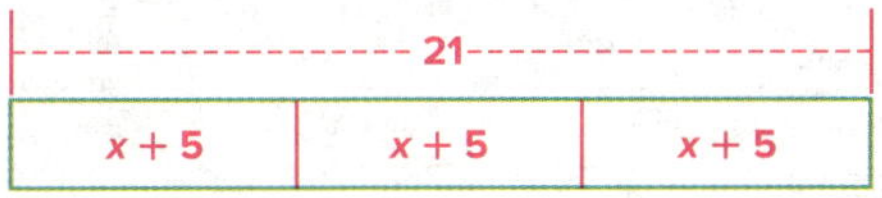

2. $2(x - 3) = 10$ $\quad x =$ 8

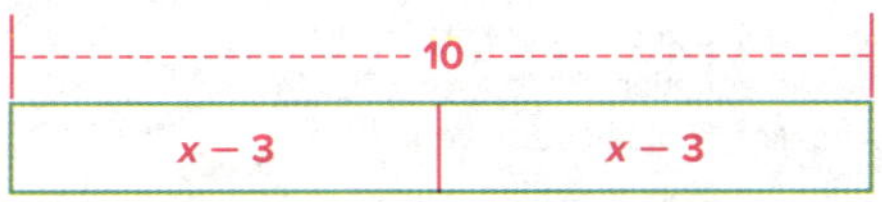

3. $4(x + 1) = 8$ $\quad x =$ 1

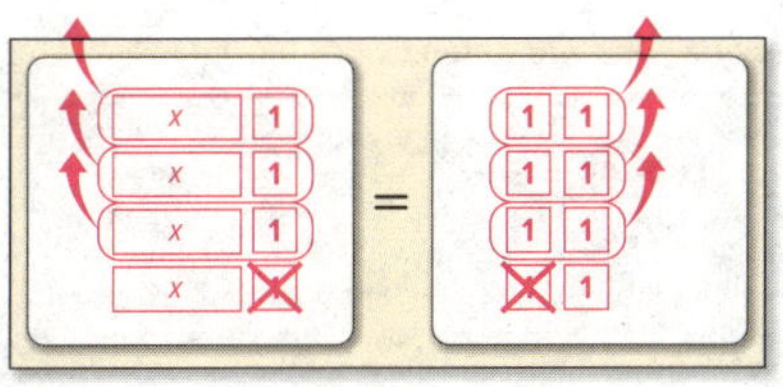

4. $3(x + 2) = -12$ $\quad x =$ −6

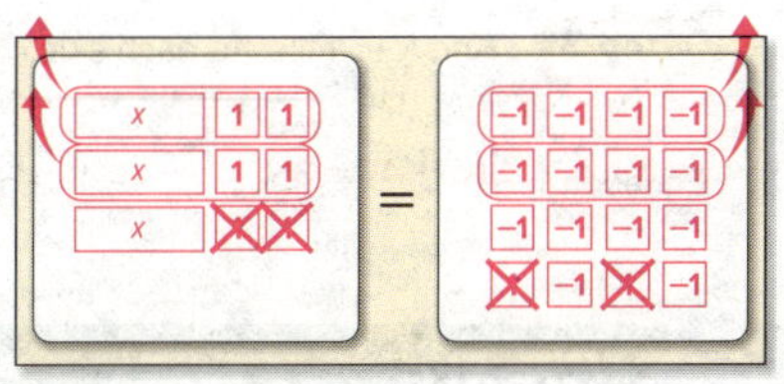

5. $2(x - 1) = 6$ $\quad x =$ 4

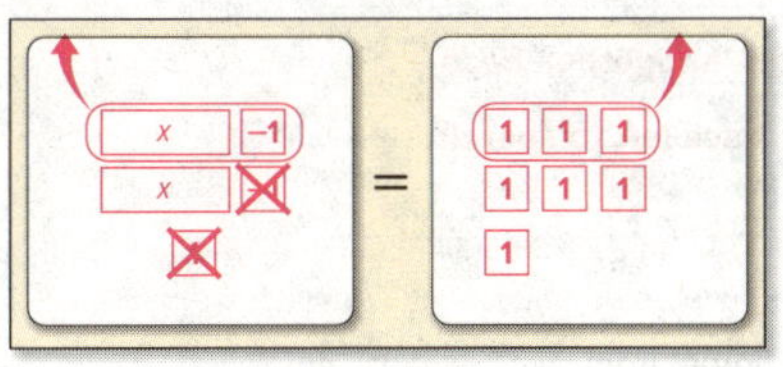

6. $3(x - 4) = -3$ $\quad x =$ 3

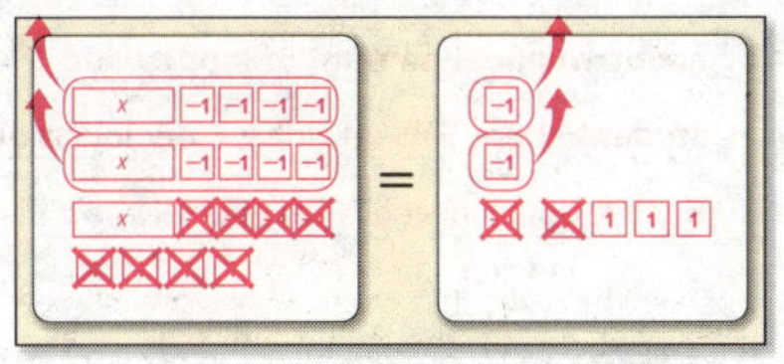

ENGAGE EXPLORE EXPLAIN ELABORATE EVALUATE

2 Collaborate

The **Investigate** and **Analyze and Reflect** sections are intended to be used as small-group investigations. The **Create** section is intended to be used as independent exercises.

Levels of Complexity

The levels of the exercises progress from 1 to 3, with Level 1 indicating the lowest level of complexity.

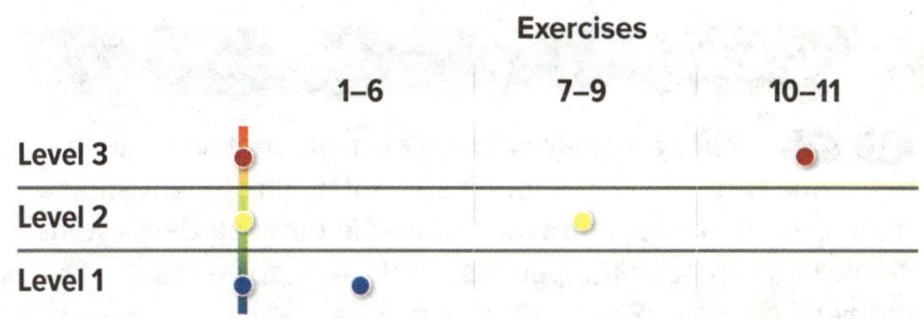

Investigate

Collaborate

AL **EL** **Circle the Sage** Designate several "sages" for Exercises 1–6. Sages should be proficient in bar diagrams, using algebra tiles, solving two-step equations, and communication skills. Have the sages stand in the front of the room. Have one student from each group report to a sage, with no two students from the same group reporting to the same sage, if possible. Sages lead the discussion to complete each exercise. Then have students report back to their original groups and compare what they learned from each sage. Students may use manipulatives, such as a paper bag and counters, if algebra tiles are not readily available. MP 1, 2, 5

BL **EL** **Trade-a-Problem** Have students create their own equation in the form $p(x + q) = r$. Then have them trade equations with a partner. Partners should either draw a bar diagram or use algebra tiles to solve the equation. Each partner checks and verifies the other student's work. MP 1, 2, 5

Analyze and Reflect

Collaborate

AL EL **Pairs to Groups** Arrange students in pairs to complete Exercises 7–9. Students may use manipulatives, such as algebra tiles, to complete Exercise 9. Then, have each pair join with another pair to form a group of 4. Have each pair share their responses and processes they used to complete each exercise. Have the group discuss and resolve any discrepancies. Have groups share their final responses with the class. MP 1, 2, 4, 5, 7

Create

On Your Own

BL EL **Share-a-Problem** Have each student share their real-world problem with another student. Each student should read aloud their word problem, while the other student listens carefully. Then have the pair discuss how to solve each problem. MP 1, 3

BL EL **Mix and Match** Have students write equations in the form $p(x + q) = r$ on index cards. Then have them use the Distributive Property to rewrite the same equation without using parentheses on other index cards. Have them shuffle the index cards and lay them face down. Students will play a game in which they take turns turning two cards face up. If the equations are equivalent, they remove those cards from the set and earn a point. If the equations are not equivalent, they return the cards face down to the pile. The student with the most points wins the game. MP 1, 2, 7

Inquiry Students should be able to answer "HOW are equations in $p(x + q) = r$ form different from $px + q = r$ equations?" Check for student understanding and provide guidance, if needed.

Analyze and Reflect

Collaborate

Work with a partner to write and solve an equation that represents each problem.

7. Refer to Activity 1. If Mark worked four days a week and made $360, how much did he earn babysitting each day?

   $4(x + 30) = 360$; $60

8. Refer to Activity 2. If Vijay and his brother spent a total of $15, how much did each lemonade cost?

   $2(x + 6) = 15$; $1.50

9. MP **Reason Inductively** After modeling an equation using algebra tiles, Angelina used the steps shown below to solve the equation. Write two different equations in $p(x + q) = r$ form that Angelina could have solved.

   Step 1 Divide the tiles into three equal groups on both sides of the mat.

   Step 2 Remove two groups from each side.

   Step 3 Add four 1-tiles to each side. **Sample equations are given.**

   Equation 1: **$3(x - 4) = 3$** Equation 2: **$3(x - 4) = 6$**

Create

On Your Own

10. MP **Model with Mathematics** Write a real-world problem that can be represented by the equation $4(x + 15) = 140$. Then solve the problem.

    Sample answer: Beng and three friends went to a festival. The students spent an equal amount of money and $140 dollars altogether. Each student spent $15 on rides. How much did each have left to spend?; Each student had $20 to spend.

11. Inquiry HOW are equations in $p(x + q) = r$ form different from $px + q = r$ equations?

    Sample answer: The order of operations states to multiply before adding or subtracting. To solve an equation in $p(x + q) = r$ form, first divide to undo the multiplication.

PLAN ONLINE: PD | RtI | Watch | Worksheets | Vocab | Tutor | Tools | Check | English Learners | Sketchpad

PRESENT: IWB

An Interactive Whiteboard Ready presentation is available for each lesson in the chapter.

Lesson 5

More Two-Step Equations

Real-World Link

Watch

Museums A new exhibit about dinosaurs is being constructed. The exhibit is a rectangle that is 36 feet long. It has a perimeter of 114 feet. Follow the steps to write an equation that can be used to find the width of the museum exhibit.

Step 1 Draw a diagram to help visualize the exhibit.

Label the length and width. Let *w* represent the width.

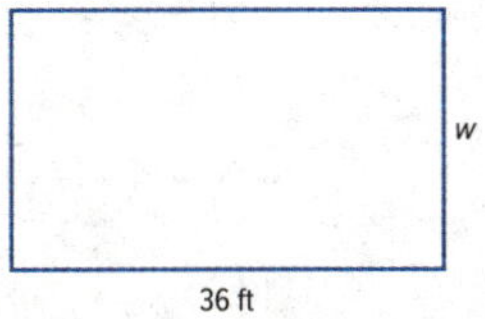

Step 2 Write an expression that represents the sum of the length and width of the exhibit. $36 + w$

Step 3 Write an expression that represents twice the sum of the length and width. $2(36 + w)$

Step 4 Write an equation that represents the perimeter of the exhibit. $2(36 + w) = 114$

Essential Question

WHAT does it mean to say two quantities are equal?

Content Standards
7.EE.4, 7.EE.4a

MP Mathematical Practices
1, 2, 3, 4

Which **MP Mathematical Practices** did you use? Shade the circle(s) that applies.

① Persevere with Problems
② Reason Abstractly
③ Construct an Argument
④ Model with Mathematics
⑤ Use Math Tools
⑥ Attend to Precision
⑦ Make Use of Structure
⑧ Use Repeated Reasoning

Focus narrowing the scope

Objective Solve two-step equations of the form $p(x + q) = r$.

Coherence connecting within and across grades

Previous Students modeled and solved equations in the form $p(x + q) = r$.

Now Students solve two-step equations in the form $p(x + q) = r$.

Next Students will model and solve inequalities.

Rigor pursuing concepts, fluency, and applications

See the Levels of Complexity chart on page 485.

ENGAGE EXPLORE EXPLAIN ELABORATE EVALUATE

1 Launch the Lesson

Ideas for Use

You may wish to launch the lesson using a whole group, small group, think-pair-share activity, or independent activity.

EL **Teams-Pairs-Solo** Have students work in small teams to complete Steps 1 and 2, ensuring that each team member understands how to generate the expression in Step 2. Then have the team divide into pairs to complete Steps 3 and 4. Then have them rejoin their original team to compare answers. MP 1, 2, 7

Alternate Strategies

AL Review the perimeter formula for rectangles and what perimeter means.

BL Have students explain how the equation in Step 4 would change if the rectangular exhibit was 40 feet long and had a perimeter of 120 feet. MP 1, 3

2 Teach the Concept

Ask the scaffolded questions for each example to differentiate instruction.

Examples

IWB

1. Solve two-step equations in the form $p(x + q) = r$.

AL
- *What operation is indicated by the number outside the parentheses?* multiplication
- *How could you undo this multiplication by 3?* Divide by 3.

OL
- *What property allows you to divide both sides by 3?* Division Property of Equality
- *After dividing by 3, what is the final step in solving the equation?* Subtract 5 from both sides.

BL
- *Which method do you prefer to use to solve the equation?* See students' work.

Need Another Example?
Solve $2(x + 4) = 18$. 5

2. Solve two-step equations in the form $p(x + q) = r$.

AL
- *What operation is indicated by the number outside the parentheses?* multiplication
- *How could you undo this multiplication by 5?* Divide by 5.

OL
- *What property allows you to divide both sides by 5?* Division Property of Equality
- *After dividing by 5, what is the final step in solving the equation?* Add 2 to both sides.

BL
- *Describe another way to solve the equation.* Sample answer: Use the Distributive Property to rewrite the equation without parentheses. The new equation becomes $5n - 10 = -30$. Then add 10 to both sides and divide both sides by 5.

Need Another Example?
Solve $4(5 + b) = -12$. −8

Work Zone

Solve Two-Step Equations

An equation like $2(w + 36) = 114$ is in the form $p(x + q) = r$. It contains two factors, p and $(x + q)$, and is considered a two-step equation. Solve these equations using the properties of equality.

Examples

Tutor

1. Solve $3(x + 5) = 45$.

Method 1 Solve arithmetically.

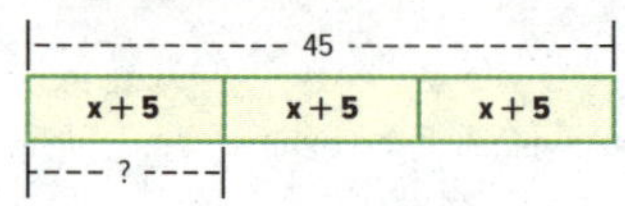

Draw a bar diagram. From the diagram, you can see that $x + 5 = 45 \div 3$ or 15. So, $x = 15 - 5$ or 10.

Method 2 Solve algebraically.

$3(x + 5) = 45$	Write the equation.
$\frac{3(x+5)}{3} = \frac{45}{3}$	Division Property of Equality
$x + 5 = 15$	Simplify.
$-5 = -5$	Subtraction Property of Equality
$x = 10$	Simplify.

2. Solve $5(n - 2) = -30$.

$5(n - 2) = -30$	Write the equation.
$\frac{5(n-2)}{5} = \frac{-30}{5}$	Division Property of Equality
$n - 2 = -6$	Simplify.
$+2 = +2$	Addition Property of Equality
$n = -4$	Simplify. Check the solution.

Check Your Work
Remember to plug your solution back into the original equation to see if it makes a true statement.

Got it? Do these problems to find out.

a. $2(x + 4) = 20$ **b.** $3(b - 6) = 12$ **c.** $-7(6 + d) = 49$

Show your work.

a. 6

b. 10

c. −13

Equations with Rational Coefficients

Sometimes the factor p, in $p(x + q)$, will be a fraction or decimal.

Examples

Tutor

3. **Solve $\frac{2}{3}(n + 6) = 10$. Check your solution.**

$\frac{2}{3}(n + 6) = 10$ — Write the equation.

$\frac{3}{2} \cdot \frac{2}{3}(n + 6) = \frac{3}{2} \cdot 10$ — Multiplication Property of Equality

$(n + 6) = \frac{3}{2} \cdot \left(\frac{10}{1}\right)$ — $\frac{2}{3} \cdot \frac{3}{2} = 1$; write 10 as $\frac{10}{1}$.

$n + 6 = 15$ — Simplify.

$-6 = -6$ — Subtraction Property of Equality

$n = 9$ — Simplify.

Check

$\frac{2}{3}(n + 6) = 10$ — Write the original equation.

$\frac{2}{3}(9 + 6) \stackrel{?}{=} 10$ — Replace n with 9. Is this sentence true?

$10 = 10$ ✓ — The sentence is true.

4. **Solve $0.2(c - 3) = -10$. Check your solution.**

$0.2(c - 3) = -10$ — Write the equation.

$\frac{0.2(c - 3)}{0.2} = \frac{-10}{0.2}$ — Division Property of Equality

$c - 3 = -50$ — Simplify.

$+3 = +3$ — Addition Property of Equality

$c = -47$ — Simplify.

Check $0.2(c - 3) = -10$ — Write the original equation.

$0.2(-47 - 3) \stackrel{?}{=} -10$ — Replace c with -47. Is this sentence true?

$-10 = -10$ ✓ — The sentence is true.

Got it? Do these problems to find out.

d. $\frac{1}{4}(d - 3) = -15$ **e.** $0.75(6 + d) = 12$ **f.** $(t + 3)\frac{5}{9} = 40$

Reciprocals
The product of a number and its reciprocal is 1.

show your work.

d. −57

e. 10

f. 69

Examples

IWB

3. **Solve two-step equations in the form $p(x + q) = r$.**

AL
- *What do you notice about the number being multiplied outside of the parentheses?* It is a fraction.
- *How could you undo this multiplication by $\frac{2}{3}$?* Multiply by its reciprocal.

OL
- *What property allows you to multiply by the reciprocal?* Multiplication Property of Equality
- *What is $\frac{3}{2} \cdot 10$?* 15

BL
- *Describe another way to solve the equation.* Sample answer: Multiply both sides of the equation by 3 to eliminate the denominator of 3. The new equation becomes $2(n + 6) = 30$. Divide both sides by 2. Then subtract 6 from each side.

Need Another Example?

Solve $\frac{1}{2}(w - 4) = 5$. Check your solution. 14

4. **Solve two-step equations in the form $p(x + q) = r$.**

AL
- *What do you notice about the number being multiplied outside of the parentheses?* It is a decimal.
- *How could you undo this multiplication by 0.2?* Divide by 0.2.

OL
- *What property allows you to divide both sides by 0.2?* Division Property of Equality
- *What is $-10 \div 0.2$?* −50

BL
- *Describe another way to solve the equation.* Sample answer: Use the Distributive Property to rewrite the equation without parentheses. The new equation becomes $0.2c - 0.6 = -10$. Then add 0.6 to both sides and divide both sides by 0.2.

Need Another Example?

Solve $0.4(w - 7) = 18$. Check your solution. 52

Example

IWB

5. **Write and solve a two-step equation for a real-world problem.**

AL
- *What are you trying to find?* the amount of money each boy received
- *What variable is used to represent this unknown?* m

OL
- *What does $(m - 15)$ represent?* the amount of money each boy had after spending \$15
- *What does $3(m - 15)$ represent?* the amount of money altogether after each boy spent \$15; there are three boys

BL
- *What percentage of his money did each boy spend?* \$15 of \$25 is 60%

Need Another Example?
Javier bought 3 bags of balloons for a party. He used 8 balloons from each bag. Write and solve an equation to determine how many balloons were originally in each bag if there were 21 balloons left over. $3(b - 8) = 21$; 15 balloons

Guided Practice

Formative Assessment Use these exercises to assess students' understanding of the concepts in this lesson.

If some of your students are not ready for assignments, use the differentiated activities below.

AL EL **Rally Coach** Have students work with a partner to complete Exercises 1–6. Have Student 1 talk through their procedure for solving the equation, while Student 2 watches, listens, coaches, and encourages. Have students trade roles for each successive exercise. MP 1, 2, 7

BL EL **Trade-a-Problem** Have students work in pairs to write a real-world problem that can be represented by a two-step equation in the form $p(x + q) = r$. Have them trade their problems with a partner and each partner writes and solve the equation. Have each partner check each other's work. MP 1, 2, 4, 7

STOP and Reflect

Solve the problem in Example 5 arithmetically. How does the arithmetic solution compare to the algebraic solution? Write your answer below.

They are the same.

Real World Example

Tutor

5. **Jamal and two cousins received the same amount of money to go to a movie. Each boy spent \$15. Afterward, the boys had \$30 altogether. Write and solve an equation to find the amount of money each boy received.**

Let m represent the amount of money each boy received.

$3(m - 15) = 30$	Write the equation.
$\frac{3(m - 15)}{3} = \frac{30}{3}$	Division Property of Equality
$m - 15 = 10$	Simplify.
$+15 = +15$	Addition Property of Equality
$m = 25$	Simplify.

So, each boy received \$25.

Guided Practice

Check

Solve each equation. Check your solution. (Examples 1–4)

1. $2(p + 7) = 18$ 2

2. $(4 + g)(-11) = 121$ -15

3. $(v + 5)\left(-\frac{1}{9}\right) = 6$ -59

4. $0.8(m - 5) = 10$ 17.5

5. Mr. Singh had three sheets of stickers. He gave 20 stickers from each sheet to his students and has 12 total stickers left. Write and solve an equation to find how many stickers were originally on each sheet. (Example 5)

Equation: $3(s - 20) = 12$;

Solution: 24 stickers

6. **Building on the Essential Question** What is the difference between $px + q = r$ and $p(x + q) = r$?

Sample answer: Equations in the form $px + q = r$ indicate that q is added to the product px. Equations in the form $p(x + q) = r$ indicate that both x and q are multiplied by p.

Rate Yourself!

Are you ready to move on? Shade the section that applies.

For more help, go online to access a Personal Tutor.

Tutor

FOLDABLES Time to update your Foldable!

Name ______________________ My Homework ______________________

Independent Practice

Go online for Step-by-Step Solutions eHelp

Solve each equation. Check your solution. (Examples 1–4)

1. $8(s + 3) = 72$ **6**

2. $-7(z - 6) = -70$ **16**

3. $(t + 8)(-2) = 12$ **−14**

4. $\frac{8}{11}(n - 10) = 64$ **98**

5. $-0.6(r + 0.2) = 1.8$ **−3.2**

6. $\left(w - \frac{4}{9}\right)\left(-\frac{2}{3}\right) = -\frac{4}{5}$ **$\frac{74}{45}$ or $1\frac{29}{45}$**

7. The length of each side of an equilateral triangle is increased by 5 inches, so the perimeter is now 60 inches. Write and solve an equation to find the original length of each side of the equilateral triangle. (Example 5)

Equation: **$3(\ell + 5) = 60$** Solution: **15 in.**

8. MP **Multiple Representations** Miguel and three of his friends went to the movies. They originally had a total of \$40. Each boy had the same amount of money and spent \$7.50 on a ticket. How much money did each boy have left after buying his ticket?

a. **Model** Draw a bar diagram that represents the situation.

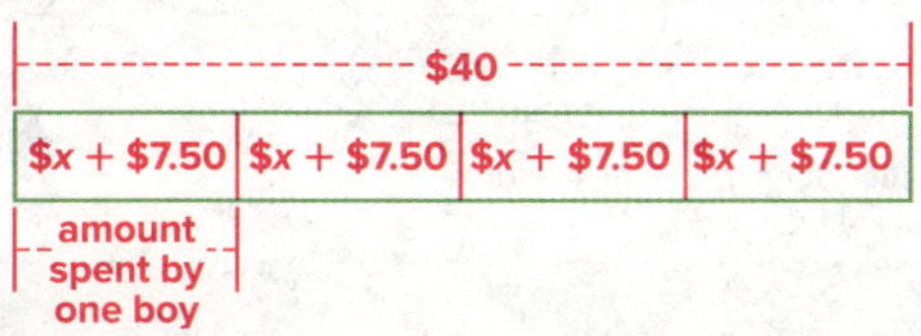

b. **Algebra** Write and solve an equation that represents the situation.
$4(x + 7.50) = 40$; \$2.50

c. **Words** Explain how you solved your equation.
I divided each side of the equation by 4. Then I subtracted 7.50 from each side.

d. **Words** Compare the arithmetic solution and the algebraic solution.
Sample answer: Both solutions use the same inverse operations. Arithmetic solutions use numbers. Algebraic solutions use equations.

ENGAGE EXPLORE EXPLAIN ELABORATE EVALUATE

3 Practice and Apply

Independent Practice and Extra Practice

The Independent Practice pages are meant to be used as the homework assignment. The Extra Practice page can be used for additional reinforcement or as a second-day assignment.

Levels of Complexity

The levels of the exercises progress from 1 to 3, with Level 1 indicating the lowest level of complexity.

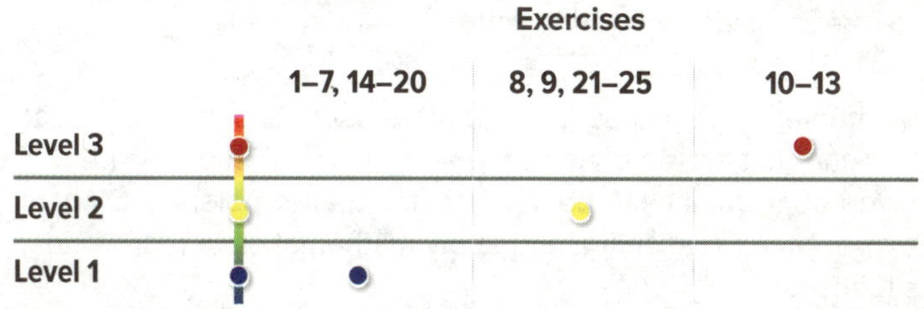

Suggested Assignments

You can use the table below that includes exercises of all complexity levels to select appropriate exercises for your students' needs.

Differentiated Homework Options		
AL	Approaching Level	1–7, 9–11, 13, 24, 25
OL	On Level	1–7 odd, 8–11, 13, 24, 25
BL	Beyond Level	8–13, 24, 25

ALEKS® can provide additional remediation support with personalized instruction and practice.

MP MATHEMATICAL PRACTICES

Emphasis On	Exercise(s)
1 Make sense of problems and persevere in solving them.	12
2 Reason abstractly and quantitatively.	20
3 Construct viable arguments and critique the reasoning of others.	8, 11
4 Model with mathematics.	10
5 Use appropriate tools strategically.	13

Mathematical Practices 1, 3, and 4 are aspects of mathematical thinking that are emphasized in every lesson. Students are given opportunities to be persistent in their problem solving, to express their reasoning, and to apply mathematics to real-world situations.

Formative Assessment
Use this activity as a closing formative assessment before dismissing students from your class.

TICKET Out the Door

Solve the equation $4(s + 3) = 52$. 10

Watch Out!

Common Error Students may forget the negative sign when dividing each side of an equation by a negative number. Suggest that they write the negative number inside parentheses.

9. Mrs. Sorenstam bought one ruler, one compass, and one mechanical pencil at the prices shown in the table for each of her 12 students.

Item	Price ($)
compass	1.49
mechanical pencil	0.59
ruler	0.49

a. Suppose Mrs. Sorenstam had 36 cents left after buying the school supplies. Write an equation to find the amount of money Mrs. Sorenstam initially had to spend on each student.

$12(m - 2.57) = 0.36$

b. Describe a two-step process you could use to solve your equation. Then solve the equation.

Sample answer: I first divided each side by 12 and then added 2.57 to each side; $2.60.

H.O.T. Problems Higher Order Thinking

10. MP **Model with Mathematics** Write a real-world situation that can be represented by the equation $2(n + 20) = 110$.

Sample answer: For the past two weeks, Jamal has saved an additional $20 from his paycheck. He saved $110 during this time period. How much does Jamal typically save from each paycheck?

11. MP **Find the Error** Marisol is solving the equation $6(x + 3) = 21$. Find her mistake and correct it.

Sample answer: Marisol should have divided by six before subtracting three; $6(x + 3) = 21$, $x + 3 = 3.5$, $x = 3.5 - 3$, $x = 0.5$

12. MP **Persevere with Problems** Solve $p(x + q) = r$ for x.

$x = \frac{r}{p} - q$

13. MP **Use Math Tools** Write an equation to represent the bar diagram at the right. Then write a real-world problem that can be represented by the equation and the diagram.

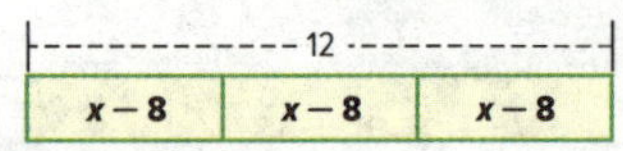

$3(x - 8) = 12$; Sample answer: Valeria bought a new collar for each of her three dogs. She paid $8 for each necklace. Suppose she had $12 left. How much money did Valeria have initially to spend on each dog collar?; $12 per collar

Name ______________________ My Homework ______________________

Extra Practice

Solve each equation. Check your solution.

14. $0.25(3 + a) = 0.5$

Homework Help

$0.25(3 + a) = 0.5$

$\frac{0.25(3 + a)}{0.25} = \frac{0.5}{0.25}$

$3 + a = 2$

$a = -1$

15. $12(x - 20) = -48$ **16**

16. $-28 = 7(n + 3)$ **−7**

17. $(t + 9)20 = 140$ **−2**

18. $\frac{5}{9}(8 + c) = -20$ **−44**

19. $(d - 3)\frac{2}{5} = 30$ **78**

20. MP **Reason Abstractly** Anne bought a necklace for each of her three sisters. She paid $7 for each necklace. Suppose she had $9 left. Write and solve an equation to find how much money Anne had initially to spend on each sister.

Equation: **$3(m - 7) = 9$**

Solution: **$10**

Solve each equation. Check your solution.

21. $1\frac{3}{5}(t - 6) = -0.4$ **$5\frac{3}{4}$ or 5.75**

22. $\left(x + 5\frac{1}{2}\right)0.75 = \frac{5}{8}$ **$-4\frac{2}{3}$ or $-4.\overline{6}$**

23. Mr. Gomez bought fruit to make fruit salad. He bought $2\frac{1}{2}$ pounds of apples and spent $4.50 on apples and oranges. Write and solve an equation to determine the number of pounds of oranges Mr. Gomez bought.

$1.20\left(n + 2\frac{1}{2}\right) = 4.50$; 1.25 or $1\frac{1}{4}$ pounds

Fruit	Price per Pound ($)
apples	1.20
bananas	0.50
grapes	1.50
oranges	1.20

Create Your Own Homework Online

eSolutionsManual™ can be used to create worksheets for the suggested assignments on page 485, or create your own worksheets for differentiated homework or review.

Power Up! Test Practice

Exercises 24 and 25 prepare students for more rigorous thinking needed for the state assessment.

24.

This test item requires students to analyze and solve complex real-world problems through the use of mathematical tools and models.	
Depth of Knowledge	DOK2
Content Standard	7.EE.4, 7.EE.4a
Mathematical Practice	MP1, MP4
Online Experience	Students will be required to type their responses in boxes.
Scoring Rubric	
2 points	Students complete the model of the classroom, write correct expressions and find the width.
1 point	Students correctly model the classroom and complete two or three of the other four blanks OR students fail to correctly model the classroom, but correctly complete the other blanks.

25.

This test item requires students to explain and apply mathematical concepts and solve problems with precision, while making use of structure.	
Depth of Knowledge	DOK1
Content Standard	7.EE.4a
Mathematical Practice	MP1
Online Experience	Students will be required to click on the bubbles to select all answers that are correct.
Scoring Rubric	
1 point	Students correctly answer the question.

Power Up! Test Practice

24. A rectangular classroom is 32 feet long and has a perimeter of 120 feet. Label the drawing with the correct values to represent the situation. Let w represent the width of the classroom.

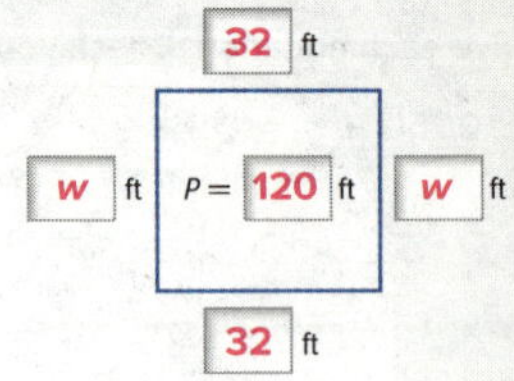

Write an expression that represents the sum of the length and width. $w + 32$

Write an expression that represents twice the sum of the length and width. $2(w + 32)$

Write an equation you could use to find the perimeter of the classroom. $2(w + 32) = 120$

What is the width of the classroom? 28 ft

25. Which of the following are operations that you should use to solve the equation $p(x - q) = r$ for x? Select all that apply.

- ☐ Subtract q from both sides.
- ☐ Multiply both sides by p.
- ☑ Divide both sides by p.
- ☑ Add q to both sides.

Spiral Review

Solve each equation. 6.EE.6

26. $x + 3 = 5$ 2

27. $x - 2 = -6$ −4

28. $4x = 12$ 3

29. $-6x = -24$ 4

30. $\frac{x}{2} = -1$ −2

31. $\frac{x}{-3} = 1$ −3

Write the number or numbers from the set {−3, −2, −1, 0, 1, 2, 3} that make each statement true. 6.EE.5

32. $4m = 12$ 3

33. $y - 1 = 1$ 2

34. $v > 0$ 1, 2, 3

35. $r \leq 0$ −3, −2, −1, 0

PLAN ONLINE

PD | RtI | Watch | Worksheets | Vocab | Tutor | Tools | Check | English Learners | Sketchpad

PRESENT

IWB

An Interactive Whiteboard Ready presentation is available for each lesson in the chapter.

Expressions and Equations

MP **Problem-Solving Investigation**

Work Backward

Case #1 Yard Work

Mike earned extra money by doing yard work for his neighbor. Then he spent \$5.50 at the convenience store and four times that amount at the bookstore. Now he has \$7.75 left.

How much money did Mike have before he went to the convenience store and the bookstore?

Content Standards
7.EE.3

MP **Mathematical Practices**
1, 3, 4

1 Understand *What are the facts?*

You know Mike has \$7.75 left. You need to find the amount before his purchases.

2 Plan *What is your strategy to solve this problem?*

Start with the end result and work backward.

3 Solve *How can you apply the strategy?*

He has \$7.75 left.

Undo the four times \$5.50 spent at the bookstore. Since \$5.50 × 4 is \$22, add \$7.75 and \$22.

$$\begin{array}{r} \$7.75 \\ +\ \$22.00 \\ \hline \$29.75 \\ +\ \$5.50 \\ \hline \$35.25 \end{array}$$

Undo the \$5.50 spent at the convenience store.

Add \$5.50 and **\$29.75**.

So, Mike's starting amount was **\$35.25**.

4 Check *Does the answer make sense?*

Assume Mike started with \$35.25. He spent \$5.50 and \$22. He had \$35 − \$5.50 − \$22 or **\$7.75** left. So, 35.25 is correct. ✓

Analyze the Strategy Watch Tutor

MP **Construct an Argument** Describe how to solve a problem by working backward. **Sample answer: Begin by taking the last value in the problem and perform opposite operations with each subsequent value until you arrive at the initial value.**

Focus narrowing the scope

Objective Solve problems by working backward. This lesson emphasizes MP **Mathematical Practice 3** Construct an Argument.

Work Backward Working backward is not only useful in problem solving but has a strong link to solving equations. Students have used the reverse process when solving addition, subtraction, and multiplication equations.

Coherence connecting within and across grades

Now
Students solve non-routine problems.

Next
Students will apply the work backward strategy to solve inequalities.

Rigor pursuing concepts, fluency, and applications

See the Levels of Complexity chart on page 491.

ENGAGE EXPLORE EXPLAIN ELABORATE EVALUATE

1 Launch the Lesson

The problems on pages 489 and 490 are intended to be used as a whole-group discussion on how to solve non-routine problems and are designed to provide scaffolded guidance. The problem on page 489 walks students through the solution, while the problem on page 490 asks students to come up with their own solutions.

Case #1 Yard Work

BL Have students extend the problem by having them answer the question below.

Ask:

- *Write an equation with a variable that could be used to solve the problem in a different way.* $m - 5.50 - 22 = 7.75$ or $m - 27.50 = 7.75$

Case #2 Money

AL **EL** **Rally Coach** Have students work in pairs to complete Step 3 using the *work backward* strategy. Have Student 1 complete the first step, speaking out loud, while Student 2 listens carefully, coaches, and praises. Next have Student complete the second step while Student 1 listens carefully, coaches, and praises. Partners take turns until they have completed all of the steps. MP 1, 6

BL **EL** **Trade-a-Problem** Have students create their own problem that uses the *work backward* strategy. Students trade their problems with a partner, solve each other's problem, and compare solutions. If the solutions do not agree, students work together to determine any errors. MP 1, 4

Need Another Example?
Fiona has a brother who is 8 years younger than she is. Her younger sister is 10 years old and is 3 years older than her younger brother. How old is Fiona? 15 years old

Case #2 Money
Marisa spent $8 on a movie ticket. Then she spent $5 on popcorn and one half of what was left on a drink. She had $2 left.

How much did she have initially?

1 Understand

Read the problem. What are you being asked to find?

I need to find the amount of money Marisa had initially.

Underline key words and values. What information do you know?

I know Marisa has $2 left and that she spent $8, $5, and half of what was left.

Is there any information that you do *not* need to know?

I do not need to know the actual items that she bought.

2 Plan

Choose a problem-solving strategy.

I will use the work backward strategy.

3 Solve

Use your problem-solving strategy to solve the problem.
Marisa has $2 left.

Undo the half-of-what-was-left amount. Multiply by 2. $2 \times 2 = 4$

Undo the spent $5. Add $5. $4 + 5 = 9$

Undo the spent $8. Add $8. $9 + 8 = 17$

So, Marisa had $17 initially.

4 Check

Use information from the problem to check your answer.

Marisa's initial amount: $17

Amount after spending $8: $17 − $8 = $9

Amount after spending $5: $9 − $5 = $4

Amount after spending half of what was left: $4 ÷ 2 = $2

Expressions and Equations

Collaborate

Work with a small group to solve the following cases. Show your work on a separate piece of paper.

Case #3 Waterfalls

Angel Falls in Venezuela is 3,212 feet high. It is 29 yards higher than 2.5 times the architectural height of the Empire State Building.

Find the architectural height, in feet, of the Empire State Building.

1,250 ft

Case #4 Number Theory

Travis works at a kite factory. He checks all the kites before they are packaged. Travis discovered that of the 28 kites that he inspected, 7 kites did not pass: 4 kites did not have tails, and 3 kites had the wrong colors.

Of the 476 kites Travis examined, how many did not have tails and how many had the wrong colors?

68 did not have tails and 51 had the wrong colors

Case #5 Time

Timothy's morning schedule is shown.

At what time does Timothy wake up if he arrives at school at 7:35 A.M.?

Timothy's Schedule	
Activity	**Time**
Wake up	■
Get ready for school – $\frac{3}{4}$ h	■
Walk to school – $\frac{5}{12}$ h	7:35 A.M.

6:25 A.M.

Use any strategy!

Case #6 Money

Antonio has saved $28 to spend at the arcade.

If he has 5 bills, how many of each kind of bill does he have?

1 twenty-dollar bill, 1 five-dollar bill, and 3 one-dollar bills

ENGAGE EXPLORE **EXPLAIN** **ELABORATE** EVALUATE

2 Collaborate

Levels of Complexity

The levels of the exercises progress from 1 to 3, with Level 1 indicating the lowest level of complexity.

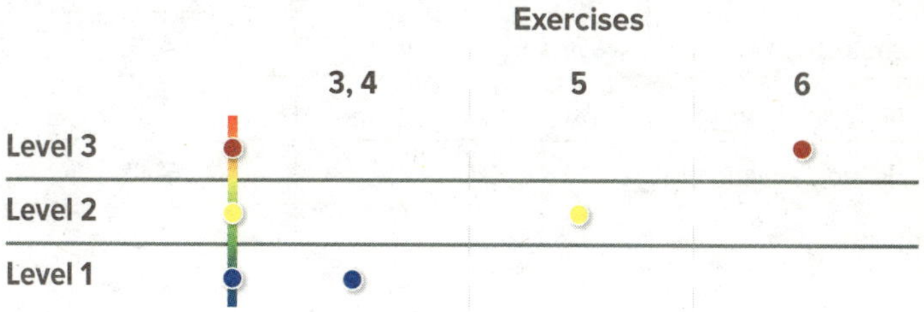

AL EL **Pairs Discussion** Have students work in pairs to answer the following questions related to Case 4. MP 1, 2, 4

Ask:

- *How can you solve the question?* Sample answer: I can use a proportion and cross multiply. $\frac{3}{28} = \frac{x}{476}$; $x = 51$; $\frac{4}{28} = \frac{x}{476}$; $x = 68$; Of the kites Travis examined, 68 did not have tails and 51 had the wrong color.
- *What is another method to solve the problem? Which method do you prefer? Explain.* Sample answer: I could solve the problem by making a table. The proportion is more efficient and quicker.

BL EL **Think-Pair-Share** Have students work in pairs to answer the following extension questions related to Case 3. MP 1, 2

Ask:

- *Write an equation you could use to solve Case 3.* Sample answer: $2.5h + 87 = 3{,}212$
- *Pikes Peak is 265 feet shorter than 11.5 times the architectural height of the Empire State Building. Find the height of Pikes Peak in feet.* 14,110 ft

Mid-Chapter Check

If students have trouble with Exercises 1–10, they may need help with the following concepts.

Concept	Exercise(s)
addition equations (Lesson 1)	1, 3
subtraction equations (Lesson 1)	4, 9
multiplication equations (Lesson 2)	2, 5
division equations (Lesson 2)	6, 10
two-step equations (Lessons 4 and 5)	7, 8

Vocabulary Activity

EL **Rally Coach** Have students work in pairs to complete Exercise 1. Have Student 1 speak aloud about what an equation means, while Student 2 listens, coaches, and encourages. If students are having trouble remembering the definition of an equation, have them discuss different equations they have solved and the parts that make up an equation. MP 1, 2, 6

McGraw Hill Education **ALEKS**® provides additional remediation support with personalized instruction and practice for those who are struggling, while providing enhanced learning for those who have mastered the concepts.

Alternate Stategies

AL EL Have students refer back to Lesson 1 to review the definition of equation and look for examples of equations. Have students circle examples of equations they find throughout the lesson. MP 1, 6

BL Have students verbally give two examples of equations that are two-step equations that use two different operations. For example, $2x + 6 = 13$ is a two-step equation that uses multiplication and addition. MP 1, 6

Mid-Chapter Check

Vocabulary Check

Vocab

1. Define *equation*. Give an example of two equivalent equations. (Lesson 1)

An equation is a sentence stating that two quantities are equal;

Sample answer: $x = 5$ and $x + 1 = 6$.

2. Fill in the blank with the correct term. (Lesson 2)

A **coefficient** is the numerical factor of a multiplication expression like $3x$.

Skills Check and Problem Solving

Solve each equation. Check your solution. (Lessons 1–5)

3. $21 + m = 33$ **12**

4. $a - 5 = -12$ **−7**

5. $5f = -75$ **−15**

Show your work.

6. $15 = \frac{b}{15}$ **225**

7. $19 = 4p + 5$ **3.5 or $\frac{7}{2}$**

8. $3(n - 7) = -30$ **−3**

9. Cameron has 11 adult Fantail goldfish. This is 7 fewer Fantail goldfish than his friend Julia has. Write and solve a subtraction equation to determine the number of Fantail goldfish g that Julia has. (Lesson 1)

Equation: **$11 = g - 7$** Solution: **18 Fantail goldfish**

10. MP **Persevere with Problems** The pentagon shown is a regular pentagon, so each side has the same length. The perimeter of the pentagon is 22.5 centimeters. What is the value of x? **6 cm**

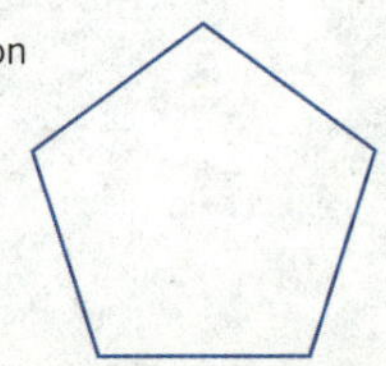

$(x - 1.5)$ cm

IWB An Interactive Whiteboard Ready presentation is available for each lesson in the chapter.

Inquiry Lab
Solve Inequalities

Inquiry **HOW** is an inequality like an equation? How is it different?

Content Standards
7.EE.4, 7.EE.4b

MP Mathematical Practices
1, 2, 3, 4

Mr. Numkena volunteered to drive Hinto and his friends to the school dance. The car can carry up to 5 people, including the driver. How many friends can ride in the car with Hinto?

What do you know? The car can carry up to 5 people. Mr. Numkena and Hinto will be in the car.

What do you need to find? the number of friends that can ride in the car with Hinto

Hands-On Activity 1

Tools

The real-world situation described above can be represented by the inequality $x + 2 \leq 5$. Let x represent the friends that can ride with Hinto.

$$x + 2 \leq 5$$

Mr. Numkena, Hinto, and friends → $x + 2$

Maximum number of people → 5

You can use a balance to model and solve the inequality $x + 2 \leq 5$.

Step 1 On one side of a balance, place a paper bag and **2** cubes to model $x + 2$.

Step 2 On the other side of a balance, place **5** cubes.

Add one cube to the bag at a time. Then complete the table.

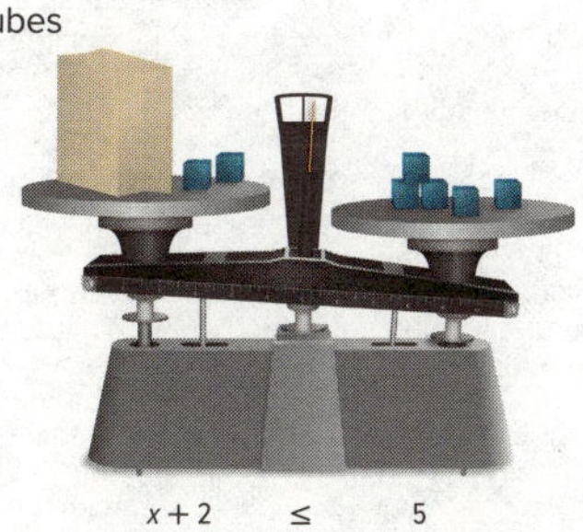

Number of Friends, x	$x + 2$	Less than or equal to 5?
1	3	yes
2	4	yes
3	5	yes
4	6	No

So, up to **3** friends can ride with Hinto to the school dance.

Focus narrowing the scope

Objective Use models to solve problems involving inequalities. 7.EE.4, 7.EE.4b

Coherence connecting within and across grades

Now
Students use models to solve one-step inequalities.

Next
Students will use Properties of Inequality to solve one-step inequalities.

Rigor pursuing concepts, fluency, and applications

See the Levels of Complexity chart on page 495.

ENGAGE EXPLORE EXPLAIN ELABORATE EVALUATE

1 Launch the Lab

Activity 1 is intended to be used as a whole-group activity. Activity 1 is designed to provide more guidance than Activity 2.

Hands-On Activity 1

AL **EL** Explain to students that because the car can hold no more than 5 people, the number of people in the car must be less than or equal to 5.

Ask:

- *What does the symbol ≤ mean?* less than or equal to
- *Is 0 + 2 less than or equal to 5?* yes
- *Is 1 + 2 less than or equal to 5?* yes
- *Is 2 + 2 less than or equal to 5?* yes
- *Is 3 + 2 less than or equal to 5?* yes
- *Is 4 + 2 less than or equal to 5?* no

Hands-On Activity 2

AL **EL** Tell students to work together to draw the bar diagram and discuss what each part of the diagram represents.
MP 1, 3, 4, 5

Ask:

- *How much does Mia's suitcase weigh without the shoes?* 35 pounds
- *What is the unknown?* the weight of her shoes
- *What symbol is used to represent less than or equal to?* ≤

An *inequality* is a mathematical sentence that compares quantities. The table shows two examples of inequalities.

Words	Symbols
x is less than two	$x < 2$
x is greater than or equal to four	$x \geq 4$

To solve an inequality means to find values for the variable that make the sentence true. You can use bar diagrams to solve inequalities.

Hands-On Activity 2

An airline charges for checked luggage that weighs more than 50 pounds. Mia's suitcase currently weighs 35 pounds and she still needs to pack her shoes. Find the maximum amount her shoes can weigh so Mia will not be charged a fee.

Step 1 In the bar diagram, write the maximum weight Mia's luggage can be without a fee. Label the weight of Mia's luggage without her shoes.

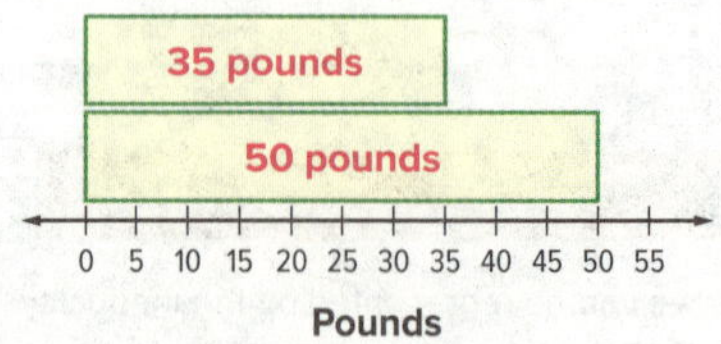

Step 2 In the bar diagram, write an x beside the bar that represents the weight of Mia's luggage.

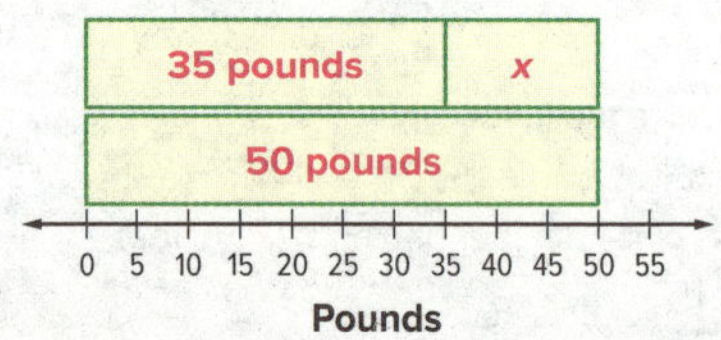

The weight of Mia's suitcase plus the weight of her shoes must be less than or equal to the maximum luggage weight.
This can be written as $35 + x \leq 50$.

Using the bar diagram, Mia's shoes cannot weigh more than $50 - 35$ or 15 pounds.

Investigate

Collaborate

Work with a partner to solve the following problems.

MP **Reason Inductively** For Exercises 1–3, assume the paper bag is weightless. Write the inequality represented by each balance. Then write the different possible numbers of cubes in the paper bag if the sides of each balance remain unlevel.

1. 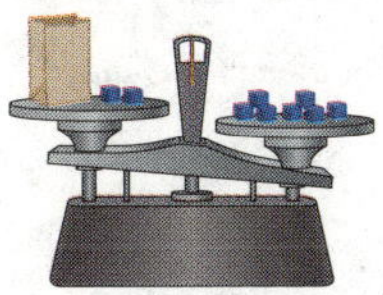

Inequality: $x + 2 < 7$

Number of Cubes: 0, 1, 2, 3, or 4

2. 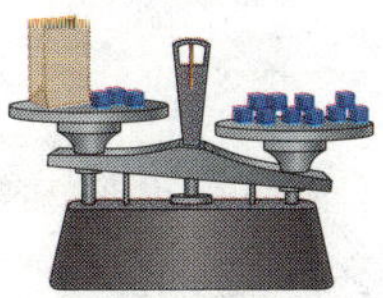

Inequality: $x + 3 < 10$

Number of Cubes: 0, 1, 2, 3, 4, 5, or 6

3. 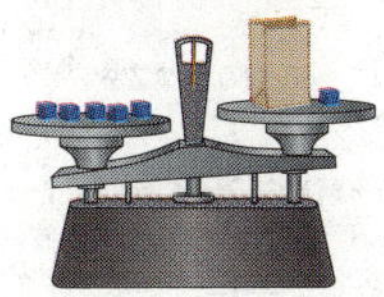

Inequality: $5 > x + 1$ or $x + 1 < 5$

Number of Cubes: 0, 1, 2, or 3

4. MP **Reason Abstractly** At an amusement park, roller coaster riders are required to be at least 48 inches tall. Last year, Myron was 42 inches tall. Complete the bar diagram to determine the number of inches x Myron needed to grow this year to be able to ride the roller coaster. Then write an inequality to represent the situation.

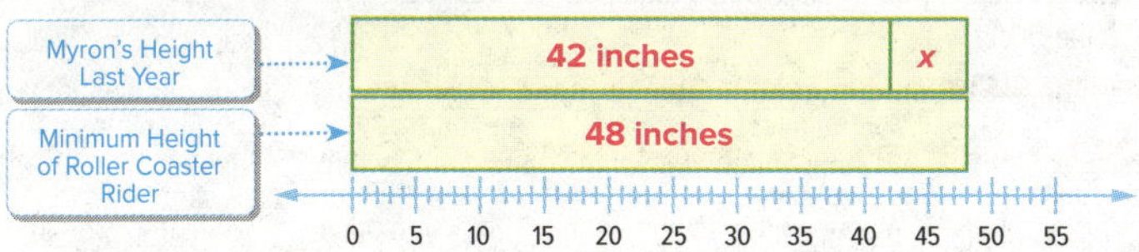

So, Myron needed to grow at least 6 inches.

Inequality: $42 + x \geq 48$

ENGAGE EXPLORE EXPLAIN ELABORATE EVALUATE

2 Collaborate

The **Investigate** and **Analyze and Reflect** sections are intended to be used as small-group investigations. The **Create** section is intended to be used as independent exercises.

Levels of Complexity

The levels of the exercises progress from 1 to 3, with Level 1 indicating the lowest level of complexity.

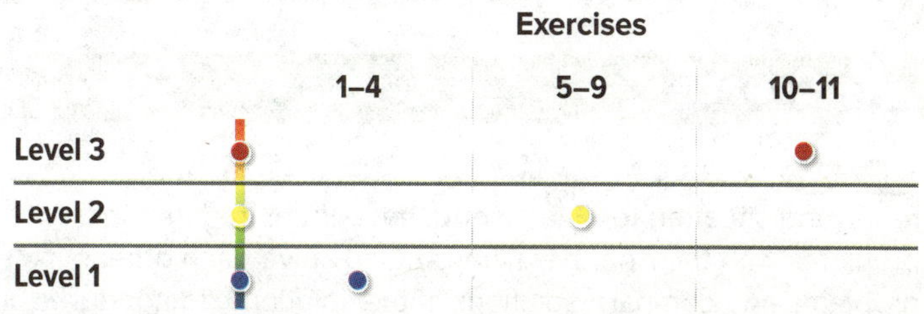

Investigate

Collaborate

AL EL **Pairs Discussion** Have students work in pairs to complete Exercises 1–4. Have them trade their solutions with another pair of students and discuss any differences. MP 1, 2, 5

BL EL **Trade-a-Problem** Have students create their own problem, similar to Exercises 1–4. Students trade their problems, solve each other's problem, and compare solutions. If the solutions do not agree, students work together to find the errors. MP 1, 2, 4

Analyze and Reflect

Collaborate

AL EL **Think-Pair-Share** Have students work in pairs. Give students one minute to think through their responses to Exercises 5–9. Have them share their responses with their partner. Then call on one student to share their response within a small group or large group discussion. MP 1, 2, 4

BL EL **Pairs Discussion** Have students work in pairs to complete Exercises 5–9. Have them trade their solutions with another pair of students and discuss any differences. MP 1, 2

Create

On Your Own

BL EL **Trade-a-Problem** After students create their own real-world situation for Exercise 10, have them trade their problems with their partner. They should solve each other's problems and compare solutions. If the solutions do not agree, students work together to find the errors. MP 1, 4

Inquiry Students should be able to answer "HOW is an inequality like an equation? How is it different?" Check for student understanding and provide guidance, if needed.

Analyze and Reflect

Collaborate

Work with a partner to circle the correct inequality for each situation. The first one is done for you.

	Real-World Situation	Inequalities	
	Yolanda wants to score at least 84% on the next history test.	$x \leq 84$	$x \geq 84$ (circled)
5.	To see a certain movie, you must be at least 13 years old.	$n \leq 13$	$n \geq 13$ (circled)
6.	Kai has \$4.99 left on a music download gift card. She has a download costing \$1.99 in her online shopping cart. How much money does Kai have left to spend?	$x + 1.99 \leq 4.99$ (circled)	$x + 1.99 > 4.99$
7.	In some states, teens must be at least 16 years old to obtain a driver's license.	$x < 16$ $x \leq 16$	$x > 16$ $x \geq 16$ (circled)
8.	The Walter family budgets a maximum amount of \$125 per week for groceries. Mr. Walter already spent \$40. How much more can the Walter family spend on groceries?	$x + 40 < 125$ $x + 40 \leq 125$ (circled)	$x + 40 > 125$ $x + 40 \geq 125$
9.	Miles pays \$30 for a ticket to an amusement park. He cannot spend more than \$50. How much more money can Miles spend at the amusement park?	$x + 30 < 50$ $x + 30 \leq 50$ (circled)	$x + 30 > 50$ $x + 30 \geq 50$

Create

On Your Own

10. MP **Model with Mathematics** Write a real-world situation that could be represented by $x + 20 \geq 50$.

Sample answer: Josefina wants to save at least \$50 for a school jacket. If she has saved \$20, how much more does Josefina have to save?

11. Inquiry HOW is an inequality like an equation? How is it different?

Sample answer: An inequality is like an equation because it is a comparison of two quantities. In an equation, the two quantities are equal. In an inequality, one quantity may be less than or greater than the other quantity.

PLAN ONLINE

PD | RtI | Watch | Worksheets | Vocab | Tutor | Tools | Check | English Learners | Sketchpad

PRESENT

IWB An Interactive Whiteboard Ready presentation is available for each lesson in the chapter.

Expressions and Equations

Lesson 6

Solve Inequalities by Addition or Subtraction

Real-World Link

Mail A first class stamp can be used for letters and packages weighing thirteen ounces or less. Fisher is mailing pictures to his grandmother, and only has a first class stamp. His envelope weighs 2 ounces. Follow the steps to determine how much the pictures can weigh so that Fisher can use the stamp.

Step 1 Let x represent the weight of the pictures. Write and solve an equation to find the maximum weight of the pictures.

weight of the envelope		weight of the pictures		maximum weight of the package
2	+	x	=	13

Solve for x.

So, the maximum weight of the pictures is 11 ounces.

Step 2 Replace the equals sign in your equation with the less than or equal to symbol, ≤.

$2 + x \leq 13$

Refer to Step 2. Name three possible values of x that will result in a true sentence.

Sample answer: 9, 10, and 11

Which MP **Mathematical Practices** did you use? Shade the circle(s) that applies.

1. Persevere with Problems
2. Reason Abstractly
3. Construct an Argument
4. Model with Mathematics
5. Use Math Tools
6. Attend to Precision
7. Make Use of Structure
8. Use Repeated Reasoning

Essential Question

WHAT does it mean to say two quantities are equal?

Vocabulary

Subtraction Property of Inequality
Addition Property of Inequality
inequality

Content Standards
7.EE.4, 7.EE.4b

MP **Mathematical Practices**
1, 2, 3, 4

Focus narrowing the scope

Objective Solve inequalities by using the Addition and Subtraction Properties of Inequality. 7.EE.4, 7.EE.4b

Coherence connecting within and across grades

Previous Students solved one-step addition and subtraction equations.

Now Students solve one-step addition and subtraction inequalities.

Next Students will solve one-step multiplication and division inequalities.

Rigor pursuing concepts, fluency, and applications

See the Levels of Complexity chart on page 501.

ENGAGE EXPLORE EXPLAIN ELABORATE EVALUATE

1 Launch the Lesson

Ideas for Use

You may wish to launch the lesson using a whole group, small group, think-pair-share activity, or independent activity.

BL EL **Find the Fib** Have students work in pairs. Each student should write a problem that is similar to the Real-World Link and supply three possible solutions to the problem. Two should be correct and one incorrect. The job of each partner is to determine which one is incorrect. MP 1, 3

Alternate Strategy

AL Review the symbols used for inequalities and what they mean. Have students come up with key words or phrases that can be used for each symbol. Then ask them how they know that the ≤ symbol should be used for the problem in the Real-World Link. MP 1, 2, 3

ENGAGE EXPLORE **EXPLAIN** ELABORATE EVALUATE

2 Teach the Concept

Ask the scaffolded questions for each example to differentiate instruction.

Example

IWB

1. Solve an inequality.

AL
- *What is the variable?* x
- *What number is on the same side of the inequality sign as the variable?* 3
- *What operation is used between x and 3?* addition
- *How will you undo adding 3?* subtract 3 from each side of the inequality

OL
- *Does subtracting 3 from each side of the inequality change the solution of the inequality?* no
- *What is the first step to solving the inequality?* Subtract 3 from each side of the inequality.
- *Can 7.5 be a solution? Explain.* yes; It is greater than 7.

BL
- *Is 7 part of the solution? Explain.* no; The inequality is greater than, not greater than or equal to.
- *How can you check that the solution is correct?* Replace x with a number greater than 7 in the original inequality, simplify, and determine if the resulting statement is true.

Need Another Example?
Solve $x + 5 > 12$. $x > 7$

Work Zone

Key Concept Solve Inequalities

Words You can solve inequalities by using the **Addition Property of Inequalities** and the **Subtraction Property of Inequalities**. When you add or subtract the same number from each side of an inequality, the inequality remains true.

Symbols For all numbers a, b, and c,

1. if $a > b$, then $a + c > b + c$ and $a - c > b - c$.
2. if $a < b$, then $a + c < b + c$ and $a - c < b - c$.

Examples

$$\begin{array}{rr} 2 < & 4 \\ +3 & +3 \\ \hline 5 < & 7 \end{array} \qquad \begin{array}{rr} 6 > & 3 \\ -4 & -4 \\ \hline 2 > & -1 \end{array}$$

An **inequality** is a mathematical sentence that compares quantities. Solving an inequality means finding values for the variable that make the inequality true.

The table below gives some examples of the words you might use when describing different inequalities.

Inequalities				
Words	• is less than • is fewer than	• is greater than • is more than • exceeds	• is less than or equal to • is no more than • is at most	• is greater than or equal to • is no less than • is at least
Symbols	$<$	$>$	$\leq$	$\geq$

Examples

Tutor

1. Solve $x + 3 > 10$.

$x + 3 > 10$ Write the inequality.

$-3 \quad -3$ Subtract 3 from each side.

$x > 7$ Simplify.

Therefore, the solution is $x > 7$.

You can check this solution by substituting a number greater than 7 into the original inequality. Try using 8.

Check $x + 3 > 10$ Write the inequality.

$8 + 3 \overset{?}{>} 10$ Replace x with 8. Is this sentence true?

$11 > 10$ This is a true statement. ✓

Expressions and Equations

2. Solve $-6 \geq n - 5$.

$-6 \geq n - 5$ Write the inequality.

$\underline{+5 \quad\quad +5}$ Add 5 to each side.

$-1 \geq n$ Simplify.

The solution is $-1 \geq n$ or $n \leq -1$.

You can check this solution by substituting -1 or a number less than -1 into the original inequality.

Got it? Do these problems to find out.

Solve each inequality.

a. $a - 3 < 8$ **b.** $0.4 + y \geq 7$

Show your work.

a. $a < 11$

b. $y \geq 6.6$

Example

Tutor

3. Solve $a + \frac{1}{2} < 2$. Graph the solution set on a number line.

$a + \frac{1}{2} < 2$ Write the inequality.

$\underline{-\frac{1}{2} \quad -\frac{1}{2}}$ Subtract $\frac{1}{2}$ from each side.

$a < 1\frac{1}{2}$ Simplify.

The solution is $a < 1\frac{1}{2}$. Check your solution.

Graph the solution.

Place an open dot at $1\frac{1}{2}$. Draw a line and an arrow to the left.

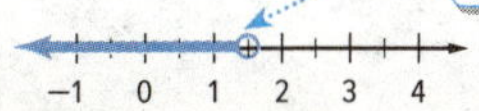

Open and Closed Dots

When graphing inequalities, an open dot is used when the value should not be included in the solution, as with > and < inequalities. A closed dot indicates the value is included in the solution, as with ≤ and ≥ inequalities.

Got it? Do these problems to find out.

Solve each inequality. Graph the solution set on the number line provided.

c. $h + 4 > 4$ **d.** $x - 6 \leq 4$

c. $h > 0$

d. $x \leq 10$

IWB

Examples

2. Solve an inequality.

AL
- *What number is on the same side of the inequality sign as the variable?* 5
- *What operation is used between n and 5?* subtraction
- *How will you undo subtracting 5?* Add 5 to each side.
- *What is $5 + (-6)$?* -1

OL
- *What is the first step to solve the inequality?* Add 5 to each side.
- *Is -1 one of the solutions to the inequality? Explain.* yes; when you substitute -1 in for n, you get $-6 \geq -6$, which is a true statement.
- *Name one other possible solution.* Sample answer: -5

BL
- *Which is easier to understand, $-1 \geq n$ or $n \leq -1$? Explain.* See students' work.

Need Another Example?

Solve $-8 \geq y + 3$. $-11 \geq y$ or $y \leq -11$

3. Solve and graph an inequality.

AL
- *What is the first step to solve the inequality?* Subtract $\frac{1}{2}$ from each side.
- *Does the inequality symbol contain an "or equal to"?* no
- *Will the circle on the graph be open or closed?* open

OL
- *To graph the solution on a number line, do you draw an open dot or a closed dot for the inequality? Explain.* Since the sign is < and not ≤, you use an open dot because $1\frac{1}{2}$ is not included in the solution.
- *Does the arrow point to the right or to the left?* left

BL
- *Since the values are less than $1\frac{1}{2}$, why isn't the arrow started at 1?* Sample answer: The solution includes any values less than $1\frac{1}{2}$, this could include numbers like $1\frac{1}{2}$

Need Another Example?

Solve $n + \frac{3}{4} > 2$. Graph the solution set on a number line.

$n > 1\frac{1}{4}$

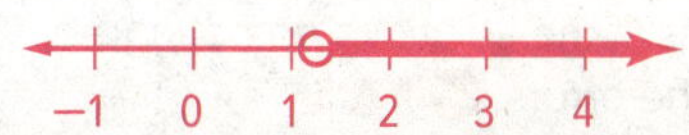

Example

IWB

4. Write and interpret inequalities.

AL • *What do you need to find?* The most Dylan can spend on games.

• *What word or phrase indicates which inequality symbol to use?* the most he can spend

• *What inequality symbol will you use?* $\leq$

OL • *What inequality can be used to find the amount of money he can spend on games without spending more than $18?* $5.5 + x \leq 18$

BL • *If each game costs $0.75, what is maximum number of games Dylan can play?* 16

Need Another Example?

Jerome took $20 to the store to buy a book and some CDs. If he buys a book that costs $4.50, write and solve an inequality to find the most he could spend on CDs. Interpret the solution. $4.50 + x \leq 20$; $x \leq 15.50$; The most Jerome can spend on CDs is $15.50.

Guided Practice

Formative Assessment Use these exercises to assess students' understanding of the concepts in this lesson.

If some of your students are not ready for assignments, use the differentiated activities below.

AL EL **Paired Heads Together** Have students work in pairs to solve Exercises 1–3. Students complete the first exercise, then turn to their partner and discuss their answers, paying particular attention to the graphs. Students should check to make sure the correct dot and arrow direction were used. Students repeat this process for Exercises 2 and 3. MP 1, 2, 5

BL EL **Trade-a-Problem** Have students create their own problem, similar to Exercise 3, using either addition or subtraction, and requiring a graph as part of the answer. Challenge students to use fractions with unlike denominators in their problems. Students trade their problems, solve each other's problem, and compare solutions. If the solutions do not agree, students work together to find the errors. MP 1, 4, 5

Write Inequalities

Inequalities can be used to represent real-world situations. You will want to first identify a variable to represent the unknown value.

Real World Example

Tutor

4. Dylan has $18 to ride go-karts and play games at the state fair. Suppose the go-karts cost $5.50. Write and solve an inequality to find the most he can spend on games.

Words	Cost of go-kart	plus	cost of games	must be less than or equal to	total amount.
Symbols	Let x = the cost of the games.				
Inequality	5.5	+	x	$\leq$	18

$5.5 + x \leq 18$ Write the inequality. (5.50 = 5.5)

$-5.5 \quad -5.5$ Subtract 5.5 from each side.

$x \leq 12.5$ Simplify.

So, the most Dylan can spend on games is $12.50.

Guided Practice

Check

Solve each inequality. Graph the solution set on a number line. (Examples 1–3)

1. $6 + h \geq 12$ $h \geq 6$

2. $14 + t > 5$ $t > -9$

3. An elevator can hold 2,800 pounds or less. Write and solve an inequality that describes how much more weight the elevator can hold if it is currently holding 2,375 pounds. Interpret the solution. (Example 4)

$x + 2{,}375 \leq 2{,}800$; $x \leq 425$; The elevator can hold 425 more pounds or less.

4. **Building on the Essential Question** Explain when you would use addition and when you would use subtraction to solve an inequality. Sample answer: Use the opposite operation as what appears in the inequality.

Rate Yourself!

Are you ready to move on? Shade the section that applies.

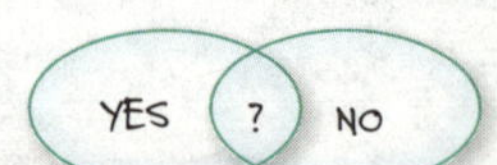

For more help, go online to access a Personal Tutor.

Tutor

Name ______________________ My Homework ______________________

Independent Practice

Go online for Step-by-Step Solutions eHelp

Solve each inequality. (Examples 1 and 2)

1. $h - 16 \leq -24$ $h \leq -8$
2. $y + 6 \geq -13$ $y \geq -19$
3. $-3 < n - 8$ $5 < n$

Show your work.

4. $3 \leq m + 1.4$ $1.6 \leq m$
5. $x + 0.7 > -0.3$ $x > -1$
6. $w - 8 \geq 5.6$ $w \geq 13.6$

Solve each inequality. Graph the solution set on a number line. (Example 3)

7. $m + 5 \geq -1$ $m \geq -6$

8. $-11 > t + 7$ $-18 > t$ or $t < -18$

MP **Reason Abstractly** **Write an inequality and solve each problem. For Exercises 11 and 12, interpret the solution.** (Example 4)

9. Four more than a number is more than 13.

Inequality: $n + 4 > 13$

Solution: $n > 9$

10. The sum of a number and 19 is at least 8.2.

Inequality: $n + 19 \geq 8.2$

Solution: $n \geq -10.8$

11. The high school soccer team can have no more than 26 players. Write and solve an inequality to determine how many more players can make the team if the coach has already chosen 17 players.

Inequality: $p + 17 \leq 26$ Solution: $p \leq 9$

Interpretation: Nine additional players or fewer can make the team.

12. Lalo has 1,500 minutes per month on his cell phone plan. How many more minutes can he use if he has already talked for 785 minutes?

Inequality: $785 + m \leq 1{,}500$ Solution: $m \leq 715$

Interpretation: Lalo can talk for an additional 715 minutes or less.

ENGAGE EXPLORE **EXPLAIN** **ELABORATE** **EVALUATE**

3 Practice and Apply

Independent Practice and Extra Practice

The Independent Practice pages are meant to be used as the homework assignment. The Extra Practice page can be used for additional reinforcement or as a second-day assignment.

Levels of Complexity

The levels of the exercises progress from 1 to 3, with Level 1 indicating the lowest level of complexity.

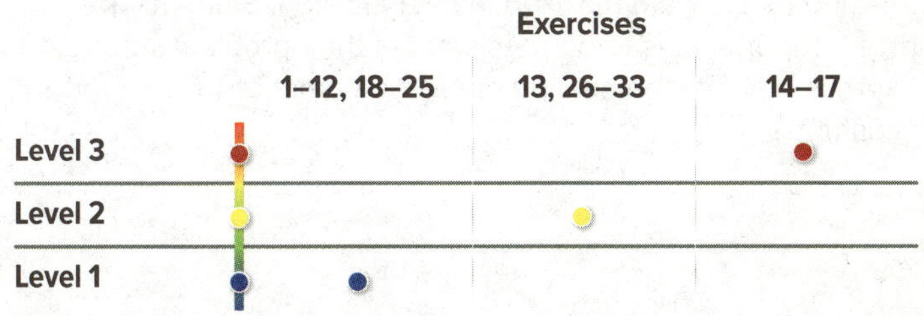

Suggested Assignments

You can use the table below that includes exercises of all complexity levels to select appropriate exercises for your students' needs.

Differentiated Homework Options		
AL	Approaching Level	1–15, 17, 32, 33
OL	On Level	1–11 odd, 13–15, 17, 32, 33
BL	Beyond Level	13–17, 32, 33

McGraw Hill Education **ALEKS**® can provide additional remediation support with personalized instruction and practice.

Watch Out!

Common Error When working with fractions or decimals, student may neglect to consider the signs. Remind students that signed rational numbers follow the same rules as signed integers. Emphasize the importance of checking their answers.

MP MATHEMATICAL PRACTICES	
Emphasis On	**Exercise(s)**
1 Make sense of problems and persevere in solving them.	16
2 Reason abstractly and quantitatively.	9–12
3 Construct viable arguments and critique the reasoning of others.	14, 17
4 Model with mathematics.	15, 21, 22

Mathematical Practices 1, 3, and 4 are aspects of mathematical thinking that are emphasized in every lesson. Students are given opportunities to be persistent in their problem solving, to express their reasoning, and apply mathematics to real-world situations.

Formative Assessment

Use this activity as a closing formative assessment before dismissing students from your class.

TICKET Out the Door

Write an inequality on the board, such as $x + 5 < 12$. Draw four different graphs labeled A–D, with only one being the correct graph of the solution set for the inequality. Ask students to write the letter of the graph that shows the correct answer on a small piece of paper and hand it to you as they leave the room. See students' work.

13. Refer to the diagram below.

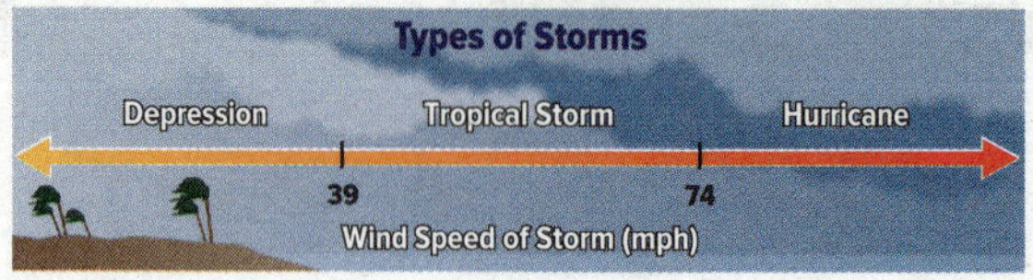

a. A hurricane has winds that are at least 74 miles per hour. Suppose a tropical storm has winds that are 42 miles per hour. Write and solve an inequality to find how much the winds must increase before the storm becomes a hurricane.

Inequality: $42 + x \geq 74$ Solution: $x \geq 32$

b. A *major storm* has wind speeds that are at least 110 miles per hour. Write and solve an inequality that describes how much greater these wind speeds are than the slowest hurricane.

Inequality: $74 + y \geq 110$ Solution: $y \geq 36$

H.O.T. Problems Higher Order Thinking

14. MP **Reason Inductively** Compare and contrast the solutions of $a - 3 = 15$ and $a - 3 \geq 15$. Sample answer: $a - 3 = 15$ only has one solution, $a = 18$; $a - 3 \geq 15$ has an infinite number of solutions.

15. MP **Model with Mathematics** Write an addition inequality for the solution set graphed below.

Sample answer: $x + 3 < 25$

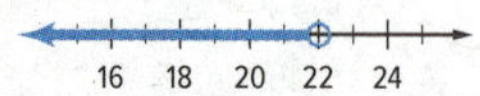

16. MP **Persevere with Problems** Solve $x + b > c$ for x.

$x > c - b$

17. MP **Reason Inductively** Does the graph shown at the right show the solution set of the inequality $x + 3 \geq 2$? If not, explain how you would change the graph to show the actual solution set. no; Sample answer: The solution is $x \geq -1$, so the graph should have a closed dot above -1 and the arrow should point to the right, not the left.

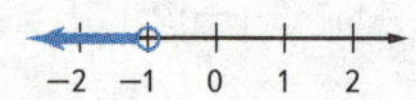

Name ________________ My Homework ________________

Extra Practice

Solve each inequality.

18. $10 < b - 8$ $18 < b$

Homework Help

$10 < b - 8$
$+8 \quad +8$
$18 < b$

19. $1.2 + m \leq 5.5$ $m \leq 4.3$

20. $c - 1\frac{1}{4} > -2\frac{1}{2}$ $c > -1\frac{1}{4}$

MP Model with Mathematics **Solve each inequality. Graph the solution set on a number line.**

21. $-21 < a - 16$ $-5 < a$

22. $t - 6.2 < 4$ $t < 10.2$

Write an inequality and solve each problem.

23. Eight less than a number is less than 10.

Inequality: $n - 8 < 10$

Solution: $n < 18$

24. The difference between a number and $21\frac{1}{2}$ is no more than $14\frac{1}{4}$.

Inequality: $n - 21\frac{1}{2} \leq 14\frac{1}{4}$

Solution: $n \leq 35\frac{3}{4}$

25. There were a total of 125 cars at a car dealership. A salesperson sold 68 of the cars in one month. Write and solve an inequality that describes how many more cars, at most, the salesman has left to sell. Interpret the solution.

Inequality: $68 + c \leq 125$ Solution: $c \leq 57$

Interpretation: The salesman has 57 cars or less left to sell.

Copy and Solve **Solve each inequality. Graph the solution set on a number line. Show your work on a separate sheet of paper.** 26–31. See students' work for number lines.

26. $n - \frac{1}{5} \leq \frac{3}{10}$ $n \leq \frac{1}{2}$

27. $6 > x + 3\frac{1}{3}$ $2\frac{2}{3} > x$ or $x < 2\frac{2}{3}$

28. $c + 1\frac{1}{4} < 5$ $c < 3\frac{3}{4}$

29. $9 \leq m - 2\frac{1}{5}$ $m \geq 11\frac{1}{5}$

30. $\frac{3}{4} + d > 4\frac{1}{2}$ $d > 3\frac{3}{4}$

31. $-\frac{7}{8} \leq n + 3\frac{5}{16}$ $n \geq -4\frac{3}{16}$

Create Your Own Homework Online

eSolutionsManual™ can be used to create worksheets for the suggested assignments on page 501, or create your own worksheets for differentiated homework or review.

Power Up! Test Practice

Exercises 32 and 33 prepare students for more rigorous thinking needed for the state assessment.

32.

This test item requires students to analyze and solve complex real-world problems through the use of mathematical tools and models.	
Depth of Knowledge	DOK3
Content Standard	7.EE.4, 7.EE.4b
Mathematical Practice	MP1, MP3, MP4
Online Experience	Students will graph on a number line and type their responses in the boxes.
Scoring Rubric	
3 points	Students correctly write, solve, graph, and interpret the solution to an inequality.
2 points	Students correctly complete three of the four parts.
1 point	Students correctly complete two of the four parts.

33.

This test item requires students to explain and apply mathematical concepts and solve problems with precision, while making use of structure.	
Depth of Knowledge	DOK1
Content Standard	7.EE.4b
Mathematical Practice	MP1
Online Experience	Students will be required to click on the bubbles to select all answers that are correct.
Scoring Rubric	
1 point	Students correctly answer each part of the question.

Power Up! Test Practice

32. Joaquin can send up to 250 text messages each month. So far this month, he has sent 141 text messages. Let t represent the number of text messages Joaquin can send during the rest of the month.

Write an inequality to model the situation $t + 141 \leq 250$

Solve the inequality for t. $t \leq 109$

Graph the solution on the number line.

Interpret the solution to the inequality. Explain your reasoning.

Sample answer: The solution $t \leq 109$ means that Joaquin can send up to 109 more text messages this month and stay within his limit.

33. Which inequality has the solution set shown in the number line below? Select all that apply.

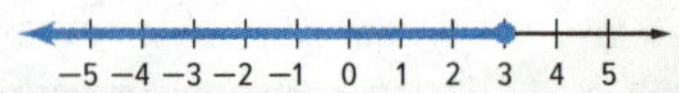

- [x] $x + 4 \leq 7$
- [ ] $12 > x + 9$
- [ ] $x + 1 \leq 2$
- [x] $-7 \geq x - 10$

Spiral Review

Solve each equation. Then graph each solution on the number line below. 6.EE.6

34. $x + 2 = 1$ **−1**

35. $x - 1 = -5$ **−4**

36. $2x = 10$ **5**

37. $-2x = 4$ **−2**

38. $\frac{x}{2} = 1$ **2**

39. $\frac{x}{-2} = 3$ **−6**

PLAN ONLINE

PD | RtI | Watch | Worksheets | Vocab | Tutor | Tools | Check | English Learners | Sketchpad

PRESENT

IWB

An Interactive Whiteboard Ready presentation is available for each lesson in the chapter.

Lesson 7

Solve Inequalities by Multiplication or Division

Real-World Link

Science An astronaut in a space suit weighs about 300 pounds on Earth, but only 50 pounds on the Moon.

weight on Earth		weight on Moon
300 lb	>	50 lb

1. If the astronaut and space suit each weighed half as much, would the inequality still be true?

$$\frac{300}{2} > \frac{50}{2}$$ Divide each side by 2.

$$150 > 25$$

Is the inequality still true? Circle yes or no.

Yes (circled) No

2. Is the weight of one astronaut greater on Pluto or Earth? Would the weight of 5 astronauts be greater on Pluto or on Earth? Explain by using an inequality.
Earth; Earth; 300 > 67, so 5(300) > 5(67)

Location	Weight of Astronaut (lb)
Earth	300
Moon	50
Pluto	67
Jupiter	796

3. Is the weight of one astronaut greater on Jupiter or on Earth? Would the weight of 5 astronauts be greater on Jupiter or on Earth? Explain by using an inequality.
Jupiter; Jupiter; 796 > 300, so 5(796) > 5(300)

Which MP **Mathematical Practices** did you use? Shade the circle(s) that applies.

1. Persevere with Problems
2. Reason Abstractly
3. Construct an Argument
4. Model with Mathematics
5. Use Math Tools
6. Attend to Precision
7. Make Use of Structure
8. Use Repeated Reasoning

Essential Question

WHAT does it mean to say two quantities are equal?

Vocabulary

Multiplication Property of Inequality
Division Property of Inequality

Content Standards
7.EE.4, 7.EE.4b

MP Mathematical Practices
1, 2, 3, 4, 7

Focus narrowing the scope

Objective Solve inequalities by using the Multiplication or Division Properties of Inequality. 7.EE.4, 7.EE.4b

Coherence connecting within and across grades

Previous Students solved and graphed one-step addition and subtraction inequalities.

Now Students solve and graph one-step multiplication and division inequalities

Next Students will solve two-step inequalities

Rigor pursuing concepts, fluency, and applications

See the Levels of Complexity chart on page 509.

ENGAGE EXPLORE EXPLAIN ELABORATE EVALUATE

1 Launch the Lesson

Ideas for Use

You may wish to launch the lesson using a whole group, small group, think-pair-share activity, or independent activity.

BL EL **Pairs Discussions** Have students work in pairs. Ask students to extend the Real-World Link by comparing the weights of an astronaut on the moon and on Earth by using an inequality. Then have them write another inequality after multiplying the weights by −2. Pairs should discuss what happened, make other comparisons, and then make a conjecture about multiplying by a negative number. Have them trade their conjectures with another pair of students and discuss any differences. MP 1, 2, 7

ENGAGE EXPLORE **EXPLAIN** ELABORATE EVALUATE

2 Teach the Concept

Ask the scaffolded questions for each example to differentiate instruction.

Examples

IWB

1. Solve an inequality.

AL
- *What is the variable?* x
- *What number is on the same side of the inequality sign as the variable?* 8
- *What operation is used between x and 8?* multiplication
- *What operation will undo multiplication?* division

OL
- *If you were solving the equation $8x = 40$, what would be your first step?* Divide each side by 8.
- *Based on that, what is the first step to solve this inequality?* Divide each side by 8.

BL
- *How can you check that the solution is correct?* Replace x with 5 or a number less than 5 in the original inequality, simplify, and determine if the resulting statement is true.

Need Another Example?
Solve $5x > 30$. $x > 6$

2. Solve an inequality.

AL
- *What number is on the same side of the inequality sign as the variable?* 2
- *What operation is used between d and 2?* division
- *What operation will undo division?* multiplication

OL
- *What is the first step to solve the inequality?* Multiply each side of the inequality by 2.

BL
- *Are the statements $d > 14$ and $14 < d$ equivalent? Explain.* yes; Sample answer: They both state that the solution is more than 14.

Need Another Example?
Solve $3 \geq \frac{h}{4}$. $12 \geq h$ or $h \leq 12$

Key Concept

Multiplication and Division Properties of Inequality, Positive Number

Words The **Multiplication Property of Inequality** and the **Division Property of Inequality** state that an inequality remains true when you multiply or divide each side of an inequality by a positive number.

Symbols For all numbers a, b, and c, where $c > 0$,
1. if $a > b$, then $ac > bc$ and $\frac{a}{c} > \frac{b}{c}$.
2. if $a < b$, then $ac < bc$ and $\frac{a}{c} < \frac{b}{c}$.

These properties are also true for $a \geq b$ and $a \leq b$.

Work Zone

STOP and Reflect
What does the inequality $c > 0$ mean? Explain below.

It means that c is a positive number.

You can solve inequalities by using the Multiplication Property of Inequality and the Division Property of Inequality.

Examples

Tutor

1. Solve $8x \leq 40$.

$8x \leq 40$ Write the inequality.

$\frac{8x}{8} \leq \frac{40}{8}$ Divide each side by 8.

$x \leq 5$ Simplify.

The solution is $x \leq 5$. You can check this solution by substituting 5 or a number less than 5 into the inequality.

2. Solve $\frac{d}{2} > 7$.

$\frac{d}{2} > 7$ Write the inequality.

$2\left(\frac{d}{2}\right) > 2(7)$ Multiply each side by 2.

$d > 14$ Simplify.

The solution is $d > 14$. You can check this solution by substituting a number greater than 14 into the inequality.

Got it? Do these problems to find out.

a. $4x < 40$ **b.** $6 \geq \frac{x}{7}$

Show your work.

a. $x < 10$

b. $42 \geq x$ or $x \leq 42$

Multiplication and Division Properties of Inequality, Negative Number

Key Concept

Words When you multiply or divide each side of an inequality by a negative number, the inequality symbol must be reversed for the inequality to remain true.

Symbols For all numbers a, b, and c, where $c < 0$,

1. if $a > b$, then $ac < bc$ and $\frac{a}{c} < \frac{b}{c}$.
2. if $a < b$, then $ac > bc$ and $\frac{a}{c} > \frac{b}{c}$.

Examples

$7 > 1$ | $-4 < 16$
$-2(7) < -2(1)$ Reverse the symbols. $\frac{-4}{-4} > \frac{16}{-4}$
$-14 < -2$ | $1 > -4$

These properties are also true for $a \geq b$ and $a \leq b$.

STOP and Reflect

What does the inequality $c < 0$ mean? Expain below.

It means that c is a negative number.

Examples

Tutor

3. Solve $-2g < 10$. Graph the solution set on a number line.

$-2g < 10$ Write the inequality.

$\frac{-2g}{-2} > \frac{10}{-2}$ Divide each side by -2 and reverse the symbol.

Simplify.

$g > -5$

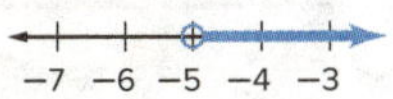

4. Solve $\frac{x}{-3} \leq 4$. Graph the solution set on a number line.

$\frac{x}{-3} \leq 4$ Write the inequality.

$-3\left(\frac{x}{-3}\right) \geq -3(4)$ Multiply each side by -3 and reverse the symbol.

$x \geq -12$ Simplify.

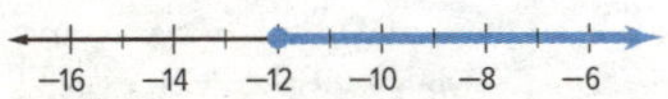

Got it? Do these problems to find out.

c. $\frac{k}{-2} < 9$

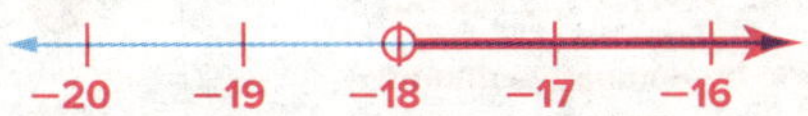

c. $k > -18$

Examples

IWB

3. Solve a multiplication inequality.

AL
- *What number is on the same side of the inequality sign as the variable?* -2
- *What operation is used between g and -2?* multiplication
- *How will you undo multiplying by -2?* divide each side of the inequality by -2

OL
- *What is the first step to solve the inequality?* Divide each side of the inequality by -2.
- *Since you are dividing by a negative number, what do you need to do?* Reverse the direction of the inequality symbol.

BL
- *Do you draw an open or closed dot on the graph of the solution set? Explain.* open; When the symbol is just $>$ or $<$, the dot is open.

Need Another Example?

Solve $-4x \leq 4$. Graph the solution set on a number line.

See Answer Appendix.

4. Solve a division inequality.

AL
- *What is the first step to solve the inequality?* Multiply each side by -3.
- *Since you are multiplying by a negative number, what do you need to do?* Reverse the direction of the inequality symbol.

OL
- *Do you need to reverse the inequality symbol? Explain.* Yes; since you are multiplying both sides by a negative number, you need to reverse the symbol.
- *What is the new symbol?* $\geq$

BL
- *Consider the inequality $\frac{x}{6} \geq -4$. Since you will be multiplying 6 and -4, do you need to reverse the inequality symbol when solving the inequality? Explain.* No; you only need to reverse the symbol when both sides are multiplied by a negative number.

Need Another Example?

Solve $\frac{x}{-4} > -5$. Graph the solution set on a number line.

See Answer Appendix.

Example

IWB

5. **Write and interpret inequalities.**

AL • *What do you need to find?* The number of hours Ling needs to work to make at least $120

• *What word or phrase indicates which inequality symbol to use?* at least

• *What inequality symbol will you use?* $\geq$

OL • *What inequality can be used to find the number of hours Ling must work to earn at least $120?* $8x \geq 120$

BL • *Do you need to reverse the inequality symbol? Explain.* No, because you are not dividing both sides by a negative number.

Need Another Example?

A plate weighs $\frac{1}{4}$ pound. A shelf can hold at most 20 pounds. Write and solve an inequality to find how many plates the shelf can hold. Interpret the solution. $\frac{1}{4}x \leq 20$; $x \leq 80$; The shelf can hold at most 80 plates.

Guided Practice

Formative Assessment Use these exercises to assess students' understanding of the concepts in this lesson.

If some of your students are not ready for assignments, use the differentiated activities below.

AL EL **Pairs Check** Have students work in pairs to solve Exercise 1. One partner solves the problem while the other coaches, paying particular attention to multiplying or dividing by a negative number. Students switch roles for the next two problems. After the three problems are done, the pairs check their answers with another pair. MP 1, 2, 7

BL EL **Pairs Consult** Have students work in pairs to write a one-step inequality about the graph shown. Then pairs write a real-world problem for the inequality. Pairs trade their problems to check that the solutions do apply to the real-world problems written. MP 1, 2, 4

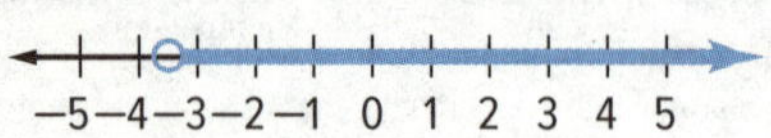

Real World

Example

Tutor

5. **Ling earns $8 per hour working at the zoo. Write and solve an inequality that can be used to find how many hours she must work in a week to earn at least $120. Interpret the solution.**

Words	Amount earned per hour	times	number of hours	is at least	amount earned each week.
Variable	Let x represent the number of hours.				
Inequality	8	$\cdot$	x	$\geq$	120

$8x \geq 120$ Write the inequality.

$\frac{8x}{8} \geq \frac{120}{8}$ Divide each side by 8.

$x \geq 15$ Simplify.

So, Ling must work at least 15 hours.

Guided Practice

Check

Solve each inequality. Graph the solution set on a number line. (Examples 1–4)

1. $-3n \leq -22$ $n \geq 7\frac{1}{3}$

2. $\frac{t}{-4} < -11$ $t > 44$

3. At a baseball game you can get a single hot dog for $2. You have $10 to spend. Write and solve an inequality to find the number of hot dogs you can buy. Interpret the solution. (Example 5) $2x \leq 10$; $x \leq 5$; You can buy five hot dogs or fewer.

4. **Building on the Essential Question** Explain when you should reverse the inequality symbol when solving an inequality. Sample answer: Reverse the symbol when multiplying or dividing by a negative number.

Rate Yourself!

How confident are you about solving multiplication and division inequalities? Check the box that applies.

For more help, go online to access a Personal Tutor.

Tutor

Name ______________________ My Homework ______________________

Independent Practice

Go online for Step-by-Step Solutions eHelp

Solve each inequality. (Examples 1 and 2)

1. $6y < 18$ $y < 3$
2. $-3s \geq 33$ $s \leq -11$
3. $60 \leq \frac{m}{3}$ $180 \leq m$

Show your work.

4. $\frac{t}{-2} < 6$ $t > -12$
5. $\frac{m}{-14} \leq -4$ $m \geq 56$
6. $-56 \leq -8x$ $x \leq 7$
7. $12n \leq 54$ $n \leq 4.5$
8. $\frac{h}{9} > \frac{1}{4}$ $h > 2\frac{1}{4}$
9. $\frac{w}{-5} \geq 9$ $w \leq -45$

Solve each inequality. Graph the solution set on a number line. (Examples 3 and 4)

10. $4x \geq 36$ $x \geq 9$

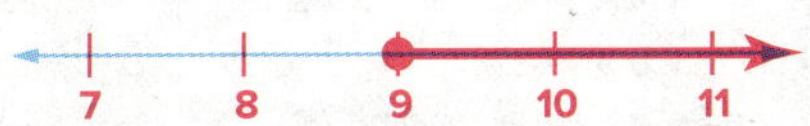

11. $20 < 5t$ $4 < t$

12. $\frac{s}{-6} > -16$ $s < 96$

13. $\frac{x}{-4} \geq 8$ $x \leq -32$

14. A pool charges $4 each visit, or you can buy a membership. Write and solve an inequality to find how many times a person should use the pool so that a membership is less expensive than paying each time. Interpret the solution. (Example 5)

Inequality: $4x > 100$ Solution: $x > 25$

Interpretation: You would need to use the pool more than 25 times in three months.

ENGAGE EXPLORE EXPLAIN ELABORATE EVALUATE

3 Practice and Apply

Independent Practice and Extra Practice

The Independent Practice pages are meant to be used as the homework assignment. The Extra Practice page can be used for additional reinforcement or as a second-day assignment.

Levels of Complexity

The levels of the exercises progress from 1 to 3, with Level 1 indicating the lowest level of complexity.

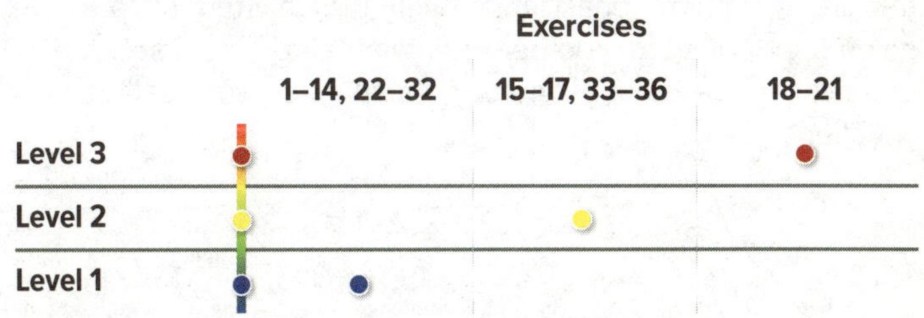

Suggested Assignments

You can use the table below that includes exercises of all complexity levels to select appropriate exercises for your students' needs.

Differentiated Homework Options		
AL	Approaching Level	1–15, 17, 18, 20, 35, 36
OL	On Level	1–13 odd, 15–18, 20, 35, 36
BL	Beyond Level	15–21, 35, 36

McGraw Hill Education ALEKS® can provide additional remediation support with personalized instruction and practice.

MATHEMATICAL PRACTICES

Emphasis On	Exercise(s)
1 Make sense of problems and persevere in solving them.	19, 21
2 Reason abstractly and quantitatively.	32
3 Construct viable arguments and critique the reasoning of others.	15, 20
7 Look for and make use of structure.	18

Mathematical Practices 1, 3, and 4 are aspects of mathematical thinking that are emphasized in every lesson. Students are given opportunities to be persistent in their problem solving, to express their reasoning, and apply mathematics to real-world situations.

Formative Assessment

Use this activity as a closing formative assessment before dismissing students from your class.

TICKET Out the Door

Have students write how yesterday's lesson, solving inequalities by adding or subtracting, helped them with the content of today's lesson. See student's work.

15. **Reason Inductively** Cross out the inequality that does not belong in the organizer shown at the right. Then explain your reasoning.

Sample answer: The inequalities $-2x > 12$, $\frac{x}{2} < -3$, and $-7 > x - 1$ are equal to $x < -6$. The inequality $-2 < x + 4$ is equal to $x > -6$.

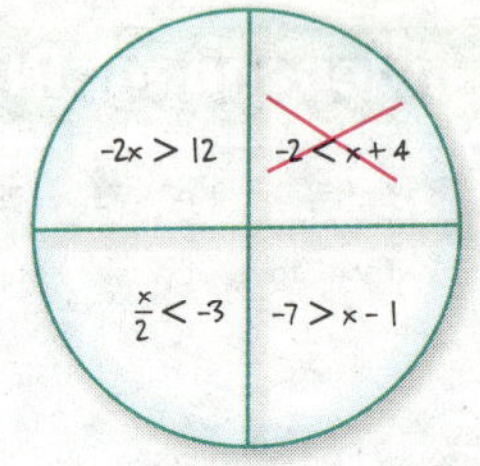

Write an inequality for each sentence. Then solve the inequality.

16. Sixteen is less than eight times a number.

Inequality: $16 < 8n$

Solution: $2 < n$ or $n > 2$

17. The product of a number and five is at the most 30.

Inequality: $5n \leq 30$

Solution: $n \leq 6$

H.O.T. Problems Higher Order Thinking

18. **Identify Structure** Write two different inequalities that have the solution $y > 6$. One inequality should be solved using multiplication properties, and the other should be solved using division properties.

Sample answer: $7y > 42$ and $\frac{1}{2}y > 3$

19. **Persevere with Problems** You score 15, 16, 17, 14, and 19 points out of 20 possible points on five tests. What must you score on the sixth test to have an average of at least 16 points?

at least a 15

20. **Reason Inductively** The inequalities $3x > 2$ and $9x > 6$ are equivalent inequalities. Write another inequality that is equivalent to $3x > 2$ and $9x > 6$.

Sample answer: $12x > 8$

21. **Persevere with Problems** Consider the inequalities $b \geq 4$ and $b \leq 13$.

a. Graph each inequality on the number line.

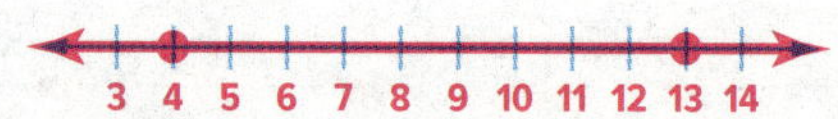

b. Do the solution sets of the two inequalities overlap? If so, what does this overlapping area represent?

yes; It represents the solutions that satisfy both inequalities.

c. A compound inequality is an inequality that combines two inequalities. Write a compound inequality for the situation.

$4 \leq b \leq 13$

d. Look back at the graph of the solutions for both inequalities. Make another graph that shows only the solution of the compound inequality.

Name ____________________ My Homework ____________________

Extra Practice

Solve each inequality.

22. $-10n > -20$ $n < 2$

Homework Help

$-10n > -20$

$\frac{-10n}{-10} < \frac{-20}{-10}$

$n < 2$

23. $-7y < 35$ $y > -5$

24. $15 < 3r$ $5 < r$ or $r > 5$

25. $12p \geq -72$ $p \geq -6$

26. $\frac{t}{-7} > 10$ $t < -70$

27. $-8 < \frac{y}{5}$ $-40 < y$ or $y > -40$

Solve each inequality. Graph the solution set on a number line.

28. $\frac{h}{5} \leq -12$ $h \leq -60$

29. $-3w < -39$ $w > 13$

30. $15 < 4x$ $3.75 < x$ or $x > 3.75$

31. $10 \leq \frac{t}{-2}$ $-20 \geq t$ or $t \leq -20$

32. MP **Reason Abstractly** Each game at a carnival costs \$0.50, or you can pay \$15 and play an unlimited amount of games. Write and solve an inequality to find how many times you should play a game so that the unlimited game play is less expensive than paying each time. Interpret the solution.

Inequality: $0.5x > 15$ Solution: $x > 30$

Interpretation: A person should play more than 30 games.

Write an inequality for each sentence. Then solve the inequality.

33. The product of a number and 4 is at least −12.

Inequality: $4n \geq -12$

Solution: $n \geq -3$

34. Five times a number is less than −45.

Inequality: $5n < -45$

Solution: $n < -9$

Create Your Own Homework Online

eSolutionsManual™ can be used to create worksheets for the suggested assignments on page 509, or create your own worksheets for differentiated homework or review.

Power Up! Test Practice

Exercises 35 and 36 prepare students for more rigorous thinking needed for the state assessment.

35.

This test item requires students to reason abstractly and quantitatively when problem solving.	
Depth of Knowledge	DOK1
Content Standard	7.EE.4, 7.EE.4b
Mathematical Practice	MP1
Online Experience	Students will be required to click on the bubbles to select all answers that are correct.
Scoring Rubric	
1 point	Students correctly answer each part of the question.

36.

This test item requires students to analyze and solve complex real-world problems through the use of mathematical tools and models.	
Depth of Knowledge	DOK2
Content Standard	7.EE.4, 7.EE.4b
Mathematical Practice	MP1, MP4
Online Experience	Students will graph on a number line and type their responses in the boxes.
Scoring Rubric	
2 points	Students correctly write, solve, and graph an inequality and list the solution.
1 point	Students correctly complete two or three of the four parts.

Power Up! Test Practice

35. Caitlin earns $7 per hour babysitting. She wants to earn at least $105 for a camping trip. Determine if each statement is true or false.

a. The inequality $\frac{h}{7} \geq 105$ models how many hours Caitlin must babysit to earn at least $105. ☐ True ■ False

b. The inequality $7h \geq 105$ models how many hours Caitlin must babysit to earn at least $105. ■ True ☐ False

c. Caitlin must babysit up to 15 hours in order to earn at least $105. ☐ True ■ False

36. Soccer balls cost $24 each at Sports Emporium. Coach Neville can spend at most $120 on equipment for the soccer team. Let *b* represent the number of soccer balls Coach Neville can buy.

Write an inequality to model the situation. $24b \leq 120$

Solve the inequality for *b*. $b \leq 5$

Graph the solution on the number line.

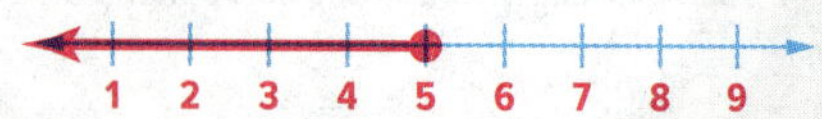

How many soccer balls can Coach Neville buy? List all of the possible answers.

0, 1, 2, 3, 4, or 5 soccer balls

Spiral Review

Solve each equation. Check your solution. 6.EE.6

37. $5k + 6 = 16$ **2**

38. $-14 = 2x - 8$ **−3**

39. $-4n + 3 = 13$ **−2.5**

40. $25 = 7m + 4$ **3**

41. $10.5 + h = 22.5$ **12**

42. $14n - 32 = 22$ $3\frac{6}{7}$

PLAN ONLINE

PD · RtI · Watch · Worksheets · Vocab · Tutor · Tools · Check · English Learners · Sketchpad

PRESENT

IWB

An Interactive Whiteboard Ready presentation is available for each lesson in the chapter.

Lesson 8

Solve Two-Step Inequalities

Real-World Link

Newspapers Kaitlyn is placing an ad in the local newspaper for a pottery class. The cost of placing an ad is shown in the table.

Service	Cost ($)
10-day ad with 3 lines	38.00
each additional line	9.00

1. Complete the equation to find the total cost c of an ad with 4 or more lines. Use x as the variable.

cost of a 10-day add with only 3 lines		cost of each additional line		total cost
38	+	9 x	=	c

2. How much will it cost to place the ad if it is 5 lines long?
$56

3. Suppose Kaitlyn can spend only $50 on the ad. Does she have enough money to place the ad? Circle yes or no.
yes   no (circled)
If the answer is no, how much more money will Kaitlyn need? Explain. **She needs $6 more. The ad costs $56 and she only has $50. $56 − $50 = $6.**

Essential Question

WHAT does it mean to say two quantities are equal?

Vocabulary

two-step inequality

Content Standards
7.EE.4, 7.EE.4b

MP Mathematical Practices
1, 2, 3, 4, 5

Which **MP Mathematical Practices** did you use? Shade the circle(s) that applies.

① Persevere with Problems
② Reason Abstractly
③ Construct an Argument
④ Model with Mathematics
⑤ Use Math Tools
⑥ Attend to Precision
⑦ Make Use of Structure
⑧ Use Repeated Reasoning

Focus narrowing the scope

Objective Model and solve two-step inequalities and represent the solution on the number line. 7.EE.4, 7.EE.4b

Coherence connecting within and across grades

Previous Students solved one-step inequalities.

Now Students model and solve two-step inequalities.

Next Students will write and solve multi-step equations.

Rigor pursuing concepts, fluency, and applications

See the Levels of Complexity chart on page 517.

ENGAGE EXPLORE EXPLAIN ELABORATE EVALUATE

1 Launch the Lesson

Ideas for Use

You may wish to launch the lesson using a whole group, small group, think-pair-share activity, or independent activity.

EL Think-Pair-Share Give students one minute to individually think through their responses to Exercises 1–3. Then have them complete the exercises with a partner, ensuring that each student understands how to write the two-step inequality. Call on one pair of students to share their responses with the class. MP 1, 2

Alternate Strategies

AL Have students create a table that shows the rates for having a 3-, 4-, and 5-line advertisement printed. MP 1, 4, 5

BL Have students write an inequality to represent how many lines Kaitlyn can place in the ad if she only has $50. MP 1, 4

ENGAGE EXPLORE **EXPLAIN** ELABORATE EVALUATE

2 Teach the Concept

Ask the scaffolded questions for each example to differentiate instruction.

Examples

IWB

1. Solve a two-step inequality and represent the solution on the number line.

- AL • *What are the two operations in the inequality?* multiplication and addition
- OL • *What is the coefficient of the variable?* 3
  - • *Will the dot be open or closed? Explain.* closed; the inequality includes 4
- BL • *How many solutions are there to this inequality? Explain.* There are an infinite number of solutions; any value greater than or equal to 4 is a solution.

Need Another Example?

Solve $2x + 1 < 11$. Graph the solution set on a number line

$x < 5$

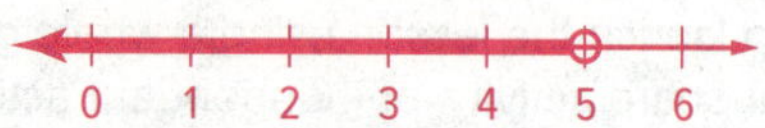

2. Solve a two-step inequality.

- AL • *What are the inverse operations for these operations?* division and subtraction
- OL • *Will the dot be open or closed? Explain.* open; The inequality does not include 7.
- BL • *How many solutions are there to this inequality? Explain.* There are an infinite number of solutions; any value less than 7 is a solution.

Need Another Example?

Solve $8 + 3x > 14$. Graph the solution set on a number line.

$x > 2$

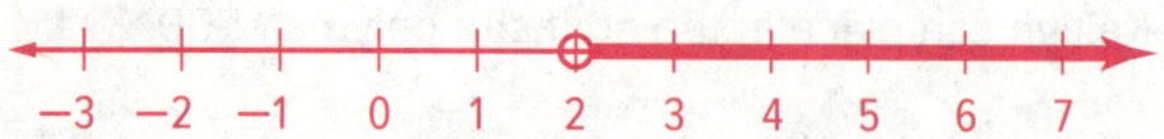

Work Zone

Solve a Two-Step Inequality

A **two-step inequality** is an inequality that contains two operations. To solve a two-step inequality, use inverse operations to undo each operation in reverse order of the order of operations.

Examples

Tutor

1. Solve $3x + 4 \geq 16$. Graph the solution set on a number line.

$3x + 4 \geq 16$	Write the inequality.
$-4 \quad -4$	Subtract 4 from each side
$3x \geq 12$	Simplify.
$\frac{3x}{3} \geq \frac{12}{3}$	Divide each side by 3.
$x \geq 4$	Simplify.

Graph the solution set.

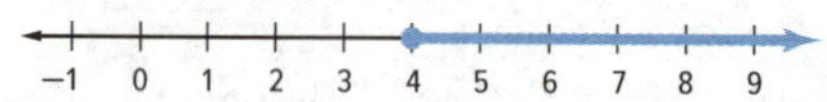

Draw a closed dot at 4 with an arrow to the right.

2. Solve $5 + 4x < 33$. Graph the solution set on a number line.

$5 + 4x < 33$	Write the inequality.
$-5 \quad -5$	Subtract 5 from each side.
$4x < 28$	Simplify.
$\frac{4x}{4} < \frac{28}{4}$	Divide each side by 4.
$x < 7$	Simplify.

Graph the solution set.

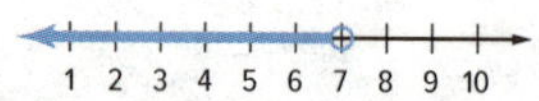

Draw an open dot at 7 with an arrow to the left.

Got it? **Do this problem to find out.**

Show your work.

a. Solve $2x + 8 > 24$. Graph the solution on the number line provided.

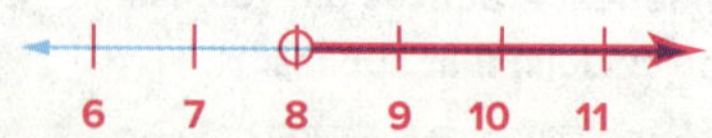

a. $x > 8$

Examples

3. Solve $7 - 2x > 11$. Graph the solution set on a number line.

$7 - 2x > 11$	Write the inequality.
$-7 \quad -7$	Subtract 7 from each side.
$-2x > 4$	Simplify.
$\frac{-2x}{-2} < \frac{4}{-2}$	Divide each side by −2. Reverse inequality symbol.
$x < -2$	Simplify. Check your solution.

Graph the solution set.

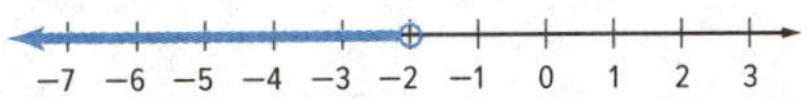

Draw an open dot at −2 with an arrow to the left.

You can check the solution by substituting a number less than −2 into the original inequality. Try using −3.

Check	$7 - 2x > 11$	Write the inequality.
	$7 - 2(-3) \overset{?}{>} 11$	Replace *x* with −3. Is the sentence true?
	$13 > 11$	This is a true statement. ✓

4. Solve $\frac{x}{2} - 5 < -8$. Graph the solution set on a number line.

$\frac{x}{2} - 5 < -8$	Write the inequality.
$+5 \quad +5$	Add 5 to each side.
$\frac{x}{2} < -3$	Simplify.
$\frac{x}{2}(2) < -3(2)$	Multiply each side by 2.
$x < -6$	Simplify. Check your solution.

Graph the solution set.

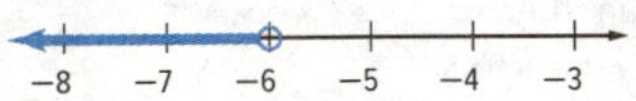

Draw an open dot at −6 with an arrow to the left.

Got it? Do these problems to find out.

Solve each inequality. Graph the solution set on the number line provided.

b. $\frac{x}{2} + 9 \geq 5$

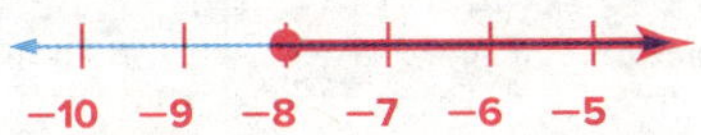

c. $8 - \frac{x}{3} \leq 7$

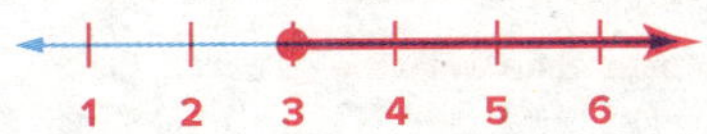

Solving Inequalities

Remember that if multiplying or dividing by a negative number when solving inequalities, reverse the direction of the inequality symbol.

Show your work.

b. $x \geq -8$

c. $x \geq 3$

IWB

Examples

3. Solve a two-step inequality.

AL
- *What are the inverse operations for the operations in the inequality?* division and subtraction

OL
- *What are the steps to solve the inequality?* Subtract 7 from each side. Then divide each side by −2.
- *Will the dot be open or closed? Explain.* open; The inequality does not include −2.

BL
- *How many solutions are there to this inequality? Explain.* There are an infinite number of solutions; any value less than −2 is a solution.

Need Another Example?

Solve $6 - 3x < 9$. Graph the solution set on a number line.

$x \geq -1$

4. Solve a two-step inequality.

AL
- *What are the two operations in the inequality?* division and subtraction
- *What is the inverse operation for these operations?* multiplication and addition

OL
- *What are the steps to solve the inequality?* Add 5 to each side. Then multiply each side by 2.
- *Will the dot be open or closed? Explain.* open; The inequality does not include −6.

BL
- *How many solutions are there to this inequality? Explain.* There are an infinite number of solutions; any value less than −6 is a solution.

Need Another Example?

Solve $\frac{x}{4} + 3 \geq 7$. Graph the solution set on a number line.

$x \geq 16$

Example

IWB

5. **Write and solve an inequality for a real-world problem.**

AL • *What are you trying to find?* how many more games it will take for Steward to have at least 61 strikes

• *What phrase indicates an inequality?* at least

OL • *What expression represents 2 strikes per game?* $2g$

• *What expression represents the total number of strikes?* $34 + 2g$

BL • *Why does Stewart need 14 more games?* We have to round up from 13.5 because we can't have 0.5 of a game.

Need Another Example?

Tim has already earned $40 mowing lawns. He earns $10 per lawn. Write and solve an inequality to determine how many more lawns he will have to mow to have at least $95 for a new lawn mower. Interpret the solution. $40 + 10x \geq 95$, $x \geq 5.5$. Tim will have at least $95 after mowing 6 more lawns.

Guided Practice

Formative Assessment Use these exercises to assess students' understanding of the concepts in this lesson.

If some of your students are not ready for assignments, use the differentiated activities below.

AL EL **Talking Chips** Have students work in small groups to discuss and complete Exercises 1–4. Provide each student with 5 chips. Students must place a chip in the center of the table as they contribute to the discussion. After they have used all of their chips, they may not contribute. All students must use all of their chips. MP 1, 2, 5

BL EL **Trade-a-Problem** Have students work in pairs to write a real-world problem that can be represented by a two-step inequality. Have them trade their problems with a partner and each partner writes and solves the inequality. Have each partner check each other's work. MP 1, 2, 4

Real-World Example

Tutor

5. **Halfway through the bowling league season, Stewart has 34 strikes. He averages 2 strikes per game. Write and solve an inequality to find how many more games it will take for Stewart to have at least 61 strikes, the league record. Interpret the solution.**

The number of strikes plus two strikes per game is at least 61. Let g represent the number of games he needs to bowl.

$$34 + 2g \geq 61 \quad \text{Write the inequality.}$$
$$-34 \quad -34 \quad \text{Subtract 34 from each side.}$$
$$2g \geq 27 \quad \text{Simplify.}$$
$$\frac{2g}{2} \geq \frac{27}{2} \quad \text{Divide each side by 2.}$$
$$g \geq 13.5 \quad \text{Simplify.}$$

Stewart should have at least 61 strikes after 14 more games.

Guided Practice

Check

Solve each inequality. Graph the solution set on a number line. (Examples 1–4)

1. $5x - 7 \geq 43 =$ $x \geq 10$

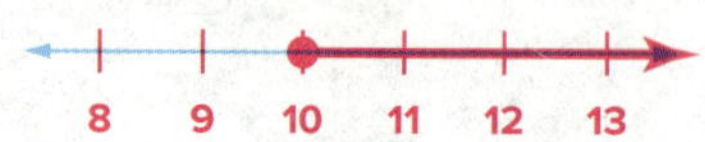

2. $11 \leq 7 + \frac{x}{5}$ $x \geq 20$

3. **Financial Literacy** A rental car company charges $45 plus $0.20 per mile to rent a car. Mr. Lawrence does not want to spend more than $100 for his rental car. Write and solve an inequality to find how many miles he can drive and not spend more than $100. Interpret the solution. (Example 5)

$45 + 0.2d \leq 100$; $d \leq 275$; He can drive no more than 275 miles.

4. **Building on the Essential Question** Compare $2x + 8 > 18$ and $2x + 8 \leq 18$.

$x > 5$; $x \leq 5$; Sample answer: Both inequalities contain the same terms. However, one is greater than while the other also includes equals.

Rate Yourself!

How well do you understand solving two-step inequalities? Circle the image that applies.

Clear Somewhat Clear Not So Clear

For more help, go online to access a Personal Tutor.

Tutor

Name ______________________ My Homework ______________________

Independent Practice

Go online for Step-by-Step Solutions eHelp

Solve each inequality. Graph the solution set on a number line. (Examples 1–4)

1. $6x + 14 \geq 20$ $x \geq 1$

Show your work.

2. $4x - 13 < 11$ $x < 6$

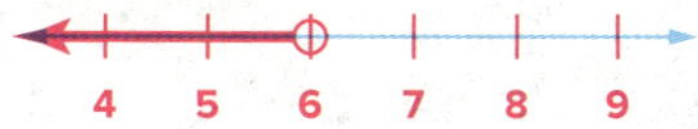

3. $-20 > -2x + 4$ $x > 12$

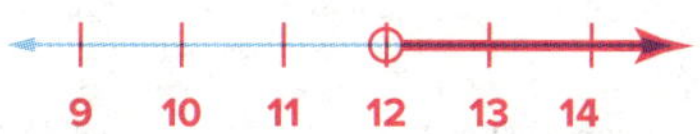

4. $\frac{x}{13} + 3 \geq 4$ $x \geq 13$

5. Tyler needs at least $205 for a new video game system. He has already saved $30. He earns $7 an hour at his job. Write and solve an inequality to find how many hours he will need to work to buy the system. Interpret the solution. (Example 5)

Inequality: $30 + 7x \geq 205$ Solution: $x \geq 25$ hours

Interpretation: He will have to work at least 25 hours.

MP Reason Abstractly **Write and solve an inequality for each sentence.**

6. Three times a number increased by four is less than −62.
$3x + 4 < -62$; $x < -22$

7. The quotient of a number and −5 increased by one is at most 7.
$\frac{x}{-5} + 1 \leq 7$; $x \geq -30$

8. The quotient of a number and 3 minus two is at least −12.
$\frac{x}{3} - 2 \geq -12$; $x \geq -30$

9. The product of −2 and a number minus six is greater than −18.
$-2x - 6 > -18$; $x < 6$

ENGAGE EXPLORE **EXPLAIN** **ELABORATE** **EVALUATE**

3 Practice and Apply

Independent Practice and Extra Practice

The Independent Practice pages are meant to be used as the homework assignment. The Extra Practice page can be used for additional reinforcement or as a second-day assignment.

Levels of Complexity

The levels of the exercises progress from 1 to 3, with Level 1 indicating the lowest level of complexity.

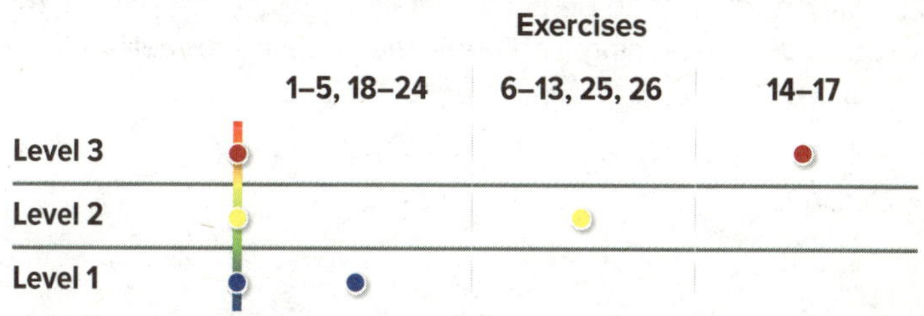

Suggested Assignments

You can use the table below that includes exercises of all complexity levels to select appropriate exercises for your students' needs.

Differentiated Homework Options		
AL	Approaching Level	1–5, 7–13 odd, 14, 16, 17, 25, 26
OL	On Level	1–5 odd, 6–14, 16, 17, 25, 26
BL	Beyond Level	6–17, 25, 26

McGraw Hill Education **ALEKS**® can provide additional remediation support with personalized instruction and practice.

MP MATHEMATICAL PRACTICES

Emphasis On	Exercise(s)
1 Make sense of problems and persevere in solving them.	15
2 Reason abstractly and quantitatively.	6–9, 23
4 Model with mathematics.	14, 17
5 Use appropriate tools strategically.	16

Mathematical Practices 1, 3, and 4 are aspects of mathematical thinking that are emphasized in every lesson. Students are given opportunities to be persistent in their problem solving, to express their reasoning, and apply mathematics to real-world situations.

Formative Assessment
Use this activity as a closing formative assessment before dismissing students from your class.

TICKET Out the Door

Have students write about the similarities and differences between solving two-step equations and two-step inequalities. See students' work.

Watch Out!

Common Error Some students may forget that they are solving an inequality and use an equals sign. Remind them that each step of their solution should contain an inequality symbol as the one in the original inequality, or the reverse symbol if they multiplied or divided by a negative number.

Write a two-step inequality that could be represented by each number line.

10.
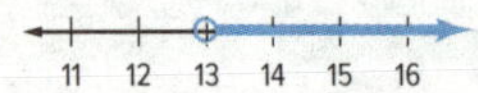

Sample answer: $4x + 1 > 53$

11.
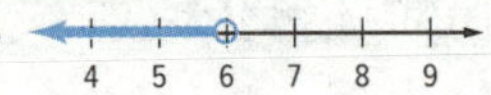

Sample answer: $-2x + 5 > -7$

12.
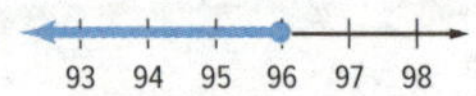

Sample answer: $2x - 6 \leq 186$

13.
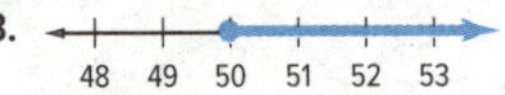

Sample answer: $\frac{x}{2} + 5 \geq 30$

H.O.T. Problems Higher Order Thinking

14. MP **Model with Mathematics** Write a real-world example that could be solved by using the inequality $4x + 8 \geq 32$. Then solve the inequality.

Sample answer: Felicia plans on spending at least \$32 on a new purse. She has already saved \$8. If she earns \$4 an hour tutoring, how many hours will she need to tutor to save at least \$32?; $x \geq 6$; at least 6 hours

15. MP **Persevere with Problems** In five games, you score 16, 12, 15, 13, and 17 points. Write and solve an inequality to determine how many points you must score in the sixth game to have an average of at least 15 points.

$\frac{73 + x}{6} \geq 15$; $x \geq 17$; at least 17 points

16. MP **Use Math Tools** Solve $-x + 6 > -(2x + 4)$. Then graph the solution set on the number line.

Solution: $x > -10$

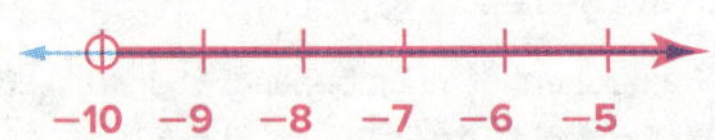

17. MP **Model with Mathematics** Write and solve a real-world problem that can be represented by the inequality $4(x - 2.8) \leq 45$.

Sample answer: At the electronics store, CDs were marked down \$2.80 from their regular price. Orlando has \$45 to spend on 4 CDs. How much can he spend on each CD?; \$14.05

Name ______________________ My Homework ______________________

Extra Practice

Solve each inequality. Graph the solution set on a number line.

18. $4x - 15 \le 5$ $x \le 5$

Homework Help

$4x - 15 \le 5$
$+15 + 15$
$4x \le 20$
$x \le 5$

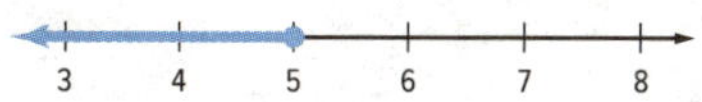

19. $-73 \ge 15 + 11x$ $x \le -8$

20. $\frac{x}{5} - 2 > 1$ $x > 15$

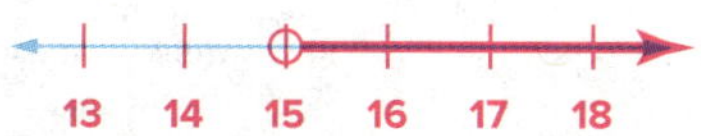

21. $9 \le \frac{x}{14} + 6$ $x \ge 42$

22. Catie is starting a babysitting business. She spent $26 to make signs to advertise. She charges an initial fee of $5 and then $3 for each hour of service. Write and solve an inequality to find the number of hours she will have to babysit to make a profit. Interpret the solution.

Inequality: $5 + 3h > 26$ Solution: $h > 7$

Interpretation: Catie must babysit more than 7 hours to make a profit.

23. MP **Reason Abstractly** As a salesperson, Audrey earns $75 per week plus $5 per sale. This week, she wants her pay to be at least $125. Write and solve an inequality for the number of sales Audrey needs to make. Interpret the solution.

Inequality: $75 + 5s \ge 125$ Solution: $s \ge 10$

Interpretation: Audrey needs to make at least 10 sales for her pay to be $125.

24. Elijah and his sister went to the movies. They had $34 altogether and spent $9.50 per ticket. Elijah and his sister bought the same snacks. Write and solve an inequality for the amount that each person spent on snacks. Interpret the solution.

Inequality: $19 + 2a \le 34$ Solution: $a \le 7.5$

Interpretation: Each person spent a maximum of $7.50 on snacks.

Create Your Own Homework Online

eSolutionsManual™ can be used to create worksheets for the suggested assignments on page 517, or create your own worksheets for differentiated homework or review.

Power Up! Test Practice

Exercises 25 and 26 prepare students for more rigorous thinking needed for the state assessment.

25. This test item requires students to explain and apply mathematical concepts and solve problems with precision, while making use of structure.

Depth of Knowledge	DOK1
Content Standard	7.EE.4b
Mathematical Practice	MP1
Online Experience	Students will be required to click on the bubbles to select all answers that are correct.
Scoring Rubric	
1 point	Students correctly answer the question.

26. This test item requires students to reason abstractly and quantitatively when problem solving.

Depth of Knowledge	DOK2
Content Standard	7.EE.4, 7.EE.4b
Mathematical Practice	MP1, MP4
Online Experience	Students will drag values to model the inequality and type their response in the box.
Scoring Rubric	
2 points	Students correctly model the inequality and solve it.
1 point	Students correctly model the inequality OR solve it.

Power Up! Test Practice

25. Which of the following are operations that you should use to solve $-2x - 5 < 7$ for x? Select all that apply.

- [ ] Subtract 7 from both sides.
- [x] Divide both sides by -2.
- [x] Add 5 to both sides.
- [x] Reverse the inequality symbol.

26. The table shows the cost of renting a jet ski.

Rental Period	Cost ($)
First hour	$55
Each additional 15-minutes	$10

Jeremy can spend no more than $105 on a jet ski rental. Let x represent the number of additional 15-minute increments. Fill in each box to write an inequality to represent the situation.

$10x$	10
$55x$	55
$105x$	105
$<$	$\leq$
$>$	$\geq$

$55 + 10x \leq 105$

What is the greatest length of time Jeremy can rent the jet ski?

135 minutes, or 2 hours 15 minutes

Spiral Review

Solve and graph each inequality. 7.EE.4b

27. $n + 1 > -2$

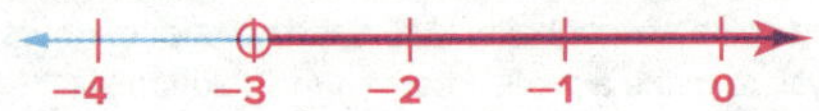

Solution: $n > -3$

28. $-2y > 12$

Solution: $y < -6$

29. $\frac{t}{-1} > -2$

Solution: $t < 2$

Solve each equation. Check your solution. 7.EE.4a

30. $5y + 6 = 46$ 8

31. $-4k - 1 = 47$ -12

32. $5 = 8m + 1$ $\frac{1}{2}$

33. Michael's dad is 30 years of age. He is 2 years more than four times Michael's age m. Write and solve a two-step equation to determine Michael's age. 6.EE.7

Equation: $4m + 2 = 30$ Solution: 7 years

PLAN ONLINE

PD | RtI | Watch | Worksheets | Vocab | Tutor | Tools | Check | English Learners | Sketchpad

PRESENT

College & Career READINESS

21ST CENTURY CAREER in Veterinary Medicine

Veterinary Technician

If you love being around animals, enjoy working with your hands, and are good at analyzing problems, a challenging career in veterinary medicine might be a perfect fit for you. Veterinary technicians help veterinarians by helping to diagnose and treat medical conditions. They may work in private clinics, animal hospitals, zoos, aquariums, or wildlife rehabilitation centers.

College & Career READINESS

Is This the Career for You?

Are you interested in a career as a veterinary technician? Take some of the following courses in high school.

- Algebra
- Animal Science
- Biology
- Chemistry
- Veterinary Assisting

Find out how math relates to a career in Veterinary Medicine.

Focus narrowing the scope

Objective Apply mathematics to problems arising in the workplace.

This lesson emphasizes MP **Mathematical Practice 4** Model with Mathematics.

Coherence connecting within and across grades

Previous
Students wrote and solved equations to represent real-world problems.

Now
Students apply the content standard to solve problems in the workplace.

Rigor pursuing concepts, fluency, and applications

See the Career Project on page 522.

ENGAGE EXPLORE EXPLAIN ELABORATE EVALUATE

1 Launch the Lesson

Ask students to read the information on the student page about veterinary medicine and answer the following questions.

Ask:

- *What does a veterinary technician do?* helps the veterinarian by recording case histories, conducting medical tests, and helping to diagnose and treat animals
- *What kinds of classes should you take to be a veterinary technician?* Algebra, Animal Sciences and Services, Biology, Veterinary Assisting, Chemistry

College & Career READINESS

Help students connect what they do today to their futures. Direct them to the Internet or another source to explore, learn, and plan for college and future careers.

2 Collaborate

AL EL Trade-a-Problem Have students create their own problem using the information in the tables. Have students trade their problems with a partner, solve each other's problem, and compare solutions. If the solutions do not agree, students work together to find any errors. MP 1, 2, 4

BL EL Pairs Discussion Have students work in pairs to answer the following extension question. MP 1, 2, 4

Ask:

- *Cotton-top tamarins can cover up to 1.1 miles per day while searching for food. If they move about 0.15 mile per hour, write and solve an equation to determine about how many hours it takes them to travel 1.1 miles.* $1.1 = 0.15t$; about 7.3 hours

Career Portfolio

When students complete this page, have them add it to their Career Portfolio.

Career Facts

A similar career to a veterinary technician is a veterinary technologist. Both careers involve similar job responsibilities, but different educational requirements. Veterinary technicians attend accredited, two-year veterinary technology programs and usually earn Associate degrees. Veterinary technologists attend four year programs and usually earn Bachelor's degrees.

MP Vet Techs Don't Monkey Around

For each problem, use the information in the tables to write an equation. Then solve the equation.

1. The minimum tail length of an emperor tamarin is 1.6 inches greater than that of a golden lion tamarin. What is the minimum tail length of a golden lion tamarin? $14 = t + 1.6$; 12.4 in.
2. The minimum body length of a golden lion tamarin is 5.3 inches less than the maximum body length. What is the maximum body length? $7.9 = \ell - 5.3$; 13.2 in.
3. Tamarins live an average of 15 years. This is 13 years less than the years that one tamarin in captivity lived. How long did the tamarin in captivity live? $15 = y - 13$; 28 yr
4. The maximum weight of a golden lion tamarin is about 1.97 times the maximum weight of an emperor tamarin. What is the maximum weight of an emperor tamarin? Round to the nearest tenth. $28 = 1.97w$; 14.2 oz
5. For an emperor tamarin, the maximum total length, including the body and tail, is 27 inches. What is the maximum body length of an emperor tamarin? $b + 16.6 = 27$; 10.4 in.

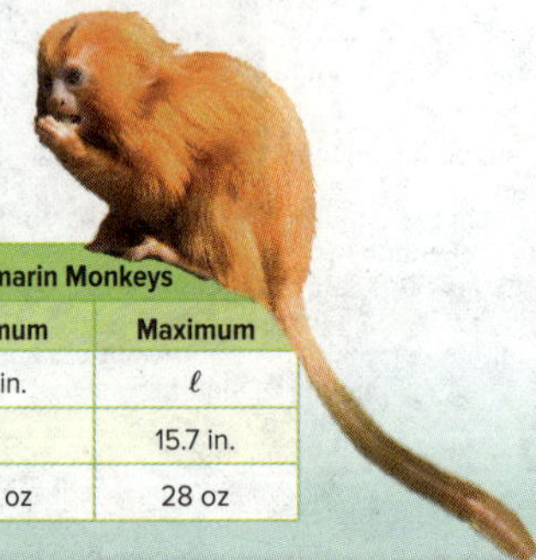

Golden Lion Tamarin Monkeys

Measure	Minimum	Maximum
Body length	7.9 in.	ℓ
Tail length	t	15.7 in.
Weight	12.7 oz	28 oz

Emperor Tamarin Monkeys

Measure	Minimum	Maximum
Body length	9.2 in.	b
Tail length	14 in.	16.6 in.
Weight	10.7 oz	w

MP Career Project

It's time to update your career portfolio! Go to the Occupational Outlook Handbook online and research a career as a veterinary technician. Include brief descriptions of the work environment, education and training requirements, and the job outlook.

Do you think you would enjoy a career as a veterinary technician? Why or why not?

-
-
-
-
-

Chapter Review

Vocabulary Check

Unscramble each of the clue words.

TOW-SETP

T W O – S T E P (7 under T)

PYORERPT

P R O P E R T Y (8 under Y)

DODTIINA

A D D I T I O N (6 under T)

NIIOSDIV

D I V I S I O N

LABVIERA

V A R I A B L E (5 under L)

AILEYQUITN

I N E Q U A L I T Y (2 under Q)

BISTAUTORNC

S U B T R A C T I O N (3 under U)

NUATIEQO

E Q U A T I O N (1 under E)

TIULINTICPOLMA

M U L T I P L I C A T I O N (4 under A)

Use the numbered letters to find another vocabulary term from this chapter.

E	Q	U	A	L	I	T	Y
1	2	3	4	5	6	7	8

Vocabulary Check

EL **Find the Fib** Have students work in small groups to complete the Vocabulary Check. Have students write two facts and one fib, relating to the vocabulary terms. For example, one fact could be that a variable represents an unknown quantity. One fib could be that $3x = 15$ is an example of a two-step equation. Then have each student read aloud what they wrote to the group. The group will discuss each fact and fib, identify the fibs, and correct them so that they become facts.
MP 1, 3, 6

Alternate Strategy

AL EL To help students, you may wish to give them a vocabulary list from which they can choose their answers. A vocabulary list for this activity would include the following terms.

- Addition Property of Equality (Lesson 1)
- Addition Property of Inequality (Lesson 6)
- Division Property of Equality (Lesson 2)
- Division Property of Inequality (Lesson 7)
- Multiplication Property of Equality (Lesson 2)
- Multiplication Property of Inequality (Lesson 7)
- Subtraction Property of Equality (Lesson 1)
- Subtraction Property of Inequality (Lesson 6)
- two-step equation (Lesson 4)
- two-step inequality (Lesson 8)
- variable (Lesson 5–1)

Key Concept Check

FOLDABLES EL A completed Foldable for this chapter should include a review of solving two-step equations.

If you choose not to use this Foldable, have students write a brief review of the Key Concepts found throughout the chapter and give an example of each.

Ideas for Use

EL Have students work in pairs to discuss their Foldables. Have them practice speaking in a collaborative setting by sharing how they have completed their Foldable thus far and how they could finish it. Have each student complete their Foldable and trade with their partner to discuss any similarities and differences. MP 1, 3, 5

Got It?

If students have trouble with Exercises 1–4, they may need help with the following concept(s).

Concept	Exercise(s)
equations (Lesson 1)	1, 3, 4
coefficients (Lesson 2)	2

ALEKS® provides additional support with personalized instruction and practice for those who are struggling, while providing enhanced learning for those who have mastered the concepts.

Key Concept Check

Use Your FOLDABLES

Use your Foldable to help review the chapter.

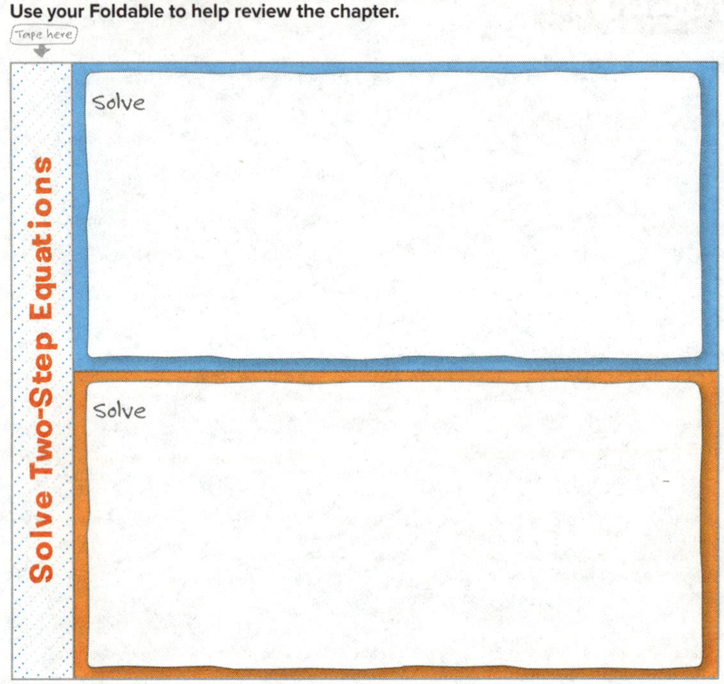

Got it?

Match each phrase with the correct term.

1. the value of a variable that makes an equation true
2. the numerical factor in a multiplication expression
3. equations that have the same solution
4. a sentence stating that two quantities are equal

a. equivalent equations
b. equation
c. Addition Property of Equality
d. coefficient
e. formula
f. solution

Power Up! Performance Task

Fall Reading

Gordon's English teacher assigned a book to be read by October 31st. The students may select a book from the table, and Gordon chose *City Streets*.

Book	Number of Pages
City Streets	387
Life and Time	411
Myopia	435

Write your answers on another piece of paper. Show all of your work to receive full credit.

Part A
By October 19th, Gordon had read 35 pages. Starting on October 20th, he decides to read the same number of pages each day until he finishes the book on October 30th. Write and solve an equation to represent the situation. Let p represent the number of pages read per day. How many pages does Gordon read per day?

Part B
Gordon's friend, Kendrick, selected *Myopia*. He read eight pages in class on October 19th and begins reading again on October 23rd. He needs to read at least 350 pages by the end of the day on October 28th. Write and solve an inequality to represent this situation and graph the solution on a number line. Let p represent the number of pages read per day. How many pages must Kendrick read per day to accomplish his goal?

Power Up! Performance Task

This Performance-Based Assessment requires students to solve multi-step problems through abstract reasoning, precision, and perseverance. This practice scenario can be used to help students prepare for the thinking skills that will be used on the State Assessment.

A complete scoring rubric with answers to the Exercises can be found on page PT2.

Answering the Essential Question

Before answering the Essential Question, have students review their answers to the **Building on the Essential Question** exercises found in each lesson of the chapter.

- What are two methods for solving a real-world problem that can be represented by an equation? (p. 440)
- How is the process for solving multiplication and division one-step equations like solving one-step addition and subtraction equations? (p. 450)
- What is the process for solving a multiplication equation with a rational coefficient? (p. 460)
- Why is it important to perform identical operations on each side of the equals sign? (p. 472)
- What is the difference between $px + q = r$ and $p(x + q) = r$? (p. 484)
- When would you use addition or subtraction to solve an inequality? (p. 500)
- When do you reverse the inequality symbol when solving an inequality? (p. 508)
- How are the inequalities and solutions of $2x + 8 > 18$ and $2x + 8 \leq 18$ similar and how are they different? (p. 516)

Ideas for Use

EL **Think-Pair-Share** Have students work in pairs. Pose the Essential Question. Give students about one minute to think about how they could complete the graphic organizer. Then have them share their responses with their partner before they complete the graphic organizer. MP 1, 7

Reflect

Answering the Essential Question

Use what you learned about equations and inequalities to complete the graphic organizer.

When do you use an equals sign?

Sample answer: Use an equals sign to indicate that one expression is equal to another expression. Apply the properties of equality to solve an equation.

Essential Question

WHAT does it mean to say two quantities are equal?

When do you use an inequality symbol?

Sample answer: Use an inequality symbol when one expression is greater than, greater than or equal to, less than, or less than or equal to another expression. Apply the properties of inequality to solve an inequality.

Answer the Essential Question. WHAT does it mean to say two quantities are equal?

See students' work.

UNIT PROJECT

Watch

Stand Up and Be Counted The U.S. Census is used to determine the number of U.S. House of Representative members that each state is assigned. In this project you will:

- **Collaborate** with your classmates as you research Census data and the U.S. House of Representatives.
- **Share** the results of your research in a creative way.
- **Reflect** on how you can communicate mathematical ideas effectively.

Collaborate

Go Online Work with your group to research and complete each activity. You will use your results in the Share section on the following page.

1. Explore the official U.S. Census web site to find the 2010 state populations. There will be interactive maps that display this information. Write down a few facts you find interesting.

2. Create a table that displays the population and the number of U.S. Representatives for your state and three other states. Then create a line plot for the number of U.S. Representatives.

3. Write an equation that uses any state's population x and its number of U.S. Representative members y to describes the number of people per U.S. Representative z.

4. Use your equation from Exercise 3 to determine the approximate number of people per U.S. Representative for the four states you chose. Interpret the results.

5. Look at the 2000 and 2010 census. How did the population of your state and states in your region change? Did the population change affect the number of U.S. Representatives assigned?

6. States can be categorized by population size and density. Write at least two inequalities that compare the states using these categories.

Expressions and Equations

Watch the Project Video

Go online to watch a video to launch this unit project.

Launch the Project

Objective Research the United States Census and how it affects the number of members in the House of Representatives.

Stand Up and Be Counted

This project is designed to be completed by a group of 4 or 5 students over several days or several weeks. It utilizes concepts from the Ratios and Proportional Relationships domain. You may choose to complete this project after completing the chapters within this domain.

Collaborate

Have students work in teams to research each activity. Together, they should be able to gather the necessary information to complete Exercises 1–6. Students should show their work on a separate piece of paper.

Share
Collaborate

After each group gives their presentation, allow students to ask questions to the presenters.

21st Century Skills

You may want your students to connect their projects to a 21st century skill. Check out the suggestion below and on the student page.

connect with Language Arts

Civic Literacy Research and write an essay about one aspect of the U.S. Census. Some questions to consider are:

- Why is the U.S. Census taken?
- How could the U.S. Census become more accurate?

Reflect
On Your Own

Students should work on their own to reflect on how the chapters from this unit and the objective of the project relate to the Essential Question.

Share
Collaborate

With your group, decide on a way to share what you have learned about the U.S. House of Representatives and state populations. Some suggestions are listed below, but you can also think of other creative ways to present your information. Remember to show how you used mathematics to complete each of the activities in this project!

- Act as a Census representative and create a presentation to encourage people to participate in the census and explain why it is important.
- Write a letter or email to your Representative about what you learned in this project and how it can be used to improve your community.

Check out the note on the right to connect this project with other subjects.

connect with Social Studies

Civic Literacy Research the Electoral College. Some questions to consider are:

- Why was it established?
- What is the relationship between the United States House of Representatives and the Electoral College?

Reflect
On Your Own

7. **Answer the Essential Question** How can you communicate mathematical ideas effectively? **See students' work.**

 a. How did you use what you learned about expressions to help you communicate mathematical ideas effectively in this project?

 b. How did you use what you learned about equations and inequalities to help you communicate mathematical ideas effectively in this project?

UNIT 4 Geometry

Essential Question

HOW can you use different measurements to solve real-life problems?

Chapter 7 Geometric Figures

Geometric shapes can be drawn freehand, with a ruler and protractor, or using technology. In this chapter, you will draw two- and three-dimensional figures. You will also solve problems involving scale drawings of geometric figures.

Chapter 8 Measure Figures

Real-life problems involving area, surface area, and volume can be solved by using formulas. In this chapter, you will use formulas to find the area and circumference of a circle and to find the surface area and volume of prisms and pyramids.

Plan Online connectED.mcgraw-hill.com

You can use the resources available online to plan for this unit.

Essential Question

At the end of this unit, students should be able to answer "How can you use different measurements to solve real-life problems?"

Each chapter explores a different essential question that assists students in answering the unit question. The lessons in each chapter include exercises that lead students to various aspects of the essential question.

This unit focuses on the Geometry. The chapters address the following grade 7 standards:

Draw, construct, and describe geometrical figures and describe the relationships between them.

1. Solve problems involving scale drawings of geometric figures, including computing actual lengths and areas from a scale drawing and reproducing a scale drawing at a different scale. (7.G.1)
2. Draw (freehand, with ruler and protractor, and with technology) geometric shapes with given conditions. Focus on constructing triangles from three measures of angles or sides, noticing when the conditions determine a unique triangle, more than one triangle, or no triangle. (7.G.2)
3. Describe the two-dimensional figures that result from slicing threedimensional figures, as in plane sections of right rectangular prisms and right rectangular pyramids. (7.G.3)

continued on page 530

Solve real-life and mathematical problems involving angle measure, area, surface area, and volume.

4. Know the formulas for the area and circumference of a circle and use them to solve problems; give an informal derivation of the relationship between the circumference and area of a circle. (7.G.4)
5. Use facts about supplementary, complementary, vertical, and adjacent angles in a multi-step problem to write and solve simple equations for an unknown angle in a figure. (7.G.5)
6. Solve real-world and mathematical problems involving area, volume and surface area of two- and three-dimensional objects composed of triangles, quadrilaterals, polygons, cubes, and right prisms. (7.G.6)

Unit Project Preview

Collaborate

Ask students what they know about the structure of leaves.

Have students estimate the area of their leaf by counting whole squares as 1 square unit and partial squares as $\frac{1}{2}$ square unit.

The Unit Project can be found on pages 703–704.

Video Play the Unit Project video to give students some background information on the topic and to generate excitement for the upcoming project.

Unit Project Preview

Collaborate

Watch

Turn Over a New Leaf Leaves serve an important purpose for plants and trees, and there are scientific reasons why they are flat.

Make a sketch of a leaf. Estimate the area of the leaf in square units.

At the end of Chapter 8, you'll complete a project to investigate the relationship between the volume and surface area of a leaf. So, put on your hiking shoes, and don't forget to bring along your measuring tools. You're about to go on a nature hike!

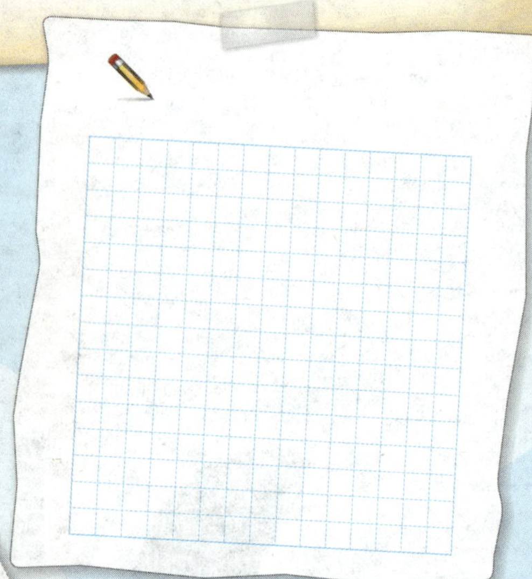

PLAN ONLINE

PD | RtI | Watch | Worksheets | Vocab | Tutor | Tools | Check | English Learners | Sketchpad

PRESENT

IWB

An Interactive Whiteboard Ready presentation is available for each lesson in the chapter.

Geometry

Chapter 7
Geometric Figures

Essential Question

HOW does geometry help us describe real-world objects?

Content Standards
7.G.1, 7.G.2, 7.G.3, 7.G.5

MP Mathematical Practices
1, 2, 3, 4, 5, 6, 7, 8

Math in the Real World

Robots that could be programmed and digitally operated were invented by George Devol in 1954.

The actual length of the robot's arm is 15 inches. A drawing of the robot is $\frac{1}{5}$ the size of the actual robot. Fill in the blank below with the correct measurement for the robot's arm.

FOLDABLES® Study Organizer

1. Cut out the Foldable on page FL7 of this book.
2. Place your Foldable on page 604.
3. Use the Foldable throughout this chapter to help you learn about geometric figures.

Focus narrowing the scope

This chapter focuses on content from the **Geometry** (G) domain.

Mathematical Background Additional information about the mathematical background for this chapter can be found online at connectED.mcgraw-hill.com.

Coherence connecting within and across grades

Previous Students simplified expressions and solved equations.

Now Students create and draw two- and three-dimensional figures.

Next Students will use various methods to measure figures.

Rigor pursuing concepts, fluency, and applications

The Levels of Complexity charts located throughout this chapter indicate how the exercises progress from conceptual understanding and procedural skills and fluency, to application and critical thinking.

Launch the Chapter

Math in the Real World

Robots Tell students that to find the length of the robot's arm on the drawing, they can write and solve a proportion.

What Tools Do You Need?

Vocabulary Activity

EL As you proceed through the chapter, introduce each vocabulary term using the following routine. Ask the students to say each term aloud after you say it.

Define: Supplementary angles are two angles with measures that have a sum of 180°.

Example: $m\angle A = 120°$ and $m\angle B = 60°$, so they are supplementary angles.

Ask:

- *What is the measure of an angle supplementary to an angle with a measure of 56°?* **124°**

Reading Math

EL Have students read the Reading Math section. Students will learn about mathematical vocabulary that also have meanings in science or everyday usage. Have students read about the language of mathematics. Have them suggest words that they believe have meaning in both mathematics and in everyday or scientific use.

Ask:

- *What are the everyday and mathematical meanings for "side"?* **Sample answer: a position held in a dispute; a segment that forms part of a geometric figure**

What Tools Do You Need?

Vocabulary

acute angle
acute triangle
adjacent angles
base
complementary angles
cone
congruent
congruent segments
coplanar
cross section
cylinder
diagonal
edge
equilateral triangle
face
isosceles triangle
obtuse angle
obtuse triangle
plane
polyhedron
prism
pyramid
right angle
right triangle
scale
scale drawing
scale factor
scale model
scalene triangle
skew line
straight angle
supplementary angles
triangle
vertex
vertical angles

Study Skill: Reading Math

The Language of Mathematics Many of the words you use in math and science are also used in everyday language, such as the leg of a person and the leg of a right triangle.

Usage	Example
Some words are used in science and in mathematics, but the meanings are different.	$x + 4 = -2$ $x = -6$ solution 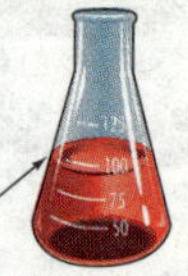
Some words are used only in mathematics.	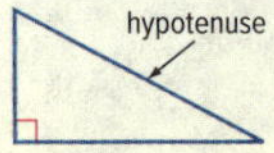

Explain how the everyday meaning of *face* is different than its mathematical meaning.

Everyday meaning: **Sample answer: the front part of a human head including the eyes, nose, mouth, and chin**

Mathematical meaning: **any surface that forms a side or a base of a prism**

What Do You Already Know?

Read each statement. Decide whether you agree (A) or disagree (D). Place a checkmark in the appropriate column and then justify your reasoning. See students' work.

Geometric Figures			
Statement	A	D	Why?
The common endpoint shared by the two sides of an angle is called the origin.			
A pair of adjacent supplementary angles forms a right angle.			
The sum of the measures of the angles in any triangle is 180°.			
A scale drawing/model represents an object that is too large or too small to be drawn at actual size.			
An isosceles triangle has three congruent sides.			
A cylinder has two parallel congruent circular bases.			

When Will You Use This?

Here are a few examples of how scale drawings are used in the real world.

Activity 1 Use the Internet to find a map of the area where you live. Find the map distance, in inches, between your school and your home. Describe a method you could use to find the actual distance once you know the map distance.

See students' work.

Activity 2 Go online at connectED.mcgraw-hill.com to read the graphic novel ***Campfire Song***. On the map, how many units long is the line connecting the cabin to the lake?

4 units

What Do You Already Know?

In this activity students assess their prior knowledge by determining whether they agree or disagree with each statement about concepts in this chapter.

- You may want to add a third option of "I don't know" for those students who do not have any prior knowledge of the content of the statement.
- After completing the chapter, have students return to this page and see if any of their responses would change now that they have finished the chapter.

When Will You Use This?

Activity 1

Students use a real-world situation involving maps to understand scale drawings.

Activity 2

Use the Graphic Novel to help students learn about scale maps and drawings.

Ask:

- *How far would Raul, Caitlyn, and Jamar have to walk if they went straight to the campfire after the lake?* Sample answer: $\frac{1 \text{ square}}{75 \text{ yards}} = \frac{7 \text{ squares}}{x \text{ yards}}$, $x = (75)(7) = 525$

Are You Ready?

Use this page to determine if students have skills that are needed for the chapter.

Quick Review
Students with strong math backgrounds may opt to go directly to Quick Check.

QUICK REVIEW		
Example	**Skill**	**Standard**
1	Find Measures of Angles	4.MD.6
2	Area of a Triangle	6.G.1

Quick Check
If students have difficulty with the exercises, present an additional example to clarify any misconceptions.

Exercises 1–3
Use a protractor to find the measure of the angle shown. 30°

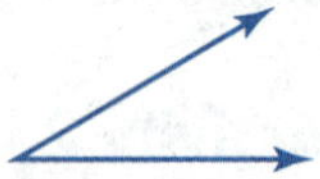

Exercises 4–5
Find the area of a triangle with a base of 8 meters and a height of 5.2 meters. 20.8 m^2

RtI Response to Intervention
Go online at connectED.mcgraw-hill.com for resources to differentiate remediation for Tier 1, Tier 2, and Tier 3 students.

ALEKS® can provide additional remediation support with personalized instruction and practice. See pages T8 and T9 for more information.

Are You Ready?

Try the Quick Check below.
Or, take the Online Readiness Quiz. Check

Quick Review
4.MD.6, 6.G.1

Example 1
Use a protractor to measure angle *ABC*.

Align the center of the protractor with the vertex of the angle.

Make sure one ray of the angle passes through zero on the protractor.

Read the measure on the protractor where the other ray crosses the protractor.

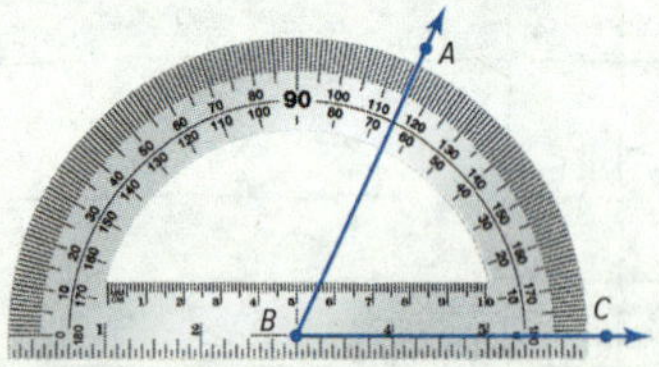

The angle measures 65°.

Example 2
Find the area of the triangle.

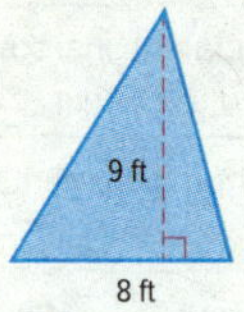

$A = \frac{1}{2}bh$ Area of a triangle

$A = \frac{1}{2}(8 \cdot 9)$ Replace *b* with 8 and *h* with 9.

$A = 36$ Simplify.

The area of the triangle is 36 square feet.

Quick Check

Angle Measures Use a protractor to measure each angle.

1. 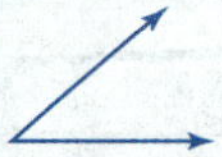 40°

2. 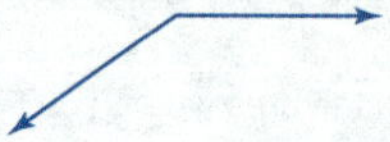 145°

3. 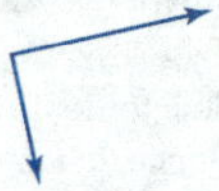 90°

Area Find the area of each triangle.

4. 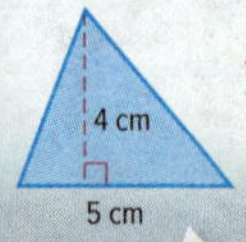

10 cm^2

5. base: 3.2 yd
height: 4.2 yd 6.72 yd^2

How Did You Do? Which problems did you answer correctly in the Quick Check? Shade those exercise numbers below.

1 2 3 4 5

PLAN ONLINE

PD | RtI | Watch | Worksheets | Vocab | Tutor | Tools | Check | English Learners | Sketchpad

PRESENT

IWB

An Interactive Whiteboard Ready presentation is available for each lesson in the chapter.

Geometry

Lesson 1

Classify Angles

Vocabulary Start-Up

An angle is formed by two rays that share a common endpoint. The **vertex** is the point where the two rays meet.

Complete the table by drawing the hands of a clock to represent each angle. Sample answers are given.

Type of Angle			
Right	Acute	Obtuse	Straight
exactly 90°	less than 90°	greater than 90°	exactly 180°

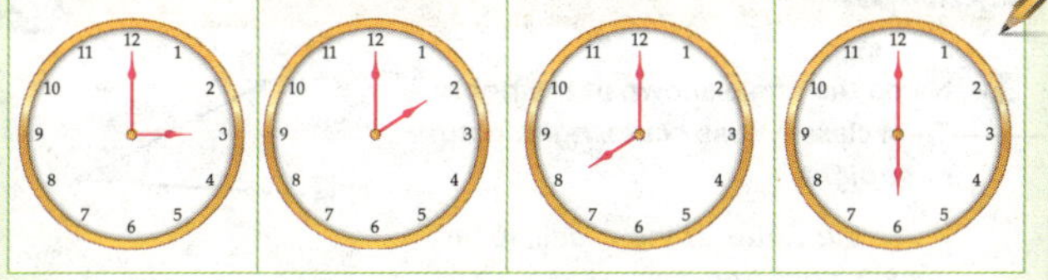

Essential Question

HOW does geometry help us describe real-world objects?

Vocabulary

vertex
right angle
acute angle
obtuse angle
straight angle
vertical angles
congruent
adjacent angles

Math Symbols

∠
≅

Content Standards
7.G.5

MP Mathematical Practices
1, 3, 4, 7

Real-World Link

The angle formed by a bike ramp is shown.

1. What type of angle is formed?
   acute

2. Estimate the measure of the angle.
   Sample answer: 20°

Which MP **Mathematical Practices** did you use? Shade the circle(s) that applies.

① Persevere with Problems
② Reason Abstractly
③ Construct an Argument
④ Model with Mathematics
⑤ Use Math Tools
⑥ Attend to Precision
⑦ Make Use of Structure
⑧ Use Repeated Reasoning

Focus narrowing the scope

Objective Classify angles and identify vertical and adjacent angles. 7.G.5

Coherence connecting within and across grades

Previous Students identified types of two-dimensional figures.

Now Students identify and classify different types of angles.

Next Students will compare angle relationships.

Rigor pursuing concepts, fluency, and applications

See the Levels of Complexity chart on page 539.

ENGAGE EXPLORE EXPLAIN ELABORATE EVALUATE

1 Launch the Lesson

Ideas for Use

You may wish to launch the lesson using a whole group, small group, think-pair-share activity, or independent activity.

EL **Pairs Discussion** Have students work with a partner to complete the table and complete Exercises 1 and 2 in the Real-World Link. Have students draw several different possibilities for each type of angle. Call on one pair of students to share their responses with the class. MP 1, 6

Alternate Strategy

AL EL Have students work in pairs to create vocabulary cards using the terms *vertex*, *acute*, *right*, *obtuse*, and *straight*. Have students draw an example for each word. Have them use these cards as a reference throughout the chapter. MP 1, 4, 6

ENGAGE EXPLORE **EXPLAIN** ELABORATE EVALUATE

2 Teach the Concept

Ask the scaffolded questions for each example to differentiate instruction.

Example

IWB

1. Name and classify angles.

AL
- *How would you name the angle using a number?* ∠1
- *What is the vertex of the angle?* Y
- *What is a vertex?* the point common to two sides of an angle

OL
- *How can you name the angle using only its vertex?* ∠Y
- *How can you name the angle using its vertex and a point from each ray?* ∠XYZ or ∠ZYX
- *How would you classify the angle?* an acute angle

BL
- *Estimate the measure of ∠1.* Sample answer: about 30°
- *If there were another point on ray YX, and this point was labeled P, give two other possibilities for naming this angle.* ∠PYZ or ∠ZYP

Need Another Example?
Name the angle shown in four ways. Then classify it as *acute*, *right*, *obtuse*, or *straight*. ∠FGH, ∠HGF, ∠G, ∠2; acute

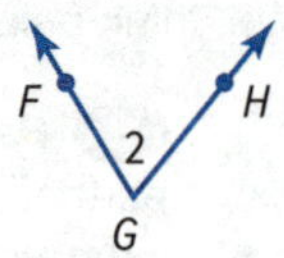

Key Concept

Name and Identify Angles

Words	Models	Symbols
Two angles are **vertical** if they are opposite angles formed by the intersection of two lines. Vertical angles are **congruent** or have the same measure.	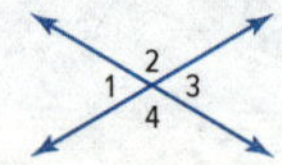 ∠1 and ∠3, ∠2 and ∠4	∠1 ≅ ∠3 ∠2 ≅ ∠4
Two angles are **adjacent** if they share a common vertex, a common side, and do not overlap.	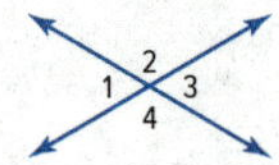	Adjacent angle pairs are ∠1 and ∠2, ∠2 and ∠3, ∠3 and ∠4, and ∠4 and ∠1.

You can name an angle by its vertex and by its points.

Work Zone

Symbols
The symbol for angle is ∠.
The symbol ≅ means is congruent to.

Example

Tutor

1. Name the angle shown at the right. Then classify it as *acute, right, obtuse,* or *straight*.

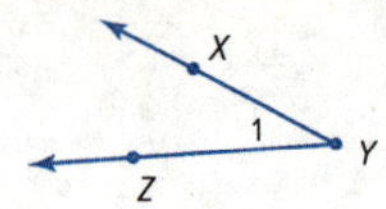

- Use the vertex as the middle letter and a point from each side, ∠XYZ or ∠ZYX.
- Use the vertex only, ∠Y.
- Use a number, ∠1.

Since the angle is less than 90°, it is an acute angle.

Got it? **Do these problems to find out.**

Name each angle in four ways. Then classify each angle as *acute, right, obtuse,* or *straight*.

a. 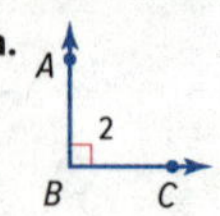

b. 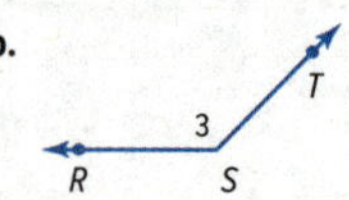

c. 

Show your work.

a. ∠ABC, ∠CBA, ∠B, ∠2; right

b. ∠RST, ∠TSR, ∠S, ∠3; obtuse

c. ∠LMN, ∠NML, ∠M, ∠4; straight

Example

2. Identify a pair of vertical angles and adjacent angles in the diagram at the right. Justify your response.

Since $\angle 2$ and $\angle 4$ are opposite angles formed by the intersection of two lines, they are vertical angles.

Since $\angle 1$ and $\angle 2$ share a common side and vertex, and they do not overlap, they are adjacent angles.

Got it? **Do this problem to find out.**

d. Refer to the diagram in Example 2. Identify different pairs of vertical and adjacent angles. Justify your response.

Show your work.

d. Sample answer: $\angle 1$ and $\angle 3$ are vertical angles because $\angle 1$ and $\angle 3$ are opposite angles formed by the intersection of two lines. $\angle 2$ and $\angle 3$ are adjacent angles because $\angle 2$ and $\angle 3$ share a common vertex, a common side, and do not overlap.

Find a Missing Measure

You can use what you learned about vertical and adjacent angles to find the value of a missing measure.

Example

3. What is the value of *x* in the figure?

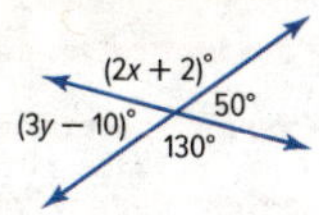

The angle labeled $(2x + 2)°$ and the angle labeled 130° are vertical angles.

Since vertical angles are congruent, $(2x + 2)°$ equals 130°.

$2x + 2 = 130$ — Write the equation.

$-2 = -2$ — Subtract 2 from each side.

$\frac{2x}{2} = \frac{128}{2}$ — Divide each side by 2.

$x = 64$

So, the value of *x* is 64.

Got it? **Do this problem to find out.**

e. What is the value of *y* in the figure in Example 2?

e. 20

Geometry

IWB

Examples

2. Identify vertical angles and adjacent angles.

AL • *Which pairs of angles are vertical?* $\angle 1$ and $\angle 3$, $\angle 2$ and $\angle 4$

• *What kind of angle is formed by $\angle 1$ and $\angle 2$?* straight angle

OL • *What do you know about the measures of $\angle 1$ and $\angle 3$, and $\angle 2$ and $\angle 4$?* They have the same measure.

BL • *If $m\angle 1 = 75°$, what is $m\angle 2$? Explain.* 105°, because $\angle 1$ and $\angle 2$ form a straight line and the sum is equal to 180°.

Need Another Example?

Identify a pair of vertical angles and adjacent angles in the diagram. Justify your response. Sample answer: $\angle 3$ and $\angle 5$ are vertical because they are opposite angles formed by intersecting lines; $\angle 4$ and $\angle 5$ are adjacent because they share a common side and do not overlap.

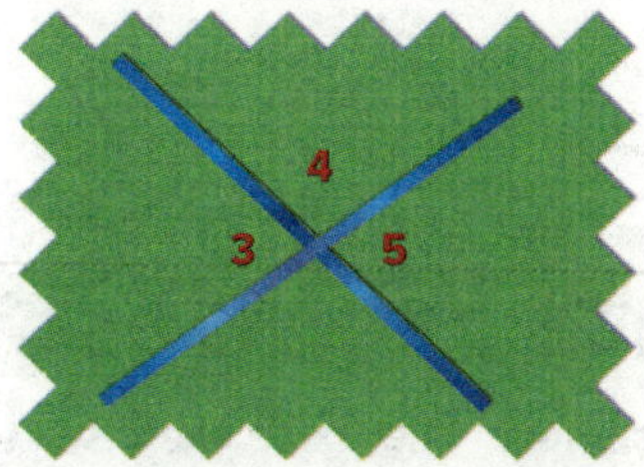

3. Find missing measures.

AL • *What type of angles are the 130° angle and the angle labeled $(2x + 2)°$?* They are vertical angles.

OL • *What is true about the measures of vertical angles?* They are equal.

• *What angles are adjacent to the 50° angle?* the ones with measures of 130° and $(2x + 2)°$

BL • *What equation could you use to solve for y?* $3y - 10 = 50$

• *What is the value of y?* $y = 20$

Need Another Example?

What is the value of *x* in the figure? 60

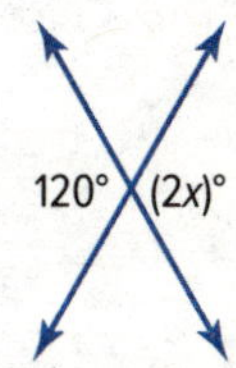

IWB

Example

4. **Write and solve an equation to find a missing measure.**

AL • *What do you know about the two labeled angles?* They are adjacent angles that form a straight angle.

• *What is the degree value of a straight angle?* 180°

OL • *What is the equation that we can use to find the value of x?* $115 + 5x = 180$

• *What is the measure of the angle labeled (5x)? Explain.* 65°; Since $x = 13$ and $5 \times 13 = 65$, the measure of the angle labeled (5x) is 65°.

BL • *Explain why you set the addition equation equal to 180°.* The line and ray drawn (not the streets themselves), form adjacent angles that together make a straight angle of 180°.

Need Another Example?
What is the value of x in the figure shown? 10

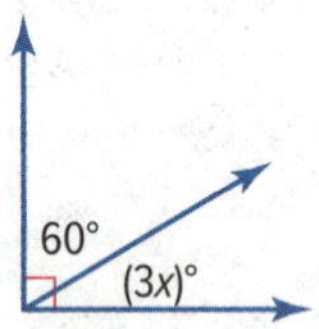

Guided Practice

Formative Assessment Use these exercises to assess students' understanding of the concepts in this lesson.

If some of your students are not ready for assignments, use the differentiated activity below.

AL EL **Pairs Consult** Have students work in pairs to complete Exercises 1–3. Prior to completing the exercises, you may wish to have them create a graphic organizer or other visual display to help them record the types of angles and angle relationships they learned in this lesson. They can use this as a reference to aid them in completing the exercises.

MP 1, 5, 6

Real World

Example

Tutor

4. **What is the value of x shown in the sidewalk?**

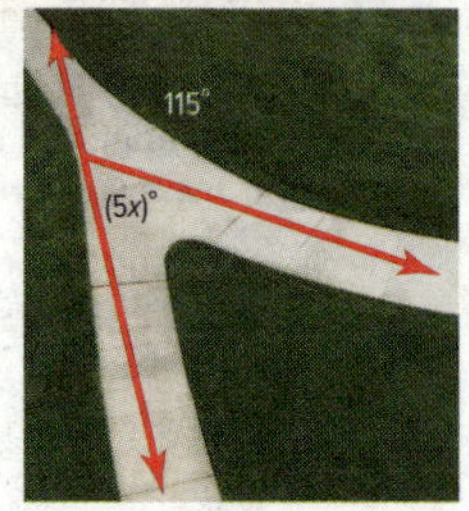

The angle labeled 115° and the angle labeled $5x$ are adjacent angles. Together they form a straight angle or 180°.

$115 + 5x = 180$ Write the equation.
$-115 \quad = -115$ Subtract 115 from each side.
$\frac{5x}{5} = \frac{65}{5}$ Divide each side by 5.
$x = 13$

So, the value of x is 13.

Guided Practice

Check

1. Name the angle below in four ways. Then classify it as *acute, right, obtuse,* or *straight.* (Example 1)

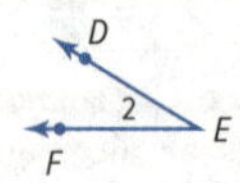

∠DEF, ∠FED, ∠E, ∠2; acute

2. Find the value of x in the figure. (Examples 3–4)

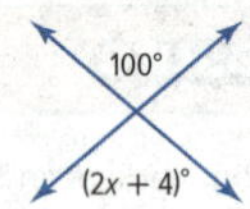

48

3. Identify a pair of vertical angles and adjacent angles on the railroad crossing sign. Justify your response. (Example 2)

Show your work.

Sample answer: ∠1 and ∠3 are vertical angles because they are opposite angles formed by the intersection of two lines. ∠2 and ∠3 are adjacent angles because they share a common vertex and common side, and they do not overlap.

4. **Building on the Essential Question** Describe the differences between vertical and adjacent angles.

Sample answer: Vertical angles are opposite angles formed by the intersection of two lines. Adjacent angles can be formed by the intersection of two lines but must share a common side and vertex.

Rate Yourself!

How confident are you about classifying angles? Check the box that applies.

For more help, go online to access a Personal Tutor.

Tutor

FOLDABLES Time to update your Foldable!

Name ______________________ My Homework ______________________

Independent Practice

Go online for Step-by-Step Solutions eHelp

Name each angle in four ways. Then classify the angle as *acute, right, obtuse,* or *straight*. (Example 1)

1.
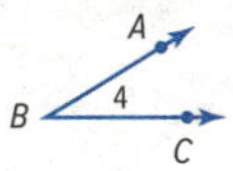

∠ABC, ∠CBA, ∠B, ∠4; acute

2.
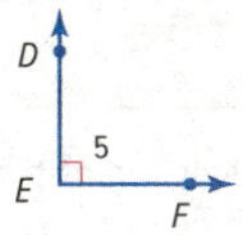

∠DEF, ∠FED, ∠E, ∠5; right

3.
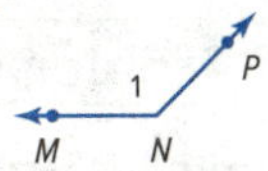

∠MNP, ∠PNM, ∠N, ∠1; obtuse

MP Identify Structure Refer to the diagram at the right. Identify each angle pair as *adjacent, vertical,* or *neither*. (Example 2)

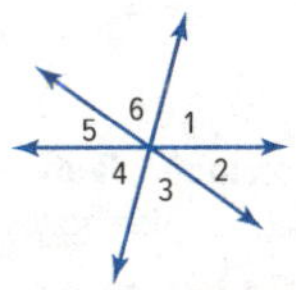

4. ∠2 and ∠5 vertical

5. ∠4 and ∠6 neither

6. ∠3 and ∠4 adjacent

7. ∠5 and ∠6 adjacent

8. ∠1 and ∠3 neither

9. ∠1 and ∠4 vertical

10. What is the value of x in the figure at the right? (Examples 3 and 4) 37

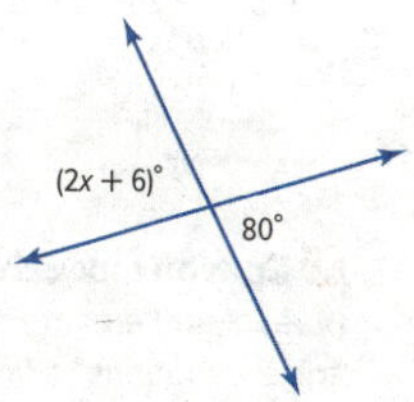

11. What is the value of x in the figure at the right? (Examples 3 and 4) 11

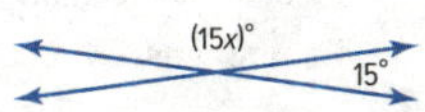

ENGAGE EXPLORE **EXPLAIN ELABORATE EVALUATE**

3 Practice and Apply

Independent Practice and Extra Practice

The Independent Practice pages are meant to be used as the homework assignment. The Extra Practice page can be used for additional reinforcement or as a second-day assignment.

Levels of Complexity

The levels of the exercises progress from 1 to 3, with Level 1 indicating the lowest level of complexity.

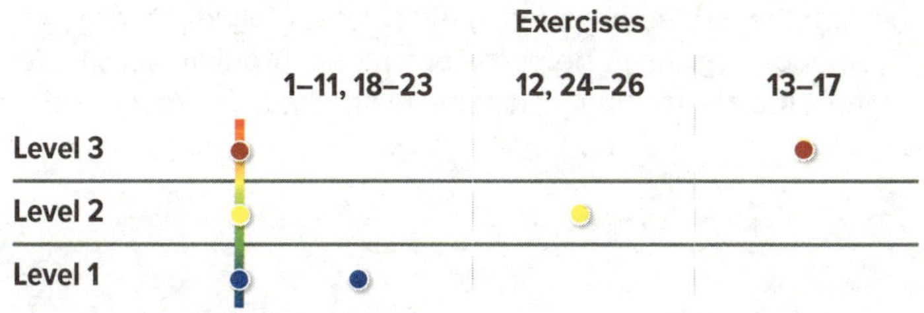

Suggested Assignments

You can use the table below that includes exercises of all complexity levels to select appropriate exercises for your students' needs.

Differentiated Homework Options		
AL	Approaching Level	1–11, 13, 14, 17, 25, 26
OL	On Level	1–11 odd, 12–14, 17, 25, 26
BL	Beyond Level	12–17, 25, 26

McGraw Hill Education **ALEKS®** can provide additional remediation support with personalized instruction and practice

Watch Out!

Common Error When more than two lines intersect, students may mistakenly identify angle pairs as being vertical when they are neither vertical nor adjacent. When classifying angle pairs with multiple intersecting lines, have students first identify the lines that intersect to create each angle. If the same straight lines are used to create both angles, then the angles are vertical.

MATHEMATICAL PRACTICES

Emphasis On	Exercise(s)
1 Make sense of problems and persevere in solving them.	15, 16
3 Construct viable arguments and critique the reasoning of others.	14, 17
4 Model with mathematics.	13
7 Look for and make use of structure.	4–9, 24

Mathematical Practices 1, 3, and 4 are aspects of mathematical thinking that are emphasized in every lesson. Students are given opportunities to be persistent in their problem solving, to express their reasoning, and apply mathematics to real-world situations.

Formative Assessment

Use this activity as a closing formative assessment before dismissing students from your class.

TICKET Out the Door

Ask students to use their own words to write a definition for vertical and adjacent angles. See students' work.

12. Angles *ABC* and *DBE* are vertical angles. If the measure of ∠*ABC* is 40°, what is the measure of ∠*ABD*?

140°

H.O.T. Problems Higher Order Thinking

13. **MP Model with Mathematics** Draw examples of angles that represent real-world objects. Be sure to include at least three of the following angles: acute, right, obtuse, straight, vertical, and adjacent. Verify by measuring the angles.

See students' work.

14. **MP Reason Inductively** Explain how you can use a protractor to measure the angle shown. Find the measure of the angle.

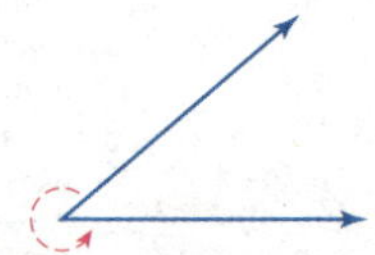

Sample answer: Since a full circle measures 360°, measure the smaller angle, then subtract that measure from 360; 320°.

MP Persevere with Problems **Determine whether each statement is *true* or *false*. If the statement is true, provide a diagram to support it. If the statement is false, explain why.**

15. A pair of obtuse angles can also be vertical angles.

True; Sample answer:

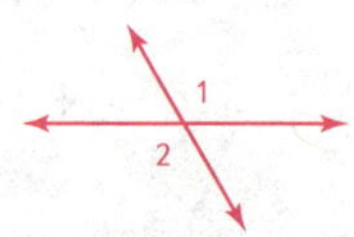

Show your work.

16. A pair of straight angles can also be adjacent angles.

True; Sample answer:

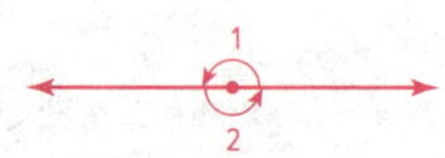

Show your work.

17. **MP Reason Inductively** Lines ℓ and *k* shown at the right are parallel and are intersected by line *j*. Explain how you can write and solve equations to find the measure of each angle. Then find the measure of each angle.

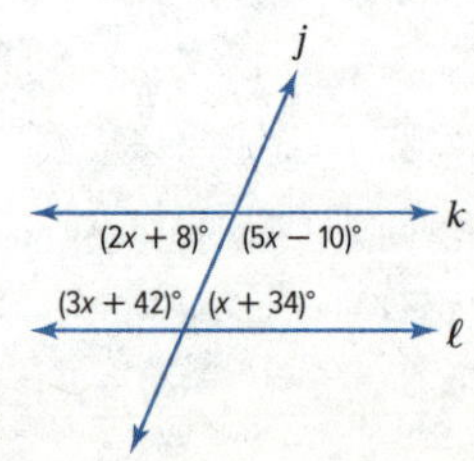

Sample answer: Each pair of angles is adjacent and forms a straight angle. So $(2x + 8) + (5x - 10) = 180$ and $(3x + 42) + (x + 34) = 180$. When you solve both equations, $x = 26$. The angle measures are 60°, 120°, 120°, and 60°.

Name ______________________ My Homework ______________________

Extra Practice

Name each angle in four ways. Then classify the angle as *acute, right, obtuse,* or *straight*.

18. 

Homework Help

∠MNP, ∠PNM, ∠N, ∠7;
straight

19. 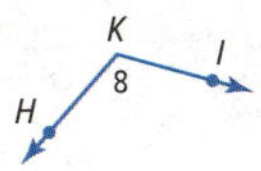

∠HKI, ∠IKH, ∠K, ∠8;
obtuse

20. 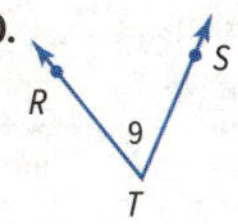

∠RTS, ∠STR, ∠T, ∠9;
acute

21. The corner where the states of Utah, Arizona, New Mexico, and Colorado meet is called the Four Corners.

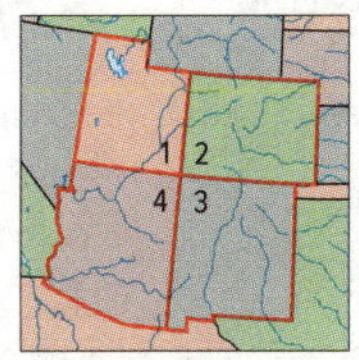

a. Identify a pair of vertical angles. Justify your response.
Sample answer: ∠1 and ∠3; Since ∠1 and ∠3 are opposite angles formed by the intersection of two lines, they are vertical angles.

b. Identify a pair of adjacent angles. Justify your response.
Sample answer: ∠1 and ∠2; Since ∠1 and ∠2 share a common vertex, a common side, and do not overlap, they are adjacent angles.

22. What is the value of x in the figure at the right?
26

23. What is the value of x in the figure at the right?
9

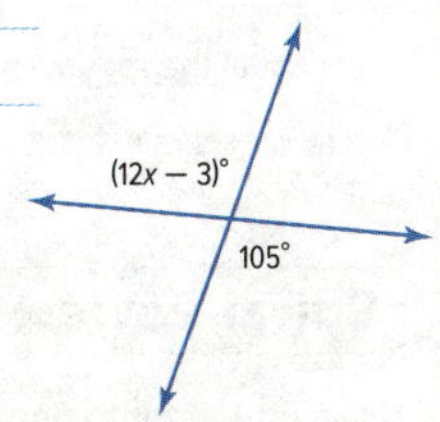

24. MP **Identify Structure** The John Hancock Center in Chicago is shown at the right. Classify each pair of angles.

a. ∠1 and ∠2 adjacent

b. ∠2 and ∠4 vertical

c. ∠3 and ∠4 adjacent

d. ∠1 and ∠3 vertical

e. If the measure of ∠2 is 66°, what are the measures of the other angles? ∠1 measures 114°, ∠4 measures 66°, ∠3 measures 114°

Create Your Own Homework Online

eSolutionsManual™ can be used to create worksheets for the suggested assignments on page 539, or create your own worksheets for differentiated homework or review.

Power Up! Test Practice

Exercises 25 and 26 prepare students for more rigorous thinking needed for the state assessment.

25.

This test item requires students to explain and apply mathematical concepts and solve problems with precision, while making use of structure.	
Depth of Knowledge	DOK1
Content Standard	7.G.5
Mathematical Practice	MP1
Online Experience	Students will be required to type their responses in the boxes.
Scoring Rubric	
1 point	Students correctly answer each part of the question.

26.

This test item requires students to reason abstractly and quantitatively when problem solving.	
Depth of Knowledge	DOK1
Content Standard	7.G.5
Mathematical Practice	MP1, MP4
Online Experience	Students drag values to complete the equation and type in the box.
Scoring Rubric	
2 points	Students correctly model the equation and find the measure of the angle.
1 point	Students correctly model the equation OR find the measure of the angle.

Power Up! Test Practice

25. Refer to the figure at the right.

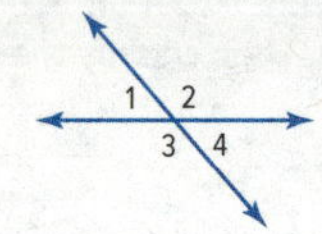

Fill in each box to make a true statement.

a. ∠1 and ∠4 are **vertical** angles.

b. ∠3 and ∠4 are **adjacent** angles.

c. ∠2 and ∠4 are **adjacent** angles.

d. ∠2 and ∠3 are **vertical** angles.

26. In the figure below, ∠*OLN* and ∠*PLR* are vertical angles.

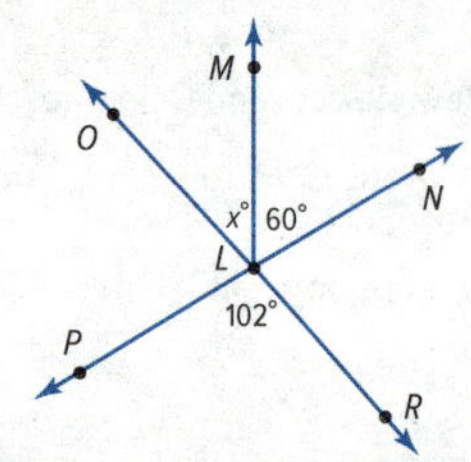

Select values to complete the equation to find the measure of ∠*MLO*.

x°	30°	60°
90°	102°	180°

x° + **60°** = **102°**

What is the measure of ∠*MLO*? **42°**

Spiral Review

Use a protractor to find the measure of each angle. 4.MD.6

27.

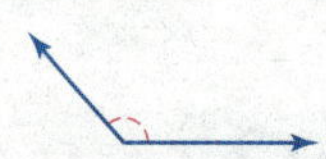

134°

28.

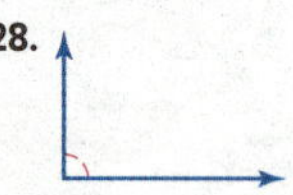

90°

29.

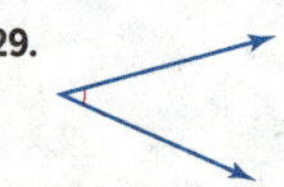

38°

30. Name the line segment at the right in two ways. 5.G.4

$\overline{AB}$, $\overline{BA}$

31. What is the name for a quadrilateral with all right angles and opposite sides that are parallel and congruent? 5.G.3

rectangle

PRESENT

IWB An Interactive Whiteboard Ready presentation is available for each lesson in the chapter.

Lesson 2

Complementary and Supplementary Angles

Real-World Link

Bridges Engineers use angles to construct bridges. The Golden Gate Bridge is created by combining angles as shown.

1. What types of angles make up the two angles marked in the drawing of the bridge? right angles

2. What is the sum of the two angles marked in the drawing of the bridge? 180°

3. In the space below, draw a figure that contains two angles that have a sum of 90°. **Sample answer:**

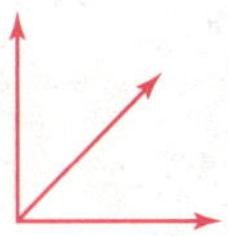

Show your work.

Essential Question

HOW does geometry help us describe real-world objects?

Vocabulary

complementary angles
supplementary angles

Math Symbols

$m\angle 1$

Content Standards

7.G.5

MP Mathematical Practices

1, 3, 4, 7

Which MP **Mathematical Practices** did you use?
Shade the circle(s) that applies.

① Persevere with Problems
② Reason Abstractly
③ Construct an Argument
④ Model with Mathematics
⑤ Use Math Tools
⑥ Attend to Precision
⑦ Make Use of Structure
⑧ Use Repeated Reasoning

Focus narrowing the scope

Objective Identify pairs of complementary and supplementary angles. 7.G.5

Coherence connecting within and across grades

Previous Students identified and classified vertical and adjacent angles.

Now Students identify complementary and supplementary angles and find missing angle measures.

Next Students will find missing angles measures of triangles.

Rigor pursuing concepts, fluency, and applications

See the Levels of Complexity chart on page 547.

ENGAGE EXPLORE EXPLAIN ELABORATE EVALUATE

1 Launch the Lesson

Ideas for Use

You may wish to launch the lesson using a whole group, small group, think-pair-share activity, or independent activity.

EL **Pairs Discussion** Have students work with a partner to complete Exercises 1–3. For Exercise 3, have them brainstorm different ways to draw the figure. Have them list several pairs of angle measures with a sum of 90°. MP 1, 5, 6

Alternate Strategy

AL EL Have students explain the meanings of *complementary and supplementary* outside of mathematics. Have them relate these meanings to the meanings of the terms within mathematics. Have them come up with a way that will help them remember the meanings of the terms as they relate to angle relationships. MP 1, 6

2 Teach the Concept

Ask the scaffolded questions for each example to differentiate instruction.

IWB

Examples

1. Identify complementary and supplementary angles.

- AL • *What kind of line do ∠1 and ∠2 form?* a straight line
- OL • *Are the angles complementary, supplementary, or neither? Explain.* supplementary; They form a straight angle, so the sum of their angle measures is 180°.
- BL • *Estimate the measures of each angle?* $\angle 1 \approx 135°$, $\angle 2 \approx 45°$
  • *Suppose the* $m\angle 1 = 135°$, *what is* $m\angle 2$? *Explain.* $m\angle 1 + m\angle 2 = 180°$; therefore, $m\angle 2 = 45°$

Need Another Example?
Identify the pair of angles as *complementary*, *supplementary*, or *neither*. supplementary

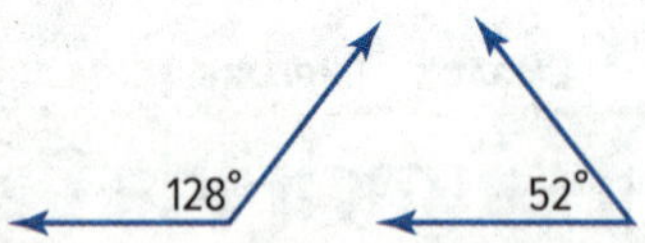

2. Identify complementary and supplementary angles.

- AL • *Are the angles adjacent? Explain.* no; They do not share a common vertex.
- OL • *Are the angles complementary, supplementary, or neither? Explain.* complementary; The sum of their angle measures is 90°.
- BL • *Can two angles be complementary, if they are not adjacent? Explain.* Yes, as long as the sum of their measures equals 90°.

Need Another Example?
Identify ∠1 and ∠2 as *complementary*, *supplementary*, or *neither*. complementary

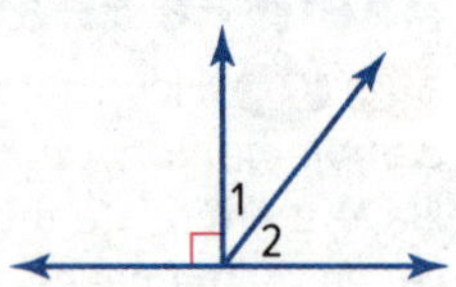

Key Concept

Pairs of Angles

Words	Models	Symbols
Two angles are **complementary** if the sum of their measures is 90°.	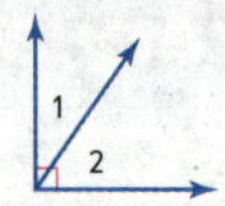	$m\angle 1 + m\angle 2 = 90°$
Two angles are **supplementary** if the sum of their measures is 180°.	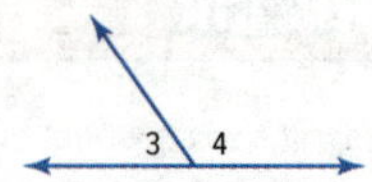	$m\angle 3 + m\angle 4 = 180°$

Work Zone

A special relationship exists between two angles with a sum of 90°. A special relationship also exists between two angles with a sum of 180°. The symbol $m\angle 1$ means *the measure of angle 1.*

Examples

Tutor

Identify each pair of angles as *complementary, supplementary,* or *neither*.

1.

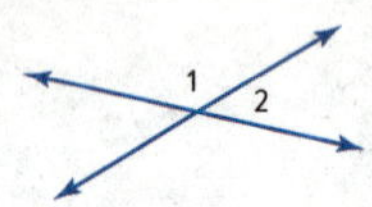

∠1 and ∠2 form a straight angle. So, the angles are supplementary.

2.

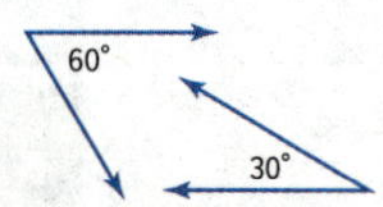

60° + 30° = 90° The angles are complementary.

Adjacent
As shown in Example 2, angles do not need to be adjacent to be complementary or supplementary angles.

Got it? **Do these problems to find out.**

a.

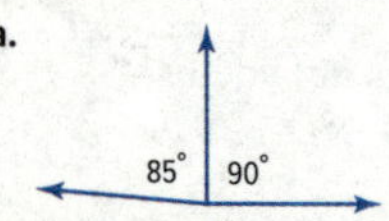

b.

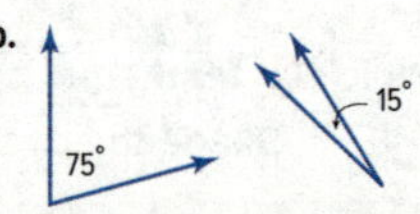

Show your work.

a. neither

b. complementary

Find a Missing Measure

You can use angle relationships to find missing measures.

Examples

Watch Tutor

3. Find the value of *x*.

Since the two angles form a right angle, they are complementary.

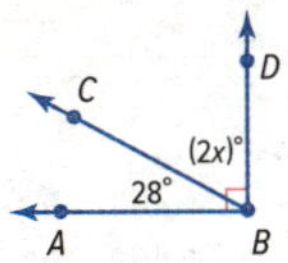

Words	The sum of the measures of ∠ABC and ∠CBD	is	90°.
Variable	Let 2x represent the measure of ∠CBD.		
Equation	28 + 2x	=	90

$28 + 2x = 90$ Write the equation.

$-28 \quad = -28$ Subtract 28 from each side.

$\frac{2x}{2} = \frac{62}{2}$ Divide each side by 2.

$x = 31$

So, the value of *x* is 31.

4. The angles shown are supplementary. Find the value of *x*.

$123 + 3x = 180$ Write the equation.

$-123 \quad = -123$ Subtract 123 from each side.

$\frac{3x}{3} = \frac{57}{3}$ Divide each side by 3.

$x = 19$

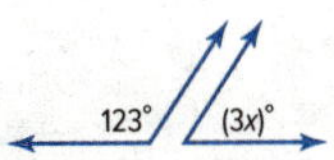

So, the value of *x* is 19.

Got it? Do this problem to find out.

c. Find the value of *x*.

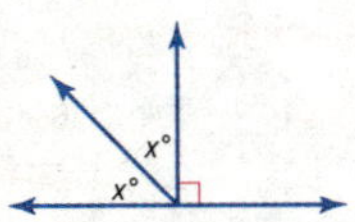

STOP and Reflect

Circle true or false.
The sum of two angles that are supplementary is 180°.

True False

Show your work.

c. 45

Examples

IWB

3. Find missing measures.

AL
- *Are the angles complementary or supplementary?* complementary
- *What is the sum of the measures of the two angles?* 90°

OL
- *What equation can we use to find the value of x?* $28 + 2x = 90$
- *What steps do we use to solve the equation?* First, subtract 28 from both sides. Then divide both sides by 2.

BL
- *If the value of x is 31, what is m∠CBD? Explain.* You have to substitute the value back into the expression 2*x*; *m*∠*CBD* = 62°.

Need Another Example?
Find the value of *x*. 62

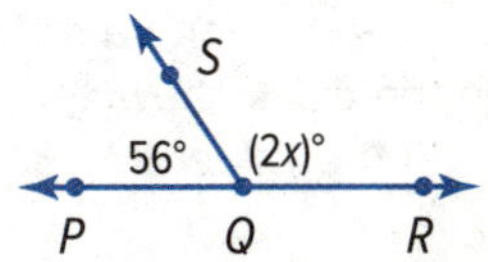

4. Find missing measures.

AL
- *If the angles are supplementary, what is the sum of their measures?* 180°
- *What is the measure of the angle we are given?* 123°
- *What is the algebraic expression for the other angle measure we are given?* (3*x*)°

OL
- *What equation can we use to find the value of x?* $123 + 3x = 180$
- *What steps do we use to solve the equation?* First, subtract 123 from both sides. Then divide both sides by 3.

BL
- *How can you tell, by looking at the diagrams of the angles, that the angles are not complementary?* Sample answer: One of the angles is obtuse, which means that angle measure is already greater than 90°.

Need Another Example?
The angles shown are complementary. Find the value of *x*. 9

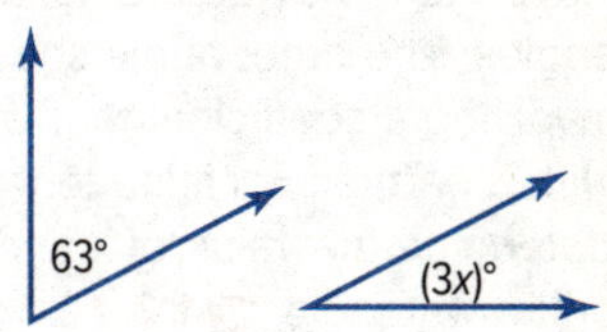

Example

IWB

5. Find missing measures.

AL • *If the angles are supplementary, what is their sum?* 180°

• *What is the algebraic expression for the other angle measure we are given?* $(10x)°$

OL • *What equation can we use to find the value of x?* $80 + 10x = 180$

• *What steps do we use to solve the equation?* First, subtract 80 from both sides. Then divide both sides by 10.

BL • *What is the measure of the angle labeled $(10x)°$?* 100°

Need Another Example?
The hour, minute, and second hands make up two adjacent angles that form a right angle in the clock shown. Find the value of x. 3

Guided Practice

Formative Assessment Use these exercises to assess students' understanding of the concepts in this lesson.

If some of your students are not ready for assignments, use the differentiated activities below.

AL EL **Pairs Check** Have students complete Exercises 1–4 in pairs. Then have them join another pair to check their work and discuss and resolve any discrepancies. MP 1, 6

BL EL **Trade-a-Problem** Have students draw their own diagram using either complementary or supplementary angles. Have them provide the numerical measure of one of the angles. The other angle should be an algebraic expression involving a coefficient that is not 1. Have them trade diagrams with a partner. Each student writes and solves an equation to determine the value of x and then finds the measure of the unknown angle. MP 1, 2, 7

Real World Example

Tutor

5. The picture shows a support brace for a gate. Find the value of x.

The angle labeled 80° and the angle labeled $10x$ are supplementary angles.

$$80 + 10x = 180 \quad \text{Write the equation.}$$
$$-80 \quad = -80 \quad \text{Subtract 80 from each side.}$$
$$\frac{10x}{10} = \frac{100}{10} \quad \text{Divide each side by 10.}$$
$$x = 10$$

So, the value of x is 10.

Got it? Do this problem to find out.

Show your work.

d. A pair of scissors forms the angles shown. What is the value of x?

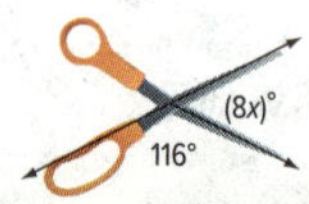

d. 8

Guided Practice

Check

Identify each pair of angles as *complementary*, *supplementary*, or *neither*. (Examples 1 and 2)

1.

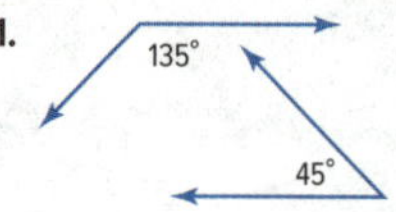

supplementary

2.

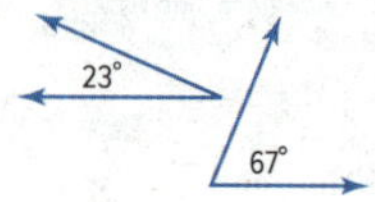

complementary

3. Find the value of x. (Examples 3–5)

45

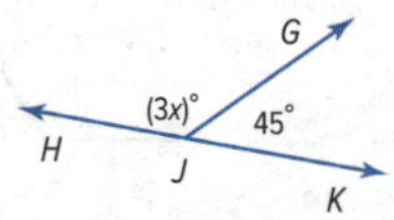

4. **Building on the Essential Question** How are vertical, adjacent, complementary, and supplementary angles related? Sample answer: Adjacent angles are two angles that share a common side and vertex and do not overlap. Vertical angles will never be adjacent. Complementary and supplementary angles may or may not be adjacent.

Rate Yourself!

Are you ready to move on? Shade the section that applies.

For more help, go online to access a Personal Tutor.

Tutor

Image Source/Superstock

Name ____________ My Homework ____________

Independent Practice

Go online for Step-by-Step Solutions eHelp

Identify each pair of angles as *complementary, supplementary,* or *neither.* (Examples 1 and 2)

1. 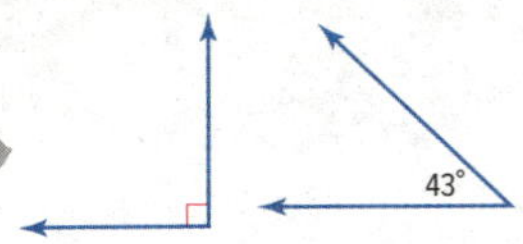

neither

2. 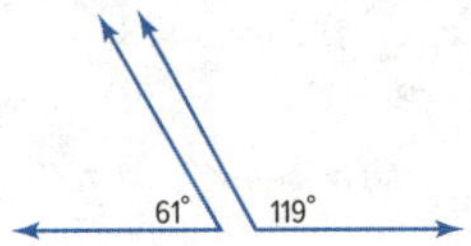

supplementary

3. 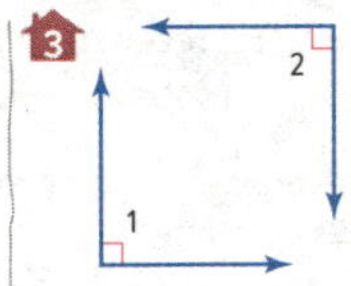

supplementary

Find the measure of *x* in each figure. (Examples 3 and 4)

4. 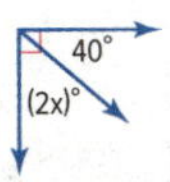

25

5. 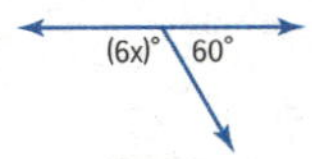

20

6. ∠*A* and ∠*B* are complementary angles. The measure of ∠*B* is (4*x*)°, and the measure of ∠*A* is 50°. What is the value of *x*? (Example 5)

10

7. A skateboard ramp forms a 42° angle as shown. Find the value of *x*. (Example 5)

23

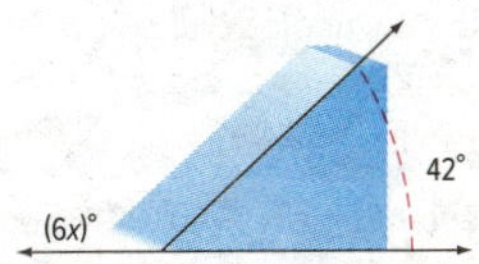

Use the figure at the right to name the following.

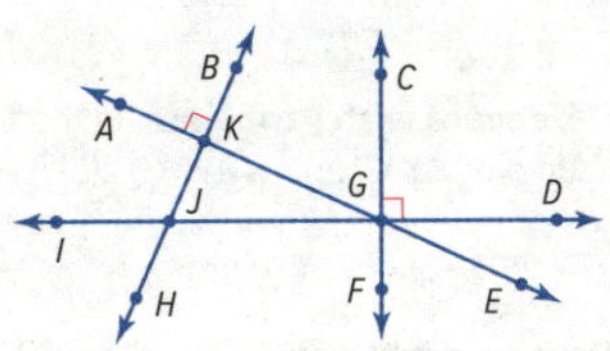

8. a pair of supplementary angles

Sample answer: ∠*IJK*, ∠*KJG*

9. a pair of complementary angles

Sample answer: ∠*CGK*, ∠*KGJ*

10. a pair of vertical angles

Sample answer: ∠*AKB*, ∠*JKG*

ENGAGE EXPLORE **EXPLAIN** **ELABORATE** **EVALUATE**

3 Practice and Apply

Independent Practice and Extra Practice

The Independent Practice pages are meant to be used as the homework assignment. The Extra Practice page can be used for additional reinforcement or as a second-day assignment.

Levels of Complexity

The levels of the exercises progress from 1 to 3, with Level 1 indicating the lowest level of complexity.

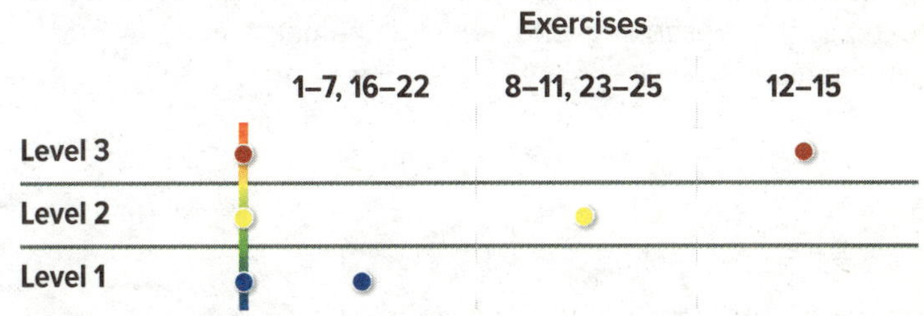

Suggested Assignments

You can use the table below that includes exercises of all complexity levels to select appropriate exercises for your students' needs.

Differentiated Homework Options		
AL	Approaching Level	1–7, 9, 11, 12, 15, 24, 25
OL	On Level	1–7 odd, 8–12, 15, 24, 25
BL	Beyond Level	8–15, 24, 25

ALEKS® can provide additional remediation support with personalized instruction and practice.

MATHEMATICAL PRACTICES

Emphasis On	Exercise(s)
1 Make sense of problems and persevere in solving them.	13, 14
3 Construct viable arguments and critique the reasoning of others.	12, 15, 23
7 Look for and make use of structure.	21, 22

Mathematical Practices 1, 3, and 4 are aspects of mathematical thinking that are emphasized in every lesson. Students are given opportunities to be persistent in their problem solving, to express their reasoning, and apply mathematics to real-world situations.

Formative Assessment
Use this activity as a closing formative assessment before dismissing students from your class.

TICKET Out the Door

Tell students that ∠1 and ∠2 are complementary, ∠1 measures 48°, and ∠2 measures (3*x*)°. Have students write and solve an equation to find the value of *x*.
$48 + 3x = 90; x = 14$

Watch Out!

Common Error Students may confuse the terms *complementary* and *supplementary*. Provide students with a mnemonic device to help them remember the definition of supplementary, such as supplementary: straight.

11. Use the figure at the right.

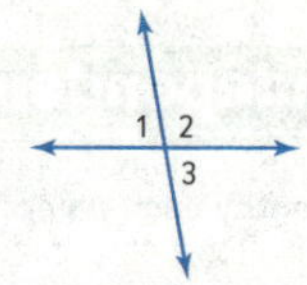

a. Are ∠1 and ∠2 vertical angles, adjacent angles, or neither? ∠2 and ∠3? ∠1 and ∠3?

adjacent; adjacent; vertical

b. Write an equation representing the sum of $m\angle1$ and $m\angle2$. Then write an equation representing the sum of $m\angle2$ and $m\angle3$.

$m\angle1 + m\angle2 = 180°$; $m\angle2 + m\angle3 = 180°$

c. Solve the equations you wrote in part **b** for $m\angle1$ and $m\angle3$, respectively. What do you notice?

$m\angle1 = 180° - m\angle2$; $m\angle3 = 180° - m\angle2$; Sample answer: $m\angle1$ and $m\angle3$ are equal.

d. MP **Make a Conjecture** Use your answer from part **c** to make a conjecture as to the relationship between vertical angles.

Sample answer: Vertical angles are congruent.

H.O.T. Problems Higher Order Thinking

12. MP **Reason Inductively** When a basketball hits a hard, level surface, it bounces off at the same angle at which it hits. Use the figure to find the angle at which the ball hit the floor.

55°

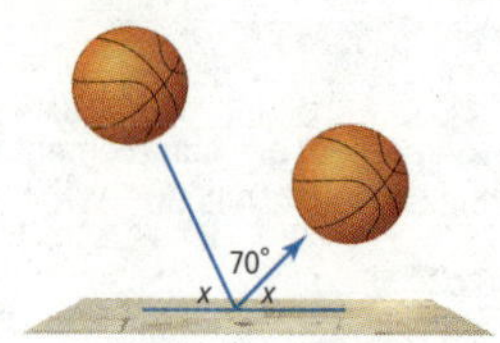

13. MP **Persevere with Problems** Find the measure of each angle in the given situation.

a. complementary angles *E* and *F*, where $m\angle E = (x - 10)°$ and $m\angle F = (x + 2)°$

$m\angle E = 39°$; $m\angle F = 51°$

b. supplementary angles *B* and *C*, where $m\angle B = (2x - 40)°$ and $m\angle C = (2x + 20)°$

$m\angle B = 60°$; $m\angle C = 120°$

14. MP **Persevere with Problems** In the figure shown, the sum of the measures of ∠*YXZ* and ∠*WXV* is 75°. What is the measure of ∠*ZXW*?

105°

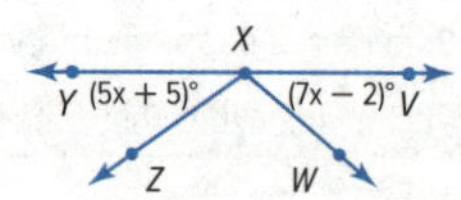

15. MP **Reason Inductively** Is the statement below *always*, *sometimes*, or *never* true? Explain.

If two angles are right angles, they must be supplementary.

Sample answer: Right angles have a measure of 90°, so two right angles will always have a sum of 180°. This is the definition of supplementary angles.

Name ______________________ My Homework ______________________

Extra Practice

Identify each pair of angles as *complementary, supplementary,* or *neither*.

16. 

Homework Help

∠1 and ∠2 form a straight angle. So, the angles are supplementary.

17. 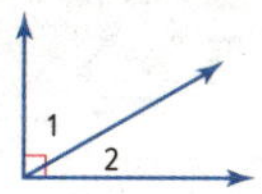

complementary

18. 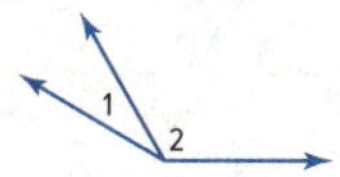

neither

19. ∠*J* and ∠*K* are supplementary. The measure of ∠*J* is $(9x)°$ and the measure of ∠*K* is 45°. What is the value of *x*?

15

20. ∠*C* and ∠*D* are complementary. The measure of ∠*C* is $(4x)°$ and the measure of ∠*D* is 26°. What is the value of *x*?

16

MP **Identify Structure** **Determine whether each statement is *always, sometimes,* or *never* true. Explain your reasoning.**

21. Two obtuse angles are supplementary.

never; Sample answer: Since an obtuse angle is greater than 90°, the sum of two obtuse angles must be greater than, not equal to, 180°.

22. Two vertical angles are complementary.

sometimes; Sample answer: If the measure of each angle is 45°, then the two angles are complementary.

23. MP **Multiple Representations** Line *a* passes through (1, 4) and (−4, −1). Line *b* passes through (−3, 4) and (2, −1).

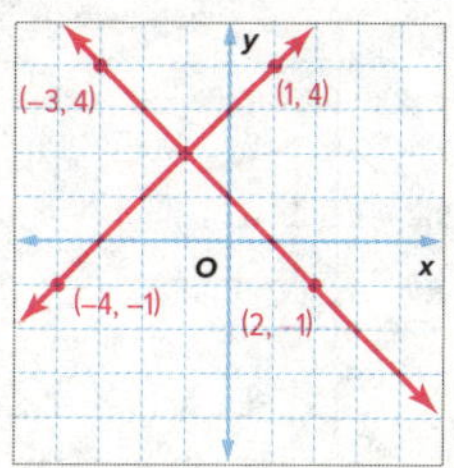

a. Graphs Graph each line on the same coordinate plane.

b. Words Describe the lines.

The lines appear to be perpendicular.

c. Numbers What is the slope of each line?

line *a*: 1; line *b*: −1

Create Your Own Homework Online

eSolutionsManual™ can be used to create worksheets for the suggested assignments on page 547, or create your own worksheets for differentiated homework or review.

Power Up! Test Practice

Exercises 24 and 25 prepare students for more rigorous thinking needed for the state assessment.

24. This test item requires students to reason abstractly and quantitatively when problem solving.

Depth of Knowledge	DOK1
Content Standard	7.G.5
Mathematical Practice	MP1
Online Experience	Students will be required to click on the bubbles to select all answers that are correct.
Scoring Rubric	
1 point	Students correctly answer the question.

25. This test item requires students to explain and apply mathematical concepts and solve problems with precision, while making use of structure.

Depth of Knowledge	DOK1
Content Standard	7.G.5
Mathematical Practices	MP1, MP4
Online Experience	Students will drag values to model the equation and type their responses in boxes.
Scoring Rubric	
2 points	Students correctly model the equation and find each measure.
1 point	Students correctly model the equation but fail to find both measures OR students find both measures but fail to correctly model the equation.

Power Up! Test Practice

24. Which angle pairs below are supplementary? Select all that apply.

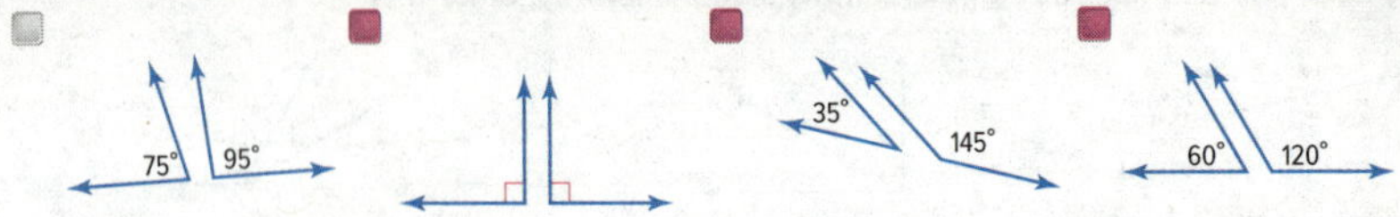

25. The angle at which the light ray hits the water is equal to the angle at which the light ray is reflected from the water.

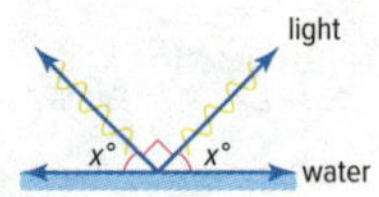

Select values to complete the equation below to find the value of x.

2 × [x°] + [90°] = [180°]

x°
45°
60°
90°
180°

What is the measure of the angle at which the light ray hits the water?

[45°]

What is the measure of the angle at which the light ray is reflected from the water?

[45°]

Spiral Review

Graph each figure with the given vertices on the coordinate plane. Then classify each figure. 6.G.3

26. (1, 3), (1, 6), (5, 5), and (5, 3)

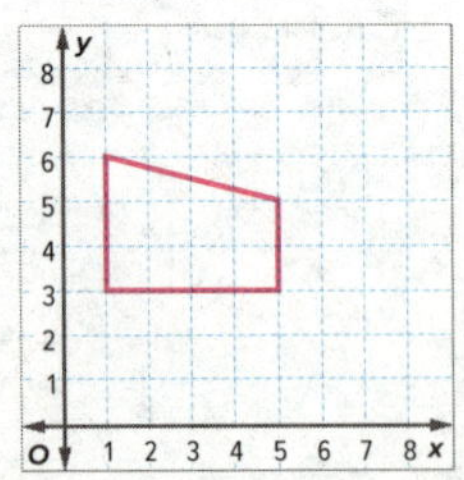

trapezoid

27. (1, 2), (5, 2), (5, 6), and (1, 6)

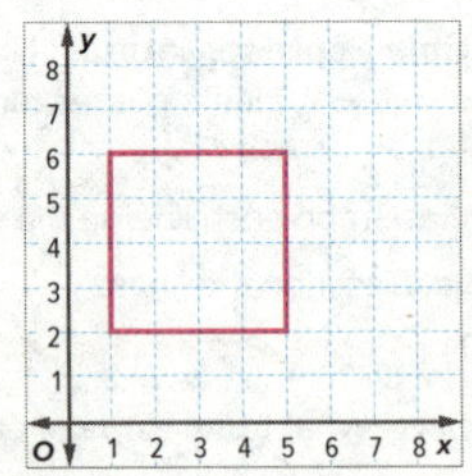

square

PLAN ONLINE

PD | RtI | Watch | Worksheets | Vocab | Tutor | Tools | Check | English Learners | Sketchpad

PRESENT

IWB

An Interactive Whiteboard Ready presentation is available for each lesson in the chapter.

Inquiry Lab
Create Triangles

Inquiry WHAT do you notice about the measures of the sides or the measures of the angles that form triangles?

Content Standards
7.G.2

MP Mathematical Practices
1, 3, 5, 8

Dennis has a sailboat. The sail on his boat is in the shape of a triangle with side lengths of 6 feet, 8 feet, and 10 feet. These dimensions work to form a triangle, but not just any three lengths form a triangle. Complete the Activity below to determine which side lengths form triangles.

Hands-On Activity 1

Step 1 Measure and cut several plastic straws into lengths that equal 3, 4, 4, 5, 8, 8, 8, 13, 15, 15, 15, and 15 centimeters.

Step 2 Arrange three of the pieces that each measure 15 centimeters to see if you can form a triangle.

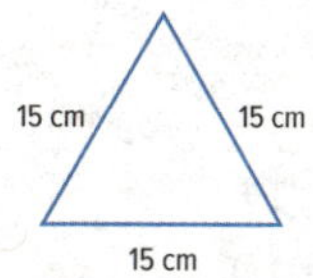

So, you can form a triangle with side lengths of 15 centimeters, 15 centimeters, and 15 centimeters.

Step 3 Continue using pieces of straw to try to form triangles using the different combinations of side lengths given. Determine whether or not the lengths form a triangle. Complete the table.

Side 1	Side 2	Side 3	Do the sides form a triangle?
15 cm	15 cm	15 cm	yes
3 cm	4 cm	5 cm	yes
8 cm	8 cm	13 cm	yes
3 cm	4 cm	8 cm	no
4 cm	4 cm	5 cm	yes
8 cm	3 cm	15 cm	no
4 cm	8 cm	15 cm	no

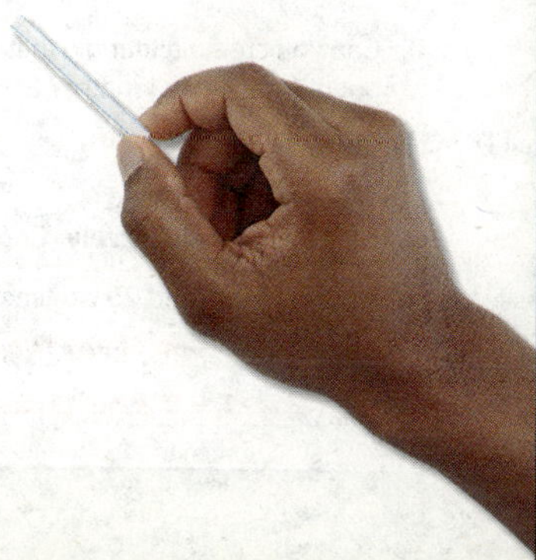

Focus narrowing the scope

Objective Draw triangles using given angles or side lengths. 7.G.2

Materials: plastic drinking straws, patty paper, protractor

Coherence connecting within and across grades

Now
Students use manipulatives to try to create triangles from given angle measurements or given side measurements.

Next
Students will find the measure of an unknown angle in a triangle.

Rigor pursuing concepts, fluency, and applications

See the Levels of Complexity chart on page 552.

ENGAGE EXPLORE EXPLAIN ELABORATE EVALUATE

1 Launch the Lab

Activity 1 is intended to be used as a whole-group activity. Activity 1 is designed to provide more guidance than Activity 2.

Hands-On Activity 1

AL **EL** Explain to students that when measuring the straws, it is very important that they measure their straws carefully. Precise measurements are important in completing this Activity. MP 1, 6

BL Omit Activities 1 and 2 and proceed directly to the Investigate section.

2 Collaborate

The **Investigate** and **Analyze and Reflect** sections are intended to be used as small-group investigations. The **Create** section is intended to be used as independent exercises.

Levels of Complexity

The levels of the exercises progress from 1 to 3, with Level 1 indicating the lowest level of complexity.

Exercises	1–3, 8, 9	4, 5, 10	6, 7, 11, 12
Level 3			●
Level 2		●	
Level 1	●		

Investigate

Collaborate

AL **EL** **Pairs Discussion** Have students work in pairs to complete Exercises 1–3. Have them trade their solutions with another pair of students and discuss any differences. MP 1, 5

Analyze and Reflect

Collaborate

AL **EL** **Think-Pair-Share** Have students work in pairs. Give students one minute to think through their responses to Exercises 4 and 5. Have them share their responses with their partner. Then call on one student to share their response within a small group or large group discussion. MP 1, 7

Create

On Your Own

BL **EL** **Brainstorm** Have students brainstorm different side lengths that might make a triangle. Have students explain why or why not their measurements could be used to make a triangle. MP 1, 7

Investigate

Collaborate

Work with a partner. Try to create triangles using the given side lengths. Circle *yes* if you can make a triangle or *no* if you cannot.

1. 5 cm, 8 cm, 15 cm

Yes or (No)

2. 13 cm, 8 cm, 15 cm

(Yes) or No

3. 13 cm, 4 cm, 4 cm

Yes or (No)

Analyze and Reflect

Collaborate

Work with a partner.

4. The table below contains the dimensions you used in Step 3 of the Activity. Transfer your results from the Investigation into the fourth column and then complete the fifth column.

Side 1	Side 2	Side 3	Do the sides form a triangle?	Is Side 1 + Side 2 greater than or less than Side 3?
15 cm	15 cm	15 cm	yes	greater than
3 cm	4 cm	5 cm	yes	greater than
8 cm	8 cm	13 cm	yes	greater than
3 cm	4 cm	8 cm	no	less than
4 cm	4 cm	5 cm	yes	greater than
8 cm	3 cm	15 cm	no	less than
4 cm	8 cm	15 cm	no	less than

5. What do you notice about the figures with a Side 1 and Side 2 sum that is less than the length of Side 3? Sample answer: They do not form triangles.

Create

On Your Own

6. Can you create a triangle that has the same shape as the triangle in the Activity, but different side lengths? Explain.

Yes; 8 cm, 8 cm, 8 cm

7. MP **Reason Inductively** Could you form a triangle using the side lengths of 7, 8, and 25 centimeters? Explain. No; Sample answer: To form a triangle, the sum of any two sides must be greater than the length of the third side. 7 + 8 is not greater than 25.

Geometry

Hands-On Activity 2

Use angles of different sizes to determine which ones form a triangle.

Step 1 Draw two sets of angles measuring 30°, 45°, 60°, and 90° on different pieces of patty paper. Extend the rays of each angle to the edges of the patty paper.

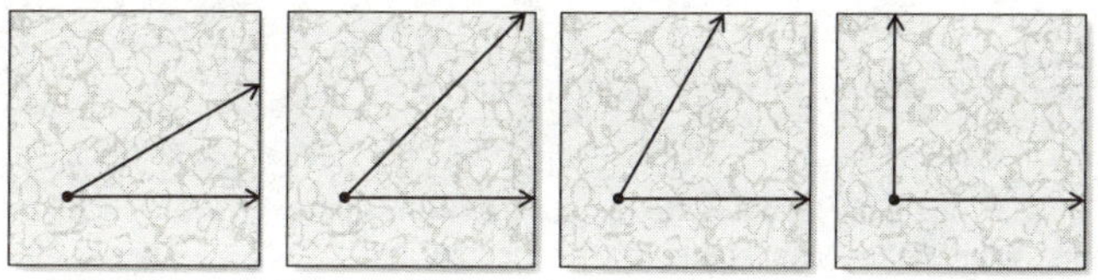

30° 45° 60° 90°

Step 2 Try to form a triangle with one 90° angle and two 45° angles.

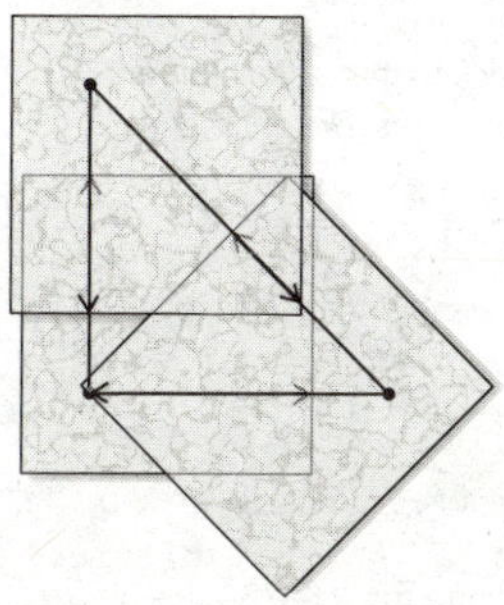

So, a 90° angle and two 45° angles form a triangle.

Step 3 Try to form triangles using the angle measures that are given in the table. Fill in *yes* or *no* in the fourth column of the table.

Angle 1	Angle 2	Angle 3	Do the angles form a triangle?
90°	45°	45°	yes
30°	60°	90°	yes
30°	45°	60°	no
30°	30°	60°	no

Hands-On Activity 2

AL EL **Three Stay, One Stray** Have students work in groups of four to complete Steps 1–3. Upon completion of Step 3, have one student from each group stray to another group to share ideas and results. Have students return to their original groups to share results and revise their solutions, if necessary. MP 1, 5

BL EL **Find the Fib** Have students work in pairs to write two facts and one fib about the Activity. For example, one fact could be that angle measures of 90°, 45°, and 45° make a triangle. One fib could be that angle measures of 30°, 45°, and 60° make a triangle. Have students trade facts and fibs with another pair of students. Each pair identifies the facts and fibs and shares their responses with the original pair of students to resolve any disagreements. MP 1, 3, 7

Investigate

AL EL **Talking Chips** Have students work in groups of 3–4 to complete Exercises 8 and 9. Provide each student with 4 talking chips. As students discuss each exercise, they should place a chip in the center of the table every time they verbally contribute a response or ask a clarifying question. After they have placed all of their chips in the center of the table, they may not contribute. Students must use all of their chips. MP 1, 5

BL EL **Circle the Sage** Separate students into groups of 4. Teacher should select a "sage" to lead the discussion for each group through Exercises 8 and 9. The sage should be a student that is proficient in triangle sums and is able to communicate ideas to the group and lead a discussion. Sages are responsible for ensuring that each team member contributes to the discussion and that each team member understands how to complete the exercises. MP 1, 7

Analyze and Reflect

AL EL **Pairs Check** Have students work in pairs to complete Exercise 10. Have students discuss differences in responses and make corrections, if necessary. Have pairs share their responses and reasoning with the class. MP 1, 8

Create

BL EL **Trade-a-Problem** Have students draw and measure three angles on their own. Students trade their angles with a partner and determine if the angles could be used to form a triangle. If they do not form a triangle, students work together to find an angle that would work. MP 1, 5, 7

Inquiry Students should be able to answer "WHAT do you notice about the measures of the sides or the measures of the angles that form triangles?" Check for student understanding and provide guidance, if needed.

Investigate

Work with a partner.

8. Draw another 60° angle on a piece of patty paper. Describe the angles and side lengths of the figure you form using three 60° angles.

Show your work.

The figure is a triangle with three equal angles and three equal side lengths.

9. Draw angles measuring 20°, 70°, and 90° on pieces of patty paper.

a. Do the angles form a triangle? yes

b. Can you create more than one triangle that is the same shape with different side lengths? What are the side lengths of your triangle?

yes; Student answers will vary.

Analyze and Reflect

10. MP **Identify Repeated Reasoning** Refer back to the table in Step 3 of Activity 2. Compare the sum of the angle measures. Describe any patterns that are found.

To form a triangle, the sum of the angles must equal 180°.

Create

11. MP **Use Math Tools** Use a protractor to measure the three angles below. Would you be able to form a triangle from these angles? Explain.

Yes. The angles measure 65°, 25°, 90°. The sum of these angles equals 180°.

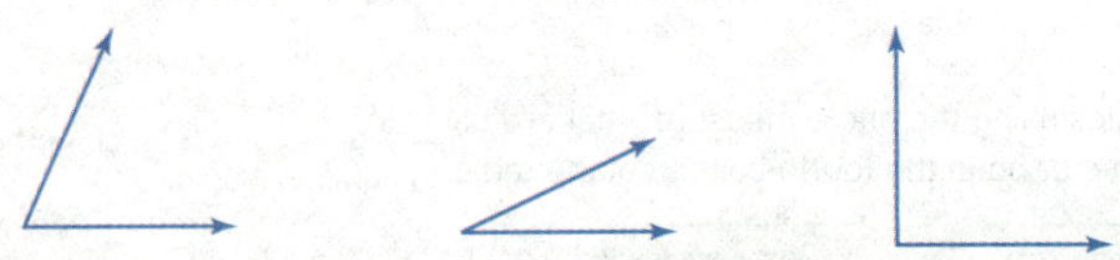

12. Inquiry WHAT do you notice about the measures of the sides or the measures of the angles that form triangles?

The sum of the lengths of any two sides of a triangle must be greater than the length of the third side. The sum of the three angles of a triangle must equal 180°.

PLAN ONLINE: PD · RtI · Watch · Worksheets · Vocab · Tutor · Tools · Check · English Learners · Sketchpad

PRESENT: IWB — An Interactive Whiteboard Ready presentation is available for each lesson in the chapter.

Lesson 3

Triangles

Real-World Link

Ramps Julia practices jumping on a ski ramp. The front of the ramp is a triangle like the one shown below.

1. Draw an X through the type of angle that is not shown in the triangle.

   right acute ~~obtuse~~

2. Measure the unknown angle. Describe the relationship between the 80° angle and the unknown angle. **10°; Sample answer: The angles are complementary.**

3. Draw a triangle with one obtuse angle. **Sample answer:**

Show your work.

4. Is it possible to draw a triangle with two obtuse angles? Explain.
   No; When you have two obtuse angles the rays of the angles can not connect.

Which MP **Mathematical Practices** did you use? Shade the circle(s) that applies.

1. Persevere with Problems
2. Reason Abstractly
3. Construct an Argument
4. Model with Mathematics
5. Use Math Tools
6. Attend to Precision
7. Make Use of Structure
8. Use Repeated Reasoning

Essential Question

HOW does geometry help us describe real-world objects?

Vocabulary

acute triangle
right triangle
obtuse triangle
scalene triangle
isosceles triangle
equilateral triangle
triangle
congruent segments

Math Symbols

△

Content Standards
7.G.2

MP **Mathematical Practices**
1, 2, 3, 4

Focus narrowing the scope

Objective Idenify and classify triangles and find missing angle measures. 7.G.2

Coherence connecting within and across grades

Previous Students used properties of angles to find missing angle measures.

Now Students classify different types of triangles and find missing angle measures in triangles.

Next Students will classify quadrilaterals and find missing angle measures of quadrilaterals.

Rigor pursuing concepts, fluency, and applications

See the Levels of Complexity chart on page 559.

ENGAGE EXPLORE EXPLAIN ELABORATE EVALUATE

1 Launch the Lesson

Ideas for Use

You may wish to launch the lesson using a whole group, small group, think-pair-share activity, or independent activity.

EL **Think-Pair-Draw** Give students one minute to think through their responses to Exercises 1–4. Then have them discuss their ideas and responses with a partner. Call on one set of partners to explain their responses to the class. MP 1, 5, 7

Alternate Strategy

BL Have students explain whether it is possible to draw a triangle with two right triangles. Have them verify their response by using logical reasoning. MP 1, 3, 7

2 Teach the Concept

Ask the scaffolded questions for each example to differentiate instruction.

IWB

Example

1. Draw and classify triangles.

AL
- *Describe what you know about an obtuse angle.* Sample answer: Its angle measure is greater than 90° and less than 180°.
- *How can you draw an obtuse angle?* Sample answer: Use a ruler or straightedge to draw one side. Then use a protractor to draw a second side so that the angle formed is more than a right angle but less than a straight angle.

OL
- *If a triangle has one obtuse angle, what types of angles are the other two angles?* acute angles
- *Since the triangle has one obtuse angle, how would you classify the triangle by its angles?* obtuse
- *Since the triangle has no congruent sides, how can you classify the triangle by its sides?* scalene

BL
- *When drawing the triangle, how can you be certain that it will be scalene?* Sample answer: make sure that the three sides drawn are all different lengths

Need Another Example?
Draw a triangle with three acute angles and two congruent sides. Then classify the triangle. Sample answer: acute isosceles

Key Concept **Classify Triangles**

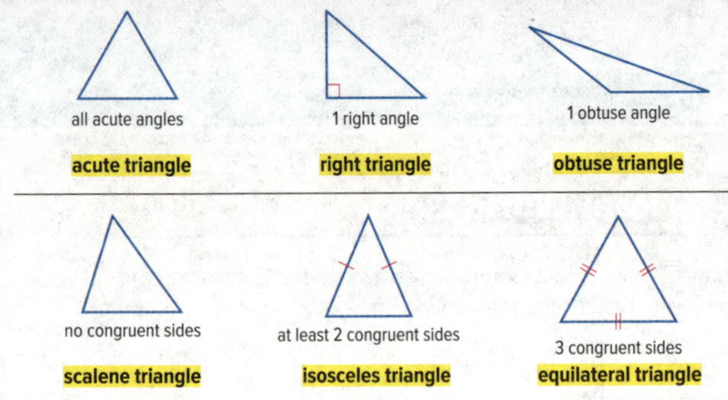

Work Zone

Congruent Segments
The tick marks on the sides of the triangle indicate that those sides are congruent.

A **triangle** is a figure with three sides and three angles. The symbol for triangle is △.

Every triangle has at least two acute angles. One way you can classify a triangle is by using the third angle. Another way to classify triangles is by their sides. Sides with the same length are **congruent segments**.

Example

Tutor

1. Draw a triangle with one obtuse angle and no congruent sides. Then classify the triangle.

Draw an obtuse angle. The two segments of the angle should have different lengths.

Connect the two segments to form a triangle.

The triangle is an obtuse scalene triangle.

Show your work.

Got it? **Do this problem to find out.**

Draw a triangle that satisfies the set of conditions below. Then classify the triangle.

a. a triangle with one right angle and two congruent sides

Sample answer: right isosceles

a.

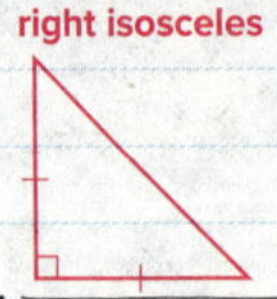

Example

Real World

Watch Tutor

2. **Classify the triangle on the house by its angles and by its sides.**

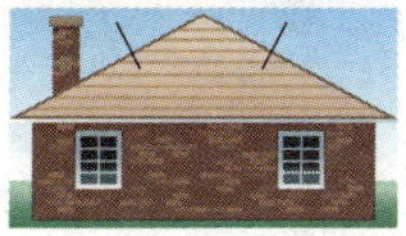

The triangle has one obtuse angle and two congruent sides. So, it is an obtuse isosceles triangle.

Got it? **Do this problem to find out.**

b. Classify the triangle shown by its angles and by its sides.

STOP and Reflect

How would you classify a triangle with a right angle and two congruent sides?

right isosceles

b. right scalene

Angles of a Triangle

Key Concept

Words The sum of the measures of the angles of a triangle is 180°.

Algebra $x + y + z = 180$

Model

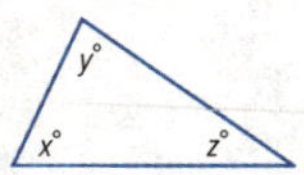

You can write and solve an equation to find the missing angle measure of a triangle.

Example

Tutor

3. **Find $m\angle Z$.**

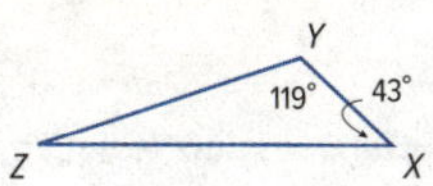

The sum of the angle measures in a triangle is 180°.

$m\angle Z + 43° + 119° = 180°$ Write the equation.

$m\angle Z + 162° = 180°$ Simplify.

$-162° = -162°$ Subtract 162° from each side.

$m\angle Z = 18°$

So, $m\angle Z$ is 18°.

Got it? **Do this problem to find out.**

c. In $\triangle ABC$, if $m\angle A = 25°$ and $m\angle B = 108°$, what is $m\angle C$?

c. 47°

Examples

IWB

2. **Classify triangles.**

AL
- *What do the tic marks indicate?* The tic marks indicate congruent sides.
- *What type of triangle has two congruent sides?* isosceles

OL
- *What type of angle does the top angle appear to be?* obtuse
- *If one angle in a triangle is obtuse, what do you know about the other two angles?* They have to be acute.

BL
- *What do the congruent sides indicate about the angles that are opposite each side?* Angles that are opposite congruent sides are also congruent.

Need Another Example?
Classify the marked triangle by its angles and by its sides. right scalene

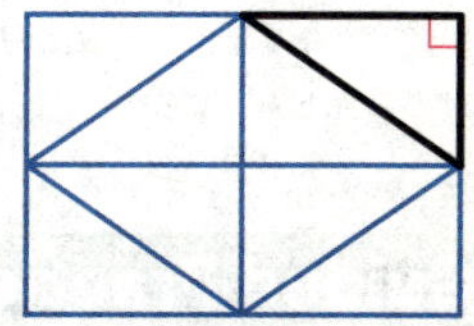

3. **Find missing measures.**

AL
- *What is the sum of the measures of the angles in a triangle?* 180°
- *What is the sum of the measures of the two known angles?* $119° + 43° = 162°$

OL
- *What equation can you write to use to find the value of $\angle Z$?* $m\angle Z + 43 + 119 = 180$
- *What steps can you use to solve the equation?* First, add 43 and 119, which is 162. Then subtract 162 from each side.

BL
- *Classify this triangle by its angles and by its sides.* obtuse, scalene

Need Another Example?
In triangle ABC, $m\angle B = 50°$ and $m\angle C = 80°$. What is $m\angle A$? 50°

Example

IWB

4. Find missing measures.

AL • *What is the sum of the angles of a triangle?* 180°

• *What angle measures are you given?* 110° and 35°

OL • *What equation can you write to find the value of x?*
$x + 110 + 35 = 180$

• *What are the steps you can do to solve the equation?* First, add 110 and 35, which is 145. Then subtract 145 from each side.

BL • *Using what you know about the angle measures of this triangle, classify the triangle by both its angles and its sides.* obtuse, isosceles

Need Another Example?
Find the value of *x* in the triangle shown. 32

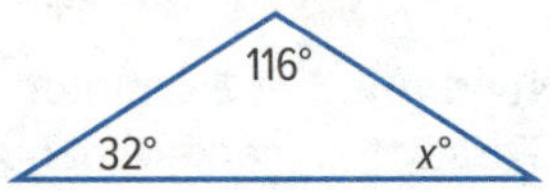

Guided Practice

Formative Assessment Use these exercises to assess students' understanding of the concepts in this lesson.

If some of your students are not ready for assignments, use the differentiated activity below.

AL EL **Pair-to-Pair to Compare** Arrange students in pairs to complete Exercises 1–4. Students may benefit from drawing the triangle described in Exercise 2. Have students switch partners to form new pairs to compare their solutions to each exercise. This step may be repeated. Then call on one student to share their response to a given exercise. MP 1, 5, 7

Real World Example

Tutor

4. The Alabama state flag is shown. What is the missing measure in the triangle?

To find the missing measure, write and solve an equation.

$x + 110 + 35 = 180$ The sum of the measures is 180.

$x + 145 = 180$ Simplify.

$-145 = -145$ Subtract 145 from each side.

$x = 35$

The missing measure is 35°.

Guided Practice

Check

1. Draw a triangle with three acute angles and two congruent sides. Classify the triangle. (Examples 1 and 2) acute isosceles

Sample answer:

Show your work.

2. Find $m\angle T$ in $\triangle RST$ if $m\angle R = 37°$ and $m\angle S = 55°$. (Example 3) 88°

3. A triangle is used in the game of pool to rack the pool balls. Find the missing measure of the triangle. (Example 4)

60°

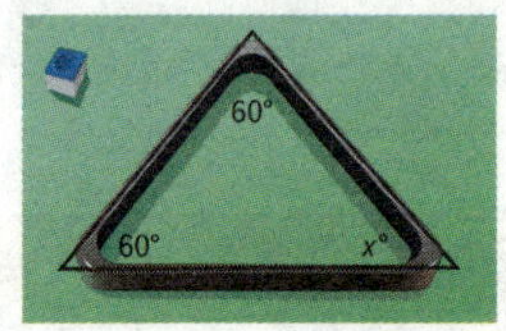

4. **Building on the Essential Question** How can triangles be classified?

Sample answer: Triangles can be classified as acute, right or obtuse using angle measures or as scalene, isosceles, or equilateral using side lengths.

Rate Yourself!

Are you ready to move on? Shade the section that applies.

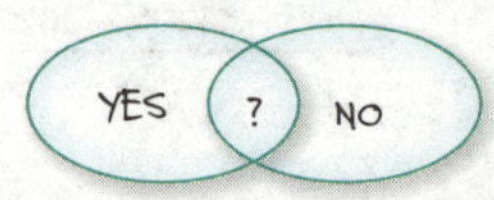

For more help, go online to access a Personal Tutor.

Tutor

FOLDABLES Time to update your Foldable!

Name ______________________ My Homework

Independent Practice

Go online for Step-by-Step Solutions eHelp

Draw a triangle that satisfies each set of conditions. Then classify the triangle. (Example 1)

1. a triangle with three acute angles and three congruent sides **acute equilateral**

Sample answer:

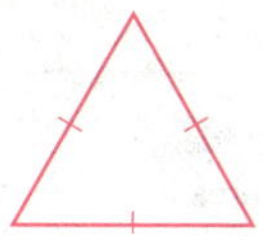

2. a triangle with one right angle and no congruent sides **right scalene**

Sample answer:

Classify the marked triangle by its angles and by its sides. (Example 2)

3.

acute equilateral

4.

acute equilateral

5.

obtuse isosceles

Find the value of *x*. (Examples 3 and 4)

6. **60**

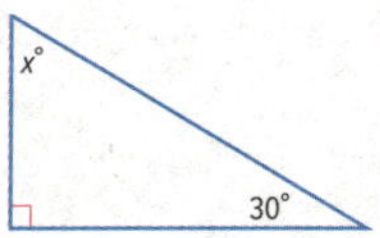

7. **118**

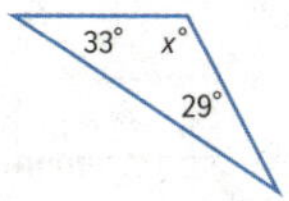

8. **27**

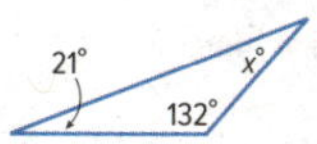

9. MP **Model with Mathematics** Refer to the graphic novel below. Classify the triangle formed by the cabin, ropes course, and mess hall by its angles and sides.

acute isosceles

ENGAGE EXPLORE **EXPLAIN** **ELABORATE** **EVALUATE**

3 Practice and Apply

Independent Practice and Extra Practice

The Independent Practice pages are meant to be used as the homework assignment. The Extra Practice page can be used for additional reinforcement or as a second-day assignment.

Levels of Complexity

The levels of the exercises progress from 1 to 3, with Level 1 indicating the lowest level of complexity.

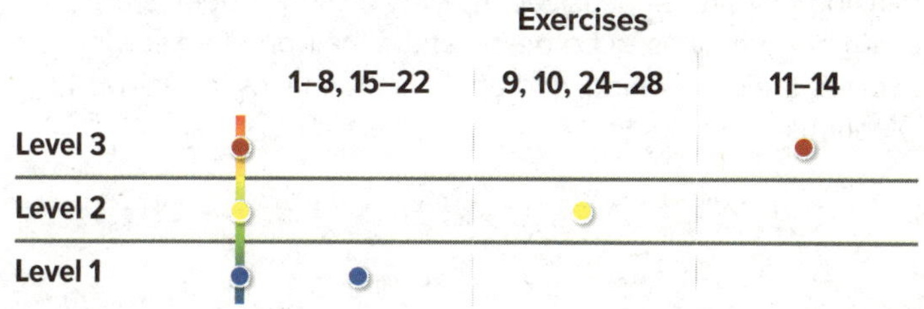

Suggested Assignments

You can use the table below that includes exercises of all complexity levels to select appropriate exercises for your students' needs.

Differentiated Homework Options		
AL	Approaching Level	1–9, 12–14, 27, 28
OL	On Level	1–9 odd, 10, 12–14, 27, 28
BL	Beyond Level	9–14, 27, 28

ALEKS® can provide additional remediation support with personalized instruction and practice.

MP MATHEMATICAL PRACTICES	
Emphasis On	**Exercise(s)**
1 Make sense of problems and persevere in solving them.	11
2 Reason abstractly and quantitatively.	24–26
3 Construct viable arguments and critique the reasoning of others.	13, 14
4 Model with mathematics.	9, 12

Mathematical Practices 1, 3, and 4 are aspects of mathematical thinking that are emphasized in every lesson. Students are given opportunities to be persistent in their problem solving, to express their reasoning, and apply mathematics to real-world situations.

Formative Assessment
Use this activity as a closing formative assessment before dismissing students from your class.

TICKET Out the Door

Have students explain how classifying angles helps to classify a triangle as *acute*, *right*, or *obtuse*. See students' work.

Watch Out!

Common Error Students need to read the instruction line and problems carefully. Students may not find the measure of the angle in the triangle and only find the value of x. Some problems ask for the value of x, while others ask them to find the missing measure.

10. Triangle ABC is formed by two parallel lines and two other intersecting lines. Find the measure of each angle A, B, and C of the triangle.

$m\angle A = 61°$, $m\angle B = 72°$, $m\angle C = 47°$

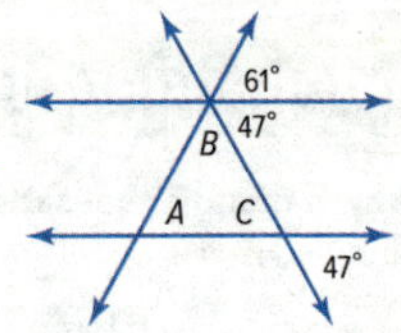

H.O.T. Problems Higher Order Thinking

11. MP **Persevere with Problems** Apply what you know about triangles to write and solve equations to find the missing angle measures in the figure.

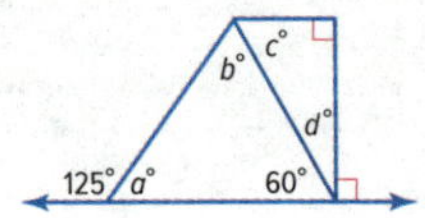

$125 + a = 180$, so $a = 55$; $a + b + 60 = 180$, so $b = 65$; $60 + d = 90$, so $d = 30$; $c + d + 90 = 180$, so $c = 60$

12. MP **Model with Mathematics** Draw an acute scalene triangle. Describe the angles and sides of the triangle.

Sample answer: All of the angles are acute and there are no congruent sides.

13. MP **Justify Conclusions** Determine whether each statement is *sometimes*, *always*, or *never* true. Justify your answer.

a. It is possible for a triangle to have two right angles.

never; Sample answer: The sum of the interior angles of a triangle is 180°. Two right angles have a sum of 180°. This means the third angle would equal 0°, which is not possible.

b. It is possible for a triangle to have two obtuse angles.

never; Sample answer: The sum of the interior angles of a triangle is 180°. The measure of an obtuse angle is greater than 90°. So, a triangle cannot have more than one obtuse angle.

14. MP **Reason Inductively** Miguel says that an equilateral triangle is sometimes an obtuse triangle. Jane says that an equilateral triangle is always an acute triangle. Is either of them correct? Explain your reasoning.

Jane; sample answer: An equilateral triangle has all sides congruent. So, each angle measures 60. Therefore, an equilateral triangle is always acute.

Name ______________________ My Homework ______________________

Extra Practice

Classify the marked triangle in each object by its angles and by its sides.

15. Homework Help

The triangle has all acute angles and two congruent sides. It is an acute isosceles triangle.

16.

obtuse isosceles

17.

right scalene

Draw a triangle that satisfies each set of conditions. Then classify the triangle.

18. a triangle with three acute angles and no congruent sides acute scalene

Sample answer:

Show your work.

19. a triangle with one obtuse angle and two congruent sides obtuse isosceles

Sample answer:

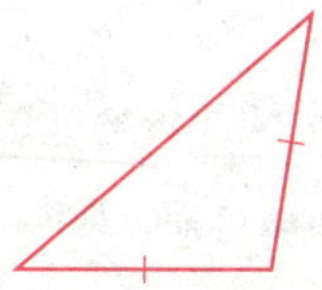

Find the value of *x*.

20.

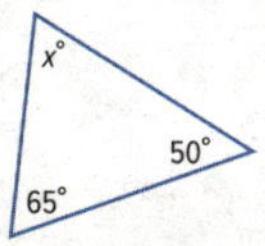

65

21.

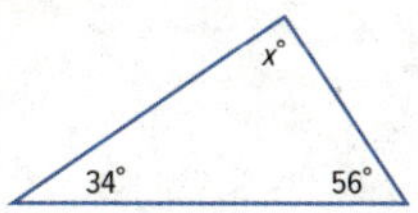

90

22.

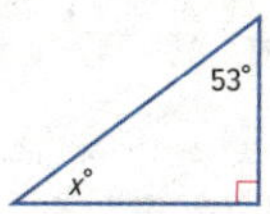

37

23. Find $m\angle Q$ in $\triangle QRS$ if $m\angle R = 25°$ and $m\angle S = 102°$. 53°

MP **Reason Abstractly** Find the value of *x* in each triangle.

24.

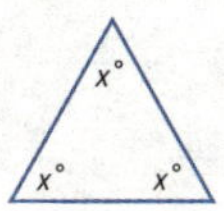

60

25.

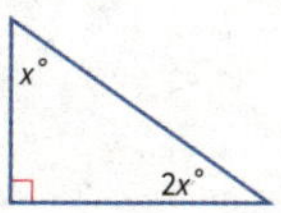

30

26.

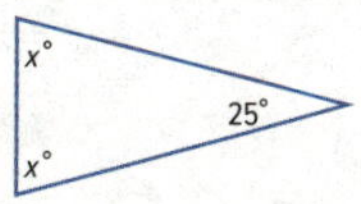

77.5

Create Your Own Homework Online

eSolutionsManual can be used to create worksheets for the suggested assignments on page 559, or create your own worksheets for differentiated homework or review.

Power Up! Test Practice

Exercises 27 and 28 prepare students for more rigorous thinking needed for the state assessment.

27.

This test item requires students to reason abstractly and quantitatively when problem solving.	
Depth of Knowledge	DOK1
Content Standard	7.G.2
Mathematical Practices	MP1, MP7
Online Experience	Students will be required to click on the bubbles to select all answers that are correct.
Scoring Rubric	
1 point	Students correctly answer each part of the question.

28.

This test item requires students to analyze and solve complex real-world problems through the use of mathematical tools and models.	
Depth of Knowledge	DOK2
Content Standard	7.G.2
Mathematical Practices	MP1, MP4
Online Experience	Students will draw a diagram and type their response in the box.
Scoring Rubric	
2 points	Students correctly model the right triangle and find the missing angle.
1 point	Students correctly model the right triangle OR find the missing angle.

Power Up! Test Practice

27. Refer to the figure shown. Determine if each statement is true or false.

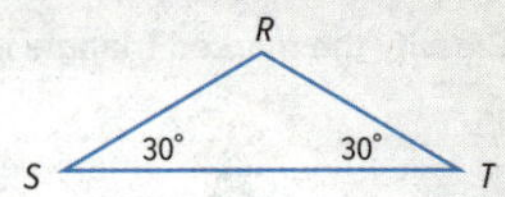

a. To find $m\angle R$, subtract 30° from 90°. ☐ True ■ False

b. The measure of $\angle R$ is 120°. ■ True ☐ False

c. Triangle *RST* is an acute triangle. ☐ True ■ False

28. In a right triangle, the measure of one of the angles is 43°. Sketch a diagram to represent this situation. **Sample answer:**

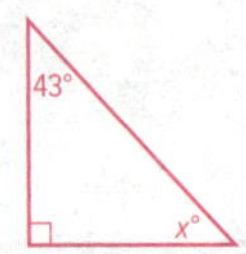

What is the measure of the other angle? **47°**

Spiral Review

Find the area of each figure. 6.G.1

29. **25 in²**

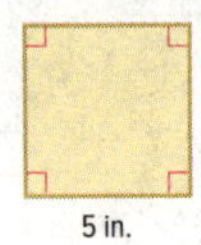

30. **32 ft²**

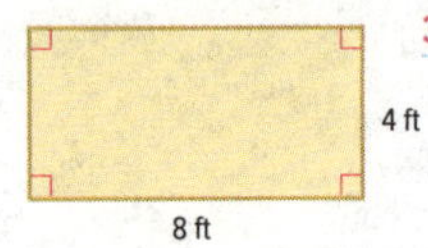

31. **35 cm²**

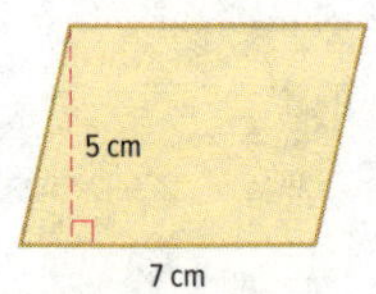

32. **25 m²**

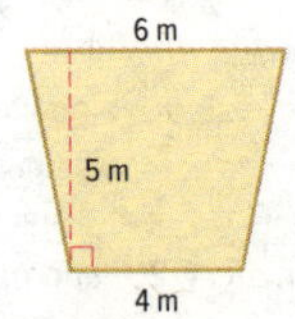

33. **9 yd²**

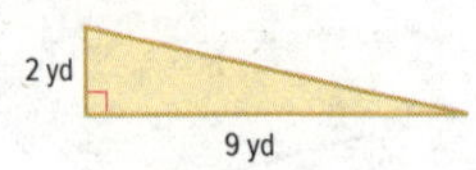

34. **36 in²**

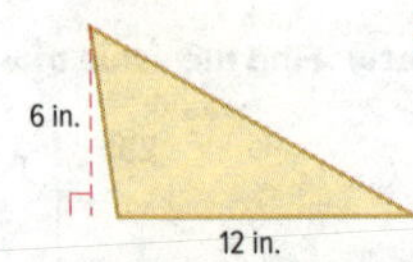

PLAN ONLINE

PD | RtI | Watch | Worksheets | Vocab | Tutor | Tools | Check | English Learners | Sketchpad

Inquiry Lab
Draw Triangles

Inquiry HOW can you use technology to draw geometric shapes?

Content Standards
7.G.2

MP Mathematical Practices
1, 3, 5

The Spirit Club is selling triangular-shaped pennants for Homecoming. Teresa is making a poster to advertise the pennants. She wants to use a computer program to draw a model of the pennant.

Hands-On Activity 1

You can use dynamic geometry software such as The Geometer's Sketchpad® to draw triangles given three angle measures. In this investigation, you will draw a triangle with angle measures of 30°, 60°, and 90°.

Step 1 First, click on **Edit**. Go to **Preferences**. Change the angle precision from *hundredths* to *units*. Next, use the **Straightedge (segment)** tool. Click and drag three times to create a triangle like the one shown.

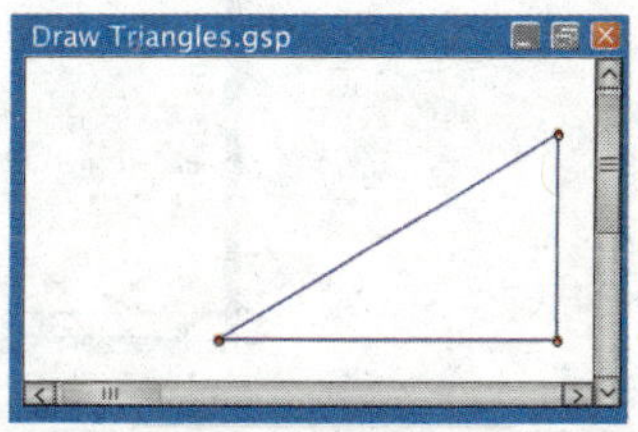

Step 2 Using the **Selection Arrow**, click on each of the vertex points *A*, *B*, and *C*. Then select **Measure** and **Angle**. Labels will automatically be assigned to the vertices. You found that the measure of ∠*ABC* is 90°.

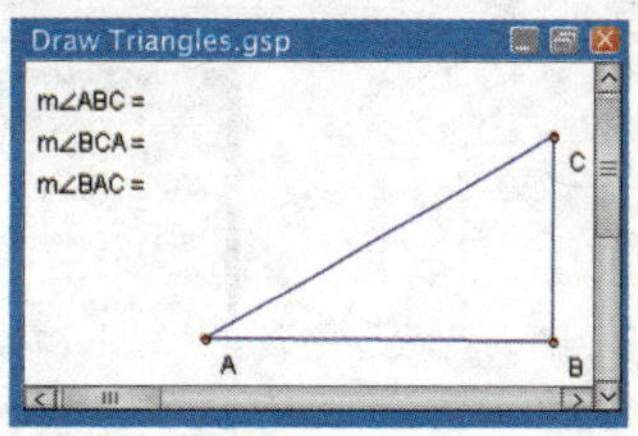

Step 3 Click on points *B*, *C*, and *A*. Click **Measure** and **Angle** again. Repeat for points *B*, *A*, and *C*. The angle measures should be displayed on your screen.

Step 4 If the angles do not measure 30°, 60°, and 90°, use the **Selection Arrow** to move the vertices. Click and drag one or more points so that the angles move.

PRESENT

IWB An Interactive Whiteboard Ready presentation is available for each lesson in the chapter.

Focus narrowing the scope

Objective Draw triangles. 7.G.2

Materials: computer with Geometer's Sketchpad® software or other dynamic geometry software

Coherence connecting within and across grades

Now
Students will use dynamic geometry software to draw triangles.

Next
Students will solve problems involving scale models.

Rigor pursuing concepts, fluency, and applications

See the Levels of Complexity chart on page 565.

ENGAGE EXPLORE EXPLAIN ELABORATE EVALUATE

1 Launch the Lab

Activities 1 and 2 are intended to be used as whole-group activities. Activity 1 is designed to provide more guidance to students than Activity 2.

Hands-On Activity 1

AL EL Think-Pair-Draw As an alternative to the Activity, have students draw a right triangle. Have student pairs use protractors to measure the angles, then find the sum of the angles. Pairs will share their sums with others to find a rule for the sum of the measures of a triangle. MP 1, 5, 7

BL EL Think-Pair-Draw Have students draw a square or rectangle. Have students find the sum of the angle measures in their figure. Have students apply the information for the sum of the interior angles of squares and rectangles to find the sum of the measure of the interior angles of a triangle, by drawing a diagonal and creating two congruent triangles. MP 1, 5, 7

Hands-On Activity 2

AL EL **Pairs to Groups** Arrange students in pairs to complete the activity. Have one student read each step aloud, while the other student performs the actions using The Geometer's Sketchpad®. Have students alternate roles for each step. Upon completion of the activity, have students join with another pair to verify the sum of the angle measures in their triangle. MP 1, 5

BL EL **Pairs Consult** Have students work in pairs. After completing the activity, have pairs write down the side lengths of a possible triangle, then try to create the triangle using the geometry software to verify if their choices worked. Have pairs try to create two more triangles using chosen side lengths and then come up with a rule for the lengths of the sides of a triangle. MP 1, 5, 7

Watch Out!

Common Error Since dynamic geometry software rounds measurements for display, choosing the proper level of precision in measurement is important. In this Activity, if students chose *units* instead of *hundredths*, they could create numerous triangles with side lengths of 3 centimeters, 4 centimeters, and 5 centimeters.

Hands-On Activity 2

You can also use The Geometer's Sketchpad® to draw triangles given three side measures. In this Activity, you will draw a triangle with side measures of 3 centimeters, 4 centimeters, and 5 centimeters.

Step 1 First, click on **Edit**. Go to **Preferences**. Check that the distance precision is set to hundredths. Using the **Straightedge (segment)** tool, click and drag to create a line segment with endpoints *A* and *B*. Use the **Selection Arrow** to select the segment. Click on **Measure** and **Length**. Then drag one of the endpoints so that the line segment measures 5 centimeters.

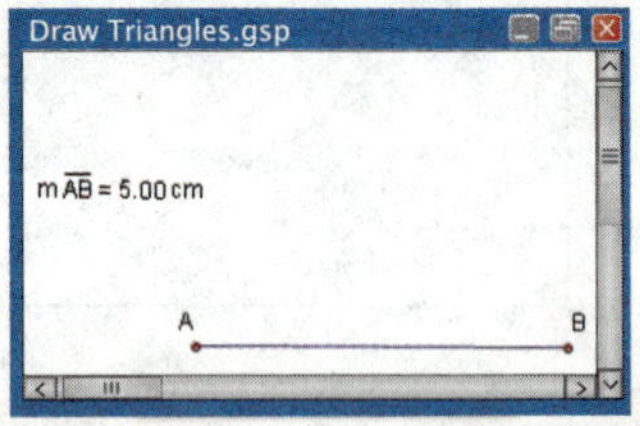

Step 2 Next, create a line segment from point *A* that is 4 centimeters long using the **Straightedge (segment)** tool. Draw the segment first and then measure it to make sure it is 4 centimeters.

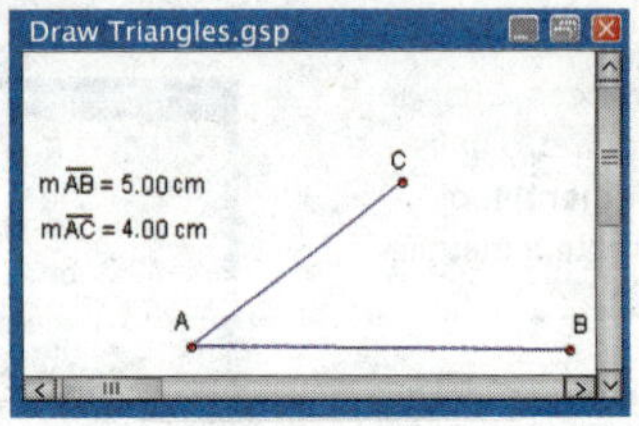

Step 3 Finally, connect points *C* and *B* with a line segment that is 3 centimeters long.

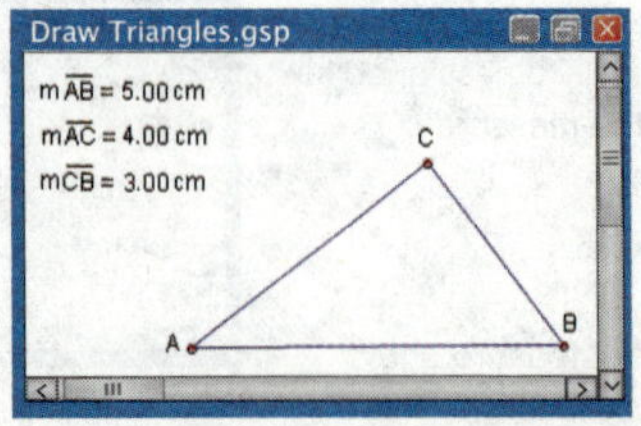

You have created a triangle with side lengths of 3 centimeters, 4 centimeters, and 5 centimeters.

Investigate

Collaborate

MP Use Math Tools Work with a partner to construct each triangle. Once you have constructed a triangle, draw the text and image that appears on your display.

1. $\angle ABC = 90°$
$\angle BCA = 70°$
$\angle BAC = 20°$

Show your work.

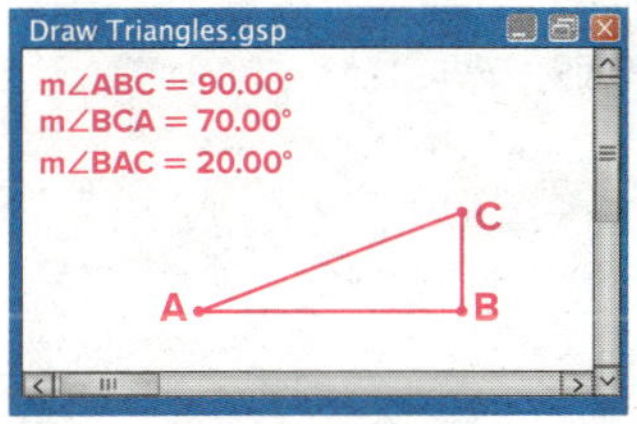

2. $\angle ABC = 90°$
$\angle BCA = 45°$
$\angle BAC = 45°$

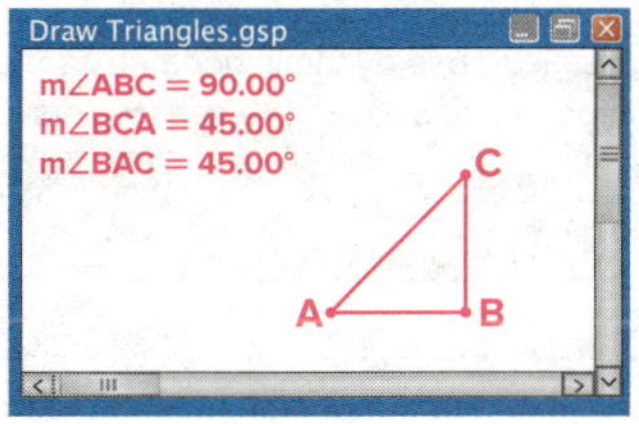

3. Explain the steps you would take to create a triangle if you were given the measures of all three angles.

Sample answer: Use a geometry program to draw and measure three angles of a triangle. Then drag one or more vertices to get the specified angle measurements.

4. $\overline{AB} = 4$ centimeters
$\overline{AC} = 6$ centimeters
$\overline{CB} = 9$ centimeters

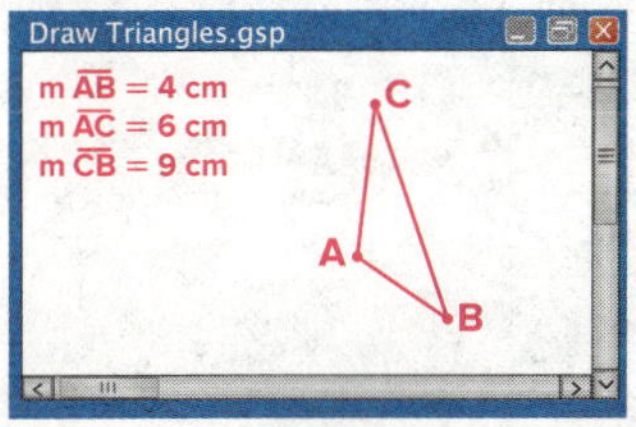

5. $\overline{AB} = 2$ centimeters
$\overline{AC} = 5$ centimeters
$\overline{CB} = 4$ centimeters

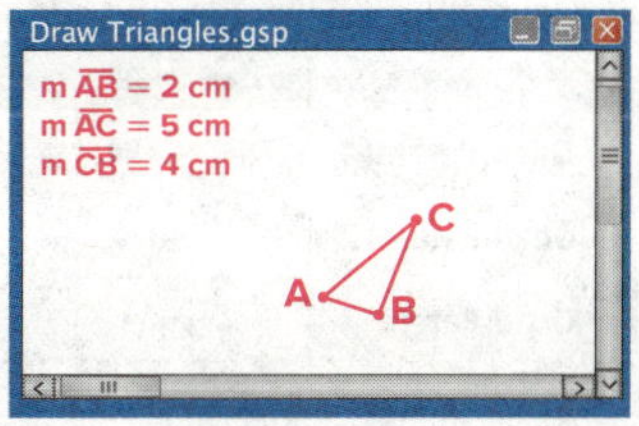

6. MP Justify Conclusions Explain the steps you would take to create a triangle if you were given the lengths of all three sides.

Sample answer: Use a geometry program to draw and measure the three sides of a triangle. Then drag one or more vertices to get the specified side lengths.

ENGAGE EXPLORE EXPLAIN ELABORATE EVALUATE

2 Collaborate

The **Investigate** and **Analyze and Reflect** sections are intended to be used as small-group investigations. The **Create** section is intended to be used as independent exercises.

Levels of Complexity

The levels of the exercises progress from 1 to 3, with Level 1 indicating the lowest level of complexity.

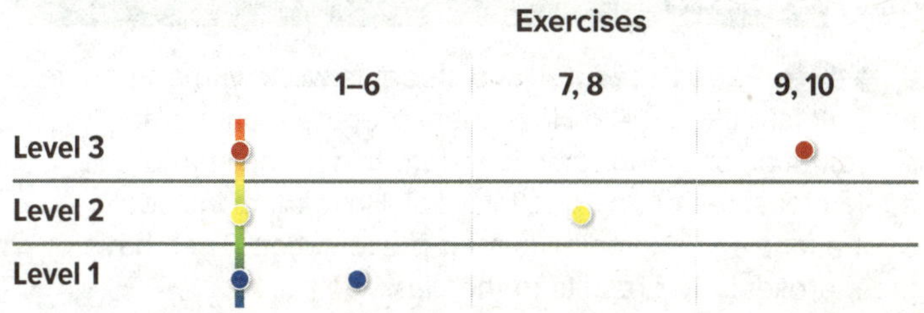

Investigate

Collaborate

AL EL Team-Pair-Solo Have students work in small teams to complete Exercises 1–3. If the technology is unavailable, have students use protractors to construct triangles with the specified angle measurements for each exercise. Have students label each vertex. Students should name each angle with its corresponding measurement. Have the teams divide into pairs to complete Exercises 4 and 5. Then have students work alone to complete Exercise 6. Upon completion, have them rejoin their original team to verify answers and discuss and compare solutions. MP 1, 5, 6

BL EL Pairs Present Have students work with a partner to come up with a rule for how to find the third angle measure of a triangle when the first two angle measures are known. Have them use illustrations and drawings, including The Geometer's Sketchpad®, if available. Have them present their results to the class. MP 1, 7

Analyze and Reflect

Collaborate

AL **EL** **Pairs Discussion** Have students discuss and complete Exercises 7 and 8. If students are having trouble answering the questions, have them respond to the following question. MP 1, 5, 7

Ask:

- *What is the sum of the interior angles of any triangle?* 180°

Create

On Your Own

BL **EL** **Pairs Present** Have students work with a partner to complete Exercise 9. Have them prepare a brief oral presentation showing how they determined the sum of the angle measures of any quadrilateral. Have them include illustrations and examples in their presentation. Then have them present their results to the class. MP 1, 5, 7, 8

Inquiry Students should be able to answer "HOW can you use technology to draw geometric shapes?" Check for student understanding and provide guidance, if needed.

Analyze and Reflect

Collaborate

Work with a partner to answer each of the following questions.

7. Is it possible to use dynamic geometry software to draw a triangle with angles of 50°, 65°, and 70°? Explain.

No; the sum of the three interior angles of a triangle is always 180°.

8. Is it possible to use dynamic geometry software to draw a triangle with side measures of 3, 6, and 10 centimeters? Explain.

No; the sum of the lengths of the two shorter sides must be greater than the longer side in order to form a triangle.

Create

On Your Own

9. MP **Reason Inductively** You know the rule to find the sum of the interior angles of a triangle. Does a similar rule exist for the sum of the interior angles of a quadrilateral? Use dynamic geometry software to draw four different quadrilaterals and complete the table below to find out. (*Hint:* Do not draw more than one square or rectangle.)

Sample answer: The sum of the interior angles of a quadrilateral is 360°.

See students' work for angle measurements.

	$m\angle 1$	$m\angle 2$	$m\angle 3$	$m\angle 4$	Sum of Angles
Quadrilateral 1					360°
Quadrilateral 2					360°
Quadrilateral 3					360°
Quadrilateral 4					360°

10. Inquiry HOW can you use technology to draw geometric shapes?

Sample answer: You can use the Straightedge Tool to draw segments that form a polygon, such as a triangle. You can use the measure tool to check the measures of sides and angles. Then you can adjust the shape.

IWB

An Interactive Whiteboard Ready presentation is available for each lesson in the chapter.

Geometry

MP **Problem-Solving Investigation**

Make a Model

Content Standards
7.G.1

MP **Mathematical Practices**
1, 4, 6

Case #1 Science Project

Jordan is making a model of Mount Saint Helens for a science project. The height of the actual volcano is about 2,500 meters. She uses a scale of 250 meters equals 1 centimeter.

What is the height of the volcano in Jordan's model?

1 Understand *What are the facts?*

- The height of the actual volcano is about 2,500 meters.
- The scale for her model is 250 meters = 1 centimeter.

2 Plan *What is your strategy to solve this problem?*

Draw a model that represents the actual volcano and Jordan's volcano to help you visualize the problem.

3 Solve *How can you apply the strategy?*

The scale is 250 meters = 1 centimeter.
Write and solve a proportion using the scale.

$$\frac{250 \text{ m}}{1 \text{ cm}} = \frac{2{,}500 \text{ m}}{x \text{ cm}}$$

$$250 \cdot x = 1 \cdot 2{,}500$$

$$x = 10 \text{ cm}$$

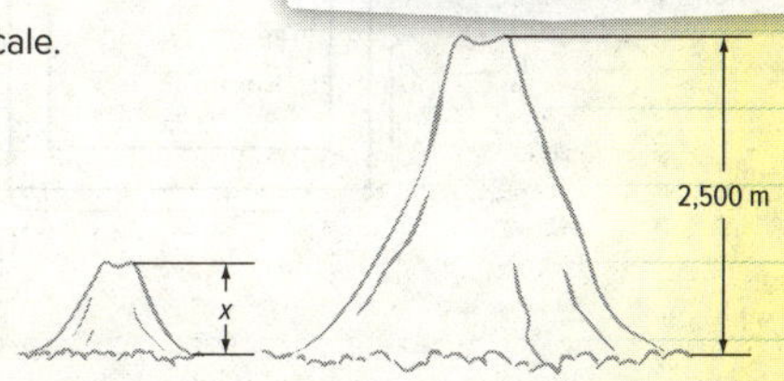

So, Jordan's model has a height of 10 centimeters.

4 Check *Does the answer make sense?*

Multiply the height of the model by 250 to see if it matches the actual height.

Analyze the Strategy Tutor

MP **Be Precise** The height of Mount Saint Helens is about 8,500 feet. What scale could Jordan use to represent the model in the U.S. Customary System?

Sample answer: 1 in. = 850 ft

Focus narrowing the scope

Objective Solve problems by making a model. This lesson emphasizes MP **Mathematical Practice 4** Model with Mathematics.

Make a Model Making a model can help students visualize the information given in a problem. A model may consist of a drawing or a figure made of counters, algebra tiles, or cubes.

Coherence connecting within and across grades

Now
Students solve non-routine problems.

Next
Students will apply the Make a Model strategy to three-dimensional figures.

Rigor pursuing concepts, fluency, and applications

See the Levels of Complexity chart on page 569.

ENGAGE EXPLORE EXPLAIN ELABORATE EVALUATE

1 Launch the Lesson

The problems on pages 567 and 568 are intended to be used as a whole-group discussion on how to solve non-routine problems and are designed to provide scaffolded guidance. The problem on page 567 walks students through the solution, while the problem on page 568 asks students to come up with their own solutions.

Case #1 Science Project

BL Have students extend the problem by having them answer the question below.

Ask:

- *Where have you seen scale models used in real life? How are they useful?* See student responses.

Case #2 Portraits

AL **EL** **Trade-a-Problem** Have students create a problem similar to the Portraits problem. Allow them to work in pairs. Have students take turns where one student speaks aloud the problem and their solution while the other listens and asks clarifying questions to help answer the problem. MP 1, 4, 5

BL **EL** **Draw-Pair-Share** Have students complete the exercise individually and draw their model on a piece of paper. Have students work in pairs to share their models and any differences. MP 1, 5

Need Another Example?

A rectangular garden is 12 feet long and 10 feet wide. A stone path around the garden is 2 feet wide. How much area is covered by the garden and the path? Use the *make a model* strategy. 224 ft^2

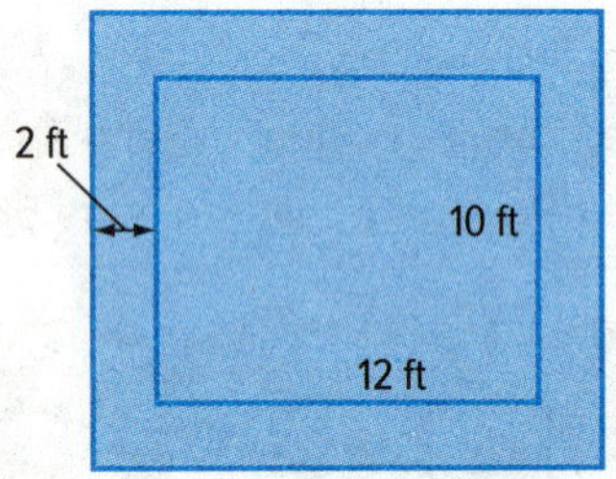

Case #2 Portraits

Alicia created a portrait that is 10 inches wide by 13 inches long. She wants to put it in a frame that is $2\frac{1}{4}$ inches wide on each side.

What is the area of the framed portrait?

1 Understand

Read the problem. What are you being asked to find?

I need to find the area of the framed portrait.

2 Plan

What is your strategy to solve this problem?

I will use the make a model strategy.

3 Solve

How can you apply the strategy?

I will draw a model of the portrait and the frame and label the dimensions.

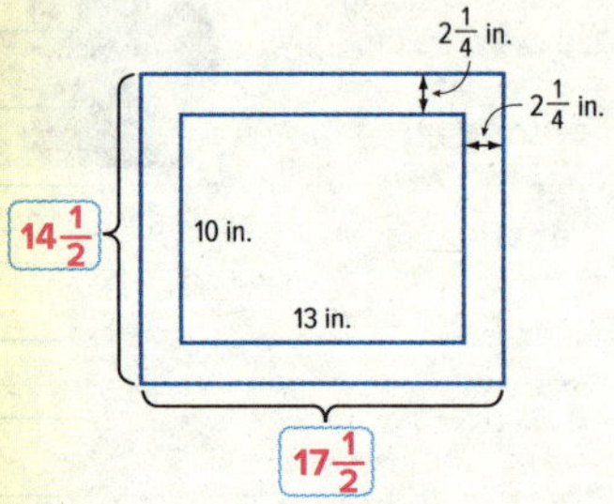

The inner rectangle is the portrait and the outer rectangle is the frame.

Label the combined length and width of the portrait and the frame.

The area of the framed portrait is $17\frac{1}{2}$ inches × $14\frac{1}{2}$ inches or $253\frac{3}{4}$ square inches.

4 Check

Estimate the product of the length and width of the framed portrait to determine if your answer is reasonable.

Sample answer: 17 × 14 = 238. Since 238 is close to my answer, my answer is reasonable.

Collaborate

Work with a small group to solve the following cases. Show your work on a separate piece of paper.

Case #3 Tables

Members of Student Council are setting up tables end-to-end for an awards banquet. Each table will seat one person on each side.

How many square tables will they need to put together for 32 people? Explain your method.

15 tables; 2 people can sit on the ends. Then divide the remaining people by 2. $(32 - 2) \div 2 = 15$.

Case #4 Tile

The diagram shows the design of a tile border around a rectangular swimming pool that measures 10.5 meters by 6 meters. Each tile is a square measuring 1.5 meter on each side.

Explain a method you could use to find the area of just the tile border. Then solve.

Subtract the area of the pool from the total area. $198 - 63 = 135\text{m}^2$

Case #5 Classes

Faith, Sarah, and Guadalupe take French, Spanish, and German. No person's language class begins with the same letter as their first name. Sarah's best friend takes French.

Which language does each person take?

Faith: Spanish; Sarah: German; Guadalupe: French

Case #6 Money

Corri received money for her birthday. She let Lakisha borrow \$4.50 and spent half of the remaining money. The next day she received \$10 from her uncle. After spending \$12.50 at the movies, she still had \$7.75 left.

How much money did she receive for her birthday?

\$25

2 Collaborate

Levels of Complexity

The levels of the exercises progress from 1 to 3, with Level 1 indicating the lowest level of complexity.

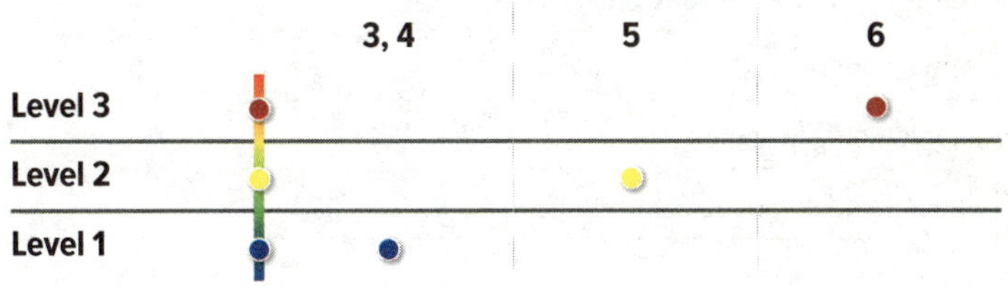

AL **EL** **Pairs Check** Have students work in pairs to complete Cases 3–6. One partner solves the problem while the other listens and coaches. Students switch roles until all exercises are complete. After every two problems, the pairs check their answers with another pair and resolve any differences. MP 1, 5

BL **EL** **Stand Up, Hand Up, Pair Up** Give students time to complete Cases 3–6 individually. Call out, "Stand up, hand up, pair up." As students do so, allow them to choose a partner in a different area of the classroom to discuss their answers. Use the following questions to help guide the discussion. MP 1, 5

Ask:

- *How does the diagram in Case 4 help you solve the problem?* **Sample answer: The diagram helps you find the area of the pool by using tiles in the diagram.**
- *What type of model could you use to solve Case 5?* **Sample answer: You could use a table and list to find what language each person takes.**

Mid-Chapter Check

If students have trouble with Exercises 1–7, they may need help with the following concepts.

Concept	Exercise(s)
complementary angles (Lesson 2)	1
classifying triangles (Lesson 3)	2, 7
vertical angles (Lesson 1)	3, 5
supplementary angles (Lesson 2)	4
find missing angle measures in triangles (Lesson 3)	6

Vocabulary Activity

EL **Numbered Heads Together** Have students work in a small group to complete Exercise 1. Each student is assigned a number. Students are responsible to ensure that each group member understands the meaning of attributes of similar figures. Students should ask each other for clarification and assistance, as needed. Call on one numbered student to share their definition with the class. MP 1, 6

ALEKS® provides additional remediation support with personalized instruction and practice for those who are struggling, while providing enhanced learning for those who have mastered the concepts.

Alternate Strategies

AL Have students look up the definition of attribute. To help students understand the term, have them list attributes of themselves. Then transition them back to attributes of angles and triangles. MP 1, 6

BL Have students verbally explain the method they would use to analyze angles they encounter in the real-world to determine if they are vertical angles, complementary angles or supplementary angles. MP 1, 4

Mid-Chapter Check

Vocabulary Check

1. MP **Be Precise** Define *complementary angles*. Give an example of two angles that would be complementary. (Lesson 2)

   Two angles are complementary if the sum of their measures is 90°. Sample answer: Two 45° angles would be complementary.

2. Fill in the blank in the sentence below with the correct term. (Lesson 3)

   A right scalene triangle is made up of one right angle and no congruent sides.

Skills Check and Problem Solving

Refer to the figure below for Exercises 3–5. (Lessons 1 and 2)

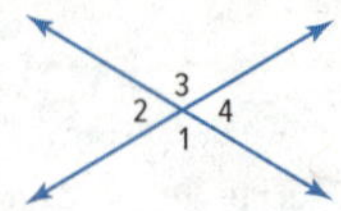

3. Identify a pair of vertical angles.

   Sample answer: $\angle 1$ and $\angle 3$

4. Identify a pair of supplementary angles.

   Sample answer: $\angle 1$ and $\angle 2$

5. Suppose $m\angle 1 = 127°$. Find the measures of the other angles.

   $m\angle 2 = 53°$ $m\angle 3 = 127°$ $m\angle 4 = 53°$

6. What is $m\angle A$ in $\triangle ABC$ if $m\angle B = 35°$ and $m\angle C = 92°$? 53°

7. MP **Reason Inductively** Classify the triangle that satisfies each set of conditions.

   a. one right angle and two congruent sides right isosceles

   b. one obtuse angle and no congruent sides obtuse scalene

   c. three acute angles and three congruent sides acute equilateral

An Interactive Whiteboard Ready presentation is available for each lesson in the chapter.

Geometry

Inquiry Lab

Investigate Online Maps and Scale Drawings

Inquiry **HOW is the zoom feature of an online map like the scale of a drawing?**

Content Standards
7.G.1

MP Mathematical Practices
1, 3, 4, 5

Maps and blueprints are *scale drawings* of the locations and buildings they represent. Unlike maps printed on paper, online map services allow users the opportunity to view a location from different distances.

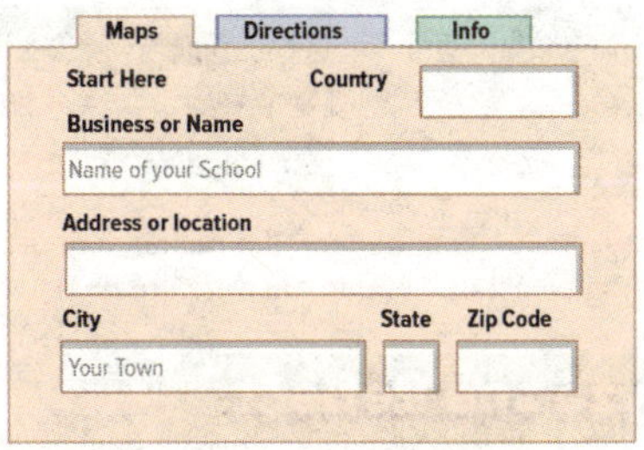

Hands-On Activity 1

Step 1 Use the online map service provided to you by your teacher. Locate your school on a map.

Step 2 Measure the length of the scale bar in centimeters on the online map. Find the scale distance of the map. Write these values in the Original View table in Step 4.

Step 3 Click on the satellite or aerial view. Use the zoom feature to zoom in until your school shows up on the map.

Step 4 Measure the length of the scale bar in centimeters. Find the new scale distance for the map. Write these values in the Zoom View table. **Answers will vary depending on the online map program used. Sample answers are given.**

Original View	
Scale Bar	2.8 cm
Scale Distance	800 m

Zoom View	
Scale Bar	2.8 cm
Scale Distance	30 m

What happens when you use the zoom feature?

Sample answer: The map zooms in and zooms out.

Describe the appearance of the map as you zoomed in.

Sample answer: The map images became larger.

Focus narrowing the scope

Objective Use online maps to reproduce a scale drawing at a different scale. 7.G.1

Coherence connecting within and across grades

Now
Students will solve real-world problems involving scale drawings.

Next
Students will solve mathematical and real-world problems involving scale drawings.

Rigor pursuing concepts, fluency, and applications

See the Levels of Complexity chart on page 572.

ENGAGE EXPLORE EXPLAIN ELABORATE EVALUATE

1 Launch the Lab

Activities 1 and 2 are intended to be used as whole-group activities. Activity 1 is designed to provide more guidance to students than Activity 2.

Materials: computer with Internet access

Hands-On Activity 1

AL EL **Teammates Consult** Have students work in small teams to complete Activity 1. Have each student alternate leading the discussion by reading each step aloud and guiding the rest of the team in completing that step. Then have the team discuss and respond to the questions. MP 1, 5, 6

BL EL **Pairs Discussion** Have students determine how many times they need to zoom in to reach a certain scale distance. MP 1, 6

2 Collaborate

The **Investigate** and **Analyze and Reflect** sections are intended to be used as small-group investigations. The **Create** section is intended to be used as independent exercises.

Levels of Complexity

The levels of the exercises progress from 1 to 3, with Level 1 indicating the lowest level of complexity.

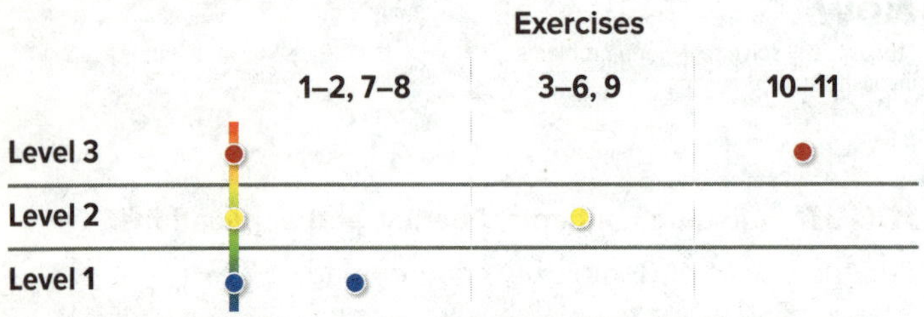

Investigate

AL EL **Pairs Check** Have students work in pairs to complete Exercises 1 and 2. Then have them trade online maps with another pair of students to check each other's work. MP 1, 5, 6

Analyze and Reflect

BL EL **Teams Present** Have students work in a small team of 3–4 students to complete Exercises 3–6 and prepare a brief oral presentation about how the zoom feature on an online map affects the scale of the map. Have them present to the class while the rest of the class listens carefully and asks for clarifying questions at the end. MP 1, 6

Investigate

MP **Use Math Tools** Work with a partner to answer the following questions about using an online map service.

1. Locate the local public library on the map. Write the scale bar and scale distance values in the Original View table below Exercise 2.

2. Click on the satellite or aerial view. Use the zoom feature to zoom in until the building shows up on the map. Write the scale bar and scale distance values in the Zoom View table.

Original View	
Scale Bar	2.8 cm
Scale Distance	400 m

Zoom View	
Scale Bar	2.8 cm
Scale Distance	200 m

Answers will vary depending on the online map program used and location selected. Sample answers are given.

Analyze and Reflect

Work with a partner to answer the following questions about using an online map.

3. Refer to Activity 1. Write a ratio $\frac{\text{scale bar}}{\text{scale distance}}$ for the original view and the zoom view. Sample answers given.

Original View: $\frac{2.8 \text{ centimeters}}{800 \text{ meters}}$ Zoom View: $\frac{2.8 \text{ centimeters}}{30 \text{ meters}}$

4. How many times bigger is the zoom view? Sample answer: The scale distance of the original view is about 27 times larger than the scale distance of the zoom view. The zoom view is about 27 times bigger.

5. How does zooming in affect the scale on the map? Sample answer: As you zoom in, the scale distance decreases.

6. When using the zoom feature on an online map, what changes and what stays the same? Sample answer: The scale distance changes as you zoom in or zoom out. Zooming in will result in the images on the map becoming larger. The window in which you view the map always stays the same.

Geometry

Hands-On Activity 2

The diagram shown represents a garden. The scale is 1 centimeter = 30 meters. That means that each square on the grid measures 1 centimeter by 1 centimeter or 30 meters by 30 meters.

Step 1 Write the length and width of the drawing of the garden.

Length: 4 centimeters Width: 1.5 centimeters

Step 2 Use the scale to find the dimensions of the garden.

Length: 120 meters Width: 45 meters

Step 3 On the grid below, draw the garden so that the scale is 1 centimeter = 10 meters. Write the dimensions of your drawing.

Length: 12 centimeters Width: 4.5 centimeters

Step 4 Use the scale on your drawing to compute the dimensions of the garden. How do the dimensions compare to the dimensions in Step 2?

Length: 120 meters Width: 45 meters

The dimensions are the same.

Hands-On Activity 2

AL EL **Three-Step Interview** Have students work in a team of 3–4 students. Student 1 reads aloud the boldface directions for Activity 2, then interviews Student 2, asking Student 2 to find the length and width of the drawing of the garden to complete Step 1. Then Student 2 interviews Student 3 by asking them to use the scale to find the dimensions of the garden in Step 2. Student 3 interviews Student 4 (or Student 1 if there are only 3 students in the group) to complete Step 3. Then the team works together to complete Step 4. MP 1, 5, 6

BL EL **Pairs Discussion** Have students work in pairs to extend Activity 2 by reproducing the scale drawing using a new scale. Have them decide on a scale and use grid paper to draw the new scale drawing. Have them write the dimensions of their drawing and use the scale to compute the actual dimensions of the garden and compare it to the actual dimensions of the garden in Activity 2. MP 1, 5, 6

Ask:

- *How do you know that your scale and drawing are accurate?* **Sample answer: By finding the actual dimensions of the garden using our scale and drawing, they should be the same dimensions of the garden in Activity 2.**

Investigate

AL EL **Think-Pair-Draw** Have students work in pairs to complete Exercises 7–8. Give them one minute to think through how they would draw the baseball diamond in Exercise 7 using the new scale. Then have them discuss their thinking with their partner, without actually completing the drawing. Finally, have students work individually to complete the drawing and share their drawings with their partner to resolve any differences. MP 1, 6

Ask:

- *How do you know that the drawing, using the new scale, will be smaller than the original drawing?* Sample answer: The new scale has 1 unit = 30 feet, so each unit on the grid will represent a greater distance; therefore, the drawing will be smaller.

Analyze and Reflect

BL EL **Find the Fib** Have students with a partner to write two facts and one fib for Exercise 9. For example, one fact could be the scale of the drawing is 1 unit = 2 feet. One fib could be that the triangle is an equilateral triangle. Have students trade papers with another set of paired students. Each pair identifies the facts and fib of the other pair. MP 1, 3, 6

Create

AL EL **Gallery Walk** Have students work in pairs to complete Exercise 10. Then post the scale drawings around the room. Have students walk around the room and select a scale drawing, other than their own. Have them determine the actual measurements of the room indicated in the drawing. MP 1, 4

Inquiry Students should be able to answer "HOW is the zoom feature of an online map like the scale of a drawing?" Check for student understanding and provide guidance, if needed.

Investigate

Work with a partner to answer the following questions about reproducing a scale drawing.

7. Recreate the drawing of the baseball diamond below using the new scale.

current scale: 1 unit = 15 ft
new scale: 1 unit = 30 ft

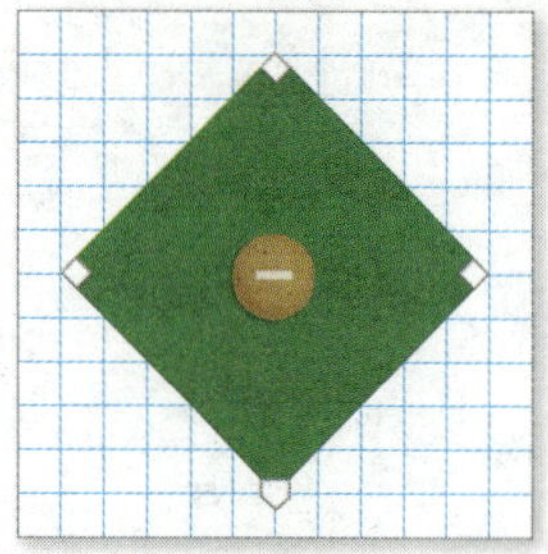

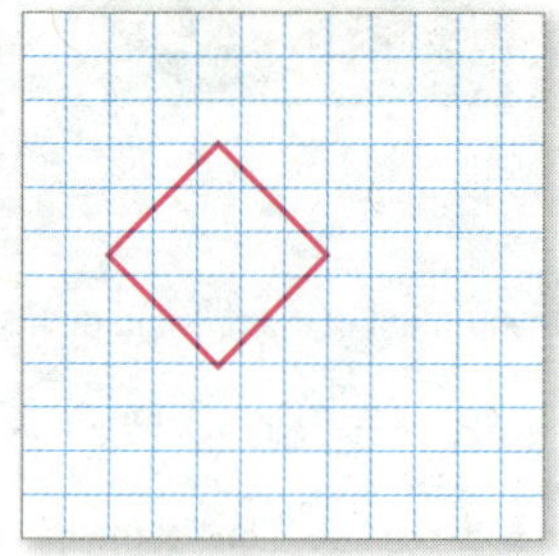

8. A drawing of the Statue of Liberty is 3 inches tall. The scale is 1 inch = 50 feet. How tall would the drawing be if the scale were 0.5 inch = 100 feet? 0.75 in.

Analyze and Reflect

9. MP **Reason Inductively** The triangle shown in the drawing has an area of 40 square feet. What is the scale of the drawing? 1 unit = 2 feet

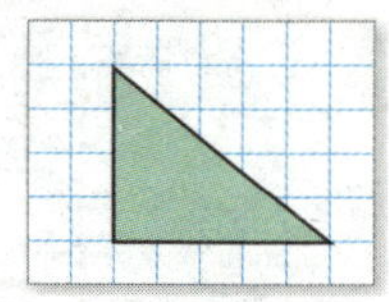

Create

10. MP **Model with Mathematics** Using a separate piece of grid paper, create a map of your classroom or a room in your home. Identify the scale you used.

See students' work.

11. Inquiry How is the zoom feature of an online map like the scale of a drawing?

Sample answer: Zooming is like changing the scale. The image will become larger or smaller depending on the scale used.

PLAN ONLINE

PD | RtI | Watch | Worksheets | Vocab | Tutor | Tools | Check | English Learners | Sketchpad

PRESENT

IWB

An Interactive Whiteboard Ready presentation is available for each lesson in the chapter.

Geometry

Lesson 4

Scale Drawings

Real-World Link

Room Model Architects make detailed drawings of rooms and buildings. Conner made a drawing of a bedroom. Follow the steps below to make a model of a room of your choosing.

See students' work.

Step 1 Measure the length of three objects in the room. Record each length to the nearest $\frac{1}{2}$ foot in the table below.

Object	Length (ft)	Length (units)

Step 2 Let 1 unit represent 2 feet. So, 4 units = 8 feet. Convert all your measurements to units. Record these values.

Step 3 On grid paper, make a drawing of your room like the one shown.

Which MP **Mathematical Practices** did you use?
Shade the circle(s) that applies.

1. Persevere with Problems
2. Reason Abstractly
3. Construct an Argument
4. Model with Mathematics
5. Use Math Tools
6. Attend to Precision
7. Make Use of Structure
8. Use Repeated Reasoning

Essential Question

HOW does geometry help us describe real-world objects?

Vocabulary

scale drawing
scale model
scale
scale factor

Content Standards
7.G.1

MP **Mathematical Practices**
1, 2, 3, 4, 5

Focus narrowing the scope

Objective Solve problems involving scale drawings. 7.G.1

Coherence connecting within and across grades

Previous
Students used proportions to solve real-world problems.

Now
Students solve real-world problems involving scale drawings.

Next
Students will use scale factors to enlarge and reduce figures on the coordinate plane.

Rigor pursuing concepts, fluency, and applications

See the Levels of Complexity chart on page 579.

ENGAGE EXPLORE EXPLAIN ELABORATE EVALUATE

1 Launch the Lesson

Ideas for Use

You may wish to launch the lesson using a whole group, small group, think-pair-share activity, or independent activity.

EL **Gallery Walk** Have students work in small groups to complete the activity in the Real-World Link. Have them display their drawings they created in Step 3 around the room. Have students walk around the room to look at each drawing. Then have them select a drawing to determine what a reasonable unit of measurement would be for the length of each grid square. MP 1, 5, 6

2 Teach the Concept

Ask the scaffolded questions for each example to differentiate instruction.

IWB

Example

1. Find the actual distance.

AL
- *What is the scale?* 1 cm = 24 miles
- *What do we need to find?* the actual distance between the cities

OL
- *What is the distance on the map?* about 4 cm
- *What proportion can we use?* $\frac{1 \text{ cm}}{24 \text{ miles}} = \frac{4 \text{ cm}}{d \text{ miles}}$
- *What is the actual distance between the cities?* about 96 miles

BL
- *What is another way we can set up the proportion?* $\frac{1 \text{ cm}}{4 \text{ cm}} = \frac{24 \text{ miles}}{d \text{ miles}}$

Need Another Example?
Refer to the map of Florida below. What is the actual distance between Daytona Beach and Orlando? Use a ruler to measure. about 51 mi

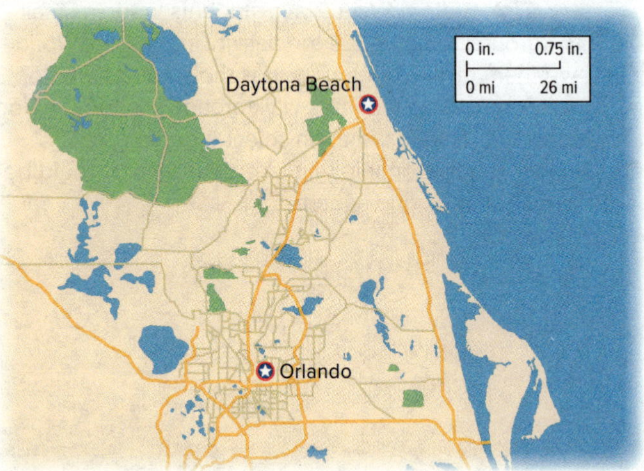

Work Zone

Use a Scale Drawing or a Scale Model

Scale drawings and **scale models** are used to represent objects that are too large or too small to be drawn or built at actual size. The **scale** gives the ratio that compares the measurements of the drawing or model to the measurements of the real object. The measurements on a drawing or model are proportional to the measurements on the actual object.

Example

Tutor

1. What is the actual distance between Hagerstown and Annapolis?

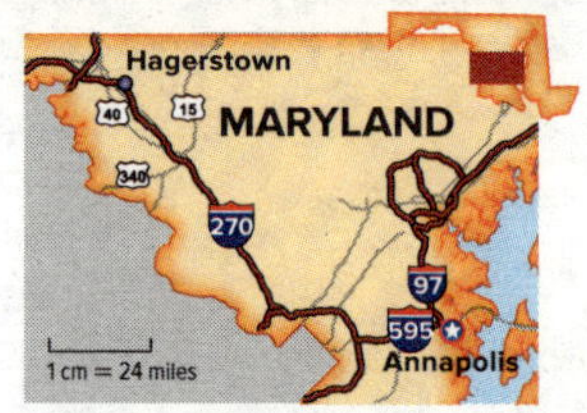

Step 1 Use a centimeter ruler to find the map distance between the two cities. The map distance is about 4 centimeters.

Step 2 Write and solve a proportion using the scale. Let *d* represent the actual distance between the cities.

	Scale		Length	
map →	1 centimeter	=	4 centimeter	← map
actual →	24 miles		*d* miles	← actual

$1 \times d = 24 \times 4$ Cross products

$d = 96$ Simplify.

The distance between the cities is about 96 miles.

Scale
A map scale can be written in different ways, including the following:
1 cm = 20 mi
1 cm : 20 mi
$\frac{1 \text{ cm}}{20 \text{ mi}}$

Got it? **Do this problem to find out.**

Show your work.

a. about 80 mi

a. On the map of Arkansas shown, find the actual distance between Clarksville and Little Rock. Use a ruler to measure.

Geometry

Example

Tutor

2. **A graphic artist is creating an advertisement for this cell phone. If she uses a scale of 5 inches = 1 inch, what is the length of the cell phone on the advertisement?**

Write a proportion using the scale. Let a represent the length of the advertisement cell phone.

	Scale		Length	
advertisement →	5 inches	=	a inches	← advertisement
actual →	1 inch		4 inches	← actual

$5 \cdot 4 = 1 \cdot a$ Cross products

$20 = a$ Simplify.

The length of the cell phone on the advertisement is 20 inches long.

Got it? **Do this problem to find out.**

b. A scooter is $3\frac{1}{2}$ feet long. Find the length of a scale model of the scooter if the scale is 1 inch = $\frac{3}{4}$ feet.

Scale
The scale is the ratio of the drawing/model measure to the actual measure. It is not always the ratio of a smaller measure to a larger measure.

Show your work.

b. $4\frac{2}{3}$ in.

Find a Scale Factor

A scale written as a ratio without units in simplest form is called the **scale factor.**

Example

Tutor

3. **Find the scale factor of a model sailboat if the scale is 1 inch = 6 feet.**

$\frac{1 \text{ inch}}{6 \text{ feet}} = \frac{1 \text{ inch}}{72 \text{ inches}}$ Convert 6 feet to inches.

$= \frac{1}{72}$ Divide out the common units.

The scale factor is $\frac{1}{72}$.

Got it? **Do this problem to find out.**

c. What is the scale factor of a model car if the scale is 1 inch = 2 feet?

c. $\frac{1}{24}$

Examples

IWB

2. **Find the distance on the scale drawing.**

AL
- *What is the scale?* 5 inches = 1 inch
- *What do we need to find?* the length of the cell phone on the advertisement
- *Will the length on the ad be less than or greater than the actual length?* greater than; the scale is 5 inches = 1 inch

OL
- *What proportion can we use?* $\frac{5 \text{ inches}}{1 \text{ inches}} = \frac{a \text{ inches}}{4 \text{ inches}}$
- *What is the length of the cell phone on the advertisement?* 20 in.

BL
- *If the width of the actual cell phone was 1.5 in., what would be the width of the cell phone on the advertisement?* 7.5 in.

Need Another Example?
An artist is painting a large mural of flowers on the side of a school. If she uses the scale 4 inches = 1 inch, how large will the mural painting of a rose bloom be if the actual height of the rose bloom is $6\frac{1}{4}$ inches? 25 in.

3. **Find the scale factor.**

AL
- *How is the scale factor different from the scale?* The scale factor is written as a ratio, without units, in simplest form.
- *What is the scale?* 1 inch = 6 feet

OL
- *Write the scale as a ratio.* $\frac{1 \text{ inch}}{6 \text{ feet}}$
- *How do we eliminate the units?* Convert 6 feet to inches.
- *What is the ratio written without units?* $\frac{1}{72}$
- *Where does the 72 come from?* 6 feet = 72 inches

BL
- *If the model sailboat was 8 inches in length, what is the actual length of the sailboat in feet? in inches?* 48 ft; 576 in.
- *How does the scale factor help you determine the actual length?* 1 inch on the model is 72 inches on the actual sailboat, so 8 inches × 72 = 576 inches

Need Another Example?
Find the scale factor of a blueprint if the scale is 1 inch = 3 feet. $\frac{1}{36}$

Example

IWB

4. Solve a problem involving a scale drawing.

AL
- *What is the scale?* $\frac{1}{2}$ inch = 3 feet
- *What do we need to find?* the area of Bedroom 1

OL
- *How do you know that this problem requires multiple steps to solve?* First we need to find the dimensions of Bedroom 1. Then we need to find the area of Bedroom 1.
- *To find the length of Bedroom 1, why do we put the variable in the denominator of the second fraction?* It corresponds to 3 feet in the scale.

BL
- *What is the actual perimeter of Bedroom 1?* 60 feet

Need Another Example?
Refer to the diagram on the student page. What is the actual area of the hallway? 108 ft^2

Guided Practice

Formative Assessment Use these exercises to assess students' understanding of the concepts in this lesson.

If some of your students are not ready for assignments, use the differentiated activities below.

AL EL **Pairs Consult** Have students work in pairs to complete Exercises 1–4. For Exercises 1–3, have them create a drawing to aid them in completing each problem. MP 1, 4

BL EL **Trade-a-Problem** Have students work in pairs to create their own multi-step real-world problem involving a scale drawing. Have them trade their problems with another pair of students. Each pair solves the other pair's problem. Then have them meet back together to discuss and resolve any differences. MP 1, 4

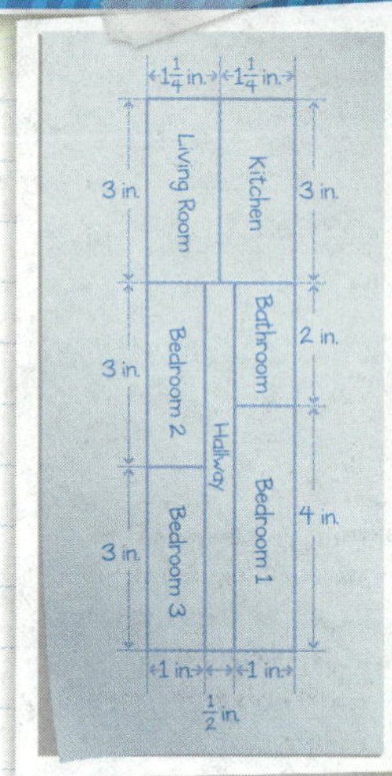

Show your work.

d. 108 ft^2

Real-World Example

Watch Tutor

4. A floor plan for a home is shown at the left where $\frac{1}{2}$ inch represents 3 feet of the actual home. What is the actual area of bedroom 1?

Length of Bedroom 1.

$\dfrac{\frac{1}{2} \text{ in.}}{3 \text{ ft}} = \dfrac{4 \text{ in.}}{w}$ ← floor plan ← actual

$\frac{1}{2}w = 12$ Find cross products.

$w = 24$ Divide each side by $\frac{1}{2}$.

Width of Bedroom 1.

$\dfrac{\frac{1}{2} \text{ in.}}{3 \text{ ft}} = \dfrac{1 \text{ in.}}{x}$ ← floor plan ← actual

$\frac{1}{2}x = 3$ Find cross products.

$x = 6$ Divide each side by $\frac{1}{2}$.

So, the area of bedroom 1 is 24 × 6 or 144 square feet.

Got it? Do this problem to find out.

d. What is the actual area of bedroom 3?

Guided Practice

Check

1. On a map, the distance from Akron to Cleveland measures 2 centimeters. What is the actual distance if the scale of the map shows that 1 centimeter is equal to 30 kilometers? (Example 1)

60 km

2. An engineer makes a model of a bridge using a scale of 1 inch = 3 yards. The length of the actual bridge is 50 yards. What is the length of the model? (Example 2)

$16\frac{2}{3}$ in.

3. Julie is constructing a scale model of her room. The rectangular room is $10\frac{1}{4}$ inches by 8 inches. If 1 inch represents 2 feet of the actual room, what is the scale factor and the actual area of the room? (Examples 3 and 4)

$\frac{1}{24}$; 328 ft^2

4. **Building on the Essential Question** Explain how you could use a map to estimate the actual distance between Miami, Florida, and Atlanta, Georgia.

Sample answer: Use the scale given on the map to estimate the actual distance.

Rate Yourself!

How well do you understand scale drawings? Circle the image that applies.

For more help, go online to access a Personal Tutor.

Tutor

Name ______________________ My Homework ______________________

Independent Practice

Go online for Step-by-Step Solutions eHelp

MP Use Math Tools **Find the actual distance between each pair of locations in South Carolina. Use a ruler to measure.** (Example 1) 1–2. Approximate distances are given.

1. Columbia and Charleston 102.6 mi

2. Hollywood and Sumter 81 mi

Show your work.

Find the length of each model. Then find the scale factor. (Examples 2 and 3)

3. 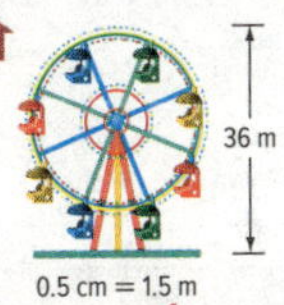

12 cm; $\frac{1}{300}$

4. 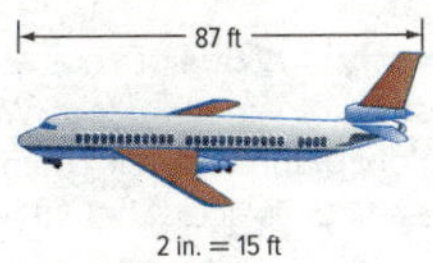

$11\frac{3}{5}$ in.; $\frac{1}{90}$

5. A model of an apartment is shown where $\frac{1}{4}$ inch represents 3 feet in the actual apartment. Find the actual area of the master bedroom. (Example 4)

108 ft^2

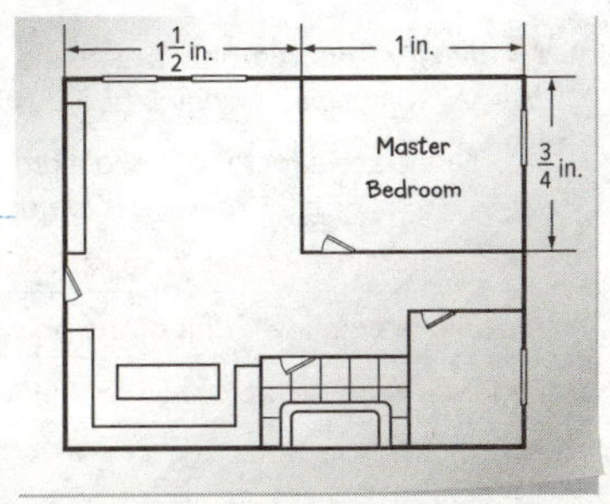

ENGAGE EXPLORE **EXPLAIN** **ELABORATE** **EVALUATE**

3 Practice and Apply

Independent Practice and Extra Practice

The Independent Practice pages are meant to be used as the homework assignment. The Extra Practice page can be used for additional reinforcement or as a second-day assignment.

Levels of Complexity

The levels of the exercises progress from 1 to 3, with Level 1 indicating the lowest level of complexity.

Exercises	1–5, 10–16	6, 17–19	7–9
Level 3			●
Level 2		●	
Level 1	●		

Suggested Assignments

You can use the table below that includes exercises of all complexity levels to select appropriate exercises for your students' needs.

Differentiated Homework Options		
AL	Approaching Level	1–5, 7–9, 18, 19
OL	On Level	1–5 odd, 6–9, 18, 19
BL	Beyond Level	6–9, 18, 19

ALEKS® can provide additional remediation support with personalized instruction and practice.

MP MATHEMATICAL PRACTICES

Emphasis On	Exercise(s)
2 Reason abstractly and quantitatively.	8
3 Construct viable arguments and critique the reasoning of others.	9
4 Model with mathematics.	6, 7
5 Use appropriate tools strategically.	1, 2, 10–13

Mathematical Practices 1, 3, and 4 are aspects of mathematical thinking that are emphasized in every lesson. Students are given opportunities to be persistent in their problem solving, to express their reasoning, and apply mathematics to real-world situations.

Formative Assessment
Use this activity as a closing formative assessment before dismissing students from your class.

TICKET Out the Door

Tell students that a map has a scale of 1 inch = 125 miles. Have students write how they could find the actual distance between two points shown on the map. See students' work.

Watch Out!

Common Error Students may incorrectly set up their proportions to find the measurements for the actual object. Have students check their answers to make sure they are reasonable.

6. MP **Model with Mathematics** Refer to the graphic novel frames below. The scale on the map shows that 1 centimeter is equal to 75 yards. If the red line represents the path they took, how far have Raul, Caitlyn, and Jamar traveled since they left the lake? Each square on the map is 1 centimeter long.
1,275 yards

H.O.T. Problems Higher Order Thinking

7. MP **Model with Mathematics** On the grid paper, create a scale drawing of a room in your home. Include the scale that you used. See students' work.

8. MP **Reason Abstractly** A statue of Thomas Jefferson was made using a scale of 3 feet = 1 foot. Write an expression to represent the height of the statue if Thomas Jefferson is *x* feet in height. Then find his actual height if the height of the statue is 19 feet.
$3x$; about $6\frac{1}{3}$ ft or 6 feet 4 in.

9. MP **Justify Conclusions** Determine whether the following statement is *always*, *sometimes*, or *never* true. Justify your reasoning.

If the scale factor of a scale drawing is greater than one, the scale drawing is larger than the actual object.

always; Sample answer: A scale factor of $\frac{3}{1}$ means that 3 units of the drawing is equal to 1 unit of the object, so the scale drawing or model will be larger than the actual object.

Name ______________________ My Homework ______________

Extra Practice

MP **Use Math Tools** **Find the actual distance between each pair of cities in New Mexico. Use a ruler to measure.** 10–13. Approximate distances are given.

10. Carlsbad and Artesia 50 km

Homework Help

$\frac{1 \text{ cm}}{25 \text{ km}} = \frac{2 \text{ cm}}{d \text{ km}}$

$1 \times d = 25 \times 2$

$d = 50$

11. Hobbs and Eunice 30 km

12. Artesia and Eunice 130 km

13. Lovington and Carlsbad 102.5 km

14. Find the length of the model. Then find the scale factor. The length of an actual bird is shown at the right. $11\frac{3}{4}$ in.; $\frac{2}{1}$

1 in. = 0.5 in.

Copy and Solve **Show your work on a separate piece of paper.**

15. A model of a tree is made using a scale of 1 inch = 25 feet. What is the height of the actual tree if the height of the model is $4\frac{3}{8}$ inches? $109\frac{3}{8}$ ft

16. A map of Bakersfield has a scale of 1 inch = 5 miles. If the city is $5\frac{1}{5}$ inches across on the map, what is the actual distance across the city? 26 mi

17. Tyson is creating a scale drawing of the area of his school. The rectangular drawing shows the length as 20 inches and the width as 19 inches. The drawing uses a scale of 1 inch = 3 feet. What is the actual area of the school in square feet? 3,420 ft^2

Create Your Own Homework Online

eSolutionsManual™ can be used to create worksheets for the suggested assignments on page 579, or create your own worksheets for differentiated homework or review.

Power Up! Test Practice

Exercises 18 and 19 prepare students for more rigorous thinking needed for the state assessment.

18.

This test item requires students to explain and apply mathematical concepts and solve problems with precision, while making use of structure.	
Depth of Knowledge	DOK2
Content Standard	7.G.1
Mathematical Practice	MP1
Online Experience	Students will be required to type their responses in the boxes.
Scoring Rubric	
1 point	Students correctly answer the question.

19.

This test item requires students to support their reasoning or evaluate the reasoning of others by justifying their response and constructing arguments.	
Depth of Knowledge	DOK3
Content Standard	7.G.1
Mathematical Practices	MP1, MP3
Online Experience	Students will be required to type their response in the box.
Scoring Rubric	
2 points	Students find the dimensions and explain their answer.
1 point	Students find the dimensions but fail to explain their answer OR students have a mathematical error in finding the dimensions but explain their answer based on the mathematical error.

Power Up! Test Practice

18. A landscape designer created a scale drawing of a bench that will be in a garden as shown. The actual width of the bench is 6 feet, and the actual height is 3 feet. Fill in each box to complete the following statements.

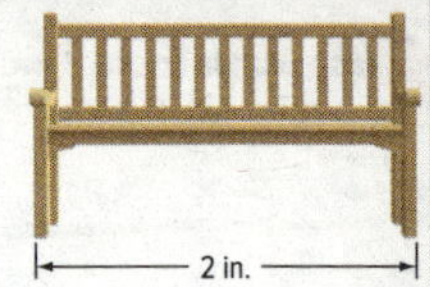

a. The scale of the drawing is [1] inch(es) = [3] feet.

b. The height of the scale drawing is [1] inch(es).

19. A scale drawing of a doctor's office is shown. What are the actual dimensions of the doctor's office? Explain how you found your answer.

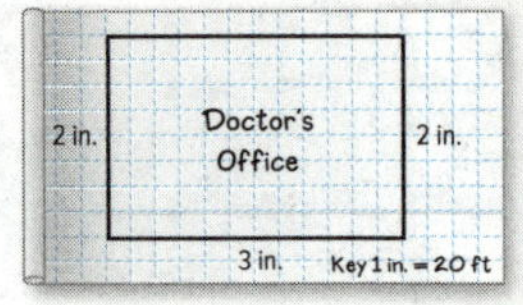

40 ft by 60 ft; Sample answer: Set up and solve proportions to find the actual length and width: $\frac{1 \text{ in.}}{20 \text{ ft}} = \frac{2 \text{ in.}}{w \text{ ft}}$ and $\frac{1 \text{ in.}}{20 \text{ ft}} = \frac{3 \text{ in.}}{\ell \text{ ft}}$

Spiral Review

20. A carpenter sawed a piece of wood into 3 pieces. The ratio of wood pieces is 1:3:6. The longest piece is 2.5 feet longer than the shortest piece. Use the *draw a diagram* strategy to find the length of the original piece. 6.RP.1

5 feet

Solve each proportion. 7.RP.2C

21. $\frac{2}{5} = \frac{b}{25}$ **10**

22. $\frac{3}{7} = \frac{a}{49}$ **21**

23. $\frac{2}{9} = \frac{x}{99}$ **22**

24. Dante has 60 baseball cards. This is at least six more than three times as many cards as Anna. Write and solve an inequality to represent the situation. 7.EE.4b

$3a + 6 \leq 60$; $a \leq 18$

PLAN ONLINE: PD | RtI | Watch | Worksheets | Vocab | Tutor | Tools | Check | English Learners | Sketchpad

PRESENT: IWB — An Interactive Whiteboard Ready presentation is available for each lesson in the chapter.

Geometry

Inquiry Lab
Scale Drawings

Inquiry **WHAT happens to the size of a scale drawing when it is reproduced using a different scale?**

MP Mathematical Practices 1, 3, 5

The owner of the miniature golf course wants to create a sign with an image of the 18th hole on it. Use the dimensions shown to create a scale drawing using the Geometer's Sketchpad®. Use the scale 1 centimeter = 3 meters.

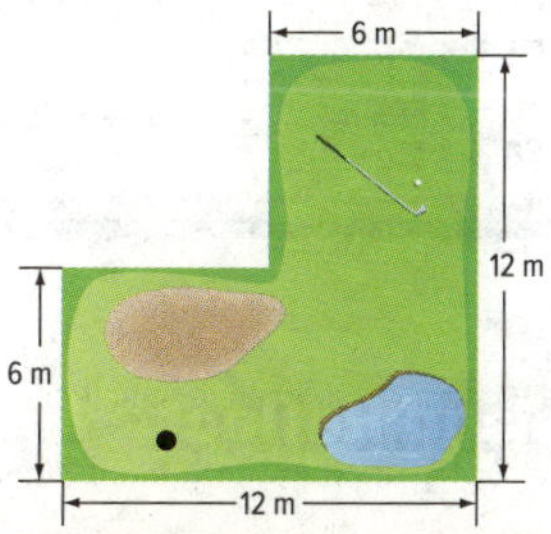

Hands-On Activity

Step 1 Determine the length the 6 meter side and the 12 meter side will be in the drawing.

Scale	Length	Scale	Length
$\frac{1 \text{ cm}}{3 \text{ m}} = \frac{x \text{ cm}}{6 \text{ m}}$		$\frac{1 \text{ cm}}{3 \text{ m}} = \frac{x \text{ cm}}{12 \text{ m}}$	

$1 \cdot 6 = 3 \cdot x$ $\qquad$ $1 \cdot 12 = 3 \cdot x$

$x = $ **2** $\qquad$ $x = $ **4**

So, the 6 meter side will be **2** centimeters and the 12 meter side will be **4** centimeters in the drawing.

Step 2 Create the drawing using a dynamic geometry software. Then fill in the correct length for each line segment.

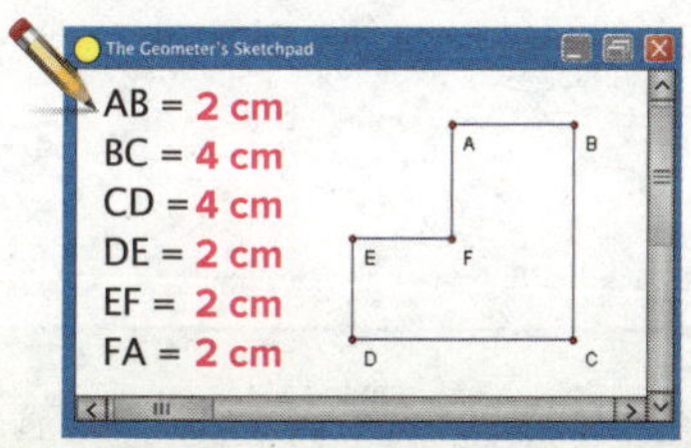

Focus narrowing the scope

Objective Use Geometer's Sketchpad® to calculate measurements for scale drawings.

Materials: computer with Geometer's Sketchpad® software or other dynamic geometry software

Coherence connecting within and across grades

Now
Students use Geometer's Sketchpad® to calculate measurements for scale drawings.

Next
Students will use scale factor to reduce and enlarge figures on the coordinate plane.

Rigor pursuing concepts, fluency, and applications

See the Levels of Complexity chart on page 584.

ENGAGE EXPLORE EXPLAIN ELABORATE EVALUATE

1 Launch the Lab

The Activity is intended to be used as a whole-group activity.

Hands-On Activity

AL EL Explain to students that the scale is 1 centimeter = 3 meters because they need to use a unit that makes sense for a scale drawing.

Ask:
- *What ratio represents the length of the 6-meter side in the Sketchpad drawing to the actual length of the miniature golf course?* $\frac{x \text{ cm}}{6 \text{ m}}$
- *How will you find the length?* Write a proportion, cross multiply, and then simplify.

2 Collaborate

The **Investigate** and **Analyze and Reflect** sections are intended to be used as small-group investigations. The **Create** section is intended to be used as independent exercises.

Levels of Complexity

The levels of the exercises progress from 1 to 3, with Level 1 indicating the lowest level of complexity.

	Exercises 1	Exercises 2	Exercises 3–4
Level 3			●
Level 2		●	
Level 1	●		

Investigate

Collaborate

AL **EL** **Pairs Discussion** Have students work in pairs to complete Exercise 1. Have them show their solutions to another pair of students and discuss any differences. MP 1, 5

Analyze and Reflect

Collaborate

BL **EL** **Gallery Walk** Have students work in pairs to draw a scale drawing of something in the classroom. Then post the scale drawings around the room. Have students walk around the room and select a scale drawing. Have them determine the actual measurements of the item shown in the drawing. MP 1, 4, 5

Create

On Your Own

Inquiry Students should be able to answer "WHAT happens to the size of a scale drawing when it is reproduced using a different scale?" Check for student understanding and provide guidance, if needed.

Investigate

Collaborate

Work with a partner. Use a dynamic geometry software.

1. MP **Use Math Tools** The owner wants a different size image of the 18th hole to place on the scorecards. Use the scale 1 centimeter = 6 meters. Fill in the new lengths of the line segments and draw the new scale drawing on the screen below. (*Hint:* You don't have to redraw the figure. Try clicking and dragging on the sides of your first drawing to adjust the side lengths.)

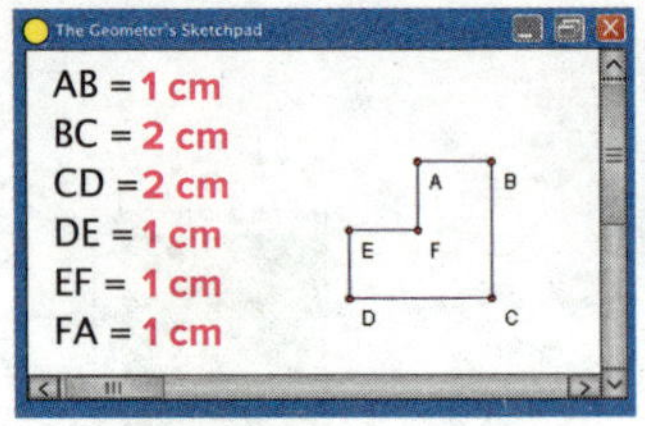

Analyze and Reflect

Collaborate

2. What happened to the size of the scale drawing when the scale changed from 1 centimeter = 3 meters to 1 centimeter = 6 meters?

The drawing became smaller.

Create

On Your Own

3. MP **Reason Inductively** Suppose you drew the miniature golf hole again at the scale 1 centimeter = 2 meters. Would the size of your drawing be larger or smaller than the drawing in the Activity? Explain.

Sample answer: The drawing would be larger because one centimeter would represent a lesser length of the actual golf hole.

4. Inquiry WHAT happens to the size of a scale drawing when it is reproduced using a different scale?

Sample answer: The drawing will be larger if a single unit of represents a lesser length. The drawing will be smaller if a single unit represents a greater length.

PLAN ONLINE

PD | RtI | Watch | Worksheets | Vocab | Tutor | Tools | Check | English Learners | Sketchpad

PRESENT

IWB

An Interactive Whiteboard Ready presentation is available for each lesson in the chapter.

Geometry

Lesson 5

Draw Three-Dimensional Figures

Real-World Link

New York City In art class, Rasheed studied buildings known for their unusual architecture. He studied the Flatiron Building shown.

Three-dimensional figures, such as the Flatiron Building, have length, width, and height. They can be viewed from different perspectives, including the *side* view and the *top* view.

Essential Question

HOW does geometry help us describe real-world objects?

Content Standards
Preparation for 7.G.3

MP Mathematical Practices
1, 3, 4

1. What is the two-dimensional figure that makes up the side view?
rectangle

2. What is the two-dimensional figure that makes up the top view?
triangle

3. Sketch the side view of the Flatiron Building.

4. Sketch the top view of the Flatiron Building.

Show your work.

5. The top view, side view, and front view of a three-dimensional figure are shown below. Sketch the figure.

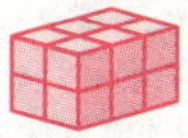

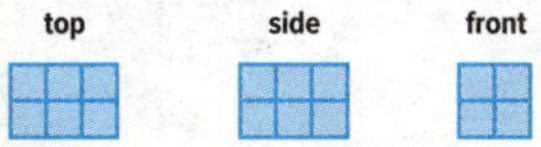

Which MP **Mathematical Practices** did you use?
Shade the circle(s) that applies.

① Persevere with Problems
② Reason Abstractly
③ Construct an Argument
④ Model with Mathematics
⑤ Use Math Tools
⑥ Attend to Precision
⑦ Make Use of Structure
⑧ Use Repeated Reasoning

Focus narrowing the scope

Objective Draw three-dimensional figures given the top, side, and front views. Preparation for 7.G.3

Coherence connecting within and across grades

Previous Students found the volume and surface area of three-dimensional figures.

Now Students draw different views of three-dimensional figures.

Next Students will examine the shapes of different cross sections of three-dimensional figures.

Rigor pursuing concepts, fluency, and applications

See the Levels of Complexity chart on page 589.

ENGAGE EXPLORE EXPLAIN ELABORATE EVALUATE

1 Launch the Lesson

Ideas for Use

You may wish to launch the lesson using a whole group, small group, think-pair-share activity, or independent activity.

BL Before beginning the Real-World Link, give students concrete objects such as a water glass, a can, or a geometric solid. Ask them to hold the object at eye level, draw the two-dimensional figure they see, and label what side they were viewing. They should repeat the process for different views. MP 1, 5

2 Teach the Concept

Ask the scaffolded questions for each example to differentiate instruction.

Examples

IWB

1. Draw top, front, and side views of a three-dimensional figure.

AL
- *How many line segments does the top have?* 3
- *What two-dimensional figure has three line segments?* triangle
- *What shape is the top and bottom of the figure?* triangle

OL
- *What figure would you see from above?* triangle *the side?* rectangle *the front?* rectangle

BL
- *Name the figure in Example 1.* triangular prism

2. Draw top, front, and side views of a three-dimensional figure.

AL
- *Form a cone with a piece of paper. Fold the paper so the bottom is flat, then hold the cone so you can view it from above. What shape do you see?* a circle
- *Look at the cone from the front. What shape do you see?* a triangle
- *What shape is the side?* a triangle

OL
- *What figure would you see from above?* circle *the side?* triangle *the front?* triangle

BL
- *Name the figure in Example 2.* cone

Need Another Example?

Draw a top, a side, and a front view of the figure. See Answer Appendix.

Work Zone

Draw a Three-Dimensional Figure

You can draw different views of three-dimensional figures. The most common views drawn are the top, side, and front views.

The top, side, and front views of a three-dimensional figure can be used to draw a corner view of the figure.

Examples

Tutor

1. Draw a top, a side, and a front view of the figure at the right.

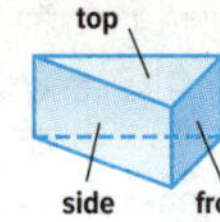

The top view is a triangle.

The side and front view are rectangles.

2. Draw a top, a side, and a front view of the figure at the right.

The top view is a circle.

The side and front view are triangles.

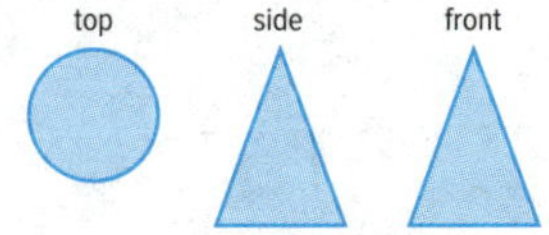

Show your work.

Got it? **Do this problem to find out.**

a. Draw a top, a side, and a front view of the figure at the right.

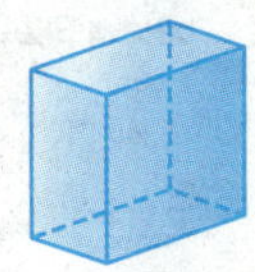

Sample answer:

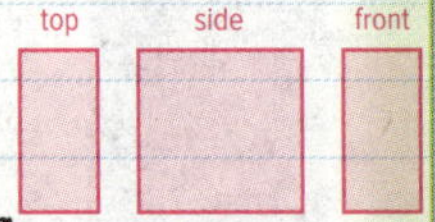

a. ________

Example

Tutor

3. **Draw a top, a side, and a front view of the video console shown.**

The top view is a rectangle.

The side and front views are also rectangles.

> **Plane Figures**
> In geometry, three-dimensional figures are solids and two-dimensional figures such as triangles, circles, and squares are plane figures.

Got it? **Do this problem to find out.**

b. Draw a top, a side, and a front view of the tent shown.

Show your work.

b. 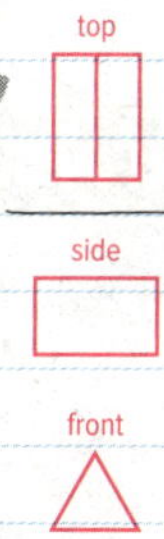

Example

Watch Tutor

4. **Draw a corner view of the three-dimensional figure whose top, side, and front views are shown.**

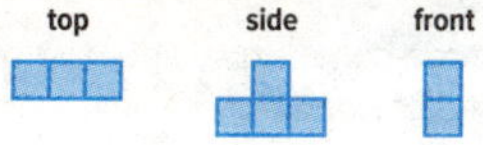

Step 1 Use the top view to draw the base of the figure, a 1-by-3 rectangle.

Step 2 Add edges to make the base a solid figure.

Step 3 Use the side and front views to complete the figure.

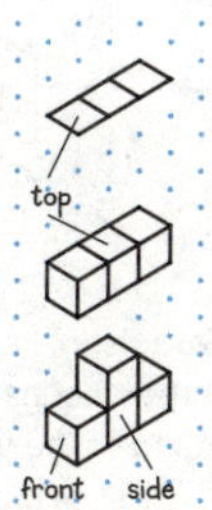

Got it? **Do this problem to find out.**

c. Draw a corner view of the three-dimensional figure whose top, side, and front views are shown.

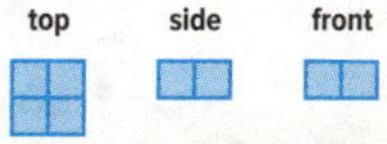

c. 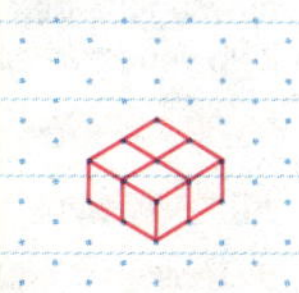

IWB

Examples

3. **Draw top, front, and side views of a three-dimensional figure.**

AL • *What figure do you see from above?* rectangle *the side?* rectangle *the front?* rectangle

OL • *Name the figure.* rectangular prism

BL • *Which faces are congruent?* opposite faces are congruent; top and bottom, left side and right side, front and back

• *What other characteristics do the opposite faces share?* Sample answer: They are parallel.

Need Another Example?
Draw a top, a side, and a front view of the figure. See Answer Appendix.

4. **Draw a three-dimensional figure.**

AL • *Use centimeter cubes to build the figure. How do you know the figure is two cubes tall in the middle?* The middle of the side view is two tall.

• *Why is the front view two cubes tall?* It shows that the middle

OL • *What part of the figure does the top view represent?* the base

• *What are the dimensions of the rectangle?* 1 by 3

• *How does the side view help you complete the drawing?* The side view shows the only part that is 2 cubes tall is the middle.

BL • *How does using isometric dot paper make it easier to draw a corner view of a three-dimensional figure?* See students' work.

Need Another Example?
Draw a corner view of the three-dimensional figure whose top, side, and front views are shown. See Answer Appendix.

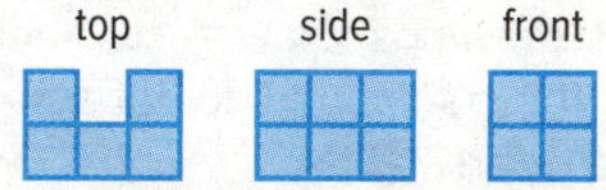

Example

5. Draw a three-dimensional figure.

AL • *Use centimeter cubes to build the figure. How does the top view help you build it?* The top view shows the base of the figure.

OL • *What part of the figure does the top view represent?* the base

• *What are the dimensions of the rectangle?* 2 by 4

• *How does the side view help you complete the drawing?* The side view shows the only parts that are 2 cubes tall are at the back.

BL • *Could you draw this figure using only the top and front views? Explain.* No, the side view shows that the figure is only one cube tall in some sections.

Need Another Example? Draw a corner view of the three-dimensional figure whose top, side, and front views are shown. See Answer Appendix.

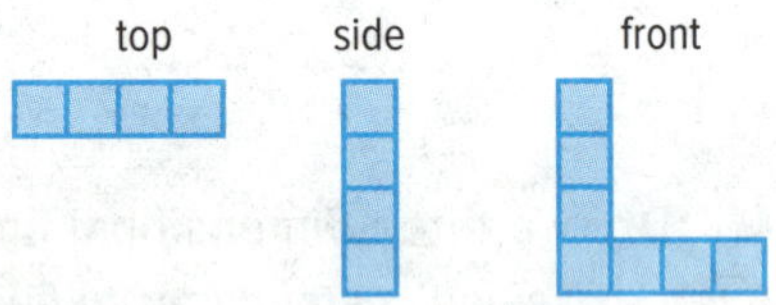

Guided Practice

Formative Assessment Use these exercises to assess students' understanding of the concepts in this lesson.

If some of your students are not ready for assignments, use the differentiated activities below.

AL EL Paired Heads Together Have students work in pairs to solve Exercises 1 and 2. Allow students to use concrete materials as needed. Students complete the first exercise, then turn to their partner and discuss their answers. Students repeat this process for Exercise 2, building the figure with cubes first before drawing it on dot paper. MP 1, 4

BL EL Trade-a-Problem Have students create their own top, side, and front view of a figure, similar to Exercise 2. Students trade their drawings, draw each other's figure, and compare solutions. If the solutions do not agree, students work together to find the errors. MP 1, 4

Example

5. **Draw a corner view of the three-dimensional figure whose top view, side view, and front view are shown.**

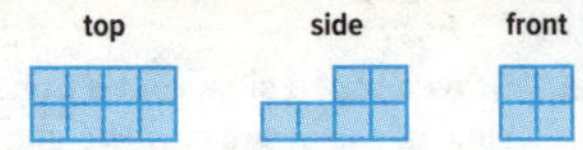

Step 1 Use the top view to draw the base of the figure, a 2-by-4 rectangle.

Step 2 Add edges to make the base a solid figure.

Step 3 Use the side and front views to complete the figure.

Guided Practice

1. Draw a top, a side, and a front view of the figure. (Examples 1–3)

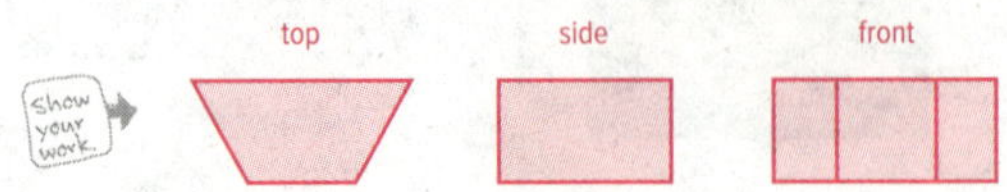

2. Draw a corner view of the three-dimensional figure whose top view, side view, and front view are shown. (Examples 4–5)

3. **Building on the Essential Question** How does drawing the different views of a three-dimensional figure help you have a better understanding of the figure?

Sample answer: The different views help you to see what two-dimensional shapes make up the three-dimensional figure.

Rate Yourself!

How confident are you about drawing three-dimensional figures? Check the box that applies.

For more help, go online to access a Personal Tutor.

Name ______________________ My Homework ______________________

Independent Practice

Go online for Step-by-Step Solutions eHelp

Draw a top, a side, and a front view of each figure. (Examples 1–2)

1.

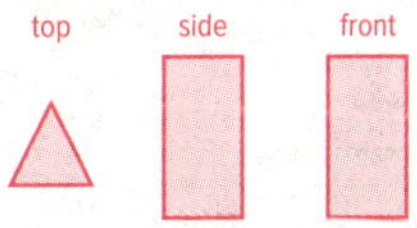

2.

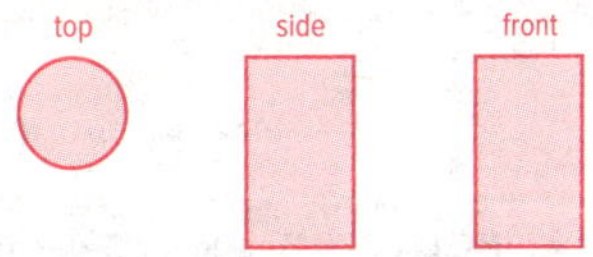

3. Draw a top, a side, and a front view of the eraser shown. (Example 3)

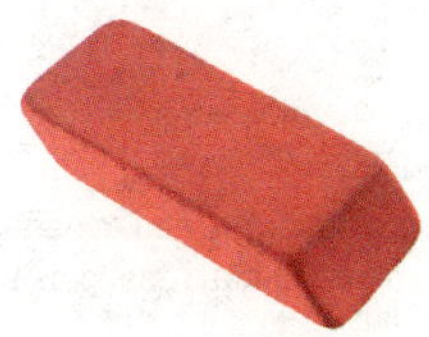

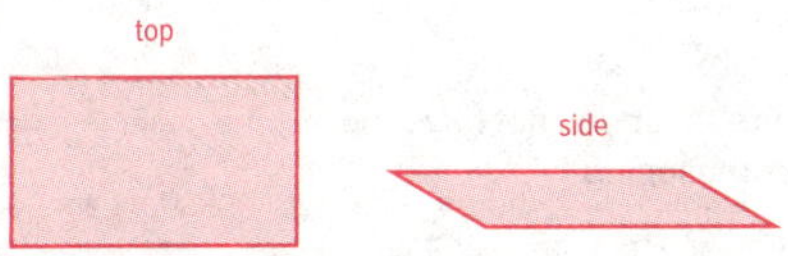

Draw a corner view of each three-dimensional figure whose top view, side view, and front view are shown. (Examples 4–5)

4.

5.
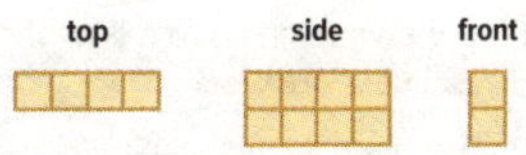

6. Name a real-world object that has a top view of a triangle, and a side and front view that are each rectangles. **See students' work.**

ENGAGE EXPLORE **EXPLAIN** **ELABORATE** **EVALUATE**

3 Practice and Apply

Independent Practice and Extra Practice

The Independent Practice pages are meant to be used as the homework assignment. The Extra Practice page can be used for additional reinforcement or as a second-day assignment.

Levels of Complexity

The levels of the exercises progress from 1 to 3, with Level 1 indicating the lowest level of complexity.

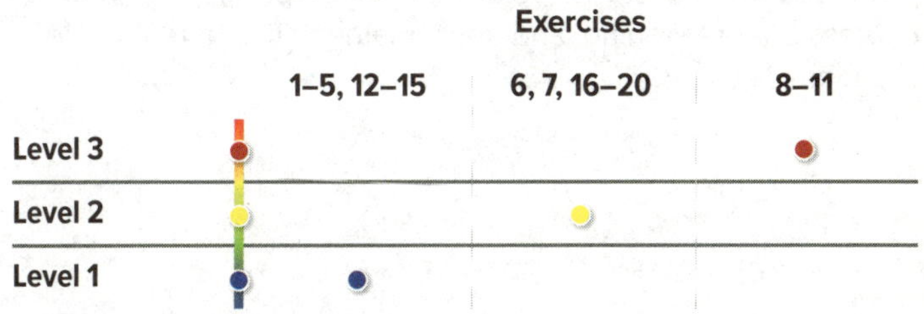

Suggested Assignments

You can use the table below that includes exercises of all complexity levels to select appropriate exercises for your students' needs.

Differentiated Homework Options		
AL	Approaching Level	1–5, 7–9, 11, 19, 20
OL	On Level	1–5 odd, 6–9, 11, 19, 20
BL	Beyond Level	6–11, 19, 20

McGraw Hill Education **ALEKS**® can provide additional remediation support with personalized instruction and practice.

MATHEMATICAL PRACTICES

Emphasis On	Exercise(s)
1 Make sense of problems and persevere in solving them.	10
3 Construct viable arguments and critique the reasoning of others.	9, 11, 18
4 Model with mathematics.	7, 8

Mathematical Practices 1, 3, and 4 are aspects of mathematical thinking that are emphasized in every lesson. Students are given opportunities to be persistent in their problem solving, to express their reasoning, and apply mathematics to real-world situations.

Formative Assessment

Use this activity as a closing formative assessment before dismissing students from your class.

TICKET Out the Door

Have students write how knowing how to draw three-dimensional figures helps in finding the volume of three-dimensional figures. See students' work.

7. **Model with Mathematics** The Quetzalcoatl pyramid in Mexico is shown. Use the photo to sketch views from the top, side, and front of the pyramid.

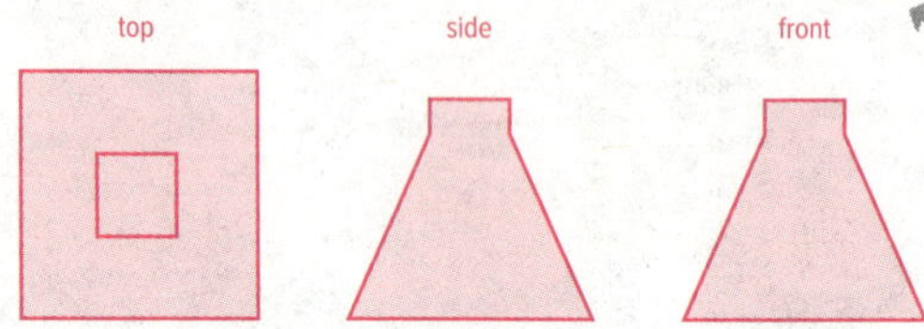

Show your work.

H.O.T. Problems Higher Order Thinking

8. **Model with Mathematics** Choose an object in your classroom or in your home. Sketch any view of the object. Choose among a top, a side, or a front view. See students' work.

9. **Which One Doesn't Belong?** Identify the figure that does not have the same characteristic as the other three. Explain your reasoning.

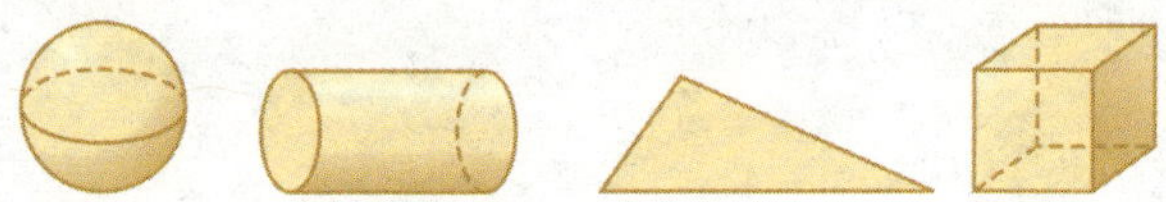

triangle; It is the only two-dimensional figure.

10. **Persevere with Problems** Draw a three-dimensional figure in which the front and top views each have a line of symmetry but the side view does not. Sample answer:

11. **Reason Inductively** Determine whether each statement is *always*, *sometimes*, or *never* true.

    a. The bases of a cylinder have different radii. never

    b. Two planes intersect in a single point. never

    c. Three planes do not intersect in a point. sometimes

Name ______________________ My Homework ______________________

Extra Practice

Draw a top, a side, and a front view of each figure.

12.

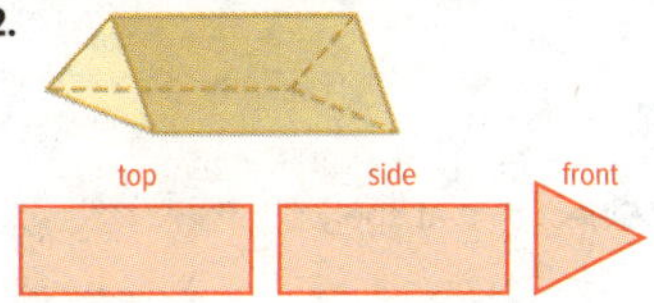

Homework Help

13.

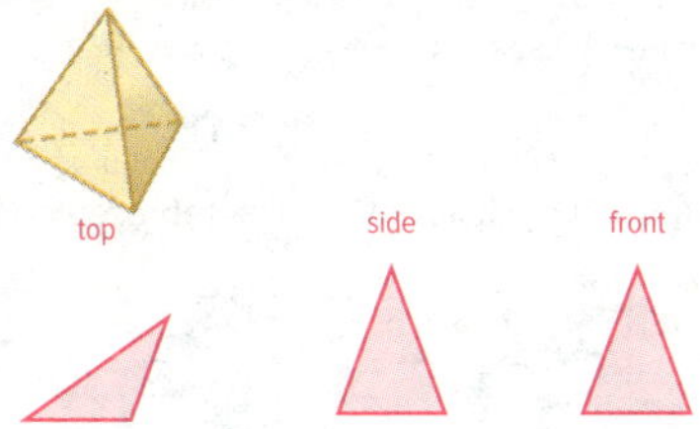

Draw a corner view of each three-dimensional figure whose top view, side view, and and front view are shown.

14.

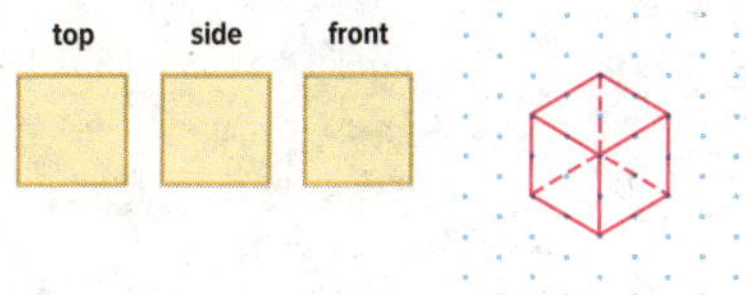

15.

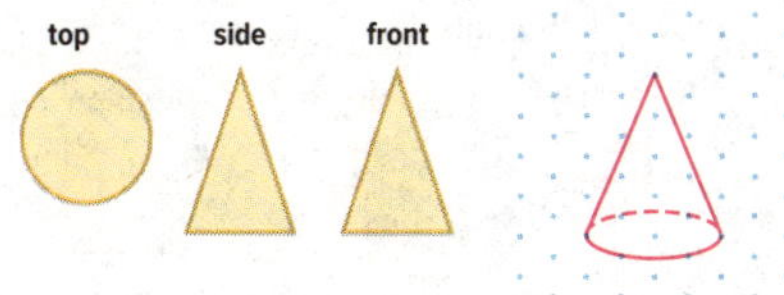

Draw a top, a side, and a front view of each figure.

16.

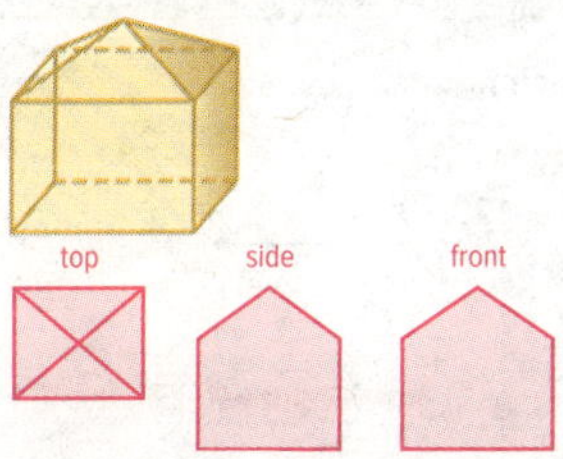

17.

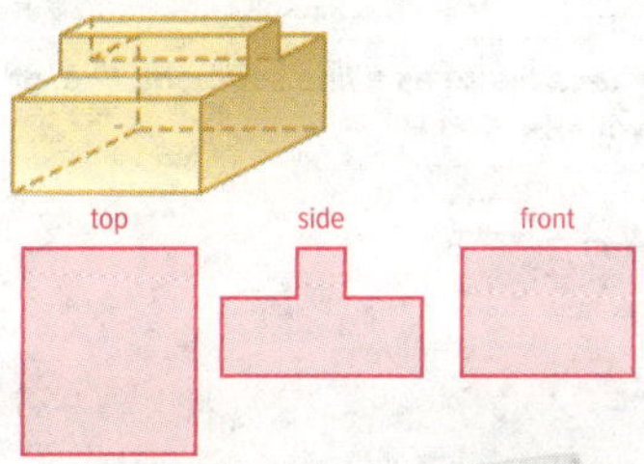

18. MP **Find the Error** Raul drew the side, top, and front view of the figure shown at the right. Find his mistake and correct it.

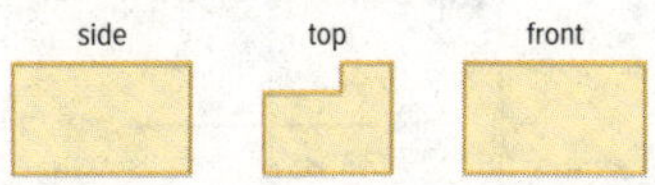

The top and side view should be switched.

Create Your Own Homework Online

eSolutionsManual™ can be used to create worksheets for the suggested assignments on page 589, or create your own worksheets for differentiated homework or review.

Watch Out!

Find the Error In Exercise 18, Raul mixed up the top view and the side view. Suggest to students that they imagine looking down on the figure from above to see the correct top view of the drawing.

Power Up! Test Practice

Exercises 19 and 20 prepare students for more rigorous thinking needed for the state assessment.

19.

This test item requires students to explain and apply mathematical concepts and solve problems with precision, while making use of structure.	
Depth of Knowledge	DOK1
Content Standard	7.G.3
Mathematical Practices	MP1, MP4
Online Experience	Students will be required to click on the bubbles to select all answers that are correct.
Scoring Rubric	
1 point	Students correctly answer the question.

20.

This test item requires students to analyze and solve complex real-world problems through the use of mathematical tools and models.	
Depth of Knowledge	DOK3
Content Standard	7.G.3
Mathematical Practices	MP1, MP4
Online Experience	Students will draw each view.
Scoring Rubric	
2 points	Students correctly draw each view of the figure.
1 point	Students correctly draw two of the views of the figure.

Power Up! Test Practice

19. The top, side, and front view of a figure made of cubes are shown.

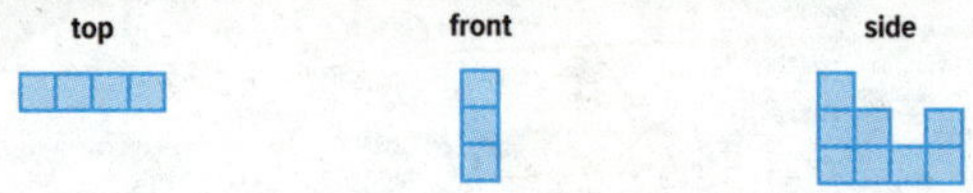

Which of the following can be represented by these views? Select all that apply.

20. Draw the front, top, and side views of the three-dimensional figure shown at the right.

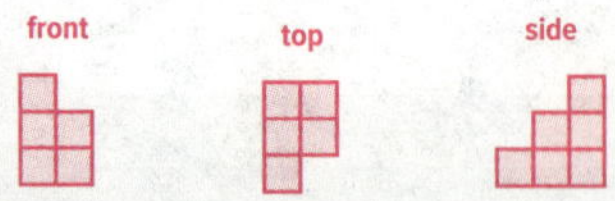

Spiral Review

Identify each figure as a *line segment*, *line*, or *ray*. Then name each figure using symbols. 5.G.3

21.

line; $\overleftrightarrow{WX}$ or $\overleftrightarrow{XW}$

22.

ray; $\overrightarrow{QR}$

23.

line segment; $\overline{EF}$ or $\overline{FE}$

Describe each pair of lines as *intersecting*, *perpendicular*, or *parallel*. Choose the most specific term. 5.G.3

24.

intersecting

25.

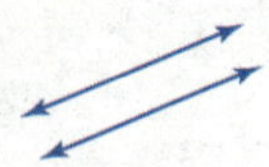

parallel

26.

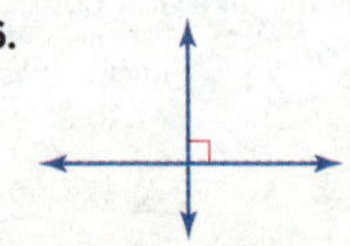

perpendicular

An Interactive Whiteboard Ready presentation is available for each lesson in the chapter.

Geometry

Lesson 6

Cross Sections

Vocabulary Start-Up

A **prism** is a three-dimensional figure with at least two parallel, congruent faces called **bases** that are polygons. A **pyramid** is a three-dimensional figure with one base that is a polygon. Its other faces are triangles.

Write *prism* or *pyramid* on the line below each figure.

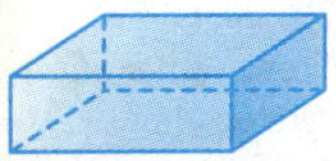

prism

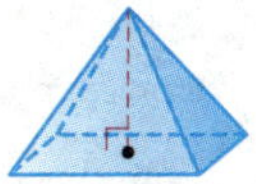

pyramid

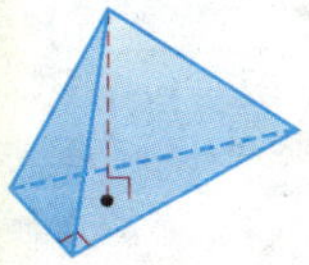

pyramid

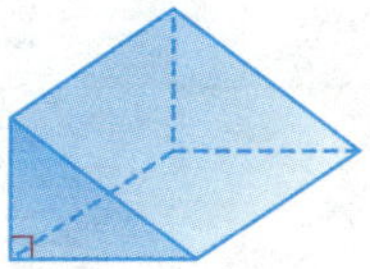

prism

Real-World Link

The Rock and Roll Hall of Fame is shown below. Is the shape of the building a *prism* or *pyramid*? Explain.

pyramid; Sample answer: The shape has one base with triangular faces.

Which MP **Mathematical Practices** did you use?
Shade the circle(s) that applies.

1. Persevere with Problems
2. Reason Abstractly
3. Construct an Argument
4. Model with Mathematics
5. Use Math Tools
6. Attend to Precision
7. Make Use of Structure
8. Use Repeated Reasoning

Essential Question

HOW does geometry help us describe real-world objects?

Vocabulary

prism
bases
pyramid
plane
coplanar
parallel
polyhedron
edge
face
vertex
diagonal
skew lines
cylinder
cone
cross section

Content Standards
7.G.3

MP Mathematical Practices
1, 3, 4

Focus narrowing the scope

Objective Identify and draw three-dimensional figures. 7.G.3

Coherence connecting within and across grades

Previous Students drew different views of three-dimensional figures.

Now Students name parts of three-dimensional figures and identify the shape of a cross section of the figure.

Next Students will draw and use nets of three-dimensional figures to find surface area.

Rigor pursuing concepts, fluency, and applications

See the Levels of Complexity chart on page 597.

ENGAGE EXPLORE EXPLAIN ELABORATE EVALUATE

1 Launch the Lesson

Ideas for Use

You may wish to launch the lesson using a whole group, small group, think-pair-share activity, or independent activity.

EL **Circle the Sage** Poll the class on which students know the vocabulary words in the list. Have those students, the sages, spread out in the room. The rest of the class each surround a sage. The sage explains what he or she knows, while the other students listen and ask questions. Students return to their seats and report on what they learned. MP 1, 6

Alternate Strategy

AL Have students work in pairs. Provide each pair with a net of the objects in the activity. Students cut out the figures and tape the edges together. Then discuss how to name the figures and what the base(s) might be. MP 1, 3, 5

2 Teach the Concept

Ask the scaffolded questions for each example to differentiate instruction.

IWB

Example

1. Identify figures.

AL
- *How many bases does the figure have?* **1**
- *What shape is the base?* **pentagon**
- *Is the base considered one of the faces?* **yes**
- *How many faces does the figure have?* **6**

OL
- *Does the figure have parallel bases?* **no**
- *Is the figure a prism or pyramid?* **pyramid**
- *Identify the pyramid.* **pentagonal pyramid**

BL
- *What are skew lines?* **Lines in the same plane that do not intersect.**
- *Since they do not intersect, are $\overline{RS}$ and $\overline{TU}$ skew lines? Explain.* **No; they are not skew because the lines that contain those segments do intersect.**

Need Another Example?
Identify the figure. Then name the bases, faces, edges, and vertices. **See Answer Appendix.**

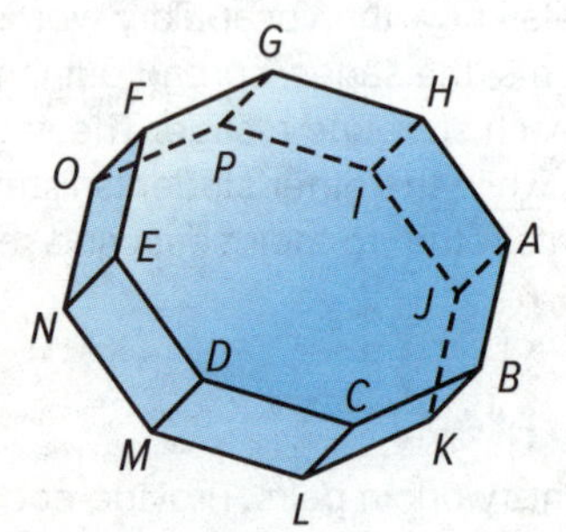

Work Zone

Identify Three-Dimensional Figures

A **plane** is a flat surface that goes on forever in all directions. The figure at the right shows rectangle *ABCD*. Line segments *AB* and *DC* are **coplanar** because they lie in the same plane. They are also **parallel** because they will never intersect, no matter how far they are extended.

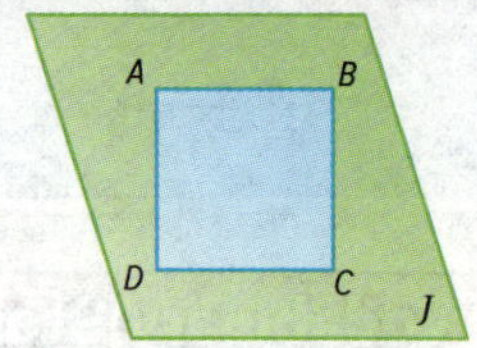

Just as two lines in a plane can intersect or be parallel, there are different ways that planes may be related in space.

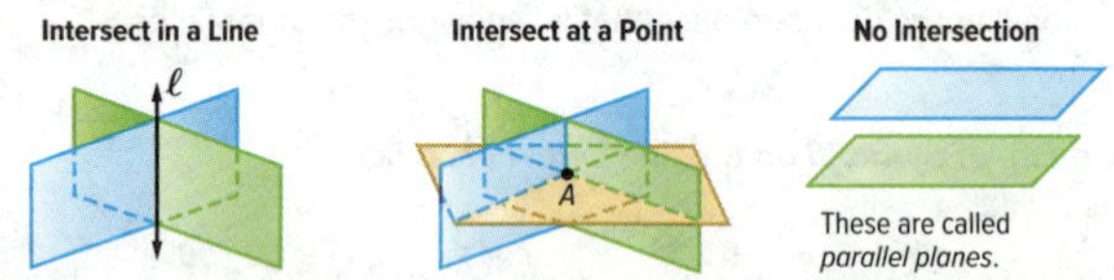

Intersecting planes can form three-dimensional figures. A **polyhedron** is a three-dimensional figure with flat surfaces that are polygons. Prisms and pyramids are both polyhedrons. Some terms associated with three-dimensional figures are *edge, face, vertex*, and *diagonal*.

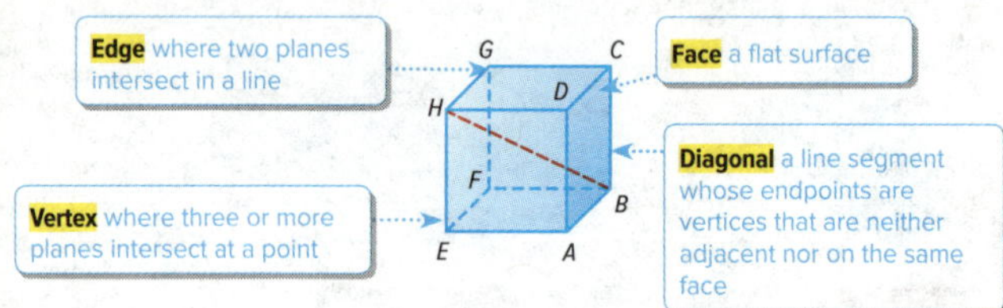

Polygons
The table below lists some common names of polygons.

Sides	Name
5	pentagon
6	hexagon
7	heptagon
8	octagon
9	nonagon
10	decagon

Notice in the figure above, $\overline{GC}$ and $\overline{DA}$ do not intersect. These segments are not parallel because they do not lie in the same plane. Lines that do not intersect and are not coplanar are called **skew lines**.

There are also solids that are not polyhedrons. A **cylinder** is a three-dimensional figure with two parallel congruent circular bases connected by a curved surface. A **cone** has one circular base connected by a curved side to a single vertex.

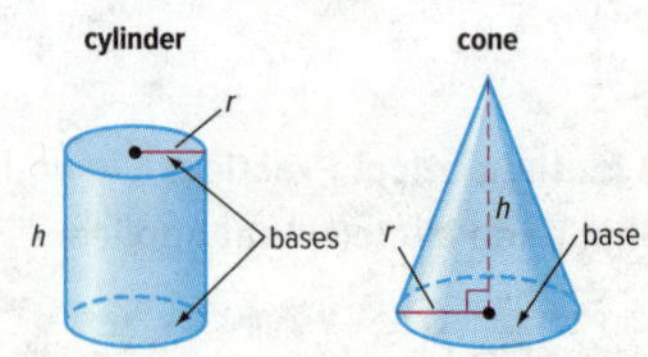

Examples

Tutor

Identify the figure. Name the bases, faces, edges, and vertices. Then, identify a pair of skew lines.

1.

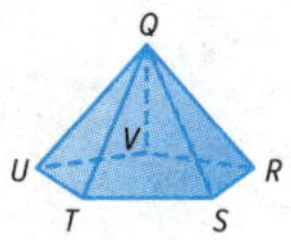

The figure has one base that is a pentagon, so it is a pentagonal pyramid.

base: *RSTUV*

faces: *RSTUV, QVR, QRS, QST, QTU, QUV*

edges: $\overline{QR}$, $\overline{QS}$, $\overline{QT}$, $\overline{QU}$, $\overline{QV}$, $\overline{VR}$, $\overline{RS}$, $\overline{ST}$, $\overline{TU}$, $\overline{UV}$

vertices: *Q, R, S, T, U, V*

skew lines: $\overline{QV}$ and $\overline{TS}$

2.

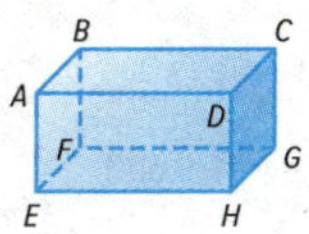

The figure has rectangular bases that are parallel and congruent, so it is a rectangular prism.

bases: *ABCD* and *EFGH*, *ABFE* and *DCGH*, *ADHE* and *BCGF*

faces: *ABCD, EFGH, ABFE, DCGH, ADHE, BCGF*

edges: $\overline{AB}$, $\overline{BC}$, $\overline{CD}$, $\overline{AD}$, $\overline{EF}$, $\overline{FG}$, $\overline{GH}$, $\overline{EH}$, $\overline{AE}$, $\overline{BF}$, $\overline{CG}$, $\overline{DH}$

vertices: *A, B, C, D, E, F, G, H*

skew lines: $\overline{AE}$ and $\overline{FG}$

Got it? Do this problem to find out.

a.

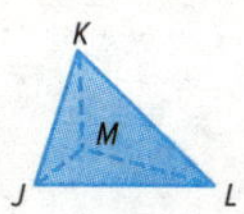

figure name: triangular pyramid

base: *JML*

faces: *JML, JKM, KML, JKL*

edges: $\overline{JK}$, $\overline{KL}$, $\overline{JL}$, $\overline{JM}$, $\overline{KM}$, $\overline{LM}$

vertices: *J, K, L, M*

skew lines: Sample answer: $\overline{KM}$ and $\overline{JL}$

Identify Cross Sections

The intersection of a solid and a plane is called a **cross section** of the solid.

Common Error

In the drawing of a rectangular prism, the bases do not have to be on the top and bottom. Any two parallel rectangles are bases. In a triangular pyramid, any face is a base.

Example

IWB

2. Identify figures.

AL

- *How many bases does the figure have?* 2
- *What shape are the bases?* rectangles
- *Are the bases considered two of the faces?* yes
- *How many faces does the figure have?* 6
- *Two faces that can be considered bases are ABCD and EFGH. Are there any other faces that can be called bases? If so, what are they?* yes; *ABFE* and *DCGH*, *ADHE* and *BCGF*

OL

- *Does the figure have parallel bases?* yes
- *How many different sets of bases can this figure have?* 3
- *Is the figure a prism or pyramid?* prism
- *Identify the prism.* rectangular prism
- *$\overline{AE}$ and $\overline{FG}$ are two skew lines. Name another pair of skew lines.* Sample answer: $\overline{BF}$ and $\overline{GH}$

BL

- *In three-dimensional space, can there be skew planes? Explain your reasoning.* no; Sample answer: Lines are two-dimensional figures, so they need three-dimensional space to be skew. Planes would need four-dimensional space in order to be skew.

Need Another Example?

Identify the figure. Then name the bases, faces, edges, and vertices. See Answer Appendix.

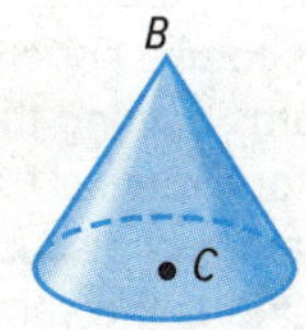

Example

IWB

3. Identify cross sections.

AL • *In your own words, what is a cross section?* See students' work.

• *What is the shape of the base of the pyramid?* square

• *If you slice the pyramid parallel to the base, what shape will result?* square

OL • *If you slice a square pyramid at an angle, what shape will you see?* trapezoid

BL • *Describe a real-world example of the use of a cross section.* See students' work; examples may include cutting down a tree and counting the rings, or slicing vegetables.

Need Another Example?
Describe the shape resulting from a vertical, angled, and horizontal cross section of a triangular prism. vertical: rectangle; angled: trapezoid; horizontal; triangle

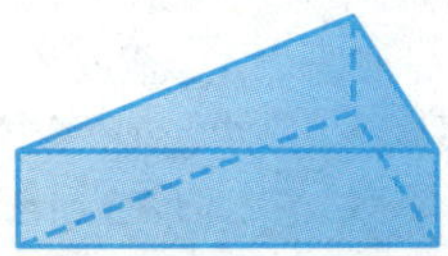

Guided Practice

Formative Assessment Use these exercises to assess students' understanding of the concepts in this lesson.

If some of your students are not ready for assignments, use the differentiated activities below.

AL EL **Rally Table** Have students work in teams to solve Exercise 1. Allow students to use concrete materials as needed. Students take turns naming the bases, faces, edges, vertices, and skew lines for Exercise 1. Have them trade their solutions with another team and discuss any differences. Remind students that $\triangle QRS$ is the same as $\triangle RSQ$. MP 1, 4

BL EL **Pairs Discussion** Have students work in pairs to research the Platonic solids and construct the solids out of paper. Then have them discuss and draw vertical and horizontal cross sections of the solids. Have them trade their drawings with another pair of students and discuss any differences. Remind students that the cross sections may look different depending on how the solid is sitting. MP 1, 4

Example

Tutor

3. Describe the shape resulting from a vertical, angled, and horizontal cross section of a square pyramid.

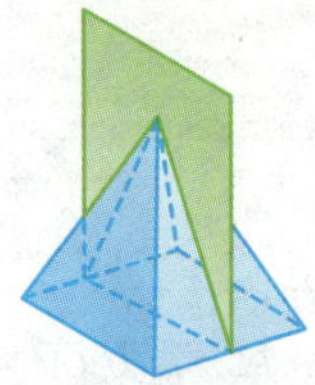

Vertical Slice

The cross section is a triangle.

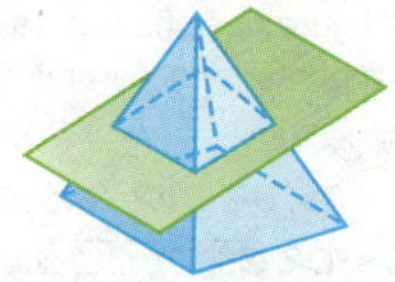

Angled Slice

The cross section is a trapezoid.

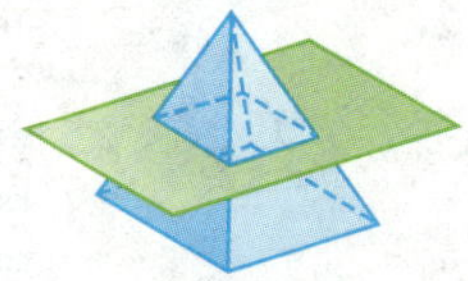

Horizontal Slice

The cross section is a square.

Got it? Do this problem to find out.

b. Describe the shape resulting from a vertical, angled, and horizontal cross section of a cylinder.

Show your work.

b. Sample answer: vertical: rectangle; angled: oval; horizontal: circle

Guided Practice

Check

1. Identify the figure. Then name the bases, faces, edges, and vertices. Then, identify a pair of skew lines. (Examples 1–2)

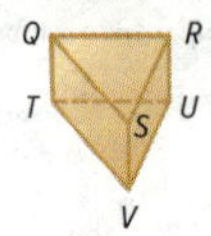

figure name: triangular prism

bases: QRS and TUV

faces: QRS, TUV, QSVT, SRUV, RQTU

edges: $\overline{QR}$, $\overline{RS}$, $\overline{QS}$, $\overline{TU}$, $\overline{UV}$, $\overline{TV}$, $\overline{QT}$, $\overline{RU}$, $\overline{SV}$

vertices: Q, R, S, T, U, V

skew lines: Sample answer: $\overline{SV}$ and $\overline{TU}$

2. Describe the shape resulting from the cross section shown. (Example 3) triangle

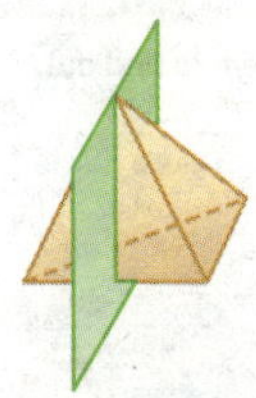

3. **Building on the Essential Question** How can knowing the shape of the base of a three-dimensional figure help you name the figure?

Sample answer: Some three-dimensional figures are named by their base.

Rate Yourself!

Are you ready to move on? Shade the section that applies.

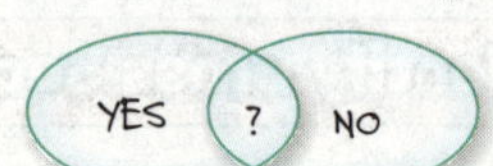

For more help, go online to access a Personal Tutor.

Tutor

Name ________________________ My Homework ________________________

Independent Practice

Go online for Step-by-Step Solutions eHelp

Identify each figure. Name the bases, faces, edges, and vertices. Then, identify a pair of skew lines. (Examples 1–2)

1.

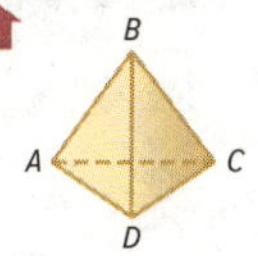

figure name: triangular pyramid

bases: *ACD*

faces: *ACD, ABD, ABC, DBC*

edges: $\overline{AB}, \overline{BC}, \overline{CD}, \overline{AD}, \overline{AC}, \overline{BD}$

vertices: *A, B, C, D*

skew lines: Sample answer: $\overline{BD}$ and $\overline{AC}$

2.

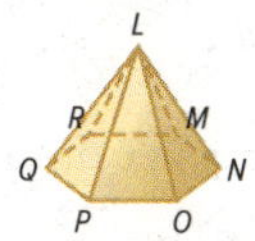

figure name: hexagonal pyramid

bases: *MNOPQR*

faces: *MNOPQR, LMN, LNO, LOP, LPQ, LQR, LRM*

edges: $\overline{LM}, \overline{LN}, \overline{LO}, \overline{LP}, \overline{LQ}, \overline{LR}, \overline{MN}, \overline{NO}, \overline{OP}, \overline{PQ}, \overline{QR}, \overline{RM}$

vertices: *L, M, N, O, P, Q, R*

skew lines Sample answer: $\overline{LM}$ and $\overline{PO}$

Describe the shape resulting from each cross section. (Example 3)

3.

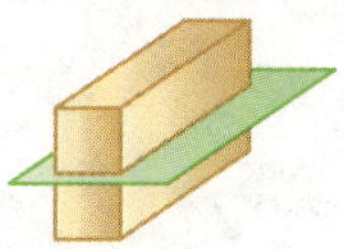

rectangle

4.

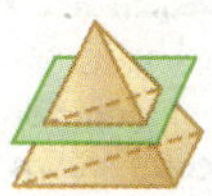

triangle

5.

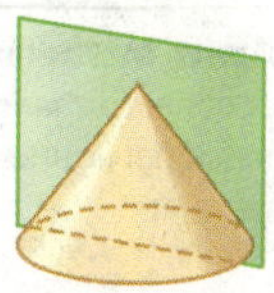

triangle

6. A basketball is shaped like a *sphere*.

a. Draw a basketball with a vertical, angled, and horizontal slice.

Show your work.

vertical: angled: horizontal:

b. Describe the cross section made by each slice.

All cross sections are circles.

c. Is the basketball a polyhedron? Explain.

No. It has no flat surfaces that are polygons.

ENGAGE EXPLORE **EXPLAIN** **ELABORATE** **EVALUATE**

3 Practice and Apply

Independent Practice and Extra Practice

The Independent Practice pages are meant to be used as the homework assignment. The Extra Practice page can be used for additional reinforcement or as a second-day assignment.

Levels of Complexity

The levels of the exercises progress from 1 to 3, with Level 1 indicating the lowest level of complexity.

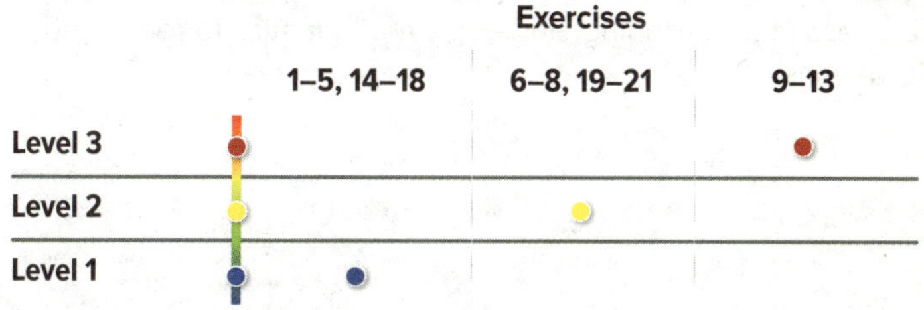

Suggested Assignments

You can use the table below that includes exercises fo all complexity levels to select appropriate exercises for your students' needs.

Differentiated Homework Options		
AL	Approaching Level	1–5, 7–9, 20, 21
OL	On Level	1–5 odd, 6–9, 20, 21
BL	Beyond Level	6–13, 20, 21

McGraw Hill Education **ALEKS**® can provide additional remediation support with personalized instruction and practice.

Watch Out!

Common Error Students may have trouble with naming all the faces of a solid. Suggest students start with the first letter of the alphabet used to name a vertex. Name each side with the letters moving from one side to the other in a clockwise manner.

MP MATHEMATICAL PRACTICES

Emphasis On	Exercise(s)
1 Make sense of problems and persevere in solving them.	10–13
3 Construct viable arguments and critique the reasoning of others.	7, 19
4 Model with mathematics.	9

Mathematical Practices 1, 3, and 4 are aspects of mathematical thinking that are emphasized in every lesson. Students are given opportunities to be persistent in their problem solving, to express their reasoning, and apply mathematics to real-world situations.

Formative Assessment
Use this activity as a closing formative assessment before dismissing students from your class.

TICKET Out the Door

Have students explain how to identify skew lines in a figure.
See students' work.

7. MP **Use a Counterexample** State whether the following conjecture is *true* or *false*. If *false*, provide a counterexample.

Two planes in three-dimensional space can intersect at one point.

False; two planes intersect at a line, which is an infinite number of points.

8. Draw and label a hexagonal prism. Then identify each of the following.
Sample answers are given.

a. parallel planes *GHJKLM* and *ABCDEF*

b. skew lines $\overline{JH}$ and $\overline{LE}$

c. intersecting planes *GHBA* and *ABCDEF*

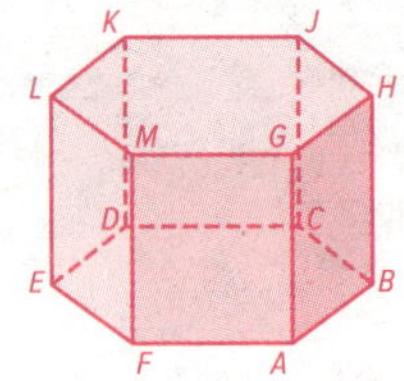

Show your work.

H.O.T. Problems Higher Order Thinking

9. MP **Model with Mathematics** Draw the cross sections of a polyhedron, cylinder, or cone. Exchange papers with another student. Identify the three-dimensional figures represented by the cross sections. See students' work.

Show your work.

MP **Persevere with Problems** **Determine whether each statement is *always*, *sometimes*, or *never* true. Explain your reasoning.**

10. A pyramid has parallel faces.
never; A pyramid has all faces, except the base, intersecting at one vertex.

11. A prism has 2 bases and 4 faces.
sometimes; A rectangular prism has 2 bases and 4 faces, but a triangular prism has 2 bases and 3 faces.

12. A parallelogram cannot be a cross section of a triangular prism.
always; The cross section of a triangular prism will be a triangle, rectangle, or trapezoid.

13. A pyramid has a rectangular base.
sometimes; A triangular pyramid has a triangle for its base.

Name ______________________ My Homework ______________________

Extra Practice

Identify each figure. Then name the bases, faces, edges, and vertices. Then identify a pair of skew lines.

14.

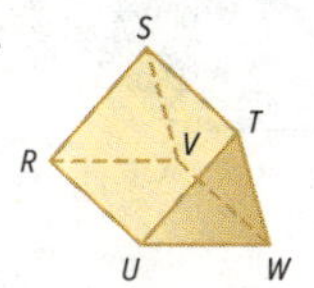

figure name: triangular prism

Homework Help

bases: RSV and UTW

faces: RSV, UTW, RSTU, SVWT, VRUW

edges: $\overline{RS}$, $\overline{SV}$, $\overline{RV}$, $\overline{UT}$, $\overline{TW}$, $\overline{UW}$, $\overline{RU}$, $\overline{VW}$, $\overline{ST}$

vertices: R, S, T, U, V, W

skew lines: Sample answer: $\overline{TU}$ and $\overline{WV}$

15.

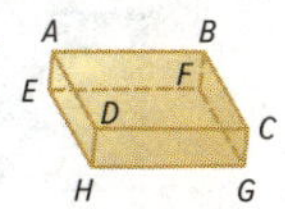

figure name: rectangular prism

bases: ABCD, EFGH, ABFE, DCGH, ADHE, BCGF

faces: ABCD, EFGH, ABFE, DCGH, ADHE, BCGF

edges: $\overline{AB}$, $\overline{BC}$, $\overline{CD}$, $\overline{AD}$, $\overline{EF}$, $\overline{FG}$, $\overline{GH}$, $\overline{EH}$, $\overline{AE}$, $\overline{BF}$, $\overline{CG}$, $\overline{DH}$

vertices: A, B, C, D, E, F, G, H

skew lines: Sample answers: $\overline{DH}$ and $\overline{GF}$

Describe the shape resulting from each cross section. (Example 4)

16.

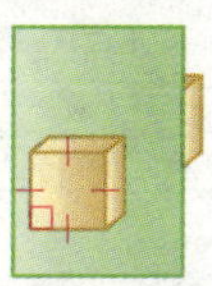

square

17.

curve

18.

triangle

19. MP **Find the Error** Hannah is identifying the figure at the right. Find her mistake and correct it.

Because there are two parallel, congruent triangular bases, it is a triangular prism.

Create Your Own Homework Online

eSolutionsManual™ can be used to create worksheets for the suggested assignments on page 597, or create your own worksheets for differentiated homework or review.

Watch Out!

Find the Error In Exercise 19, Hannah incorrectly named the figure. Suggest to students that they think of pyramids as having a common point, or vertex, at which all faces meet except the base. Have students think of prisms as having two bases that are opposite and parallel to each other.

Power Up! Test Practice

Exercises 20 and 21 prepare students for more rigorous thinking needed for the state assessment.

20.

This test item requires students to explain and apply mathematical concepts and solve problems with precision, while making use of structure.	
Depth of Knowledge	DOK1
Content Standard	7.G.3
Mathematical Practice	MP1
Online Experience	Students will be required to click on the bubbles to select all answers that are correct.
Scoring Rubric	
1 point	Students correctly answer the question.

21.

This test item requires students to explain and apply mathematical concepts and solve problems with precision, while making use of structure.	
Depth of Knowledge	DOK1
Content Standard	7.G.3
Mathematical Practice	MP1
Online Experience	Students will drag the boxes to the correct descriptions of the figure.
Scoring Rubric	
2 points	Students correctly match all three figures.
1 point	Students correctly match two of the three figures.

Power Up! Test Practice

20. The figure shown is a square pyramid. Which of the following are cross sections of the pyramid? Select all that apply.

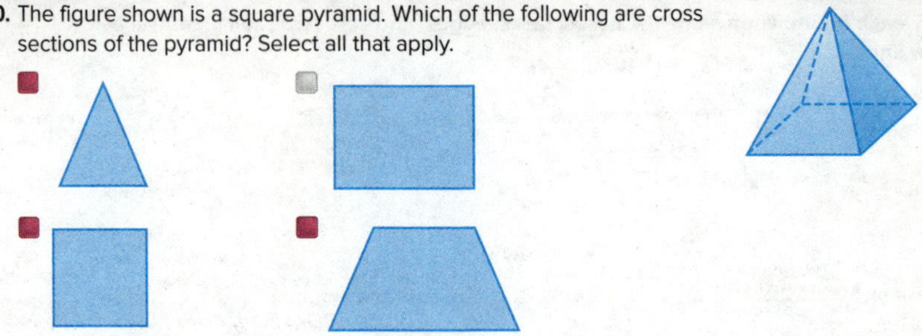

21. Match each number of faces, edges, and vertices to the correct solid figure.

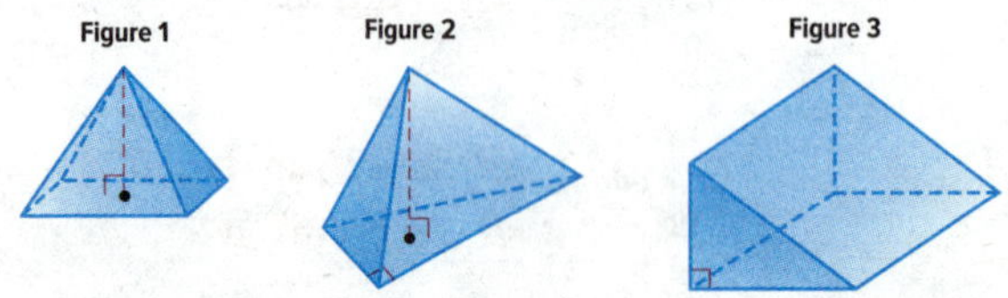

Figure 1
Figure 2
Figure 3

a. 4 faces, 6 edges, 4 vertices — Figure 2

b. 5 faces, 8 edges, 5 vertices — Figure 1

c. 5 faces, 9 edges, 6 vertices — Figure 3

Spiral Review

Name each polygon. 5.G.3

22.

trapezoid

23.

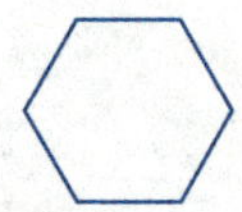

hexagon

24.

parallelogram

25. Find the measure of the missing angle of the polygon. 5.G.3 90°

College & Career READINESS

21ST CENTURY CAREER in Design Engineering

Roller Coaster Designer

If you have a passion for amusement parks, a great imagination, and enjoy building things, you might want to consider a career in roller coaster design. Roller coaster designers combine creativity, engineering, mathematics, and physics to develop rides that are both exciting and safe. In order to analyze data and make precise calculations, a roller coaster designer must have a solid background in high school math and science.

College & Career READINESS

Is This the Career for You?

Are you interested in a career as a roller coaster designer? Take some of the following courses in high school to get started in the right direction.

- Algebra
- Calculus
- Geometry
- Physics
- Trigonometry

Turn the page to find out how math relates to a career in Design Engineering.

Focus narrowing the scope

Objective Apply mathematics to problems arising in the workplace. This lesson emphasizes MP **Mathematical Practice 4** Model with Mathematics.

Coherence connecting within and across grades

Previous Students solved problems involving scale drawings.

Now Students apply the content standard to solve problems in the workplace.

Rigor pursuing concepts, fluency, and applications

See the Career Project on page 602.

ENGAGE EXPLORE EXPLAIN ELABORATE EVALUATE

1 Launch the Lesson

Ask students to read the information on the student page about roller coaster designers and answer the following questions.

Ask:

- *What kinds of classes should you take to be a roller coaster designer?* Sample answer: math and science courses like Algebra, Physics, Calculus, Geometry, Trigonometry
- *What are some important things a roller coaster designer needs to consider when designing a new coaster?* Sample answer: how to make the coaster exciting, but still safe

College & Career READINESS

Help students connect what they do today to their futures. Direct them to the Internet or another source to explore, learn, and plan for college and future careers.

2 Collaborate

AL EL Think-Write-Share Have students write a real-world word problem using information from the table. Then have students work in pairs to share their problem and discuss any changes that may need to be made to their word problem and/or solution. MP 1, 4

BL EL Timed Roundrobin Divide the class into team of 3 or 4. Give students five minutes to complete Exercises 1–5. Each student contributes at least once in the completion of each of the exercises. When the teams have finished, have students in a whole class setting or a large group setting discuss the solutions. MP 1, 6

Career Portfolio

When students complete this page, have them add it to their Career Portfolio.

Career Facts

Design engineers use tricks to make coasters more exciting. For example, when a coaster travels close to the ground, the ground acts as a reference point and makes riders feel like they are going faster than they really are. In another example, in 2007 designers updated SheiKra so that its cars became "floorless." Although the coaster's 200-foot, 90-degree drop did not change, it became even more thrilling because there was no floor against which riders could brace themselves.

MP A Thrilling Ride

Use the information in the table to solve each problem.

1. In a scale drawing of SheiKra, a designer uses a scale of 1 inch = 16 feet. What is the height of the roller coaster in the drawing? $12\frac{1}{2}$ in.
2. On a model of Montu, the height of the loop is 13 inches. What is the scale? 1 in. = 8 ft
3. In a scale drawing of Montu, the height of the roller coaster is 10 inches. What is the scale factor? $\frac{1}{180}$
4. SheiKra has a hill that goes through a tunnel. On a model of the roller coaster, the hill is 23 inches tall and the scale is 1 inch = 6 feet. What is the actual height of the tunnel hill? 138 ft
5. An engineer is building a model of SheiKra. She wants the model to be about 32 inches high. Choose an appropriate scale for the model. Then use it to find the loop height of the model. Sample answer: 1 in. = 6.25 ft; 23.2 in.

Busch Gardens Tampa

Roller Coaster	Coaster Height (ft)	Loop Height (ft)
SheiKra	200	145
Montu	150	104

MP Career Project

It's time to update your career portfolio! Describe a roller coaster that you, as a roller coaster designer, would create. Include the height and angle of the tallest drop, the total length, maximum speed, number of loops and tunnels, and color scheme. Be sure to include the name of your roller coaster.

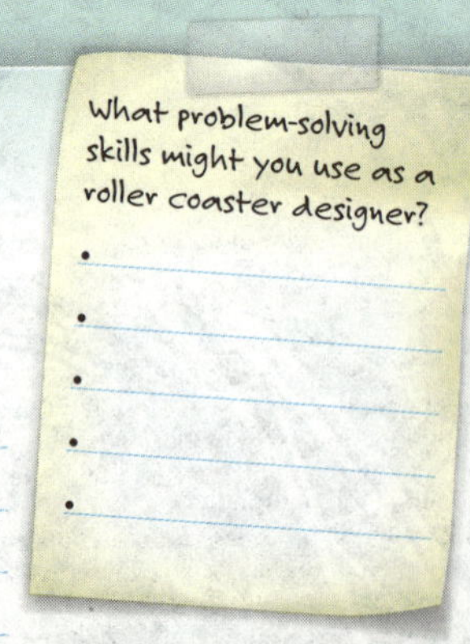

Chapter Review

Check

Vocabulary Check

Vocab

Complete the crossword puzzle using the vocabulary list at the beginning of the chapter.

Across

2. a three-dimensional figure with two parallel, congruent bases that are polygons

4. a triangle with an angle greater than 90 degrees and less than 180 degrees

8. a three-dimensional figure with two parallel congruent circular bases connected by a curved surface

11. a triangle with three congruent sides

12. segments with the same length

14. used to represent an object that is too large to be built at actual size (2 words)

15. two angles with a sum of 90 degrees

Down

1. angles that share a common vertex, a common side, and do not overlap

3. two angles with a sum of 180 degrees

5. a figure with three sides and three angles

6. the ratio that compares the measurements of a model and the real object

7. opposite angles that are formed by the intersection of two lines

8. a three-dimensional figure with one circular base connected by a curved side to a single vertex

9. an angle less than 90 degrees

10. where two rays meet to form an angle

13. a 90 degree angle

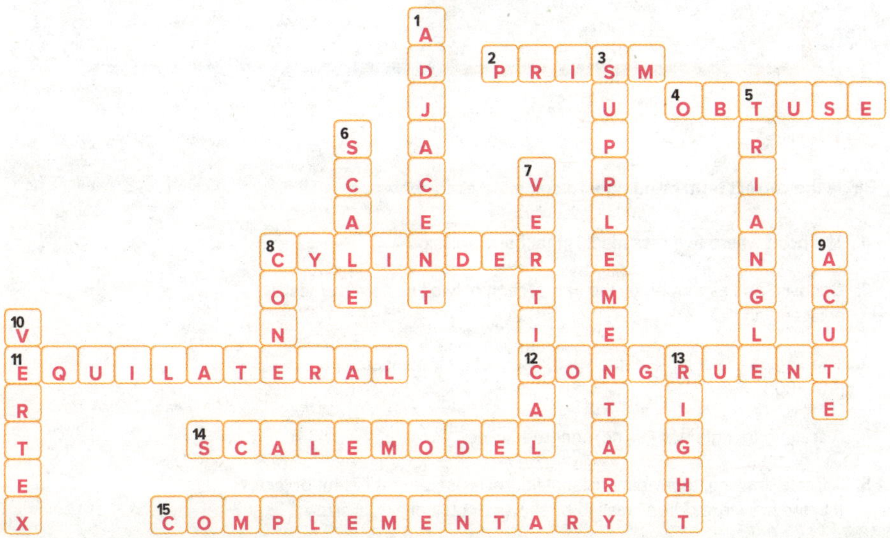

Vocabulary Check

EL **Paired Heads Together** Have students work in pairs to complete the Vocabulary Check exercises, ensuring that each partner understands. Each student is assigned a number, 1 or 2. Randomly call on a numbered student to share their responses with the class. MP 1, 6

Alternate Strategy

AL EL To help students, you may wish to give them a vocabulary list from which they can choose their answers. A vocabulary list for this activity would include the following terms. MP 1, 6

- acute angle (Lesson 1)
- adjacent angles (Lesson 1)
- complementary angles (Lesson 2)
- cone (Lesson 6)
- congruent segments (Lesson 3)
- cylinder (Lesson 6)
- equilateral triangle (Lesson 3)
- obtuse angle (Lesson 1)
- prism (Lesson 6)
- right angle (Lesson 1)
- scale (Lesson 4)
- scale model (Lesson 4)
- supplementary angles (Lesson 2)
- triangle (Lesson 3)
- vertex (Lesson 1)
- vertical angles (Lesson 1)

Key Concept Check

FOLDABLES EL A completed Foldable for this chapter should include a review of similar figures and scale drawings.

If you choose not to use this Foldable, have students write a brief review of the Key Concepts found throughout the chapter and give an example of each.

Ideas for Use

EL Have students work in pairs to discuss their Foldables. Have them practice speaking in a collaborative setting by sharing how they have completed their Foldable thus far and how they could finish it. Have each student complete their Foldable and trade with their partner to discuss any similarities and differences. MP 1, 3, 5

Got It?

If students have trouble with Exercises 1–5, they may need help with the following concept(s).

Concept	Exercise(s)
vertical angles (Lesson 1)	1, 2
complementary angles (Lesson 2)	3
classifying triangles (Lesson 3)	4
scale drawings (Lesson 4)	5

ALEKS® provides additional support with personalized instruction and practice for those who are struggling, while providing enhanced learning for those who have mastered the concepts.

Key Concept Check

Use Your FOLDABLES

Use your Foldable to help review the chapter.

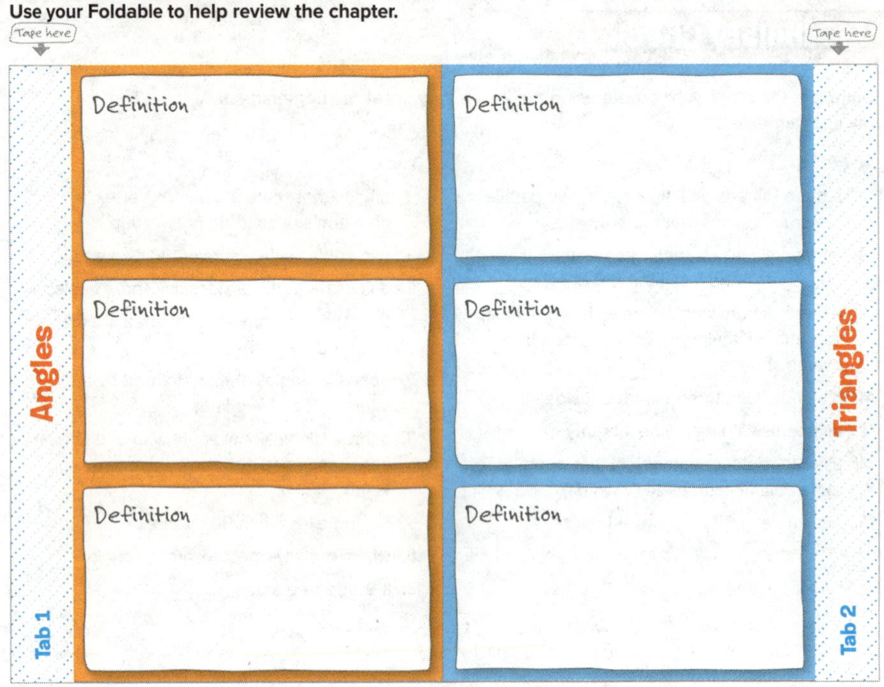

Got it?

Circle the correct term or number to complete each sentence.

1. The point where two rays meet is the (base, vertex).
2. Opposite angles formed by the intersection of two lines are (vertical, adjacent) angles.
3. Two angles are complementary if the sum of their measures is (90°, 180°).
4. A scalene triangle has (all, no) congruent sides.
5. A (scale drawing, three-dimensional figure) is used to represent objects that are too large or too small to be drawn or built at actual size.

Geometry

Power Up! Performance Task

Stacking Triangles

Thompson has drawn two different triangles.

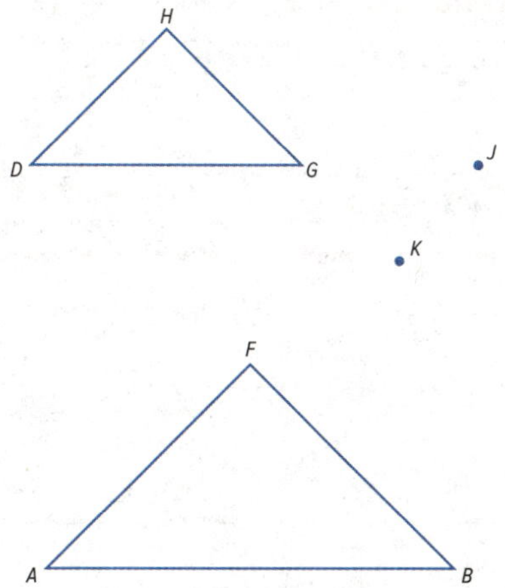

Write your answers on another piece of paper. Show all of your work to receive full credit.

Part A
Triangle *DHG* is a scale drawing of triangle *AFB*. Use a ruler. Measure and label the side lengths of triangle *AFB* and triangle *DHG*. What scale factor was used to make triangle *DHG*?

Part B
Use a scale factor of 2 to make a new scale drawing of triangle *DHG*. Label the new triangle *XYZ*.

Part C
Extend line *DG* though point *J* and extend line *HG* through point *K*. Find the measure of angle *HGJ* and angle *JGK*. Name a pair of complementary or supplementary angles. Justify your response.

Power Up! Performance Task

This Performance-Based Assessment requires students to solve multi-step problems through abstract reasoning, precision, and perseverance. This practice scenario can be used to help students prepare for the thinking skills that will be used on the State Assessment.

A complete scoring rubric with answers to the Exercises can be found on page PT3.

Answering the Essential Question

Before answering the Essential Question, have students review their answers to the **Building on the Essential Question** exercises found in each lesson of the chapter.

- What are the differences between vertical and adjacent angles. (p. 538)
- How are vertical, adjacent, complementary, and supplementary angles related? (p. 546)
- How can triangles be classified? (p. 558)
- How can you use a map to estimate the actual distance between Miami, Florida, and Atlanta, Georgia? (p. 578)
- How does drawing the different views of a three-dimensional figure help you have a better understanding of the figure? (p. 588)
- How can knowing the shape of the base of a three-dimensional figure help you name the figure? (p. 596)

Ideas for Use

EL **Think-Pair-Share** Have students work in pairs. Pose the Essential Question. Give students about one minute to think about how they could complete the graphic organizer and answer the Essential Question. Then have them share their responses with their partner, ensuring that each partner understands. Have pairs volunteer to share their responses with the class. MP 1, 4

Reflect

Answering the Essential Question

Use what you learned about geometric figures to complete the graphic organizer.

How do polygons help us describe real-world objects?

Sample answer: A polygon is a closed figure formed by three or more line segments. Triangles, squares, and rectangles are types of polygons. Polygons can be used to represent flat objects, such as a sheet of paper, or the surface of an object, such as the shape of the lid of a box.

Essential Question

HOW does geometry help us describe real-world objects?

How do polyhedrons help us describe real-world objects?

Sample answer: A polyhedron is a solid with flat surfaces that are polygons. Prisms and pyramids are types of polyhedrons. Polyhedrons can be used to represent three-dimensional objects, such as containers and buildings.

Answer the Essential Question. HOW does geometry help us describe real-world objects?

See students' work.

PLAN ONLINE: PD | RtI | Watch | Worksheets | Vocab | Tutor | Tools | Check | English Learners | Sketchpad

PRESENT: IWB

An Interactive Whiteboard Ready presentation is available for each lesson in the chapter.

Chapter 8

Measure Figures

Essential Question

How do measurements help you describe real-world objects?

Content Standards
7.G.4, 7.G.6

MP Mathematical Practices
1, 2, 3, 4, 5, 6, 8

Math in the Real World

Soccer is a sport that is played on a rectangular field. The dimensions of a regulation size soccer field are 100 yards long and 60 yards wide.

What is the area of the soccer field shown?

$A =$ 6,000 square yards

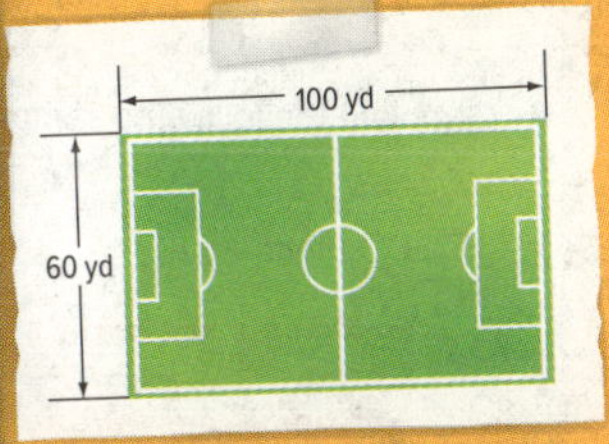

FOLDABLES® Study Organizer

1. Cut out the Foldable on page FL9 of this book.
2. Place your Foldable on page 700.
3. Use the Foldable throughout this chapter to help you learn about measuring figures.

Focus narrowing the scope

This chapter focuses on content from the **Geometry** (G) domain.

Mathematical Background Additional information about the mathematical background for this chapter can be found online at connectED.mcgraw-hill.com.

Coherence connecting within and across grades

Previous	Now	Next
Students simplified expressions and solved equations.	Students find the area of circles and composite figures and the volume of prisms and pyramids.	Students will find the surface area and volume of cylinders, cones, and spheres.

Rigor pursuing concepts, fluency, and applications

The Levels of Complexity charts located throughout this chapter indicate how the exercises progress from conceptual understanding and procedural skills and fluency, to application and critical thinking.

Launch the Chapter

Math in the Real World

Soccer Tell students that to find the area of the soccer field they need to use the formula for the area of a rectangle, $A = \ell w$.

What Tools Do You Need?

Vocabulary Activity

EL As you proceed through the chapter, introduce each vocabulary term using the following routine. Ask the students to say each term aloud after you say it.

Define: Volume is the number of cubic units needed to fill the space occupied by a solid.

Example:

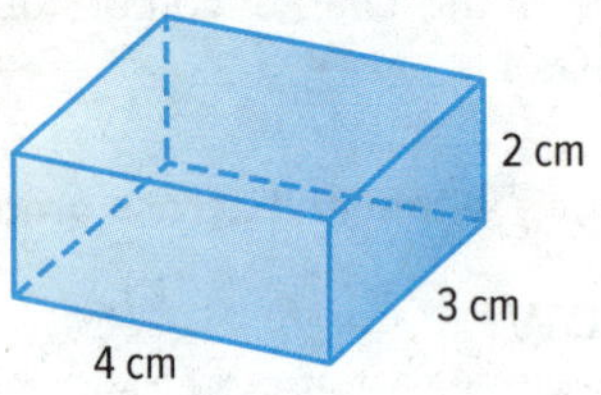

Ask:

- *What is the volume of the figure shown?* 24 cm^3

Studying Math

EL Have students read the Power Notes section.

Ask:

- *How are lesson outlines and power notes similar?* Sample answer: Power notes and lesson outlines both arrange information in layers.
- *How do power notes and lesson outlines differ?* Sample answer: Power notes use a system of powers to indicate the main idea, one or more details about the main idea, and less formal than a lesson outline.

What Tools Do You Need?

Vocabulary

center	lateral face	semicircle
circle	lateral surface area	slant height
circumference	pi	surface area
composite figure	radius	volume
diameter	regular pyramid	

Study Skill: Studying Math

Power Notes *Power notes* are similar to lesson outlines, but they are simpler to organize. Power notes use the numbers 1, 2, 3, and so on. You can have more than one detail under each power. You can even add drawings or examples to your power notes.

Power 1: This is the main idea.
Power 2: This provides details about the main idea.
Power 3: This provides details about Power 2.
and so on...

Complete the following sample of power notes for this chapter.

1: Circles
2: Circumference
3: Sample answer: $2\pi r$
3: Sample answer: πd
2: Area
3: πr^2

What Do You Already Know?

Place a checkmark below the face that expresses how much you know about each concept. Then scan the chapter to find a definition or example of it. See students' work.

I have no clue. I've heard of it. I know it!

Integers				
Concept				Definition or Example
area of a circle				
area of composite figures				
lateral surface area				
pi (π)				
total surface area				
volume				

When Will You Use This?

Here are a few examples of how volume and surface area are used in the real world.

Activity 1 When wrapping a present, how do you determine how much paper to use? Describe a method that you could use to make sure that you cut the right size piece of wrapping paper.

See students' work.

Activity 2 Go online at **connectED.mcgraw-hill.com** to read the graphic novel ***The Dunk Tank***. How many square feet of metal sheeting do they have to build the dunk tank?

160 square feet

What Do You Already Know?

In this activity students assess their prior knowledge choosing a face to represent their knowledge about concepts in the chapter.

After completing the chapter, have students return to this page and have them reevaluate their knowledge level about the content.

When Will You Use This?

Activity 1

Students discover when and how to use the dimensions to find surface area and volume of an object.

Activity 2

Use the Graphic Novel to help students learn about writing and solving equations.

Ask:

- *What measurements do Caitlyn, Dario, and Hannah need to know in order to find the surface area and volume of the dunk tank?* Sample answer: base, width, and height

Are You Ready?

Use this page to determine if students have skills that are needed for the chapter.

Quick Review
Students with strong math backgrounds may opt to go directly to the Quick Check.

QUICK REVIEW		
Examples	Skill	Standard
1	Area of Rectangles	6.G.1
2	Area of Triangles	6.G.1

Quick Check
If students have difficulty with the exercises, present an additional example to clarify any misconceptions.

Exercise 1
Find the area of a rectangle that has a width of 7 meters and length of 3 meters. $21\ m^2$

Exercises 2–4
Find the area of a triangle with a base of 8 inches and a height of 4 inches. $16\ in^2$

RtI Response to Intervention
Go online at connectED.mcgraw-hill.com for resources to differentiate remediation for Tier 1, Tier 2, and Tier 3 students.

ALEKS® can provide additional remediation support with personalized instruction and practice. See pages T8 and T9 for more information.

Are You Ready?

Try the Quick Check below.
Or, take the Online Readiness Quiz.

Quick Review

6.G.1

Example 1

Find the area of the rectangle.

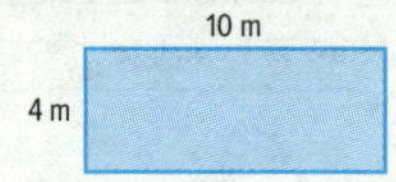

$A = \ell w$ — Area of a rectangle
$A = (10)(4)$ — Replace ℓ with 10 and w with 4.
$A = 40$ — Simplify.

The area of the rectangle is 40 square meters.

Example 2

Find the area of the triangle.

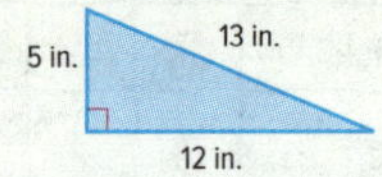

$A = \frac{1}{2}bh$ — Area of a triangle
$A = \frac{1}{2}(12)(5)$ — Replace b with 12 and h with 5.
$A = \frac{1}{2}(60)$ — Multiply.
$A = 30$ — Simplify.

The area of the triangle is 30 square inches.

Quick Check

Area **Find the area of each figure.**

1. 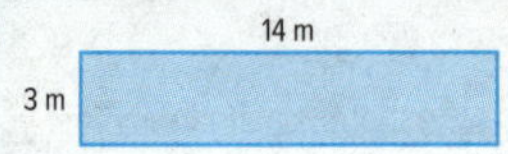

$A =$ 42 sq m

2. 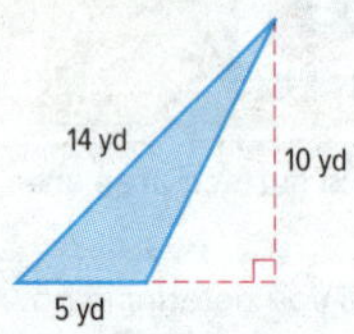

$A =$ 25 sq yd

3. 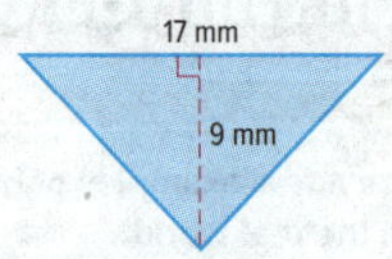

$A =$ 76.5 sq mm

4. Anita's yard is in the shape of a triangle. It has a height of 35 feet and a base of 50 feet. What is the area of the yard?
875 sq ft

How Did You Do?

Which problems did you answer correctly in the Quick Check? Shade those exercise numbers below.

① ② ③ ④

PRESENT
IWB
An Interactive Whiteboard Ready presentation is available for each lesson in the chapter.

Geometry

Inquiry Lab
Circumference

Inquiry HOW is the circumference of a circle related to its diameter?

Content Standards
7.G.4
MP **Mathematical Practices**
1, 3, 6

The distance around a flying disc, or its *circumference*, is 37.7 centimeters. The distance across the disc through its center, or its *diameter*, is 12 centimeters. How is the circumference of a circular object, such as a flying disc, related to its diameter?

Hands-On Activity

Step 1 Cut a piece of string the length of the circumference of a circular object such as a jar lid. Use a centimeter ruler to measure the length of the string to the nearest tenth of a centimeter. Record this measurement in the table below. **See students' work.**

Object	Circumference (C)	Diameter (d)	$\frac{C}{d}$
Disc	37.7 cm	12 cm	3.14

Step 2 Measure and record the diameter of the lid.

Step 3 Use a calculator to find the ratio of the circumference of the flying disc to its diameter. Repeat for the circular object you measured in Steps 1 and 2. Round answers to the nearest hundredth.

Step 4 Repeat Steps 1 through 3 for other circular objects.

Describe the ratios $\frac{C}{d}$ you found. Identify the number that is closest to the value of each ratio. **Sample answer: The ratios $\frac{C}{d}$ are a little more than 3. The number closest is about 3.14.**

Write a rule in the form $\frac{C}{d} \approx$ ■, where ■ is the number you identified in the question above. **Sample answer: $\frac{C}{d} \approx 3.14$**

Focus narrowing the scope

Objective Describe the relationship between the diameter and circumference of a circle. 7.G.4

Coherence connecting within and across grades

Now
Students use models to determine how the circumference of a circle is related to its diameter.

Next
Students will find the circumference of a circle given the radius or diameter.

Rigor pursuing concepts, fluency, and applications

See the Levels of Complexity chart on page 612.

ENGAGE EXPLORE EXPLAIN ELABORATE EVALUATE

1 Launch the Lab

The Activity is intended to be used as a whole-group activity.

Hands-On Activity

AL EL **Pairs Discussion** Have students work with a partner to complete the activity. Students may benefit from hearing the terms *circumference* and *diameter* out loud and practice the pronunciation of these terms by having them speak the terms aloud as well. MP 1, 5, 6

BL EL **Pairs Consult** Have students work in pairs to write the rule for the exercises. Have them consult with another pair to discuss and resolve any differences in the value of the ratio $\frac{C}{d}$. Have them list a variety of approximate rules, such as $\frac{C}{d} \approx 3$, $\frac{C}{d} \approx 3.14$, and so on. MP 1, 6

2 Collaborate

The **Investigate** and **Analyze and Reflect** sections are intended to be used as small-group investigations. The **Create** section is intended to be used as independent exercises.

Levels of Complexity

The levels of the exercises progress from 1 to 3, with Level 1 indicating the lowest level of complexity.

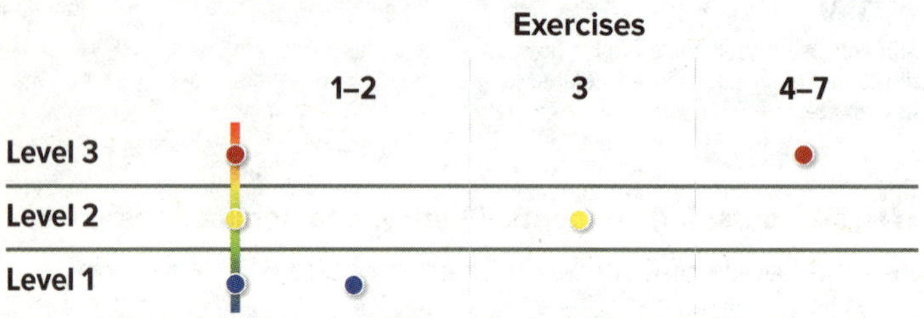

Investigate

Collaborate

AL **EL** **Rally Coach** Have students work with a partner to complete Exercises 1 and 2. Have Student 1 complete Exercise 1, talking aloud through their process, while Student 2 watches, listens, and encourages. Have them trade roles for Exercise 2. MP 1, 5, 6, 7

Create

On Your Own

BL **EL** **Pairs Present** Have pairs work together to complete Exercises 4–7. Then have them make a brief oral presentation to the class on how they generated their formula for the circumference of a circle, providing examples, models, and illustrations. MP 1, 2, 7

Inquiry Students should be able to answer "HOW is the circumference of a circle related to its diameter?" Check for student understanding and provide guidance, if needed.

Investigate

Collaborate

MP **Make a Prediction** Work with a partner. Measure the diameter of two different circular objects. Predict each circumference. Check your predictions by measuring. Then find each ratio $\frac{C}{d}$. Record your values to the nearest hundredth in the table below. See students' work.

	Object	Diameter (d)	Predicted Circumference	Measured Circumference (C)	Ratio $\frac{C}{d}$
1.					
2.					

Analyze and Reflect

Collaborate

3. MP **Reason Inductively** How do the ratios $\frac{C}{d}$ in the table compare to the ones in the Activity? Identify the number that is closest to the value of all of the ratios.
Sample answer: The ratios are all about the same. The number closest to the value of each ratio is 3.14.

Create

On Your Own

4. MP **Reason Abstractly** Write a formula in the form $\frac{C}{d} = \blacksquare$, that gives the approximate ratio of the circumference C of a circle to its diameter d, where $\blacksquare$ is the number you identified in Exercise 3. Sample answer: $\frac{C}{d} = 3.14$

5. MP **Reason Abstractly** Multiply both sides of your formula by d to write an equivalent formula in the form $C = \blacksquare \times d$ *that gives the approximate circumference* C if you know the diameter d of a circle.
Sample answer: $C = 3.14 \cdot d$

6. MP **Reason Abstractly** The radius of a circle is one half of its diameter. Write a formula that relates the circumference C of a circle to its radius r.
Sample answer: $C = 2 \cdot 3.14 \cdot r$

7. **Inquiry** HOW is the circumference of a circle related to its diameter?
Sample answer: The circumference is about 3 times the diameter.

PLAN ONLINE: PD | RtI | Watch | Worksheets | Vocab | Tutor | Tools | Check | English Learners | Sketchpad

PRESENT

IWB An Interactive Whiteboard Ready presentation is available for each lesson in the chapter.

Geometry

Lesson 1

Circumference

Vocabulary Start-Up

A **circle** is the set of all points in a plane that are the same distance from a point, called the **center**. The **circumference** is the distance around a circle. The **diameter** is the distance across a circle through its center. The **radius** is the distance from the center to any point on the circle.

Fill in each box with one of the following terms: *center*, *diameter*, and *radius*.

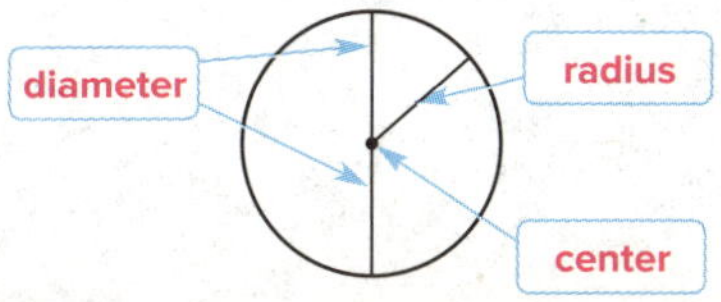

Real-World Link

1. The table shows the approximate measurements of two sizes of hula hoops.

Size	Radius (in.)	Diameter (in.)	Circumference (in.)
child	14	28	88
adult	20	40	126

a. Describe the relationship between the diameter and radius of each hula hoop. Sample answer: the diameter is twice the radius.

b. Describe the relationship between the circumference and diameter of each hula hoop. Sample answer: circumference is about three times the diameter.

Which MP **Mathematical Practices** did you use? Shade the circle(s) that applies.

1. Persevere with Problems
2. Reason Abstractly
3. Construct an Argument
4. Model with Mathematics
5. Use Math Tools
6. Attend to Precision
7. Make Use of Structure
8. Use Repeated Reasoning

Essential Question

HOW do measurements help you describe real-world objects?

Vocabulary

circle
center
circumference
diameter
radius
pi π

Content Standards
7.G.4

MP Mathematical Practices
1, 3, 4, 6, 8

Focus narrowing the scope

Objective Find the circumference of circles. 7.G.4

Coherence connecting within and across grades

Previous Students used models to determine how the circumference of a circle is related to its diameter.

Now Students find the circumference of circles given the radius or diameter.

Next Students will find the area of circles given the radius or diameter.

Rigor pursuing concepts, fluency, and applications

See the Levels of Complexity chart on page 617.

ENGAGE EXPLORE EXPLAIN ELABORATE EVALUATE

1 Launch the Lesson

Ideas for Use

You may wish to launch the lesson using a whole group, small group, think-pair-share activity, or independent activity.

EL **Circle the Sage** Poll the class to see who has a good understanding of circumference. These students will be the sages. Spread the sages around the room. The rest of the class is organized into groups. Each group member goes to a different sage. The sages lead the Vocabulary activity and Real-World Link discussion. Have students return to their original groups to discuss and resolve any differences. MP 1, 6

2 Teach the Concept

Ask the scaffolded questions for each example to differentiate instruction.

IWB

Examples

1. Use the diameter to find the radius of a circle.

AL
- *Are we given the radius or the diameter?* diameter
- *What do we need to find?* radius

OL
- *How does the radius of a circle relate to its diameter?* The radius is half the diameter.
- *What formula can we use to find the radius?* $r = \frac{d}{2}$

BL
- *What are some other words that have the same root as the word radius?* Sample answers: radial, radiant

Need Another Example?
The diameter of a circle is 48 centimeters. Find the radius.
24 cm

2. Use the radius to find the diameter of a circle.

AL
- *Are we given the radius or the diameter?* radius
- *What do we need to find?* diameter

OL
- *How does the diameter of a circle relate to its radius?* The diameter is twice the radius.
- *What formula can we use to find the diameter?* $d = 2r$

BL
- *What are some other words that have the same root as the word diameter?* Sample answers: diagonal, diamond

Need Another Example?
The radius of a circle is 9 inches. Find the diameter. 18 in.

Work Zone

Key Concept

Radius and Diameter

Words The diameter d of a circle is twice its radius r. The radius r of a circle is half of its diameter d.

Symbols $d = 2r$ $r = \frac{d}{2}$

Examples

Tutor

1. The diameter of a circle is 14 inches. Find the radius.

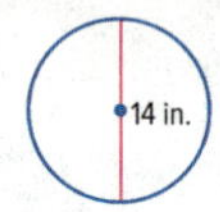

$r = \frac{d}{2}$ Radius of circle

$r = \frac{14}{2}$ Replace d with 14.

$r = 7$ Divide.

The radius is 7 inches.

2. The radius of a circle is 8 feet. Find the diameter.

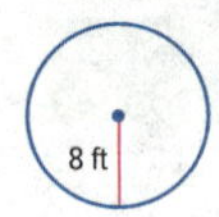

$d = 2r$ Diameter of circle

$d = 2 \cdot 8$ Replace r with 8.

$d = 16$ Multiply.

The diameter is 16 feet.

STOP and Reflect

The diameter of a circle is 36 inches. Circle the radius.

72 in. 18 in.

Got it? Do these problems to find out.

Find the radius or diameter of each circle with the given dimension.

a. $d = 23$ cm **b.** $r = 3$ in.

c. $d = 16$ yd **d.** $r = 5.2$

Show your work.

a. 11.5 cm

b. 6 in.

c. 8 yd

d. 10.4

Circumference

Key Concept

Words The circumference of a circle is equal to π times its diameter or π times twice its radius.

Model

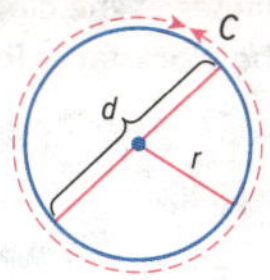

Symbols $C = \pi d$ or $C = 2\pi r$

In the Inquiry Lab, you learned that $\frac{C}{d} \approx 3$. The exact ratio is represented by the Greek letter **π (pi)**. The value of π is 3.1415926… . The decimal never ends, but it is often approximated as 3.14.

Another approximation for π is $\frac{22}{7}$. Use this value when the radius or diameter is a multiple of 7 or has a multiple of 7 in its numerator if the radius is a fraction.

Estimation
To estimate the circumference of a circle, you can use 3 for π since $\pi \approx 3$.

Example

Tutor

3. Find the circumference of a circle with a radius of 21 inches.

Since 21 is a multiple of 7, use $\frac{22}{7}$ for π.

$C = 2\pi r$	Circumference of a circle
$C \approx 2 \cdot \frac{22}{7} \cdot 21$	Replace π with $\frac{22}{7}$ and r with 21.
$C \approx 2 \cdot \frac{22}{\cancel{7}_1} \cdot \frac{\cancel{21}^3}{1}$	Divide by the GCF, 7.
$C \approx 132$	Simplify.

The circumference of the circle is about 132 inches.

Got it? Do these problems to find out.

Find the circumference of each circle. Use $\frac{22}{7}$ for π.

e.

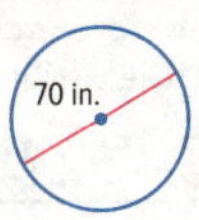

f.

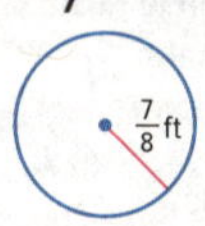

Show your work.

e. 220 in.

f. $5\frac{1}{2}$ ft

Example

IWB

3. Find the circumference of a circle.

AL
- *Are we given the radius or the diameter?* radius
- *What formula for the circumference should we use?* $C = 2\pi r$

OL
- *Why can we use $\frac{22}{7}$ as an approximation for π?* 21 is a multiple of 7.
- *Why do we divide 21 and 7 by the GCF?* to allow for easier multiplication and a simplified answer

BL
- *What would be the approximation of the circumference if we used 3.14 instead?* 131.88 in.
- *Is either approximation correct? Explain.* Yes, we can use either 3.14 or $\frac{22}{7}$ to approximate π, since both approximations are close to the exact value.

Need Another Example?
Find the circumference of a circle with a radius of 35 inches. about 220 in.

Watch Out!

Common Error Some students may use the incorrect formula for circumference by substituting the diameter for radius into $C = 2\pi r$ or substituting the radius for the diameter into $C = \pi d$. Remind students that they have learned two formulas for circumference in this lesson: $C = 2\pi r$ and $C = \pi d$. They should realize that since $2r = d$, these are actually the same formula. As students apply these two formulas, they can use 3.14 for π and round their answers to the nearest tenth after the calculation is complete.

Example

4. Find the circumference.

AL
- *Are we given the radius or the diameter?* diameter
- *What formula for the circumference should we use?* $C = \pi d$

OL
- *Is 3.14 the exact value of π or an approximation? Explain.* an approximation because the exact value goes on forever
- *What is the approximate distance around the clock?* about 72.2 feet

BL
- *How far does the tip of the minute hand of Big Ben travel in one hour?* 72.2 feet
- *How far does the tip of the minute hand of Big Ben travel in one day?* 1,732.8 feet

Need Another Example?
John is making a circular table that has a top with a diameter of 24 inches. Find the circumference of the table. Round to the nearest tenth. 75.4 in.

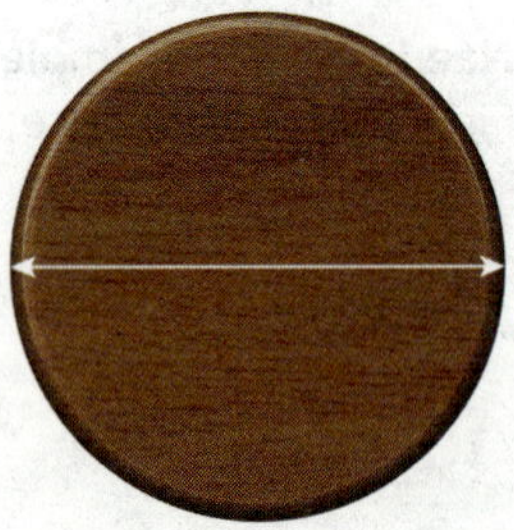

Guided Practice

Formative Assessment Use these exercises to assess students' understanding of the concepts in this lesson.

If some of your students are not ready for assignments, use the differentiated activity below.

AL EL **Group-Pair-Solo** Have students work in small groups to complete Exercises 1–3. Then have them divide into pairs to complete Exercises 4 and 5. Have students work individually to complete Exercises 6. Have them regroup to discuss their responses and resolve any differences. MP 1, 6, 7

Real-World Example

4. Big Ben is a famous clock tower in London, England. The diameter of the clock face is 23 feet. Find the circumference of the clock face. Round to the nearest tenth.

$C = \pi d$	Circumference of a circle
$C \approx 3.14(23)$	Replace π with 3.14 and d with 23.
$C \approx 72.2$	Multiply.

So, the distance around the clock is about 72.2 feet.

Got it? Do this problem to find out.

g. A circular fence is being placed to surround a tree. The diameter of the fence is 4 feet. How much fencing is used? Use 3.14 for π. Round to the nearest tenth if necessary.

Show your work.

g. 12.6 ft

Guided Practice

Find the radius or diameter of each circle with the given dimension. (Examples 1 and 2)

Show your work.

1. $d = 3$ m 1.5 m
2. $r = 14$ ft 28 ft
3. $d = 20$ in. 10 in.

Find the circumference of each circle. Use 3.14 or $\frac{22}{7}$ for π. Round to the nearest tenth if necessary. (Examples 3 and 4)

4. 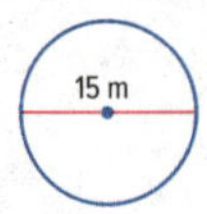

$3.14 \times 15 = 47.1$ m

5. 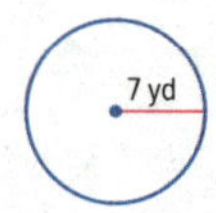

$\frac{22}{7} \times 14 = 44$ yd

6. **Building on the Essential Question** A circle has a circumference of about 16.3 meters and a diameter of about 5.2 meters. What is the relationship between the circumference and diameter of this circle?
Sample answer: The circumference is about 3 times the measure of the diameter.

Rate Yourself!

How confident are you about finding the circumference? Check the box that applies.

For more help, go online to access a Personal Tutor.

Name ______________________ My Homework ______________________

Independent Practice

Go online for Step-by-Step Solutions eHelp

Find the radius or diameter of each circle with the given dimensions. (Examples 1 and 2)

1. $d = 5$ mm **2.5 mm**
2. $d = 24$ ft **12 ft**
3. $r = 17$ cm **34 cm**

Show your work.

Find the circumference of each circle. Use 3.14 or $\frac{22}{7}$ for π. Round to the nearest tenth if necessary. (Example 3)

4. 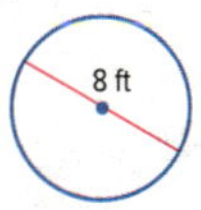

3.14 × 8 = 25.1 ft

5. 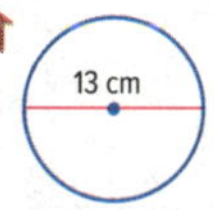

3.14 × 13 = 40.8 cm

6. 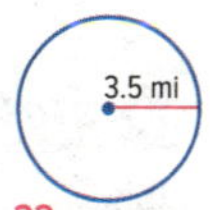

$\frac{22}{7} \times 7 = 22$ **mi**

7. The largest tree in the world by volume is in Sequoia National Park. The diameter at the base is 36 feet. If a person with outstretched arms can reach 6 feet, how many people would it take to reach around the base of the tree? (Example 4)
19 people

8. The Belknap shield volcano is located in the Cascade Range in Oregon. The volcano is circular and has a diameter of 5 miles. What is the circumference of this volcano. Round your answer to the nearest tenth? (Example 4)
15.7 mi

9. MP **Be Precise** Refer to the circle at the right.

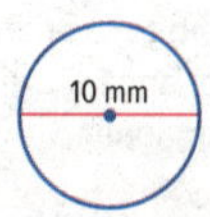

a. Find the circumference of the circle. Use 3 as the estimate of π.
30 mm

b. Find the circumference of the circle using 3.14 for π.
31.4 mm

c. Another estimate of π is 3.14159. Find the circumference using this estimate.
31.4159 mm

d. What do you notice about the estimate used for π and the circumference of the circle?
Sample answer: The more decimal places of the estimate of π, the more precise the circumference.

ENGAGE EXPLORE **EXPLAIN ELABORATE EVALUATE**

3 Practice and Apply

Independent Practice and Extra Practice

The Independent Practice pages are meant to be used as the homework assignment. The Extra Practice page can be used for additional reinforcement or as a second-day assignment.

Levels of Complexity

The levels of the exercises progress from 1 to 3, with Level 1 indicating the lowest level of complexity.

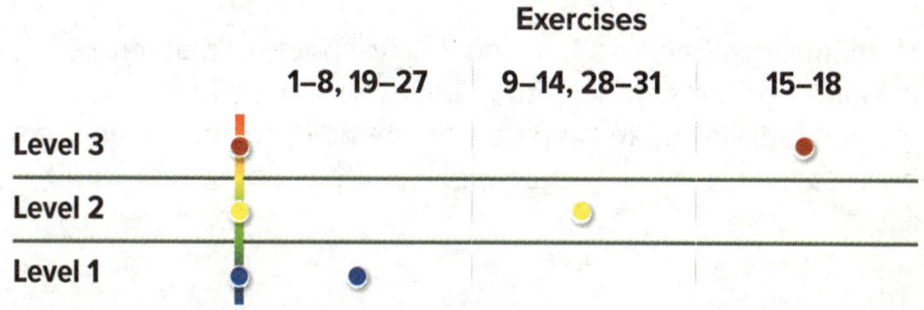

Suggested Assignments

You can use the table below that includes exercises of all complexity levels to select appropriate exercises for your students' needs.

Differentiated Homework Options		
AL	Approaching Level	1–9, 11, 13, 15, 16, 18, 30, 31
OL	On Level	1–9 odd, 10–16, 18, 30, 31
BL	Beyond Level	9–18, 30, 31

McGraw Hill Education **ALEKS®** can provide additional remediation support with personalized instruction and practice.

MP MATHEMATICAL PRACTICES

Emphasis On	Exercise(s)
1 Make sense of problems and persevere in solving them.	17
3 Construct viable arguments and critique the reasoning of others.	15, 18
4 Model with mathematics.	16
6 Attend to precision.	9
8 Look for and express regularity in repeated reasoning.	29

Mathematical Practices 1, 3, and 4 are aspects of mathematical thinking that are emphasized in every lesson. Students are given opportunities to be persistent in their problem solving, to express their reasoning, and apply mathematics to real-world situations.

Formative Assessment
Use this activity as a closing formative assessment before dismissing students from your class.

TICKET Out the Door

Have students find the diameter and circumference of a circle with a radius of 5 miles to the nearest tenth.
diameter: 10 mi; circumference: 31.4 mi

Copy and Solve **For Exercises 10–14, show your work on a separate piece of paper.**

Find the diameter given each circumference. Use 3.14 for π.

10. a satellite dish with a circumference of 957.7 meters **305 m**

11. a basketball hoop with a circumference of 56.52 inches **18 in.**

12. a nickel with a circumference of about 65.94 millimeters **21 mm**

Find the distance around each figure. Use 3.14 for π.

13. **257 cm**

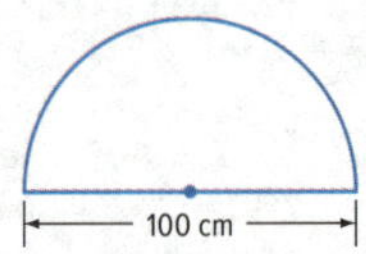

14. **33.55 ft**

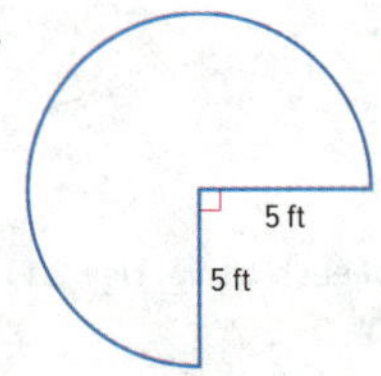

H.O.T. Problems Higher Order Thinking

15. MP **Justify Conclusions** Determine if the circumference of a circle with a radius of 4 feet will be greater or less than 24 feet. Explain.
Greater than; Sample answer: Since the radius is 4 feet, the diameter is 8 feet. Since π is a little more than 3, the circumference will be a little more than 3 times 8, or 24 feet.

16. MP **Model with Mathematics** Draw and label a circle that has a diameter more than 5 inches, but less than 10 inches. Estimate its circumference and then find its circumference using a calculator. Compare your results.
Estimated circumference: 21 in.; using calculator: 22.0. The estimate is close to the value found on the calculator.

Sample answer:

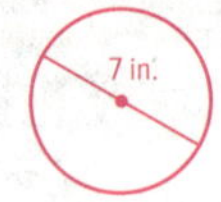

Show your work.

17. MP **Persevere with Problems** Analyze how the circumference of a circle would change if the diameter was doubled. Provide an example to support your explanation.
The circumference would double. For example, with a diameter of 4 feet, the circumference is about 12.6 feet. With a diameter of 8 feet, the circumference is about 25.1 feet.

18. MP **Justify Conclusions** Determine whether the relationship between the circumference of a circle and its diameter is a direct variation. If so, identify the constant of proportionality. Justify your response.
yes; Sample answer: The formula for the circumference C of a circle related to its diameter d is $C = \pi d$. The two variables C and d have a constant ratio, π. The constant of proportionality is π.

Name ______________ My Homework ______________

Extra Practice

Find the radius or diameter of each circle with the given dimensions.

19. $d = 7$ in. 3.5 in.

Homework Help

$r = \frac{d}{2}$

$r = \frac{7}{2}$ or 3.5

20. $d = 30$ m 15 m

21. $r = 36$ ft 72 ft

Find the circumference of each circle. Use 3.14 or $\frac{22}{7}$ for π.

22.

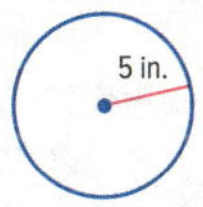

$3.14 \times 2(5) = 31.4$ in.

23.

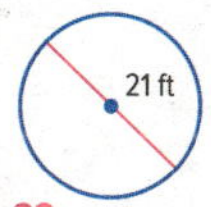

$\frac{22}{7} \times 21 = 66$ ft

24.

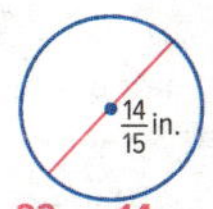

$\frac{22}{7} \times \frac{14}{15} = 2\frac{14}{15}$ in.

25. a button with a radius of 21 millimeters $\frac{22}{7} \times 42 = 132$ mm

26. a dunk tank with a radius of 36 inches $3.14 \times 72 = 226.08$ in.

27. The diameter of a music CD is 12 centimeters. Find the circumference of a CD to the nearest tenth. 37.7 cm

28. At a local park, Sara can choose between two circular paths to walk. One path has a diameter of 120 yards, and the other has a radius of 45 yards. How much farther can Sara walk on the longer path than the shorter path if she walks around the path once? about 94.2 yd

29. MP **Identify Repeated Reasoning** The diagram at the right is made up of circles with the same center. The innermost circle has a diameter of 1 unit. Each circle moving outward has a diameter one more unit than the previous. Without calculating, how much longer is the circumference of each circle? Each is π, or about 3.14, units longer than the previous circle.

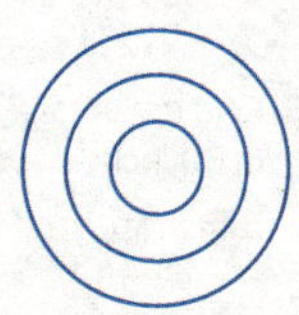

Create Your Own Homework Online

eSolutionsManual™ can be used to create worksheets for the suggested assignments on page 617, or create your own worksheets for differentiated homework or review.

Power Up! Test Practice

Exercises 30 and 31 prepare students for more rigorous thinking needed for the state assessment.

30.

This test item requires students to analyze and solve complex real-world problems through the use of mathematical tools and models.	
Depth of Knowledge	DOK2
Content Standard	7.G.4
Mathematical Practice	MP1, MP4
Online Experience	Students will drag values to model the equation and type their response in the box.
Scoring Rubric	
2 points	Students correctly model the equation and find how far the tire rolls.
1 point	Students correctly model the equation but fail to find how far the tire rolls OR students find how far the tire roles, but fail to model the equation OR students incorrectly model the equation but find how far the tire roles based on the incorrect equation.

31.

This test item requires students to reason abstractly and quantitatively when problem solving.	
Depth of Knowledge	DOK1
Content Standard	7.G.4
Mathematical Practice	MP1
Online Experience	Students will be required to click on the bubbles to select all answers that are correct.
Scoring Rubric	
1 point	Students correctly answer each part of the question.

Power Up! Test Practice

30. A bicycle tire has a radius of 12.5 inches. Select values to complete the equation below to find the circumference of the wheel. Use 3.14 for π.

0.5	4
2	12.5
3.14	25

$C \approx$ [2] × [12.5] × [3.14]

How far does the tire roll in one complete revolution?

[78.5 in.]

31. A circle with center at point O is shown. Determine if each statement is true or false.

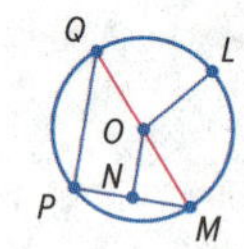

		True	False
a.	$\overline{ON}$ is a radius of the circle.	☐ True	■ False
b.	$\overline{QM}$ is a diameter of the circle.	■ True	☐ False
c.	To find the circumference, multiply the length of $\overline{OL}$ by π.	☐ True	■ False

Spiral Review

Find the area of each trapezoid. 6.G.1

32. 315 cm²

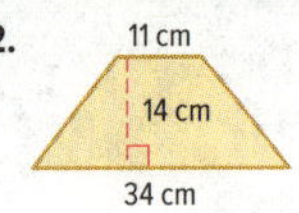

33. 12.74 m²

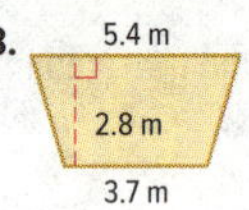

34. 2,015 mm²

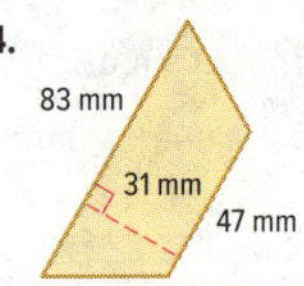

35. Find the area of glass used on the side of the parallelogram-shaped building shown. 6.G.1

36,946 ft²

36. Find the area of a triangle with a base of 25 inches and a height of 30 inches. 6.G.1

375 in²

PRESENT

IWB An Interactive Whiteboard Ready presentation is available for each lesson in the chapter.

Inquiry Lab
Area of Circles

Inquiry HOW are the circumference and area of a circle related?

Content Standards
7.G.4

MP Mathematical Practices
1, 3, 6

Mrs. Allende wants to create a family message center on a wall in her house. There are 4 family members, including Mrs. Allende. She decides to paint 1 circle for each family member using magnetic paint. Each circle will have a 12-inch radius. How do you find the area of a circle?

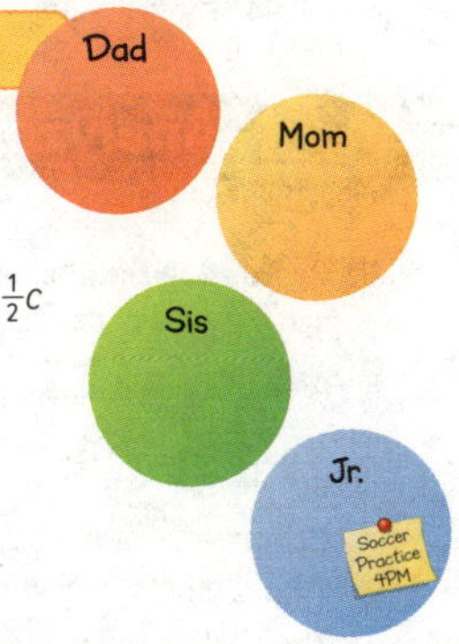

Hands-On Activity

Let's develop a formula for finding the area of a circle.

Step 1 Fold a paper plate in half four times to divide it into 16 equal sections.

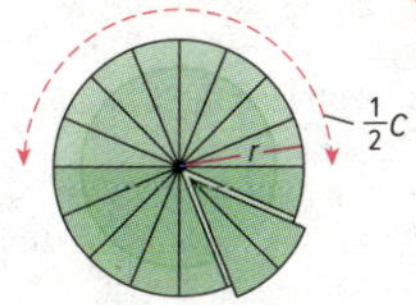

Step 2 Label the radius r as shown. Let C represent the circumference of the circle.

Step 3 Cut out each section. Reassemble the sections to form a parallelogram-shaped figure.

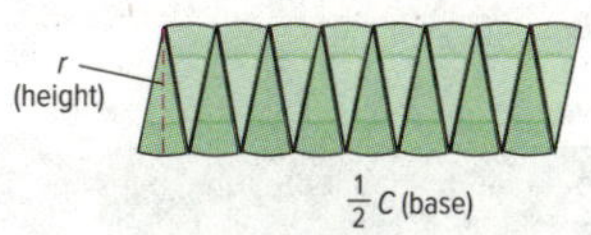

What expressions represent the measurements of the base and the height?

Base: $\frac{1}{2}C$ Height: r

Substitute these values into the formula for the area of a parallelogram, $A = b \times h$. Write the new formula. $A = \frac{1}{2}Cr$

Replace C with the expression for the circumference of a circle, $2\pi r$. Simplify the equation and describe what it represents.

$A = \frac{1}{2}(2\pi r)(r)$; $A = \pi r^2$; the area of a circle

Focus narrowing the scope

Objective Develop the formula for the area of a circle. 7.G.4

Coherence connecting within and across grades

Now
Students use models to develop the approximate formula for the area of a circle.

Next
Students will find the area of circles given the radius or diameter.

Rigor pursuing concepts, fluency, and applications

See the Levels of Complexity chart on page 622.

ENGAGE EXPLORE EXPLAIN ELABORATE EVALUATE

1 Launch the Lab

The activity is intended to be used as a whole-group activity.

Hands-On Activity

AL EL Pairs to Groups Allow students to complete Steps 1–3 in pairs. Have students recall the definitions for the radius and diameter of a circle and how they are related. They may benefit from a review of the formulas for the circumference of a circle and area of a parallelogram. Then, have pairs join to form groups of 4 to complete the questions. Have groups share their responses with the rest of the class. MP 1, 2, 6, 7

BL EL Pairs Consult Have students work with a partner to explain why the base of the parallelogram is represented by $\frac{1}{2}C$. Have them find what simplified expression is equivalent to $\frac{1}{2}C$. MP 1, 2, 6, 7

ENGAGE EXPLORE EXPLAIN ELABORATE EVALUATE

2 Collaborate

The **Investigate** and **Analyze and Reflect** sections are intended to be used as small-group investigations. The **Create** section is intended to be used as independent exercises.

Levels of Complexity

The levels of the exercises progress from 1 to 3, with Level 1 indicating the lowest level of complexity.

Exercises

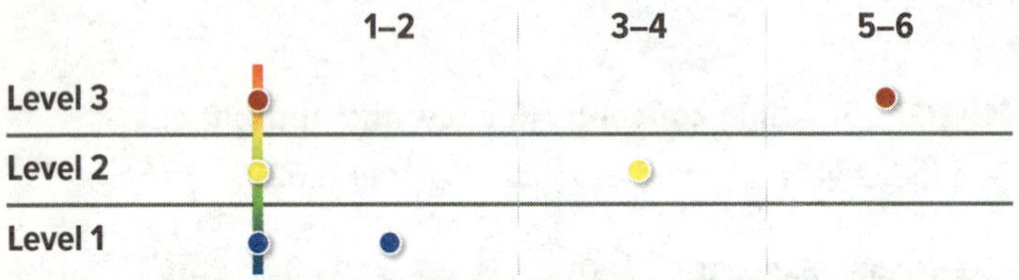

Investigate

Collaborate

AL EL Pairs Discussion Have students complete Exercises 1 and 2 in pairs. Allow them to construct circles using a compass, cut out the circles, and reassemble them as a parallelogram, if needed. Have students compare their results with another pair and resolve any discrepancies. MP 1, 6, 7

Analyze and Reflect

Collaborate

BL EL Think-Pair-Share Have students use a protractor to measure the angles of the parallelograms in Exercises 1 and 2. Tell students that a circle measures 360°. Compare the measures of the angles. Students should determine that the sum of the angles in the parallelograms equal 360°. MP 1, 5, 7

Create

On Your Own

Inquiry Students should be able to answer "HOW are the circumference and area of a circle related?" Check for student understanding and provide guidance, if needed.

Investigate

Collaborate

Work with a partner. Use the circle to draw and label a parallelogram that would result from cutting and reassembling the circle. Use 3.14 for π.

1.

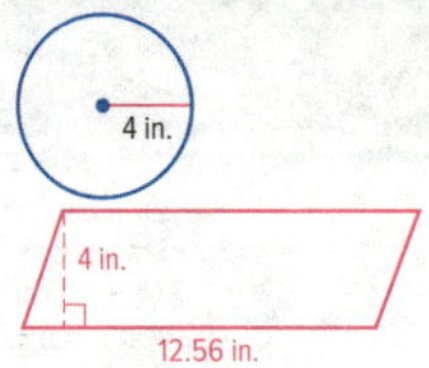

Base: 12.56 in.

Height: 4 in.

Area of Parallelogram: 50.24 in^2

2.

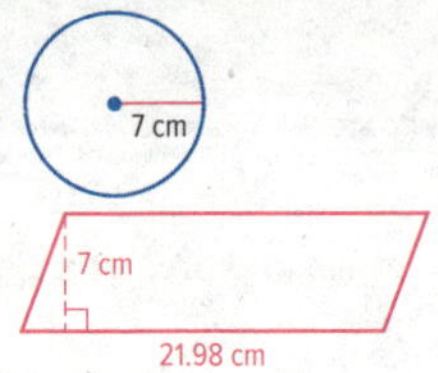

Base: 21.98 cm

Height: 7 cm

Area of Parallelogram: 153.86 cm^2

Analyze and Reflect

Collaborate

3. MP **Reason Inductively** Use the formula you wrote on the previous page to find the area of the circles in Exercises 1 and 2 above. Use 3.14 for π.

Area of circle in Exercise 1: 50.24 in^2

Area of circle in Exercise 2: 153.86 cm^2

4. Compare the area of the circles you found in Exercise 3 to the area of the parallelograms in Exercises 1 and 2. What do you notice? Explain.

They are the same. Sample answer: I can reassemble a circle to form a parallelogram that has an equivalent area.

Create

On Your Own

5. MP **Model with Mathematics** Find a real-world example of a circle. Measure the radius of the circle. Draw a resulting parallelogram from reassembling the circle. Then calculate the circle's area. See students' work.

6. Inquiry HOW are the circumference and area of a circle related?

Sample answer: Sections of the area can be arranged to form a parallelogram with a base that is $\frac{1}{2}$ of the circumference.

PLAN ONLINE

PD | RtI | Watch | Worksheets | Vocab | Tutor | Tools | Check | English Learners | Sketchpad

PRESENT

IWB

An Interactive Whiteboard Ready presentation is available for each lesson in the chapter.

Lesson 2

Area of Circles

Real-World Link

Pets Adrienne bought an 8-foot leash for her dog.

1. Adrienne wants to find the distance the dog runs when it runs one circle with the leash fully extended. Should she calculate the circumference or area? Explain.
   Circumference; the circumference is the distance around a circle.

2. Suppose she wants to find the amount of running room the dog has with the leash fully extended. Should she calculate the circumference or area? Explain.
   Area; the area is the interior region of an enclosed figure measured in square units.

3. Describe a real-world situation that would involve finding the area of a circle.
   Sample answer: comparing the amount of pizza in 10-inch and 12-inch pizzas

4. Describe a real-world situation that would involve finding the circumference of a circle.
   Sample answer: measuring distance around your head for a school play costume

Essential Question

HOW do measurements help you describe real-world objects?

Vocabulary

semicircle

Content Standards
7.G.4

MP Mathematical Practices
1, 3, 4

Which MP **Mathematical Practices** did you use? Shade the circle(s) that applies.

1. Persevere with Problems
2. Reason Abstractly
3. Construct an Argument
4. Model with Mathematics
5. Use Math Tools
6. Attend to Precision
7. Make Use of Structure
8. Use Repeated Reasoning

Focus narrowing the scope

Objective Find the area of circles. 7.G.4

Coherence connecting within and across grades

Previous Students used models to develop the approximate formula for the area of a circle.

Now Students find the area of circles given the radius or diameter.

Next Students will find the area of composite figures.

Rigor pursuing concepts, fluency, and applications

See the Levels of Complexity chart on page 627.

ENGAGE EXPLORE EXPLAIN ELABORATE EVALUATE

1 Launch the Lesson

Ideas for Use

You may wish to launch the lesson using a whole group, small group, think-pair-share activity, or independent activity.

EL **Pairs Discussion** Have students complete Exercises 1–4 in pairs. Be sure they understand how the area formula for a parallelogram helps them find the area formula for a circle before proceeding with the lesson. MP 1, 6, 7

Alternate Strategy

AL EL If students are struggling to connect models to the formula, have them cut out a circle using construction paper, cut it into eight sections, and reassemble those sections to form a parallelogram. Have them use the area formula for a parallelogram to help them find the area formula for a circle. MP 1, 4

2 Teach the Concept

Ask the scaffolded questions for each example to differentiate instruction.

Examples

IWB

1. Find the area of a circle.

AL
- *What is the formula for the area of a circle?* $A = \pi r^2$
- *What is the radius?* 2 in.
- *What is 2^2?* 4

OL
- *How can you check your answer for reasonableness?* Sample answer: Use estimation; $3 \times 2^2 = 12$.

BL
- *How are the radius and the diameter related?* The radius is half of the diameter. The diameter is twice the radius.

Need Another Example?
Find the area of the circle.
Use 3.14 for π. 50.24 cm^2

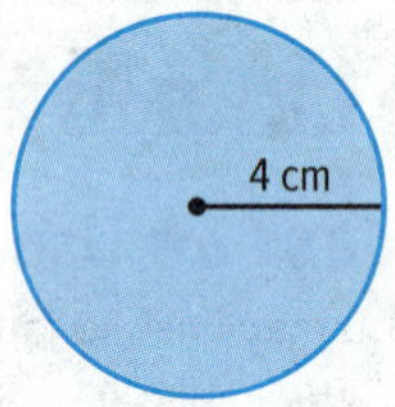

2. Find the area of a circle.

AL
- *What does the r represent in the area formula?* radius
- *What is the radius of this circle?* 14 cm

OL
- *Why can we approximate π as $\frac{22}{7}$?* It is close to the exact value of π.
- *How can you check your answer for reasonableness?* Sample answer: Use estimation; $3 \times 14^2 = 588$, so the answer is reasonable.

BL
- *If you were given the diameter instead of the radius, what would you need to do first before determining the area of the circle?* Divide the diameter by 2 to obtain the radius.

Need Another Example?
Find the area of a circle with a radius of 7 meters. Use $\frac{22}{7}$ for π. 154 m^2

Work Zone

Key Concept — Find the Area of a Circle

Words The area A of a circle equals the product of π and the square of its radius r.

Symbols $A = \pi r^2$

Model

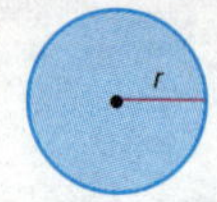

Examples

Tutor

1. Find the area of the circle. Use 3.14 for π.

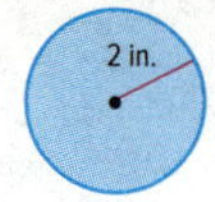

Estimate $3 \times 2 \times 2 = 12$

$A = \pi r^2$	Area of a circle
$A \approx 3.14 \cdot 2^2$	Replace r with 2.
$A \approx 3.14 \cdot 4$	$2^2 = 2 \cdot 2$ or 4
$A \approx 12.56$	Multiply.

Check for Reasonableness $12.56 \approx 12$ ✓

The area of the circle is approximately 12.56 square inches.

2. Find the area of a circle with a radius of 14 centimeters. Use $\frac{22}{7}$ for π.

Estimate $3 \times 14 \times 14 = 588$

$A = \pi r^2$	Area of a circle
$A \approx \frac{22}{7} \cdot 14^2$	Replace π with $\frac{22}{7}$ and r with 14.
$A \approx \frac{22}{7} \cdot 196$	$14^2 = 14 \cdot 14$ or 196
$A \approx \frac{22}{\cancel{7}_1} \cdot \cancel{196}^{28}$	Divide by the GCF, 7.
$A \approx 616$	Multiply.

Check for Reasonableness $616 \approx 588$ ✓

The area of the circle is approximately 616 square centimeters.

STOP and Reflect

Cross out the formula that is not used for finding the area of a circle.

$A = \pi r^2$ $A = 3.14r^2$

$A = \frac{22}{7}r^2$ ~~$A = \frac{1}{2}bh$~~

Got it? Do this problem to find out.

a. Find the area of a circle with a radius of 3.2 centimeters. Round to the nearest tenth.

Show your work.

a. 32.2 cm^2

Example

3. Find the area of the face of the Virginia quarter with a diameter of 24 millimeters. Use 3.14 for π. Round to the nearest tenth if necessary.

The radius is $\frac{1}{2}(24)$ or 12 millimeters.

$A = \pi r^2$ — Area of a circle

$A \approx 3.14 \cdot 12^2$ — Replace r with 12.

$A \approx 452.16$ — Multiply.

The area is approximately 452.2 square millimeters.

Calculating with π
When evaluating expressions involving π, using the π key on a calculator will result in a different approximation.

Got it? **Do this problem to find out.**

b. The bottom of a circular swimming pool with a diameter of 30 feet is painted blue. How many square feet are blue?

Show your work.

b. 706.5 ft^2

Area of Semicircles

A **semicircle** is half of a circle. The formula for the area of a semicircle is $A = \frac{1}{2}\pi r^2$.

Example

4. Find the area of the semicircle. Use 3.14 for π. Round to the nearest tenth.

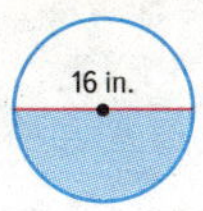

$A = \frac{1}{2}\pi r^2$ — Area of a semicircle

$A \approx \frac{1}{2}(3.14)8^2$ — Replace r with 8.

$A \approx 0.5(3.14)(64)$ — $8^2 = 8 \cdot 8$ or 64

$A \approx 100.5$ — Simplify.

The area of the semicircle is approximately 100.5 square inches.

Got it? **Do this problem to find out.**

c. Find the approximate area of a semicircle with a radius of 6 centimeters.

c. 56.5 cm^2

Examples

IWB

3. Find the area of a circle.

AL • *Are you given the radius or the diameter?* diameter

OL • *What is the formula for the area of a circle?* $A = \pi r^2$

BL • *How can you use estimation to determine if your answer is reasonable?* Sample answer: Half of 24 is 12. Approximate π as 3. Since $3 \cdot 12^2 = 432$ the answer of 452.2 is reasonable.

Need Another Example?
Find the area covered by the fountain.
Use 3.14 for π. Round to the nearest tenth.
21.2 m^2

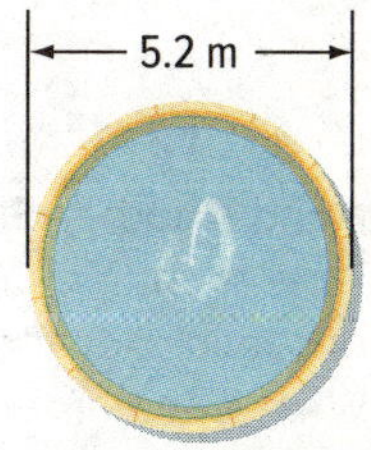

4. Find the area of a semicircle.

AL • *What does semicircle mean?* half of a circle

• *Are you given the radius or the diameter?* diameter

OL • *What is the formula for the area of a circle?* $A = \pi r^2$

• *What is the formula for the area of a semicircle?* $A = \frac{1}{2}\pi r^2$

BL • *How can you use estimation to determine if your answer is reasonable?* Sample answer: Half of 16 is 8. Approximate π as 3. Since $3 \cdot 8^2 = 192$ and half of 192 is 96, the answer of 100.5 is reasonable.

Need Another Example?
Find the area of the semicircle.
Use 3.14 for π. Round to the nearest tenth. 31.8 cm^2

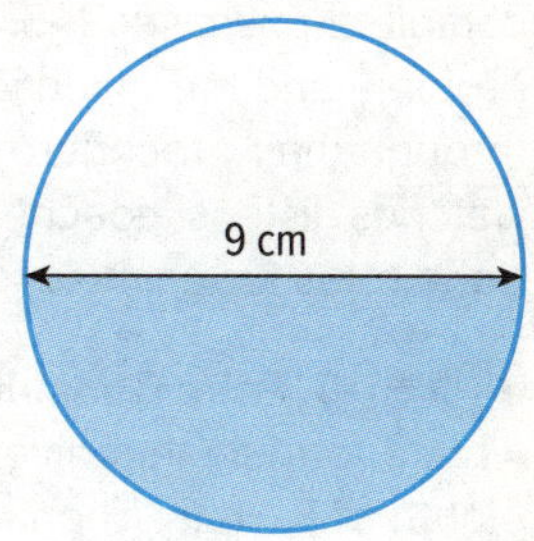

Example

IWB

5. Find the area of a semicircle.

AL • *What do you need to find?* the area of the semicircle

• *What is the radius?* 6 ft

OL • *What is the formula for the area of a circle?* $A = \pi r^2$

• *What is the formula for the area of a semicircle?* $A = \frac{1}{2}\pi r^2$

BL • *What would the diameter represent in this situation?* the length of the free-throw line

• *What is the length of the free-throw line?* 12 ft

Need Another Example?
Tarie is cutting material in the shape of semicircles for her craft project. What is the area of the semicircle? Use 3.14 for π. Round to the nearest tenth if necessary. 100.5 cm²

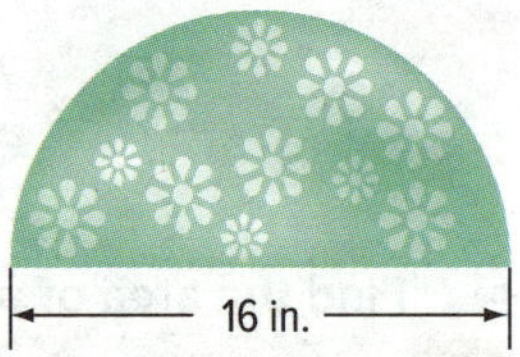

Guided Practice

Formative Assessment Use these exercises to assess students' understanding of the concepts in this lesson.

If some of your students are not ready for assignments, use the differentiated activities below.

AL EL **Rally Coach** Have students work in pairs to complete Exercises 1–5. Have Student 1 read aloud the problem and the given information. Then Student 1 talks through their procedure for finding the area, while Student 2 watches, listens, coaches, and encourages. Have students trade roles for each successive exercise. MP 1, 6, 7

BL EL **Pairs Consult** Have students work with a partner to write a formula that gives the area of one-fourth and one-eighth of a circle. Then have them draw what one-fourth and one-eighth of a circle would look like. Explain to them that any fraction of a circle is considered a *sector* of a circle. Have them use the Internet or another source to research sectors of circles and what other information is related to the sector of a circle. MP 1, 2, 7

Real World Example

Tutor

5. On a basketball court, there is a semicircle above the free-throw line that has a radius of 6 feet. Find the area of the semicircle. Use 3.14 for π. Round to the nearest tenth.

$A = \frac{1}{2}\pi r^2$ Area of a semicircle

$A \approx 0.5(3.14)(6^2)$ Replace π with 3.14 and r with 6.

$A \approx 0.5(3.14)(36)$ $6^2 = 6 \cdot 6$ or 36

$A \approx 56.5$ Multiply.

So, the area of the semicircle is approximately 56.5 square feet.

Guided Practice

Check

Find the area of each circle. Round to the nearest tenth. Use 3.14 or $\frac{22}{7}$ for π. (Examples 1–3)

1. Show your work.

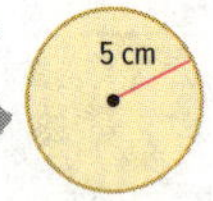

$3.14 \times 5 \times 5 = 78.5$ cm²

2.

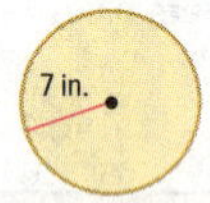

$\frac{22}{7} \times 7 \times 7 = 154$ in²

3. diameter = 16 m

$3.14 \times 8 \times 8 = 201.0$ m²

4. Rondell draws the semicircle shown at the right. What is the area of the semicircle? Use 3.14 for π. (Examples 4 and 5)

307.72 yd²

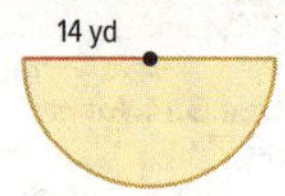

5. **Building on the Essential Question** Name one way the circumference and area of a circle are the same and one way they are different. Sample answer: They are the same in that they are both measurements of a circle. They are different in that circumference is measured in linear units while area is measured in square units.

Rate Yourself!

Are you ready to move on? Shade the section that applies.

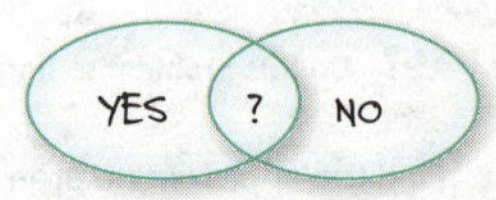

For more help, go online to access a Personal Tutor.

Tutor

Name ______________________ My Homework ______________________

Independent Practice

Go online for Step-by-Step Solutions eHelp

Find the area of each circle. Round to the nearest tenth. Use 3.14 or $\frac{22}{7}$ for π. (Examples 1–3)

1. 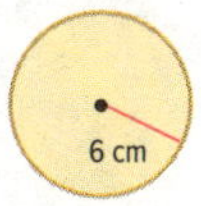

Show your work.

$3.14 \times 6 \times 6 = 113.0$ cm^2

2. 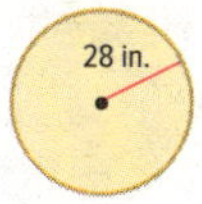

$\frac{22}{7} \times 28 \times 28 = 2{,}464$ in^2

3. 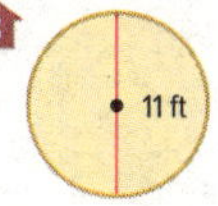

$3.14 \times 5.5 \times 5.5 = 95.0$ ft^2

4. diameter = 10.5 in.
$3.14 \times 5.25 \times 5.25 = 86.5$ in^2

5. radius = 6.3 mm
$3.14 \times 6.3 \times 6.3 =$
124.6 mm^2

6. radius = $3\frac{1}{4}$ yd
$3.14 \times 3.25 \times 3.25 =$
33.2 yd^2

7. Refer to the pets problem at the beginning of this lesson. Find the area, to the nearest tenth, of grass that Adrianne's dog may run in if the leash is 9 feet long. (Example 3) 254.3 ft^2

8. A rotating sprinkler that sprays water at a radius of 11 feet is used to water a lawn. Find the area of the lawn that is watered. Use 3.14 for π. (Example 3) 379.94 ft^2

Find the area of each semicircle. Round to the nearest tenth. Use 3.14 for π. (Example 4)

9. 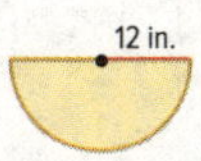

226.1 in^2

10. 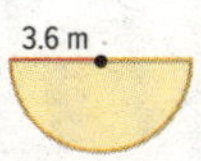

20.3 m^2

11. 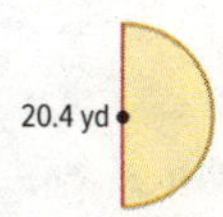

163.3 yd^2

12. The tunnel opening shown is a semicircle. Find the area, to the nearest tenth, of the opening of the tunnel enclosed by the semicircle. (Example 5)
207.6 ft^2

ENGAGE EXPLORE **EXPLAIN** **ELABORATE** **EVALUATE**

3 Practice and Apply

Independent Practice and Extra Practice

The Independent Practice pages are meant to be used as the homework assignment. The Extra Practice page can be used for additional reinforcement or as a second-day assignment.

Levels of Complexity

The levels of the exercises progress from 1 to 3, with Level 1 indicating the lowest level of complexity.

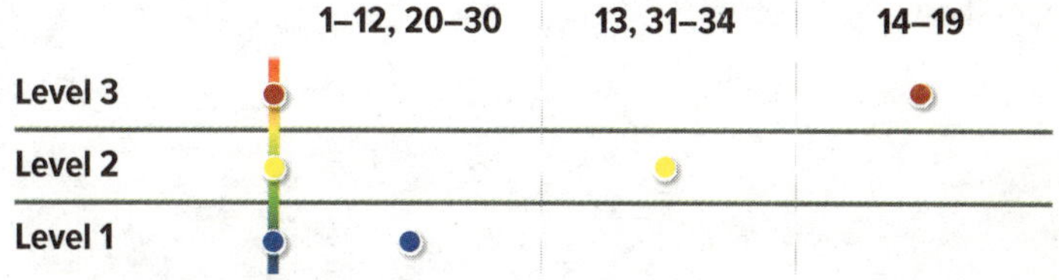

Suggested Assignments

You can use the table below that includes exercises of all complexity levels to select appropriate exercises for your students' needs.

Differentiated Homework Options		
AL	Approaching Level	1–15, 33, 34
OL	On Level	1–11 odd, 13–15, 33, 34
BL	Beyond Level	13–19, 33, 34

McGraw Hill Education ALEKS® can provide additional remediation support with personalized instruction and practice.

MATHEMATICAL PRACTICES

Emphasis On	Exercise(s)
1 Make sense of problems and persevere in solving them.	16–19
3 Construct viable arguments and critique the reasoning of others.	13, 15, 31
4 Model with mathematics.	14

Mathematical Practices 1, 3, and 4 are aspects of mathematical thinking that are emphasized in every lesson. Students are given opportunities to be persistent in their problem solving, to express their reasoning, and apply mathematics to real-world situations.

Formative Assessment
Use this activity as a closing formative assessment before dismissing students from your class.

TICKET Out the Door

Tell students you have a circular rug in your living room. Have students describe how they would find the area of the rug and which measure they would need to know in order to find its area. See students' work.

Watch Out!

Common Error Remind students to check which measurement is given in a problem and, if the diameter is given, to find the radius before using the area formula.

13. **Justify Conclusions** Harry's Pizzeria is having a sale on medium and large pizzas. Medium pizzas are 10 inches in diameter and cost $7.99. Large pizzas are 14 inches in diameter and cost $14.99. Which size pizza is the better deal? Explain. (*Hint*: Find the cost per square inch of each pizza.)
The large pizza; the medium pizza's area is 78.5 square inches and costs $0.102 per square inch. The large pizza's area is 153.86 square inches and costs $0.097 per square inch.

H.O.T. Problems Higher Order Thinking

14. **Model with Mathematics** Write a real-world problem that involves finding the area of two circles. Then solve your problem.
Sample answer: The interior of a circular dirt bike track has a 25-foot radius. There is a 40-foot radius from the center of the interior to the outer edge of the track. What is the area of the track?; 3,061.5 ft^2

15. **Reason Inductively** If the length of the radius of a circle is doubled, how does that affect the circumference and area? Explain.
When the radius of a circle is doubled, the circumference doubles and the area is 4 times as large. In the formula for area of a circle, the radius is squared, so when the radius of a circle is doubled, the area is 2^2 or 4 times as large.

Persevere with Problems Find the area of the shaded region in each figure. Round to the nearest tenth.

16. 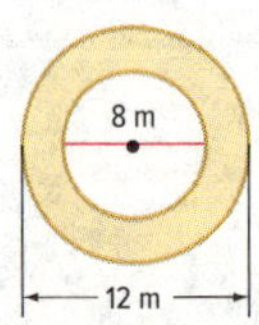

62.8 m^2

17. 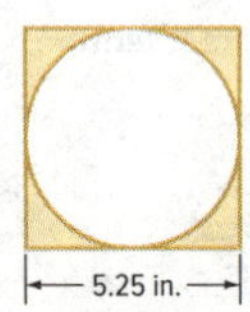

5.9 in^2

18. 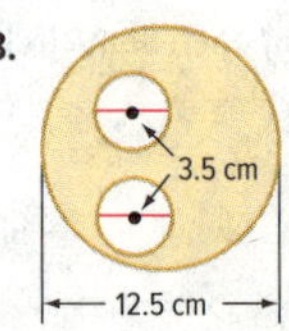

103.4 cm^2

19. **Persevere with Problems** Explain how you could find the area of the quarter circle shown at the right. Then write a formula that could be used to find the area of a quarter circle and use the formula to find the area to the nearest tenth.

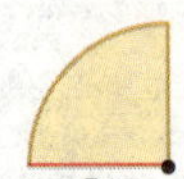

Sample answer: To find the area of the quarter circle, multiply the area of the entire circle by $\frac{1}{4}$; $A = \frac{1}{4}\pi r^2$; 19.6 in^2

Name ______________________ My Homework ______________________

Extra Practice

Find the area of each circle. Round to the nearest tenth. Use 3.14 or $\frac{22}{7}$ for π.

20.

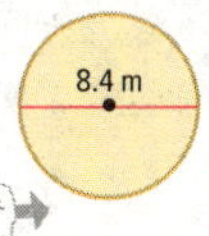

$A = \pi r^2$

$A = 3.14 \bullet 4.2^2$

$A = 55.4\ m^2$

Homework Help

$3.14 \times 4.2 \times 4.2 = 55.4\ m^2$

21.

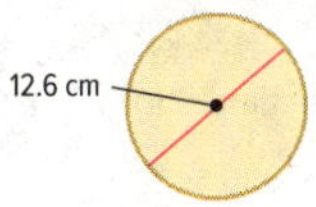

$3.14 \times 6.3 \times 6.3 =$ $124.6\ cm^2$

22.

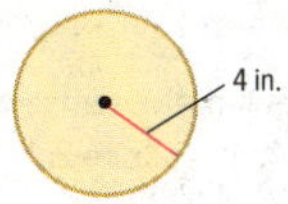

$3.14 \times 4 \times 4 = 50.2\ in^2$

23. diameter = 10.8 yd

$3.14 \times 5.4 \times 5.4 = 91.6\ yd^2$

24. radius = $3\frac{4}{5}$ ft

$3.14 \times 3.8 \times 3.8 = 45.3\ ft^2$

25. radius = 9.3 mm

$3.14 \times 9.3 \times 9.3 = 271.6\ mm^2$

26. Find the area of the Girl Scout patch shown if the diameter is 1.25 inches. Round to the nearest tenth.

$1.2\ in^2$

Find the area of each semicircle. Round to the nearest tenth. Use 3.14 for π.

27.

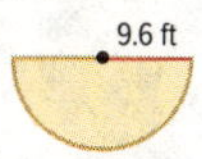

$144.7\ ft^2$

28.

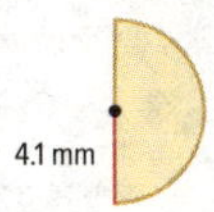

$26.4\ mm^2$

29.

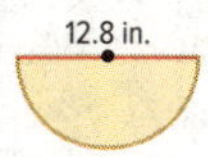

$64.3\ in^2$

30. A window that is in the shape of a semicircle has a diameter of 28 inches. Find the area of the window. Round to the nearest tenth.

$307.7\ in^2$

31. MP **Justify Conclusions** Which has a greater area, a triangle with a base of 100 feet and a height of 100 feet or a circle with diameter of 100 feet? Justify your selection.

circle; $\frac{1}{2} \bullet 100 \bullet 100 < 3 \bullet 50 \bullet 50$

32. A radio station sends a signal in a circular area with an 80-mile radius. Find the approximate area in square kilometers that receives the signal. (*Hint*: 1 square mile ≈ 2.6 square kilometers)

$52{,}249.6\ km^2$

Create Your Own Homework Online

eSolutionsManual™ can be used to create worksheets for the suggested assignments on page 627, or create your own worksheets for differentiated homework or review.

Power Up! Test Practice

Exercises 33 and 34 prepare students for more rigorous thinking needed for the state assessment.

33.

This test item requires students to support their reasoning or evaluate the reasoning of others by justifying their response and constructing arguments.	
Depth of Knowledge	DOK2
Content Standard	7.G.4
Mathematical Practice	MP1, MP3
Online Experience	Students will be required to type their response in the box.
Scoring Rubric	
2 points	Students find the area and explain their response.
1 point	Students find the area but fail to explain their response OR students explain the response but fail to find the correct area.

34.

This test item requires students to explain and apply mathematical concepts and solve problems with precision, while making use of structure.	
Depth of Knowledge	DOK1
Content Standard	7.G.4
Mathematical Practice	MP1
Online Experience	Students will be required to click on the bubbles to select all answers that are correct.
Scoring Rubric	
1 point	Students correctly answer the question.

Power Up! Test Practice

33. A large pizza at a restaurant has the dimensions shown. Find the area of the pizza. Use $\frac{22}{7}$ for π.

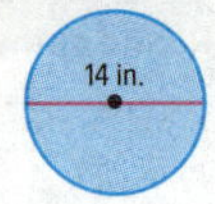

154 in²

Why does it make sense to use $\frac{22}{7}$ as the estimate for π? Explain your reasoning.

Sample answer: Using $\frac{22}{7}$ makes the computation easier since the radius is 7. The 7s cancel out in the multiplication.

34. Refer to the figures shown below. Which figures have the same area? Select all that apply.

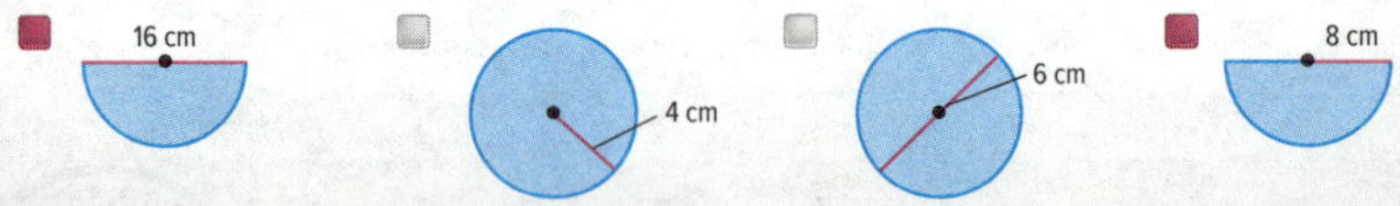

Spiral Review

35. A frame for a collage of pictures is in the shape of a trapezoid. The two bases are 15 inches and 20 inches. The height of the trapezoid is 12 inches. What is the area enclosed by the frame? 6.G.1 **210 in²**

Find the area of each parallelogram. Round to the nearest tenth if necessary. 6.G.1

36.

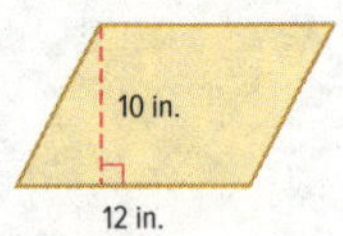

120 in²

37.

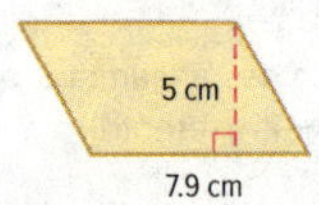

39.5 cm²

38.

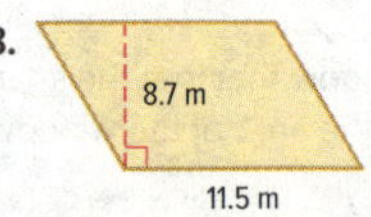

100.1 m²

An Interactive Whiteboard Ready presentation is available for each lesson in the chapter.

Lesson 3

Area of Composite Figures

Real-World Link

Stained Glass Windows An image of a stained glass window is shown below.

1. Identify two of the shapes that make up the window.
   triangles and circles

2. How could you find the area of the entire window except for the shapes you identified in Exercise 1?
   Sample answer: Multiply the length and width of the window. Subtract the areas of the circles and triangles.

3. Draw a figure that is made up of a triangle and a rectangle on the grid below. Then find the area of your figure by counting square units.
   See students' work.

Area: ________ square units

Essential Question

HOW do measurements help you describe real-world objects?

Vocabulary

composite figure

Content Standards
7.G.4, 7.G.6

MP Mathematical Practices
1, 2, 3, 4

Which MP **Mathematical Practices** did you use? Shade the circle(s) that applies.

① Persevere with Problems
② Reason Abstractly
③ Construct an Argument
④ Model with Mathematics
⑤ Use Math Tools
⑥ Attend to Precision
⑦ Make Use of Structure
⑧ Use Repeated Reasoning

Focus narrowing the scope

Objective Find the area of composite figures. 7.G.4, 7.G.6

Coherence connecting within and across grades

Previous Students found the circumference and area of circles.

Now Students find the area of composite figures.

Next Students will solve problems involving the volume of rectangular and triangular prisms.

Rigor pursuing concepts, fluency, and applications

See the Levels of Complexity chart on page 635.

ENGAGE EXPLORE EXPLAIN ELABORATE EVALUATE

1 Launch the Lesson

Ideas for Use

You may wish to launch the lesson using a whole group, small group, think-pair-share activity, or independent activity.

EL **Think-Pair-Draw** Have students read through Exercises 1–3 on their own, thinking about how they would respond to each exercise. Then have them work with a partner to complete the exercises. Have them draw two different figures for Exercise 3. MP 1, 7

Alternate Strategy

BL Have students draw a figure, using grid paper, that is made up of a rectangle and a semicircle. Have them determine the approximate area of the composite figure by counting square units. Then have them make a conjecture as how to determine the area by using area formulas. MP 1, 3, 4

ENGAGE EXPLORE **EXPLAIN** ELABORATE EVALUATE

2 Teach the Concept

Ask the scaffolded questions for each example to differentiate instruction.

IWB

Example

1. Find the area of a composite figure.

AL
- *What two figures form the composite figure?* a semicircle and a triangle
- *After you find the area of each shape, what will you need to do?* Add the areas together.

OL
- *What is the formula for the area of a semicircle? What is the area of this semicircle?* $A = \frac{1}{2}\pi r^2$; 14.1 m^2
- *What is the formula for the area of a triangle? What is the area of this triangle?* $A = \frac{1}{2}bh$; 33m^2

BL
- *Describe some real-world applications for finding the area of a composite figure.* Sample answers: buying and laying carpet, painting, art, interior/exterior design, building and construction

Need Another Example?
Find the area of the composite figure. Round to the nearest tenth. 86.1 cm^2

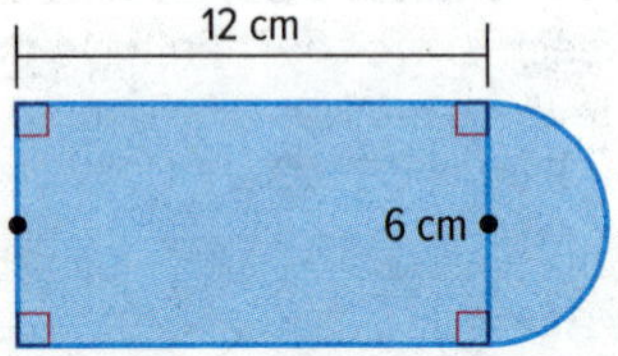

Work Zone

Find the Area of a Composite Figure

A **composite figure** is made up of two or more shapes.

To find the area of a composite figure, decompose the figure into shapes with areas you know. Then find the sum of these areas.

Shape	Words	Formula
Parallelogram	The area A of a parallelogram is the product of any base b and its height h.	$A = bh$
Triangle	The area A of a triangle is half the product of any base b and its height h.	$A = \frac{1}{2}bh$
Trapezoid	The area A of a trapezoid is half the product of the height h and the sum of the bases, b_1 and b_2.	$A = \frac{1}{2}h(b_1 + b_2)$
Circle	The area A of a circle is equal to π times the square of the radius r.	$A = \pi r^2$

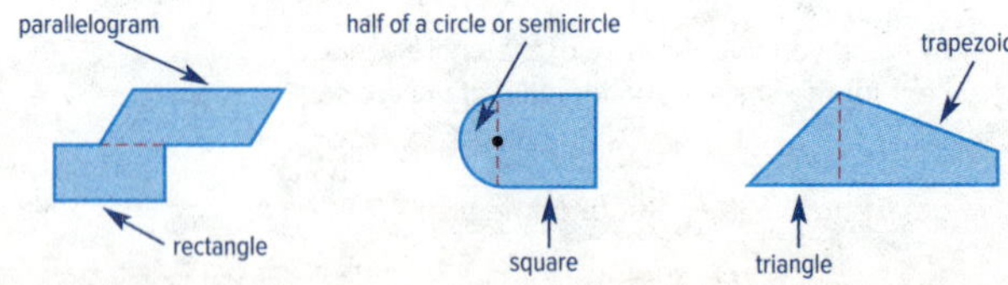

Example

Tutor

1. Find the area of the composite figure.

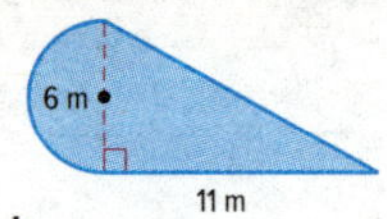

The figure can be separated into a semicircle and a triangle.

Area of semicircle

$A = \frac{1}{2}\pi r^2$

$A \approx \frac{1}{2} \cdot 3.14 \cdot 3^2$

$A \approx 14.1$

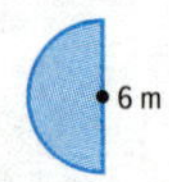

Area of triangle

$A = \frac{1}{2}bh$

$A = \frac{1}{2} \cdot 11 \cdot 6$

$A = 33$

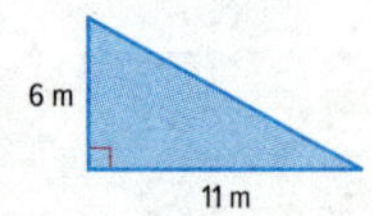

The area of the figure is about 14.1 + 33 or 47.1 square meters.

Got it? Do this problem to find out.

Show your work.

a. Find the area of the figure. Round to the nearest tenth if necessary.

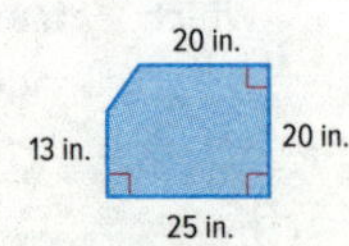

a. 482.5 in^2

Real World Example

Watch Tutor

2. **A miniature golf hole is composed of a trapezoid and a parallelogram. How many square feet of turf does the hole cover?**

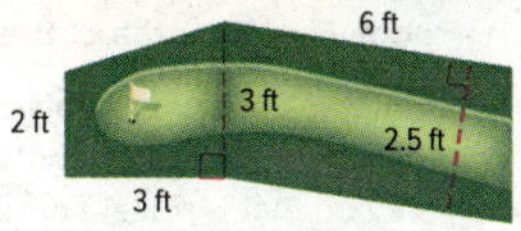

Area of trapezoid

$A = \frac{1}{2}h(b_1 + b_2)$

$A = \frac{1}{2}(3)(2 + 3)$

$A = 7.5$

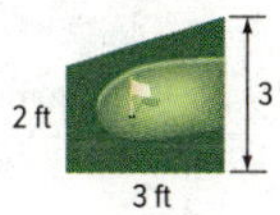

Area of parallelogram

$A = bh$

$A = 6 \cdot 2.5$

$A = 15$

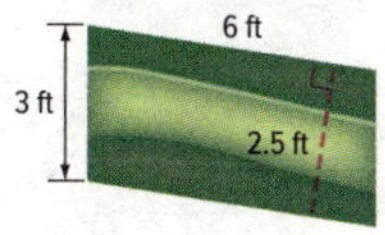

So, 7.5 + 15 or 22.5 square feet of turf will be needed.

Got it? **Do this problem to find out.**

b. Pedro's father is building a shed. How many square feet of wood are needed to build the back of the shed shown at the right?

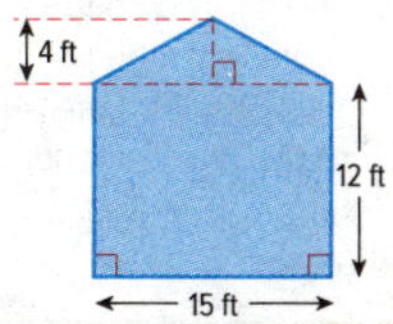

Show your work.

b. 210 ft^2

Find the Area of a Shaded Region

Use the areas you know to find the area of a shaded region.

Examples

Tutor

3. **Find the area of the shaded region.**

Find the area of the rectangle and subtract the area of the four congruent triangles.

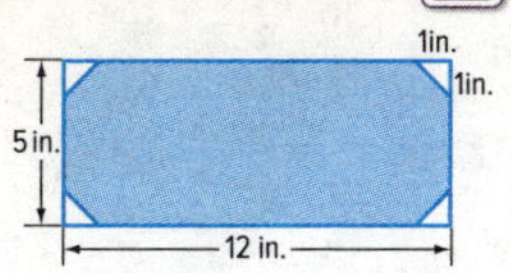

Area of rectangle

$A = \ell w$

$A = 12 \cdot 5$ $\quad \ell = 12, w = 5$

$A = 60$ $\quad$ Simplify.

Area of triangles

$A = 4 \cdot \left(\frac{1}{2}bh\right)$

$A = 4 \cdot \frac{1}{2} \cdot 1 \cdot 1$ $\quad b = 1, h = 1$

$A = 2$ $\quad$ Simplify.

The area of the shaded region is 60 − 2 or 58 square inches.

Congruent Triangles

Congruent triangles have corresponding sides and angles that are congruent.

Examples

IWB

2. **Find the area of a composite figure.**

AL
- *What are the two shapes in the figure?* a trapezoid and a parallelogram.
- *How can you find the area of a parallelogram?* Multiply the base by the height

OL
- *How can you find the area of the trapezoid?* $\frac{1}{2}h(b_1 + b_2)$.

BL
- *If turf costs $22 per square foot, how much will the golf hole cost? Explain.* $495; Multiply 22.5 square feet by $22.

Need Another Example?

The back of a dog house is composed of a square and a triangle. How much wood is needed for the back of the dog house to the nearest tenth of a square foot? 8.1 ft^2

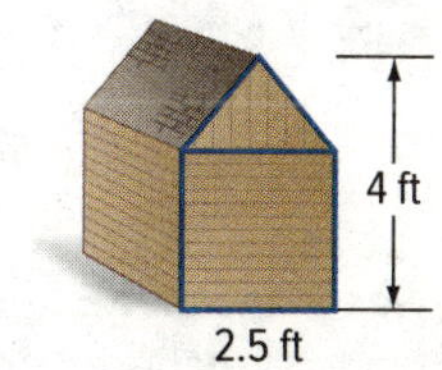

3. **Find the area of the shaded region.**

AL
- *What are the shapes in the figure?* a rectangle and four congruent triangles
- *How can you find the area of the rectangle?* Multiply the base by the height.

OL
- *How can you find the area of the triangles?* $4\left(\frac{1}{2}bh\right)$

BL
- *To find the area of the shaded region, what should you do? Explain.* Subtract the area of the triangles from the area of the rectangle.

Need Another Example?

Two congruent triangles are cut from a rectangle. Find the area of the shaded region. Round to the nearest tenth if necessary? 144 in^2

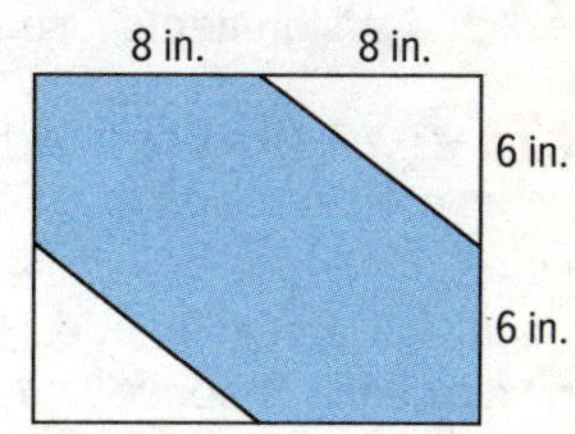

Example

IWB

4. Find the area of a shaded region.

AL • *Into what shapes can this composite figure be split?* rectangles

• *What is the formula for the area of a rectangle?* $A = \ell w$

OL • *What are the dimensions and the area of the rectangle that is not shaded?* 22 m and 20 m; 440 m^2

• *What are the dimensions and the area of the entire rectangle?* 42 m and 25 m; 1,050 m^2

• *How can you find the area of the shaded region?* Subtract 440 from 1,050, which is 610 square meters.

BL • *Describe another method you can use to find the area of the shaded region.* Sample answer: Divide the shaded region into three rectangles. Find the area of each one. Then find the sum.

Need Another Example?
Mario sketched a drawing of a dirt bike track he wants his dad to build. The brown area represents the track. Find the area of the track. Round to the nearest tenth. 2,590.5 ft^2

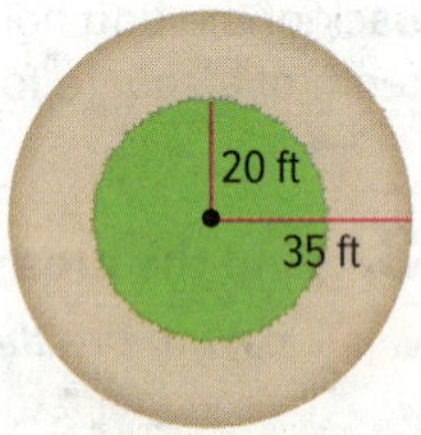

Guided Practice

Formative Assessment Use these exercises to assess students' understanding of the concepts in this lesson.

If some of your students are not ready for assignments, use the differentiated activities below.

AL EL **Pairs Consult** Have students work in pairs to complete Exercises 1–3. For Exercises 1 and 2, have them use colored markers or highlighters to show how they will decompose each shape. Have them write the area formulas next to each shape. MP 1, 7

BL EL **Trade-a-Problem** Have students draw a composite figure and label the necessary dimensions. Then have them trade with a partner to determine the total area. MP 1, 7

4. **The blueprint for a hotel swimming area is represented by the figure shown. The shaded area represents the pool. Find the area of the pool.**

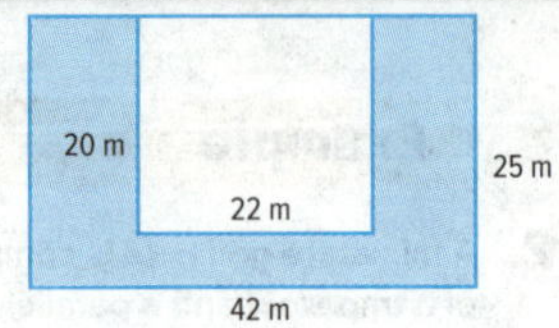

Find the area of the entire rectangle and subtract the section that is not shaded.

Area of the entire rectangle	**Area not shaded**
$A = \ell w$	$A = \ell w$
$A = 42 \cdot 25$ or 1,050	$A = 22 \cdot 20$ or 440

The area of the shaded region is 1,050 − 440 or 610 square meters.

Got it? **Do this problem to find out.**

Show your work.

c. A diagram for a park is shown. The shaded area represents the picnic sections. Find the area of the picnic sections.

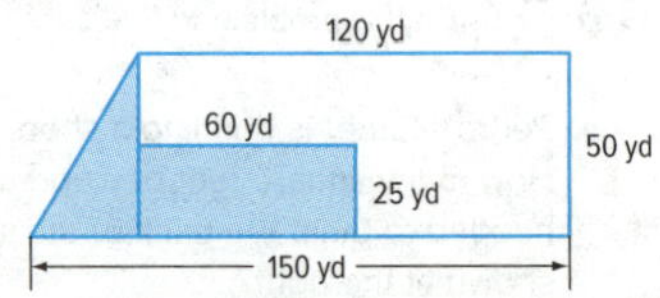

c. 2,250 yd^2

Guided Practice

Check

1. Mike installed the window shown. How many square feet is the window? Round to the nearest tenth. Use 3.14 for π.

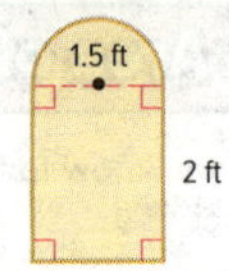

Show your work. (Examples 1 and 2) 3.9 ft^2

2. A triangle is cut from a rectangle. Find the area of the shaded region.

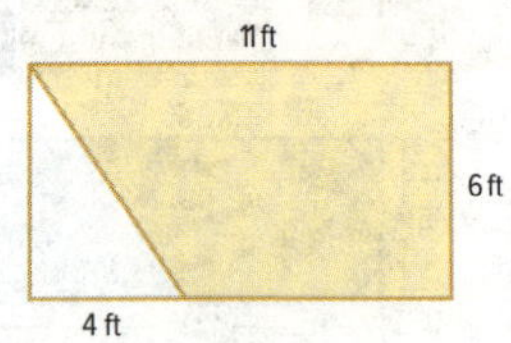

(Examples 3 and 4) 54 ft^2

3. **Building on the Essential Question** Is your answer to Exercise 1 an exact or approximate answer? Explain.

approximate; Sample answer: Since 3.14 is an approximation for pi, the answer will also be an approximation.

Rate Yourself!

How confident are you about finding the area of composite figures? Check the box that applies.

For more help, go online to access a Personal Tutor.

Tutor

ENGAGE EXPLORE **EXPLAIN** **ELABORATE** **EVALUATE**

3 Practice and Apply

Name ______________________ My Homework ______________________

Independent Practice

Go online for Step-by-Step Solutions eHelp

Find the area of each figure. Round to the nearest tenth if necessary. (Example 1) Unless otherwise specified, answers were computed using 3.14.

1. 64 cm^2

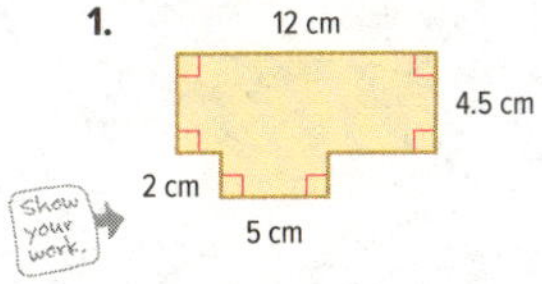

2. 240 yd^2

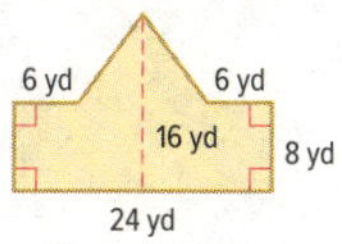

3. 220.5 cm^2

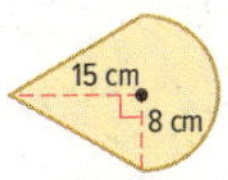

4. 193.3 m^2

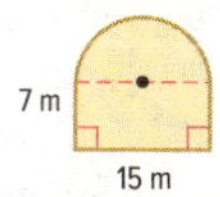

5. 38.6 ft^2

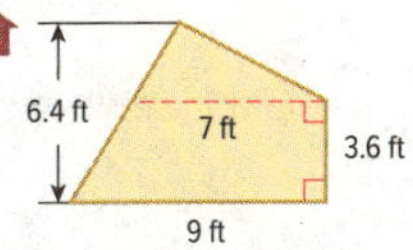

6. 78.1 yd^2

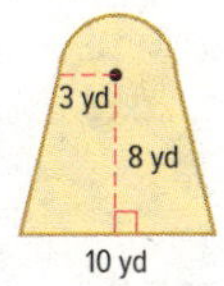

7. Daniel is constructing a deck like the one shown. What is the area of the deck? (Example 2)

119.5 ft^2

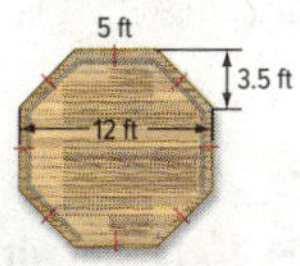

Find the area of the shaded region. Round to the nearest tenth if necessary. (Examples 3 and 4)

8.

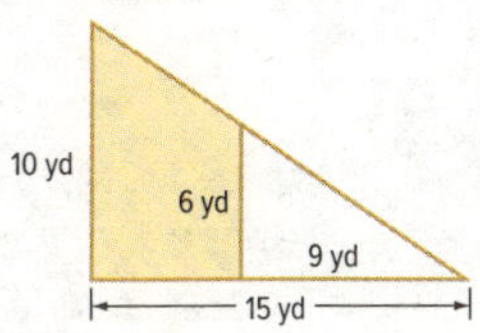

48 yd^2

9.

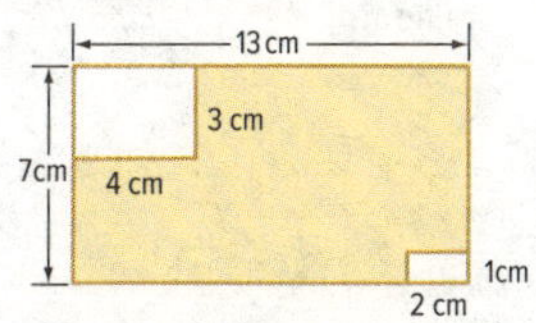

77 cm^2

Independent Practice and Extra Practice

The Independent Practice pages are meant to be used as the homework assignment. The Extra Practice page can be used for additional reinforcement or as a second-day assignment.

Levels of Complexity

The levels of the exercises progress from 1 to 3, with Level 1 indicating the lowest level of complexity.

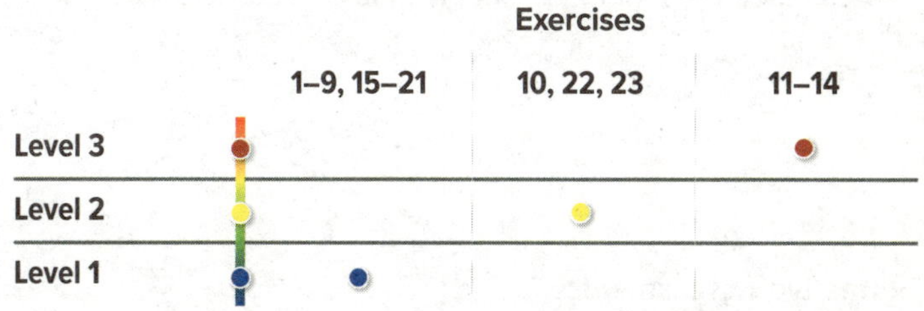

Suggested Assignments

You can use the table below that includes exercises of all complexity levels to select appropriate exercises for your students' needs.

Differentiated Homework Options		
AL	Approaching Level	1–9, 12, 14, 22, 23
OL	On Level	1–9 odd, 10, 12, 14, 22, 23
BL	Beyond Level	10–14, 22, 23

McGraw Hill Education **ALEKS**® can provide additional remediation support with personalized instruction and practice.

MATHEMATICAL PRACTICES

Emphasis On	Exercise(s)
1 Make sense of problems and persevere in solving them.	10, 11, 13
2 Reason abstractly and quantitatively.	12
4 Model with mathematics.	14

Mathematical Practices 1, 3, and 4 are aspects of mathematical thinking that are emphasized in every lesson. Students are given opportunities to be persistent in their problem solving, to express their reasoning, and apply mathematics to real-world situations.

Formative Assessment

Use this activity as a closing formative assessment before dismissing students from your class.

TICKET Out the Door

Draw the composite figure shown on the board, without labeling any measurements. Have students write what measurements they would need to know in order to find the area of the composite figure and what steps they would take to find its area. See students' work.

Watch Out!

Common Error Students may make mistakes in finding the area of composite figures, because they overlook one or more measurements when they find the length of an unmarked side. Suggest that students sketch and label each shape in the composite figure, recheck that the side lengths are accurate, then find the area of the figure.

10. **Persevere with Problems** Zoe's mom is carpeting her bedroom and needs to know the amount of floor space. How many square feet of carpeting are needed for the room? If she is also installing baseboards on the bottom of all the walls, how many feet of baseboards are needed? 218 ft^2; 66 ft

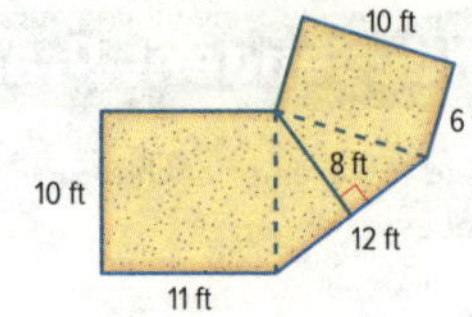

H.O.T. Problems Higher Order Thinking

11. **Persevere with Problems** The composite figure shown is made from a rectangle and part of a circle. Find the approximate area and perimeter of the entire figure. Round to the nearest tenth.
44.6 ft^2; 30.3 ft

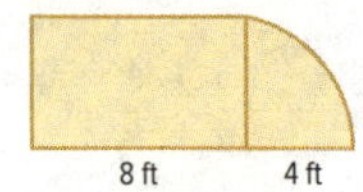

12. **Reason Abstractly** The side length of the square in the figure at the right is x units. Write expressions that represent the perimeter and area of the figure.
Perimeter: $3x + \frac{1}{2}\pi x$; Area: $x^2 + \frac{1}{2}\pi\left(\frac{x}{2}\right)^2$

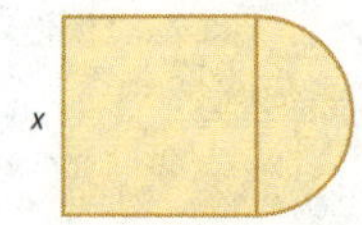

13. **Persevere with Problems** In the diagram shown at the right, a 2-foot-wide flower border surrounds the heart-shaped pond. What is the area of the border?
110.8 ft^2

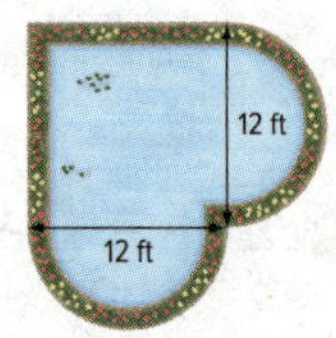

14. **Model with Mathematics** Find a real-world object that is a composite figure. Measure the dimensions of the figure. Draw a model of the figure with appropriate labels. Then find the area of the composite figure. See students' work.

Show your work.

Name ______________________ My Homework ______________________

Extra Practice

Find the area of each figure. Round to the nearest tenth if necessary.

15. 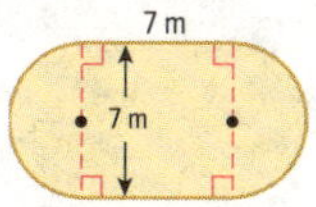

$87.5\ m^2$

Homework Help

Area of circle

$A = \pi r^2$

$A = 3.14 \cdot 3.5^2$ or 38.5

Area of square

$A = lw$

$A = 7 \cdot 7$ or 49

$38.5 + 49 = 87.5$

16. 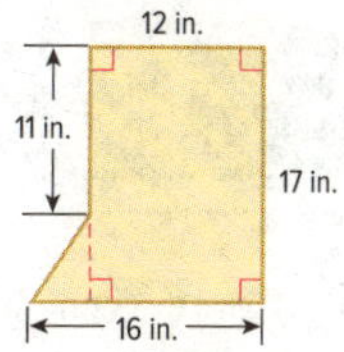

$216\ in^2$

17. 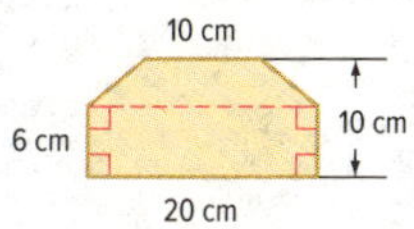

$180\ cm^2$

18. 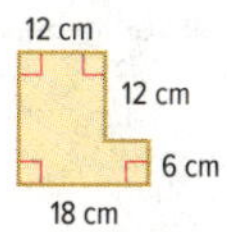

$252\ cm^2$

19. A necklace comes with a gold pendant. What is the area of the pendant in square centimeters? $9\ cm^2$

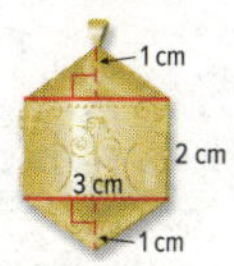

Find the area of the shaded region. Round to the nearest tenth if necessary.

20. 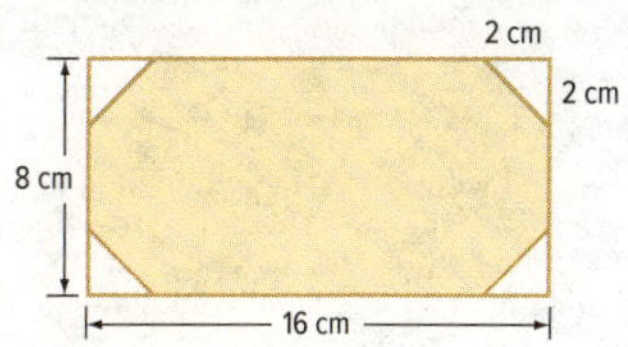

$120\ cm^2$

21. 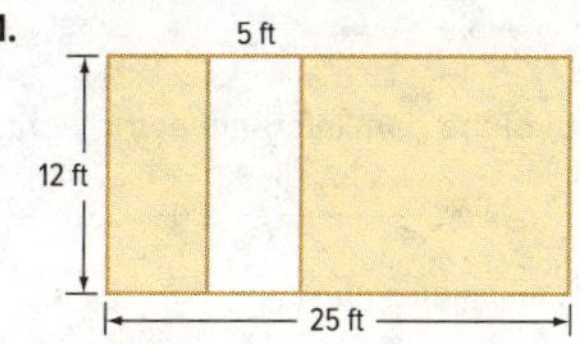

$240\ ft^2$

Create Your Own Homework Online

eSolutionsManual™ can be used to create worksheets for the suggested assignments on page 635, or create your own worksheets for differentiated homework or review.

Power Up! Test Practice

Exercises 22 and 23 prepare students for more rigorous thinking needed for the state assessment.

22.

This test item requires students to explain and apply mathematical concepts and solve problems with precision, while making use of structure.	
Depth of Knowledge	DOK1
Content Standard	7.G.6
Mathematical Practice	MP1
Online Experience	Students will drag values to find the area and type their response in the box.
Scoring Rubric	
2 points	Students correctly find each area as well as the area not used.
1 point	Students find each area but fail to find the area not used OR students find two of the three areas and the area not being used OR students have a mathematical error in one of the areas that impacts the rest of the calculations.

23.

This test item requires students to explain and apply mathematical concepts and solve problems with precision, while making use of structure.	
Depth of Knowledge	DOK1
Content Standard	7.G.4, 7.G.6
Mathematical Practice	MP1
Online Experience	Students will be required to type their responses in the boxes.
Scoring Rubric	
2 points	Students correctly answer each part of the question.
1 point	Students correctly answer two of the three parts OR students have a calculation error in a or b and their answer for c is based on that error.

Power Up! Test Practice

22. The Patel's backyard has a rectangular vegetable garden and a triangular pet exercise area.

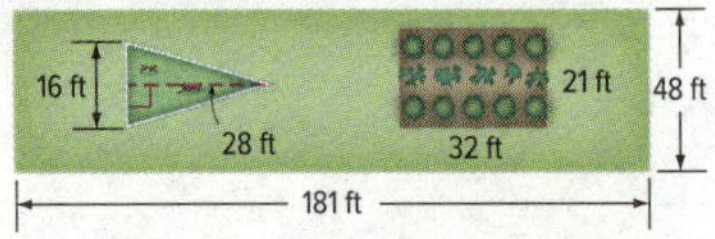

Match each part of the yard with the correct area.

Pet Exercise Area: **224** ft^2

Vegetable Garden Area: **672** ft^2

Total Backyard Area: **8,688** ft^2

106	672
224	1,092
458	7,520
544	8,688

How much of the backyard is not being used for the vegetable garden or pet exercise area?

7,792 ft^2

23. The figure is made up of a square and four semicircles. Fill in each box to complete each statement. Round to the nearest hundredth.

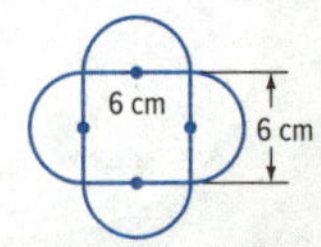

a. The area of the square is **36** cm^2.

b. The area of each semicircle is about **14.14** cm^2.

c. The total area of the figure is about **92.56** cm^2.

Spiral Review

24. What is the area of a triangle with a base of 52 feet and a height of 38 feet? 6.G.1 **988 ft^2**

25. Find the area of the parallelogram at the right. Round to the nearest tenth. 6.G.1 **3.7 cm^2**

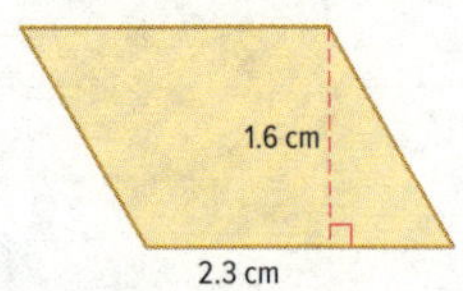

26. Find the height of a parallelogram with an area of 104 square yards and a base of 8 yards. 6.G.1

13 yd

27. Find the base of a parallelogram with a height of 3.2 meters and an area of 15.04 square meters. 6.G.1

4.7 m

PD | RtI | Watch | Worksheets | Vocab | Tutor | Tools | Check | English Learners | Sketchpad

PRESENT

IWB

An Interactive Whiteboard Ready presentation is available for each lesson in the chapter.

Geometry

Lesson 4

Volume of Prisms

Vocabulary Start-Up

Vocab

Recall that a prism is a polyhedron with two parallel, congruent bases. The bases of a *rectangular prism* are rectangles, and the bases of a *triangular prism* are triangles.

Write *rectangular prism* or *triangular prism* on the line below each figure.

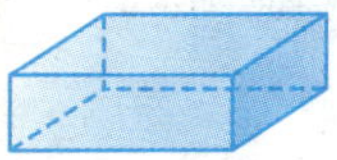

rectangular prism

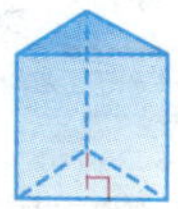

triangular prism

Essential Question

HOW do measurements help you describe real-world objects?

Vocabulary

volume

Content Standards
7.G.6

MP Mathematical Practices
1, 2, 3, 4

Real-World Link

1. Suppose you observed the camping tent shown from directly above. What geometric figure would you see?

   rectangle

2. What formula would you use to find the area of the figure?

   $A = \ell w$

Which MP **Mathematical Practices** did you use? Shade the circle(s) that applies.

① Persevere with Problems
② Reason Abstractly
③ Construct an Argument
④ Model with Mathematics
⑤ Use Math Tools
⑥ Attend to Precision
⑦ Make Use of Structure
⑧ Use Repeated Reasoning

Focus narrowing the scope

Objective Find the volume of prisms. 7.G.6

Coherence connecting within and across grades

Previous Students found the area of composite figures.

Now Students find the volume of prisms.

Next Students will find the volume of pyramids.

Rigor pursuing concepts, fluency, and applications

See the Levels of Complexity chart on page 643.

ENGAGE EXPLORE EXPLAIN ELABORATE EVALUATE

1 Launch the Lesson

Ideas for Use

You may wish to launch the lesson using a whole group, small group, think-pair-share activity, or independent activity.

EL **Pairs Check** Have students complete Exercises 1 and 2 with a partner. Then have each pair of students team up with another pair to compare answers and discuss and resolve any differences. MP 1, 6

Alternate Strategy

AL Have students construct a net for a triangular prism. Have students label the bases and explain why the bases are the triangular faces and not the other rectangular faces. MP 1, 3, 4

ENGAGE EXPLORE **EXPLAIN** ELABORATE EVALUATE

2 Teach the Concept

Ask the scaffolded questions for each example to differentiate instruction.

IWB

Example

1. Find the volume of a rectangular prism.

AL
- *What is the formula for the volume of a rectangular prism?* $V = Bh$ or $V = \ell wh$
- *What are the dimensions of the base? The area of the base?* $5 \text{ cm} \times 4 \text{ cm} = 20 \text{ cm}^2$

OL
- *In the formulas $V = Bh$ or $V = \ell wh$, what is an expression that is equivalent to B? Explain.* B is equivalent to ℓw, which is the area of the base.
- *What is the height of the figure?* 3 cm

BL
- *If the prism were turned on its side and the base became a different face, will the volume change? Explain.* no; The volume will not change regardless of the orientation of the prism. Multiplication is commutative, so the order in which we multiply does not matter.
- *What is another way to think of the height of a rectangular prism?* Sample answer: the number of layers of the base

Need Another Example?

Find the volume of the rectangular prism. 24 cm^3

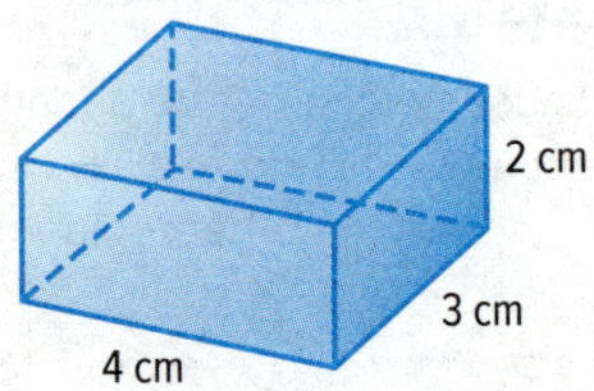

Key Concept **Volume of a Rectangular Prism**

Work Zone

Words The volume V of a rectangular prism is the product of the length ℓ, the width w, and the height h. It is also the area of the base B times the height h.

Model

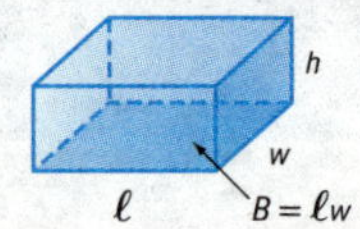

Symbols $V = \ell wh$ or $V = Bh$

The **volume** of a three-dimensional figure is the measure of space it occupies. It is measured in cubic units such as cubic centimeters (cm^3) or cubic inches (in^3).

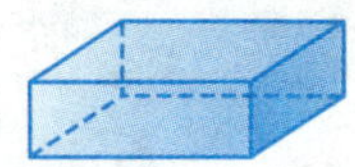

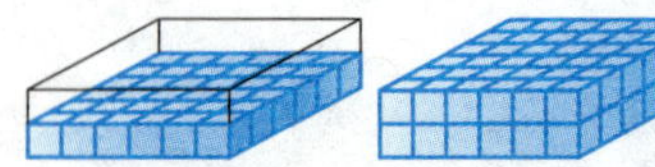

It takes 2 layers of 36 cubes to fill the box. So, the volume of the box is 72 cubic centimeters.

Decomposing Figures

Think of the volume of the three prism as consisting of three congruent slices. Each slice contains the base area, 20 square centimeters, and a height of 1 centimeter.

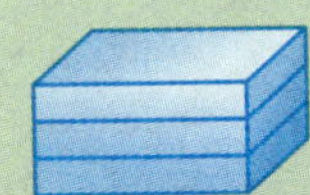

Example

Tutor

1. Find the volume of the rectangular prism.

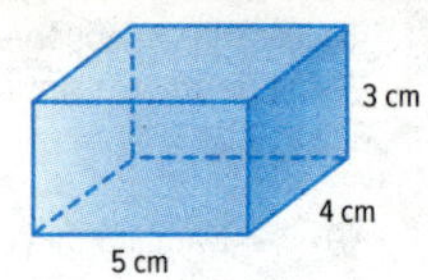

$V = \ell wh$ Volume of a prism

$V = 5 \cdot 4 \cdot 3$ $\ell = 5$, $w = 4$, and $h = 3$

$V = 60$ Multiply.

The volume is 60 cubic centimeters or 60 cm^3.

Got it? **Do this problem to find out.**

a. Find the volume of the rectangular prism shown below.

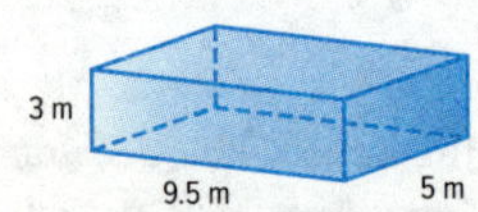

Show your work.

a. 142.5 m^3

Volume of a Triangular Prism

Key Concept

Words The volume V of a triangular prism is the area of the base B times the height h.

Model

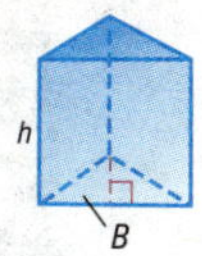

Symbols $V = Bh$, where B is the area of the base.

Height
Do not confuse the height of the triangular base with the height of the prism.

The diagram below shows that the volume of a triangular prism is also the product of the area of the base B and the height h of the prism.

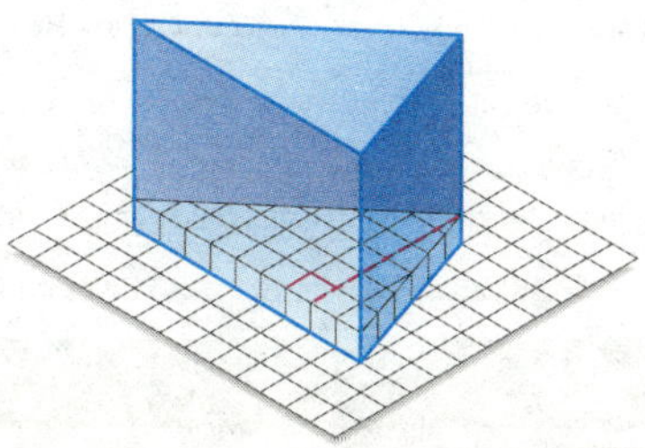

Example

Tutor

2. Find the volume of the triangular prism shown.

The area of the triangle is $\frac{1}{2} \cdot 6 \cdot 8$, so replace B with $\frac{1}{2} \cdot 6 \cdot 8$.

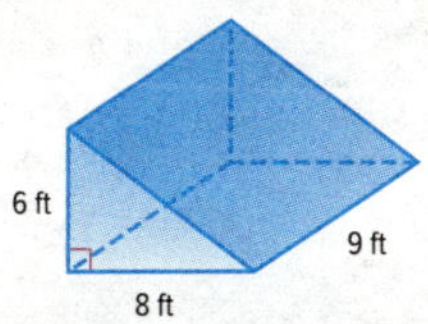

$V = Bh$	Volume of a prism
$V = \left(\frac{1}{2} \cdot 6 \cdot 8\right)h$	Replace B with $\frac{1}{2} \cdot 6 \cdot 8$.
$V = \left(\frac{1}{2} \cdot 6 \cdot 8\right)9$	The height of the prism is 9.
$V = 216$	Multiply.

The volume is 216 cubic feet or 216 ft^3.

Before finding the volume of a prism, identify the base. In Example 2, the base is a triangle, so you replace B with $\frac{1}{2}bh$.

Got it? **Do this problem to find out.**

b. Find the volume of the triangular prism.

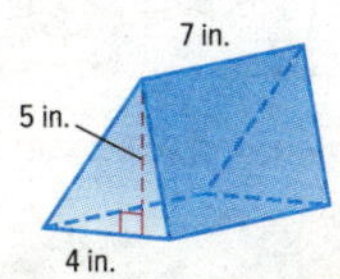

Show your work.

b. 70 in^3

Example

IWB

2. Find the volume of a triangular prism.

AL
- *What is the formula for the volume of a prism?* $V = bh$ or $V = \ell wh$
- *What does volume mean?* Sample answer: the amount of space inside a three-dimensional figure measured in cubic units

OL
- *What is the shape of the base of the prism?* a triangle
- *What is the formula for the area of a triangle?* $A = \frac{1}{2}bh$
- *What are the shapes of the other faces of the triangular prism?* rectangles

BL
- *How do you know that the bases are triangles?* The base of a prism are parallel and congruent. The only faces of this prism that are parallel and congruent are the two triangular faces.

Need Another Example?
Find the volume of the triangular prism. 315 m^3

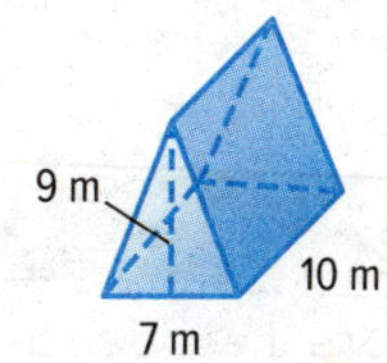

Watch Out!

Common Error Students may automatically multiply the three given dimensions to find the volume of a triangular prism. Remind students that the area of the base of a triangular prism is $B = \frac{1}{2}bh$. Encourage them to first identify the base of each triangular prism, then substitute the values into the volume formula.

Example

3. Solve a real-world problem involving volume.

AL
- *What is the formula for volume of a rectangular prism?* $V = bh$ or $V = \ell wh$
- *What is the shape of each lunch box?* rectangular prism

OL
- *What are the dimensions of the base for lunch box A as shown? lunch box B as shown?* 3.75 in. × 7.5 in.; 3.75 in. × 8 in.

BL
- *How do you know that this problem requires multiple steps to solve?* Sample answer: First I need to find the volume of each prism. Then I need to compare the volumes.

Need Another Example?
The game Planet Bugs comes in a box with the dimensions shown. The game Fire and Ice comes in a box that measures 9 inches by 5 inches by $4\frac{1}{2}$ inches. Which game box has the greater volume? Planet Bugs

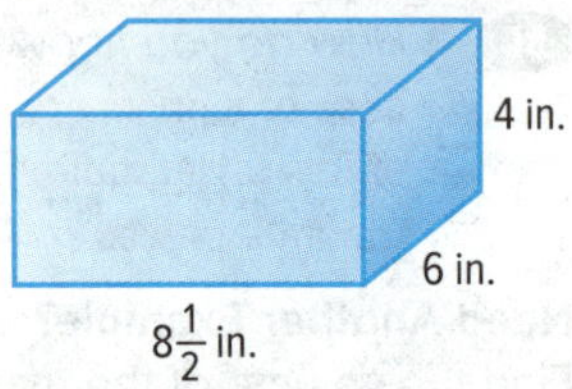

Guided Practice

Formative Assessment Use these exercises to assess students' understanding of the concepts in this lesson.

If some of your students are not ready for assignments, use the differentiated activities below.

AL EL **Pairs Discussion** Have students work in pairs to complete Exercises 1–4. Have students label the dimensions of each base and find the area of each base prior to finding the volume of each prism. MP 1, 7

BL EL **Pairs Consult** Have students work backward to find a missing dimension given the volume of a rectangular prism. Have students share their procedures with another pair of students. MP 1, 7

Example

3. Which lunch box holds more food?

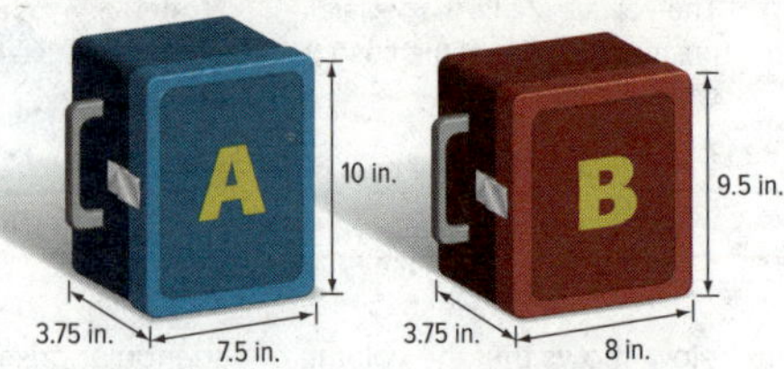

Find the volume of each lunch box. Then compare.

Lunch Box A	Lunch Box B
$V = \ell wh$	$V = \ell wh$
$V = 7.5 \cdot 3.75 \cdot 10$	$V = 8 \cdot 3.75 \cdot 9.5$
$V = 281.25 \text{ in}^3$	$V = 285 \text{ in}^3$

Since $285 \text{ in}^3 > 281.25 \text{ in}^3$, Lunch Box B holds more food.

Guided Practice

Find the volume of each prism. Round to the nearest tenth if necessary. (Examples 1–2)

1. 220 in^3

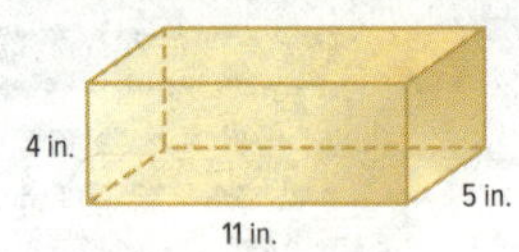

2. 63 yd^3

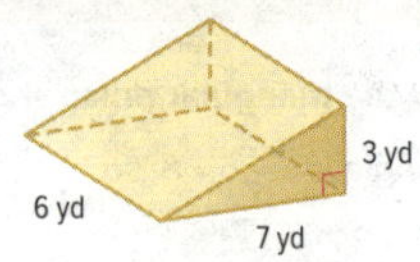

Show your work.

3. One cabinet measures 3 feet by 2.5 feet by 5 feet. A second measures 4 feet by 3.5 feet by 4.5 feet. Which volume is greater? Explain. (Example 3)
second cabinet; $37.5 \text{ ft}^3 < 63 \text{ ft}^3$

4. **Building on the Essential Question** Compare and contrast finding the volume of a rectangular prism and a triangular prism. Sample answer: They are both the product of the area of the base and the prism height. They differ in how to find the area of the base.

Rate Yourself!

How confident are you about finding volume for prisms? Check the box that applies.

For more help, go online to access a Personal Tutor.

FOLDABLES Time to update your Foldable!

Name ______________________ My Homework ______________________

Independent Practice

Go online for Step-by-Step Solutions eHelp

Find the volume of each prism. Round to the nearest tenth if necessary. (Examples 1–2)

1. 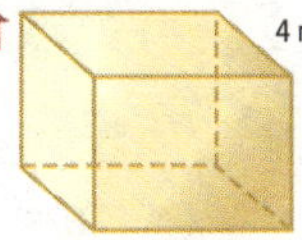

192 m^3

2. 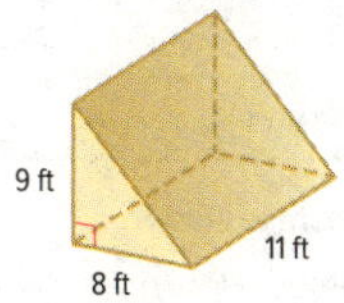

396 ft^3

3. 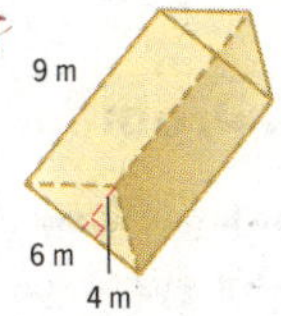

108 m^3

Show your work.

4. Which container holds more detergent? Justify your answer. (Example 3)

Soapy Suds; 1,248 $in^3 > 468$ in^3

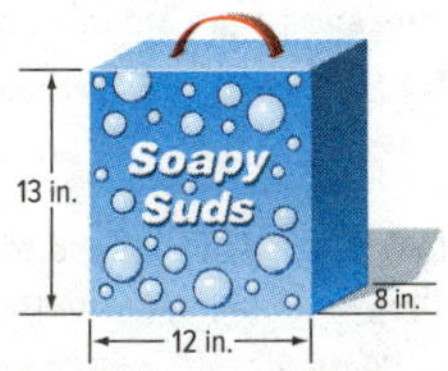

5. MP **Model with Mathematics** Refer to the graphic novel frame below. The table shows possible dimensions for the dunk tank.

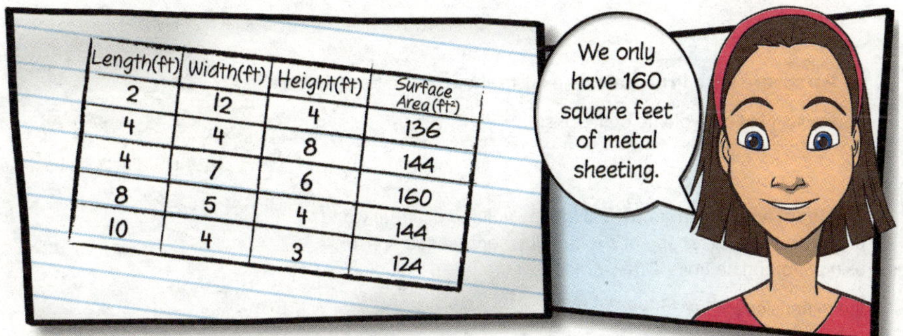

Length(ft)	Width(ft)	Height(ft)	Surface Area(ft^2)
2	12	4	136
4	4	8	144
4	7	6	160
8	5	4	144
10	4	3	124

a. Find the volume of each given dunk tank.

96 ft^3; 128 ft^3; 168 ft^3; 160 ft^3; 120 ft^3

b. Which dimensions are reasonable for a dunk tank? Explain.

The height must allow the water to be deep enough for someone to get wet and the length and width must allow a person to fit. So the first and last sets of dimensions would not work.

ENGAGE EXPLORE **EXPLAIN** **ELABORATE** **EVALUATE**

3 Practice and Apply

Independent Practice and Extra Practice

The Independent Practice pages are meant to be used as the homework assignment. The Extra Practice page can be used for additional reinforcement or as a second-day assignment.

Levels of Complexity

The levels of the exercises progress from 1 to 3, with Level 1 indicating the lowest level of complexity.

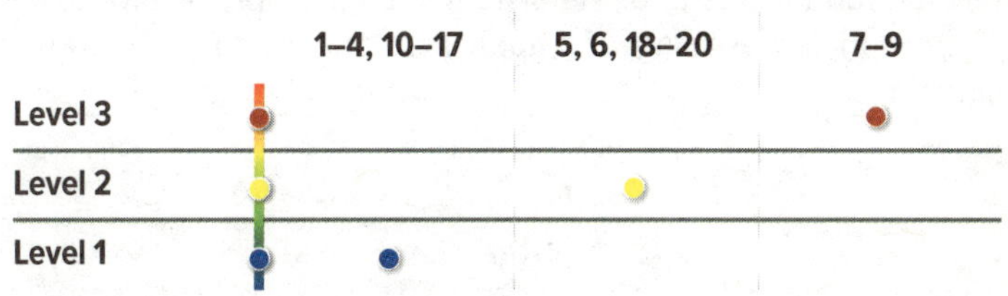

Suggested Assignments

You can use the table below that includes exercises of all complexity levels to select appropriate exercises for your students' needs.

Differentiated Homework Options		
AL	Approaching Level	1–5, 7, 9, 19, 20
OL	On Level	1–5 odd, 6, 7, 9, 19, 20
BL	Beyond Level	5–9, 19, 20

ALEKS® can provide additional remediation support with personalized instruction and practice.

MP MATHEMATICAL PRACTICES

Emphasis On	Exercise(s)
1 Make sense of problems and persevere in solving them.	8
2 Reason abstractly and quantitatively.	18
3 Construct viable arguments and critique the reasoning of others.	7
4 Model with mathematics.	5, 9

Mathematical Practices 1, 3, and 4 are aspects of mathematical thinking that are emphasized in every lesson. Students are given opportunities to be persistent in their problem solving, to express their reasoning, and apply mathematics to real-world situations.

Formative Assessment
Use this activity as a closing formative assessment before dismissing students from your class.

TICKET Out the Door

Ask students to measure and find the volume of a rectangular or triangular prism found in the classroom. See students' work.

6. The diagram shows the dimensions of an office. It costs about \$0.11 per year to air condition one cubic foot of space. On average, how much does it cost to air condition the office for one month? \$88

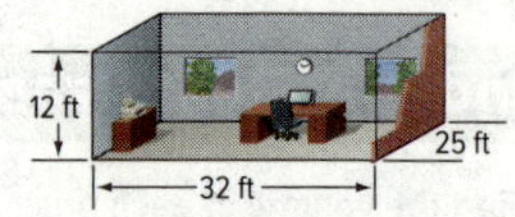

H.O.T. Problems Higher Order Thinking

7. MP **Reason Inductively** A rectangular prism is shown.

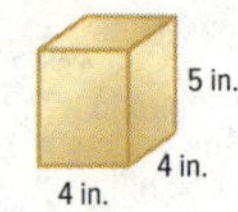

a. Suppose the length of the prism is doubled. How does the volume change? Explain your reasoning. Sample answer: There is a direct relationship between the volume and the length. Since the length is doubled, the volume is also doubled.

b. Suppose the length, width, and height are each doubled. How does the volume change? The volume is eight times greater.

c. Which will have a greater effect on the volume of the prism: doubling the height or doubling the width? Explain your reasoning.
Neither; Sample answer: doubling the height will result in a volume of $4 \cdot 4 \cdot 10$ or 160 in^3; doubling the width will result in a volume of $4 \cdot 8 \cdot 5$ or 160 in^3.

8. MP **Persevere with Problems** The prism shown has a base that is a trapezoid. Find the volume of the prism. 364 in^3

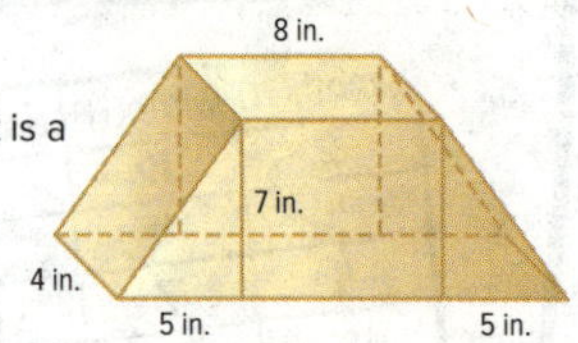

9. MP **Model with Mathematics** Find the volume of a real-world object that is in the shape of a rectangular or triangular prism using appropriate units. Draw a model of the prism including the dimensions. See students' work.

Show your work.

Name ______________________ My Homework ______________________

Extra Practice

Find the volume of each prism. Round to the nearest tenth if necessary.

10. Homework Help

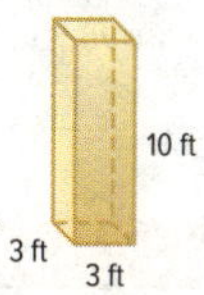

90 ft^3

V = lwh

V = 3 · 3 · 10

V = 90

11.

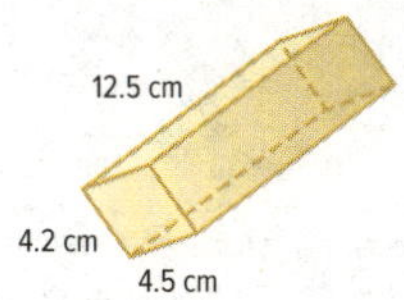

236.3 cm^3

12.

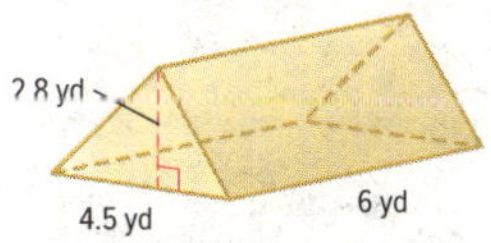

37.8 yd^3

13.

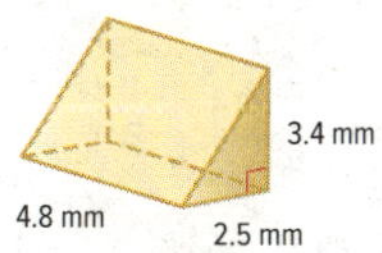

20.4 mm^3

14. A toy company makes rectangular sandboxes that measure 6 feet by 5 feet by 1.2 feet. A customer buys a sandbox and 40 cubic feet of sand. Did the customer buy too much or too little sand? Justify your answer.

40 ft^3 > 36 ft^3, so too much was bought.

15. The base of a rectangular prism has an area of 19.4 square meters and the prism has a volume of 306.52 cubic meters. Write an equation that can be used to find the height *h* of the prism. Then find the height of the prism.

306.52 = 19.4*h*; 15.8 m

Find the volume of each prism.

16.

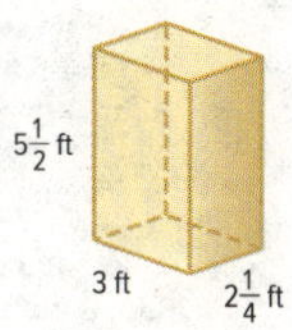

$37\frac{1}{8}$ ft^3

17.

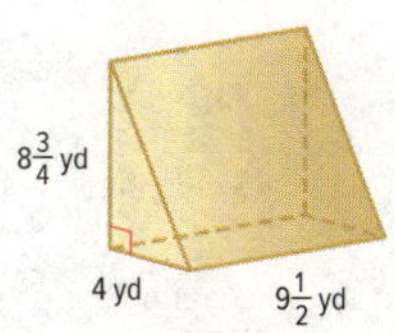

$166\frac{1}{4}$ yd^3

18. MP **Reason Abstractly** Write a formula for finding the volume of a cube. Use an exponent and the variable *s* to represent the side lengths. Then use the formula to find the volume of a cube with side lengths of 7 inches.

$V = s^3$; 343 in^3

Create Your Own Homework Online

eSolutionsManual™ can be used to create worksheets for the suggested assignments on page 643, or create your own worksheets for differentiated homework or review.

Power Up! Test Practice

Exercises 19 and 20 prepare students for more rigorous thinking needed for the state assessment.

19.

This test item requires students to explain and apply mathematical concepts and solve problems with precision, while making use of structure.	
Depth of Knowledge	DOK1
Content Standard	7.G.6
Mathematical Practice	MP1
Online Experience	Students will be required to click on the bubbles to select all answers that are correct.
Scoring Rubric	
1 point	Students correctly answer the question.

20.

This test item requires students to explain and apply mathematical concepts and solve problems with precision, while making use of structure.	
Depth of Knowledge	DOK2
Content Standard	7.G.6
Mathematical Practice	MP1
Online Experience	Students will be required to type their responses in the boxes.
Scoring Rubric	
2 points	Students correctly order each container, give the corresponding volume and list the container with the greatest volume.
1 point	Students correctly complete the table but fail to list the greatest volume OR students correctly order all of the container, list the container with the greatest volume, but fail to find the corresponding volume for each OR students correctly order three of the four containers and find their corresponding volumes.

Power Up! Test Practice

19. The volume of a paperclip box is 1.5 cubic inches. Which of the following are possible dimensions of the box? Select all that apply.

- [x] 2 in. by 1.5 in. by 0.5 in.
- [ ] 3 in. by 0.5 in. by 1.5 in.
- [ ] 2 in. by 1 in. by 1 in.
- [x] 3 in. by 1 in. by 0.5 in.

20. The table shows the dimensions of 4 mailing containers. Sort the containers from least to greatest volume.

Container	ℓ (ft)	w (ft)	h (ft)
A	2	2	2
B	1	3	3
C	3	4	0.5
D	3	2	0.5

	Container	Volume (ft^3)
Least	D	3
	C	6
	A	8
Greatest	B	9

Which container has the greatest volume? Container B

Spiral Review

Find the perimeter of each figure. 4.MD.3

21.

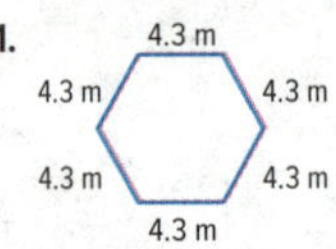

25.8 m

22.

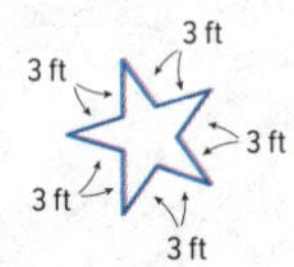

30 ft

23.

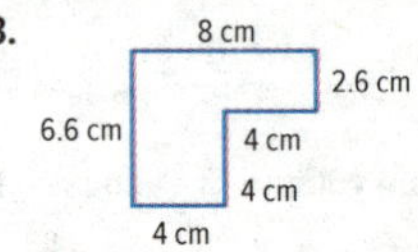

29.2 cm

24. Write a formula for finding the perimeter of a square. Use your formula to find the perimeter of a square with side length of 0.5 inch. 6.G.3

$p = 4s$; 2 in.

PD | RtI | Watch | Worksheets | Vocab | Tutor | Tools | Check | English Learners | Sketchpad

PRESENT

IWB

An Interactive Whiteboard Ready presentation is available for each lesson in the chapter.

MP **Problem-Solving Investigation**

Solve a Simpler Problem

Content Standards
7.G.4, 7.G.6

MP **Mathematical Practices**
1, 3

Case #1 Playgrounds

Liam is helping to mulch the play area at the community center. The diagram shows the dimensions of the play area.

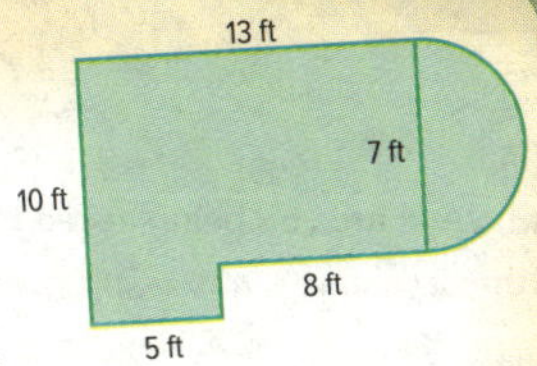

What is the area of the play area to be mulched? Round to the nearest tenth if necessary.

1 Understand *What are the facts?*

You know the shape and dimensions of the play area.

2 Plan *What is your strategy to solve this problem?*

Find the area of the two rectangles and the semi-circle, and then add.

3 Solve *How can you apply the strategy?*

Area of Rectangle 1	Area of Rectangle 2	Area of Semi-Circle
$A = \ell w$	$A = \ell w$	$A = \frac{\pi r^2}{2}$
$A = 5 \cdot 10$	$A = 8 \cdot 7$	$A = \frac{3.14 \cdot (3.5)^2}{2}$
$A =$ 50	$A =$ 56	$A =$ 19.2

The total area is 50 + 56 + 19.2 or 125.2 square feet.

4 Check *Does the answer make sense?*

The play area is about 13 • 10 or 130 square feet. So, an answer of 125.2 square feet is reasonable.

Analyze the Strategy

Tutor

MP **Reason Inductively** Why is breaking this problem into simpler parts a good strategy to solve it?

Sample answer: Finding the areas of the separate geometric figures and then adding is easier than trying to find the area of the whole figure at once.

Focus narrowing the scope

Objective Solve problems by solving a simpler problem. This lesson emphasizes MP **Mathematical Practice 1** Persevere with Problems.

Solve a Simpler Problem Many problems are composed of several connected problems. By breaking such problems into parts, students can solve them more easily.

Coherence connecting within and across grades

Now
Students solve non-routine problems.

Next
Students will apply the solve a simpler problem strategy to find volume.

Rigor pursuing concepts, fluency, and applications

See the Levels of Complexity chart on page 649.

ENGAGE EXPLORE EXPLAIN ELABORATE EVALUATE

1 Launch the Lesson

The problems on pages 647 and 648 are intended to be used as a whole-group discussion on how to solve non-routine problems and are designed to provide scaffolded guidance. The problem on page 647 walks students through the solution, while the problem on page 648 asks students to solve.

Case #1 Playgrounds

BL Have students extend the problem by having them answer the question below.

Ask:

- *Cari solved the problem by subtracting the area of the 3 × 8 rectangle from the area of the 10 × 13 rectangle and adding the area of the semi-circle. Explain her strategy.* She made a larger rectangle with shaded and unshaded regions. She found the width of the unshaded rectangle by subtracting 10 − 7.

Case #2 Wallpaper

AL EL **Circle the Sage** Poll the class to see which students have some knowledge of the *solve a simpler problem* strategy. Those students (the sages) spread out around the room. Assign the rest of the students to teams. Have the teams split up with each team member going to a different sage, if possible. Have the sages lead the discussion of each step for *Paint*. When the problem is complete, have students return to their teams and compare solutions. Have them discuss how the sages may have explained the steps differently. MP 1, 5, 7

BL EL **Roundtable** In teams of four, have one student be responsible to complete one of the four steps. The first student will complete Step 1 and record their answer in their text. Have that student pass their text clockwise to the next student and that student records Step 2. Continue until all four steps are completed. Then have students discuss their answers to each step. MP 1, 5, 7

Need Another Example?
Ben and Sheila are going to paint the wall of a room as shown in the diagram. What is the area that will be painted? 67 ft^2

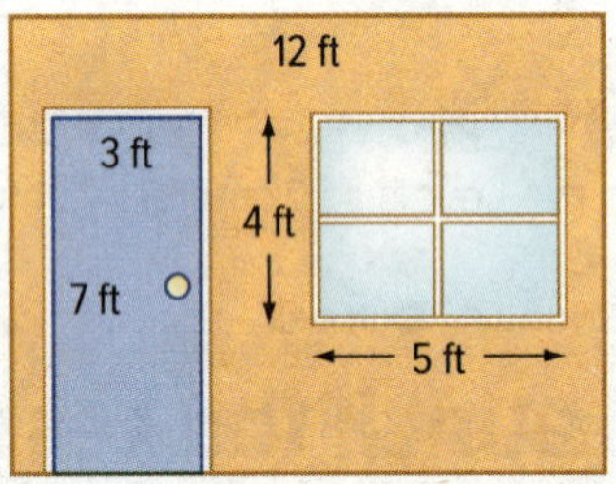

Case #2 Wallpaper

Dora is painting a wall in her house.

What is the area that will be painted?

1 Understand

Read the problem. What are you being asked to find?

I need to find the area of the wall being painted.

What information do you know?

The picture shows the wall is 12 feet long and 10 feet high.

There is a window that is 2 feet by 3 feet.

2 Plan

Choose a problem-solving strategy.

I will use the solve a simpler problem strategy.

3 Solve

Use your problem-solving strategy to solve the problem.

Find the area of the wall. Then subtract the area of the window.

The dimensions of the wall are 12 feet by 10 feet.

So, the area of the wall is $12 \times 10 = 120$ ft^2.

The dimensions of the window are 2 feet by 3 feet.

So, the area of the window is $2 \times 3 = 6$ ft^2.

$120 - 6 = 114$

So, the area of the wall to be painted is 114 ft^2.

4 Check

Use information from the problem to check your answer.

Use estimation to check the reasonableness of your answer. The area of the wall is approximately $10 \times 12 = 120$ ft^2. The answer is reasonable.

Work with a small group to solve the following cases. Show your work on a separate piece of paper.

Case #3 Woodworking

Two workers can make two chairs in two days.

How many chairs can 8 workers working at the same rate make in 20 days?

80 chairs

Case #4 Tips

Ebony wants to leave an 18% tip for a $19.82 restaurant bill. The tax is 6.25%, which is added to the bill before the tip.

How much money does Ebony spend at the restaurant? Explain.

$24.63; Add the percent of tax and percent of tip to find the total percent, $0.18 + 0.0625 = 0.2425$. Multiply the bill by the tax, $19.82 \cdot 0.2425 = 4.81$. Add 19.82 and 4.81. The total is $24.63.

Case #5 Continents

The land area of Earth is 57,505,708 square miles.

To the nearest tenth, how much larger is the land area of Asia than North America? Explain.

7,763,270.6 mi^2; Sample answer: The area of Asia is about 17,251,712.4 mi^2 and the area of North America is about 9,488,441.8 mi^2.
$17,251,712.4 - 9,488,441.8 = 7,763,270.6$

Continent	Percent of Earth's Land
Asia	30
Africa	20.2
North America	16.5

Use any strategy!

Case #6 Fountains

Mr. Flores has a circular fountain with a radius of 5 feet. He plans on installing a brick path around the fountain.

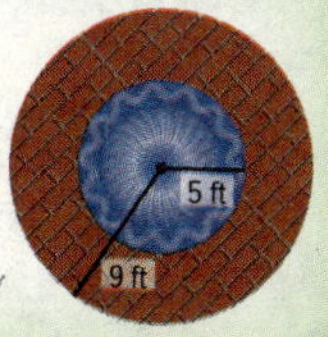

If each brick covers 2 square feet, how many bricks will he need to buy?.

88 bricks

ENGAGE EXPLORE **EXPLAIN** **ELABORATE** EVALUATE

2 Collaborate

Levels of Complexity

The levels of the exercises progress from 1 to 3, with Level 1 indicating the lowest level of complexity.

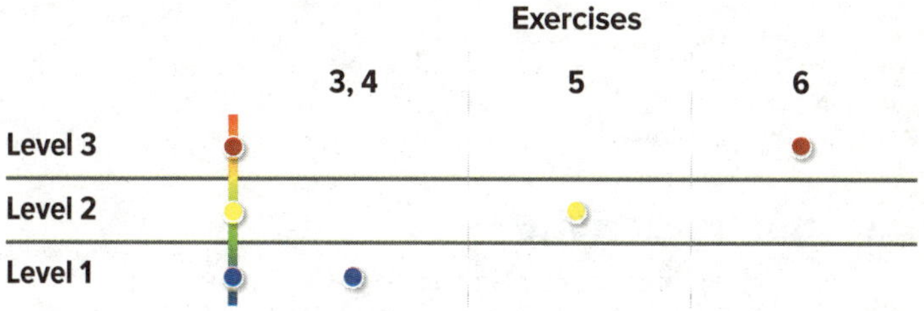

AL **EL** **Pairs Discussion** Have students complete Cases 3–6 individually. After they have completed the Cases, have them work in pairs and discuss their answers. Each partner takes turns speaking their answers aloud and listening to the other present their answers. Be sure to have students address any incorrect answers. MP 1, 4, 5, 6

BL **EL** **Trade-a-Problem** Have students write a real-world problem that is similar to Case 6. Students trade their problems and have partners solve using the *solve a simpler problem* strategy. MP 1, 4

Mid-Chapter Check

If students have trouble with Exercises 1–7, they may need help with the following concepts.

Concept	Exercise(s)
circumference and area of circles (Lesson 1 and 2)	1, 3–5
area of composite figures (Lesson 3)	2, 7
volume of a prism (Lesson 4)	6

Vocabulary Activity

EL **Numbered Heads Together** Have students work in a small group to complete Exercise 1. Each student is assigned a number. Students are responsible to ensure that each group member understands the meaning of a complementary angles. Students should ask each other for clarification and assistance, as needed. Call on one numbered student to share their definition with the class. MP 1, 6

ALEKS® provides additional remediation support with personalized instruction and practice for those who are struggling, while providing enhanced learning for those who have mastered the concepts.

Alternate Strategies

AL EL Have students refer back to Lesson 1 to review the definition of circumference.

BL EL Have students look for examples of circles around the classroom. Then use a ruler to find the diameter and find the circumferences of the circles.

Mid-Chapter Check

Vocabulary Check

1. MP **Be Precise** Define *circumference*. Explain how to find the circumference of a circle. (Lesson 1)
Circumference is the distance around a circle. Find circumference by using the formula $C = \pi d$ where d represents the diameter of the circle or the formula $C = 2\pi r$ where r represents its radius.

2. Fill in the blank in the sentence below with the correct term. (Lesson 3)
A composite figure is made up of two or more shapes.

Skills Check and Problem Solving

Find the circumference and area of each circle. Use 3.14 for π. Round to the nearest tenth if necessary. (Lessons 1 and 2)

3. circumference = 50.2 in.
area = 201.0 in^2

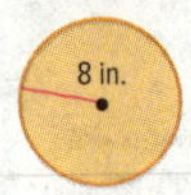

4. circumference = 28.3 cm
area = 63.6 cm^2

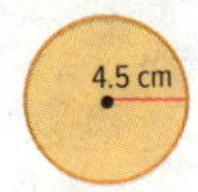

5. circumference = 52.8 mi
area = 221.6 mi^2

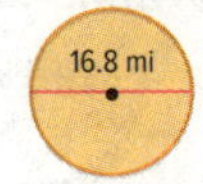

6. The dimensions of a cardboard box are shown in the figure at the right. What is the volume of the box? (Lesson 4)
440 ft^3

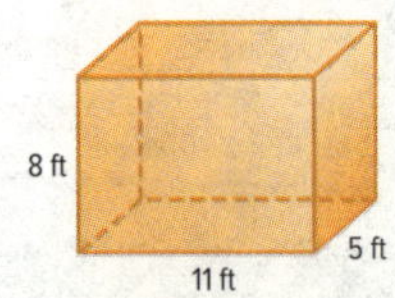

7. MP **Persevere with Problems** The figure at the right represents the design for a new hole for a miniature golf course. The new turf to cover the hole costs $1.50 per square foot. How much will it cost to cover the entire area? (Lesson 3)
$52.71

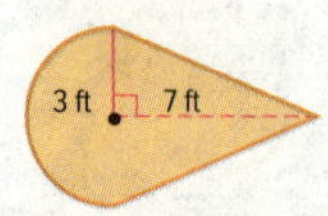

PD | RtI | Watch | Worksheets | Vocab | Tutor | Tools | Check | English Learners | Sketchpad

PRESENT

IWB

An Interactive Whiteboard Ready presentation is available for each lesson in the chapter.

Inquiry Lab
Volume of Pyramids

Inquiry WHAT is the relationship between the volume of a prism and the volume of a pyramid with the same base area and height?

Content Standards
7.G.6

MP Mathematical Practices
1, 3, 5

A movie theater offers two different containers of popcorn: a square prism and a square pyramid. Both containers are 4 inches tall and have a base area of 16 square inches. Determine the container that holds more popcorn.

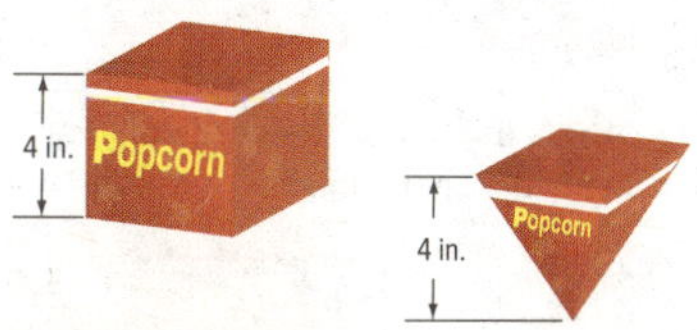

Hands-On Activity

Nets are two-dimensional patterns of three-dimensional figures.

Step 1 Draw the nets of the popcorn containers shown below onto card stock. Cut out and tape each net to form its shape. The prism and pyramid will be open. The pyramid is composed of [4] congruent isosceles triangles with bases of 4 inches and heights of $4\frac{1}{2}$ inches.

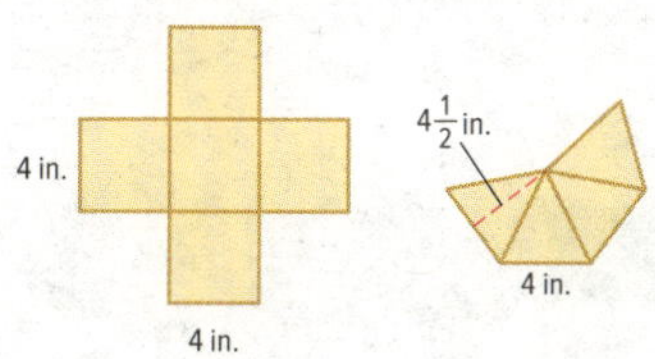

Step 2 Fill the pyramid with rice. Pour the rice from the pyramid into the prism and repeat until the prism is full. Slide a ruler across the top to level the amount.

It took [3] pyramids of rice to fill the prism.

So, the square prism container holds more popcorn than the square pyramid container.

Focus narrowing the scope

Objective Justify formulas for the volume of pyramids. 7.G.6

Coherence connecting within and across grades

Now
Students justify formulas for the volume of pyramids.

Next
Students will use a formula to find the volume of a pyramid.

Rigor pursuing concepts, fluency, and applications

See the Levels of Complexity chart on page 652.

ENGAGE EXPLORE EXPLAIN ELABORATE EVALUATE

1 Launch the Lab

The Activity is intended to be used as a whole-group activity.

Materials: card stock, uncooked rice

Hands-On Activity

AL EL **Paired Heads Together** Have students work in pairs to complete the Activity. Assign each student a number. Pairs should ensure that each partner understands the activity. Call up on a numbered student to share their responses with the class. MP 1, 5, 7

BL Omit the Activity and proceed directly to the Investigate section.

2 Collaborate

The **Investigate** and **Analyze and Reflect** sections are intended to be used as small-group investigations. The **Create** section is intended to be used as independent exercises.

Levels of Complexity

The levels of the exercises progress from 1 to 3, with Level 1 indicating the lowest level of complexity.

	Exercises 1–3	Exercises 4, 5	Exercises 6, 7
Level 3			●
Level 2		●	
Level 1	●		

Investigate

AL EL Team-Pair-Solo Have students work in groups of 4 to complete Exercise 1. Then have each group split into two pairs to complete Exercises 2 and 3, ensuring that each partner understands. Finally, call on one random student to explain their responses to Exercises 1–3. MP 1, 5, 7

Analyze and Reflect

AL EL Pairs Check Have students work in pairs to complete Exercises 4 and 5 and trade their answers with another pair of students to check their work. MP 1

Create

Inquiry Students should be able to answer "WHAT is the relationship between the volume of a prism and the volume of a pyramid with the same base area and height?" Check for student understanding and provide guidance, if needed.

Investigate

MP Use Math Tools **Work with a partner to repeat the Activity with the rectangular prism and the rectangular pyramid shown.**

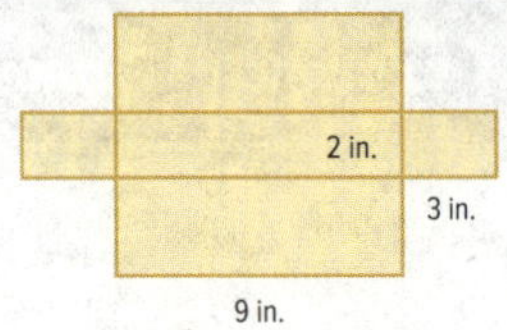

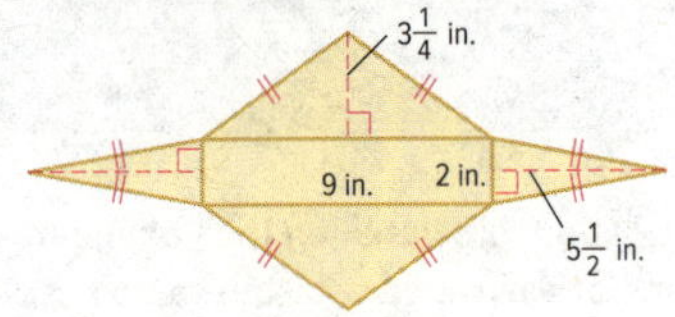

1. How many pyramids of rice did it take to fill the prism?
   Sample answer: It took three pyramids of rice to fill the prism.

2. What is true about the bases of your rectangular prism and rectangular pyramid? the heights?
   Sample answer: The bases and the heights appear to be the same.

3. Refer to the Activity. What is true about the bases of the square prism and square pyramid? the heights?
   Sample answer: The bases and the heights are the same.

Analyze and Reflect

4. What fraction of the volume of the rectangular prism is the volume of the rectangular pyramid? $\frac{1}{3}$

5. Refer to the Activity. What fraction of the volume of the square prism is the volume of the square pyramid? $\frac{1}{3}$

Create

6. **MP Reason Inductively** How can you find volume of a pyramid given a prism with the same base area and height? Write a formula for the volume of a pyramid based on the formula for the volume of a prism.
   Sample answer: Multiply the volume of the prism by $\frac{1}{3}$; $V = \frac{1}{3}Bh$

7. **Inquiry** WHAT is the relationship between the volume of a prism and the volume of a pyramid with the same base area and height?
   Sample answer: The volume of the pyramid is $\frac{1}{3}$ the volume of the prism.

IWB

An Interactive Whiteboard Ready presentation is available for each lesson in the chapter.

Geometry

Lesson 5

Volume of Pyramids

Real-World Link

Sand Sculpture Dion is helping his mother build a sand sculpture at the beach in the shape of a pyramid. The square pyramid has a base with a length and width of 12 inches each and a height of 14 inches.

1. Label the dimensions of the sand sculpture on the square pyramid below.

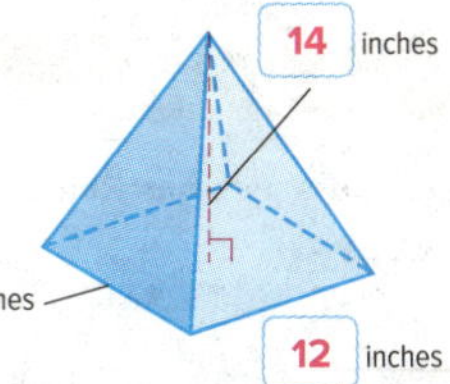

2. What is the area of the base of the pyramid?
   144 in^2

3. What is the volume of a square prism with the same dimensions as the pyramid?
   $2{,}016 \text{ in}^3$

Essential Question

HOW do measurements help you describe real-world objects?

Vocabulary

lateral face

Content Standards
7.G.6

MP Mathematical Practices
1, 3, 4, 6

Which MP **Mathematical Practices** did you use? Shade the circle(s) that applies.

1. Persevere with Problems
2. Reason Abstractly
3. Construct an Argument
4. Model with Mathematics
5. Use Math Tools
6. Attend to Precision
7. Make Use of Structure
8. Use Repeated Reasoning

Focus narrowing the scope

Objective Find the volume of pyramids. 7.G.6

Coherence connecting within and across grades

Previous Students found the volume of a prism.

Now Students will find the volume of pyramids.

Next Students will find the lateral area and total surface area of prisms and pyramids.

Rigor pursuing concepts, fluency, and applications

See the Levels of Complexity chart on page 657.

ENGAGE EXPLORE EXPLAIN ELABORATE EVALUATE

1 Launch the Lesson

Ideas for Use

You may wish to launch the lesson using a whole group, small group, think-pair-share activity, or independent activity.

EL **Team-Pair-Solo** Have students work in a small team to complete Exercise 1, ensuring that each team member understands how to draw the prism. Then have the team divide into pairs to complete Exercise 2. Finally, have them work alone to complete Exercise 3. Have them rejoin their original team to compare answers to Exercises 1–3. MP 1, 7

Alternate Strategy

AL You may wish to have the square prism in Exercise 3 already drawn and labeled for students.

2 Teach the Concept

Ask the scaffolded questions for each example to differentiate instruction.

Examples

IWB

1. Find the volume of a pyramid.

AL
- *What is the shape of the base?* rectangle
- *What are the shapes of the lateral faces?* triangles

OL
- *What is the formula for the area of the base?* $A = bh$
- *What is the area of the base?* 3.2 in. × 1.4 in. = 4.48 in^2

BL
- *Why do we multiply by $\frac{1}{3}$?* The volume of a pyramid is one-third the volume of a prism with the same base area and height.

Need Another Example?
Find the volume of a pyramid that has a height of 3.3 inches and a rectangular base with a length of 4.2 inches and a width of 2.1 inches. Round to the nearest tenth. 9.7 in^3

2. Find the volume of a pyramid.

AL
- *What is the shape of the base?* triangle
- *What are the shapes of the lateral faces?* triangles

OL
- *What is the formula for the area of a triangle? What is the area of the base?* $A = \frac{1}{2}bh$; 25.92 m^2
- *What is the height of the pyramid?* 11 m

BL
- *How are the lateral faces of a prism different from the lateral faces of a pyramid?* The lateral faces of a prism are rectangles. The lateral faces of a pyramid are triangles.

Need Another Example?
Find the volume of the pyramid. Round to the nearest tenth.
119.2 ft^3

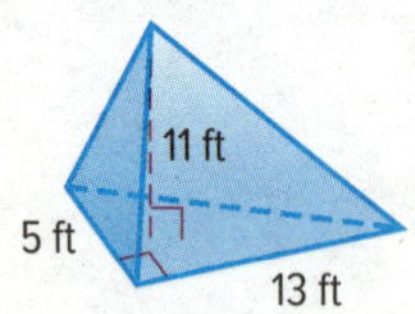

Key Concept

Volume of a Pyramid

Words The volume V of a pyramid is one third the area of the base B times the height of the pyramid h.

Symbols $V = \frac{1}{3}Bh$

Model

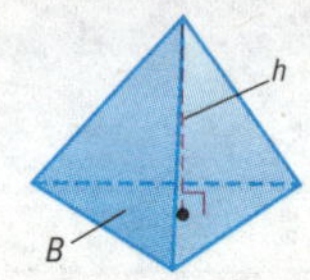

Work Zone

In a polyhedron, any face that is not a base is called a **lateral face**. The lateral faces of a pyramid meet at a common vertex. The height of a pyramid is the distance from the vertex perpendicular to the base.

Examples

Tutor

1. Find the volume of the pyramid. Round to the nearest tenth.

$V = \frac{1}{3}Bh$ — Volume of a pyramid

$V = \frac{1}{3}(3.2 \cdot 1.4)2.8$ — $B = 3.2 \cdot 1.4$, $h = 2.8$

$V \approx 4.2$ — Simplify.

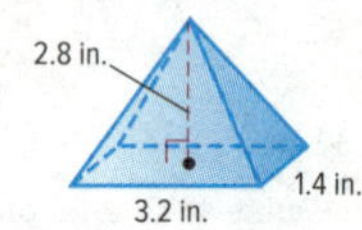

The volume is about 4.2 cubic inches.

2. Find the volume of the pyramid. Round to the nearest tenth.

$V = \frac{1}{3}Bh$ — Volume of a pyramid

$V = \frac{1}{3}\left(\frac{1}{2} \cdot 8.1 \cdot 6.4\right)11$ — $B = \frac{1}{2} \cdot 8.1 \cdot 6.4$, $h = 11$

$V = 95.04$ — Simplify.

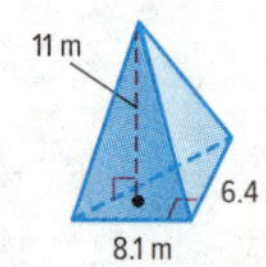

The volume is about 95.0 cubic meters.

Got it? Do this problem to find out.

Show your work.

a. Find the volume of a pyramid that has a height of 9 centimeters and a rectangular base with a length of 7 centimeters and a width of 3 centimeters.

a. 63 cm^3

Find the Height of a Pyramid

You can also use the formula for the volume of a pyramid to find a missing height.

Examples

3. **The rectangular pyramid shown has a volume of 90 cubic inches. Find the height of the pyramid.**

$V = \frac{1}{3}Bh$ Volume of a pyramid

$90 = \frac{1}{3}(9 \cdot 5)h$ $V = 90, B = 9 \cdot 5$

$90 = 15h$ Multiply.

$\frac{90}{15} = \frac{15h}{15}$ Divide by 15.

$6 = h$ Simplify.

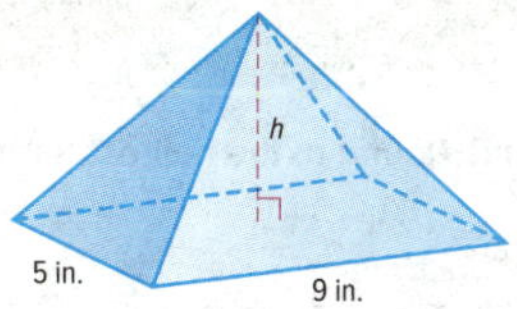

The height of the pyramid is 6 inches.

4. **A triangular pyramid has a volume of 44 cubic meters. It has an 8-meter base and a 3-meter height. Find the height of the pyramid.**

$V = \frac{1}{3}Bh$ Volume of a pyramid

$44 = \frac{1}{3}\left(\frac{1}{2} \cdot 8 \cdot 3\right)h$ $V = 44, B = \frac{1}{2} \cdot 8 \cdot 3$

$44 = 4h$ Multiply.

$\frac{44}{4} = \frac{4h}{4}$ Divide by 4.

$11 = h$ Simplify.

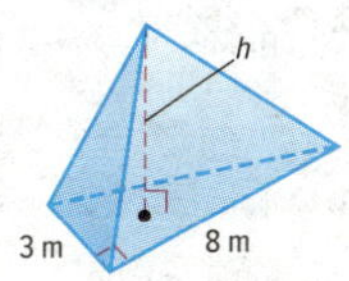

The height of the pyramid is 11 meters.

Multiplying Fractions

To find $\frac{1}{3} \cdot \frac{1}{2} \cdot 8 \cdot 3$, multiply $\frac{1}{3} \cdot \frac{1}{2}$ and $8 \cdot 3$ to get $\frac{1}{6}$ and 24, then find $\frac{1}{6}$ of 24.

Got it? **Do these problems to find out.**

b. A triangular pyramid has a volume of 840 cubic inches. The triangular base has a base length of 20 inches and a height of 21 inches. Find the height of the pyramid.

c. A rectangular pyramid has a volume of 525 cubic feet. It has a base of 25 feet by 18 feet. Find the height of the pyramid.

Show your work.

b. 12 in.

c. 3.5 ft

IWB

Examples

3. **Find the height of a pyramid.**

AL
- *What is the shape of the base?* rectangle
- *What is the volume of the rectangular pyramid?* 90 in^3

OL
- *What is the area of the base?* 45 in^2
- *What is one third of the area of the base?* 15 in^2
- *Why do we divide both sides by 15?* to isolate *h*

BL
- *How can you determine if your answer is accurate?* Substitute the value 6 for the height of the prism and determine if the volume is 90 in^3.

Need Another Example?
The triangular pyramid shown has a volume of 110 cubic centimeters. What is the height of the pyramid? 6 cm

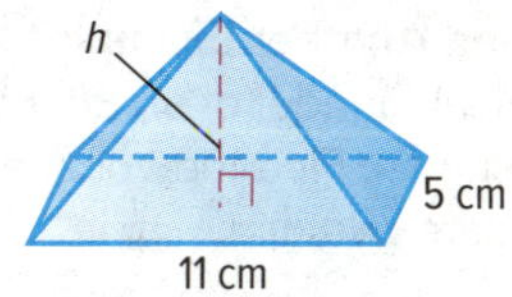

4. **Find the height of a pyramid.**

AL
- *What is the shape of the base?* triangle
- *What is the volume of the triangular pyramid?* 44 m^3

OL
- *What is the area of the base?* 12 m^2
- *What is one third of the area of the base?* 4 m^2
- *Why do we divide both sides by 4?* to isolate *h*

BL
- *How can you determine if your answer is accurate?* Substitute the value 11 for the height of the prism and determine if the volume is 44 m^3.

Need Another Example?
A triangular pyramid has a volume of 12 cubic inches. The triangular base has a 4-inch base and a 3-inch height. Find the height of the pyramid. 6 in.

IWB

Example

5. Find the volume of a pyramid.

AL • *What are the dimensions of the base?* 12 in. × 12 in.

• *What is the shape of the base?* square

OL • *What is the height of the pyramid?* 12 in.

• *In a square pyramid, what are the shapes of the lateral faces?* triangles

BL • *What is another way to express 12 × 12 × 12?* 12^3

• *What would be the volume of a square prism with the same base area and prism height?* 576 in^3

Need Another Example?
A scale model of an Egyptian pyramid is shown. Find the volume of the square pyramid. 216 in^3

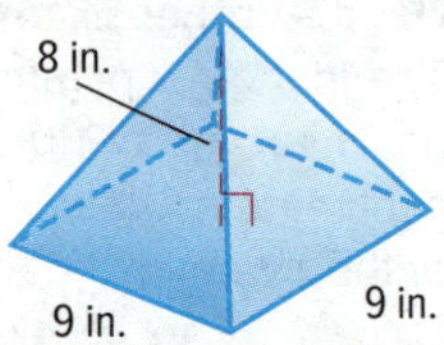

Guided Practice

Formative Assessment Use these exercises to assess students' understanding of the concepts in this lesson.

If some of your students are not ready for assignments, use the differentiated activities below.

AL EL **Rally Coach** Have students work in pairs to complete Exercises 1–6. As one student verbally describes each step, their partner listens, coaches, and praises. Students alternate roles for each exercise. MP 1, 2, 7

BL EL **Pairs Consult** Have students rewrite the volume formula in Exercises 3 and 4, so that the variable *h* is isolated on one side of the equal sign. MP 1, 2, 7

Real World

Example

Tutor

5. Kamilah is making a model of the Food Guide Pyramid for a class project. Find the volume of the square pyramid.

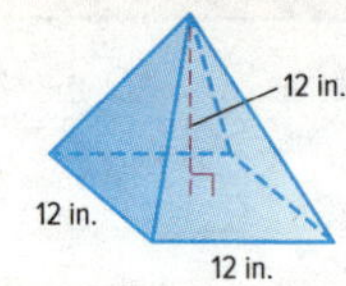

$V = \frac{1}{3}Bh$ — Volume of a pyramid

$V = \frac{1}{3}(12 \cdot 12)12$ — $B = 12 \cdot 12$, $h = 12$

$V = 576$ — Multiply.

The volume is 576 cubic inches.

Guided Practice

Check

Find the volume of each pyramid. Round to the nearest tenth if necessary. (Examples 1 and 2)

1. 2,683.3 yd^3

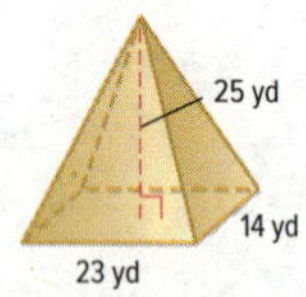

2. 3.8 cm^3

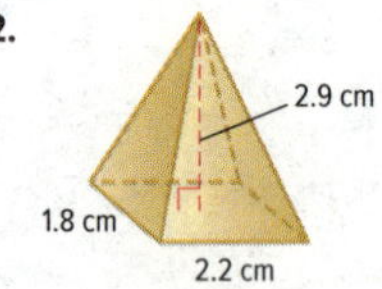

Find the height of each pyramid. (Examples 3 and 4)

3. square pyramid: volume 1,024 cm^3; base edge 16 cm 12 cm

4. triangular pyramid: volume 48 in^3; base edge 9 in.; base height 4 in. 8 in.

Show your work.

5. The Transamerica Pyramid is a skyscraper in San Francisco. The rectangular base has a length of 175 feet and a width of 120 feet. The height is 853 feet. Find the volume of the building. (Example 5) 5,971,000 ft^3

6. **Building on the Essential Question** When you are finding the volume of a pyramid, why is it important to know the shape of the base of the pyramid?
Sample answer: In the formula $V = \frac{1}{3}Bh$, B will be different depending on the shape of the base.

Rate Yourself!

How well do you understand volume of pyramids? Circle the image that applies.

For more help, go online to access a Personal Tutor.

Tutor

FOLDABLES Time to update your Foldable!

Mitch Hrdlicka/Getty Images

Name ______________________ My Homework ______________________

Independent Practice

Go online for Step-by-Step Solutions eHelp

Find the volume of each pyramid. Round to the nearest tenth if necessary. (Examples 1 and 2)

1. 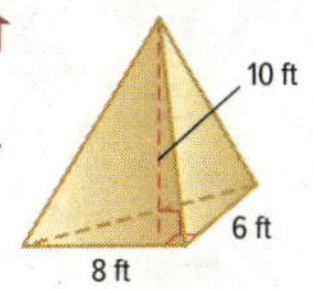

Show your work.

80 ft^3

2. 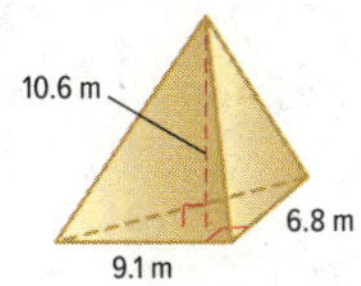

109.3 m^3

3. 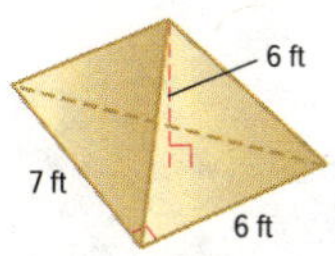

42 ft^3

4. 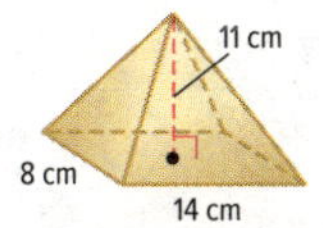

410.7 cm^3

Find the height of each pyramid. (Examples 3 and 4)

5. rectangular pyramid: volume 448 in^3; base edge 12 in.; base length 8 in.

14 in.

6. triangular pyramid: volume 270 cm^3; base edge 15 cm; height of base 4 cm

27 cm

7. A glass pyramid has a height of 4 inches. Its rectangular base has a length of 3 inches and a width of 2.5 inches. Find the volume of glass used to create the pyramid. (Example 5)

10 in^3

8. The Pyramid Arena in Memphis, Tennessee, is a square pyramid that is 321 feet tall. The base has 600-foot sides. Find the volume of the pyramid. (Example 5)

38,520,000 ft^3

ENGAGE EXPLORE **EXPLAIN** **ELABORATE** **EVALUATE**

3 Practice and Apply

Independent Practice and Extra Practice

The Independent Practice pages are meant to be used as the homework assignment. The Extra Practice page can be used for additional reinforcement or as a second-day assignment.

Levels of Complexity

The levels of the exercises progress from 1 to 3, with Level 1 indicating the lowest level of complexity.

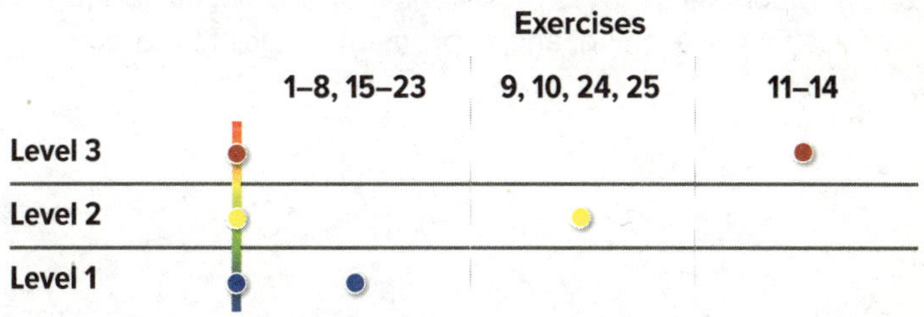

Suggested Assignments

You can use the table below that includes exercises of all complexity levels to select appropriate exercises for your students' needs.

Differentiated Homework Options		
AL	Approaching Level	1–9, 11, 13, 14, 24, 25
OL	On Level	1–7 odd, 9–11, 13, 14, 24, 25
BL	Beyond Level	9–14, 24, 25

McGraw Hill Education ALEKS® can provide additional remediation support with personalized instruction and practice.

MP MATHEMATICAL PRACTICES

Emphasis On	Exercise(s)
1 Make sense of problems and persevere in solving them.	12
3 Construct viable arguments and critique the reasoning of others.	9, 13, 14
6 Attend to precision.	11

Mathematical Practices 1, 3, and 4 are aspects of mathematical thinking that are emphasized in every lesson. Students are given opportunities to be persistent in their problem solving, to express their reasoning, and apply mathematics to real-world situations.

Formative Assessment

Use this activity as a closing formative assessment before dismissing students from your class.

TICKET Out the Door

Have students write the steps to how they would find the volume of a triangular pyramid. See students' work.

Watch Out!

Common Error Students may forget to multiply the product of the base and height by one-half when calculating the volume of triangular pyramids. Remind students that the formula for finding the area of the base of a pyramid, B, differs depending on the shape of the base. It can be $B = \ell w$ for a rectangle, $B = s^2$ for a square, or $B = \frac{1}{2}bh$ for a triangle.

9. MP **Reason Inductively** A rectangular pyramid has a length of 14 centimeters, a width of 9 centimeters, and a height of 10 centimeters. Explain the effect on the volume if each dimension were doubled.

The volume is eight times greater; Sample answer: Since each dimension is two times greater, the volume is $2 \times 2 \times 2$ or eight times greater.

10. Find the height of a square pyramid that has a volume of $25\frac{3}{5}$ meters and a base with 4 meter sides.

$4\frac{4}{5}$ meters

H.O.T. Problems Higher Order Thinking

11. MP **Be Precise** A rectangular pyramid has a volume of 160 cubic feet. Find two possible sets of measurements for the base area and height of the pyramid. Sample answer: first set: area of the base, 40 ft^2; height of the pyramid, 12 ft; second set: area of the base, 30 ft^2; height of the pyramid, 16 ft

12. MP **Persevere with Problems** A square pyramid and a cube have the same bases and volumes. How are their heights related? Explain.

The height of the pyramid is 3 times the height of the cube.

13. MP **Reason Inductively** The two figures shown have congruent bases. How does the volume of the two square pyramids in Figure B compare to the volume of the square pyramid in Figure A?

The volumes are the same.

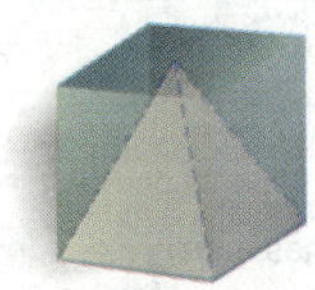

Figure A

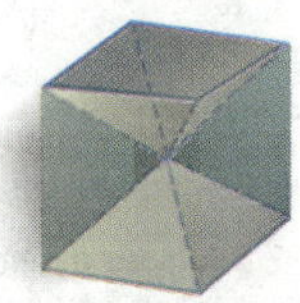

Figure B

14. MP **Reason Inductively** Determine whether the following statement is *true* or *false*. Explain your reasoning.

The volumes of a rectangular-based pyramid and a triangular-based pyramid with congruent heights and equal base areas are equal.

true; Sample answer: Both volumes are found using the formula $V = \frac{1}{3}Bh$. If the base area and the height are congruent, then the volumes are also congruent.

Name ______________________ My Homework ______________________

Extra Practice

Find the volume of each pyramid. Round to the nearest tenth if necessary.

15. 60 in^3

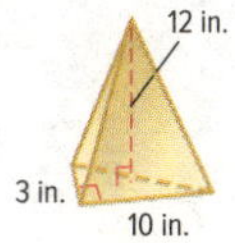

Homework Help

$V = \frac{1}{3}Bh$

$V = \frac{1}{3}\left(\frac{1}{2} \cdot 10 \cdot 3\right)12$

$V = 60$

16. 43.3 in^3

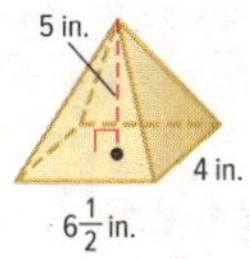

17. 195 yd^3

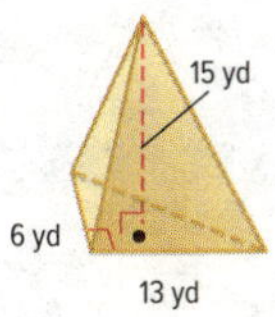

18. 61.4 cm^3

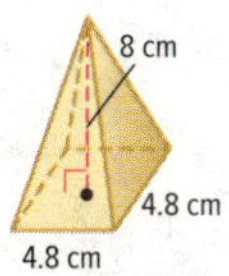

Find the height of each pyramid.

19. square pyramid: volume 297 ft^3; area of the base 81 ft^2

11 ft

20. hexagonal pyramid: volume 1,320 ft^3; area of the base 120 ft^2

33 ft

21. square pyramid: volume 550 in^3; area of the base 75 in^2

22 in.

22. rectangular pyramid: volume 3,800 m^3; area of the base 300 m^2

38 m

23. An ancient stone pyramid has a height of 13.6 meters. The edges of the square base are 16.5 meters. Find the volume of the stone pyramid.

$1{,}234.2 \text{ m}^3$

Create Your Own Homework Online

eSolutions Manual™ can be used to create worksheets for the suggested assignments on page 657, or create your own worksheets for differentiated homework or review.

Power Up! Test Practice

Exercises 24 and 25 prepare students for more rigorous thinking needed for the state assessment.

24.

This test item requires students to explain and apply mathematical concepts and solve problems with precision, while making use of structure.	
Depth of Knowledge	DOK2
Content Standard	7.G.6
Mathematical Practice	MP1
Online Experience	Students type their responses in the boxes.
Scoring Rubric	
2 points	Students correctly order each pyramid, give the corresponding volume and list the pyramid with the greatest volume.
1 point	Students complete the table but fail to list the greatest volume OR students order all of the pyramids and list the one with the greatest volume, but fail to find the volume for each OR students correctly order three of the four and find their volumes.

25.

This test item requires students to support their reasoning or evaluate the reasoning of others by justifying their response and constructing arguments.	
Depth of Knowledge	DOK2
Content Standard	7.G.3
Mathematical Practice	MP1, MP3
Online Experience	Students type their response in the box.
Scoring Rubric	
2 points	Students find the height of the pyramid and explain their response.
1 point	Students find the height but fail to explain their response OR students have a calculation error in the height but a correct mathematical explanation.

Power Up! Test Practice

24. The table shows the base dimensions and heights of 4 rectangular pyramids. Sort the pyramids from least to greatest volume.

Pyramid	ℓ (yd)	w (yd)	h (yd)
A	4	9	5
B	6	6	7
C	5	5	9
D	3	6	12

	Pyramid	Volume (yd^3)
Least	A	60
	D	72
	C	75
Greatest	B	84

Which pyramid has the greatest volume? Pyramid B

25. The rectangular pyramid shown has a volume of 1,560 cubic inches. What is the height of the pyramid? Explain how you found your answer.

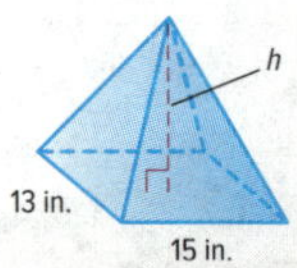

24 in.; Sample answer: Replace V with 1,560 and B with 13×15 in the formula $V = \frac{1}{3}Bh$. Then solve for h.

Spiral Review

Convert each length to feet. Then find the area of each figure in square feet.
5.MD.1

26. 135 ft^2

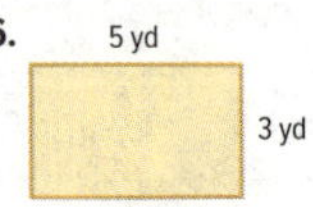

27. 1.5 ft^2

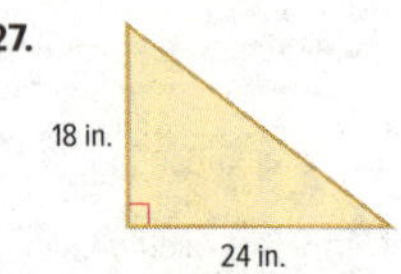

28. 1,462.5 ft^2

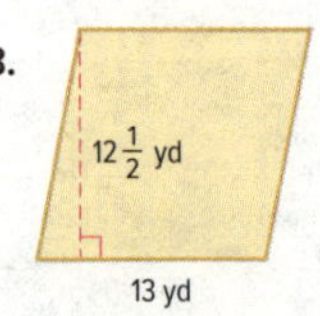

29. 28.75 ft^2

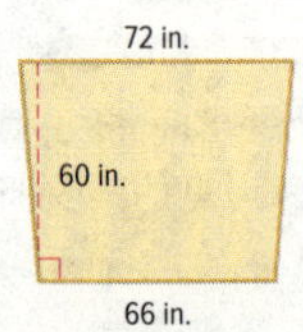

An Interactive Whiteboard Ready presentation is available for each lesson in the chapter.

Inquiry Lab

Nets of Three-Dimensional Figures

Inquiry **HOW** can models and nets help you find the surface area of prisms?

Content Standards
7.G.6

MP **Mathematical Practices**
1, 3, 6

Nets are used to design and manufacture items such as boxes and labels. Find the shapes that make up the net of a cereal box.

Hands-On Activity 1

Make a net from a rectangular prism.

Step 1 Use an empty cereal box. Cut off one of the two top flaps. The remaining top flap is the top face.

Step 2 Label the top and bottom faces using a green marker. Label the front and back faces using a blue marker. Label the left and right faces using a red marker.

Step 3 Carefully cut along the three edges of the top face. Then cut down each vertical edge.

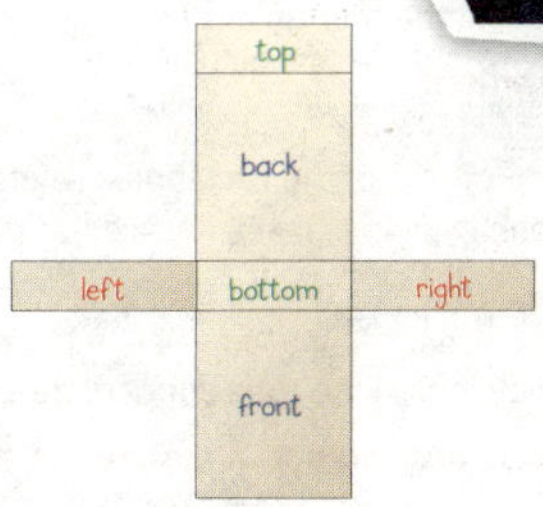

The net of a cereal box is made up of a total of 6 rectangles.

What do you notice about the top and bottom faces, the left and right faces, and the front and back faces?

They are congruent.

Focus narrowing the scope

Objective Find the total surface area of a prism using models and nets. 7.G.6

Coherence connecting within and across grades

Now
Students use nets to find the total surface area of prisms.

Next
Students will use a formula to find the lateral and total surface area of a prism.

Rigor pursuing concepts, fluency, and applications

See the Levels of Complexity chart on page 663.

ENGAGE EXPLORE EXPLAIN ELABORATE EVALUATE

1 Launch the Lab

Activities 1 and 2 are intended to be used as whole-group activities. Activity 1 is designed to provide more guidance to students than Activity 2.

Materials: empty cereal box, card stock

Hands-On Activity 1

AL EL **Pairs Consult** Provide each pair of students with an empty box. Have them work together to complete the activity. Have them pause between each step and verify with another pair that they are cutting along the correct edges and labeling the correct faces. MP 1, 5, 7

BL EL **Pairs Consult** Have students label the faces before cutting the box. After opening the box and laying it flat, have them verify if their labels were correct. MP 1, 5

Hands-On Activity 2

AL **EL** **Teammates Consult** Have students work in small teams to complete the activity. You may wish to have preprinted triangular prism nets for students to cut out. Have one student from each team demonstrate each step prior to the rest of the team completing the step. Pause between each step and have students check each other's work to verify that they are folding and taping the correct edges. MP 1, 4

BL **EL** **Pairs Discussion** After completing the activity, have students work with a partner to draw a new net where the perimeter of the base does not match the length of the rectangle formed by the left, middle, and right faces (for example the base has a perimeter of 18, but the rectangle has a length of 20). Have them attempt to fold and tape the net into a prism. Then have them explain why it does not work and why the side lengths of the faces must be congruent to the side lengths of the bases. MP 1, 4, 7

Hands-On Activity 2

Make a triangular prism from a net.

Step 1 Draw a net on a piece of card stock with the dimensions shown below.

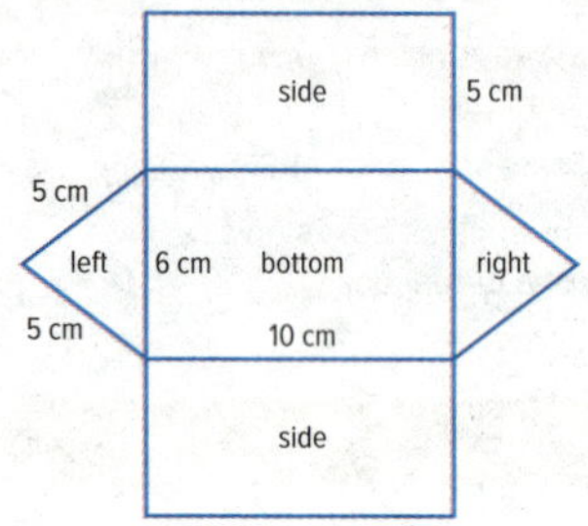

Step 2 Fold the net into a triangular prism. Tape together adjacent edges.

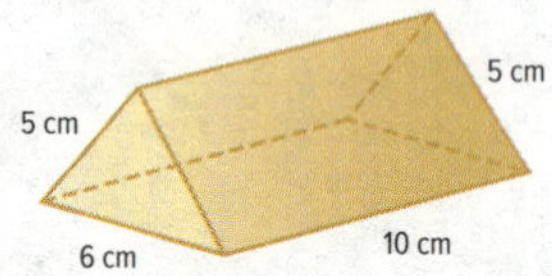

The triangular prism is made up of **2** triangles and **3** rectangles.

What is true about the triangular bases?

They are congruent.

How is the side of one of the rectangles related to the base of one of the triangles?

They are congruent.

Explain one way to find the total surface area of a triangular prism.

Sample answer: You could find the area of all five faces and add them together.

Investigate

Collaborate

Work with a partner to solve each problem.

1. A net of a rectangular prism that is 24 inches by 18 inches by 4 inches is shown. The net of the prism is labeled with *top*, *bottom*, *side*, and *end*. Fill in the boxes to find the total area of the rectangular prism.

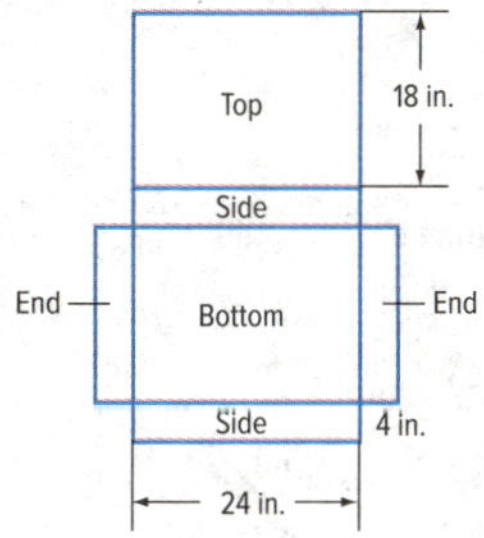

Area of Top and Bottom → 864 in^2

Area of Both Sides → 192 in^2

Area of Both Ends → + 144 in^2

Total Area → 1,200 in^2

2. Describe in words how you could find the total surface area of a rectangular prism.

Sample answer: Find the sum of the areas of each section.

3. A net of a triangular prism is shown. Fill in the boxes to find the total area of the triangular prism.

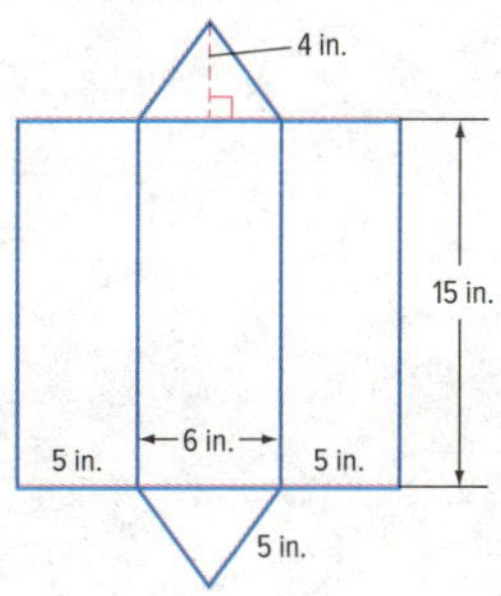

Area of Center Rectangle → 90 in^2

Area of Left and Right Rectangles → 150 in^2

Area of Triangles → + 24 in^2

Total Area → 264 in^2

4. Describe in words how you could find the total surface area of a triangular prism.

Sample answer: Find the sum of the areas of each section.

ENGAGE EXPLORE EXPLAIN ELABORATE EVALUATE

2 Collaborate

The **Investigate** and **Analyze and Reflect** sections are intended to be used as small-group investigations. The **Create** section is intended to be used as independent exercises.

Levels of Complexity

The levels of the exercises progress from 1 to 3, with Level 1 indicating the lowest level of complexity.

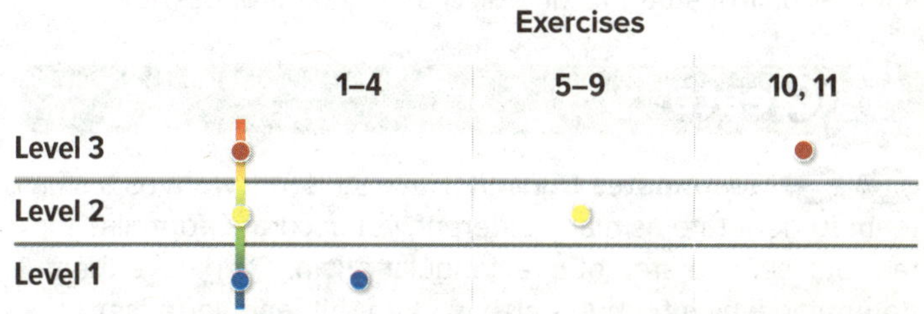

Investigate

AL EL **Group-Solo** Work together as a class to complete Exercise 1 while you, or a student volunteer, demonstrates how to find the area of each individual piece of the prism. Then have students complete Exercises 2–4 individually. MP 1, 7

BL EL **Pairs Consult** Have students work with a partner to extend the exercises by responding to the following question. MP 1, 7

Ask:

- *In Exercise 1, how can you tell what the area of the end on the right is without multiplying?* Sample answer: The two ends are the same shape and size so the area of the end on the right is the same as the area of the end on the left.

Analyze and Reflect

AL EL Pairs Discussion Have students work with a partner to complete the table. Have one partner take notes on what methods or techniques they used to complete each section of the table while the other partner keeps track of the final solutions. MP 1, 7

BL EL Pairs Discussion Have students work in pairs to complete Exercises 5–9. Have them trade their solutions with another pair of students and discuss any differences. MP 1, 7

Create

BL EL Teammates Consult Have students work as a small team to generate as many different, yet accurate, formulas for the total surface area of a rectangular prism. Then have them determine which formulas also work for a triangular prism. MP 1, 2, 7

Inquiry Students should be able to answer "HOW can models and nets help you find the surface area of prisms?" Check for student understanding and provide guidance, if needed.

Analyze and Reflect

Collaborate

Work with a partner.

5. MP **Reason Inductively** Suppose Ladell wants to wrap a present in a container that is a rectangular prism. How can he determine the amount of wrapping paper that he will need? Sample answer: Find and add the areas of the top, bottom, sides and ends of the box.

Circle each correct surface area. Draw and label the net for each figure if needed. The first one is done for you.

	Prism	Measures	Surface Area		
	Rectangular	Length: 10 cm Width: 8 cm Height: 5 cm	170 cm^2	(circled) 340 cm^2	400 cm^2
6.	Rectangular	Length: 3 ft Width: 2 ft Height: 5 ft	30 ft^2	31 ft^2	(circled) 62 ft^2
7.	Rectangular	Length: 2 m Width: 1 m Height: 1.5 m	3 m^2	6.5 m^2	(circled) 13 m^2
8.	Triangular	Area of Top and Bottom Triangles: 3 mm^2 Area of Center Rectangle: 12 mm^2 Area of Left and Right Rectangles: 10 mm^2	25 mm^2	28 mm^2	(circled) 38 mm^2
9.	Triangular	Area of Top and Bottom Triangles: 6 in^2 Area of Center Rectangle: 50.4 in^2 Area of Left and Right Rectangles: 56 in^2	(circled) 174.4 in^2	118.4 in^2	112.4 in^2

Create

On Your Own

10. MP **Be Precise** *Surface area* is the sum of the areas of all the surfaces of a three-dimensional figure. Write the formula for the total surface area of a rectangular prism.

$S.A. = 2\ell h + 2\ell w + 2hw$

11. Inquiry HOW can models and nets help you find the surface area of prisms? Models and nets show all of the faces. They provide a visual reference for finding the area of each face.

PLAN ONLINE

PD | RtI | Watch | Worksheets | Vocab | Tutor | Tools | Check | English Learners | Sketchpad

PRESENT

IWB

An Interactive Whiteboard Ready presentation is available for each lesson in the chapter.

Geometry

Lesson 6

Surface Area of Prisms

Real-World Link

Message Board Members of a local recreation center are permitted to post messages on 8.5-inch by 11-inch paper on the board. Assume the signs are posted vertically and do not overlap, as shown below.

1. Suppose 6 messages fit across the board widthwise.

   What is the width of the board in inches? 51 inches

2. Suppose 3 messages fit down the board lengthwise.

   What is the length of the board in inches? 33 inches

3. What is the area in square inches of the message board?

   1,683 in^2

4. Messages can also be posted on the other side of the board. What is the total area of the front and back of the board in square inches?

   3,366 in^2

Essential Question

HOW do measurements help you describe real-world objects?

Vocabulary

surface area

Content Standards
7.G.6

MP Mathematical Practices
1, 3, 4, 6

Which MP **Mathematical Practices** did you use? Shade the circle(s) that applies.

1. Persevere with Problems
2. Reason Abstractly
3. Construct an Argument
4. Model with Mathematics
5. Use Math Tools
6. Attend to Precision
7. Make Use of Structure
8. Use Repeated Reasoning

Focus narrowing the scope

Objective Find the surface area of prisms. 7.G.6

Coherence connecting within and across grades

Previous Students found the surface area of prisms using models and nets.

Now Students find the lateral area and total surface area of prisms.

Next Students will find the lateral area and total surface area of pyramids.

Rigor pursuing concepts, fluency, and applications

See the Levels of Complexity chart on page 669.

ENGAGE EXPLORE EXPLAIN ELABORATE EVALUATE

1 Launch the Lesson

Ideas for Use

You may wish to launch the lesson using a whole group, small group, think-pair-share activity, or independent activity.

EL **Pairs Consult** Give each pair of students a piece of 8.5 in. by 11 in. paper to decorate or write a message. Have them post their papers on an empty bulletin board without leaving space or overlapping papers. Ask how they can find the area of the bulletin board. Then have pairs complete Exercises 1–4. MP 1, 4, 7

Alternate Strategy

BL Extend the activity by giving this scenario: Another nearby message board has four sides that can be filled with notices. What is the total surface area of the message board? MP 1, 7

ENGAGE EXPLORE **EXPLAIN** ELABORATE EVALUATE

2 Teach the Concept

Ask the scaffolded questions for each example to differentiate instruction.

Example

IWB

1. Find the surface area of a rectangular prism.

AL • *What is the formula for total surface area?*
S.A. = 2ℓh + 2ℓw + 2hw

OL • *To find the surface area, what should you do?*
Substitute 9 for ℓ, 7 for w, and 13 for h in the formula and then evaluate.

BL • *By using the formula, what are you actually finding?*
Sample answer: We are finding the surface area of each of the three different sized faces. Because each face is a pair, we multiply each area by 2, then add all of them together.

Need Another Example?
Find the surface area of the rectangular prism. 72 cm^2

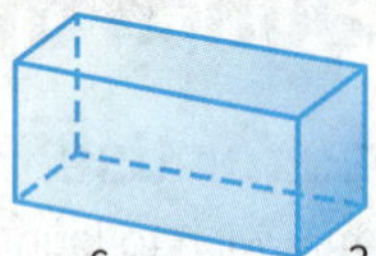

Work Zone

Key Concept

Surface Area of a Rectangular Prism

Words The surface area *S.A.* of a rectangular prism with base ℓ, width *w*, and height *h* is the sum of the areas of its faces.

Model

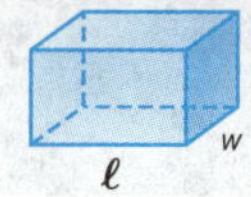

Symbols $S.A. = 2\ell h + 2\ell w + 2hw$

The sum of the areas of all the surfaces, or faces, of a three-dimensional figure is the **surface area**. In the previous Inquiry Lab, you used a net to find the surface area of a rectangular prism. You can also use a formula to find surface area.

When you find the surface area of a three-dimensional figure, the units are square units, not cubic units.

Example

Watch Tutor

1. Find the surface area of the rectangular prism shown at the right.

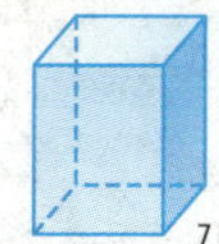

Replace ℓ with 9, *w* with 7, and *h* with 13.

$$\text{surface area} = 2\ell h + 2\ell w + 2hw$$
$$= 2 \cdot 9 \cdot 13 + 2 \cdot 9 \cdot 7 + 2 \cdot 13 \cdot 7$$
$$= 234 + 126 + 182 \quad \text{Multiply first. Then add.}$$
$$= 542$$

The surface area of the prism is 542 square inches.

Got it? **Do these problems to find out.**

Show your work.

Find the surface area of each rectangular prism.

a.

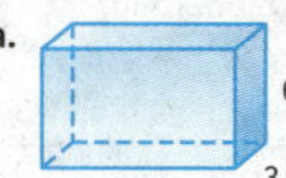

b.

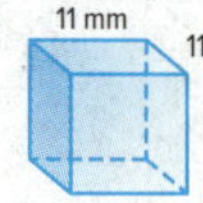

a. 216 m^2

b. 726 mm^2

Real-World Example

2. **Domingo built a toy box 60 inches long, 24 inches wide, and 36 inches high. He has 1 quart of paint that covers about 87 square feet of surface. Does he have enough to paint the outside of the toy box? Justify your answer.**

Step 1 Find the surface area of the toy box.

Replace ℓ with 60, w with 24, and h with 36.

$$\text{surface area} = 2\ell h + 2\ell w + 2hw$$
$$= 2 \cdot 60 \cdot 36 + 2 \cdot 60 \cdot 24 + 2 \cdot 36 \cdot 24$$
$$= 8{,}928 \text{ in}^2$$

Step 2 Find the number of square inches the paint will cover.

$1 \text{ ft}^2 = 1 \text{ ft} \times 1 \text{ ft}$ — Replace 1 ft with 12 in.

$= 12 \text{ in.} \times 12 \text{ in.}$ — Multiply.

$= 144 \text{ in}^2$

So, 87 square feet is equal to 87×144 or 12,528 square inches.

Since $12{,}528 > 8{,}928$, Domingo has enough paint.

Consistent Units
Since the surface area of the toy box is expressed in inches, convert 87 ft^2 to square inches so that all measurements are expressed using the same units.

Got it? **Do this problem to find out.**

c. The largest corrugated cardboard box ever constructed measured about 23 feet long, 9 feet high, and 8 feet wide. Would 950 square feet of paper be enough to cover the box? Justify your answer.

Show your work.

c. Yes; the surface area of the box is 926 ft^2 and $950 \text{ ft}^2 > 926 \text{ ft}^2$.

Surface Area of Triangular Prisms

To find the surface area of a triangular prism, it is more efficient to find the area of each face and calculate the sum of all of the faces rather than using a formula.

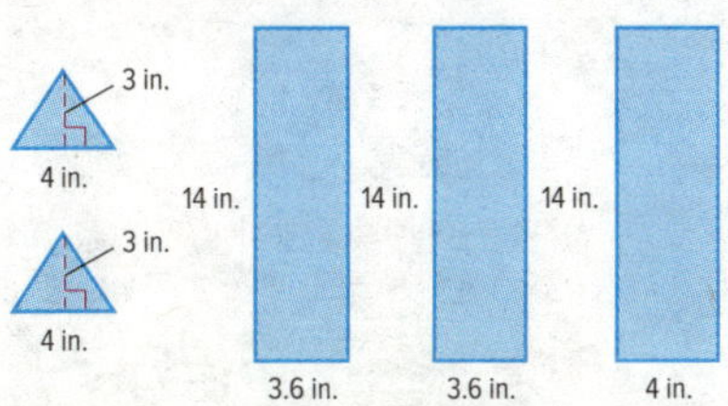

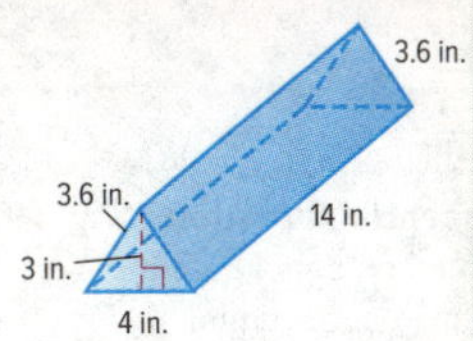

Example

IWB

2. Solve a real-world example involving the surface area of a rectangular prism.

AL
- *What do you need to find?* if Domingo has enough paint to paint the toy box
- *What do you notice about the units for the dimensions of the toy box and the units for the area that one quart of paint will cover?* The dimensions of the toy box are given in inches and the area that one quart of paint will cover are given in square feet.
- *How many inches are in one foot?* 12 in.

OL
- *How do you know this problem requires multiple steps to solve?* First, we need to find the surface area of the toy box. Then we need to convert the number of square feet that 1 quart of paint will cover to square inches. Then compare to determine if Domingo has enough paint.
- *What is the total surface area of the toy box?* 8,928 in^2
- *How many square inches are in 1 square foot? Explain.* 144; There are 12 inches in one foot, so there are 12^2, or 144, square inches in one square foot.

BL
- *If Domingo wanted to use two coats of paint to cover the toy box, does he have enough paint? Explain.* No; $8{,}928 \times 2 = 17{,}856$, which is more than 12,528.

Need Another Example?
Diana has a gift box that is 11 inches long, 8 inches wide, and 6 inches tall. She has a sheet of wrapping paper that is 4 feet long by 1 foot wide. Does she have enough wrapping paper to wrap the box? Justify your answer. yes; Since $404 < 576$, Diana has enough paper.

Example

3. Find the surface area of a triangular prism.

AL • *What is the shape of the shipping container?* triangular prism

OL • *How do you find the total surface area?* Find the area of each face and add them together. The total surface area is 168.8 in^2.

BL • *If each square inch of cardboard costs \$0.02, how much would it cost to produce the shipping container, to the nearest penny?* \$3.38

Need Another Example?
Valerie's tent is in the shape of a triangular prism. How much fabric was used to make the tent? 396.4 ft^2

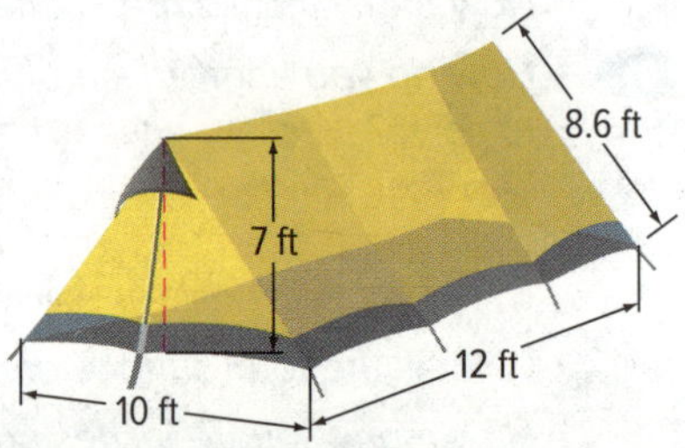

Guided Practice

Formative Assessment Use these exercises to assess students' understanding of the concepts in this lesson.

If some of your students are not ready for assignments, use the differentiated activities below.

AL EL **Pairs Discussion** For Exercises 1 and 2, have students draw the nets of the prisms to help make the connection between the nets and the formulas for lateral and total surface area. MP 1, 4, 7

BL EL **Pairs Present** Have students prepare a brief oral presentation on how their knowledge of nets and surface area connect to the formulas. Have them include diagrams and examples. Have them present their results to the class, while the rest of the class listens carefully and asks clarifying questions, if needed. MP 1, 7

Real-World Example

3. **Marty is mailing his aunt the package shown. How much cardboard is used to create the shipping container?**

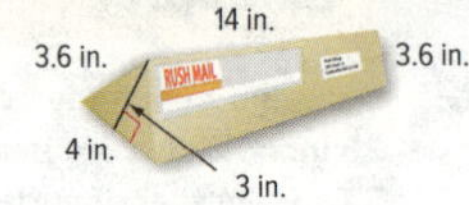

Find the area of each face and add.

The area of each triangle is $\frac{1}{2} \cdot 4 \cdot 3$ or 6.

The area of two of the rectangles is $14 \cdot 3.6$ or 50.4. The area of the third rectangle is $14 \cdot 4$ or 56.

The sum of the areas of the faces is $6 + 6 + 50.4 + 50.4 + 56$ or 168.8 square inches.

Got it? Do this problem to find out.

d. Find the surface area of the triangular prism.

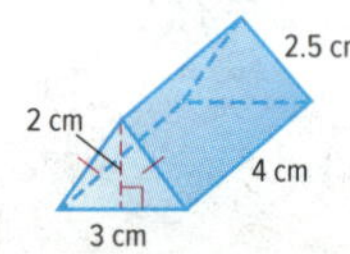

d. 38 cm^2

Guided Practice

Find the surface area of each prism. (Examples 1–3)

1.

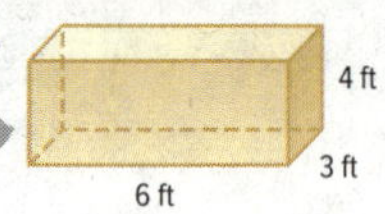

108 ft^2

2.

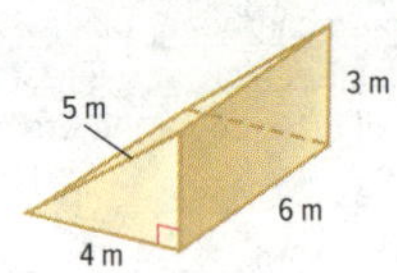

84 m^2

3. **Building on the Essential Question** Why is the surface area of a three-dimensional figure measured in square units rather than in cubic units?

Sample answer: Surface area measures the area of the faces, and area is measured in square units.

Rate Yourself!

Are you ready to move on?
Shade the section that applies.

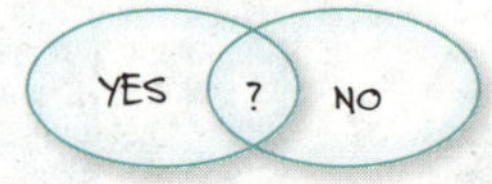

For more help, go online to access a Personal Tutor.

FOLDABLES Time to update your Foldable!

Name ____________ My Homework ____________

Independent Practice

Go online for Step-by-Step Solutions eHelp

Find the surface area of each rectangular prism. Round to the nearest tenth if necessary. (Example 1)

1. 314 cm^2

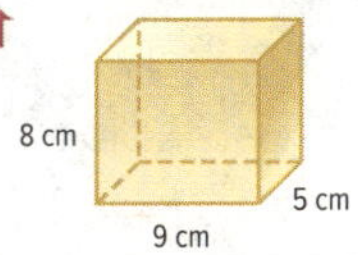

Show your work.

2. 216.2 ft^2

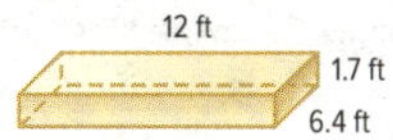

3. When making a book cover, Anwar adds an additional 20 square inches to the surface area to allow for overlap. How many square inches of paper will Anwar use to make a book cover for a book 11 inches long, 8 inches wide, and 1 inch high? (Example 2) 207 in^2

Find the surface area of each triangular prism. (Example 3)

4. 192 cm^2

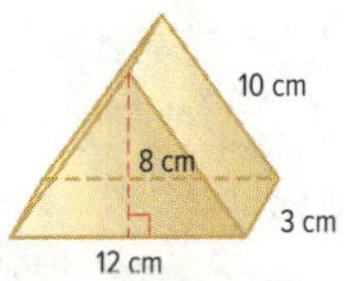

5. 180 in^2

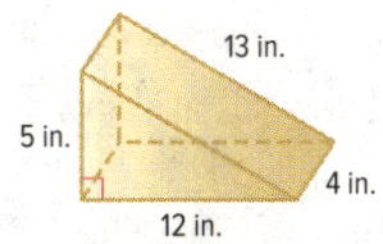

6. MP **Model with Mathematics** Refer to the graphic novel frame below. What whole number dimensions would allow the students to maximize the volume while keeping the surface area at most 160 square feet? Explain. 4 ft by 7 ft by 6 ft; The dimensions of the dunk tank are sufficient for a person to fall in and get wet.

ENGAGE EXPLORE EXPLAIN ELABORATE EVALUATE

3 Practice and Apply

Independent Practice and Extra Practice

The Independent Practice pages are meant to be used as the homework assignment. The Extra Practice page can be used for additional reinforcement or as a second-day assignment.

Levels of Complexity

The levels of the exercises progress from 1 to 3, with Level 1 indicating the lowest level of complexity.

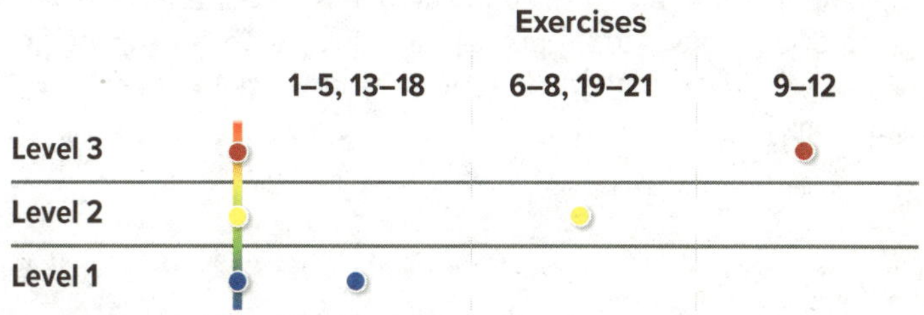

Suggested Assignments

You can use the table below that includes exercises of all complexity levels to select appropriate exercises for your students' needs.

Differentiated Homework Options		
AL	Approaching Level	1–5, 7, 9, 10, 12, 20, 21
OL	On Level	1, 3, 5–10, 12, 20, 21
BL	Beyond Level	6–12, 20, 21

McGraw Hill Education ALEKS® can provide additional remediation support with personalized instruction and practice.

Watch Out!

Common Error Students may accidentally leave out the area of a face when calculating surface area. Remind them that rectangular prisms have six faces and triangular prisms have five.

MATHEMATICAL PRACTICES

Emphasis On	Exercise(s)
1 Make sense of problems and persevere in solving them.	11
3 Construct viable arguments and critique the reasoning of others.	9, 10
4 Model with mathematics.	6, 12
6 Attend to precision.	19

Mathematical Practices 1, 3, and 4 are aspects of mathematical thinking that are emphasized in every lesson. Students are given opportunities to be persistent in their problem solving, to express their reasoning, and apply mathematics to real-world situations.

Formative Assessment
Use this activity as a closing formative assessment before dismissing students from your class.

TICKET Out the Door

Ask students to write the steps to describe how to find the surface area of a prism. See students' work.

7. Write a formula for the surface area *S.A.* of a cube in which each side measures x units.
$S.A. = 6x^2$

8. A company will make a cereal box with whole number dimensions and a volume of 100 cubic centimeters. If cardboard costs $0.05 per 100 square centimeters, what is the least cost to make 100 boxes?
$6.50

H.O.T. Problems Higher Order Thinking

9. **Reason Inductively** Determine if the following statement is *true* or *false*. Explain your reasoning.
If you double one of the dimensions of a rectangular prism, the surface area will double.
false; Sample answer: A $9 \times 7 \times 13$ rectangular prism has a surface area of $2(9 \times 13) + 2(9 \times 7) + 2(13 \times 7)$ or 542 square units. Doubling the length, the surface area is $2(18 \times 13) + 2(18 \times 7) + 2(13 \times 7)$ or 902 square units. $2 \times 542 \neq 902$

10. **Reason Inductively** A prism with a base that is a regular hexagon is shown. How would you find the surface area of the hexagonal prism if the area of the base of the prism is x square centimeters?
Sample answer: I would add the lateral area, $48y$, to the area of the bases, $2x^2$.

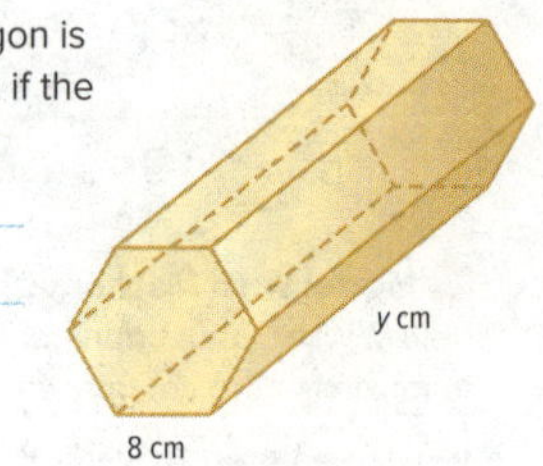

11. **Persevere with Problems** The figure at the right is made by placing a cube with 12-centimeter sides on top of another cube with 15-centimeter sides. Find the surface area of the figure.
$1{,}926\text{ cm}^2$

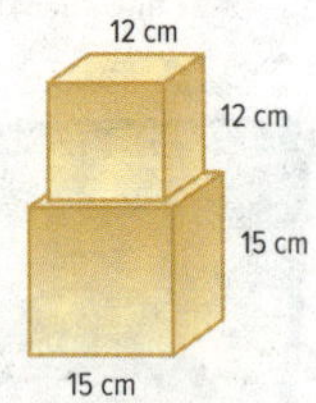

12. **Model with Mathematics** Draw and label a rectangular prism that has a total surface area between 100 and 200 square units. Then find the surface area of your prism. See students' work.

Show your work.

Name ______________________ My Homework

Extra Practice

Find the surface area of each prism. Round to the nearest tenth if necessary.

13. 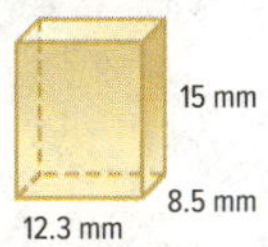

833.1 mm^2

S.A. = 2lh + 2lw + 2hw

Homework Help

= 2 • 12.3 • 15 + 2 • 12.3 • 8.5 + 2 • 15 • 8.5

= 369 + 209.1 + 255

= 833.1

14. 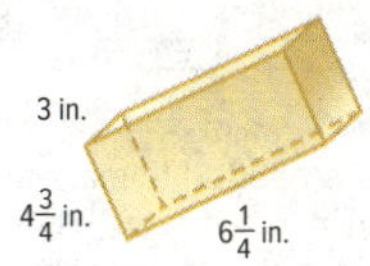

125.4 in^2

15. 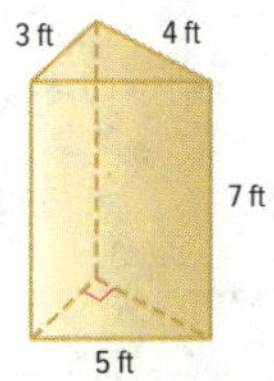

96 ft^2

16. 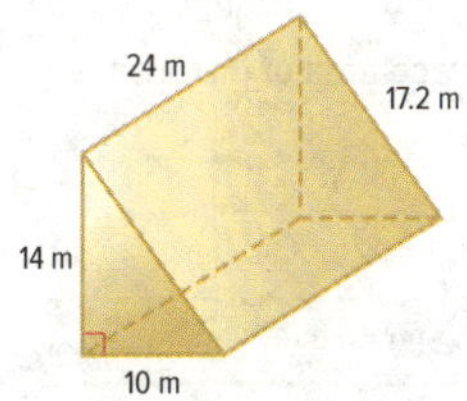

$1{,}128.8 \text{ m}^2$

17. If one gallon of paint covers 350 square feet, will 8 gallons of paint be enough to paint the inside and outside of the fence shown once? Explain.

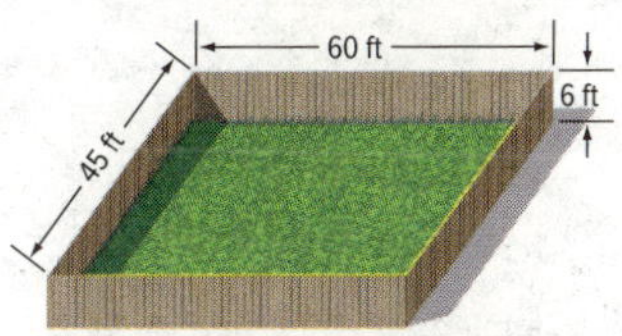

Yes; there are 2,520 ft^2 of fencing. Since 8 gallons of paint will cover 350 • 8 or 2,800 ft^2 and 2,800 ft^2 > 2,520 ft^2, 8 gallons is enough paint.

18. The attic shown is a triangular prism. Insulation will be placed inside all walls, not including the floor. Find the surface area that will be covered with insulation.

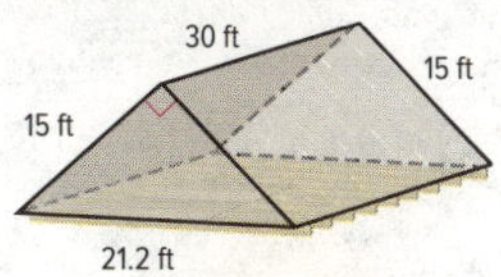

$1{,}125 \text{ ft}^2$

19. MP **Be Precise** To the nearest tenth, find the approximate amount of plastic covering the outside of the CD case.

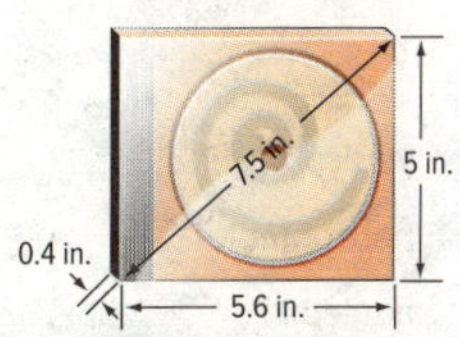

64.5 in^2

Create Your Own Homework Online

eSolutionsManual™ can be used to create worksheets for the suggested assignments on page 669, or create your own worksheets for differentiated homework or review.

Power Up! Test Practice

Exercises 20 and 21 prepare students for more rigorous thinking needed for the state assessment.

20.

This test item requires students to analyze and solve complex real-world problems through the use of mathematical tools and models.	
Depth of Knowledge	DOK2
Content Standard	7.G.6
Mathematical Practice	MP1, MP4
Online Experience	Students will drag values to model the equation and type their response in the box.
Scoring Rubric	
2 points	Students correctly model and solve the equation.
1 point	Students correctly model OR solve the equation.

21.

This test item requires students to explain and apply mathematical concepts and solve problems with precision, while making use of structure.	
Depth of Knowledge	DOK1
Content Standard	7.G.6
Mathematical Practice	MP1
Online Experience	Students will be required to type their responses in the boxes.
Scoring Rubric	
2 points	Students correctly complete all four statements.
1 point	Students correctly complete three of the four statements.

Power Up! Test Practice

20. A cardboard box has the dimensions shown. Select the correct values to complete the formula to find the surface area of the box.

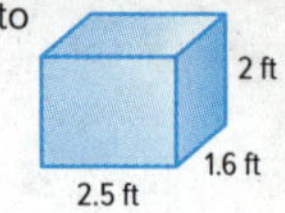

1.6
2
2.5

$SA =$ 2 · 2.5 · 2 + 2 · 2.5 · 1.6 + 2 · 2 · 1.6

How much cardboard is needed to make the box? 24.4 ft^2

21. A triangular prism has the dimensions shown. Fill in each box to complete each statement.

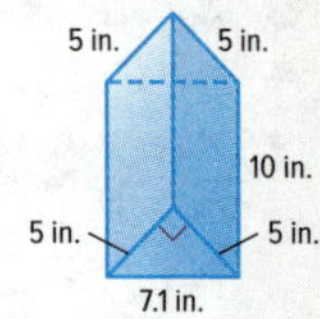

a. The area of each triangular base is 12.5 square inches.

b. The area of each of the two congruent rectangular faces is 50 square inches.

c. The area of the third rectangular face is 71 square inches.

d. The total surface area of the prism is 196 square inches.

Spiral Review

Describe the shape resulting from a vertical, horizontal, and angled cross section for each figure. 7.G.3

22.

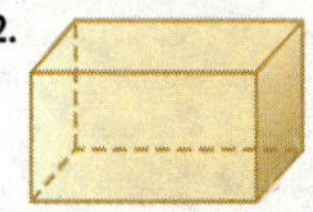

vertical: rectangle

horizontal: rectangle

angled: rectangle

23.

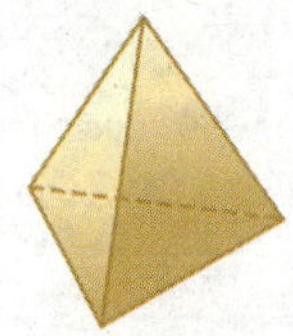

vertical: triangle

horizontal: triangle

angled: triangle

24.

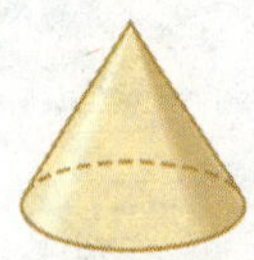

vertical: triangle

horizontal: circle

angled: oval

25.

vertical: rectangle

horizontal: circle

angled: oval

An Interactive Whiteboard Ready presentation is available for each lesson in the chapter.

Inquiry Lab
Relate Surface Area and Volume

Inquiry HOW does the shape of a rectangular prism affect its volume and surface area?

Content Standards
7.G.6

MP Mathematical Practices
1, 3, 4

You can arrange blocks in many ways. How can you arrange 8 blocks to create the least possible surface area?

What do you know? Eight blocks are being arranged.

What do you need to find? How are the blocks arranged to create the least possible surface area?

Hands-On Activity 1

Tools

Step 1 Create a rectangular prism using 8 centimeter cubes. Record the dimensions in the table below. Find and record the volume and surface area of the prism.

Rectangular Prism	Length (cm)	Width (cm)	Height (cm)	Volume (cm^3)	Surface Area (cm^2)
1	2	2	2	8	24
2	4	2	1	8	28
3	8	1	1	8	34

Step 2 Repeat Step 1 for as many different rectangular prisms as you can create with 8 cubes.

Does the volume change when the prism changes? Explain.
No; the volume is always 8 cm^3.

The rectangular prism measuring 2 × 2 × 2 has the least surface area.

Focus narrowing the scope

Objective Compare surface area and volume of rectangular prisms. 7.G.6

Coherence connecting within and across grades

Now
Students compare the surface area and volume of rectangular prisms.

Next
Students will find the lateral area and total surface area of pyramids.

Rigor pursuing concepts, fluency, and applications

See the Levels of Complexity chart on page 675.

ENGAGE EXPLORE EXPLAIN ELABORATE EVALUATE

1 Launch the Lab

Activities 1 and 2 are intended to be used as whole-group activities. Activity 1 is designed to provide more guidance to students than Activity 2.

Hands-On Activity 1

AL EL **Think-Pair-Create** Give students one minute to think through how they would respond to Steps 1 and 2. Then have them work with a partner to complete the steps. Have students draw the net of each prism to help them find the surface area. MP 1, 4, 7, 8

BL EL **Pairs Consult** Upon completion of the activity, have students work with a partner to respond to the following extension question: Why does the volume remain the same, but the surface area changes? MP 1, 7

Hands-On Activity 2

AL **EL** **Pairs to Groups** Have students work in pairs to complete Steps 1–3 of Activity 2. Allow students to use grid paper to draw a net of each prism to help them find the surface area. Then have pairs join with another pair to share their responses and discuss and resolve any discrepancies.
MP 1, 5, 7

BL **EL** **Pairs Discussion** Have students work with a partner to predict which figure will have the lesser surface area prior to completing Activity 2. Then have them complete the activity and check their prediction against the actual results.
MP 1, 7

Hands-On Activity 2

Suppose you make structures in the shape of the ones shown below. What is the volume of each structure? Which structure has the lesser surface area? Draw a net if necessary.

Figure 1

Figure 2

Step 1 Use centimeter cubes to create the rectangular prism shown in Figure 1. Write its dimensions, volume, and surface area in the table below.

Rectangular Prism	Length (cm)	Width (cm)	Height (cm)	Volume (cm^3)	Surface Area (cm^2)
Figure 1	3	2	2	12	32
Figure 2	6	1	2	12	40

Step 2 Use centimeter cubes to create the rectangular prism shown in Figure 2. Write its dimensions, volume, and surface area in the table.

Step 3 Compare the volume and surface areas of Figure 1 and Figure 2.

What do you notice about the volume of Figure 1 and Figure 2?
The volume of each figure is 12 cubic centimeters.

The surface area of Figure 1 is 32 square centimeters.
The surface area of Figure 2 is 40 square centimeters.
Compare the surface areas using an inequality.

32 square centimeters < 40 square centimeters

So, Figure 1 has the lesser surface area.

Investigate

Collaborate

Work with a partner. Compare the two figures that have the same volume. Then determine which figure has a greater surface area. Draw a net if necessary.

Show your work.

1.

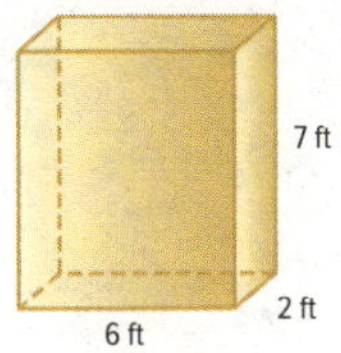

Figure 1

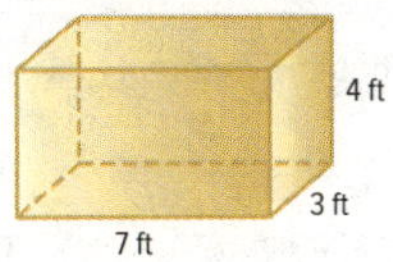

Figure 2

Surface Area: 136 ft^2

Surface Area: 122 ft^2

Sample answer: Since 136 > 122, Figure 1 has the greater surface area.

2.

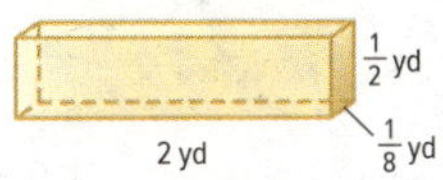

Figure 1

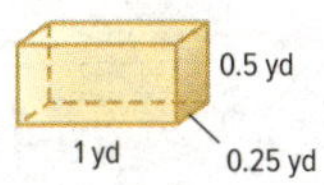

Figure 2

Surface Area: $2\frac{5}{8}$ yd^2

Surface Area: $1\frac{3}{4}$ yd^2

Sample answer: Since $2\frac{5}{8} > 1\frac{3}{4}$, Figure 1 has the greater surface area.

3.

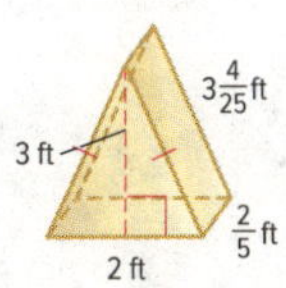

Figure 1

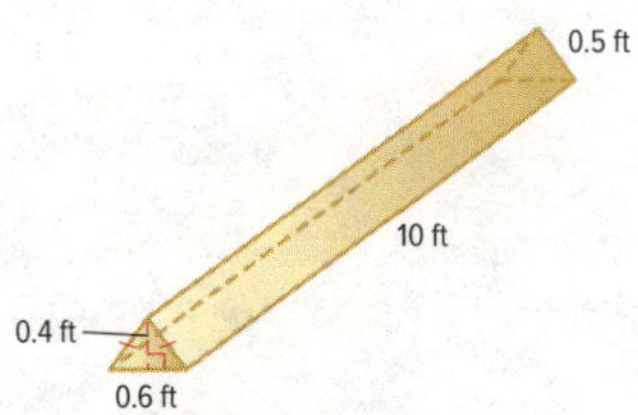

Figure 2

Surface Area: $9\frac{41}{125}$ or 9.33 ft^2

Surface Area: 16.24 ft^2

Sample answer: Since $16.24 > 9\frac{41}{125}$, Figure 2 has the greater surface area.

ENGAGE EXPLORE EXPLAIN ELABORATE EVALUATE

2 Collaborate

The **Investigate** and **Analyze and Reflect** sections are intended to be used as small-group investigations. The **Create** section is intended to be used as independent exercises.

Levels of Complexity

The levels of the exercises progress from 1 to 3, with Level 1 indicating the lowest level of complexity.

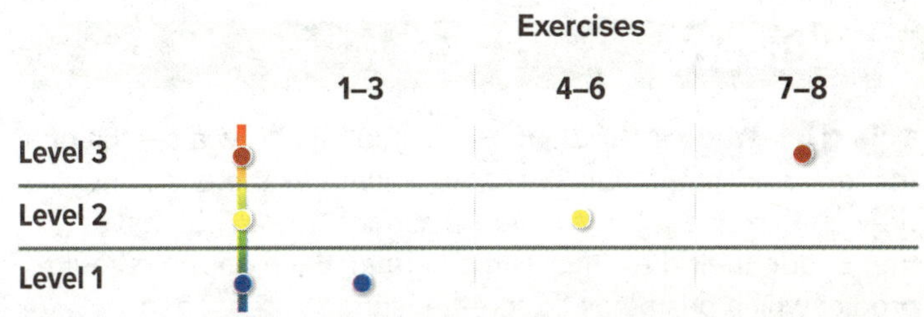

Investigate

Collaborate

AL EL **Team-Pair-Solo** Have students work in small teams of four students to complete Exercise 1, ensuring that each team member understands how to determine which figure has the greater surface area. Students should have a clear understanding that each figure has the same volume. Then have teams divide into pairs to complete Exercise 2. Finally, have students work on their own to complete Exercise 3. Then have students rejoin their original team to compare responses. MP 1, 4, 7

BL EL **Pairs Consult** Have students work in pairs to complete Exercises 1–3. Prior to beginning each exercise, have students make a prediction as to which figure will have the greater surface area. They should provide a justification for their prediction. Then have them complete the exercises and compare the actual results to their predictions. MP 1, 4, 7

Analyze and Reflect

Collaborate

AL EL **Teammates Consult** In groups of three, have students complete Exercises 4–6. Each student in the group will lead the discussion for one of the exercises. Give students ample time to discuss and ask questions of their teammates. After a thorough discussion, each student will silently, independently submit their own response to the exercise. Call on one student to share their response with the class. MP 1, 3, 4, 7

Create

On Your Own

BL EL **Trade-a-Problem** Have students draw a sketch of a triangular prism that has the same volume as the prism they drew in Exercise 7, but a different surface area. Then have them trade their drawings with a partner. Each partner should predict which prism has the greater surface area. Then partners should verify their predictions by determining the actual surface area. MP 1, 7

Inquiry Students should be able to answer "HOW does the shape of a rectangular prism affect its volume and surface area?" Check for student understanding and provide guidance, if needed.

Analyze and Reflect

Collaborate

Work with a partner to solve the following problems. Draw a net if necessary.

4. Monique sews together pieces of fabric to make rectangular gift boxes. She only uses whole numbers. What are the dimensions of a box with a volume of 50 cubic inches that has the greatest amount of surface area?

50 in. by 1 in. by 1 in.

5. Thomas is creating a decorative container to fill with colored sand. He uses only whole numbers. The top of the container is open. What are the dimensions of the rectangular prism that holds 100 cubic inches with the least amount of surface area?

5 in. by 4 in. by 5 in.

6. MP **Construct an Argument** Zack needs to melt a stick of butter that measures 5 inches by 1 inch by 1 inch. He is going to put the butter in a pan on top of the stove. Explain why cutting the butter into smaller pieces will help the butter melt faster. **Sample answer: He can cut the butter into smaller pieces. Using smaller pieces increases the surface area that will be heated.**

Create

On Your Own

7. MP **Model with Mathematics** Draw a sketch of a triangular prism with a volume of 120 cubic units and a surface area of 184 square units.

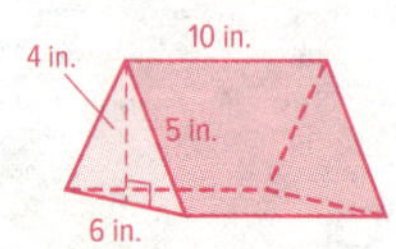

Show your work.

8. Inquiry HOW does the shape of a rectangular prism affect its volume and surface area?

Sample answer: The volume is not affected. Suppose you have a cube and a rectangular prism of equal volume made from centimeter cubes. The structure that has more faces located in the interior will have the lesser surface area.

PLAN ONLINE: PD | RtI | Watch | Worksheets | Vocab | Tutor | Tools | Check | English Learners | Sketchpad

PRESENT: IWB — An Interactive Whiteboard Ready presentation is available for each lesson in the chapter.

Geometry

Lesson 7

Surface Area of Pyramids

Vocabulary Start-Up

Vocab | Watch

Pyramids Ancient Egyptians built pyramids, such as the one shown in the photo below. A right square pyramid has a square base and four isosceles triangles that make up the lateral faces. The **lateral surface area** is the sum of the areas of all its lateral faces. The height of each lateral face is called **slant height**.

1. Fill in the blanks on the diagram below with the terms *slant height* and *lateral face*.

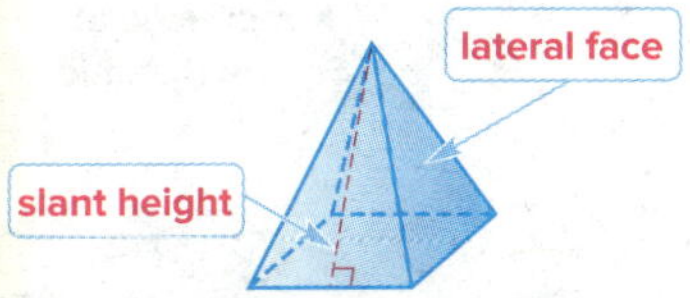

2. Draw a net of a square pyramid.
Sample answer:

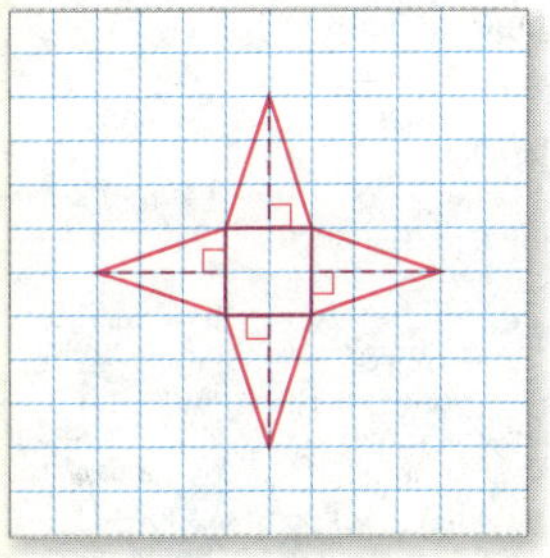

Essential Question

HOW do measurements help you describe real-world objects?

Vocabulary

lateral surface area
slant height
regular pyramid

Content Standards
7.G.6

MP Mathematical Practices
1, 3, 4, 5

Which MP **Mathematical Practices** did you use?
Shade the circle(s) that applies.

1. Persevere with Problems
2. Reason Abstractly
3. Construct an Argument
4. Model with Mathematics
5. Use Math Tools
6. Attend to Precision
7. Make Use of Structure
8. Use Repeated Reasoning

Focus narrowing the scope

Objective Find the surface areas of pyramids. 7.G.6

Coherence connecting within and across grades

Previous Students found the lateral area and total surface area of prisms.

Now Students use a formula to find the surface area of pyramids.

Next Students will use formulas to find the surface area of composite figures.

Rigor pursuing concepts, fluency, and applications

See the Levels of Complexity chart on page 681.

ENGAGE EXPLORE EXPLAIN ELABORATE EVALUATE

1 Launch the Lesson

Ideas for Use

You may wish to launch the lesson using a whole group, small group, think-pair-share activity, or independent activity.

BL EL **Find the Fib** Students write down two facts and one fib about the net or surface area of a pyramid. The job of the remainder of the class or team is to identify the fib. MP 1, 3

Alternate Strategy

AL Have students work in pairs. Provide each pair with a net of a square pyramid, rectangular prism, and triangular pyramid. Students should cut out the figure and label the base and lateral faces. Then have students identify the shape of the lateral faces.

2 Teach the Concept

Ask the scaffolded questions for each example to differentiate instruction.

Example

IWB

1. Find the surface area of a pyramid.

AL
- *What is the formula for the surface area of a pyramid?* $S.A. = B + \frac{1}{2}P\ell$
- *What does B represent?* the area of the base
- *What does P represent?* the perimeter of the base
- *What does ℓ represent?* the slant height

OL
- *What is the shape of the base?* square
- *How do you find the area of a square?* multiply the length of two sides
- *What is the area of the base?* 16 in^2
- *What is the perimeter of the square?* 16 in.
- *What is the slant height of the pyramid?* 9 in.

BL
- *Explain why in a square pyramid, $\frac{1}{2}(4s)\ell = \frac{1}{2}P\ell$.* 4*s* represents the perimeter *P* of the square

Need Another Example?

Find the total surface area of the pyramid. Round to the nearest tenth. 51 in^2

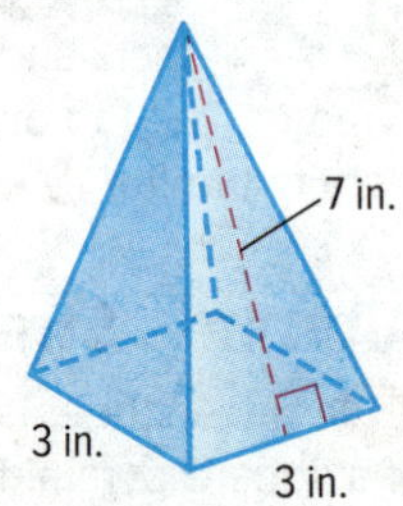

Work Zone

Key Concept

Surface Area of a Pyramid

Lateral Area

Words The lateral surface area *L.A.* of a regular pyramid is half the perimeter *P* of the base times the slant height ℓ.

Model

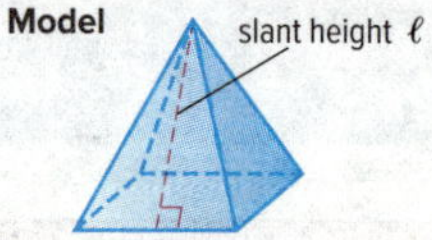

Symbols $L.A. = \frac{1}{2}P\ell$

Total Surface Area

Words The total surface area *S.A.* of a regular pyramid is the lateral area *L.A.* plus the area of the base *B*.

Symbols $S.A. = B + L.A.$ or $S.A. = B + \frac{1}{2}P\ell$

A **regular pyramid** is a pyramid with a base that is a regular polygon.

Model of Regular Square Pyramid

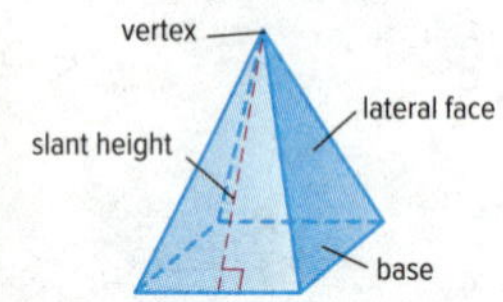

Net of Regular Square Pyramid

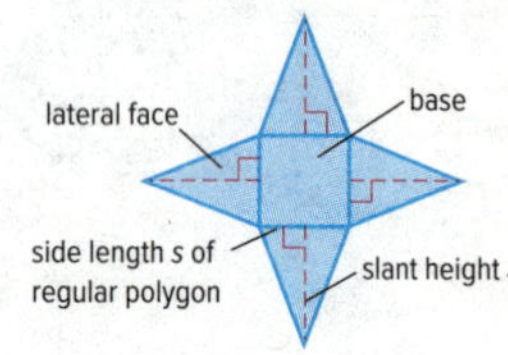

To find the lateral area *L.A.* of a regular pyramid, refer to the net. The lateral area is the sum of the areas of the triangles.

$L.A. = 4\left(\frac{1}{2}s\ell\right)$ Area of the lateral faces

$L.A. = \frac{1}{2}(4s)\ell$ Commutative Property of Multiplication

$L.A. = \frac{1}{2}P\ell$ The perimeter of the base *P* is 4*s*.

The total surface area of a regular pyramid is the lateral surface area *L.A.* plus the area of the base *B*.

$$S.A. = B + \frac{1}{2}P\ell$$

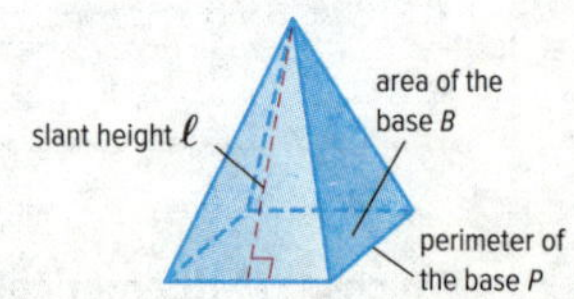

Examples

Tutor

1. Find the total surface area of the pyramid. Round to the nearest tenth.

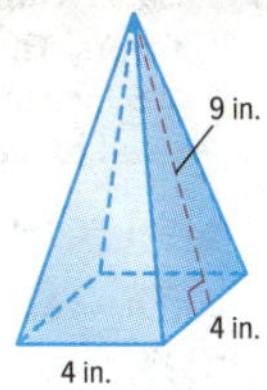

$S.A. = B + \frac{1}{2}P\ell$ — Surface area of a pyramid

$S.A. = 16 + \frac{1}{2}(16 \cdot 9)$ — $B = 4 \cdot 4$, $P = 4 \cdot 4$ or 16, $\ell = 9$

$S.A. = 88$ — Simplify.

The surface area is 88 square inches.

2. Find the total surface area of the pyramid with a base area of 111 square meters.

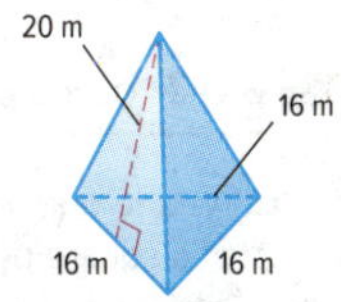

$S.A. = B + \frac{1}{2}P\ell$ — Surface area of a pyramid

$S.A. = 111 + \frac{1}{2}(48 \cdot 20)$ — $B = 111$, $P = 16 + 16 + 16$ or 48, $\ell = 20$

$S.A. = 591$ — Simplify.

The surface area of the pyramid is 591 square meters.

3. Find the total surface area of the pyramid.

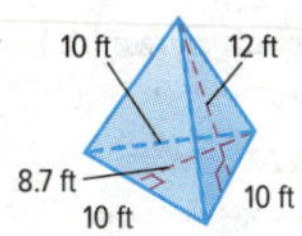

$S.A. = B + \frac{1}{2}P\ell$ — Surface area of a pyramid

$S.A. = 43.5 + \frac{1}{2}P\ell$ — $B = \frac{1}{2} \cdot 10 \cdot 8.7$ or 43.5

$S.A. = 43.5 + \frac{1}{2}(30 \cdot 12)$ — $P = 10 + 10 + 10$ or 30, $\ell = 12$

$S.A. = 223.5$ — Simplify.

The surface area is 223.5 square feet.

Perimeter of a Square

The formula for the perimeter of a square is $P = 4s$.

Got it? **Do these problems to find out.**

a. Find the surface area of a square pyramid that has a slant height of 8 centimeters and a base length of 5 centimeters.

b. Find the total surface area of the pyramid shown.

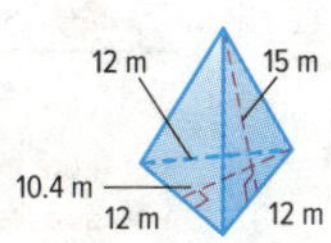

Show your work.

a. 105 cm^2

b. 332.4 m^2

Examples

IWB

2. Find the surface area of a pyramid.

AL
- *What is the shape of the base of the pyramid?* triangle
- *What is the area of the base?* 111 m^2

OL
- *What is the perimeter of the base?* 48 m
- *What is the slant height of the pyramid?* 20 m

BL
- *If you did not know the area of the triangular base, could you find it using the given information?* See students' work; it is possible if students know the properties of an equilateral triangle and the Pythagorean Theorem.

Need Another Example?
Find the total surface area of the pyramid with a base area of 73.2 square centimeters.
424.2 cm^2

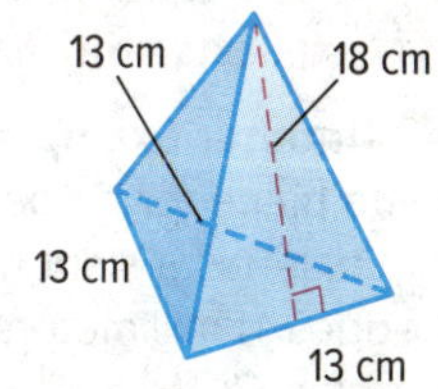

3. Find the surface area of a pyramid.

AL
- *What is the shape of the base of the pyramid?* triangle
- *What is the formula for the area of a triangle?* $\frac{1}{2}bh$
- *What is the height of the base triangle?* 8.7 ft
- *What is the length of the base of the base triangle?* 10 ft

OL
- *What is the perimeter of the base?* 30 ft
- *What is the lateral surface area of the pyramid?* 180 ft^2

BL
- *Suppose this figure is a tent without a bottom. What is the surface area of the tent? Explain.* 180 ft^2; You only need to find the lateral surface area.

Need Another Example?
Find the total surface area of the triangular pyramid. 70.8 in^2

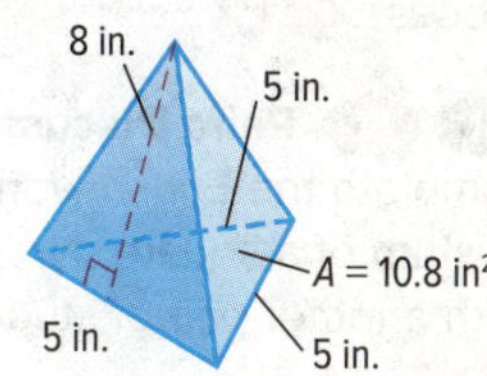

Example

IWB

4. Find the surface area of a pyramid.

AL
- *What is the shape of the base?* square
- *What is the formula for the area of a square?* $A = s^2$
- *What is the length of one side of the square?* 2.5 in.

OL
- *What is the area of the base?* 6.25 in^2
- *What is the perimeter of the square?* 10 in.
- *What is the lateral surface area of the pyramid?* 15 in^2

BL
- *Could the gift boxes have a rectangular base that is not a square? If so, draw one. If not, why not?* yes; See students' work for sketch.

Need Another Example?

A game piece for a board game is shaped like a square pyramid. It has a slant height of 15 millimeters and the base has edges 11 millimeters long. What is the surface area of the game piece? 451 mm^2

Guided Practice

Formative Assessment Use these exercises to assess students' understanding of the concepts in this lesson.

If some of your students are not ready for assignments, use the differentiated activities below.

AL EL **Rally Table** Have students work in teams to solve Exercises 1–3. Students take turns drawing and labeling one part of the net for Exercise 1, or finding one part of the formula for total surface area. Then, students find the appropriate surface area, compare answer, and discuss any differences. They then move on to Exercises 2 and 3, repeating the process. MP 1, 7

BL EL **Pairs Discussion** Have students work in pairs to complete the Enrich worksheet on the surface area of a frustum of a square pyramid. Have them trade their solutions with another pair of students and discuss any differences. MP 1, 7

Real World Example

Tutor

4. **Sal is wrapping gift boxes that are square pyramids for party favors. They have a slant height of 3 inches and base edges 2.5 inches long. How many square inches of card stock are used to make one gift box?**

$S.A. = B + \frac{1}{2}P\ell$ Surface area of a pyramid

$S.A. = 6.25 + \frac{1}{2}(10 \cdot 3)$ $B = 2.5^2$ or 6.25, $P = 4(2.5)$ or 10, $\ell = 3$

$S.A. = 21.25$ Simplify.

So, 21.25 square inches of card stock are used to make one gift box.

Got it? **Do this problem to find out.**

c. Amado purchased a bottle of perfume that is in the shape of a square pyramid. The slant height of the bottle is 4.5 inches and the base is 2 inches. Find the surface area.

Show your work.

c. 22 in^2

Guided Practice

Check

Find the total surface area of each pyramid. Round to the nearest tenth. (Examples 1–3)

1. 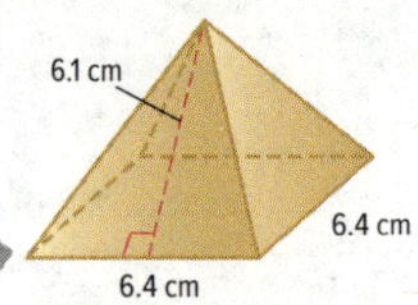

119.0 cm^2

Show your work.

2. 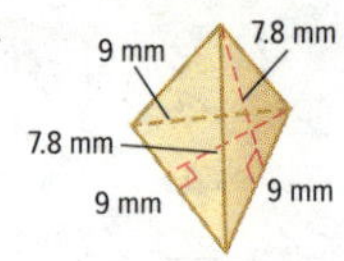

140.4 mm^2

3. The Washington Monument is an obelisk with a square pyramid top. The slant height of the pyramid is 55.5 feet, and the square base has sides of 34.5 feet. Find the lateral area of the pyramid. (Example 4) 3,829.5 ft^2

4. **Building on the Essential Question** Justify the formula for the surface area of a pyramid.
The formula is based on finding the area of each face and the base and then adding them.

Rate Yourself!

ow confident are you about finding the surface area of pyramids? Check the box that applies.

For more help, go online to access a Personal Tutor. Tutor

FOLDABLES Time to update your Foldable!

Name ______________________ My Homework ______________________

Independent Practice

Go online for Step-by-Step Solutions eHelp

Find the total surface area of each pyramid. Round to the nearest tenth. (Examples 1–3)

1. 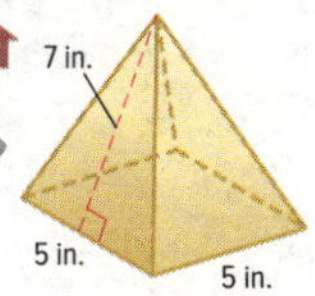

95 in^2

2. 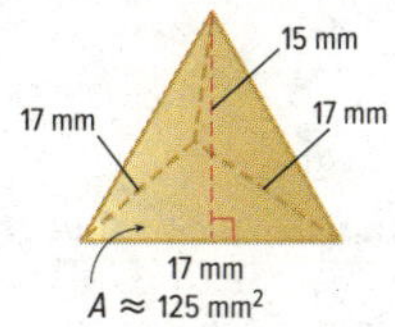

507.5 mm^2

3. 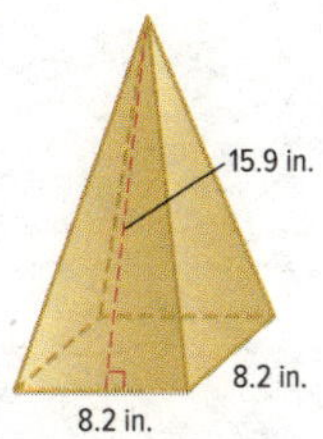

328 in^2

4. 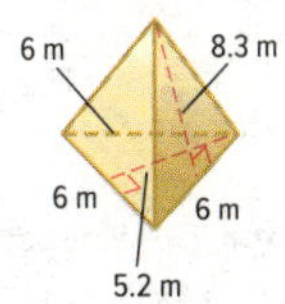

90.3 m^2

5. A triangular pyramid has a slant height of 0.75 foot. The equilateral triangular base has a perimeter of 1.2 feet and an area of about 0.07 square foot. Find the approximate surface area. (Example 4)
0.52 ft^2

6. The gemstone shown is a square pyramid that has a base with sides 3.4 inches long. The slant height of the pyramid is 3.8 inches. Find the surface area of the gemstone. (Example 4)
37.4 in^2

7. Isaac is building a birdhouse for a class project. The birdhouse is a regular hexagonal pyramid. The base has side lengths of 3 inches and an area of about 24 square inches. The slant height is 6 inches. Find the approximate surface area of the birdhouse. (Example 4)
78 in^2

ENGAGE EXPLORE **EXPLAIN** **ELABORATE** **EVALUATE**

3 Practice and Apply

Independent Practice and Extra Practice

The Independent Practice pages are meant to be used as the homework assignment. The Extra Practice page can be used for additional reinforcement or as a second-day assignment.

Levels of Complexity

The levels of the exercises progress from 1 to 3, with Level 1 indicating the lowest level of complexity.

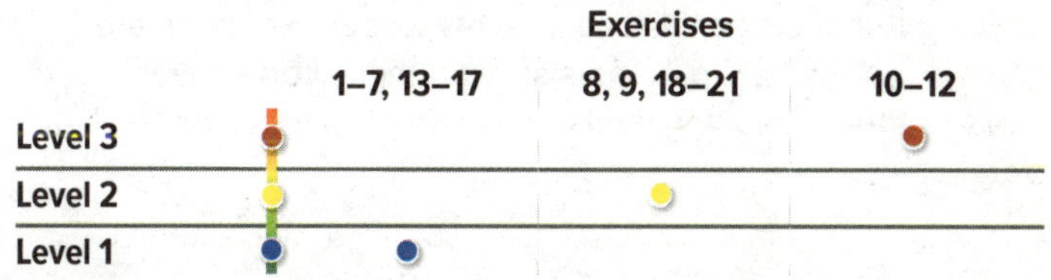

Suggested Assignments

You can use the table below that includes exercises of all complexity levels to select appropriate exercises for your students' needs.

Differentiated Homework Options		
AL	Approaching Level	1–7, 9–11, 20, 21
OL	On Level	1–7 odd, 8–11, 20, 21
BL	Beyond Level	8–12, 20, 21

ALEKS® can provide additional remediation support with personalized instruction and practice.

Watch Out!

Common Error Students may use the wrong dimensions to calculate the area of the base of a triangular pyramid. For Exercise 2, point out that the area of the triangular base is already given.

Common Error For Exercise 7, remind students that a regular hexagon is a six-sided polygon with equal sides and angles.

MP MATHEMATICAL PRACTICES

Emphasis On	Exercise(s)
1 Make sense of problems and persevere in solving them.	8, 12
3 Construct viable arguments and critique the reasoning of others.	10
4 Model with mathematics.	11
5 Use appropriate tools strategically.	19

Mathematical Practices 1, 3, and 4 are aspects of mathematical thinking that are emphasized in every lesson. Students are given opportunities to be persistent in their problem solving, to express their reasoning, and apply mathematics to real-world situations.

Formative Assessment
Use this activity as a closing formative assessment before dismissing students from your class.

TICKET Out the Door

Have students write a paragraph describing how what they learned about surface area of prisms helped them with finding the surface area of pyramids. See students' work.

8. MP **Persevere with Problems** A square pyramid has a surface area of 175 square inches. The square base has side lengths of 5 inches. Find the slant height of the pyramid.

15 in.

9. A square pyramid has a lateral area of 107.25 square centimeters and a slant height of 8.25 centimeters. Find the length of each side of its base.

6.5 cm

H.O.T. Problems Higher Order Thinking

10. MP **Justify Conclusions** Suppose you could climb to the top of the Great Pyramid of Giza in Egypt. Which path would be shorter, climbing a lateral edge or the slant height? Justify your response.

It would be shorter to climb up the slant height. The bottom of the slant height is closer to the center of the base of the pyramid than the bottom of the lateral edge.

11. MP **Model with Mathematics** Draw a rectangular pyramid and a square pyramid. Explain the differences between the two.

Rectangular Pyramid

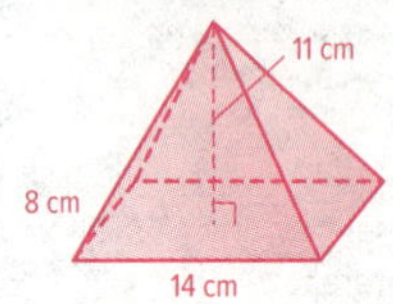

Square Pyramid

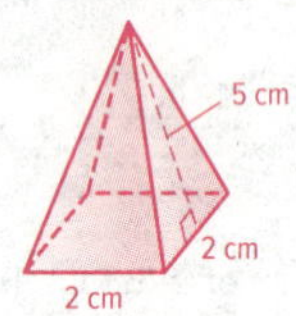

Show your work.

Sample answer: Both a square pyramid and a rectangular pyramid have isosceles triangles as their lateral faces. All the lateral faces are congruent on a square pyramid but, on a rectangular pyramid, the opposite pairs of lateral faces are congruent.

12. MP **Persevere with Problems** The total height of the figure shown is 20 inches and the slant height is 17 inches. Which has a greater surface area, the prism or the pyramid? Explain your reasoning.

The prism; the surface area of the prism is 576 in^2 and the lateral surface area of the pyramid is 544 in^2.

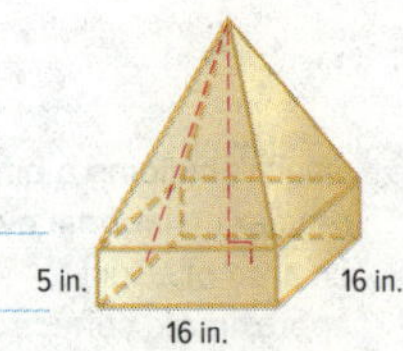

Name ______________________ My Homework ______________________

Extra Practice

Find the total surface area of each pyramid. Round to the nearest tenth.

13. 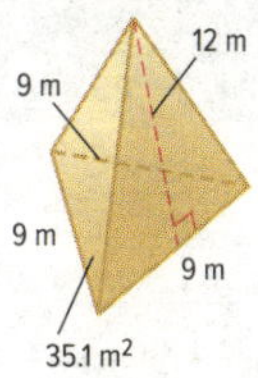

197.1 m^2

S.A. $= B + \frac{1}{2}Pl$

S.A. $= 35.1 + \frac{1}{2}(27 \cdot 12)$

S.A. $= 197.1$

Homework Help

14. 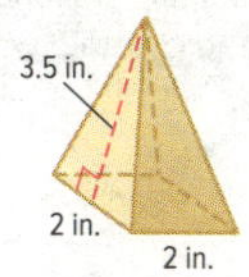

18 in^2

15. 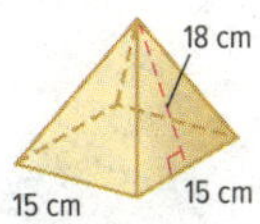

765 cm^2

16. 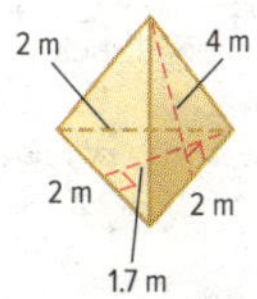

13.7 m^2

17. A square pyramid has a slant height of $4\frac{2}{3}$ feet. The base has side lengths of $2\frac{1}{4}$ feet. Find the surface area. 26.1 ft^2

18. A building in San Francisco is shaped like a square pyramid. It has a slant height of 856.1 feet and each side of its base is 145 feet long. Find the lateral area of the building. 248,269 ft^2

19. MP **Use Math Tools** Complete the organizer below to help you remember what each part of the formula for the surface area of a pyramid represents.

Area of the base → B

Slant height → ℓ

S.A. $= B + \frac{1}{2}P\ell$

Perimeter of the base → P

Create Your Own Homework Online

eSolutionsManual™ can be used to create worksheets for the suggested assignments on page 681, or create your own worksheets for differentiated homework or review.

Power Up! Test Practice

Exercises 20 and 21 prepare students for more rigorous thinking needed for the state assessment.

20. This test item requires students to explain and apply mathematical concepts and solve problems with precision, while making use of structure.

Depth of Knowledge	DOK1
Content Standard	7.G.6
Mathematical Practice	MP1
Online Experience	Students will drag values to label the net and type their response in the box.
Scoring Rubric	
2 points	Students correctly label the net and find the surface area of the pyramid.
1 point	Students correctly label the net OR find the surface area of the pyramid.

21. This test item requires students to reason abstractly and quantitatively when problem solving.

Depth of Knowledge	DOK1
Content Standard	7.G.6
Mathematical Practice	MP1
Online Experience	Students will be required to click on the bubbles to select all answers that are correct.
Scoring Rubric	
1 point	Students correctly answer each part of the question.

Power Up! Test Practice

20. The base of a square pyramid has a perimeter of 28 centimeters. The height of the pyramid is 2.1 centimeters longer than the side length of the base. Label the net of the pyramid with the correct dimensions.

2.1 cm	7 cm
4 cm	9.1 cm
4.9 cm	28 cm

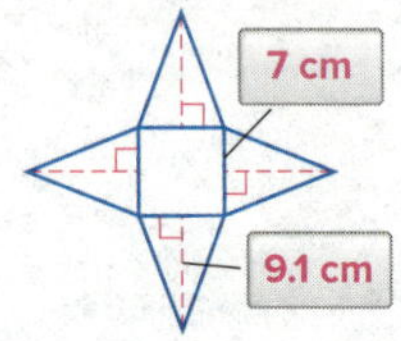

What is the total surface area of the pyramid? 176.4 cm²

21. An entertainment company is constructing a tent in the shape of a square pyramid, without a floor, to be used at a party. Determine if each statement is true or false.

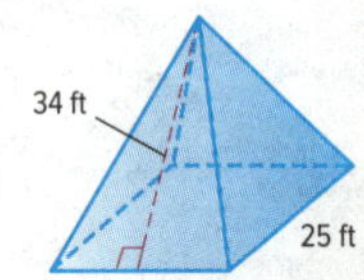

a. The area of the ground covered by the tent is 625 square feet. ■ True ☐ False

b. The area of each triangular face of the tent is 425 square feet. ■ True ☐ False

c. The amount of material needed to make the tent is 2,325 square feet. ☐ True ■ False

Spiral Review

Find the surface area of each prism. 7.G.6

22. 13,890 cm²

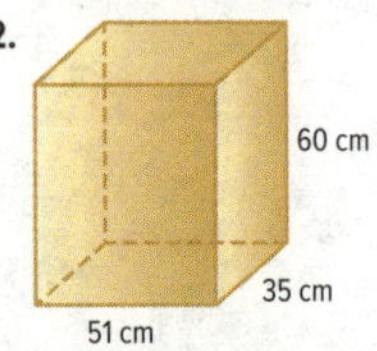

23. 456 ft²

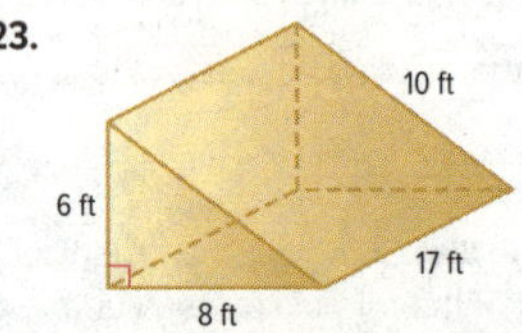

24. The volume of the prism shown below is 140 cubic meters. Find the height of the prism. 7.G.6 5 m

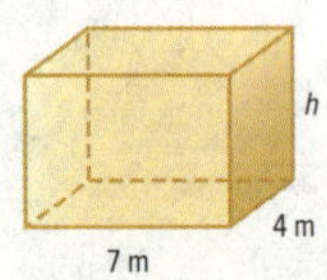

25. The volume of the prism shown below is 10,360 cubic feet. Find the width of the prism. 7.G.6 10 ft

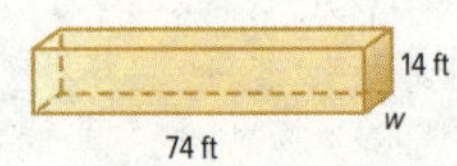

PD | RtI | Watch | Worksheets | Vocab | Tutor | Tools | Check | English Learners | Sketchpad

PRESENT

IWB

An Interactive Whiteboard Ready presentation is available for each lesson in the chapter.

Inquiry Lab
Composite Figures

Inquiry HOW can you find the volume and surface area of a composite figure?

Content Standards
7.G.6

MP **Mathematical Practices**
1, 3, 4

A company made a model of a new office building. The building is composed of rectangular prisms. You can use centimeter cubes to find the volume of the building model.

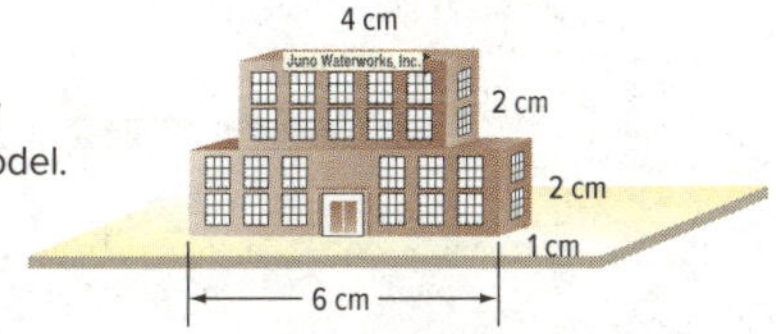

Hands-On Activity 1

Tools

The model is a *composite figure* because it is made from two rectangular prisms.

Step 1 Model the top and bottom rectangular prisms using cubes.

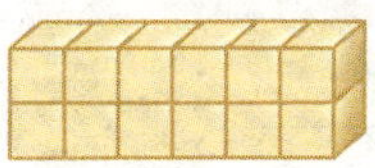
Bottom

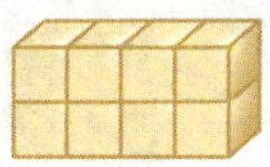
Top

Step 2 Count the cubes to find the dimensions. Write the dimensions in the table below. Then use the cube models to find the volume of both prisms. Write these measures in the table below step 3.

Step 3 Use the table to find the volume of the entire building model. Write these measures in the composite row of the table.

Model	Length (cm)	Width (cm)	Height (cm)	Volume (cm^3)
Bottom	6	1	2	12
Top	4	1	2	8
Composite				20

Focus narrowing the scope

Objective Find the volume and surface area of composite figures. 7.G.6

Materials: centimeter cubes

Coherence connecting within and across grades

Now
Students find the volume and surface area of composite figures.

Next
Students will use formulas to find the volume and surface area of composite figures.

Rigor pursuing concepts, fluency, and applications

See the Levels of Complexity chart on page 687.

ENGAGE EXPLORE EXPLAIN ELABORATE EVALUATE

1 Launch the Lab

Activities 1 and 2 are intended to be used as whole-group activities.

Hands-On Activity 1

AL EL **Pairs Discussion** Have students work in pairs to complete the activity and respond to the following questions. MP 1, 7

Ask:

- *What are the length, width, and height of the bottom figure?* 6 cm; 1 cm; 2 cm *the top figure?* 4 cm; 1 cm; 2 cm
- *What is the volume of one cube?* 1 cm^3
- *How can you find the volume of each figure using the cubes?* count the number of cubes

BL Omit the Activities and proceed directly to the Investigate section.

Hands-On Activity 2

AL EL **Paired Heads Together** Have students work in pairs to complete Activity 2. Assign each student a number. Pairs should ensure that each partner understands the activity. Call on a numbered student to share their responses with the class. MP 1, 7

Ask:

- *What two figures comprise the figure?* **a rectangular prism and a triangular prism**
- *What are the length, width, and height of the rectangular prism?* **4 cm; 3 cm; 3 cm**
- *What are the length, base, and height of the triangular prism?* **4 cm; 3 cm; 2 cm**
- *What is the volume of the rectangular prism?* **36 cm^3**
- *What is the volume of the triangular prism?* **12 cm^3**
- *How will you find the total volume?* **Add the volumes together.**
- *What is the surface area of the rectangular prism?* **66 cm^2**
- *What is the surface area of the triangular prism?* **38 cm^2**
- *How will you find the total surface area?* **Add the surfaces together and subtract the area where the figures overlap.**

Mr. Wendell's class made a model of a house. The model was composed of a rectangular prism and a triangular prism. Determine the volume and surface area of the model house.

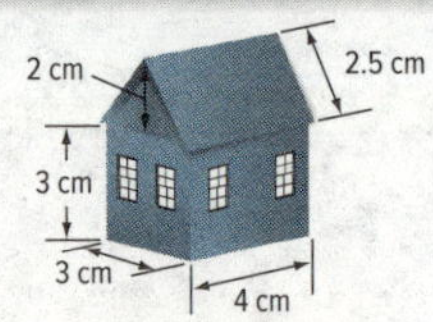

Hands-On Activity 2

Step 1 Use a rectangular prism to model the bottom of the house. Use a triangular prism to model the top of the house.

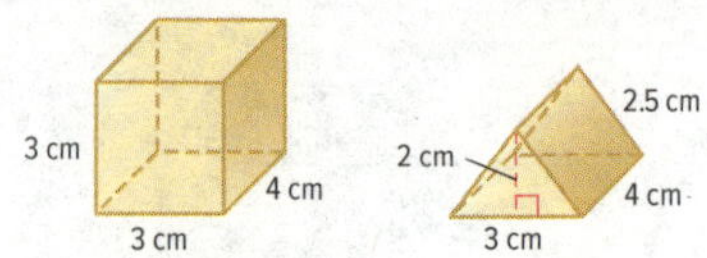

Step 2 Complete the tables below using the models from Step 1.

Prism	Length (cm)	Width (cm)	Height (cm)
Rectangular	4	3	3

Prism	Length (cm)	Base (cm)	Height (cm)
Triangular	4	3	2

Step 3 Use the information from the tables and the models to find the total volume of the model house.

36 cm^3 + **12** cm^3 = **48** cm^3

Volume of Rectangular Prism; Volume of Triangular Prism; Total Volume

Step 4 Use the information from the tables and the models to find the total surface area of the model house.

66 cm^2 + **38** cm^2 − **24** cm^2 = **80** cm^2

Surface Area of Rectangular Prism; Surface Area of Triangular Prism; Areas where Prisms Connect; Total Surface Area

The total volume of the model house is **48** cubic centimeters. The total surface area is **80** square centimeters.

Investigate

Collaborate

Work with a partner.

1. MP **Model with Mathematics** Use the top, side, and front views to build a figure using centimeter cubes. **See students' work for model.**

Show your work.

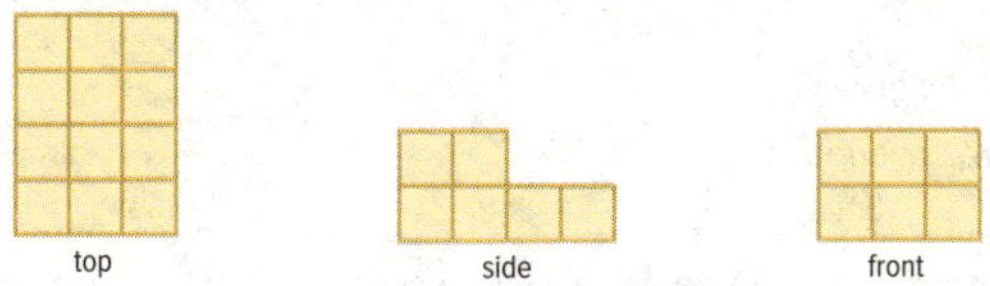

   a. Make a sketch of the figure you built.

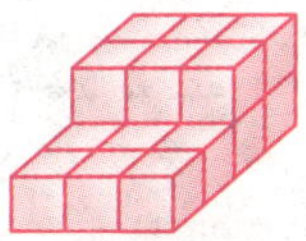

Show your work.

   b. Find the volume and surface area of the figure.

   Volume: **18 cm^3** Surface Area: **48cm^2, including the bottom**

Refer to the figure at the right for Exercises 2–4.

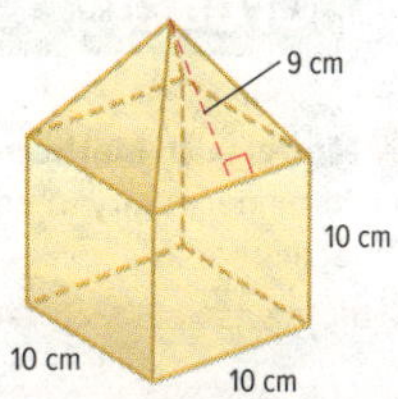

2. The figure is comprised of a **cube** and a square **pyramid**.

3. Complete the following to find the volume of the figure.

   a. The volume of the cube is **1,000** cubic centimeters.

   b. The volume of the square pyramid is 250 cubic centimeters.

   c. So, the volume of the composite figure is **1,250** cubic centimeters.

4. Complete the following to find the surface area of the figure.

   a. The surface area of the cube is **600** square centimeters.

   b. The surface area of the square pyramid is **280** square centimeters.

   c. The area where the figures overlap is **200** square centimeters.

   d. The surface area of the composite figure is **680** square centimeters.

ENGAGE EXPLORE EXPLAIN ELABORATE EVALUATE

2 Collaborate

The **Investigate** and **Analyze and Reflect** sections are intended to be used as small-group investigations. The **Create** section is intended to be used as independent exercises.

Levels of Complexity

The levels of the exercises progress from 1 to 3, with Level 1 indicating the lowest level of complexity.

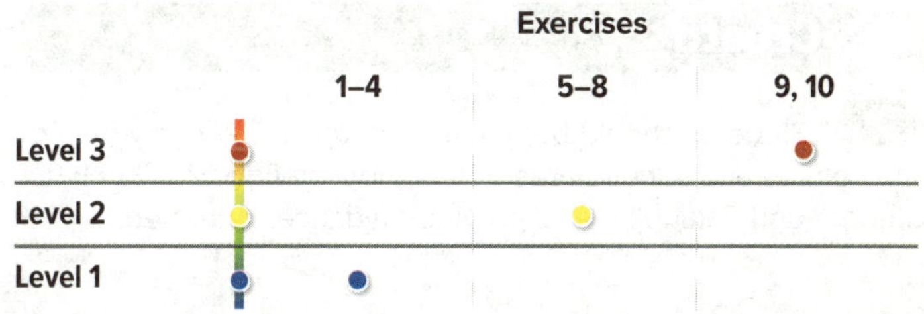

Investigate

Collaborate

AL EL **Team-Pair-Solo** Have students work in groups of 4 to complete Exercise 1, ensuring that each group member understands how to create the three-dimensional figure. Then have each group split into two pairs to complete Exercises 2–4, ensuring that each partner understands. Finally, call on one random student to explain their responses to Exercise 1–4. MP 1, 3, 4, 7

BL EL **Trade-a-Problem** Have students draw their own three-dimensional composite figure, using isometric dot paper. Then have them trade drawings with a partner. Each partner determines the volume and surface are of the composite figure. Have pairs work together to discuss and resolve any discrepancies. MP 1, 4, 7

Analyze and Reflect

Collaborate

AL EL **Pairs Discussion** Have students work with a partner to complete Exercises 5–8. Have one partner take notes on how they determined where each statement should be placed in the diagram. MP 1, 3, 4

BL EL **Pairs Discussion** Have students work in pairs to complete Exercises 5–8. Have them trade their solutions with another pair of students and discuss any differences. MP 1, 3, 4

Create

On Your Own

Inquiry Students should be able to answer "HOW can you find the volume and surface area of a composite figure?" Check for student understanding and provide guidance, if needed.

Analyze and Reflect

Collaborate

MP **Reason Inductively** Work with a partner. Write each of the following statements in the correct location. One statement is done for you.

5. *measured in square units*

6. *measured in cubic units*

7. *involves adding measures of each figure*

8. *involves subtracting where figures overlap*

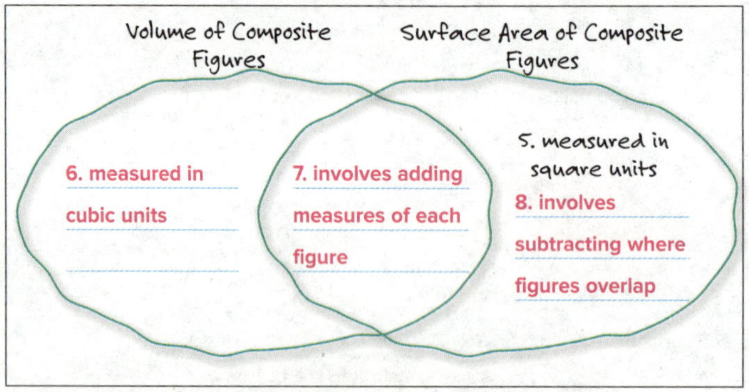

Create

On Your Own

9. MP **Model with Mathematics** Describe a real-world situation where it might be necessary to use a model or a drawing to find the volume or surface area.

Sample answer: Architects use models and drawings to determine volume and surface area of large buildings.

10. Inquiry HOW can you find the volume and surface area of a composite figure?

Sample answer: Add the volumes and surface areas of the figures that make up the composite figure. When finding surface area, be sure to subtract the overlapping areas.

An Interactive Whiteboard Ready presentation is available for each lesson in the chapter.

Lesson 8

Volume and Surface Area of Composite Figures

Real-World Link

Kaylee and Miles are making a bat house for their backyard like the one shown. They need to determine the surface area to find how much wood they will need.

1. Look at the largest bat house. What three-dimensional figures make up the bat house?
   rectangular prism; triangular prism

2. What method could you use to find the surface area of the bat house?
   Find the area of each face and add. Then subtract the faces that overlap.

3. Suppose you wanted to find the volume of the bat house. What method could you use?
   Find the volume of each shape separately and then add.

Essential Question

HOW do measurements help you describe real-world objects?

Content Standards
7.G.6

MP Mathematical Practices
1, 3, 4

Which MP **Mathematical Practices** did you use? Shade the circle(s) that applies.

1. Persevere with Problems
2. Reason Abstractly
3. Construct an Argument
4. Model with Mathematics
5. Use Math Tools
6. Attend to Precision
7. Make Use of Structure
8. Use Repeated Reasoning

Focus narrowing the scope

Objective Find the volume and surface area of a composite figure. 7.G.6

Coherence connecting within and across grades

Previous Students found the volume and surface area of prisms and pyramids.

Now Students find the volume and surface area of composite solids composed of prisms and pyramids.

Next Students will find the volume and surface area of figures that are circular in nature.

Rigor pursuing concepts, fluency, and applications

See the Levels of Complexity chart on page 693.

ENGAGE EXPLORE EXPLAIN ELABORATE EVALUATE

1 Launch the Lesson

Ideas for Use

You may wish to launch the lesson using a whole group, small group, think-pair-share activity, or independent activity.

AL EL **Trade a Problem** Have students work in pairs. Give students base-ten unit cubes, and ask them to construct a composite figure using the cubes. Pairs trade their problems, identify the component figures that make up the composite figures, and find the volume of the component figures. Pairs then compare solution. If the solutions do not agree, students work together to find the errors. MP 1, 4

ENGAGE EXPLORE **EXPLAIN** ELABORATE EVALUATE

2 Teach the Concept

Ask the scaffolded questions for each example to differentiate instruction.

Examples

IWB

1. Find the volume of a composite figure.

AL • *Into what two figures can the composite figure be separated?* rectangular prisms

• *What is the formula for the volume of a rectangular prism?* $V = \ell wh$

OL • *After finding the volume of each figure, what should you do?* Add the volumes.

BL • *Is there another way to decompose the figure? Explain.* See students' work.

Need Another Example?
Find the volume of the figure. 2,184 in^3

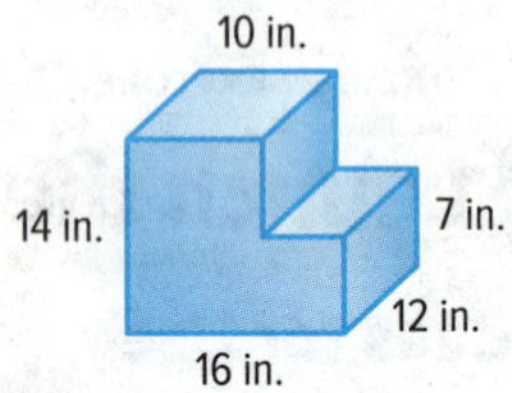

2. Find the volume of a composite figure.

AL • *Into what two figures can the composite figure be separated?* a cube and a pyramid

OL • *What is the formula for the volume of a cube?* $V = s^3$ *volume of a pyramid?* $V = \frac{1}{3}Bh$

BL • *Is there another way to decompose the figure? Explain.* See students' work.

Need Another Example?
Find the volume of the figure. 560 ft^3

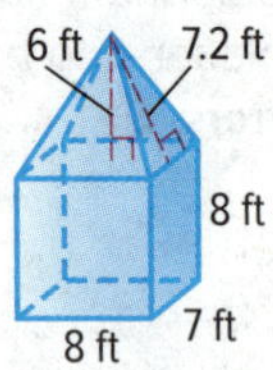

Work Zone

Volume of a Composite Figure

The volume of a composite figure can be found by decomposing the figure into solids whose volumes you know how to find.

Examples

Tutor

1. Find the volume of the composite figure.

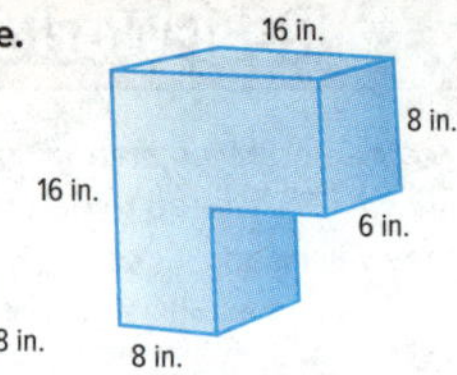

Find the volume of each prism.

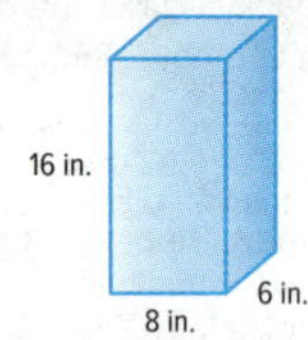

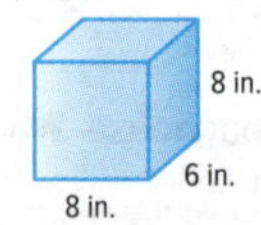

$V = \ell wh$ $\quad$ $V = \ell wh$

$V = 8 \cdot 6 \cdot 16$ or 768 $\quad$ $V = 8 \cdot 6 \cdot 8$ or 384

The volume is 768 + 384 or 1,152 cubic inches.

2. Find the volume of the composite figure.

Find the volume of the cube and the pyramid. Round to the nearest tenth.

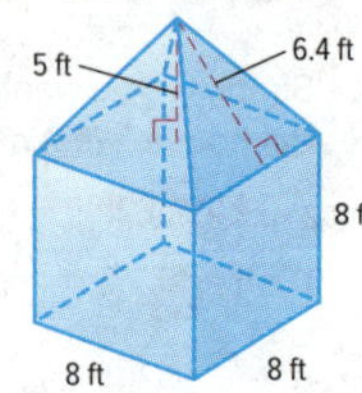

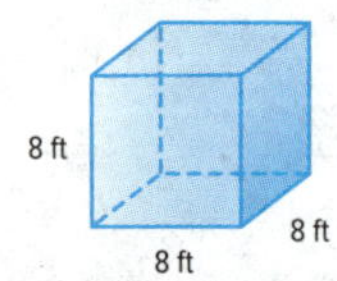

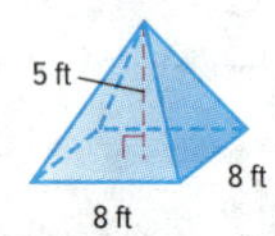

$V = \ell wh$ $\quad$ $V = \frac{1}{3}Bh$

$V = 8 \cdot 8 \cdot 8$ or 512 $\quad$ $V = \frac{1}{3}(8 \cdot 8)5$ or 106.7

The volume is 512 + 106.7 or 618.7 cubic feet.

Show your work.

Got it? **Do this problem to find out.**

a. Find the volume of the composite figure.

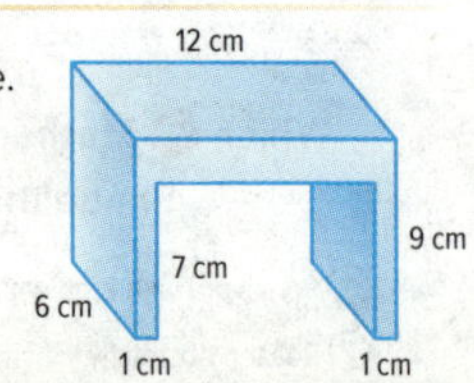

a. 228 cm^3

Surface Area of a Composite Figure

You can also find the surface area of composite figures by finding the areas of the faces that make up the composite figure.

Examples

Tutor

3. Find the surface area of the figure in Example 1.

The surface is made up of three different polygons.

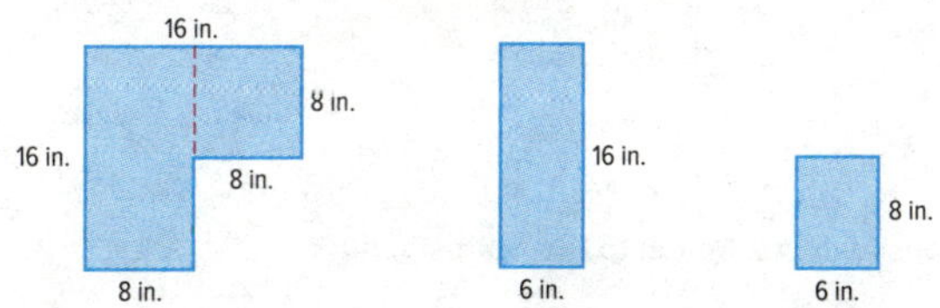

$A = \ell w + \ell w$	$A = \ell w$	$A = \ell w$
$A = (8 \cdot 16) + (8 \cdot 8)$	$A = 6 \cdot 16$	$A = 6 \cdot 8$
$A = 128 + 64$ or 192	$A = 96$	$A = 48$

The total surface area is $2(192) + 2(96) + 4(48)$ or 768 square inches.

4. Find the surface area of the composite figure in Example 2.

The figure is made up of two different polygons.

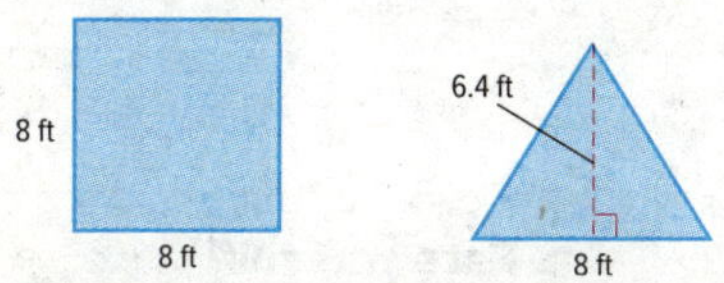

$A = \ell w$	$A = \frac{1}{2}bh$
$A = 8 \cdot 8$ or 64	$A = \frac{1}{2} \cdot 8 \cdot 6.4$ or 25.6

The total surface area is $5(64) + 4(25.6)$ or 422.4 square feet.

Got it? Do this problem to find out.

b. Find the surface area of the steps that are represented by the composite figure shown.

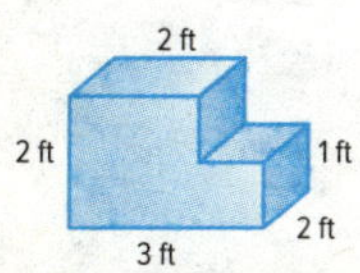

Surface Area
To make it easier to see each face, sketch the faces and label the dimensions of each.

Show your work.

b. 30 ft^2

Examples

IWB

3. Find the surface area of a composite figure.

AL
- *What polygons make up the surfaces of the figure?* squares and rectangles
- *How many 6 inch by 8 inch rectangles are there?* 2 *6 inch by 16 inch rectangles?* 2
- *How many 16 inch by 8 inch rectangles are there?* 2 *8 inch by 8 inch squares?* 2

OL
- *How many faces are there to the figure?* 6
- *After you find the area of each face, what do you do?* Add the areas together.

BL
- *Describe how to use the surface areas of the individual prisms from Example 1 to find the surface area of the composite figure.* See students' work.

Need Another Example?
Find the surface area of the figure.
1,084 in^2

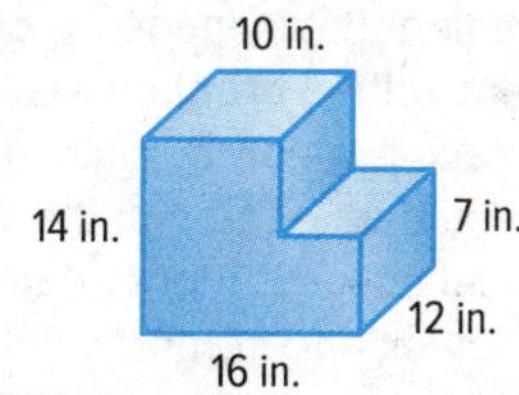

4. Find the surface area of a composite figure.

AL
- *What polygons make up the surfaces of the figure?* squares and triangles
- *How many squares are there?* 5 *triangles?* 4

OL
- *What is the formula for the area of a square?* $A = s^2$
- *What is the formula for the area of a triangle?* $A = \frac{1}{2}bh$

BL
- *Describe how to use the surface areas of the individual prisms from Example 2 to find the surface area of the composite figure.* See students' work.

Need Another Example?
Find the surface area of the figure. 373.8 ft^2

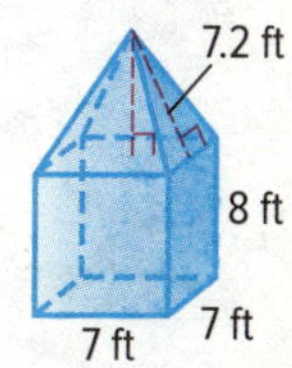

Guided Practice

Formative Assessment Use these exercises to assess students' understanding of the concepts in this lesson.

If some of your students are not ready for assignments, use the differentiated activities below.

AL EL Think-Draw-Pair Have students work in pairs to solve Exercises 1 and 3. Give students one minute to think about how to decompose each figure. Have them draw each separate figure. Students take turns finding one part of the formula for total volume or total surface area. Then, students find the appropriate measure, compare answers, and discuss any differences. They then move on to Exercises 2 and 4, repeating the process. MP 1, 4, 7

BL EL Trade-a-Problem Have students research a famous building that is made up of more than one shape. Then have them write a problem that would involve using the volume or surface area of the building (i.e. find how many gallons of paint it would take to paint the outside and how much the paint would cost.) Students trade their problems solve each other's problem, and compare solutions. If the solutions do not agree, students work together to find the errors. MP 1, 4, 7

Guided Practice

Check

Find the volume of each composite figure. Round to the nearest tenth if necessary. (Examples 1 and 2)

1. 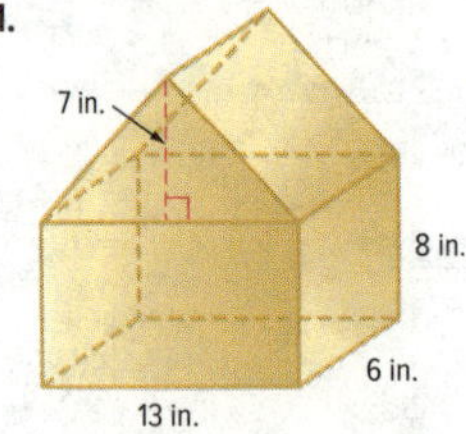

897 in^3

Show your work.

2. 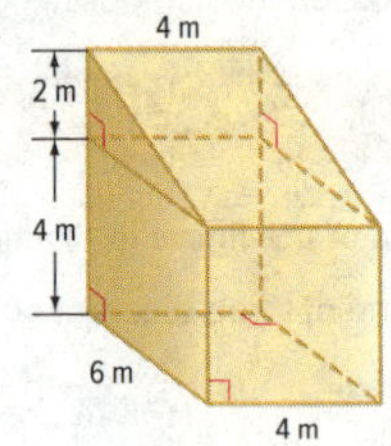

120 m^3

Find the surface area of each composite figure. Round to the nearest tenth if necessary. (Examples 3 and 4)

3. 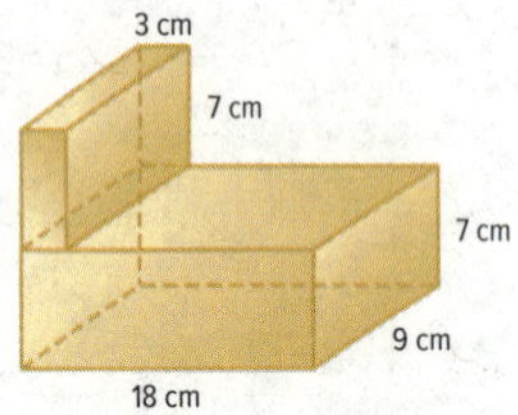

870 cm^2

4. 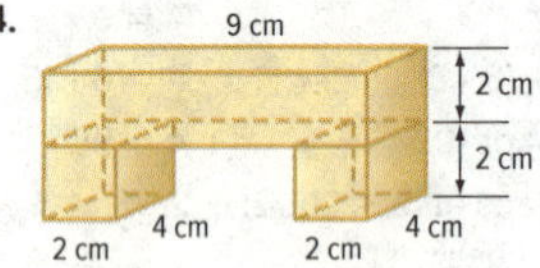

172 cm^2

5. **Building on the Essential Question** How do the previous lessons in this chapter help you find the surface area and volume of a composite figure?

Sample answer: We can decompose the composite figure into three-dimensional shapes for which we already know how to find the surface area and volume.

Rate Yourself!

Are you ready to move on? Shade the section that applies.

For more help, go online to access a Personal Tutor.

Tutor

Name ________________ My Homework ________________

Independent Practice

Go online for Step-by-Step Solutions eHelp

Find the volume of each composite figure. Round to the nearest tenth if necessary. (Examples 1 and 2)

1. 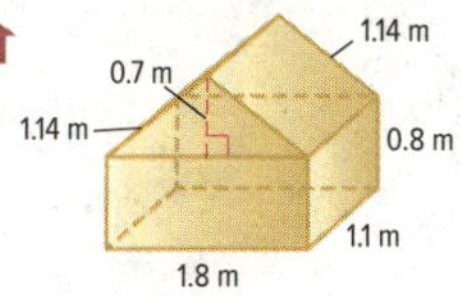

2.3 m^3

2. 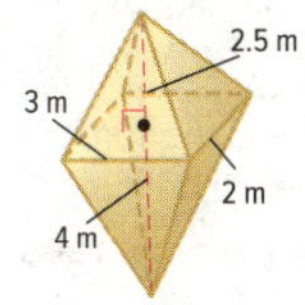

13 m^3

Find the surface area of each composite figure. Round to the nearest tenth if necessary. (Examples 3 and 4)

3. 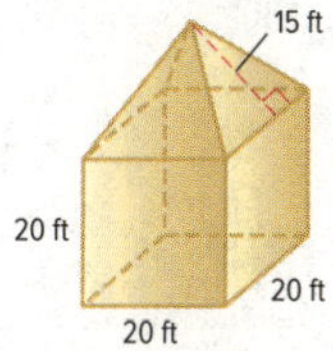

2,600 ft^2

4. 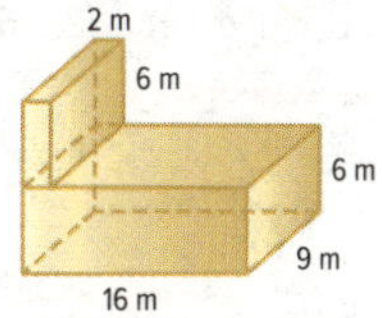

720 m^2

5. Find the volume of the figure at the right in cubic feet. Round to the nearest tenth. (Examples 1 and 2)

0.5 ft^3

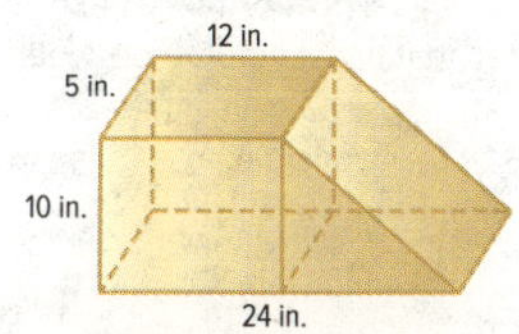

6. MP **Reason Inductively** The swimming pool at the right is being filled with water. Find the number of cubic feet that it will take to fill the swimming pool. (*Hint:* The area of a trapezoid is $A = \frac{1}{2}h(b_1 + b_2)$.) (Examples 1 and 2)

2,400 ft^3

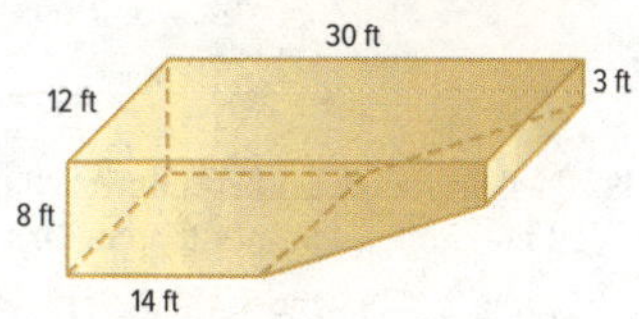

Copy and Solve **For Exercises 7–8, show your work on a separate piece of paper. Round to the nearest tenth.** (Examples 1–4)

7. Find the surface area of the figure in Exercise 1. 10.4 m^2

8. Find the volume of the figure in Exercise 4. 972 m^3

ENGAGE EXPLORE **EXPLAIN** **ELABORATE** **EVALUATE**

3 Practice and Apply

Independent Practice and Extra Practice

The Independent Practice pages are meant to be used as the homework assignment. The Extra Practice page can be used for additional reinforcement or as a second-day assignment.

Levels of Complexity

The levels of the exercises progress from 1 to 3, with Level 1 indicating the lowest level of complexity.

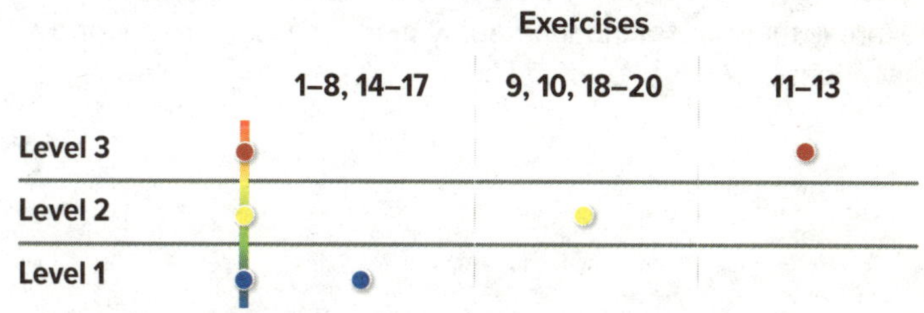

Suggested Assignments

You can use the table below that includes exercises of all complexity levels to select appropriate exercises for your students' needs.

Differentiated Homework Options		
AL	Approaching Level	1–8, 9, 11, 13, 19, 20
OL	On Level	1–7 odd, 9–11, 13, 19, 20
BL	Beyond Level	9–13, 19, 20

McGraw Hill Education **ALEKS**® can provide additional remediation support with personalized instruction and practice.

Watch Out!

Common Error When finding surface areas of composite figures, students may erroneously find the surface areas of each simpler figure and add them together. Remind students that not every surface of a simpler figure is part of the surface area of the composite figure.

MP MATHEMATICAL PRACTICES	
Emphasis On	**Exercise(s)**
1 Make sense of problems and persevere in solving them.	12
3 Construct viable arguments and critique the reasoning of others.	6, 13, 18
4 Model with mathematics.	11

Mathematical Practices 1, 3, and 4 are aspects of mathematical thinking that are emphasized in every lesson. Students are given opportunities to be persistent in their problem solving, to express their reasoning, and apply mathematics to real-world situations.

Formative Assessment

Use this activity as a closing formative assessment before dismissing students from your class.

TICKET Out the Door

Have students write about how they used the *solve a simpler problem* strategy to solve problems involving volume and surface area of composite figures. See students' work.

9. A carryout container is shown. The bottom base is a 4-inch square and the top base is a 4-inch by 6-inch rectangle. The height of the container is 5 inches. Find the volume of food that it holds. 100 in^3

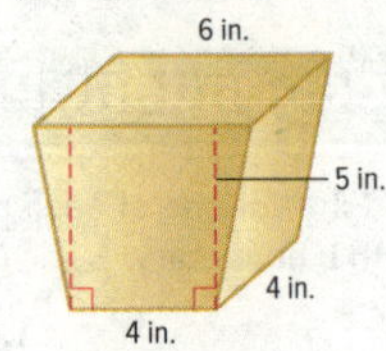

10. Refer to the house shown. Find the surface area and volume of the house. Do not include the bottom of the house when calculating the surface area. volume: $1{,}380 \text{ m}^3$; surface area: 616.4 m^2

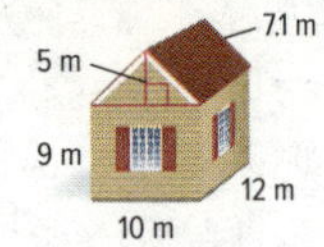

H.O.T. Problems Higher Order Thinking

11. MP **Model with Mathematics** Draw a composite figure that is made up of a cube and a square pyramid. Label its dimensions and find the volume of the figure. See students' work.

Show your work.

12. MP **Persevere with Problems** Draw an example of a composite figure that has a volume between 250 and 300 cubic units. See students' work.

13. MP **Construct an Argument** Will the surface area of the figure at the right be greater than or less than 180 square inches? Explain your reasoning. less than; Sample answer: The combined surface area of the two separate prisms is 180 in^2. Since they share a surface, the area of that surface is not included in the total surface area. The total surface area will be less than 180 in^2.

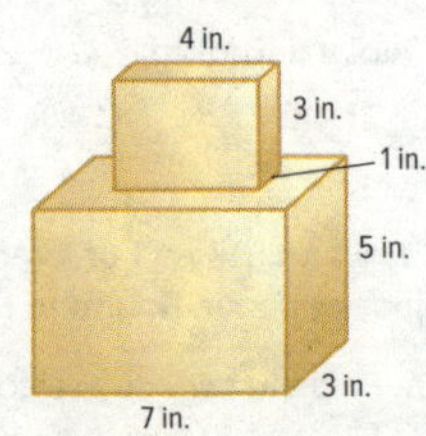

Name ____________________ My Homework ____________________

Extra Practice

Find the volume of each composite figure. Round to the nearest tenth if necessary.

14. $450\ in^3$

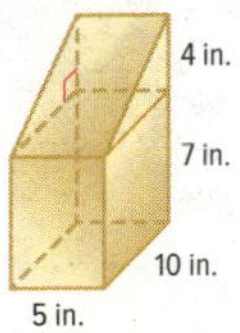

Homework Help

Rectangular Prism

$V = lwh$

$V = 5 \cdot 10 \cdot 7$

$V = 350$

Triangular Prism

$V = Bh$

$V = \frac{1}{2} \cdot 10 \cdot 4 \cdot 5$

$V = 100$

Total Volume $= 350 + 100$ or $450\ in^3$

15. $100\ in^3$

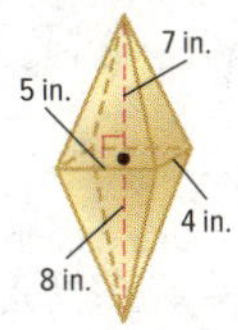

Find the surface area of each composite figure. Round to the nearest tenth if necessary.

16. $292\ yd^2$

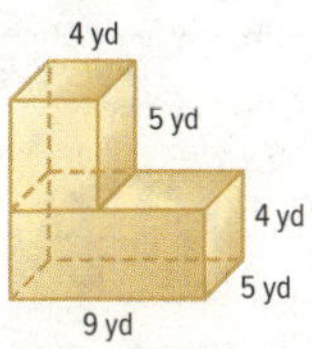

17. $280.2\ cm^2$

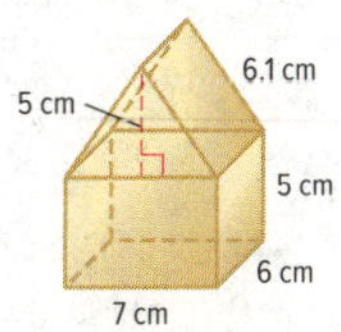

18. MP **Find the Error** Seth is finding the surface area of the composite figure shown. Find his mistake and correct it.

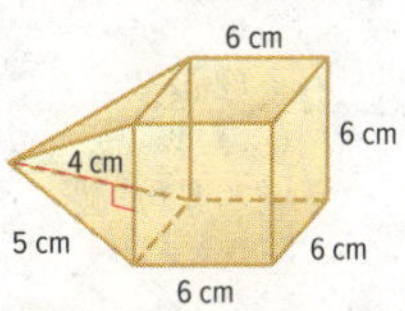

Seth incorrectly found the volume of the composite figure instead of the surface area. The actual surface area is $228\ cm^2$.

Create Your Own Homework Online

eSolutionsManual™ can be used to create worksheets for the suggested assignments on page 693, or create your own worksheets for differentiated homework or review.

Watch Out!

Find the Error For Exercise 18, students may not realize that although Seth's calculation for the volume of the figure is correct, he was asked to find its surface area. Encourage students to read the problem again carefully to discover his error.

Power Up! Test Practice

Exercises 19 and 20 prepare students for more rigorous thinking needed for the state assessment.

19.

This test item requires students to explain and apply mathematical concepts and solve problems with precision, while making use of structure.	
Depth of Knowledge	DOK1
Content Standard	7.G.6
Mathematical Practice	MP1
Online Experience	Students will be required to type their responses in the boxes.
Scoring Rubric	
1 point	Students correctly answer each part of the question.

20.

This test item requires students to analyze and solve complex real-world problems through the use of mathematical tools and models.	
Depth of Knowledge	DOK2
Content Standard	7.G.6
Mathematical Practice	MP1, MP4
Online Experience	Students will drag values to model the equation and type their response in the box.
Scoring Rubric	
2 points	Students correctly model the equation and find the volume of the figure.
1 point	Students correctly model the equation OR find the volume of the figure.

Power Up! Test Practice

19. Refer to the composite figure with the dimensions shown. Fill in the boxes to complete each statement.

a. The volume of the composite figure is [1.68 ft³].

b. The total surface area of the composite figure is [19.28 ft²].

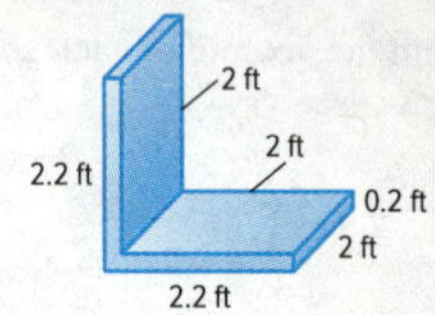

20. Refer to the composite figure with the dimensions shown.

Select the correct values to complete the expression to find the volume of the figure.

$V = \boxed{2} \cdot \frac{1}{3} \cdot \boxed{6} \cdot \boxed{6} \cdot \boxed{8}$

What is the volume of the composite figure?

[192 mm³]

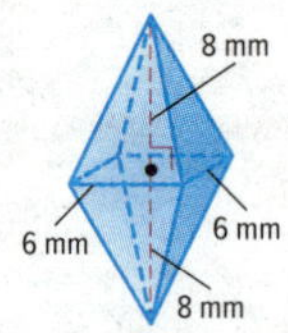

2
3
4
6
8

Spiral Review

Draw a net for each figure. 6.G.4

21.

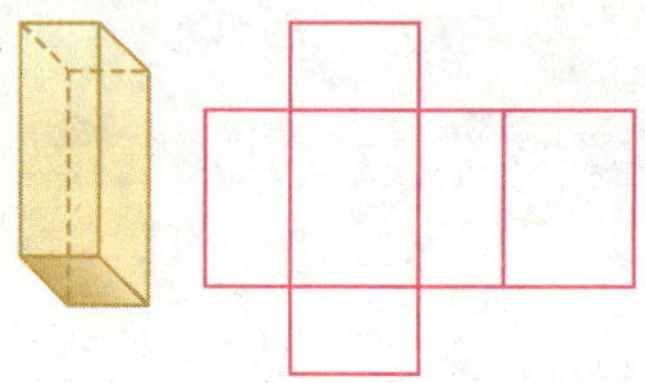

Show your work.

22.

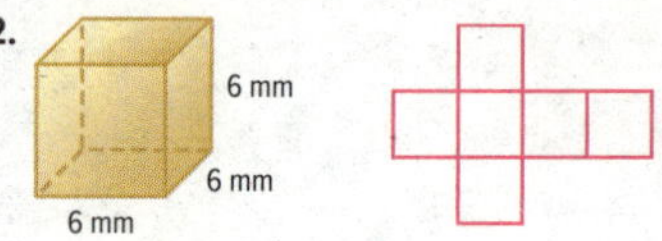

23.

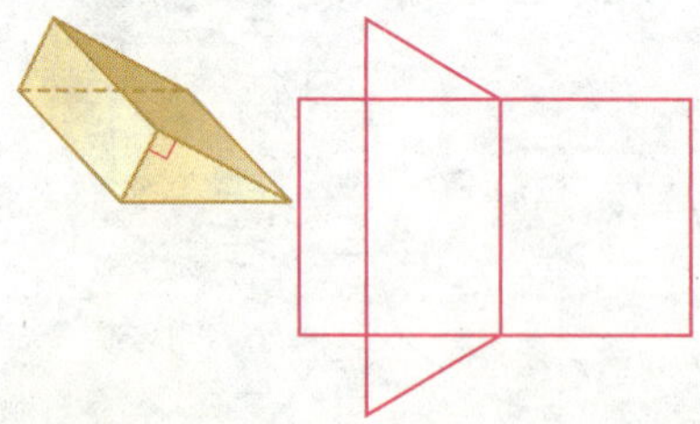

24.

PRESENT

College & Career READINESS

Focus narrowing the scope

Objective Apply mathematics to problems arising in the workplace. This lesson emphasizes MP **Mathematical Practice 4** Model with Mathematics.

Coherence connecting within and across grades

Previous
Students use formulas to find circumberence, area, volume, and surface area.

Now
Students apply the content standard to solve problems in the workplace.

Rigor pursuing concepts, fluency, and applications

See the Career Project on page 698.

21ST CENTURY CAREER in Landscape Architecture

Landscape Architect

Do you have an artistic side, and do you enjoy being outdoors? If so, a career in landscape design might be a perfect fit for you. Landscape architects design outside areas such as yards, parks, playgrounds, campuses, shopping centers, and golf courses. Their designed areas are not only meant to be beautiful, but also functional and compatible with the natural environment. A landscape architect must be proficient in mathematics, science, and the use of computer-aided design.

College & Career READINESS

Is This the Career for You?

Are you interested in a career as a landscape architect? Take some of the following courses in high school.

- **Algebra**
- **Architectural Design**
- **Botany**
- **Drafting/Illustrative Design Technology**
- **Geometry**

Find out how math relates to a career in Landscape Architecture.

ENGAGE EXPLORE EXPLAIN ELABORATE EVALUATE

1 Launch the Lesson

Ask students to read the information on the student page about landscape architects and answer the following questions.

Ask:

- *What responsibilities does a landscape architect have?* **Sample answer: design an area that looks nice, is easy for people to use, and matches the natural environment**
- *What subjects must a landscape architect understand well?* **Sample answers: Algebra, Architectural Design, Botany, Drafting/Illustrative Design Technology, Geometry**

College & Career READINESS

Help students connect what they do today to their futures. Direct them to the Internet or another source to explore, learn, and plan for college and future careers.

ENGAGE EXPLORE **EXPLAIN** **ELABORATE** EVALUATE

2 Collaborate

AL EL **Pairs Check** Have students work in pairs to complete Exercises 1–6. One partner solves the problem while the other coaches. Students switch roles for the next problem. After every two problems, the pairs check their answers with another pair and discuss and resolve any discrepancies. Use the following questions to guide students' reviews. MP 1, 6, 7

Ask:

- *To find the answer to Exercise 1, what do you need to know?* Sample answer: The radius of a circle is half of the diameter.
- *In Exercise 6, what variable should you solve for in the problem?* r

BL EL **Numbered Heads Together** Assign students to a 3-person learning team. Each member is assigned a number from 1 to 3. Each team completes Exercises 1–6 where each student is responsible for two exercises. Give the teams time to review their answers to make sure all team members understand the solution. At this point, every student should be able to answer any exercise. Call out an exercise number and a number from one team. That team member should explain the solution and solution method to that exercise. MP 1, 6, 7

Career Portfolio

When students complete this page, have them add it to their Career Portfolio.

Career Facts

According to the U.S. Bureau of Labor Statistics, there are more than 61 colleges and universities that offer undergraduate and graduate programs in landscape architecture.

MP Planting in Circles

For each problem, use the information in the designs.

1. In Design 2, what is the radius of the larger grassy area? 5 m
2. The small circular fountain in Design 1 is surrounded by a stone wall. Find the circumference of the wall. Use $\frac{22}{7}$ for π. $18\frac{6}{7}$ ft
3. Find the circumference of the smaller grassy area in Design 2. Use 3.14 for π. 25.12 m
4. In Design 2, how much greater is the lawn area in the larger circle than in the smaller circle? Use 3.14 for π. 28.26 m^2
5. In Design 2, the smaller circle is surrounded by a path 1 meter wide. What is the outer circumference of the path? Use the π key on a calculator and round to the nearest tenth. 31.4 m
6. In Design 1, the area of the large circular patio is about 201.1 square feet. What is the radius of the patio? Round to the nearest foot. 8 ft

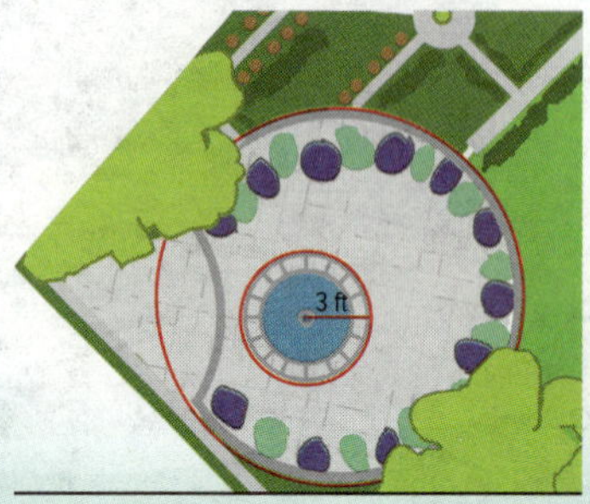

Design 1

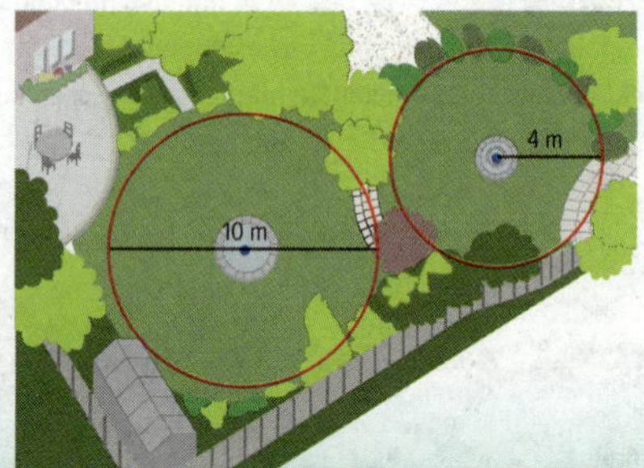

Design 2

MP Career Project

It's time to update your career portfolio! Download free landscaping software from the Internet and use it to create your own landscape design. Include a list of all the plants, materials, and hard elements used in your design. Also, provide an estimate of the total cost of the landscaping project.

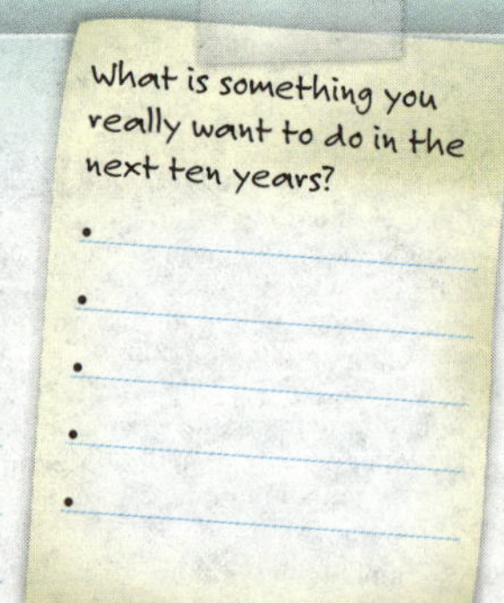

Chapter Review

Vocabulary Check

Vocab

Complete each sentence using the vocabulary list at the beginning of the chapter. Then circle the word that completes the sentence in the word search.

1. The distance across a circle through its center is called the **diameter**.
2. The **radius** is the distance from the center to any point on the circle.
3. A **circle** is the set of all points in a plane that are the same distance from a point.
4. The point in a circle from which all other points are equidistant is called the **center**.
5. The distance around a circle is the **circumference**.
6. The ratio of circumference to diameter is called **pi**.
7. A **semicircle** is half of a circle.
8. A **composite** figure is made up of two or more shapes.
9. The **volume** of a three-dimensional figure is the measure of the space it occupies.
10. The sum of the areas of all the faces of a three-dimensional figure is the **surface** area.
11. The triangular faces of a pyramid that are not bases are **lateral** faces.
12. The height of each lateral face of a pyramid is called the **slant** height.

G	U	H	M	I	R	H	X	P	E	S	F	S	S	Q	W	C	P	A	C	O	Q
P	I	B	A	E	V	O	L	U	M	E	E	V	W	Z	A	X	S	D	O	O	C
P	G	J	T	V	C	T	Y	A	G	E	R	M	R	Q	A	Q	I	E	M	I	O
C	N	N	C	D	E	D	Z	M	M	L	R	L	I	I	N	A	D	P	P	I	D
M	E	Z	C	K	G	H	N	L	O	C	P	I	V	C	M	C	W	Z	O	C	Z
C	H	C	I	R	C	U	M	F	E	R	E	N	C	E	I	P	M	C	S	N	P
X	E	O	V	G	B	L	H	V	Z	I	B	B	T	P	T	R	S	O	I	C	N
S	Y	V	T	D	K	L	A	B	W	C	O	E	E	T	J	L	C	V	T	D	L
S	P	M	T	Y	S	U	Z	R	I	T	R	J	Q	O	R	Y	B	L	E	Y	Q
Y	P	V	S	Z	B	E	Z	O	E	H	N	W	G	J	C	T	T	Q	E	H	S
P	R	D	B	T	T	L	D	W	T	T	N	W	Y	X	Z	S	V	J	X	L	J
E	K	A	J	N	J	G	W	C	M	P	A	C	D	M	K	L	M	O	S	L	P
A	I	Y	D	A	Z	X	F	Q	F	C	X	L	Y	M	Y	A	W	X	F	Z	F
V	X	Y	M	I	N	H	P	I	W	D	U	Z	L	A	T	N	Q	L	O	Q	J
Z	U	O	Y	M	U	U	K	K	K	L	I	C	E	W	H	T	A	J	M	U	H
E	C	A	F	R	U	S	G	Z	E	X	K	W	S	T	R	X	J	X	K	I	K

Vocabulary Check

EL **Group Check** Have students work in groups of four to complete the Vocabulary Check. Students take turns completing each exercise. After every four exercises, the group checks their answers with each other. All group members must agree on the same answer. Students continue this until all the exercises have been completed. MP 1, 6

Alternate Strategy

AL EL To help students, you may wish to give them a vocabulary list from which they can choose their answers. A vocabulary list for this activity would include the following terms.

- center (Lesson 1)
- circle (Lesson 1)
- circumference (Lesson 1)
- composite figure (Lesson 3)
- diameter (Lesson 1)
- lateral face (Lesson 5)
- pi (Lesson 1)
- radius (Lesson 1)
- semicircle (Lesson 2)
- slant height (Lesson 7)
- surface area (Lesson 6)
- volume (Lesson 4)

Key Concept Check

FOLDABLES **EL** A completed Foldable for this chapter should include a review of finding the volume and surface area of prisms and pyramids.

If you choose not to use this Foldable, have students write a brief review of the Key Concepts found throughout the chapter and give an example of each.

Ideas for Use

EL Have students work in pairs to discuss their Foldables. Have them practice speaking in a collaborative setting by sharing how they have completed their Foldable thus far and how they could finish it. Have each student complete their Foldable and trade with their partner to discuss any similarities and differences.

Got It?

If students have trouble with Exercises 1–4, they may need help with the following concept(s).

Concept	Exercise(s)
circles (Lessons 1 and 2)	1, 2
volume of prisms (Lesson 4)	3
surface area of prisms (Lesson 6)	4

ALEKS® provides additional support with personalized instruction and practice for those who are struggling, while providing enhanced learning for those who have mastered the concepts.

Key Concept Check

Use Your FOLDABLES

Use your Foldable to help review the chapter.

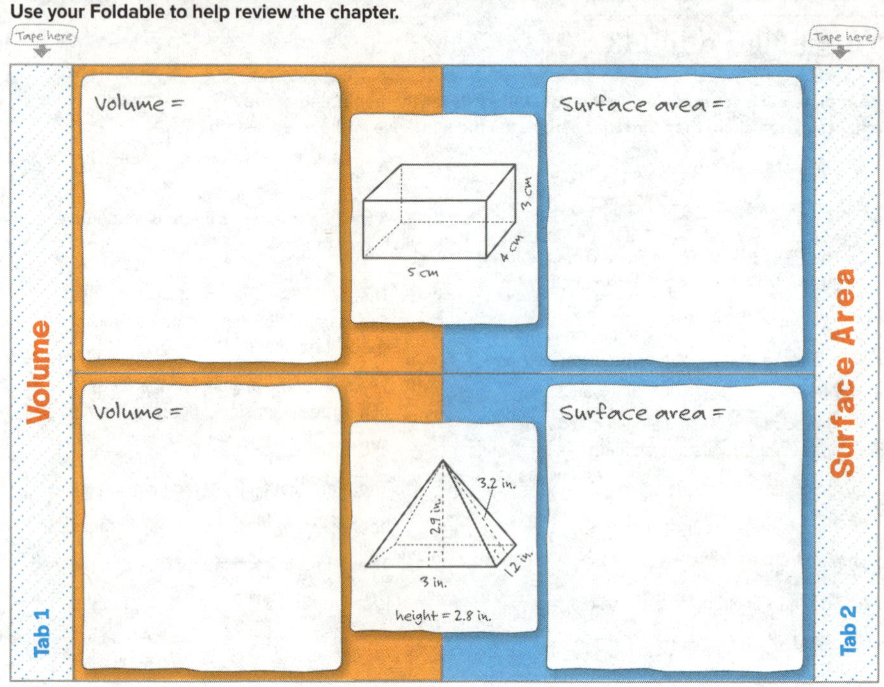

Got it?

Circle the correct term or number to complete each sentence.

1. The diameter of a circle is (twice, three times) its radius.
2. The area of a circle equals the product of pi and the square of its (radius, diameter).
3. The volume of a rectangular prism can be found by multiplying the area of the base times the (length, height).
4. To find the surface area of a triangular prism, find the area of each face and calculate the (sum, product) of all the faces.

Power Up! Performance Task

Juice Box Packaging

Supreme Packaging Company manufactures juice boxes for juice companies. They are examining different ways to make the juice boxes using various lengths, widths, and heights. The measurements of one juice box are shown.

Write your answers on another piece of paper. Show all of your to receive full credit.

Part A
What is the volume of the juice box shown? The company received an order to make a jumbo juice box that has twice the volume as the one shown. Could you double the current dimensions to make the jumbo juice box at the suggested volume? Explain.

Part B
Draw and label a net to find the surface area of the original juice box. It costs Supreme Packaging $0.02 per square inch to create one juice box. The company groups eight juice boxes together as one package. How much does it cost to create one package?

Part C
An artist created the picture of the citrus fruit on the label. The picture is a circle and has an area of 12.56 square inches. Will the artist's picture fit on the juice box label? Explain. Use 3.14 for π.

Power Up! Performance Task

This Performance-Based Assessment requires students to solve multi-step problems through abstract reasoning, precision, and perseverance. This practice scenario can be used to help students prepare for the thinking skills that will be used on the State Assessment.

A complete scoring rubric with answers to the Exercises can be found on page PT4.

Answering the Essential Question

Before answering the Essential Question, have students review their answers to the **Building on the Essential Question** exercises found in each lesson of the chapter.

- What is the relationship between the circumference and diameter of a circle (p. 616)
- How are the circumference and area of a circle alike? How are they different? (p. 626)
- How can you tell if an answer is exact or an approximation? (p. 634)
- How is finding the volume of a rectangular prism and the volume of a triangular prism alike? different? (p. 642)
- When you are finding the volume of a pyramid, why is it important to know the shape of the base of the pyramid? (p. 656)
- Why is the surface area of a three-dimensional figure measured in square units instead of cubic units? (p. 668)
- How can you justify the formula for the surface area of a pyramid? (p. 680)
- How do the previous lessons in this chapter help you find the surface area and volume of a composite figure? (p. 692)

Ideas for Use

EL **Think-Pair-Share** Have students work in pairs. Pose the Essential Question. Give students about one minute to think about how they could complete the graphic organizer. Then have them share their responses with their partner before they complete the graphic organizer. MP 1, 6, 7

Reflect

Answering the Essential Question

Use what you learned about measuring figures to complete the graphic organizer. Sample answers are given.

Circumference

Circumference is the distance around a circular object, such as a car tire.

Area

Area is the space covered by a two-dimensional object, such as the size of a rug.

Essential Question

HOW do measurements help you describe real-world objects?

Volume

Volume is the amount a three-dimensional object can hold, such as the liquid in a beverage container.

Surface Area

Surface area is the amount needed to cover a three-dimensional object, such as wrapping a present.

Answer the Essential Question. HOW do measurements help you describe real-world objects?

See students' work.

UNIT PROJECT

Turn Over a New Leaf The flatness of leaves serves an important purpose. In this project you will:

- **Collaborate** with your classmates as you research the primary function of leaves.
- **Share** the results of your research in a creative way.
- **Reflect** on how you use different measurements to solve real-life problems.

Collaborate

Go Online Work with your group to research and complete each activity. You will use your results in the Share section on the following page.

1. Suppose you have a cube that is 10 centimeters on each side. Find the volume, surface area, and surface area to volume ratio.

2. Disassemble the cube from Exercise 1 into centimeter cubes. Arrange the cubes in a 50-by-20-by-1 prism. Find the volume, surface area, and surface area to volume ratio.

3. Compare and contrast the volume, surface area, and surface area to volume ratio from Exercises 1 and 2.

4. Trace the outline of a leaf onto centimeter grid paper. Estimate the volume of the leaf. (Assume the height of your leaf is 0.1 centimeter.) Estimate the surface area. (You can ignore the edge of the leaf.) Find the surface area to volume ratio.

5. Do research to find the primary function of a leaf. Explain how the surface area to volume ratio of a leaf aids in its function.

6. Find examples from nature or man-made objects that have a small surface area to volume ratio. Explain the benefits.

Watch the Project Video

Go online to watch a video to launch this unit project.

Launch the Project

Objective Research the implications of a leaf's surface area to volume ratio.

Turn Over a New Leaf

This project is designed to be completed by a group of 4 or 5 students over several days or several weeks. It utilizes concepts from the Geometry domain. You may choose to complete this project after completing the chapters within this domain.

Collaborate

Have students work in teams to research each activity. Together, they should be able to gather the necessary information to complete Exercises 1–6. Students should show their work on a separate piece of paper.

Share

Collaborate

After each group gives their presentation, ask students to discuss the most challenging part of this project. How did they handle this part of the project? What could they have done differently to make it less challenging?

21st Century Skills

You may want your students to connect their projects to a 21st century skill. Check out the suggestion below and on the student page.

connect with Science

Investigate the surface area to volume ratio for large and small animals. Write an essay that describes your findings. Some questions to consider are:

- Which animals have a large surface area to volume ratio?
- How does an animal's surface area to volume ratio affect its body temperature?

Reflect

On Your Own

Students should work on their own to reflect on how the chapters from this unit and the objective of the project relate to the Essential Question.

Share

Collaborate

With your group, decide on a way to share what you have learned about the surface area to volume ratio of leaves. Some suggestions are listed below, but you could also think of other creative ways to present your information. Remember to show how you used mathematics to complete each of the activities in this project!

- Create a digital presentation that compares two types of leaves. Use what you learned about surface area to volume ratios in your presentation.
- Imagine you discovered a new type of leaf. Create an annotated diagram of your leaf. The annotations should include the type of information you learned in this project.

Check out the note on the right to connect this project with other subjects.

connect with Science

Environmental Literacy Write a paragraph detailing facts about the leaves you researched. Some questions to consider are:

- What are the names of the trees that dropped these leaves?
- Are these types of trees common in your state?

Reflect

On Your Own

6. **Answer the Essential Question** How can you use different measurements to solve real-life problems? **See students' work.**

   a. How did what you learned about geometric figures help you use different measurements to solve real-life problems in this project?

   b. How did what you learned about measuring figures to help you use different measurements to solve real-life problems in this project?

UNIT 5 Statistics and Probability

Essential Question

WHY is learning mathematics important?

Chapter 9 Probability

Probability describes the likelihood of an event occurring. In this chapter, you will develop probability models and find probabilities of simple and compound events.

Chapter 10 Statistics

Statistics can be used to draw conclusions about a population. In this chapter, you will use random samples to make predictions and compare populations.

Plan Online connectED.mcgraw-hill.com

You can use the resources available online to plan for this unit.

Essential Question

At the end of this unit, students should be able to answer "Why is learning mathematics important?"

Each chapter explores a different essential question that assists students in answering the unit question. The lessons in each chapter include exercises that lead students to various aspects of the essential question.

This unit focuses on the Statistics and Probability. The chapters address the following grade 7 standards:

Use random sampling to draw inferences about a population.

1. Understand that statistics can be used to gain information about a population by examining a sample of the population; generalizations about a population from a sample are valid only if the sample is representative of that population. Understand that random sampling tends to produce representative samples and support valid inferences. (7.SP.1)
2. Use data from a random sample to draw inferences about a population with an unknown characteristic of interest. Generate multiple samples (or simulated samples) of the same size to gauge the variation in estimates or predictions. (7.SP.2)

continued on page 706

Draw informal comparative inferences about two populations.

4. Use measures of center and measures of variability for numerical data from random samples to draw informal comparative inferences about two populations. (7.SP.4)

Investigate chance processes and develop, use, and evaluate probability models.

5. Understand that the probability of a chance event is a number between 0 and 1 that expresses the likelihood of the event occurring. Larger numbers indicate greater likelihood. A probability near 0 indicates an unlikely event, a probability around 1/2 indicates an event that is neither unlikely nor likely, and a probability near 1 indicates a likely event. (7.SP.5)

6. Approximate the probability of a chance event by collecting data on the chance process that produces it and observing its long-run relative frequency, and predict the approximate relative frequency given the probability. (7.SP.6)

7. Develop a probability model and use it to find probabilities of events. Compare probabilities from a model to observed frequencies; if the agreement is not good, explain possible sources of the discrepancy. (7.SP.7)

8. Find probabilities of compound events using organized lists, tables, tree diagrams, and simulation. (7.SP.8)

Unit Project Preview

Collaborate

Ask students what they know about genetics and Punnett Squares.

Have students fill in each square by combining the letters in the column and row for that square.

The Unit Project can be found on pages 853–854.

Video Play the Unit Project video to give students some background information on the topic and to generate excitement for the upcoming project.

Unit Project Preview

Collaborate

Watch

Math Genes A *Punnett Square* is a diagram that is used to predict the genetic traits of offspring.

A pea plant can be tall (described by TT, TS, or ST) or short (described by SS). Complete the Punnett Square below. What percent of the outcomes indicate that the offspring will be short? 25%

At the end of Chapter 10, you'll complete a project in which you use pets' traits to make predictions about their offspring. Put on your lab coat and grab your math tool kit to begin this adventure!

Pea Plants

Parent 2 \ Parent 1	T	S
T	TT	TS
S	ST	SS

PLAN ONLINE

PD | RtI | Watch | Worksheets | Vocab | Tutor | Tools | Check | English Learners | Sketchpad

PRESENT

IWB An Interactive Whiteboard Ready presentation is available for each lesson in the chapter.

Chapter 9
Probability

Essential Question

HOW can you predict the outcome of future events?

Content Standards
7.SP.5, 7.SP.6, 7.SP.7, 7.SP.7a, 7.SP.7b, 7.SP.8, 7.SP.8a, 7.SP.8b, 7.SP.8c

MP Mathematical Practices
1, 3, 4, 5

Math in the Real World

Probability is the likelihood or chance of an event occurring.

At the beginning of a football game, a coin is tossed to determine which team receives the ball first. Fill in the table below to indicate the number of times a team would expect to win the coin toss based on the number of games played.

Number of Games	Number of Coin Toss Wins
4	2
10	5
22	11
50	25

FOLDABLES® Study Organizer

1. Cut out the Foldable on page FL11 of this book.
2. Place your Foldable on page 786.
3. Use the Foldable throughout this chapter to help you learn about probability.

Focus narrowing the scope

This chapter focuses on content from the **Statistics and Probability** (SP) domain.

Mathematical Background Additional information about the mathematical background for this chapter can be found online at connectED.mcgraw-hill.com.

Coherence connecting within and across grades

Previous Students computed with rational numbers.

Now Students find the probability of simple and compound events.

Next Students will analyze samples and interpret the data.

Rigor pursuing concepts, fluency, and applications

The Levels of Complexity charts located throughout this chapter indicate how the exercises progress from conceptual understanding and procedural skills and fluency, to application and critical thinking.

Launch the Chapter

Math in the Real World

Probability Explain that there is an equally likely chance of tossing heads as tossing tails. So, you could expect to win the coin toss 50% of the time.

What Tools Do You Need?

Vocabulary Activity

EL As you proceed through the chapter, introduce each vocabulary term using the following routine. Ask the students to say each term aloud after you say it.

Define: Probability is the chance that an event will happen. It is the ratio of the number of favorable outcomes to the number of possible outcomes.

Example: Peter has a blue, a black, and a red pen in his schoolbag. The probability that he will pull a blue pen out of his schoolbag is 1:3.

Ask:

- *What is the probability that a coin, when tossed, will land on tails?* **$\frac{1}{2}$, 0.5, or 50%**

Review Vocabulary

EL Have students read the Review Vocabulary section.

Ask:

- *How do you write a fraction as a decimal?* **Sample answer: Perform long division to express the fraction as a decimal.**
- *How do you write a decimal as a percent?* **Sample answer: Multiply the decimal by 100, which is the same as moving the decimal point two places to the right, then add the % sign.**

What Tools Do You Need?

Vocabulary

complementary events	outcome	simple event
compound event	permutation	simulation
dependent events	probability	theoretical probability
experimental probability	random	tree diagram
fair	relative frequency	uniform probability model
Fundamental Counting Principle	sample space	unfair
independent events		

Review Vocabulary

Fractions, Decimals, and Percents Equivalent rational numbers are numbers that have the same value. For example, three-fourths is equivalent to 0.75 or 75%.

A probability can be expressed as a fraction, decimal, or percent. For each rational number, write the missing equivalent values. Write fractions in simplest form.

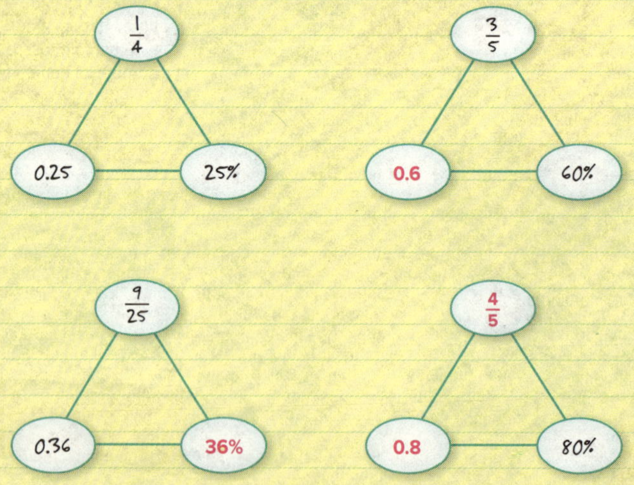

What Do You Already Know?

List three things you already know about probability in the first section. Then list three things you would like to learn about probability in the second section. See students' work.

Probability

What I know	What I want to find out

When Will You Use This?

Here are a few examples of how probability is used in the real world.

Activity 1 Have you ever read something like "The chances of winning are 75%." or "30% of the people surveyed said that they prefer vanilla ice cream."? Use the Internet to find an example like the ones given. Describe your example and what it means to you.

See students' work.

Activity 2 Go online at connectED.mcgraw-hill.com to read the graphic novel ***Radio Surveys***. What type of information do Jamar and Theresa want to learn from their survey?

The types of music teens listen to.

What Do You Already Know?

In this activity students assess their prior knowledge by listing three things they already know and three things they would like to learn about concepts in the chapter.

- You may want to add a third option of "I don't know" for those students who do not have any prior knowledge of the topic.
- After completing the chapter, have students return to this page and have them add three new facts that they learned about the topic.

When Will You Use This?

Activity 1

Students may not realize the vast examples of probability that exist in the real-world. Students will use the Internet to discover examples.

Activity 2

Use the Graphic Novel to help students learn about using rational numbers to solve problems.

Ask:

- *What are other ways that Jamar and Theresa could collect data?* **Sample answer: They could survey all the students in their homerooms.**

Are You Ready?

Use this page to determine if students have skills that are needed for the chapter.

Quick Review

Students with strong math backgrounds may opt to go directly to the Quick Check.

QUICK REVIEW		
Example	Skill	Standard
1	Simplify fractions.	6.NS.4
2	Multiply whole numbers.	5.NBT.5

Quick Check

If students have difficulty with the exercises, present an additional example to clarify any misconceptions.

Exercises 1–4

Write $\frac{4}{16}$ in simplest form. $\frac{1}{4}$

Exercises 5–8

Find $11 \times 10 \times 9$. 990

RtI Response to Intervention

Go online at connectED.mcgraw-hill.com for resources to differentiate remediation for Tier 1, Tier 2, and Tier 3 students.

ALEKS® can provide additional remediation support with personalized instruction and practice. See page T8 and T9 for more information.

Are You Ready?

Try the Quick Check below. Or, take the Online Readiness Quiz. Check

Quick Review

5.NBT.5, 6.NS.4

Example 1

Write $\frac{21}{28}$ in simplest form.

$\frac{21}{28} = \frac{3}{4}$ (÷7)

Divide the numerator and denominator by the GCF, 7.

Example 2

Find 7 • 6 • 5 • 4.

$7 \cdot 6 \cdot 5 \cdot 4 = 42 \cdot 5 \cdot 4$
$= 210 \cdot 4$
$= 840$

Multiply from left to right.

Quick Check

Fractions Write each fraction in simplest form.

1. $\frac{5}{15} = \frac{1}{3}$
2. $\frac{3}{18} = \frac{1}{6}$
3. $\frac{8}{12} = \frac{2}{3}$
4. $\frac{12}{20} = \frac{3}{5}$

Show your work.

Products Find each product.

5. $6 \cdot 5 =$ 30
6. $10 \cdot 9 \cdot 8 =$ 720
7. $4 \cdot 3 \cdot 2 \cdot 1 =$ 24

8. Suppose you listen to 9 songs each hour for 5 hours every day this week. How many songs will you have listened to this week?
315 songs

How Did You Do?

Which problems did you answer correctly in the Quick Check? Shade those exercise numbers below.

1 2 3 4 5 6 7 8

PLAN ONLINE

PD | RtI | Watch | Worksheets | Vocab | Tutor | Tools | Check | English Learners | Sketchpad

PRESENT

IWB

An Interactive Whiteboard Ready presentation is available for each lesson in the chapter.

Lesson 1

Probability of Simple Events

Vocabulary Start-Up

Probability is the chance that some event will occur. A **simple event** is one outcome or a collection of outcomes. What is an **outcome**?

Math Definition		Real-World Definition
A possible result in a probability experiment.	Outcome	The way that something turns out.

Essential Question

HOW can you predict the outcome of future events?

Vocabulary

probability
outcome
simple event
random
complementary events

Content Standards
7.SP.5, 7.SP.7, 7.SP.7a

MP Mathematical Practices
1, 3, 4

Real-World Link

For a sledding trip, you randomly select one of the four hats shown. Complete the table to show the possible outcomes.

Hat Selection Outcomes			
Outcome 1	green hat	Outcome 3	red hat
Outcome 2	blue hat	Outcome 4	purple hat

1. Write a ratio that compares the number of blue hats to the total number of hats. $\frac{1}{4}$

2. Describe a hat display in which you would have a better chance of selecting a red hat.
Sample answer: a display containing 4 red hats and 2 blue hats

Which MP **Mathematical Practices** did you use?
Shade the circle(s) that applies.

① Persevere with Problems
② Reason Abstractly
③ Construct an Argument
④ Model with Mathematics
⑤ Use Math Tools
⑥ Attend to Precision
⑦ Make Use of Structure
⑧ Use Repeated Reasoning

Focus narrowing the scope

Objective Find the probability of a simple event and its complement. 7.SP.5, 7.SP.7, 7.SP.7a

Coherence connecting within and across grades

Previous Students wrote rational number in different forms.

Now Students will find the probability of simple events and compund events.

Next Students will solve problems using predictions and comparisons from simple experiments.

Rigor pursuing concepts, fluency, and applications

See the Levels of Complexity chart on page 715.

ENGAGE EXPLORE EXPLAIN ELABORATE EVALUATE

1 Launch the Lesson

Ideas for Use

You may wish to launch the lesson using a whole group, small group, think-pair-share activity, or independent activity.

EL **Pairs Consult** Have students think of real-world experiences they have encountered in which they described the probability of an event occurring, such as weather or sporting events. Then have them work with a partner to complete the Real-World Link. MP 1, 4, 6

Alternate Strategy

AL EL Have students relate how the term *probably* helps them to remember the meaning of the term *probability*. MP 1, 6

2 Teach the Concept

Ask the scaffolded questions for each example to differentiate instruction.

IWB

Example

1. Find the probability of an event.

AL
- *What outcomes are favorable?* 6
- *How many outcomes are favorable?* 1
- *What outcomes are possible?* 1, 2, 3, 4, 5, or 6
- *How many outcomes are possible?* 6

OL
- *What is the formula for the probability ratio?* $\frac{\text{favorable outcomes}}{\text{possible outcomes}}$

BL
- *Determine P(prime) when rolling a number cube. Explain.* $\frac{1}{2}$; There are 3 prime numbers (2, 3, 5) out of the 6 possible outcomes.
- *Does any number have a better chance than another of being rolled? Explain.* Each number has the same chance, $\frac{1}{6}$, of being rolled.

Need Another Example?

A spinner is divided into 8 equal sections numbered 1–8. Find the probability of spinning a 1. Write your answer as a fraction, percent, and decimal. $\frac{1}{8}$, 12.5%, 0.125

Watch Out!

Common Error Remind students that when they express probabilities as fractions, they should express the fractions in simplest form.

Key Concept **Probability**

Words The probability of an event is a ratio that compares the number of favorable outcomes to the number of possible outcomes.

Symbols $P(event) = \frac{\text{number of favorable outcomes}}{\text{number of possible outcomes}}$

Work Zone

STOP and Reflect

In the space below, describe an example of a simple event that is certain to occur.

Sample answer: Rolling a number less than 7 on a number cube.

The probability of a chance event is a number between 0 and 1 that expresses the likelihood of the event occurring. Greater numbers indicate greater likelihood. A probability near 0 indicates an unlikely event, a probability around $\frac{1}{2}$ indicates an event that is neither unlikely nor likely, and a probability near 1 indicates a likely event.

Probability can be written as a fraction, decimal, or percent.

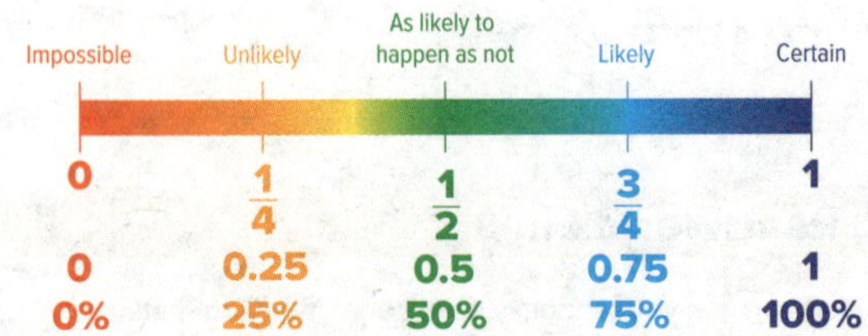

Outcomes occur at **random** if each outcome is equally likely to occur.

Example

Tools Tutor

There are six equally likely outcomes if a number cube with sides labeled 1 through 6 is rolled.

1. Find *P*(6) or the probability of rolling a 6.

There is only one 6 on the number cube.

$$P(6) = \frac{\text{number of favorable outcomes}}{\text{number of possible outcomes}}$$
$$= \frac{1}{6}$$

The probability of rolling a 6 is $\frac{1}{6}$, or about 17%, or about 0.17.

Got it? Do this problem to find out.

a. A coin is tossed. Find the probability of the coin landing on heads. Write your answer as a fraction, percent, and decimal.

Show your work.

a. $\frac{1}{2}$, 50%, or 0.5

Example

Tutor

2. Find the probability of rolling a 2, 3, or 4 on the number cube.

The word *or* indicates that the number of favorable outcomes needs to include the numbers 2, 3, and 4.

$P(2, 3, \text{or } 4) = \dfrac{\text{number of favorable outcomes}}{\text{number of possible outcomes}}$

$= \dfrac{3}{6} \text{ or } \dfrac{1}{2}$ Simplify.

The probability of rolling a 2, 3, or 4 is $\frac{1}{2}$, 50%, or 0.5.

Got it? **Do these problems to find out.**

The spinner at the right is spun once. Find the probability of each event. Write each answer as a fraction, percent, and decimal.

b. *P*(F) **c.** *P*(D or G) **d.** *P*(vowel)

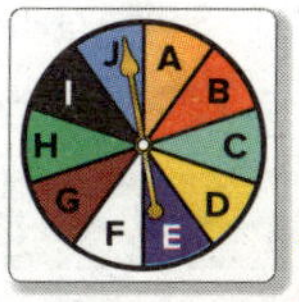

Show your work.

b. $\frac{1}{10}$, 10%, or 0.1

c. $\frac{1}{5}$, 20%, or 0.2

d. $\frac{3}{10}$, 30%, or 0.3

Find Probability of the Complement

Complementary events are two events in which either one or the other must happen, but they cannot happen at the same time. For example, a coin can either land on heads or *not* land on heads. The sum of the probability of an event and its complement is 1 or 100%.

Complement
In everyday language complement means the quantity required to make something complete. This is similar to the math meaning.

Example

Tutor

3. Find the probability of *not* rolling a 6 in Example 1.

The probability of *not* rolling a 6 and the probability of rolling a 6 are complementary. So, the sum of the probabilities is 1.

$P(6) + P(\text{not } 6) = 1$ *P*(6) and *P*(*not* 6) are complements.

$\frac{1}{6} + P(\text{not } 6) = 1$ Replace *P*(6) with $\frac{1}{6}$.

$\frac{1}{6} + \frac{5}{6} = 1$ THINK $\frac{1}{6}$ plus what number equals 1?

The probability of *not* rolling a 6 is $\frac{5}{6}$, or about 83% or 0.83.

Got it? **Do this problem to find out.**

e. A bag contains 5 blue, 8 red, and 7 green marbles. A marble is selected at random. Find the probability the marble is *not* red.

e. $\frac{3}{5}$, 60%, or 0.6

Examples

IWB

2. Find the probability of an event.

AL
- *What outcomes are favorable?* 2, 3, or a 4
- *How many outcomes are favorable?* 3
- *What outcomes are possible?* 1, 2, 3, 4, 5, or 6
- *How many outcomes are possible?* 6

OL
- *What percentage of a chance do you have to roll a 2, 3, or 4?* 50%

BL
- *Name another probability with a 50% chance of happening.* Sample answers: *P*(1, 5, or 6) *P*(odd), *P*(even)

Need Another Example?
A spinner is divided into eight equal sections numbered 1–8. Find the probability of spinning a 2 or 4. Write as a fraction, percent, and decimal. $\frac{1}{4}$, 25%, 0.25

3. Write the probability of the complement of an event.

AL
- *What is the probability of rolling a 6?* $\frac{1}{6}$
- *What are the other possible outcomes, other than 6?* 1, 2, 3, 4, 5

OL
- *In your own words, what does complement mean?* See students' responses.
- *What is always the sum of a probability and its complement?* 1

BL
- *Using the probability of some event, write an equation you can use to determine the probability of its complement.* *P*(complement) = 1 − *P*(event)

Need Another Example?
A spinner is divided into eight equal sections numbered 1–8. Find the probability of *not* spinning a 5. Write as a fraction, percent, and decimal. $\frac{7}{8}$, 87.5%, 0.875

Example

4. Identify the complement and find its probability.

AL • *What is the complement to P(blue eyes)?* P(*not* blue eyes)

• *What is the fraction equivalent to P(blue eyes)?* P(blue eyes) = $\frac{3}{10}$

OL • *The sum of the probability and its complement is what percent?* 100%

• *If 30% have blue eyes, what percent do not have blue eyes?* 70%

BL • *Describe the likelihood of the event and its complement.* Sample answer: The probability of having blue eyes is unlikely. The probability of not having blue eyes is likely.

Need Another Example?

A sportscaster predicted that the Tigers have a 75% chance of winning tonight. Identify the complement of this event and find its probability. The complement of the Tigers winning tonight is the Tigers *not* winning tonight. The probability that the Tigers will *not* win tonight is 25%, 0.25, or $\frac{1}{4}$.

Guided Practice

Formative Assessment Use these exercises to assess students' understanding of the concepts in this lesson.

If some of your students are not ready for assignments, use the differentiated activities below.

AL EL **Pairs Discussion** Have students use index cards to create letter cards for each letter in a given phrase, such as in Exercises 1–3. Have students find different probabilities, such as *P*(vowel), *P*(consonant), *P*(specific letter). Then have students describe the qualitative probabilities, such as likely, unlikely, or impossible. MP 1, 4, 6

BL EL **Pairs Consult** Have students work with a partner to discuss why the following two events are *not* complements: randomly selecting a prime number among the digits 0, 1, 2, 3, 4, 5, 6, 7, 8, and 9 and randomly selecting a composite number among the same digits. MP 1, 7

Real World Example

4. Mr. Harada surveyed his class and discovered that 30% of his students have blue eyes. Identify the complement of this event. Then find its probability.

The complement of having blue eyes is *not* having blue eyes. The sum of the probabilities is 100%.

P(blue eyes) + *P*(*not* blue eyes) = 100%	*P*(blue eyes) and *P*(*not* blue eyes) are complements.
30% + *P*(*not* blue eyes) = 100%	Replace *P*(blue eyes) with 30%.
30% + 70% = 100%	**THINK** 30% plus what number equals 100%?

So, the probability that a student does *not* have blue eyes is 70%, 0.7, or $\frac{7}{10}$.

Guided Practice

A letter tile is chosen randomly. Find the probability of each event. Write each answer as a fraction, percent, and decimal. (Examples 1–3)

1. *P*(D) $\frac{1}{9}$, about 11%, or about 0.11

2. *P*(S, V, or L) $\frac{1}{3}$, about 33%, or about 0.33

3. *P*(*not* D) $\frac{8}{9}$, about 89%, or about 0.89

4. The probability of choosing a "Go Back 1 Space" card in a board game is 25%. Describe the complement of this event and find its probability. (Example 4) The complement of selecting a "Go Back 1 Space" card is selecting any card other than that card. Its probability is $\frac{3}{4}$, 0.75, or 75%.

5. **Building on the Essential Question** Explain the relationship between the probability of an event and its complement. Give an example.
Sample answer: The probability of an event occurring or its complement occurring is certain to happen. If there is a 30% chance of rain, then the complement is a 70% chance of no rain.

Rate Yourself!

How confident are you about finding the probability of simple events? Shade the ring on the target.

For more help, go online to access a Personal Tutor.

FOLDABLES Time to update your Foldable!

Name ______________________ My Homework ______________________

Independent Practice

Go online for Step-by-Step Solutions eHelp

The spinner shown is spun once. Find the probability of each event. Write each answer as a fraction, percent, and decimal. (Examples 1–3)

1. *P*(blue)

$\frac{1}{4}$, 25%, or 0.25

2. *P*(red or yellow)

$\frac{3}{8}$, 37.5%, or 0.375

3. *P*(*not* brown)

$\frac{1}{1}$, 100%, or 1

4. *P*(*not* green)

$\frac{5}{8}$, 62.5%, or 0.625

5. Refer to the table on air travel at selected airports. Suppose a flight that arrived at El Centro is selected at random. What is the probability that the flight did *not* arrive on time? Write the answer as a fraction, decimal, and percent. Explain your reasoning. (Example 4)

$\frac{1}{5}$, 0.2, or 20%; Sample answer: Since 80% arrive on time, that means that 20% do not arrive on time.

Air Travel	
Airport	Arrivals (Percent on-time)
El Centro (CA)	80
Baltimore (MD)	82

6. MP **Model with Mathematics** Refer to the graphic novel frame below. Jamar and Theresa decide to create a music mix and include an equal number of songs from each genre. What is the probability that any given song would be from the hip-hop genre? $\frac{1}{5}$

ENGAGE EXPLORE **EXPLAIN** **ELABORATE** **EVALUATE**

3 Practice and Apply

Independent Practice and Extra Practice

The Independent Practice pages are meant to be used as the homework assignment. The Extra Practice page can be used for additional reinforcement or as a second-day assignment.

Levels of Complexity

The levels of the exercises progress from 1 to 3, with Level 1 indicating the lowest level of complexity.

	Exercises		
	1–5, 12–22	6–8, 23–25	9–11
Level 3			●
Level 2		●	
Level 1	●		

Suggested Assignments

You can use the table below that includes exercises of all complexity levels to select appropriate exercises for your students' needs.

Differentiated Homework Options		
AL	Approaching Level	1–5, 7, 11, 24, 25
OL	On Level	1–5 odd, 6–8, 11, 24, 25
BL	Beyond Level	6–11, 24, 25

McGraw Hill Education **ALEKS**® can provide additional remediation support with personalized instruction and practice.

MP MATHEMATICAL PRACTICES	
Emphasis On	**Exercise(s)**
1 Make sense of problems and persevere in solving them.	9, 10, 23
3 Construct viable arguments and critique the reasoning of others.	11
4 Model with mathematics.	6

Mathematical Practices 1, 3, and 4 are aspects of mathematical thinking that are emphasized in every lesson. Students are given opportunities to be persistent in their problem solving, to express their reasoning, and apply mathematics to real-world situations.

Formative Assessment

Use this activity as a closing formative assessment before dismissing students from your class.

TICKET Out the Door

Tell the students the probability of drawing a purple marble from a bag is $\frac{3}{8}$. Have them describe the complement of the event and find the probability of the complement.
The complement is drawing a marble that is *not* purple; $\frac{5}{8}$.

One jelly bean is picked, without looking, from the dish. Write a sentence that explains how likely it is for each event to happen.

7. black

Picking a black jelly bean is impossible since the probability of picking a black jelly bean is 0%.

8. purple, red, or yellow

This is very likely to happen since the probability of picking a purple, red, or yellow jelly bean is 90%, $\frac{9}{10}$, or 0.9.

H.O.T. Problems Higher Order Thinking

9. MP **Persevere with Problems** The probability of landing in a certain section on a spinner can be found by considering the size of the angle formed by that section. On spinner shown, the angle formed by the yellow section is one-fourth of the angle formed by the entire circle. So, $P(\text{yellow}) = \frac{1}{4}$, 0.25, or 25%.

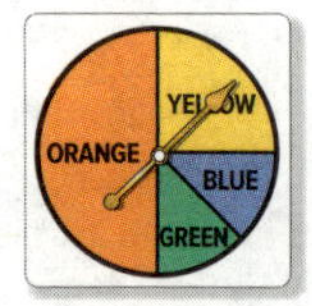

a. Determine P(green) and P(orange) for the spinner. Write the probabilities as fractions, decimals, and percents.
$\frac{1}{8}$, 0.125, 12.5%; $\frac{1}{2}$, 0.5, 50%

b. Determine P(*not* yellow).
$\frac{3}{4}$, 0.75, 75%

10. MP **Persevere with Problems** A bag contains 6 red, 4 blue, and 8 green marbles. How many marbles of each color should be added so that the total number of marbles is 27, but the probability of randomly selecting one marble of each color remains unchanged? Sample answer: There are 18 marbles in the bag. Nine marbles should be added. To do so without changing the probability, add 3 red, 2 blue, and 4 green marbles.

11. MP **Which One Doesn't Belong?** Circle the pair of probabilities that does not belong with the other three. Explain your reasoning.

0.625, $\frac{3}{8}$	0.38, 62%	$\frac{7}{8}$, 0.125	70%, $\frac{1}{3}$

70%, $\frac{1}{3}$; Sample answer: 70% and $\frac{1}{3}$ are probabilities that are not complementary because $0.7 + 0.\overline{3} \neq 1$. The other sets of probabilities are complementary.

Name ______________________ My Homework ______________________

Extra Practice

Ten cards numbered 1 through 10 are mixed together and then one card is drawn. Find the probability of each event. Write each answer as a fraction, percent, and decimal.

12. *P*(8)
$\frac{1}{10}$, 10%, or 0.1

Only 1 card has an 8. So, P(8) is $\frac{1}{10}$, 10%, or 0.1.

Homework Help

13. *P*(7 or 9)
$\frac{1}{5}$, 20%, or 0.2

There is 1 card with a 7 and 1 card with a 9. So, P(7 or 9) is $\frac{1}{5}$, or 20%, or 0.2.

14. *P*(less than 5)
$\frac{2}{5}$, 40%, or 0.4

15. *P*(greater than 3)
$\frac{7}{10}$, 70%, or 0.7

16. *P*(odd)
$\frac{1}{2}$, 50%, or 0.50

17. *P*(even)
$\frac{1}{2}$, 50%, or 0.5

18. *P*(*not* a multiple of 4)
$\frac{4}{5}$, 80%, or 0.8

19. *P*(*not* 5, 6, 7, or 8)
$\frac{3}{5}$, 60%, or 0.6

20. *P*(divisible by 3)
$\frac{3}{10}$, 30%, or 0.3

21. Of the students at Grant Middle School, 63% are girls. The school newspaper is randomly selecting a student to be interviewed. Describe the complement of selecting a girl and find the probability of the complement. Write the answer as a fraction, decimal, and percent.
The complement of selecting a girl is selecting a boy. The probability of the complement is $\frac{37}{100}$, 0.37, or 37%.

22. The table shows the number of dogs and cats at a groomer. If a pet is selected at random to be groomed, find the probability that Patches the cat will be selected. Then find the probability that a cat will be selected.
$\frac{1}{28}$, about 0.04, or about 4%; $\frac{3}{7}$, about 43%, or about 0.43

Pets at the Groomer	
Cats	**Dogs**
12	16

23. MP **Persevere with Problems** For a certain game, the probability of choosing a card with the number 13 is $\frac{8}{1,000}$. Find the probability of *not* choosing a card with the number 13. Then describe the likelihood of the event occurring.
$\frac{124}{125}$, 99.2%, or 0.992; It is very likely that card 13 will *not* be chosen.

Create Your Own Homework Online

eSolutionsManual™ can be used to create worksheets for the suggested assignments on page 715, or create your own worksheets for differentiated homework or review.

Power Up! Test Practice

Exercises 24 and 25 prepare students for more rigorous thinking needed for the state assessment.

24. This test item requires students to analyze and solve complex real-world problems through the use of mathematical tools and models.

Depth of Knowledge	DOK2
Content Standard	7.SP.5
Mathematical Practices	MP1, MP4
Online Experience	Students will be required to type their responses in the boxes.
Scoring Rubric	
1 point	Students correctly model and solve the equation.

25. This test item requires students to explain and apply mathematical concepts and solve problems with precision, while making use of structure.

Depth of Knowledge	DOK1
Content Standard	7.SP.5
Mathematical Practice	MP1
Online Experience	Students will be required to click on the bubbles to select all answers that are correct.
Scoring Rubric	
1 point	Students correctly answer the question.

Power Up! Test Practice

24. The types of songs on Max's MP3 player are shown on the graph. Max will play one of the songs at random. Complete the model below to find *P*(country or R&B).

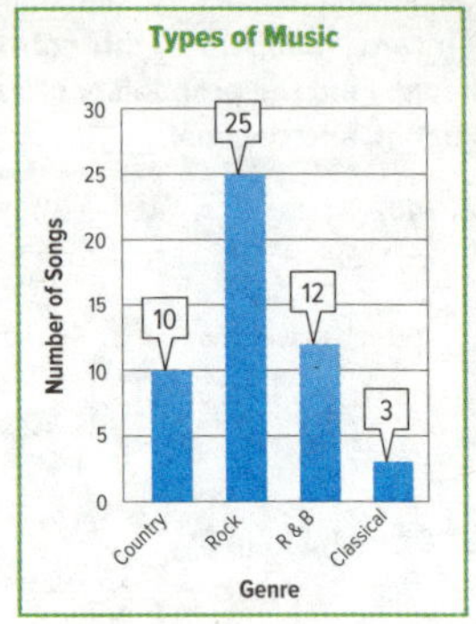

P(country or R&B) =

$$\frac{10 + 12}{10 + 25 + 12 + 3} = 0.44$$

25. Joel has a bowl containing the numbers of colored candies shown in the table. Which of the following probabilities are correct? Select all that apply.

Color	Number
Red	5
Orange	3
Yellow	1
Green	6

- ☐ $P(\text{red}) = \frac{1}{4}$
- ☐ $P(\text{yellow}) = \frac{1}{10}$
- ■ $P(\text{orange}) = \frac{1}{5}$
- ■ $P(\text{green}) = \frac{2}{5}$

Spiral Review

Compare each decimal using <, >, or =. 5.NBT.3b

26. 0.2 (<) 0.3

27. 0.75 (>) 0.7

28. 5.89 (<) 5.899

29. Dwayne misses 12% of his foul shots and Bryan misses 0.2 of his foul shots. Write 12% and 0.2 as fractions in simplest form. Then compare the fractions to determine who misses more foul shots. 6.NS.7b

$\frac{3}{25}$; $\frac{1}{5}$; Bryan misses more foul shots than Dwayne.

PLAN ONLINE: PD | RtI | Watch | Worksheets | Vocab | Tutor | Tools | Check | English Learners | Sketchpad

PRESENT: IWB

An Interactive Whiteboard Ready presentation is available for each lesson in the chapter.

Inquiry Lab
Relative Frequency

Content Standards
7.SP.6, 7.SP.7, 7.SP.7a

MP Mathematical Practices
1, 3

Inquiry HOW is probability related to relative frequency?

In a board game, you get an extra turn if you roll doubles or two of the same number.

You can conduct an experiment to find the relative frequency of rolling doubles using two number cubes. **Relative frequency** is the ratio of the number of experimental successes to the number of experimental attempts.

Hands-On Activity

Tools

Step 1 Complete the table to show all of the possible outcomes for rolling two number cubes. Shade all of the possible outcomes that are doubles.

(1, 1)	(2, 1)	(3, 1)	(4, 1)	(5, 1)	(6, 1)
(1, 2)	(2, 2)	(3, 2)	(4, 2)	(5, 2)	(6, 2)
(1, 3)	(2, 3)	(3, 3)	(4, 3)	(5, 3)	(6, 3)
(1, 4)	(2, 4)	(3, 4)	(4, 4)	(5, 4)	(6, 4)
(1, 5)	(2, 5)	(3, 5)	(4, 5)	(5, 5)	(6, 5)
(1, 6)	(2, 6)	(3, 6)	(4, 6)	(5, 6)	(6, 6)

The probability of rolling doubles is $\frac{6}{36}$ or $\frac{1}{6}$.

How many times would you expect doubles to be rolled if you roll the number cubes 50 times? Explain. Sample answer: I would expect to roll doubles about 8 or 9 times because $\frac{1}{6} \times 50 = 8\frac{1}{3}$.

Step 2 Roll two number cubes and record the number of doubles in the table. Repeat the experiment 50 times.

Number of Rolls	50
Number of Doubles	See students' work.

Step 3 Find the relative frequency of rolling doubles. Use the ratio $\frac{\text{number of times doubles were rolled}}{\text{number of rolls}}$. See students' work.

Compare the ratios in Steps 1 and 3. What do you notice? Explain.

Sample answer: My ratios are about the same.

Suppose the number cubes are rolled 100 times. Would you expect the results to be the same? Explain why or why not.

Sample answer: The results should be closer to $\frac{1}{6}$.

Focus narrowing the scope

Objective Use an experiment to determine relative frequency. 7.SP.6, 7.SP.7, 7.SP.7a

Materials: number cubes

Coherence connecting within and across grades

Now Students conduct an experiment to find relative frequency using number cubes.

Next Students will find and compare theoretical and experimental probabilities.

Rigor pursuing concepts, fluency, and applications

See the Levels of Complexity chart on page 720.

ENGAGE EXPLORE EXPLAIN ELABORATE EVALUATE

1 Launch the Lab

The Activity is intended to be used as a whole-group activity.

Hands-On Activity

AL EL **Pairs Discussion** Have students work in pairs to complete the activity and respond to the following questions. MP 1, 5, 8

Ask:

- *If a 1 is rolled on the first roll, what are the possibilities for the second roll?* 1, 2, 3, 4, 5, 6
- *How many possible outcomes are there if both number cubes are rolled once? twice? three times? 50 times?* 36 outcomes; 72 outcomes; 108 outcomes; 1,800 outcomes
- *How would you find the probability of rolling doubles?* $\frac{\text{favorable outcomes}}{\text{possible outcomes}} = \frac{6}{36}$ or $\frac{1}{6}$

2 Collaborate

The **Investigate** and **Analyze and Reflect** sections are intended to be used as small-group investigations. The **Create** section is intended to be used as independent exercises.

Levels of Complexity

The levels of the exercises progress from 1 to 3, with Level 1 indicating the lowest level of complexity.

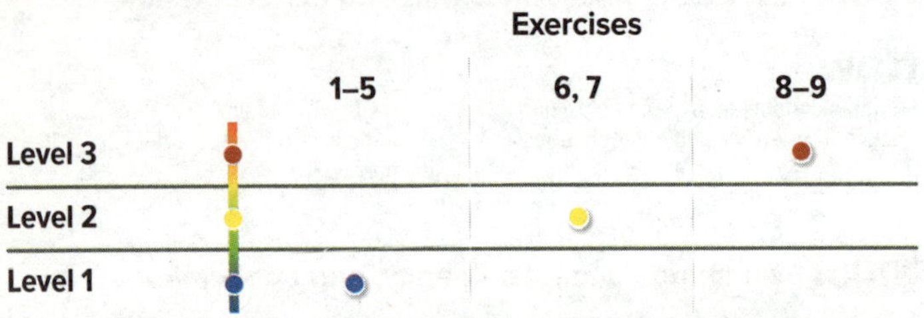

Investigate

AL Numbered Heads Together Have students arrange in groups of 4 to complete Exercises 1–5, ensuring that each member understands. Each student is assigned a number from 1–4. Teacher calls on a student number from each group to report their group results to the class. MP 1, 5

Analyze and Reflect

BL Trade-a-Problem Arrange students in pairs to create a spinner board with more than 4 possible outcomes. Have pairs of students generate more than one *P(event)* using their spinner board. Pairs will trade with other pairs to make qualitative and quantitative predictions. MP 1, 5

Create

Inquiry Students should be able to answer "HOW is probability related to relative frequency?" Check for student understanding and provide guidance, if needed.

Investigate

Work with a partner.

1. Place a paperclip around the tip of a pencil. Then place the tip on the center of the spinner. Spin the paperclip 40 times. Record the results in the table below.

Section	A	B	C	D
Frequency	See students' work.			
Relative Frequency				

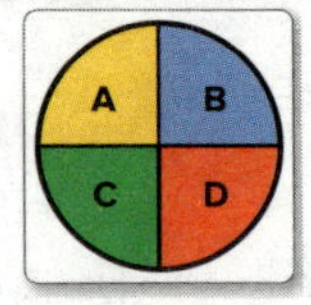

The spinner above is spun once. Find the probability of each event.

2. $P(A)$ $\frac{1}{4}$

3. $P(B)$ $\frac{1}{4}$

4. $P(C)$ $\frac{1}{4}$

5. $P(D)$ $\frac{1}{4}$

Analyze and Reflect

6. Based on your results from the spinner experiment, are the outcomes of A, B, C, or D equally likely? See students' work.

7. MP **Reason Inductively** What would you expect to happen to the long-run relative frequency of spinning an A as you increase the number of spins from 40 to 1,000? Sample answer: It would get closer to the probability of $\frac{1}{4}$.

Create

8. MP **Justify Conclusions** If you rolled a number cube 600 times, approximate the relative frequency of rolling a 3 or 6. Explain your reasoning to a classmate. about 200 times

9. **Inquiry** HOW is probability related to relative frequency? Sample answer: As the number of trials increase, the relative frequency of the event is closer to the probability.

PLAN ONLINE

PD | RtI | Watch | Worksheets | Vocab | Tutor | Tools | Check | English Learners | Sketchpad

PRESENT

IWB

An Interactive Whiteboard Ready presentation is available for each lesson in the chapter.

Lesson 2

Theoretical and Experimental Probability

Real-World Link

Watch

Carnival Games The prize wheels for a carnival game are shown. You receive a less expensive prize if you spin and win on wheel A. You receive a more expensive prize if you spin and win on wheel B.

In a **uniform probability model**, each outcome has an equal probability of happening.

1. Which wheel has uniform probability? wheel A

2. Use a paperclip and the tip of your pencil to spin each wheel 4 times. Record your results.

Spin	Wheel A	Wheel B
1		
2		
3		
4		

See students' work.

3. Why do you think winners on wheel A receive a less expensive prize than winners on wheel B?
Sample answer: There is a better chance of winning on wheel A.

Essential Question

HOW can you predict the outcome of future events?

Vocabulary

uniform probability model
theoretical probability
experimental probability

Content Standards
7.SP.7, 7.SP.7a, 7.SP.7b

MP Mathematical Practices
1, 3, 4

Which MP **Mathematical Practices** did you use?
Shade the circle(s) that applies.

① Persevere with Problems
② Reason Abstractly
③ Construct an Argument
④ Model with Mathematics
⑤ Use Math Tools
⑥ Attend to Precision
⑦ Make Use of Structure
⑧ Use Repeated Reasoning

Focus narrowing the scope

Objective Find and compare experimental and theoretical probabilities. 7.SP.7, 7.SP.7a, 7.SP.7b

Coherence connecting within and across grades

Previous Students solved problems using predictions and comparisons from simple experiments.

Now Students find experimental and theoretical probabilities related to simple and compound events.

Next Students will make predictions and determine solutions for compound events.

Rigor pursuing concepts, fluency, and applications

See the Levels of Complexity chart on page 725.

ENGAGE EXPLORE EXPLAIN ELABORATE EVALUATE

1 Launch the Lesson

Ideas for Use

You may wish to launch the lesson using a whole group, small group, think-pair-share activity, or independent activity.

EL **Paired Heads Together** Have students work in pairs to complete Exercises 1–3, ensuring that each student understands why Wheel B does not display uniform probability. Then randomly call on students to share their responses with the class. MP 1, 7

Alternate Strategy

AL EL Have students think of how the meaning of the word *uniform* in everyday life will help them understand the meaning of *uniform probability*. MP 1, 6

Engage Explore **Explain** Elaborate Evaluate

2 Teach the Concept

Ask the scaffolded questions to differentiate instruction.

Examples

IWB

1–2. Find experimental probability using data.

AL
- *What is the favorable outcome? How many times did it occur?* spinning red; 24 times
- *What was the total number of spins?* 60

OL
- *What is the experimental probability of spinning red?* $\frac{2}{5}$
- *What is the theoretical probability of spinning any color?* $\frac{1}{3}$
- *How can you use the experimental probability to predict the number of times the spinner will land on red if the spinner is spun 500 times?* Multiply the experimental probability by 500.

BL
- *How could you use the theoretical probability to predict the number times the spinner will land on red if the spinner is spun 500 times?* Sample answer: The spinner has three equal sections, so the theoretical probability of spinning red is $\frac{1}{3}$. Since $\frac{1}{3} \times 500 = 166\frac{2}{3}$, a prediction is that the spinner will land on red 167 times.

Need Another Example?
The graph shows the results of an experiment in which a number cube is rolled 50 times. Find the experimental probability of rolling a 4. Then compare the experimental probability to its theoretical probability. $\frac{9}{50}$; The experimental probability is close to the theoretical probability since $\frac{9}{50} \approx \frac{1}{6}$

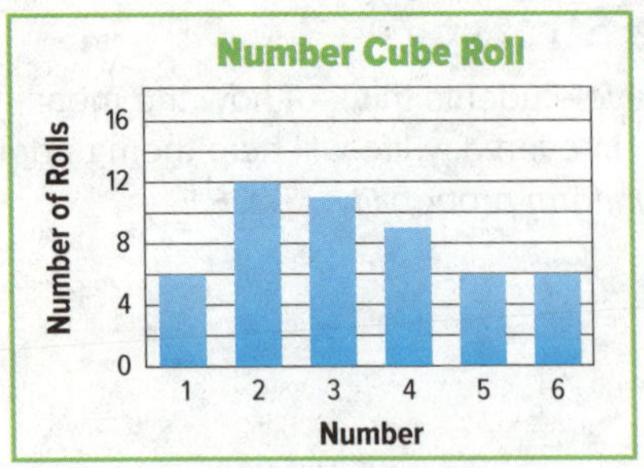

Work Zone

Trials
A trial is one experiment in a series of successive experiments.

Experimental and Theoretical Probability

Theoretical probability is based on uniform probability — what *should* happen when conducting a probability experiment. **Experimental probability** is based on relative frequency — what *actually* occurs during such an experiment.

The theoretical probability and the experimental probability of an event may or may not be the same. As the number of attempts increases, the theoretical probability and the experimental probability should become closer in value.

Real World Examples

Tools Tutor

1. The graph shows the results of an experiment in which a spinner with 3 equal sections is spun sixty times. Find the experimental probability of spinning red for this experiment.

The graph indicates that the spinner landed on red 24 times, blue 15 times, and green 21 times.

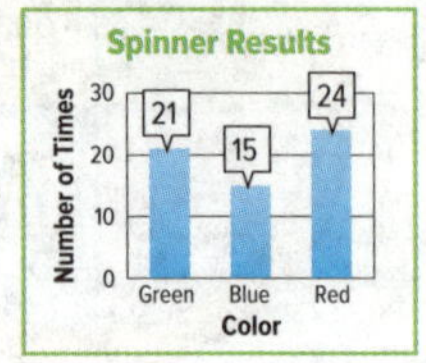

$$P(\text{red}) = \frac{\text{number of times red occurs}}{\text{total number of spins}}$$
$$= \frac{24}{60} \text{ or } \frac{2}{5}$$

The experimental probability of spinning red is $\frac{2}{5}$.

2. Compare the experimental probability you found in Example 1 to its theoretical probability.

The spinner has three equal sections: red, blue, and green. So, the theoretical probability of spinning red is $\frac{1}{3}$. Since $\frac{2}{5} \approx \frac{1}{3}$, the experimental probability is close to the theoretical probability.

Got it? **Do these problems to find out.**

a. Refer to Example 1. If the spinner was spun 3 more times and landed on green each time, find the experimental probability of spinning green for this experiment.

b. Compare the experimental probability you found in Exercise **a** to its theoretical probability.

Show your work.

a. $\frac{8}{21}$

b. The experimental probability is close to the theoretical probability since $\frac{8}{21} \approx \frac{1}{3}$.

Statistics and Probability

Examples

Tutor

3. Two number cubes are rolled together 20 times. A sum of 9 is rolled 8 times. What is the experimental probability of rolling a sum of 9?

$P(9) = \frac{\text{number of times a sum of 9 occurs}}{\text{total number of rolls}}$

$= \frac{8}{20}$ or $\frac{2}{5}$

The experimental probability of rolling a sum of 9 is $\frac{2}{5}$.

4. Compare the experimental probability you found in Example 3 to its theoretical probability. If the probabilities are not close, explain a possible reason for the discrepancy.

When rolling two number cubes, there are 36 possible outcomes.

The theoretical probability of rolling a sum of 9 is $\frac{4}{36}$ or $\frac{1}{9}$.

Rolls with Sum of 9

First Cube	Second Cube
3	6
4	5
5	4
6	3

Since $\frac{1}{9}$ is not close to $\frac{2}{5}$, the experimental probability is *not* close to the theoretical probability. One possible explanation is that there were not enough trials.

Got it? Do these problems to find out.

c. In Example 3, what is the experimental probability of rolling a sum that is *not* 9?

d. Two coins are tossed 10 times. Both coins land on heads 6 times. Compare the experimental probability to the theoretical probability. If the probabilities are not close, explain a possible reason for the discrepancy.

e. Suppose three coins are tossed 10 times. All three coins land on heads 1 time. Compare the experimental probability to the theoretical probability. If the probabilities are not close, explain a possible reason for the discrepancy.

Show your work.

c. $\frac{3}{5}$

d. Sample answer: $\frac{3}{5}$ is not close to $\frac{1}{4}$. One possible explanation is that there were not enough trials.

e. Sample answer: $\frac{1}{10}$ is close to $\frac{1}{8}$.

IWB

Examples

3. Find experimental probability using data.

AL • *What is the number of possible outcomes (number of rolls)?* 20

• *How many times did a favorable result occur?* 8

OL • *What is the P(sum of 9) as a decimal? percent?* 0.4; 40%

BL • *What is the complement of P(sum of 9)?* $\frac{3}{5}$

• *Do you think this outcome is typical? Explain.* Sample answer: It seems too high to get a sum of 9 on 40% of the rolls. If two number cubes are rolled, there are 36 possible sums. A sum of 9 only has four favorable outcomes, (3, 6), (4, 5), (5, 4), (6, 3), and 40% is higher than $\frac{4}{36}$ or $\frac{1}{9}$.

Need Another Example?

A coin is tossed 45 times. Heads appears 21 times. Find the experimental probability for heads, *P*(heads). $\frac{7}{15}$

4. Compare experimental and theoretical probability.

AL • *What are the four favorable outcomes for rolling a sum of 9?* (3, 6), (4, 5), (5, 4), (6, 3)

OL • *How does the theoretical probability compare to the experimental probability from Example 2?* Sample answer: The probabilities are not close, since $\frac{1}{9}$ is not close to $\frac{2}{5}$.

• *Why is there a wide discrepancy between the experimental and theoretical probabilities?* Sample answer: In an experiment, a result can occur any amount of times, even though it may not be likely.

BL • *When rolling two numbered cubes, which sum has the best chance of occurring? Explain.* 7, because it has the most combinations that could equal 7

Need Another Example?

A spinner that is divided into four equal sections is spun 100 times and it lands on green 32 times. Compare the experimental probability to the theoretical probability.

Experimental: $\frac{8}{25}$; Theoretical: $\frac{1}{4}$; Sample answer: The probabilities are not the same, but they are close to each other.

Example

5. Use probability to predict future events.

AL
- *How many DVDs were sold altogether?* 2,000
- *What is the experimental probability?* $\frac{580}{2,000}$ or $\frac{29}{100}$.

OL
- *Describe two different ways to find the value of x in the proportion.* Sample answer: Determine the cross products and divide each side by 100. Or generate an equivalent ratio. Since $100 \times 50 = 5,000$, multiply 29 by 50.

BL
- *Would your projected comedy DVD sales differ if you did not simplify the probability ratio $\frac{580}{2,000}$ first? Explain.* No, the ratios are still equivalent.

Need Another Example?

A survey of Mrs. Ramirez's students showed that 30 students will have pizza for lunch, 17 will have macaroni and cheese, 12 will have a hamburger, and 5 will have chicken fingers. Suppose Mrs. Ramirez surveys all 1,200 students in the school. How many students can she expect to choose hamburgers for lunch? 225 students

Guided Practice

Formative Assessment Use these exercises to assess students' understanding of the concepts in this lesson.

If some of your students are not ready for assignments, use the differentiated activities below.

AL EL **Team-Pair-Solo** Have students work in small teams to complete Exercise 1, ensuring that each team member understands. Then have students work in pairs to complete Exercise 2. Have them work on their own to complete Exercise 3. Then have them rejoin their original teams to discuss and share their responses. MP 1, 7

BL EL **Pairs Discussion** Have students work in pairs to extend Exercise 2 by having them predict how many customers out of 580 would *not* be expected to buy a banana muffin. MP 1, 7

Predict Future Events

Theoretical and experimental probability can be used to make predictions about future events.

Solving Proportions

The cross products of any proportion are equal.

$\frac{29}{100} = \frac{x}{5,000}$

Real World Example

5. Last year, a DVD store sold 670 action DVDs, 580 comedy DVDs, 450 drama DVDs, and 300 horror DVDs. A media buyer expects to sell 5,000 DVDs this year. Based on these results, how many comedy DVDs should she buy? Explain.

2,000 DVDs were sold and 580 were comedy. So, the probability is $\frac{580}{2,000}$ or $\frac{29}{100}$.

$\frac{29}{100} = \frac{x}{5,000}$	Write a proportion.
$29 \cdot 5,000 = 100 \cdot x$	Find the cross products.
$145,000 = 100x$	Multiply.
$1,450 = x$	Divide each side by 100.

She should buy about 1,450 comedy DVDs.

Guided Practice

1. A coin is tossed 50 times, and it lands on heads 28 times. Find the experimental probability and the theoretical probability of the coin landing on heads. Then, compare the experimental and theoretical probabilities. (Examples 1–4)

   $\frac{14}{25}$, $\frac{1}{2}$; The experimental probability, $\frac{14}{25}$ or 56%, is close to its theoretical probability of $\frac{1}{2}$ or 50%.

2. Yesterday, 50 bakery customers bought muffins and 11 of those customers bought banana muffins. If 100 customers buy muffins tomorrow, how many would you expect to buy a banana muffin? (Example 5)

   22 people

3. **Building on the Essential Question** How are experimental probability and theoretical probability alike?

   Sample answer: Both probabilities can be written as ratios.

Rate Yourself!

Are you ready to move on? Shade the section that applies.

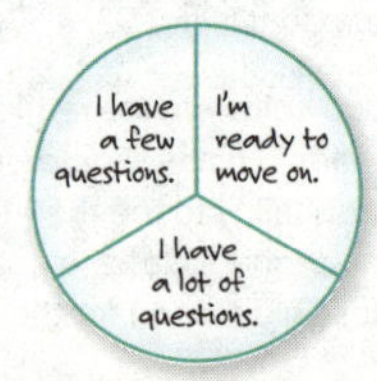

For more help, go online to access a Personal Tutor.

FOLDABLES Time to update your Foldable!

Name ______________________ My Homework ______________________

Independent Practice

Go online for Step-by-Step Solutions (eHelp)

1. A number cube is rolled 20 times and lands on 1 two times and on 5 four times. Find each experimental probability. Then compare the experimental probability to the theoretical probability. (Examples 1–4)

 a. landing on 5

 $\frac{1}{5}$; The experimental probability is close to the theoretical probability of $\frac{1}{6}$.

 b. *not* landing on 1

 $\frac{9}{10}$; The experimental probability is close to the theoretical probability of $\frac{5}{6}$.

2. The spinner at the right is spun 12 times. It lands on blue 1 time. (Examples 1–4)

 a. What is the experimental probability of the spinner landing on blue?

 $\frac{1}{12}$

 b. Compare the experimental and theoretical probabilities of the spinner landing on blue. If the probabilities are not close, explain a possible reason for the discrepancy.

 Sample answer: $\frac{1}{12}$ is not close to $\frac{1}{4}$. One possible explanation is that there were not enough trials.

3. The frequency table shows the results of a survey of 70 zoo visitors who were asked to name their favorite animal exhibit. (Example 5)

 a. Suppose 540 people visit the zoo. Predict how many people will choose the monkey exhibit as their favorite. 162 people

 b. Suppose 720 people visit the zoo. Predict how many people will choose the penguin exhibit as their favorite. about 134 people

What is your Favorite Animal Exhibit?

Exhibit	Tally	Frequency
Bears	卌 I	6
Elephants	卌 卌 卌 II	17
Monkeys	卌 卌 卌 卌 I	21
Penguins	卌 卌 III	13
Snakes	卌 卌 III	13

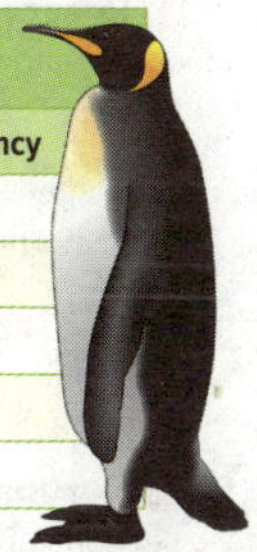

4. MP **Make a Conjecture** Cross out the part of the concept circle that does *not* belong. Then describe the relationship among the remaining parts.

 Sample answer: The crossed out section describes theoretical probability. The rest of the sections describe experimental probability.

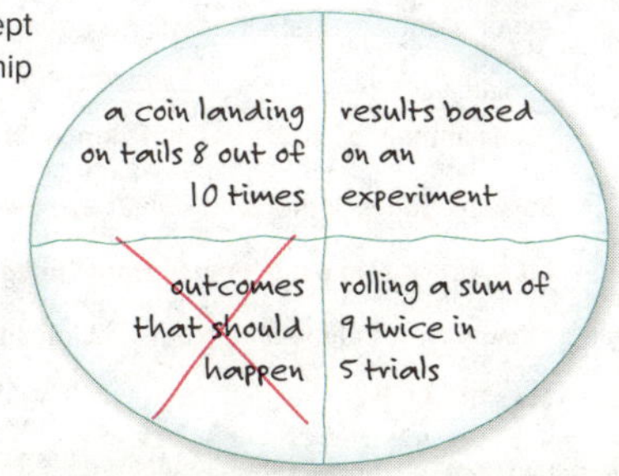

ENGAGE EXPLORE **EXPLAIN** **ELABORATE** **EVALUATE**

3 Practice and Apply

Independent Practice and Extra Practice

The Independent Practice pages are meant to be used as the homework assignment. The Extra Practice page can be used for additional reinforcement or as a second-day assignment.

Levels of Complexity

The levels of the exercises progress from 1 to 3, with Level 1 indicating the lowest level of complexity.

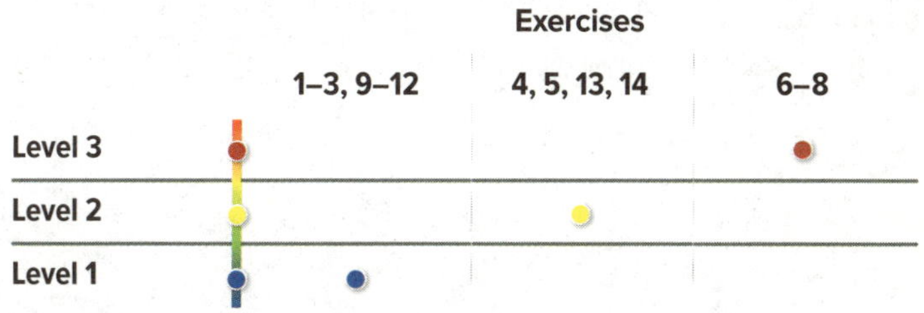

Suggested Assignments

You can use the table below that includes exercises of all complexity levels to select appropriate exercises for your students' needs.

Differentiated Homework Options		
AL	Approaching Level	1–3, 5, 7, 8, 13, 14
OL	On Level	1, 3–5, 7, 8, 13, 14
BL	Beyond Level	4–8, 13, 14

ALEKS® can provide additional remediation support with personalized instruction and practice.

MP MATHEMATICAL PRACTICES

Emphasis On	Exercise(s)
1 Make sense of problems and persevere in solving them.	6
3 Construct viable arguments and critique the reasoning of others.	4, 5, 7, 8

Mathematical Practices 1, 3, and 4 are aspects of mathematical thinking that are emphasized in every lesson. Students are given opportunities to be persistent in their problem solving, to express their reasoning, and apply mathematics to real-world situations.

Formative Assessment
Use this activity as a closing formative assessment before dismissing students from your class.

TICKET Out the Door

Have students find the theoretical probability of rolling a sum of 10 when rolling two number cubes. $\frac{1}{12}$

Watch Out!

Common Error Remind students that experimental probabilities will fluctuate while theoretical probabilities remain constant. Every time an experiment is conducted, the probability results will vary, but as more trials are conducted in an experiment, the experimental probabilities will move closer to the theoretical probabilities.

5. MP **Multiple Representations** A spinner with three equal-sized sections marked A, B, and C is spun 100 times.

a. **Numbers** What is the theoretical probability of landing on A?
$\frac{1}{3}$

b. **Numbers** The results of the experiment are shown in the table. What is the experimental probability of landing on A? on C?
$\frac{6}{25}$; $\frac{13}{50}$

Section	Frequency
A	24
B	50
C	26

c. **Models** Make a drawing of what the spinner might look like based on its experimental probabilities. Explain.
Sample answer: Section B should be one half of the spinner and sections A and C should each be one fourth of the spinner.

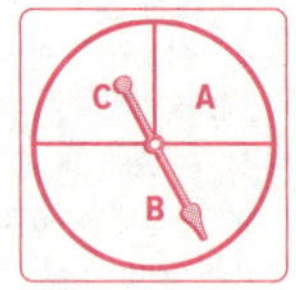

H.O.T. Problems Higher Order Thinking

6. MP **Persevere with Problems** The experimental probability of a coin landing on heads is $\frac{7}{12}$. If the coin landed on tails 30 times, find the number of tosses.
72 tosses

7. MP **Reason Inductively** Twenty sharpened pencils are placed in a box containing an unknown number of unsharpened pencils. Suppose 15 pencils are removed at random and five of the removed pencils are sharpened. Based on this, is it reasonable to assume that the number of unsharpened pencils was 40? Explain your reasoning. Yes; Sample answer: $\frac{5 \text{ sharpened}}{10 \text{ unsharpened}} = \frac{20 \text{ sharpened}}{x \text{ unsharpened}}$. So, $x = 40$.

8. MP **Reason Inductively** The results of spinning a spinner with six equal sections are shown. Determine the minimum number of additional spins needed and their frequency of landing on each color so that the experimental probabilities will be equal to the theoretical probabilities. Explain your reasoning. 24 more spins; Sample answer: The theoretical probability is $\frac{1}{6}$, so the experimental probability also needs to be $\frac{1}{6}$. Each frequency needs to be 12. So, the spinner will need to land on blue 4 more times, green 6 more times, purple 2 more times, red 4 more times, yellow 8 more times, and the frequency for orange will stay the same.

Color	Frequency
Blue	8
Green	6
Orange	12
Purple	10
Red	8
Yellow	4

Name ______________________ My Homework ______________________

Extra Practice

For Exercises 9 and 10, find each experimental probability. Then compare the experimental probability to its theoretical probability. If the probabilities are not close, explain a possible reason for the discrepancy.

9. A coin is tossed 20 times. It lands on heads 9 times.

Homework Help

$P(\text{heads}) = \frac{\text{number of times heads occurs}}{\text{total number of coin tosses}} = \frac{9}{20}$

The experimental probability of $\frac{9}{20}$ is close to the theoretical probability of $\frac{1}{2}$.

10. A heart is randomly chosen 7 out of 12 times from the cards shown.

$\frac{7}{12}$; Sample answer: The experimental probability of $\frac{7}{12}$ is not close to the theoretical probability of $\frac{1}{4}$. One possible explanation is that there were not enough trials.

Solve.

11. Last month, customers at a gift shop bought 40 birthday cards, 19 congratulations cards, 20 holiday cards, and 21 thank you cards. Suppose 125 customers buy greeting cards next month. How many would you expect to buy a birthday card?

50 customers

12. Use the graph at the right.

a. What is the probability that a mother received a gift of flowers or plants? Write the probability as a fraction in simplest form.

$\frac{7}{25}$

b. Suppose 400 mothers will receive a gift. Predict how many will receive flowers or plants.

112 mothers

Create Your Own Homework Online

eSolutionsManual™ can be used to create worksheets for the suggested assignments on page 725, or create your own worksheets for differentiated homework or review.

Power Up! Test Practice

Exercises 13 and 14 prepare students for more rigorous thinking needed for the state assessment.

13.

This test item requires students to explain and apply mathematical concepts and solve problems with precision, while making use of structure.	
Depth of Knowledge	DOK2
Content Standard	7.SP.7
Mathematical Practice	MP1
Online Experience	Students will be required to type their response in the box.
Scoring Rubric	
2 points	Students correctly answer each part of the question.
1 point	Students correctly fill in two of the three blanks.

14.

This test item requires students to reason abstractly and quantitatively when problem solving.	
Depth of Knowledge	DOK1
Content Standard	7.SP.7
Mathematical Practice	MP1
Online Experience	Students will be required to click on the bubbles to select all answers that are correct.
Scoring Rubric	
1 point	Students correctly answer each part of the question.

Power Up! Test Practice

13. J.R. tossed a coin 100 times. Fill in the boxes to complete each statement.

Based on J.R.'s results, the [experimental] probability of tossing heads is [40] %. This is [less] than the theoretical probability of tossing heads with a coin.

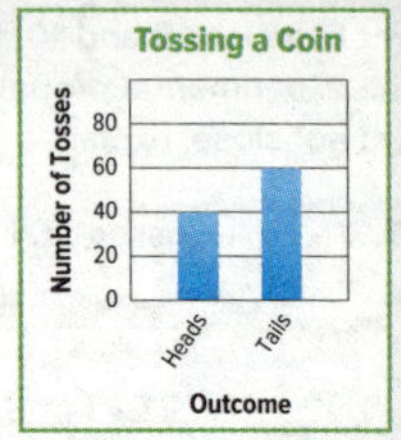

14. Determine if each situation represents experimental or theoretical probability.

a. Saul flips a coin 20 times and determines that the probability of flipping heads is 0.55. ■ experimental ☐ theoretical

b. Kelly has made 16 out of 25 free throws. The probability that she will make her next free throw is 64%. ■ experimental ☐ theoretical

c. There are 4 pennies, 2 nickels, 5 dimes, and 5 quarters in a jar. The probability that a randomly selected coin is a penny is $\frac{1}{4}$. ☐ experimental ■ theoretical

Spiral Review

For Exercises 15 and 16, circle the greater probability. 7.SP.5

15. The spinner at the right is spun.
P(red)   (*P*(not red))

16. A number cube is rolled.
P(multiple of 3)   (*P*(prime number))

17. A restaurant offers three flavors of ice cream on its dessert menu: vanilla, chocolate, and strawberry. Dessert options are sundaes or ice cream cones. List all of the possible desserts. Then determine if it is likely, unlikely, or equally likely of randomly choosing a sundae.
7.SP.5 **vanilla sundae, vanilla cone, chocolate sundae, chocolate cone, strawberry sundae, strawberry cone; equally likely**

PLAN ONLINE: PD, RtI, Watch, Worksheets, Vocab, Tutor, Tools, Check, English Learners, Sketchpad

PRESENT

IWB

An Interactive Whiteboard Ready presentation is available for each lesson in the chapter.

Statistics and Probability

Inquiry Lab

Fair and Unfair Games

Inquiry HOW can you determine if a game is fair?

Content Standards
7.SP.7, 7.SP.7a, 7.SP.7b

MP **Mathematical Practices**
1, 3

In a counter-toss game, players toss three two-color counters. The winner of each game is determined by how many counters land with either the red or yellow side facing up. Find out if this game is fair or unfair.

Mathematically speaking, a two-player game is **fair** if each player has an equal chance of winning. A game is **unfair** if there is not such a chance.

Hands-On Activity 1

Tools

Work in pairs to play the game described above.

Step 1 Player 1 tosses the counters. If 2 or 3 counters land red-side up, Player 1 wins. If 2 or 3 counters land yellow-side up, Player 2 wins. Record the results in the table below. Place a check in the winner's column for each game. **See students' work.**

Game	Player 1	Player 2	Game	Player 1	Player 2
1			6		
2			7		
3			8		
4			9		
5			10		

Step 2 Player 2 then tosses the counters and the results are recorded.

Step 3 Continue alternating turns until the counters have been tossed 10 times.

Based on your results, do you think the game is fair or unfair? Circle your response below.

Fair Unfair

Focus narrowing the scope

Objective Use experimental and theoretical probabilities to decide whether a game is fair or unfair. 7.SP.7, 7.SP.7a, 7.SP.7b

Coherence connecting within and across grades

Now
Students will make predictions and find solutions for experimental data and for simple and compound events.

Next
Students will find probabilities of compound events using data and sample spaces.

Rigor pursuing concepts, fluency, and applications

See the Levels of Complexity chart on page 730.

ENGAGE EXPLORE EXPLAIN ELABORATE EVALUATE

1 Launch the Lab

Activities 1 and 2 are intended to be used as whole-group activities. Activity 1 is designed to provide more guidance to students than Activity 2.

Materials: counters, plastic cups, number cubes

Hands-On Activity 1

AL EL **Solo to Pairs** Review rules of the game with students and have them individually write down their prediction as to whether the game is fair or unfair. Arrange students in pairs to complete Steps 1–3. Pairs should discuss how the rules and outcomes determine whether the game is fair or unfair. MP 1, 4, 7

2 Collaborate

The **Investigate** and **Analyze and Reflect** sections are intended to be used as small-group investigations. The **Create** section is intended to be used as independent exercises.

Levels of Complexity

The levels of the exercises progress from 1 to 3, with Level 1 indicating the lowest level of complexity.

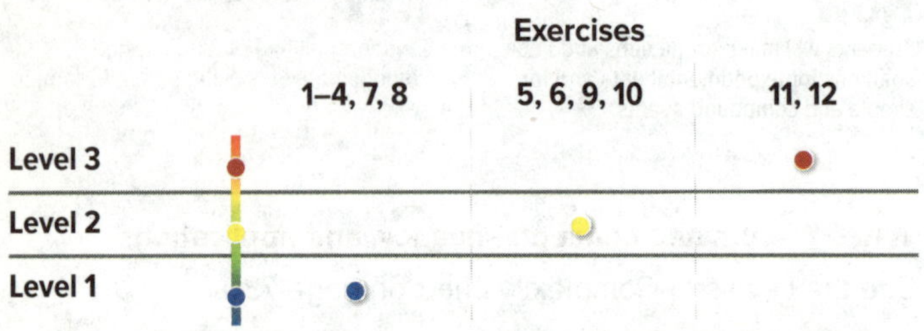

Investigate

AL EL **Think-Pair-Share** Give students 1–2 minutes to individually think through their responses for Exercises 1–4. Then have students discuss their results with a partner. Have pairs report results to the class. Students may want to create a tree diagram to help determine the list of all possible outcomes. Remind students to keep their list organized and that each unique response may be recorded only once. MP 1, 4

BL EL **Pairs Consult** Have students work with a partner to alter the rules of the game so that it is no longer fair. Have them play the new game numerous times and verify that the game is not fair. MP 1, 4, 7

Investigate

Work with a partner.

1. Complete the organized list of all the possible outcomes resulting from one toss of the three counters described in Activity 1.

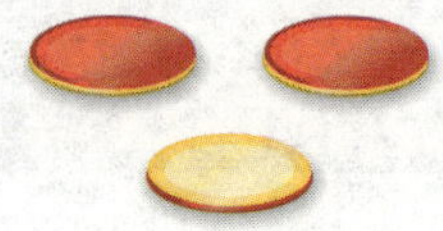

Counter 1	Counter 2	Counter 3	Outcome
red	red	red	red, red, red
red	red	yellow	red, red, yellow
red	yellow	yellow	red, yellow, yellow
red	yellow	red	red, yellow, red
yellow	yellow	yellow	yellow, yellow, yellow
yellow	yellow	red	yellow, yellow, red
yellow	red	red	yellow, red, red
yellow	red	yellow	yellow, red, yellow

2. In the outcome column of the table above, draw a circle around the outcomes that are a win for Player 1. Draw a box around the outcomes that are a win for Player 2. **See table above.**

3. Calculate the theoretical probability of each player winning. Write each probability as a fraction and as a percent. Is the game fair or unfair?
$P(\text{Player 1}) = \frac{1}{2}$ or 50%, $P(\text{Player 2}) = \frac{1}{2}$ or 50%; The game is fair.

4. Use your results from Activity 1 to calculate the experimental probability of each player winning.
See students' work.

Analyze and Reflect

5. MP **Justify Conclusions** Compare the probabilities you found in Exercises 3 and 4. Explain any discrepancies. **See students' work.**

6. MP **Reason Inductively** Predict the number of times Player 1 would win if the game were played 100 times. Explain your reasoning. **50 times**

David and Lyn made up a game using a plastic cup. A cup is tossed. If it lands right-side up or open-end down, David wins. If it lands on its side, Lyn wins. Is this game fair?

Hands-On Activity 2

Work in pairs to play the game and determine if David and Lyn created a fair game.

Step 1 Player 1 tosses the cup. If it lands right-side up or open-end down, Player 1 gets a point. If the cup lands on its side, Player 2 gets a point. Record your results in the table below. **See students' work.**

Toss	Player 1	Player 2	Toss	Player 1	Player 2
1			6		
2			7		
3			8		
4			9		
5			10		

Step 2 Player 2 then tosses the cup and the results are recorded.

Step 3 Continue alternating turns until there is a total of 10 tosses.

Based on your results, do you think the game David and Lyn created is fair or unfair? Circle your response below.

Fair   Unfair

There are three possible outcomes when tossing the cup and David wins if two of those outcomes happen. It may appear that David has a better chance of winning, however this is not necessarily true.

Explain why Lyn actually has a better chance at winning the game.

Sample answer: The game that they created does not take into account that it is more likely for the cup to land on its side.

What was the experimental probability for the cup landing right-side up or open-end down?

See students' work.

Hands-On Activity 2

AL **EL** **Predict-Pair-Write** After reviewing the rules to the game, give students 1–2 minutes to predict whether the game is fair or unfair. In pairs, have students complete Steps 1–3. Have students switch roles as Player 1 or Player 2 and play the game a second time. Have pairs complete Exercises 7 and 8. Then have them choose whether they would rather be Player 1 or Player 2 for a third game and justify their response. MP **1, 4, 7**

BL **EL** **Pairs Consult** Have students work with a partner to create a game involving either counters or plastic cups in which the game is unfair. Then have them alter the rules of the game so that it is fair. Have them present their games to another pair of students. Each pair plays the game more than once to verify whether they agree that the game is fair or unfair. MP **1, 4, 7**

Analyze and Reflect

Collaborate

AL EL **Pairs to Groups** Have students work in pairs to complete Exercises 9 and 10, ensuring that each student understands how to complete the table to show the sample space and which outcomes result in Player 1 winning. Then have the pair assemble with another pair to form a group to check the experimental probability of the game. Have them play the game numerous times to see if their experimental results are close to the theoretical results. Have them explain any discrepancies. Have groups report results to the class. MP 1, 8

Ask:

- *How do you know that the game is unfair simply by looking at the table in Exercises 10–11?* **Sample answer: There are 21 outcomes in which Player 2 wins and only 15 outcomes in which Player 1 wins.**
- *If you played the game 36 times, does this mean that Player 1 would always win 21 of those games? Explain.* **No; Sample answer: It is possible that Player 1 would win more than 21 games or less than 21 games. But we would expect that Player 1 would win about 21 games based on the theoretical probability.**

BL EL **Brainstorm** Have students work in a small group to brainstorm how the game could be altered to be a four-player game and a fair game. Then have the group play the game to verify their results. MP 1, 4, 7

Create

On Your Own

Inquiry Students should be able to answer "HOW can you determine if a game is fair?" Check for student understanding and provide guidance, if needed.

Investigate

Collaborate

Work with a partner.

7. A game involves rolling two number cubes. Player 1 wins the game if the total of the numbers rolled is 5 or if a 5 is shown on one or both number cubes. Otherwise, Player 2 wins. Fill in the table for all of the possible outcomes of rolling two number cubes.

	1	2	3	4	5	6
1	1 + 1 = 2	1 + 2 = 3	1 + 3 = 4	1 + 4 = 5	1 + 5 = 6	1 + 6 = 7
2	2 + 1 = 3	2 + 2 = 4	2 + 3 = 5	2 + 4 = 6	2 + 5 = 7	2 + 6 = 8
3	3 + 1 = 4	3 + 2 = 5	3 + 3 = 6	3 + 4 = 7	3 + 5 = 8	3 + 6 = 9
4	4 + 1 = 5	4 + 2 = 6	4 + 3 = 7	4 + 4 = 8	4 + 5 = 9	4 + 6 = 10
5	5 + 1 = 6	5 + 2 = 7	5 + 3 = 8	5 + 4 = 9	5 + 5 = 10	5 + 6 = 11
6	6 + 1 = 7	6 + 2 = 8	6 + 3 = 9	6 + 4 = 10	6 + 5 = 11	6 + 6 = 12

8. Shade in the cells of the table in which Player 1 is a winner.

Analyze and Reflect

Collaborate

9. For the number cube game, calculate the theoretical probability of each player winning. Write each probability as a fraction and as a percent.
P(Player 1 wins) $= \frac{15}{36} = \frac{5}{12}$ or about 42%, P(Player 2 wins) $= \frac{21}{36} = \frac{7}{12}$ or about 58%

10. MP **Justify Conclusions** Is the number cube game fair? Explain.
No. Player 2 has a $\frac{7}{12}$ chance of winning and Player 1 has a $\frac{5}{12}$ chance of winning. So, Player 2 is more likely to win.

Create

On Your Own

11. MP **Model with Mathematics** Design and describe a game in which the outcome is not fair. Then explain how you could change the game to make it fair. **See students' work.**

12. Inquiry HOW can you determine if a game is fair? **Sample answer: There are no factors that give one player an advantage over another player.**

PLAN ONLINE

PD | RtI | Watch | Worksheets | Vocab | Tutor | Tools | Check | English Learners | Sketchpad

PRESENT

IWB

An Interactive Whiteboard Ready presentation is available for each lesson in the chapter.

Lesson 3

Probability of Compound Events

Real-World Link

Travel Aimee wants to pack enough items to create 6 different outfits. She packs 1 jacket, 3 shirts, and 2 pairs of jeans. Can Aimee create 6 different outfits from her clothing items?

1. Complete the table below.

Outfit	Clothing Items
1	jacket, shirt 1, jeans 1
2	jacket, shirt 1, jeans 2
3	jacket, shirt 2, jeans 1
4	jacket, shirt 2, jeans 2
5	jacket, shirt 3, jeans 1
6	jacket, shirt 3, jeans 2

2. The table is an example of an organized list. What is another way to show the different outfits that Aimee can create?
Sample answer: Make a diagram.

3. Describe another situation for which you might want to list all of the possible outcomes.
Sample answer: the number of lunches you could make from a choice of salads, sandwiches, and desserts

Essential Question

HOW can you predict the outcome of future events?

Vocabulary

sample space
tree diagram
compound event

Mathematical Practices
1, 3, 4, 5

Which **Mathematical Practices** did you use? Shade the circle(s) that applies.

1 Persevere with Problems
2 Reason Abstractly
3 Construct an Argument
4 Model with Mathematics
5 Use Math Tools
6 Attend to Precision
7 Make Use of Structure
8 Use Repeated Reasoning

Focus narrowing the scope

Objective Find probabilities of compound events.

Coherence connecting within and across grades

Previous Students made predictions and found solutions using experimental data for simple and compound events.

Now Students will find theoretical probabilities related to compound events using sample spaces.

Next Students will select and use different simulations to represent simple and compound events.

Rigor pursuing concepts, fluency, and applications

See the Levels of Complexity chart on page 737.

ENGAGE EXPLORE EXPLAIN ELABORATE EVALUATE

1 Launch the Lesson

Ideas for Use

You may wish to launch the lesson using a whole group, small group, think-pair-share activity, or independent activity.

EL **Pairs Discussion** Have students write the clothing items on slips of paper. For example, write JACKET, SHIRT 1, SHIRT 2, SHIRT 3, JEANS 1 and JEANS 2 on different slips of paper. Then have them create outfits by arranging the slips of paper. Have one student create an outfit, while the other student records the outfit in the table. Have them come up with another way to show the total number of different outfits that can be made. MP 1, 4, 5

Alternate Strategy

AL EL Bring in clothing items to represent the items in the activity. Have students create different outfits and record the total number of outfits that can be made. MP 1, 4, 5

2 Teach the Concept

Ask the scaffolded questions to differentiate instruction.

Examples

IWB

1. Find the sample space by making a list.

AL • *How many ways are listed with Adrienne seated first? second? third?* 2, 2, 2

• *What does ACG mean in the context of this problem?* The order of the students sitting in the row is Adrienne, Carlos, and Greg.

OL • *How do you know you have listed all possible outcomes?* Each person is represented the same amount of times in each position (1st, 2nd, 3rd).

BL • *How many outcomes are there if 4 students sit in the first row? Explain.* 24; See students' work.

Need Another Example?
Melinda has four pictures that she wants to place in a column in her scrapbook. Use a list to represent the sample space for the different ways she can place the pictures. 1234, 1243, 1324, 1342, 1423, 1432, 2134, 2143, 2314, 2341, 2413, 2431, 3124, 3142, 3214, 3241, 3412, 3421, 4123, 4132, 4213, 4231, 4312, 4321

2. Find the sample space by making a table or tree diagram.

AL • *How many options are possible for the color? top?* 4; 2

OL • *How many outcomes are possible in the sample space?* 8

BL • *Compare and contrast using a list or a tree diagram.* Sample answer: Both show all the possible outcomes. A tree diagram shows how each outcome in the second event branches from the outcome in the first event.

Need Another Example?
An Italian ice shop sells lime, cherry, blueberry, and watermelon Italian ice. It is served plain, mixed with ice cream, or as a drink. Use a table or tree diagram to find the sample space for the different orders that can be made. LP, LI, LD, CP, CI, CD, BP, BI, BD, WP, WI, WD; See students' work.

Work Zone

Find a Sample Space

The set of all of the possible outcomes in a probability experiment is called the **sample space**. Organized lists, tables, and **tree diagrams** can be used to represent the sample space.

Examples

Tutor

1. **The three students chosen to represent Mr. Balderick's class in a school assembly are shown. All three of them need to sit in a row on the stage. Use a list to find the sample space for the different ways they can sit in a row.**

Students
Adrienne
Carlos
Greg

Use A for Adrienne, C for Carlos, and G for Greg. Use each letter exactly once.

ACG AGC CAG CGA GAC GCA

So, the sample space consists of 6 outcomes.

2. **A car can be purchased in blue, silver, red, or purple. It also comes as a convertible or hardtop. Use a table or a tree diagram to find the sample space for the different styles in which the car can be purchased.**

Color	Top
blue	convertible
blue	hardtop
silver	convertible
silver	hardtop
red	convertible
red	hardtop
purple	convertible
purple	hardtop

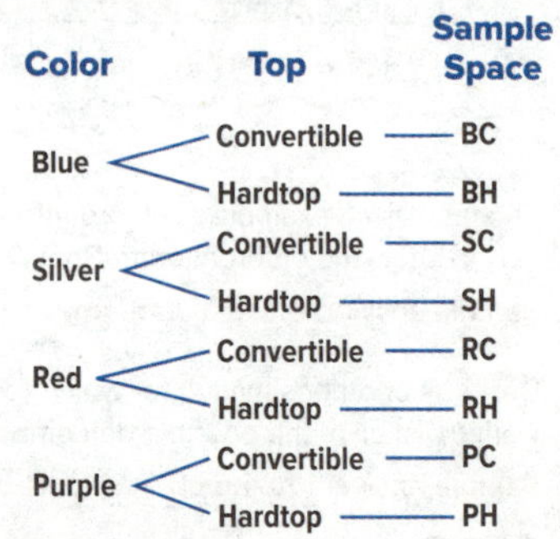

Using either method, the sample space consists of 8 outcomes.

Got it? **Do this problem to find out.**

a. The table shows the sandwich choices for a picnic. Find the sample space using a list, table, or tree diagram for a sandwich consisting one type of meat and one type of bread.

Meat	Bread
ham turkey	rye sourdough white

Show your work.

a. HR, HS, HW, TR, TS, TW

Find Probability

A **compound event** consists of two or more simple events. The probability of a compound event, just as with simple events, is the fraction of outcomes in the sample space for which the compound event occurs.

Example

3. Suppose you toss a quarter, a dime, and a nickel. Find the sample space. What is the probability of getting three tails?

Make a tree diagram to show the sample space.

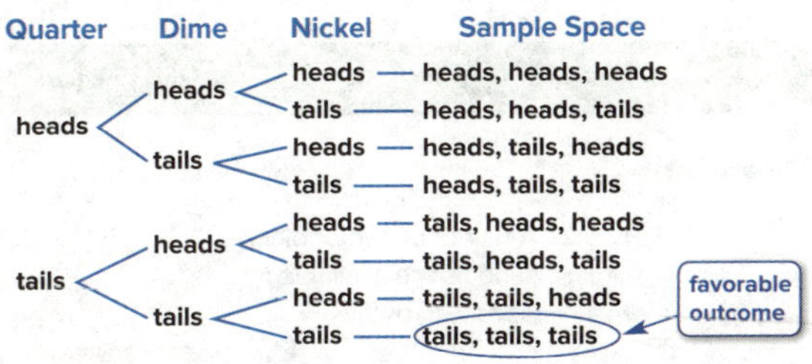

$P(3 \text{ tails}) = \frac{1}{8}$ ← number of favorable outcomes / ← number of possible outcomes

So, the probability of getting three tails is $\frac{1}{8}$.

Got it? **Do this problem to find out.**

b. The animal shelter has both male and female Labrador Retrievers in yellow, brown, or black. There is an equal number of each kind. What is the probability of choosing a female yellow Labrador Retriever? Show your work in the space below.

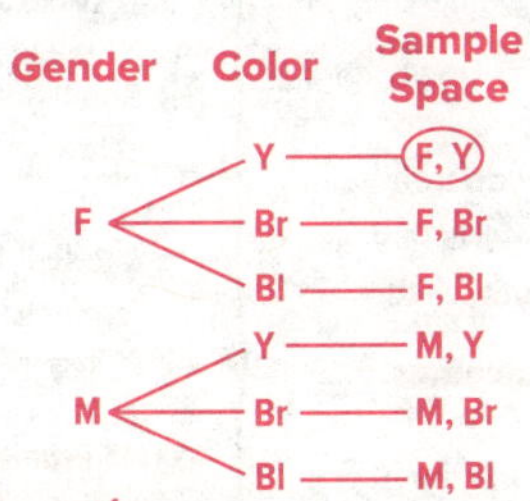

$P(\text{female yellow lab}) = \frac{1}{6}$

Random
When choosing an outcome, assume that each outcome is chosen randomly.

Example

3. Find the probability of a compound event.

AL • *How many possible outcomes are there for each coin? What are they?* 2; heads or tails

• *How many coins are being flipped?* 3

OL • *How many outcomes are listed in the sample space?* 8

• *What is the probability of getting three tails?* $\frac{1}{8}$

BL • *What is the probability of getting at least one tail?* $\frac{7}{8}$

Need Another Example?

The school cafeteria gives students two choices of snacks: carrot sticks and pretzels. They also offer a beverage choice of apple juice, low-fat milk, or bottled water. Find the sample space for all possible orders of one snack with one beverage. What is the probability of someone getting pretzels and apple juice? $\frac{1}{6}$

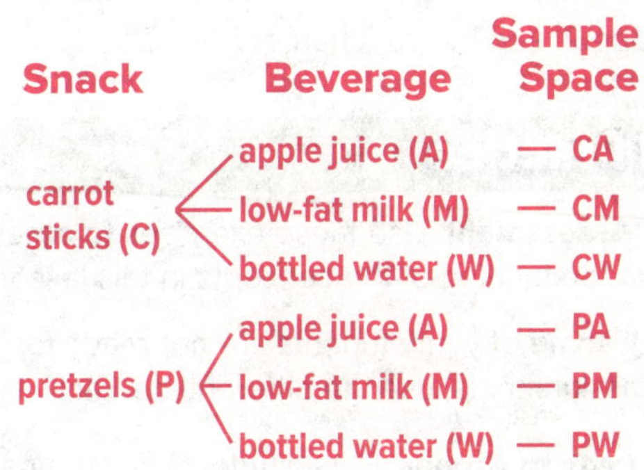

Watch Out!

Common Error When students use and interpret a tree diagram, remind them to follow along the branches on a path through the tree to identify all of the joint outcomes.

Example

4. Find the probability of compound events.

AL
- *How many door options are there?* 3
- *How many color options?* 3

OL
- *How many total outcomes are possible?* 9
- *How many outcomes are favorable?* 2
- *What is the probability that the prize is in the blue or yellow box behind door 2?* $\frac{2}{9}$

BL
- *Name another outcome that has the same probability.* Sample answer: The prize is in the red or blue box behind door 3.

Need Another Example?
A cell phone company is offering a special deal. If you choose from payment plans A, B, and C and one of four different phones, you can choose a free gift of a case, a car charger, or a memory card. What is the probability that Jamal will choose plan A, phone 2, and the car charger? $\frac{1}{36}$

Guided Practice

Formative Assessment Use these exercises to assess students' understanding of the concepts in this lesson.

If some of your students are not ready for assignments, use the differentiated activities below.

AL EL **Pairs to Groups** Have students work in pairs to complete Exercises 1–4. Have pairs join to form groups of 4. Groups should discuss ideas, procedures, and results, ensuring that each member understands how to find the sample space of a compound event and the probability of a compound event. Have groups share responses with the class. MP 1, 4, 7

BL EL **Think-Pair-Write** Have students think about how they would respond to Exercise 4 individually. Then have them discuss their responses with a partner. Finally, have them write their response to the exercise individually. MP 1, 4

Real World Example

4. To win a carnival prize, you need to choose one of 3 doors labeled 1 through 3. Then you need to choose a red, yellow, or blue box behind each door. What is the probability that the prize is in the blue or yellow box behind door 2?

The table shows that there are 9 total outcomes. Two of the outcomes are favorable.

So, the probability that the prize is in a blue or yellow box behind door 2 is $\frac{2}{9}$.

Outcomes	
door 1	red box
door 1	yellow box
door 1	blue box
door 2	red box
door 2	yellow box
door 2	blue box
door 3	red box
door 3	yellow box
door 3	blue box

Guided Practice

For each situation, find the sample space. (Examples 1–2)

1. A coin is tossed twice.

Coin 1	Coin 2	Sample Space
heads	heads	heads, heads
	tails	heads, tails
tails	heads	tails, heads
	tails	tails, tails

2. A pair of brown or black sandals are available in sizes 7, 8, or 9.

Brown	7
Brown	8
Brown	9
Black	7
Black	8
Black	9

3. Gerardo spins a spinner with four equal sections, labeled A, B, C, and D, twice. If letter A is spun at least once, Gerardo wins. Otherwise, Odell wins. Use a list to find the sample space. Then find the probability that Odell wins. (Examples 3–4)
AA, AB, AC, AD, BA, BB, BC, BD, CA, CB, CC, CD, DA, DB, DC, DD; $\frac{9}{16}$

4. **Bulding on the Essential Question** How do tree diagrams, tables, and lists help you find the probability of a compound event? Sample answer: They help you visualize and organize the total number of outcomes.

Rate Yourself!

☐ I understand how to show a sample space.

Great! You're ready to move on!

☐ I still have questions about showing a sample space.

No Problem! Go online to access a Personal Tutor.

Name ________________ My Homework

Independent Practice

Go online for Step-by-Step Solutions eHelp

For each situation, find the sample space. (Examples 1–2)

1. tossing a coin and spinning the spinner at the right

H1, H2, H3, H4, H5,

T1, T2, T3, T4, T5

2. picking a number from 1 to 5 and choosing the color red, white, or blue

1 red, 1 white, 1 blue, 2 red,

2 white, 2 blue, 3 red, 3 white,

3 blue, 4 red, 4 white, 4 blue,

5 red, 5 white, 5 blue

3 choosing a purple, green, black, or silver bike having 10, 18, 21, or 24 speeds

purple 10, purple 18, purple 21, purple 24,

green 10, green 18, green 21, green 24,

black 10, black 18, black 21, black 24,

silver 10, silver 18, silver 21, silver 24

4. choosing a letter from the word SPACE and choosing a consonant from the word MATH

SM, ST, SH, PM, PT,

PH, AM, AT, AH, CM,

CT, CH, EM, ET, EH

For each game, find the sample space. Then find the indicated probability. (Examples 3–4)

5. Alana tosses 2 number cubes. She wins if she rolls double sixes.

Find *P*(Alana wins). $\frac{1}{36}$

1, 1	1, 2	1, 3	1, 4	1, 5	1, 6
2, 1	2, 2	2, 3	2, 4	2, 5	2, 6
3, 1	3, 2	3, 3	3, 4	3, 5	3, 6
4, 1	4, 2	4, 3	4, 4	4, 5	4, 6
5, 1	5, 2	5, 3	5, 4	5, 5	5, 6
6, 1	6, 2	6, 3	6, 4	6, 5	6, 6

6. Ming rolls a number cube, tosses a coin, and chooses a card from two cards marked A and B. If an even number and heads appears, Ming wins, no matter which card is chosen. Otherwise Lashonda wins.

Find *P*(Ming wins). $\frac{6}{24}$ or $\frac{1}{4}$

1HA, 1HB, 1TA, 1TB, 2HA, 2HB, 2TA, 2TB, 3HA, 3HB, 3TA, 3TB,

4HA, 4HB, 4TA, 4TB, 5HA, 5HB, 5TA, 5TB, 6HA, 6HB, 6TA, 6TB

ENGAGE EXPLORE **EXPLAIN** **ELABORATE** **EVALUATE**

3 Practice and Apply

Independent Practice and Extra Practice

The Independent Practice pages are meant to be used as the homework assignment. The Extra Practice page can be used for additional reinforcement or as a second-day assignment.

Levels of Complexity

The levels of the exercises progress from 1 to 3, with Level 1 indicating the lowest level of complexity.

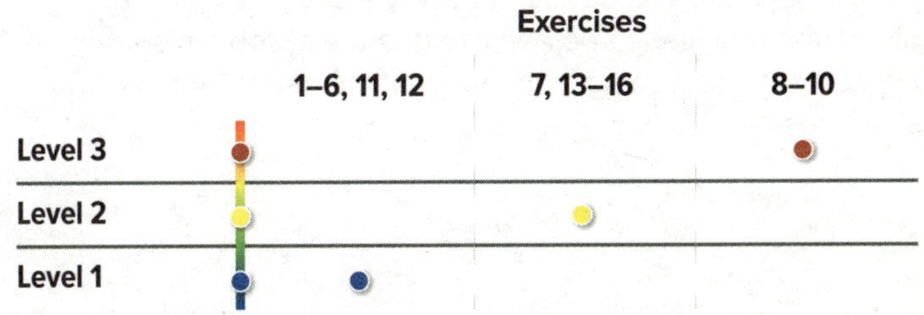

Suggested Assignments

You can use the table below that includes exercises of all complexity levels to select appropriate exercises for your students' needs.

Differentiated Homework Options		
AL	Approaching Level	1–7, 9, 10, 15, 16
OL	On Level	1–5 odd, 7, 9, 10, 15, 16
BL	Beyond Level	7–10, 15, 16

ALEKS® can provide additional remediation support with personalized instruction and practice.

MP MATHEMATICAL PRACTICES

Emphasis On	Exercise(s)
1 Make sense of problems and persevere in solving them.	7, 8
3 Construct viable arguments and critique the reasoning of others.	9
4 Model with mathematics.	10
5 Use appropriate tools strategically.	14

Mathematical Practices 1, 3, and 4 are aspects of mathematical thinking that are emphasized in every lesson. Students are given opportunities to be persistent in their problem solving, to express their reasoning, and apply mathematics to real-world situations.

Formative Assessment

Use this activity as a closing formative assessment before dismissing students from your class.

TICKET Out the Door

Have students use any method to give the sample space for rolling a number cube and flipping a coin. 1H, 2H, 3H, 4H, 5H, 6H, 1T, 2T, 3T, 4T, 5T, 6T (H = heads and T = tails)

7. MP **Persevere with Problems** The following is a game for two players.
- Three counters are labeled according to the table at the right.
- Toss the three counters.
- If exactly 2 counters match, Player 1 scores a point. Otherwise, Player 2 scores a point.

Counters	Side 1	Side 2
Counter 1	red	blue
Counter 2	red	yellow
Counter 3	blue	yellow

Find the probability that each player scores a point.

$P(\text{Player 1}) = \frac{6}{8}$ or $\frac{3}{4}$; $P(\text{Player 2}) = \frac{2}{8}$ or $\frac{1}{4}$

RRB, RYB, RRY, RYY, BRB, BYB, BYY, BRY

H.O.T. Problems Higher Order Thinking

8. MP **Persevere with Problems** Refer to Exercise 7. Do the two players both have an equal chance of winning? Explain.

Sample answer: No, Player 1 has a better chance of winning because $\frac{3}{4} > \frac{1}{4}$.

9. MP **Find the Error** Caitlyn wants to determine the probability of guessing correctly on two true-false questions on her history test. She draws the tree diagram below using C for correct and I for incorrect. Find her mistake and correct it.

The first outcome in the I bracket should be IC.

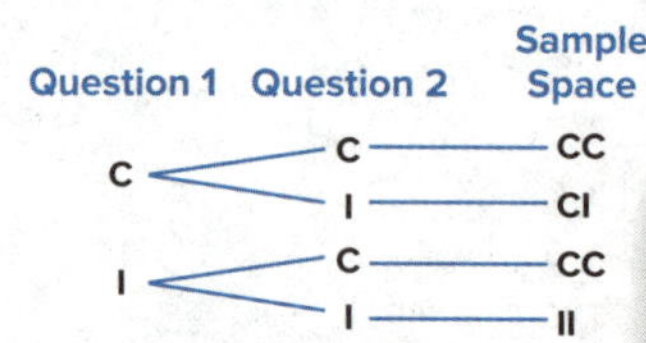

10. MP **Model with Mathematics** Write a real-world problem in which the probability of a compound event occurring is 0.25.

Sample answer: If a coin is tossed and a number cube is rolled, what is the probability of heads and an odd number?

Name ______________________ My Homework ______________________

Extra Practice

11. Three-course dinners can be made from the menu shown. Find the sample space for a dinner consisting of an appetizer, entrée, and dessert.

Appetizers	Entrees	Desserts
Soup	Steak	Carrot cake
Salad	Chicken	Apple pie

Homework Help

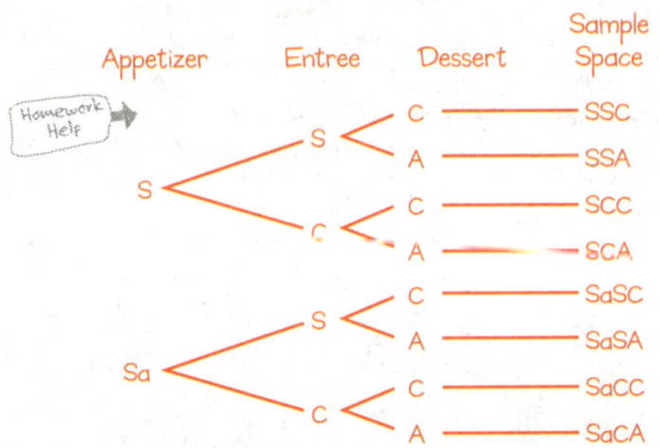

12. Mr. and Mrs. Romero are expecting triplets. Suppose the chance of each child being a boy is 50% and of being a girl is 50%. Find the probability of each event.
BBB, BGB, BGG, BBG GGG, GGB, GBB, GBG

a. *P*(all three children will be boys) $\frac{1}{8}$

b. *P*(at least one boy and one girl) $\frac{3}{4}$

c. *P*(two boys and one girl) $\frac{3}{8}$

d. *P*(at least two girls) $\frac{1}{2}$

Copy and Solve **For Exercises 13 and 14, show your work on a separate piece of paper.** 13c. See margin for tree diagram.

13. The University of Oregon's football team has many different uniforms. The coach can choose from four colors of jerseys and pants: green, yellow, white, and black. There are three helmet options: green, white, and yellow. Also, there are the same four colors of socks and two colors of shoes, black and yellow.

a. How many jersey/pant combinations are there? 16 combinations

b. If the coach picks a jersey/pant combination at random, what is the probability he will pick a yellow jersey with green pants? $\frac{1}{16}$

c. Use a tree diagram to find all of the possible shoe and sock combinations. 8 combinations

14. MP **Use Math Tools** Use the Internet or another source to find the top five best-selling animated movies. Then create a list of the possibilities for choosing a movie and choosing a wide-screen or full-screen version. See students' work.

Create Your Own Homework Online

eSolutionsManual™ can be used to create worksheets for the suggested assignments on page 737, or create your own worksheets for differentiated homework or review.

Additional Answer

13c.

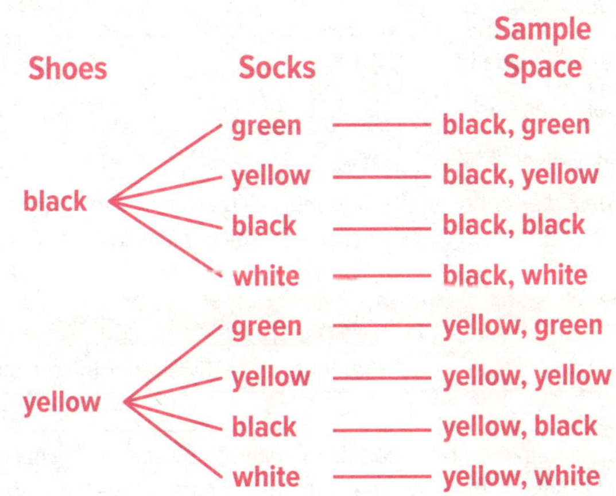

Power Up! Test Practice

Exercises 15 and 16 prepare students for more rigorous thinking needed for the state assessment.

15.

This test item requires students to explain and apply mathematical concepts and solve problems with precision, while making use of structure.	
Depth of Knowledge	DOK1
Content Standard	7.SP.8b
Mathematical Practice	MP1
Online Experience	Students will be required to click on the bubbles to select all answers that are correct.
Scoring Rubric	
1 point	Students correctly answer the question.

16.

This test item requires students to analyze and solve complex real-world problems through the use of mathematical tools and models.	
Depth of Knowledge	DOK3
Content Standard	7.SP.8, 7.SP.8b
Mathematical Practice	MP1, MP5
Online Experience	Students will be required to type their responses in the boxes.
Scoring Rubric	
2 points	Students correctly list the sample space and find the probability.
1 point	Students correctly list the sample space but fail to find the probability OR students find the probability but have errors in listing the sample space OR students have errors in the sample space and base their probability on the sample space they have listed.

Power Up! Test Practice

15. Mr. Skeels will choose one student from each of the two groups to present their history report to the class. Which of the following represent possible outcomes? Select all that apply.

Group 1	Group 2
Ava	Mario
Antoine	Brooke
Greg	

- ■ (Ava, Brooke)
- ■ (Greg, Brooke)
- □ (Antoine, Greg)
- ■ (Antoine, Mario)

16. Campers choose one activity from each of the morning, afternoon, and evening activities shown below.

Morning	Afternoon	Evening
Hiking (H)	Archery (A)	Horseback Riding (R)
Canoeing (C)	Bird Watching (B)	Campfire Building (F)
		Navigating (N)

Make a list to show the sample space for the possible morning, afternoon, and evening activities.

HAR, HAF, HAN, HBR, HBF, HBN, CAR, CAF, CAN, CBR, CBF, CBN

What is the probability that a randomly selected camper will be horseback riding in the evening? $\frac{1}{3}$

Spiral Review

Eight cards numbered 1–8 are shuffled together. A card is drawn at random. Find the probability of each event. 7.SP.5

17. $P(8)$ $\frac{1}{8}$

18. $P(\text{greater than } 5)$ $\frac{3}{8}$

19. $P(\text{even})$ $\frac{1}{2}$

20. $P(3 \text{ or } 7)$ $\frac{1}{4}$

21. What is the probability of rolling a number greater than 4 on a number cube? Explain. 7.SP.5

$\frac{1}{3}$; There are 2 numbers out of 6 on a number cube that are greater than 4. $\frac{2}{6} = \frac{1}{3}$

PLAN ONLINE: PD | RtI | Watch | Worksheets | Vocab | Tutor | Tools | Check | English Learners | Sketchpad

PRESENT: IWB — An Interactive Whiteboard Ready presentation is available for each lesson in the chapter.

Lesson 4

Simulations

Real-World Link

Music Downloads A new electronics store is opening at the mall. One out of six new customers will receive a free music download. The winners are chosen at random. On Monday, the store had 50 customers. You can act out or *simulate* 50 random customers by using the random number generator on a graphing calculator.

Type in the following keystrokes to set 1 as the lower bound and 6 as the upper bound for 50 trials.

Keystrokes: MATH ◀ 5 1 , 6 , 50) ENTER

The screen should look similar to the screen shown below.

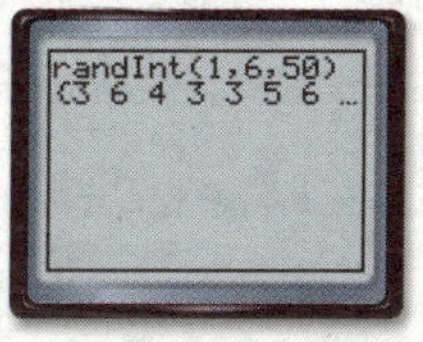

A set of 50 numbers ranging from 1 to 6 appears. Use the right arrow key to see the next number in the set.

1. Let the number 3 represent a customer who wins a free download. Write the experimental probability of winning a download.
   See students' work.

2. Compare the experimental probabilities found in Exercise 1 to the theoretical probability of winning a download.
   Sample answer: The theoretical probability is $\frac{1}{6}$. See students' work for their experimental probabilities.

Essential Question

HOW can you predict the outcome of future events?

Vocabulary

simulation

Content Standards
7.SP.8, 7.SP.8c

Mathematical Practices
1, 3, 4

Which **Mathematical Practices** did you use? Shade the circle(s) that applies.

① Persevere with Problems
② Reason Abstractly
③ Construct an Argument
④ Model with Mathematics
⑤ Use Math Tools
⑥ Attend to Precision
⑦ Make Use of Structure
⑧ Use Repeated Reasoning

Focus narrowing the scope

Objective Perform probability simulations to model real-world situations involving uncertainty. 7.SP.8, 7.SP.8c

Coherence connecting within and across grades

Previous Students found theoretical probabilities related to compound events using sample spaces.

Now Students select and use different simulations to represent simple events.

Next Students will select and use different simulations to represent simple and compound events.

Rigor pursuing concepts, fluency, and applications

See the Levels of Complexity chart on page 745.

ENGAGE EXPLORE EXPLAIN ELABORATE EVALUATE

1 Launch the Lesson

Ideas for Use

You may wish to launch the lesson using a whole group, small group, think-pair-share activity, or independent activity.

EL **Paired Heads Together** Arrange students, numbered 1 or 2, in pairs to complete Exercises 1 and 2, ensuring that each partner understands how to use the random number generator on the graphing calculator. MP 1, 5

Alternate Strategy

AL Have students explain how the experimental probability is affected if the number 4 was chosen to represent a customer winning a free download. MP 1, 4, 7

2 Teach the Concept

Ask the scaffolded questions for each example to differentiate instruction.

IWB

Example

1. Describe a simulation.

AL
- *How many trading cards are there?* 8
- *Why would tossing three coins be an appropriate model?* There are 8 possible outcomes when tossing three coins (HHH, HHT, HTH, THH, HTT, THT, TTH, TTT).

OL
- *If you tossed all three coins and got the result THT, what toy was assigned to this outcome?* Card 7
- *Could we have assigned these 8 outcomes differently? Explain.* yes; Sample answer: THT could have been assigned as Card 2.
- *How many times do we need to toss all three coins to simulate the trading cards we would find in 15 boxes of cereal?* 15
- *Is it possible to get Card 4 every time? Explain.* It is possible, but not very likely.

BL
- *Does the theoretical probability change when the experiment is repeated? Explain.* no; Theoretically you still have a 1 in 8 chance of getting any card number in each box of cereal.

Need Another Example?

A supermarket is issuing one of six different in-store discount coupons to each customer who enters the store. If the coupons are given out randomly, describe a model that could be used to simulate which coupons would be given to the first 100 customers. Sample answer: Assign each face of a number cube to a type of coupon and roll the number cube 100 times.

Work Zone

Model Equally Likely Outcomes

A **simulation** is an experiment that is designed to model the action in a given situation. For example, you used a random number generator to simulate rolling a number cube. Simulations often use models to act out an event that would be impractical to perform.

Real World

Example

Tutor

1. **A cereal company is placing one of eight different trading cards in its boxes of cereal. If each card is equally likely to appear in a box of cereal, describe a model that could be used to simulate the cards you would find in 15 boxes of cereal.**

Choose a method that has 8 possible outcomes, such as tossing 3 coins. Let each outcome represent a different card.

For example, the outcome of all three coins landing heads up could simulate finding card 1.

Toss 3 coins to simulate the cards that might be in 15 boxes of cereal. Repeat 15 times.

Coin Toss Simulation

Outcome	Card	Outcome	Card
HHH	1	TTT	5
HHT	2	TTH	6
HTH	3	THT	7
HTT	4	THH	8

Got it? Do this problem to find out.

Show your work.

a. A restaurant is giving away 1 of 5 different toys with its children's meals. If the toys are given out randomly, describe a model that could be used to simulate which toys would be given with 6 children's meals.

a. Sample answer: Use a spinner with 5 equal sections, assigning each toy to a section. Then spin the spinner 6 times.

Statistics and Probability

Real World Example

Tools Tutor

2. **Every student who volunteers at the concession stand during basketball games will receive a free school T-shirt. The T-shirts come in 3 different designs.**

Design a simulation that could be used to model this situation. Use your simulation to find how many times a student must volunteer in order to get all 3 T-shirts.

Use a spinner divided into 3 equal sections. Assign each section one of the T-shirts. Spin the spinner until you land on each section.

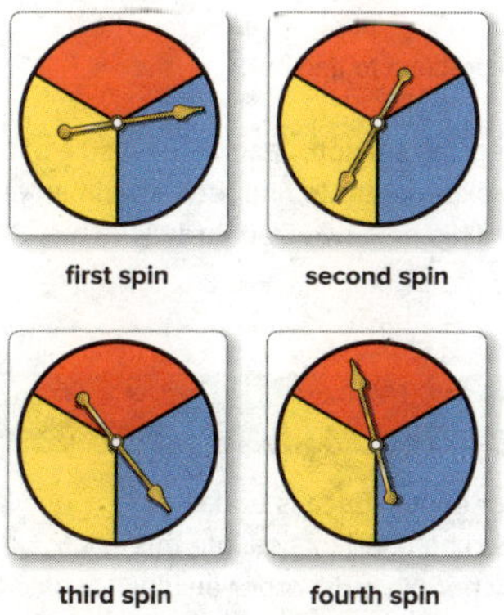

Based on this simulation, a student should volunteer 4 times in order to get all 3 T-shirts.

Got it? **Do this problem to find out.**

Show your work.

b. Mr. Chen must wear a dress shirt and a tie to work. Each day he picks one of his 6 ties at random. Design a simulation that could be used to model this situation. Use your simulation to find how many days Mr. Chen must work in order to wear all of his ties.

b. Sample answer: Roll a number cube. Each number represents a different tie. Repeat the simulation until all possible ties are selected. See students' work.

Model Unequally Likely Outcomes

Simulations can also be used to model events in which the outcomes are not equally likely.

Example

IWB

2. **Design and use a simulation.**

AL
- *Why is the spinner split into 3 sections?* because there are 3 different shirt designs
- *Does it matter which section we assign to which shirt design? Explain.* no; Sample answer: As long as we are consistent within the simulation, it does not matter which section is assigned to which shirt design.

OL
- *Is it possible that a student could receive all 3 designs in 3 games? Explain.* Yes, it is possible that the student could receive a different design each game.
- *Is it possible that a student would receive the same shirt design over any number of games? Explain.* yes; It is possible because the shirt designs are handed out randomly.

BL
- *If you repeated this simulation, would you always get the three sections in 4 spins? Explain.* no; It described one simulation, but any simulation could generate different results.

Need Another Example?

Every marathon runner that passes the halfway point gets an energy gel pack. There are four different flavors available and they are given out randomly. Describe a model that could be used to simulate this situation. Based on your simulation, how many runners will get gel packs before all four flavors are given out? Sample answer: Spin a spinner that has four equal sections until each section is spun once.

Watch Out!

Common Error Students may have a difficult time determining a model that can be used to simulate an experiment. Encourage students to use manipulatives or models to help them solve the problem.

Example

3. Use a simulation to model unequally likely events.

AL • *Is it more likely to rain or not rain? Explain.* more likely to rain, but only by a small margin

• *Why will 3 red and 2 blue marbles be a good model to simulate this event?* The total is 5 marbles, and 3 out of 5 is 60%.

OL • *What does selecting a red marble represent? blue?* Selecting a red marble indicates that it will rain. Selecting a blue marble indicates that it will not rain.

• *Why replace the marble back into the bag?* The next day will start with the same chance (percentage) of rain.

BL • *What would happen if you did not replace the marble back in the bag?* If you do not replace the marble, there would no longer be a 60% chance of selecting a red marble on the second draw.

Need Another Example?
During the regular season, Keisha had base hits in 40% of her times at bat. Describe an experiment she could use to simulate her next 20 times at bat. Sample answer: $40\% = \frac{2}{5}$, so Keisha could use a spinner with 5 sections, 2 representing making a base hit and 3 representing a failure to make a base hit. She would spin the spinner 20 times.

Guided Practice

Formative Assessment Use these exercises to assess students' understanding of the concepts in this lesson.

If some of your students are not ready for assignments, use the differentiated activity below.

AL EL **Give One, Get One** Have students complete Exercises 1–3 in pairs. Have students copy responses on a second sheet of paper to submit to a common pile in the classroom. Distribute the copies to different pairs, so that students may consider other simulations and responses.
MP 1, 4, 5

STOP and Reflect

How could you simulate a 20% chance? Write your answer below.

Sample answer: Use 1 red marble and 4 blue marbles.

Real World

Example

3. There is a 60% chance of rain for each of the next two days. Describe a method you could use to find the experimental probability of having rain on both of the next two days.

Place 3 red and 2 blue marbles in a bag. Let 60% or $\frac{3}{5}$ of them represent rain. Let 40% or $\frac{2}{5}$ of them represent no rain.

Randomly pick one marble to simulate the first day. Replace the marble and pick again to simulate the second day. Find the probability of rain on both days.

Got it? Do this problem to find out.

c. During the regular season, Jason made 80% of his free throws. Describe an experiment to find the experimental probability of Jason making his next two free throws.

Show your work.

c. Sample answer: Use a spinner in which 80% or $\frac{4}{5}$ represents making a free throw. Spin the spinner twice.

Guided Practice

1. An ice cream store offers waffle cones or sugar cones. Each is equally likely to be chosen. Describe a model that could be used to simulate this situation. Based on your simulation, how many people must order an ice cream cone in order to sell all possible combinations? (Examples 1 and 2)
Sample answer: Toss a coin. Repeat the simulation until all possible cones are obtained. See students' work.

2. An electronics store has determined that 45% of its customers buy a wide-screen television. Describe a model that you could use to find the experimental probability that the next three television-buying customers will buy a wide-screen television. (Example 3)
Sample answer: Use 9 white marbles to represent buying a wide screen and 11 red marbles to represent not buying a wide screen. Draw 3 marbles, replacing each marble.

3. **Building on the Essential Question** Explain how using a simulation is related to experimental probability.
Sample answer: A simulation is a process to collect data from which experimental probabilities can be calculated.

Rate Yourself!

How well do you understand simulations? Circle the image that applies.

For more help, go online to access a Personal Tutor.

Name ______________________ My Homework ______________________

Independent Practice

Go online for Step-by-Step Solutions eHelp

1. The questions on a multiple-choice test each have 4 answer choices. Describe a model that you could use to simulate the outcome of guessing the correct answers to a 50-question test. (Example 1)

   Sample answer: Spin a spinner with 4 equal-size sections 50 times.

2. A game requires drawing balls numbered 0 through 9 for each of four digits to determine the winning number. Describe a model that could be used to simulate the selection of the number. (Example 1)

   Sample answer: Repeat the random number function of a graphing calculator 4 times.

MP **Model with Mathematics** **Describe a model you could use to simulate each event.**

3. A jar of cookies contains 18 different types of cookies. Each type is equally likely to be chosen. Based on your simulation, how many times must a cookie be chosen in order to get each type? (Example 2)

   Sample answer: Spin a spinner divided into 3 equal sections and roll a number cube. Repeat the simulation until all types of cookies are obtained.

4. A cooler contains 5 bottles of lemonade, 4 bottles of water, and 3 bottles of juice. Each type is equally likely to be chosen. Based on your simulation, how many times must a drink be chosen in order to get each type? (Example 3)

   Sample answer: Spin a spinner divided into 12 equal sections. Five sections represent lemonade, 4 represent water, and 3 represent juice. Repeat until all types of drinks are obtained.

5. Players at a carnival game win about 30% of the time. Based on your simulation, what is the experimental probability that the next four players will win. (Example 3)

   Sample answer: Use 3 red marbles to represent winning and 7 blue marbles to represent losing. Draw 1 marble 4 times, replacing the marble each time.

ENGAGE EXPLORE **EXPLAIN** **ELABORATE** **EVALUATE**

3 Practice and Apply

Independent Practice and Extra Practice

The Independent Practice pages are meant to be used as the homework assignment. The Extra Practice page can be used for additional reinforcement or as a second-day assignment.

Levels of Complexity

The levels of the exercises progress from 1 to 3, with Level 1 indicating the lowest level of complexity.

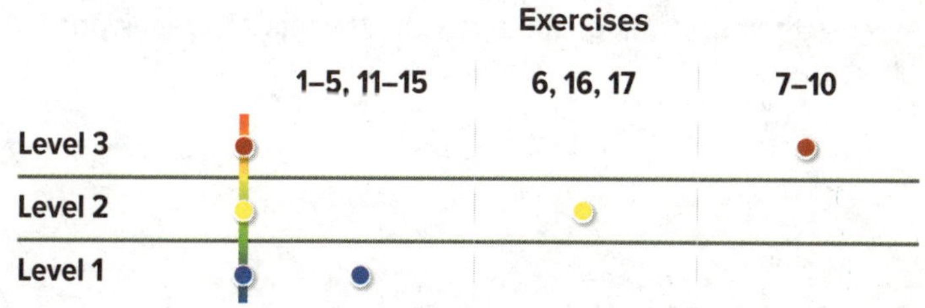

Suggested Assignments

You can use the table below that includes exercises of all complexity levels to select appropriate exercises for your students' needs.

Differentiated Homework Options		
AL	Approaching Level	1–5, 7, 9, 10, 16, 17
OL	On Level	1–5 odd, 6, 7, 9, 10, 16,17
BL	Beyond Level	6–10, 16, 17

ALEKS® can provide additional remediation support with personalized instruction and practice.

MP MATHEMATICAL PRACTICES

Emphasis On	Exercise(s)
1 Make sense of problems and persevere in solving them.	8
3 Construct viable arguments and critique the reasoning of others.	9, 10
4 Model with mathematics.	3–7, 13–15

Mathematical Practices 1, 3, and 4 are aspects of mathematical thinking that are emphasized in every lesson. Students are given opportunities to be persistent in their problem solving, to express their reasoning, and apply mathematics to real-world situations.

Formative Assessment
Use this activity as a closing formative assessment before dismissing students from your class.

TICKET Out the Door

Have students describe a simulation they may have used in another class. Answers will vary.

6. MP **Model with Mathematics** Suppose a mouse is placed in the maze at the right. If each decision about direction is made at random, create a simulation to determine the probability that the mouse will find its way out before coming to a dead end or going out the In opening.

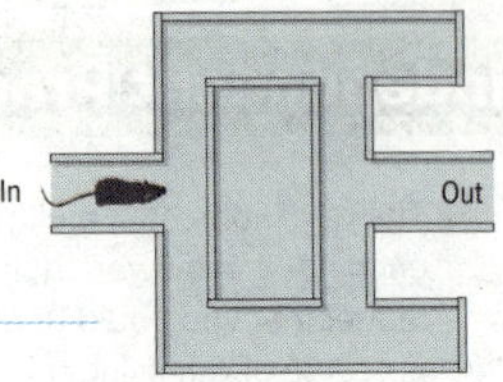

Sample answer: Use a coin to decide which way the mouse will go at each intersection. Record whether the mouse goes out the Out opening, goes out the In opening, or comes to a dead end. Repeat numerous times.

H.O.T. Problems Higher Order Thinking

7. MP **Model with Mathematics** Describe a situation that could be represented by a simulation. What objects could be used in your simulation?

Sample answer: a survey of 100 people voting on whether or not to enact a tax increase, where each person is equally likely to vote yes or no. Toss a coin 100 times.

8. MP **Persevere with Problems** A simulation uses cards numbered 0 through 9 to generate five 2-digit numbers. A card is selected for the tens digit and not replaced. Then a card for the ones digit is drawn and not replaced. The process is repeated until all the cards are used. If the simulation is performed 10 times, about how many times could you expect a 2-digit number to begin with a 5? Explain.

1 time; Sample answer: 9 out of 81 possibilities begin with 5 and $\frac{1}{9}$ of $10 \approx 1$.

9. MP **Justify Conclusions** Determine whether the following statement is *sometimes*, *always*, or *never* true. Justify your answer.

A spinner can be used to model equally likely outcomes.

Sample answer: sometimes; The spinner must have equal-sized sections.

10. MP **Justify Conclusions** Barton believes that the coin his teacher uses for an experiment gives an advantage to one team of students. His teacher has students toss the coin 50 times each and record their results. Based on the results in the table, do you think the coin is fair? Explain.

Student	Heads	Tails
1	17	33
2	22	28
3	28	22
4	21	29
5	13	37
6	20	30

no; Sample answer: There were 121 heads out of 300 tosses. The experimental probability of heads is about 40%.

Name ______________________ My Homework ______________________

Extra Practice

11. A store employee randomly gives scratch-off discount cards to the first 50 customers. The cards offer discounts of 10%, 20%, 25%, 30%, or 40%. There is an equal chance of receiving any of the 5 cards. Describe a model that could be used to simulate the discount received by 4 customers.

Homework Help

Use a spinner with 5 equal sections to represent the 5 different discounts. Spin 4 times to simulate 4 customers receiving cards.

12. On average, 75% of the days in Henderson county are sunny, with little or no cloud cover. Describe a model that you could use to find the experimental probability of sunny days each day for a week in Henderson county.

Sample answer: Use a spinner divided into 4 equal sections. Three sections represent sunny days and 1 section represents cloudy days. Spin the spinner 7 times.

MP **Model with Mathematics** **Describe a model you could use to simulate each event.**

13. Every student who participated in field day activities received a water bottle. The water bottles came in 2 different colors. Based on your simulation, how many students had to receive a water bottle in order to distribute water bottles in both colors?

Sample answer: Toss a coin. Heads represents one color and tails represents the other color. Repeat until both colors are selected.

14. A field hockey team wins 80% of its games. Based on your simulation, what is the experimental probability of the team winning its next 3 games?

Sample answer: Place 5 marbles in a bag. Four red marbles represent winning and 1 blue marble represents losing. Randomly pick one marble to simulate the first game. Replace the marble. Repeat for the next two games.

15. There are 4 different magazines on Hannah's nightstand. Each evening, she randomly selects one magazine to read. Based on your simulation, how many days must she select a magazine in order to read all 4 magazines?

Sample answer: Spin a spinner with 4 equal sections. Each section represents one of the magazines. Repeat the simulation until all possible magazines are selected.

Create Your Own Homework Online

eSolutionsManual™ can be used to create worksheets for the suggested assignments on page 745, or create your own worksheets for differentiated homework or review.

Power Up! Test Practice

Exercises 16 and 17 prepare students for more rigorous thinking needed for the state assessment.

16. This test item requires students to support their reasoning or evaluate the reasoning of others by justifying their response and constructing arguments.

Depth of Knowledge	DOK3
Content Standard	7.SP.8c
Mathematical Practice	MP1, MP3
Online Experience	Students will drag values to complete the sentences and type their response in the box.
Scoring Rubric	
2 points	Students correctly place values, answer the question, and explain their response.
1 point	Students correctly place all five values but fail to explain their response OR students fully explain their response but fail to correctly place all five values.

17. This test item requires students to explain and apply mathematical concepts and solve problems with precision, while making use of structure.

Depth of Knowledge	DOK2
Content Standard	7.SP.8c
Mathematical Practice	MP1
Online Experience	Students will be required to click on the bubbles to select all answers that are correct.
Scoring Rubric	
1 point	Students correctly answer the question.

Power Up! Test Practice

16. The table shows the chance of rain this weekend. Select values to fill in the boxes in the model below to describe a method you could use to find the experimental probability of having rain on both days.

Day	Saturday	Sunday
Chance of Rain	30%	30%

2	4	6	7	red
10	30	60	70	blue

Place 3 red and **7** blue marbles in a bag. Let the **red** marbles represent rain since **30** % of the marbles are this color. Let the **blue** marbles represent no rain since **70** % of the marbles are this color.

Randomly pick one marble to simulate the first day. Replace the marble and pick again to simulate the second day. Find the experimental probability of rain on both days. Do you think it matters how many trials of the simulation you conduct? Will conducting more trials result in a better prediction? Explain your reasoning.

Sample answer: Yes, as more trials of the simulation are conducted, the experimental probability will get closer to the theoretical probability, and the prediction will be more accurate.

17. At a restaurant, 1 out of every 6 kids' meals wins a prize. Determine which probability models could be used to simulate winning a prize. Select all that apply.

- ☐ Toss a coin. Let tossing heads represent winning a prize and let tossing tails represent not winning a prize.
- ■ Spin a spinner with equal size spaces labeled A, B, C, D, E, and F. Let spinning A represent winning a prize and let spinning other letters represent not winning a prize.
- ■ Roll a number cube. Let rolling a 1 represent winning a prize and let rolling a 2, 3, 4, 5, or 6 represent not winning a prize.

Spiral Review

18. A local video store has advertised that one out of every four customers will receive a free box of popcorn with their video rental. So far, 15 out of 75 customers have received popcorn. Compare the experimental and theoretical probabilities of receiving popcorn. 7.SP.5, 7.SP.7

The experimental probability is $\frac{1}{5}$ and the theoretical probability is $\frac{1}{4}$.

The experimental probability is less than the theoretical probability.

PLAN ONLINE

PD | RtI | Watch | Worksheets | Vocab | Tutor | Tools | Check | English Learners | Sketchpad

PRESENT

IWB

An Interactive Whiteboard Ready presentation is available for each lesson in the chapter.

Inquiry Lab

Simulate Compound Events

Inquiry **HOW** do simulations help you understand the probability of events happening?

Content Standards
7.SP.8, 7.SP.8c

MP **Mathematical Practices**
1, 3

A local shop randomly gives coupons to 3 out of every 8 customers. Use a spinner to determine the probability that a customer will receive a coupon two days in a row.

Hands-On Activity 1

Tools

Step 1 A spinner with eight equal sections can be used to simulate the situation. Label three of the sections with the letter C to represent the people that receive a coupon. Label five of the sections with the letter D to represent the people that do not receive a coupon.

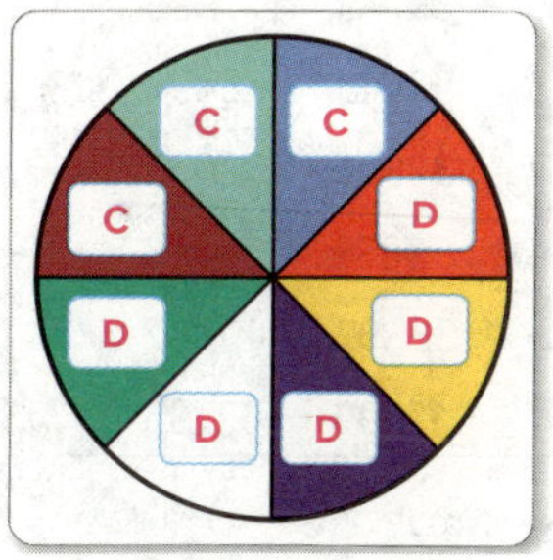

Step 2 Every two spins of the spinner represents one trial. Use a paperclip and the tip of your pencil to spin the spinner twice and record the results in the table. Perform a total of 15 trials.
See students' work.

Trial	Spin 1	Spin 2	Trial	Spin 1	Spin 2	Trial	Spin 1	Spin 2
1			6			11		
2			7			12		
3			8			13		
4			9			14		
5			10			15		

Based on your results, what is the experimental probability that a customer will receive a coupon two days in a row?

See students' work.

Focus narrowing the scope

Objective Use a simulation to generate frequencies for a compound event. 7.SP.8, 7.SP.8c

Coherence connecting within and across grades

Now
Students use simulations to produce compound events and find the probability.

Next
Students will use the Fundamental Counting Principle to find the probability of events.

Rigor pursuing concepts, fluency, and applications

See the Levels of Complexity chart on page 751.

ENGAGE EXPLORE EXPLAIN ELABORATE EVALUATE

1 Launch the Lab

Activities 1 and 2 are intended to be used as whole-group activities. Activity 1 is designed to provide more guidance than Activity 2.

Materials: random number table, spinner

Hands-On Activity 1

AL EL **Elbow Partners** Students can work with their nearest neighbor to complete Steps 1 and 2 and the follow-up question. Have students repeat the experiment to compare probabilities. MP 1, 4, 5

BL EL **Elbow Partners** Students can work with their nearest neighbor to complete Steps 1 and 2. Have students repeat the experiment to compare probabilities. Have partners present findings to compare results with the class. Have partners discuss the follow-up question with another pair. MP 1, 4, 5, 7

Hands-On Activity 2

AL EL Pairs Discussion Have students work in pairs to complete Activity 2. After they have completed the activity, use the following questions to guide their discussion and check their answers. MP 1, 4, 5, 7

Ask:

- *Why did we divide the random number table into numbers with 2 units?* to represent the two days
- *The number 19 appears in the second row of the table. Why is it not circled?* It only represents rain on Sundays. The second digit would have to be a 1 or 2 to represent rain on Monday also.
- *What does the number 61 represent in the random number table?* rain on Monday but not on Sunday

BL EL Think-Pair-Draw Have students work in pairs to complete Activity 2. After they have completed the activity, have them work together to draw and describe a spinner that could be used to represent the situation. MP 1, 4, 5, 7

You can also use a random number table to simulate a compound event.

There is a 10% chance of rain for a city on Sunday and a 20% chance of rain on Monday. Use a random number table to find the probability that it will rain on both days.

Hands-On Activity 2

Step 1 A random number table has random digits in rows that can be grouped in different combinations as needed. These digits are arranged in groups of 5, but the grouping often does not matter. Since the situation we want to represent involves two days, continue drawing lines to separate the numbers into two-digit numbers.

48587	49460	89640	30270
19507	87835	99812	52353
11364	35645	90087	64254
87045	39769	77995	14316
69913	93449	68497	31270
81827	32901	82033	43714
33386	99637	25725	31900
41575	86692	40882	44123
77351	12790	62795	77307

Step 2 Using the digits 0 through 9, assign one digit in the tens place for rain on Sunday and assign two different digits in the ones place for rain on Monday. For example, the digit 1 in the tens place can represent rain occurring on Sunday and the digits 1 and 2 in the ones place can represent rain occurring on Monday.

Step 3 Find the numbers in the table that have a 1 in the tens place and either a 1 or 2 in the ones place. Those numbers are 11 and 12. Circle those numbers in the table.

Step 4 Find the probability using the numbers found in Step 3.

There were 3 instances of the random numbers 11 and 12 occurring out of 90 random numbers.

So, the probability that it will rain on both days is $\frac{3}{90}$ or $3\frac{1}{3}\%$.

Investigate

Collaborate

Work with a partner.

1. Luke plays goalie on his soccer team. He usually stops 2 out of every 6 penalty kicks. Label the sections of the spinner at the right. Then use the spinner to determine the experimental probability that Luke stops 2 penalty kicks in a row.

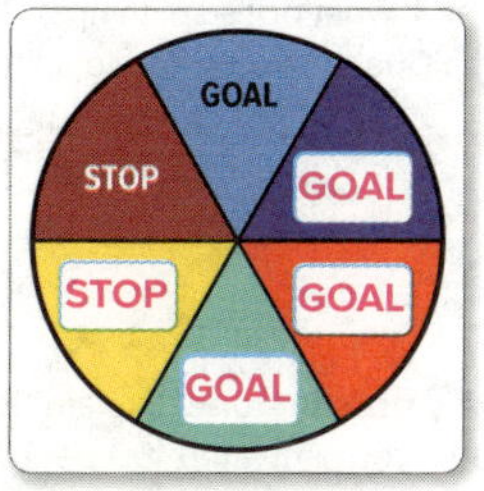

Trial	Spin 1	Spin 2	Trial	Spin 1	Spin 2	Trial	Spin 1	Spin 2
1			6			11		
2			7			12		
3			8			13		
4			9			14		
5			10			15		

The experimental probability is See students' work. .

2. Suppose 40% of customers who enter a pet store own a cat. What is the probability that it will take at least 4 customers before a cat owner enters the store? Use a random number table to simulate this compound event.

In the table below, separate the numbers into groups of 4. Then use the digits 0, 1, 2, and 3 to represent people who own cats. You are looking for groups of 4 numbers that do *not* contain a 0, 1, 2, or 3. Circle those groups.

18771	47374	36541	83454
97907	40978	34947	78482
26071	12644	94567	35467
02459	78467	06161	85897
44480	71716	13166	44096
72769	18974	24186	50866
35842	78478	45468	15441
58438	37487	16187	89892
83711	54631	19846	08483

In this case, the probability is $\frac{7}{45}$ or 15.6%.

So, the experimental probability that it takes at least 4 customers before a cat owner enters the store is 15.6%.

ENGAGE EXPLORE EXPLAIN ELABORATE EVALUATE

2 Collaborate

The **Investigate** and **Analyze and Reflect** sections are intended to be used as small-group investigations. The **Create** section is intended to be used as independent exercises.

Levels of Complexity

The levels of the exercises progress from 1 to 3, with Level 1 indicating the lowest level of complexity.

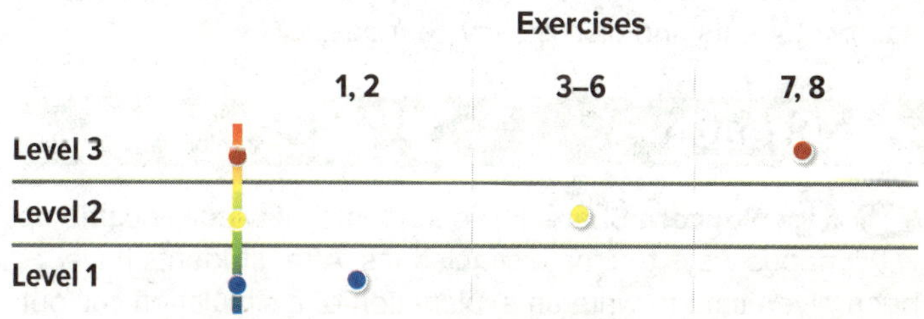

Investigate

Collaborate

AL EL **Three-Step-Interview** Have students work in teams of four. Within each team of four students will work in pairs. Partner A interviews Partner B and asks how they answered Exercise 1 and why. Partner B interviews Partner A and asks how they answered Exercise 2 and why. After interviews have been completed, each of the four-team members introduces his or her partner to the team and summarizes the information that was shared during the interview. MP 1, 3

BL EL **Three-Stay One-Stray** In teams of four, have students complete Exercises 1 and 2. After the exercises are completed, each team chooses one member to rotate to another team as a "visitor." The visitors explains to their new teams how they solved the exercises. Students discuss the answers and make any necessary corrections and changes. MP 1, 3, 4

Analyze and Reflect

Collaborate

AL EL **Teammates Consult** Students work in pairs to complete Exercises 3–6. Each person takes turn leading the discussion and recording the answers for the exercises. MP 1, 3, 4, 7

BL EL **Pairs Check** Have students work in pairs to complete Exercises 3–6. One partner solves the problem while the other coaches. Students switch roles until all exercises are completed. Have them then trade their answers with another pair of students and discuss any changes. MP 1, 3, 4

Create

On Your Own

BL EL **Popcorn Share** Have students individually come up with various ways to create simulations. After students have been given time to write an explanation of a simulation call out "Popcorn!" Students should then voluntarily pop up from their chairs one at a time to share their ideas. MP 1, 4, 5

Inquiry Students should be able to answer "HOW do simulations help you understand the probability of events happening? Check for student understanding and provide guidance, if needed.

Analyze and Reflect

Collaborate

3. In Exercise 1, what does spinning a Stop on your first spin, and spinning a Goal on your second spin represent in this situation?

   It represents Luke stopping the first penalty kick, but not stopping the second penalty kick.

4. MP **Justify Conclusions** Explain how your results might change for Exercise 1 if you simulated 100 penalty kicks.

   Sample answer: The simulated probability would be closer to the actual probability.

5. In Exercise 2, why were the numbers from the random number table separated into groups of four?

   Sample answer: To represent at least 4 people entering the store.

6. In Exercise 2, you could have used any 4 numbers to represent cat owners. Complete the simulation four more times using the numbers in the table to represent the cat owners.

Numbers that Represent Cat Owners	Experimental Probability
4, 5, 6, 7	$\frac{3}{45}$
0, 1, 8, 9	$\frac{6}{45}$
3, 4, 5, 6	$\frac{6}{45}$

Create

On Your Own

7. MP **Model with Mathematics** Design a simulation that could be used to predict the probability of taking a four question multiple-choice test with four answer choices and getting all four questions correct by guessing. Conduct 50 trials of the experiment. Then calculate the experimental probability of getting all four questions correct by guessing. See students' work.

8. Inquiry HOW do simulations help you understand the probability of events happening?

   Sample answer: Simulations help you visualize the probability of events. They also show that the more trials of an event, the closer the experimental probability will be to the theoretical probability.

PLAN ONLINE: PD | RtI | Watch | Worksheets | Vocab | Tutor | Tools | Check | English Learners | Sketchpad

PRESENT: IWB — **An Interactive Whiteboard Ready presentation is available for each lesson in the chapter.**

MP **Problem-Solving Investigation**

Act It Out

Content Standards
7.SP.8, 7.SP.8c

MP **Mathematical Practices**
1, 3, 4

Case #1 Winning Serves

Edie has been practicing her volleyball serve every day after school. Sho hits a good serve an average of 3 out of 4 times.

What is the probability that Edie will hit two good serves in a row?

1 Understand *What are the facts?*

You know that Edie hits a good serve an average of 3 out of 4 times. Act it out with a spinner.

2 Plan *What is your strategy?*

Spin a spinner, numbered 1 to 4, two times. If the spinner lands on 1, 2, or 3, she hits a good serve. If the spinner lands on 4, she doesn't. Repeat the experiment 10 times.

3 Solve *How can you apply the strategy?*

Here are some possible results. Circle the columns that show two good serves. The first two are done for you.

Trials	1	2	3	4	5	6	7	8	9	10
First Spin	4	1	4	3	1	2	2	1	3	2
Second Spin	2	3	3	2	1	4	1	4	3	3

The circled columns show that six out of 10 trials resulted in two good serves in a row. So, the probability is 60 %.

4 Check *Does the answer make sense?*

Repeat the experiment several times to see whether the results agree.

Analyze the Strategy (Watch, Tutor)

MP **Reason Inductively** Describe an advantage of using the *act it out* strategy?

Sample answer: Acting it out lets you find the experimental probability in a more practical way than what is in the scenerio.

Focus narrowing the scope

Objective Solve problems by acting them out. This lesson emphasizes MP **Mathematical Practice 4** Model with Mathematics.

Act It Out Students can solve many probability problems by acting them out. They can also use number cubes, coins, and spinners to perform probability experiments and simulations.

You actually do the action in the *act it out* strategy. In a simulation, you represent the action using something else.

Coherence connecting within and across grades

Now
Students solve non-routine problems.

Next
Students will apply the act it out strategy to find probability.

Rigor pursuing concepts, fluency, and applications

See the Levels of Complexity chart on page 755.

ENGAGE EXPLORE EXPLAIN ELABORATE EVALUATE

1 Launch the Lesson

The problems on pages 753 and 754 are for a whole-group discussion on how to solve non-routine problems and provide scaffolded guidance. The problem on page 753 walks students through the solution, while the problem on page 754 asks students to come up with their own solutions.

Materials: spinners, number cubes, coins

Case #1 Winning Serves

BL Have students extend the problem by having them answer the question below. MP 1, 5

Ask:

- *What is the probability that Edie will hit three good serves in a row?* See students' work.

Case #2 Books

AL EL Pairs Discussion If students have difficulty determining how to solve in step 3, have them work in pairs to answer the following scaffolded questions. MP 1, 5

Ask:

- *What do the colors on the spinner represent?* The answer choices to the multiple-choice quiz.
- *If you are trying to determine experimental probability, how can you get more reliable results?* Sample answer: You need a good sample, so you should run the simulation many times.

BL EL Trade-a-Problem Have students write their own real-world probability problem involving the spinner. Students trade their problems and solve. If the solutions do not agree, students work together to determine the errors. MP 1, 4, 5

Need Another Example?
Julia has two towels and three swimsuits to choose from to take to the swimming pool. How many different combinations of a swimsuit and a towel can she make from one towel and one swimsuit? 6 different combinations

Case #2 Tests

Tools

James uses a spinner with four equal sections to answer a five-question multiple-choice quiz. Each question has choices A, B, C, and D.

Is this a good way to answer the quiz questions?

1 Understand

- **Read the problem. What are you being asked to find?**

I need to find if using a spinner with 4 equal sections is a good way to answer a 5-question multiple-choice quiz with choices A, B, C, and D.

- **What information do you know?**

The spinner has 4 equal parts. There are 5 multiple-choice questions.

The answer choices are A, B, C, and D.

2 Plan

- **Choose a problem-solving strategy.**

I will use the act it out strategy.

3 Solve

Use your problem-solving strategy to solve the problem.
Spin a spinner with four equal parts labeled A, B, C, and D five times.
Repeat the experiment two times. Make a table of the results.
Sample results given.

Question	1	2	3	4	5
Trial 1	B	C	B	C	A
Trial 2	A	D	C	D	B

With each spin there is an equal chance of landing on any section. Since the probability of an answer being A, B, C, or D is equally likely, any answer choice is possible.

Is using a spinner to answer a multiple-choice question a good idea? no

4 Check

Use information from the problem to check your answer.
Repeat the experiment several times to see if the results agree.

Collaborate

Work with a small group to solve the following cases. Show your work on a separate piece of paper.

Case #3 Chess

A chess tournament will be held and 32 students will participate. If a player loses one match, he or she will be eliminated.

How many total games will be played in the tournament?

31

Case #4 Running

Six runners are entered in a race. Assume there are no ties.

In how many ways can first and second places be awarded?

30

Case #5 Fair Games

Karla and Jason are playing a game with number cubes. Each number cube is numbered 1 to 6. They roll both number cubes. If the product is a multiple of 3, Jason wins. If the product is a multiple of 4, Karla wins.

Is this game fair or unfair? Justify your response.

unfair; Sample answer: There are 20 out of 36 outcomes that are multiples of 3 and only 15 that are multiples of 4. Jason has a greater chance of winning.

Use any strategy!

Case #6 Algebra

The figure shown at the right is known as Pascal's Triangle.

Make a conjecture for the numbers in the 6th and 7th rows.

The 6th row should have the numbers 1, 5, 10, 10, 5, 1 and the 7th row should have the numbers 1, 6, 15, 20, 15, 6, 1.

ENGAGE EXPLORE **EXPLAIN** **ELABORATE** EVALUATE

2 Collaborate

Levels of Complexity

The levels of the cases progress from 1 to 3, with Level 1 indicating the lowest level of complexity.

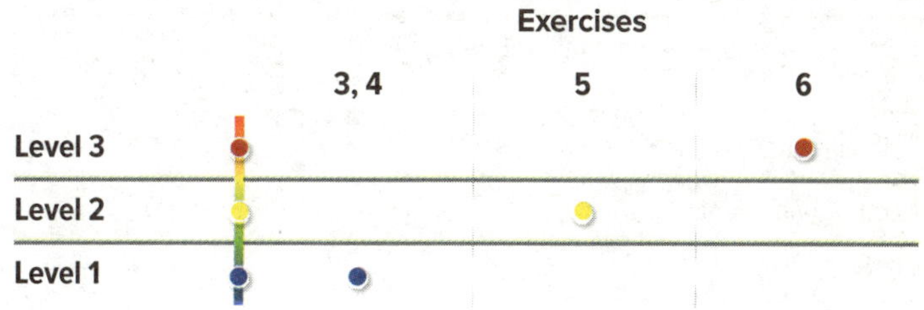

AL EL Team Project Assign students to 6-person learning teams. Ask each team to act out Case #4. Teams should discuss their strategy and ask clarifying questions as they act out the problem. Call on one student from each team to share what they learned aloud to the class. MP 1, 5

BL EL Rally Robin Have students work in groups to complete Cases #3–6, making sure that every member understands. Then, take turns calling on a member from a group to explain an Exercise to the rest of the class. Repeat and continue until all Exercises have been explained. MP 1, 5

Mid-Chapter Check

If students have trouble with Exercises 1–7, they may need help with the following concepts.

Concept	Exercise(s)
simple events (Lesson 1)	1, 3, 4
theoretical and experimental probability (Lesson 2)	5
simulations (Lesson 4)	2, 6
compound events (Lesson 3)	7

Vocabulary Activity

EL **Think-Pair-Share** Have students work in pairs to complete Exercise 1 and 2. Give them about one minute to individually think through their response. Then have them share their responses with a partner. Call on one set of pairs to share their responses with the class. MP 1, 6, 7

ALEKS® provides additional remediation support with personalized instruction and practice for those who are struggling, while providing enhanced learning for those who have mastered the concepts.

Alternate Strategies

AL Provide students, in groups of 3, with different probability events and have the students create sample spaces using different methods for each event. Have students compare the situations to determine why a particular sample space method could be most useful for that situation.

BL In groups of 3, have students create an experiment. Each student within each group can utilize a different sample space method to show the sample space in three different ways. Have students justify why his/her method is most useful.

Mid-Chapter Check

Vocabulary Check

1. Define *probability*. Give an example of the probability of a simple event. (Lesson 1)
   Probability is the chance that an event will happen. Sample answer: The probability of a tossed coin landing heads is $\frac{1}{2}$.

2. Fill in the blank in the sentence below with the correct term. (Lesson 4)
   A(n) simulation is an experiment that is designed to act out a given situation.

Skills Check and Problem Solving

The table shows the number of science fiction, action, and comedy movies Jason has in his collection. Suppose one movie is selected at random. Find each probability. Write as a fraction in simplest form. (Lesson 1)

Type of Movie	
Science Fiction	10
Action	7
Comedy	3

3. *P*(science fiction) $\frac{1}{2}$

4. *P*(*not* action) $\frac{13}{20}$

5. A coin is tossed 20 times. It lands heads 4 times. Compare the experimental probability to its theoretical probability. If the probabilities are not close, explain a possible reason for the discrepancy. (Lesson 2)
   Sample answer: $\frac{1}{5}$ is not close to $\frac{1}{2}$. One possible reason for the discrepancy is that there were not many trials.

6. A weather forecaster predicts a 30% chance of rain for each of the next three days. Describe a way to simulate the chance that it will rain the next three days. (Lesson 4) Sample answer: Place 3 red marbles and 7 white marbles in a bag. Let the red marbles represent the chance of rain. Randomly select 1 marble to simulate the chance of rain on day 1. Replace the marble. Repeat for days 2 and 3.

7. MP **Persevere with Problems** Without looking, Santiago took a handful of multi-colored candies from a bag and found that 20% of the candies were yellow and 15% were green. Suppose there were 480 candies in the bag. Based on Santiago's results, how many more yellow candies would you expect there to be than green candies? (Lesson 1) 24

PLAN ONLINE

PD | RtI | Watch | Worksheets | Vocab | Tutor | Tools | Check | English Learners | Sketchpad

PRESENT

IWB

An Interactive Whiteboard Ready presentation is available for each lesson in the chapter.

Statistics and Probability

Lesson 5

Fundamental Counting Principle

Real-World Link

Classes Tyler wants to take a class at the community center. The table shows the class options he is considering. All of the classes are offered only on Monday and Tuesday.

Class	Day
Drawing Martial Arts Dance	Monday Tuesday

1. According to the table, how many classes is he considering? 3

2. How many days are the classes offered?
2

3. Complete the tree diagram to find the number of different class and day outcomes.

Class	Day	Sample Space
Drawing	Monday	Drawing, Monday
	Tuesday	Drawing, Tuesday
Martial Arts	Monday	Martial Arts, Monday
	Tuesday	Martial Arts, Tuesday
Dance	Monday	Dance, Monday
	Tuesday	Dance, Tuesday

4. Find the product of the two numbers you found in Exercises 1 and 2. How does the number of outcomes compare to the product?
6; They are the same.

Which MP **Mathematical Practices** did you use?
Shade the circle(s) that applies.

① Persevere with Problems
② Reason Abstractly
③ Construct an Argument
④ Model with Mathematics
⑤ Use Math Tools
⑥ Attend to Precision
⑦ Make Use of Structure
⑧ Use Repeated Reasoning

Essential Question

HOW can you predict the outcome of future events?

Vocabulary

Fundamental Counting Principle

Content Standards
7.SP.5, 7.SP.8, 7.SP.8a, 7.SP.8b

MP Mathematical Practices
1, 3, 4

Focus narrowing the scope

Objective Use multiplication to count the number of outcomes and find probabilities. 7.SP.5, 7.SP.8, 7.SP.8a, 7.SP.8b

Coherence connecting within and across grades

Previous Students found outcomes of compound events by using lists and tree diagrams.

Now Students find number of outcomes of compound events by using the Fundamental Counting Principle.

Next Students will use the Fundamental Counting Principle to find permutations.

Rigor pursuing concepts, fluency, and applications

See the Levels of Complexity chart on page 761.

ENGAGE EXPLORE EXPLAIN ELABORATE EVALUATE

1 Launch the Lesson

Ideas for Use

You may wish to launch the lesson using a whole group, small group, think-pair-share activity, or independent activity.

AL EL **Pairs Consult** Have students work in pairs. Give each pair a different set of manipulatives that they have used in learning about probability, such as coins, spinners, marbles, and so on. Have each group design a simple probability experiment using the manipulatives to determine the sample space and find the probability of different outcomes. MP 1, 4, 5

Alternate Strategy

BL Extend the activity by adding a fourth class to the choices. Then ask how this compares to the product of the number of classes and the number of days. MP 1, 7

ENGAGE EXPLORE **EXPLAIN** ELABORATE EVALUATE

2 Teach the Concept

Ask the scaffolded questions for each example to differentiate instruction.

Example

IWB

1. Find the number of outcomes.

AL
- *How many outcomes are possible when tossing a coin?* 2
- *How many outcomes are possible when rolling a number cube?* 6

OL
- *Does the Fundamental Counting Principle show what the outcomes are? Explain.* No, the Fundamental Counting Principle only determines the number of outcomes, not what the outcomes are.

BL
- *How does the tree diagram demonstrate why the Fundamental Counting Principle works?* Sample answer: The branches show the multiplication. The two branches separate into 6 branches each or $2 \cdot 6 = 12$.

Need Another Example?

Find the total number of outcomes when a number from 0 to 9 is randomly chosen, then a letter from A to D is randomly chosen. 40

Work Zone

Key Concept

Fundamental Counting Principle

If event *M* has *m* possible outcomes and event *N* has *n* possible outcomes, then event *M* followed by event *N* has $m \times n$ possible outcomes.

You can use multiplication instead of making a tree diagram to find the number of possible outcomes in a sample space. This is called the **Fundamental Counting Principle**.

Real World

Example

Tools Tutor

1. Find the total number of outcomes when a coin is tossed and a number cube is rolled.

A coin has 2 possible outcomes. A number cube has 6 possible outcomes. Multiply the possible outcomes of each event.

coin | number cube | total

$2 \cdot 6 = 12$ Fundamental Counting Principle

There are 12 different outcomes.

Check Draw a tree diagram to show the sample space.

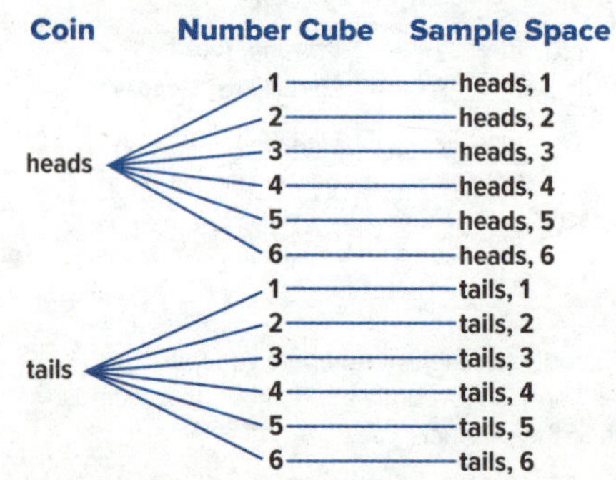

The tree diagram also shows that there are 12 outcomes. ✓

Got it? **Do this problem to find out.**

Show your work.

a. Find the total number of outcomes when choosing from bike helmets that come in three colors and two styles.

a. 6

Statistics and Probability

Find Probability

You can use the Fundamental Counting Principle to help find the probability of events.

Examples

2. **Find the total number of outcomes from rolling a number cube with sides labeled 1–6 and choosing a letter from the word NUMBERS. Then find the probability of rolling a 6 and choosing an M.**

number cube | letters | total

$6 \cdot 7 = 42$ Fundamental Counting Principle

There are 42 different outcomes.

There is only one favorable outcome. So, the probability of rolling a 6 and choosing an M is $\frac{1}{42}$ or about 2%.

3. **Find the number of different jeans available at The Jeans Shop. Then find the probability of randomly selecting a size 32 × 34 slim fit. Is it likely or unlikely that the jeans would be chosen?**

The Jeans Shop

Waist Size	Length (in.)	Style
30	30	slim fit
32	32	bootcut
34	34	loose fit
36		
38		

Jean Size
In men's jeans, the size is labeled waist × length. So, a 32 × 34 is a 32-inch waist with a 34-inch length.

size | length | style | total

$5 \cdot 3 \cdot 3 = 45$ Fundamental Counting Principle

There are 45 different types of jeans to choose. Out of the 45 possible outcomes, only one is favorable. So, the probability of randomly selecting a 32 × 34 slim fit is $\frac{1}{45}$ or about 2%.

It is very unlikely that the size would be chosen at random.

Got it? **Do this problem to find out.**

b. Two number cubes are rolled. What is the probability that the sum of the numbers on the cubes is 12? How likely is it that the sum would be 12?

Show your work.

b. $\frac{1}{36}$ or about 3%; very unlikely

Examples

IWB

2. **Find probability.**

AL
- *How many outcomes are possible when rolling a number cube?* 6
- *How many outcomes are possible when choosing a letter from the word NUMBERS?* 7
- *How many total outcomes are possible?* 42

OL
- *What is the probability of rolling a 6 and choosing an M?* $\frac{1}{42}$ or about 2%.

BL
- *What is the probability of rolling an even number and choosing a vowel?* $\frac{1}{7}$ or about 14%

Need Another Example?

A pizzeria has two different types of crust, 3 types of cheese, and 4 toppings. A personal pizza can only have one type of cheese and one topping. What is the probability of choosing a thin crust pizza with parmesan cheese and pepperoni? $\frac{1}{24}$

3. **Find probability.**

AL
- *How many different waist sizes are offered?* 5
- *How many different lengths are offered?* 3
- *How many different styles are offered?* 3

OL
- *How many total outcomes are possible?* 45
- *What is the probability of selecting a particular pair of jeans?* $\frac{1}{45}$

BL
- *Suppose you only wanted bootcut jean. How would the problem change?* You would only have 5 • 3 or 15 outcomes.

Need Another Example?

A shoe store sells sneakers, loafers, and boots in narrow, medium, and wide widths. They are available in sizes 6, 6.5, 7, 7.5, 8, 8.5, 9, 9.5, 10, and 10.5. Find the number of pairs of shoes available. Then find the probability of selecting a size 8 in medium width sneakers. Is it likely or unlikely that the size would be chosen? 90, $\frac{1}{90}$ or about 1.1%; It is very unlikely that the size would be chosen at random.

Example

4. Find probability.

AL • *How many different colors are there?* 5

• *How many different action figures are there?* 2

• *How could you find the total number of outcomes?* multiply 5 by 2

OL • *What is the probability of selecting an orange car and a female action figure?* $\frac{1}{10}$

BL • *If you wanted a larger sample space, should you add a car color or an action figure? Explain.* If you added another car color, you would have 6 • 2 or 12 outcomes. If you added an action figure, you would have 5 • 3 or 15 outcomes, so you should add another action figure.

Need Another Example?

The two spinners below are spun. What is the probability that the product of the numbers spun is 12? How likely is it that the product would be 12? $\frac{1}{25}$ or 4%; very unlikely

Guided Practice

Formative Assessment Use these exercises to assess students' understanding of the concepts in this lesson.

If some of your students are not ready for assignments, use the differentiated activities below.

AL EL **Pairs Discussion** Have students work in pairs to solve Exercises 1–3. Students should list the number of outcomes for each simple event before finding the total number of outcomes. Have them trade their solutions with another pair of students and discuss any differences. MP 1, 7

Real World Example

4. **A box of toy cars contains blue, orange, yellow, red, and black cars. A separate box contains a male and a female action figure. What is the probability of randomly choosing an orange car and a female action figure? Is it likely or unlikely that this combination is chosen?**

First, find the number of possible outcomes.

There are 5 choices for the car and 2 choices for the action figure.

5 • 2 = 10 Fundamental Counting Principal

There are 10 possible outcomes. There is one way to choose an orange car and a female action figure. It is very unlikely that this combination is chosen at random.

P(orange car, female action figure) = $\frac{1}{10}$ or 10%.

Guided Practice

1. Use the Fundamental Counting Principle to find the number of outcomes from tossing a quarter, a dime, and a nickel. (Example 1)
   8

2. How many outcomes are possible when rolling a number cube and picking a cube from 4 different colored cubes? (Example 1)
   24

3. Find the number of different outfits that can be made from 3 sweaters, 4 blouses, and 6 skirts. Then find the probability of randomly selecting a particular sweater-blouse-skirt outfit. Is the probability of this event likely or unlikely? (Examples 2–4)
   72; $\frac{1}{72}$ or about 1.4%; unlikely

4. **Building on the Essential Question** Compare and contrast tree diagrams and the Fundamental Counting Principle.
   Sample answer: Tree diagrams show specific outcomes. The Fundamental Counting Principle is a faster way to obtain the number of outcomes.

Rate Yourself!

How confident are you about using the Fundamental Counting Principle? Shade the ring on the target.

For more help, go online to access a Personal Tutor.

Name ________________ My Homework ________________

Independent Practice

Go online for Step-by-Step Solutions eHelp

Use the Fundamental Counting Principle to find the total number of outcomes for each situation. (Example 1)

1. choosing a bagel with one type of cream cheese from the list shown in the table

12

Bagels	Cream Cheese
Plain Blueberry Cinnamon raisin Garlic	Plain Chive Sun-dried tomato

2. choosing a sandwich and a side from the list shown in the table

20

Sandwiches	Sides
Ham Turkey Roast Beef Tuna Salad Vegetarian	Pasta Salad Fruit Cup Potato Chips Side Salad

3. picking a month of the year and a day of the week 84

4. choosing from a comedy, horror, or action movie each shown in four different theaters

12

5. Find the number of possible routes from Eastland to Johnstown that pass through Harping. Then find the probability that State and Fairview will be used if a route is selected at random. State the probability as a fraction and percent. (Examples 2–3)

6 possible routes; $\frac{1}{6}$ or about 17%

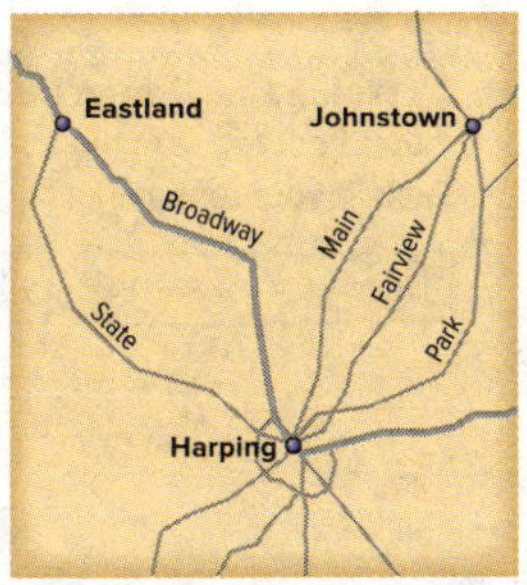

6. Find the number of possible choices for a 2-digit number that is greater than 19. Then find the number of possible choices for a 4-digit Personal Identification Number (PIN) if the digits cannot be repeated. (Example 1)

80; 5,040

7. An electronics company makes educational apps for 5 subjects, including math. The app has 10 versions, with a different avatar in each version. One version has an avatar that looks similar to a lion. The company is randomly giving free apps to its customers. Find the probability of randomly receiving a math app with a lion avatar. How likely is the probability of receiving this app at random? (Examples 2–4)

$\frac{1}{50}$; very unlikely

ENGAGE EXPLORE **EXPLAIN** **ELABORATE** **EVALUATE**

3 Practice and Apply

Independent Practice and Extra Practice

The Independent Practice pages are meant to be used as the homework assignment. The Extra Practice page can be used for additional reinforcement or as a second-day assignment.

Levels of Complexity

The levels of the exercises progress from 1 to 3, with Level 1 indicating the lowest level of complexity.

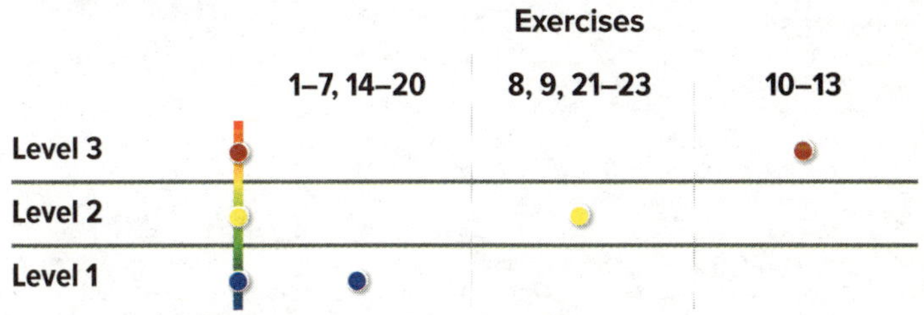

Suggested Assignments

You can use the table below that includes exercises of all complexity levels to select appropriate exercises for your students' needs.

Differentiated Homework Options		
AL	Approaching Level	1–7, 9, 11, 12, 22, 23
OL	On Level	1–7 odd, 8, 9, 11, 12, 22, 23
BL	Beyond Level	8–13, 22, 23

ALEKS® can provide additional remediation support with personalized instruction and practice.

MATHEMATICAL PRACTICES

Emphasis On	Exercise(s)
1 Make sense of problems and persevere in solving them.	10, 13
3 Construct viable arguments and critique the reasoning of others.	9, 11, 12, 21

Mathematical Practices 1, 3, and 4 are aspects of mathematical thinking that are emphasized in every lesson. Students are given opportunities to be persistent in their problem solving, to express their reasoning, and apply mathematics to real-world situations.

Formative Assessment
Use this activity as a closing formative assessment before dismissing students from your class.

TICKET Out the Door

Tell students that you have four kinds of cereal (A, B, C, and D) and two kinds of berries (strawberries and blueberries) to put on the cereal. Have students describe the method they would use to find the sample space. Then have students find the probability of having cereal A with strawberries.
use a tree diagram to find the sample space; $\frac{1}{8}$

8. A sandwich shop offers 4 different meats and 2 different cheeses. Suppose the sandwich shop offers 24 different meat-cheese sandwiches. How many different breads does the sandwich shop use?

3 different breads

9. **Justify Conclusions** A store offers 32 different T-shirt designs and 11 choices of color. Is the store's advertisement true? Explain.

No; the number of selections is 32 · 11 or 352, which is less than 365.

H.O.T. Problems Higher Order Thinking

10. **Persevere with Problems** Determine the number of possible outcomes when tossing one coin, two coins, and three coins. Then determine the number of possible outcomes for tossing *n* coins. Describe the strategy you used.

2; 4; 8; 2^n; Sample answer: I used a pattern to determine the number of outcomes for *n* coins. One coin: 2^1 outcomes, two coins: 2 • 2 or 2^2 outcomes, three coins: 2 • 2 • 2 or 2^3 outcomes, *n* coins: 2^n outcomes.

11. **Which One Doesn't Belong?** Identify the choices for events *M* and *N* that do not result in the same number of outcomes as the other two. Explain your reasoning.

9 drinks, 8 desserts	18 shirts, 4 pants	10 groups, 8 activities

10 groups, 8 activities have 80 outcomes; the other two have 72 outcomes.

12. **Justify Conclusions** Marcus has a choice of a white, gray, or black shirt to wear with a choice of tan, black, brown, or denim pants. Without calculating the number of possible outcomes, how many more outfits can he make if he buys a green shirt? Explain your reasoning to a classmate.

4 more outfits; Sample answer: He will have four different pairs of pants that he can wear with the green shirt.

13. **Persevere with Problems** Write an algebraic expression to find the number of outcomes if a number cube is rolled *x* times.

6^x

Name ______ My Homework ______

Extra Practice

Use the Fundamental Counting Principle to find the total number of outcomes for each situation.

14. rolling a number cube and spinning a spinner with eight equal sections 48

$6 \cdot 8 = 48$

Homework Help

15. tossing a coin and selecting one letter from the word MATH 8

16. selecting one sweatshirt from a choice of five sweatshirts and one pair of pants from a choice of four pairs of pants 20

17. selecting one entrée from a choice of nine entrées and one dessert from a choice of three desserts 27

18. rolling a number cube and tossing two coins 24

19. choosing tea in regular, raspberry, lemon, or peach; sweetened or unsweetened; and in a glass or bottle 16

20. A cafeteria offers oranges, apples, or bananas as its fruit option. It offers peas, green beans, or carrots as the vegetable option. Find the number of fruit and vegetable options. If the fruit and the vegetable are chosen at random, what is the probability of getting an orange and carrots? Is it likely or unlikely that a customer would get an orange and carrots?

9 options; $\frac{1}{9}$ or about 11.1%; unlikely

21. MP **Justify Conclusions** The table shows cell phone options offered by a wireless phone company. If a phone with one payment plan and one accessory is given away at random, predict the probability that it will be Brand B and have a headset. Explain your reasoning.

Phone Brands	Payment Plans	Accessories
Brand A	Individual	Leather case
Brand B	Family	Car mount
Brand C	Business	Headset
	Government	Travel charger

$\frac{4}{48}$ or $\frac{1}{12}$; Sample answer: There are $3 \cdot 4 \cdot 4$ or 48 different possible outcomes of a phone plan. There are $1 \cdot 4 \cdot 1$ or 4 different possible outcomes of a phone plan that includes Brand B and has a headset.

Create Your Own Homework Online

SolutionsManual™ can be used to create worksheets for the suggested assignments on page 761, or create your own worksheets for differentiated homework or review.

Power Up! Test Practice

Exercises 22 and 23 prepare students for more rigorous thinking needed for the state assessment.

22.

This test item requires students to explain and apply mathematical concepts and solve problems with precision, while making use of structure.	
Depth of Knowledge	DOK1
Content Standard	7.SP.8b
Mathematical Practice	MP1
Online Experience	Students will be required to click on the bubbles to select all answers that are correct.
Scoring Rubric	
1 point	Students correctly answer the question.

23.

This test item requires students to explain and apply mathematical concepts and solve problems with precision, while making use of structure.	
Depth of Knowledge	DOK2
Content Standard	7.SP.8b
Mathematical Practice	MP1
Online Experience	Students will drag values to model the equation and type their response in the box.
Scoring Rubric	
2 points	Students correctly model the equation and determine the how many hats the company makes.
1 point	Students correctly model the equation OR determine the how many hats the company makes.

Power Up! Test Practice

22. A restaurant has 24 different lunch combinations. Which of the following could describe the lunch options? Select all that apply.

- [x] 3 drink sizes, 4 main dishes, 2 side dishes
- [ ] 2 appetizers, 6 main dishes, 3 desserts
- [x] 3 kinds of bread, 8 kinds of sandwiches
- [ ] 2 drink sizes, 7 appetizers, 2 main dishes

23. Hat Shack sells 9 different styles of hats in several different colors for 2 different sports teams. The company makes 108 kinds of hats in all. Select the correct values to complete the formula below to find the number of different color hats the Hat Shack makes.

Hat Shack		
Styles	Colors	Teams
9	?	2

108 = 9 × c × 2

Choices: 2, 9, 108, c

How many different colors does the company use for hats?

6 colors

Spiral Review

Find each probability. 7.SP.8

24. A coin is tossed and a spinner with 4 equal sections labeled W–Z is spun. Find *P*(heads and Z).

$\frac{1}{8}$

25. A pizza shop offers a single item pizza with choice of pepperoni, green peppers, pineapple, sausage, or mushroom toppings. The pizza can be thick crust or thin crust. Find *P*(thick crust).

$\frac{1}{2}$

Describe a model that could be used to simulate each situation. 7.SP.8c

26. There is a fifty percent chance of rain on Monday.

Sample answer: Toss a coin.

27. A restaurant randomly gives away 1 of 6 toys. Determine the number of times a child needs to visit the restaurant to receive all 6 toys.

Sample answer: Assign each number of a number cube to a toy. Roll the number cube. Repeat until all numbers are rolled.

PLAN ONLINE: PD · RtI · Watch · Worksheets · Vocab · Tutor · Tools · Check · English Learners · Sketchpad

PRESENT: IWB

An Interactive Whiteboard Ready presentation is available for each lesson in the chapter.

Statistics and Probability

Lesson 6

Permutations

Real-World Link

Scheduling Colt is planning his Saturday. He wants to mow the grass, go swimming, and do his homework. How many different ways are there to arrange what he wants to do?

Fill in the blanks of the organized list below to find all of the possible arrangements of the activities.

1: Mowing	2: Swimming	3: Homework
1: Mowing	2: Homework	3: Swimming
1: Swimming	2: Mowing	3: Homework
1: Swimming	2: Homework	3: Mowing
1: Homework	2: Mowing	3: Swimming
1: Homework	2: Swimming	3: Mowing

1. How many choices does Colt have for his first activity?
   3
2. Once the first activity is selected, how many choices does Colt have for the second activity?
   2
3. Once the first and second activities are selected, how many choices does Colt have for the third activity?
   1

Which MP **Mathematical Practices** did you use?
Shade the circle(s) that applies.

① Persevere with Problems
② Reason Abstractly
③ Construct an Argument
④ Model with Mathematics
⑤ Use Math Tools
⑥ Attend to Precision
⑦ Make Use of Structure
⑧ Use Repeated Reasoning

Essential Question

HOW can you predict the outcome of future events?

Vocabulary

permutation

Content Standards
7.SP.8, 7.SP.8a

MP **Mathematical Practices**
1, 3, 4

Focus narrowing the scope

Objective Find the number of permutations of a set of objects and find probabilities. 7.SP.8, 7.SP.8a

Coherence connecting within and across grades

Previous Students used the Fundamental Counting Principle to find the number of outcomes.

Now Students use the Fundamental Counting Principle to find the number of permutations.

Next Students will find probabilities of dependent and independent events.

Rigor pursuing concepts, fluency, and applications

See the Levels of Complexity chart on page 769.

ENGAGE EXPLORE EXPLAIN ELABORATE EVALUATE

1 Launch the Lesson

Ideas for Use

You may wish to launch the lesson using a whole group, small group, think-pair-share activity, or independent activity.

BL **Pairs Discussion** In pairs, ask students to discuss if the activities in the list are really different. Have one student from each pair write down their response. Have them trade their response with another pair of students. MP 1, 6, 7

Alternate Strategy

AL Before beginning the Real-World Link, place two chairs in the front of the room. Have three students come to the front. Have the class determine how many ways there are for two students to sit in the first and second chairs. Then ask the class to determine how many ways there are for the three students to sit in the two chairs. MP 1, 7

ENGAGE EXPLORE **EXPLAIN** ELABORATE EVALUATE

2 Teach the Concept

Ask the scaffolded questions for each example to differentiate instruction.

Examples

IWB

1. Find a permutation.

AL • *How many choices are possible for the first class?* 3

• *Having chosen one class, how many choices are possible for the second class?* 2

OL • *How do you use the Fundamental Counting Principle to solve this problem?* You multiply the number of outcomes for each event to find the total number of outcomes for a compound event.

BL • *Suppose there are four different courses. How many ways can Julia schedule her first three classes?* 24 ways

Need Another Example?
There are five people on a bowling team. If they bowl one at a time, in how many different ways can they order the team? 120

2. Find a permutation.

AL • *How many choices are possible for the first scoop?* 31

• *How many outcomes are possible for the second scoop?* 30

OL • *How can you find the total number of ways Carlos could create using three scoops of ice cream?* Multiply the number of choices for each scoop.

BL • *Would it be advantageous to create a tree diagram for this situation? Explain.* No, there are too many choices for each scoop to be able to draw a tree diagram.

Need Another Example?
Fifteen students are running for seventh grade student council. In how many different ways can the president, vice-president, and secretary be chosen? 2,730

Work Zone

Find a Permutation

A **permutation** is an arrangement, or listing, of objects in which order is important.

Mowing
Swimming
Homework → Different Orders ← Swimming
Mowing
Homework

You can use the Fundamental Counting Principle to find the number of permutations.

Real World

Examples

Tutor

1. Julia is scheduling her first three classes. Her choices are math, science, and language arts. Use the Fundamental Counting Principle to find the number of different ways Julia can schedule her first three classes.

There are **3** choices for the first class.
There are **2** choices that remain for the second class.
There is **1** choice that remains for the third class.

$3 \cdot 2 \cdot 1 = 6$ ← the number of permutations of 3 classes

There are 6 possible arrangements, or permutations, of the 3 classes.

2. An ice cream shop has 31 flavors. Carlos wants to buy a three-scoop cone with three different flavors. How many cones could he buy if the order of the flavors is important?

There are 31 choices for the first scoop, 30 choices for the second scoop, and 29 choices for the third scoop.

Use the Fundamental Counting Principle.

$31 \cdot 30 \cdot 29 = 26{,}970$

Carlos could buy 26,970 different cones.

Got it? **Do these problems to find out.**

Show your work.

a. In how many ways can the starting six players of a volleyball team stand in a row for a picture?

b. In a race with 7 runners, in how many ways can the runners end up in first, second, and third place?

a. 720

b. 210

The symbol $P(31, 3)$ represents the number of permutations of 31 things taken 3 at a time.

Start with 31.

$$P(31, 3) = 31 \cdot 30 \cdot 29$$

Use three factors.

Example

Tutor

3. Find $P(8, 3)$.

$P(8, 3) = 8 \cdot 7 \cdot 6$ or 336 — 8 things taken 3 at a time

Got it? **Do these problems to find out.**

c. $P(12, 2)$ d. $P(4, 4)$ e. $P(10, 5)$

c. 132

d. 24

Show your work

e. 30,240

Find Probability

Permutations can be used when finding probabilities of real-world situations.

Examples

Tutor

4. Ashley's MP3 player has a setting that allows the songs to play in a random order. She has a playlist that contains 10 songs. What is the probability that the MP3 player will randomly play the first three songs in order?

First find the permutation of ten things taken three at a time or $P(10, 3)$.

10 songs — Choose 3

$$P(10, 3) = 10 \cdot 9 \cdot 8$$
$$= 720$$

10 choices for the 1st song
9 choices for the 2nd song
8 choices for the 3rd song

So, there are 720 different ways to play the first 3 songs. Since you want the first three songs in order, there is only 1 out of the 720 ways to do this.

So, the probability that the first 3 songs will play in order is $\frac{1}{720}$.

Notation
In Example 4, the notation $P(10, 3)$ indicates a permutation while the notation P(playing the first three songs in order) indicates probability.

IWB

Examples

3. Use permutation notation.

AL
- *Suppose you had 8 different pencils and chose a pencil 3 times. In how many ways could you make the first choice?* 8
- *If you don't replace the pencil, in how many ways could you make the second choice? the third?* 7; 6
- *The notation $P(8, 3)$ represents this situation. How would you find $P(8, 3)$?* multiply $8 \cdot 7 \cdot 6$

OL
- *What does the notation $P(8, 3)$ mean?* the number of permutations of 8 things taken 3 at a time

BL
- *Can you find $P(3, 8)$? Explain.* No, $P(3, 8)$ means three things taken eight at a time. The most you can do is three things taken three at a time.

Need Another Example?
Find $P(7, 2)$. 42

4. Find probability.

AL
- *What does $P(10, 3)$ represent in this situation?* the number of ways the first three songs can be arranged out of a total of 10 songs
- *How do you find $P(10, 3)$?* multiply $10 \cdot 9 \cdot 8$

OL
- *How would you find the probability of randomly picking the first three songs in order?* find the ratio of the number of possible outcomes, 1, to the total number of outcomes, 720

BL
- *Suppose you programmed the first song to be a specific song. What is the probability that the MP3 player will randomly play the next two songs in order?* $\frac{1}{72}$

Need Another Example?
Consider all of the five-digit numbers that can be formed using the digits 1, 2, 3, 4, and 5, where no digit is used twice. Find the probability that one of these numbers picked at random ends with a 5. $\frac{1}{5}$ or 20%

Example

5. Find probability.

AL • *What does P(8, 2) represent in this situation?* the number of ways the first two places in a swimming event can happen if there are 8 swimmers

• *How do you find P(8, 2)?* multiply 8 • 7

OL • *How would you find the probability of randomly picking the first two swimmers in order?* find the ratio of the number of possible outcomes, 1, to the total number of outcomes, 56

BL • *Why is order important in this problem?* The problem is asking for a certain person to win first place and another to win second place.

Need Another Example?

A school fair holds a raffle with 1st, 2nd, and 3rd prizes. Seven people enter the raffle, including Marc, Lilly, and Heather. What is the probability that Marc will win the 1st prize, Lilly will win the 2nd prize, and Heather will win the 3rd prize? $\frac{1}{210}$

Guided Practice

Formative Assessment Use these exercises to assess students' understanding of the concepts in this lesson.

If some of your students are not ready for assignments, use the differentiated activities below.

AL **Think-Pair-Share** Have students work in pairs to solve Exercises 1–3. Give students one minute to write a blank for the number of positions. Then they can fill in the blanks with the number of choices for each position, and arrive at the answer. Have them share their responses with their partner. Call on one student to share their answer within a small group discussion. MP 1, 7

BL **Circle the Sage** Have some students research combinations and the difference between a permutation and a combination. Those students (the sages) spread out in the room. The rest of the class split up, surround a sage, take notes about what the sage says, and return to their seats. Then the class can discuss what they learned. MP 1, 6

5. **A swimming event features 8 swimmers. If each swimmer has an equally likely chance of finishing in the top two, what is the probability that Yumii will be in first place and Paquita in second place?**

Swimmers	
Octavia	Eden
Natasha	Paquita
Calista	Samantha
Yumii	Lorena

First find the permutation of 8 things taken two at a time or *P*(8, 2).

$P(8, 2) = 8 \cdot 7$

$= 56$

There are 56 possible arrangements, or permutations, of the two places. Since there is only one way of having Yumii come in first and Paquita second, the probability of this event is $\frac{1}{56}$.

Reasonable Answers

A possible probability of $\frac{1}{56}$ indicates that it is very unlikely that Yumii will finish first and Paquita will finish second.

Got it? **Do this problem to find out.**

f. Two different letters are randomly selected from the letters in the word *math*. What is the probability that the first letter selected is *m* and the second letter is *h*?

Show your work.

f. $\frac{1}{12}$

Guided Practice

Check

1. In how many ways can a president, vice president, and secretary be randomly selected from a class of 25 students? (Examples 1 and 2) 13,800

2. Find the value of *P*(5, 3). (Example 3) 60

3. Adrianne, Julián, and two of their friends will sit in a row at a baseball game. If each friend is equally likely to sit in any seat, what is the probability that Adrianne will sit in the first seat and Julián will sit in the second seat? (Examples 4 and 5) $\frac{1}{12}$

4. **Building on the Essential Question** HOW can you find the number of permutations of a set of objects? Sample answer: The Fundamental Counting Principle can be used to find the number of permutations of a set of objects.

Rate Yourself!

☐ I understand how to find permutations.

Great! You're ready to move on!

☐ I still have questions about finding permutations.

No Problem! Go online to access a Personal Tutor.

Tutor

Name ______________________ My Homework ______________________

Independent Practice

Go online for Step-by-Step Solutions eHelp

1. In the Battle of the Bands contest, in how many ways can the four participating bands perform? (Examples 1 and 2)
   24

2. A garage door code has 5 digits. If no digit is repeated, how many codes are possible?
   30,240

Find each value. Use a calculator if needed. (Example 3)

3. $P(7, 4)$ 840

4. $P(12, 5)$ 95,040

5. $P(8, 8)$ 40,320

6. You have five seasons of your favorite TV show on DVD. If you randomly select two of them from a shelf, what is the probability that you will select season one first and season two second? (Examples 4 and 5)
   $\frac{1}{20}$

7. MP **Model with Mathematics** The graphic novel frame below explains how the survey has students rank their favorite kinds of music. In how many ways can the survey be answered? 120 ways

ENGAGE EXPLORE **EXPLAIN** **ELABORATE** **EVALUATE**

3 Practice and Apply

Independent Practice and Extra Practice

The Independent Practice pages are meant to be used as the homework assignment. The Extra Practice page can be used for additional reinforcement or as a second-day assignment.

Levels of Complexity

The levels of the exercises progress from 1 to 3, with Level 1 indicating the lowest level of complexity.

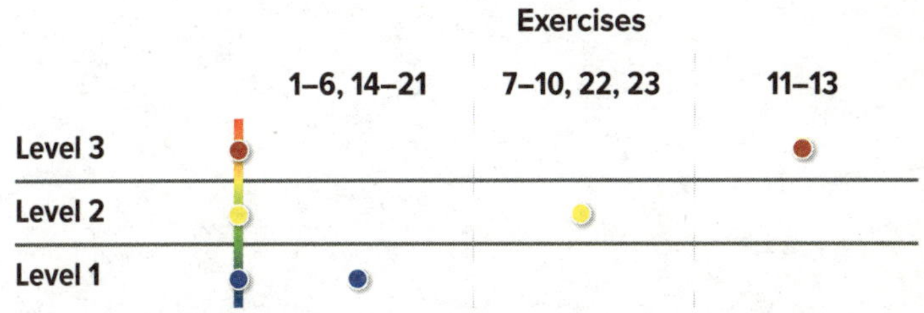

Suggested Assignments

You can use the table below that includes exercises of all complexity levels to select appropriate exercises for your students' needs.

Differentiated Homework Options		
AL	Approaching Level	1–7, 9, 11, 22, 23
OL	On Level	1–7 odd, 8–11, 22, 23
BL	Beyond Level	8–13, 22, 23

ALEKS® can provide additional remediation support with personalized instruction and practice.

Watch Out!

Common Error In Exercises 1 and 2, students may multiply without taking into account that no objects can be repeated. Remind students that in a permutation, the number of choices for each place is less than the number of choices for the previous place.

MP MATHEMATICAL PRACTICES	
Emphasis On	**Exercise(s)**
1 Make sense of problems and persevere in solving them.	12, 13
4 Model with mathematics.	7, 11

Mathematical Practices 1, 3, and 4 are aspects of mathematical thinking that are emphasized in every lesson. Students are given opportunities to be persistent in their problem solving, to express their reasoning, and apply mathematics to real-world situations.

Formative Assessment

Use this activity as a closing formative assessment before dismissing students from your class.

TICKET Out the Door

Remind students that yesterday's lesson was about using the Fundamental Counting Principle to find the number of possible outcomes in a sample space. Have students write how yesterday's concepts helped them with today's material. See students' work.

8. A certain number of friends are waiting in line to board a new roller coaster. They can board the ride in 5,040 different ways. How many friends are in line?

7

9. The Coughlin family discovered they can stand in a row for their family portrait in 720 different ways. How many members are in the Coughlin family? 6

10. Howland Middle School assigns a four-digit identification number to each student. The number is made from the digits 1, 2, 3, and 4, and no digit is repeated. If assigned randomly, what is the probability that an ID number will end with a 3? $\frac{1}{4}$

H.O.T. Problems Higher Order Thinking

11. MP **Model with Mathematics** Describe a real-world situation that has 6 permutations.

Sample answer: The number of ways you can order 3 books on a shelf is 3 • 2 • 1 or 6.

12. MP **Persevere with Problems** There are 1,320 ways for three students to win first, second, and third place during a debate match. How many students are there on the debate team? Explain your reasoning.

12 students; Since 12 • 11 • 10 = 1,320, there must be 12 students on the debate team.

13. MP **Persevere with Problems** A *combination* is an arrangement where order is *not* important. You can find the number of combinations of items by dividing the number of permutations by the number of ways the smaller set can be arranged. The combination at the right shows the number of combinations if you choose 2 flavors of ice cream out of 5 flavors. Use this method to find each value.

From 5 flavors take 2 at a time.

$C(5, 2) = \frac{5 \cdot 4}{2 \cdot 1}$ or 10

There are 2 • 1 ways to order 2 flavors.

a. $C(6, 4)$ 15

b. $C(10, 3)$ 120

c. $C(5, 3)$ 10

d. $C(8, 6)$ 28

Name ______________________ My Homework ______________________

Extra Practice

14. How many permutations are possible of the letters in the word FRIEND? 720

Homework Help → $6 \cdot 5 \cdot 4 \cdot 3 \cdot 2 \cdot 1 = 720$

15. How many different 3-digit numbers can be formed using the digits 9, 3, 4, 7, and 6? Assume no number can be used more than once. 60

Find each value. Use a calculator if needed.

16. $P(9, 2)$ 72

17. $P(5, 5)$ 120

18. $P(7, 7)$ 5,040

19. The members of the Evergreen Junior High Quiz Bowl team are listed in the table. If a captain and an assistant captain are chosen at random, what is the probability that Walter is selected as captain and Mi-Ling as co-captain? $\frac{1}{90}$

Evergreen Junior High Quiz Bowl Team	
Jamil	Luanda
Savannah	Mi-Ling
Tucker	Booker
Ferdinand	Nina
Walter	Meghan

20. Alex, Aiden, Dexter, and Dion are playing a video game. If they each have an equally likely chance of getting the highest score, what is the probability that Dion will get the highest score and Alex the second highest? $\frac{1}{12}$

21. A child has wooden blocks with the letters shown. Find the probability that the child randomly arranges the letters in the order TIGER. $\frac{1}{120}$

Create Your Own Homework Online

eSolutionsManual™ can be used to create worksheets for the suggested assignments on page 769, or create your own worksheets for differentiated homework or review.

Power Up! Test Practice

Exercises 22 and 23 prepare students for more rigorous thinking needed for the state assessment.

22.

This test item requires students to analyze and solve complex real-world problems through the use of mathematical tools and models.	
Depth of Knowledge	DOK2
Content Standard	7.SP.8, 7.SP.8a
Mathematical Practice	MP1, MP4
Online Experience	Students will drag values to model the equation and outcome.
Scoring Rubric	
2 points	Students correctly answer each part of the question.
1 point	Students correctly model the equation but fail to correctly complete the remainder of the question OR students correctly state the number of ways and the probability but fail to correctly model the probability.

23.

This test item requires students to reason abstractly and quantitatively when problem solving.	
Depth of Knowledge	DOK1
Content Standard	7.SP.8, 7.SP.8a
Mathematical Practice	MP1
Online Experience	Students will be required to click on the bubbles to select all answers that are correct.
Scoring Rubric	
1 point	Students correctly answer each part of the question.

Power Up! Test Practice

22. The schools listed in the table are finalists in a science competition. First through third places will win a prize. Each school is equally likely to win the competition. Select values to complete the model below to find the probability that Lincoln wins first place, River Valley wins second place, and Glenwood wins third place.

Finalists
Chester Middle School
Glenwood Middle School
Lincoln Middle School
River Valley Middle School
South Middle School

Find the number of ways the schools can finish in first, second, and third place:

P(5 , 3) = 60

1	2	3	4	5
10	20	30	60	90

The number of ways that Lincoln can finish first, River Valley second, and Glenwood third is equal to 1.

P(Lincoln first, River Valley second, Glenwood third) = $\frac{1}{60}$

23. The five finalists in a writing contest are Cesar, Teresa, Sean, Nikita, and Alfonso. There will be a first place award and a second place award. Each finalist is equally likely to win an award. Determine if each statement is true or false.

a. There are 10 permutations of 5 finalists taken 2 at a time. ☐ True ■ False

b. There is only 1 way that Teresa can earn first place and Sean can earn second place. ■ True ☐ False

c. The probability that Teresa earns first place and Sean earns second place is 0.05. ■ True ☐ False

Spiral Review

A card is pulled from a stack of 30 cards labeled 1–30. Find each probability. Write as a fraction in simplest form. 7.SP.5

24. P(greater than 5) $\frac{5}{6}$

25. P(*not* 1) $\frac{29}{30}$

26. P(an even number) $\frac{1}{2}$

27. A cross country athlete has a white, a red, and a gray sweatshirt. She has black and gray running pants. Make a list to show the possible combinations of training outfits. 7.SP.8b WB, WG, RB, RG, GB, GG

PLAN ONLINE

PD | RtI | Watch | Worksheets | Vocab | Tutor | Tools | Check | English Learners | Sketchpad

PRESENT

IWB

An Interactive Whiteboard Ready presentation is available for each lesson in the chapter.

Statistics and Probability

Inquiry Lab

Independent and Dependent Events

Inquiry HOW can one event impact a second event in a probability experiment?

Content Standards
7.SP.8, 7.SP.8b, 7.SP.8c

MP Mathematical Practices
1, 3

Jeanie wants to go to the movies and Kate wants to go skating. They decide by doing a simulation. They place two red counters in a bag to represent going to the movies and two white counters to represent going skating. If they draw or remove two red counters, they will go to the movies. If they draw two white counters they will go skating. If they draw a red and a white counter, they will stay home.

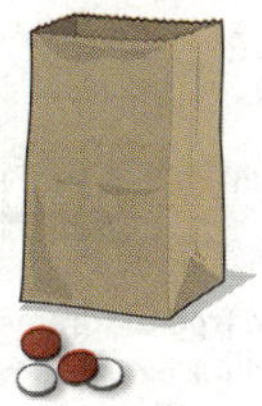

You can simulate this activity using counters.

Hands-On Activity

Step 1 Place two red counters and two white counters in a paper bag.

Step 2 Without looking, draw a counter from the bag and record its color in the table below. Place the counter back in the bag.

Step 3 Without looking, draw a second counter and record its color in the table. The two colors are one trial. Place the counter back in the bag.

Step 4 Repeat until you have 18 trials. See students' work.

Trial	1st Color	2nd Color	Trial	1st Color	2nd Color	Trial	1st Color	2nd Color
1			7			13		
2			8			14		
3			9			15		
4			10			16		
5			11			17		
6			12			18		

What is the experimental probability that the girls will go to the movies?

See students' work.

Focus narrowing the scope

Objective Explore the probability of dependent and independent events. 7.SP.8, 7.SP.8b, 7.SP.8c

Materials: paper bags, two-color counters

Coherence connecting within and across grades

Now
Students will select and use simulations to represent compound events without technology.

Next
Students will make predictions and determine solutions using theoretical probability for simple and compound events.

Rigor pursuing concepts, fluency, and applications

See the Levels of Complexity chart on page 774.

ENGAGE EXPLORE EXPLAIN ELABORATE EVALUATE

1 Launch the Lab

Activity 1 is intended to be used as a whole-group activity.

Hands-On Activity

AL EL Think-Pair-Write Give students 1-2 minutes to think about the activity and the possible results they could record in Step 4. Have students write down their predictions for the probability for the movies, skating, or staying home. Next, arrange students in pairs to complete Steps 1–4. Have students compare their experimental results to their predictions. MP 1, 4, 7

BL EL Pairs Consult Have students determine the sample space by creating an organized list. Then have them use the sample space to determine the probability that the girls will go to the movies. MP 1, 4, 7

2 Collaborate

The **Investigate** and **Analyze and Reflect** sections are intended to be used as small-group investigations. The **Create** section is intended to be used as independent exercises.

Levels of Complexity

The levels of the exercises progress from 1 to 3, with Level 1 indicating the lowest level of complexity.

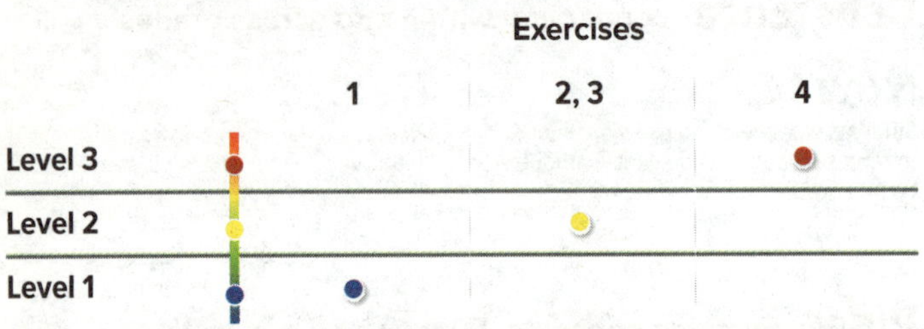

Investigate

Collaborate

AL **EL** **Pairs to Groups** Have students work in pairs to complete Exercise 1. Upon completion, have pairs team up with another pair to form groups of four. Have groups discuss their results from Exercise 1. Have each group complete Exercises 2and 3 and share their results with the class. MP 1, 4, 7

Create

On Your Own

Inquiry Students should be able to answer "HOW can one event impact a second event in a probability experiment?" Check for student understanding and provide guidance, if needed.

Investigate

Collaborate

Work with a partner.

1. Complete the same experiment from the Activity. Except do not replace the counter after the first draw for each trial. Record your results.

Trial	1st Color	2nd Color	Trial	1st Color	2nd Color	Trial	1st Color	2nd Color
1			7			13		
2			8			14		
3			9			15		
4			10			16		
5			11			17		
6			12			18		

What is the experimental probability that the girls will go to the movies?

See students' work.

Analyze and Reflect

Collaborate

3–4. Sample answers are given.

The tree diagrams below represent the possible outcomes for the Activity and for Exercise 1. Use the diagrams to answer Exercises 2–3.

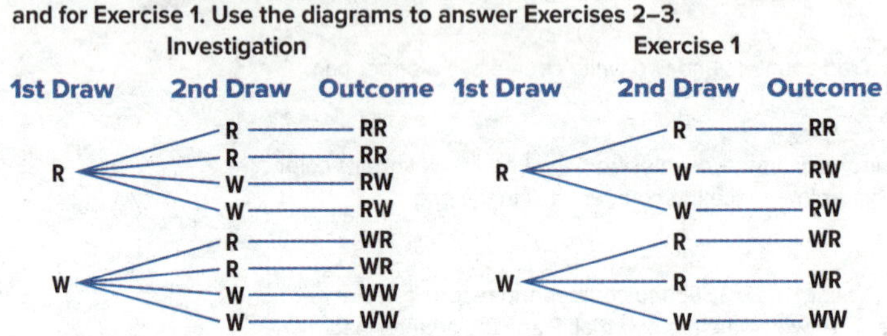

2. What is the theoretical probability of drawing two reds in the Investigation? In Exercise 1? $\frac{1}{4}$, $\frac{1}{6}$

3. MP **Reason Inductively** Is there a better chance that the girls will go to the movies if the counters are replaced after the first draw? Explain.
There is a better chance if the counters are replaced. $\frac{1}{4} > \frac{1}{6}$.

Create

On Your Own

4. Inquiry HOW can one event impact a second event in a probability experiment?
This happens if something in the first event changes what could happen in the second event.

PLAN ONLINE: PD | RtI | Watch | Worksheets | Vocab | Tutor | Tools | Check | English Learners | Sketchpad

PRESENT — IWB: An Interactive Whiteboard Ready presentation is available for each lesson in the chapter.

Lesson 7

Independent and Dependent Events

Vocabulary Start-Up

When one event does not affect the outcome of the other event, the events are **independent events**. For example, if you toss a coin twice, the first toss has no affect on the second toss. Complete the graphic organizer below.

Sample answers are given.

Independent Events

Picture It	List an Example	Describe It
 Event 1 Event 2	spinning a spinner and rolling a number cube	when a first event does not affect a second event

Essential Question

HOW can you predict the outcome of future events?

Vocabulary

independent events
dependent events

Content Standards
7.SP.8, 7.SP.8a, 7.SP.8b

MP Mathematical Practices
1, 3, 4

Real-World Link

Independent is a common word in the English language. Use a dictionary to look up its definition. Explain how the dictionary definition can help you remember the mathematical definition of *independent*. Sample answer: not under the control of others; In mathematics, an independent event is not controlled by the outcome of another event.

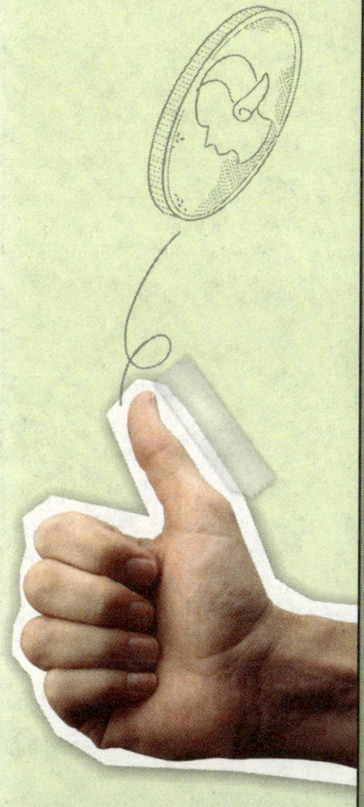

Which MP **Mathematical Practices** did you use? Shade the circle(s) that applies.

1. Persevere with Problems
2. Reason Abstractly
3. Construct an Argument
4. Model with Mathematics
5. Use Math Tools
6. Attend to Precision
7. Make Use of Structure
8. Use Repeated Reasoning

Focus narrowing the scope

Objective Find the probability of independent and dependent events. 7.SP.8, 7.SP.8a, 7.SP.8b

Coherence connecting within and across grades

Previous Students selected and used different simulations to represent simple and compound events.

Now Students will determine solutions for theoretical probability for compound events.

Next Students will make predictions, interpret, compare and analyze data.

Rigor pursuing concepts, fluency, and applications

See the Levels of Complexity chart on page 779.

ENGAGE EXPLORE EXPLAIN ELABORATE EVALUATE

1 Launch the Lesson

Ideas for Use

You may wish to launch the lesson using a whole group, small group, think-pair-share activity, or independent activity.

EL **Three Stay, One Stray** Arrange students in groups of 4 to complete the Vocabulary Start-Up. Have one student from each group stray to a different group to discuss differences and similarities. This step may be repeated. Have students return to his or her original group to further discuss responses. MP 1, 6

Alternate Strategy

AL EL Have students explain what the word *independent* means in everyday life and how that meaning helps them understand what *independent events* are in mathematics. MP 1, 6, 7

ENGAGE EXPLORE **EXPLAIN** ELABORATE EVALUATE

2 Teach the Concept

Ask the scaffolded questions for each example to differentiate instruction.

IWB

Example

1. Find the probability of independent events.

AL
- *Why are these events independent?* The outcome when spinning the spinner is not affected by the outcome of choosing a lettered tile.
- *How many total outcomes are shown by the tree diagram?* 12
- *How many favorable outcomes are shown by the tree diagram?* 2

OL
- *What is P(vowel) for the tiles?* $\frac{1}{2}$
- *What is P(vowel) for the spinner?* $\frac{1}{3}$
- *When would a tree diagram be more useful than multiplying?* when you need to know the other outcomes
- *When would multiplying the probabilities be more useful?* when you do not need to know the other outcomes

BL
- *What is P(at least one vowel)?* $\frac{2}{3}$
- *What is the probability of drawing double letters?* $\frac{1}{6}$

Need Another Example?
The two spinners below are spun. What is the probability that both spinners will show a number greater than 6? $\frac{9}{100}$

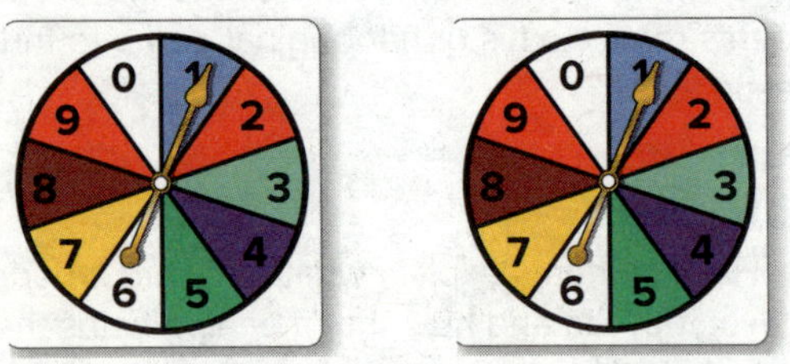

Key Concept

Probability of Independent Events

Words	The probability of two independent events can be found by multiplying the probability of the first event by the probability of the second event.
Symbols	$P(A \text{ and } B) = P(A) \cdot P(B)$

Work Zone

You can use organized lists, tables, tree diagrams, or multiplication to find the probability of compound events.

Examples

Tools Tutor

1. One letter tile is selected and the spinner is spun. What is the probability that both will be a vowel?

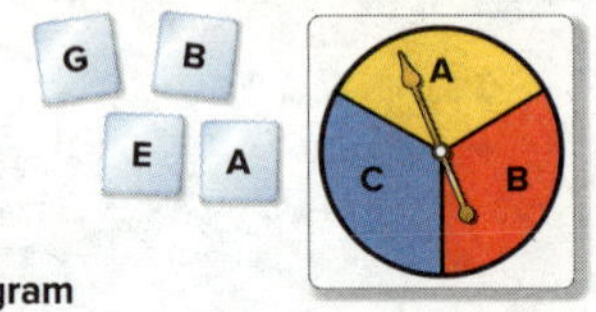

Method 1 Make a Tree Diagram

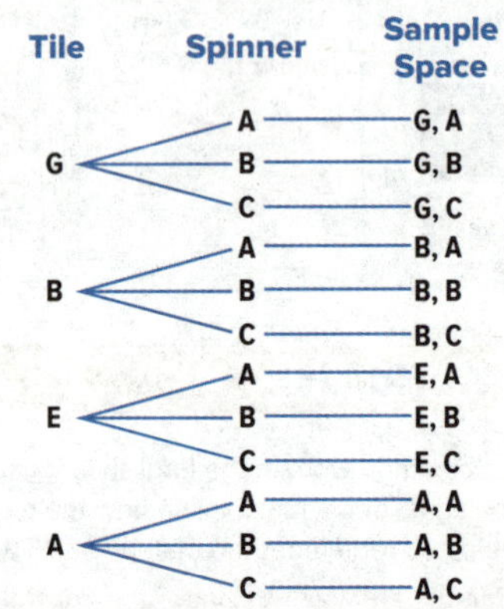

There are 12 outcomes. Two outcomes contain only vowels. The probability that both will be a vowel is $\frac{2}{12}$ or $\frac{1}{6}$.

Method 2 Use Multiplication

$P(\text{selecting a vowel}) = \frac{2}{4}$ or $\frac{1}{2}$. $P(\text{spinning a vowel}) = \frac{1}{3}$.

$P(\text{both vowels}) = \frac{1}{2} \cdot \frac{1}{3}$ or $\frac{1}{6}$. Multiply the probabilities.

So, using either method the probability is $\frac{1}{6}$.

2. **The spinner and number cube shown are used in a game. What is the probability of a player *not* spinning blue and then rolling a 3 or 4?**

You are asked to find the probability of the spinner *not* landing on blue and rolling a 3 or 4 on a number cube. The events are independent because spinning the spinner does not affect the outcome of rolling a number cube.

First, find the probability of each event.

$P(\text{not blue}) = \frac{4}{5}$ ← number of ways not to spin blue / number of possible outcomes

$P(3 \text{ or } 4) = \frac{2}{6} \text{ or } \frac{1}{3}$ ← number of ways to roll 3 or 4 / number of possible outcomes

Then, find the probability of both events occurring.

$P(\text{not blue and 3 or 4}) = \frac{4}{5} \cdot \frac{1}{3}$ — $P(A \text{ and } B) = P(A) \cdot P(B)$

$= \frac{4}{15}$ — Multiply.

The probability is $\frac{4}{15}$.

Check Make an organized list, table, or a tree diagram to show the sample space.

Got it? **Do this problem to find out.**

a. A game requires players to roll two number cubes to move the game pieces. The faces of the cubes are labeled 1 through 6. What is the probability of rolling a 2 or 4 on the first number cube and then rolling a 5 on the second?

Show your work.

a. $\frac{1}{18}$

Probability of Dependent Events

Key Concept

Words If two events *A* and *B* are dependent, then the probability of both events occurring is the product of the probability of *A* and the probability of *B* after *A* occurs.

Symbols $P(A \text{ and } B) = P(A) \cdot P(B \text{ following } A)$

If the outcome of one event affects the outcome of another event, the events are called **dependent events**. For example, you have a bag with blue and green marbles. You pick one marble, do not replace it, and pick another one.

IWB

Example

2. Find the probability of independent events.

AL
- *What is P(not blue) for the spinner?* $\frac{4}{5}$
- *What is P(3 or 4) for the number cube?* $\frac{1}{3}$

OL
- *How can you find the probability of a not spinning blue and rolling a 3 or 4?* Multiply the probabilities of the two independent events together; $\frac{4}{5} \times \frac{1}{3} = \frac{4}{15}$.
- *What is probability of spinning red or yellow and then rolling an even number?* $\frac{2}{5} \times \frac{1}{2} = \frac{1}{5}$

BL
- *When spinning the spinner and then rolling the number cube, how many possible outcomes are there? Explain.* 30; 5 possibilities on the spinner multiplied by 6 possibilities for the number cube

Need Another Example?

A red number cube and a white number cube are rolled. The faces of both cubes are numbered from 1 to 6. What is the probability of *not* rolling a 3 on the red number cube and rolling the number 3 or less on the white number cube? $\frac{5}{12}$

Watch Out!

Common Error Students need to be able to fluently multiply fractions to solve problems in this lesson. It may be helpful to review multiplying fractions and simplifying their answers before completing the exercises independently.

Example

IWB

3. Determine the probability of dependent events.

AL
- *Why is this a dependent event?* The probability of the second selection depends on the outcome of the first selection; the totals change after the first selection because the fruit is not put back for the next selection.
- *How many pieces of fruit are in the basket?* 16
- *How many favorable outcomes (apples) are in the basket?* 5

OL
- *What is the probability of selecting an apple?* $\frac{5}{16}$
- *After an apple is selected and not replaced, how many total pieces of fruit remain in the basket? how many apples?* There will be 15 total pieces of fruit and 4 apples.

BL
- *How could you find the probability of randomly selecting 2 apples and 1 banana?* Multiply $\frac{5}{16} \times \frac{4}{15} \times \frac{7}{14}$. The probability is $\frac{1}{24}$.

Need Another Example?
There are 4 red, 8 yellow, and 6 blue socks mixed up in a drawer. Once a sock is selected, it is not replaced. Find the probability of reaching into the drawer without looking and choosing 2 blue socks. $\frac{5}{51}$.

Guided Practice

Formative Assessment Use these exercises to assess students' understanding of the concepts in this lesson.

If some of your students are not ready for assignments, use the differentiated activities below.

AL EL **Rally Coach** Have students work with a partner to complete Exercises 1–4. Student 1 talks through their process for completing Exercise 1, while Student 2 watches, listens, and encourages. Students trade roles for each successive exercise. MP 1, 7

BL EL **Pairs Present** Have students work in pairs to create and demonstrate an independent and a dependent event. Have pairs present their events to the entire class. MP 1, 7

Real World Example

Watch Tutor

3. There are 4 oranges, 7 bananas, and 5 apples in a fruit basket. Ignacio selects a piece of fruit at random and then Terrance selects a piece of fruit at random. Find the probability that two apples are chosen.

Since the first piece of fruit is not replaced, the first event affects the second event. These are dependent events.

$P(\text{first piece is an apple}) = \frac{5}{16}$ ← number of apples / total pieces of fruit

$P(\text{second piece is an apple}) = \frac{4}{15}$ ← number of apples left / total pieces of fruit left

$P(\text{two apples}) = \frac{\overset{1}{\cancel{5}}}{\underset{4}{\cancel{16}}} \cdot \frac{\overset{1}{\cancel{4}}}{\underset{3}{\cancel{15}}}$ or $\frac{1}{12}$.

The probability that two apples are chosen is $\frac{1}{12}$.

Got it? Do these problems to find out.

Refer to the situation above. Find each probability.

b. P(two bananas) $\frac{7}{40}$

c. P(orange then apple) $\frac{1}{12}$

Show your work.

Guided Practice

Check

A penny is tossed and a number cube is rolled. Find each probability. (Examples 1–2)

1. P(tails and 3) $\frac{1}{12}$

2. P(heads and odd) $\frac{1}{4}$

3. Cards labeled 5, 6, 7, 8, and 9 are in a stack. A card is drawn and not replaced. Then, a second card is drawn at random. Find the probability of drawing two even numbers. (Example 3) $\frac{1}{10}$

4. **Building on the Essential Question** Explain the difference between independent events and dependent events.
Sample answer: Independent events do not affect each other. Dependent events affect each other.

Rate Yourself!

Are you ready to move on? Shade the section that applies.

For more help, go online to access a Personal Tutor.

Tutor

Name ______________________ My Homework ______________________

Independent Practice

Go online for Step-by-Step Solutions eHelp

A number cube is rolled and a marble is selected at random from the bag at the right. Find each probability. Show your work. (Example 1)

1. P(1 and red) $\frac{1}{24}$
2. P(3 and purple) $\frac{1}{48}$

Show your work.

3. P(even and yellow) $\frac{1}{8}$
4. P(odd and *not* green) $\frac{3}{8}$

5. A carnival game wheel has 12 equal sections. One of the sections contains a star. To win a prize, players must land on the section with the star on two consecutive spins. What is the probability of a player winning? (Example 2) $\frac{1}{144}$

6. A standard set of dominoes contains 28 tiles, with each tile having two sides of dots from 0 to 6. Of these tiles, 7 have the same number of dots on each side. If four players each randomly choose a tile, without replacement, what is the probability that each chooses a tile with the same number of dots on each side? (Example 3) $\frac{1}{585}$

Mrs. Ameldo's class has 5 students with blue eyes, 7 with brown eyes, 4 with hazel eyes, and 4 with green eyes. Two students are selected at random. Find each probability. (Example 3)

7. P(green then brown) $\frac{7}{95}$
8. P(two blue) $\frac{1}{19}$
9. P(hazel then blue) $\frac{1}{19}$
10. P(brown then blue) $\frac{7}{76}$

ENGAGE EXPLORE **EXPLAIN** **ELABORATE** **EVALUATE**

3 Practice and Apply

Independent Practice and Extra Practice

The Independent Practice pages are meant to be used as the homework assignment. The Extra Practice page can be used for additional reinforcement or as a second-day assignment.

Levels of Complexity

The levels of the exercises progress from 1 to 3, with Level 1 indicating the lowest level of complexity.

Exercises	1–10, 16–28	11, 29, 30	12–15
Level 3			●
Level 2		●	
Level 1	●		

Suggested Assignments

You can use the table below to select appropriate exercises for your students' needs.

Differentiated Homework Options		
AL	Approaching Level	1–14, 29, 30
OL	On Level	1–9 odd, 11–14, 29, 30
BL	Beyond Level	11–15, 29, 30

McGraw Hill Education | **ALEKS**® can provide additional remediation support with personalized instruction and practice.

MP MATHEMATICAL PRACTICES

Emphasis On	Exercise(s)
1 Make sense of problems and persevere in solving them.	15, 20
3 Construct viable arguments and critique the reasoning of others.	11, 13, 14
4 Model with mathematics.	12

Mathematical Practices 1, 3, and 4 are aspects of mathematical thinking that are emphasized in every lesson. Students are given opportunities to be persistent in their problem solving, to express their reasoning, and apply mathematics to real-world situations.

Formative Assessment
Use this activity as a closing formative assessment before dismissing students from your class.

TICKET Out the Door

Have students write an explanation of how to determine the probability of two independent events occurring. **See students' work.**

11. **MP Reason Inductively** You and a friend plan to see 2 movies over the weekend. You can choose from 6 comedy, 2 drama, 4 romance, 1 science fiction, or 3 action movies. You write the movie titles on pieces of paper, place them in a bag, and each randomly select a movie. What is the probability that neither of you selects a comedy? Is this a dependent or independent event? Explain.
$\frac{3}{8}$; dependent event; after the first piece of paper is chosen, there is one less from which to choose.

H.O.T. Problems Higher Order Thinking

12. **MP Model with Mathematics** There are 9 marbles representing 3 different colors. Write a problem where 2 marbles are selected at random without replacement and the probability is $\frac{1}{6}$.
Sample answer: There are 4 red marbles, 3 green marbles, and 2 blue marbles in a bag. Two marbles are picked at random without replacement. The probability of 2 red marbles is $\frac{4}{9} \cdot \frac{3}{8}$ or $\frac{1}{6}$.

13. **MP Find the Error** A spinner with equal sections numbered from 1 to 5 is spun twice. Raul is finding the probability that both spins will result in an even number. Find his mistake and correct it.
Sample answer: Spinning the spinner twice represents two independent events. The probability of getting an even number is $\frac{2}{5}$ each time; $\frac{2}{5} \cdot \frac{2}{5}$ or $\frac{4}{25}$.

14. **MP Justify Conclusions** Determine whether the following statement is *true* or *false*. If false, provide a counterexample.
If two events are independent, then the probability of both events is less than 1. **False; sample answer: The probability of tossing heads or tails on a coin and rolling a 6 or less on a number cube.**

15. **MP Persevere with Problems** A company has determined that 2% of the pudding cups it produces are defective in some way. The pudding cups are sold in packages of two.
   a. What is the probability that both pudding cups in a package are defective?
   0.0004 or 0.04%
   b. The company produces 1,000,000 packages each year. Predict the number of packages in which both cups are defective.
   about 400 packages

Name ______ My Homework ______

Extra Practice

A number cube is rolled and a letter is selected from the word AMERICA. Find each probability. Show your work.

16. *P*(less than 4 and vowel) $\frac{1}{7}$

Homework Help

P(less than 4) = $\frac{1}{2}$

P(vowel) = $\frac{4}{7}$

$\frac{1}{2} \cdot \frac{4}{7} = \frac{4}{14}$ or $\frac{1}{7}$

17. *P*(greater than 1 and a consonant) $\frac{5}{14}$

18. A number cube is rolled and a coin is tossed. What is the probability of the cube landing on 5 or 6 and the coin landing on heads? $\frac{1}{6}$

19. A laundry basket contains 18 blue socks and 24 black socks. What is the probability of randomly picking 2 black socks, without replacement, from the basket? $\frac{92}{287}$

20. MP **Persevere with Problems** Corbin is playing a board game that requires rolling two number cubes to move a game piece. He needs to roll a sum of 6 on his first turn and then a sum of 10 on his second turn to land on the next two bonus spaces. What is the probability that Corbin will roll a sum of 6 and then a sum of 10 on his next two turns? $\frac{5}{432}$

Copy and Solve **Solve Exercises 21–28 on a separate sheet of paper.**

A card is pulled from a stack of 15 cards labeled 1–15 and the spinner shown is spun. Find each probability.

21. *P*(less than 10 and red) $\frac{3}{20}$

22. *P*(odd and red or blue) $\frac{4}{15}$

23. *P*(even and blue) $\frac{7}{60}$

24. *P*(prime number and blue) $\frac{1}{10}$

Maddie is packing for a trip. In her closet, there are 3 red, 4 black, 2 green, and 2 yellow blouses. She randomly selects 2 blouses. Find each probability.

25. *P*(red and red) $\frac{3}{55}$

26. *P*(black and yellow) $\frac{4}{55}$

27. *P*(red and black) $\frac{6}{55}$

28. *P*(green and green) $\frac{1}{55}$

Create Your Own Homework Online

eSolutionsManual™ can be used to create worksheets for the suggested assignments on page 779, or create your own worksheets for differentiated homework or review.

Power Up! Test Practice

Exercises 29 and 30 prepare students for more rigorous thinking needed for the state assessment.

29.

This test item requires students to reason abstractly and quantitatively when problem solving.	
Depth of Knowledge	DOK2
Content Standard	7.SP.8, 7.SP.8a
Mathematical Practice	MP1
Online Experience	Students will be required to click on the bubbles to select all answers that are correct.
Scoring Rubric	
1 point	Students correctly answer each part of the question.

30.

This test item requires students to analyze and solve complex real-world problems through the use of mathematical tools and models.	
Depth of Knowledge	DOK2
Content Standard	7.SP.8, 7.SP.8a
Mathematical Practice	MP1, MP4
Online Experience	Students will drag values to model the probability and type their response in the box.
Scoring Rubric	
2 points	Students correctly model the probability and answer the question.
1 point	Students correctly model the probability OR answer the question.

Power Up! Test Practice

29. A bag contains letter tiles. There are 6 vowels in the bag and 14 consonants. On Michael's next turn, he will select a letter tile at random from the bag. Without replacing the first tile, he will then select a second letter tile. Determine if each of the following probabilities is true or false.

a. $P(\text{vowel then vowel}) = \frac{3}{38}$ ■ True □ False

b. $P(\text{vowel then consonant}) = \frac{21}{95}$ ■ True □ False

c. $P(\text{consonant then consonant}) = \frac{49}{100}$ □ True ■ False

30. The spinners are each spun once.

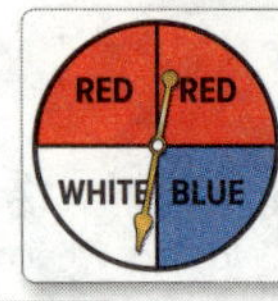

Do the two spins represent independent or dependent events? Independent

Select the correct values to complete the model below to find $P(2 \text{ and white})$.

$P(2 \text{ and white}) = \frac{2}{8} \times \frac{1}{4} = \frac{1}{16}$

1	6
2	8
3	12
4	16

Spiral Review

Solve each proportion. 6.RP.1, 6.RP.3

31. $\frac{1}{4} = \frac{x}{72}$ $x =$ 18

32. $\frac{8}{n} = \frac{0.5}{0.9}$ $n =$ 14.4

33. $\frac{1}{3} = \frac{m}{153}$ $m =$ 51

34. $\frac{0.2}{a} = \frac{1.8}{18}$ $a =$ 2

35. 9 is 15% of what number? Write an equation. Then solve. 6.RP.3

9 = 0.15x; 60

36. A school librarian surveyed students about their favorite type of novel. The results are shown in the table at the right. What percent of students chose science fiction as their favorite type of novel? Round to the nearest whole percent. 6.RP.3c

45%

Type of Novel	Number of Students
mystery	18
romance	10
science fiction	26
other	4

PLAN ONLINE

PD | RtI | Watch | Worksheets | Vocab | Tutor | Tools | Check | English Learners | Sketchpad

PRESENT

College & Career READINESS

21ST CENTURY CAREER in Medicine

Pediatricians

Do you have compassion, a sense of humor, and the ability to analyze data? You might want to consider a career in medicine. Pediatricians care for the health of infants, children, and teenagers. They diagnose illnesses, interpret diagnostic tests, and prescribe and administer treatment.

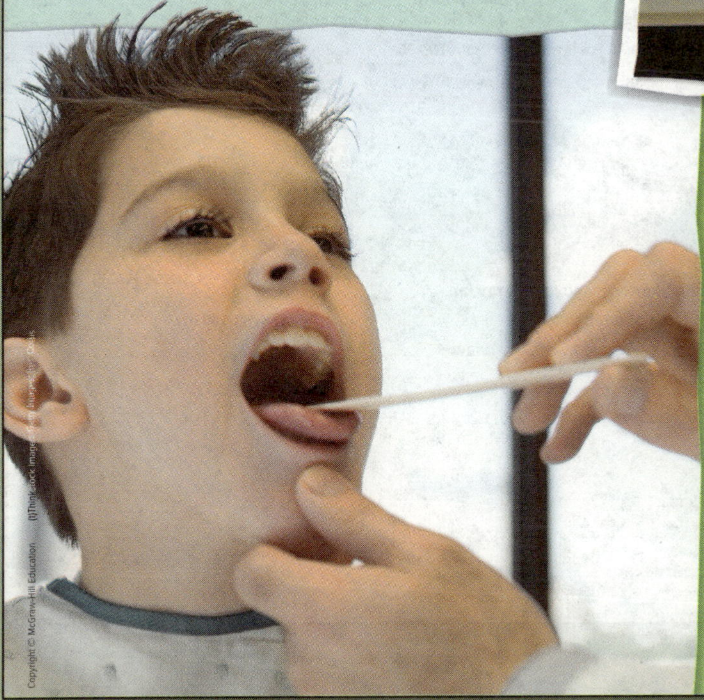

College & Career READINESS

Is This the Career for You?

Are you interested in a career as a pediatrician? Take some of the following courses in high school.

- Algebra
- Biology
- Calculus
- Chemistry
- Psychology

Find out how math relates to a career in Medicine.

Focus narrowing the scope

Objective Apply mathematics to problems arising in the workplace. This lesson emphasizes MP **Mathematical Practice 4** Model with Mathematics.

Coherence connecting within and across grades

Previous
Students used data to find the probabilities of simple and compound events..

Now
Students apply the content standard to solve problems in the workplace.

Rigor pursuing concepts, fluency, and applications

See the Career Project on page 784.

ENGAGE EXPLORE EXPLAIN ELABORATE EVALUATE

1 Launch the Lesson

Ask students to read the information on the student page about pediatric medicine and answer the following questions.

Ask:

- *What type of doctor does a child see when they get a checkup?* pediatrician
- *What are some common reasons that people take children to see a doctor?* Sample answers: sore throat, fever, broken bones, physicals

College & Career READINESS

Help students connect what they do today to their futures. Direct them to the Internet or another source to explore, learn, and plan for college and future careers.

ENGAGE EXPLORE **EXPLAIN** **ELABORATE** EVALUATE

2 Collaborate

AL **Think-Pair-Share** Have students work in pairs to complete Exercises 1–7 using the following scaffolded questions. Sample answers shown are for Exercise 1.
MP 1, 6, 7

Ask:

- *What information from the table do you need to solve this problem? Explain.* the number of true positive and the number of false negative; Sample answer: Both groups have strep throat.
- *Write the steps you can use to solve this problem.* Find the probability of having strep throat, which is $\frac{98}{200}$, or 49%.

BL **Trade-a-Problem** Have students create their own real-world problem using the data in the table. Students trade their problems, solve, and compare solutions. If the solutions do not agree, students should work together to determine the errors.
MP 1, 4

Career Portfolio

When students complete this page, have them add it to their Career Portfolio.

Career Facts

There are many types of specialties in pediatric medicine. For example, pediatric sports medicine specialists have the expertise to treat sports-related needs of children and teens, including sprains, dislocations, stress fractures, exercise-induced asthma, and concussions.

MP On Call for Kids

Use the information in the table below to solve each problem. Write each answer as a percent rounded to the nearest whole number.

1. What is the probability that one of the patients tested has strep throat? 49%
2. If a patient has strep throat, what is the probability that they have a positive test? 92%
3. What is the probability that a patient with the disease has a negative test? 8%
4. If a patient does not have the disease, what is the probability that they have a positive test? 17%
5. What is the probability that a patient that does *not* have strep throat tested negative for the disease? 83%
6. The *positive predictive value,* or *PPV,* is the probability that a patient with a positive test result will have the disease. What is the PPV? 84%
7. The *negative predictive value,* or *NPV,* is the probability that a patient with a negative test result will not have the disease. What is the NPV? 91%

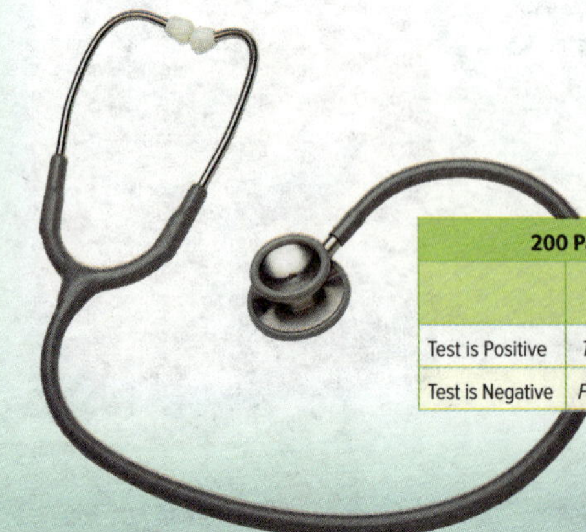

200 Patients Tested for Strep Throat		
	Patients Have Strep Throat	Patients do *Not* Have Strep Throat
Test is Positive	*True Positive (TP)* 90	*False Positive (FP)* 17
Test is Negative	*False Negative (FN)* 8	*True Negative (TN)* 85

MP Career Project

It's time to update your career portfolio! Interview your pediatrician. Be sure to ask what he or she enjoys most about being a pediatrician and what is most challenging. Include all the interview questions and answers in your portfolio.

What are some short term goals you need to achieve to become a pediatrician?

-
-
-
-
-

Statistics and Probability

Chapter Review

Vocabulary Check

Unscramble each of the clue words. After unscrambling all of the terms, use the numbered letters to find a sentence associated with probability.

HELATCORTEI

T	H	E	O	R	E	T	I	C	A	L
							8		5	

PORTUNMETAI

P	E	R	M	U	T	A	T	I	O	N
									2	9

LEAPMS ECPAS

S	A	M	P	L	E		S	P	A	C	E
4							3			6	

COAPELMERTMYN

C	O	M	P	L	E	M	E	N	T	A	R	Y
	7								1			

T	O	S	S		A		C	O	I	N
1	2	3	4		5		6	7	8	9

Complete each sentence using one of the unscrambled words above.

1. The sample space is the set of all of the possible outcomes of a probability experiment.
2. A permutation is an arrangement, or listing, of objects in which order is important.
3. The theoretical probability is based on what should happen when conducting a probability experiment.
4. Two events in which one or the other must happen, but they cannot happen at the same time are complementary.

Vocabulary Check

EL **Roundrobin** Have students work in pairs, taking turns to complete the Vocabulary Check. Make sure each student understands the terms and definitions. Students should speak each vocabulary term aloud to ensure they know how to pronounce it and recognize it when it is heard. MP 1, 6

Alternate Strategy

AL EL To help students, you may wish to give them a vocabulary list from which they can choose their answers. A vocabulary list for this activity would include the following terms.

- complementary events (Lesson 1)
- permutation (Lesson 6)
- sample space (Lesson 3)
- theoretical probability (Lesson 2)

Key Concept Check

FOLDABLES **EL** A completed Foldable for this chapter should include a review of simple and compound events.

If you choose not to use this Foldable, have students write a brief review of the Key Concepts found throughout the chapter and give an example of each.

Ideas for Use

EL **Gallery Walk** Have students work with a partner to share their completed Foldables. Then have each student add or adjust anything in their Foldable based on the discussion with their partner. Display all of the Foldables around the room and have students walk around the room studying each Foldable. Have them determine if they should add anything to their Foldable based upon what they saw in others' Foldables.

Got It?

If students have trouble with Exercises 1–4, they may need help with the following concept(s).

Concept	Exercise(s)
experimental probability (Lesson 2)	1
dependent events (Lesson 7)	2
compound events (Lesson 3)	3
sample space (Lesson 3)	4

ALEKS® provides additional support with personalized instruction and practice for those who are struggling, while providing enhanced learning for those who have mastered the concepts.

Key Concept Check

Use Your FOLDABLES

Use your Foldable to help review the chapter.

Tape here

Probability

Example	Example
Picture	Picture

Got it?

Match each term or phrase on the left with the words on the right.

1. Based on what actually occurred in a probability experiment
2. The outcome of one event affects the outcome of a separate event
3. Consists of two or more simple events
4. Can be used to find the sample space

a. compound event
b. experimental probability
c. Fundamental Counting Principle
d. dependent event
e. tree diagrams
f. organized lists

Power Up! Performance Task

Carnival Prizes

Kelli is in charge of a game booth at the school carnival. The game has two simple rules.

- Randomly pick one blue card and one red card.
- If the product of the two numbers is greater than or equal to 45, you win a prize.

3	5	8	10
4	7	9	

Write your answers on another piece of paper. Show all of your work to receive full credit.

Part A
Create a sample space and find the product of each combination. What is the probability that a person wins the game? Express your answer as a fraction in lowest terms and as a percent rounded to the nearest whole number.

Part B
The sponsor of the booth determines that they are giving away too many prizes. Recommend a minimum winning number that lowers the chance of winning to 25%. Explain your reasoning.

Part C
Participants achieving a winning score of 70 or higher in four consecutive attempts will receive a large stuffed animal. What is the probability of this occurring?

Part D
After changing the game rules, patrons and onlookers are disappointed when the first five games yield products of 12, 21, 32, 35, and 12. Recommend a statement that the sponsor can use to reassure customers that the game is fair.

Power Up! Performance Task

This Performance-Based Assessment requires students to solve multi-step problems through abstract reasoning, precision, and perseverance. This practice scenario can be used to help students prepare for the thinking skills that will be used on the State Assessment.

A complete scoring rubric with answers to the Exercises can be found on page PT5.

Answering the Essential Question

Before answering the Essential Question, have students review their answers to the **Building on the Essential Question** exercises found in each lesson of the chapter.

- What is the relationship between the probability of an event and its complement? (p. 714)
- How are experimental probability and theoretical probability alike? (p. 724)
- How do tree diagrams, tables, and lists help you find the probability of a compound event? (p. 736)
- How is using a simulation related to experimental probability? (p. 744)
- How does using the Fundamental Counting Principle compare to making a tree diagram? (p. 760)
- How can you find the number of permutations of a set of objects? (p. 768)
- What is the difference between independent and dependent events? (p. 778)

Ideas for Use

EL **Teammates Consult** Place students in 3- or 4-person learning teams. Have each team designate a leader. The leader guides a discussion, posing the essential question for each category: theoretical probability, experimental probability, sample space, and simulation. All team members must contribute. When everyone on the team is ready with an answer to the Essential Question, they each write a response in their textbooks. MP 1, 6, 7

Reflect

Answering the Essential Question

Use what you learned about probability to complete the graphic organizer.

Sample answers are given.

Theoretical Probability
Sample answer: Use theoretical probability to make predictions based on what should happen in a given situation.

Experimental Probability
Sample answer: Use experimental probability to make predictions based on what has happened in the past.

Essential Question
HOW can you predict the outcome of future events?

Sample Space
Sample answer: Make a list or tree diagram to show all possible outcomes, or sample space.

Simulation
Sample answer: Use a simulation to model the likelihood of an event happening.

Answer the Essential Question. HOW can you predict the outcome of future events?

See students' work.

PLAN ONLINE

PD | RtI | Watch | Worksheets | Vocab | Tutor | Tools | Check | English Learners | Sketchpad

PRESENT

IWB

An Interactive Whiteboard Ready presentation is available for each lesson in the chapter.

Chapter 10 Statistics

Essential Question

HOW do you know which type of graph to use when displaying data?

Content Standards
7.SP.1, 7.SP.2, 7.SP.3, 7.SP.4

MP Mathematical Practices
1, 3, 4, 5, 6,

Math in the Real World

Surveys are used to collect information. Survey results can be shown in graphs.

The results of a survey of 50 middle school students are shown in the table. On the circle graph, write the percent of students who preferred each activity.

Activity	Number of Students
Gaming	22
Social Networking	18
Viewing Movies	6
Other	4

FOLDABLES Study Organizer

1. Cut out the Foldable on page FL13 of this book.
2. Place your Foldable on page 850.
3. Use the Foldable throughout this chapter to help you learn about statistics.

Focus narrowing the scope

This chapter focuses on content from the **Statistics and Probability** (SP) domain.

Mathematical Background Additional information about the mathematical background for this chapter can be found online at connectED.mcgraw-hill.com.

Coherence connecting within and across grades

Previous
Students found the probability of simple and compound events.

Now
Students analyze samples and interpret the data.

Next
Students will determine if a relationship exists between sets of bivariate data.

Rigor pursuing concepts, fluency, and applications

The Levels of Complexity charts located throughout this chapter indicate how the exercises progress from conceptual understanding and procedural skills and fluency, to application and critical thinking.

Launch the Chapter

Math in the Real World

Surveys Remind students that to find the percent for each activity first write each activity as a fraction. The numerator should be the number of students who preferred that activity and the denominator should be the total number of students surveyed. Then divide.

What Tools Do You Need?

Vocabulary Activity

EL As you proceed through the chapter, introduce each vocabulary term using the following routine. Ask the students to say each term aloud after you say it.

Define: A sample is a randomly selected group chosen for the purpose of collecting data.

Example: The sixth-grade students are a sample of all students in a school.

Ask:

- *Which of the following would be an appropriate sample for the cars in a city: all of the cars in the city or the cars in a parking garage?* **the cars in a parking garage**

Writing Math

EL Have students read about the ways to describe data in the Writing Math section. Display the following table.

Types of Advertising	Percent of teens
Television	80
Magazine	62
Product in a movie	48
E-mail	24

Ask:

- *How do the percents for advertising a product in a movie and E-mail compare?* **Sample answer: Twice as many teens paid attention to products in a movie than E-mail.**
- *Which type of advertising seems to attract the greatest number of teens?* **television**

What Tools Do You Need?

Vocabulary

biased sample	population	survey
convenience sample	sample	systematic random sample
double box plot	simple random sample	unbiased sample
double dot plot	statistics	voluntary response sample

Study Skill: Writing Math

Describe Data When you *describe* something, you represent it in words.

The table shows the prices for takeout orders at Lombardo's Restaurant.

Takeout	Price ($)
Main Dish	8.00
Side Dish	2.50
Dessert	4.00

Use the table to complete the following statements.

1. The price of a dessert is **$4**.
2. The price of a main dish is twice the price of **a dessert**.
3. A **side dish** is the least expensive item.

Write two other statements that describe the data. **Sample answers given.**

4. **A main dish is the most expensive item.**
5. **If you buy one of each item, the cost is more than $10.**

What Do You Already Know?

Read each statement. Decide whether you agree (A) or disagree (D). Place a checkmark in the appropriate column and then justify your reasoning. See students' work.

Statistics			
Statement	A	D	Why?
Statistics deal with collecting, organizing, and interpreting data.			
A sample is the same thing as the entire population.			
A biased sample accurately represents the entire population.			
Graphs are sometimes made to influence conclusions by misrepresenting the data.			
A double box plot consists of two box plots that are drawn on the same number line.			
Any type of display can be used to represent data.			

When Will You Use This?

Here are a few examples of how statistics are used in the real world.

Activity 1 Find the average monthly high and low temperatures for the city where you live. Then find the average monthly high and low temperatures for another city. How do these temperatures compare to the temperatures for your city?

See students' work.

Activity 2 Go online at connectED.mcgraw-hill.com to read the graphic novel ***Record Highs***. Blake, Hannah, and Jamar need to compare the record high temperatures for two different cities. What cities do they use? Phoenix, AZ, and Key West, FL

What Do You Already Know?

In this activity students assess their prior knowledge by determining whether they agree or disagree with each statement about concepts in this chapter.

- You may want to add a third option of "I don't know" for those students who do not have any prior knowledge of the content of the statement.
- After completing the chapter, have students return to this page and see if any of their responses would change now that they have finished the chapter.

When Will You Use This?

Activity 1

Students use a real-world situation involving high and low temperatures to understand the connection to statistics.

Activity 2

Use the Graphic Novel to help students learn about scale maps and drawings.

Ask:

- *Do these lists give an accurate picture of the temperatures in each city?* No; They represent record highs only, not average temperatures for each month.

Are You Ready?

Use this page to determine if students have skills that are needed for the chapter.

Quick Review

Students with strong math backgrounds may opt to go directly to the Quick Check.

QUICK REVIEW		
Example	**Skill**	**Standard**
1	Interpret Graphs	6.SP.5c
2	Make Predictions	6.NS.4

Quick Check

If students have difficulty with the exercises, present an additional example to clarify any misconceptions.

Exercises 1–3

Refer to the bar graph for Exercises 1 and 2. What was the average number of items obtained by all five students? 12.6 items

RtI Response to Intervention

Go online at connectED.mcgraw-hill.com for resources to differentiate remediation for Tier 1, Tier 2, and Tier 3 students.

ALEKS® can provide additional remediation support with personalized instruction and practice. See pages T8 and T9 for more information.

Are You Ready?

Try the Quick Check below. Or, take the Online Readiness Quiz.

Quick Review

6.SP.5c, 6.NS.4

Example 1

Which players averaged more than 10 points per game?

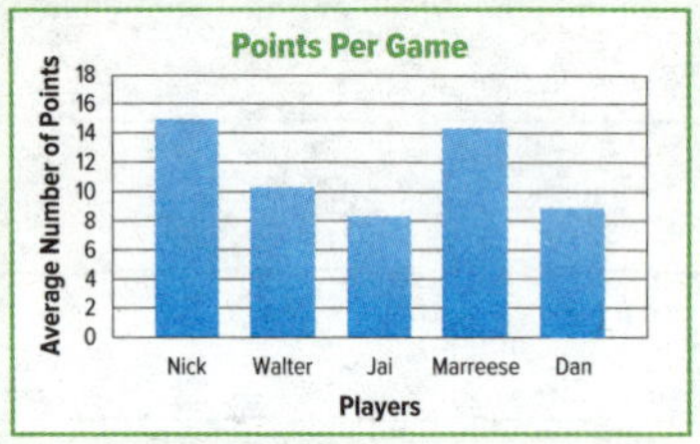

Nick, Walter, and Marreese averaged more than 10 points per game.

Example 2

Use the circle graph. Suppose 300 people were surveyed. How many people have two accounts?

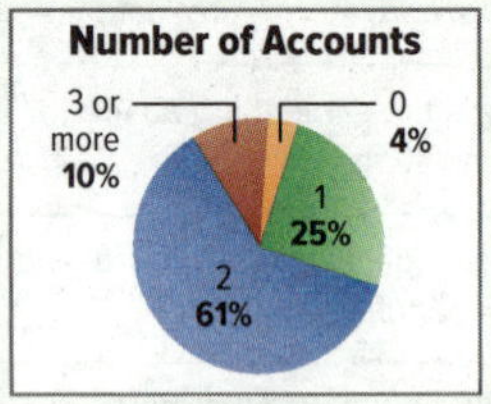

Find 61% of 300.

61% of $300 = 61\% \times 300$

$= 0.61 \times 300$ or 183

So, 183 people have two accounts.

Quick Check

Graphs **The bar graph at the right shows the number of items each student obtained during a scavenger hunt.**

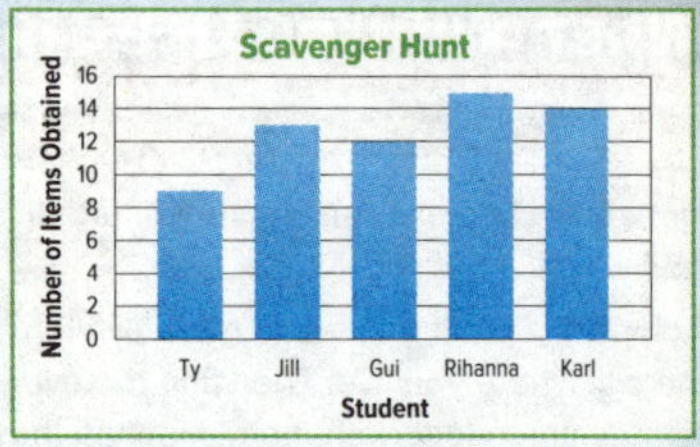

1. Who obtained the most items?

Rihanna

2. Who obtained the least items?

Ty

3. Refer to the circle graph in Example 2. Suppose 300 people were surveyed. How many people have 1 account?

75

How Did You Do?

Which problems did you answer correctly in the Quick Check? Shade those exercise numbers below.

① ② ③

PLAN ONLINE

PD | RtI | Watch | Worksheets | Vocab | Tutor | Tools | Check | English Learners | Sketchpad

PRESENT

IWB

An Interactive Whiteboard Ready presentation is available for each lesson in the chapter.

Lesson 1

Make Predictions

Vocabulary Start-Up

Statistics deal with collecting, organizing, and interpreting data. A **survey** is a method of collecting information. The group being studied is the **population**. Sometimes the population is very large. To save time and money, part of the group, called a **sample**, is surveyed.

For each survey topic, determine which set represents the population and which represents a sample of the population. Write *population* or *sample*.

	Survey Topic	Set A	Set B
1.	dress code changes	the students in a middle school population	the seventh graders in the middle school sample
2.	favorite flavors of ice cream	the customers at an ice cream shop in the town sample	the residents of a town population

Essential Question

HOW do you know which type of graph to use when displaying data?

Vocabulary

statistics
survey
population
sample

Content Standards
7.SP.1, 7.SP.2

MP Mathematical Practices
1, 3, 4

Real-World Link

Logan wants to survey students in his school about their favorite and least favorite zoo exhibit. Describe a possible sample Logan could survey instead of surveying the entire school.

Sample answer: He could survey every 20th student entering the cafeteria.

Which MP **Mathematical Practices** did you use? Shade the circle(s) that applies.

1. Persevere with Problems
2. Reason Abstractly
3. Construct an Argument
4. Model with Mathematics
5. Use Math Tools
6. Attend to Precision
7. Make Use of Structure
8. Use Repeated Reasoning

Focus narrowing the scope

Objective Predict actions of a larger group by using a sample.
7.SP.1, 7.SP.2

Coherence connecting within and across grades

Previous
Students solved problems using data presented in bar graphs and dot plots.

Now
Students use data to make predictions about a population.

Next
Students will use data from a random sample to make inferences about a population.

Rigor pursuing concepts, fluency, and applications

See the Levels of Complexity chart on page 797.

ENGAGE EXPLORE EXPLAIN ELABORATE EVALUATE

1 Launch the Lesson

Ideas for Use

You may wish to launch the lesson using a whole group, small group, think-pair-share activity, or independent activity.

EL **Pairs Consult** In pairs, have students complete Exercises 1 and 2. Make sure they understand the difference between a sample and a population. MP 1, 6

Alternate Strategy

AL Have the class stand up. Tell students that the class is a *population*. Then have everyone sit down. Ask every third person to stand up. The students that are standing represent a *sample* of the population. MP 1, 6

ENGAGE EXPLORE **EXPLAIN** ELABORATE EVALUATE

2 Teach the Concept

Ask the scaffolded questions for each example to differentiate instruction.

Examples

IWB

1. Make predictions using ratios.

AL
- *How many students brought a photo taken at a theme park?* 11
- *What is the total number of students?* 28

OL
- *What is the ratio for this probability?* $\frac{11}{28}$
- *Express this probability as a decimal and a percent.* $0.3928 \approx 39\%$

BL
- *What is the probability that a student did not bring a photo taken at the beach?* $\frac{22}{28} = \frac{11}{14}$

2. Make predictions using ratios.

AL
- *What is the sample? population?* The sample is Mr. Blackwell's class, and the 560 students at the school is the population.
- *What will s represent in the equivalent ratios?* the number of theme park photos

OL
- *Why do we multiply by 20?* Since $28 \times 20 = 560$, we have to multiply the numerator of 11 by 20 to maintain equivalence.

BL
- *About how many students can be expected not to bring in a photo taken at a theme park? Explain.* about 560 − 220, or 340 students

Need Another Example?

Every sixth person in the school cafeteria was asked to name where he or she would like to go for the school's spring outing. Fifteen chose an amusement park, 10 chose a baseball game, 10 chose a water park, and 5 chose an art museum. What is the probability that a student prefers to go to an amusement park? $\frac{3}{8}$ Suppose there are 408 students at Julia's school. Predict how many students prefer going to an amusement park. about 153 students

Work Zone

Make Predictions Using Ratios

You can use the results of a survey or past actions to predict the actions of a larger group. Since the ratios of the responses of a good sample are often the same as the ratios of the responses of the population.

Real World

Examples

Tutor

The students in Mr. Blackwell's class brought photos from their summer break. The table shows how many students brought each type of photo.

Summer Break Photos	
Location	**Students**
beach	6
campground	4
home	7
theme park	11

1. What is the probability that a student brought a photo taken at a theme park?

$$P(\text{theme park}) = \frac{\text{number of theme park photos}}{\text{number of students with a photo}} = \frac{11}{28}$$

So, the probability of a theme park photo is $\frac{11}{28}$.

2. There are 560 students at the school where Mr. Blackwell teaches. Predict how many students would bring in a photo taken at a theme park.

Let s represent the number of theme park photos.

$\frac{11}{28} = \frac{s}{560}$ Write an equivalent ratio.

$\frac{11}{28} = \frac{s}{560}$ (×20, ×20) Since $28 \times 20 = 560$, multiply 11 by 20 to find s.

$\frac{11}{28} = \frac{220}{560}$ $s = 220$

Of the 560 students, you can expect about 220 to bring a photo from a theme park.

Show your work.

Got it? **Do these problems to find out.**

A survey found that 6 out of every 10 students have a blog.

a. What is the probability that a student at the school has a blog?

b. Suppose there are about 250 students at the school. About how many have a blog?

a. $\frac{3}{5}$, 0.6, or 60%

b. about 150 students

Make Predictions Using Equations

You can also use the percent equation to make predictions.

Examples

Watch Tutor

3. **A survey found that 85% of people use emoticons on their instant messengers. Predict how many of the 2,450 students at Washington Middle School use emoticons.**

Words	What number of students is 85% of 2,450 students?
Variable	Let n represent the number of students.
Equation	$n \quad = \quad 0.85 \quad \cdot \quad 2{,}450$

$n = 0.85 \cdot 2{,}450$ Write the percent equation.

$n = 2{,}082.5$ Multiply.

About 2,083 of the students use emoticons.

4. **The circle graph shows the results of a survey in which children ages 8 to 12 were asked whether they have a television in their bedroom. Predict how many out of 1,725 students would not have a television in their bedroom.**

TV's in the Bedroom

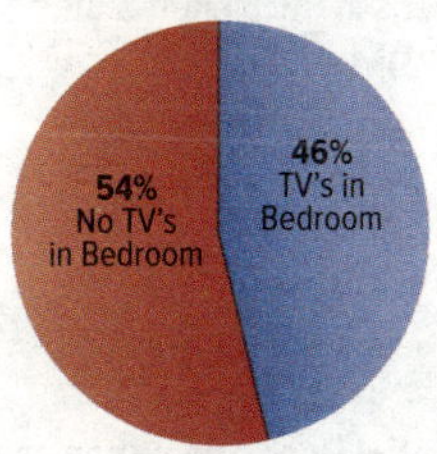

You can use the percent equation and the survey results to predict what part p of the 1,725 students have no TV in their bedroom.

part = percent · whole

$p = 0.54 \cdot 1{,}725$ Survey results: 54%

$p = 931.5$ Multiply.

About 932 students do not have a television in their bedroom.

STOP and Reflect

What proportion could you use to solve Example 4? Write your answer below.

$\frac{p}{1{,}725} = \frac{54}{100}$

Got it? **Do this problem to find out.**

c. Refer to Example 4. Predict how many out of 1,370 students have a television in their bedroom.

Show your work.

c. about 630 students

IWB

Examples

3. Make predictions using equations.

AL
- *How would you write 85% as a decimal?* 0.85
- *How can you find 85% of 2,450?* Multiply 0.85 by 2,450.

OL
- *What does n represent in the equation $n = 0.85 \cdot 2{,}450$?* the number of students that use emoticons
- *Why do we round the answer to 2,083?* The number of students must be a whole number.

BL
- *Predict how many students do not use emoticons. Explain.* Sample answer: about 367; 2,450 − 2,083 = 367

Need Another Example?

According to one survey, 25% of high school students reported that they would not get summer jobs. Predict how many of the 948 students at Mohawk High School will not get a summer job. about 237 students

4. Make predictions using equations.

AL
- *What percent of those surveyed have a TV in their bedroom?* 46%
- *What percent of those surveyed don't have a TV in their bedroom?* 54%

OL
- *What does p represent in the equation?* part of the whole
- *What is the prediction for how many more students would not have a television in their bedroom than those who do have a television in their bedroom?* about 138 students

BL
- *Once you know the part of the whole that would not have a television in their bedroom, what is another way you could determine the part of the whole that would have a television in their bedroom?* Sample answer: Subtract 931.5 from 1,725, which is 793.5.

Need Another Example?

The table shows the results of a survey in which people were asked whether their house pets watch television. There are 540 students at McCloskey Middle School who own pets. Predict how many of them would say their pets watch TV. about 205

Does your pet watch TV?	
Response	**Percent**
yes	38%
no	60%
don't know	2%

Guided Practice

Formative Assessment Use these exercises to assess students' understanding of the concepts in this lesson.

If some of your students are not ready for assignments, use the differentiated activities below.

AL EL Numbered Heads Together Have students work in groups of 4 to complete Exercises 1–7. Assign each student a number, from 1 to 4. Groups must work together to ensure that each student understands how to use the bar graph to find probabilities and make predictions and how to use the circle graph to make predictions. Students are responsible to ask questions if they do not understand. Upon completion of the exercises, randomly call on one numbered student to share their group's responses with the class. MP 1, 7

BL EL Roundrobin In groups of 4, have students go around in a circle. Each student writes a prediction problem, similar to Exercises 4–6 that can be solved by either using the data in the bar graph or the circle graph. Have groups trade problems with another group. Each student is assigned to solve one of the problems. Have groups reconvene to discuss responses and resolve any discrepancies. MP 1, 4, 7

Watch Out!

Common Error Remind students that equivalent ratios are ratios that have the same value. To write an equivalent ratio, multiply the numerator and denominator of a ratio by the same number.

Guided Practice

Check

The table shows the results of a survey of Hamilton Middle School seventh graders. Use the table to find the following probabilities. (Examples 1 and 2)

Career Field	Students
Entertainment	17
Education	14
Medicine	11
Public service	6
Sports	2

1. the probability of choosing a career in public service
   Show your work.
   $\frac{3}{25}$, 0.12, or 12%

2. the probability of choosing a career in education
   $\frac{7}{25}$, 0.28, or 28%

3. the probability of choosing a career in sports
   $\frac{1}{25}$, 0.04, or 4%

4. Predict how many students out of 400 will enter the education field.
   112 students

5. Predict how many students out of 500 will enter the medical field.
   110 students

6. Use the circle graph that shows the results of a poll to which 60,000 teens responded. Predict how many of the approximately 28 million teens in the United States would buy a music CD if they were given $20. (Examples 3 and 4)
   about 8.96 million teens

How Would You Spend a Gift of $20?

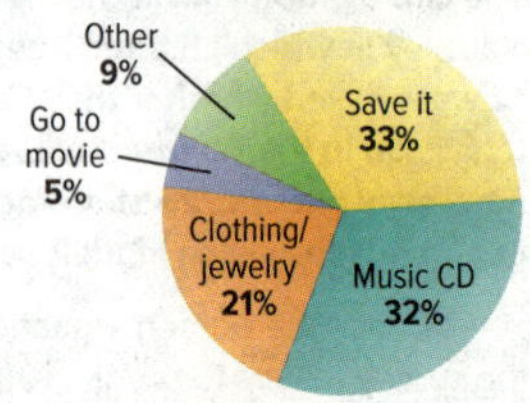

7. **Building on the Essential Question** When can statistics be used to gain information about a population from a sample?
   Sample answer: If a sample is representative of the population, valid inferences can be drawn from the sample that apply to the population.

Rate Yourself!

How confident are you about making predictions? Check the box that applies.

For more help, go online to access a Personal Tutor.

Tutor

Name ______________________ My Homework ______________

Independent Practice

Go online for Step-by-Step Solutions eHelp

The table shows the results of a survey of 150 students. Use the table to find the probability of a student participating in each sport. (Example 1)

Sport	Students
Baseball/softball	36
Basketball	30
Football	45
Gymnastics	12
Tennis	18
Volleyball	9

1. football
   $\frac{3}{10}$, 0.3, or 30%

2. tennis
   $\frac{3}{25}$, 0.12, or 12%

3. gymnastics
   $\frac{2}{25}$, 0.08, or 8%

4. volleyball
   $\frac{3}{50}$, 0.06, or 6%

5. Three out of every 10 students ages 6–14 have a magazine subscription. Suppose there are 30 students in Annabelle's class. About how many will have a magazine subscription? (Example 2)
   9 students

6. Use the graph that shows the percent of cat owners who train their cats in each category. (Examples 3 and 4)

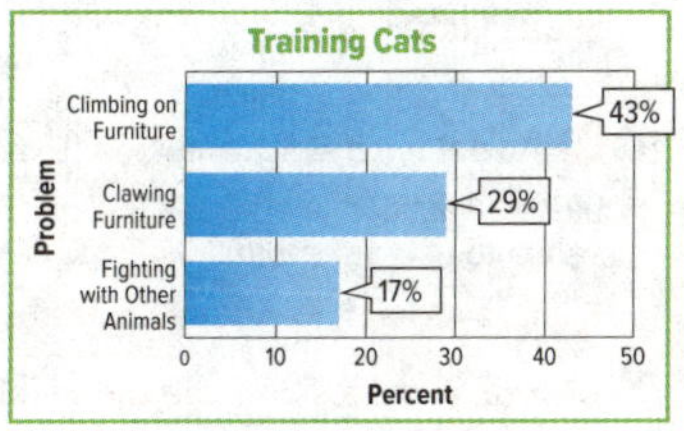

   a. Out of 255 cat owners, predict how many owners trained their cat not to climb on furniture.
   about 110 people

   b. Out of 316 cat owners, predict how many cat owners trained their cat not to claw on furniture.
   about 92 people

7. MP **Make a Prediction** The school librarian recorded the types of books students checked out on a typical day. Suppose there are 605 students enrolled at the school. Predict the number of students that prefer humor books. Compare this to the number of students at the school who prefer nonfiction.
   About 143 students prefer humor books, and the number of students that prefer nonfiction is 88. So, there are about 55 more students who prefer humor books to nonfiction books.

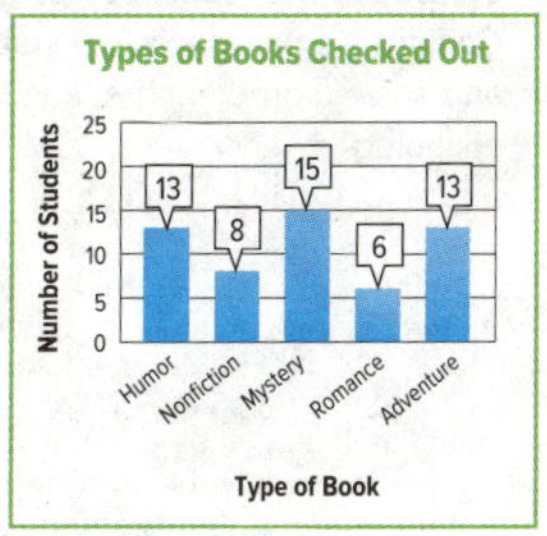

ENGAGE EXPLORE EXPLAIN ELABORATE EVALUATE

3 Practice and Apply

Independent Practice and Extra Practice

The Independent Practice pages are meant to be used as the homework assignment. The Extra Practice page can be used for additional reinforcement or as a second-day assignment.

Levels of Complexity

The levels of the exercises progress from 1 to 3, with Level 1 indicating the lowest level of complexity.

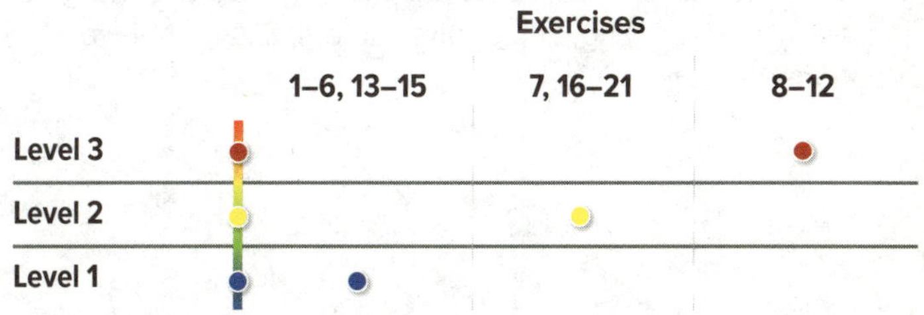

Suggested Assignments

You can use the table below that includes exercises of all complexity levels to select appropriate exercises for your students' needs.

Differentiated Homework Options		
AL	Approaching Level	1–8, 11, 12, 20, 21
OL	On Level	1–7 odd, 8, 11, 12, 20, 21
BL	Beyond Level	7–12, 20, 21

McGraw Hill Education ALEKS® can provide additional remediation support with personalized instruction and practice.

MATHEMATICAL PRACTICES

Emphasis On	Exercise(s)
1 Make sense of problems and persevere in solving them.	9, 10
3 Construct viable arguments and critique the reasoning of others.	7, 8, 16
4 Model with mathematics.	11, 12

Mathematical Practices 1, 3, and 4 are aspects of mathematical thinking that are emphasized in every lesson. Students are given opportunities to be persistent in their problem solving, to express their reasoning, and apply mathematics to real-world situations.

Formative Assessment
Use this activity as a closing formative assessment before dismissing students from your class.

TICKET Out the Door

Pose the following question to students: If 16 students in this class chose math as their favorite subject, what is *P*(math)? See students' work.

H.O.T. Problems Higher Order Thinking

8. **Find the Error** A survey of a seventh-grade class showed that 4 out of every 10 students are taking a trip during spring break. There are 150 students in the seventh grade. Caitlyn is trying to determine how many of the seventh-grade students can be expected to take a trip during spring break. Find her mistake and correct it.

Caitlyn set up the proportion incorrectly, it should be $\frac{4}{10} = \frac{x}{150}$; $x = 60$ students

9. **Persevere with Problems** One letter tile is drawn from the bag and replaced 300 times. Predict how many times a consonant will *not* be picked.

about 100 times

10. **Persevere with Problems** A survey found that 80% of teens enjoy going to the movies in their free time. Out of 5,200 teens, predict how many said that they do not enjoy going to the movies in their free time.

about 1,040 teens

11. **Model with Mathematics** Explain how to use a sample to predict what a group of people prefer. Then give an example of a situation in which it makes sense to use a sample.

Sample answer: Randomly select a part of the group to get a sample. Determine their preferences and use the results to determine the percent of the total group. It makes sense to use a sample when surveying the population of a city.

12. **Model with Mathematics** Design a survey to give to your classmates. Construct a bar graph in the space below to represent your data. Then write and solve a problem that involves a prediction based on the data you collected.

See students' work.

Show your work.

Name ______________________ My Homework ______________________

Extra Practice

Solve.

13. Luther won 12 of the last 20 video games he played. Find the probability of Luther winning the next game he plays. $\frac{3}{5}$, 0.6, or 60%

Homework Help

$P(\text{winning}) = \frac{\text{number of games won}}{\text{number of games played}}$

$= \frac{12}{20}$ or $\frac{3}{5}$

14. Refer to Exercise 13. Suppose Luther plays a total of 60 games with his friends over the next month. Predict how many of these games Luther will win. 36 games

15. Use the graph that shows the number of times teens volunteer.

How Often Teens Volunteer

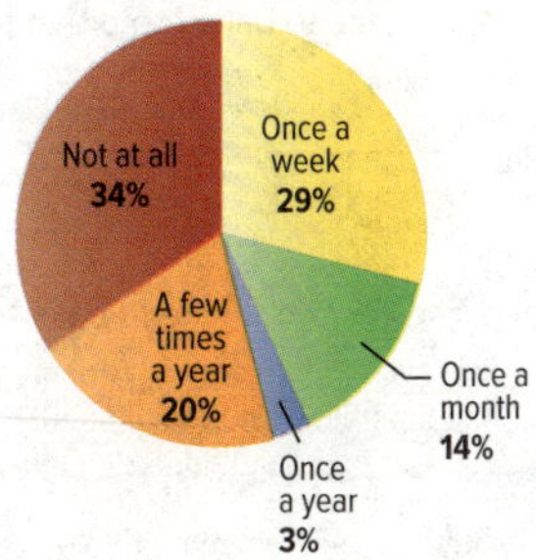

a. About 300,000 teens ages 12–14 live in Virginia. Predict the number of teens in this age group who volunteer a few times a year.

about 60,000

b. Tennessee has about 250,000 teens ages 12–14. Predict the number of teens in this age group who volunteer once a week.

about 72,500

c. About 240,000 teens ages 12–14 live in Missouri. Predict the number of teens in this age group who volunteer once a year.

about 7,200

16. MP **Make a Prediction** The probability of Jaden making a free throw is 15%. Predict the number of free throws that he can expect to make if he attempts 40 free throws.

about 6 free throws

Draw a line to match each situation with the appropriate equation or proportion.

17. 27 MP3s is what percent of 238 MP3s?

18. 238% of 27 is what number?

19. 27% of MP3 owners download music weekly. Predict how many MP3 owners out of 238 owners download music weekly.

a. $n = 27 \cdot 2.38$

b. $\frac{27}{100} = \frac{p}{238}$

c. $\frac{27}{238} = \frac{n}{100}$

Create Your Own Homework Online

eSolutions Manual can be used to create worksheets for the suggested assignments on page 797, or create your own worksheets for differentiated homework or review.

Power Up! Test Practice

Exercises 20 and 21 prepare students for more rigorous thinking needed for the State assessment.

20.

This test item requires students to explain and apply mathematical concepts and solve problems with precision, while making use of structure.	
Depth of Knowledge	DOK1
Content Standard	7.SP.2
Mathematical Practice	MP1
Online Experience	Students will be required to click on the bubbles to select all answers that are correct.
Scoring Rubric	
1 point	Students answer the question.

21.

This test item requires students to reason abstractly and quantitatively when problem solving.	
Depth of Knowledge	DOK2
Content Standard	7.SP.2
Mathematical Practices	MP1, MP4
Online Experience	Students will drag values to model the question and type their response in the box.
Scoring Rubric	
2 points	Students correctly model the equation and find how long it will take to bake the bread.
1 point	Students correctly model the equation OR find how long it will take to bake the bread.

Power Up! Test Practice

20. There were 515 students surveyed on how they spend time with their families. Which of the following estimates are accurate? Select all that apply.

- ■ About 175 students spend time with their family eating dinner.
- ■ About 72 students spend time with their family playing sports.
- □ About 50 students spend time with their family watching TV.
- □ About 38 students spend time with their family taking walks.

How Students Spend Time with Family	
Eating Dinner	34%
Watching TV	20%
Talking	14%
Playing Sports	14%
Talking Walks	4%
Other	14%

21. Yesterday a bakery baked 54 loaves of bread in 20 minutes. Today the bakery needs to bake 405 loaves of bread at the same rate. Select values to complete the model below to predict how long it will take to bake the bread today.

$$\frac{54}{20} = \frac{405}{x}$$

20

54

405

x

How long will it take to bake the bread today?

150 minutes, or 2.5 hours

Spiral Review

22. A magazine rack contains 5 sports magazines, 7 news magazines, and 10 fashion magazines. After a magazine is chosen, it is *not* replaced. Find the probability of randomly choosing two fashion magazines. 7.SP.8a

$\frac{15}{77}$

23. Each week, Ryan's mother has him randomly choose a chore that he must complete from the list shown. The first week, he chose washing the dishes. What is the probability that Ryan will choose washing the dishes two more weeks in a row? 7.SP.5

$\frac{1}{25}$

Weekly Chores
Collecting the trash
Folding the laundry
Cleaning the house
Washing the dishes
Cutting the grass

24. In how many different orders can a person watch 3 different movies? Use a list to show the sample space. 7.SP.8b

6 ways; 123, 132, 213, 231, 312, 321

PLAN ONLINE: PD · RtI · Watch · Worksheets · Vocab · Tutor · Tools · Check · English Learners · Sketchpad

PRESENT: IWB — **An Interactive Whiteboard Ready presentation is available for each lesson in the chapter.**

Statistics and Probability

Lesson 2

Unbiased and Biased Samples

Real-World Link

Watch

Entertainment A T.V. programming manager wants to conduct a survey to determine which reality television show is the favorite of viewers in a certain viewing area. He is considering the three samples shown. Draw an X through the two samples that would not fairly represent all of the people in the viewing area.

Sample 1
100 people that are trying out for a reality show

Sample 2
100 students at your middle school

Sample 3
Every 100th person at a shopping mall

Explain why the two samples that you crossed out do *not* fairly represent all of the people in the viewing area? Explain.

Sample answer: People who are trying out to be on a reality show are probably fans of that show. Only a narrow age group would be represented at a middle school.

Which MP **Mathematical Practices** did you use? Shade the circle(s) that applies.

1. Persevere with Problems
2. Reason Abstractly
3. Construct an Argument
4. Model with Mathematics
5. Use Math Tools
6. Attend to Precision
7. Make Use of Structure
8. Use Repeated Reasoning

Essential Question

HOW do you know which type of graph to use when displaying data?

Vocabulary

unbiased sample
simple random sample
systematic random sample
biased sample
convenience sample
voluntary response sample

Content Standards
7.SP.1, 7.SP.2

MP Mathematical Practices
1, 3, 4, 5

Focus narrowing the scope

Objective Determine whether sampling methods are valid.
7.SP.1, 7.SP.2

Coherence connecting within and across grades

Previous
Students used data to make predictions about a population.

Now
Students use data from a random sample to make inferences about a population.

Next
Students will evaluate graphs to determine whether or not they are misleading.

Rigor pursuing concepts, fluency, and applications

See the Levels of Complexity chart on page 805.

ENGAGE EXPLORE EXPLAIN ELABORATE EVALUATE

1 Launch the Lesson

Ideas for Use

You may wish to launch the lesson using a whole group, small group, think-pair-share activity, or independent activity.

EL **Think-Pair-Write** Give students 1–2 minutes to read through the directions in Real-World Link and to think about how they would respond to Exercise 1. Then have them work with a partner to discuss their responses, prior to writing down their response. Students should individually write their own response to Exercise 1. MP 1, 7

Alternate Strategy

BL Have students write additional examples of samples that do not fairly represent all of the people in the viewing area. Have them share their examples with the class and justify why their chosen examples are not representative of the population. MP 1, 3, 4, 7

ENGAGE EXPLORE **EXPLAIN** ELABORATE EVALUATE

2 Teach the Concept

Ask the scaffolded questions for each example to differentiate instruction.

IWB

Example

1. Determine the validity of conclusions.

AL
- *Describe the sample.* random sample of students at a middle school
- *Describe the population.* all students at the middle school

OL
- *What does it mean to take a random sample?* Sample answer: Each student is as likely to be surveyed as every other student.
- *How many students were surveyed altogether?* 50 students
- *Is the conclusion valid? Explain.* yes; Sample answer: 25 out of 50 students surveyed prefer no music while they exercise. This is equal to half of the students. This is an unbiased sample, so the conclusion is valid.

BL
- *Generate a conclusion about the students that prefer listening to rock music while they exercise.* Sample answer: One-fifth of the students prefer listening to rock music while they exercise.

Need Another Example?
One classroom of students is surveyed to determine the theme for the spring dance. Out of 25 students, 15 chose Blast from the Past. The dance committee concluded that 60% of the students like this theme best. Is the sample method valid? Justify your answer. The conclusion is not valid. This is a biased convenience sample because only one classroom is surveyed.

Watch Out!

Common Error Surveys may be biased if the respondents are self-selected, that is, they can choose whether or not to respond.

Work Zone

Biased and Unbiased Samples

To get valid results, a sample must be chosen very carefully. An **unbiased sample** is selected so that it accurately represents the entire population. Two ways to pick an unbiased sample are listed below.

Unbiased Samples		
Type	**Description**	**Example**
Simple Random Sample	Each item or person in the population is as likely to be chosen as any other.	Each student's name is written on a piece of paper. The names are placed in a bowl, and names are picked without looking.
Systematic Random Sample	The items or people are selected according to a specific time or item interval.	Every 20th person is chosen from an alphabetical list of all students attending a school.

Everyday Use
Bias is a tendency or prejudice

Math Use
Bias is an error introduced by selecting or encouraging a specific outcome

In a **biased sample**, one or more parts of the population are favored over others. Two ways to pick a biased sample are listed below.

Biased Samples		
Type	**Description**	**Example**
Convenience Sample	A convenience sample consists of members of a population that are easily accessed.	To represent all the students attending a school, the principal surveys the students in one math class.
Voluntary Response Sample	A voluntary response sample involves only those who want to participate in the sampling.	Students at a school who wish to express their opinions complete an online survey.

Examples

Tutor

Determine whether the conclusion is valid. Justify your answer.

1. A random sample of students at a middle school shows that 10 students prefer listening to rock, 15 students prefer listening to hip hop, and 25 students prefer no music while they exercise. It can be concluded that half the students prefer no music while they exercise.

This is a simple random sample. So, the sample is unbiased and the conclusion is valid.

Determine whether each conclusion is valid. Justify your answer.

2. **Every tenth person who walks into a department store is surveyed to determine his or her music preference. Out of 150 customers, 70 stated that they prefer rock music. The manager concludes that about half of all customers prefer rock music.**

Since the population is every tenth customer of a department store, the sample is an unbiased, systematic random sample. The conclusion is valid.

3. **The customers of a music store are surveyed to determine their favorite leisure time activity. The results are shown in the graph. The store manager concludes that most people prefer to listen to music in their leisure time.**

Leisure Time Activities

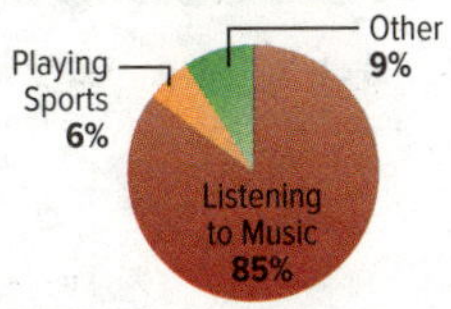

The customers of a music store probably like to listen to music in their leisure time. The sample is a biased, convenience sample since all of the people surveyed are in one specific location. The conclusion is not valid.

Got it? **Do this problem to find out.**

a. A radio station asks its listeners to indicate their preference for one of two candidates in an upcoming election. Seventy-two percent of the listeners who responded preferred candidate A, so the radio station announced that candidate A would win the election. Is the conclusion valid? Justify your answer.

show your work.

a. The conclusion is not valid. The population is restricted to listeners of a radio station and it is a voluntary response sample.

Use Sampling to Predict

A valid sampling method uses unbiased samples. If a sampling method is valid, you can make generalizations about the population.

IWB

Examples

2. Determine the validity of conclusions.

AL
- *Describe the sample.* every tenth person who walks into a department store
- *Describe the population.* all of the customers

OL
- *What fraction of customers surveyed preferred rock music?* $\frac{70}{150} = \frac{7}{15}$
- *Did the manager make a valid conclusion? Explain.* yes; Sample answer: The sample is unbiased. Since 70 out of 150 is about one half, the conclusion is valid.

BL
- *Do you think this sample should determine the outcome for other locations of the same department store?* Sample answer: Not necessarily, the various locations will have different types of shoppers.

Need Another Example?
Every tenth student who walked into the cafeteria was surveyed to determine his or her favorite lunch. Out of 40 students, 19 students stated that they liked hamburgers best. The staff concluded that about 50% of the students like hamburgers. Is the sample method valid? Justify your answer. The conclusion is valid. This is a unbiased systematic random sample.

3. Determine the validity of conclusions.

AL
- *Describe the sample.* customers of a music store
- *Describe the population.* all people

OL
- *Why is this sample biased?* The shoppers are in a specialty shop, and each response would likely favor that specialty.
- *What kind of sample is this?* biased, convenience sample

BL
- *How could you alter the survey to make it unbiased?* Sample answer: Survey every tenth person in a grocery store.

Need Another Example?
Janet surveyed the athletes on the girls' field hockey team to determine which sports teenagers like best. Of these, 65% said that they like field hockey best. Janet concluded that over half of teenagers like field hockey best. Is the sample method valid? Justify your answer. The conclusion is not valid. This is a biased sample, because Janet used a convenience sample.

Example

4. **Use sampling to predict.**

AL
- *How do you know that this is a random sample?* The customers were randomly selected to participate in the survey.
- *How many survey responses favored jeans?* 25

OL
- *What fraction of the total number of survey response were for jeans?* $\frac{25}{50} = \frac{1}{2}$
- *How can we determine how many jeans should be ordered if 450 pairs of pants are ordered?* Determine $\frac{1}{2}$ of 450, which is 225.

BL
- *The store manager decides to order 700 pairs of pants. She orders 350 pairs of capris. Was this a good decision? Explain.* no; Sample answer: Based on the survey results, she should only have ordered 0.3 × 700, or 210 pairs of capris.

Need Another Example?
The library is trying to decide what types of books to sell at its book fair. It surveyed 40 students at random. The results are in the table. If 220 books are to be sold at the book fair, how many should be mysteries? 66 books

Book Type	Number of Students
adventure novel	9
mystery	12
short stories	8
sport	11

Guided Practice

Formative Assessment Use these exercises to assess students' understanding of the concepts in this lesson.

If some of your students are not ready for assignments, use the differentiated activity below.

AL EL **Pairs to Groups** Arrange students in pairs to complete Exercises 1–3. Have students list reasons why the sample is biased or unbiased. Have students generate a scenario that would make the sample valid (if it is invalid) or invalid (if it is valid). Have pairs join with another pair to compare responses and discuss and resolve any discrepancies. MP 1, 4, 6

Real-World Example

4. **A store sells 3 types of pants: jeans, capris, and cargos. The store workers survey 50 customers at random about their favorite type of pants. The survey responses are indicated at the right. If 450 pairs of pants are ordered, how many should be jeans?**

Type	Number
Jeans	25
Capris	15
Cargos	10

First, determine whether the sample method is valid. The sample is a simple random sample since customers were randomly selected. Thus, the sample method is valid.

$\frac{25}{50}$ or 50% of the customers prefer jeans. So, find 50% of 450.

0.5 × 450 = 225, so about 225 pairs of jeans should be ordered.

Guided Practice

1. Zach is trying to decide which of three golf courses is the best. He randomly surveyed people at a sports store and recorded the results in the table. Is the sample method valid? If so, suppose Zach surveyed 150 more people. How many people would be expected to vote for Rolling Meadows? (Example 4)

Course	Number
Whispering Trail	10
Tall Pines	8
Rolling Meadows	7

This is a simple random sample. So, the sample is valid; 42 people.

2. To find how much money the average American family spends to cool their home, 100 Alaskan families are surveyed at random. Of the families, 85 said that they spend less than $75 per month on cooling. The researcher concluded that the average American family spends less than $75 on cooling per month. Is the conclusion valid? Explain. (Examples 1–3)

The conclusion is not valid. This is a biased, convenience sample, since people in other states would spend much more than those in Alaska.

3. **Building on the Essential Question** How is using a survey one way to determine experimental probability?

Sample answer: A survey uses an actual sample to predict the results in a population.

Rate Yourself!

Are you ready to move on?
Shade the section that applies.

YES ? NO

For more help, go online to access a Personal Tutor.

FOLDABLES Time to update your Foldable!

Name ______________________ My Homework ______________________

Independent Practice

Go online for Step-by-Step Solutions eHelp

Determine whether each conclusion is valid. Justify your answer. (Examples 1–3)

1. To evaluate the quality of their product, a manufacturer of cell phones checks every 50th phone off the assembly line. Out of 200 phones tested, 4 are defective. The manager concludes that about 2% of the cell phones produced will be defective.

Show your work.

The conclusion is valid. This is an unbiased systematic random sample.

2. To determine whether the students will attend an arts festival at the school, Oliver surveys his friends in the art club. All of Oliver's friends plan to attend. So, Oliver assumes that all the students at his school will also attend.

The conclusion is not valid. This is a biased convenience sample, since only art club members were surveyed.

3. A random sample of people at a mall shows that 22 prefer to take a family trip by car, 18 prefer to travel by plane, and 4 prefer to travel by bus. Is the sample method valid? If so, how many people out of 500 would you expect to say they prefer to travel by plane? (Example 4)

This is a simple random sample. So, the sample is valid; about 205 people.

Preferred Ways to Travel

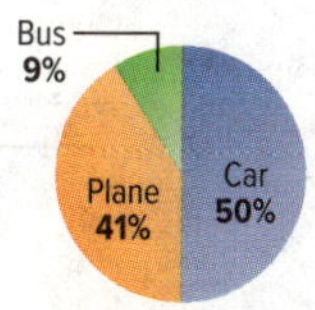

4. **MP Use Math Tools** Use the organizer to determine whether the conclusion is valid.

Step 1: Read the situation.	Marcus wants to predict the next student council president. He polls every fourth person from each grade level as they exit the cafeteria. In his poll, 65% chose Sophia. So, Marcus predicts Sophia will win the election.
Step 2: Determine the type of sample taken.	The sample is an unbiased, systematic random sample.
Step 3: Determine if the conclusion is valid.	Yes; the conclusion is valid.

ENGAGE EXPLORE **EXPLAIN** **ELABORATE** **EVALUATE**

3 Practice and Apply

Independent Practice and Extra Practice

The Independent Practice pages are meant to be used as the homework assignment. The Extra Practice page can be used for additional reinforcement or as a second-day assignment.

Levels of Complexity

The levels of the exercises progress from 1 to 3, with Level 1 indicating the lowest level of complexity.

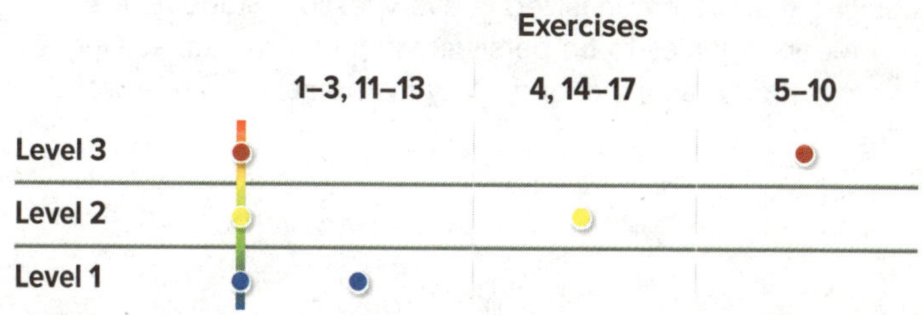

Suggested Assignments

You can use the table below that includes exercises of all complexity levels to select appropriate exercises for your students' needs.

Differentiated Homework Options		
AL	Approaching Level	1–3, 6–10, 16, 17
OL	On Level	1, 3, 4, 6–10, 16, 17
BL	Beyond Level	4–10, 16, 17

McGraw Hill Education ALEKS® can provide additional remediation support with personalized instruction and practice.

MP MATHEMATICAL PRACTICES

Emphasis On	Exercise(s)
1 Make sense of problems and persevere in solving them.	5
3 Construct viable arguments and critique the reasoning of others.	6–9, 14, 15
4 Model with mathematics.	10
5 Use appropriate tools strategically.	4

Mathematical Practices 1, 3, and 4 are aspects of mathematical thinking that are emphasized in every lesson. Students are given opportunities to be persistent in their problem solving, to express their reasoning, and apply mathematics to real-world situations.

Formative Assessment

Use this activity as a closing formative assessment before dismissing students from your class.

TICKET Out the Door

Have students name one type of a biased sample and explain the bias. See students' work.

H.O.T. Problems Higher Order Thinking

5. MP **Persevere with Problems** How could the wording of a question or the tone of voice of the interviewer affect a survey? Provide an example.
   Sample answer: Questions should be asked in a neutral manner. For example, the question "You really don't like Brand X, do you?" might not get the same answer as the question "Do you prefer Brand X or Brand Y?"

MP **Justify Conclusions** Determine whether each statement is *sometimes*, *always*, or *never* true. Explain your reasoning to a classmate.

6. A biased sample is valid.
   Never; Sample answer: A biased sample favors one or more parts of the population over others.

7. A simple random sample is valid.
   Sometimes; Sample answer: The sample needs to represent the entire population to be valid.

8. A voluntary response sample is valid.
   Never; Sample answer: A voluntary response sample involves only those who want to participate in the sampling.

9. MP **Find the Error** Marisol wants to determine how many students plan to attend the girls' varsity basketball game. Find her mistake and correct it.
   Sample answer: The sample will be biased because it is a convenience sample. Marisol will be asking only basketball fans.

10. MP **Model with Mathematics** Give an example of a data set from a random sample. Then make an inference about the population represented by the sample.
    See students' work.

Name ______________________ My Homework ______________

Extra Practice

Determine whether each conclusion is valid. Justify your answer.

11. To determine what people in California think about a proposed law, 5,000 people from the state are randomly surveyed. Of the people surveyed, 58% are against the law. The legislature concludes that the law should not be passed.

This is an unbiased, simple random sample because randomly selected Californians were surveyed. So, the conclusion is valid.

Homework Help

12. A magazine asks its readers to complete and return a questionnaire about popular television actors. The majority of those who replied liked one actor the most, so the magazine decides to write more articles about that actor.

This is a biased sample, since only voluntary responses are used. So, the conclusion is not valid.

13. The Student Council advisor asked every tenth student in the lunch line how they preferred to be contacted with school news. The results are shown in the table. Is this a random sample? If yes, suppose there are 684 students at the school. How many can be expected to prefer E-mail?

This is an unbiased, systematic random sample. So, the conclusion is valid; 304 students.

Method	Number
E-mail	16
Newsletter	12
Announcement	5
Telephone	3

MP **Justify Conclusions** **Each of the following surveys results in a biased sample. For each situation, explain why the survey is biased. Then explain how you would change the survey to obtain an unbiased sample.**

14. A store manager sends an E-mail survey to customers who have registered at the store's Web site.

The survey results in a voluntary response sample; Sample answer: The manager could distribute surveys to every fifth customer who enters the store.

15. A school district surveys the family of every tenth student to determine if they would vote in favor of the construction of a new school building.

The survey results in a convenience sample; Sample answer: The school district should survey every tenth family living within the school district's boundaries.

Create Your Own Homework Online

eSolutionsManual can be used to create worksheets for the suggested assignments on page 805, or create your own worksheets for differentiated homework or review.

Power Up! Test Practice

Exercises 16 and 17 prepare students for more rigorous thinking needed for the State assessment.

16.

This test item requires students to support their reasoning or evaluate the reasoning of others by justifying their response and constructing arguments.	
Depth of Knowledge	DOK3
Content Standard	7.SP.1
Mathematical Practices	MP1, MP3
Online Experience	Students will be required to type their response in the box.
Scoring Rubric	
2 points	Students correctly explain their response and offer an alternative.
1 point	Students correctly explain their response OR offer an alternative.

17.

This test item requires students to reason abstractly and quantitatively when problem solving.	
Depth of Knowledge	DOK1
Content Standard	7.SP.2
Mathematical Practice	MP1
Online Experience	Students will be required to click on the bubbles to select all answers that are correct.
Scoring Rubric	
1 point	Students correctly answer each part of the question.

Power Up! Test Practice

16. Maci surveyed all the members of her softball team about their favorite sport. Based on these results, Maci concludes that softball is the favorite sport among all her classmates. Explain why Maci's conclusion might *not* be valid. How could she change the survey to achieve a more valid conclusion?

Sport	Number of Members
Softball	12
Basketball	5
Soccer	3
Volleyball	8

Sample answer: Since Maci surveyed the members of her softball team, the sample is not representative of all her classmates. The members of the softball team represent a biased sample who might favor softball. Maci could survey randomly selected classmates standing in the lunch line.

17. Ms. Hernandez determined that 60% of the students in her classes brought an umbrella to school when the weather forecast predicted rain. She has a total of 150 students in her classes. Determine if each statement represents a valid or invalid conclusion.

a. On days when rain is forecasted, less than $\frac{2}{5}$ of her students bring an umbrella to school. ☐ Valid ■ Invalid

b. On days when rain is forecasted, about 90 of her students bring an umbrella to school. ■ Valid ☐ Invalid

c. On days when rain is forecasted, more than $\frac{1}{2}$ of her students bring an umbrella to school. ■ Valid ☐ Invalid

Spiral Review

For Exercises 18 and 19, use the table that shows Alana's first six math test scores. 6.SP.3

Test	1	2	3	4	5	6
Score	88%	92%	70%	96%	84%	96%

18. Find the mean, median, and mode of Alana's test scores. Round to the nearest tenth if necessary.

mean: **87.7** median: **90** mode: **96**

19. Determine which measure of center best represents Alana's performance. Justify your reasoning.

median; Sample answer: She scored better than the mean on four of the tests. She scored lower than the mode on four of the tests.

PLAN ONLINE

PD | RtI | Watch | Worksheets | Vocab | Tutor | Tools | Check | English Learners | Sketchpad

PRESENT

IWB

An Interactive Whiteboard Ready presentation is available for each lesson in the chapter.

Statistics and Probability

Inquiry Lab

Multiple Samples of Data

Inquiry WHY is it important to analyze multiple samples of data before making predictions?

Content Standards
7.SP.2

MP **Mathematical Practices**
1, 3, 4, 5

A hostess at a restaurant randomly hands out crayons to young children. There are three different color crayons: green (G), red (R), and blue (B). The server gives out the green crayon 40% of the time, the red crayon 40% of the time, and the blue crayon 20% of the time.

Hands-On Activity 1

Tools

When you draw a conclusion about a population from a sample of data, you are making *inferences* about that population. Sometimes, making inferences about a population from only one sample is not as accurate as using multiple samples of data.

Use a spinner to simulate the situation above.

Step 1 Create a spinner with five equal sections. Label two sections G. Label another two sections R and label one section B.

Step 2 Each spin of the spinner represents a young child receiving a crayon. Spin the spinner 20 times. Record the number of times each color of crayon was received in the column labeled Sample 1 in the table below. Repeat two more times. Record the results in the columns labeled Sample 2 and Sample 3 in the table.
See students' work for sample frequencies.

Color	Sample 1 Frequency	Sample 2 Frequency	Sample 3 Frequency
Green			
Red			
Blue			

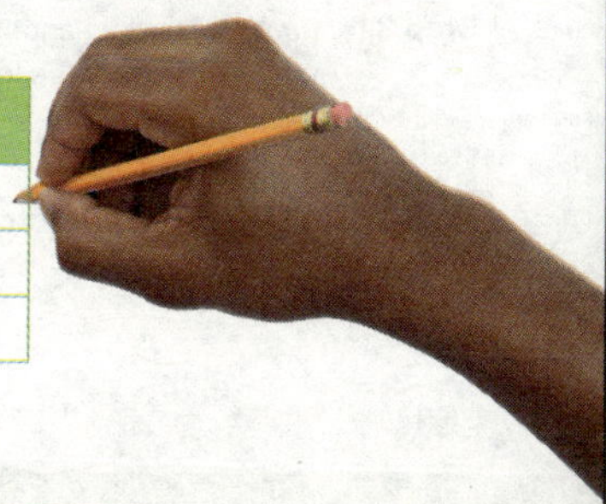

Compare the results of the 3 samples. Do you notice any differences?
Sample answer: The blue crayon is handed out less frequently.

Focus narrowing the scope

Objective Analyze the variation in multiple samples of data.
7.SP.2

Coherence connecting within and across grades

Now
Students analyze multiple samples of data to make predictions about the sample.

Next
Students will determine whether or not a data display is misleading.

Rigor pursuing concepts, fluency, and applications

See the Levels of Complexity chart on page 811.

ENGAGE EXPLORE EXPLAIN ELABORATE EVALUATE

1 Launch the Lab

Activities 1 and 2 are intended to be used as whole-group activities. Activity 1 is designed to provide more guidance to students than Activity 2.

Hands-On Activity 1

AL BL EL **Team Project** Have students work in small teams to complete the activity. Make sure teams are assigned so that there are a variety of ability levels in each team. Have each team prepare a brief oral presentation sharing the results of their simulations and their responses to the final question.
MP 1, 4, 5

Hands-On Activity 2

AL BL EL **Team Project** Have students work in small teams to complete the activity. Have them work in different teams than they did in Activity 1. Make sure teams are assigned so that there is a variety of ability levels in each team. Have each team prepare a brief oral presentation sharing the results of their samples for Steps 2 and 3, and their responses to the following questions. MP 1, 5

Ask:

- *What is the most common letter in each of your samples?* See students' work.
- *Complete the ratio for each sample:* $\frac{\text{most common letter frequency}}{\text{total letters}}$. See students' work.
- *What percentage of all letters (for each sample) are vowels? Assume there are 5 vowels: a, e, i, o, and u.* See students' work.

The most commonly used keyboard is the QWERTY keyboard. However, there is another type of keyboard called the Dvorak keyboard that is based on letter frequency. Complete the Activity below about letter frequencies.

Hands-On Activity 2

The table at the right contains fifteen randomly selected words from the English language dictionary.

Sample 1		
airport	juggle	sewer
blueberry	lemon	standard
costume	mileage	thread
doorstop	percentage	vacuum
instrument	print	whale

Step 1 Find the frequency of each letter. Record the frequencies in the Sample 1 rows of the tables below.

Letter	a	b	c	d	e	f	g	h	i	j	k	l	m
Sample 1 Frequency	8	2	3	4	15	0	4	2	4	1	0	5	5
Sample 2 Frequency													
Sample 3 Frequency													

Letter	n	o	p	q	r	s	t	u	v	w	x	y	z
Sample 1 Frequency	6	6	4	0	11	5	9	6	1	2	0	1	0
Sample 2 Frequency													
Sample 3 Frequency													

Step 2 Randomly select another 15 words from a dictionary. Record the frequency of the letters in the rows labeled Sample 2 in the tables above. See students' work.

Step 3 Repeat Step 2. Record the frequency of the letters in the rows labeled Sample 3. See students' work.

Collaborate Investigate

Work with a partner to collect multiple samples based on the following situation.

Janet and Masao are making centerpieces for their school's fall dance. They randomly select a ribbon to use in each centerpiece. There are four different colors of ribbon to choose from: brown (B), green (G), orange (O), and yellow (Y).

1. MP **Model with Mathematics** Design a method to simulate how many times each ribbon will be selected. Describe your simulation.

   Show your work.

   Sample answer: Use a spinner with 4 equal sections. Label the sections B, G, O, and Y.

2. Use the method you described in Exercise 1 to simulate the ribbon selection 20 times. Record the frequency of each color selection in the Sample 1 Frequency column of the table below. **2–5. See students' work.**

Color	Sample 1 Frequency	Sample 2 Frequency	Sample 3 Frequency
Brown			
Green			
Orange			
Yellow			

3. Repeat the process described in Exercise 2 two more times. Record the frequencies of each color selection in the Sample 2 and Sample 3 columns.

4. Make an inference to determine which color was selected the most often in each sample.

5. The *relative frequency* of a color being selected is the ratio of the number of times the color was selected to the total number of selections. Find the relative frequency of an orange ribbon being selected for each sample.

   Sample 1: ______ Sample 2: ______ Sample 3: ______

6. Masao predicts that 5 out of 10 centerpieces will have an orange ribbon. How far off is Masao's prediction? Explain.

   Sample answer: Orange will likely occur 25% of the time. Masao's estimate is off by 25%.

ENGAGE EXPLORE EXPLAIN ELABORATE EVALUATE

2 Collaborate

The **Investigate** and **Analyze and Reflect** sections are intended to be used as small-group investigations. The **Create** section is intended to be used as independent exercises.

Levels of Complexity

The levels of the exercises progress from 1 to 3, with Level 1 indicating the lowest level of complexity.

	Exercises 1–6	7–10	11, 12
Level 3			●
Level 2		●	
Level 1	●		

Collaborate Investigate

AL BL EL **Team Project** Have students work in small teams to complete Exercises 1–6. Have them work in different teams than they did in Activities 1 or 2. Make sure teams are assigned so that there is a variety of ability levels in each team. Have each team prepare a brief oral presentation sharing their results and responses to each exercise. Have them also respond to the following questions. MP 1, 5

Ask:

- *Was each sample similar? What were the similarities?* See students' work.
- *What were some differences in the samples?* See students' work.
- *Describe some unexpected results.* See students' work.
- *What are some other methods (you) used to randomly select ribbons?* See students' work.
- *What was the theoretical probability for each color?* $\frac{1}{4}$
- *What were your experimental probability results?* See students' work.

Analyze and Reflect

Collaborate

AL EL Pairs to Groups Have students work in pairs to complete Exercises 7–8. Each partner should ensure that the other partner understands how to determine the relative frequency and mean relative frequency. Then have pairs join with another pair to share responses and discuss and resolve any differences. Have the group complete Exercises 9 and 10, ensuring that all students contribute and understand. Then call on one student to share their group's responses to Exercises 9–10 with the class. MP 1, 4

Create

On Your Own

BL EL Pair Predictions In pairs, have students generate predictions for letter frequencies for words in the English language. Have students compare their predictions with actual experimental results, using at least three samples. Then have them compare their predictions and experimental results with results they locate on the Internet. MP 1, 8

Inquiry Students should be able to answer "WHY is it important to analyze multiple samples of data before making predictions?" Check for student understanding and provide guidance, if needed.

Analyze and Reflect

Collaborate

Work with a partner to answer the following questions. Refer to Activity 2.

7. What is the relative frequency for the letter e for each sample? Round to the nearest hundredth. **See students' work for Samples 2 and 3.**

   Sample 1: $\frac{15}{104}$ or about 0.14 Sample 2: ______ Sample 3: ______

8. What is the mean relative frequency of the letter e for the three samples? the median relative frequency? Round to the nearest tenth if necessary. **See students' work.**

   mean relative frequency: ______ median relative frequency: ______

9. MP **Use Math Tools** Research on the Internet to find the actual relative frequency of the letter e for words in the English language. How do your sample results compare to the actual relative frequency?

   See students' work.

10. MP **Reason Inductively** Write a few sentences describing the inferences you can make about the frequency of letters in the words in the English language using your three samples.

    Sample answer: According to my samples, the three most frequently occurring letters were e, *r*, and *t*. The three least frequently occurring letters were *q*, *x*, and *z*.

Create

On Your Own

11. MP **Justify Conclusions** Research on the Internet to find the relative frequency of other letters in words in the English language. Write how your sample results compare to the actual frequencies. Note any differences.

    Sample answer: The three letters that occur the most often are e, *t*, and *a*. I correctly predicted two of the top three. The three letters that occur the least frequently are *q*, *x*, and *z*. I correctly predicted all three.

12. Inquiry WHY is it important to analyze multiple samples of data before making predictions?

    Sample answer: Multiple samples tend to produce more reliable results.

PLAN ONLINE: PD | RtI | Watch | Worksheets | Vocab | Tutor | Tools | Check | English Learners | Sketchpad

PRESENT: IWB

An Interactive Whiteboard Ready presentation is available for each lesson in the chapter.

Lesson 3

Misleading Graphs and Statistics

Real-World Link

Hockey The Stanley Cup is awarded annually to the champion team in the National Hockey League. The graph shows the total number of points scored in Stanley Cup playoff games by three players during their careers.

1. According to the size of the players, how many times more points does Messier appear to have than Kurri?
   Sample answer: about 2 times as many; Messier's image is twice the height of Kurri's image.

2. Do you think this is representative of the players' number of points? Explain.
   Sample answer: No, the graph is misleading. Messier has only about 50 more points than Kurri.

3. What reason could someone have for intentionally creating a misleading Stanley Cup graph?
   Sample answer: Someone might want the point total for Wayne Gretzky to appear greater than it is actually is.

Essential Question

HOW do you know which type of graph to use when displaying data?

Content Standards
Extension of 7.SP.1

MP Mathematical Practices
1, 3, 4

Which **MP Mathematical Practices** did you use? Shade the circle(s) that applies.

① Persevere with Problems
② Reason Abstractly
③ Construct an Argument
④ Model with Mathematics
⑤ Use Math Tools
⑥ Attend to Precision
⑦ Make Use of Structure
⑧ Use Repeated Reasoning

Focus narrowing the scope

Objective Identify misleading graphs and statistics.

Extension of 7.SP.1

Coherence connecting within and across grades

Previous
Students used data from a random sample to make inferences about a population.

Now
Students identify whether or not a graph is misleading and solve problems using data represented in graphs.

Next
Students will compare two groups of numeric data using comparative dot plots or box plots by comparing their shapes, centers, and spreads.

Rigor pursuing concepts, fluency, and applications

See the Levels of Complexity chart on page 817.

ENGAGE EXPLORE EXPLAIN ELABORATE EVALUATE

1 Launch the Lesson

Ideas for Use

You may wish to launch the lesson using a whole group, small group, think-pair-share activity, or independent activity.

EL **Think-Pair-Write** Give students one to two minutes to think about how they would respond to Exercises 1–3. Then have them work with a partner to discuss their responses, and write down their response. MP 1, 3, 7

Alternate Strategy

AL BL EL Have students use the Internet, magazines, or newspapers, to locate examples of graphs that may be misleading. Have them determine whether or not the graph might be misleading and share their responses with the class. They should provide a justification for their determination. MP 1, 3, 4, 7

2 Teach the Concept

Ask the scaffolded questions for each example to differentiate instruction.

Example

IWB

1. Explain how graphs may be misleading.

AL
- *What is an interval?* the gaps in the scale used to count
- *Do both graphs show the same prices for each year?* yes

OL
- *How are the graphs different?* Graph A uses an interval of 4, and Graph B uses an interval of 2.
- *How do the different intervals display a different interpretation?* Sample answer: Graph A makes it appear the price has not changed much over time; Graph B makes it appear that the price has changed a lot over time.
- *What could account for our different interpretations of graphs that show the same data?* Sample answer: We make assumptions with our eyes before examining the data.

BL
- *Describe a scenario in which the Student Council would want to use Graph B.* Sample answer: to show they have increased their revenue a lot from year to year

Need Another Example?
The line graphs show the sales for a local bakery. Which graph makes it appear that the sales declined only slightly? Is this a valid conclusion? Explain.
Graph A; Sample answer: The intervals are not the same on both graphs. Graph A appears to show a slight decline while Graph B shows a sharp decline.

Graph A

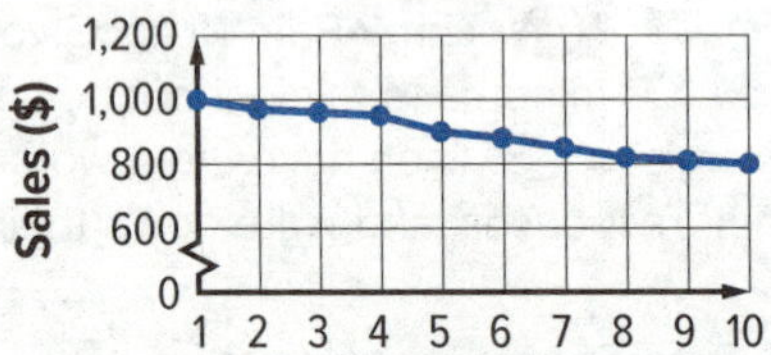

Graph B

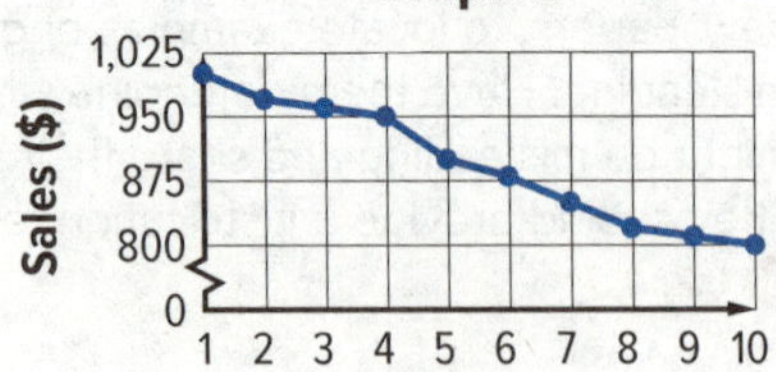

Work Zone

Changing Scales
To emphasize a change over time, reduce the scale interval on the vertical axis.

Identify a Misleading Graph

Graphs let readers analyze data easily, but are sometimes made to influence conclusions by misrepresenting the data.

Real World

Example

Tutor

1. Explain how the graphs differ.

Graph A

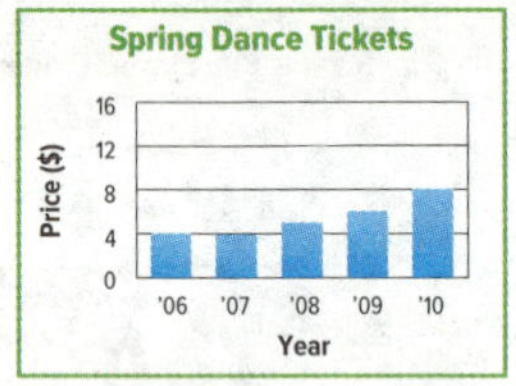

Graph B

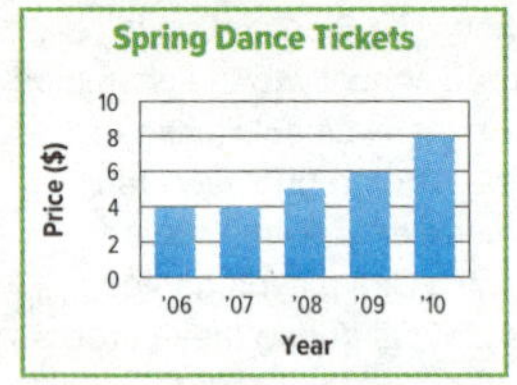

The graphs show the same data. However, the graphs differ in that Graph A uses an interval of 4, and Graph B uses an interval of 2.

Which graph appears to show a sharper increase in price?
Graph B makes it appear that the prices increased more rapidly even though the price increase is the same.

Which graph might the Student Council use to show that while ticket prices have risen, the increase is not significant? Why?
They might use Graph A. The scale used on the vertical axis of this graph makes the increase appear less significant.

Got it? **Do this problem to find out.**

a. The line graphs show monthly profits of a company from October to March. Which graph suggests that the business is extremely profitable? Is this a valid conclusion? Explain.

Graph A

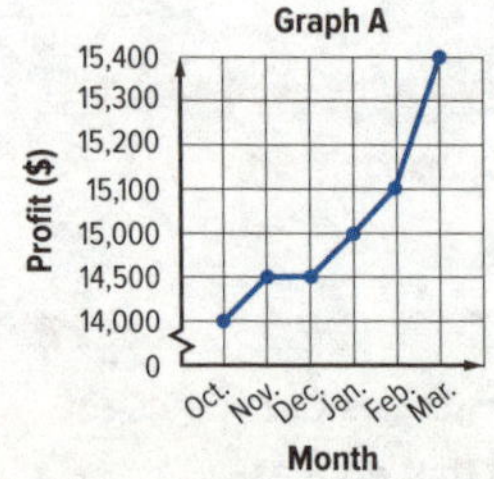

Graph B

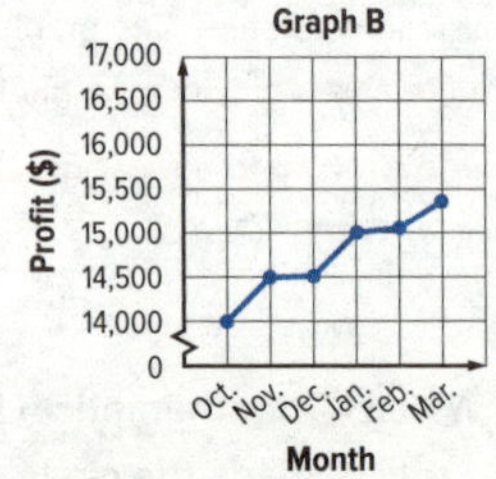

Show your work.

a. Sample answer: Although both graphs show a profit, in Graph A, the increase in profits is exaggerated due to the intervals of both $500 and $100.

Misleading Statistics

Statistics can also be used to influence conclusions.

Example

2. **An amusement park boasts that the average height of their roller coasters is 170 feet. Explain how this might be misleading.**

Park Roller Coaster Heights	
Coaster	Height (ft)
Viper	109
Monster	135
Red Zip	115
Tornado	365
Riptide	126

Mean $\frac{109 + 135 + 115 + 365 + 126}{5} = \frac{850}{5}$

$= 170$

Median 109, 115, 126, 135, 365

Mode none

The average used by the park was the mean. This measure is much greater than most of the heights listed because of the coaster that is 365 feet. So, it is misleading to use this measure to attract visitors.

A more appropriate measure to describe the data is the median, 126 feet, which is closer to the height of most of the coasters.

Mode

The mode is the number or numbers that appear most often in a set of data.

Got it? **Do this problem to find out.**

b. Find the mean, median, and mode of the sofa prices shown in the table. Which measurement might be misleading in describing the average cost of a sofa? Explain.

Sofa Prices	
Sofa Style	Cost
leather	$1,700
reclining	$1,400
DIY assembly	$350
sectional	$1,600
micro-fiber	$1,400

Show your work.

b. mean: $1,290; median: $1,400; mode: $1,400; Sample answer: The mean would be misleading because the value of the mean is lower than most of the data.

IWB

Example

2. **Explain how statistics may be misleading.**

AL

- *What measures can we use that can be represented by the term "average"?* the measures of center: mean, median, and mode
- *What is the mean height of the roller coasters?* 170 feet
- *What is the median height of the roller coasters?* 126 feet
- *Is there a mode?* no

OL

- *Which measure did the park use to describe the average?* the mean
- *Why is the mean not an appropriate measure to use?* It is affected by the data value of 365 feet.
- *Why would the median be a more appropriate measure to use?* Sample answer: It is not affected by 365 feet.

BL

- *Why do you think the amusement park might want to use the mean to describe the average height of the roller coasters?* Sample answer: They have one roller coaster that is very tall. By using the mean, the average is affected by the outlier and it makes it seem that they have higher roller coasters.
- *What is the mean height, not including the Tornado outlier?* about 121 feet

Need Another Example?

Michael and Melissa both claim to be earning a C average—70% to 79%—in their Latin class. One student is wrong. Which one? Explain how he or she is using a misleading statistic. Michael is wrong. He claimed to be earning a C because the median of his test grades was 70%. But his mean, or average, is much less than 70%.

Test	Michael's Grades (%)	Melissa's Grades (%)
1	80	88
2	76	83
3	73	75
4	70	70
5	40	60
6	25	65
7	10	62

	Michael	Melissa
mean	53.4%	71.9%
median	70%	70%

Guided Practice

Formative Assessment Use these exercises to assess students' understanding of the concepts in this lesson.

If some of your students are not ready for assignments, use the differentiated activities below.

AL **EL** **Three Stay, One Stray** Arrange students in groups of 4 students, with each student numbered 1–4. Have groups complete Exercise 1. Upon completion of the exercise, have one student stray to a new group to compare responses and discuss and resolve any discrepancies. The new group then completes Exercise 2. Upon completion, have a different student stray to a new group to compare responses. Repeat this step for each exercise. Upon completion of all four exercise, have the students return to their original groups to finalize responses. MP 1, 3

BL **EL** **Trade-a-Problem** Have students work with a partner to create a graph that is misleading. Then have them trade their graphs with another pair of students. Each pair of students determines why the graph is misleading. Pairs discuss and resolve any discrepancies. MP 1, 4

Watch Out!

Common Error Remind students that when figures are used in graphs to represent quantities, they should be drawn to scale. Otherwise, the representations are not accurate, as in the graph in lesson opener.

Guided Practice

Check

1. The graph suggests that Cy Young had three times as many wins as Jim Galvin. Is this a valid conclusion? Explain. (Example 1)

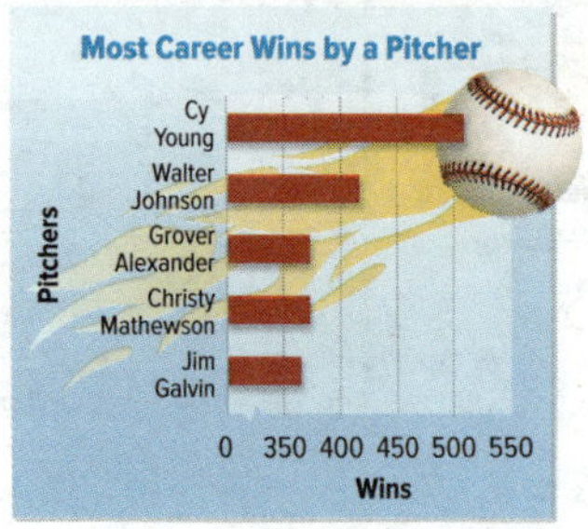

From the length of the bars, it appears that Cy Young had about 3 times as many wins as Jim Galvin. However, Jim Galvin had 365 wins and Cy Young had 511 wins. So, the conclusion is not valid.

2. The graph at the right shows the results of a survey to determine students' favorite pets. Why is the graph misleading? (Example 1)

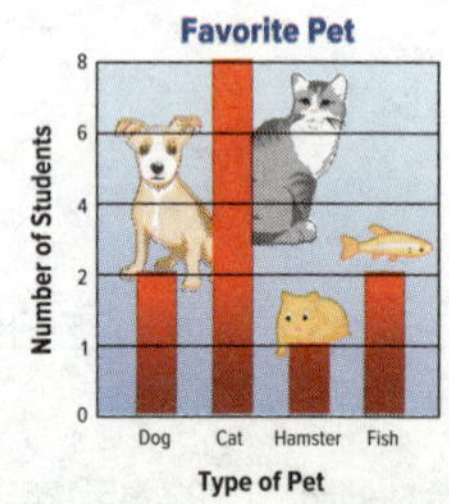

Sample answer: The intervals do not break the scale into equal sections. It appears that there are only 3 more students that voted for cats than dogs, but there are actually 6 more votes.

3. The table lists the five largest land vehicle tunnels in the United States. Write a convincing argument for which measure of center you would use to emphasize the average length of the tunnels. (Example 2)

U.S. Vehicle Tunnels	Length (ft)
Anton Anderson Memorial	13,300
E. Johnson Memorial	8,959
Eisenhower Memorial	8,941
Allegheny	6,072
Liberty Tubes	5,920

Sample answer: The mean is 8,638 and the median is 8,941. Since the median is greater than the mean, use the median to emphasize the average length.

4. **Building on the Essential Question** Describe at least two ways in which the display of data can influence the conclusions reached.

Sample answer: Outliers may distort measures of center; data shown in graphs may be exaggerated or minimized by manipulating scales and intervals.

Rate Yourself!

How well do you understand misleading graphs and statistics? Circle the image that applies.

Clear | Somewhat Clear | Not So Clear

For more help, go online to access a Personal Tutor.

Tutor

Name ______________________ My Homework ______________________

Independent Practice

Go online for Step-by-Step Solutions eHelp

1 Which graph could be used to indicate a greater increase in monthly gas prices? Explain. (Example 1)

Show your work.

Graph B; Sample answer: The ratio of the area of the gas pumps in the graph on the right are not proportional to the cost of gas.

Graph A

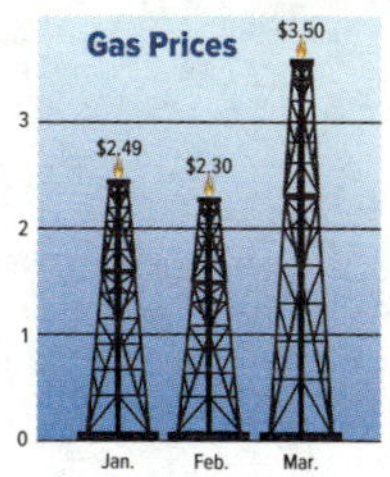

Graph B

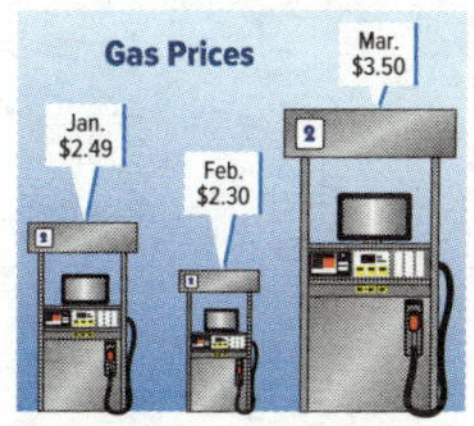

For Exercises 2 and 3, use the table. (Example 2)

Annual Sight-Seeing Visitors	
Sight	**Visitors**
Cape Cod	4,600,000
Grand Canyon	4,500,000
Lincoln Memorial	4,000,000
Castle Clinton	4,600,000
Smoky Mountains	10,200,000

2. Find the mean, median, and mode of the data. Which measure might be misleading in describing the average annual number of visitors who visit these sights? Explain.

5,580,000; 4,600,000; 4,600,000; The mean because the value of the mean is much higher in value than most of the data.

3 Which measure would be best if you wanted a value close to the most number of visitors? Explain.

The median or the mode because they are much closer in value to most of the data.

4. MP **Model with Mathematics** Refer to the graphic novel frame below. Which measure of center should the students use? Mode; The mode is 116° F. Since this measure of center is higher than the mean and median, it will greater emphasize how hot the weather is in Phoenix.

ENGAGE EXPLORE **EXPLAIN** **ELABORATE** **EVALUATE**

3 Practice and Apply

Independent Practice and Extra Practice

The Independent Practice pages are meant to be used as the homework assignment. The Extra Practice page can be used for additional reinforcement or as a second-day assignment.

Levels of Complexity

The levels of the exercises progress from 1 to 3, with Level 1 indicating the lowest level of complexity.

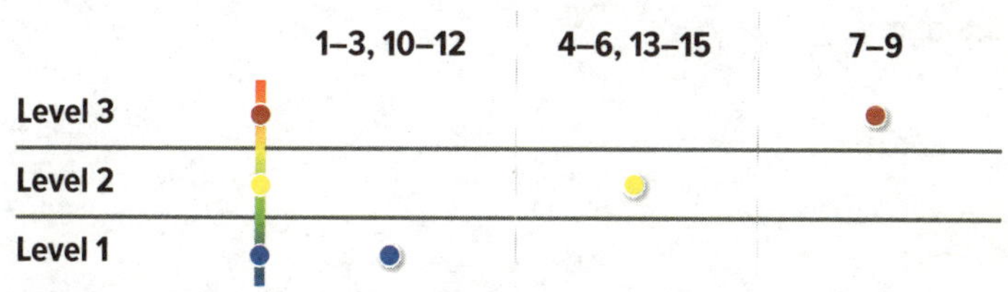

Suggested Assignments

You can use the table below that includes exercises of all complexity levels to select appropriate exercises for your students' needs.

Differentiated Homework Options		
AL	Approaching Level	1–5, 7, 9, 14, 15
OL	On Level	1, 3–7, 9, 14, 15
BL	Beyond Level	4–9, 14, 15

McGraw Hill Education ALEKS® can provide additional remediation support with personalized instruction and practice.

MATHEMATICAL PRACTICES

Emphasis On	Exercise(s)
1 Make sense of problems and persevere in solving them.	8
3 Construct viable arguments and critique the reasoning of others.	7, 9, 12
4 Model with mathematics.	4

Mathematical Practices 1, 3, and 4 are aspects of mathematical thinking that are emphasized in every lesson. Students are given opportunities to be persistent in their problem solving, to express their reasoning, and apply mathematics to real-world situations.

Formative Assessment

Use this activity as a closing formative assessment before dismissing students from your class.

TICKET Out the Door

Have students list some of the things they should look for when determining whether a graph or statistical measure is misleading. See students' work.

For Exercises 5 and 6, create a display that would support each argument. The monthly costs to rent an apartment for the last five years are $500, $525, $560, $585, and $605.

5. Rent has remained fairly stable.

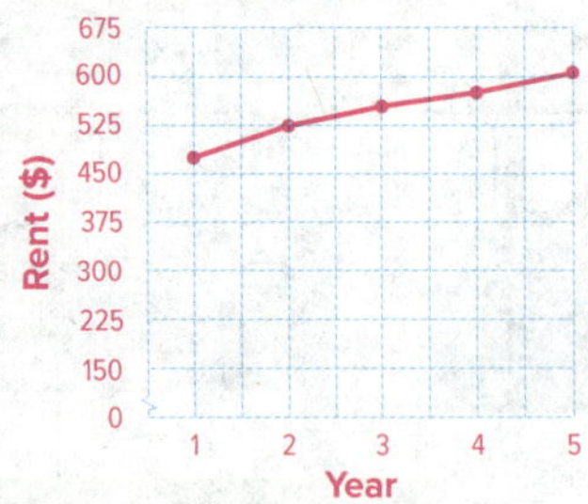

6. Rent has increased dramatically.

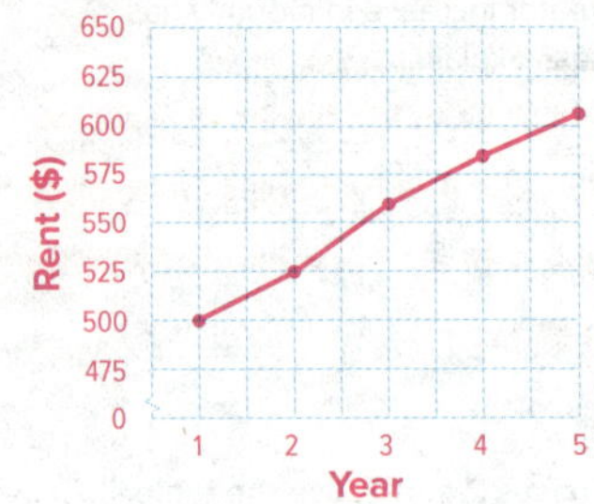

H.O.T. Problems Higher Order Thinking

7. MP **Reason Inductively** How could the graph you created in Exercise 5 help influence someone's decision to rent the apartment?

Sample answer: Since the graph makes it seem as if rent has been stable, a person may choose to become a tenant.

8. MP **Persevere with Problems** Does adding values that are much greater or much less than the other values in a set of data affect the median of the set? Give an example to support your answer.

Not usually; for example, the median of 9, 10, 11, 12, 100 is the same as the median of 9, 10, 11, 12, 13. However, the median of 1, 17, 23 is not the same as the median of 1, 17, 23, 400.

9. MP **Reason Inductively** The circle graph shows the results of a survey. In what way is this graph misleading? Explain.

Sample answer: The graph makes it appear that the Fall section is greater than the Spring section. This is because the perspective of the graph makes it appear greater, when, in fact , they are equal in size.

Favorite Time of Year

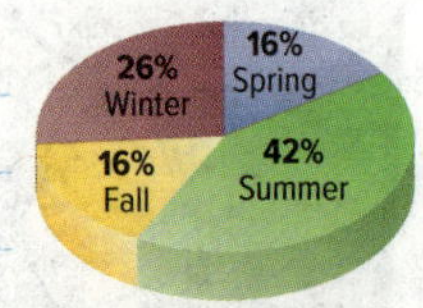

Name ________________ My Homework ________________

Extra Practice

10. To determine how often his students are tardy, Mr. Kessler considered the attendance record for his first period class. Why is this graph misleading?

Homework Help

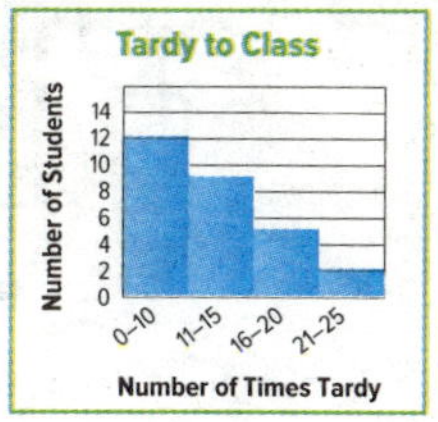

There are not equal intervals on the horizontal axis. So, the height of the bars is not representative of the sample.

11. The graph shows the height of a plant after 9 weeks of growth. Why is the graph misleading?

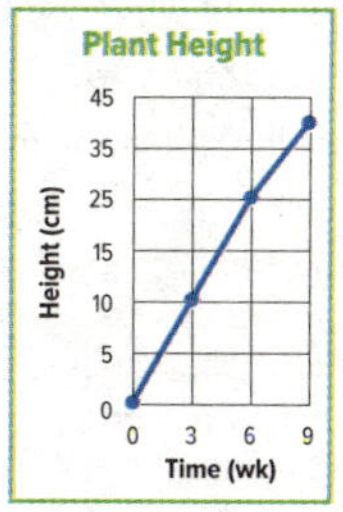

Sample answer: The scale of the graph is not divided into equal intervals, so differences in heights appear less than they actually are.

12. MP **Justify Conclusions** Each of the graphs below show the distance Romerio travels on his bike. Romerio wants to impress his friends with the distance he travels. Which graph should he show his friends? Explain.

Graph A

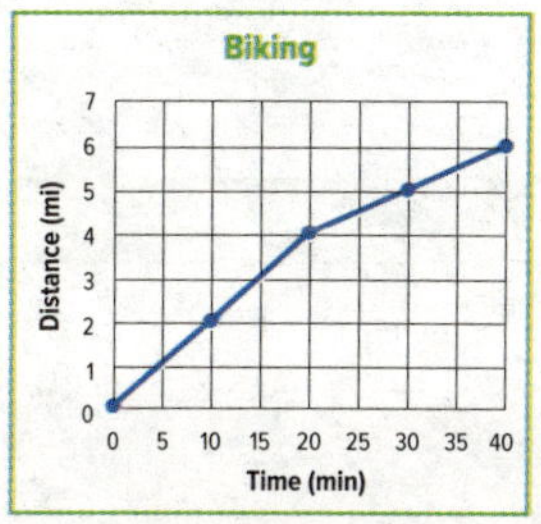

Graph B

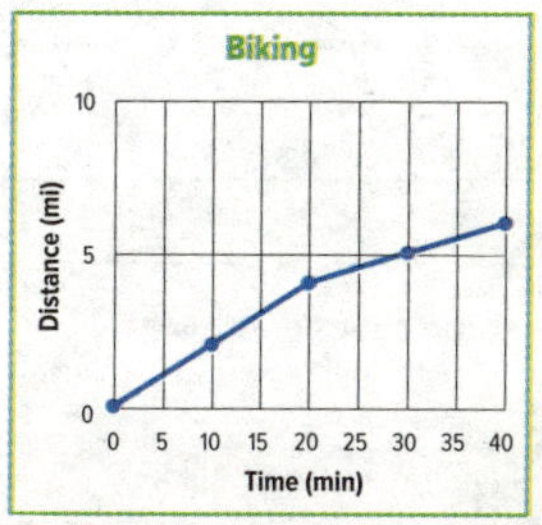

Sample answer: Romerio should show his friends Graph A because it shows the increase of the distance better than Graph B. The scale of Graph B makes it hard to determine the change in distance.

13. The scores Emily received on her math tests were 80, 90, 85, 100, 100, and 84. Why might it be misleading for Emily to say that most of the time she receives a score of 100?

Sample answer: The mode is 100, but she only received 100 two times out of 6 tests.

Create Your Own Homework Online

eSolutionsManual™ can be used to create worksheets for the suggested assignments on page 817, or create your own worksheets for differentiated homework or review.

Power Up! Test Practice

Exercises 14 and 15 prepare students for more rigorous thinking needed for the State assessment.

14.

This test item requires students to support their reasoning or evaluate the reasoning of others by justifying their response and constructing arguments.	
Depth of Knowledge	DOK3
Content Standard	7.SP.1
Mathematical Practices	MP1, MP3
Online Experience	Students will be required to type their responses in the boxes.
Scoring Rubric	
2 points	Students determine how many more minutes per month and fully explain why the display might be misleading.
1 point	Students determine how many more minutes per month OR fully explain why the display might be misleading.

15.

This test item requires students to explain and apply mathematical concepts and solve problems with precision, while making use of structure.	
Depth of Knowledge	DOK1
Content Standard	7.SP.1
Mathematical Practice	MP1
Online Experience	Students will be required to click on the bubbles to select all answers that are correct.
Scoring Rubric	
1 point	Students correctly answer the question.

Power Up! Test Practice

14. Phones For All uses the display shown at the right to compare the number of minutes that they offer per month versus their competitor.

a. How many more minutes per month does Phones For All offer than its competitor? **225 min**

b. Why might the display be misleading?

Sample answer: The display might be misleading because the phone used for Phones For All's information is much larger than the one used for Phonetastic, which might make it seem like the difference in minutes offered is larger than it actually is.

15. The graph shows the average number of hours each week that certain students spend on extracurricular activities after school. Which of the following describe reasons why the graph may be misleading? Select all that apply.

- ☐ The graph does not show the number of hours each student spent on extracurricular activities.
- ■ The intervals on the vertical scale are inconsistent.
- ☐ The graph's title is misleading.

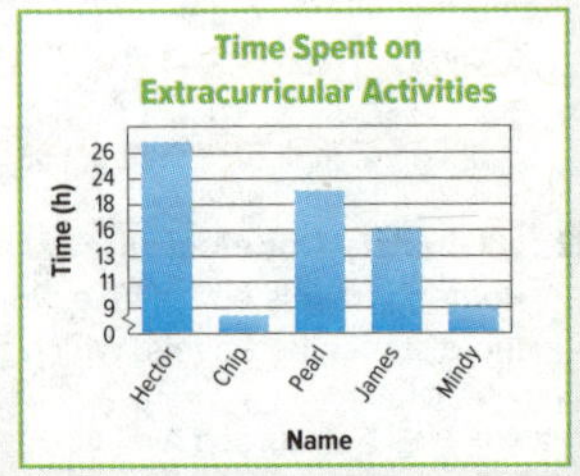

Spiral Review

Draw a histogram to represent the set of data. 6.SP.4

16.

Test Scores		
Percent	**Tally**	**Frequency**
50–59	|	1
60–69	||	2
70–79	||||	4
80–89	𝍸 𝍸 |	11
90–99	𝍸 |||	8

Show your work.

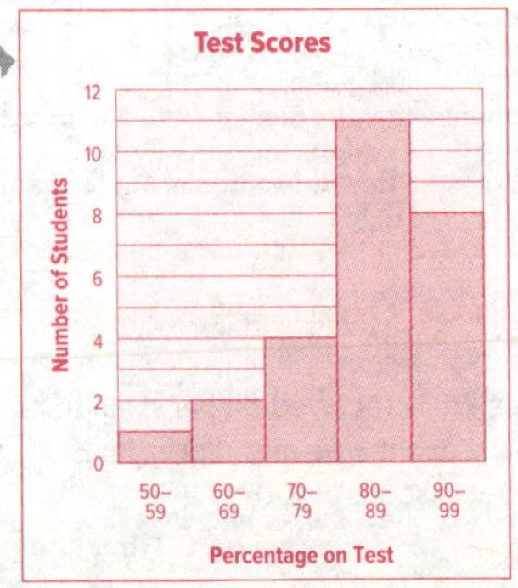

PLAN ONLINE: PD | RtI | Watch | Worksheets | Vocab | Tutor | Tools | Check | English Learners | Sketchpad

PRESENT: IWB — **An Interactive Whiteboard Ready presentation is available for each lesson in the chapter.**

MP **Problem-Solving Investigation**

Use a Graph

Content Standards
7.SP.1

MP Mathematical Practices
1, 3, 4

Case #1 Fishy Waters

Tess recently purchased a saltwater aquarium. She needs to add 1 tablespoon of sea salt for every 5 gallons of water.

Sea Salt Requirements						
Tablespoons of Sea Salt	1	2	3	4	5	6
Capacity of Tank (gallons)	5	10	15	20	25	30

How can she use a graph to show the number of tablespoons of salt required for a 50-gallon saltwater fish tank?

1 Understand *What are the facts?*

You know the number of gallons of the tank. You need to show the number of tablespoons of sea salt.

2 Plan *What is your strategy to solve this problem?*

Organize the rest of the data in a graph so you can easily see any trends.

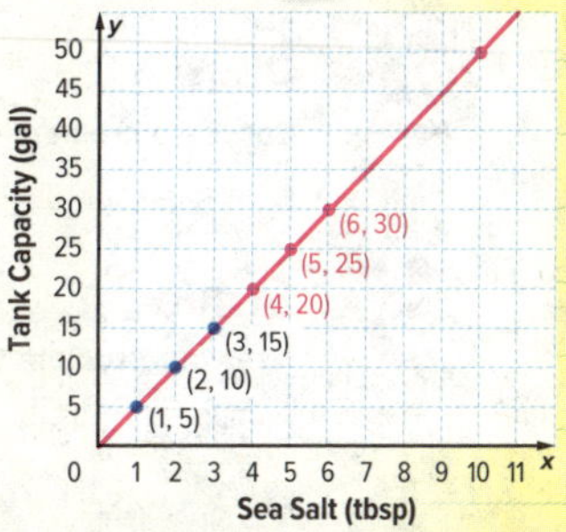

3 Solve *How can you apply the strategy?*

Continue the graph until you align horizontally with 50 gallons. Graph a point. What value of sea salt corresponds with the point?

10 tbsp

4 Check *Does the answer make sense?*

Find the unit rate of tablespoons of sea salt per gallon of water. Multiply the unit rate by the number of gallons to find the number of tablespoons of sea salt.

$$\frac{0.2 \text{ tbsp salt}}{1 \text{ gal water}} \times \frac{50 \text{ gal water}}{1} = \boxed{10} \text{ tbsp salt } ✓$$

Analyze the Strategy (Tutor)

MP **Make a Prediction** Suppose the tank holds 32 gallons. Predict how much sea salt is required.

about $6\frac{1}{2}$ tablespoons

Focus narrowing the scope

Objective Solve problems by using a graph. This lesson emphasizes MP **Mathematical Practice 4** Model with Mathematics.

Use a Graph Students have learned to solve problems and make inferences about data by analyzing graphs. Students will use this to make predictions from line graphs and scatter plots.

Coherence connecting within and across grades

Now
Students solve non-routine problems.

Next
Students will apply the Use a Graph strategy to compare different populations.

Rigor pursuing concepts, fluency, and applications

See the Levels of Complexity chart on page 823.

ENGAGE EXPLORE EXPLAIN ELABORATE EVALUATE

1 Launch the Lesson

The problems on pages 821 and 822 are intended to be used as a whole-group discussion on how to solve non-routine problems and are designed to provide scaffolded guidance. The problem on page 821 walks students through the solution, while the problem on page 822 asks students to come up with their own solutions.

Case #1 Fishy Waters

BL Have students extend the problem by having them answer the question below.

Ask:

- *Why is a line graph appropriate in this case, as opposed to a bar graph?* Sample answer: There can be partial gallons of water or partial tablespoons of salt and a line graph shows continuous numbers. A bar graph would only be appropriate if the tank could have only whole numbers of gallons or tablespoons.

Case #2 Calories

AL **EL** **Talking Chips** Have students work in groups to complete the problem. Give each student 5 chips. Each time a student contributes to the discussion, they must place a chip in the center of the table. Once they have used all of their chips, they may no longer contribute to the discussion. All students must use all their chips. MP 1, 5, 8

Need Another Example?
Based on the information in the table, how many VCRs would you expect to be sold in 2015?

Year	2003	2004	2005	2006	2007	2008	2009	2010
VCRs Sold (millions)	65	63	64	52	44	12	7	4

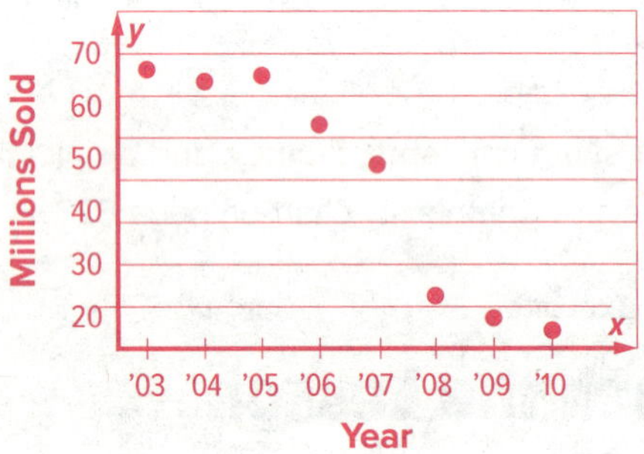

The graph shows a rapid downward trend. If it continued, no VCRs would be sold in 2015.

Case #2 Calories

The table shows the average number of Calories burned while sleeping for various numbers of hours. Assume the trend continues.

Calories Burned While Sleeping	
Hours	**Calories**
6	386
7	450
8	514
9	579

Make a graph to determine the approximate number of Calories that are burned by sleeping for 10 hours.

1 Understand

Read the problem. What are you being asked to find?

I need to find how many Calories are burned while sleeping for 10 hours.

What information do you know?

There is an average of 386 Calories burned while sleeping for 6 hours and 514 Calories burned while sleeping for 8 hours.

2 Plan

Choose a problem-solving strategy.

I will use the use a graph strategy.

3 Solve

Use your problem-solving strategy to solve the problem.

Continue the graph until it is aligned vertically with 10 hours. Graph a point. Find what value of Calories corresponds with the point. So, about 645 Calories are burned while sleeping for 10 hours.

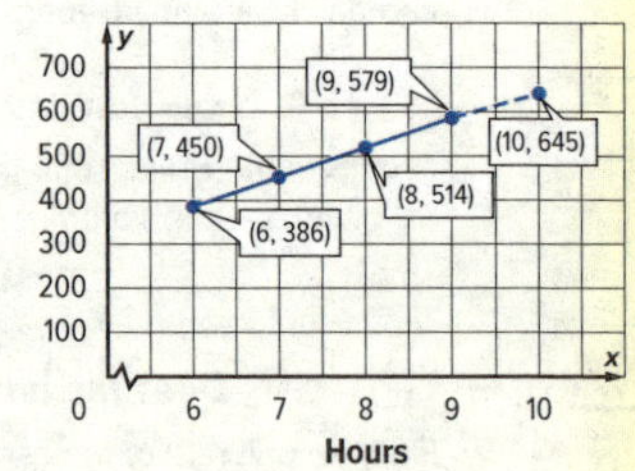

4 Check

Review the data in the table.

450 − 386 = 64; 514 − 450 = 64; 579 − 514 = 65. 645 − 579 = 66.

So, the answer seems reasonable.

Statistics and Probability

Collaborate

Work with a small group to solve the following cases. Show your work on a separate piece of paper.

Case #3 Postage

The table shows the postage stamp rate from 1999 to 2009.

Make a graph of the data. Predict the year the postage rate will reach $0.52.

Sample answer: 2017

Postage Stamp Rates	
Year	**Cost ($)**
1999	0.33
2001	0.34
2002	0.37
2006	0.39
2007	0.41
2008	0.42
2009	0.44

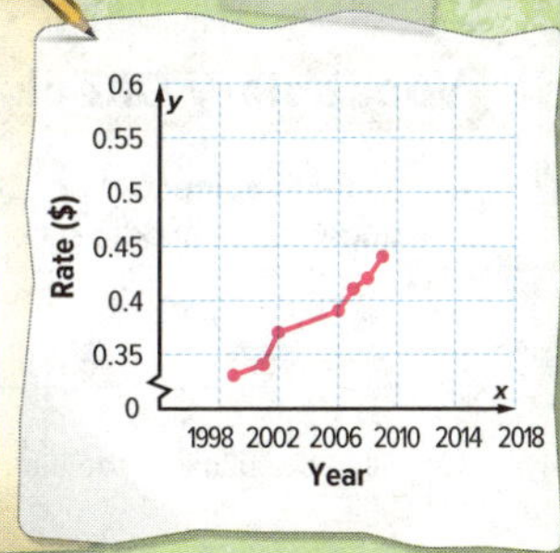

Case #4 Trains

The lengths of various train rides are 4, 1, 2, 3, 6, 2, 3, 2, 5, 8, and 4 hours.

Draw a box plot for the data set. What percent of the train rides are longer than 3 hours?

50%

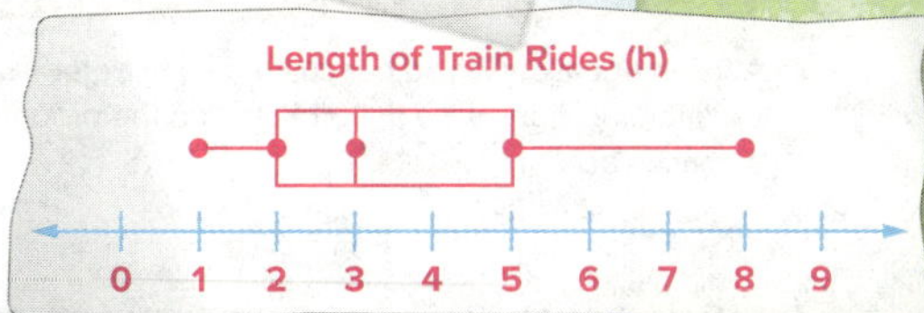

Case #5 Advertising

A local newspaper charges $14.50 for every three lines of a classified ad plus a 7% sales tax.

What is the cost of a 7-line ad? Round to the nearest hundredth.

$36.20

Use any strategy!

Case #6 Anatomy

Each human hand has 27 bones. There are 6 more bones in the fingers than in the wrist. There are 3 fewer bones in the palm than in the wrist.

How many bones are in each part of the hand?

bones in wrist: 8; bones in fingers: 14; bones in palm: 5

ENGAGE EXPLORE **EXPLAIN** **ELABORATE** EVALUATE

2 Collaborate

Levels of Complexity

The levels of the exercises progress from 1 to 3, with Level 1 indicating the lowest level of complexity.

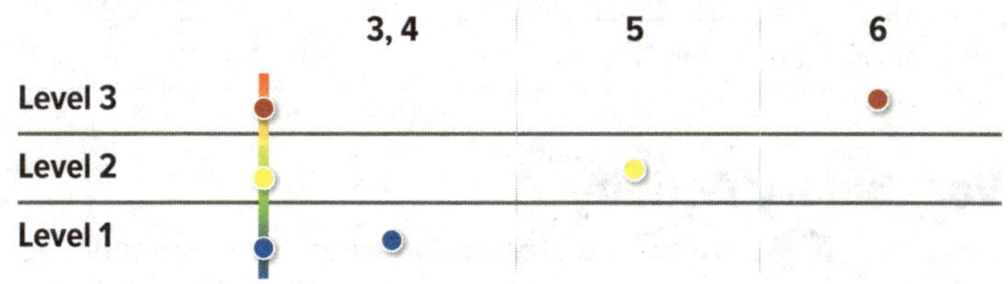

AL EL **Rally Coach** Have students work in pairs to complete Cases 3–6. Have Student 1 complete Case 3, speaking aloud, while Student 2 listens carefully, coaches, and praises. Have students trade roles for each exercise. MP 1, 5

BL EL **Trade-a-Problem** Have students use the Internet or another source to locate information that can be used to create their own real-world problem similar to Case 6. Have students trade their problems, solve each other's problem, and compare solutions. If the solutions do not agree, students work together to find the errors. MP 1, 4, 5

Mid-Chapter Check

If students have trouble with Exercises 1–7, they may need help with the following concepts.

Concept	Exercise(s)
make predictions from data (Lesson 1)	1, 3, 4, 6
biased and unbiased samples (Lesson 2)	2, 7
misleading data (Lesson 3)	5

Vocabulary Activity

EL **Numbered Heads Together** Have students work in small groups to complete Exercise 1. Each student is assigned a number. Students are responsible to ensure that each group member understands the meaning of a sample. Students should ask each other for clarification and assistance, as needed. Call on one numbered student to share their definition with the class. MP 1, 6

McGraw Hill Education **ALEKS®** provides additional remediation support with personalized instruction and practice for those who are struggling, while providing enhanced learning for those who have mastered the concepts.

Alternate Strategies

AL EL Have students refer back to Lesson 2 to review unbiased and biased samples. Have students think of additional examples of each type of sample. Remind students that making an inference is the same as making a conclusion about something. MP 1, 6, 7

BL EL Have students design and conduct an unbiased sample based on their example given. Then give a brief oral presentation of their results to their classmates. MP 1, 4, 7

Mid-Chapter Check

Vocabulary Check

Vocab

1. MP **Be Precise** Define *sample*. Give an example of a sample of the students in a middle school. (Lesson 1)

   A sample is a smaller group of the population. Sample answer: every fourth student listed in the school directory

2. Fill in the blank in the sentence below with the correct terms. (Lesson 2)

   Simple random and systematic random are two types of unbiased samples.

Skills Check and Problem-Solving

3. A travel agent surveyed her customers to determine their favorite vacation locations. Use the table to find the probability of choosing a beach vacation. (Lesson 1)

   Show your work.

   $\frac{11}{25}$, 0.44, or 44%

Vacation Locations

Location	Customers
amusement park	2
beach	11
campground	8
national park	4

4. Refer to the table. Suppose 120 customers are planning vacations. Predict how many will plan a national park vacation. (Lesson 1)

   about 19

5. The number of points Emerson scored in 5 basketball games is 10, 8, 9, 8, and 30. Why might it be misleading for Emerson to say that she averages 13 points per game? (Lesson 3)

   Sample answer: The mean is 13, but she only scored over 10 points once in five games.

6. MP **Persevere with Problems** An online gaming site conducted a survey to determine the types of games people play online. The results are shown in the circle graph. If 1,500 people participated in the study, how many more would play card games than arcade games? (Lesson 1) 315 people

Games People Play Online

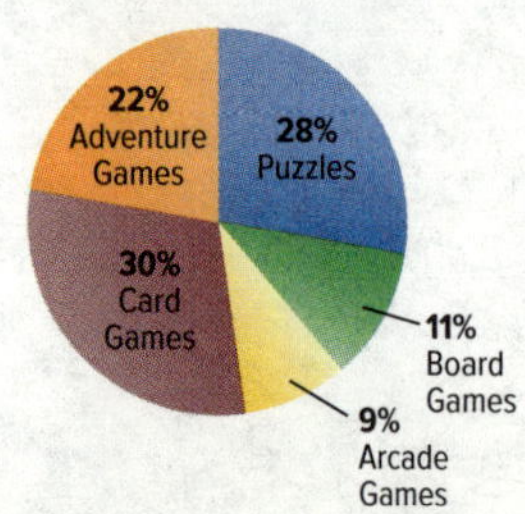

7. An owner of a restaurant wants to conduct a survey about possible menu changes. Give an example of a sampling method that would produce a valid sample. (Lesson 2)

   Sample answer: survey every fifth person entering the mall

PLAN ONLINE: PD | RtI | Watch | Worksheets | Vocab | Tutor | Tools | Check | English Learners | Sketchpad

PRESENT: IWB

An Interactive Whiteboard Ready presentation is available for each lesson in the chapter.

Inquiry Lab
Collect Data

Inquiry HOW can you use the measures of center and the range to compare two populations?

Content Standards 7.SP.3, 7.SP.4

MP Mathematical Practices 1, 3, 4

Studies show that teens need around 9 hours of sleep each night to stay healthy.

Hands-On Activity

Step 1 The results of a survey that asked 24 teens how many hours they slept last night are shown below. The teens were split into two populations, male and female.

Males	7	7	6	8	6	8	7	6	7	6	8	6
Females	8	8	7	6	8	7	6	6	7	8	9	7

Step 2 Graph the data for each population on a single line plot.

Number of Hours of Sleep

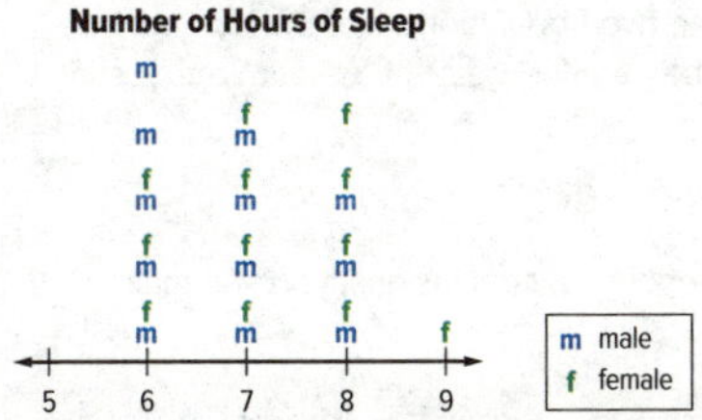

Step 3 Find the measures of center and range for each population.

	Mean	Median	Mode	Range
Males	$6.8\overline{3}$	7	6	2
Females	7.25	7	7 and 8	3

Are the data for males more or less varied than females?

less

Which measure most accurately represents the data of the whole class?

Explain. Sample answer: The median most accurately represents the data of the whole class because the value appears to be where most data are clustered.

Focus narrowing the scope

Objective Use measures of center and the range to compare two populations. 7.SP.3, 7.SP.4

Coherence connecting within and across grades

Now

Students use the measures of center and the range to compare two groups of numeric data.

Next

Students will compare two groups of numeric data using comparative dot plots or box plots by comparing their shapes, centers, and spreads.

Rigor pursuing concepts, fluency, and applications

See the Levels of Complexity chart on page 826.

ENGAGE EXPLORE EXPLAIN ELABORATE EVALUATE

1 Launch the Lab

The activity is intended to be used as a whole-group activity.

Hands-On Activity

BL EL **Think-Pair-Share** Give students one to two minutes to think about how they would perform the actions in Steps 1–3. Then arrange students in pairs to complete each step. Have students determine which measure of center will most accurately represent the whole class data. Have them justify their response. Call on one set of students to share their responses with the class. MP 1, 3, 5

2 Collaborate

The **Investigate** and **Analyze and Reflect** sections are intended to be used as small-group investigations. The **Create** section is intended to be used as independent exercises.

Levels of Complexity

The levels of the exercises progress from 1 to 3, with Level 1 indicating the lowest level of complexity.

	Exercises 1	Exercises 2–4	Exercises 5
Level 3			●
Level 2		●	
Level 1	●		

Investigate

Collaborate

AL **EL** **Solo to Pairs** Have the whole class brainstorm survey questions to complete the Investigate and Create section. Then assign questions to students (2 students with the same question) to survey their classmates. Each student generates a prediction and conducts the survey. Students with the same survey question will then form pairs to complete the remaining steps. MP 1, 4

Analyze and Reflect

Collaborate

AL **EL** **Pairs Check** In pairs, students will complete Exercises 2–4. One student submits the pair's answer for each exercise while the other student monitors and checks the work. Students alternate roles for each exercise. MP 1, 3

Create

On Your Own

Inquiry Students should be able to answer "HOW can you use the measures of center and the range to compare two populations?" Check for student understanding and provide guidance, if needed.

Investigate

Collaborate

1. Work with a partner to design your own survey that meets the following guidelines. **See students' work.**
   - Create a survey question that involves two populations. For example, you might want to know about how many hours of sleep per night male students get in your school versus female students. Write your survey question below.
   - Survey a random sample that is representative of your school's population. Survey at least 25 people. Collect the data and record your results in a table on a separate piece of paper.
   - Create a display of your data. Be sure that the display shows the two populations.

Analyze and Reflect

Collaborate

Work with a partner to complete the exercises below based on the data you collected above. **2–4. See students' work.**

2. Determine the measures of center (mean, median, and mode) and the range for each population's set of data.

3. MP **Reason Inductively** Compare the two populations. Are the data for one population more or less varied than the data for the other population? Justify your response.

4. Describe any other comparative inferences, or conclusions, you can make about differences in the two populations.

Create

On Your Own

5. Inquiry HOW can you use the measures of center and the range to compare two populations?

Sample answer: Gather numerical data from random samples. Graph the data to see how scattered it is. Determine which measure of center best represents the data.

PLAN ONLINE

PD | RtI | Watch | Worksheets | Vocab | Tutor | Tools | Check | English Learners | Sketchpad

PRESENT

IWB

An Interactive Whiteboard Ready presentation is available for each lesson in the chapter.

Lesson 4

Compare Populations

Real-World Link

Exercise Mr. Singh surveyed the students in his first period gym class to find out how many times they exercised this month. The box plot below shows the results.

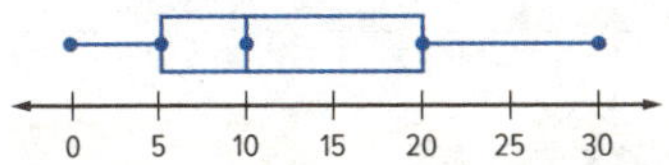

1. Find the following values.

Minimum: 0 First Quartile: 5

Maximum: 30 Third Quartile: 20

Range: 30 Interquartile Range: 15

2. What is the median? What does the median represent?
10; Half of the students exercised fewer than 10 times during the month and half exercised more than 10 times.

3. Write a conclusion that you can make from the box plot.
Sample answer: Twenty-five percent of the students exercised between 5 and 10 times.

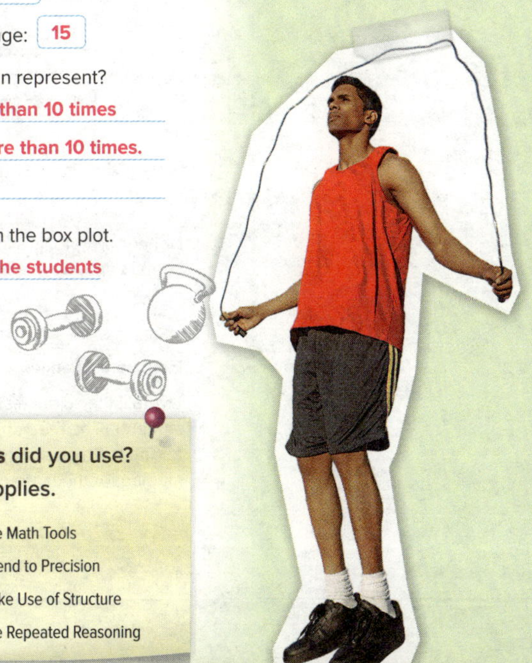

Essential Question

HOW do you know which type of graph to use when displaying data?

Vocabulary

double box plot
double dot plot

Content Standards
7.SP.4

MP Mathematical Practices
1, 3, 4, 6

Which **MP Mathematical Practices** did you use? Shade the circle(s) that applies.

① Persevere with Problems
② Reason Abstractly
③ Construct an Argument
④ Model with Mathematics
⑤ Use Math Tools
⑥ Attend to Precision
⑦ Make Use of Structure
⑧ Use Repeated Reasoning

Focus narrowing the scope

Objective Compare two populations. 7.SP.4

Coherence connecting within and across grades

Previous
Students used graphs to make predictions about a population.

Now
Students compare two sets of data using dot plots or box plots by comparing their shapes, centers, and spreads.

Next
Students will select an appropriate display to represent differents types of data.

Rigor pursuing concepts, fluency, and applications

See the Levels of Complexity chart on page 833.

ENGAGE EXPLORE EXPLAIN ELABORATE EVALUATE

1 Launch the Lesson

Ideas for Use

You may wish to launch the lesson using a whole group, small group, think-pair-share activity, or independent activity.

EL **Teammates Consult** Arrange students in groups of 3 to complete Exercises 1–3. Assign each teammate to lead the discussion on one exercise, ensuring that all teammates understand each exercise. Call on one teammate from each group to share their responses to the exercises. MP 1, 3, 7

Alternate Strategy

AL Students may benefit from a review of how to determine the quartiles and interquartile range of a box plot and what those measures indicate.

ENGAGE EXPLORE **EXPLAIN** ELABORATE EVALUATE

2 Teach the Concept

Ask the scaffolded questions for each example to differentiate instruction.

IWB

Example

1. Compare two populations.

AL
- *What does the top box plot show? the bottom plot?* **Math Class blogs; Science Class blogs**
- *Is either plot symmetrical? Explain.* **Neither plot is symmetrical, because the left side of each plot does not look like the right side.**

OL
- *Why do we use the median and interquartile range?* **because the plots are not symmetrical**
- *What is the median for each set of data?* **Math: 10; Science: 20**

BL
- *What do the medians tell you about the data?* **Sample answer: Science has a greater median, so overall, the science students posted more blogs.**
- *What do the interquartile ranges tell you about the data?* **Sample answer: The IQR is greater for math, so there is a greater spread, or variation, around the median for the math class than the science class.**

Need Another Example? Refer to the double box plot shown. Compare their centers and variations. Write an inference you can draw about the two populations.

Walk-a-thon Money Raised ($)

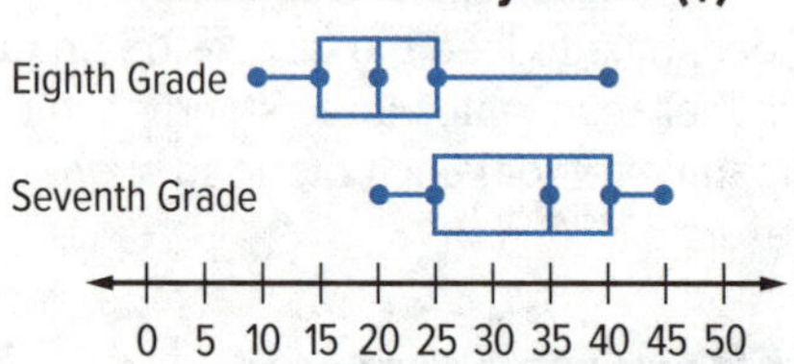

Sample answer: The median amount of money raised by the eighth graders is $20 with a variation of $10. The median amount of money raised by the seventh graders is $35 with a variation of $15. In general, the seventh graders raised more money than the eighth graders, but the variation is also greater, which means the amounts raised were more spread out.

Work Zone

Box plots

A box plot is symmetric if the data are balanced at the center.

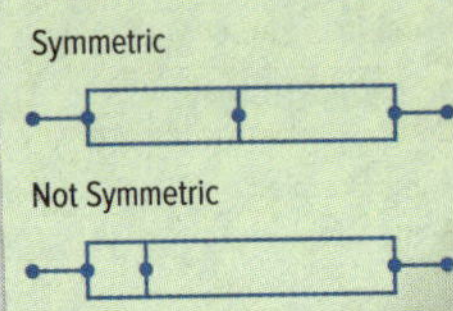

Compare Two Populations

A **double box plot** consists of two box plots graphed on the same number line. A **double dot plot** consists of two dot plots that are drawn on the same number line. You can draw inferences about two populations in a double box plot or double dot plot by comparing their centers and variations. The centers and variations to use are shown.

Most Appropriate Measures			
	Both sets of data are symmetric.	Neither set of data is symmetric.	Only one set of data is symmetric.
Measure of Center	mean	median	median
Measure of Variation	mean absolute deviation	interquartile range	interquartile range

Real World

Example

Tutor

1. Kacey surveyed a different group of students in her science and math classes. The double box plot shows the results for both classes. Compare their centers and variations. Write an inference you can draw about the two populations.

How Many Times Have You Posted A Blog This Month?

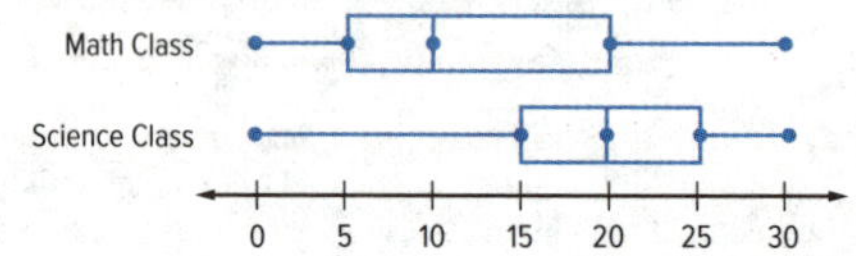

Neither box plot is symmetric. Use the median to compare the centers and the interquartile range to compare the variations.

	Math Class	Science Class
Median	10	20
Interquartile Range	20 − 5, or 15	25 − 15, or 10

Overall, the science students posted more blogs than the math students. The median for the science class is twice the median for the math class. There is a greater spread of data around the median for the math class than the science class.

Got it? Do this problem to find out.

Show your work.

a. The double box plot shows the costs of MP3 players at two different stores. Compare the centers and variations of the two populations. Write an inference you can draw about the two populations.

Cost of MP3 Players ($)

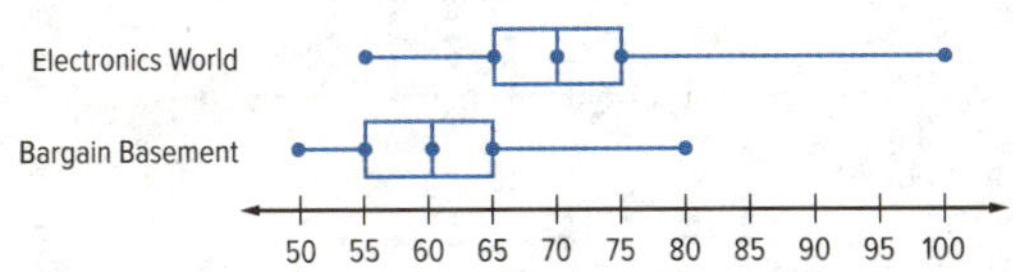

a. Sample answer: The median price at Electronics World is $10 more than at Bargain Basement. The interquartile range is the same for both stores, $10. Generally, MP3 players are more expensive at Electronics World.

Real World

Example

Tutor

2. The double dot plot below shows the daily high temperatures for two cities for thirteen days. Compare the centers and variations of the two populations. Write an inference you can draw about the two populations.

Daily High Temperatures (°F)

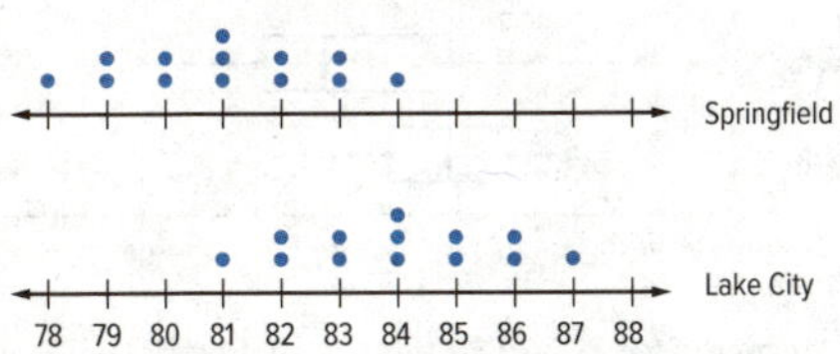

Both dot plots are symmetric. Use the mean to compare the centers and use the mean absolute deviation, rounded to the nearest tenth, to compare the variations.

	Springfield	Lake City
Mean	81	84
Mean Absolute Deviation	1.4	1.4

While both cities have the same variation, or spread of data about each of their means, Lake City has a greater mean temperature than Springfield.

Mean Absolute Deviation

To find the mean absolute deviation, find the absolute values of the differences between each value and the mean. Then find the average of those differences.

IWB

Example

2. Compare two populations.

AL
- *What does each plot show?* The top plot shows the daily high temperatures for Springfield; the bottom shows the daily high temperatures for Lake City.
- *How many data values are reported on each plot?* 13

OL
- *Are the plots symmetrical? Explain.* yes; Both plots are symmetrical because the left side of each plot looks like the right side.
- *Why do we use the mean as the measure of center?* the plots are symmetrical
- *Which city has a greater mean temperature?* Lake City
- *Describe the spread of data for the cities.* They both have the same variation, or spread of data, around the center.

BL
- *In these examples, describe how the medians compare to the means.* The medians and means are equivalent.

Need Another Example?

The double dot plot shows the daily number of fruit smoothies sold at two different places during a two-week period. Compare the shapes, centers, and spreads of the two populations. Write an inference you can draw about the two populations.

Number of Fruit Smoothies Sold

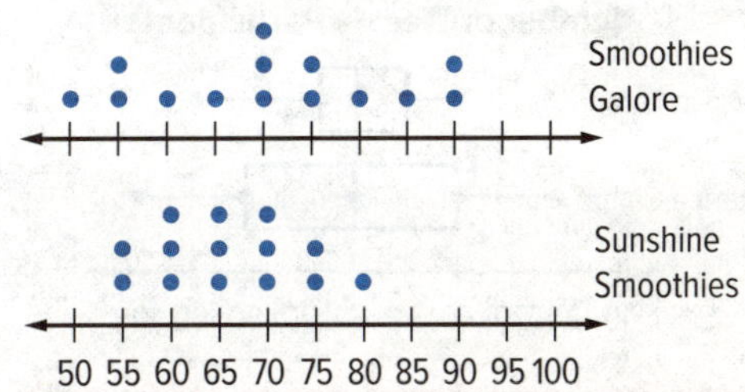

Sample answer: Neither plot is symmetric. The median of Smoothies Galore's data is 70 with a variation of 20. The median for Sunshine Smoothie's data is 65 with a variation of 10. So, Sunshine Smoothies generally sells fewer fruit smoothies per day, but there is less variation, which means the numbers sold at Sunshine Smoothies are more consistent than the numbers sold at Smoothies Galore.

IWB

Example

3. Compare two populations.

AL • *Is either plot symmetrical?* Zip Adventures is symmetrical, but Treetop Tours is not symmetrical.

• *Which measure of center should we use? Explain.* median; One of the data sets is not symmetrical.

OL • *What do the medians tell you about the data?* Sample answer: Treetop Tours has a greater number of daily participants overall.

• *What do the interquartile ranges tell you about the data?* Sample answer: Treetop Tours has a greater spread, or variation. It is more difficult to predict how many participants they may have each day.

• *What does the asterisk (*) at 125 mean?* It is an outlier.

BL • *How would the outlier affect the data?* The outlier would increase the mean.

• *What are some important measures that you cannot determine using a box plot?* Sample answers: the number of data values, the mean, the mode

Need Another Example?

The double box plot shows the number of weekly participants at two community center summer camps. Compare the centers and variations of the two populations. Which camp had the greater number of weekly participants?

Number of Weekly Participants

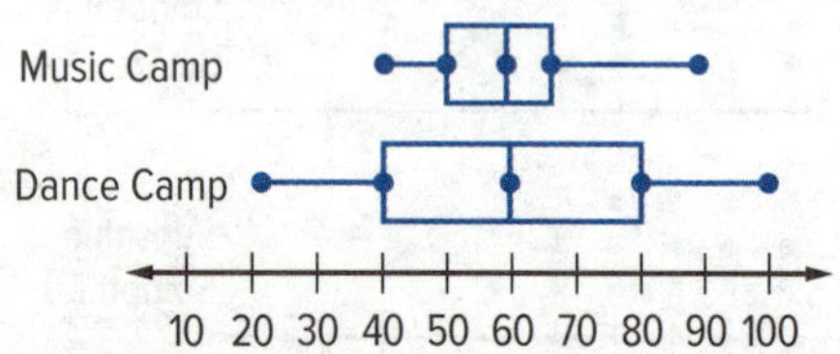

Sample answer: Both camps have a median of 60 weekly participants, but the dance camp has a greater variation. The music camp data is more consistent; Dance Camp had more participants.

Got it? Do this problem to find out.

b. The double dot plot shows the number of new E-mails in each of Pedro's and Annika's inboxes for sixteen days. Compare the centers and variations of the two populations. Write an inference you can draw about the two populations.

Number of E-mails in Inbox

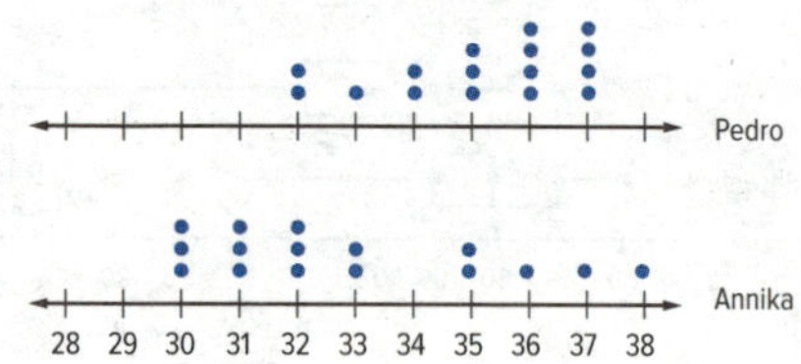

Show your work.

b. Sample answer: The median of Pedro's data is 35.5 E-mails with an interquartile range of 2.5 E-mails. The median for Annika's data is 32 E-mails with an interquartile range of 4 E-mails. There is a greater spead of data around Annika's E-mails, but Pedro's data centers around a higher number of E-mails. So, you normally would expect him to have more E-mails.

Real World

Examples

Tutor

3. The double box plot shows the daily participants for two zip line companies for one month. Compare the centers and variations of the two populations. Which company has the greater number of daily participants?

Number of Daily Participants

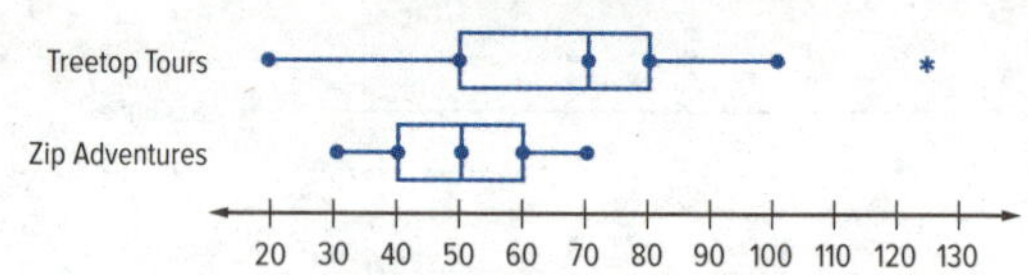

The distribution for Zip Adventures is symmetric, while the distribution for Treetop Tours is not symmetric. Use the median and the interquartile range to compare the populations.

	Treetop Tours	Zip Adventures
Median	70	50
Interquartile Range	30	20

Overall, Treetop Tours has a greater number of daily participants. However, Treetop Tours also has a greater variation, so it is more difficult to predict how many participants they may have each day. Zip Adventures has a greater consistency in their distribution.

STOP and Reflect

What can you tell about the set of data for Zip Adventures by looking at its box plot? Write your answer in the space below.

Sample answer: It is symmetrical.

4. The double dot plot shows Jada's and Angel's number of hours worked in two weeks at their part-time jobs. Compare the centers and variations of the two populations. Who typically works the greater number of hours in a week?

Hours Worked

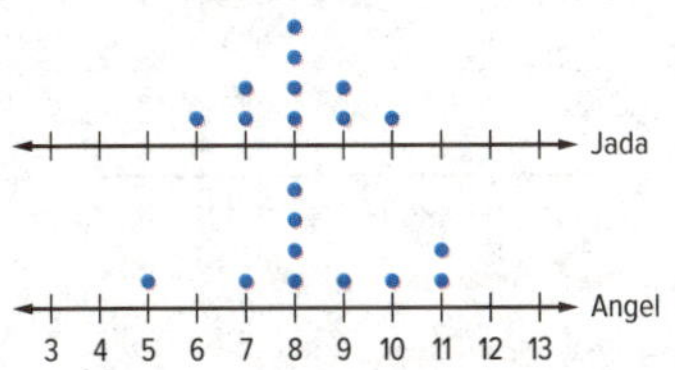

The distribution for Jada's number of hours is symmetric, while the distribution for Angel's number of hours is not symmetric. Use the median and interquartile range to compare the populations.

	Jada	Angel
Median	8	8
Interquartile Range	2	2

The median and interquartile range for both sets of data are the same. However, the interquartile range for Angel's number of hours worked is the difference of 10 and 8, while the interquartile range for Jada's number of hours is the difference of 9 and 7. So, Angel typically works more per week.

Got it? **Do this problem to find out.**

c. The double dot plot shows Kareem's and Martin's race times for a three-mile race. Compare the centers and variations of the two populations. Which runner is more likely to run a faster race?

Race Times (min)

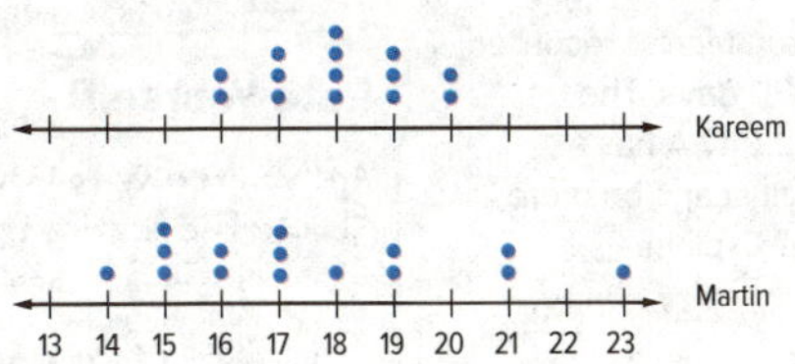

Show your work.

c. Martin; Sample answer: Kareem's data centers around 18 minutes with an interquartile range of 2 minutes. Martin's data centers around 17 minutes with an interquartile range of 4 minutes. So, Martin typically runs a faster race. However, his race times are not as consistent as Kareem's times.

IWB

Example

4. **Compare two populations.**

AL
- *Is either plot symmetrical?* Jada's dot plot is symmetrical, but Angel's dot plot is not symmetrical.
- *Which measure of center should we use? Explain.* median; One of the data sets is not symmetrical.

OL
- *What do the medians tell you about the data?* Sample answer: The medians are the same, so the data are centered around 8 hours worked for both Jada and Angel.
- *What do the interquartile ranges tell you about the data?* Sample answer: The IQRs are the same, but the IQR for Angel is the difference of 10 and 8, while the IQR for Jada is the difference of 9 and 7. So, Angel typically works more hours per week.

BL
- *Is the data value of 5 in Angel's dot plot an outlier? Explain.* Sample answer: It is not an outlier, but it is on the border for an outlier. If the data value were 4, it would be an outlier.

Need Another Example?

The double dot plot shows Katie's and Danielle's resting heart rates in beats per minute (bpm). Compare the shapes, centers, and spreads of the two populations. Which person typically would have a greater resting heat rate? Katie has a median heart rate of 66, and Danielle has a median heart rate of 71. Katie's heart rate varies more. Danielle has the greater resting heart rate.

Katie's Heart Rate (bpm)

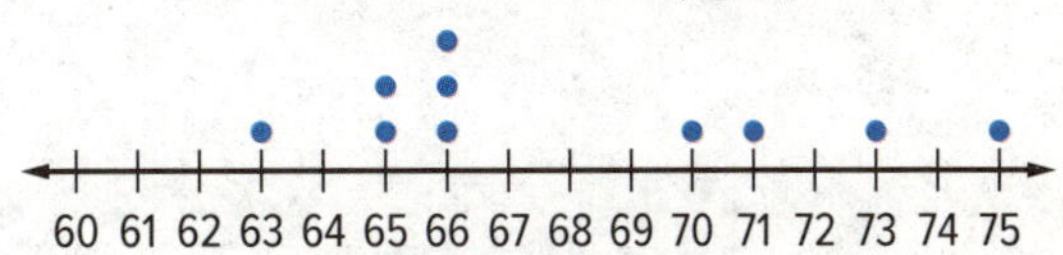

Danielle's Heart Rate (bpm)

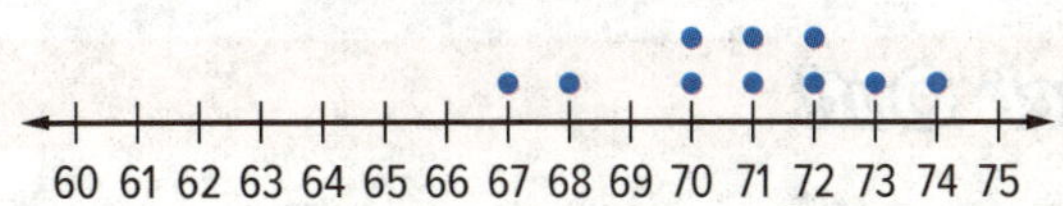

Guided Practice

Formative Assessment Use these exercises to assess students' understanding of the concepts in this lesson.

If some of your students are not ready for assignments, use the differentiated activity below.

AL EL **Team-Pair-Solo** Have students work in small teams to complete Exercise 1, ensuring that all team members contribute and understand how to compare two dot plots. Then have teams divide into pairs to complete Exercise 2, ensuring that both partners contribute and understand how to compare two box plots. Then have students work alone to think about how they would respond to Exercise 3. Have them rejoin their original team to discuss and compare responses to Exercises 1–3. If they are struggling, have them keep a list of the following guiding questions they can use to compare two populations. MP 1, 3, 7

Ask:

- *Are the plots symmetrical?* See students' work.
- *What measure of center should be used to compare the data? Why?* See students' work.
- *Which plot has a greater measure of center? What does this tell you about the data?* See students' work.
- *Which plot has a greater measure of spread? What does this tell you about the data?* See students' work.

Watch Out!

Common Error Students will need to review quartiles and interquartile range to solve problems in this lesson. Calculations in this lesson require a lot of space. Encourage students to use a separate sheet of paper to solve problems.

Guided Practice

Check

1. The double dot plot at the right shows the quiz scores out of 20 points for two different class periods. Compare the centers and variations of the two populations. Round to the nearest tenth. Write an inference you can draw about the two populations. (Examples 1 and 2)

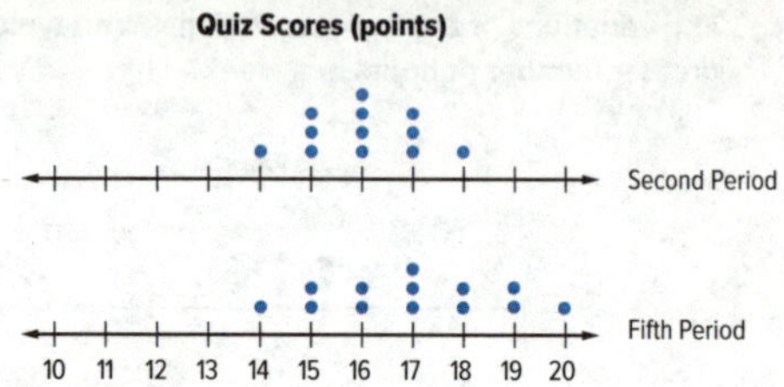

Show your work.

Sample answer: Second period's data has a mean of 16 points with a mean absolute deviation of about 0.8 points. Fifth period's data has a mean of 17 points with a mean absolute deviation of about 1.4 points. Fifth period's scores centered around a higher value. However, the variation is also greater, which means the scores were more spread out.

2. The double box plot shows the speeds of cars recorded on two different roads in Hamilton County. Compare the centers and variations of the two populations. On which road are the speeds greater? (Examples 3 and 4)

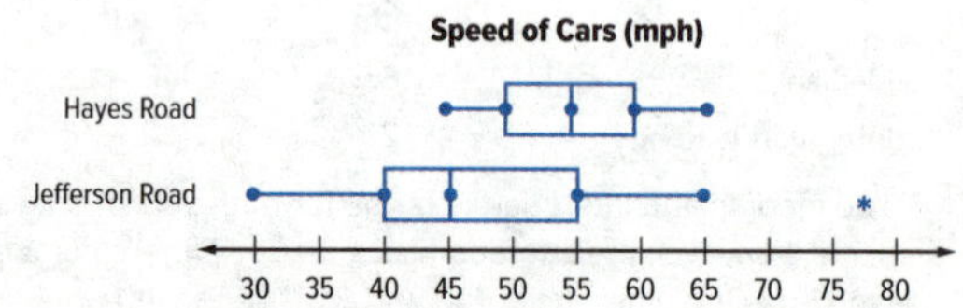

The speeds recorded on Hayes Road have a median of 55 miles per hour with an interquartile range of 10 miles per hour. Jefferson Road speeds have a median of 45 miles per hours with an interquartile range of 15 miles per hour. The Hayes Road speeds are centered around a higher value, but the variation is less. So, Hayes Road speeds are more consistent.

3. **Building on the Essential Question** Marcia recorded the daily temperatures for two cities for 30 days. The two populations have similar centers, but City A has a greater variation than City B. For which city can you more accurately predict the daily temperature? Explain.

City B; Sample answer: City A has a greater variation than City B, so its temperatures are more spread out. City B temperatures are more consistent. Predictions are made more accurately from consistent data.

Rate Yourself!

Are you ready to move on? Shade the section that applies.

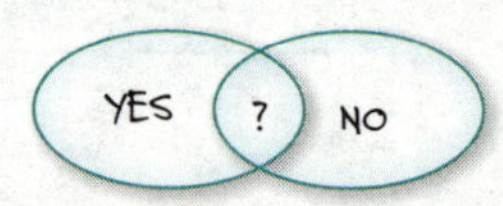

For more help, go online to access a Personal Tutor.

Tutor

Name ______________________ My Homework ______________________

Independent Practice

Go online for Step-by-Step Solutions eHelp

1. Jordan randomly asked customers at two different restaurants how long they waited for a table before they were seated. The double box plot shows the results. Compare their centers and variations. Write an inference you can draw about the two populations. (Examples 1 and 2)

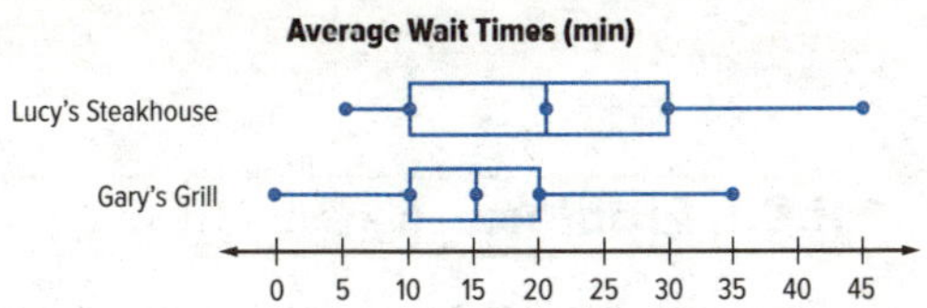

Show your work.

Sample answer: The times at Lucy's Steakhouse have a median of 20 minutes with an interquartile range of 20 minutes. The times at Gary's Grill have a median of 15 minutes with an interquartile range of 10 minutes. In general, a customer will wait longer at Lucy's Steakhouse.

2. The double dot plot shows the times, in hours, for flights of two different airlines flying out of the same airport. Compare the centers and variations of the two populations. Which airline's flights had shorter flight times? (Examples 3 and 4)

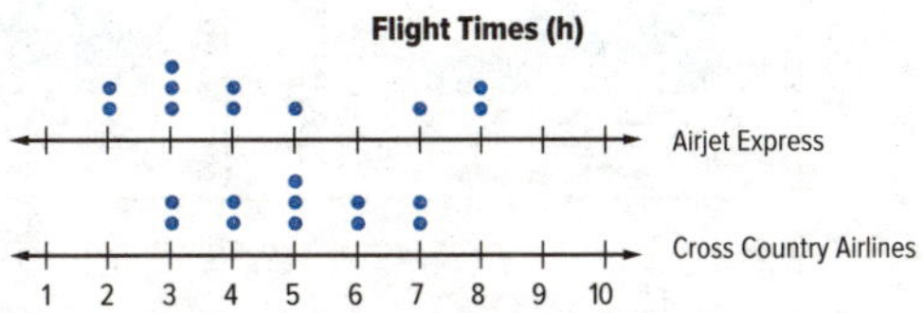

Airjet Express; Sample answer: The data for Airjet Express has a median of 4 hours with an interquartile range of 4 hours. The data for Cross Country Airlines has a median of 5 hours with an interquartile range of 2 hours. The flights of Airjet Express vary more in their flight times, yet overall their flight times are less than those of Cross Country Airlines.

Copy and Solve **Write your answers for Exercise 3 on a separate piece of paper.**

3. MP **Multiple Representations** For a science project, Mackenzie is measuring the growth of two plants.

Weekly Plant Growth (cm)

	Week 1	Week 2	Week 3	Week 4	Week 5	Week 6	Week 7	Week 8
Plant A	2	3	2	2.5	3.4	3	2.5	3
Plant B	3	2.5	3	3.4	3.2	3.8	3.5	2.5

a. **Numbers** Find the median and interquartile range for both plants. 3a. Plant A: 2.75, 0.75; Plant B: 3.1; 0.7

b. **Graphs** Graph the data using a double box plot. See Answer Appendix for 3b and 3c.

c. **Words** Write an inference you can draw about the two populations.

ENGAGE EXPLORE **EXPLAIN** **ELABORATE** **EVALUATE**

3 Practice and Apply

Independent Practice and Extra Practice

The Independent Practice pages are meant to be used as the homework assignment. The Extra Practice page can be used for additional reinforcement or as a second-day assignment.

Levels of Complexity

The levels of the exercises progress from 1 to 3, with Level 1 indicating the lowest level of complexity.

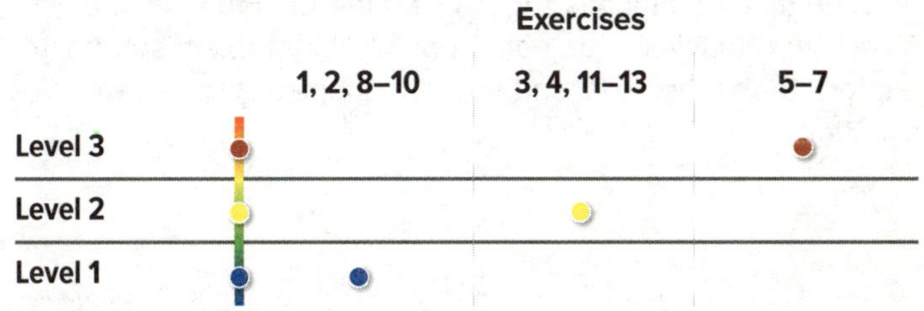

Suggested Assignments

You can use the table below that includes exercises of all complexity levels to select appropriate exercises for your students' needs.

Differentiated Homework Options

AL	Approaching Level	1–3, 6, 7, 12, 13
OL	On Level	1, 3, 4, 6, 7, 12, 13
BL	Beyond Level	3–7, 12, 13

ALEKS® can provide additional remediation support with personalized instruction and practice.

MP MATHEMATICAL PRACTICES

Emphasis On	Exercise(s)
1 Make sense of problems and persevere in solving them.	5
3 Construct viable arguments and critique the reasoning of others.	3
4 Model with mathematics.	6, 7
6 Attend to precision.	11

Mathematical Practices 1, 3, and 4 are aspects of mathematical thinking that are emphasized in every lesson. Students are given opportunities to be persistent in their problem solving, to express their reasoning, and to apply mathematics to real-world situations.

Formative Assessment
Use this activity as a closing formative assessment before dismissing students from your class.

TICKET Out the Door

Ask students to generate an example of how a measure of center or a measure of variation can be used to compare two populations. See students' work.

4. The median and interquartile range of a set of data is shown. Write a set of data consisting of seven values for the pair of measures.

Median: 6 Interquartile Range: 5

Sample answer: 3, 5, 6, 6, 8, 10, 13

H.O.T. Problems Higher Order Thinking

5. MP **Persevere with Problems** The histograms below show the number of tall buildings for two cities. Explain why you cannot describe the specific location of the centers and spreads of the histograms.

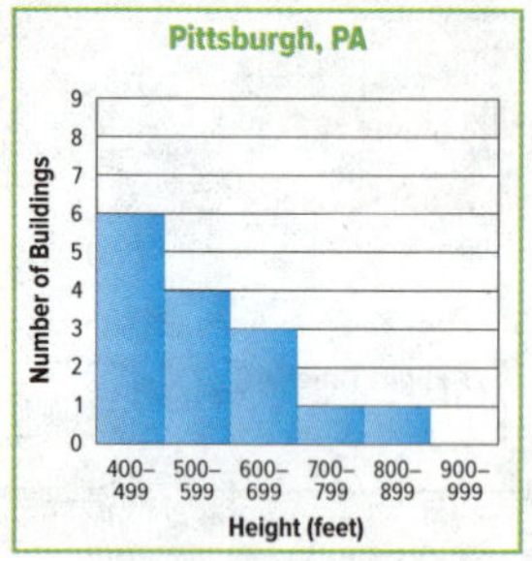

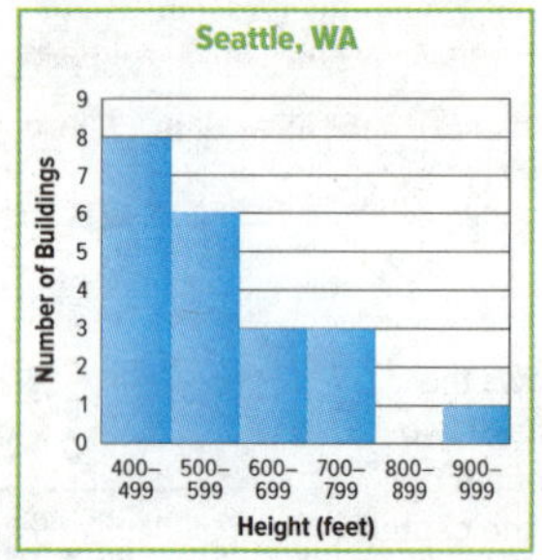

The data shown in the histograms are only shown in intervals. Specific values are not shown.

6. MP **Model with Mathematics** Refer to Exercise 1. What is a specific question you could ask about the two populations? Sample answer: At which restaurant can a customer expect a longer wait time?

7. MP **Model with Mathematics** Two hockey teams, the Warriors and the Bulldogs, played 15 games each during a month. Both scored a minimum of 0 goals and a maximum of 8 goals. The Bulldogs generally scored fewer goals than the Warriors. Draw a double box plot that could represent the situation.
See students' work.

Name ____________________ My Homework ____________________

Extra Practice

8. The double dot plot shows the heights in inches for the girls and boys in Franklin's math class. Compare the centers and variations of the two populations. Round to the nearest tenth. Write an inference you can draw about the two populations.

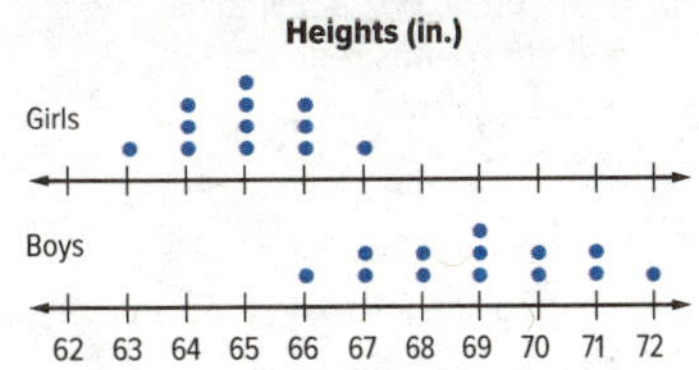

Homework Help

Both plots are symmetric. The girls' heights have a mean of 65 inches with a mean absolute deviation of about 0.8 inch. The boys' heights have a mean of 69 inches with a mean absolute deviation of about 1.4 inches. Overall, the girls' heights are lower than the boys' heights and are also more consistently grouped together.

9. The double box plot shows the number of points scored by the football team for two seasons. Compare the centers and variations of the two populations. During which season was the team's performance more consistent?

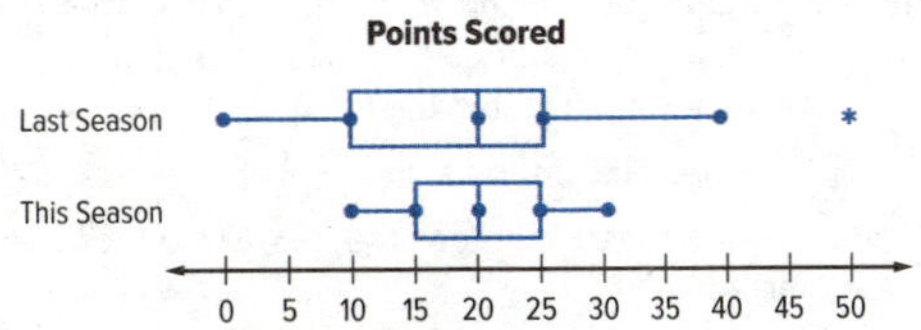

this season; Sample answer: Both seasons' scores have a median of 20 points, but last season's scores have an interquartile range of 15 points while this season's interquartile range is 10 points. So, the football team's performance was more consistent this season.

10. The double box plot shows the number of daily visitors to two different parks. Compare the centers and variations of the two populations. In general, which park has more daily visitors?

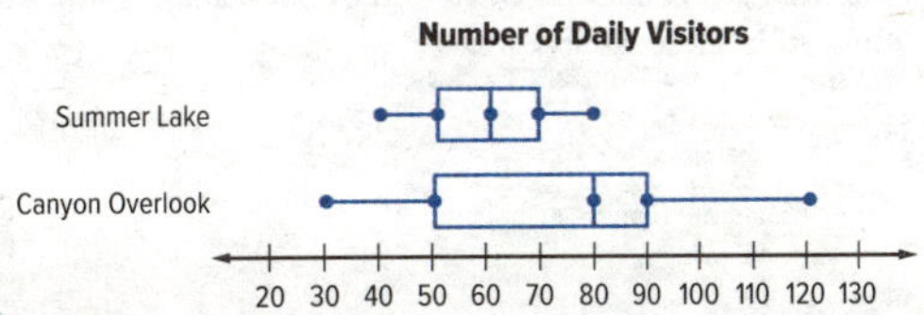

Canyon Overlook; Sample answer: During half of the days, there were at least 80 visitors to the park. On any given day, there were no more than 80 visitors to Summer Lake.

11. MP **Be Precise** The median and interquartile range of a set of data is shown. Write a set of data consisting of seven values for the pair of measures.

Median: 5 Interquartile Range: 5

Sample answer: 2, 4, 4, 5, 8, 9, 10

Create Your Own Homework Online

eSolutionsManual™ can be used to create worksheets for the suggested assignments on page 833, or create your own worksheets for differentiated homework or review.

Power Up! Test Practice

Exercises 12 and 13 prepare students for more rigorous thinking needed for the State assessment.

12.

This test item requires students to explain and apply mathematical concepts and solve problems with precision, while making use of structure.	
Depth of Knowledge	DOK1
Content Standard	7.SP.4
Mathematical Practice	MP1
Online Experience	Students will be required to click on the bubbles to select all answers that are correct.
Scoring Rubric	
1 point	Students correctly answer the question.

13.

This test item requires students to reason abstractly and quantitatively when problem solving.	
Depth of Knowledge	DOK1
Content Standard	7.SP.4
Mathematical Practice	MP1
Online Experience	Students will be required to click on the bubbles to select all answers that are correct.
Scoring Rubric	
1 point	Students correctly answer each part of the question.

Power Up! Test Practice

12. The double box plot shows the top speeds reached by wood and steel roller coasters.

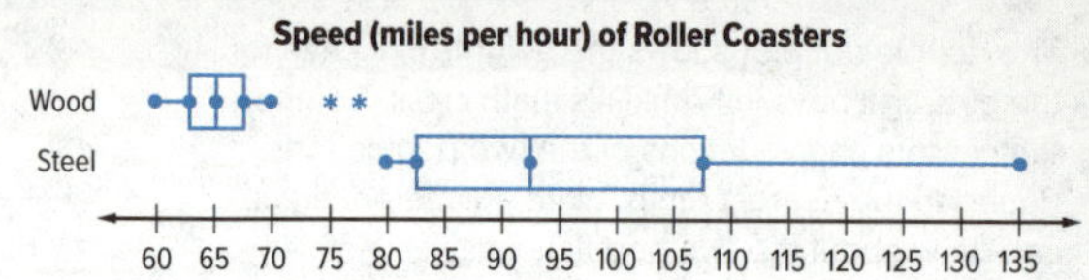

Which of the following is not true about the double box plot? Select all that apply.

- [x] The data for steel coasters is symmetric.
- [x] The data for wood coasters is symmetric.
- [ ] The top speed of the fastest steel coaster is 135 miles per hour.
- [ ] The top speed of the slowest wooden coaster is 60 miles per hour.

13. The double dot plot shows the daily low temperatures of two cities in January over a two week period. Determine if each statement is true or false

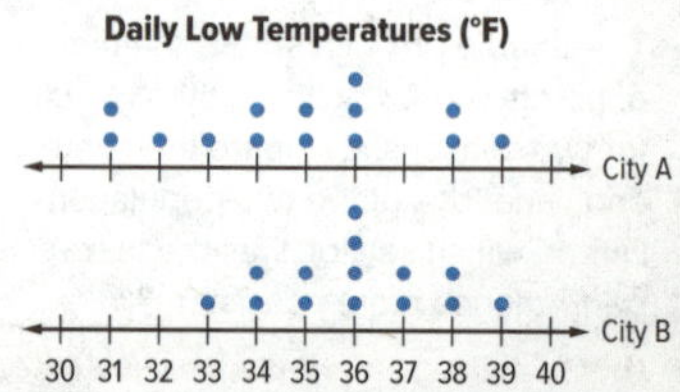

a. The medians are the same. [ ] True [x] False

b. The interquartile ranges are the same. [ ] True [x] False

c. The temperatures for City B are more consistent. [x] True [ ] False

Spiral Review

Find the mean absolute deviation of each set of data. Round to the nearest hundredth if necessary. 6.SP.5c

14. 12.5 mph

Maximum Speeds of Boats (mph)			
40	48	58	60
66	72	80	88

15. 1.74 million

Populations of Largest U.S. Cities (millions)			
1.3	3.8	1.5	8.4
0.9	1.4	2.3	1.3

16. Refer to the graph in Exercise 2. Describe the shape of the distribution of the data for Airjet Express. 6.SP.5d

Sample answer: There is a peak at 3 and a gap between 5 and 7.

17. Refer to the graph in Exercise 10. Describe the shape of the distribution of the data for Canyon Overlook. 6.SP.5d

Sample answer: The shape of the distribution is not symmetric since the lengths of each box and whisker are not the same. There are no outliers.

IWB An Interactive Whiteboard Ready presentation is available for each lesson in the chapter.

Inquiry Lab
Visual Overlap of Data Distributions

Inquiry WHAT does the ratio $\frac{\text{difference in means}}{\text{mean absolute deviation}}$ tell you about how much visual overlap there is between two distributions with similar variation?

Content Standards
7.SP.3

MP Mathematical Practices
1, 3

A survey was done. The tables below show the number of text messages sent and received daily for two different age groups.

Text Messages Ages 12–15

70	90	80	90
85	75	85	80
90	80	75	95
100	85	95	85

Text Messages Ages 16–19

85	75	80	70
75	80	65	75
85	70	90	80
70	75	60	65

Hands-On Activity

You can compare two numerical data sets by comparing the shape of their distributions. The **visual overlap** of two distributions with similar variation is a visual demonstration that compares their centers to their variation, or spread.

Step 1 Use a double dot plot to display the data in each table.

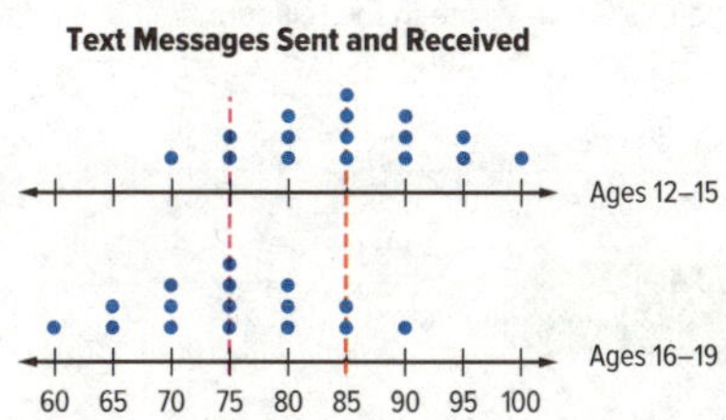

Step 2 Find the mean number of text messages for each age group.

Ages 12–15 mean = 85 **Ages 16–19 mean =** 75

Step 3 A red dotted line has been drawn through both dot plots that corresponds to the mean for the age group, 12–15 years. Draw a vertical dotted line through both dot plots that corresponds to the mean for the age group, 16–19 years. The dotted lines show the visual overlap between the centers.

Focus narrowing the scope

Objective Analyze the visual overlap of two numerical data distributions. 7.SP.3

Coherence connecting within and across grades

Now
Students will compare two populations to determine if there is a visual ovelap of the data.

Next
Students will select an appropriate display to represent different types of data.

Rigor pursuing concepts, fluency, and applications

See the Levels of Complexity chart on page 838.

ENGAGE EXPLORE EXPLAIN ELABORATE EVALUATE

1 Launch the Lab

The activity is intended to be used as a whole-group activity.

Hands-On Activity

AL EL Pairs Discussion Have pairs of students complete Steps 1–3. Students should find the mean, median, mode, and range for each dot plot. Have students discuss how the mean, median, mode, and range of each plot can be seen visually, and not just by mathematical computation. MP 1, 6, 7

BL EL Pairs Consult Have students generate a possible real-world reason for why the means of the data plots might be different. MP 1, 4

ENGAGE EXPLORE EXPLAIN ELABORATE EVALUATE

2 Collaborate

The **Investigate** and **Analyze and Reflect** sections are intended to be used as small-group investigations. The **Create** section is intended to be used as independent exercises.

Levels of Complexity

The levels of the exercises progress from 1 to 3, with Level 1 indicating the lowest level of complexity.

	Exercises 1, 2	Exercises 3–5	Exercises 6
Level 3			●
Level 2		●	
Level 1	●		

Investigate

AL BL EL **Three Stay, One Stray** Have students work in groups of 4. Make sure there are a variety of ability levels in each group. Assign each student a number, from 1–4. Groups should complete Exercises 1–6. After Exercises 1 and 2 have been completed by each group, call on one numbered student from each group to stray to a new group to share responses and resolve any discrepancies. Repeat this process for Exercises 3 and 4, and then again for Exercises 5 and 6. Have students return to their original group to compare responses to all of the exercises. MP 1, 3, 6

Create

Inquiry Students should be able to answer "WHAT does the ratio $\frac{\text{difference in means}}{\text{mean absolute deviation}}$ tell you about how much visual overlap there is between two distributions with similar variation?" Check for student understanding and provide guidance, if needed.

Investigate

Work with a partner. The double dot plot compares the number of text messages sent and received by a third age group to the age group, 12–15 years.

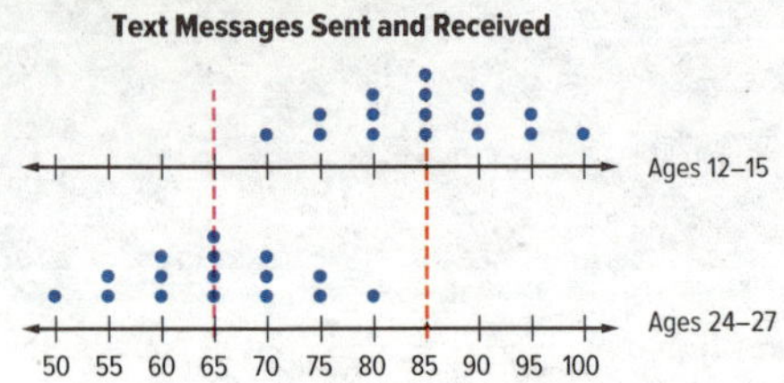

1. What is the mean number of texts for the age group, 24–27 years?
   65 texts

2. In the graph above, draw a vertical dotted line through both dot plots that corresponds to the mean for the age group, 24–27 years.

Analyze and Reflect

Work with a partner.

3. What is the difference between the means of the distributions for the Activity? for Exercise 1?
   85 − 75, or 10 text messages; 85 − 65 or 20 text messages

4. The mean absolute deviation of each distribution is 6.25 texts. For the Activity and Exercise 1, write the difference between the means and the mean absolute deviation as a ratio. Express the ratio as a decimal.
   $\frac{10}{6.25} = 1.6$; $\frac{20}{6.25} = 3.2$

5. MP **Reason Inductively** Compare the ratios you wrote in Exercise 4.
   Sample answer: The ratio written for Exercise 1 is twice as large as the ratio written for the Investigation.

Create

6. Inquiry What does the ratio $\frac{\text{difference in means}}{\text{mean absolute deviation}}$ tell you about how much visual overlap there is between two distributions with similar variation?
   Sample answer: The ratio, $\frac{\text{difference in means}}{\text{mean absolute devation}}$, will be smaller if there is more visual overlap between the distributions. As the ratio gets larger, the centers of the distributions become farther apart.

PLAN ONLINE

PD | RtI | Watch | Worksheets | Vocab | Tutor | Tools | Check | English Learners | Sketchpad

PRESENT

IWB

An Interactive Whiteboard Ready presentation is available for each lesson in the chapter.

Lesson 5

Select an Appropriate Display

Real-World Link

There are many different types of graphs that are used to display all kinds of statistical data. List all of the types of graphs you can think of below.

Sample answer: bar graph, line graph, box plot, histogram, circle graph, pictograph, line plot

The graphs below display the total number of pounds of plastic recycled each week during a ten-week period in different ways.

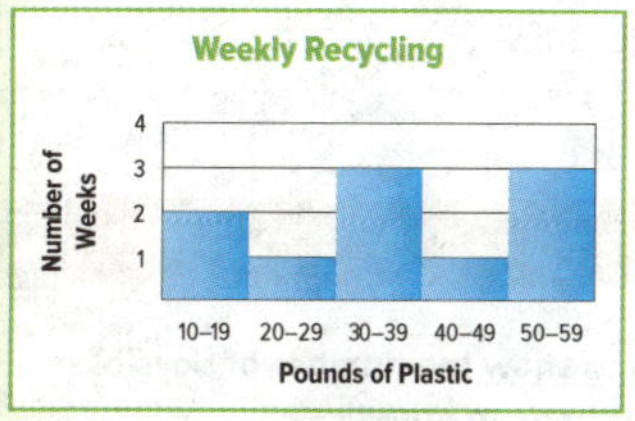

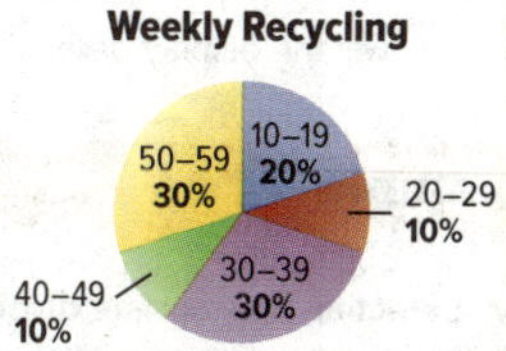

histogram   circle graph

1. On the line below each graph, write the type of graph used.
2. Which display more easily shows the number of weeks the class collected between 30 and 39 pounds of plastic? histogram
3. Which display more easily shows the percent of time that 40 to 49 pounds of plastic was recycled? circle graph

Essential Question

HOW do you know which type of graph to use when displaying data?

Content Standards
Extension of 7.SP.1

MP Mathematical Practices
1, 3, 4

Which MP **Mathematical Practices** did you use? Shade the circle(s) that applies.

① Persevere with Problems
② Reason Abstractly
③ Construct an Argument
④ Model with Mathematics
⑤ Use Math Tools
⑥ Attend to Precision
⑦ Make Use of Structure
⑧ Use Repeated Reasoning

Focus narrowing the scope

Objective Select, organize and construct appropriate data displays. 7.SP.1

Coherence connecting within and across grades

Previous
Students used different types of displays to represent data.

Now
Students select an appropriate display to represent different types of data.

Next
Students will determine whether or not a relationship exists between sets of bivariate data.

Rigor pursuing concepts, fluency, and applications

See the Levels of Complexity chart on page 843.

ENGAGE EXPLORE EXPLAIN ELABORATE EVALUATE

1 Launch the Lesson

Ideas for Use

You may wish to launch the lesson using a whole group, small group, think-pair-share activity, or independent activity.

EL **Think-Pair-Share** Give students 1–2 minutes to think about how they would respond to Exercises 1–3. Then have them share their responses with a partner. Call on one student to share their responses with the class. MP 1

Alternate Strategies

AL Have students use the Internet to locate examples of histograms and circle graphs. Have them explain how each display helps them to see the data that is presented. MP 1, 3, 5, 7

BL Have students explain how they could use the histogram to find the percent of each category. MP 1, 3, 7

2 Teach the Concept

Ask the scaffolded questions for each example to differentiate instruction.

IWB

Example

1. Select an appropriate display.

AL
- *What do you want the graph to show?* the number of boys of different age ranges that participate in athletics
- *Why is a histogram an appropriate display?* A histogram would show intervals.

OL
- *Why would a line graph not be an appropriate display?* Sample response: We are not showing change over time.
- *Why would a circle graph not be an appropriate display?* Sample response: We are not asked to show parts of the whole.

BL
- *Generate an inference you can make about the data presented in the histogram.* Sample answer: More boys ages 5–9 participate in athletics than any other age range.

Need Another Example?
Select an appropriate display to compare the percents of students in seventh grade who traveled to school this morning by bus, by car, or by foot. circle graph

Watch Out!

Common Error Students may choose a display that is not the most appropriate statistical display for the data. Have students choose a different type of display for the data if necessary. Then have them compare the two displays and decide which one allows them to interpret the data more easily.

Key Concept

Select an Appropriate Display

Type of Display	Best Used to...
Bar Graph	show the number of items in specific categories
Box Plot	show measures of variation for a set of data; also useful for very large sets of data
Circle Graph	compare parts of the data to the whole
Double Bar Graph	compare two sets of categorical data
Histogram	show frequency of data divided into equal intervals
Line Graph	show change over a period of time
Line Plot	show frequency of data with a number line

Work Zone

Data Displays
Many situations have more than one appropriate display.

When deciding what type of display to use, ask these questions.
- What type of information is given?
- What do you want the display to show?
- How will the display be analyzed?

Example

Tutor

1. Select an appropriate display to show the number of boys of different age ranges that participate in athletics.

Since the display will show an interval, a histogram like the one below would be an appropriate display to represent this data.

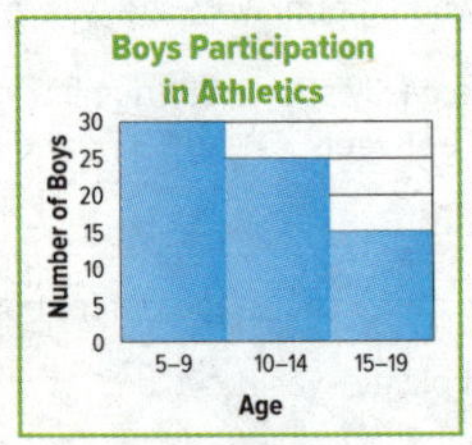

Got it? Do this problem to find out.

Show your work.

a. Select an appropriate display for the percent of students in each grade at a middle school.

a. circle graph

Statistics and Probability

Real World

Example

Tutor

2. **Select an appropriate type of display to compare the percent of ethanol production by state. Justify your reasoning. Then construct the display. What can you conclude from your display?**

Ethanol Production by State Per Year						
State	Iowa	Nebraska	Illinois	Minnesota	Indiana	Other
Gallons (millions)	3,534	1,665	1,135	1,102	1,074	5,098

You are asked to compare parts to a whole. A circle graph would be an appropriate display.

Ethanol Production by State

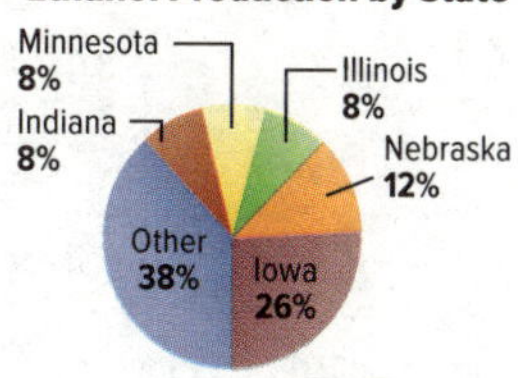

Indiana, Minnesota, and Illinois produce about the same amount of ethanol.

Got it? **Do this problem to find out.**

b. The table lists the ticket prices for school musicals during recent years. Select an appropriate display to predict the price of a ticket in 2013. Justify your reasoning. Then construct the display. What can you conclude from your display?

Ticket Prices	
Year	**Price ($)**
2009	5.00
2010	5.50
2011	6.50
2012	7.00

Show your work.

A line graph would be an appropriate graph because the data is organized by time. The graph shows that there is a steady increase of ticket prices over time.

IWB

Example

2. **Select an appropriate display.**

AL
- *What do you want the display to show?* a comparison of percents
- *What kind of display compares percents, or parts of a whole?* circle graph

OL
- *Explain how you can find the percentage of gallons of ethanol for each category.* Divide the number of gallons by the total number of gallons, then multiply by 100 and add the % symbol.
- *Explain how you would use the percentages to create the circle graph.* Multiply 360° by each percent to find the measure of the angle for each section of the circle. Draw each section using the center of the circle for the angle vertex. Then shade and label each section.

BL
- *Explain why a line graph is not an appropriate display for this data.* Sample answer: A line graph is used to show changes over time. A graph for this type of data should show parts of a whole.

Need Another Example?

Select an appropriate display to compare the percent of girls who play in the soccer league by age range. Justify your reasoning. Then construct the display. Round each percent to the nearest whole percent, if necessary. What can you conclude from your display?

Girls in Soccer League	
Ages (years)	**Number**
6–8	10
9–11	29
12–14	22
15–17	15

Sample answer: A circle graph would be an appropriate way to compare the percents to the total number of girls in the soccer league. About 38% of the girls are ages 9 to 11.

Number of Girls by Age

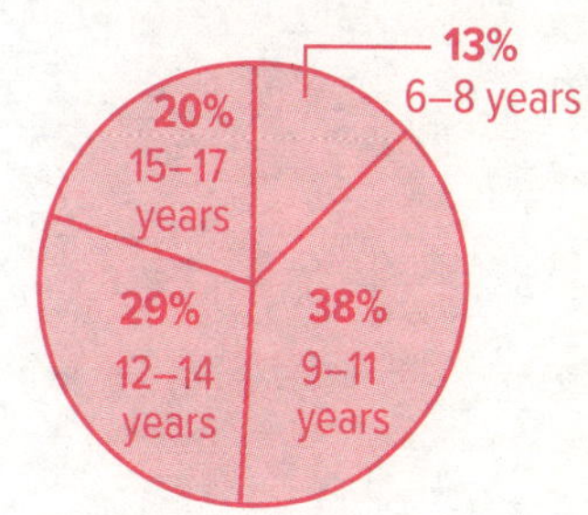

Guided Practice

Formative Assessment Use these exercises to assess students' understanding of the concepts in this lesson.

If some of your students are not ready for assignments, use the differentiated activities below.

AL EL Pairs to Groups Have students work in pairs to complete Exercises 1–2. Each partner should ensure that the other partner understands how to select an appropriate display for each situation. Then have pairs join with another pair to share responses and discuss and resolve any differences. Have the group complete Exercises 3–5, ensuring that all students contribute and understand how to select and create an appropriate display for each situation. Then call on one student to share their group's responses to Exercises 1–5 with the class. MP 1, 3, 4

BL EL Find the Fib Have students work with a partner to write two facts and one fib regarding the data in Exercise 3 or 4. For example, one fact could be that one-third of the sandwiches in Exercise 3 are priced in the interval \$3.00–\$3.99. One fib could be that more than one-half of the sandwiches are priced in the interval \$2.00–\$2.99. Then have students trade facts and fibs with another pair of students. Each pair should correctly identify each fact and fib. MP 1, 3

Guided Practice

Check

Select an appropriate display for each situation. Justify your reasoning. (Example 1) **1–4. Sample answers are given.**

1. the number of people who have different kinds of pets

   bar graph; groups values into categories

2. the percent of different ways electricity is generated

   circle graph; compares parts to a whole

3. The prices of sandwiches at a restaurant are \$4.50, \$5.59, \$3.99, \$2.50, \$4.99, \$3.75, \$2.99, \$3.29, and \$4.19. Select an appropriate display to determine how many sandwiches range from \$3.00 to \$3.99. Justify your reasoning. Then construct the display. What can you conclude from your display? (Example 2)

   A histogram would be an appropriate graph to show the data divided into equal intervals. The graph shows that most sandwiches fall between \$3.00–\$4.99.

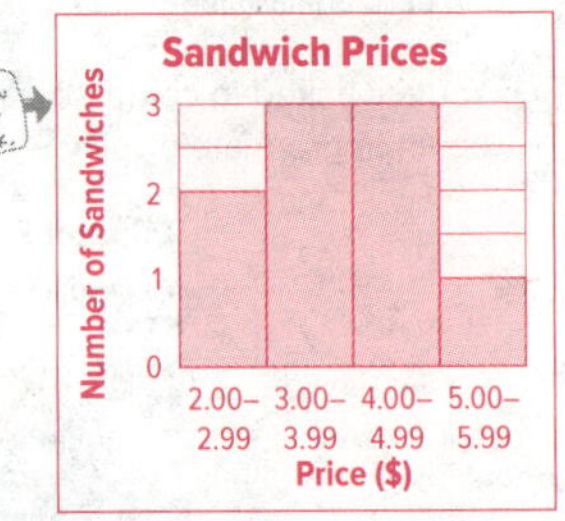

4. A survey asked teens which subject they felt was most difficult. Of those who responded, 25 said English, 39 said social studies, 17 said science, and 19 said other. Construct an appropriate display of the data. Justify your reasoning. Then name one thing you can conclude from the display. (Example 2)

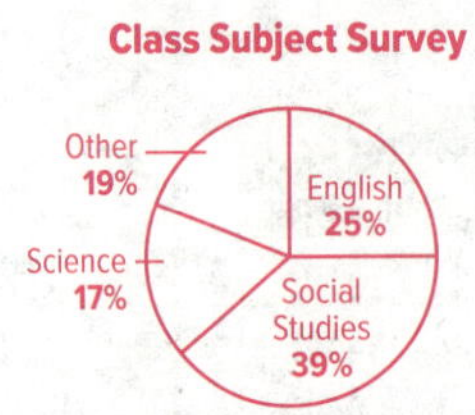

   A circle graph compares parts to a whole. English represents $\frac{1}{4}$ of the responses.

5. **Building on the Essential Question** What are some of the factors to consider when selecting an appropriate display for a set of data?

   What type of data is given? How will the data be analyzed?

Rate Yourself!

How confident are you about selecting an appropriate display? Shade the ring on the target.

For more help, go online to access a Personal Tutor.

Tutor

Name ______________________ My Homework ______________________

Independent Practice

Go online for Step-by-Step Solutions eHelp

Select an appropriate display for each situation. Justify your reasoning. (Example 1)

1. the median age of members in a community band

box plot; shows the median

2. the number of students that favor chocolate or vanilla as a frosting

bar graph; shows the number of items per category

3. Select an appropriate display for the data. Justify your reasoning. Then construct the display. What can you conclude from your display? (Example 2)

Number of Push-ups			
45	35	42	37
44	40	36	42
45	40	42	39
44	43	36	39

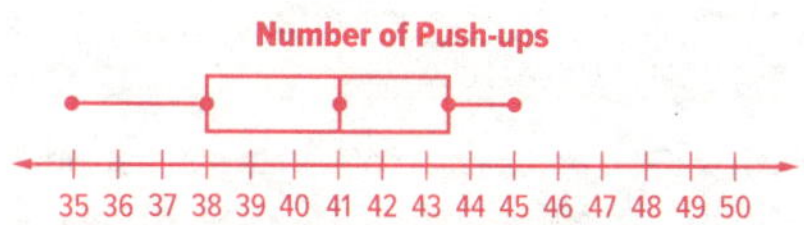

A box plot is an appropriate graph because there is a large set of data and it will show the measures of variation of the data set. This graph has a median of 41.

4. **MP Model with Mathematics** Refer to the graphic novel frame below. What is the best type of display to use for this data? Explain.

box plot; Sample answer: It can be used to find the median and range easily.

ENGAGE EXPLORE EXPLAIN ELABORATE EVALUATE

3 Practice and Apply

Independent Practice and Extra Practice

The Independent Practice pages are meant to be used as the homework assignment. The Extra Practice page can be used for additional reinforcement or as a second-day assignment.

Levels of Complexity

The levels of the exercises progress from 1 to 3, with Level 1 indicating the lowest level of complexity.

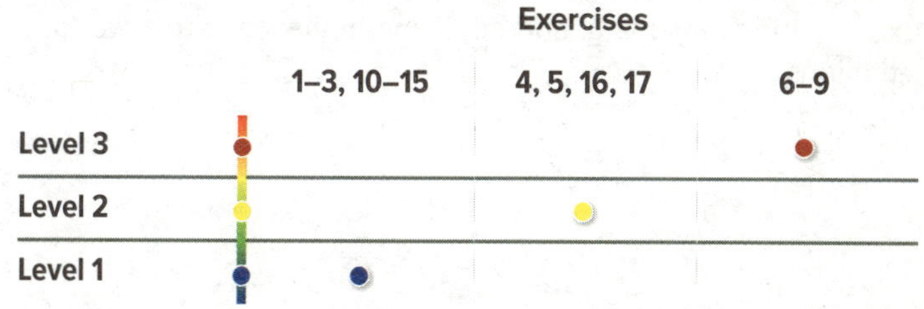

Suggested Assignments

You can use the table below that includes exercises of all complexity levels to select appropriate exercises for your students' needs.

Differentiated Homework Options		
AL	Approaching Level	1–3, 5–7, 9, 16, 17
OL	On Level	1, 3, 4–7, 9, 16, 17
BL	Beyond Level	4–9, 16, 17

ALEKS® can provide additional remediation support with personalized instruction and practice.

MP MATHEMATICAL PRACTICES

Emphasis On	Exercise(s)
1 Make sense of problems and persevere in solving them.	8
3 Construct viable arguments and critique the reasoning of others.	7, 9, 10–12
4 Model with mathematics.	4, 6

Mathematical Practices 1, 3, and 4 are aspects of mathematical thinking that are emphasized in every lesson. Students are given opportunities to be persistent in their problem solving, to express their reasoning, and apply mathematics to real-world situations.

Formative Assessment
Use this activity as a closing formative assessment before dismissing students from your class.

TICKET Out the Door

Have students identify the type of statistical display that they think is most appropriate for showing the change in a city's population over the course of 20 years. Have them justify their reasoning. See students' work.

5. Refer to the situations described below.

Situation A	Situation B
the number of customers ages 12–19 compared to all age groups	the number of customers ages 12, 13, 14, 15, and 16 who made a purchase

a. Which situation involves data that is best displayed in a bar graph? Explain your reasoning. Situation B; Sample answer: A bar graph can show the number of customers who made a purchase by each individual age.

b. Refer to the situation you selected in part **a.** Could you display the data using another type of display? If so, which display? Explain.
Yes; Sample answer: line plot; A line plot shows the frequency of data on a number line.

H.O.T. Problems Higher Order Thinking

6. MP **Model with Mathematics** Give an example of a data set that would be best represented in a line graph. Sample answer: The population of polar bears over the last 10 years.

7. MP **Reason Inductively** Determine if the following statement is *always*, *sometimes*, or *never* true. Justify your response.

A circle graph can be used to display data from a bar graph.

always; Sample answer: The sections of the circle graph can be taken from the bars of the graph and the percents can be found by dividing each bar's value by the total number of data values.

8. MP **Persevere with Problems** Determine if the following statement is *true* or *false*. Explain your reasoning.

A line plot can be used to display data from a histogram.

false; Sample answer: A histogram gives frequency of data in intervals. So, you cannot determine how many times a single number occurs.

9. MP **Reason Inductively** Compare and contrast bar graphs and histograms. Explain when it is appropriate to use a histogram rather than a bar graph.
Sample answer: Both graphs use bars to show how many things are in each category. A histogram shows the frequency of data that has been organized into equal intervals, so there is no space between the bars. It would be appropriate to use a histogram instead of a bar graph when the data can be organized into equal intervals.

Name ______________________ My Homework ______________________

Extra Practice

MP Justify Conclusions **Select an appropriate display for each situation. Justify your reasoning.**

10. the resale value of a person's car over time

line graph; A line graph compares change over time.

11. the percent of people that drink 0, 1, 2, 3, or more than 3 glasses of water a day

circle graph; compares parts to a whole

12. the number of different colored cars at a car dealership

bar graph: shows the number of items per category

13. The circle graph shows the approximate percent of the total volume of each Great Lake.

a. Display the data using another type of display.

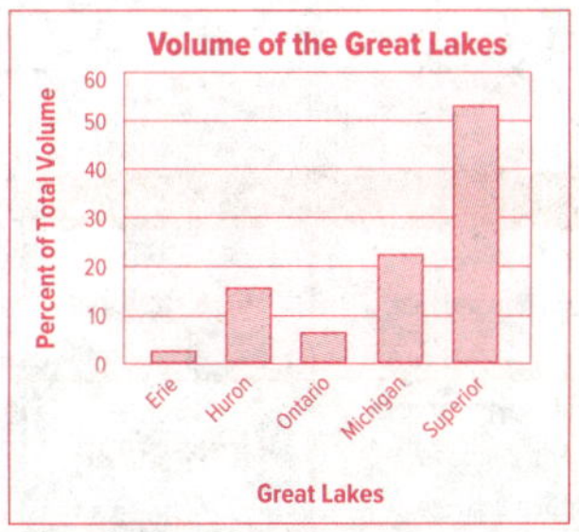

Volume of the Great Lakes

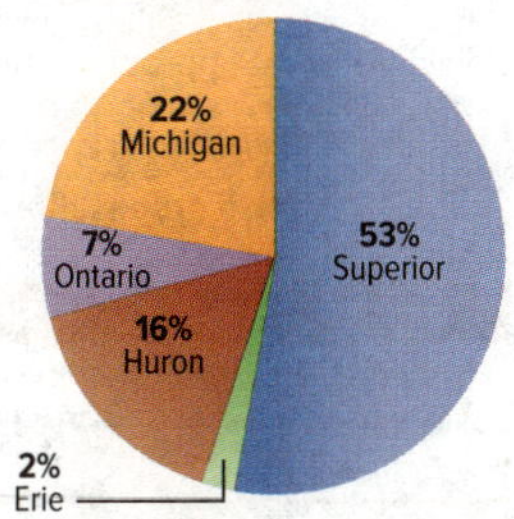

b. Write a convincing argument telling which display is more appropriate.

Sample answer: The circle graph is most appropriate because it shows how each lake compares to the whole.

Copy and Solve **Select an appropriate display for each situation. Then justify your reasoning and construct the display on a separate sheet of paper. What can you conclude from your display?** 14–15. See margin for graphs.

14.

Favorite Movies	
Type of Movie	Number of People
Comedy	48
Action	17
Drama	5
Horror	2

A bar graph would be an appropriate graph to show the number of people in categories. The graph shows that comedies are liked by the majority of people.

15.

Age Group	Number of Texts per Day
11–15	25
16–20	23
21–25	17
26–30	10

A histogram is an appropriate graph because the data is given in intervals. The graph shows people ages 26–30 text the least amount.

Create Your Own Homework Online

eSolutionsManual™ can be used to create worksheets for the suggested assignments on page 843, or create your own worksheets for differentiated homework or review.

Additional Answers

14.

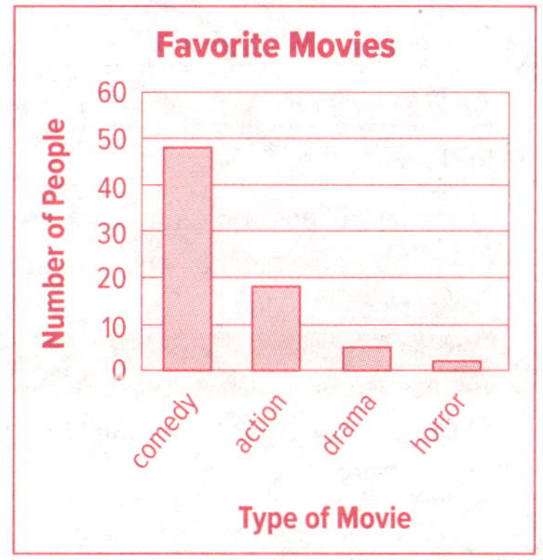

15.

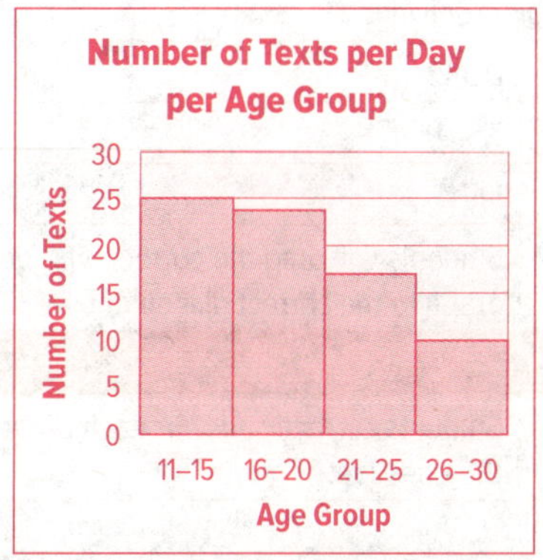

Power Up! Test Practice

Exercises 16 and 17 prepare students for more rigorous thinking needed for the State assessment.

16.

This test item requires students to reason abstractly and quantitatively when problem solving.	
Depth of Knowledge	DOK1
Content Standard	7.SP.1
Mathematical Practice	MP1
Online Experience	Students will be required to click on the bubbles to select all answers that are correct.
Scoring Rubric	
1 point	Students correctly answer each part of the question.

17.

This test item requires students to reason abstractly and quantitatively when problem solving.	
Depth of Knowledge	DOK2
Content Standard	7.SP.1
Mathematical Practice	MP1
Online Experience	Students will drag the correct type of graph to the correct placement.
Scoring Rubric	
1 point	Students correctly answer each part of the question.

Power Up! Test Practice

16. The number of home runs hit by each player of a professional baseball team is shown in the table.

Home Runs					
10	15	5	10	12	5
12	12	4	5	10	7

Determine if each statement is true or false.

a. A line plot would be most appropriate for showing the frequency of the data on a number line. ■ True ☐ False

b. A histogram would be most appropriate for showing the frequency of the data in equal intervals. ■ True ☐ False

c. A circle graph would be most appropriate for showing how the number of home runs changes over time. ☐ True ■ False

17. Select the most appropriate type of display for each situation.

bar graph | histogram | line plot | circle graph | line graph

Situation	Type of Graph
Mr. Reynolds measured the amount of rain that had fallen every 15 minutes during a storm. He wants to show how the amount of rain fallen changed over time during the storm.	line graph
Alexandria recorded how many hours of her free time she spent playing sports, watching TV, talking with her friends, or playing video games. She wants to compare the percentages of her free time that she spends on each activity.	circle graph
Rachel collected data on how many of her classmates ride the bus, get a ride, or walk to school. She wants to compare how many students are in each category.	bar graph

Spiral Review

Use the graph to answer Exercises 18–20. The graph shows the number of male and the number of female students that chose certain occupations to research. 6.SP.5

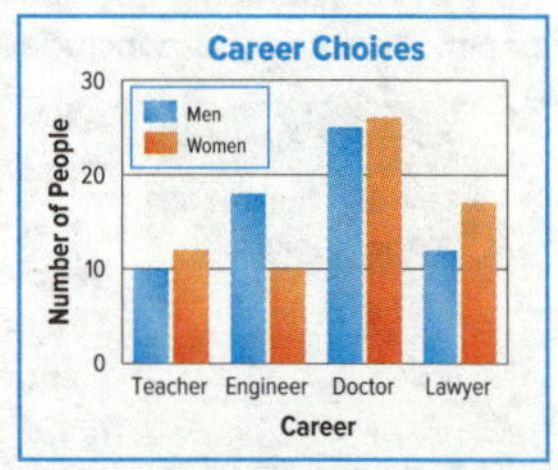

18. About how many people are represented in the graph? 133

19. About how many men and how many women are represented in the graph? 65 men; 65 women

20. How many more women chose to research law? 5

College & Career READINESS

21ST CENTURY CAREER in Market Research

Market Research Analyst

Do you think that gathering and analyzing information about people's opinions, tastes, likes, and dislikes sounds interesting? If so, then you should consider a career in market research. Market research analysts help companies understand what types of products and services consumers want. They design Internet, telephone, or mail response surveys and then analyze the data, identify trends, and present their conclusions and recommendations. Market research analysts must be analytical, creative problem-solvers, have strong backgrounds in mathematics, and have good written and verbal communication skills.

College & Career READINESS

Is This the Career for You?

Are you interested in a career as a market research analyst? Take some of the following courses in high school.

- Algebra
- Calculus
- Computer Science
- English
- Statistics

Find out how math relates to a career in Market Research.

Focus narrowing the scope

Objective Apply mathematics to problems arising in the workplace. This lesson emphasizes MP **Mathematical Practice 4** Model with Mathematics.

Coherence connecting within and across grades

Previous
Students used graphs to analyze and display data.

Now
Students apply the content standard to solve problems in the workplace.

Rigor pursuing concepts, fluency, and applications

See the Career Project on page 847.

ENGAGE EXPLORE EXPLAIN ELABORATE EVALUATE

1 Launch the Lesson

Ask students to read the information on the student page about market research and answer the following questions.

Ask:

- *What kinds of classes should you take if you want to be a market research analyst?* Sample answers: Algebra, Calculus, Computer Science, English, and Statistics
- *What are some of the tasks that a market research analyst does?* Sample answers: designs surveys and analyzes data, identifies trends and presents conclusions, makes recommendations based on the results of market research
- *What skills are helpful for becoming a market research analyst?* Sample answers: being analytical, and a creative problem-solver; having good written and verbal communication skills

College & Career READINESS

Help students connect what they do today to their futures. Direct them to the Internet or another source to explore, learn, and plan for college and future careers.

2 Collaborate

AL **Circle the Sage** Poll the class to see which students feel comfortable with their knowledge of proportions. Those students (the sages) spread out around the room. Assign the rest of the students to teams. Have the teams split up, with each team member going to a different sage, if possible. Have the sages lead the discussion for Exercises 1 and 2. When the exercises are complete, students report back to their original teams and compare solutions. Students discuss how the sages may have explained the steps differently. MP 1, 5, 7

BL **Team Project** Have students work in learning teams to use the Internet, newspapers, or magazines to locate examples of how math is used in advertising and marketing claims. Teams should analyze the validity of the claims and give a presentation to the class outlining the claims and whether they think the claims are accurate or misleading. MP 1, 3, 4

Career Portfolio

When students complete this page, have them add it to their Career Portfolio.

Career Facts

Market research analysts are employed in many different types of industries. These include computer systems design companies, software publishers, financial services organizations, health care institutions, and advertising firms.

MP Keeping Your Eye on the Target Market!

Use the results of the survey in the table below to solve each problem.

1. At Hastings Middle School, 560 of the students use social networking sites. Predict how many of them use the sites to make plans with friends. about 403

2. Suppose 17.9 million teens use online social networks. Predict how many will be using the sites to make new friends. about 8.8 million

3. According to the survey, what percent of a teen's networking site friends are people they regularly see? about 43.4%

4. Landon randomly selects a friend from his social networking site. What is the probability that it is someone he never sees in person? Write as a percent. about 33.3%

5. Paris wants to leave a message on 8 of her friends' social networking sites. In how many ways can she leave a message on her friends' sites? 40,320

Survey Results: Teens and Social Networking	
Reason to Use Social Networks	**Percent of Respondents**
Stay in touch with friends	91%
Make plans with friends	72%
Make new friends	49%
Friends on Social Networking Sites	**Average Number**
People who are regularly seen	43
People who are occasionally seen	23
People who are never seen in person	33
Total	99

MP Career Project

It's time to update your career portfolio! Use the Internet or another source to research a career as a market research analyst. Write a paragraph that summarizes your findings.

What skills would you need to improve to succeed in this career?

-
-
-
-
-

Statistics and Probability

Chapter Review

Vocabulary Check

Complete the crossword puzzle using the vocabulary list at the beginning of the chapter.

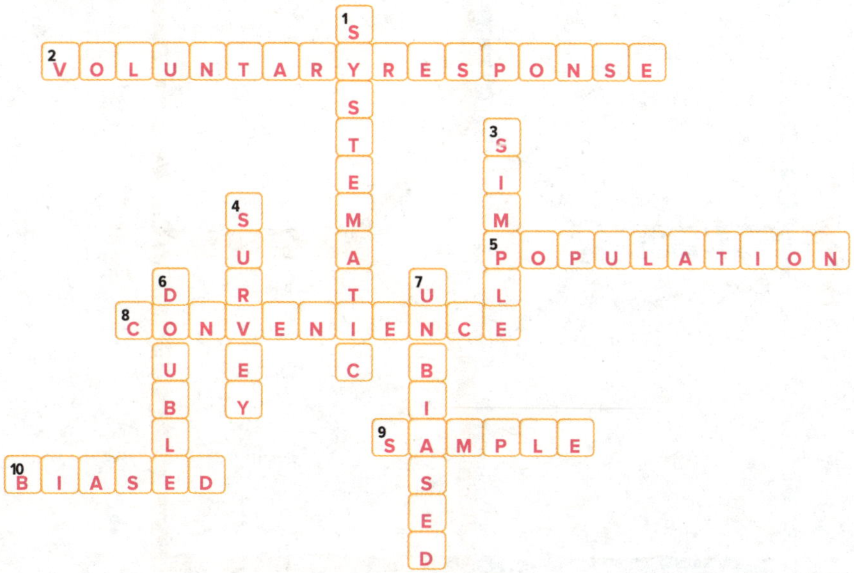

Across

2. sample involving only those who want to participate (two words)
5. the group being studied
8. sample in which members of a population are easily accessed
9. part of a group
10. sample in which one or more parts of the population are favored over other parts

Down

1. random sample in which items are selected according to a specific time or interval
3. random sample in which each item is as likely to be chosen as any other item
4. a method of collecting information
6. two box plots on the same number line
7. sample that represents the entire population

Vocabulary Check

EL Roundrobin Have students work in pairs, taking turns to complete the Vocabulary Check. Make sure each student understands the terms and definitions. Students should speak each vocabulary term aloud to ensure they know how to pronounce it and recognize it when it is heard. MP 1, 6

Alternate Strategy

AL EL To help students, you may wish to give them a vocabulary list from which they can choose their answers. A vocabulary list for this activity would include the following terms.

- biased sample (Lesson 2)
- convenience sample (Lesson 2)
- double box plot (Lesson 4)
- population (Lesson 1)
- sample (Lesson 1)
- simple random sample (Lesson 2)
- survey (Lesson 1)
- systematic random sample (Lesson 2)
- unbiased sample (Lesson 2)
- voluntary response sample (Lesson 2)

Key Concept Check

FOLDABLES EL A completed Foldable for this chapter should include a review of how to represent and compare proportional and nonproportional relationships using tables, graphs, and equations.

If you choose not to use this Foldable, have students write a brief review of the Key Concepts found throughout the chapter and give an example of each.

Ideas for Use

EL **Gallery Walk** Have students work with a partner to complete the graphic organizers in Exercises 1 and 2. Then have each student add or adjust anything in their graphic organizers based on the discussion with their partner. Display all of the graphic organizers around the room and have students walk around the room studying each one. Have them determine if they should add anything to their graphic organizer based upon what they saw in others' graphic organizers.

Got It?

If students have trouble with Exercises 1–4, they may need help with the following concept(s).

Concept	Exercise(s)
surveys (Lesson 1)	1, 2
biased and unbiased samples (Lesson 2)	3, 4

ALEKS® can provides additional support with personalized instruction and practice for those who are struggling, while providing enhanced learning for those who have mastered the concepts.

Key Concept Check

Use Your FOLDABLES

Use your Foldable to help review the chapter.

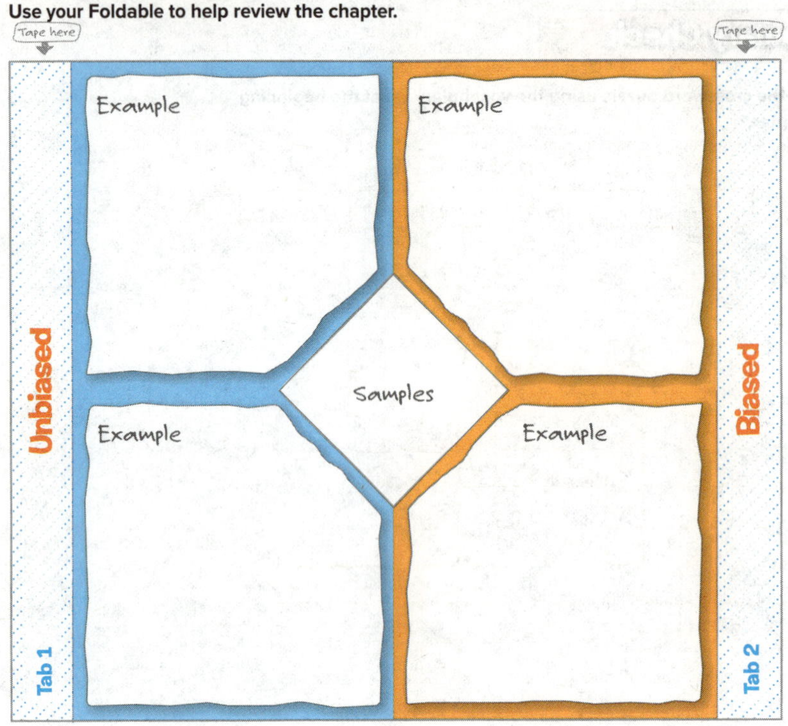

Got it?

Match each phrase with the correct term.

1. a method of collecting information
2. the group being studied
3. when one or more parts of the population is favored
4. a sample that involves only those who want to participate

a. voluntary response sample
b. biased sample
c. survey
d. population
e. convenience sample

Power Up! Performance Task

Class Evaluation

Mr. Fuentes is analyzing his student's grades over the last three years. He has had approximately 65 students each year. To simplify his analysis, he has decided to use a random sample of data from only ten students from 2012 and 2013. He had no records of the grades from 2014, so he asked students to bring in transcripts. He used the first few transcripts he received for his 2014 data.

	Student Grades									
2012	?	58	86	78	82	79	84	83	82	72
2013	83	85	85	85	87	87	88	90	91	91
2014	79	83	84	88	88	90	93	93	94	95

Write your answers on another piece of paper. Show all of your work to receive full credit.

Part A
Is the above information likely to be a legitimate representation of all the students of each respective year? Is the 2012 data biased or unbiased? Explain your answers.

Part B
In the year 2012, one of the grades is missing. If the mean was 80.1, what is the missing grade?

Part C
Considering the years 2013 and 2014, in which year were the grades the most consistent? Which of the two years had the better scores? What type of display would best show the data? Justify your responses.

Part D
Mr. Fuentes wants to submit the data from one year for a Teacher of the Year award. Choose a year. Could the data be seen as misleading? Explain.

Power Up! Performance Task

This Performance-Based Assessment requires students to solve multi-step problems through abstract reasoning, precision, and perseverance. This practice scenario can be used to help students prepare for the thinking skills that will be used on the stae Assessment.

A complete scoring rubric with answers to the Exercises can be found on page PT6.

Answering the Essential Question

Before answering the Essential Question, have students review their answers to the **Building on the Essential Question** exercises found in each lesson of the chapter.

- When can statistics be used to gain information about a population from a sample? (p. 796)
- How is using a survey one way to determine experimental probability? (p. 804)
- What are ways in which the display of data can influence conclusions? (p. 816)
- How can you use data displays to compare two populations? (p. 832)
- What are some of the factors to consider when selecting an appropriate display for a data set? (p. 842)

Ideas for Use

EL **Think-Pair-Share** Have students work in pairs. Pose the Essential Question. Give students about one minute to think about how they could complete the graphic organizer. Then have them share their responses with their partner before they complete the graphic organizer. MP 1, 7

Reflect

Answering the Essential Question

Use what you learned about statistics to complete the graphic organizer.
Sample answers given.

Bar Graph
A bar graph shows the number of items in a specific category.

Line Graph
A line graph shows change over time.

Essential Question
HOW do you know which type of graph to use when displaying data?

Double Dot Plot
A double dot plot shows the frequency in a distribution of two sets of data values.

Double Box Plot
A double box plot shows the measures of variation for two sets of data on a single number line.

Answer the Essential Question. HOW do you know which type of graph to use when displaying data?
See students' work.

UNIT PROJECT

Math Genes A Punnett Square is a graphical way to predict the genetic traits of offspring. In this project you will:

- **Collaborate** with your classmates as you research genetics and the Punnet Square.
- **Share** the results of your research in a creative way.
- **Reflect** on why learning mathematics is important.

Complete the activities below and discover the fun you can have with genetics.

Collaborate

Go Online Work with your group to research and complete each activity. You will use your results in the Share section on the following page.

1. Use the Internet to research Punnett Squares and their role in genetics. Write a paragraph describing your findings.

2. Create sample genes for pet traits. Then create a Punnett Square using those traits. Describe what each outcome represents. Include a graph with your explanation.

3. Refer to Exercise 2. How many different genetic outcomes are possible according to your Punnett Square? What is the probability of each outcome occurring?

4. Create three word problems that involve using probability and the Punnett Squares to help answer the questions.

5. Collect two or more genetic-related information samples about students in your class. For example, you can collect data on attached/unattached earlobes. Analyze the data and make a prediction about the genetics of the entire school. Draw an appropriate graph of your results.

Statistics and Probability

Watch the Project Video

Go online to watch a video to launch this unit project.

Launch the Project

Objective Research genetic traits and the Punnett Square.

Math Genes

This project is designed to be completed by a group of 4 or 5 students over several days or several weeks. It utilizes concepts from the Statistics and Probability domain. You may choose to complete this project after completing the chapters within this domain.

Collaborate

Have students work in teams to research each activity. Together, they should be able to gather the necessary information to complete Exercises 1-5. Students should show their work on a separate piece of paper.

Share

Collaborate

After each group gives their presentation, ask students to discuss the most challenging part of this project. How did they handle this part of the project? What could they have done differently to make it less challenging?

21st Century Skills

You may want your students to connect their projects to a 21st century skill. Check out the suggestion below and on the student page.

connect with Language Arts

Health Literacy Research the theories of genetics. Write an essay about genes. Some questions to consider are:

- How do genes work?
- What does it mean for a trait to be dominant or recessive?

Reflect

On Your Own

Students should work on their own to reflect on how the chapters from this unit and the objective of the project relate to the Essential Question.

Share

Collaborate

With your group, decide on a way to share what you have learned about genetics and Punnett Squares. Some suggestions are listed below, but you can also think of other creative ways to your present your information. Remember to show how you used mathematics to complete each of the activities in this project.

- Create a digital presentation of the facts you learned about genetics.
- Act as a genetic scientist. Write a journal entry that explains your current research on predicting traits passed down from generations.

Check out the note on the right to connect this project with other subjects.

connect with Health

Health Literacy Select a health condition or disease and research how genetics may play a part in the disease. Write 1-2 paragraphs explaining how genetics may influence someone's risk of getting the disease and steps that can be taken to reduce the risk factors.

Reflect

On Your Own

6. **Answer the Essential Question** Why is learning mathematics important?

   a. How did what you learned about probability help you to understand why learning mathematics is important?

   See students' work.

   b. How did what you learned about statistics help you to understand why learning mathematics is important?

   See students' work.

Glossary/Glosario

Go online for the eGlossary.

The eGlossary contains words and definitions in the following 13 languages:

Arabic	**Cantonese**	**Hmong**	**Spanish**	**Urdu**
Bengali	**English**	**Korean**	**Tagalog**	**Vietnamese**
Brazilian Portuguese	**Haitian Creole**	**Russian**		

English

Aa

absolute value The distance the number is from zero on a number line.

acute angle An angle with a measure greater than 0° and less than 90°.

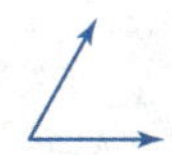

acute triangle A triangle having three acute angles.

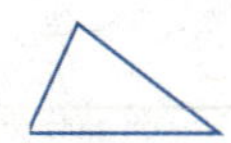

Addition Property of Equality If you add the same number to each side of an equation, the two sides remain equal.

Addition Property of Inequality If you add the same number to each side of an inequality, the inequality remains true.

Additive Identity Property The sum of any number and zero is the number.

additive inverse Two integers that are opposites. The sum of an integer and its additive inverse is zero.

adjacent angles Angles that have the same vertex, share a common side, and do not overlap.

algebra A branch of mathematics that involves expressions with variables.

algebraic expression A combination of variables, numbers, and at least one operation.

Español

valor absoluto Distancia a la que se encuentra un número de cero en la recta numérica.

ángulo agudo Ángulo que mide más de 0° y menos de 90°.

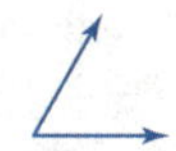

triángulo acutángulo Triángulo con tres ángulos agudos.

propiedad de adición de la igualdad Si sumas el mismo número a ambos lados de una ecuación, los dos lados permanecen iguales.

propiedad de desigualdad en la suma Si se suma el mismo número a cada lado de una desigualdad, la desigualdad sigue siendo verdadera.

propiedad de identidad de la suma La suma de cualquier número y cero es el mismo número.

inverso aditivo Dos enteros opuestos.

ángulos adyacentes Ángulos que comparten el mismo vértice y un común lado, pero no se sobreponen.

álgebra Rama de las matemáticas que trata de las expresiones con variables.

expresión algebraica Combinación de variables, números y por lo menos una operación.

alternate exterior angles Angles that are on opposite sides of the transversal and outside the parallel lines.

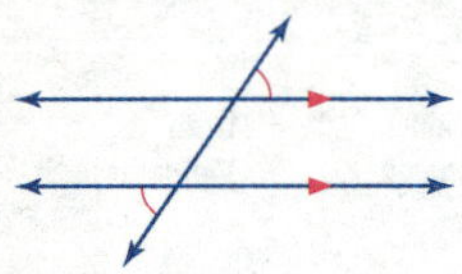

ángulos alternos externos Ángulos en lados opuestos de la trasversal y afuera de las rectas paralelas.

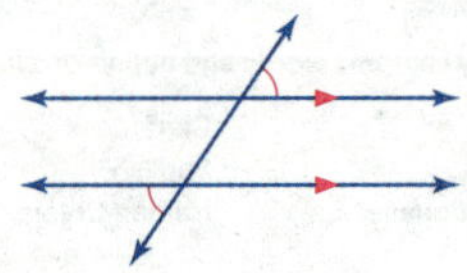

alternate interior angles Angles that are on opposite sides of the transversal and inside the parallel lines.

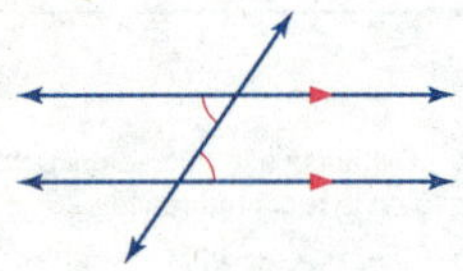

ángulos alternos internos Ángulos en lados opuestos de la trasversal y dentro de las rectas paralelas.

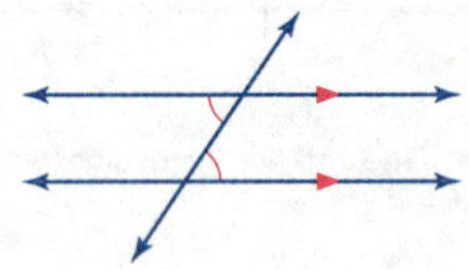

angle Two rays with a common endpoint form an angle. The rays and vertex are used to name the angle.

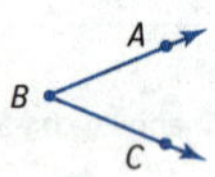

$\angle ABC$, $\angle CBA$, or $\angle B$

ángulo Dos rayos con un extremo común forman un ángulo. Los rayos y el vértice se usan para nombrar el ángulo.

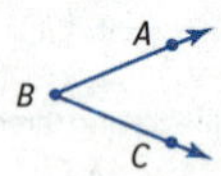

$\angle ABC$, $\angle CBA$ o $\angle B$

arithmetic sequence A sequence in which the difference between any two consecutive terms is the same.

sucesión aritmética Sucesión en la cual la diferencia entre dos términos consecutivos es constante.

Associative Property The way in which numbers are grouped does not change their sum or product.

propiedad asociativa La forma en que se agrupan números al sumarlos o multiplicarlos no altera su suma o producto.

Bb

bar notation In repeating decimals, the line or bar placed over the digits that repeat. For example, $2.\overline{63}$ indicates that the digits 63 repeat.

notación de barra Línea o barra que se coloca sobre los dígitos que se repiten en decimales periódicos. Por ejemplo, $2.\overline{63}$ indica que los dígitos 63 se repiten.

base In a power, the number used as a factor. In 10^3, the base is 10. That is, $10^3 = 10 \times 10 \times 10$.

base En una potencia, el número usado como factor. En 10^3, la base es 10. Es decir, $10^3 = 10 \times 10 \times 10$.

base One of the two parallel congruent faces of a prism.

base Una de las dos caras paralelas congruentes de un prisma.

biased sample A sample drawn in such a way that one or more parts of the population are favored over others.

muestra sesgada Muestra en que se favorece una o más partes de una población.

box plot A method of visually displaying a distribution of data values by using the median, quartiles, and extremes of the data set. A box shows the middle 50% of the data.

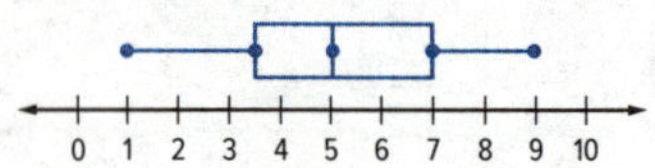

diagrama de caja Un método de mostrar visualmente una distribución de valores usando la mediana, cuartiles y extremos del conjunto de datos. Una caja muestra el 50% del medio de los datos.

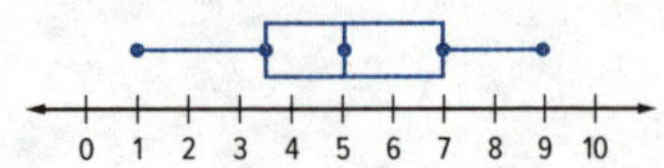

Cc

center The point from which all points on circle are the same distance.

centro El punto desde el cual todos los puntos en una circunferencia están a la misma distancia.

circle The set of all points in a plane that are the same distance from a given point called the center.

círculo Conjunto de todos los puntos de un plano que están a la misma distancia de un punto dado denominado "centro".

circle graph A graph that shows data as parts of a whole. In a circle graph, the percents add up to 100.

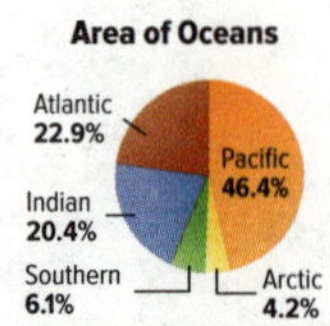

gráfica circular Gráfica que muestra los datos como partes de un todo. En una gráfica circular los porcentajes suman 100.

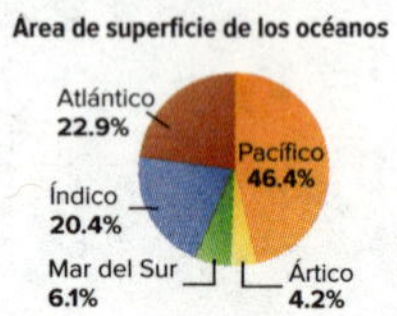

circumference The distance around a circle.

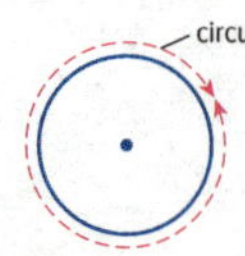

circunferencia Distancia en torno a un círculo.

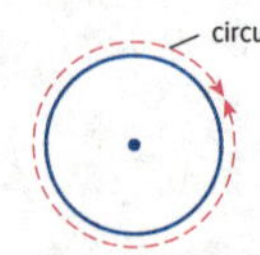

coefficient The numerical factor of a term that contains a variable.

coeficiente El factor numérico de un término que contiene una variable.

common denominator A common multiple of the denominators of two or more fractions. 24 is a common denominator for $\frac{1}{3}$, $\frac{5}{8}$, and $\frac{3}{4}$ because 24 is the LCM of 3, 8, and 4.

común denominador El múltiplo común de los denominadores de dos o más fracciones. 24 es un denominador común para $\frac{1}{3}$, $\frac{5}{8}$ y $\frac{3}{4}$ porque 24 es el mcm de 3, 8 y 4.

Commutative Property The order in which two numbers are added or multiplied does not change their sum or product.

propiedad conmutativa El orden en que se suman o multiplican dos números no altera el resultado.

complementary angles Two angles are complementary if the sum of their measures is 90°.

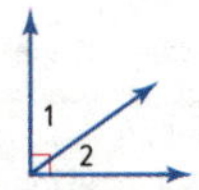

∠1 and ∠2 are complementary angles.

complementary events The events of one outcome happening and that outcome not happening. The sum of the probabilities of an event and its complement is 1 or 100%. In symbols, $P(\text{A}) + P(not \text{ A}) = 1$.

complex fraction A fraction $\frac{A}{B}$ where A or B are fractions and B does not equal zero.

composite figure A figure that is made up of two or more three-dimensional figures.

compound event An event consisting of two or more simple events.

cone A three-dimensional figure with one circular base connected by a curved surface to a single vertex.

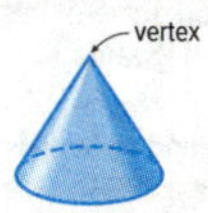

congruent Having the same measure.

congruent angles Angles that have the same measure.

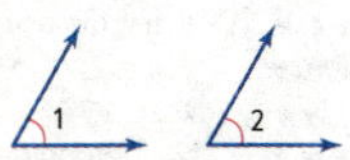

∠1 and ∠2 are congruent angles.

congruent figures Figures that have the same size and same shape and corresponding sides and angles with equal measure.

congruent segments Sides with the same length.

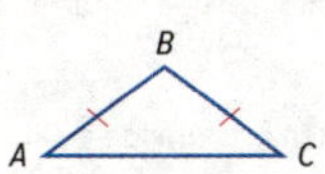

Side $\overline{AB}$ is congruent to side $\overline{BC}$.

ángulos complementarios Dos ángulos son complementarios si la suma de sus medidas es 90°.

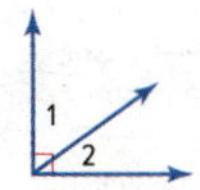

∠1 y ∠2 son complementarios.

eventos complementarios Los eventos de un resultado que ocurre y ese resultado que no ocurre. La suma de las probabilidades de un evento y su complemento es 1 ó 100. En símbolos $P(\text{A}) + P(no \text{ A}) = 1$.

fracción compleja Una fracción $\frac{A}{B}$ en la cual A o B son fracciones y B no es igual a cero.

figura compuesta Figura formada por dos o más figuras tridimensionales.

evento compuesto Un evento que consiste en dos o más eventos simples.

cono Una figura tridimensional con una base circular conectada por una superficie curva para un solo vértice.

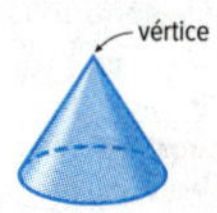

congruente Que tiene la misma medida.

ángulos congruentes Ángulos que tienen la misma medida.

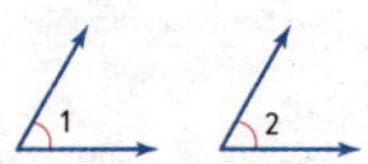

∠1 y ∠2 son congruentes.

figuras congruentes Figuras que tienen el mismo tamaño y la misma forma y los lados y los ángulos correspondientes tienen igual medida.

segmentos congruentes Lados con la misma longitud.

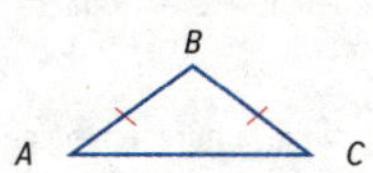

$\overline{AB}$ es congruente a $\overline{BC}$.

constant A term that does not contain a variable.

constant of proportionality A constant ratio or unit rate of two variable quantities. It is also called the constant of variation.

constant of variation The constant ratio in a direct variation. It is also called the constant of proportionality.

constant rate of change The rate of change in a linear relationship.

continuous data Data that take on any real number value. It can be determined by considering what numbers are reasonable as part of the domain.

convenience sample A sample which consists of members of a population that are easily accessed.

coordinate plane A plane in which a horizontal number line and a vertical number line intersect at their zero points. Also called a coordinate grid.

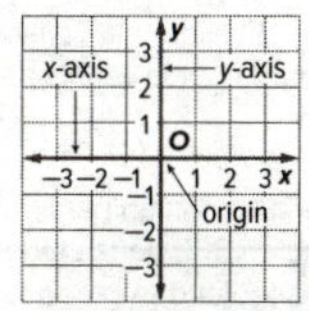

coplanar Lines or points that lie in the same plane.

corresponding angles Angles in the same position on parallel lines in relation to a transversal.

corresponding sides The sides of similar figures that are in the same relative position.

counterexample A specific case which proves a statement false.

cross product The product of the numerator of one ratio and the denominator of the other ratio. The cross products of any proportion are equal.

cross section The cross section of a solid and a plane.

constante Término que no contiene ninguna variable.

constante de proporcionalidad Una razón constante o tasa por unidad de dos cantidades variables. También se llama constante de variación.

constante de variación Una razón constante o tasa por unidad de dos cantidades variables. También se llama constante de proporcionalidad.

razón constante de cambio Tasa de cambio en una relación lineal.

datos continuos Datos que asumen cualquier valor numérico real. Se pueden determinar al considerar qué números son razonables como parte del dominio.

muestra de conveniencia Muestra que incluye miembros de una población fácilmente accesibles.

plano de coordenadas Plano en el cual se han trazado dos rectas numéricas, una horizontal y una vertical, que se intersecan en sus puntos cero. También conocido como sistema de coordenadas.

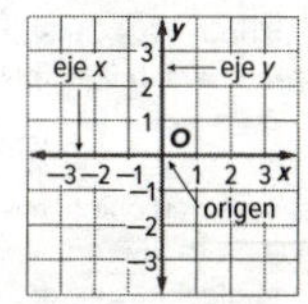

coplanar Líneas o puntos situados en el mismo plano.

ángulos correspondientes Ángulos que están en la misma posición sobre rectas paralelas en relación con la transversal.

lados correspondientes Lados de figuras semejantes que estan en la misma posición.

contraejemplo Caso específico que demuestra la falsedad de un enunciado.

producto cruzado Producto del numerador de una razón por el denominador de la otra razón. Los productos cruzados de cualquier proporción son iguales.

sección transversal Intersección de un sólido con un plano.

cube root One of three equal factors of a number. If $a^3 = b$, then a is the cube root of b. The cube root of 125 is 5 since $5^3 = 125$.

cubed The product in which a number is a factor three times. Two cubed is 8 because $2 \times 2 \times 2 = 8$.

cylinder A three-dimensional figure with two parallel congruent circular bases connected by a curved surface.

raíz cúbica Uno de tres factores iguales de un número. Si $a^3 = b$, entonces a es la raíz cúbica de b. La raíz cúbica de 125 es 5, dado que $5^3 = 125$.

al cubo El producto de un número por sí mismo, tres veces. Dos al cubo es 8 porque $2 \times 2 \times 2 = 8$.

cilindro Una figura tridimensional con dos paralelas congruentes circulares bases conectados por una superficie curva.

Dd

decagon A polygon having ten sides.

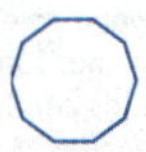

defining a variable Choosing a variable and a quantity for the variable to represent in an expression or equation.

degrees The most common unit of measure for angles. If a circle were divided into 360 equal-sized parts, each part would have an angle measure of 1 degree.

dependent events Two or more events in which the outcome of one event affects the outcome of the other event(s).

dependent variable The variable in a relation with a value that depends on the value of the independent variable.

derived unit A unit that is derived from a measurement system base unit, such as length, mass, or time.

diagonal A line segment that connects two nonconsecutive vertices.

diameter The distance across a circle through its center.

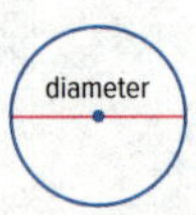

decágono Un polígono con diez lados.

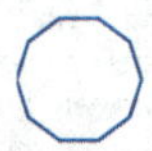

definir una variable El elegir una variable y una cantidad que esté representada por la variable en una expresión o en una ecuacion.

grados La unidad más común para medir ángulos. Si un círculo se divide en 360 partes iguales, cada parte tiene una medida angular de 1 grado.

eventos dependientes Dos o más eventos en que el resultado de un evento afecta el resultado de otro u otros eventos.

variable dependiente La variable en una relación cuyo valor depende del valor de la variable independiente.

unidad derivada Unidad que se deriva de una unidad básica de un sistema de medidas, como la longitud, la masa o el tiempo.

diagonal Segmento de recta que une dos vértices no consecutivos de un polígono.

diámetro Segmento que pasa por el centro de un círculo y lo divide en dos partes iguales.

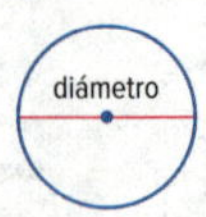

dimensional analysis The process of including units of measurement when you compute.

direct variation The relationship between two variable quantities that have a constant ratio.

discount The amount by which the regular price of an item is reduced.

discrete data When solutions of a function are only integer values. It can be determined by considering what numbers are reasonable as part of the domain.

disjoint events Events that cannot happen at the same time.

Distributive Property To multiply a sum by a number, multiply each addend of the sum by the number outside the parentheses. For any numbers a, b, and c, $a(b + c) = ab + ac$ and $a(b - c) = ab - ac$.

Example: $2(5 + 3) = (2 \times 5) + (2 \times 3)$ and $2(5 - 3) = (2 \times 5) - (2 \times 3)$

Division Property of Equality If you divide each side of an equation by the same nonzero number, the two sides remain equal.

Division Property of Inequality When you divide each side of an inequality by a negative number, the inequality symbol must be reversed for the inequality to remain true.

domain The set of input values for a function.

double box plot Two box plots graphed on the same number line.

double dot plot A method of visually displaying a distribution of two sets of data values where each value is shown as a dot above a number line.

análisis dimensional Proceso que incluye las unidades de medida al hacer cálculos.

variación directa Relación entre las cantidades de dos variables que tienen una tasa constante.

descuento Cantidad que se le rebaja al precio regular de un artículo.

datos discretos Cuando las soluciones de una función son solo valores enteros. Se pueden determinar considerando qué números son razonables como parte del dominio.

eventos disjuntos Eventos que no pueden ocurrir al mismo tiempo.

propiedad distributiva Para multiplicar una suma por un número, multiplíquese cada sumando de la suma por el número que está fuera del paréntesis. Sean cuales fuere los números a, b, y c, $a(b + c) = ab + ac$ y $a(b - c) = ab - ac$.

Ejemplo: $2(5 + 3) = (2 \cdot 5) + (2 \cdot 3)$ y $2(5 - 3) = (2 \cdot 5) - (2 \cdot 3)$

propiedad de igualdad de la división Si divides ambos lados de una ecuación entre el mismo número no nulo, los lados permanecen iguales.

propiedad de desigualdad en la división Cuando se divide cada lado de una desigualdad entre un número negativo, el símbolo de desigualdad debe invertirse para que la desigualdad siga siendo verdadera.

dominio El conjunto de valores de entrada de una función.

doble diagrama de caja Dos diagramas de caja sobre la misma recta numérica.

doble diagrama de puntos Un método de mostrar visualmente una distribución de dos conjuntos de valores donde cada valor se muestra como un punto arriba de una recta numérica.

Ee

edge The line segment where two faces of a polyhedron intersect.

enlargement An image larger than the original.

equation A mathematical sentence that contains an equals sign, =, stating that two quantities are equal.

borde El segmento de línea donde se cruzan dos caras de un poliedro.

ampliación Imagen más grande que la original.

ecuación Enunciado matemático que contiene el signo de igualdad = indicando que dos cantidades son iguales.

equiangular In a polygon, all of the angles are congruent.

equilateral In a polygon, all of the sides are congruent.

equilateral triangle A triangle having three congruent sides.

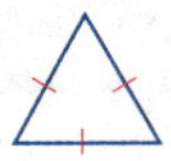

equivalent equations Two or more equations with the same solution.

equivalent expressions Expressions that have the same value.

equivalent ratios Two ratios that have the same value.

evaluate To find the value of an expression.

experimental probability An estimated probability based on the relative frequency of positive outcomes occurring during an experiment. It is based on what *actually* occurred during such an experiment.

exponent In a power, the number that tells how many times the base is used as a factor. In 5^3, the exponent is 3. That is, $5^3 = 5 \times 5 \times 5$.

exponential form Numbers written with exponents.

equiangular En un polígono, todos los ángulos son congruentes.

equilátero En un polígono, todos los lados son congruentes.

triángulo equilátero Triángulo con tres lados congruentes.

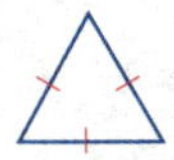

ecuaciones equivalentes Dos o más ecuaciones con la misma solución.

expresiones equivalentes Expresiones que tienen el mismo valor.

razones equivalentes Dos razones que tienen el mismo valor.

evaluar Calcular el valor de una expresión.

probabilidad experimental Probabilidad estimada que se basa en la frecuencia relativa de los resultados positivos que ocurren durante un experimento. Se basa en lo que *en realidad* ocurre durante dicho experimento.

exponente En una potencia, el número que indica las veces que la base se usa como factor. En 5^3, el exponente es 3. Es decir, $5^3 = 5 \times 5 \times 5$.

forma exponencial Números escritos usando exponentes.

Ff

face A flat surface of a polyhedron.

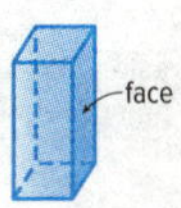

factor To write a number as a product of its factors.

factored form An expression expressed as the product of its factors.

factors Two or more numbers that are multiplied together to form a product.

cara Una superficie plana de un poliedro.

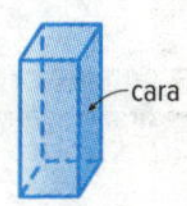

factorizar Escribir un número como el producto de sus factores.

forma factorizada Una expresión expresada como el producto de sus factores.

factores Dos o más números que se multiplican entre sí para formar un producto.

fair game A game where each player has an equally likely chance of winning.

first quartile For a data set with median *M*, the first quartile is the median of the data values less than *M*.

formula An equation that shows the relationship among certain quantities.

function A relationship which assigns exactly one output value for each input value.

function rule The operation performed on the input of a function.

function table A table used to organize the input numbers, output numbers, and the function rule.

Fundamental Counting Principle Uses multiplication of the number of ways each event in an experiment can occur to find the number of possible outcomes in a sample space.

juego justo Juego donde cada jugador tiene igual posibilidad de ganar.

primer cuartil Para un conjunto de datos con la mediana *M*, el primer cuartil es la mediana de los valores menores que *M*.

fórmula Ecuación que muestra la relación entre ciertas cantidades.

función Relación que asigna exactamente un valor de salida a cada valor de entrada.

regla de función Operación que se efectúa en el valor de entrada.

tabla de funciones Tabla que organiza las entradas, la regla y las salidas de una función.

Principio Fundamental de Contar Este principio usa la multiplicación del número de veces que puede ocurrir cada evento en un experimento para calcular el número de posibles resultados en un espacio muestral.

Gg

gram A unit of mass in the metric system equivalent to 0.001 kilogram. The amount of matter an object can hold.

graph The process of placing a point on a number line or on a coordinate plane at its proper location.

gratuity Also known as a tip. It is a small amount of money in return for a service.

gramo Unidad de masa en el sistema métrico que equivale a 0.001 de kilogramo. La cantidad de materia que puede contener un objeto.

graficar Proceso de dibujar o trazar un punto en una recta numérica o en un plano de coordenadas en su ubicación correcta.

gratificación También conocida como propina. Es una cantidad pequeña de dinero en retribución por un servicio.

Hh

heptagon A polygon having seven sides.

hexagon A polygon having six sides.

heptágono Polígono con siete lados.

hexágono Polígono con seis lados.

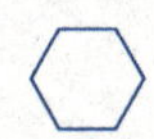

histogram A type of bar graph used to display numerical data that have been organized into equal intervals.

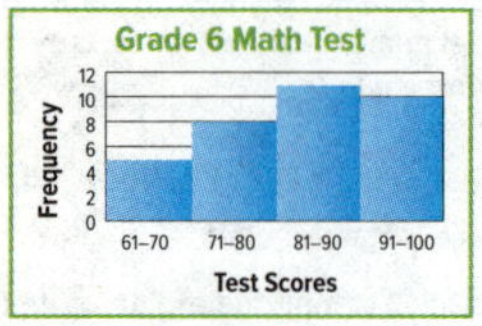

histograma Tipo de gráfica de barras que se usa para exhibir datos que se han organizado en intervalos iguales.

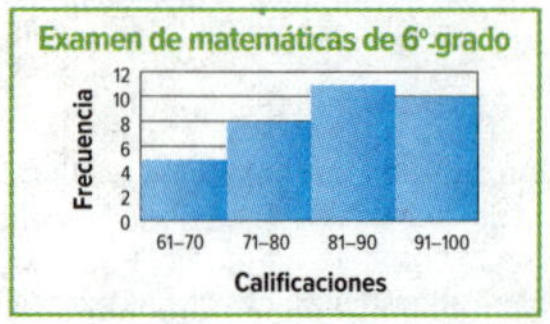

Ii

Identity Property of Zero The sum of an addend and zero is the addend. Example: $5 + 0 = 5$

propiedad de identidad del cero La suma de un sumando y cero es igual al sumando. Ejemplo: $5 + 0 = 5$

independent events Two or more events in which the outcome of one event does not affect the outcome of the other event(s).

eventos independientes Dos o más eventos en los cuales el resultado de uno de ellos no afecta el resultado de los otros eventos.

independent variable The variable in a function with a value that is subject to choice.

variable independiente Variable en una función cuyo valor está sujeto a elección.

indirect measurement Finding a measurement using similar figures to find the length, width, or height of objects that are too difficult to measure directly.

medición indirecta Hallar una medición usando figuras semejantes para calcular el largo, ancho o altura de objetos que son difíciles de medir directamente.

inequality An open sentence that uses $<, >, \neq, \leq$, or $\geq$ to compare two quantities.

desigualdad Enunciado abierto que usa $<, >, \neq, \leq$ o $\geq$ para comparar dos cantidades.

integer Any number from the set $\{\ldots, -4, -3, -2, -1, 0, 1, 2, 3, 4, \ldots\}$, where … means continues without end.

entero Cualquier número del conjunto $\{\ldots, -4, -3, -2, -1, 0, 1, 2, 3, 4, \ldots\}$, donde … significa que continúa sin fin.

interquartile range A measure of variation in a set of numerical data. It is the distance between first and third quartiles of the data set.

rango intercuartil Una medida de la variación en un conjunto de datos numéricos. Es la distancia entre el primer y el tercer cuartiles del conjunto de datos.

inverse variation A relationship where the product of x and y is a constant k. As x increases in value, y decreases in value, or as y decreases in value, x increases in value.

variación inversa Relación en la cual el producto de x y y es una constante k. A medida que aumenta el valor de x, disminuye el valor de y o a medida que disminuye el valor de y, aumenta el valor de x.

irrational number A number that cannot be expressed as the ratio of two integers.

número irracional Número que no se puede expresar como el razón de dos enteros.

isosceles triangle A triangle having at least two congruent sides.

triángulo isósceles Triángulo que tiene por lo menos dos lados congruentes.

Kk

kilogram The base unit of mass in the metric system. One kilogram equals 1,000 grams.

kilogramo Unidad básica de masa del sistema métrico. Un kilogramo equivale a 1,000 gramos.

Ll

lateral face In a polyhedron, a face that is not a base.

cara lateral En un poliedro, las caras que no forman las bases.

lateral surface area The sum of the areas of all of the lateral faces of a solid.

área de superficie lateral Suma de las áreas de todas las caras de un sólido.

least common denominator (LCD) The least common multiple of the denominators of two or more fractions. You can use the LCD to compare fractions.

mínimo común denominador (mcd) El menor de los múltiplos de los denominadores de dos o más fracciones. Puedes usar el mínimo común denominador para comparar fracciones.

like fractions Fractions that have the same denominators.

fracciones semejantes Fracciones que tienen los mismos denominadores.

like terms Terms that contain the same variables raised to the same power. Example: $5x$ and $6x$ are like terms.

términos semejante Términos que contienen las mismas variables elevadas a la misma potencia. Ejemplo: $5x$ y $6x$ son *términos semejante*.

line graph A type of statistical graph using lines to show how values change over a period of time.

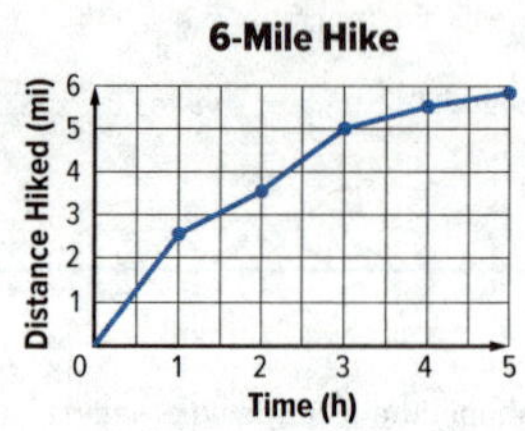

gráfica lineal Tipo de gráfica estadística que usa segmentos de recta para mostrar cómo cambian los valores durante un período de tiempo.

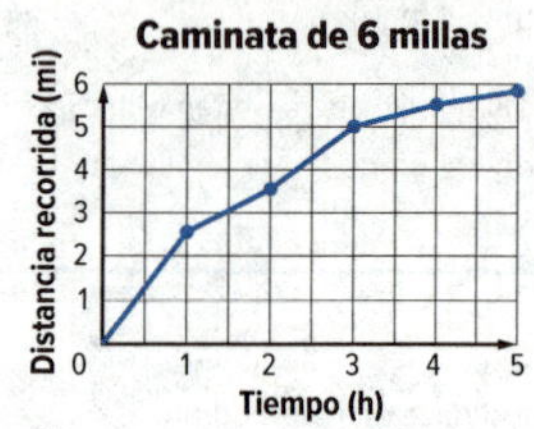

linear expression An algebraic expression in which the variable is raised to the first power, and variables are not multiplied nor divided.

expresión lineal Expresión algebraica en la cual la variable se eleva a la primera potencia.

linear function A function for which the graph is a straight line.

función lineal Función cuya gráfica es una recta.

linear relationship A relationship for which the graph is a straight line.

relación lineal Una relación para la cual la gráfica es una línea recta.

liter The base unit of capacity in the metric system. The amount of dry or liquid material an object can hold.

litro Unidad básica de capacidad del sistema métrico. La cantidad de materia líquida o sólida que puede contener un objeto.

Mm

markdown An amount by which the regular price of an item is reduced.

rebaja Una cantidad por la cual el precio regular de un artículo se reduce.

markup The amount the price of an item is increased above the price the store paid for the item.

margen de utilidad Cantidad de aumento en el precio de un artículo por encima del precio que paga la tienda por dicho artículo.

mean The sum of the data divided by the number of items in the data set.

media La suma de los datos dividida entre el número total de artículos en el conjunto de datos.

mean absolute deviation A measure of variation in a set of numerical data, computed by adding the distances between each data value and the mean, then dividing by the number of data values.

desviación media absoluta Una medida de variación en un conjunto de datos numéricos que se calcula sumando las distancias entre el valor de cada dato y la media, y luego dividiendo entre el número de valores.

measures of center Numbers that are used to describe the center of a set of data. These measures include the mean, median, and mode.

medidas del centro Números que se usan para describir el centro de un conjunto de datos. Estas medidas incluyen la media, la mediana y la moda.

measures of variation A measure used to describe the distribution of data.

medidas de variación Medida usada para describir la distribución de los datos.

median A measure of center in a set of numerical data. The median of a list of values is the value appearing at the center of a sorted version of the list—or the mean of the two central values, if the list contains an even number of values.

mediana Una medida del centro en un conjunto de dados numéricos. La mediana de una lista de valores es el valor que aparace en el centro de una versíon ordenada de la lista, o la media de dos valores centrales si la lista contiene un número par de valores.

meter The base unit of length in the metric system.

metro Unidad fundamental de longitud del sistema métrico.

metric system A decimal system of measures. The prefixes commonly used in this system are kilo-, centi-, and milli-.

sistema métrico Sistema decimal de medidas. Los prefijos más comunes son kilo-, centi- y mili-.

mode The number or numbers that appear most often in a set of data. If there are two or more numbers that occur most often, all of them are modes.

moda El número o números que aparece con más frecuencia en un conjunto de datos. Si hay dos o más números que ocurren con más frecuencia, todosellos son modas.

monomial A number, variable, or product of a number and one or more variables.

monomio Número, variable o producto de un número y una o más variables.

Multiplication Property of Equality If you multiply each side of an equation by the same nonzero number, the two sides remain equal.

propiedad de multiplicación de la igualdad Si multiplicas ambos lados de una ecuación por el mismo número no nulo, lo lados permanecen iguales.

Multiplication Property of Inequality When you multiply each side of an inequality by a negative number, the inequality symbol must be reversed for the inequality to remain true.

propiedad de desigualdad en la multiplicación Cuando se multiplica cada lado de una desigualdad por un número negativo, el símbolo de desigualdad debe invertirse para que la desigualdad siga siendo verdadera.

Multiplicative Identity Property The product of any number and one is the number.

propiedad de identidad de la multiplicación El producto de cualquier número y uno es el mismo número.

Multiplicative Property of Zero The product of any number and zero is zero.

propiedad del cero en la multiplicación El producto de cualquier número y cero es cero.

multiplicative inverse Two numbers with a product of 1. For example, the multiplicative inverse of $\frac{2}{3}$ is $\frac{3}{2}$.

inverso multiplicativo Dos números cuyo producto es 1. Por ejemplo, el inverso multiplicativo de $\frac{2}{3}$ es $\frac{3}{2}$.

Nn

negative exponent Any nonzero number to the negative *n* power. It is the multiplicative inverse of its *n*th power.

exponente negativo Cualquier número que no sea cero a la potencia negative de *n*. Es el inverso multiplicativo de su *enésimo* potencia.

negative integer An integer that is less than zero. Negative integers are written with a − sign.

entero negativo Número menor que cero. Se escriben con el signo −.

net A two-dimensional figure that can be used to build a three-dimensional figure.

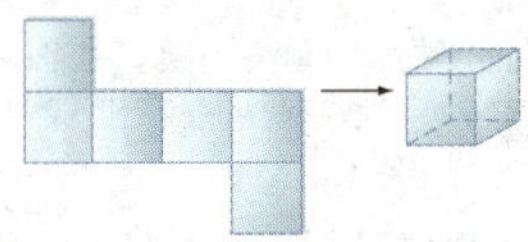

red Figura bidimensional que sirve para hacer una figura tridimensional.

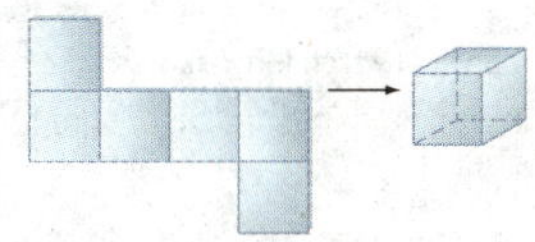

nonagon A polygon having nine sides.

enágono Polígono que tiene nueve lados.

nonlinear function A function for which the graph is *not* a straight line.

nonlinear function Función cuya gráfica *no* es una línea recta.

nonproportional The relationship between two ratios with a rate or ratio that is not constant.

no proporcional Relación entre dos razones cuya tasa o razón no es constante.

numerical expression A combination of numbers and operations.

expresión numérica Combinación de números y operaciones.

Oo

obtuse angle Any angle that measures greater than 90° but less than 180°.

ángulo obtuso Cualquier ángulo que mide más de 90° pero menos de 180°.

obtuse triangle A triangle having one obtuse angle.

triángulo obtusángulo Triángulo que tiene un ángulo obtuso.

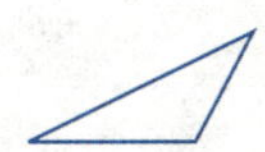

octagon A polygon having eight sides.

opposites Two integers are opposites if they are represented on the number line by points that are the same distance from zero, but on opposite sides of zero. The sum of two opposites is zero.

order of operations The rules to follow when more than one operation is used in a numerical expression.

1. Evaluate the expressions inside grouping symbols.
2. Evaluate all powers.
3. Multiply and divide in order from left to right.
4. Add and subtract in order from left to right.

ordered pair A pair of numbers used to locate a point in the coordinate plane. An ordered pair is written in the form (*x*-coordinate, *y*-coordinate).

origin The point at which the *x*-axis and the *y*-axis intersect in a coordinate plane. The origin is at (0, 0).

outcome Any one of the possible results of an action. For example, 4 is an outcome when a number cube is rolled.

outlier A data value that is either much *greater* or much *less* than the median.

octágono Polígono que tiene ocho lados.

opuestos Dos enteros son opuestos si, en la recta numérica, están representados por puntos que equidistan de cero, pero en direcciones opuestas. La suma de dos opuestos es cero.

orden de las operaciones Reglas a seguir cuando se usa más de una operación en una expresión numérica.

1. Primero, evalúa las expresiones dentro de los símbolos de agrupación.
2. Evalúa todas las potencias.
3. Multiplica y divide en orden de izquierda a derecha.
4. Suma y resta en orden de izquierda a derecha.

par ordenado Par de números que se utiliza para ubicar un punto en un plano de coordenadas. Se escribe de la siguiente forma: (coordenada *x*, coordenada *y*).

origen Punto en que el eje *x* y el eje *y* se intersecan en un plano de coordenadas. El origen está ubicado en (0, 0).

resultado Cualquiera de los resultados posibles de una acción. Por ejemplo, 4 puede ser un resultado al lanzar un cubo numerado.

valor atípico Valor de los datos que es mucho *mayor* o mucho *menor* que la mediana.

Pp

parallel lines Lines in a plane that never intersect.

parallelogram A quadrilateral with opposite sides parallel and opposite sides congruent.

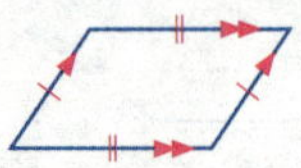

rectas paralelas Rectas en un plano que nunca se intersecan.

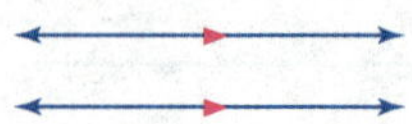

paralelogramo Cuadrilátero cuyos lados opuestos son paralelos y congruentes.

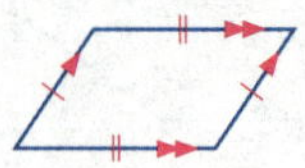

pentagon A polygon having five sides.

percent equation An equation that describes the relationship between the part, whole, and percent.

part = percent • whole

percent error A ratio that compares the inaccuracy of an estimate (amount of error) to the actual amount.

percent of change A ratio that compares the change in a quantity to the original amount.

$$\text{percent of change} = \frac{\text{amount of change}}{\text{original amount}}$$

percent of decrease A negative percent of change.

percent of increase A positive percent of change.

percent proportion One ratio or fraction that compares part of a quantity to the whole quantity. The other ratio is the equivalent percent written as a fraction with a denominator of 100.

$$\frac{\text{part}}{\text{whole}} = \frac{\text{percent}}{100}$$

perfect squares Numbers with square roots that are whole numbers. 25 is a perfect square because the square root of 25 is 5.

permutation An arrangement, or listing, of objects in which order is important.

perpendicular lines Lines that meet or cross each other to form right angles.

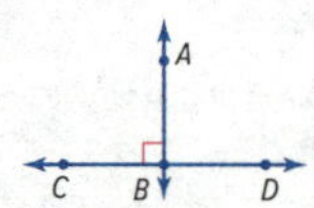

pi The ratio of the circumference of a circle to its diameter. The Greek letter π represents this number. The value of pi is 3.1415926. . . . Approximations for pi are 3.14 and $\frac{22}{7}$.

plane A two-dimensional flat surface that extends in all directions.

pentágono Polígono que tiene cinco lados.

ecuación porcentual Ecuación que describe la relación entre la parte, el todo y el por ciento.

parte = por ciento • todo

porcentaje de error Una razón que compara la inexactitud de una estimación (cantidad del error) con la cantidad real.

porcentaje de cambio Razón que compara el cambio en una cantidad a la cantidad original.

$$\text{porcentaje de cambio} = \frac{\text{cantidad del cambio}}{\text{cantidad original}}$$

porcentaje de disminución Porcentaje de cambio negativo.

porcentaje de aumento Porcentaje de cambio positivo.

proporción porcentual Razón o fracción que compara parte de una cantidad a toda la cantidad. La otra razón es el porcentaje equivalente escrito como fracción con 100 de denominador.

$$\frac{\text{parte}}{\text{todo}} = \frac{\text{porcentaje}}{100}$$

cuadrados perfectos Números cuya raíz cuadrada es un número entero. 25 es un cuadrado perfecto porque la raíz cuadrada de 25 es 5.

permutación Arreglo o lista de objetos en la cual el orden es importante.

rectas perpendiculares Rectas que al encontrarse o cruzarse forman ángulos rectos.

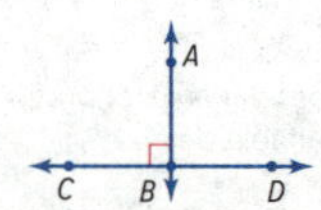

pi Relación entre la circunferencia de un círculo y su diámetro. La letra griega π representa este número. El valor de pi es 3.1415926. . . . Las aproximaciones de pi son 3.14 y $\frac{22}{7}$.

plano Superficie bidimensional que se extiende en todas direcciones.

polygon A simple closed figure formed by three or more straight line segments.

polyhedron A three-dimensional figure with faces that are polygons.

population The entire group of items or individuals from which the samples under consideration are taken.

positive integer An integer that is greater than zero. They are written with or without a + sign.

powers Numbers expressed using exponents. The power 3^2 is read *three to the second power,* or *three squared.*

precision The ability of a measurement to be consistently reproduced.

principal The amount of money deposited or borrowed.

prism A polyhedron with two parallel congruent faces called bases.

probability The chance that some event will happen. It is the ratio of the number of favorable outcomes to the number of possible outcomes.

probability model A model used to assign probabilities to outcomes of a chance process by examining the nature of the process.

properties Statements that are true for any number or variable.

proportion An equation stating that two ratios or rates are equivalent.

proportional The relationship between two ratios with a constant rate or ratio.

pyramid A polyhedron with one base that is a polygon and three or more triangular faces that meet at a common vertex.

polígono Figura cerrada simple formada por tres o más segmentos de recta.

poliedro Una figura tridimensional con caras que son polígonos.

población El grupo total de individuos o de artículos del cual se toman las muestras bajo estudio.

entero positivo Entero que es mayor que cero; se escribe con o sin el signo +.

potencias Números que se expresan usando exponentes. La potencia 3^2 se lee *tres a la segunda potencia o tres al cuadrado.*

precisión Capacidad que tiene una medición de poder reproducirse consistentemente.

capital Cantidad de dinero que se deposita o se toma prestada.

prisma Un poliedro con dos caras congruentes paralelas llamadas bases.

probabilidad La posibilidad de que suceda un evento. Es la razón del número de resultados favorables al número de resultados posibles.

modelo de probabilidad Un modelo usado para asignar probabilidades a resultados de un proceso aleatorio examinando la naturaleza del proceso.

propiedades Enunciados que son verdaderos para cualquier número o variable.

proporción Ecuación que indica que dos razones o tasas son equivalentes.

proporcional Relación entre dos razones con una tasa o razón constante.

pirámide Un poliedro con una base que es un polígono y tres o más caras triangulares que se encuentran en un vértice común.

Qq

quadrant One of the four regions into which the two perpendicular number lines of the coordinate plane separate the plane.

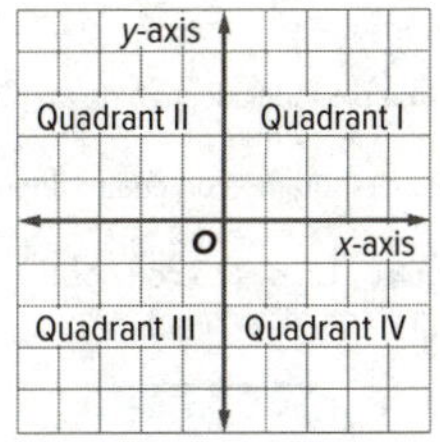

quadrilateral A closed figure having four sides and four angles.

quartile A value that divides the data set into four equal parts.

cuadrante Una de las cuatro regiones en que dos rectas numéricas perpendiculares dividen el plano de coordenadas.

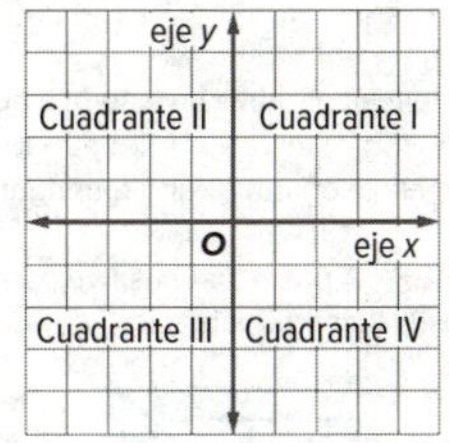

cuadrilátero Figura cerrada que tiene cuatro lados y cuatro ángulos.

cuartil Valor que divide el conjunto de datos en cuatro partes iguales.

Rr

radical sign The symbol used to indicate a nonnegative square root, $\sqrt{\ }$.

radius The distance from the center of a circle to any point on the circle.

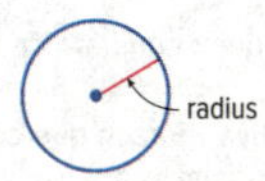

random Outcomes occur at random if each outcome occurs by chance. For example, rolling a number on a number cube occurs at random.

range The set of output values for a function.

range The difference between the greatest and least data value.

rate A ratio that compares two quantities with different kinds of units.

rate of change A rate that describes how one quantity changes in relation to another. A rate of change is usually expressed as a unit rate.

signo radical Símbolo que se usa para indicar una raíz cuadrada no negativa, $\sqrt{\ }$.

radio Distancia desde el centro de un círculo hasta cualquiera de sus puntos.

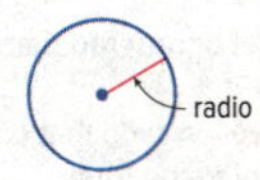

azar Los resultados ocurren aleatoriamente si cada resultado ocurre por casualidad. Por ejemplo, sacar un número en un cubo numerado ocurre al azar.

rango Conjunto de valores de salida para una función.

rango La diferencia entre el número mayor y el menor en un conjunto de datos.

tasa Razón que compara dos cantidades que tienen distintas unidades de medida.

tasa de cambio Tasa que describe cómo cambia una cantidad con respecto a otra. Por lo general, se expresa como tasa unitaria.

rational numbers The set of numbers that can be written in the form $\frac{a}{b}$, where a and b are integers and $b \neq 0$.
Examples: $1 = \frac{1}{1}, \frac{2}{9}, -2.3 = -2\frac{3}{10}$

real numbers A set made up of rational and irrational numbers.

reciprocal The multiplicative inverse of a number.

rectangle A parallelogram having four right angles.

rectangular prism A prism that has two parallel congruent bases that are rectangles.

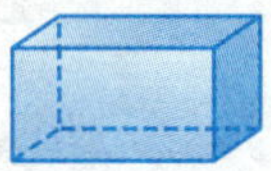

reduction An image smaller than the original.

regular polygon A polygon that has all sides congruent and all angles congruent.

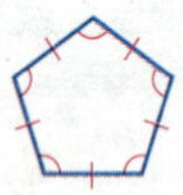

regular pyramid A pyramid whose base is a regular polygon and in which the segment from the vertex to the center of the base is the altitude.

relation Any set of ordered pairs.

relative frequency A ratio that compares the frequency of each category to the total.

repeating decimal The decimal form of a rational number.

rhombus A parallelogram having four congruent sides.

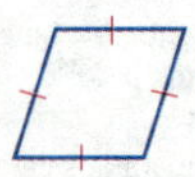

right angle An angle that measures exactly 90°.

números racionales Conjunto de números que puede escribirse en la forma $\frac{a}{b}$ donde a y b son números enteros y $b \neq 0$.
Ejemplos: $1 = \frac{1}{1}, \frac{2}{9}, -2.3 = -2\frac{3}{10}$

números reales Conjunto de números racionales e irracionales.

recíproco El inverso multiplicativo de un número.

rectángulo Paralelogramo con cuatro ángulos rectos.

prisma rectangular Un prisma con dos bases paralelas congruentes que son rectángulos.

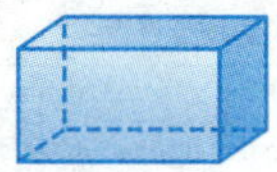

reducción Imagen más pequeña que la original.

polígono regular Polígono con todos los lados y todos los ángulos congruentes.

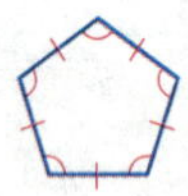

pirámide regular Pirámide cuya base es un polígono regular y en la cual el segmento desde el vértice hasta el centro de la base es la altura.

relación Cualquier conjunto de pares ordenados.

frecuencia relativa Razón que compara la frecuencia de cada categoría al total.

decimal periódico La forma decimal de un número racional.

rombo Paralelogramo que tiene cuatro lados congruentes.

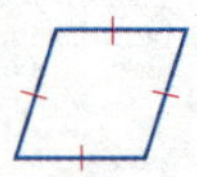

ángulo recto Ángulo que mide exactamente 90°.

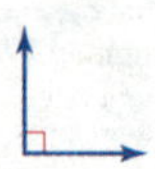

right triangle A triangle having one right angle.

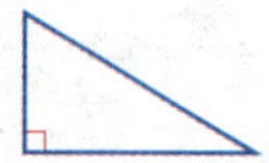

triángulo rectángulo Triángulo que tiene un ángulo recto.

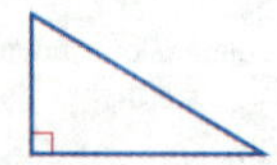

Ss

sales tax An additional amount of money charged on items that people buy.

sample A randomly selected group chosen for the purpose of collecting data.

sample space The set of all possible outcomes of a probability experiment.

scale The scale that gives the ratio that compares the measurements of a drawing or model to the measurements of the real object.

scale drawing A drawing that is used to represent objects that are too large or too small to be drawn at actual size.

scale factor A scale written as a ratio without units in simplest form.

scale model A model used to represent objects that are too large or too small to be built at actual size.

scalene triangle A triangle having no congruent sides.

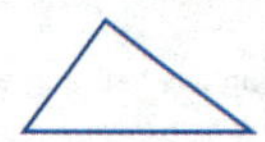

scatter plot In a scatter plot, two sets of related data are plotted as ordered pairs on the same graph.

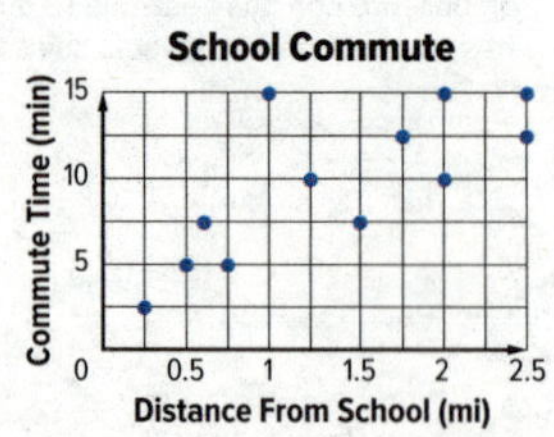

impuesto sobre las ventas Cantidad de dinero adicional que se cobra por los artículos que se compran.

muestra Grupo escogido al azar o aleatoriamente que se usa con el propósito de recoger datos.

espacio muestral Conjunto de todos los resultados posibles de un experimento probabilístico.

escala Razón que compara las medidas de un dibujo o modelo a las medidas del objeto real.

dibujo a escala Dibujo que se usa para representar objetos que son demasiado grandes o demasiado pequeños como para dibujarlos de tamaño natural.

factor de escala Escala escrita como una razón sin unidades en forma simplificada.

modelo a escala Réplica de un objeto real, el cual es demasiado grande o demasiado pequeño como para construirlo de tamaño natural.

triángulo escaleno Triángulo sin lados congruentes.

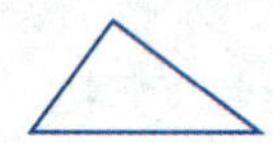

diagrama de dispersión Diagrama en que dos conjuntos de datos relacionados aparecen graficados como pares ordenados en la misma gráfica.

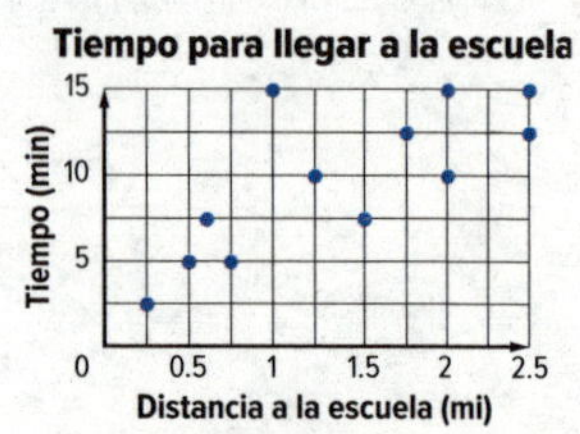

selling price The amount the customer pays for an item.

semicircle Half of a circle. The formula for the area of a semicircle is $A = \frac{1}{2}\pi r^2$.

sequence An ordered list of numbers, such as 0, 1, 2, 3 or 2, 4, 6, 8.

similar figures Figures that have the same shape but not necessarily the same size.

similar solids Solids with the same shape. Their corresponding linear measures are proportional.

simple event One outcome or a collection of outcomes.

simple interest The amount paid or earned for the use of money. The formula for simple interest is $I = prt$.

simple random sample An unbiased sample where each item or person in the population is as likely to be chosen as any other.

simplest form An expression is in simplest form when it is replaced by an equivalent expression having no like terms or parentheses.

simplify Write an expression in simplest form.

simulation An experiment that is designed to model the action in a given situation.

skew lines Lines that do not intersect and are not coplanar.

slant height The height of each lateral face.

slope The rate of change between any two points on a line. It is the ratio of vertical change to horizontal change. The slope tells how steep the line is.

solution A replacement value for the variable in an open sentence. A value for the variable that makes an equation true. Example: The *solution* of $12 = x + 7$ is 5.

precio de venta Cantidad de dinero que paga un consumidor por un artículo.

semicírculo Medio círculo La fórmula para el área de un semicírculo es $A = \frac{1}{2}\pi r^2$.

sucesión Lista ordenada de números, como 0, 1, 2, 3 ó 2, 4, 6, 8.

figuras semejantes Figuras que tienen la misma forma, pero no necesariamente el mismo tamaño.

sólidos semejantes Sólidos con la misma forma. Sus medidas lineales correspondientes son proporcionales.

eventos simples Un resultado o una colección de resultados.

interés simple Cantidad que se paga o que se gana por el uso del dinero. La fórmula para calcular el interés simple es $I = prt$.

muestra aleatoria simple Muestra de una población que tiene la misma probabilidad de escogerse que cualquier otra.

expresión mínima Expresión en su forma más simple cuando es reemplazada por una expresión equivalente que no tiene términos similares ni paréntesis.

simplificar Escribir una expresión en su forma más simple.

simulación Un experimento diseñado para modelar la acción en una situación dada.

rectas alabeadas Rectas que no se intersecan y que no son coplanares.

altura oblicua Altura de cada cara lateral.

pendiente Razón de cambio entre cualquier par de puntos en una recta. Es la razón del cambio vertical al cambio horizontal. La pendiente indica el grado de inclinación de la recta.

solución Valor de reemplazo de la variable en un enunciado abierto. Valor de la variable que hace que una ecuación sea verdadera. Ejemplo: La *solución* de $12 = x + 7$ es 5.

square The product of a number and itself. 36 is the square of 6.

square A parallelogram having four right angles and four congruent sides.

square root The factors multiplied to form perfect squares.

squared The product of a number and itself. 36 is the square of 6.

standard form Numbers written without exponents.

statistics The study of collecting, organizing, and interpreting data.

straight angle An angle that measures exactly 180°.

Subtraction Property of Equality If you subtract the same number from each side of an equation, the two sides remain equal.

Subtraction Property of Inequality If you subtract the same number from each side of an inequality, the inequality remains true.

supplementary angles Two angles are supplementary if the sum of their measures is 180°.

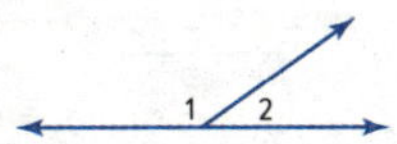

∠1 and ∠2 are supplementary angles.

surface area The sum of the areas of all the surfaces (faces) of a three-dimensional figure.

survey A question or set of questions designed to collect data about a specific group of people, or population.

systematic random sample A sample where the items or people are selected according to a specific time or item interval.

cuadrado Producto de un número por sí mismo. 36 es el cuadrado de 6.

cuadrado Paralelogramo con cuatro ángulos rectos y cuatro lados congruentes.

al cuadrado Factores multiplicados para formar cuadrados perfectos.

raíz cuadrada El producto de un número por sí mismo. 36 es el cuadrado de 6.

forma estándar Números escritos sin exponentes.

estadística Estudio que consiste en recopilar, organizar e interpretar datos.

ángulo llano Ángulo que mide exactamente 180°.

propiedad de sustracción de la igualdad Si restas el mismo número de ambos lados de una ecuación, los dos lados permanecen iguales.

propiedad de desigualdad en la resta Si se resta el mismo número a cada lado de una desigualdad, la desigualdad sigue siendo verdadera.

ángulos suplementarios Dos ángulos son suplementarios si la suma de sus medidas es 180°.

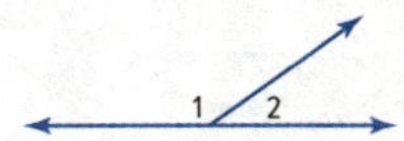

∠1 y ∠2 son suplementarios.

área de superficie La suma de las áreas de todas las superficies (caras) de una figura tridimensional.

encuesta Pregunta o conjunto de preguntas diseñadas para recoger datos sobre un grupo específico de personas o población.

muestra aleatoria sistemática Muestra en que los elementos o personas se eligen según un intervalo de tiempo o elemento específico.

Tt

term Each number in a sequence.

term A number, a variable, or a product or quotient of numbers and variables.

término Cada número en una sucesión.

término Número, variable, producto o cociente de números y de variables.

terminating decimal A repeating decimal which has a repeating digit of 0.

decimal finito Un decimal periódico que tiene un dígito que se repite que es 0.

theoretical probability The ratio of the number of ways an event can occur to the number of possible outcomes. It is based on what *should* happen when conducting a probability experiment.

probabilidad teórica Razón del número de maneras en que puede ocurrir un evento al número de resultados posibles. Se basa en lo que *debería* pasar cuando se conduce un experimento probabilístico.

three-dimensional figure A figure with length, width, and height.

figura tridimensional Figura que tiene largo, ancho y alto.

third quartile For a data set with median *M*, the third quartile is the median of the data values greater than *M*.

tercer cuartil Para un conjunto de datos con la mediana *M*, el tercer cuartil es la mediana de los valores mayores que *M*.

tip Also known as a gratuity, it is a small amount of money in return for a service.

propina También conocida como gratificación; es una cantidad pequeña de dinero en recompensa por un servicio.

transversal The third line formed when two parallel lines are intersected.

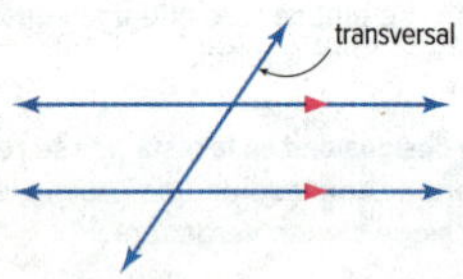

transversal Tercera recta que se forma cuando se intersecan dos rectas paralelas.

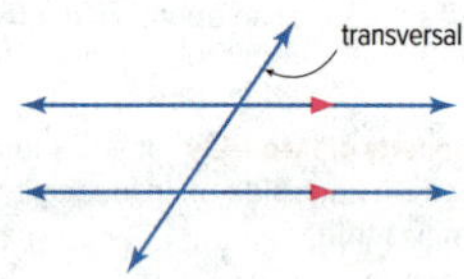

trapezoid A quadrilateral with one pair of parallel sides.

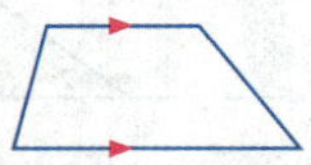

trapecio Cuadrilátero con un único par de lados paralelos.

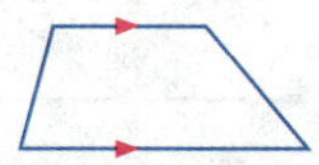

tree diagram A diagram used to show the sample space.

diagrama de árbol Diagrama que se usa para mostrar el espacio muestral.

triangle A figure with three sides and three angles.

triángulo Figura con tres lados y tres ángulos.

triangular prism A prism that has two parallel congruent bases that are triangles.

prisma triangular Un prisma que tiene dos bases congruentes paralelas que triángulos.

two-step equation An equation having two different operations.

ecuación de dos pasos Ecuación que contiene dos operaciones distintas.

two-step inequality An inequality than contains two operations.

desigualdad de dos pasos Desigualdad que contiene dos operaciones.

Uu

unbiased sample A sample representative of the entire population.

muestra no sesgada Muestra que se selecciona de modo que se representativa de la población entera.

unfair game A game where there is not a chance of each player being equally likely to win.

juego injusto Juego donde cada jugador no tiene la misma posibilidad de ganar.

uniform probability model A probability model which assigns equal probability to all outcomes.

modelo de probabilidad uniforme Un modelo de probabilidad que asigna igual probabilidad a todos los resultados.

unit rate A rate that is simplified so that it has a denominator of 1 unit.

tasa unitaria Tasa simplificada para que tenga un denominador igual a 1.

unit ratio A unit rate where the denominator is one unit.

razón unitaria Tasa unitaria en que el denominador es la unidad.

unlike fractions Fractions with different denominators.

fracciones con distinto denominador Fracciones cuyos denominadores son diferentes.

Vv

variable A symbol, usually a letter, used to represent a number in mathematical expressions or sentences.

variable Símbolo, por lo general una letra, que se usa para representar un número en expresiones o enunciados matemáticos.

vertex A vertex of an angle is the common endpoint of the rays forming the angle.

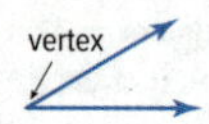

vértice El vértice de un ángulo es el extremo común de los rayos que lo forman.

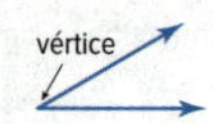

vertex The point where three or more faces of a polyhedron intersect.

vértice El punto donde tres o más caras de un poliedro se cruzan.

vertex The point at the tip of a cone.

vértice El punto en la punta de un cono.

vertical angles Opposite angles formed by the intersection of two lines. Vertical angles are congruent.

$\angle 1$ and $\angle 2$ are vertical angles.

ángulos opuestos por el vértice Ángulos opuestos formados por la intersección de dos rectas. Los ángulos opuestos por el vértice son congruentes.

$\angle 1$ y $\angle 2$ son ángulos opuestos por el vértice.

visual overlap A visual demonstration that compares the centers of two distributions with their variation, or spread.

superposición visual Una demostración visual que compara los centros de dos distribuciones con su variación, o magnitud.

volume The number of cubic units needed to fill the space occupied by a solid.

voluntary response sample A sample which involves only those who want to participate in the sampling.

volumen Número de unidades cúbicas que se requieren para llenar el espacio que ocupa un sólido.

muestra de respuesta voluntaria Muestra que involucra sólo aquellos que quieren participar en el muestreo.

Xx

***x*-axis** The horizontal number line in a coordinate plane.

***x*-coordinate** The first number of an ordered pair. It corresponds to a number on the *x*-axis.

eje *x* La recta numérica horizontal en el plano de coordenadas.

coordenada *x* El primer número de un par ordenado. Corresponde a un número en el eje *x*.

Yy

***y*-axis** The vertical number line in a coordinate plane.

***y*-coordinate** The second number of an ordered pair. It corresponds to a number on the *y*-axis.

eje *y* La recta numérica vertical en el plano de coordenadas.

coordenada *y* El segundo número de un par ordenado. Corresponde a un número en el eje *y*.

Zz

zero pair The result when one positive counter is paired with one negative counter. The value of a zero pair is 0.

par nulo Resultado de hacer coordinar una ficha positiva con una negativa. El valor de un par nulo es 0.

Selected Answers

Go online for Step-by-Step Solutions. eHelp

Chapter 5 Expressions

Page 348 Chapter 5 Are You Ready?

1. 16 **3.** 16 **5.** −50 **7.** −25

Pages 353–354 Lesson 5-1 Independent Practice

1. 34 **3.** 3 **5.** 3 **7.** 2 **9.** −1 **11.** $50 + 0.17m$; $75.50 **13.** 9.1 **15.** 37.85 **17.** Sample answer: The fee to rent a bicycle is $10 plus $5 for each hour. The expression $5x + 10$ represents the total cost for renting a bicycle for x hours. **19.** Sample answer: $2n + 4$; $2(n + 2)$

Pages 355–356 Lesson 5-1 Extra Practice

21. 4 **23.** −12 **25.** 5 **27.** $8.75 **29a.** True **29b.** False **29c.** True **31.** Let p = the number of hours Palla worked; $p + 8$ **33.** Let n = Nathan's age; $n - 3$

Pages 361–362 Lesson 5-2 Independent Practice

1. 7 is added to the previous term; 28, 35, 42 **3.** 8 is added to the previous term; 58, 66, 74 **5.** 0.8 is added to the previous term; 5.6, 6.4, 7.2 **7.** $3n$; 36 in.

9a.

x	1	2	3	4	5
y	3	6	9	12	15

9b. $3n$

9c.

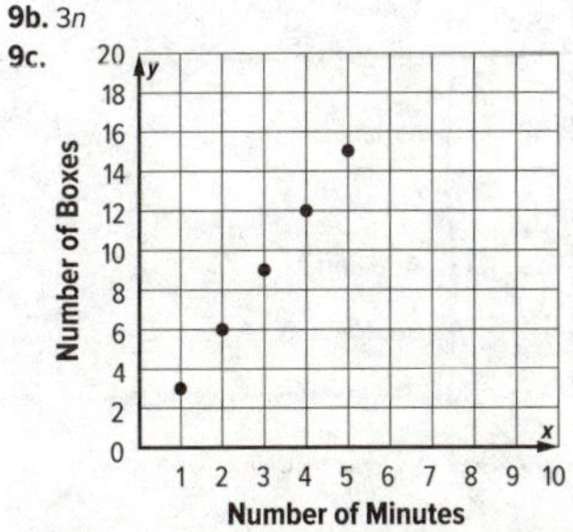

Sample answer: The number of boxes increases by 3 each minute. The points appear to fall in a straight line passing through the origin. **9d.** 135 boxes **11.** + 1, + 2, + 3, + 4, ...; 16, 22, 29 **13.** 81; Sample answer: The multiples of 6 from 41 to 523 can be represented by the sequence 42, 48, 54, ... 522. The expression $6n + 36$ represents this sequence. When $n = 81$, the value of the expression is 522. So, the 81st term of the sequence is 522. There are 81 multiples of 6 between 41 and 523.

Pages 363–364 Lesson 5-2 Extra Practice

15. 10 is added to the previous term; 46, 56, 66 **17.** 1.5 is added to the previous term; 10.5, 12.0, 13.5 **19.** 4 is added to the previous term; 20.6, 24.6, 28.6 **21.** 25 is added to the previous term; 120, 145, 170 **23a.** Each figure is 8 less than the previous figure. **23b.** 40, 32 **25.** 33, 30, 27 **27a.** True **27b.** True **27c.** False **29.** 1 **31.** 64 **33.** 5 **35.** $1.50

Pages 371–372 Lesson 5-3 Independent Practice

1. Commutative (+) **3.** Associative (+) **5.** false; Sample answer: $(24 \div 4) \div 2 \neq 24 \div (4 \div 2)$

7.

$= (15 + 12) + 8a$	Associative (+)
$= 27 + 8a$	Simplify.

9.

$= 3x \cdot (x \cdot 7)$	Commutative (×)
$= (3x \cdot x) \cdot 7$	Associative (×)
$= 3x^2 \cdot 7$	Simplify.
$= 3 \cdot 7 \cdot x^2$	Commutative (×)
$= (3 \cdot 7) \cdot x^2$	Associative (×)
$= 21x^2$	Simplify.

11. $[7 + (47 + 3)][5 \cdot (2 \cdot 3)]$, Associative (+); $(7 + 50)[5 \cdot (2 \cdot 3)]$, Simplify; $57[5 \cdot (2 \cdot 3)]$, Simplify; $57[(5 \cdot 2) \cdot 3]$, Associative (×); $57 \cdot 10 \cdot 3$, Simplify; $(57 \cdot 10) \cdot 3$, Associative (×); $570 \cdot 3$, Simplify; 1,710 **13.** Blake incorrectly multiplied both the 5 and m by 4. He should have used the Associative Property to group the 5 and 4 together, simplify, and then multiply by m. $4 \cdot (5 \cdot m) = 20m$ **15a.** no; Sample answer: $2 - 3 = -1$ and −1 is not a whole number **15b.** no; Sample answer: $1 + 1 = 2$ and 2 is not a member of the set.

Pages 373–374 Lesson 5-3 Extra Practice

17. Commutative (×) **19.** Associative (+) **21.** 48 s; Sample answer: $12.4 + 12.6 = 25$ and $11.8 + 11.2 = 23$, $25 + 23 = 48$

23.

$= (18 + 5) + 6m$	Associative (+)
$= 23 + 6m$	Simplify.

25.

$= 10 \cdot 7 \cdot y$	Commutative (×)
$= (10 \cdot 7) \cdot y$	Associative (×)
$= 70y$	Simplify.

27. 2(2.29) + 2(2.21) + 2.50; 2(2.29) + 2.50 + 2(2.21); 2.50 + 2(2.21 + 2.29) **29.** 36 **31.** 226 **33.** 74 **35.** $1.25(3) + $0.45(2); $4.65

Pages 379–380 Lesson 5-4 Independent Practice

1. 33 **3.** −30 **5.** 4 **7.** $-12x + 24$ **9.** $30 - 6q$ **11.** $-15 + 3b$ **13.** $27.40; 4($7.00 − $0.15) = $4 \cdot 7 - 4 \cdot 0.15$

15. 315;

$$9(30 + 5) = 9(30) + 9(5)$$
$$= 270 + 45$$

17. 672;

$$\begin{aligned}(100 + 12)6 &= 100(6) + 12(6)\\ &= 600 + 72\end{aligned}$$

19. 488;

$$\begin{aligned}4(120 + 2) &= 4(120) + 4(2)\\ &= 480 + 8\end{aligned}$$

21. Sample answer: $6(2a + 3b - c)$ **23.** $2a + ay + 2b + by$
25. No; $3 + (4 \cdot 5) = 23$ but $(3 + 4) \cdot (3 + 5) = 56$

Pages 381–382 Lesson 5-4 Extra Practice

27. 24 **29.** $-8a - 8b$ **31.** $-2p - 14$ **33.** $n(4.75 + 2.50) + 30$; $7.25n + 30$ **35.** $-12ab - 30ac$ **37.** $6y + 12z$
39. $-72p + 48n$ **41.** $3 \times (\$18.95 + \$14.95 + \$9.95)$; \$131.55; Sample answer: The ticket prices can be added first and then the sum can be multiplied by 3. This requires fewer steps and easier computations than multiplying each price by 3 and then adding the resulting products. **43.** −46 **45.** −47

Page 385 Problem-Solving Investigation Make a Table

Case 3. 26 containers **Case 5.** $2n + 2$; 18 toothpicks

Pages 391–392 Lesson 5-5 Independent Practice

1. terms: 2, $3a$, $9a$; like terms: $3a$, $9a$; coefficients: 3, 9; constant: 2 **3.** terms: 9, $-z$, 3, $-2z$; like terms: 9 and 3, $-z$ and $-2z$; coefficients: −1, −2; constants: 9, 3 **5.** $11c$ **7.** $1.03t$; \$74.16
9. $2x + 30$ **11. a.** $7 + 5x + 4y + 2z$ **b.** \$43 **13.** $16a + 8b + 4$ **15.** Sample answer: $3x + x - 7$; coefficients: 3, 1; constant: −7 **17.** $18x - 3$; $18x - 3 = 18(2) - 3 = 33$ and $8x - 2x + 12x - 3 = 8(2) - 2(2) + 12(2) - 3 = 33$

Pages 393–394 Lesson 5-5 Extra Practice

19. terms: 4, $5y$, $-6y$, y; like terms: $5y$, $-6y$, y; coefficients: 5, −6, 1; constant: 4 **21.** terms: $-3d$, 8, $-d$, −2; like terms: $-3d$ and $-d$, 8 and −2; coefficients: −3, −1; constants: 8, −2
23. $2 + 4d$ **25.** $2m - 2$ **27.** $7m - 20$ **29.** $20x + 9$
31. $38g + 36h - 38$ **33.** $5a + 9b$ **35.** t = hours Tricia volunteered; $t + 9$ **37.** 10 **39.** 13

Pages 399–400 Lesson 5-6 Independent Practice

1. $11x + 11$ **3.** $4x - 16$ **5.** $4x + 14$ **7.** $(22x + 10)$ mm; 230 mm **9.** $-x + 2$ **11.** $8.7x - 1.6$ **13.** Sample answer: $(10x + 2)$ and $(-15x + 2)$ **15.** $2x + 1$; The expression $2x + 1$ will always be odd when x is an integer because when an integer is doubled, the result is always even. Adding one to the result will give an odd number.

Pages 401–402 Lesson 5-6 Extra Practice

17. $-4x + 16$ **19.** $-2x - 2$ **21.** $-6x + 5$ **23.** $(24x + 9)$ yd; 177 yd **25a.** False **25b.** False **25c.** True **27.** 35 **29.** 85

Pages 407–408 Lesson 5-7 Independent Practice

1. $5x + 2$ **3.** $2x + 2$ **5.** $8x - 12$ **7.** $5x - 2$; 248 customers **9.** $x + 0.51$ **11.** Sample answer: The additive inverse of $(2x + 1)$ is $(-2x - 1)$.

$$\begin{aligned}(5x + 3) - (2x + 1) &= (5x + 3) + (-2x - 1)\\ &= 5x + 3 + (-2x) + (-1)\\ &= 5x + (-2x) + 3 + (-1)\\ &= 3x + 2\end{aligned}$$

13. $-x + 5$ **15.** Sample answer: The rule is to add the inverse when subtracting integers, and is applied to each term in the linear expression that is subtracted.

Pages 409–410 Lesson 5-7 Extra Practice

17. $-3x + 6$ **19.** $-16x + 2$ **21.** $-4x - 7$ **23.** $0.8x + 0.6$
25. $-x + 2$ **27.** $12 + 1.50t - (10 + 1.25t) = 2 + 0.25t$
29. $(12x - 4)$ ft; 32 ft **31.** $-\frac{1}{4}$ **33.** $\frac{1}{8}$ **35.** $\frac{2}{3}$

Pages 419–420 Lesson 5-8 Independent Practice

1. 24 **3.** $36k$ **5.** cannot be factored **7.** 4 units by $(x - 2)$ units **9.** $(x + 2)$ dollars **11.** $5(x + 4)$ units^2
13. $4(5x + 19)$ units^2 **15.** Sample answer: $20m$ and $12mn$
17. $6(4x - y)$

Pages 421–422 Lesson 5-8 Extra Practice

19. $6rs$ **21.** $20x$ **23.** $25xy$ **25.** $6(3x + 1)$ **27.** $5(2x - 7)$
29. $10(3x - 4)$ **31.** $(2x + 5)$ in. **33.** $\frac{2}{3}(x + 9)$ **35.** $\frac{5}{6}(x - 36)$
37. $\frac{3}{8}(x + 48)$ **39.** $16ab$, $12a$; $28a$, $20a$ **41.** $3a + 30$
43.

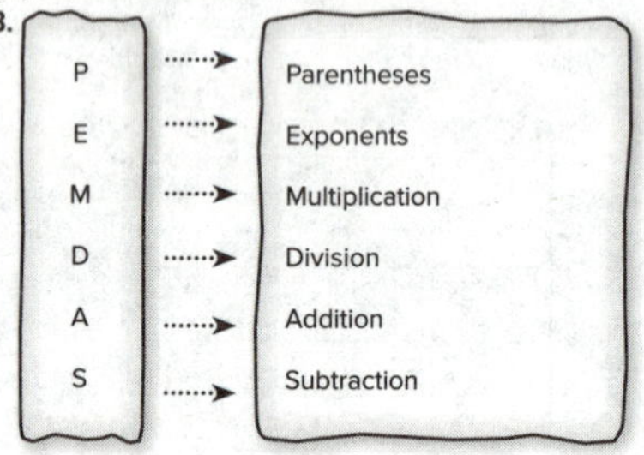

Page 425 Chapter Review Vocabulary Check

Across
3. simplest form **7.** sequence **11.** counterexample
13. define
Down
1. equivalent **5.** variable **9.** term

Page 426 Chapter Review Key Concept Check

1. $1 + 3$ **3.** $2x - 4$ **5.** $3(x + 7)$

Chapter 6 Equations and Inequalities

Page 432 Chapter 6 Are You Ready?

1. $p + 3$ **3.** $g + 10$ **5.** 17 **7.** 1 **9.** 35

Pages 441–442 Lesson 6-1 Independent Practice

1. 7 **3.** 17 **5.** −1
7.

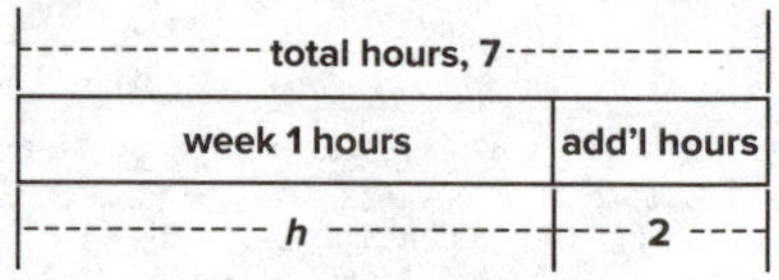

$7 = h + 2$; 5 h **9a.** $s - 65 = 5$; 70 mph
9b.

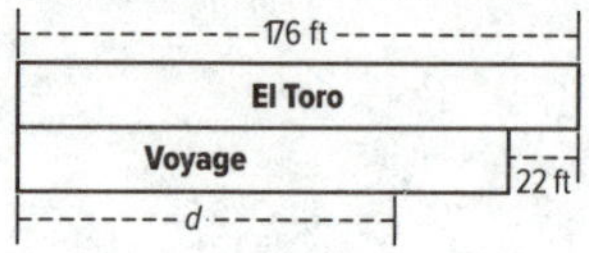

$d + 22 = 176$; 154 ft **9c.** The solution of each equation is 197; Colossos is 197 feet tall. **11.** $115 + 115 + 65 + x = 360$; 65 **13.** She should have subtracted 5 from each side; −13
15. $x + 2 = 8$; The solution for the other equations is −6.

Pages 443–444 Lesson 6-1 Extra Practice

17. −9 **19.** −12 **21.** 7
23.

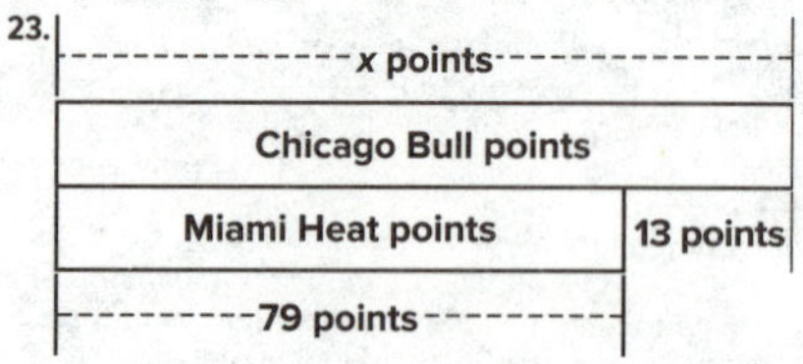

$x - 13 = 79$; 92 points **25.** $-1 + (-3) + s + 2 = 0$; +2
27. −1.25 **29.** 12.3 **31.** 5.8 **33.** $-\frac{1}{12}$ **35a.** True
35b. False **35c.** True **37.** −20 **39.** 60 **41.** −36
43. $3h = -3$; $h = -1$

Pages 451–452 Lesson 6-2 Independent Practice

1. 7 **3.** 8 **5.** 80 **7.** −5 **9.** −90 **11.** $205 = \frac{d}{3}$; 615 mi
13a.

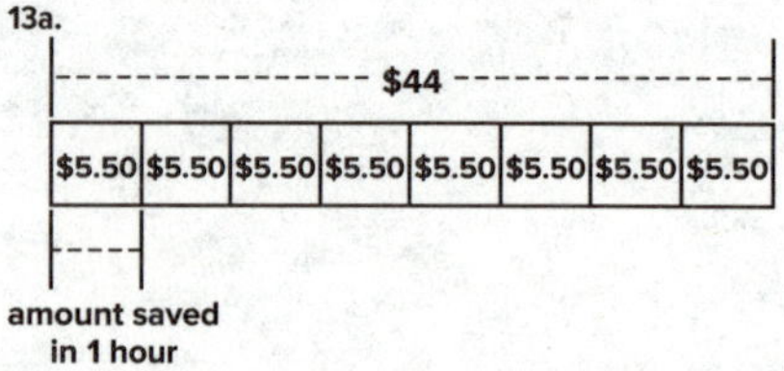

13b. $5.5x = 44$ **13c.** Sample answer: Divide each side by 5.5. Then simplify. $x = 8$ **15.** True; Sample answer: Multiply each side of the equation by $\frac{1}{5}$ instead of dividing each side by 5.
17. Sample answer: Multiply both sides by x, then divide both sides of the equation by 6; −5.

Pages 453–454 Lesson 6-2 Extra Practice

19. 4 **21.** 70 **23.** −120 **25.** $50 = 25t$; 2 s **27.** 8 in.
29. $3\frac{1}{3}$ **31.** $1\frac{1}{100}$ **33.** $\frac{13}{4}$ **35.** 4 **37.** 2.1 **39.** $\frac{21}{4}$ or $5\frac{1}{4}$

Pages 461–462 Lesson 6-3 Independent Practice

1. 5 **3.** 3 **5.** $\frac{20}{3}$ or $6\frac{2}{3}$ **7.** $\frac{3}{4}p = 46.50$; \$62 **9.** Emily's homeroom class; Sample answer: Write and solve the equations $0.75e = 15$ and $\frac{2}{3}s = 12$; $e = 20$ and $s = 18$; Since $20 > 18$, Emily's homeroom class has more students. **11.** 20; Sample answer: Solve $8 = \frac{m}{4}$ to find that $m = 32$. So, replace m with 32 to find $32 - 12 = 20$. **13.** Sample answer: Multiply each side by 2. Then divide each side by $(b_1 + b_2)$. So, $\frac{2A}{b_1 + b_2} = h$.

Pages 463–464 Lesson 6-3 Extra Practice

15. 7 **17.** −3.8 **19.** $-\frac{125}{12}$ or $-10\frac{5}{12}$
21.

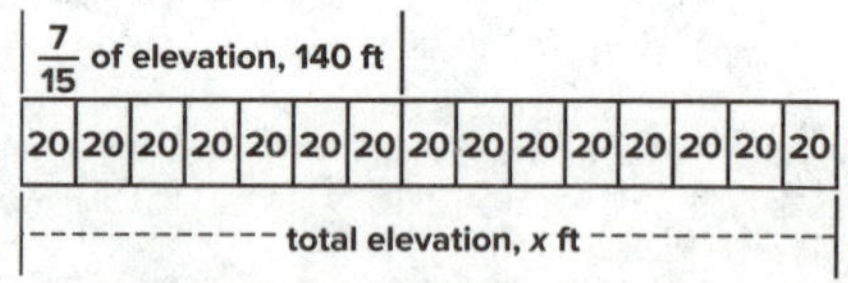

$140 = \frac{7}{15}x$; 300 ft
23. a train that travels 100 miles in $\frac{2}{3}$ hour; a train that travels 90 miles in $\frac{3}{5}$ hour **25.** 22 **27.** 2 **29.** $3 \times \$0.25 + 5 \times \$0.50$; \$3.25

Pages 473–474 Lesson 6-4 Independent Practice

1. 3 **3.** 7 **5.** −3
7.

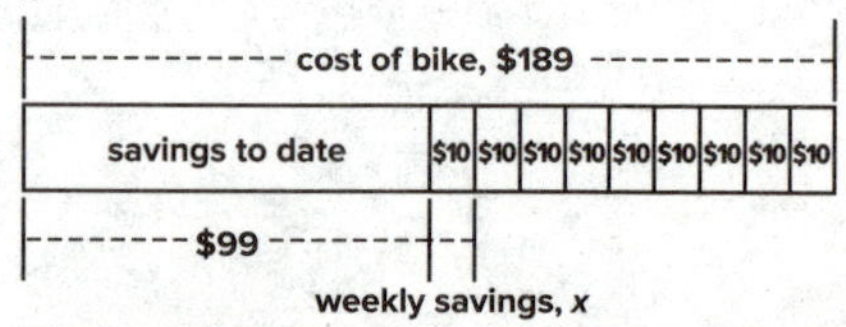

$189 = 10x + 99$; 9 weeks
9. 2.25 **11. a.** −9°C **b.** 92.2°F **13.** No, none of the Fahrenheit temperatures convert to the same temperature in Celsius. Only −40°F = −40°C. **15.** Sample answer: Cameron found the area of a trapezoid to be 52 square inches. One base was 12 inches long and the other was 14 inches long. What is the height h of the trapezoid?; 4 in.

Pages 475–476 Lesson 6-4 Extra Practice

17. −4 **19.** 4 **21.** 36

23a.

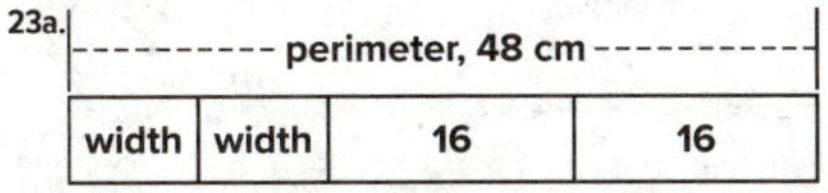

23b. $48 = 32 + 2w$; 8 cm **23c.** Sample answer: Using either method, you would subtract first and then divide **25.** $c = 30 + 0.05m$; 395 mi **27.** $6 \cdot 10 + 6 \cdot n$ or $60 + 6n$ **29.** $5(x + 7)$ **31.** $10(t + 3)$

Pages 485–486 Lesson 6-5 Independent Practice

1. 6 **3.** −14 **5.** −3.2 **7.** $3(\ell + 5) = 60$; 15 in. **9a.** $12(m - 2.57) = 0.36$ **9b.** Sample answer: I first divided each side by 12 and then added 2.57 to each side; \$2.60. **11.** Sample answer: Marisol should have divided by six before subtracting three; $6(x + 3) = 21$, $x + 3 = 3.5$, $x = 3.5 - 3$, $x = 0.5$ **13.** $3(x - 8) = 12$; Sample answer: Valeria bought a new collar for each of her three dogs. She paid \$8 for each necklace. Suppose she had \$12 left. How much money did Valeria have initially to spend on each dog collar?; \$12 per collar

Pages 487–488 Lesson 6-5 Extra Practice

15. 16 **17.** −2 **19.** 78 **21.** $5\frac{3}{4}$ or 5.75 **23.** $1.20\left(n + 2\frac{1}{2}\right) = 4.50$; 1.25 or $1\frac{1}{4}$ pounds **25.** Divide both sides by p; Add q to both sides. **27.** −4 **29.** 4 **31.** −3 **33.** 2 **35.** −3, −2, −1, 0

Page 491 Problem-Solving Investigation Work Backward

Case 3. 1,250 ft **Case 5.** 6:25 A.M.

Pages 501–502 Lesson 6-6 Independent Practice

1. $h \le -8$ **3.** $5 < n$ **5.** $x > -1$
7. $m \ge -6$;

9. $n + 4 > 13$; $n > 9$ **11.** $p + 17 \le 26$; $p \le 9$; Nine additional players or fewer can make the team. **13a.** $42 + x \ge 74$; $x \ge 32$ **13b.** $74 + y \ge 110$; $y \ge 36$ **15.** Sample answer: $x + 3 < 25$ **17.** no; Sample answer: The solution is $x \ge -1$, so the graph should have a closed dot above −1 and the arrow should point to the right, not the left.

Pages 503–504 Lesson 6-6 Extra Practice

19. $m \le 4.3$
21. $-5 < a$

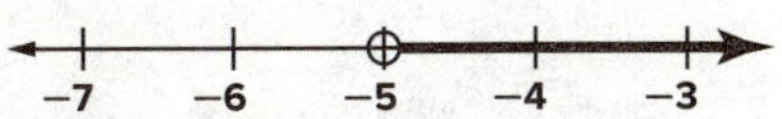

23. $n - 8 < 10$; $n < 18$ **25.** $68 + c \le 125$; $c \le 57$; The salesman has 57 cars or less left to sell.

27. $2\frac{2}{3} > x$ or $x < 2\frac{2}{3}$

29. $m \ge 11\frac{1}{5}$

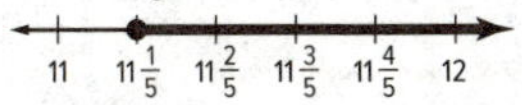

31. $n \ge -4\frac{3}{16}$

33. $x + 4 \le 7$; $-7 \ge x - 10$ **35.** −4; See answer 39 for graph. **37.** −2; See answer 39 for graph. **39.** −6;

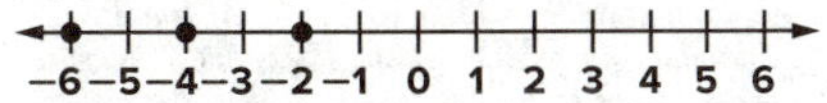

Pages 509–510 Lesson 6-7 Independent Practice

1. $y < 3$ **3.** $180 \le m$ **5.** $m \ge 56$ **7.** $n \le 4.5$
9. $w \le -45$
11. $4 < t$

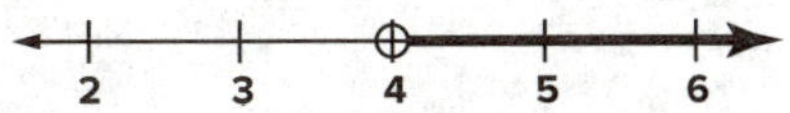

13. $x \le -32$

15. Sample answer: The inequalities $-2x > 12$, $\frac{x}{2} < -3$, and $-7 > x - 1$ are equal to $x < -6$. The inequality $-2 < x + 4$ is equal to $x > -6$. **17.** $5n \le 30$; $n \le 6$ **19.** at least a 15
21a.

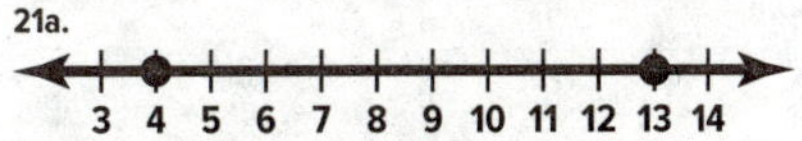

21b. yes; It represents the solutions that satisfy both inequalities. **21c.** $4 \le b \le 13$
21d.

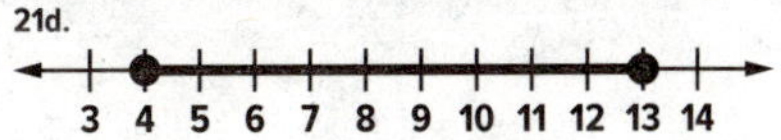

Pages 511–512 Lesson 6-7 Extra Practice

23. $y > -5$ **25.** $p \ge -6$ **27.** $-40 < y$ or $y > -40$
29. $w > 13$

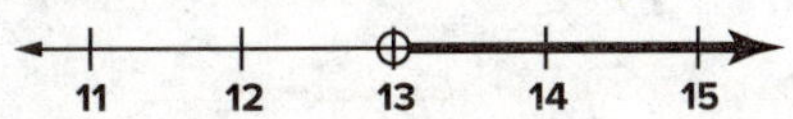

31. $-20 \ge t$ or $t \le -20$

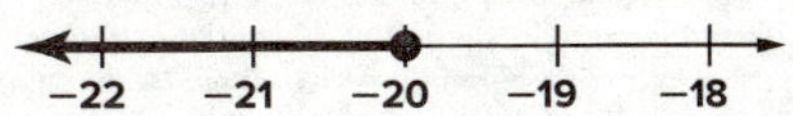

33. $4n \ge -12$; $n \ge -3$ **35a.** False **35b.** True **35c.** False **37.** 2 **39.** −2.5 **41.** 12

Pages 517–518 Lesson 6-8 Independent Practice

1. $x \ge 1$;

3. $x > 12$

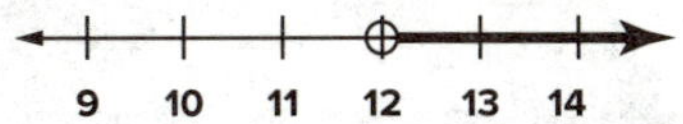

5. $30 + 7x \ge 205$; $x \ge 25$ hours; He will have to work at least 25 hours **7.** $\frac{x}{-5} + 1 \le 7$; $x \ge -30$ **9.** $-2x - 6 > -18$; $x < 6$ **11.** Sample answer: $-2x + 5 > -7$ **13.** Sample answer: $\frac{x}{2} + 5 \ge 30$ **15.** $\frac{73 + x}{6} \ge 15$; $x \ge 17$; at least 17 points **17.** Sample answer: At the electronics store, CDs were marked down \$2.80 from their regular price. Orlando has \$45 to spend on 4 CDs. How much can he spend on each CD?; \$14.05

Pages 519–520 Lesson 6-8 Extra Practice

19. $x \le -8$

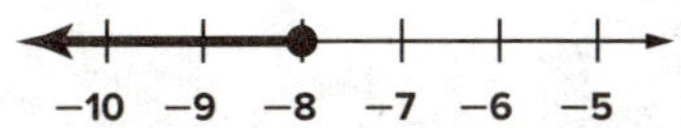

21. $x \ge 42$

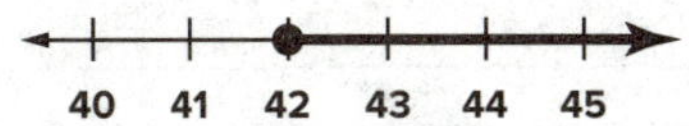

23. $75 + 5s \ge 125$; $s \ge 10$; Audrey needs to make at least 10 sales for her pay to be \$125. **25.** Add 5 to both sides; Divide both sides by −2; Reverse the inequality symbol.
27. $n > -3$

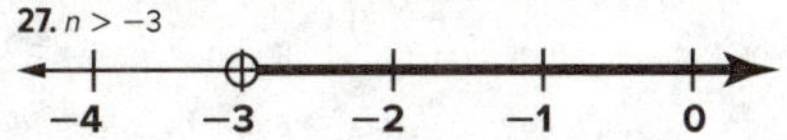

29. $t < 2$

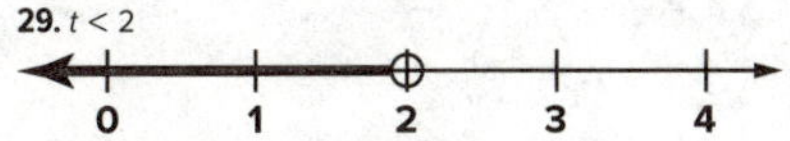

31. −12 **33.** $4m + 2 = 30$; 7 years

Page 524 Chapter Review Key Concept Check

1. solution **3.** equivalent equations

Chapter 7 Geometric Figures

Page 534 Chapter 7 Are You Ready?

1. 40° **3.** 90° **5.** 6.72 yd^2

Pages 539–540 Lesson 7-1 Independent Practice

1. ∠ABC, ∠CBA, ∠B, ∠4; acute **3.** ∠MNP, ∠PNM, ∠N, ∠1; obtuse **5.** neither **7.** adjacent **9.** vertical **11.** 11
15. True; Sample answer:

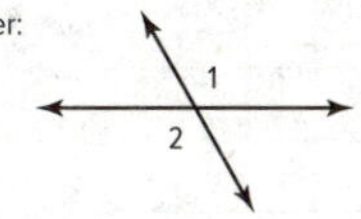

17. Sample answer: Each pair of angles is adjacent and forms a straight angle. So $(2x + 8) + (5x - 10) = 180$ and $(3x + 42) + (x + 34) = 180$. When you solve both equations, $x = 26$. The angle measures are 60°, 120°, 120°, and 60°.

Pages 541–542 Lesson 7-1 Extra Practice

19. ∠HKI, ∠IKH, ∠K, ∠8; obtuse **21a.** Sample answer: ∠1 and ∠3; Since ∠1 and ∠3 are opposite angles formed by the intersection of two lines, they are vertical angles. **21b.** Sample answer: ∠1 and ∠2; Since ∠1 and ∠2 share a common vertex, a common side, and do not overlap, they are adjacent angles. **23.** 9 **25a.** vertical **25b.** adjacent **25c.** adjacent **25d.** vertical **27.** 134° **29.** 38° **31.** rectangle

Pages 547–548 Lesson 7-2 Independent Practice

1. neither **3.** supplementary **5.** 20 **7.** 23 **9.** Sample answer: ∠CGK, ∠KGJ **11a.** adjacent; adjacent; vertical **11b.** $m\angle 1 + m\angle 2 = 180°$; $m\angle 2 + m\angle 3 = 180°$ **11c.** $m\angle 1 = 180° - m\angle 2$; $m\angle 3 = 180° - m\angle 2$; Sample answer: $m\angle 1$ and $m\angle 3$ are equal. **11d.** Sample answer: Vertical angles are congruent. **13a.** $m\angle E = 39°$; $m\angle F = 51°$ **13b.** $m\angle B = 60°$; $m\angle C = 120°$ **15.** Sample answer: Right angles have a measure of 90°, so two right angles will always have a sum of 180°. This is the definition of supplementary angles.

Pages 549–550 Lesson 7-2 Extra Practice

17. complementary **19.** 15 **21.** never; Sample answer: Since an obtuse angle is greater than 90°, the sum of two obtuse angles must be greater than, not equal to, 180°.
23a.

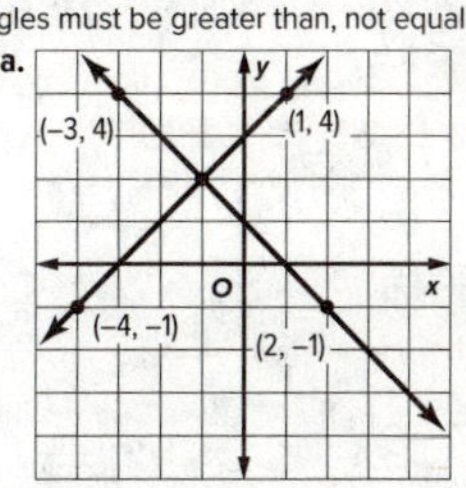

23b. The lines appear to be perpendicular. **23c.** line a: 1; line b: −1 **25.** $x°$; 90°; 180°; 45°; 45°

27. 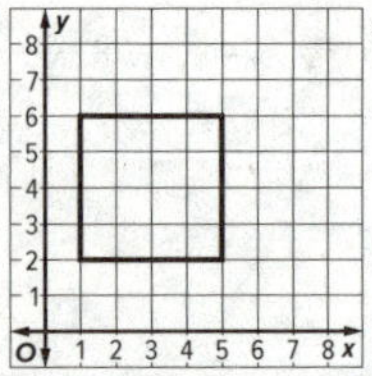

square

Pages 559–560 Lesson 7-3 Independent Practice

1 acute equilateral; Sample answer:

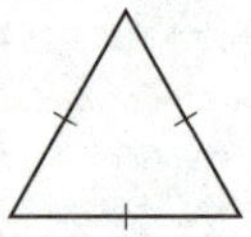

3 acute equilateral **5.** obtuse isosceles **7.** 118 **9.** acute isosceles **11.** $125 + a = 180$, so $a = 55$; $a + b + 60 = 180$, so $b = 65$; $60 + d = 90$, so $d = 30$; $c + d + 90 = 180$, so $c = 60$ **13a.** never; Sample answer: The sum of the interior angles of a triangle is 180°. Two right angles have a sum of 180°. This means the third angle would equal 0°, which is not possible. **13b.** never; Sample answer: The sum of the interior angles of a triangle is 180°. The measure of an obtuse angle is greater than 90°. So, a triangle cannot have more than one obtuse angle.

Pages 561–562 Lesson 7-3 Extra Practice

15. acute isosceles **17.** right scalene **19.** obtuse isosceles; Sample answer:

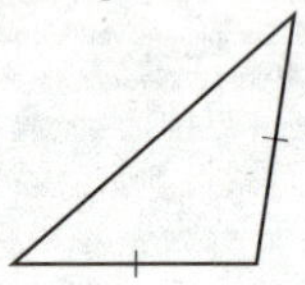

21. 90 **23.** 53° **25.** 30 **27a.** False **27b.** True **27c.** False **29.** 25 in^2 **31.** 35 cm^2 **33.** 9 yd^2

Page 569 Problem-Solving Investigation Make a Model

Case 3. 15 tables; 2 people can sit on the ends. Then divide the remaining people by 2. $(32 - 2) \div 2 = 15$. **Case 5.** Faith: Spanish; Sarah: German; Guadalupe: French

Pages 579–580 Lesson 7-4 Independent Practice

1 102.6 mi **3** 12 cm; $\frac{1}{300}$ **5.** 108 ft^2 **9.** always; Sample answer: A scale factor of $\frac{3}{1}$ means that 3 units of the drawing is equal to 1 unit of the object, so the scale drawing or model will be larger than the actual object.

Pages 581–582 Lesson 7-4 Extra Practice

11. 30 km **13.** 102.5 km **15.** $109\frac{3}{8}$ ft **17.** 3,420 ft^2 **19.** 40 ft by 60 ft; Sample answer: Set up and solve proportions to find the actual length and width: $\frac{1 \text{ in.}}{20 \text{ ft}} = \frac{2 \text{ in.}}{w \text{ ft}}$ and $\frac{1 \text{ in.}}{20 \text{ ft}} = \frac{3 \text{ in.}}{\ell \text{ ft}}$ **21.** 10 **23.** 22

Pages 589–590 Lesson 7-5 Independent Practice

1 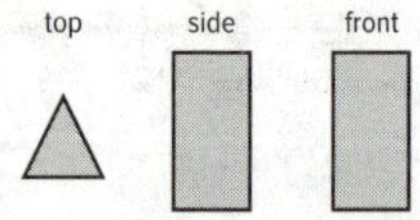

3 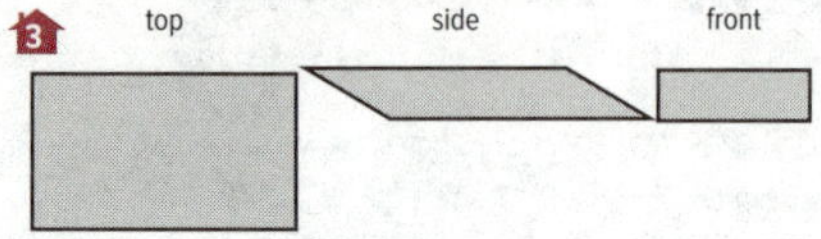

5. 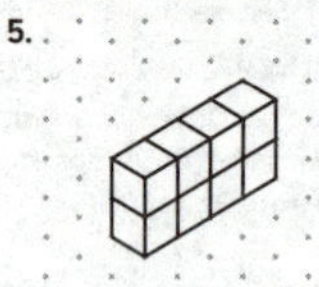

7. 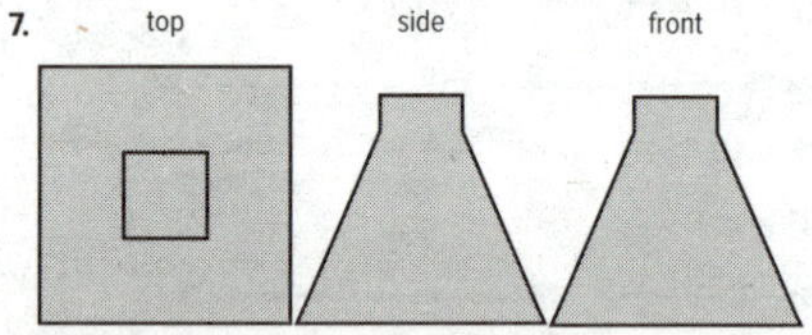

9. triangle; It is the only two-dimensional figure. **11a.** never **11b.** never **11c.** sometimes

Pages 591–592 Lesson 7-5 Extra Practice

13. 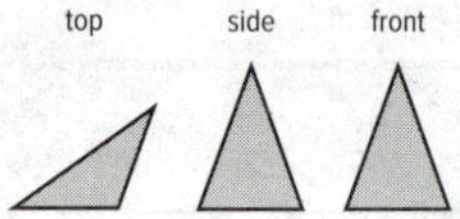

15. 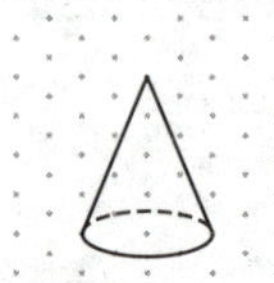

17. 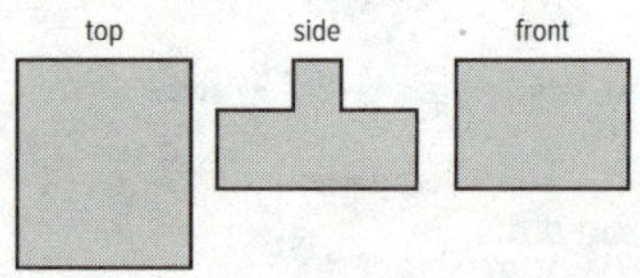

19. 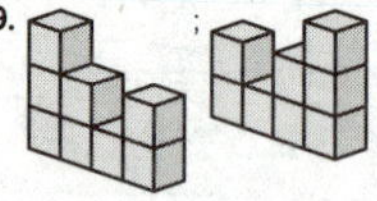

21. line; $\overleftrightarrow{WX}$ or $\overleftrightarrow{XW}$ **23.** line segment; $\overline{EF}$ or $\overline{FE}$ **25.** parallel

Pages 597–598 Lesson 7-6 Independent Practice

1 **figure name:** triangular pyramid
bases: *ACD*
faces: *ACD, ABD, ABC, DBC*
edges: $\overline{AB}, \overline{BC}, \overline{CD}, \overline{AD}, \overline{AC}, \overline{BD}$
vertices: *A, B, C, D*
skew lines: Sample answer: $\overline{BD}$ and $\overline{AC}$

3 rectangle **5.** triangle **7.** False; two planes intersect at a line, which is an infinite number of points. **11.** sometimes; A rectangular prism has 2 bases and 4 faces, but a triangular prism has 2 bases and 3 faces. **13.** sometimes; A triangular pyramid has a triangle for its base.

Pages 599–600 Lesson 7-6 Extra Practice

15. **figure name:** rectangular prism
bases: *ABCD, EFGH, ABFE, DCGH, ADHE, BCGF*
faces: *ABCD, EFGH, ABFE, DCGH, ADHE, BCGF*
edges: $\overline{AB}, \overline{BC}, \overline{CD}, \overline{AD}, \overline{EF}, \overline{FG}, \overline{GH}, \overline{EH}, \overline{AE}, \overline{BF}, \overline{CG}, \overline{DH}$
vertices: *A, B, C, D, E, F, G, H*
skew lines: Sample answer: $\overline{DH}$ and $\overline{GF}$

17. curve **19.** Because there are two parallel, congruent triangular bases, it is a triangular prism. **21a.** Figure 2 **21b.** Figure 1 **21c.** Figure 3 **23.** hexagon **25.** 90°

Page 603 Chapter Review Vocabulary Check

Across
11. equilateral **15.** complementary
Down
1. adjacent **3.** supplementary **5.** triangle **7.** vertical **9.** acute **13.** right

Page 604 Chapter Review Key Concept Check

1. vertex **3.** 90° **5.** scale drawing

Chapter 8 Measure Figures

Page 610 Chapter 8 Are You Ready?

1. 42 sq m **3.** 76.5 sq mm

Pages 617–618 Lesson 8-1 Independent Practice

1. 2.5 mm **3.** 34 cm **5** $3.14 \times 13 = 40.8$ cm **7** 19 people **9a.** 30 mm **9b.** 31.4 mm **9c.** 31.4159 mm **9d.** Sample answer: The more decimal places of the estimate of π, the more precise the circumference. **11.** 18 in. **13.** 257 cm **15.** Greater than; Sample answer: Since the radius is 4 feet, the diameter is 8 feet. Since π is a little more than 3, the circumference will be a little more than 3 times 8, or 24 feet. **17.** The circumference would double. For example, with a diameter of 4 feet, the circumference is about 12.6 feet. With a diameter of 8 feet, the circumference is about 25.1 feet.

Pages 619–620 Lesson 8-1 Extra Practice

19. 3.5 in. **21.** 72 ft **23.** $\frac{22}{7} \times 21 = 66$ ft **25.** $\frac{22}{7} \times 42 = 132$ mm **27.** 37.7 cm **29.** Each is π, or about 3.14, units longer than the previous circle. **31a.** False **31b.** True **31c.** False **33.** 12.74 m^2 **35.** 36,976 ft^2

Pages 627–628 Lesson 8-2 Independent Practice

1. $3.14 \times 6 \times 6 = 113.0$ cm^2 **3** $3.14 \times 5.5 \times 5.5 = 95.0$ ft^2 **5.** $3.14 \times 6.3 \times 6.3 = 124.6$ mm^2 **7.** 254.3 ft^2 **9** 226.1 in^2 **11.** 163.3 yd^2 **13.** The large pizza; the medium pizza's area is 78.5 square inches and costs $0.102 per square inch. The large pizza's area is 153.86 square inches and costs $0.097 per square inch. **15.** When the radius of a circle is doubled, the circumference doubles and the area is 4 times as large. In the formula for area of a circle, the radius is squared, so when the radius of a circle is doubled, the area is 2^2 or 4 times as large. **17.** 5.9 in^2 **19.** Sample answer: To find the area of the quarter circle, multiply the area of the entire circle by $\frac{1}{4}$; $A = \frac{1}{4}\pi r^2$; 19.6 in^2

Pages 629–630 Lesson 8-2 Extra Practice

21. $3.14 \times 6.3 \times 6.3 = 124.6$ cm^2 **23.** $3.14 \times 5.4 \times 5.4 = 91.6$ yd^2 **25.** $3.14 \times 9.3 \times 9.3 = 271.6$ mm^2 **27.** 144.7 ft^2 **29.** 64.3 in^2 **31.** circle; $\frac{1}{2} \cdot 100 \cdot 100 < 3 \cdot 50 \cdot 50$ **33.** 154 in^2; Sample answer: Using $\frac{22}{7}$ makes the computation easier since the radius is 7. The 7s cancel out in the multiplication. **35.** 210 in^2 **37.** 39.5 cm^2

Pages 635–636 Lesson 8-3 Independent Practice

1. 64 cm^2 **3.** 220.5 cm^2 **5** 38.6 ft^2 **7** 119.5 ft^2 **9.** 77 cm^2 **11.** 44.6 ft^2; 30.3 ft **13.** 110.8 ft^2

Pages 637–638 Lesson 8-3 Extra Practice

15. 87.5 m^2 **17.** 180 cm^2 **19.** 9 cm^2 **21.** 240 ft^2 **23a.** 36 **23b.** 14.14 **23c.** 92.56 **25.** 3.7 cm^2 **27.** 4.7 m

Pages 643–644 Lesson 8-4 Independent Practice

1 192 m^3 **3** 108 m^3 **5a.** 96 ft^3; 128 ft^3; 168 ft^3; 160 ft^3; 120 ft^3 **5b.** The height must allow the water to be deep enough for someone to get wet and the length and width must allow a person to fit. So the first and last sets of dimensions would not work. **7a.** Sample answer: There is a direct relationship between the volume and the length. Since the length is doubled, the volume is also doubled. **7b.** The volume is eight times greater. **7c.** Neither; Sample answer: doubling the height will result in a volume of $4 \cdot 4 \cdot 10$ or 160 in^3; doubling the width will result in a volume of $4 \cdot 8 \cdot 5$ or 160 in^3.

Pages 645–646 Lesson 8-4 Extra Practice

11. 236.3 cm^3 **13.** 20.4 mm^3 **15.** 306.52 = 19.4*h*; 15.8 m **17.** $166\frac{1}{4}$ yd^3 **19.** 2 in. by 1.5 in. by 0.5 in.; 3 in. by 1 in. by 0.5 in. **21.** 25.8 m **23.** 29.2 cm

Page 649 Problem-Solving Investigation Solve a Simpler Problem

Case 3. 80 chairs **Case 5.** 7,763,270.6 mi^2; Sample answer: The area of Asia is about 17,251,712.4 mi^2 and the area of North America is about 9,488,441.8 mi^2. 17,251,712.4 – 9,488,441.8 = 7,763,270.6

Pages 657–658 Lesson 8-5 Independent Practice

1. 80 ft^3 **3.** 42 ft^3 **5.** 14 in. **7.** 10 in^3 **9.** The volume is eight times greater; Sample answer: Since each dimension is two times greater, the volume is 2 × 2 × 2 or eight times greater. **11.** Sample answer: first set: area of the base, 40 ft^2; height of the pyramid, 12 ft; second set: area of the base, 30 ft^2; height of the pyramid, 16 ft **13.** The volumes are the same.

Pages 659–660 Lesson 8-5 Extra Practice

15. 60 in^3 **17.** 195 yd^3 **19.** 11 ft **21.** 22 in. **23.** 1,234.2 m^3 **25.** 24 in.; Sample answer: Replace *V* with 1,560 and *B* with 13 × 15 in the formula $V = \frac{1}{3}Bh$. Then solve for *h*. **27.** 1.5 ft^2 **29.** 28.75 ft^2

Pages 669–670 Lesson 8-6 Independent Practice

1. 314 cm^2 **3.** 207 in^2 **5.** 180 in^2 **7.** $S.A. = 6x^2$
9. False; Sample answer: A 9 × 7 × 13 rectangular prism has a surface area of 2(9 × 13) + 2(9 × 7) + 2(13 × 7) or 542 square units. Doubling the length, the surface area is 2(18 × 13) + 2(18 × 7) + 2(13 × 7) or 902 square units. 2 × 542 ≠ 902
11. 1,926 cm^2

Pages 671–672 Lesson 8-6 Extra Practice

13. 833.1 mm^2 **15.** 96 ft^2 **17.** Yes; there are 2,520 ft^2 of fencing. Since 8 gallons of paint will cover 350 • 8 or 2,800 ft^2 and 2,800 ft^2 > 2,520 ft^2, 8 gallons is enough paint.
19. 64.5 in^2 **21a.** 12.5 **21b.** 50 **21c.** 71 **21d.** 196
23. triangle; triangle; triangle **25.** rectangle; circle; oval

Pages 681–682 Lesson 8-7 Independent Practice

1. 95 in^2 **3.** 328 in^2 **5.** 0.52 ft^2 **7.** 78 in^2
9. 6.5 cm
11.

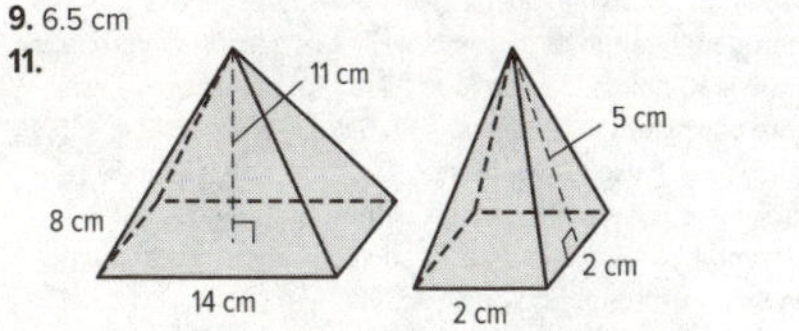

Sample answer: Both a square pyramid and a rectangular pyramid have isosceles triangles as their lateral faces. All the lateral faces are congruent on a square pyramid but, on a rectangular pyramid, the opposite pairs of lateral faces are congruent.

Pages 683–684 Lesson 8-7 Extra Practice

13. 197.1 m^2 **15.** 765 cm^2 **17.** 26.1 ft^2
19.

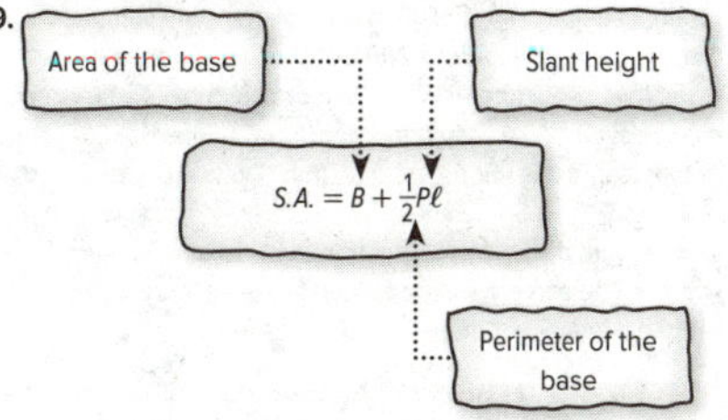

21a. True **21b.** True **21c.** False **23.** 456 ft^2 **25.** 10 ft

Pages 693–694 Lesson 8-8 Independent Practice

1. 2.3 m^3 **3.** 2,600 ft^2 **5.** 0.5 ft^3 **7.** 10.4 m^2 **9.** 100 in^3 **13.** less than; Sample answer: The combined surface area of the two prisms is 180 in^2. Since they share a common surface, the area of that surface is not included in the total surface area.

Pages 695–696 Lesson 8-8 Extra Practice

15. 100 in^3 **17.** 280.2 cm^2 **19a.** 1.68 ft^3 **19b.** 19.28 ft^2
21.

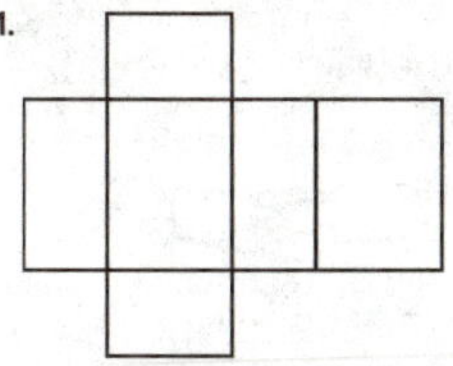

23.

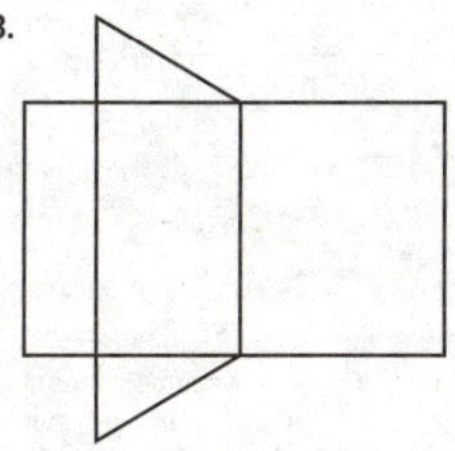

Page 699 Chapter Review Vocabulary Check

1. diameter **3.** circle **5.** circumference **7.** semicircle **9.** volume **11.** lateral

Page 700 Chapter Review Key Concept Check

1. twice **3.** height

Chapter 9 Probability

Page 710 Chapter 9 Are You Ready?

1. $\frac{1}{3}$ **3.** $\frac{2}{3}$ **5.** 30 **7.** 24

Pages 715–716 Lesson 9-1 Independent Practice

1. $\frac{1}{4}$, 25%, or 0.25 **3.** $\frac{1}{1}$, 100%, or 1 **5.** $\frac{1}{5}$, 0.2, or 20%; Sample answer: Since 80% arrive on time, that means that 20% do not arrive on time. **7.** Picking a black jelly bean is impossible since the probability of picking a black jelly bean is 0%. **9a.** $\frac{1}{8}$, 0.125, 12.5%; $\frac{1}{2}$, 0.5, 50% **9b.** $\frac{3}{4}$, 0.75, 75%
11. 70%, $\frac{1}{3}$; Sample answer: 70% and $\frac{1}{3}$ are probabilities that are not complementary because $0.7 + 0.\overline{3} \neq 1$. The other sets of probability are complementary.

Pages 717–718 Lesson 9-1 Extra Practice

13. $\frac{1}{5}$, 20%, or 0.2 **15.** $\frac{7}{10}$, 70%, or 0.7 **17.** $\frac{1}{2}$, 50%, or 0.5
19. $\frac{3}{5}$, 60%, or 0.6 **21.** The complement of selecting a girl is selecting a boy. The probability of the complement is $\frac{37}{100}$, 0.37, or 37%. **23.** $\frac{124}{125}$, 99.2%, or 0.992; It is very likely that card 13 will *not* be chosen. **25.** *P*(orange) = $\frac{1}{5}$; *P*(green) = $\frac{2}{5}$ **27.** >
29. $\frac{3}{25}$; $\frac{1}{5}$; Bryan misses more foul shots than Dwayne.

Pages 725–726 Lesson 9-2 Independent Practice

1. a. $\frac{1}{5}$; The experimental probability is close to the theoretical probability of $\frac{1}{6}$. **b.** $\frac{9}{10}$; The experimental probability is close to the theoretical probability of $\frac{5}{6}$.
3a. 162 people **3b.** about 134 people **5. a.** $\frac{1}{3}$
b. $\frac{6}{25}$; $\frac{13}{50}$
c.

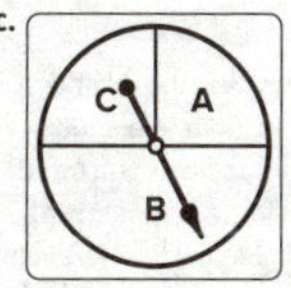

Sample answer: Section B should be one half of the spinner and sections A and C should each be one fourth of the spinner.
7. Yes; Sample answer: $\frac{5 \text{ sharpened}}{10 \text{ unsharpened}} = \frac{20 \text{ sharpened}}{x \text{ unsharpened}}$. So, $x = 40$.

Pages 727–728 Lesson 9-2 Extra Practice

9. $\frac{9}{20}$; The experimental probability of $\frac{9}{20}$ is close to the theoretical probability of $\frac{1}{2}$. **11.** 50 customers
13. experimental; 40; less **15.** *P*(not red) **17.** vanilla sundae, vanilla cone, chocolate sundae, chocolate cone, strawberry sundae, strawberry cone; equally likely

Pages 737–738 Lesson 9-3 Independent Practice

1. H1, H2, H3, H4, H5, T1, T2, T3, T4, T5
3. purple 10, purple 18, purple 21, purple 24, green 10, green 18, green 21, green 24, black 10, black 18, black 21, black 24, silver 10, silver 18, silver 21, silver 24
5. $\frac{1}{36}$;

1, 1	1, 2	1, 3	1, 4	1, 5	1, 6
2, 1	2, 2	2, 3	2, 4	2, 5	2, 6
3, 1	3, 2	3, 3	3, 4	3, 5	3, 6
4, 1	4, 2	4, 3	4, 4	4, 5	4, 6
5, 1	5, 2	5, 3	5, 4	5, 5	5, 6
6, 1	6, 2	6, 3	6, 4	6, 5	6, 6

7. *P*(Player 1) = $\frac{6}{8}$ or $\frac{3}{4}$; *P*(Player 2) = $\frac{2}{8}$ or $\frac{1}{4}$; RRB, RYB, RRY, RYY, BRB, BYB, BYY, BRY **9.** The first outcome in the I bracket should be IC.

Pages 739–740 Lesson 9-3 Extra Practice

11.

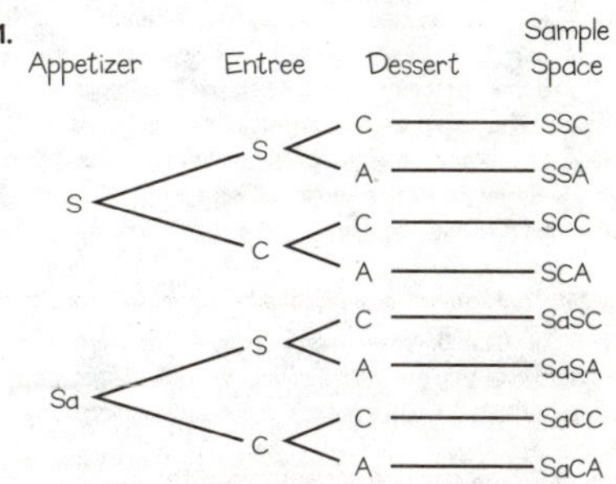

13a. 16 combinations **13b.** $\frac{1}{16}$
13c.

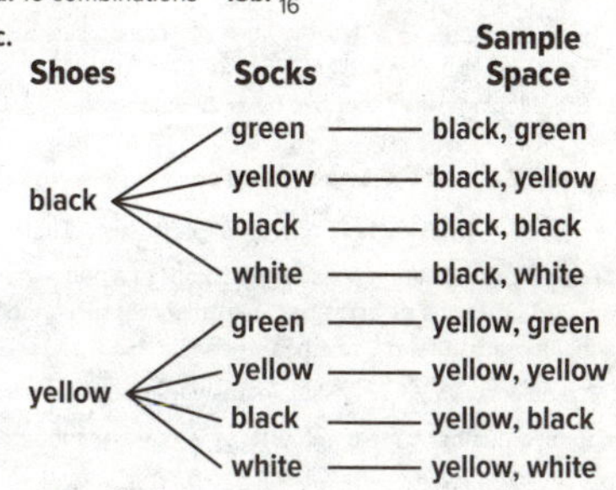

8 combinations

15. (Ava, Brooke); (Greg, Brooke); (Antoine, Mario) **17.** $\frac{1}{8}$
19. $\frac{1}{2}$ **21.** $\frac{1}{3}$; There are 2 numbers out of 6 on a number cube that are greater than 4. $\frac{2}{6} = \frac{1}{3}$

Pages 745–746 Lesson 9-4 Independent Practice

1 Sample answer: Spin a spinner with 4 equal-size sections 50 times. **3** Sample answer: Spin a spinner divided into 3 equal sections and roll a number cube. Repeat the simulation until all types of cookies are obtained. **5.** Sample answer: Use 3 red marbles to represent winning and 7 blue marbles to represent losing. Draw 1 marble 4 times, replacing the marble each time. **7.** Sample answer: a survey of 100 people voting on whether or not to enact a tax increase, where each person is equally likely to vote yes or no. Toss a coin 100 times. **9.** Sample answer: sometimes; The spinner must have equal-sized sections.

Pages 747–748 Lesson 9-4 Extra Practice

11. Sample answer: Use a spinner with 5 equal sections to represent the 5 discounts. Spin 4 times to represent 4 customers receiving cards. **13.** Sample answer: Toss a coin. Heads represents one color and tails represents the other color. Repeat until both colors are selected. **15.** Sample answer: Spin a spinner with 4 equal sections. Each section represents one of the magazines. Repeat the simulation until all possible magazines are selected. **17.** Spin a spinner with equal size spaces labeled A, B, C, D, E, and F. Let spinning A represent winning a prize and let spinning other letters represent not winning a prize; Roll a number cube. Let rolling a 1 represent winning a prize and let rolling a 2, 3, 4, 5, or 6 represent not winning a prize.

Page 755 Problem-Solving Investigation Act It Out

Case 3. 31 **Case 5.** unfair; Sample answer: There are 20 out of 36 outcomes that are multiples of 3 and only 15 that are multiples of 4. Jason has a greater chance of winning.

Pages 761–762 Lesson 9-5 Independent Practice

1 12 **3.** 84 **5.** 6 possible routes; $\frac{1}{6}$ or about 17%
7. $\frac{1}{50}$; very unlikely **9** No; the number of selections is 32 • 11 or 352, which is less than 365. **11.** 10 groups, 8 activities have 80 outcomes; the other two have 72 outcomes. **13.** 6^x

Pages 763–764 Lesson 9-5 Extra Practice

15. 8 **17.** 27 **19.** 16 **21.** $\frac{4}{48}$ or $\frac{1}{12}$; Sample answer: There are 3 • 4 • 4 or 48 different possible outcomes of a phone plan. There are 1 • 4 • 1 or 4 different possible outcomes of a phone plan that includes Brand B and has a headset. **23.** $108 = 9 \times c \times 2$; 6 colors **25.** $\frac{1}{2}$ **27.** Sample answer: Assign each number of a number cube to a toy. Roll the number cube. Repeat until all numbers are rolled.

Pages 769–770 Lesson 9-6 Independent Practice

1 24 **3.** 840 **5.** 40,320 **7.** 120 ways **9** 6
11. Sample answer: The number of ways you can order 3 books on a shelf is 3 • 2 • 1 or 6. **13a.** 15 **13b.** 120 **13c.** 10 **13d.** 28

Pages 771–772 Lesson 9-6 Extra Practice

15. 60 **17.** 120 **19.** $\frac{1}{90}$ **21.** $\frac{1}{120}$ **23a.** False **23b.** True **23c.** True **25.** $\frac{29}{30}$ **27.** WB, WG, RB, RG, GB, GG

Pages 779–780 Lesson 9-7 Independent Practice

1. $\frac{1}{24}$ **3** $\frac{1}{8}$ **5.** $\frac{1}{144}$ **7** $\frac{7}{95}$ **9.** $\frac{1}{19}$ **11.** $\frac{3}{8}$; dependent event; after the first piece of paper is chosen, there is one less from which to choose. **13.** Sample answer: Spinning the spinner twice represents two independent events. The probability of getting an even number is $\frac{2}{5}$ each time; $\frac{2}{5} \cdot \frac{2}{5}$ or $\frac{4}{25}$. **15a.** 0.0004 or 0.04% **15b.** about 400 packages

Pages 781–782 Lesson 9-7 Extra Practice

17. $\frac{5}{14}$ **19.** $\frac{92}{287}$ **21.** $\frac{3}{20}$ **23.** $\frac{7}{60}$ **25.** $\frac{3}{55}$ **27.** $\frac{6}{55}$ **29a.** True **29b.** True **29c.** False **31.** 18 **33.** 51 **35.** $9 = 0.15x$; 60

Page 785 Chapter Review Vocabulary Check

1. sample space **3.** theoretical

Page 786 Chapter Review Key Concept Check

1. experimental probability **3.** compound event

Chapter 10 Statistics

Page 792 Chapter 10 Are You Ready?

1. Rihanna **3.** 75

Pages 797–798 Lesson 10-1 Independent Practice

1. $\frac{3}{10}$, 0.3, or 30% **3** $\frac{2}{25}$, 0.08, or 8% **5** 9 students
7. About 143 students prefer humor books, and the number of students that prefer nonfiction is 88. So, there are about 55 more students who prefer humor books to nonfiction books. **9.** about 100 times **11.** Sample answer: Randomly select a part of the group to get a sample. Determine their preferences and use the results to determine the percent of the total group. It makes sense to use a sample when surveying the population of a city.

Pages 799–800 Lesson 10-1 Extra Practice

13. $\frac{3}{5}$, 0.6, or 60% **15a.** about 60,000 **15b.** about 72,500 **15c.** about 7,200 **17.** $\frac{27}{238} = \frac{n}{100}$ **19.** $\frac{27}{100} = \frac{p}{238}$ **21.** $\frac{54}{20} = \frac{405}{x}$; 150 minutes or 2.5 hours **23.** $\frac{1}{25}$

Pages 805–806 Lesson 10-2 Independent Practice

1 The conclusion is valid. This is an unbiased systematic random sample. **3** This is a simple random sample. So, the sample is valid; about 205 people. **5.** Sample answer: Questions should be asked in a neutral manner. For example, the question "You really don't like Brand X, do you?" might not get the same answer as the question "Do you prefer Brand X or Brand Y?" **7.** Sometimes; Sample answer: The sample needs to represent the entire population to be valid. **9.** Sample answer: The sample will be biased because it is a convenience sample. Marisol will be asking only basketball fans.

Pages 807–808 Lesson 10-2 Extra Practice

11. This is an unbiased, simple random sample because randomly selected Californians were surveyed. So, the conclusion is valid. **13.** This is an unbiased, systematic random sample. So, the conclusion is valid; 304 students. **15.** The survey results in a convenience sample; Sample answer: The school district should survey every tenth family living within the school district's boundaries. **17a.** Invalid **17b.** Valid **17c.** Valid **19.** median; Sample answer: She scored better than the mean on four of the tests. She scored lower than the mode on four of the tests.

Pages 817–818 Lesson 10-3 Independent Practice

1 Graph B; Sample answer: The ratio of the area of the gas pumps in the graph on the right are not proportional to the cost of gas. **3** The median or the mode because they are much closer in value to most of the data.

5.

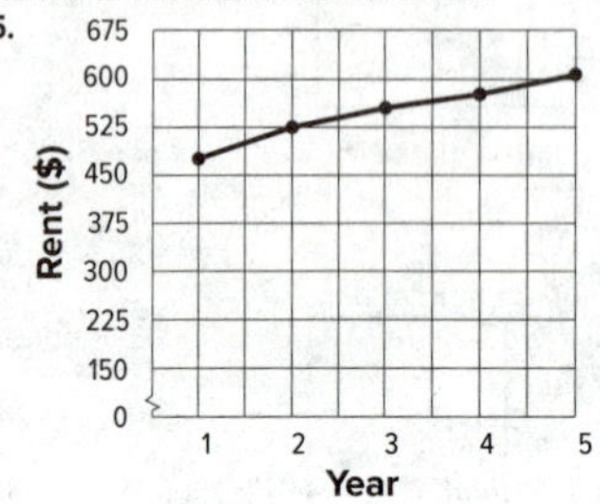

7. Sample answer: Since the graph makes it seem as if rent has been stable, a person may choose to become a tenant.
9. Sample answer: The graph makes it appear that the Fall section is greater than the Spring section. This is because the perspective of the graph makes it appear greater, when, in fact, they are equal in size.

Pages 819–820 Lesson 10-3 Extra Practice

11. Sample answer: The scale of the graph is not divided into equal intervals, so differences in heights appear less than they actually are. **13.** Sample answer: The mode is 100, but she only received 100 two times out of 6 tests. **15.** The intervals on the vertical scale are inconsistent.

Page 823 Problem-Solving Investigation Use a Graph

Case 3. Sample answer: 2017

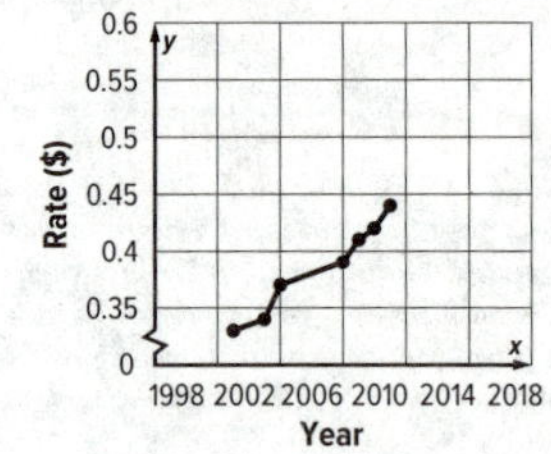

Case 5. $36.20

Pages 833–834 Lesson 10-4 Independent Practice

1 Sample answer: The times at Lucy's Steakhouse have a median of 20 minutes with an interquartile range of 20 minutes. The times at Gary's Grill have a median of 15 minutes with an interquartile range of 10 minutes. In general, a customer will wait longer at Lucy's Steakhouse.
3a. Plant A: 2.75, 0.75; Plant B: 3.1; 0.7
3b.

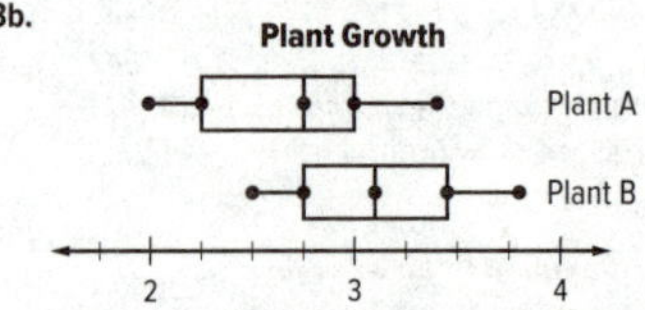

3c. Sample answer: Both populations have similar interquartile ranges. The median for Plant B is greater. So, Plant B generally showed more growth. **5.** The data shown in the histograms are only shown in intervals. Specific values are not shown.

Pages 835–836 Lesson 10-4 Extra Practice

9. this season; Sample answer: Both seasons' scores have a median of 20 points, but last season's scores have an interquartile range of 15 points while this season's interquartile range is 10 points. So, the football team's performance was more consistent this season. **11.** Sample answer: 2, 4, 4, 5, 8, 9, 10 **13a.** False **13b.** False **13c.** True **15.** 1.74 million **17.** Sample answer: The shape of the distribution is not symmetric since the lengths of each box and whisker are not the same. There are no outliers.

Pages 843–844 Lesson 10-5 Independent Practice

1 box plot; shows the median

3. A box plot is an appropriate graph because there is a large set of data and it will show the measures of variation of the data set. This graph has a median of 41.

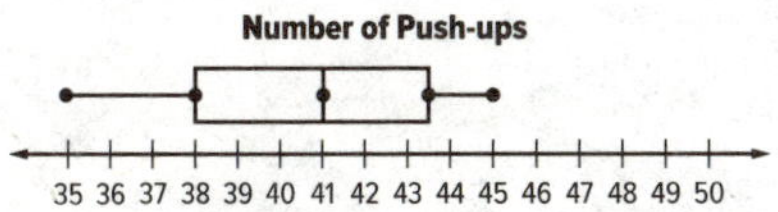

5a. Situation B; Sample answer: A bar graph can show the number of customers who made a purchase by each individual age. **5b.** Yes; Sample answer: line plot; A line plot shows the frequency of data on a number line. **7.** always; Sample answer: The sections of the circle graph can be taken from the bars of the graph and the percents can be found by dividing each bar's value by the total number of data values.

9. Sample answer: Both use bars to show how many things are in each category. A histogram shows the frequency of data that has been organized into equal intervals, so there is no space between the bars. It would be appropriate to use a histogram instead of a bar graph when the data can be organized into equal intervals.

Pages 845–846 Lesson 10-5 Extra Practice

11. circle graph; compares parts to a whole

13a.

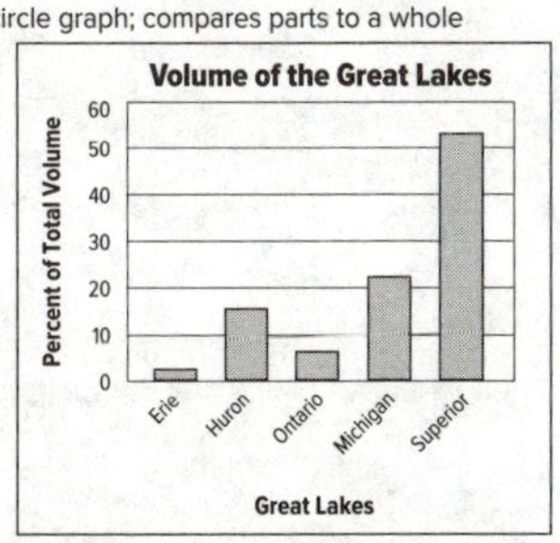

13b. Sample answer: The circle graph is most appropriate because it shows how each lake compares to the whole.

15.

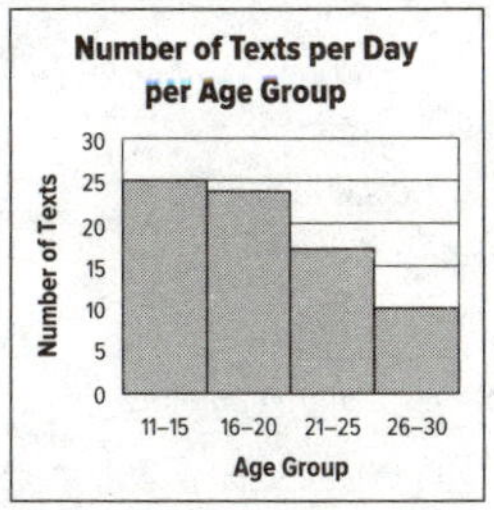

A histogram is an appropriate graph because the data is given in intervals. The graph shows people ages 26–30 text the least amount. **17.** line graph; circle graph; bar graph

19. 65 men; 65 women

Page 849 Chapter Review Vocabulary Check

Across

5. population **9.** sample

Down

1. systematic **3.** simple **7.** unbiased

Page 850 Chapter Review Key Concept Check

1. survey **3.** biased sample

Index

Dd

Ee

Kk

Ll

Mm

Nn

Oo

Pp

Qq

Rr

Ss

Tt

Uu

Vv

Ww

Xx

Yy

Zz

Work Mats

Name ______

=

Name ____________

Name ____________

Work Mats

Name ______

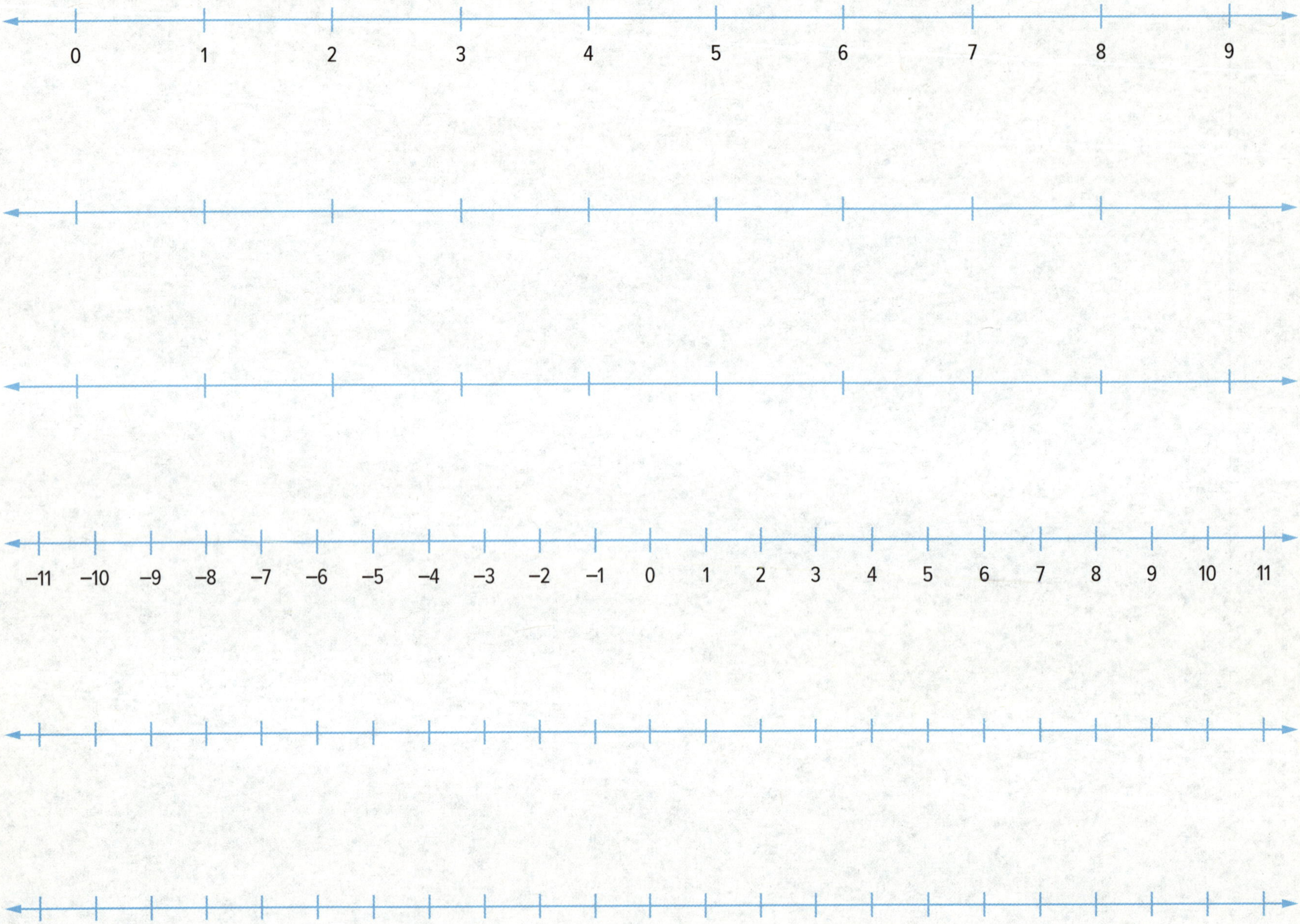

FOLDABLES® Study Organizers

What Are Foldables and How Do I Create Them?

Foldables are three-dimensional graphic organizers that help you create study guides for each chapter in your book.

Step 1 Go to the back of your book to find the Foldable for the chapter you are currently studying. Follow the cutting and assembly instructions at the top of the page.

Step 2 Go to the Key Concept Check at the end of the chapter you are currently studying. Match up the tabs and attach your Foldable to this page. Dotted tabs show where to place your Foldable. Striped tabs indicate where to tape the Foldable.

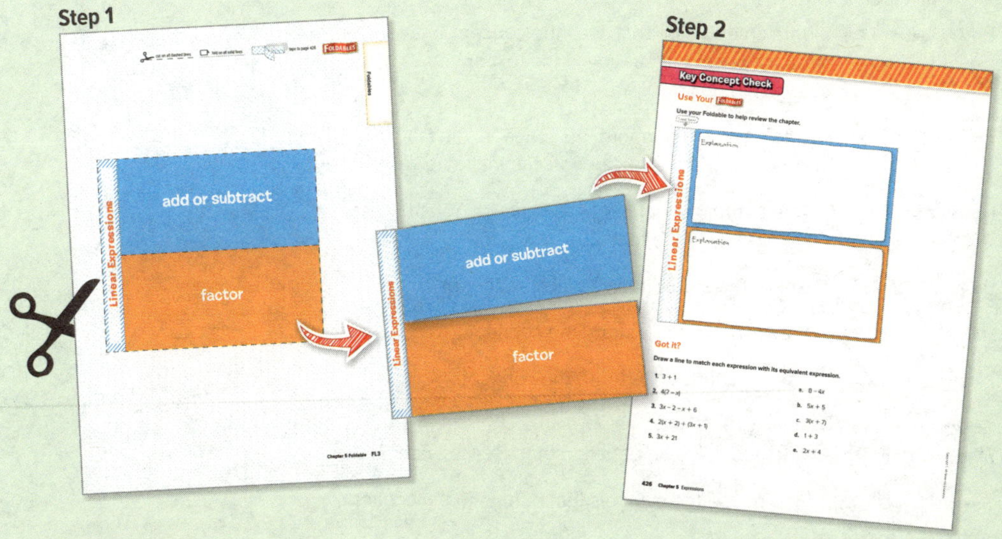

How Will I Know When to Use My Foldable?

When it's time to work on your Foldable, you will see a Foldables logo at the bottom of the **Rate Yourself!** box on the Guided Practice pages. This lets you know that it is time to update it with concepts from that lesson. Once you've completed your Foldable, use it to study for the chapter test.

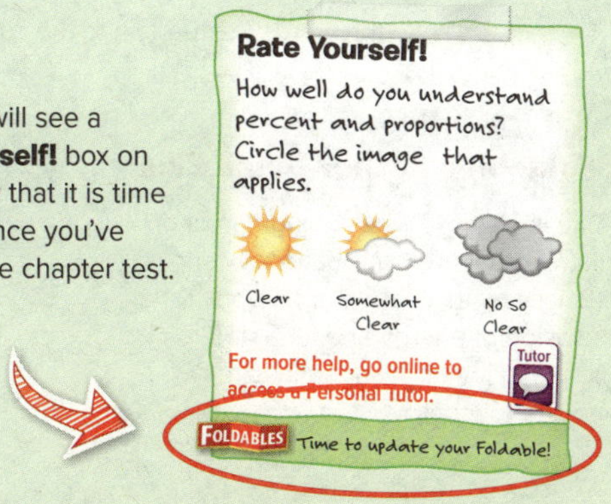

How Do I Complete My Foldable?

No two Foldables in your book will look alike. However, some will ask you to fill in similar information. Below are some of the instructions you'll see as you complete your Foldable. **HAVE FUN** learning math using Foldables!

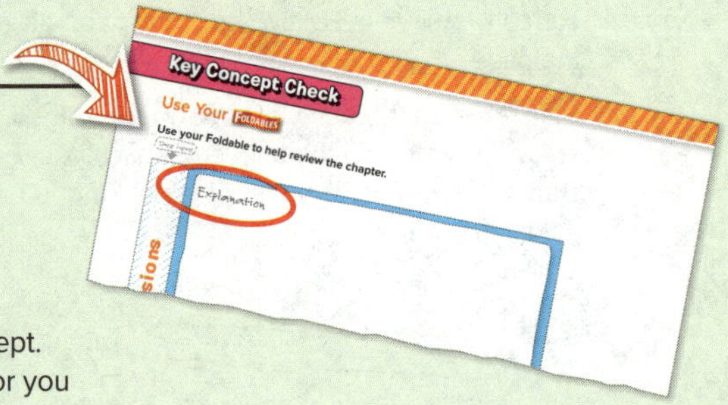

Instructions and what they mean

Best Used to...	Complete the sentence explaining when the concept should be used.
Definition	Write a definition in your own words.
Description	Describe the concept using words.
Equation	Write an equation that uses the concept. You may use one already in the text or you can make up your own.
Example	Write an example about the concept. You may use one already in the text or you can make up your own.
Formulas	Write a formula that uses the concept. You may use one already in the text.
How do I ...?	Explain the steps involved in the concept.
Models	Draw a model to illustrate the concept.
Picture	Draw a picture to illustrate the concept.
Solve Algebraically	Write and solve an equation that uses the concept.
Symbols	Write or use the symbols that pertain to the concept.
Write About It	Write a definition or description in your own words.
Words	Write the words that pertain to the concept.

Meet Foldables Author Dinah Zike

Dinah Zike is known for designing hands-on manipulatives that are used nationally and internationally by teachers and parents. Dinah is an explosion of energy and ideas. Her excitement and joy for learning inspires everyone she touches.

Courtesy of Dinah Zike

Use this Foldable with Chapter 5, page 426.

cut on all dashed lines

fold on all solid lines

tape to page 426

FOLDABLES

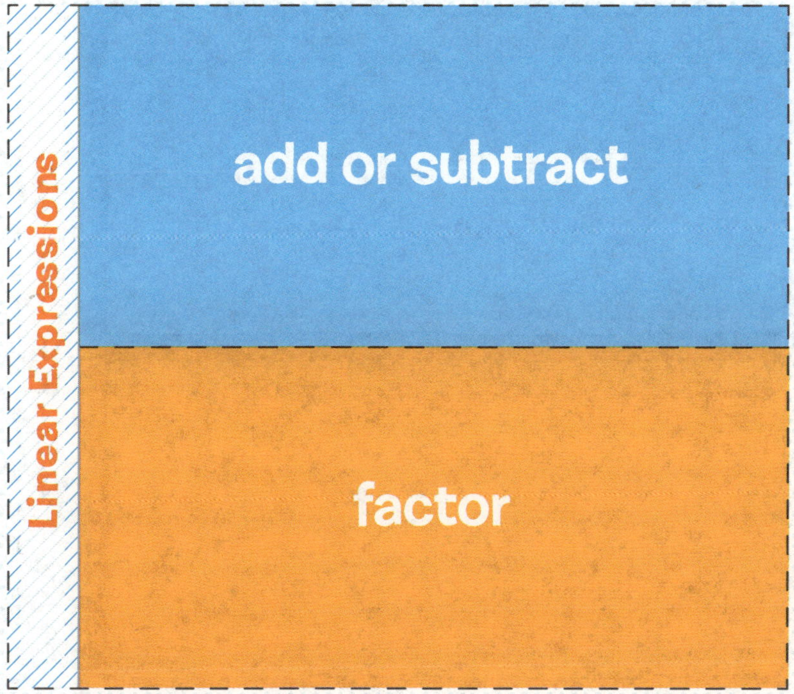

Foldables

cut on all dashed lines   fold on all solid lines   tape to page 426

FOLDABLES®

Examples

Examples

page 426

Use this Foldable with Chapter 5, page 426.

Use this Foldable with Chapter 6, page 524.

cut on all dashed lines
fold on all solid lines
tape to page 524
FOLDABLES

Foldables

Solve Two-Step Equations

$-3x + 6 = 21$

$-4(x + 9) = 24$

Foldables

cut on all dashed lines   fold on all solid lines   tape to page 524   FOLDABLES

Use this Foldable with Chapter 6, page 524.

Write About It

Write About It

page 524

Use this Foldable with Chapter 7, page 604.

cut on all dashed lines

fold on all solid lines

tape to page 604

FOLDABLES

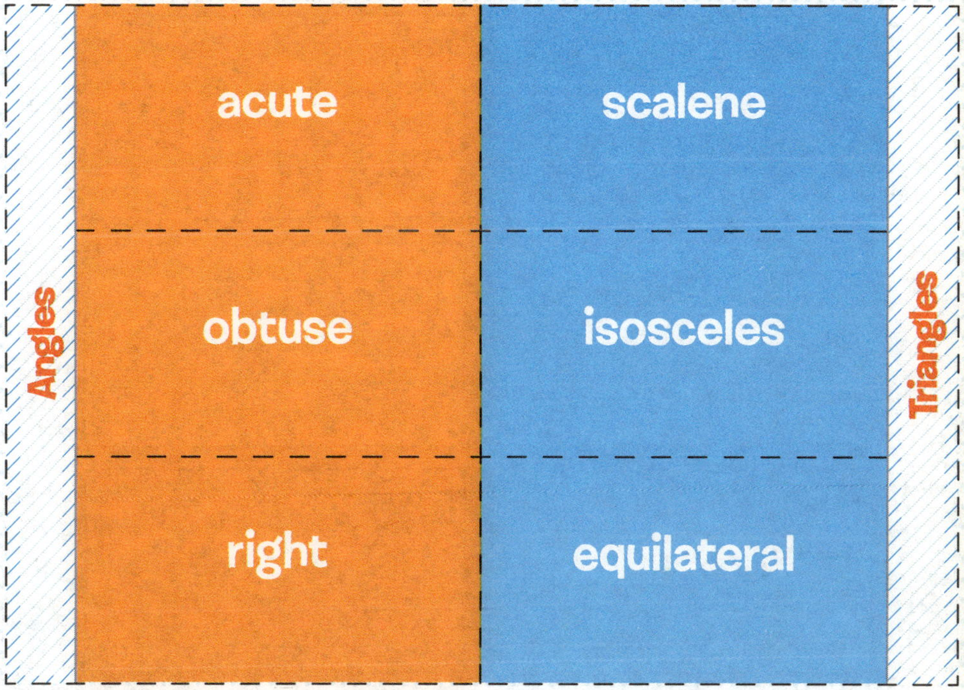

Foldables

cut on all dashed lines — fold on all solid lines — tape to page 604

FOLDABLES

Use this Foldable with Chapter 7, page 604.

Use this Foldable with Chapter 8, page 700.

cut on all dashed lines fold on all solid lines tape to page 700

FOLDABLES

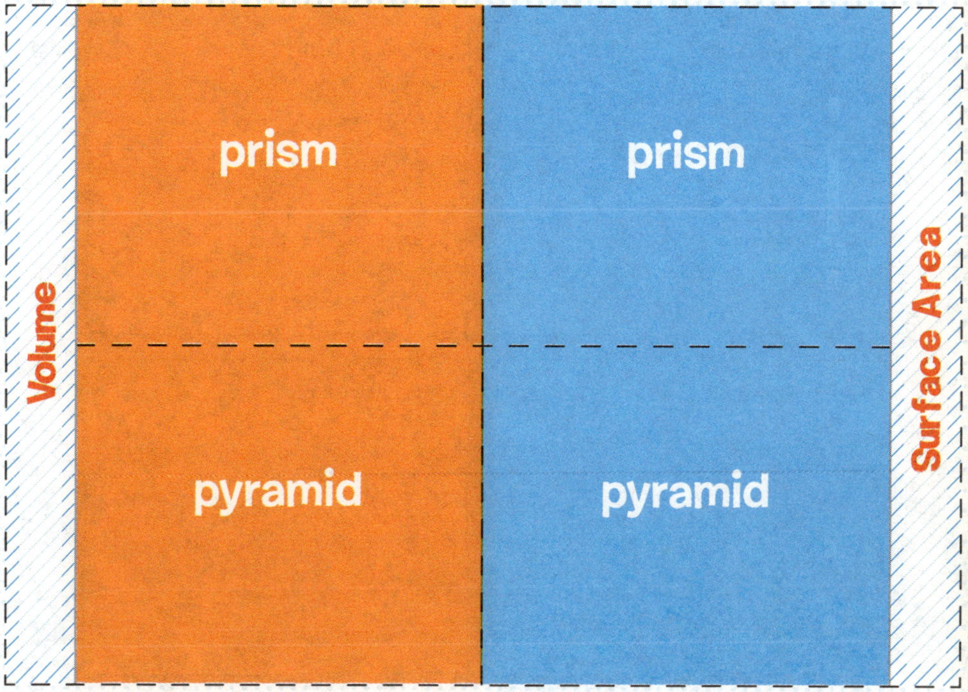

Foldables

cut on all dashed lines | fold on all solid lines | tape to page 700

FOLDABLES®

Write About It	Write About It
Write About It	Write About It

page 700 — Tab 2

page 700 — Tab 1

Use this Foldable with Chapter 8, page 700.

Use this Foldable with Chapter 9, page 786.

cut on all dashed lines fold on all solid lines tape to page 786

FOLDABLES

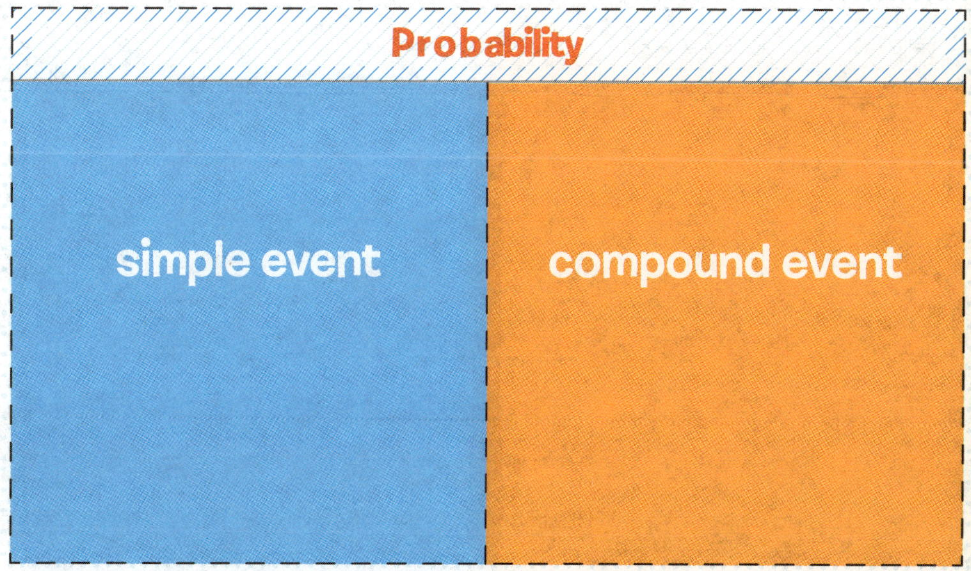

Foldables

cut on all dashed lines

fold on all solid lines

tape to page 786

FOLDABLES

Use this Foldable with Chapter 9, page 786.

page 786

Definition

Definition

Use this Foldable with Chapter 10, page 850.

cut on all dashed lines fold on all solid lines tape to page 850 FOLDABLES

Foldables

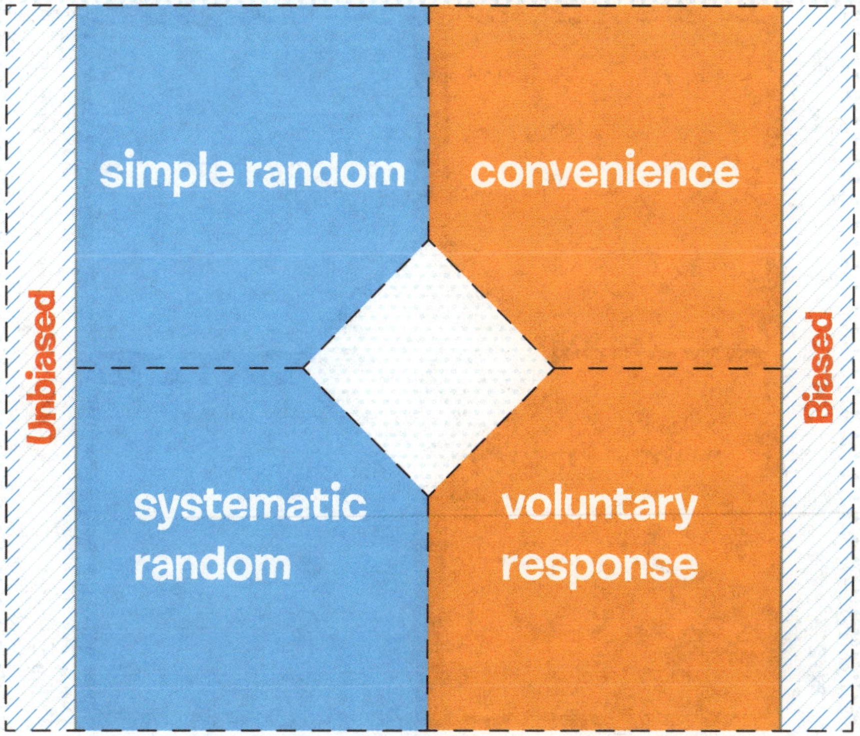

cut on all dashed lines | fold on all solid lines | tape to page 850 | FOLDABLES

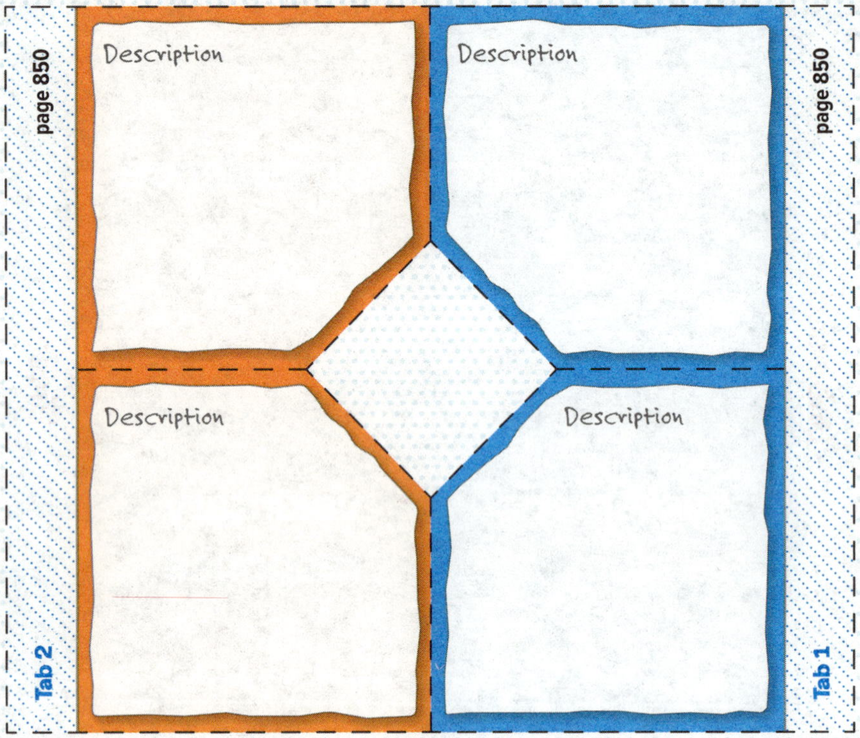

Use this Foldable with Chapter 10, page 850.

Chapter 6 Equations and Inequalities

Page 507 Lesson 6-7 Need Another Example?

3. $x \geq -1$

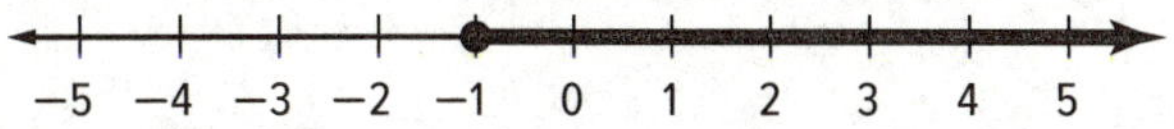

4. $x < 20$

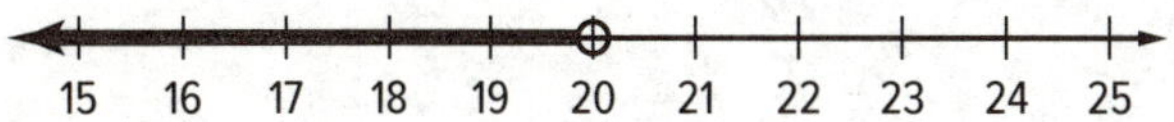

Chapter 7 Geometric Figures

Pages 586–588 Lesson 7-5 Need Another Example?

2.

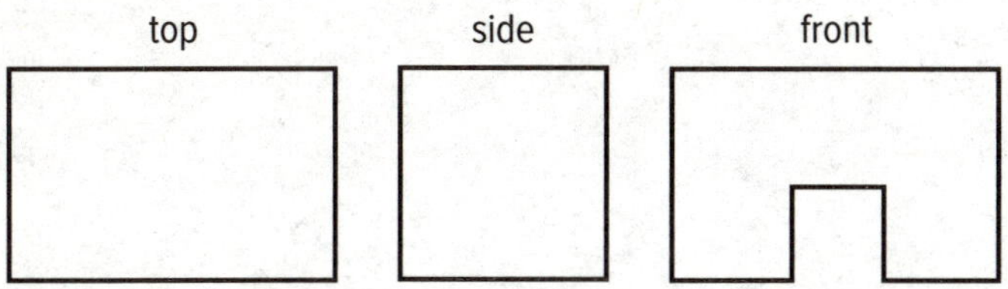

3.

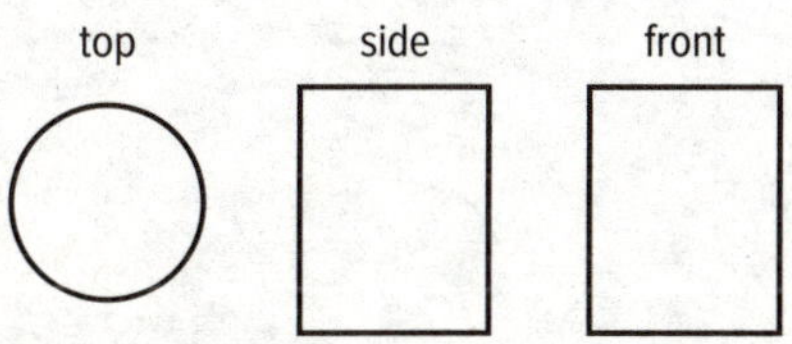

4.

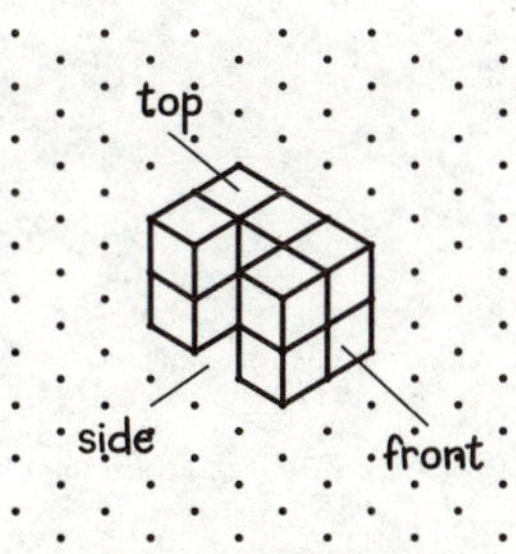

5.

Pages 594–595 Lesson 7-6 Need Another Example?

1. octagonal prism;

   bases: *ABCDEFGH, IJKLMNOP*

   faces: *ABCDEFGH, IJKLMNOP, ABKJ, BKLC, CLMD, DMNE, ENOF, FGPO, GHIP, HAJI*

   edges: $\overline{AB}$, $\overline{BC}$, $\overline{CD}$, $\overline{DE}$, $\overline{EF}$, $\overline{FG}$, $\overline{GH}$, $\overline{HA}$, $\overline{IJ}$, $\overline{JK}$, $\overline{KL}$, $\overline{LM}$, $\overline{MN}$, $\overline{NO}$, $\overline{OP}$, $\overline{PI}$, $\overline{AJ}$, $\overline{BK}$, $\overline{CL}$, $\overline{DM}$, $\overline{EN}$, $\overline{FO}$, $\overline{GP}$, $\overline{HI}$

   vertices: *A, B, C, D, E, F, G, H, I, J, K, L, M, N, O, P*

3. cone;

   base: circle *C*

   faces: none

   edges: none

   vertex: *B*

Chapter 10 Statistics

Page 833 Lesson 10-4 Independent Practice

3b.

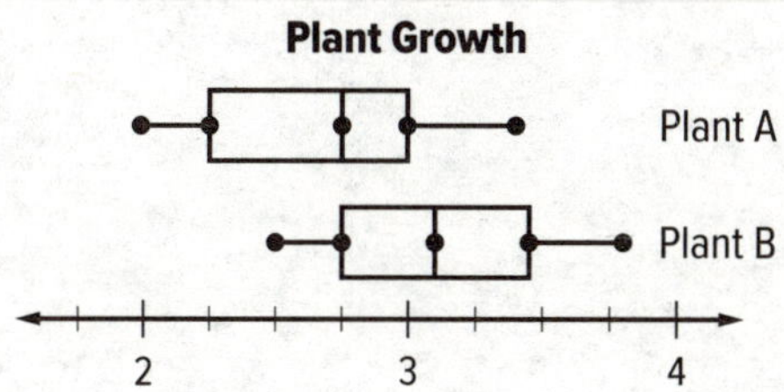

3c. Sample answer: Both populations have similar interquartile ranges. The median for Plant B is greater. So, Plant B generally showed more growth.

Chapter 5 Expressions

Page 427 Movie Time

Content Standard(s)	7.EE.1, 7.EE.2, 7.NS.3
Mathematical Practices	MP1, MP2, MP4, MP5, MP6
Depth of Knowledge	DOK3

Part	Max Points	Scoring Rubric
A	2	Full Credit: Cost $= 2(10.50 + d) + 3(6.50 + d) + p$ Cost $= 40.50 + 5d + p$ Partial Credit will be given for the correct initial expression before the Distributive Property is used. No credit will be given for an incorrect answer.
B	1	Full Credit: $2d - 5$ No credit will be given for an incorrect answer.
C	2	Full Credit: $40.50 + 5d + p + 2d - 5$; \$85.00 $40.50 + 5d + p + 2d - 5$ $= 40.50 - 5 + 5d + 2d + p$ $= 35.50 + 7d + p$ $= 35.50 + 7(6) + 7.50$ $= 35.50 + 42 + 7.50$ $= 35.50 + 7.50 + 42$ $= 43 + 42$ $= 85$ Partial Credit will be given for a correct expression. No credit will be given for an incorrect answer.
TOTAL	5	

Chapter 6 Equations and Inequalities

Page 525 Fall Reading

Content Standard(s)	7.EE.3, 7.EE.4
Mathematical Practices	MP1, MP2, MP4, MP5, MP6, MP8
Depth of Knowledge	DOK3

Part	Max Points	Scoring Rubric
A	2	Full Credit: This can be represented by the equation $11p + 35 = 387$. $11p + 35 = 387$ $11p = 352$ $p = 32$ So, Gordon reads 32 pages per day. Partial Credit will be given for the correct answer without showing work. No credit will be given for an incorrect answer.
B	3	Full Credit: This is represented by the inequality $8 + 6p \geq 350$. So, $p \geq 57$. Kendrick must read 57 pages per day. 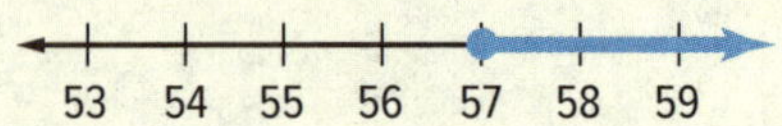 Partial Credit of 2 points will be given if the student correctly answers two of the three parts (write the inequality, solve the inequality, graph the inequality). Partial Credit of 1 point will be given if the student correctly answers one of the three parts. No credit will be given for an incorrect answer.
TOTAL	5	

Chapter 7 Geometric Figures

Page 605 Stacking Triangles

Content Standard(s)	7.G.1, 7.G.2, 7.G.5
Mathematical Practices	MP1, MP2, MP4, MP5, MP6, MP7
Depth of Knowledge	DOK3

Part	Max Points	Scoring Rubric
A	2	Full Credit will be given for correctly labeling both triangles and finding the scale factor: $\overline{AB} = 6$ cm $\overline{DG} = 4$ cm $\overline{AF} = 4.2$ cm $\overline{GH} = 2.8$ cm $\overline{BF} = 4.2$ cm $\overline{DH} = 2.8$ cm $\frac{4}{6} = \frac{2}{3}$ and $\frac{2.8}{4.2} = \frac{2}{3}$ The scale factor is $\frac{2}{3}$. Partial Credit will be given if the student finds the scale factor but does not label each triangle OR if the student incorrectly measures the side lengths of the triangles correctly calculates a scale factor based on these measurements. No credit will be given for an incorrect answer.
B	1	Full Credit will be given for the correct figure *XYZ* with measures: $\overline{XZ} = 8$ cm $\overline{XY} = 5.6$ cm $\overline{ZY} = 5.6$ cm No credit will be given for an incorrect answer.
C	3	Full Credit will be given for the correct drawing, correct angle measures, and explanation. 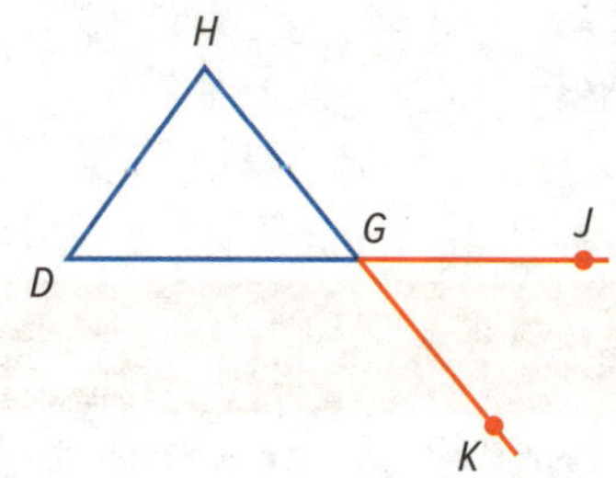 $m\angle HGJ = 135°$ $m\angle JGK = 45°$ $\angle DGH$ and $\angle HGJ$ are supplementary angles because the sum of their measures is 180°. Partial Credit: 2 points will be given if the student correctly completes any two of the three parts. 1 point will be given if the student correct completes one of the three parts. No credit will be given for an incorrect answer.
TOTAL	6	

Chapter 8 Measure Figures

Page 701 Juice Box Packaging

Content Standard(s)	7.G.4, 7.G.6
Mathematical Practices	MP1, MP2, MP4, MP6
Depth of Knowledge	DOK3

Part	Max Points	Scoring Rubric
A	2	Full Credit will be given for both correct answers of 18 in^3 with work shown and a correct response of no with an explanation. $V = \ell wh$ $V = (4)(3)(1.5)$ $V = 18$ in^3 The volume of the jumbo juice box would be 36 in^3. The new dimensions would be 3 by 6 by 8 inches, which would give a volume of 144 in^3. Therefore, the answer is no. Partial Credit will be given for either correct answer with an explanation. No credit will be given for an incorrect answer.
B	3	Full Credit: 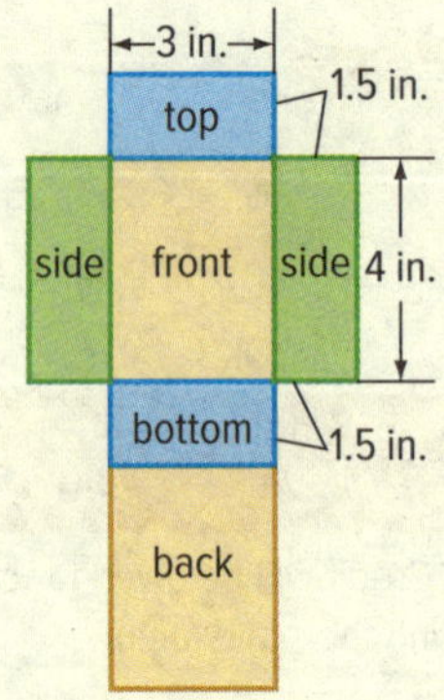 Area of front and back: $2(4)(3) = 24$ in^2 Area of top and bottom: $2(3)(1.5) = 9$ in^2 Area of sides: $2(4)(1.5) = 12$ in^2 Surface area: $24 + 9 + 12 = 45$ in^2 So, each box has a surface area of 45 in^2. Surface area of 8 boxes: 8(45) or 360 in^2 Total cost: 360($0.02) or $7.20 It will cost Supreme Packaging $7.20 for the 8 juice boxes. Partial Credit: 2 points will be given for correctly answering two of the three parts. 1 point will be given for correctly answering one of the three parts. No credit will be given for an incorrect answer.
C	1	Full Credit: $A = \pi r^2$ $12.56 = 3.14 \cdot r^2$ $\frac{12.56}{3.14} = r^2$ $2 = r$ The radius of the artist's picture is about 2 inches which makes the diameter about 4 inches. Since the front of the box is only 3 inches wide, the picture will not fit on the box. No credit will be given for an incorrect answer.
TOTAL	6	

Chapter 9 Probability

Page 787 ***Carnival Prizes***

Content Standard(s)	7.SP.5, 7.SP.7, 7.SP.8
Mathematical Practices	MP1, MP2, MP3, MP4, MP5, MP6
Depth of Knowledge	DOK4

Part	Max Points	Scoring Rubric
A	3	Full Credit will be given for a correct sample space with 12 events and a correct probability answer of $\frac{5}{12}$. Sample Space (Red Card, Blue Card) 3, 4 3, 7 3, 9 5, 4 5, 7 5, 9 8, 4 8, 7 8, 9 10, 4 10, 7 10, 9 There are 12 possible outcomes. Product of Red Card and Blue Card: $3(4) = 12$ $3(7) = 21$ $3(9) = 27$ $5(4) = 20$ $5(7) = 35$ $5(9) = 45$ $8(4) = 32$ $8(7) = 56$ $8(9) = 72$ $10(4) = 40$ $10(7) = 70$ $10(9) = 90$ There are 5 combinations of cards that produce a product greater than or equal to 45. So, the probability of winning the game is $\frac{5}{12}$ or 42%. Partial Credit: 2 points will be given for a correct sample space and an incorrect or missing probability fraction or percent. 1 point will be given for an incomplete sample space and an incorrect or missing probability fraction or percent OR for a correct probability fraction and percent with a missing sample space. No credit will be given for an incorrect answer.
B	2	Full Credit will be given for the correct answer of 70 with a proper explanation. There are only three events that produce a product of at least 70: $8(9) = 72$ $10(7) = 70$ $10(9) = 90$ $\frac{3}{12} = \frac{1}{4}$ or 25% Partial Credit will be given for a correct answer without an explanation. No credit will be given for an incorrect answer.
C	1	Full Credit: The probability of achieving a score of 70 or higher is $\frac{1}{4}$. $\left(\frac{1}{4}\right)\left(\frac{1}{4}\right)\left(\frac{1}{4}\right)\left(\frac{1}{4}\right) = \left(\frac{1}{4}\right)^4 = \frac{1}{256}$. The probability is $\frac{1}{256}$. No credit will be given for an incorrect answer.
D	1	Full Credit will be given for a statement similar to: There will be times when there will be several winners over 15–20 attempts, and there will be times when there will not be any winners over 15–20 attempts. There are several combinations, and there is not a uniform sequence concerning the outcomes. Be patient and there will be winners! No credit will be given for an incorrect answer.
TOTAL	7	

Chapter 10 Statistics

Page 851 Class Evaluation

Content Standard(s)	7.SP.1, 7.SP.2, 7.SP.4
Mathematical Practices	MP1, MP2, MP3, MP5, MP6
Depth of Knowledge	DOK3

Part	Max Points	Scoring Rubric
A	2	Full Credit: This is a legitimate representation of the grades of all the students in 2012 and 2013, since it is a random sample of all the grades in a given year. In 2014, the data might be biased because students were asked to bring in their transcripts. This is not a random sample because students who performed well might be more likely both to bring in their transcripts and also respond quickly. Partial Credit will be given if students answer but do not adequately explain their response OR if students fail to make a distinction for the 2012 data. No credit will be given for an incorrect answer.
B	2	Full Credit: $80.1 \times 10 = 801$ The sum of the 9 known values is 704. $801 - 704 = 97$. The missing grade is 97. Partial credit will be given for a correct answer without work shown. No credit will be given for an incorrect answer.
C	2	Full Credit: The grades were more consistent in 2013 because the range of scores is smaller. The median for the 2013 data is 87 and the mean is 87.2, while the median for the 2014 data is 89 and the mean is 88.7, so the scores for 2014 were better. A box plot would best display the data because it would show the median and the spread of the data. Partial Credit will be given for a correct answer without an explanation. No credit will be given for an incorrect answer.
D	1	Full Credit: Sample answer: If Mr. Fuentes submits the scores from 2014 the data would be misleading because his sample was biased and would show inflated scores. (Students might pick a different year and indicate that the data is not misleading.) No credit will be given for an incorrect answer.
TOTAL	7	

Mathematics Reference Sheet

Formulas

Area

Rectangle	$A = \ell w$	
Parallelogram	$A = bh$	
Triangle	$A = \frac{1}{2}bh$	
Trapezoid	$A = \frac{1}{2}h(b_1 + b_2)$	
Circle	$A = \pi r^2$	

Circumference

Circle	$C = \pi d$ or $C = 2\pi r$

Volume

Rectangular Prism	$V = \ell wh$
Right Circular Cylinder	$V = \pi r^2 h$

Measurement

Conversions within a System of Measure

1 yard = 3 feet
1 mile = 1760 yards = 5280 feet
1 acre = 43,560 square feet
1 minute = 60 seconds
1 hour = 60 minutes
1 year = 52 weeks = 365 days

1 liter = 1000 milliliters = 1000 cubic centimeters
1 meter = 100 centimeters = 1000 millimeters
1 kilometer = 1000 meters
1 gram = 1000 milligrams
1 kilogram = 1000 grams

1 cup = 8 fluid ounces
1 pint = 2 cups
1 quart = 2 pints
1 gallon = 4 quarts

1 pound = 16 ounces
1 ton = 2000 pounds

Conversions between Systems of Measure

1 inch ≈ 2.54 centimeters
1 foot ≈ 0.305 meter
1 mile ≈ 1.61 kilometers
1 cup ≈ 0.24 liter
1 gallon ≈ 3.785 liters
1 ounce ≈ 28.35 grams
1 pound ≈ 0.454 kilograms

1 centimeter ≈ 0.39 inch
1 meter ≈ 3.28 feet
1 kilometer ≈ 0.62 mile
1 liter ≈ 4.23 cups
1 liter ≈ 0.26 gallon
1 gram ≈ 0.035 ounce
1 kilogram ≈ 2.21 pounds

Conversions between Systems of Measure

$C = (F - 32) \div 1.8$

$F = (C \times 1.8) + 32$